LET'S GO:
Greece
& Turkey

"Its yearly revision by a new crop of Harvard students makes it as valuable as ever." **—The New York Times**

"Value-packed, unbeatable, accurate, and comprehensive." **—The Los Angeles Times**

"A world-wise traveling companion—always ready with friendly advice and helpful hints, all sprinkled with a bit of wit." **—The Philadelphia Inquirer**

"Lighthearted and sophisticated, informative and fun to read. [Let's Go] helps the novice traveler navigate like a knowledgeable old hand." **—Atlanta Journal-Constitution**

"All the essential information you need, from making a phone call to exchanging money to contacting your embassy. [Let's Go] provides maps to help you find your way from every train station to a full range of youth hostels and hotels." **—Minneapolis Star Tribune**

"Unbeatable: good sight-seeing advice; up-to-date info on restaurants, hotels, and inns; a commitment to money-saving travel; and a wry style that brightens nearly every page." **—The Washington Post**

■ Let's Go researchers have to make it on their own.

"The writers seem to have experienced every rooster-packed bus and lunar-surfaced mattress about which they write." **—The New York Times**

"Retains the spirit of the student-written publication it is: candid, opinionated, resourceful, amusing info for the traveler of limited means but broad curiosity." **—Mademoiselle**

■ No other guidebook is as comprehensive.

"Whether you're touring the United States, Europe, Southeast Asia, or Central America, a Let's Go guide will clue you in to the cheapest, yet safe, hotels and hostels, food and transportation. Going beyond the call of duty, the guides reveal a country's latest news, cultural hints, and off-beat information that any tourist is likely to miss." **—Tulsa World**

■ Let's Go is completely revised each year.

"Up-to-date travel tips for touring four continents on skimpy budgets." **—Time**

"Inimitable.... Let's Go's 24 guides are updated yearly (as opposed to the general guidebook standard of every two to three years), and in a marvelously spunky way." **—The New York Times**

Let's Go Publications

Let's Go: Alaska & The Pacific Northwest
Let's Go: Britain & Ireland
Let's Go: California
Let's Go: Central America
Let's Go: Eastern Europe
Let's Go: Ecuador & The Galápagos Islands
Let's Go: Europe
Let's Go: France
Let's Go: Germany
Let's Go: Greece & Turkey
Let's Go: India & Nepal
Let's Go: Ireland
Let's Go: Israel & Egypt
Let's Go: Italy
Let's Go: London
Let's Go: Mexico
Let's Go: New York City
Let's Go: Paris
Let's Go: Rome
Let's Go: Southeast Asia
Let's Go: Spain & Portugal
Let's Go: Switzerland & Austria
Let's Go: USA
Let's Go: Washington, D.C.

Let's Go **Map Guide:** Boston
Let's Go **Map Guide:** London
Let's Go **Map Guide:** New York City
Let's Go **Map Guide:** Paris
Let's Go **Map Guide:** San Francisco
Let's Go **Map Guide:** Washington, D.C.

LET'S GO

The Budget Guide to
Greece
& Turkey
1997

Eti Brachna Bonn
Editor

Özge Güzelsu
Associate Editor

Rachel Lebejko
Assistant Editor

St. Martin's Press ⚮ New York

HELPING LET'S GO

If you want to share your discoveries, suggestions, or corrections, please drop us a line. We read every piece of correspondence, whether a postcard, a 10-page e-mail, or a coconut. All suggestions are passed along to our researcher-writers. Please note that mail received after May 1997 may be too late for the 1998 book, but will be retained for the following edition. **Address mail to:**

**Let's Go: Greece & Turkey
67 Mt. Auburn Street
Cambridge, MA 02138
USA**

Visit Let's Go at **http://www.letsgo.com,** or send e-mail to:

**Fanmail@letsgo.com
Subject: "Let's Go: Greece & Turkey"**

In addition to the invaluable travel advice our readers share with us, many are kind enough to offer their services as researchers or editors. Unfortunately, the charter of Let's Go, Inc. enables us to employ only currently enrolled Harvard-Radcliffe students.

Maps by David Lindroth copyright © 1997, 1996, 1995, 1994, 1993, 1992, 1991, 1990, 1989, 1988 by St. Martin's Press, Inc.

Map revisions pp. 52, 53, 54, 55, 76, 77, 95, 113, 159, 178, 179, 185, 189, 197, 281, 335, 357, 381, 389, 429, 446, 447, 448, 449 by Let's Go, Inc.

Distributed outside the USA and Canada by Macmillan.

ISBN: 0-312-14654-X

First edition
10 9 8 7 6 5 4 3 2 1

Let's Go: Greece & Turkey is written by Let's Go Publications, 67 Mt. Auburn Street, Cambridge, MA 02138, USA.

About Let's Go

THIRTY-SIX YEARS OF WISDOM

Back in 1960, a few students at Harvard University banded together to produce a 20-page pamphlet offering a collection of tips on budget travel in Europe. This modest, mimeographed packet, offered as an extra to passengers on student charter flights to Europe, met with instant popularity. The following year, students traveling to Europe researched the first, full-fledged edition of *Let's Go: Europe*, a pocket-sized book featuring honest, irreverent writing and a decidedly youthful outlook on the world. Throughout the 60s, our guides reflected the times; the 1969 guide to America led off by inviting travelers to "dig the scene" at San Francisco's Haight-Ashbury. During the 70s and 80s, we gradually added regional guides and expanded coverage into the Middle East and Central America. With the addition of our in-depth city guides, handy map guides, and extensive coverage of Asia, the 90s are also proving to be a time of explosive growth for Let's Go, and there's certainly no end in sight. The first editions of *Let's Go: India & Nepal* and *Let's Go: Ecuador & The Galápagos Islands* hit the shelves this year, and research for next year's series has already begun.

We've seen a lot in 37 years. *Let's Go: Europe* is now the world's bestselling international guide, translated into seven languages. And our new guides bring Let's Go's total number of titles, with their spirit of adventure and their reputation for honesty, accuracy, and editorial integrity, to 30. But some things never change: our guides are still researched, written, and produced entirely by students who know first-hand how to see the world on the cheap.

HOW WE DO IT

Each guide is completely revised and thoroughly updated every year by a well-traveled set of 200 students. Every winter, we recruit over 120 researchers and 60 editors to write the books anew. After several months of training, Researcher-Writers hit the road for seven weeks of exploration, from Anchorage to Ankara, Estonia to El Salvador, Iceland to Indonesia. Hired for their rare combination of budget travel sense, writing ability, stamina, and courage, these adventurous travelers know that train strikes, stolen luggage, food poisoning, and marriage proposals are all part of a day's work. Back at our offices, editors work from spring to fall, massaging copy written on Himalayan bus rides into witty yet informative prose. A student staff of typesetters, cartographers, publicists, and managers keeps our lively team together. In September, the collected efforts of the summer are delivered to our printer, who turns them into books in record time, so that you have the most up-to-date information available for *your* vacation. And even as you read this, work on next year's editions is well underway.

WHY WE DO IT

At Let's Go, our goal is to give you a great vacation. We don't think of budget travel as the last recourse of the destitute; we believe that it's the only way to travel. Living cheaply and simply brings you closer to the people and places you've been saving up to visit. Our books will ease your anxieties and answer your questions about the basics—so you can get off the beaten track and explore. Once you learn the ropes, we encourage you to put Let's Go away now and then to strike out on your own. As any seasoned traveler will tell you, the best discoveries are often those you make yourself. When you find something worth sharing, drop us a line. We're Let's Go Publications, 67 Mt. Auburn St., Cambridge, MA 02138, USA (e-mail: fanmail@letsgo.com).

HAPPY TRAVELS!

Contents

Maps

Researcher-Writers

Amara Balthrop-Lewis   *Cyprus, Saronic Gulf Islands, Crete, Santorini*
Amara's fearless and enthusiastic plunge into the depths of Greece and Southern Cyprus, like Aphrodite's intrepid bathing technique, left us wondering how she did it all, so well, and so quickly. Perhaps it was the stellar Greek cuisine that kept her going (*tzatziki* 300dr), or maybe it was her secret weapon, Mike (*opa!*). In either event, we ate up every scrumptious word of her delectable copy and wish her the very best, wherever her next journey may take her.

Erik Charlson   *Kıbrıs, Peloponnese, Ionian Islands*
Erik, our hero, captured the true character and spirit of every obscure place we sent him to in one flawless copybatch after another. After hawking some clothes to lighten his load, politely fracturing some hearts, and picking up a *ligo ellinika*, Erik returned a lot blonder and a little wiser (an unusual combination). We have utmost faith that Erik, now a seasoned traveler, will be guided by his many talents beyond the Mediterranean basin. *Sağol.*

Alexis Gallagher   *Central and Northern Greece, NE Aegean Islands,*
Sporades
While merrily chit-chatting his way through Greece's less-traversed regions, Alexis proved that the art of making *kamaki*, as old as Greece itself, is alive and well. Stories of his exploits, from Thessaly to Macedonia, will live long in our memories of his passionate copybatches. Although we almost lost his invaluable services to one of the most majestic monasteries of Mount Athos, we're glad he threw off the shackles of his monastic inner self and finished his itinerary. Ευχαριστουμε, αγαπη μας.

Vicky Hatzisavvas   *Athens, Cyclades, Dodecanese*
Our Greek crown jewel, Vicky sparkled like the sun that reflects off the Aegean Sea at dusk. Her thorough research, amazing attention to detail, and stylish flair brought as many tears to our eyes as a certain sunburnt "sighting" on a beach in Mykonos brought to hers. We will long remember her warmth, good humor, and sunny attitude as she fit right in with Greece's most glamorous jet-setters. Her gracious service to her blushing country will be appreciated by oblivious tourists for years to come. Σ'αγαπουμε, κουκλα μας.

Jonathan Nelms   *Central Anatolia, Black Sea Coast, Mediterranean Coast*
Demure Jonathan's mellow nature was just what the Valley of Love needed. Rumor has it that his intimate experience with the tall, hard, 90-foot rock formations there was so unusual that the festival won't go on next year without him. Ploughing through his vacation days (and a couple hundred cold Turkish *bira*), our soft spoken stud cranked out a few extra Turkish *lira* for a taxi, but his sensitive perception of Australian-Turkish relations kept him on his toes. *Kolay gelsin.*

Suzan Sandık   *İstanbul, Aegean Coast, Mediterranean Coast*
Suzan's kick-ass coverage of Turkey's most dazzling regions never failed to make our jaws drop to the *kilim*. Living vicariously through her scandalous "mountain hikes," *mükemmel* nocturnal pursuits, and special diving lessons, we came to realize that the travel industry really does need more writers with purple hair and a Turkish-Bronx attitude. Undaunted about being stalked from İstanbul to the Mediterranean Sea, Suzan's love and pride for her *other* country shone through every glorious copybatch she sent us. *Canimiz, seni seviyoruz.*

Rosanna Gomez   *Cyprus*

Acknowledgments

Thanks Allison, for all your hard work, and *Let's Go,* for your advice. Book team: you kicked butt. Thanks for paying us, Stephen (£); Jen—you are *extraordinaire!* Your proofing rocked, Yori! Um…thanks Quentin. I&E is cool in our book.

Özge, my dearest *şiş,* thanks for the Reds, your steadfast commitment, enduring friendship, and for making the office a riot. Your talents never ceased to amaze me. Dirty M-d! Bad! Citrus (g&t)! Rachel, your contributions were extraordinary; thanks for putting up with us. Ladies (Ö&R)—we made the room HOT! Corey- Σε θελω! Stephen-omygawd! Roar, Gene! With love, I thank my family (Brachnas and Bonns), Lori *(je t'aime!),* Yoshiko, Hughes, Ween, Adam, Kepa, Nikki, Nicole, Leila, and my painter, Dirk *(hola!).* Tim, you are always my inspiration. Dad, your optimism and love see me through. Christopher and Jonathan—may you one day see the wonders of the Aegean. For my loving mother (την καρδια μου; σ'αγαπω).**—EBB**

Eti, my own Athena, I prefer you to all the beaches in Turkey. I never knew old married couples could have so much fun. Our friendship will outlast the Acropolis. Rachel, your wry humor and hard work kept us sane. To M&F, well, at least there was always beer in the fridge. Suzan, *canım,* I lived in Türkiye through you. To the Milbergs, my newly acquired second family, I love you all. Anne *ve* Baba, you provided this book with more information than any tourist office ever could have, *sağol.* And to my true love, Colin, who may have finally discovered my passions, *seni seviyorum.* I haven't read a book this summer, but I've written one.**—ÖG**

Eti and Özge, thanks for a great summer—never a dull moment. Allison, a thousand thanks for all of your help. AnneE, I'm still counting the days. Katie and Pogen, sharing a fan was fun. Corey, Sidi Bou Said has great doors. A big hug to Josh and Dave (my other half). Jen, Anne, and MEs, thanks for keeping us all going. Grant, I'm glad you have a couch. Thanks to my family (and my dogs) for their support. My beloved BJ, thank you for the gift that you have been to me.**—RL**

Editor	Eti Brachna Bonn
Associate Editor	Özge Güzelsu
Assistant Editor	Rachel Lebejko
Managing Editor	Allison Crapo
Publishing Director	Michelle C. Sullivan
Production Manager	Daniel O. Williams
Associate Production Manager	Michael S. Campbell
Cartography Manager	Amanda K. Bean
Editorial Manager	John R. Brooks
Editorial Manager	Allison Crapo
Financial Manager	Stephen P. Janiak
Personnel Manager	Alexander H. Travelli
Publicity Manager	SoRelle B. Braun
Associate Publicity Manager	David Fagundes
Associate Publicity Manager	Elisabeth Mayer
Assistant Cartographer	Jonathan D. Kibera
Assistant Cartographer	Mark C. Staloff
Office Coordinator	Jennifer L. Schuberth
Director of Advertising and Sales	Amit Tiwari
Senior Sales Executives	Andrew T. Rourke
	Nicholas A. Valtz, Charles E. Varner
General Manager	Richard Olken
Assistant General Manager	Anne E. Chisholm

How to Use This Book

The ancients had it a little easier when they traveled—they chose a picturesque spot, built a potential wonder of the world, took off their togas, and stayed a while. Modern day visitors to Greece, Turkey, and Cyprus may encounter a few more diffi-culties; that's where we at *Let's Go* can help. Whether a first-time visitor or a veteran traveler, information like hospital phone numbers and candid accommodations list-ings always come in handy. *Let's Go: Greece and Turkey 1997* has strived to bring you the most comprehensive coverage of the Mediterranean basin to date. We've added maps, revamped the index, and spruced up our already saucy prose.

"Planning" a trip to Greece, Turkey, and Cyprus may be as practical as adding a Corinthian column to the Ayasofya: transportation operates in its own time world (although schedules are often posted, delays are long, frequent, and expected), and office, store, and restaurant hours vary according to the whims (and *siesta* times) of their proprietors. Your best bet may be to prioritize what your travel objectives are—to bask on sultry beaches, stagger from snazzy bars to hip clubs, sip coffee while engrossed in endless games of backgammon, shop until you drop, view some of the world's most intriguing ancient and Byzantine sights, or discover the modern beauty of Europe's periphery. Plan in hand, start flipping through the index, reading the regional introductions and gray boxes, and brushing up on the cultures that have shaped the countries you intend to visit. Having some idea of the regional mores and folk ways is usually a warmly received sign of respect.

The **Essentials** section at the beginning of the guide, and in the beginning of the Greece, Turkey, and Cyprus sections, outline more general information which you'll need before you depart and when you're there. The **regional introductions** offer not only information on country-specific conventions that are important to get-ting around but also histories of the regions. And our **Appendix** provides a quick introduction to some useful phrases in Greek and Turkish.

Destinations are grouped by geographic location to facilitate travel planning. This year, we expanded our coverage of the Turkish Republic of Northern Cyprus and refer to it by its Turkish name, Kıbrıs. Although extensive information about travel-ing within and among regions is provided, a useful technique is to use a larger city as a base for daytrips. From here, you can venture out to some of the smaller towns that lie off the beaten path while still maintaining a high level of comfort and safety.

Within each city, our accommodations, restaurants, clubs, and even sights listings are in the order of what our researchers, in their opinion, have deemed best. We provide detailed prices, hours of operation, street addresses, directions, and phone numbers so that you can have an idea of what shape your inevitably flexible itiner-ary may take. While the capricious nature of schedules in Greece, Turkey, and Cyprus render perfect planning impossible, we provide you with the tools to find the information you will need. We wish you safe and happy travels, and without fur-ther ado: Παμε! *Hadi gidelim!* (Let's Go!)

A NOTE TO OUR READERS

The information for this book is gathered by *Let's Go*'s researchers during the late spring and summer months. Each listing is derived from the assigned researcher's opinion based upon his or her visit at a particular time. The opin-ions are expressed in a candid and forthright manner. Other travelers might dis-agree. Those traveling at a different time may have different experiences since prices, dates, hours, and conditions are always subject to change. You are urged to check beforehand to avoid inconvenience and surprises. Travel always involves a certain degree of risk, especially in low-cost areas. When traveling, especially on a budget, always take particular care to ensure your safety.

ESSENTIALS

Greece, Turkey, and Cyprus are legendary—countries that contain within their cultures, architecture, and even their geography the history of ancient civilizations and mighty empires. Centuries of foreign domination and domestic greatness form a curious juxtaposition that shapes a segue into the modern world. Tourism is a big business here. Major destinations provide a meta-touristic experience, but seclusion can also be found among ancient ruins, beaches, and remote mountain trails.

Plan ahead to get the most out of your vacation, but understand that these countries may not always be accommodating of your itinerary. An astounding amount of travel information is available to best facilitate your trip; stop by your local travel agency or library, or see Useful Information (p. 1).

> A note on nomenclature: throughout the guide, for clarity's sake, we refer to the northern 37% of Cyprus, officially called the "Turkish Republic of Northern Cyprus" (TRNC), as "Kıbrıs" (the Turkish word for Cyprus).

PLANNING YOUR TRIP

■ When To Go

Summer is high tourist season in Greece, Turkey, and Cyprus. If you visit between late July and early September, expect to run with large groups. If you feel annoyed by crowds or taxed by the frantic pace of summer travel, consider visiting during off season (Sept.-May), when inexpensive airfares are easier to obtain and lodging is cheaper. Some facilities and sights may close down, but residents are often more receptive and the weather is far more pleasant. Even during the winter months, some areas continue to be mild. These countries also have winter sports, with ski areas at Parnassos, Mt. Pelion, Metsovo, Bursa, and Troodos. Ferry schedules become more capricious in winter. Mainland travel is less affected by season. Refer to the climate chart in the appendix for average temperatures and rainfall (p. 577).

■ Useful Information

The following organizations and agencies offer a wealth of information. If you don't know where to begin, write a few polite letters. Calling offices directly (or faxing, if you have the means) is always an option and necessary if you're in a rush.

GOVERNMENT INFORMATION OFFICES

Greek National Tourist Organization (GNTO): In **Australia,** 3rd floor, 51-57 Pitt St., Sydney, NSW 2000 (tel. (2) 241 16 63; fax 235 2174). In **Canada,** Head Office, 1300 Bay St., Toronto, Ont. M5R 3K8 (tel. (416) 968-2220; fax 968-6533); 1233 rue de la Montagne, Suite 101, Montréal, Québec, H3G 1Z2 (tel. (514) 871-1535; fax 871-1498; e-mail gnto@ael.com). In **U.K.,** 4 Conduit St., London W1R 0DJ (tel. (171) 734 5997; fax 287 1369). In **U.S.,** Head Office, Olympic Tower, 645 Fifth Ave., 5th Floor, New York, NY 10022 (tel. (212) 421-5777; fax 826-6940); 168 N. Michigan Ave., 6th floor, Chicago, IL 60601 (tel. (312) 782-1084; fax 782-1091); 611 W. Sixth St. #2198, Los Angeles, CA 90017 (tel. (213) 626-6696; fax 489-9744). Provides pamphlets on different regions and tourist literature, including the booklet *General Information About Greece.*

Turkish Cultural and Information Office: In **Australia,** Suite 101, 280 George St., Sydney, NSW 2000 (tel. (2) 223 3055; fax 223 3204). In **Canada,** 360 Albert

USEFUL INFORMATION

The World At a Discount

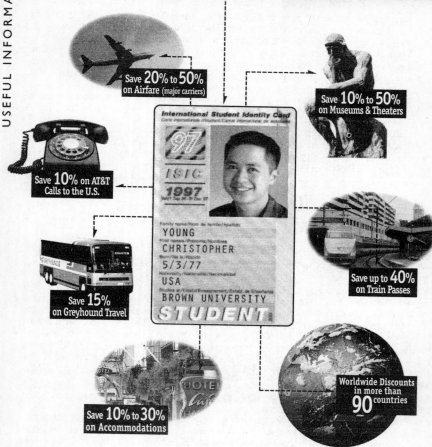

Save **20%** to **50%** on Airfare (major carriers)

Save **10%** to **50%** on Museums & Theaters

Save **10%** on AT&T Calls to the U.S.

Save up to **40%** on Train Passes

Save **15%** on Greyhound Travel

Save **10%** to **30%** on Accommodations

Worldwide Discounts in more than **90** countries

The International Student Identity Card
Your Passport to Discounts & Benefits

With the ISIC, you'll receive discounts on airfare, hotels, transportation, computer services, foreign currency exchange, phone calls, major attractions, and more. You'll also receive basic accident and sickness insurance coverage when traveling outside the U.S. and access to a 24-hour, toll-free Help Line. Call now to locate the issuing office nearest you (over 555 across the U.S.) at:

Free 40-page handbook with each card!

1-888-COUNCIL (toll-free)

For an application and complete discount list, you can also visit us at **http://www.ciee.org/**

CIEE: Council on International Educational Exchange

St., Suite 801, Ottawa, Ontario K1R 7X7 (tel. (613) 230-8654; fax 230-3683). In **U.K.,** 1st floor, Egyptian House, 170-173 Piccadilly, London, W1V 9DD (tel. (071) 355 4207; fax 491 0773; e-mail eb25@cityscape.co.uk). In **U.S.,** Turkish Centre, 821 United Nations Plaza, New York, NY 10017 (tel. (212) 687-2194; fax 599-7568; e-mail tourny@soho.ios.com); 1717 Massachusetts Ave. NW, Suite 306, Washington, D.C. 20036 (tel. (202) 429-9844; fax 429-5649). Supplies information, maps, and regional brochures.

Cyprus Tourism Organization (CCTO): In **Cyprus,** P.O. Box 4535, CY1390, Nicosia, Cyprus (tel. (2) 33 77 15; fax 33 16 64). In **U.K.,** 213 Regent St., London W1R 8DA (tel. (171) 734 25 93; fax 287 65 34; e-mail cto@cyta.com.cy). In **U.S.,** 13 E. 40th St., New York, NY 10016 (tel. (212) 683-5280; fax 683-5282; e-mail gocyprus@aol.com; http://www.wam.umd.edu/~cyprus/tourist.html). The *Cyprus Travellers Handbook* is available.

TRAVEL ORGANIZATIONS

Council on International Educational Exchange (Council), 205 East 42nd St., New York, NY 10017-5706 (888-COUNCIL; fax (212)-822-2699; e-mail info@ciee.org; http://www.ciee.org). A private, non-profit organization, Council administers work, volunteer, academic, and professional programs around the world. They also offer identity cards (including the ISIC and the GO25) and a range of publications, among them the useful magazine *Student Travels* (free). Call or write for more information.

Federation of International Youth Travel Organizations (FIYTO), Bredgade 25H, DK-1260 Copenhagen K, Denmark (tel. (45) 33 33 96 00; fax 33 93 96 76; e-mail mailbox@fiyto.org). An international organization promoting educational, cultural, and social travel for young people. FIYTO sponsors the GO25 Card.

International Student Travel Confederation, Herengracht 479, 1017 BS Amsterdam, The Netherlands (tel. (31) 20 421 2800; fax 20 421 2810; http://www.istc.org; e-mail istcinfo@istc.org). A nonprofit confederation of student travel organizations whose focus is to develop, promote, and facilitate travel among young people and students.

USEFUL PUBLICATIONS

Adventurous Traveler Bookstore, P.O. Box 1468, Williston, VT 05495 (tel. (801) 860-6776; fax 860-6607, or both at (800) 282-3963; e-mail books@atbook.com; http://www.gorp.com/atbook.htm). Free 40-page catalogue upon request. Specializes in outdoor adventure travel books and maps.

Forsyth Travel Library, P.O. Box 480800, Kansas City, MO 64148 (tel. (800) 367-7984; fax (816) 942-6969; http://www.forsyth.com). Mail order with maps, rail, ferry schedules, and rail ticket and pass sales/reservations. Sells the *Thomas Cook European Timetable* for European train departures, arrivals, and a map of routes.

Travel Books & Language Center, Inc., 4931 Cordell Ave., Bethesda, MD 20814 (tel. (800) 220-2665; fax (301) 951-8546; e-mail travelbks@aol.com). Atlases, dictionaries, cassettes, and a wide selection of maps.

INTERNET RESOURCES

There are a number of ways to access the **Internet.** Most popular are commercial internet providers, such as **America Online** (tel. (800) 827-6394) and **Compuserve** (tel. (800) 433-0389). Many employers and schools also offer gateways to the Internet, often at no cost (unlike the corporate gateways above). The Internet itself can be used in many different forms, but the most useful to'net-surfing budget travelers are the World Wide Web and Usenet newsgroups.

The World Wide Web

Increasingly the Internet forum of choice, the **World Wide Web** provides its users with graphics and sound, as well as textual information. This, and the huge proliferation of "web pages," has made the Web the most active and exciting of the destinations on the Internet. The introduction of **search engines** (services that search for web pages under specific subjects) has aided the search process. **Lycos** (http://a2z.lycos.com) and **Infoseek** (http://guide.infoseek.com) are two of the more popular. **Yahoo!** is a slightly more organized search engine; check out its travel links at http://www.yahoo.com/Recreation/Travel. It is often better to know a good site, and start "surfing" from there, through links from one web page to another.

Dr. Memory's Favorite Travel Pages (http://www.access.digex.net/~drmemory/cyber_travel.html).Links to hundreds of different travel pages.

Rent-A-Wreck's Travel Links (http://www.rent-a-wreck.com/raw/travlist.htm). Contrary to what its name implies, very good and very complete.

Big World Magazine (http://boss.cpcnet.com/personal/bigworld/bigworld.htm). A budget travel magazine with a great collection of links to travel pages.

The CIA World Factbook (http://www.odci.gov/cia/publications/95fact). Tons of vital statistics on the country you want to visit.

Shoestring Travel (http://www.stratpub.com). A travel magazine, with feature articles, links, user exchange, and accommodations information.

The Interactive Travel Guide (http://www.developnet.com/travel). Began as *Cheap Travel Page,* and has since expanded to more than low cost travel.

■ Documents and Formalities

File all applications weeks or months in advance. The agency might deem your applications inadequate and return them, so leave enough time to resubmit them. Apply off season (August to December) for speedier service.

EMBASSIES AND CONSULATES

Greek Embassy: In **Australia,** 9 Turrana St., Yarralumla, Canberra, ACT 2600 (tel. (6) 273-3011; fax 273-2620). In **Canada,** 80 MacLaren St., Ottawa, Ont. K2P 0K6 (tel. (613) 238-6271; fax 238-5676). In **Great Britain,** 1A Holland Park, London W11 3TP (tel. (171) 229 3850; fax 229 7221). In **Ireland,** One Upper Pembroke St., Dublin 2 (tel. (1) 676-7254; fax 661-8892). In **South Africa,** 995 Pretorius St., Arcadia 0083, Pretoria (tel. (12) 437-351, -3; fax 434-313). In **U.S.,** 2221 Mass. Ave. NW, Washington, D.C. 20008 (tel. (202) 939-5800; fax 939-5824, gremb@sysnet.net.com).

Greek Consulates: In **Australia:** 1st floor, 366 King William St., **Adelaide** 5000, S.A. (tel. (8) 211-8066; fax 211 8820); Stanhill House, 34 Queens Road, **Melbourne** 3004, Vic. (tel. (03) 9866-4524,-5; fax 9866-4933); 20th floor, 15 Castlereagh St., **Sydney,** N.S.W. 2000 (tel. (2) 221-2388; fax 221-1423); 16 St. George's Terrace, **Perth,** W.A. 6000 (tel. (9) 325-6608; fax 325-2940). In **Canada:** 1170 Place du Frère André, 3rd floor, **Montréal,** Québec H3B 3C6 (tel. (514) 875-2119; fax 875-8781); 365 Blue St. E, Suite 1800, **Toronto,** Ont. M4W 3L4 (tel. (416) 515-0133; fax 515-0209); 500-688 West Hastings, **Vancouver,** B.C. V6B 1P1 (tel. (604) 681-1381; fax 681-6656). In **U.S.:** 69 East 79th St., **New York,** NY 10021 (tel. (212) 988-5500; fax 734-8492); 650 North St. Clair St., **Chicago,** IL 60611 (tel. (312) 335-3915; fax 335-3958); 2441 Gough St., **San Francisco,** CA 94123 (tel. (415) 775-2102; fax 776-6815); 12424 Wilshire Blvd., Suite 800, **Los Angeles,** CA 90025 (tel. (310) 826-5555; fax 826-8670); 86 Beacon St., **Boston,** MA 02108, open Mon.-Fri. 9am-1pm, Wed. 2pm-5pm, tel. (617) 523-0100; fax 523-0511); Tower Place, Suite 1670, 3340 Peachtree Rd. NE, **Atlanta,** GA 30326 (tel. (404) 261-3391; fax 262-2798); 1360 Post Oak Blvd., Suite 2480, **Houston,** TX 77056 (tel. (713) 840-7522; fax 840-0614); World Trade Center, 2 Canal St., Suite 2318, **New Orleans,** LA 70130 (tel. (504) 523-1167; fax 524-5610). In **New Zealand,** 5-7 Willeston St., 10th floor, P.O. Box 24066, Wellington (tel. (4) 473-7775; fax 473-7441).

Turkish Embassy: In **U.S.,** 1714 Mass. Ave. NW, Washington, D.C. 20036 (tel. (202) 659-0742). In **Canada,** 197 Wurtemburg St., Ottawa, Ont. K1N 8L9 (tel. (613) 789-4044; fax 230-3683). In **U.K.,** 43 Belgrave Sq., London SW1 X8PA (tel. (171) 393 0202; fax (0171) 393 0066). In **Ireland,** 11 Clyde Rd. Ballsbridge, Dublin 4 (tel. (01) 668 5240; fax 6685 014). In **Australia,** 60 Muggaway, Red Hill ACT 2603 (tel. (6) 295 0227; fax 293 6592). In **New Zealand,** 15-17 Murphy St., P.O. Box 12248, Thorndon-Wellington (tel. (4) 472-1290 or -2; fax 472-1277). In **South Africa,** 1067 Church St., Hatfield 0083 Pretoria (tel. (12) 342 6053), or P.O. Box 56014 Arcadia 0007.

Turkish Consulates: In **U.S.:** 360 N. Michigan Ave. #1405, **Chicago,** IL 60601 (tel. (312) 263-1295; fax (312) 263-1449); 4801 Wilshire Blvd. #310, **Los Angeles,** CA 90010 (tel. (213) 937-0110; fax (213) 932-0061); 1990 Post Oak Blvd. #1300, **Houston, TX** 77056 (tel. (713) 622-5849; fax 623-6639; e-mail turcon@ix.netcom.com).

Cypriot Embassy: In **Australia,** 30 Beale Crescent, Deakin-Canberra ACT 2600 (tel. (6) 281-0832, -4; fax 281-0860). In **Canada,** Attn: Mr. Michael Paidoussis, Honorary Consul of Cyprus, 2930 Rue Edouard Mont Petit, Suite PH2, Montréal, Québec H3T 1J7 (tel. (514) 735-7233). In **U.K.,** 93 Park St., London W1Y 4ET (tel. (71) 499 82 72; fax 491 0691). In **U.S.,** 2211 R St. NW, Washington, D.C. 20008 (tel. (202) 462-5772).

Northern Cyprus Representative Offices: In **Canada,** 328 Highway East, Suite 308, Richmond Hill, Ontario L4B 3P7. In **U.K.,** 28 Cockspur St., London SW1Y 5BN (tel. (171) 839 4577; fax 830 5282). In **U.S.:** 821 United Nations Plaza, 6th floor, **New York,** NY 10017 (tel. (212) 687-2350; fax 949-6872); 1667 K St., Suite 690, **Washington,** D.C. 20006 (tel. (202) 887-6198; fax 467-0685; e-mail kktc@aol.com).

PASSPORTS

Citizens of the United States, Canada, the United Kingdom, Ireland, Australia, New Zealand, and South Africa all need valid passports to enter Greece, Turkey, and Cyprus, and to re-enter their own country. If you plan a long stay, you may want to register your passport with the nearest embassy or consulate; notify them or the police immediately if your passport is lost or stolen. Your consulate can issue you a new passport or temporary traveling papers. If you lose your passport in İstanbul, first go to your consulate to get a citizen certificate and then to the tourist police.

Before you leave, as a safeguard, photocopy the page of your passport that contains your photograph and identifying information. (Especially important is your **passport number.**) Also, copy all the pages in your passport that are stamped with visas, and leave a duplicate with a friend. Consulates recommend that you carry an expired passport or an official copy of your birth certificate in a separate part of your luggage from other documents. U.S. citizens can request a duplicate birth certificate from the Bureau of Vital Records and Statistics in their region of birth.

Losing your passport can be a nightmare. A replacement may take weeks, and may be valid only for a limited time. Immediately notify the local police and the nearest embassy or consulate of your home government. Provide all the information that you had previously recorded and photocopied, and show identification and proof of citizenship. Some consulates issue new passports within two days. In an emergency, ask for immediate temporary traveling papers that will permit you to return to your home country. Remember, your passport is a public document that belongs to your nation's government. You may have to surrender your passport to a foreign government official; if you don't get it back in a reasonable time, inform the nearest mission, consulate, or embassy of your home country.

United States Citizens may apply for a passport, valid for 10 years (five years if under 18) at any federal or state **courthouse** or **post office** authorized to accept passport applications, or at a **U.S. Passport Agency,** located in Boston, Chicago, Honolulu, Houston, Los Angeles, Miami, New Orleans, New York, Philadelphia, San Francisco, Seattle, Stamford, or Washington D.C. Potential applicants should refer to the "U.S. Government, State Department" section of the telephone directory or the local post office for addresses. The following must be submitted: (1) proof of U.S. citizenship (a certified birth certificate, certification of naturalization or of citizenship, or a previous passport); (2) identification bearing the applicant's signature and either a photograph or physical description (e.g. an unexpired driver's license or passport, student ID card, or government ID card); and (3) two identical, passport-size (2" x 2") photographs with a white or off-white background taken within the last six months. It will cost US$65 (under 18 US$40). Passports can be renewed by mail or in person for US$55. Processing takes two to four weeks. Passport agencies offer **rush service** for a surcharge of US$30, if the applicant has proof that he or she is departing within ten working days (e.g., an airplane ticket or itinerary). Abroad, a U.S. embassy or consulate can usually issue a new passport, given proof of citizenship. If a passport is lost or stolen in the U.S., it should be reported in writing to: Passport Services, U.S. Department of State, 111 19th St., NW, Washington D.C., 20522-1705 or to the nearest passport agency. For more information, contact the U.S. Passport Information's **24-hour recorded message** (tel. (202) 647-0518).

Canada Application forms in English and French are available at all **passport offices, post offices,** and most **travel agencies.** Citizens may apply in person at any one of 28 regional Passport Offices across Canada. Canadian citizens residing abroad should contact the nearest Canadian embassy or consulate. Along with the application form, a citizen must provide: (1) citizenship documentation (an original Canadian birth certificate, or a certificate of Canadian citizenship); (2) two identical passport photos taken within the last year; (3) any previous Canadian passport; and (4) a CDN$60 fee (paid in cash, money order, or certified check) to Passport Office, Ottawa, Ont. K1A OG3. All above information is outlined in both English and French on the application form. Processing takes approximately five business days for in-person applications and three weeks for mailed ones. A passport is valid for five years, and a new one must be purchased when the old one expires. If a passport is lost abroad, Canadians must be able to prove citizenship with another document. For additional information, call (800) 567-6868 (open 24hr.; from Canada only) or call the Passport Office at (819) 994-3500. In Metro Toronto, call (416) 973-3251. Montréalers should dial (514) 283-2152. Refer to the booklet *Bon Voyage, But...* for further help and a list of Canadian embassies and consulates abroad.

Britain British citizens, British Dependent Territories citizens, British Nationals (overseas), and British Overseas citizens may apply for a **full passport.** For a full passport, valid for 10 years (five years if under 16), apply in person or by mail to a passport office, located in London, Liverpool, Newport, Peterborough, Glasgow, or Belfast. The fee is UK£18. The London office offers same-day, walk-in rush service—arrive early.

Ireland Citizens can apply for a passport by mail to either the **Department of Foreign Affairs,** Passport Office, Setanta Centre, Molesworth St., Dublin 2 (tel. (1) 671 16 33), or the **Passport Office,** 1A South Mall, Cork (tel. (021) 627 25 25). Obtain an application at a local Garda station or request one from a passport office. The new **Passport Express Service** offers a two week turn-around and is available through post offices for IR£3. Passports cost IR£45 and are valid for 10 years. Citizens under 18 or over 65 can request a three-year passport that costs IR£10.

Australia Citizens must apply for a passport in person at a post office, a passport office, or an Australian diplomatic mission overseas. An appointment may be necessary. **Passport offices** are located in Adelaide, Brisbane, Canberra City, Darwin, Hobart, Melbourne, Newcastle, Perth, and Sydney. A parent may file an application for a child who is under 18 and unmarried. Application fees are adjusted frequently. For more information, call toll-free (in Australia) 13 12 32.

New Zealand Applications for passports are available in New Zealand from travel agents and **Department of Internal Affairs Link Centres,** and overseas from New Zealand embassies, high commissions, and consulates. Applications may be lodged at Link Centres and at overseas posts, or forwarded to the Passport Office,

P.O. Box 10-526, Wellington, New Zealand. Processing time is 10 working days from receipt of application. The application fee for an adult passport is NZ$80 in New Zealand, and NZ$130 overseas for applications under the standard service.

South Africa Citizens can apply for a passport at any Home Affairs Office. Two photos, either a birth certificate or an identity book, and a $12 (SAR80) fee must accompany a completed application. For further information, contact the nearest **Department of Home Affairs Office.**

ENTRANCE REQUIREMENTS AND VISAS

Citizens of the U.S., Canada, E.U. members, Australia, and New Zealand do not need to get a visa ahead of time to visit **Greece.** Non-E.U. members will be automatically granted leave for a three-month stay (not valid for employment), but South Africans do need a visa. Apply to stay longer at least 20 days prior to the three-month expiration date at the **Aliens Bureau,** 175 Alexandras Ave., Athens 11522 (tel. 642 3094), or check with a Greek embassy or consulate. Bona fide tourists with valid passports from Australia, Canada, Great Britain, Ireland, New Zealand, and the U.S. do not need a visa to enter either Cyprus or Northern Cyprus for stays of up to 90 days; South Africans and Turks do need visas (fee: C£5). It is suggested that tourists wishing to stay longer leave and then re-enter. Citizens of Australia, Canada, and New Zealand do not need a visa for visits to **Turkey** of up to three months. South African nationals need a visa, and they may stay up to one month. Three-month sticker visas, not valid for employment, are available for cash at ports of entry for citizens of the U.S. ($20), U.K. (£5), and Ireland.

CUSTOMS: ENTERING

Greece Upon entering Greece, you must declare cameras, typewriters, portable radios, and musical instruments. One of each may be brought in duty-free as long as they will be taken with you upon departure. You must also register all currency above $1000, or you may not take it with you when you leave. Duty-free limits include: 10kg of foodstuffs and beverages; 200 cigarettes, 50 cigars, or 250g tobacco; 5 boxes of matches; 2 packs of playing cards; and 1L of alcoholic beverage or 2L of wine. Children under 15 may bring in 5000dr worth of gift articles, everyone else up to 9000dr worth. Bicycles must be declared when entering; they may be used freely throughout, but they must be taken with you when exiting the country. Weapons and explosives are strictly prohibited. Prescription medications for personal use are the only admissible drugs, and even these may need to be accompanied by the prescription.

Turkey and Kıbrıs Travelers entering Turkey or Kıbrıs may bring along: one camera and five rolls of film, one video camera with five blank cassettes, one personal stereo and five cassettes or compact discs, one video player or slide projector, and no more than three musical instruments, 200 cigarettes (or 50 cigars), 200g tobacco (or 50g chewing tobacco), 1.5 kg coffee, 1.5kg instant coffee, 500g tea, 1kg chocolate, 1kg sweets, and five 100cc or seven 70cc bottles of wine and/or spirits. In addition to these allowances, it is possible to purchase 400 cigarettes, 100 cigars, and 500g pipe tobacco from Turkish duty-free shops on entering the country. No sharp instruments or firearms of any sort may be brought in, and under no circumstances should you bring any illegal drugs into Turkey or Kıbrıs (see DRUGS AND ALCOHOL, p. 16). To avoid problems when you transport prescription drugs, ensure that the bottles are clearly marked, and carry a copy of the prescription to show the customs officer.

Republic of Cyprus Cyprus allows travelers to bring in duty-free not more than 250g tobacco, 1L spirits, ¾L wine, and 0.3L perfume. Other personal effects are permitted, up to a total value of C£50. If a traveler enters Cyprus after a stay abroad of less than 72 hours, he or she is allowed to import free of duty only 250g of tobacco. Travelers importing more than $1000 worth of foreign currency should declare it on form D (NR), especially if they want to take it out of the country later. Firearms, live animals, ammunition, plants, agricultural products, and uncooked meat are prohibited. Illegal drugs, of course, are not to be imported.

CUSTOMS: GOING HOME

Upon returning home, you must declare all articles you acquired abroad and must pay a duty on the value of those articles that exceed the allowance established by your country's customs service. Holding onto **receipts** for purchases made abroad will help establish values when you return. It is absolutely forbidden to export antiques from Greece, Turkey, or Cyprus, though shopkeepers may try to convince you otherwise. Customs officials may require, even as your plane is boarding for departure, that you produce a signed statement from a museum curator stating that your purchase is not an antique. If you purchase anything really old (over 100 years) have the shop-owner draft a signed statement saying that what you bought can be legally exported. Goods and gifts purchased at duty-free shops abroad are not exempt from duty or sales tax at your return; you must declare these items as well. "Duty-free" merely means that you need not pay a tax in the country of purchase.

United States Citizens returning home may bring US$400 worth of accompanying goods duty-free and must pay a 10% tax on the next US$1000. You must declare all purchases, so have sales slips ready. Goods are considered duty-free if they are for personal or household use (this includes gifts) and cannot include more than 100 cigars, 200 cigarettes (1 carton), and 1L of wine or liquor. You must be over 21 to bring liquor into the U.S. If you mail home personal goods of U.S. origin, you can avoid duty charges by marking the package "American goods returned." For more information, consult the brochure *Know Before You Go,* available from the U.S. Customs Service, Box 7407, Washington D.C. 20044 (tel. (202) 927-6724).

Canada Citizens who remain abroad for at least one week may bring back up to CDN$500 worth of goods duty-free once per calendar year. Canadian citizens or residents who travel for a period between 48 hours and six days can bring back up to CDN$200 with the exception of tobacco and alcohol. You are permitted to ship goods except tobacco and alcohol home under this exemption as long as you declare them when you arrive. Citizens of legal age (which varies by province) may import in-person up to 200 cigarettes, 50 cigars, 400g loose tobacco, 400 tobacco sticks, 1.14L wine or alcohol, and 24 355mL cans/bottles of beer; the value of these products is included in the CDN$500. For more information, write to Canadian Customs, 2265 St. Laurent Blvd., Ottawa, Ontario K1G 4K3 (tel. (613) 993-0534).

U.K. Citizens or visitors arriving in the U.K. from outside the EU must declare any goods in excess of the following allowances: 200 cigarettes, 100 cigarillos, 50 cigars, or 250g tobacco; still table wine (2L); strong liqueurs over 22% volume (1L), or fortified or sparkling wine, other liqueurs (2L); perfume (60 cc/mL); toilet water (250 cc/mL); and UK£136 worth of all other goods including gifts and souvenirs. You must be over 17 to import liquor or tobacco. These allowances also apply to duty-free purchases within the EU, except for the last category, other goods, which then has an allowance of UK£71. For more info about U.K. customs, contact Her Majesty's Customs and Excise, Custom House, Nettleton Road, Heathrow Airport, Hounslow, Middlesex TW6 2LA (tel. (0181) 910-3744; fax 910-3765).

Ireland Citizens must declare everything in excess of IR£34 (IR£17 per traveler under 15 years of age) obtained outside the EU or duty- and tax-free in the EU above the following allowances: 200 cigarettes, 100 cigarillos, 50 cigars, or 250g tobacco; 1L liquor or 2L wine; 2L still wine; 50g perfume; and 250mL toilet water. Goods obtained duty and tax paid in another EU country up to a value of IR£460 (IR£115 per traveler under 15) will not be subject to additional customs duties. For more information, contact The Revenue Commissioners, Dublin Castle (tel. (01) 679 27 77; fax 671 20 21; e-mail taxes@ior.ie; WWW http:www.revenue.ie) or The Collector of Customs and Excise, The Custom House, Dublin 1.

Australia Citizens may import AUS$400 (under 18 AUS$200) of goods duty-free, in addition to the allowance of 1.125L alcohol and 250 cigarettes or 250g tobacco. You must be over 18 to import either of these. There is no limit to the amount of Australian and/or foreign cash that may be brought into or taken out of the country. Amounts of AUS$5000 or more, or the equivalent in foreign currency, must be reported. All foodstuffs and animal products must be declared on arrival. For information, contact the Regional Director, Australian Customs Service, GPO Box 8, Sydney NSW 2001 (tel. (02) 2132000; fax 2134000).

New Zealand Citizens may bring home up to NZ$700 worth of goods duty-free if they are intended for personal use or are unsolicited gifts. The concession is 200 cigarettes (1 carton) or 250g tobacco or 50 cigars or a combination of all three not to exceed 250g. You may also bring in 4.5L of beer or wine and 1.125L of liquor. Only travelers over 17 may bring tobacco or alcoholic beverages into the country. For more information, consult the *New Zealand Customs Guide for Travelers,* available from customs offices, or contact New Zealand Customs, 50 Anzac Ave., Box 29, Auckland (tel. (09) 377 35 20; fax 309 29 78).

South Africa Citizens may import duty-free: 400 cigarettes; 50 cigars; 250g tobacco; 2L wine; 1L of spirits; 250mL toilet water; and 50mL perfume; and other items up to a value of SAR500. Amounts exceeding this limit but not SAR10,000 are dutiable at 20%. Certain items require a duty higher than the standard 20%. Goods acquired abroad and sent to the Republic as unaccompanied baggage do not qualify for any allowances. You may not export or import South African bank notes in excess of SAR500. Persons who require more information can address their inquiries to the Commissioner for Customs and Excise, Private Bag X47, Pretoria 0001. This agency distributes the pamphlet *South African Customs Information,* for visitors and residents who travel abroad. South Africans residing in the U.S. should contact the Embassy of South Africa, 3051 Massachusetts Ave., NW, Washington D.C. 20008 (tel. (202) 232-4400; fax 244-9417) or the South African Home Annex, 3201 New Mexico Ave. #380, NW, Washington D.C. 20016 (tel. (202) 966-1650).

YOUTH, STUDENT, & TEACHER IDENTIFICATION

Always carry at least two forms of ID on your person, including at least one photo ID. A passport combined with a driver's license or birth certificate serves as adequate proof of your identity and citizenship and will help when cashing traveler's checks. Never carry your passport, ticket, identification, money, traveler's checks, insurance, and credit cards together, or you risk being left entirely without ID or funds in case of theft or loss. Carry a few extra passport-size photos.

The **International Student Identity Card (ISIC)** is the most widely accepted form of student identification. The card can procure you discounts for sights, theaters, museums, accommodations, train, ferry, and airplane travel, and other services. A school ID may also help you with student discounts in Greece, Turkey, and Cyprus, although some Turkish establishments may not accept it if they don't recognize the institution. The ISIC also provides accident insurance of up to US$3000 with no daily limit. In addition, cardholders have access to a toll-free Traveler's Assistance hotline whose staff can provide help in medical, legal, and financial emergencies.

Many student travel offices issue ISICs, including Council Travel, STA Travel, and Let's Go Travel in the U.S.; Travel CUTS in Canada; and any of the organizations under the auspices of the International Student Travel Confederation (ISTC) around the world (p. 3). When you apply for the card, request a copy of the *International*

Student Identity Card Handbook, which lists by country some of the available discounts. You can also write to Council for a copy. The card is valid from September to December of the following year. The fee is US$18. Applicants must be at least 12 years old and degree-seeking students of a secondary or post-secondary school. Because of the proliferation of phony ISICs, many airlines and some other services require other proof of student identity: a signed letter from the registrar attesting to your student status and stamped with the school seal and/or your school ID card.

Federation of International Youth Travel Organizations (FIYTO) issues a discount card to travelers who are under 26 but not students. Known as the **GO25 Card,** this one-year card offers many of the same benefits as the ISIC, and most organizations that sell the ISIC also sell the GO25 Card. To apply, you will need a passport, valid driver's license, or copy of a birth certificate; and a passport-sized photo with your name printed on the back. The fee is US$16, CDN$15, or UK£5. For information, contact Council in the U.S. or FIYTO in Denmark.

The US$19 **International Teacher Identity Card (ITIC)** offers similar but limited discounts, as well as medical insurance coverage. (WWW http:\\www.istc.org) see (p. 3).

DRIVING PERMITS AND INSURANCE

Unless you have a valid driver's license from an EU country, you must have an **International Driving Permit (IDP)** to drive in Greece, Turkey, or Cyprus. A valid driver's license from your home country must always accompany the permit. Even where you don't need an IDP to drive, having one may simplify dealings with non-English-speaking police if you're stranded or in an accident.

Your IDP must be issued in your own country before you depart. U.S. license holders can obtain an International Driving Permit (US$10), valid for one year, at any **American Automobile Association (AAA)** office or by writing to the main office, AAA Florida, Travel Agency Services Department, 1000 AAA Drive (mail stop 28), Heathrow, FL 32746-5080 (tel. (407) 444-4245; fax 444-4247). For further information, contact a local AAA office.

Canadian license holders can obtain an IDP (CDN$10) through any **Canadian Automobile Association (CAA)** branch office in Canada, or by writing to CAA Central Ontario, 60 Commerce Valley Drive East, Thornhill, Ontario L3T 7P9 (tel. (416) 221-4300).The **Greek Automobile Touring Club (ELPA),** in Athens at both 2-4 Messogion St. (tel. 779 1615) and 6 Amerikis St. (tel. 363 8632), will also issue an IDP upon presentation of a valid driver's license, passport, and one photograph.

Most credit cards cover standard insurance. If you rent, lease, or borrow a car abroad, you will need a **green card,** or **International Insurance Certificate,** to prove that you have liability insurance. Obtain it through the car rental agency; most of them include coverage in their prices. If you lease a car, you can obtain a green card from the dealer. Some travel agents offer the card, and it may be available at the border. Verify whether your auto insurance applies abroad; even if it does, you will still need a green card to certify this to foreign officials.

■ Money Matters

CURRENCY AND EXCHANGE

Before leaving home, exchange US$50 or so for the currency of Greece, Turkey, or Cyprus. You'll pay a higher exchange rate (and you may have to call your bank to find Greek *drachmae,* Turkish *lira,* or Cypriot pounds), but this will save time and exasperation, especially if you arrive when the banks are closed. When exchanging currency, you'll usually lose money due to commissions and high exchange rates; ordinarily exchange in fairly large sums in order to minimize the loss.

Greek *drachmae* are issued in both paper notes (500, 1000, 5000, and 10,000dr) and coins (10, 20, 50, and 100dr). If you're carrying more than US$1000 in cash

A note on prices: throughout the guide, we quote prices effective in the summer of 1996. Since inflation and exchange rates fluctuate considerably, be advised that listed prices could rise by an additional 10-30% by 1997. Because inflation in Turkey generally keeps pace with the devaluation of the lira, prices are quoted in U.S. dollars and should be slightly more stable than those in Greece.

when you enter Greece, you must declare it upon entry in order to export it legally (this does not apply to traveler's checks). You can bring up to US$445 worth of *drachmae* into Greece. In addition, no more than 20,000 *drachmae* can be taken out of the country when you leave. It is not difficult to exchange money in Greece. Commission-free ATMs are located in most major cities. Remember that because Greece is a member of the European Union, assorted goods are subject to the **Value-Added Tax (VAT)** of approximately 18%.

The official currency in Turkey and Kıbrıs is the Turkish *lira* (TL). Coins are divided into 50, 1000, 2500, 5000, 10,000, and 25,000 *lira* pieces, and paper currency comes in denominations of 5000, 10,000, 20,000, 50,000, 100,000, 250,000, 500,000, and 1,000,000 *lira* notes. It is hard to get change for bills of 250,000TL or more at museum entrances and cheap restaurants. Once in Turkey, currency can be exchanged almost anywhere, but you get the best rates at banks and exchange bureaus. Turkey has 24-hour currency exchanges at border crossings, major airports, and train stations; major tourist areas have places to change money on weekends. Even better, commission-free 24-hour ATM machines are centrally located in the larger cities. Hold on to exchange slips, since you may have to present them when you're re-converting your cash. If you take gifts out of Turkey, you may have to prove that they were bought with legally exchanged foreign currency. There is no limit to the amount of foreign currency that can be brought into Turkey, but no more than US$5000 in *lira* may be brought into or taken out of the country. If you are coming from Greece, exchange your money before arriving. The banks that accept *drachmae* exchange them at an absurdly high rate. Value-Added Tax (abbreviated KDV in Turkey) is roughly 15%.

The main unit of currency in the Republic of Cyprus is the pound (£), which is divided into 100 cents. Coins come in 1, 2, 5, 10, 20, and 50 cent sizes; banknotes in denominations of £1, 5, 10, and 20. Cyprus imposes no limit on the amount of foreign currency that may be imported upon entering the country, but amounts in excess of US$1000 should be declared on Customs form D (NR). No more than £50 in Cypriot currency may be brought into or taken out of the country. Cyprus charges 8% VAT, which quoted prices do not necessarily include.

TRAVELER'S CHECKS

Traveler's checks are one of the safer and lesser troublesome means of carrying funds. Several agencies and many banks sell them, usually for face value plus a 1% commission. (Members of the American Automobile Association can get American Express checks commission-free through AAA). American Express and Visa are the most widely recognized, though other major checks are sold, exchanged, cashed, and refunded with almost equal ease. Keep in mind that in small towns, traveler's checks are less readily accepted than in cities with large tourist industries. Nonetheless, there will probably be at least one place in every town where you can exchange them for local currency. If you're ordering your checks, do so well in advance, especially if you are requesting large sums. Each agency provides refunds if your checks are lost or stolen, and many provide additional services. (Note that you may need a police report verifying the loss or theft.) You should expect a fair amount of red tape and delay in the event of theft or loss of traveler's checks. To expedite the refund process, you should: keep your check receipts separate from your checks and store them in a safe place or with a traveling companion; record check numbers when you cash them and leave a list of check numbers with someone at home; and ask for a list of refund centers when you buy your checks. Keep a separate supply of cash or traveler's checks for emergencies. Be sure never to countersign your checks until you're prepared to cash them and always be sure to bring your passport with you when you plan to use the checks.

American Express: Call (800) 221-7282 in the U.S. and Canada; in the U.K. (0800) 52 13 13; in New Zealand (0800) 44 10 68; in Australia (008) 25 19 02. Elsewhere, call U.S. collect (801) 964-6665. American Express traveler's cheques are now available in 11 currencies: Australian, British, Canadian, Dutch, French, German, Japanese, Saudi Arabian, Spanish, Swiss, and U.S. They are the most widely recognized worldwide and the easiest to replace if lost or stolen. Checks can be purchased for a small fee at American Express Travel Service Offices, banks, and American Automobile Association offices (AAA members can buy the checks commission-free). Cardmembers can also purchase cheques at American Express Dispensers at Travel Service Offices at airports and by ordering them via phone (tel. (800) ORDER-TC (673-3782)). American Express offices cash their cheques commission-free (except where prohibited by national governments), although they often offer slightly worse rates than banks.

Citicorp: Call (800) 645-6556 in the U.S. and Canada; in the U.K. (44) 181 297 4781; from elsewhere call U.S. collect (813) 623-1709. Sells both Citicorp and Citicorp Visa traveler's checks in U.S., Australian, and Canadian dollars, British pounds, German marks, Spanish pesetas, and Japanese yen. Commission is 1-2% on check purchases. Checkholders are automatically enrolled for 45 days in the **Travel Assist Program** (hotline tel. (800) 250-4377 or collect (202) 296-8728) which provides travelers with English-speaking doctor, lawyer, and interpreter referrals as well as check refund assistance and general travel information. Citicorp's **World Courier Service** guarantees hand-delivery of traveler's checks when a refund location is not convenient. Call 24hr. a day, 7 days a week.

Visa: Call (800) 227-6811 in the U.S.; in the U.K. (0800) 895 492; from anywhere else in the world call (01733 318 949) which is a pay call, but you can reverse the charges. Call any of the above numbers; if you give them your zip code, they will tell you where the closest office to you is to purchase their traveler's checks. Any kind of Visa traveler's checks can be reported lost at the Visa number.

CREDIT CARDS

Credit cards can be either invaluable or a frustrating nuisance. Major credit cards—**MasterCard** and **Visa** are the most welcomed—instantly extract cash advances from associated banks and teller machines throughout Western Europe (and elsewhere, though it varies by country) in local currency. This can be a great bargain because credit card companies get the wholesale exchange rate, which is generally 5% better than the retail rate used by banks and even better than that used by other currency exchange establishments. **American Express** cards also work in some stores and ATMs, as well as at AmEx offices and major airports. All such machines require a **Personal Identification Number (PIN),** which credit cards holders in the U. S do not usually activate. You must ask American Express, MasterCard, or Visa to assign you one before you leave; without this PIN, you will be unable to withdraw cash with your card abroad. Keep in mind that MasterCard and Visa have different names elsewhere; some cashiers may not know this until they check their manuals.

American Express (tel. (800) CASH-NOW (528-4800)) has a hefty annual fee (US$55) but offers a number of services. AmEx cardholders can cash personal checks at AmEx offices abroad. U.S. Assist, a 24-hour hotline offering medical and legal assistance in emergencies, is also available (tel. (800) 554-2639 in U.S. and Canada; from abroad call U.S. collect (301) 214-8228). Cardholders can also take advantage of the American Express Travel Service; benefits include assistance in changing airline, hotel, and car rental reservations, sending mailgrams and international cables, and holding your mail at one of the more than 1700 AmEx offices around the world.

MasterCard (tel. (800) 999-0454) and **Visa** (tel. (800) 336-8472) are issued in cooperation with individual banks and some other organizations.

CASH CARDS

Cash cards—popularly called **Automated Teller Machine (ATM)** cards—are widespread in Europe and elsewhere. Depending on the system that your bank at home uses, you will probably be able to access your own personal bank account whenever you're in need of funds. Happily, the ATM machines get the same wholesale exchange rate as credit cards. Despite these perks, do some research before relying too heavily on automation. There is often a limit on the amount of money you can withdraw per day, and computer network failures are not uncommon. Be sure to memorize your PIN code in numeral form since machines abroad often don't have letters on the keys (and in Greece, they appear in the Greek alphabet). Also, if your PIN is longer than four digits, be sure to ask your bank whether the first four digits will work, or whether you need a new number.

The two international money networks you should know about are **Cirrus** (U.S. tel. (800) 4-CIRRUS (424-7787)) and **PLUS** (U.S. tel. (800) 843-7587)). Cirrus now has international cash machines in 80 countries and territories. It charges $1-2 to withdraw non-domestically, depending on your bank. PLUS is not quite as extensive, only covering 51 countries. If you can swing it, it may be a good idea to carry two cards, one linked to each network. That way you're covered regardless of which system covers your particular area.

GETTING MONEY FROM HOME

One of the easier ways to get money from home is to bring an **American Express** card. AmEx allows cardholders to draw cash from their checking accounts at any of its major offices and many of its representatives' offices, up to US$1000 every 21 days (no service charge, no interest). AmEx also offers **Express Cash,** with over 100,000 ATMs located in airports, hotels, banks, office complexes, and shopping areas around the world. Express Cash withdrawals are automatically debited from the Cardmember's specified bank account or line of credit. Cardholders may withdraw up to $1000 in a seven day period. There is a 2% transaction fee for each cash withdrawal with a $2.50 minimum. To enroll in Express Cash, Cardmembers may call (800) 227-4669 (CASH NOW). Outside the U.S. call collect (904) 565-7875.Unless using the AmEx service, avoid cashing checks in foreign currencies; they usually take weeks and a US$30 fee to clear. You can also get a **cash advance** on your MasterCard and VISA credit cards in banks.

Money can also be wired abroad through international money transfer services operated by **Western Union** (tel (800) 325-6000). In the U.S., call Western Union any time at (800) 225-5227 CALL-CASH) to cable money with your Visa or Master-Card within the domestic United States. Credit card transfers do not work overseas— you must send cash. The rates for sending cash are generally $10 cheaper than with a credit card. The money is usually available in the country you're sending it to within an hour, although in some cases this may vary.

In emergencies, U.S. citizens can have money sent via the State Department's **Overseas Citizens Service, American Citizens Services,** Consular Affairs, Public Affairs Staff, Room 4831, U.S. Department of States, Washington, D.C. 20520 (tel. (202) 647-5225; at night and on Sundays and holidays 647-4000; fax 647-3000; http://travel.state.gov). For a fee of US$15, the State Department will forward money within hours to the nearest consular office, which will then disburse it according to instructions. The office serves only Americans in the direst of straits abroad. The quickest way to have the money sent is to cable the State Department through Western Union.

■ Safety and Security

SAFETY

> Road travel in Turkey is dangerous by European standards. *Let's Go* lists emergency, police, and consulate numbers in every large city, for more information (see Turkish Buses, p. 430).

Tourists are particularly vulnerable to crime for two reasons—they often carry large amounts of cash and they are not as street savvy as locals. To avoid such unwanted attention, try to **blend in** as much as possible. Respecting local customs (in many cases, this means dressing more conservatively) can often placate would-be hecklers. Walking directly into a café or shop to check your map beats checking it on a street corner. Look over your map before leaving the hotel room so that you can act as if you know where you are going. Muggings are more often impromptu than planned. Walking with nervous, over-the-shoulder glances can be a tip that you have something valuable to protect. An obviously bewildered bodybuilder is more likely to be harassed than a stern and confident 98-pound weakling. You may consider carrying small whistle to scare off attackers and familiarizing yourself with distress calls in Greek (*vo ee thee a*) or Turkish (*imdat*).

When exploring a new city, extra vigilance may be wise, but no city should force you to turn precautions into panic. When you get to a place where you'll be spending some time, find out about unsafe areas from tourist information or from the manager of your hotel or hostel. If you are traveling alone, be sure that someone knows your itinerary. Never say that you're traveling alone. You may want to carry a small **whistles** to scare off attackers or attract attention, and it's not a bad idea to jot down the number of the police if you'll be in town for a couple days.

When **walking at night,** you should turn day-time precautions into mandates. Stick to busy, well lit streets and avoid dark alleyways. Do not attempt to cross through parks, parking lots, or any other large, deserted areas. A blissfully isolated beach can become a treacherous nightmare as soon as night falls. Whenever possible, *Let's Go* warns of unsafe neighborhoods and areas, but only your eyes can tell you for sure if you've wandered into one; buildings in disrepair, vacant lots, and general desertedness are all bad signs. Pay attention to the neighborhood that surrounds you. A district can change character drastically in the course of a single block. Many notoriously dangerous districts have safe sections; look for children playing, women walking in the open, and other signs of an active community. If you feel uncomfortable, leave as quickly and directly as you can, but don't allow your fear of the new to close off whole worlds to you.

Always wear a **seatbelt** when driving on Greek, Turkish, or Cypriot roads, which are plagued by hundreds of road accidents each year. Wearing a seatbelt is law in many areas. If you are using a **car,** learn local driving signals. The leading cause of travel deaths in many parts of the world is automobile-related injury, with deaths from motor vehicle crashes topping the list. Be sure to park your vehicle in a garage or well-traveled area. Children under 40 lbs. should ride in a specially-designed carseat, which can be obtained for a small fee from most car rental agencies. Remember, the convenience or comfort of riding unbelted will count for little if someone you care about is injured or killed in an accident. If you plan on spending a lot of time on the road, you may want to bring along some spare parts. Learn your route before you hit the road; some roads have poor (or nonexistent) shoulders, few gas stations, and loose animals. *Let's Go* does not recommend **hitchhiking,** particularly for women.

Sleeping in your car is one of the more dangerous ways to get your rest. If your car breaks down, wait for the police to assist you. If you must sleep in your car, do so as close to a police station or a 24-hour service station as possible. Sleeping out in the open can be even more dangerous—camping is recommended only in official, supervised campsites or in wilderness backcountry.

Exercise extreme caution when using pools or beaches without **lifeguards.** Hidden rocks and shallow depths may cause serious injury or even death. Heed warning signs about dangerous undertows. If you rent scuba diving equipment, make sure that it is up to par before taking the plunge.

There is no sure-fire set of precautions that will protect you from all of the situations you may encounter when you travel. A good self-defense course will give you more concrete ways to react to different types of aggression, but it might cost you more money than your trip. **Model Mugging** teaches a very effective, comprehensive course on self-defense. Contact Lynn S. Auerbach on the East Coast (tel. (617) 232-7900); Alice Tibits in the Midwest (tel. (612) 645-6189);and Cori Couture on the West Coast (tel. (415) 592-7300). Course for men and women vary from $400-500. Community colleges frequently offer self-defense courses at more affordable prices. For official **United States Department of State** travel advisories for the U.S. and/ or Canada, including crime and security, call their 24-hour hotline at 202-647-5225. To order publications, including a pamphlet entitled *A Safe Trip Abroad,* write them at Superintendent of Documents, U.S. Government Printing Office, Washington, D.C. 20402, or call (202) 783-3238.

SECURITY

Among the more colorful aspects of large cities are the **con artists.** Con artists and hustlers often work in groups, and, unfortunately, children are among the most effective at the game. Be aware of certain classics—sob stories that require money, rolls of bills "found" on the street, mustard spilled (or saliva spit) onto your shoulder distracting you for enough time to snatch your bag. Be especially alert in these situations. Do not respond or make eye contact, walk away quickly, and keep a solid grip on your belongings. Contact the police if a hustler is particularly aggressive.

Don't put money in a wallet in your back pocket. Never count your money in public, and carry as little as possible. If you carry a purse, buy a sturdy one with a secure clasp, and carry it crosswise on the side, away from the street with the clasp against you. As far as packs are concerned, buy some small combination padlocks which slip through the two zippers, securing the pack shut. (Even these precautions do not always suffice—moped riders who snatch purses and backpacks sometimes tote knives to cut the straps). A **money belt** is the best way to carry cash; you can buy one at most camping supply stores or through the Forsyth Travel Library. The best combination of convenience and invulnerability is the nylon, zippered pouch with belt that should sit inside the waist of your pants or skirt. A **neck pouch** is equally safe, although far less accessible. Refrain from pulling out your neck pouch in public; if you must, be very discreet. Do avoid keeping anything precious in a fanny-pack (or even carrying one at all)— you will be targeted as a tourist and your valuables will be highly visible and easy to steal. In city crowds and especially on public transportation, pick-pockets are amazingly deft at their craft. Rush hour is no excuse for strangers to press up against you on the metro. If somebody is standing too close for comfort, move to another car and hold your bags tightly. Also, be alert in public telephone booths. If you must say your calling-card number, do so very quietly; if you punch it in, make sure no one can look over your shoulder. Be particularly watchful of your belongings on **buses** (for example, carry your backpack in front of you where you can see it); don't check baggage on **trains** especially if you're switching lines, and don't trust anyone to "watch your bag for a second."

Let's Go lists **locker availability** in hostels and train stations, but you'll need your own padlock. Lockers are useful if you plan on sleeping outdoors or don't want to lug everything with you, but don't store valuables in them. Never leave your belongings unattended; even a demure looking hostel (monasteries included) may be a den of thieves. If you feel unsafe, look for places with either a curfew or a night attendant. Keep valuables on your person if you're staying in low-budget hotels where someone else may have a passkey and always in dormitory-style surroundings.

If you take your **car** on your travels, try not to leave valuable possessions, such as radios or luggage, in it while you're off rambling. Radios are especially tempting. If your tape deck or radio is removable, hide it in the trunk or take it with you. If it isn't, at least conceal it under a lot of junk.

Travel Assistance International by Worldwide Assistance Services, Inc. provides its members with a 24-hour hotline for emergencies and referrals. Their year-long frequent traveler package ($226) includes medical and travel insurance, financial assistance, and help in replacing lost documents. Call (800) 821-2828 or (202) 828-5894 (fax 202-828-5896), or write them at 1133 15th St. NW, Suite 400, Washington, D.C. 20005-2710. More complete information on safety while traveling may be found in *Americans Traveling Abroad: What You Should Know Before You Go,* available at Barnes and Noble booksellers across the country.

DRUGS AND ALCOHOL

If you're caught with drugs in Greece, Turkey, or Cyprus, the least you can expect is to be expelled from the country, but remember that your state department can offer little assistance in foreign courts. Possessing drugs in these countries is an *extremely* serious offense. The safest course while abroad is to stay away from drugs and never bring drugs across international borders. Buying or selling any type of drug may lead to anything from a prison sentence to the death penalty. A meek "I didn't know it was illegal" will not suffice. Remember that you are subject to the laws of the country that you are traveling in, not to those of your home country, and it is your responsibility to familiarize yourself with these laws before leaving. Should you be imprisoned, consular officers are allowed to visit you, suggest attorneys, and inform family and friends. Their benevolence ends there. As a U.S. State Department bulletin dourly states, you're virtually "on your own" if you become involved, however innocently, in drug trafficking.

Make sure you get a statement and/or prescription from your doctor if you'll be carrying insulin, syringes, or any narcotic drugs abroad. In addition, be aware that **codeine,** a painkiller commonly prescribed by U.S. physicians, is illegal in Greece. If you are on medication that contains codeine you should have the prescription from your doctor, reasons why you are taking the medication, and the directions on how to take it clearly written out and with you at all times.

The drinking age in Greece, Turkey, and Cyprus is the same (18 years), but a good rule of thumb is if you can see over the bar, they will probably serve you. Public drunkenness is a good way to get yourself labeled as a moronic tourist by the local authorities at the very least, or kicked out of the country at the very worst. Drunk driving is illegal, stupid, and incredibly dangerous. Needless to say, keep your drunken stupors private and pedestrian.

■ Health

> For **medical emergencies** in Greece, dial 166. In Turkey and Kıbrıs, dial 112 or call your consulate. In the Republic of Cyprus, dial 190.

Greece, Turkey, and Cyprus require few medical preparations. If you heat-sterilize your **contact lenses,** you should consider switching temporarily to a chemical system, as your heater will not work properly without a bulky converter, and the availability of equivalent devices in Greece or Turkey is rare. When traveling in the warmer months in Greece and Turkey, don't underestimate the dangers of sun and heat, and educate yourself about **heatstroke.** Heatstroke, sunburn, food poisoning, bladder infections, diarrhea, exotic flus—all these could strike you during your travels in Greece, Turkey, and Cyprus.

Pharmacies *(farmakeia)* in Greece and Cyprus have sophisticated staffs with more prescribing power than you may be accustomed to in the United States or Western Europe. In emergencies you will be given free treatment in state hospitals.

HEALTH

The Turkish pharmacy *(eczane)* will have remedies for minor troubles; more serious medical problems should be taken to the *klinik* (private ones tend to be much better than state-run, and are not much more expensive for foreigners, who must pay for care in any case). Pharmacies in Greek, Turkish, and Cypriot towns stay open all night on a rotating basis; each should have a sign in the window telling which is on duty that night (the open one is known as *efimerevon* in Greece, *nöbetçi* in Turkey). They sell small rectangles of mosquito repellent to be burned slowly on little heat pads which plug into the wall and light up (*bayvap* in Greece and Cyprus, *esem mat* in Turkey and Kıbrıs).

BEFORE YOU GO

For minor health problems, bring a compact **first-aid kit,** including bandages, aspirin or other pain killer, antibiotic cream, a thermometer, a Swiss Army knife, tweezers, moleskin, a decongestant for colds, allergy medication, motion sickness remedy, medicine for diarrhea or stomach problems, sunscreen, insect repellent, and burn ointment.

In your passport, write the names of any people you wish to be contacted in case of a medical emergency, and also list any allergies or medical conditions you would want doctors to be aware of. If you wear glasses or contact lenses, carry an extra prescription or arrange to have your doctor or a family member send a replacement pair in an emergency. Allergy sufferers should find out if their conditions are likely to be aggravated in the regions they plan to visit, and obtain a full supply of any necessary medication before the trip, since matching a prescription to a foreign equivalent is not always easy, safe, or possible. Carry up-to-date, legible prescriptions or a statement from your doctor, especially if you use insulin, a syringe, or a narcotic.

Take a look at your **immunization** records before you go; in addition to standard vaccinations (travelers over two years old should be sure that the following vaccines are up to date: Measles, Mumps, and Rubella (MMR); Diptheria, Tetanus, and Pertussis (DTP or DTap); Polio (OPV); Haemophilus Influenza B (HbCV). Greece requires a vaccination certificate for travelers coming from or in transit through countries where yellow fever is present. If you expect to be sexually active, if you will be a health worker, or if you will be visiting remote areas, you should strongly consider **hepatitis B vaccinations,** and Turkey recommends a series of **rabies vaccines** if you are planning to work with animals. Additionally, from March through November there is a risk of **malaria** in southeastern Anatolia (Turkey); if planning to travel through this area, a preventive chloroquinine regimen is the smart thing to do. A booster of Tetanus-diptheria (Td) is recommended once every ten years, and adults traveling to the region should consider an additional dose of **Polio** vaccine if they have not already had one during their adult years. Hepatitis A vaccine and/or Immune Globulin (IG) is recommended as well.

For up-to-date information about which vaccinations are recommended for your destination, and region-specific health data, try these resources: the **United States Centers for Disease Control and Prevention** (based in Atlanta, Georgia) maintains an international travelers' hotline (tel. (404) 332-4559; fax 332-4565; http://www.cdc.gov). Or write directly to the Centers for Disease Control and Prevention, Travelers' Health, 1600 Clifton Rd. NE, Atlanta, GA 30333. The CDC publishes the booklet *Health Information for International Travelers* (US$14), an annual global rundown of disease, immunization, and general health advice, including risks in particular countries. The **United States State Department** compiles Consular Information Sheets on health, entry requirements, and other issues for all countries of the world. For quick information on travel warnings, call the **Overseas Citizens' Services** (tel. (202) 647-5225). To receive the same Consular Information sheets by fax, dial (202) 647-3000 directly from a fax machine and follow the recorded instructions. The State Department's regional passport agencies in the U.S., field offices of the U.S. Chamber of Commerce, and U.S. embassies and consulates abroad provide the same data, or send a self-addressed, stamped envelope to the Overseas Citizens' Services, Bureau of Consular Affairs, Room 4811, U.S. Department of State, Washington, D.C. 20520. If you are HIV positive, call (202) 647-1488 for country-specific entry requirements, or write to the Bureau of Consular Affairs, CA/P/PA, Department of State, Washington, D.C. 20520. For more general health information, contact the **American Red Cross**. The ARC publishes a *First-Aid and Safety Handbook* (US $15) available for purchase by calling or writing to the American Red Cross, 285 Columbus Ave., Boston, MA 02116-5114 (tel. (800) 564-1234). In the U.S., the American Red Cross also offers many **first-aid** and **CPR courses**.

Those with medical conditions (e.g. diabetes, allergies to antibiotics, epilepsy, or heart conditions) may want to obtain a stainless steel **Medic Alert** identification tag (US$35 the first year, and $15 annually thereafter), which identifies the disease and gives a 24-hour collect-call information number. Contact Medic Alert at (800) 825-3785, or write to Medic Alert Foundation, 2323 Colorado Avenue, Turlock, CA 95382. Diabetics can contact the **American Diabetes Association**, 1600 Duke St., Alexandria, VA 22314 (tel. (800) 232-3472) to receive copies of the article "Travel and Diabetes" and a diabetic ID card, which carries messages in 18 languages explaining the carrier's diabetic status.

If you are concerned about access to medical support while traveling, contact the **International Association for Medical Assistance to Travelers (IAMAT)**, which offers a membership ID card, a directory of English-speaking doctors around the world who treat members for a set fee schedule, and detailed charts on immunization requirements and various tropical diseases. Contact chapters in the **U.S.,** 417 Center St., Lewiston, NY 14092 (tel. (716) 754-4883; fax (519) 836-3412; e-mail iamat@sentex.net; http://www.sentex.net/iamat), **Canada,** 40 Regal Road, Guelph, Ontario, N1K 1B5 (tel. (519) 836-0102) or 1287 St. Clair Avenue West, Toronto, M6E 1B8 (tel. (416) 652-0137; fax (519) 836-3412).

ON-THE-ROAD AILMENTS

You can minimize the chances of contracting a disease while traveling by taking a few precautionary measures. Always avoid animals with open wounds, and beware of touching any animal at all in developing countries. Often dogs are not given shots, so that sweet-faced pooch at your feet might very well be disease-ridden. In *tavernas* in Greece, cats have a custom of scouting underfoot for food. If you are bitten, be concerned about **rabies**—be sure to clean your wound thoroughly and seek medical help immediately to find out whether you need treatment.

Many diseases are transmitted by **insects**—mainly mosquitoes, fleas, ticks, and lice. Insect bites are always annoying, but they can also be dangerous and sometimes life-threatening. **Mosquitoes** are most active from dusk to dawn. Wear long pants and long sleeves (the fabric need not be thick or warm; tropic-weight cottons can keep you comfortable in the heat) and buy a bednet for camping. Wear shoes and socks, and tuck long pants into socks. Use **insect repellents;** DEET can be bought in spray or liquid form, but use it sparingly, especially on children. Soak or spray your gear with permethrin, which is licensed in the U.S. for use on clothing. **Natural repellents** can also be useful: taking vitamin B-12 pills regularly can eventually make you smelly to insects, as can garlic pills. Still, be sure to supplement your vitamins with repellent. Calamine lotion or topical cortisones (like Cortaid©) may stop insect bites from itching, as can a bath with a half-cup of baking soda or oatmeal.

Malaria, absent in Greece and Cyprus but present in southern Anatolia (Turkey), is transmitted by Anopheles mosquitoes. Preliminary symptoms include fever, chills, aches, and fatigue. Since early stages resemble the flu, you should see a doctor if you exhibit flu-like symptoms. Treatment drugs are available, but left untreated, malaria can cause anemia, kidney failure, coma, and death. Malaria poses an especially serious threat to pregnant women. If hiking or staying overnight in certain areas (whether camping or not), you should take weekly anti-malarial drugs.

To ensure that your food is safe, make sure that everything is cooked properly (deep-fried is good), and be positive the water you drink is clean. Avoid ordering meat "rare" and eggs "sunny-side up" (they should be thoroughly cooked).

The water is safe to drink in Greece, Turkey, and Cyprus, but the bottled water is cheap, cooler, and tastes much better. Unless you like a strong chlorine taste (Turkish water), go with the portable stuff. If you're paranoid, you can purify your own water, and to do that, bring it to a rolling boil (simmering isn't enough), or treat it with iodine drops or tablets. Stay away from salads: uncooked vegetables (including lettuce and coleslaw) are full of untreated water. Other culprits are raw shellfish, unpasteurized milk, and sauces containing raw eggs. Peel all fruits and vegetables yourself, and beware of watermelon, which is often injected with impure water. Watch out for food from markets or street vendors (such as juices and peeled fruits) that may have been washed in dirty water or fried in rancid cooking oil.

Parasites (tapeworms, etc.) also hide in unsafe water and food. *Giardia,* for example, is acquired by drinking untreated water from streams or lakes all over the world, including Greece, Turkey, and Cyprus. It can stay with you for years. Symptoms of parasitic infections in general include swollen glands or lymph nodes, fever, rashes or itchiness, digestive problems, eye problems, and anemia. Boil your water, wear shoes, avoid bugs, and eat cooked food.

Hepatitis A (distinct from B and C) is a moderately high risk in the Eastern Mediterranean. Hep. A is a viral infection of the liver acquired primarily through contaminated water, ice, shellfish, or unpeeled fruits and vegetables (as well as from sexual contact). Symptoms include fatigue, fever, loss of appetite, nausea, dark urine, jaundice, vomiting, aches and pains, and light stools. Ask your doctor about a new vaccine called "Havrix," or ask to get an injection of immune globulin (IG; formerly called Gamma Globulin).

Hepatitis B is a viral infection of the liver transmitted by sharing needles, having unprotected sex, or coming into direct contact with an infected person's lesioned skin. If you think you may be sexually active while traveling or if you are working or living in rural areas, you are typically advised to get the vaccination for Hepatitis B. Vaccination should begin six months before traveling.

Traveler's diarrhea is the dastardly consequence of ignoring the warnings against drinking untreated water. The illness can last from three to seven days, and symptoms include diarrhea, nausea, bloating, urgency, and malaise. If the nasties hit you, have quick-energy, non-sugary foods with protein and carbohydrates to keep your strength up; plain yogurt is also good. Over the counter remedies (such as Pepto-Bismol© or Immodium©) may counteract the problems, but they can complicate serious infections. Avoid anti-diarrheals if you suspect you have been exposed to contaminated food or water, which puts you at risk for other diseases. The most dangerous side effect of diarrhea is dehydration; the simplest and most effective anti-dehydration formula is eight ounces of (clean) water with a ½ teaspoon of sugar or honey and a pinch of salt. Also good are soft drinks without caffeine and salted crackers. Down several of these remedies a day, rest, and wait for the disease to run its course. If you develop a fever, or your symptoms don't go away after four or five days, consult a doctor. Consult a doctor if children develop traveler's diarrhea.

Common sense goes a long way toward preventing **heat exhaustion:** relax in hot weather, drink lots of non-alcoholic fluids, and lie down inside if you feel awful. Continuous heat stress can eventually lead to **heatstroke,** characterized by rising body temperature, severe headache, and cessation of sweating. Wear a hat, sunglasses, and a lightweight long sleeve shirt to avoid heatstroke. Victims must be cooled off with wet towels and taken to a doctor as soon as possible.

Always drink enough liquids to keep your urine clear. Alcoholic beverages are dehydrating, as are coffee, strong tea, and caffeinated sodas. If you'll be sweating a lot, be sure to eat enough salty food to prevent electrolyte depletion, which causes severe headaches. Less debilitating, but still dangerous, is **sunburn.** You should always wear sunscreen; bring it with you (it's often more expensive and harder to find when traveling), and apply it liberally and often to avoid burns and risk of skin cancer. If you get sunburned, drink more fluids than usual and use an aloe lotion.

HEALTH

WOMEN'S HEALTH

Women traveling in unsanitary conditions are vulnerable to **urinary tract** and **bladder infections,** common and severely uncomfortable bacterial diseases which cause a burning sensation and painful and sometimes frequent urination. Drink tons of vitamin-C-rich juice such as cranberry juice, plenty of clean water, and urinate frequently, especially right after any sexual intercourse. Untreated, these infections can lead to kidney infections, sterility, and even death. If symptoms persist, see a doctor. If you often develop **vaginal yeast infections,** take along an over the counter medicine. Women may also be more susceptible to vaginal thrush and cystitis, two treatable but uncomfortable illnesses. Tampons and pads are sometimes hard to find when traveling; certainly your preferred brands may not be available, so it may be advisable to take supplies along. Refer to the *Handbook for Women Travellers* by Maggie and Gemma Moss (published by Piatkus Books) or to the women's health guide *Our Bodies, Our Selves* (published by the Boston Women's Health Collective) for more extensive information specific to women's health on the road.

HIV, AIDS, AND STDS

Acquired Immune Deficiency Syndrome (AIDS) is a growing problem around the world. The easiest mode of HIV transmission is through direct blood to blood contact with an HIV positive person; *never* share intravenous drug, tattooing, or other needles. The most common mode of transmission is sexual intercourse. Health professionals recommend the use of latex condoms; follow the instructions on the packet. Since it isn't always easy to buy condoms when traveling, take a supply with you before you depart for your trip. Some countries screen incoming travelers, primarily those planning extended visits for work or study, and deny entrance to HIV positive people. Contact the consulate for information about this policy. For more information on AIDS, call the **U.S. Center for Disease Control's** 24-hour hotline at (800) 342-2437 (in Spanish (800) 344-7332, open daily 8am-2am). In Europe, write to the **World Health Organization,** Attn: Global Program on AIDS, 20 Avenue Appia, 1211 Geneva 27, Switzerland (tel. (22) 791-2111) for statistical material on AIDS internationally. Or write to the **Bureau of Consular Affairs,** CA/P/PA, Department of State, Washington, D.C. 20520.

Sexually transmitted diseases (STDs) such as gonorrhea, chlamydia, genital warts, syphilis, and herpes are a lot easier to catch than HIV and can be just as deadly. It's a wise idea to actually *look* at your partner's genitals before you have sex. If anything looks amiss, that should be a warning signal. When having sex, condoms may protect you from certain STDs, but oral or even tactile contact can lead to transmission.

BIRTH CONTROL AND ABORTION

Reliable contraceptive devices may be difficult to find while traveling. Women on **the pill** should bring enough to allow for possible loss or extended stays and should bring a prescription, since forms of the pill vary a good deal. The **sponge** is probably too bulky to be worthwhile on the road. If you use a **diaphragm,** be sure that you have enough contraceptive jelly on hand. Though **condoms** are increasingly available, you might want to bring your favorite brand or flavors before you go. The farther from a major city you go, the harder they are to find. In Greece ask for *profilaktika* or *kapotes,* in Turkey it's a *preservatif* or a *kilif.*

Abortion is legal in Greece, Turkey, and Cyprus. Women overseas who want an **abortion** can contact the **United States abortion hotline** (tel. (800) 772-9100; open Mon.-Fri. 9:30am-12:30pm and 1:30-5:30pm), 1436 U St. NW, Washington, D.C. 20009. The hotline can direct you to organizations which provide information on techniques for abortion in the region. Or contact your embassy to receive a list of ob/gyn doctors who perform abortions. For general information on contraception, condoms, and abortion worldwide, contact the **International Planned Parenthood**

Federation, European Regional Office, Regent's College Inner Circle, Regent's Park, London NW1 4NS (tel. (44-0171) 486-0741; fax 487-7950.)

■ Insurance

Beware of buying unnecessary travel coverage—your regular policies may well extend to many travel-related accidents. **Medical insurance** (especially university policies) often cover costs incurred abroad; check with your provider. **Medicare's** foreign travel coverage is valid only in Canada and Mexico. Canadians are protected by their home province's health insurance plan for up to 90 days after leaving the country; check with the provincial Ministry of Health or Health Plan Headquarters for details. Australia has **Reciprocal Health Care Agreements (RHCAs)** with several countries; when traveling in these nations Australians are entitled to many of the services that they would receive at home. The Commonwealth Department of Human Services and Health can provide more information. Your **homeowners' insurance** (or your family's coverage) often covers theft during travel. Homeowners are generally covered against loss of travel documents (passport, plane ticket, railpass, etc.) up to $500.

ISIC and **ITIC** provide US$3000 worth of accident and illness insurance and US$100 per day up to 60 days of hospitalization. They also offer up to US$1000 for accidental death or dismemberment, up to US$25,000 if injured due to an airline, and up to $25,000 for emergency evacuation due to illness. The cards also give access to a toll-free Traveler's Assistance hotline (in the U.S. and Canada tel. (800) 626-2427; elsewhere call collect to the U.S. (713) 267-2525) whose multilingual staff provides help in emergencies. **Council** offers the Trip-Safe plan with options covering medical treatment and hospitalization, accidents, and even charter flights missed due to illness; **STA** offers a more expensive, more comprehensive plan. **American Express** cardholders receive automatic car rental and travel accident insurance on flight purchases made with the card (customer service tel. (800) 528-4800).

Remember that insurance companies usually require a copy of the police report for thefts or evidence of having paid medical expenses (doctor's statements, receipts) before they will honor a claim and may have time limits on filing for reimbursement. *Always carry policy numbers and proof of insurance.* Most of the carriers listed below have 24-hour hotlines.

Access America, 6600 West Broad St., P.O. Box 11188, Richmond, VA 23230 (tel. (800) 284-8300; fax (804) 673-1491). Covers trip cancellation/interruption, on-the-spot hospital admittance costs, emergency medical evacuation, sickness, and baggage loss. 24-hr. hotline.

Globalcare Travel Insurance (GTI), 220 Broadway Lynnfield, MA 01940 (tel. (800) 821-2488; fax (617) 592-7720); e-mail global@nebc.mv.com; WWW (nebc.mv.com/globalcare). Complete medical, legal, emergency, and travel-related services. On-the-spot payments and special student programs, including benefits for trip cancellation and interruption, GTI waives pre-existing medical conditions with their Globalcare Economy Plan for cruise and travel, and provides coverage for the bankruptcy or default of cruiselines, airlines, or tour operators.

Travel Guard International, 1145 Clark St., Stevens Point, WI 54481 (tel. (800) 826-1300 or (715) 345-0505; fax (715) 345-0525). Comprehensive insurance programs starting at US$44. Programs cover trip cancellation and interruption, bankruptcy and financial default, lost luggage, medical coverage abroad, emergency assistance, accidental death. 24hr. hotline.

■ Alternatives to Tourism

Because most visitors see Greece, Turkey, and Cyprus only through the eyes of a tourist, those who go in order to study or work can expect a particularly unique and rewarding experience. There are several general resource organizations for those interested in alternatives to tourism.

ALTERNATIVES TO TOURISM

ALTERNATIVES TO TOURISM

STUDY

American Field Service (AFS), 220 E. 42nd St., 3rd floor, New York, NY 10017 (tel. (800) 237-4636 or 876-2376 (AFS-INFO); fax (212) 949-9379; http://www.afs.org/usa). AFS offers summer, semester, and year-long homestay international exchange programs for high school students and service projects for adults. Financial aid available. Exchanges in Turkey and other countries.

The Athens Centre, Archimidous 48, Athens, Greece 116 36 (tel. (01) 701 2268; fax 701 8603; e-mail athenscr@compulink.gr), offers a modern Greek language program. Semester and quarter programs on Greek civilization in affiliation with U.S. universities. Offers 4-6 week summer Classics programs, a yearly summer theater program and a Modern Greek Language program in July on Spetses.

Beaver College Center for Education Abroad, 450 S. Easton Rd., Glenside, PA 19038-3295 (tel. (800) 755-5607; fax (215) 572-2174; http://www.beaver.edu/cea). Operates summer-, semester-, and year-long programs at universities in Greece. Applicants must have completed 3 full semesters at a university.

College Year in Athens (tel. (01) 726 0749) runs a 2-semester program for undergraduates (usually juniors), which includes travel as well as classroom instruction (in English). The program has two tracks, one in Ancient Greek civilization and one in Mediterranean studies. Scholarship available. College Year in Athens also runs 2 summer programs: a 6-week program of academic study and travel, and a three-week immersion in Modern Greek Language. From the U.S. call (617) 547-6141 or write to College Year in Athens, P.O. Box 390890 Cambridge, MA 02139.

The Hellenic American Union, 22 Massalias St., Athens 10680 (tel. (01) 701 2268; fax 701 8603). Offers courses in Modern spoken Greek, studio art, business courses, translation seminar, and Greek literature. An intensive one-month Greek language course is offered in the Cyclades. For a practical education, contact the **Delta School of Technical and Business Studies,** 3 Reythmnou St., Athens 10682 (tel. (01) 822 0083).

World Learning, Inc., Summer Abroad, P.O. Box 676, Brattleboro, VT 05302 (tel. (800) 345-2929 or (802) 257-7751; http://www.worldlearning.org). Founded in 1932 as The Experiment in International Living, it offers high school programs in Greece as well as language-training programs with elective homestays. Programs are 3-5 weeks long. Positions as group leaders are available world-wide if you are over 24, have previous in-country experience, are fluent in the language, and have experience with high school students.

Your best bet for information on study in Turkey is the education office at the nearest tourist office. You may also enroll in one of several small colleges in Cyprus; contact the Department of Education in Nicosia. **Council** sponsors over 40 study abroad programs throughout the world. Contact them for more information; see travel organizations on (p. 3).

WORK AND VOLUNTEER

Volunteer jobs are readily available in Greece, Turkey, and Cyprus. You may receive room and board in exchange for your labor. Opportunities include archaeological digs and community projects. The organizations that arrange placement sometimes charge high application fees in addition to the workcamps's charges for room and board. You can sometimes avoid this extra fee by contacting the individual workcamps directly; check with the organization.

Archaeological Institute of America, 656 Beacon Street, Boston, MA 02215-2010 (tel. (617) 353-9361; fax 353-6550). Puts out the *Archaeological Fieldwork Opportunities Bulletin* (US$11 non-members) which lists over 250 field sites throughout the world. This can be purchased from Kendall/Hunt Publishing, 4050 Westmark Drive, Dubuque, Iowa 52002 (tel. (800) 228-0810).

Council Council's Voluntary Services Department, 205 E. 42nd St., New York, NY 10017 (tel. (800) COUNCIL/2686245; fax (212) 822-2699; http://www.ciee.org).

ALTERNATIVES TO TOURISM

Department also offers 2 to 4 week environmental or community service projects in over 30 countries around the globe. Participants must be at least 18 years of age. US$250-750 placement fee.

Gençtur Turizm ve Seyahat Ac. Ltd. (Tourism and Travel Agency), Head Office: Professor K. İsmail Gürkan Cad., No. 14 Flat 4, Sultanahmet, İstanbul (tel. (212) 520 5274,-5 or 512 0228; fax 5190864). Taksim Branch: İstiklal Cad., Zambak Sok., 15/5 Taksim, İstanbul (tel. (212) 2492515; fax 2492554). Organizes teenage, group, or international voluntary workcamps and study tours in Turkey.

Peace Corps, 1990 K St. NW, Washington, D.C. 20526 (tel. (800) 424-8580; fax (202) 606-4469; http://www.peacecorps.gov). Write for their "blue" brochure, which details applicant requirements. Opportunities in a variety of fields, from agriculture to business. Volunteers must be U.S. citizens with useful skills willing to make a 2-year commitment.

Finding work in Greece, Turkey, and Cyprus is difficult. Job opportunities are scarce and the governments try to restrict employment to citizens and visitors from the EU. Be persistent; the informality of local life will work to your advantage.

For long-term employment in Greece, you must first get a work permit from your employer; permits are available at the **Ministry of Labor,** 40 Pireos St., Athens 10437 (tel. (01) 523 3110). Make all arrangements and negotiations before you leave home.

For **hotel jobs** (bartending, cleaning, etc.) arrive in the spring and early summer to search for work. Most night spots have meager pay. Check the bulletin boards of hostels in Athens and the classified ads in the *Athens News.* Another possibility is to work as a farm laborer. In Greece, the **American Farm School** runs summer work and recreation programs for high school and college students. Write 1133 Broadway, New York, NY 10010 (tel. (212) 463-8434; fax (212) 463-8208; e-mail nyoffice@amerfarm.com), or in Greece, P.O. Box 23, GR-55102, Thessaloniki (tel. 30 (31) 471 803 or 471 825; fax 472345).

The brightest prospect for working in Turkey is probably **teaching English.** Students with university credentials might fare quite well, but having your credentials verified can take some time. Various organizations in the U.S. will place you in a (low-paying) teaching job, but securing a position will require patience, because teaching English abroad has become enormously popular in the past few years.

The process for obtaining a job in Cyprus is similar. Before you arrive, you must find an employer who can assert that you are particularly suited for your position due to academic interest or experience, and that there are no suitably qualified local employees available in your field.

Council publishes *Work, Study, Travel Abroad: The Whole World Handbook.* Published by St. Martin's Press (US$14). Write to Council, Marketing Services Dept., 205 E. 42nd St., New York, NY 10017-5706 (tel. (800) COUNCIL/2686245; fax (212) 822-2699; e-mail books@ciee.org; http://www.ciee.org.

Office of Overseas Schools, A/OS Room 245, SA-29, Dept. of State, Washington, D.C. 20522-2902 (tel. (703) 875-7800). Teaching jobs abroad.

Surrey Books, 230 E. Ohio St., Chicago, IL 60611 (tel. (800) 326-4430), publishes *How to Get a Job in Europe: The Insider's Guide.* Includes information on Turkey, among others.

■ Specific Concerns

WOMEN TRAVELERS

Women traveling in the Mediterranean, whether alone or in groups, are likely to experience verbal harassment which can be just as intimidating as physical abuse. However, especially in recent years, with the increase of tourism and women's fitness centers worldwide, women have been traveling safely and confidently by fol-

SPECIFIC CONCERNS

lowing a few simple guidelines. (1) If you are traveling alone it is a good idea to wear a wedding band; we've come a long way, but involvement with a male figure still commands a great deal of respect in Greece, Turkey, and Cyprus. Never admit that you are traveling alone; rather, explain that you are waiting for your "husband." (2) You may want to carry either a whistle or an alarm (available at many airports and travel stores) which emit high-pitched sounds when activated. Whistles and alarms provide good protection, especially in smaller villages where sounds like these can be heard above the braying of donkeys (as opposed to 9am rush-hour traffic). (3) You may also wish to enroll in a self-defense course before you leave which teaches the basics of physical protection (head, eye, groin) and gives you a framework of awareness (i.e., how to carry yourself with confidence). (4) Always keep in mind that the way you dress will often brand you as a foreigner from a mile away. Try to avoid wearing clothes which are overly revealing such as short shorts, halter tops, tight tank tops, and thong bikinis, especially in more rural areas where your intentions may be misinterpreted. Bear in mind that Greek, Turkish, and Cypriot women dress relatively conservatively (long skirts/dresses and jeans) and they too may frown upon your "loose manner." (5) Finally, the best strategy is to ignore catcallers, whistlers, and other tall, dark, cultural specimens. The more attention you give them, whether by giggling or responding to their inane questions, the more attention they will give you back. Be aware of your body language, avoid direct eye contact, and continue walking. If, at any time, these advances become physical, you should yell, scream, and make it your first priority to get away. In Greek, screech "vo-EE-thee-ah" (help) or "as-te-no-MEE-ah" (police). In Turkish, holler "eem-DAHT" (help) or "PO-lees" (police). Καλη τυχη. *İyi şanslar.* (Good luck.)

OLDER TRAVELERS

Greeks and Turks have a great deal of respect for their elders, so senior citizens should receive a warm welcome. Senior citizens are often offered a variety of discounts and services; **Hostelling International** sells memberships to those over 55 at a reduced rate see (p. 40). Below is a brief list of services that provide additional information:

American Association of Retired People (AARP), 601 E St. NW, Washington, D.C. 20049 (tel. (202) 434-2277). Members 50 and over receive benefits and services including the AARP Motoring Plan from Amoco (tel. (800) 334-3300), and discounts on lodging, car rental, and sight-seeing. Annual fee US$8 per couple; lifetime membership US$75.

Elderhostel, 75 Federal St., 3rd floor, Boston, MA 02110-1941 (tel. (617) 426-7788; fax 426-8351; http://www.elderhostel.org). For those 55 or over (spouse of any age). Programs at colleges, universities, and other learning centers in over 50 countries on varied subjects and lasting 1-4 weeks.

Gateway Books, 2023 Clemens Road, Oakland, CA 94602 (tel. (510) 530-0299, credit card orders (800) 669-0773; fax 530-0497; e-mail donmerwin@aol.com; http://www.hway.com/gateway/). Publishes *Europe the European Way: A traveler's Guide to Living Affordably in the World's Great Cities* (US$14) and *Adventures Abroad* (US$13), which offer general hints for the budget-conscious senior considering a long stay or retiring abroad.

BISEXUAL, GAY, AND LESBIAN TRAVELERS

Greeks and Cypriots have a relatively tolerant attitude towards homosexuality. Homosexual sex is legal, although homosexuality as a declared lifestyle is frowned upon. In Turkey and Kıbrıs, social conservatism and religious dictates keep most activity discreet. If problems arise, plan on authorities being almost uniformly unsympathetic.

In Greece, Athens in particular offers a variety of gay bars, clubs, and hotels. For further information, consult the **Greek Gay Guide'96**, Tθ 4228, Athens 10210, (tel. (01) 381 5249). Call Monday-Friday 7-9pm for an English speaker; the guide is multilingual. The islands of Hydra, Lesbos, Paros, Rhodes, and Mykonos also offer gay and lesbian resorts, hotels, bars, and clubs. Turkey's urban centers do not lack for bars and informal cruising areas (men only), although they may be less obvious. Contact Turkey's gay and lesbian organization **Lamartin,** c/o İbrahim Eren, Lamartin Cad. 23/6, Tuslim, İstanbul for more details.

Are You Two...Together? A Gay and Lesbian Travel Guide to Europe (Random House, $18). A travel guide with anecdotes and tips for gays and lesbians traveling in Europe. Includes overviews of regional laws relating to gays and lesbians, lists of gay/lesbian organizations, and establishments catering to, friendly to, or indifferent to gays and lesbians. Available in bookstores.

Gay's the Word, 66 Marchmont St., London WC1N 1AB (tel. (0171) 278 7654). The largest gay and lesbian bookstore in the U.K. Mail order service available. No catalog of listings, but they will provide a list of titles on a given subject. Open Mon.-Sat. 10am-6pm, Thurs. 10am-7pm, Sun. 2-6pm.

Giovanni's Room, 345 S. 12th St., Philadelphia, PA 19107 (tel. (215) 923-2960; fax 923-0813; e-mail gilphilp@netaxs.com). An international feminist, lesbian, and gay bookstore with mail order service. Carries many publications listed here.

International Lesbian and Gay Association (ILGA), 81 rue Marché-au-Charbon, B-1000 Bruxelles, Belgium (tel./fax 32-2-502-2471; e-mail ilga@ilga.org). Provides political information, such as homosexuality laws of individual countries.

Spartacus International Gay Guides (US$32.95), published by Bruno Gmunder, Postfach 110729, D-10837 Berlin, Germany (tel. (30) 615 00 30; fax 615-9134). Lists bars, restaurants, hotels, and bookstores around the world catering to gays. Also lists hotlines for gays in various countries and homosexuality laws for each country. Available in bookstores and in the U.S. by mail from Giovanni's Room (listed above).

Women Going Places (Inland Book Company, US$14). A women's travel and resource guide geared toward lesbians.

DISABLED TRAVELERS

Greece, Turkey, and Cyprus are only slowly beginning to respond to the needs of travelers with disabilities. Many cruise ships that sail the Greek islands are equipped to accommodate those with disabilities. Special air transportation is available aboard Olympic Airways to many of the larger islands. Some hotels, train stations, and airports have recently installed facilities for the disabled; many of the archaeological sites throughout the region, however, are still not wheelchair-accessible.

Facts on File, 11 Penn Plaza, 15th Floor, New York, NY 10001(tel. (212) 967-8800). Publishers of *Disability Resource,* a reference guide for travelers with disabilities (US$45 plus shipping). Retail bookstores or by mail order.

Graphic Language Press, P.O. Box 270, Cardiff by the Sea, CA 92007 (tel. (619) 944-9594). Publishers of *Wheelchair Through Europe* (US$13). Specifics on wheelchair-related resources and accessible sites in cities throughout Europe.

Moss Rehab Hospital Travel Information Service (tel. (215) 456-9600, TDD 456-9602)). A telephone information resource center on international travel accessibility and other travel-related concerns for those with disabilities.

Society for the Advancement of Travel for the Handicapped (SATH), 347 Fifth Ave., #610, New York, NY 10016 (tel. (212) 447-7284; fax 725-8253). Publishes quarterly travel newsletter *SATH News* and information booklets (free for members, US$13 each for nonmembers) with advice on trip planning for people with disabilities. Annual membership US$45, students and seniors US$25.

The following organizations arrange tours or trips for disabled travelers:

Directions Unlimited, 720 N. Bedford Rd., Bedford Hills, NY 10507 (tel. (800) 533-5343; in NY (914) 241-1700; fax 241-0243). Specializes in arranging individual and group vacations, tours, and cruises for the physically disabled.

Flying Wheels Travel Service, 143 W. Bridge St., Owatonne, MN 55060 (tel. (800) 535-6790; fax (507) 451-1685). Arranges trips in the U.S. and abroad for groups and individuals in wheelchairs or with other sorts of limited mobility.

The Guided Tour Inc., Elkins Park House, Suite 114B, 7900 Old York Road, Elkins Park, PA 19027-2339 (tel. (800) 783-5841 or (215) 782-1370; fax 635-2637). Organizes travel programs for persons with developmental and physical challenges and those requiring renal dialysis. Call, fax, or write for a free brochure.

VEGETARIAN AND KOSHER TRAVELERS

Vegetarians should have no problem finding suitable cuisine. Most restaurants have vegetarian selections on their menus, and some cater specifically to vegetarians. *Let's Go* often notes restaurants with good vegetarian selections in city listings. For more information, contact the **North American Vegetarian Society,** P.O. Box 72, Dolgeville, NY 13329 (518) 568-7970) and travel-related publications, such as *Transformative Adventures* (a guide to vacations and retreats US$14.95). Membership to the Society is US$20; family membership is US$26 and members receive a 10% discount on all publications.

Vegetarian dishes in Greece, Turkey, and Cyprus include succulent fruits, colorful salads, tasty breads, *fasolia* (beans, *fasülye* in Turkish), *spanakopita* (spinach-filled pastry), and *tyropitakia* (cheese-filled pastry, *börek* in Turkish). In Turkey and Cyprus, *meze* appetizers are plentiful (see Food and Drink, p. 441). In summer fresh produce abounds in the outdoor markets; vegetarians find plenty of fresh vegetables, fruits, and interesting cheeses.

Travelers who keep kosher should contact synagogues in larger cities for information on kosher restaurants; your own synagogue or college Hillel should have access to lists of Jewish institutions across the nation. If you are strict in your observance, consider preparing your own food on the road.

The European Vegetarian Guide to Restaurants and Hotels (US$13.95, plus US$1.75 shipping) is available from the Vegetarian Times Bookshelf (tel. (800) 435-9610, orders only).

The Jewish Travel Guide (US$12, postage US$1.75) lists synagogues, kosher restaurants, and Jewish institutions in over 80 countries. Available from Ballantine-Mitchell Publishers, Newbury House 890-900, Eastern Ave., Newbury Park, Ilford, Essex, U.K. IG2 7HH (tel. (0181) 599 88 66; fax 599 09 84; #10). It is available in the U.S. from Sepher-Hermon Press, 1265 46th St., Brooklyn, NY 11219 (tel. (718) 972-9010; US$13.95 plus US$2.50 shipping).

TRAVELERS WITH CHILDREN

Greeks, Turks, and Cypriots alike adore children. Expect a stream of compliments, advice, candy, and substantial discounts on transportation throughout Greece, Turkey, and Cyprus. Restaurants often have children's menus and discounts. Virtually all museums and tourist attractions also have a children's rate. Be sure that your child carries some sort of ID in case of an emergency or he or she gets lost and arrange a reunion spot in case of separation when sight-seeing (e.g., the Parthenon). Children under two generally fly for 10% of the adult airfare on international flights (this does not necessarily include a seat). International fares are usually discounted 25% for children from two to 11.

Backpacking with Babies and Small Children (US$10). Published by Wilderness Press, 2440 Bancroft Way, Berkeley, CA 94704 (tel. (800) 443-7227 or (510) 843-8080; fax 548-1355).

Take Your Kids to Europe, by Cynthia W. Harriman (US$14). A budget travel guide geared towards families. Published by Mason-Grant Publications, P.O. Box 6547, Portsmouth, NH 03802 (tel. (603) 436-1608; fax 427-0015; e-mail charriman@masongrant.com).

Travel with Children, by Maureen Wheeler (US$11.95, postage US$1.50). Published by Lonely Planet Publications, Embarcadero West, 155 Filbert St., #251, Oakland, CA 94607 (tel. (800) 275-8555 or (510) 893-8555; fax 893-8563; e-mail info@lonelyplanet.com; http://www.lonelyplanet.com). Also P.O. Box 617, Hawthorn, Victoria 3122, Australia.

TRAVELING ALONE

There are many benefits to traveling alone, among them greater independence and challenge. Without distraction, you can write a great travel log, in the grand tradition of Homer, Yaşar Kemal, and Lawrence Durrell. As a lone traveler, you have greater opportunity to meet and interact with the locals. On the other hand, you may also be a more visible target for robbery and harassment. Lone travelers need to be well organized and look confident at all times. No wandering around back alleys looking confused. Try not to stand out as a tourist. If questioned, never admit that you are traveling alone. And try to maintain regular contact with someone at home who knows your itinerary.

A **Foxy Old Woman's Guide to Traveling Alone,** by Jay Ben-Lesser (US$11), encompasses practically every specific traveling concern, offering anecdotes and tips, for anyone interested in solitary adventure. No experience is necessary. It's sold in bookstores and from Crossing Press in Freedom, CA (tel. (800) 777-1048).

■ Packing

The more you know, the less you need, so plan your packing according to the type of travel (multi-city backpacking tour, week-long stay in one place, etc.) and the high and low temperatures in the area you will be visiting (see Climate Chart, p.

PACKING

577). If you don't pack lightly, your back and wallet will suffer. The more things you have, the more you have to lose. The larger your pack, the more cumbersome it is to store safely. Before you leave, pack your bag, strap it on, and walk uphill on hot asphalt for the next three hours. (This is what it will feel like.) A good general rule is to lay out only what you absolutely need, then take half the clothes and twice the money (and underwear).

LUGGAGE

Backpack: If you plan to cover most of your itinerary by foot, the unbeatable baggage is a sturdy frame backpack. Some convert into more normal-looking suitcases. Many packs are designed specifically for travelers, while others are for hikers; consider how you will use the pack before purchasing one or the other. In either case, get a pack with a strong, padded hip belt to transfer weight from your shoulders to your hips. It is a common error to carry the weight of these packs on your shoulders—this is not necessary. When carried correctly, a pack's weight should rest entirely on your hips. Quality packs cost anywhere from US$150 to US$420.

Suitcase/trunk/other large or heavy luggage: Fine if you plan to live in one or two cities and explore from there, but a bad idea if you're going to be moving around a lot. If you do decide that it best suits your needs, make sure it has wheels and consider how much it weighs even when empty. Hard-sided luggage is more durable and doesn't wrinkle your clothes, but it is also heavier. Soft-sided luggage should have a PVC frame, a strong lining to resist bad weather and rough handling, and its seams should be triple-stitched for durability.

Shoulder bag: If you are not backpacking, an empty, lightweight duffel bag packed inside your luggage may be useful: once abroad you can fill your luggage with purchases and keep your dirty clothes in the duffel.

Daypack, rucksack, or courier bag: Bringing a smaller bag in addition to your pack or suitcase allows you to leave your big bag in the hotel while you go sightseeing. More importantly, it can be used as an airplane carry-on: keep the absolute bare essentials with you to avoid the lost-luggage blues.

Moneybelt or neck pouch: Guard your money, passport, railpass, and other important articles in either one of these, and keep it with you *at all times*. Money belts and neck pouches are available at any good camping store. See Safety and Security for more information on protecting you and your valuables (p. 14).

CLOTHING AND FOOTWEAR

Clothing: Packing lightly does not mean dressing badly (it just means dressing repetitively). When choosing your travel wardrobe, aim for versatility and comfort, and avoid fabrics that wrinkle easily (to test a fabric, hold it tightly in your fist for twenty seconds). Because you will probably be wearing the same thing several times, remember that solid colors mix best. Keep in mind that you should probably bring along something besides the basic shorts, t-shirts, and jeans, because dress codes are stricter (especially for women), so check before you go. Women should probably bring a skirt with them when traveling through Greece, Turkey, and Cyprus. Always bring a jacket or wool sweater. As the original Easy Rider Peter Fonda said, "Pack less than you'd ever imagine... there are always laundromats." (Well, at least hotel sinks.)

Walking shoes: Not a place to cut corners. Well cushioned **sneakers** are good for walking, though you may want to consider a good water-proofed pair of **hiking boots** for camping and hiking needs. A double pair of socks—light silk or polypropylene inside and thick wool outside—will cushion feet, keep them dry, and help prevent blisters. Water-proof, ever-versatile sports sandals are probably the best footwear for light travel in hot places. Bring a pair of flip-flops for protection against the foliage and fungi that inhabit some hostel showers. Talcum powder in your shoes and on your feet can prevent sores, and moleskin is great for blisters.

Rain gear: Essential. A waterproof jacket and a backpack cover will take care of you and your stuff at a moment's notice. Gore-Tex® is a miracle fabric that's both waterproof and breathable; it's all but mandatory if you plan on hiking. Avoid cotton as outer-wear, especially if you will be in the outdoors, because it is useless if wet.

MISCELLANEOUS

Only Noah had a complete list. You may find, however, the following items valuable: umbrella, reusable plastic bags (for damp clothes, soap, food, shampoo and other spillables), alarm clock, waterproof matches, sun hat, moleskin (for blisters), needle and thread, safety pins, sunglasses, a personal stereo with headphones, pocketknife, plastic water bottle, compass, string (makeshift clothesline and lashing material), towel, padlock, whistle, rubber bands, toilet paper, flashlight, cold-water soap, insect repellant, electrical tape (for patching tears), clothespins, maps and Greek and/or Turkish phrasebooks, tweezers, garbage bags, sunscreen, and vitamins. Some items not always readily available or affordable on the road: deodorant, razors, condoms, or tampons. It is always a good idea to bring along a **first-aid kit**.

Sleepsacks: If planning to stay in **youth hostels**, make the requisite sleepsack yourself (instead of paying the linen charge). Fold a full size sheet in half the long way, then sew it closed along the open long side and one of the short sides.

Washing clothes: *Let's Go* attempts to provide information on laundromats in the Practical Information listings for each city, but sometimes it may be in your best interest to just use a sink or a cheap plastic tub. Bring a small bar or tube of detergent soap, a rubber squash ball to stop up the sink, and a travel clothes line.

Electric current: The standard electrical outlet in Greece produces 220 volts AC using the two-pronged plug used in Europe. Although Turkey uses the same plug, be careful and ask the exact voltage, since both 110 volts and 220 volts are used. In Cyprus, 220 volt outlets require either the two or three-pronged outlets used in Africa and Asia. North American appliances are designed for 110 volts AC and the prong won't fit. If you're bringing a beloved electrical appliance, you'll need a converter and a three-pronged adapter, both available in department and hardware stores. Visit a hardware store for an adapter (which changes the shape of the plug) and a converter (which changes the voltage). Don't make the mistake of using only an adapter (unless appliance instructions explicitly state otherwise, as with some portable computers), or you'll melt your radio. To receive their punny pamphlet, Foreign Electricity is No Deep Dark Secret, write to Franzus Co., Murtha Industrial Park, P.O. Box 142, Beacon Falls, CT 06403 (tel. (203) 723-6664; fax 723-6666).

Film: Expensive just about everywhere, bring lots of film from home and, if you will be seriously upset if the pictures are ruined, develop it at home. If you're not a serious photographer, you might want to consider bringing a disposable camera or two rather than an expensive permanent one. Whatever kind of camera you use, be aware that, despite disclaimers, airport security X-rays can fog film, so either buy a lead-lined pouch, sold at camera stores, or ask the security to hand inspect it. Always pack it in your carry-on luggage, since higher intensity X-rays are used on checked luggage.

GETTING THERE

■ Budget Travel Agencies

These organizations help with booking flights and acquiring railpasses, student ID cards, and HI memberships.

Council Travel, the travel division of Council, is a full-service travel agency specializing in youth and budget travel. They offer discount airfares on scheduled airlines, railpasses, hostelling cards, low-cost accommodations, guidebooks, budget tours, travel gear, and international student (ISIC), youth (GO 25), and teacher (ITIC) identity cards. U.S. offices include Emory Village, 1561 N. Decatur Rd., **Atlanta,** GA 30307 (tel. (404) 377-9997); 729 Boylston St., **Boston,** MA 02116 (tel. (617) 266-1926); 1153 N. Dearborn, **Chicago,** IL 60610 (tel. (312) 951-

BY PLANE

0585); 10904 Lindbrook Dr., **Los Angeles,** CA 90024 (tel. (310) 208-3551); 205 E. 42nd St., **New York,** NY 10017 (tel. (212) 822-2700); 3606A Chestnut St., **San Diego,** CA 92109 (tel. (619) 270-6401); 530 Bush St., **San Francisco,** CA 94108 (tel. (415) 421-3473); 1314 N.E. 43rd St., **Seattle,** WA 98105 (tel. (206) 632-2448); 3300 M St. NW, **Washington, D.C.** 20007 (tel. (202) 337-65464). For U.S. cities not listed, call (800) 2-COUNCIL/226-8624. Overseas offices include: 28A Poland St. (Oxford Circus), **London,** W1V 3DB (tel. (0171) 437 7767); 22 Rue des Pyramides 75001 **Paris** (tel. 1 44 55 55 65); **Munich** (tel. (089) 39 50 22); **Tokyo** (tel. 3 35 81 55 17); **Singapore** (tel. 65 738 70 66).

STA Travel, 6560 Scottsdale Rd. #F100, Scottsdale, AZ 85253 (tel. (800) 777-0112 nationwide; fax (602) 922-0793). A student and youth travel organization with over 100 offices worldwide offering discount airfares for young travelers, railpasses, accommodations, tours, insurance, and ISICs. 16 offices in the U.S. including: 297 Newbury Street, **Boston,** MA 02115 (tel. (617) 266-6014); 429 S. Dearborn St., Chicago IL 60605 (tel. (312) 786-9050); 7202 Melrose Ave., **Los Angeles,** CA 90046 (tel. (213) 934-8722); 10 Downing St., **New York,** NY 10003 (tel. (212) 627-3111); 4341 University Way NE, Seattle, WA 98105 (tel. (206) 633-5000); 2401 Pennsylvania Ave.; **Washington, D.C.** 20037 (tel. (202) 887-0912); 51 Grant Ave., **San Francisco,** CA 94108 (tel. (415) 391-8407); **Miami,** FL 33133 (tel. (305) 461-3444). In the U.K., 6 Wrights Ln., **London** W8 6TA (tel. (0171) 938 47 11 for North American travel). In New Zealand, 10 High St., **Auckland** (tel. (09) 309 97 23). In Australia, 222 Faraday St., **Melbourne** VIC 3050 (tel. (03) 349 69 11).

Let's Go Travel, Harvard Student Agencies, 67 Mount Auburn St., Cambridge, MA 02138 (tel. 800-5-LETS GO/553-8746) or 617-495-9649). Railpasses, HI-AYH memberships, ISICs, ITICs, FIYTO cards, guidebooks, maps, bargain flights, and a complete line of budget travel gear. All items available by mail; call or write for a catalog (or see the catalog in center of this publication).

Campus Travel, 52 Grosvenor Gardens, London SW1W 0AG (http://www.campustravel.co.uk). 41 branches in the U.K. Student and youth fares on plane, train, boat, and bus travel. Flexible airline tickets. Discount and ID cards for youths, travel insurance for students and those under 35, maps, and guides. Puts out travel suggestion booklets. Telephone booking service: in Europe call (0171) 730 3402; in North America call (0171) 730 2101; worldwide call (0171) 730 8111; in Manchester call (0161) 273 1721; in Scotland call (0131) 668 3303. (http://www.campustravel.co.uk).

Council Charter: 205 E. 42nd St., New York, NY 10017 (tel. (212) 661 0311; fax 972 0194). Offers a combination of inexpensive charter and scheduled airfares from a variety of U.S. gateways to most major European destinations. One-way fares and open jaws (fly into one city and out of another) are available.

Red Bear Tours, Suite 11A, 401 St. Kilda R, Melbourne, Victoria 3004, Australia (tel. (03) 98 67 38 88; fax 98 67 10 55; e-mail bmccunn@werple.mira.net.au). Specializes in independent arrangements for travel to Turkey, Russia, India, Israel, Egypt, and New Zealand.

■ By Plane

Flexibility saves money, especially when faced with the high cost of regularly scheduled direct flights; from North America, an indirect flight through Brussels or Luxembourg may cost considerably less than a direct flight. **Off-season** travelers are faced with less competition for inexpensive seats and benefit from lower fares. **Peak-season** rates are in effect June 1-Sept. 15 and Dec. 10-24. You can save a bundle by carefully arranging your travel dates. Commissions are smaller on budget flights so some travel agents might not be eager to help you search for the cheapest fare. Scan the travel section of the Sunday papers for cheap, albeit erratic, fares. Student travel organizations such as Council, Travel CUTS, and Let's Go Travel offer special deals through ticket consolidators of which regular travel agents may not be aware. In the summer of 1996, New York-Athens roundtrip flights cost approximately US$840, and New York-İstanbul roundtrip flights cost roughly US$999.

COMMERCIAL AIRLINES

The commercial airlines' lowest regular offer is the **APEX** (Advance Purchase Excursion Fare); specials advertised in newspapers may be cheaper, but have more restrictions and fewer available seats. APEX fares provide you with confirmed reservations and allow "open-jaw" tickets (landing in and returning from different cities). Generally, reservations must be made seven to 21 days in advance, with seven- to 14-day minimum and up to 90-day maximum stay limits and hefty cancellation and change penalties (fees rise in summer). Book APEX fares early during peak season; by May you will have a hard time getting the departure date you want.

Look into flights to less-popular destinations or on smaller carriers. **Icelandair** (tel. (800) 223-5500) has last minute offers and a standby fare from New York to Luxembourg (April-June 15 and Sept.-Oct. US$398; June 15-Aug. US$598). Reservations must be made within three days of departure.

Olympic Airways (tel. (242) 838-3600) offers a round-trip New York-Athens summer fare of US$1126, 10-30% cheaper in winter. International flights also connect to airports in Crete, Rhodes, and Corfu. **Turkish Airlines' (THY)** (U.S. tel. (800) 874-8875) fares are exorbitant, but reasonably priced student tickets are sometimes available.

TICKET CONSOLIDATORS

Ticket consolidators resell unsold tickets on commercial and charter airlines at unpublished fares. The consolidator market is by and large international; domestic flights, if they do exist, are typically for popular cross-country flights like New York-Seattle. Consolidator flights are the best deals if you are traveling on short notice, (you bypass advance purchase requirements, since you aren't tangled in airline bureaucracy), on a high-priced trip to an offbeat destination, or in the peak season (when published fares are jacked way up). There is rarely a maximum age or stay limit, but unlike tickets bought through an airline, you won't be able to use your tickets on another flight if you miss yours, and you will have to go back to the consolidator to get a refund, rather than the airline.

Consolidators come in three varieties: wholesale only (who sell only to travel agencies), specialty agencies (both wholesale and retail), and **"bucket shops"** (or discount retail agencies). You, as a private consumer, can deal directly only with the latter, but you have access to a larger market if you use a travel agent, who can also get tickets from wholesale consolidators. Look for bucket shops' tiny ads in weekend papers (in the U.S., the *Sunday New York Times* is best). In London, the real bucket shop center, the Air Travel Advisory Bureau (tel. (0171) 6365000) provides a list of consolidators.

For destinations worldwide, try **Airfare Busters,** in Washington, D.C. (tel. (800) 776-0481, Boca Raton, FL (tel. (800) 881-3273), and Houston, TX (tel. (800) 232-8783); **Pennsylvania Travel,** in Paoli, PA (tel. (800) 331-0947); **Cheap Tickets,** in Los Angeles, CA, San Francisco, CA, Honolulu, HI, Overland Park, KS, and New York, NY, (tel. (800) 377-1000); **Moment's Notice,** New York, NY (tel. (718) 234-6295; fax 234-6450), air tickets, tours, and hotels; US$25 annual fee. For a processing fee, depending on the number of travelers and the itinerary, **Travel Avenue,** Chicago, IL (tel. (800) 333-3335) will search for the lowest international airfare available and even give you a rebate on fares over US$300.

Kelly Monaghan's *Consolidators: Air Travel's Bargain Basement* (US$7 plus US$2 shipping) from the Intrepid Traveler, P.O. Box 438, New York, NY 10034 (e-mail intreptrav@aol.com), is an valuable source for more information and lists of consolidators by location and destination. Cyber-resources include **World Wide** (http://www.tmn.com/wwwanderer/WWWa) and Edward Hasbrouck's incredibly informative *Airline Ticket Consolidators and Bucket Shops* (http://www.gnn.com/gnn/wic/wics/trav.97.html).

CHARTER FLIGHTS

The theory behind a **charter** is that a tour operator contracts with an airline (usually one specializing in charters) to fly extra loads of passengers to peak-season destinations. Charter flights fly less frequently than major airlines and have more restrictions, particularly on refunds. They are also almost always fully booked, and schedules and itineraries may change or be cancelled at the last moment (as late as 48 hours before the trip and without a full refund); you'll be much better off purchasing a ticket on a regularly scheduled airline. As always, pay with a credit card if you can; consider travelers insurance against trip interruption.

Try **Interworld** (tel. (305) 443-4929), **Travac** (tel. (800) 872-8800), or **Rebel,** Valencia, CA (tel. (800) 227-3235) or Orlando, FL (tel. (800) 732-3588). Don't be afraid to call every number and hunt for the best deal.

Eleventh-hour **discount clubs** and **fare brokers** offer members savings on European travel, including charter flights and tour packages. Research your options carefully. **Last Minute Travel Club,** 1249 Boylston St., Boston, MA 02215 (tel. (800) 527-8646 or (617) 267-9800), and **Discount Travel International,** New York, NY (tel. (212) 362-3636; fax 362-3236) are among the few travel clubs that don't charge a membership fee. Others include **Moment's Notice,** New York, NY (tel. (718) 234-6295; fax 234 6450), air tickets, tours, and hotels; US$25 annual fee and **Travelers Advantage,** Stamford, CT (tel. (800) 835-8747; US$49 annual fee); and **Travel Avenue** (tel. (800) 333-3335).

COURIER COMPANIES AND FREIGHTERS

Those who travel light should consider flying to Europe as a **courier.** The company hiring you will use your checked luggage space for freight; you're only allowed to bring carry-ons. You are responsible for the safe delivery of the baggage claim slips (given to you by a courier company representative) to the representative waiting for you when you arrive—don't screw up or you will be blacklisted as a courier. You will probably never see the cargo you are transporting—the company handles it all—and airport officials know that couriers are not responsible for the baggage checked for them. Restrictions to watch for: you must be over 18, have a valid passport, and procure your own visa (if necessary); most flights are roundtrip only with short fixed-length stays (usually one week); only single tickets are issued (but a companion may be able to get a next-day flight); and most flights originate from New York. Roundtrip fares to Western Europe from the U.S. range from US$250-400 (during off season) to US$400-550 (during summer). **NOW Voyager,** 74 Varick St. #307, New York, NY 10013 (tel. (212) 431-1616), acts as an agent for many courier flights worldwide primarily from New York. They offer special last-minute deals to such cities as London, Paris, Rome, and Frankfurt for as little as US$200 roundtrip plus a US$50 registration fee. Another agent to try is **Halbart Express,** 147-05 176th St., Jamaica, NY 11434 (tel. (718) 656-5000).

You can also go directly through courier companies in New York, or check your bookstore or library for handbooks such as *Air Courier Bargains* (US$15 plus US$3.50 shipping) from the Intrepid Traveler, P.O. Box 438, New York, NY 10034. *The Courier Air Travel Handbook* (US$10 plus US$3.50 shipping) explains how to travel as an air courier and contains names, phone numbers, and contact points of courier companies. It can be ordered directly from Bookmasters, Inc., P.O. Box 2039, Mansfield, OH 44905 (tel. (800) 507-2665).

■ By Train

Greece is served by a number of international train routes that connect Athens, Thessaloniki, and Larissa to most European cities. Count on at least a three-day journey from Trieste or Vienna to Athens. İstanbul, **Turkey** is accessible by rail from points in Europe. Trains are among the cheaper transportation options, but not the more convenient—Eurail is not valid in Turkey. The Turkish rail system is rivaled only by the Greek system as Europe's most antiquated and least efficient. There is no rail system in Cyprus.

■ By Ferry

Ferry travel is a popular way to get to and travel between Greece, Turkey, and Cyprus. Reservations are recommended for many ferries, especially in high season. Be warned that *ferries run on irregular schedules*. Check in at *least* two hours in advance; late boarders may find their seats gone. If you sleep on deck, bring warm clothes and a sleeping bag. Bicycles travel free, and motorcycles are transported for an additional charge (check each agency). Don't forget motion sickness medication, toilet paper, and a hand towel. Bring your own food to avoid high prices on board.

Most lines offer **discounts.** Those 26 and under and ISIC-holders 30 and under can usually obtain student deck fares for 1000dr less than regular price. A railpass or HI card may entitle you to a small discount on selected routes. Children under 12 pay half-price (those under two or four ride free, depending on the company). There are group reductions of approximately 10% on one way and 20% on roundtrip tickets (usually 10 person minimum).

The major ports of departure from Italy to Greece are Ancona and Brindisi, on the southeast coast of Italy. Bari, Otranto, and Venice also have a few connections. If coming from the north of Italy, be aware that gassing and theft are not unheard of on the overnight trains from Rome to Brindisi. Some ferry lines offer free deck passage on a space-available basis (you could get bumped by a paying passenger), but all passengers still need to pay the port tax (L10,000, or $6.25, in Brindisi) and, in high season, a supplementary fee of L19,000 ($12). Boats travel primarily to Corfu (10hr.), Igoumenitsa (12hr.), and Patras (20hr.). Prices range L50,000-105,000 ($31-66); in low season L22,000-45,000 ($13-29). For schedules from Greece to Italy, see Patras, Cephalonia, Corfu, or Igoumenitsa.

From Çeşme, Turkey, an Ertürk ferry offers service to Chios (May-June 3-4 per week, July-April 1 per week). Prices are one way $25, same-day return $30, open round-trip $35. Rhodes is connected by ferry to Marmaris (one way 10,000dr, roundtrip 12,000dr), as well as to Limassol, Cyprus (2 per week, 17hr., 18,500-22,000dr), and Haifa, Israel (2 per week, 36hr., 28,500-33,000dr). These Limassol and Haifa services provide student and youth discounts of 20% year-round.

From **Kıbrıs,** the easiest crossing is Taşucu, Turkey to Girne (Kyrenia) on the northern coast of the island (7hr.). Boats run twice per day in the summer, less frequently in winter. **Ertürk** and **Fergün** tourism companies sell discounted tickets (see Taşucu for details (p. 535). You can also cross from Mersin (10hr.).

Hydrofoils (Flying Dolphins) are a tempting mode of traveling. They run more frequently and reliably than ferries at twice their speed, but cost twice as much.

■ By Bus

Road travel in Turkey is dangerous by European and U.S. standards (see Turkish Buses p. 430).

Though European trains and railpasses are extremely popular, the long-distance bus networks of Greece and Turkey are more extensive, efficient, and often more comfortable than train services.

Eurobus offers two-week or one-, two-, or three-month passes for unlimited travel on continental-style coaches with an English-speaking driver and guide. Destinations include major cities throughout continental Europe. Travelers can hop on and off, and move on as often as they wish. The buses also stop door to door at a selection of hostels, and budget hotels, usually one per city. For more information, contact 355 Palermo Ave., Coral Gables, Florida 33134 (tel. (800) 517-7778 or, for students, (800) 727-2437). The London address is: P.O. Box 5220, London W5 1GQ (tel.

(0181) 991 5591; fax 991 1442). Another option is **Eurolines,** 4 Cardiff Rd., LUTON LU1 1PP (tel. (01582) 404 511, in London (0171) 730 82 35), which in Europe's largest operator of Europe-wide coach services, including Eastern Europe and Russia. A Eurolines Pass offers unlimited 30- or 60- day travel between 18 major tourist destinations. **Magic Travel Services** (formerly Magic Bus) offers cheap, direct bus service between major cities in Europe, competitive airfares, hotel reservations, and ferry ticket sales. Offices are located at 20 Filellinon St., Syntagma, Athens (tel. (01) 323 7471, -4; fax 322 0219). (Competent, English-speaking staff; open Mon.-Fri. 9am-6pm, Sat. 9am-2pm.) They run buslines from Athens to Belgrade, Budapest, Prague, Naples, and Rome starting at 34,000dr. roundtrip.

ONCE THERE

■ Getting Around

The Greek government frowns on tourists taking advantage of cheaper fares to Greece for easy access to Turkey, and the information you receive on how to travel between the two countries may be confusing. Contrary to what tourist authorities may lead you to believe, there's no law that prevents crossing the borders. Many travelers make one-day excursions, but you should check into regulations on longer trips. If you fly to Greece on a European charter flight, you can't travel to Turkey.

Athens and İstanbul are connected by **Euroways Eurolines** bus and by train. If you have a railpass and are traveling from Greece to Turkey, take the train as far as Alexandroupolis, and ride the bus from there. Beware: the 38-hour ride from Athens will wear out even the most seasoned traveler. The quickest but most expensive option is an Olympic Airways **flight** to İstanbul or other points in Turkey.

Those who **hitch** between Turkey and Greece say they try to make it to İstanbul in one ride from Alexandroupolis or Thessaloniki; there isn't much traffic, and people are not permitted to walk across the border. *Let's Go* does not recommend hitchhiking. Those who have decided to hitch say they made sure their driver's car license did not get stamped in their passports (but rather on some other, disposable piece of paper), or they would have needed to produce the car to leave the country.

If you bring a car into Turkey, you can drive for three months without a *Carnet de Passage*, although the vehicle will be registered on your passport. If you stay longer, you must apply for a *triptique* at the Turkish Touring and Automobile Club (see Getting Around, p. 428).

BY TRAIN

European trains retain the charm and romance their North American counterparts lost long ago, but don't forget you're in the modern world. Bring food and a water bottle you can fill at your hostel and take with you on train trips; the on-board café can be pricey, and train water undrinkable. Trains are not theft-proof; lock your compartment door if you can, and keep your valuables on your person at all times.

Many train stations have different counters for domestic and international tickets, seat reservations, and information—check before lining up. On major lines, reservations are always advisable, and often required, even with a railpass; make them at least a few hours in advance at the train station (US$3-10). Also, while use of many of Europe's high speed or quality trains (such as EuroCity, InterCity, Sweden's X2000, or France's TGV) is included in the price of a railpass, a supplement is required to ride certain other trains. You can sometimes pay for this supplement on board, but this costs a bit more.

A sleeping berth in a couchette car is an affordable luxury (about US$20; reserve at the station at least several days in advance). Very few countries give students or young people direct discounts on regular domestic rail tickets, but many will sell a

GETTING AROUND

student or youth card valid for 20-50% off all fares for an entire year. Check the introductory sections of each country chapter for details.

Railpasses Buying a railpass is both a popular and sensible option under many circumstances. Ideally conceived, a railpass allows you to jump on any train in Europe, go wherever you want, and change your plans at will. Find a travel agent with a copy of the **Eurail tariff manual** to weigh the wisdom of purchasing them. Add up the second-class fares for your routes and deduct 5% (listed prices automatically include commission) for comparison. If you're under age 26, the BIJ (Billets Internationals de Jeunesse) tickets are probably a viable option.

Eurailpass remains the best option in European rail passes for non-EU travelers. Eurailpasses are valid in most of Western Europe (not in Britain, however). Eurailpasses and Europasses are designed by the EU itself and are only purchasable by non-Europeans from non-European distributors. The EU also sets the prices, so no one travel agent is better than any other for buying a Eurailpass—they charge the same price and get the same commission.

The first-class **Eurailpass** rarely pays off; it is offered for 15 days (US$522), 21 days (US$678), one month (US$838), two months (US$1148), or three months (US$1468). If you are traveling in a group, you might prefer the **Eurail Saverpass,** which allows unlimited first-class travel for 15 days (US$452), 21 days (US$578), or one month (US$712) per person in groups of two or more (3 or more April-Sept.). Travelers under age 26 on their first day of travel can buy a **Eurail Youthpass,** good for 15 days (US$418), one month (US$598), or two months (US$798) of second-class travel. It's hard to get your money's worth from a one-month pass; the two-month pass is more economical. **Eurail Flexipasses** allow limited first-class travel within a two-month period: 10 days (US$616) and 15 days (US$812). **Youth Flexipasses,** for those under 26 who wish to travel second-class, are available for US$438 or US$588. All five passes offer free travel in Greece and 30% discounts on ferries from Brindisi to Patras on Adriatica Lines, or on Hellenic Mediterranean Lines' ferries from Piraeus to the Republic of Cyprus, Venice, Alexandria, and Turkey (Eurail passes are *not* good for intra-Greece ferries). Keep your validation slip and receipt.

The **Europass** allows travelers to combine the more popular European countries in one travel plan: France, Germany, Italy, Spain, and Switzerland. Europass offers rail travel through a number of countries determined by the number of travel days selected.

You'll almost certainly find it easiest to buy a Eurailpass before you arrive in Europe; contact Council Travel, Travel CUTS, or Let's Go Travel (see Budget Travel Agencies, p. 31.), or any of many other travel agents. If you're stuck in Europe and unable to find someone to sell you a Eurailpass, make a transatlantic call to an American railpass agent, who should be able to send a pass by express mail. Eurailpasses are not refundable once validated; you can get a replacement for a lost pass only if you have purchased insurance on it under the Pass Protection Plan (US$10) offered by railpass agents. All Eurailpasses can be purchased from a travel agent or from **Rail Europe, Inc.,** 226-230 Westchester Ave., White Plains, NY 10604 (tel. (800) 438-7245; fax (800) 432-1329 in the U.S.; and (800) 361-7245); fax (905) 602-4198 in Canada; http://www.raileurope.com), which publishes the free *Europe on Track,* providing up-to-date information on all pass options and rail travel in Europe. They sell railpasses and point-to-point tickets.

For EU citizens who cannot get Eurail passes, there are **InterRail** passes, for which six months' residence in Europe makes you eligible. The Under 26 InterRail Card allows either 15 days or 1 month of unlimited travel within 1, 2, 3, or all of the 7 zones into which InterRail divides Europe; the cost is determined by the number of zones the pass is to cover. The Over 26 InterRail Card offers unlimited second-class travel in 19 countries in Europe for 15 days or 1 month for UK£215 and £275, respectively. Tickets are available from travel agents or at main train stations.

If you plan to focus your travels in one country, Greece and Turkey both have national rail passes as well; Cyprus, unfortunately, does not. When deciding whether to purchase a railpass for travel primarily in Greece or Turkey, keep in mind that service in these countries is among the slowest in Europe, and individual tickets are among the most affordable. Railpasses in these countries rarely pay for themselves. In addition to simple railpasses, many countries (as well as Europass and Eurail) now offer rail-and-drive passes, which combine car rental days with days of rail travel—a good option for travelers who wish both to visit cities or towns accessible by rail and make side trips into the surrounding areas. Also keep in mind that several of these national and regional passes offer companion fares, allowing two adults traveling together at all times 50% off the price of one pass. Some of these passes can be bought only in Europe, some only outside of Europe, and for some it doesn't matter; check with a railpass agent or with national tourist offices.

Rail tickets For travelers under 26 on their first day of travel, **BIJ** tickets (Billets Internationals de Jeunesse, sold under the names **Wasteels, Eurotrain,** and **Route 26**) are a great alternative to railpasses. Available for international trips within Europe and for travel within France as well as most ferry services, they knock 25-40% off regular second-class fares. Tickets are all good for 60 days after purchase and allow a number of stopovers (no longer unlimited) along the normal direct route of the train journey. Issued for a specific international route between two points, they must be used in the direction and order of the designated route without side- or back-tracking. You must buy BIJ tickets in Europe. They are available from European travel agents, at Wasteels or Eurotrain offices (usually in or near train stations), or directly at the ticket counter in some nations. Contact Wasteels in London's Victoria Station, adjacent to Platform 2 (tel. (0171) 834 70 66; fax 630 76 28).

Useful Resources The ultimate reference for planning rail trips is the *Thomas Cook European Timetable* (US$28; US$39 includes a map of Europe highlighting all train and ferry routes; postage US$4.50). This timetable, updated regularly, covers all major and most minor train routes in Europe. In the U.S., order it from Forsyth Travel Library (see Useful Publications, p. 3). Available in most bookstores or from Houghton Mifflin Co., 222 Berkeley St., Boston, MA 02116 (tel. (617) 351-5974; fax 351-1113) is the annual *Eurail Guide to Train Travel in the New Europe* (US$15); giving timetables, instructions, and prices for international train trips, daytrips, and excursions in Europe. The annual railpass special edition of Rick Steves' free *Europe Through the Back Door* travel newsletter and catalog, 120 Fourth Ave. N., P.O. Box 2009, Edmonds, WA 98020 (tel. (206) 771-8303; fax 771-0833; e-mail ricksteves@aol.com; http://www.halcyon.com) provides a comprehensive comparative analysis of European railpasses with national or regional passes and point-to-point tickets sold in Europe. **Hunter Publishing,** 300 Raritan Center Parkway, Edison, NJ 08818 (tel. (908) 225-1900; fax 417-0482), offers a comprehensive catalog of rail atlases and travel guides. Titles on hand include *Britain on the Backroads, Eastern Europe by Rail,* and other country-specific materials.

■ Accommodations

HOSTELS

For those looking for friends and a unique experience minus the expense, hostels are the place. These generally feature dorm-style accommodations with large rooms and bunk beds; some allow families and couples to have private rooms—variety is the buzzword. Some have kitchens and utensils for your use, storage areas, laundry facilities, and even bike, moped, or other rentals. They're not all fun, games, and laundry though: some close during daytime "lock-out" hours, have curfews, require you to do chores (although this is less and less common), or impose a maximum stay. Prices range, on the whole, from US$5 to US$25 per night, but hostels that are part of hostel associations will often have lower rates for members. **Hostelling International** is the largest such organization, although others such as American

Association of Independent Hostels, Backpackers Resorts International, Budget Backpackers Hostels, or Federation of International Youth Hostels may be worth considering. *The Hostel Handbook for the U.S.A. & Canada* (US$3; Jim Williams, Ed., *The Hostel Handbook*, Dept.: IGH, 722 Saint Nicholas Ave., New York, NY 10031; e-mail Hostel@aol.com) lists over 500 hostels. Lastly, if you have Internet access, check out the Internet Guide to Hostelling (http://hostels.com). Reservations for HI hostels may be made via the International Booking Network (IBN), a computerized system which allows you to book to and from HI hostels (more than 300 centers worldwide) months in advance for a nominal fee. Cyprus has six hostels, Turkey two (in İstanbul and Marmaris). Unfortunately, ongoing negotiations between HI and Greece have suspended the accreditation of Greece's two dozen hostels, except for one in Athens. Don't be fooled; many hostels in Greece display the blue triangle but are not HI affiliated. For the latest information regarding these hostels, travelers are encouraged to contact the International Youth Hostel Federation Secretariat, 9 Guessens Road, Welwyn Garden City, Hertfordshire, AL8 6QW, England (tel. (1707) 324170), or the IYHF Athens International Hostel, 16 Victor Hugo St., Athens (tel. (01) 523 4170; fax 523 4015).

CAMPING

Useful Publications

A variety of publishing companies offer hiking guidebooks to meet the educational needs of novice or expert. For information about camping, hiking, and biking, write or call the publishers listed below to receive a free catalog.

Family Campers and RVers/National Campers and Hikers Association, Inc., 4804 Transit Rd., Bldg. #2, Depew, NY 14043 (tel./fax (716) 668-6242). This all volunteer conservation group publishes *Camping Today,* which comes with the US$20 fee. For US$30, you get the International Camping Carnet, which is required by some European campgrounds, but can usually be bought on the spot.

The Mountaineers Books, 1001 SW Klickitat Way, Ste. 201, Seattle, WA 98134 (tel. (800) 553-4453 or (206) 223-6303; fax 223-6306; http://mbooks@mountaineers.org). Many titles on hiking (the *100 Hikes* series), biking, mountaineering, natural history, and conservation.

REI, P.O. Box 1700, Sumner, WA 98352–0001 (tel. (800) 426-4840), publishes *Europa Camping and Caravanning* (US$20), an annually updated catalog of European campsites, and *The U.S. Outdoor Atlas* (US$17), a similar book for the U.S. Few of their books are offered via mail-order, so check their retail stores.

What You Need and Where to Get It

Purchase **equipment** before you leave. This way you'll know exactly what you have and how much it weighs. Whether buying or renting, finding sturdy, light, and inexpensive equipment is a must. Spend some time examining catalogs and talking to knowledgeable salespeople. Mail-order firms are for the most part reputable and cheap—order from them if you can't do as well locally.

Sleeping bags: What kind of sleeping bag you should buy depends on the climate of the area you'll be camping in and climbing through. Most of the better sleeping bags are rated according to the lowest outdoor temperature at which they will still keep you warm. Bags are sometimes rated by season rather than temperature: keep in mind that "summer" translates to a rating of 30-40°F, "three-season" means 20°F, and "four-season" or "winter" means below 0°F. Sleeping bags are made either of down (warmer and lighter, but miserable when wet) or of synthetic material (cheaper, heavier, more durable, and warmer when wet). While prices vary widely depending on the manufacturer, the following prices are reasonable for good bags: US$65-100 for a summer synthetic, US$135-200 for a three-season synthetic, $150-225 for a three-season down bag, and about US$250-550 for a down sleeping bag usable in the winter.

ACCOMMODATIONS

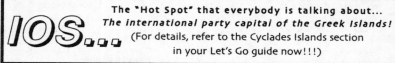

A C C O M M O D A T I O N S

Pads: If you're using a sleeping bag for serious camping, you should also have either a foam pad (US$13 and up for closed-cell foam, US$25 and up for open-cell foam) or an air mattress (US$25-50) to cushion your back and neck (and, if you're camping in a colder region, to insulate you from the ground). Another good alternative is the **Therm-A-Rest,** which is part foam and part air-mattress and inflates to full padding when you unroll it.

Tents: Just as with selecting a mate, your major considerations in selecting a tent should be shape and size. The best tents are free-standing, with their own frames and suspension systems; they set up quickly and require no staking (though staking will keep your tent from blowing away). Low profile dome tents are the best all-around. When pitched their internal space is almost entirely usable, which means little unnecessary bulk. As for size, two people *can* fit in a two-person tent but will find life more pleasant in a four-person tent. If you're traveling by car, go for the bigger tent; if you're hiking, stick with a smaller tent that weighs no more than 3.5 lbs. For especially small and lightweight models, contact **Sierra Design,** which sells the "Clip Flashlight," a two-person tent that weighs less than 1.4kg (3lb.). Good two-person tents start at about $135; $200 for a four-person. You can, however, often find last year's version for half the price. Be sure to seal the seams of your tent with waterproofer, and make sure it has a rain fly.

Backpacks: If you intend to do a lot of hiking, you should have a **frame backpack.** Buy a backpack with an internal frame if you'll be hiking on difficult trails that require a lot of bending and maneuvering—internal-frame packs mold better to your back, keep a lower center of gravity, and can flex adequately to follow you through a variety of movements. In addition, internal frame packs are more manageable on crowded planes, trains, and automobiles, and are less likely to be mangled by rough handling. External-frame packs are more comfortable for long hikes over even terrain since they keep the weight higher and distribute it more evenly. These don't travel as well; bring a duffle to protect your pack when in baggage compartments. Make sure your pack has a strong, padded hip belt, which transfers much of the weight from delicate shoulders to sturdier legs. The size of a backpack is measured in cubic inches. Any serious backpacking requires at least 4000 of them, while longer trips require around 5000. Tack on an additional 500 cubic inches for internal-frame packs, since you'll have to pack your sleeping bag inside, rather than strap it on the outside as you do with an external-frame pack. For more hints, (see Packing, p. 29). Sturdy backpacks cost anywhere from US$125-400. This is one area where it doesn't pay to economize—cheaper packs may be less comfortable, and the straps are more likely to fray or rip quickly. Test-drive a backpack for comfort before you buy it: walk around with it on, imagine walking a few miles up a rocky incline with a full pack before committing to anything that may poop out or grow uncomfortable.

Other necessities include: **battery-operated lantern** (gas is inconvenient and dangerous), **plastic groundcloth** for the floor of your tent, **nylon tarp** for general purposes, **waterproof backpack cover** (although you can forego the cover by storing your belongings in plastic bags inside your backpack), **"stuff sack"** or plastic bag to keep your sleeping bag dry. **Rain gear** should come in two pieces, a top and pants, rather than a poncho. Ponchos turns into sails when the wind kicks up, and are more bulky and unwieldy than their two-piece counterparts. **Synthetics** are of the essence in any climate: polypropylene tops, socks, and long underwear, along with a pile jacket, will keep you warm when wet. When camping in autumn, winter, or spring, bring along a **"space blanket,"** a technological wonder that helps you to retain your body heat (US$3.50-13; doubles as a groundcloth) but don't expect it to do the work of several good wool sweaters. Don't go anywhere without a **canteen** or water bottle. Plastic models keep water cooler in the hot sun than metal ones do and are virtually shatter- and leak-proof. Large, collapsible **water sacks** will significantly improve your lot in primitive campgrounds and weigh practically nothing when empty, though they can get bulky. Bring **water-purification tablets** for when you can't boil water. Although most campgrounds provide campfire sites, you may want to bring a small **metal grate** of your own, and even a grill. For those places

that forbid fires or the gathering of firewood, you'll need a **camp stove** (Coleman, the classic, starts at about US$30). Consider GAZ-powered stoves, which come with bottled propane gas that is easy to use and widely available in Europe. Make sure you have **waterproof matches,** or your stove may do you no good; it's always a good idea to have a lighter on hand. A **swiss army knife, insect repellent,** and **calamine lotion** are also essential camping items. Last but not least, **hat, hat, hat:** always have a warm hat that covers your ears.

Shop around locally before turning to mail-order firms; this allows you to get an idea of what the different items actually look like (and weigh), so that if you later decide to order by mail you'll have a more exact idea of what it is you're getting. The mail-order firms listed below offer lower prices than those you're likely to find in stores, and they can also help you determine which item you need.

> **Recreational Equipment, Inc. (REI),** 1700 45th St. E, Sumner, WA 98390 (tel. (800) 426-4840; http://www.rei.com). Stocks a wide range of the latest in camping gear and holds great seasonal sales. Many items guaranteed for life.
> **Sierra Design,** 1255 Powell St., Emeryville, CA 94608 (tel. (510) 450-9555; fax 654-0705) has a wide array (all seasons and types) of especially small and light-weight tent models. You can often find last year's version for half the price.
> **Sierra Trading Post,** 5025 Campstool Rd., Cheyenne, WY 82007-1802 (tel. (307) 775-8000; fax 307-775-8088). Savings on name brand outdoor clothing and equipment. Mail order and two locations in Cheyenne and Reno, NV.

Wilderness and Safety Concerns

The three most important things to remember when hiking or camping: stay warm, stay dry, and stay hydrated. The vast majority of life-threatening wilderness problems stem from a failure to follow this advice. If you are going on any hike, overnight or just a day hike, that will take you more than one mile from civilization, you should pack enough equipment to keep you alive should disaster befall. This includes raingear, warm layers (not cotton!) especially hat and mittens, a first-aid kit, high energy food, and water. If you are camping in the summer in Greece, Turkey, and Cyprus, the hat and mittens are (obviously) not necessary, and cotton is a good summer wear fabric.

■ Keeping In Touch

MAIL

Mail can be sent internationally through **Poste Restante** (the international phrase for General Delivery) to any city or town; it's well worth using and much more reliable than you might think. Mark the envelope "HOLD" and address it, for example, "Colin <u>MILBERG</u>, *Poste Restante,* Athens, Greece." The last name should be capitalized and underlined. The mail will go to a special desk in the central post office, unless you specify a post office by street address or postal code. As a rule, it is best to use the largest post office in the area; sometimes, mail will be sent there regardless of what you write on the envelope. When possible, it is usually safer and quicker to send mail express or registered.

It helps to use the appropriate translation of *Poste Restante* (*Postrestant* in Turkey and Northern Cyprus, *Poste Restante* in Greece and Southern Cyprus). Cyprus has official postal codes for the North, but your best bet may be to send letters via Turkey using the postal code **Mersin 10, Turkey.** When picking up your mail, bring your passport or other ID. If the clerks insist that there is nothing for you, have them check under your first name as well. *Let's Go: Greece & Turkey* lists post offices in the Practical Information section for each city and most towns.

Aerogrammes, printed sheets that fold into envelopes and travel via airmail, are available at post offices. Most post offices will charge exorbitant fees or simply

refuse to send Aerogrammes with enclosures. Airmail between Europe and the U.S. averages one to two weeks. Much depends on the national post office involved.

If regular airmail is too slow, there are a few faster, more expensive, options. Federal Express (tel. (800) 463-3339) can get a letter from New York to Paris or Tokyo in two days for a whopping US$28.50. By Uncle Sam's Express Mail, the same letter would arrive in two to three days and would cost US$21.

Surface mail is by far the cheapest and slowest way to send mail. It takes one to three months to cross the Atlantic, appropriate for sending large quantities of items you won't need to see for a while. It is vital, therefore, to distinguish your airmail from surface mail by explicitly labeling "airmail" in the appropriate language (ΑΕΡΟΠΟΡΙΚΟΣ in Greece, *uçak ile* in Turkey). When ordering books and materials from abroad, always include one or two **International Reply Coupons (IRCs)**—a way of providing the postage to cover delivery. IRCs should be available from your local post office (US$1.05).

American Express offices throughout the world will act as a mail service for cardholders if you contact them in advance. Under this free **Client Letter Service,** they will hold mail for 30 days, forward upon request, and accept telegrams. Just like *Poste Restante,* the last name of the person to whom the mail is addressed should be capitalized and underlined. Some offices will offer these services to noncardholders (especially those who have purchased AmEx Travellers's Cheques), but you must call ahead to make sure. *Let's Go: Greece & Turkey* lists AmEx office locations for most large cities. A complete list is available free from AmEx (tel. (800) 528-4800) in the booklet *Traveler's Companion.*

TELEPHONES

You can place **international calls** from most telephones. To call direct from the U.S., dial the universal international access code (011) followed by the country code, the city code, and the local number. Country codes and city codes may sometimes be listed with a zero in front (e.g., 033), but when using 011 (or whatever your international access code happens to be), drop successive zeros (e.g., 011 33). In the region, especially in small villages, you may have to go through the operator. In others, you must wait for a tone after the international access code.

You can usually make direct international calls from **pay phones,** but you may need to drop your coins as quickly as your words. In Greece, Turkey, and Cyprus some pay phones are card-operated; some even accept major credit cards. Be wary of more expensive, private pay phones; look for pay phones in public areas, especially train stations. If private pay phones are to be feared, one should all but flee from the insidious in-room hotel phone call. Although incredibly convenient, these calls invariably include a sky-high surcharge (as much as US$10 in some establishments). If you really don't want to leave your hotel, find a pay phone in the lobby.

English-speaking operators are often available for both local and international assistance. Operators will place **collect calls** for you. It's cheaper to find a pay phone and deposit just enough money to be able to say "Call me" and give your number (though some pay phones can't receive calls).

Some companies, seizing upon this "call-me-back" concept, have created callback phone services. Under these plans, you call a specified number, ring once, and hang up. The company's computer calls back and gives you a dial tone. You can then make as many calls as you want, at rates about 20-60% lower than you'd pay using credit cards or pay phones. This option is most economical for loquacious travelers, as services may include a US$10-25 minimum billing per month. For information, call America Tele-Fone (tel. (800) 321-5817), Globaltel (tel. (770) 449-1295), International Telephone (tel. (800) 638-5558), and Telegroup (tel. (800) 338-0225).

A **calling card** is another, cheaper alternative; your local long-distance phone company will have a number for you to dial while traveling (either toll-free or charged as a local call) to connect instantly to an operator in your home country. The calls (plus a small surcharge) are then billed either collect or to a calling card. For more infor-

mation, call AT&T about its **AT&T Direct** services (tel. (800) 331-1140, from abroad (412) 553-7458), **Sprint** (tel. (800) 877-4646), or **MCI WorldPhone** and **World Reach** (tel. (800) 996-7535). MCI's WorldPhone also provides access to MCI's Traveler's Assist, which gives legal and medical advice, exchange rate information, and translation services. For similar services for countries outside the U.S., contact your local phone company. In Canada, contact Bell Canada **Canada Direct** (tel. (800) 565 4708); in the U.K., British Telecom **BT Direct** (tel. (800) 34 51 44); in Ireland, Telecom Éireann **Ireland Direct** (tel. (800) 250 250); in Australia, Telstra **Australia Direct** (tel. 13 22 00); in New Zealand, **Telecom New Zealand** (tel. 123); and in South Africa, **Telkom South Africa** (tel. 09 03).

Phone rates tend to be higher in the morning, lower in the evening, and lowest on Sunday and late at night. Also, remember **time differences** when you call. Britain, Ireland, Portugal, and Iceland are on Greenwich Mean Time (GMT)—five hours ahead of Eastern Standard Time. Finland, Estonia, Latvia, Lithuania, western Russia, Romania, Bulgaria, Greece, Turkey, and Cyprus are two hours ahead of GMT. Moscow is three hours ahead. Some countries ignore daylight savings time, and fall and spring switchover times often vary among those countries that do use it.

OTHER COMMUNICATION

Domestic and international **telegrams** offer an option slower than phone but faster than post. Fill out a form at any post or telephone office; cables to North America arrive in one or two days. Telegrams can be quite expensive, so you may wish to consider **faxes,** for more immediate, personal, and cheaper communication. Major cities across Europe have bureaus where you can pay to send and receive faxes.

Between May 2 and Octoberfest, **EurAide,** P.O. Box 2375, Naperville, IL 60567 (tel. (708) 420-2343; fax 420-2369), offers **Overseas Access,** a service useful to travelers without a set itinerary. The cost is US$15 per week or US$40 per month plus a US$15 registration fee. To reach you, people call, fax, or use the internet to leave a message; you receive it by calling Munich whenever you wish, which is cheaper than calling overseas. You may also leave messages for callers to pick up by phone. For an additional US$20 per month, EurAide will forward mail sent to Munich to any addresses you specify.

Daily newspapers including the London *Times,* the *Wall Street Journal* (International Edition), *The New York Times* and the *International Herald Tribune* are available at train stations and kiosks in major European cities. *The Economist* and international versions of *Time* and *Newsweek* are also easy to find.

If you're spending a year abroad and want to keep in touch with friends or colleagues in a college or research institution, or simply are addicted to the blinking cursor of the cyber-world, **electronic mail (e-mail)** is an attractive option. With a minimum of computer knowledge and a little planning, you can beam messages anywhere for no per-message charges.

Let's Go Picks

Let's Go: Greece and Turkey can make one claim that no other book in the *Let's Go* series can make—we cover, in our unique pages, four out of the seven wonders of the ancient world: the Colossus of Rhodes (Rhodes Island, Greece), the Temple of Zeus (Olympia, Greece), the mausoleum at Halicarnassus (Bodrum, Turkey), and the Temple of Diana (Ephesus, Turkey). (In case you were wondering, the other three are: the Hanging Gardens of Babylon, the Lighthouse at Alexandria, and the Great Pyramids at Giza.) Barring all modesty, we believe that these are not the only wondrous sights to be seen in Greece, Turkey, and Cyprus. After months of deliberation, and another summer of stellar research, we have come up with a new list, which in our opinion, may someday rival that of the already overused seven wonders of the ancient world. *Let's Go Greece and Turkey 1997* is proud to present our version of the seven modern wonders of the Mediterranean basin.

Places to get the most out of a kiss: In Greece: pucker up and head to a secluded corner of the Acropolis (be respectful—Athena was a virgin), Katarrakton, the lustral (lustful) basin at the Palace of Knossos on Crete, or the sight of the discovery of the Venus de Milo. **In Cyprus:** the Baths of Aphrodite (Polis). **In Turkey:** put on your best shade of pink and row your sweetheart to the white sands of Kleopatras Island (Marmaris), or take a stroll through the ruins of Aphrodisias (dedicated to the love goddess herself). **In Kıbrıs:** the British Embassy gardens (Lefkoşa).

Places to revel in an aesthetic experience: In Greece: grab your camera, stock up on postcards, and prepare yourself to experience Delphi's Oracle, the top of the acropolis of Lindos (Rhodes), or Southern Corfu. **In Cyprus:** the Kolossi Castle (Limassol). **In Turkey:** lace up your hiking boots and climb to the Sümela Monastery (Trabzon), or bask in the glory of the blue lagoon of Ölüdeniz. **In Kıbrıs:** Kervon Saray beach, Girne.

Places to blend with the locals: In Greece: grow a beard, pick up a lyre, and saunter to Mt. Athos, the donkey stand at the caldera of Santorini, or the folk art merchants on Skyros. **In Cyprus:** the 1900 Art Café (Larnaka). **In Turkey:** buy a pack of Camels, don your fez, and hop over to Safranbolu or Artvin. **In Kıbrıs:** the Karpaz Peninsula.

Places to watch the sunset over a beverage of your choice: In Greece: grab your shades and a few thousand *drachmae*, and pay for the view at the old harbor of Chania, Crete, Oia Town, Santorini, or the waterside *tavernas* near the windmills on Mykonos. **In Cyprus:** Ktima Paphos. **In Turkey:** watch the sun dip into the Mediterranean behind the Temple of Apollo (Side) or set into the Bosphorus (İstanbul). **In Kıbrıs:** the top of Othello's Tower (Mağusa).

Places to saturate your intestines with olive oil: In Greece: spend the day hungrily sauntering amid ancient ruins, then follow the scents of Plaka (Athens), Samos's red wine, or the open-air market of Iraklion (Crete). **In Cyprus:** Berlin #2 Café at the Green Line (Nicosia). **In Turkey:** feast on a Turkish omelette at the House of Medusa (İstanbul) or Foto'nun Yeri (Kalkan). **In Kıbrıs:** Erol's Restaurant (Girne).

Places the ancients would have been proud to pour libations at: In Greece: sport your cod piece (Minoan skirt), line up with your favorite phallic vessel, and process to Thessaloniki, Hersonissis (Crete) or Ios. **In Cyprus:** Agia Napa. **In Turkey:** the Mavi Bar in Kaş or Bodrum. **In Kıbrıs:** the Sunset outdoor disco.

Reasons to cancel your ticket home, quit your day job, and raise goats: In Greece: sigh among the olive trees, kiss the ground, and move to Palaikastro (Crete), Olympos (Karpathos), or Hydra. **In Cyprus:** Kakopetria (Troodos). **In Turkey:** build a hut on the beach of Gümüşluk or Datça. **In Kıbrıs:** Lefke.

GREECE ΕΛΛΑΔΑ

US$1 = 238dr	100dr = US$0.42
CDN$1 = 172.41dr	100dr = CDN$0.58
UK£1 = 370.4dr	100dr = UK£0.27
IR£1 = 384.6dr	100dr = IR£0.26
AUS$1 = 181.82dr	100dr = AUS$0.55
NZ$1 = 161.3dr	100dr = NZ$0.62
SAR1 = 52.36dr	100dr = SAR1.91
10,000TL = 2.84dr	100dr = 352,120TL
C£1 = 123.76dr	100dr = C£0.81

Even before Odysseus made his epic voyage across the Mediterranean, Greece was a land for wanderers. The country exhibits an extraordinary range of landscapes and attractions, and even within broad categories (such as beaches, for instance), there are great variations from place to place. Greece's historical ruins are among the world's oldest and its surprisingly varied topography among the most exquisite. The uniformity of ancient classical aesthetics has given way to an extraordinary mix of popular and ethnic influences and, today, the struggles of the past remain visible in the beauty of present-day Greece.

As far as visitors are concerned, Greece is a country in which utterly hedonistic vacation pleasures and weighty cultural offerings co-exist in a rare successful relationship. Unfortunately, Greece by and large lacks the elaborate vocabulary that afflicts more "sophisticated" national tourist industries. Time here will probably be spent most happily simply soaking up Greece's offerings, natural and man-made, without high expectations for amenities or chi-chi service. Don't allow such expectations to ruin the blissful relaxation you could find while hiking, swimming late at night, eating olives, or visiting a medieval city. All these things, taken together, can be better done in Greece than anywhere else.

ESSENTIALS

■ Once There

TOURIST OFFICES

Tourism in Greece is overseen by two national organizations: the **Greek National Tourist Organization (GNTO)** and the **tourist police** *(touristiki astinomia)*. The GNTO can supply general information about sights and accommodations throughout the country. Offices in the U.S. and other countries are listed under tourist offices on p. 1; the main office is at 2 Amerikis St., Athens (tel. (01) 322 4128). Note that the GNTO is known as **EOT** in Greece. The tourist police deal with more local and immediate problems: where to find a room, what the bus schedule is, or what to do when you've lost your passport. They are open long hours and are always willing to help, although their English is often limited. Tourist information for Greece is available in English 24 hours by calling 171.

Nikis and **Filellinon Streets** in Athens are lined with agencies and organizations geared towards budget and student travelers. We also list similar establishments in different cities in the Orientation and Practical Information section for each region.

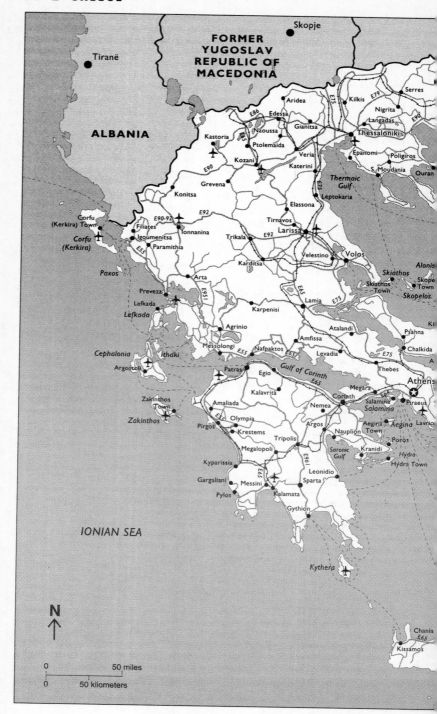

Skopje

FORMER
YUGOSLAV
REPUBLIC OF
MACEDONIA

Tiranë

ALBANIA

Aridea

Kilkis   E79   Serres

E86   Edessa   Nigrita

Kastoria   Naoussa   Gianitsa   Langadas   E90

Ptolemaïda   Thessaloniki

Kozani   Veria   Epanomi   Poligiros

Katerini   S. Moudania   Ouran

Grevena   Thermaic
Gulf

Konitsa   Elassona   Leptokaria

E90-92   E92   Tirnavos   Leptokaria

Corfu
(Kerkira) Town   Filiates   Ionnanina   Trikala   Larissa

Corfu   Igoumenitsa   E92

(Kerkira)   Paramithia   Velestino   Volos

Karditsa   Alonis

Paxos   Skiathos   Skope
Town

Arta   Skiathos-Town   Skopelos

Preveza   Lamia   E75

Lefkada   Karpenisi   Ki

Lefkada   Psahna

Agrinio   Atalandi   Chalkida

Cephalonia   Messolongi   Amfissa   A

Ithaki   Nafpaktos   Levadia   E75

Argostoli   Patras   Gulf of Corinth   Thebes

Egio   Athens

Zakinthos
Town   Kalavrita   Megara   Piraeus

Corinth   Salamina

Zakinthos   Amaliada   Nemea   Salamina   Lavrio

Olympia   Argos   Aegina

Pirgos   Krestems   Nauplion   Town   Poros

Tripolis   Kranidi   Hydra

Megalopoli   Saronic   Hydra Town

Kyparissia   Gulf

Gargaliani   Leonidio

Messini   Sparta

Pylos   Kalamata

Gythion

IONIAN SEA

Kythera

N

Chania

Kissamos

0   50 miles

0   50 kilometers

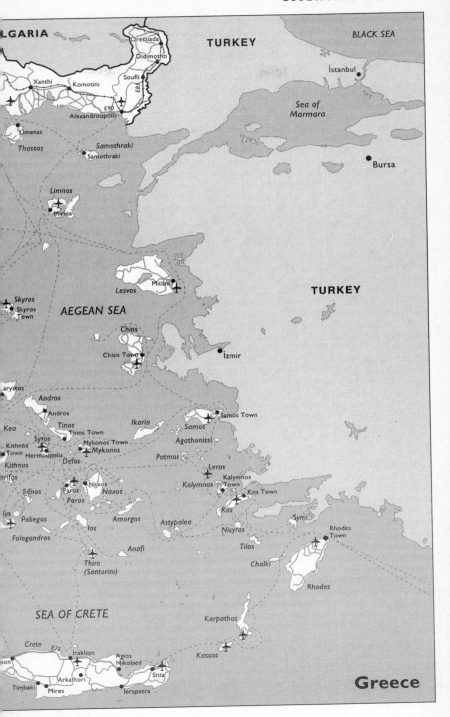

BULGARIA

TURKEY

BLACK SEA

İstanbul

Orestiada
Didimotho
Xanthi   Komotini
Soufli
E85
E90
Alexandroupolis

Sea of
Marmara

Limenas
Thassos

Samothraki
Samothraki

Bursa

Limnos
Mirina

Lesvos   Mitlini

TURKEY

Skyros
Skyros
Town

AEGEAN SEA

Chios

Chios Town

İzmir

arystos

Andros
Andros

Ikaria

Samos Town

Kea

Tinos
Tinos Town

Samos

Agathonissi

Kithnos
Town   Syros
Hermoupolis

Mykonos Town
Mykonos

Patmos

Kithnos

Delos

Leros

erifos

Kalymnos

Kalymnos
Town

Sifnos

Paros
Paros

Naxos
Naxos

Kos Town

los

Paliegos

Amorgos

Astypalea

Kos

Folegandros

los

Anafi

Nisyros

Symi

Rhodes
Town

Thiro
(Santorini)

Tilos

Chalki

SEA OF CRETE

Rhodes

Karpathos

Crete   E75   Iraklion
Agios
Nikolaos

Kassos

ion
Arkalhori   Sitia
Timbaki
Mires   Ierapetra

Greece

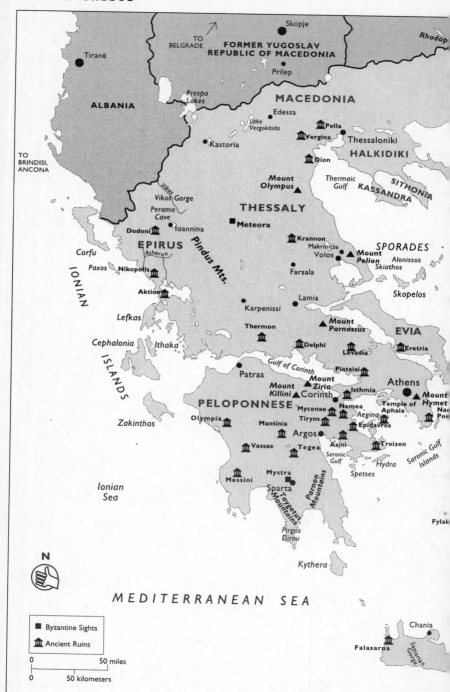

Byzantine Sights

Ancient Ruins

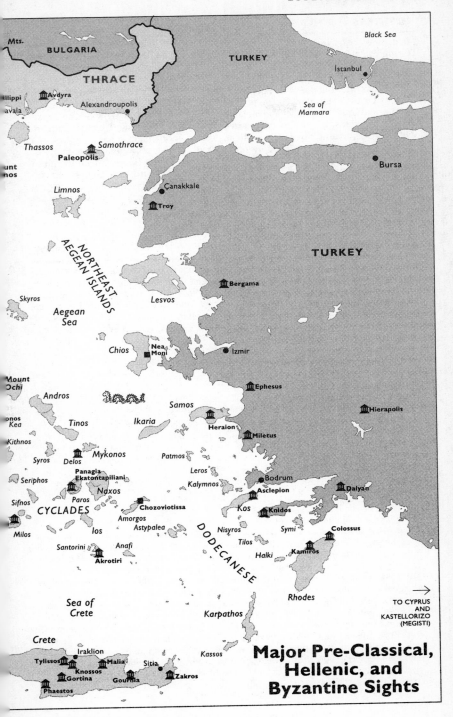

Major Pre-Classical, Hellenic, and Byzantine Sights

BUSINESS HOURS

Most **shops** close on Sundays; only restaurants, cafés, and bakeries remain open. During the week business hours vary, but most places open early (around 7am), close after 2pm for a siesta, and re-open at roughly 6pm. Most **banks** are open Monday through Friday 8am to 1:30pm, and in some larger cities, open again 3:30 to 6pm. Banks offer the best **currency exchange** rates. **Post offices** are generally open Monday through Saturday 7:30am to 2pm. The **OTE**, the Greek phone company, is often open until 7:30pm or later in larger cities. Shops and **pharmacies** are open Monday, Wednesday, and Saturday 8am to 2:30pm and Tuesday, Thursday, and Friday 8am to 1pm and 5 to 8:30pm. There's usually a pharmacy open 24 hours on a rotating basis; its address should be posted on the doors of all other pharmacies or in the local daily newspapers. **Grocery stores** have longer hours. Government-run **museums** and **archaeological sites** close on Mondays, and have slightly shorter hours from mid-October to mid-May. On holidays, sights often have Sunday opening hours and, in many cases, do not charge admission on these days. All banks and shops close on major holidays (see Holidays and Festival, p. 577). In general, travelers from time- and punctuality-obsessed countries should be aware that many establishments in Greece have flexible and variable hours.

EMERGENCIES

In each regional section, under Orientation and Practical Information, we list police telephone numbers. We also list the telephone numbers for ambulances, medical emergency centers, local hospitals, clinics, and pharmacies. Emergency phone numbers, applicable throughout most of Greece and operating 24 hours, include **police** (tel. 100), **first aid** (tel. 166), **fire** (tel. 199), **hospitals** on duty (tel. 106), and **tourist police** (171 in Athens, 922 7777 for the rest of Greece). For **U.S. citizen's emergency aid** call (01) 722 3652 or 729 4301.

■ Getting Around

BY PLANE

Olympic Airways, 96-100 Syngrou Ave., 11741 Athens (tel. (01) 929 2111), serves many large cities and islands within Greece. While flying is quickest, it may not be the most convenient or flexible option for travel; coverage in some remote areas is spotty at best. In the U.S., call the **New York** office, 645 Fifth Avenue, NY 10022 (tel. (800) 223-1226; fax 735-0215). In England, call the **London** office, 11 Conduit St., London W1R OLP (tel. (0171) 409-2400; fax 493-0563). For further flight information within Greece, check the regional Practical Information listings of airports, flight destinations, and prices, or pick up an Olympic Airways Timetable booklet at any Olympic office.

BY BUS

Spending time in Greece invariably means traveling by bus. Service is extensive in most areas, and fares are cheap. On major highways, buses tend to be more modern and efficient than in the mountainous areas of the Peloponnese or Northern Greece. The **OSE** (see By Train, p. 57) offers limited bus service from a few cities. Unless you're sticking close to train routes, **KTEL** bus service should be sufficient.

Always ask an official about scheduled departures (posted schedules are often outdated, and all services are curtailed significantly on Sat. and Sun.), and try to arrive at least 10 minutes ahead of time (Greek buses have a habit of leaving early). In major cities, KTEL bus lines have several different stations for different destinations. In villages, a café often serves as the bus station, and you must ask the proprietor for a schedule. Ask the conductor before entering the bus whether it's going to your destination (the signs on the front are often misleading or wrong), and make clear where you want to get off. If the bus passes your stop, stand up and yell *Stasi!* On the road, stand near a *Stasi* (ΣΤΑΣΗ) sign to pick up an intercity bus. KTEL buses are generally green or occasionally orange, while intercity buses are usually blue.

For long-distance rides, generally in Pullmans, you should buy your ticket beforehand in the office. (If you don't, you may have to stand throughout the journey.) For shorter trips, pay the conductor after you have boarded. Some lines offer roundtrip fares with a 20% discount. In towns and cities, local buses and trolleys charge roughly 80dr for a ride.

BY TRAIN

In general, Greek trains are not quite as comfortable as the sleek, modern lines in northern Europe and have more limited service. Service to some areas is painfully slow, and lines do not go to the west coast. Trains are not very useful for traveling to remote areas or many archaeological sites, either.

New air-conditioned intercity trains have been put into service on many lines and although they are slightly more expensive and rare, they are worth the price. **Eurail** passes are valid on Greek trains. **Hellenic Railways Organization (OSE)** connects Athens to major Greek cities. For schedules and prices in Greece, dial 145 or 147.

BY CAR

Driving might be the ideal way to tour Greece. There are highways on the mainland, and ferries take you island hopping if you pay a transport fee for the car. Drivers should be comfortable with a standard stick shift, winding mountain roads, reckless drivers (especially in Athens), and the Greek alphabet. Signs in Greek appear roughly 100m before the transliterated versions, which are placed at the turn-offs.

Agencies quote low daily rates, but these prices exclude the 20% tax and Collision Damage Waiver (CDW) insurance. Without CDW, the driver is responsible for the first 15,000dr worth of damage if theft or accident is not the driver's fault, and the full amount otherwise. CDW insurance (2000dr per day) is strongly recommended.

Read the fine print. Some places quote lower rates but hit you with hidden charges—exorbitant refueling bills if you come back with less than a full tank, 1½-2½dr per km drop-off or special charge, or 100km per day minimum mileage. Most companies won't permit driving the car outside Greece. Hertz and InterRent rent to drivers aged 21, but most other companies rent only to those 23 and older.

The cheaper and larger rental agencies are Just, InterRent, and Retca, with offices in Athens and other mainland cities, as well as on Crete and several of the islands. **Avis, Hertz, Europcar,** and **Budget** operate throughout Greece; their rates are steeper, but service is reliable. It is often cheaper to make arrangements with these companies while still in your home country.

Foreign drivers are required to have an **International Driver's License** and an **International Insurance Certificate** to drive in Greece; see International Driver's License, p. 10. The Automobile and Touring Club of Greece (ELPA), 2 Messogion St., Athens 11527 (tel. 779 7401), provides assistance and offers reciprocal membership to foreign auto club members. They also have 24-hour **emergency road assistance** (tel. 104) and an **information line** (tel. 174; open Mon.-Fri. 7am-3pm).

BY MOPED

Motorbiking is a popular way of touring Greece, especially the islands. Bikes are cheaper than cars and offer more freedom than buses, particularly for visiting remote areas. Plenty of places offer scooters or mopeds for rent, but the quality of bikes, speed of service in case of breakdown, and prices for longer periods varies drastically. Nearly all agencies are open to bargaining. Expect to pay at least 2700dr per day for a 50cc scooter, the cheapest bike still able to tackle steep mountain roads. 150cc and 200cc motorbikes cost 20% and 30% more, respectively, and usually require a Greek motorcycle license. Many agencies request your passport as a deposit, but it's wiser just to settle up in advance. If they have your passport and you have an accident or mechanical failure, they may refuse to return it until you pay for repairs. Before renting, ask if the quoted price includes the 20% tax and insurance, or you'll be hit for several hundred unexpected *drachmae*. A word of caution about travel by moped: the majority of tourist-related accidents each year occur on mopeds. Regardless of your experience driving a moped, winding, often poorly maintained mountain roads and reckless drivers make driving a moped hazardous.

BY FERRY (AND HYDROFOIL)

Ferries are the cheapest way to cross the Mediterranean, but be prepared for delays and hassle (see By Ferry, p. 35). Hydrofoils are twice as swift and twice as expensive. Ferry travel is notoriously unreliable. Always confirm your departure times with the tourist or boat office. Don't bother planning an itinerary far in advance. Although boat connections between major islands are frequent during summer, departure times fluctuate from year to year. To get to smaller islands, you often have to change boats several times, and some islands are accessible only a few times per week. Direct connections are less expensive than longer routes (the more stops, the higher the price), but also tend to be less frequent. The English-language weekly newspaper *Athens News* prints summer ferry and Athens bus schedules.

BY FOOT

Let's Go describes hikes and trails in town and city listings; local residents and fellow travelers can suggest even more. Always make sure you have comfortable shoes and a map. Remember that hiking under the hot sun at a high altitude may be more strenuous than you expect. Good sunscreen, a hat, and water are essential.

BY THUMB

Consider fully the risks involved before you decide to hitchhike. *Let's Go* does not recommend hitching as a means of travel. That said, it's hard to generalize about hitching in Greece. Greeks are not eager to pick up foreigners, and foreign cars are often full of other travelers. Sparsely populated areas have little or no traffic. Those who do hitchhike write their destination on a sign in both Greek and English letters, and try to hitch from turn-offs rather than long stretches of straight road.

■ Accommodations

Relative to the U.S. and elsewhere in Europe, Greece's accommodations remain a bargain. Off-season prices average 20-40% cheaper than during high-season. Prices quoted in the guide are from summer 1996; expect them to rise by 10-20% in 1997.

HOSTELS

Greek youth hostels are an excellent, reasonable alternative to hotels. At the time of publication, **Hostelling International (HI)** had yet to reach an agreement with Greek hostels, and they endorse only one hostel in the entire country. Nevertheless, hostels that are not currently endorsed by HI are in most cases still safe and reputable. To obtain an HI membership, please refer to Hostels on p. 40.

Greek youth hostels generally have fewer restrictions than those farther north in Europe. Most are open year-round and have midnight or 1am curfews (which are strictly enforced, and may leave you in the streets if you come back too late). In summer, they usually stay open from 6 to 10am and 1pm to midnight (shorter hours in winter). The larger hostels offer breakfast. Some hostels often have a maximum stay of five days. It's advisable to book in advance in the summer at some of the more popular hostels in Athens, Santorini, or Nauplion.

If you arrive in Greece without an HI card, you can buy an International Guest Card (2600dr), either from the Greek Youth Hostel Association, 4 Dragatsaniou St., seventh floor, Athens (tel. (01) 323 4107; fax 323 7590) or the Athens International Hostel (HI), 16 Victor Hugo St., Athens (tel. 523 1095).

HOTELS

The government oversees the construction and the seemingly random classification of most hotels. Proprietors are permitted to charge 10% extra for stays of less than three nights, and 20% extra overall in high season (July-Sept. 15). In order to get more *drachmae* out of you, they may only offer their most expensive rooms, compel you to buy breakfast, squeeze three people into a hostel-like triple and charge each for a single, or quote a price for a room that includes breakfast and private shower and then charge extra for both.

If proprietors offer a room that seems unreasonably expensive, stress that you don't want luxuries and they may tell you of a cheaper option. Late at night, in off season, or in a large town, it's a buyer's market. You may consider bargaining. As a security deposit, hotels may ask for your passport and return it when you leave. You can often leave your luggage in the reception area during the afternoon, though check-out is at 11am or noon. Be skeptical about offers to be driven to a pension or hotel. Let the driver show you the destination on a map; it may be miles out of town.

The tourist police are on your side. If a hotel flagrantly violates the prices shown by law at the front desk or on a chart behind each room's front door, or if you think you've been exploited, threaten to report the hotel to the tourist police. The threat alone often resolves "misunderstandings."

One note on Greek toilets: if a trash container is within reach of the toilet, this is where used toilet paper goes. Flushing toilet paper will probably jam the toilet. Many Greek toilets are flushed by pulling a handle that hangs from the ceiling. Also, some hotels may only have pit-toilets; check before accepting a room.

Most D- and E-class hotels start at 3500dr for singles and 5000dr for doubles. A hotel with no singles may still put you in a room by yourself. More information is available from the **Hellenic Chamber of Hotels,** 24 Stadiou St., Athens (tel. 323 7193; fax 322 5449).

"ROOMS TO LET"

Wherever there are tourists, you'll see private homes with signs offering *dhomatia* ("Rooms to Let"). As you arrive at more popular destinations, proprietors hustling their "Rooms to Let" will greet your boat or bus. Peddling rooms at bus stops or ports is illegal according to the tourist police. Generally, you should have a set destination in mind and head there. On occasion the rooms offered to you at the port or bus stop may be cheap. Nonetheless, it is imperative that you make owners pinpoint the exact location of their houses. "Ten minutes away, near the beach," can mean a 45-minute hike from the main town. Most rooms are cheap and perfectly dependable. There may not be locks, towels, or telephones, but there may be warm offers of coffee at night and friendly conversation. Then again, in the more touristed areas, there may be more locks than conversation. Prices here are especially variable, so be sure that you're paying no more than you would at a hotel. If in doubt, ask the tourist police: they'll usually set you up with a room and conduct all the negotiations themselves. Most private rooms operate only in high season, and they're a good option for those arriving without reservations. Sleeping on hotel roofs used to be a cheap option. Now it's illegal. Don't ask, tell, or pursue.

TRADITIONAL SETTLEMENTS

Greece has several traditional villages and buildings which have been preserved and restored by the government in an effort to maintain the country's architectural heritage. The restoration of some Greek villages promises to offer a taste of "small town" Greek life to visitors, and to improve the regional economy. Thus far, more than ten settlements have been converted into guesthouses: Makrinitsa and Vizitsa on Mt. Pelion, Mesta on Chios, Psara Island, Fiscardo on Cephalonia, Kapetanakos in Areopolis, and Papingo-Zagohoria in Epirus. There are 12 reconstructed towers in Vathia (Mani) and an expensive hotel in the Kastro in Monemvassia. Doubles range from 5000 to 10,000dr; tourist offices can make reservations and provide information. With the EU's new open-door policy, European businesses have been buying and tearing down traditional buildings in order to build modern hotels cheaply. In an effort to preserve traditional architecture, conservation groups have been buying traditional settlements.

CAMPING

Camping is one of the easier ways to escape the monotony of barren hotel rooms, hostel regulations, and the other limitations of conventional lodgings. More importantly, it's one of the cheapest ways to spend the night.

In Greece, the GNTO is primarily responsible for campgrounds. Most of the official GNTO campgrounds have good facilities, including drinking water, lavatories, and electricity. The Hellenic Touring Club also runs a number of campgrounds. In addition, Greece has many campgrounds run by private organizations which may include pools, discoes, minimarkets, and the like.

The prices charged at campgrounds depend on the facilities; you'll usually pay roughly 1200dr per person, plus 1000dr per tent. GNTO campgrounds tend to be ritzier and more expensive (up to 1700dr in some places).

On many islands, campers just take to the beaches. Free-lance camping outside campgrounds is illegal, but during July and August, when hotels and pensions are booked solid, illegal camping becomes commonplace. Penalties run the gamut from a stern chastisement to a 50,000dr or higher fine. At peak season when camps are crowded, the police may sometimes ignore sleeping-bagged bodies sprawled in the sand. Those who decide to free-lance camp should make sure to clean up after themselves. Many beaches offer beach huts as well as designated camping sections. We urge you to consider the safety risks inherent in free-lance camping; *Let's Go* does not recommend illegal free-lance camping.

■ Keeping In Touch

Most Greek **post offices** are open Monday through Friday from 7:30am to 2pm, although services (such as mailing parcels) may close early. Some larger offices keep longer hours. To register a letter, ask for *systemeno;* for express, *katepeegon;* for air mail, *aeroporikos,* and write "air mail" on the envelope. A letter or postcard to the U.S. costs 120dr to mail and takes as little as four days or as long as two weeks, sometimes longer from smaller villages.

Even if you have no fixed address while in Greece, you can receive mail through the Greek post office's **Poste Restante** (General Delivery) service. Mark the envelope "HOLD," and address it: "Dirk SCHNITKER, c/o Poste Restante, Main Post Office, the address of the appropriate office, the postal code, and GREECE (in capital letters)." Write "Air Mail" on the side of the envelope and use a first class stamp. If you are expecting Poste Restante to arrive for you after you leave a town, arrange at the post office to have it forwarded to another Poste Restante address. American Express offices will hold mail for up to 30 days, but often charge a small fee if you aren't a cardholder or don't use their traveler's checks.

Long-distance and collect **phone calls** and telegrams should be placed at the **OTE** (the Greek Telephone Organization) offices. In small villages, offices are usually open Monday through Friday 7:30am to 3pm, in towns 7:30am to 10pm (shorter hours or closed on weekends), and in larger cities 24 hours. If you visit one of the latter in the middle of the night, the door may be locked, but ring and they'll let you in. There's often a long line; try, if at all possible, to call early in the morning. There is no surcharge if you go to an OTE. You can also purchase a phone card **from OTE** offices or kiosks to make calls from any of the numerous card phones.

To make **direct calls** to the **U.S.** or **Canada,** dial 001 and then the area code and number. If you plan on talking for a while, ask the other party to call right back, since rates from the U.S. are cheaper. To make **direct calls** from the **U.S.** to **Greece,** dial 011-3, then the city code, then the number. If you call the U.S. collect, you'll be charged the U.S. person-to-person rate; in most cases, you'll still save money over expensive hotel surcharges. To call the U.S. **collect,** dial 008 00 13 11 (AT&T) or 008 00 12 11 (MCI). This method only works on the card phones. To use a **calling card,** dial 008 00 13 11 (AT&T only). An even better option is buying a *telekarta* for 1000dr (and up) at a kiosk or OTE; you can use it at the ubiquitous *kartotilephona* and buy a new one when it runs out. Slide the card into the phone and press "i" on the phones for English language instructions. Remember the time difference. The phone codes of the countries, cities, and towns covered in the guide can be found in the appendix on p. 580.

LIFE AND TIMES

■ History

ANCIENT GREECE

Archaeological evidence to date places the first settlements of Greece as far back as 6500 BCE. **Prehistoric,** agricultural sites were established on the mainland near Thessaloniki, on Crete, and in the Cyclades. Far from the simple-minded, playful farmers we may envision, these pioneers of Greek culture produced pottery, designed crafts, and eventually established regional and international trade routes. On the mainland and Crete, they produced terra-cotta votive figurines which they placed on the tops of mountains, or peak sanctuaries, which served as religious centers for the deities they worshiped, including a **goddess of Poppies.** In the Cyclades, they carved intricate marble statuettes, which they deposited mainly in graves.

Eventually, competition for trade routes, increased migration, and cultural diffusion led to more complex lifestyles. By the third millennium BCE, the development of weapons, government, social hierarchy, and a written script led to the construction of intricate building complexes known as palaces. During this time, the balance of power shifted to **Minoan Crete,** where the major palaces at Knossos, Gournia, Malia, Phaistos, and Zakro served both as distribution centers and the grounds for religious activities such as bull leaping and libation pouring. After an earthquake and a series of tidal waves following the eruption of the Thera volcano, the palace at **Knossos** rose to supremacy over an Aegean marine empire and remained supreme until a third trauma, probably a Mycenaean invasion, shook its walls again. The aggressive, manly **Mycenaean Era,** with war iconography at sites at Mycenae and Tyrins, was most famously chronicled in Homer's *Iliad* and *Odyssey.*

A 200-year **Dark Age,** actually not so glum, lasted approximately from the 9th to the 11th century BCE. Characterized by the Asian- and geometric-influenced pottery styles, the Dark Age actually had a great influence on its next of kin, the **Archaic Period.** Shortly thereafter, the *polis,* or city-state, became the predominant form of political organization. Despite the relative autonomy of the individual city-states, Hellenic peoples shared a sense of unity and referred to non-Hellenes as *Barbaroi,* a term that connoted foreign speech (to them, anything but Greek sounded like *bar bar bar*), rather than degree of cultural achievement. The **Olympic Games** were a source of political and athletic pride. Seafaring states like Corinth, Megara, and Miletus established colonies as far away as Spain and the Black Sea. Sparta and Athens ultimately emerged as the most powerful of the *polis.* Sparta, relatively defenseless on an agriculturally rich plain, developed an extremely militaristic culture. Children

HISTORY

Socrates: A Gentleman and a Scholar?

Following in the steps of greats like Socrates may have a meaning altogether different from what you envisioned. Socrates was certainly a great philosopher, and his technique of asking questions to steer his listener into agreeing with him even got the "method" named after him. Since Socrates himself did not write down any of his teachings, all that is known of him comes from the writings of his students, Plato and Xenophon. In *Oeconomicus*, for example, Xenophon portrays Socrates as a man with a keen knowledge of agriculture. Plato's *Symposium* depicts Socrates' scholarly gatherings that were actually drinking parties where Socrates hit on other male members of the Athenian intelligentsia undoubtedly using such witty pick-up lines as, "Is that a Doric column in your toga, or are you just happy to see me?" Perhaps this is why some scholars believe Socrates' wife, Xanthippe, had a quick temper. In one instance, an angry Xanthippe was said to have dumped a chamber pot on his head. The philosopher's only reaction was to comment dryly, "After it thunders, it usually rains." Admirers of the great philosopher might not want to consider repeating his last act. After Socrates was found guilty of corrupting the Athenian youth in 399 BC, he was condemned to death by drinking hemlock.

were separated from their parents at the age of seven to begin a military life while unhealthy babies were left to die. By contrast, life was good to Athenians, especially the wealthy. Philosophy, learning, and attempts to institute democracy were the order of the day. Despite an intense rivalry, Sparta and Athens united in defense against the Persian King Darius in the early 5th century BCE, winning victories at Salamis and Platea and saving Greece from foreign domination.

The apex of Athenian civilization, from 480 to 323 BCE, is often referred to as the **Classical Age.** In the words of classicist Edith Hamilton, "What was then produced in art and thought has never been surpassed and very rarely equalled, and the stamp of it is on all the art and all the thought of the Western world." Athens grew wealthy from trade and through its command of the Delian League that had been formed as an alliance against the Persians. The cultural achievements of this period provide a heritage that is a source of both satisfaction and frustration for modern Greeks. Athens's glorious Acropolis, including the Parthenon, dates from this period. Playwrights like Sophocles and the boisterous Aristophanes number among the pinnacle of the intellectual greats that graced Athenian streets.

Sparta's fears about Athenian ambitions culminated during the **Peloponnesian Wars,** which lasted 27 years and ended in a nominal defeat for Athens after its hopeless attack on Syracuse. Athens nonetheless retained its cultural supremacy. Some of Athens's more notable artists (Scopas, Praxiteles), philosophers (Socrates, Plato, Aristotle), and scientists (Hippocrates) flourished during this period.

In the midst of the Peloponnesian War, however, a new political force was gaining strength in **Macedonia.** Between 360 and 320 BCE, the Macedonians, under King Philip II, conquered many Greek cities. After establishing a powerful confederacy known as the Hellenic League of Corinth (in 338 BCE), Alexander the Great, King Philip's illustrious son, embarked on an historic expedition in 336 BCE to crush the extensive empire of the Persians. In only 13 years, Alexander had extended Hellenic rule and influence deep into Africa and as far east as India.

Following Alexander's death, violent conflicts ravaged his empire. During this period, however, Hellenistic culture spread and gained appreciation. In 146 BCE, after 50 years of skirmishes and political intrigue, Rome filled the Greek power vacuum. But as fast as Roman legions conquered Greece, Greek culture conquered Rome. By the middle of the 1st century CE, even Nero had a soft spot for Athens, though Alexandria and Antioch surpassed it in reputation. Two hundred years later, after the conversion of the Roman Empire to Christianity and the establishment of the **Byzantine Empire,** the focal point of Hellenic culture shifted from the

Peloponnese to Byzantium. Despite this succession of conquerors, however, Greek culture survived, as ruling forces adopted it into their own.

Although Greek culture remained strong following the Frankish conquest of Byzantium in 1204, Greece suffered a more devastating conquest in 1453, when Byzantium, renamed Constantinople after the emperor **Constantine,** fell to the Turks, ushering in four centuries of Ottoman rule. During this time, Greek culture retreated to the private sphere, centering around village life and the Greek Orthodox church, which was tolerated by the Turks.

GREEK INDEPENDENCE

After 400 years of **Turkish oppression** and numerous false starts, a revolutionary army composed of guerillas from the Peloponnese and the Aegean Islands began battling Turkish armies in early 1821, eventually declaring independence on **March 25.** The Greeks followed this success with substantial setbacks due to an outbreak of rivalry between various factions and the intervention of **Muhammad Ali,** the Ottoman governor of Egypt. Spurred on by the romantic **Lord Byron** and public sympathy for the Greeks—archaeological treasures from the Classical Age were then on display throughout Europe—European governments intervened. In 1827, at the **Battle of Navarino,** the navies of Britain, France, and Russia decimated a joint Turkish-Egyptian fleet, shattering the Ottoman grip on Greece.

France, Russia, and Britain, which had finally been persuaded to lend help to the struggle for independence, proceeded to take a controlling role in Greece's future. They drew up borders that limited the new nation to areas with an Hellenic majority, excluding many far-flung Greeks in ethnically diverse areas, as well as the most agriculturally fertile lands of northern Greece. Consequently, Greek politics for the next hundred years or so were driven by the vision of the **Megali Idhea** (Great Idea) of unifying the scattered Greek population into one enlarged, unified state. Reality, however, proved quite different.

MODERN HISTORY

Greece's fledgling democracy was thwarted by the assassination of the first elected president, Kapodistrias. After the assassination, the three allied powers intervened once more to create a monarchy. Prince Otho of Bavaria became king. In 1843, the military forced the rather heavy-handed and Germanocentric Otho to agree to a constitution, which he proceeded to ignore. He was finally unseated for good in 1862 and replaced by King George I of Denmark the following year. George I made some half-hearted attempts at land reform and tried to develop Greece's infrastructure, but the country nonetheless remained predominantly agricultural throughout the 19th century, with most capital concentrated in the hands of a few large families.

In 1910, the election of Eleftherios Venizelos as premier inaugurated a period of economic development and geographic expansion. The **Balkan Wars** of 1912-3 enabled Greece to gain Crete and parts of Thessaly and Macedonia. Owing largely to the new king's ties with Germany, Greece remained neutral during much of WWI. Venizelos, however, saw the war as a chance to push Greece's borders forward and at last realize the *Megali Idhea*. He set up his own revolutionary government, which entered the war in 1917. At Versailles, Venizelos pressed Greek claims to Smyrna (İzmir), but insufficient Allied support, Venizelos' defeat in the 1920 elections, and the disastrous Anatolian campaign against Turkey led to a crushing defeat by Atatürk in 1922. Far from gaining additional territory, Greece was forced to agree to an exchange of population with Turkey, resulting in the forced resettlement of millions of Greeks who had been living in Turkish lands.

The next decade or so saw a dizzyingly chaotic succession of monarchy, military rule, and brief intervals of democracy. The Communist Party gained in strength; meanwhile, **General Metaxas,** appointed prime minister in 1936, proceeded to develop a form of autocratic rule. Metaxas proved a fervent Greek nationalist, however, and on October 28, 1940, his famous "Όχι!" (No) to Mussolini's demand to

HISTORY

occupy Greece brought the country into WWII. In 1941 Greece fell to German invaders and, for the next four years, Greece was occupied by a group of Axis powers, resulting in widespread starvation, destruction of ancient sites, large-scale executions, and the Nazis' virtual extermination of Greece's Jewish community, which had been among the largest in the Balkans. Resistance was organized by the Communist-led EAM/ELAS, which generally received popular support. Churchill's reluctance to allow a Communist movement to ascend to power, however, made for a difficult transition to a post-liberation government, and civil war broke out in 1947. Ultimately, Greece became one of the first arenas of U.S. Cold War military intervention. The U.S. provided vast quantities of aid and numerous military advisers to the Greek government as part of the **Truman Doctrine** to contain the spread of Communism, and the last ELAS guerillas were defeated in 1949. In the next decade and a half, the U.S. maintained heavy involvement in Greek politics, which were dominated by the right-of-center Constantine Karamanlis. Greece at last attained greater stability and a decent rate of economic growth, due in part to U.S. assistance.

Left-wing stirrings continued, however, as did efforts to contain dissent. Karamanlis resigned, to be replaced by centrist Yiorgos Papandreou. On April 21, 1967, the army, feeling threatened by increasing liberalization and political disarray, staged a coup that resulted in rule by a **junta** of colonels for seven years. The junta's Metaxas-style rule included torture, censorship, and arbitrary arrest, but the regime also encouraged foreign investment and continued to enjoy U.S. support. Student demonstrations in Athens were suppressed by martial law in 1973 and, a year later, General Ionnidis's attempt to overthrow Cyprus's president provoked a Turkish invasion of Cyprus that ultimately led to the junta's downfall. Karamanlis returned from his self-imposed exile to take charge. As the new prime minister, Karamanlis skillfully orchestrated parliamentary elections and organized a referendum to determine the fate of the government. After the monarchy was defeated by a two-thirds vote, a **constitution** was drawn up in 1975 which established free general elections and a 300-member parliament charged with appointing a ceremonial president. The leader of the majority party in parliament naturally became prime minister. Greece, furthermore, worked to strengthen its memberships in NATO (having joined in 1952), the Council of Europe, and the EU.

Under **Prime Minister Andreas Papandreou,** the leftist Panhellenic Socialist Movement (PASOK) obtained landslide electoral victories in 1981 and 1985. Papandreou promised a radical break with the past and initially oversaw the passage of women's rights legislation and advances in civil liberties. But Papandreou also indulged in heavy-handed economic nationalization and finally imposed austerity measures in exchange for an EU loan. At the same time, Papandreou's heated anti-NATO rhetoric and his chumminess with Qaddafi and Arafat provoked international alarm. In September, 1988, Papandreou underwent major heart surgery. He tried to run the country while hospitalized, refusing to appoint an interim leader, thus undermining his authority within PASOK. Upon returning to work, Papandreou discovered an embezzlement scandal involving George Koskotas, the chair of the Bank of Crete, which threatened to implicate a number of government officials in corruption and bribery. After Koskotas made allegations against Papandreou himself, the beleaguered Prime Minister eked out only 125 seats in the 300-seat parliament.

In the wake of the scandals, **Tzannis Tzannetakis,** who was acceptable to both conservatives and leftists, became Prime Minister-designate through a compromise decision of the Communist-rightist coalition. As part of the compromise, the opposing conservative New Democracy (*Nea Demokratia;* ND) and the Communist Party of Greece (*Kommunistiko Komma Ellados;* KKE) forged a short-term alliance to oppose the incumbent socialist leadership. Then in 1990, after three general elections within the space of 10 months, **Constantine Mitsotakis** of the ND became Prime Minister. Although the ND was only able to obtain 47% of the total vote, the vagaries of Greek electoral law left the party with a slim majority in parliament.

Mitsotakis attempted to lead Greece into the mainstream of European politics and to solve some of the country's festering economic and diplomatic woes. To try to bring Greece's huge debt under control, he imposed a stiff austerity program that limited wage increases and began to sell state enterprises that had piled up huge losses. The state agencies, however, provided jobs for large numbers of Greeks who valued the security and undemanding nature of work in the public sector. As a result, he lost the election that was called suddenly in the fall of 1993 when a group of deputies led by former foreign minister Antonis Samaras bolted from the ND party. Andreas Papandreou returned to power, but this time with a more friendly attitude towards the West, especially the U.S., whose support he continued to court in order to deal with growing problems in the Balkans. In January 1996, Papandreou's Socialist Party named **Costas Simitis** as its new Prime Minister.

THIS YEAR'S NEWS

Early in 1996, Greece elected a new Socialist Prime Minister, **Costas Simitis**. So far, he has learned that it's not easy being green, er, gray. Tempers have flared over conflicts with Turkey concerning "gray areas" (i.e., islands near the Aegean Coast of Turkey). These regions, usually only inhabited by goats and an occasional elderly Greek couple, remain the focus of controversy because of their military and commercial strategic proximity and potential importance to both Greece and Turkey.

■ Religion

Worship of the **pantheon** of Pre-classical and Classical gods and goddesses ended after the death of the Roman Emperor Julian. In the Post-classical period, Greece saw the rise of cults associated with mysteries such as the Eleusinian and Orphic, in which members enacted rituals associated with the afterlife. Unfortunately, participants swore to keep the rituals secret, so almost all that's known of the mysteries comes from disapproving Christian authors.

The **Orthodox Church** gained ascendancy following the conversion of Constantine. The Christian faith was officially legitimized by the Edict of Milan, issued by Emperor Licinius in 313 CE, which proclaimed the toleration of Christianity. Constantine's view of the church, however, differed from that of Rome, and in 324 he founded his new capital, the city of Constantinople. Constantine also summoned the first of seven Ecumenical Councils, held in Nicaea, in order to elaborate and unify the content of the faith. During that time religion flourished in ascetic monastic communities such as those on Mount Athos and at Meteora. The schism between East and West occurred, according to some scholars, in 1054 CE when three legates of the Pope came to the Church of the Holy Wisdom (Agia Sophia) in Constantinople and placed a Bull of Excommunication at the altar. During the middle of the 9th century, Orthodox missionaries spread Christianity to Slavic peoples in Russia, Serbia, Romania, and Bulgaria. The Patriarch of Constantinople was recognized as the head of an Orthodox Christian "nation." The Ottomans tolerated the Orthodox, but Christians were treated as second-class citizens, and the church's missions were terminated. After the Greek War of Independence, the Church of Greece declared itself officially autocephalous. Today, Greek Orthodoxy is the national religion, although the constitution guarantees freedom of religion. The Church includes the archbishop of Athens, 85 bishops in 77 dioceses, and 7500 parishes. The Patriarch of Constantinople, meanwhile, still presides over Mt. Athos, the Dodecanese, and the Orthodox Church in the rest of Europe, the Americas, Australia, and East Asia.

Like the Roman Church, Orthodoxy insists upon the hierarchical structure of the church, Apostolic succession, the episcopate, and the priesthood. This, however, is where the two churches begin to diverge. Whereas Rome upholds the universal jurisdiction and infallibility of the Pope, Orthodoxy stresses the infallibility of the church as a whole and thus does not have cardinals or a pope. Much of the Orthodox position is based on its exegesis of John 15:26, in which Christ sends the Holy Spirit to man. The Spirit, Orthodox say, proceeds through the Father, while Roman theology says that the Spirit proceeds from the Father and the Son. Orthodox say that the Roman position, which confuses the source of the Trinity and God, ends up being regarded in an abstract sense, not in terms of His personality. Orthodox believe that God is highly personal, that each man can find God by looking within himself. Timothy Ware's *The Orthodox Church* provides a thorough description of both the history of the church and the exegesis behind Orthodox beliefs.

Greek Orthodox priests, who are easily discernible by their long black robes, beards, and cylindrical hats, are closely associated with their parishes and can marry, as most do (higher clergy remain celibate). Celebrations in churches include weddings, baptisms, and celebrations on the feast day of the patron saint.

■ Language

The language barrier that tourists find upon entering Greece may not crumble as easily as they may expect. Pronunciation, dialects, and vocabulary vary from region to region, from Greece to Cyprus. Although just about every Greek youth under the age of 25 speaks at least marginal English, bus destinations, many all-night pharmacies, advertisements, and street signs are, well, in Greek. It may be helpful to brush up on the **Greek alphabet** before you go—learning how to read ferry schedules may be more important than being able to ask for directions to the Acropolis if you can't understand the reply. If you're at a loss for words, most tourist agencies, and usually the trusty tourist police, speak English and are willing to help.

Be conscious of Greek body language. To indicate a negative, Greeks lift their heads back abruptly (as if they're actually nodding "yes"), while raising their eyebrows. To indicate the affirmative, they emphatically nod once. Greeks wave a hand up and down in a gesture that seems to say "stay there" when they mean "come." Be careful when waving goodbye; keep your fingers loose because gesturing with an open palm and extended fingers may be interpreted as an insult. Also, eye contact is a key way for a Greek man to communicate with a woman. Be aware that returning the intense glare is another way of saying, "yup, I'm interested—approach me."

A note on transliteration: There exists no fully satisfactory system of transliterating one alphabet to the other. Greek letters don't have an exact correspondence with English letters. Like those of the Greek government, *Let's Go's* transliterations are different for each word; the process follows no rigid rules, but is based on historical connotation, local usage, and chance. Bear in mind that when we write "ch," we're trying to form the guttural "h" sound; for a more detailed explanation, see Greek pronunciations on p. 572.

■ The Arts

DECORATIVE ARTS AND ARCHITECTURE

Ancient Greek art can be divided into periods roughly corresponding to historical eras. During the **Bronze Age** (3000-1100 BCE), the Minoans and Mycenaeans produced exquisite pottery, detailed wall paintings, intricate jewelry, bronze implements, religious icons, and earthquake-proof architecture. Bull's heads, horns of consecration, marine life, and human figures were popular Bronze Age subjects.

In the **Geometric Period** (900-700 BCE), artists developed new techniques and more expressive styles of sculpture and painting. Pottery decoration became more elaborate; jars were completely covered with bands of meanders, zigzags, and identically posed animals and people. Architects of the time created simple structures and designed one-room temples with columned porches and raised altars. Examples of Geometric architecture are concentrated at Olympia.

The **Archaic Period** (700-480 BCE) marked the transition from the Geometric Period to the more elaborate and realistic forms of the Classical Period. The cylindrical Doric column and the fluted Ionic column were developed in this period. At the end of the 7th century BCE, large-scale standing figural sculptures appeared in sanctuaries. These *kouroi* (feminine, *kori*) evolved into more graceful, simplified figures. The depiction of life and movement became prime concerns in sculpture. Vase painting similarly became more concerned with a realistic portrayal of life. The rigid friezes of marching animals and people of the Geometric Period were replaced with narrative scenes from mythology and, later, with genre scenes. The black figure technique, in which figures were glazed black and details incised into them, gave artists greater precision than before. At the end of the 6th century BCE, vase painters adopted the Attic red-figure technique in which the figures were emblazoned against a black background and the details painted in with a fine brush.

The arts flourished during the **Classical Period** (480-323 BCE), as Athens reached the pinnacle of its cultural, military, and economic power under Pericles and his successors. Sculptors such as Praxiteles and Scopas developed the heroic nude form, which idealizes the human body's severe and somber beauty. Praxiteles' statue of Hermes holding the baby Dionysus is housed in the Olympia Museum. Architecture of the Classical period, like Athens' Parthenon, features greater spaciousness, fluidity, and grace than the massive temples of the Archaic Period.

The famous Corinthian column, a fluted column with a multi-leafed top, was first designed during the **Hellenistic Period** (323-first century BCE). The Monument of Lysicrates in Athens typifies this architectural design. Several amphitheaters were built at this time, most notably those at Argos and Epidavros, where the acoustics are still so precise that more than 2000 years after their construction, a coin dropped on the stage can be heard in the theater's last row. The Romans adopted the Hellenistic style and introduced it to the rest of Europe.

In 395 CE, the Roman Empire split into the Western Empire and the Eastern, or Byzantine, Empire. The Greeks fell under the latter. As the Empire was Christianized by Constantine, Greek artists began to incorporate Christian symbols into their work. During the **Byzantine Period** (500-1200 CE), many churches were built and Christian iconography developed an elaborate repertoire of symbols. Figures of veneration generally appeared in symbolic postures, the most unusual of which is the *anapezousa*, or sleeping Christ, in which the Christ figure is depicted lying down with his eyes open, to express God's vigilance at all times. The most notable examples of Byzantine art include the monasteries built at Osios Loukas, Daphni, Mt. Athos, and Meteora, as well as the churches at Mystra. The churches were built in a cruciform style, with a narthex (small chamber) added at one end and an apse (half-dome) at the other. The transept, or crossing, of the two lengths of the church was capped by a domed ceiling. Byzantine artists created beautiful, ornate icons and mosaics to decorate their churches. A mosaic of Christ *Pantocrator* (Creator of All Things) was almost always placed in the dome or apse.

With the liberation of Greece from the Turks in 1821, nationalist sentiment impelled the government to subsidize Greek art. In 1838, the Polytechniou, Greece's first modern art school, was founded. Many artists since have gone abroad to study and **Modern Greek Art** has followed the trends of the 19th and 20th centuries. Theophilos, Alexis Kontoglou, George Bouzanis, Yiannis Spiropoulos, Sotiris Sorongas, and Michael Tombros are among the familiar modern Greek artists.

Greek **folk art** continues to fascinate both the most casual onlooker and discerning shopper. Handicrafts include hand-painted, polychromatic terra-cotta bowls and ceramics; thick, wooly woven blankets and mats; polished metalwork; intricately carved wooden furniture and gadgets; finely embroidered linens and shirts; and hand-made lace. Old women try to sell these goods on the street, and many are lured by their colorful offerings, sun-worn crinkles, and big brown eyes.

LITERATURE

The earliest appearances of the Greek language are Minoan palace record tablets inscribed in duo-syllabic scripts called **Linear A and B.** These treasury records, somewhat uninspiring in content and probably dating from the end of the Bronze Age (roughly 1100 BCE), were often preserved, ironically, by being baked hard in the fires that destroyed the palaces themselves. From the 11th to the 8th century BCE, the Greeks seem to have been largely illiterate, and it is not until the **Homeric**

Iliad and *Odyssey* that written material appears. Scholars still question whether the Homeric works were actually composed by the blind bard. While the works show evidence of origin in an oral tradition, it is possible that either Homer or a group of poets worked on the actual hard copy. Columnist Cecil Adams calls Homer "the most famous poet who may or may not have existed." Hesiod, roughly Homer's contemporary, composed *Works and Days,* a farmer's-eye view of life, as well as the *Theogony,* the first systematic account in Greek of the creation of the world and the exploits of the gods. During the 7th century BCE, Archilochus of Paros began to write anti-heroic, anti-Homeric elegies, including the often-imitated fragment in which he expresses no shame at abandoning his shield in battle to save his own life. On the island of Lesvos, during the 5th century BCE, the gifted lyric poet Sappho and her contemporary, Alcaeus, sang of love and the beauty of nature. Pindar (518-438 BCE), acclaimed by the ancients as the greatest of lyric poets, wrote Olympic odes commissioned by nobles to commemorate athletic victories.

Literature flourished in the **Classical Period.** Aeschylus, Sophocles, and Euripides developed ritualistic dramas and staged innovative tragedies, while Aristophanes produced raucous comedies (see Theater on p. 70). Orators like Gorgias practiced rhetoric, and the sophists taught methods of philosophical dialogue. Herodotus, the so-called "Father of History," captured the monumental battles and personalities of the Greco-Persian conflict in the *Persian Wars,* while Thucydides immortalized the Athenian conflict with Sparta in his *Peloponnesian War.* Callimachus (c. 305-240 BCE) wrote Alexandrian elegies, of which only fragments remain. His influence, however, was to be felt during the Alexandrian revival in Rome, when neoteric poets like Catullus took his warning *mega biblion, mega kakon* (long book, big bore) to heart. Callimachus was also the first poet to write in the vision genre, a poetic topos that holds an important place in the literature of the Middle Ages. His pupil, Apollonius of Rhodes, wrote the epic *Argonautica,* chronicling the legendary voyage of Jason and the Argonauts.

During the **Byzantine Era,** religious poetry flourished, though not necessarily to the exclusion of secular works. Photios (c. 820-893 CE), who was twice appointed Patriarch of Constantinople, admired the "pagan" works of Homer and encouraged their study. Photios himself wrote several important works, including the massive *Biblioteca,* a Byzantine cross between the *Encyclopaedia Britannica* and *Reader's Digest.* Later, under the Franks (1204-1460), Greeks developed the pseudo-historical romance, including the *Life of Alexander,* and personal love poems, such as the *Erotopaegnia* (Love Games). *Klephts* (Bandits) composed stirring folk ballads in the 16th century, when they weren't raiding Turkish installations. Byzantine heritage survived in revolt against Roman Catholic and Turkish propaganda, manifesting itself during the Period of **Religious Humanism** (1600-69).

The Ionian School (beginning with the revolution in 1821) saw the rise of Andreas Kalvos (1796-1869) and Dionysios Solomos (1798-1857). Kalvos' lyrical poetry, known for powerful tributes to freedom, earned him high esteem among modern poets. Solomos is often called the "national poet of Greece," and it was his *Hymn to Liberty* that became the Greek national anthem. During the second half of the 19th century, revolutionary hero John Makriyiannis (1797-1864) wrote his vivid *Memoirs,* considered a masterpiece of Greek literature. The 20th century has seen the emergence of a great many poets, including Angelos Sikelianos, Constantine P. Cavafy, and Kostas Varnales. Cavafy, who won the Nobel Prize in 1963, has had a wide-ranging influence, attracting the attention of writers such as E.M. Forster and W.H. Auden. Also among modern greats are Kostas Karyotakes and the lyricist Nikos Karvounes, who was the first to translate Walt Whitman's works into Greek.

Greece produced a wide variety of poetry in the 20th century. While George Seferis' poems evoke the legacy of the past, the mystical, erotic works of 1979 Nobel laureate Odysseus Elytis celebrate nature. Yiannis Ritsos blends revolutionary and mythological symbolism. Stratis Haviaris' *When The Tree Sings* depicts WWII through the eyes of a young boy. Perhaps the best known modern Greek author is Nikos Kazantzakis. His many works include *Odyssey,* a modern sequel to the Homeric epic, *Report to Greco, Zorba the Greek* (1946), and *The Last Temptation of Christ* (1951), of which the latter two were adapted for the cinema.

The landscape of Greece has also inspired some of the more inventive travel writing by English-speaking authors, such as Edward Lear's lively journals of his years in Greece, Henry Miller's classic *The Colossus of Maroussi,* and the varied works of Lawrence and Gerald Durrell, who lived in a house still visible on Corfu.

CLASSICAL MYTHOLOGY

Greek mythology is second only to the Bible in its influence on the Western imagination. Greek myths were passed from generation to generation, region to region, and gradually embellished, interpreted to reflect local concerns. The anthropomorphic gods and goddesses lived as immortal beings with divine power. Often tired of the tedium of divinity, they descended to earth to intervene romantically, mischievously, or combatively in human affairs, often disguised as animals or humans.

Traditionally, there are 14 major deities: Zeus, king of gods; his wife Hera, who watches over child-bearing and marriage; Poseidon, god of the sea; Hephaestus, god of smiths and fire; Aphrodite, goddess of love and beauty; Ares, god of war; Athena, goddess of wisdom; Apollo, god of light and music; Artemis, goddess of the hunt; Hermes, the messenger god and patron of thieves and tricksters; Hades, lord of the underworld and wealth; Demeter, goddess of the harvest; Dionysus, god of wine; and Hestia, goddess of the hearth.

In addition to the 14 gods, many **humans and minor deities** figured prominently in Greek mythology. The three Fates—Atropos, Clotho, and Lachesis—spun, measured, and snipped the threads of humans' lives; the Furies, also optimistically called *Eumenides,* or "kindly ones," punished evildoers; and the nine Muses brought inspiration to poets, artists, and musicians. Dryads and Naiads inhabited trees and streams; nymphs cavorted in the fields; Satyrs, or goat-men with long beards and tails, frolicked with Maenads in the holy groves—a good time was had by all. Humans had their place in mythology as well, though not always willingly; the talented weaver Arachne, because she dared compete with Athena, was turned into a spider, lending her name to taxonomy; Tantalus was condemned to stand in a pool in Tartarus, forever tormented by hunger and thirst and surrounded by food and water just beyond his grasp; and Europa was ravished by Zeus disguised as a bull.

The extramarital exploits of **Zeus** are even more infamous than those of less powerful but equally randy minor deities. Zeus was a sexual gymnast, ready and willing to bed down with just about anyone, as long as his baleful wife Hera wasn't looking. Zeus' mortal lovers, however, were not always willing or easily accessible: Danae, imprisoned in a tower by her father, was impregnated by Zeus in the form of a golden shower; Ganymede, a Trojan shepherd, was snatched up from earth to be the cup-bearer of the gods. Worse still for mortals, Hera, powerless to injure her husband directly, would lavish her vengeance on the object of his lust. Io was turned into a cow and chased by an enormous gadfly; Leto, pregnant with Artemis and Apollo, was forbidden to rest on solid ground until the itinerant island of Delos lent its shore for her to give birth; Callisto, who got off relatively easy, was changed into a bear. Semele, one of Zeus' voluntary cohorts, dissolved into ash when—at her request but instigated by a disguised Hera—he appeared to her in his full Olympian brilliance. The overarching lesson of stories involving Zeus and sex seems to be that mortals never win.

An accompanying book of mythology might inspire your Greek travels. Both Edith Hamilton's and Bullfinch's *Mythology* are eminently readable. Another excellent choice is Ovid's *Metamorphoses,* a principal source for our knowledge of mythology. Keep in mind that the 1st-century CE Roman poet uses the gods' Latin names (Jupiter for Zeus, Venus for Aphrodite, etc.).

THEATER

The earliest forms of drama are said to have developed in the 5th century BCE from goat songs *(tragodoi)* related to the cult of the god Dionysus. Wealthy patrons would sponsor public festivals in his honor; contests were held in open-air theaters and choruses of masked men would sing and dance. According to legend, drama was born when young Thespis, an Athenian, stepped out of the chorus to give a brief soliloquy (he was, of course, the first thespian).

One of the great tragedians, **Aeschylus** (525-456 BCE) perfected this new art form by adding a second actor and having the two actors each play several characters. His famous works include the perplexing *Prometheus Bound* and the *Oresteia*, a trilogy about Agamemnon's ill-fated return home from the Trojan war and its aftermath. **Sophocles** (496-406 BCE) created the famous *Oedipus* trilogy. **Euripides** (485-406 BC) wrote *Medea* and *The Bacchae*. "Old Comedy," a bawdy, slapstick medium, arose in the late 5th century BCE. The greatest playwright of this genre was **Aristophanes** (450-385 BCE), who wrote *The Clouds, Lysistrata,* and *The Frogs*. Unfortunately, only 11 of his 40 plays survive. **Menander,** the father of "New Comedy," wrote more mannered comedies—love stories (usually involving lovers star-crossed through cases of mistaken identity, kidnapping, etc.) with happy endings. This set the tone for later writers (hello, Shakespeare). Greek theater did not end with the Classical era; particularly on Crete, drama continues as a vital art form.

The **Athens Festival,** held from June to September, features Classical drama at the ancient **Theater of Herod Atticus** located below the Acropolis. The festival also includes concerts, opera, choruses, ballet, and modern dance. Ancient plays are staged from July to September at the **Epidavros Festival,** 78km from Athens. A language barrier won't detract from the ominous choreography of the chorus, which, in Aeschylus' time, made "boys die of fright and women have miscarriages." Tickets and programs for the theater series at both festivals are available two weeks in advance at the Athens Festival Box Office, 4 Stadiou St., inside the arcade. The same office sells tickets for a number of other smaller theaters and festivals. The **Philippi, Thassos,** and **Dodoni Festivals** all feature performances of classical drama in ancient theaters. The **Lycabettos Theater,** on Lycabettos Hill in Athens, hosts a variety of artistic events from mid-June to late August, and the **Lyric Theater,** known as the *Lyriki Skini,* presents operatic plays at 59 Akadimias St., Athens.

MUSIC AND DANCE

Musical instruments date from the Bronze Age on Crete, reinforcing scholars's belief that early poetry was often sung or chanted. As drama evolved, **choruses** played a major role in Greek plays. Before the 5th century BCE, the Greeks had no system of musical notation, yet they managed to develop a **theory of harmonics.**

Throughout the Byzantine era, **folk music and dances** assumed regional traits: the South emphasized tragic and mourning dances, the North produced war and rural harvest dances, and religious and burial dances were performed on Crete. These regional influences are still evident. For example, pontic-influenced dances like *kotsari* are danced only in the north, while islands have their own dances called *nisiotiko*. Nonetheless, dances have become somewhat more standardized. *Tsamiko* and *kalamatiano,* for example, are now danced throughout the country.

Today, it's common to see a wide circle of locals and tourists, hands joined, dancing to the tunes of *bouzouki,* clarinets, and lyre (originating in Crete). The leader of the dance performs the fancy footwork, winding around a white handkerchief and twirling around in circles, sometimes throwing in a few backward somersaults. Don't hesitate to join in; the dance steps for the followers are repetitive—you'll learn quickly. Just stamp your feet, yell *Opa,* and have fun.

To see authentic Greek dancing, check out the **Dora Stratou Folk Dance Theatre,** which performs at the open-air theater at Philopappus Theatre and on 8 Scholion St., both in Athens, at 10pm from May through September. From June through October, in the old city of Rhodes, the **Nelly Dimoglou Troupe** features dances

Cries From the Underground

Much of Greek lyric song is romantic and poetic, but at the end of the 19th century a new style of music began to develop on Turkey's western coast that would unsettle these classical notions. *Rembetika* was popularized in Greek cities by convicts who embraced the lustful strains of the music and lamented about smoking hashish and life on the run. During the exchange of populations with Turkey in the 1920s, the music was invigorated by the scores of refugees who lived in shantytowns on the outskirts of major Greek cities. This music that had been voice of the underground emerged, in its mature state, as the cry of the underclass. *Rembetika*, the music of Smyrna cafés and Greek jails, is still played on the *bouzouki* and *baglama* and features lyrics such as these from the *Little Old Monk* (1929). For more information, consult Holst's *Road to Rembetika*.

I'll become a little old monk and wear a monkish habit
And I'll carry a string of beads, sweetheart, just to please you.
Your lips tell me one thing... and your friends tell me another.
I'd rather be stabbed twice...than hear the words you're saying.
I fixed myself up as a monk, stayed in a monastery.
Then I fell into your hands, nagging bitch,
And got myself defrocked.

from northern and central Greece and the Dodecanese. The Athens and Epidavros Festivals (see Theater on p. 70) also include dancing. Greek dancing is particularly enjoyable at one of the many village or church festivals held throughout the summer in various parts of Greece. Generally, the festival is held surrounding the dates which the church's patron saint celebrates. Check the Entertainment listings in major cities for additional information and ask tourist officials about local festivals.

A grittier, more urban variety of music that developed in the 1930s, *rembetika* uses traditional Greek instruments to sing about drugs, prison, and general alienation. *Rembetika* became popular again in the 1970s but is played only in a few clubs today. Greek popular music continues to evolve, incorporating influences from *rembetika* as well as gypsy and traditional folk music.

■ Food and Drink

Greek food is simple and healthful. Recent medical studies have highlighted the Greek diet as a good model for healthy eating: its reliance upon unsaturated olive oil and vegetables has led to few heart attacks in a fairly sedentary population.

A Greek restaurant is known as a *taverna* or *estiatorio*, while a grill is a *psistaria*. Before ordering, see what others are eating. If you don't know the word for what you want, point. Most places have a few fixed-price dishes available anytime; make sure they have your dish before you sit down. Waiters will ask you if you want salad, appetizers, the works, so be careful not to wind up with mountains of food (Greek portions tend to be large). Don't be surprised if there is an extra charge for the table-cloth and bread, often listed on the menu as the *couvert*. Service is always included in the check, but it is customary to leave a few *drachmae* as an extra tip.

Breakfast can be bread, *tiropita* (cheese pie), or a pastry with *marmelada* (jam) or *meli* (honey). A particular breakfast favorite among Greeks is *patsa* (a soup made of calf or lamb tripe), served only in the early morning and particularly soothing to a travel-weary stomach. **Lunch** is eaten between noon and 3pm. The **evening meal** is a leisurely affair served late by American standards, usually after 8 or 9pm, and as late as 11pm to 1am during the summer in the larger cities. Greek restaurants divide food into two categories—*magiremeno*, meaning cooked, or *tis oras* (of the hour), indicating grilled meat. The former is generally cheaper. *Tis oras* includes grilled *moschari* (veal), *arni* (lamb), or *kotopoulo* (chicken), served with *patates* (french fries), *rizi* (rice), or *fasolia* (beans). Popular *magiremeno* dishes include *moussaka* (chopped meat and eggplant covered with a rich cream *béchamel*), *pastitsio* (a lasagna-like dish of thick noodles with *béchamel*), *yemista* (tomatoes and peppers stuffed with rice or meat), *dolmadhes* (grape leaves stuffed with rice and minced meat), and *youvarelakia* (meatballs covered with egg and lemon sauce). Fried zucchini, stuffed eggplant, *tzatziki* (spicy cucumber and yogurt salad), and/or *horta* (greens, either beet or leeks, served with oil and lemon) accompany meals at most *taverna*. Feel free to order these vegetables as the main dish. Vegetarians might also try *spanakopita* (spinach-filled pastry) or *tiropita* (cheese pie in a similar flaky crust). *Briam*, potatoes and other vegetables cooked in oil, is another delicious possibility. Seafood is as readily available as you'd expect in a such an ocean-begotten nation, but it's more expensive than you'd think. Don't leave without trying fresh *chtopodi* (octopus) marinated in olive oil and oregano. Don't miss the *taramosalata* (dip made with caviar) or the *Merenda* (Greece's version of Nutella).

You can hardly avoid *souvlaki*, a large skewer of steak, generally pork or lamb. A *souvlaki pita*, appropriately known as "the budget food of the masses," consists of a pita crammed full of skewered meat and fillings (only roughly 300dr). *Gyros* also abound in street vendor fast-food stands. *Bifteki* are a more tender, spicy version of hamburgers; you are usually served two as well as fries. For a healthy staple at a *taverna*, try a *choriatiki*, a "Greek" salad containing olives, tomatoes, onions, cucumbers, and hefty chunks of feta cheese. (Ask for it *horees ladhi* if you don't want it swimming in olive oil.) Usually accompanied by a basket of bread and a glass of water, these salads make inexpensive and satisfying meals.

Visit an **agora** (market) to stock up on the fruit available all summer. Greek fruit has few preservatives and, thus, is tastier than most fruits found in Western Europe or the U.S. The *seeka* (fresh figs) available in late August and September are delicious. After dinner, Greeks enjoy *karpouzi* (watermelon) or *peponi* (canteloupe). You should also try the freshly made *yiaourti* (yogurt), a thicker, fattier version of what most Americans are used to, with honey and melon mixed in. Sample indigenous cheeses like *feta* and *kaseri*, a yellow semi-soft cheese.

Greek pastries are delectable and available at **zacharoplastia,** or sweet shops. *Baklava*, a honey-rich, filo-dough pastry filled with chopped nuts, beats all the rest (usually 400dr); try *galaktobouriko*, a custard-filled dough; *kareedhopita*, a walnut cake; *melomakaron*, honey-nut cookies; *kataifi*, strands of angel hair wrapped around nuts and cinnamon; *koulouria*, shortbread cookies; or *kourabiedhes*, powdered sugar-coated almond cookies. Also try the fruit and cream laden *tartes*. Remember that *pasta*, in both Greek and Turkish, means pastry, not noodles.

Greek coffee is the most popular beverage. Like Turkish coffee, it's strong, sweet, and has a sludge-like consistency. Ask for *gliko* for sweet, *metrio* for medium, and *sketo* or *pikro* for a bitter, sugarless cup. *Elliniko* (Greek) coffee is usually served with a glass of water. American-style coffee (called *Nescafé*), usually instant, is also available. If you ask for **café frappé,** you'll get a tall glass of frothy iced coffee.

A favorite Greek snack is **ouzo** with **mezedhes,** tidbits of cheese, sausage, and octopus. *Ouzo* is a distilled spirit to which anise is added, lending it a licorice taste. *Ouzo* is drunk mostly in the islands, while potent *Raki* and *Tsipouro*, a grain-alcohol moonshine, are popular on the mainland and on Crete.

One of the great arts in Greece is **wine-making,** and every region has its own specialty. Long ago, the Greeks discovered that when wine is stored in pine-pitch-sealed goatskins, it develops a fresh, sappy flavor. After much deduction, they discovered that adding pine resin in varying amounts during fermentation achieves the same result. The resulting wine became known as *retsina*. Resinated wines now come in three varieties: white, rosé, and red. White *retsina* is generally cheaper than beer. To try homemade wine ask for *doppio* (local) or *spitiko* (house) *krasi*. There are also a number of non-resinated wines, including *gliko* (sweet), and *imigliko* (semi-sweet). Try the white wines of the northern Peloponnese: Rotonda, Demestika, and Santa Helena are dry. Achaïa-Clauss and Cambas Vintners are good wines. As an after-dinner aperitif, Greeks imbibe Metaxa brandy or *ouzo*.

A good place to taste various Greek wines is at a local wine festival, where you can drink all the wine you want for a flat admission fee. The wine festival in Alexandroupolis runs from early July to mid-August. On Crete, the festival in Rethymnon is held in July, while the one at the village of Dafnes (near Iraklion) runs in mid-July.

■ The Media

A decade ago much of Greek media was state-owned and thus was a propaganda tool for the government. In recent years, private organizations have bought media outlets, making the media a prisoner of the free market instead. Many Greek language **newspapers** are still sensationalistic—more akin to New York *Newsday* than to *USA Today* (which, by the way, is sold at major tourist hubs). A few reputable papers are *Eleftherotipia*, *Kathimerini* (daily) and *Bima* (published every Sun.). Unlike their newsprint counterparts, glossy Greek **magazines** are worthwhile. *Diabazo* and *Anti* are more scholarly journals; *Clique* caters to the teeny-bopper crowd; and *Taxydromos* is a more sophisticated glamour magazine. American and British magazines like *Vogue* and *Cosmopolitan* also circulate (in Greek). The most noticeable change in Greek media has been in the **television** industry. Whereas ERT1 and 2 were the original stations, both state-owned, private channels like Mega Channel and ANT-1 have brought high-tech production and, of course, more wacky American sitcoms to the Greek viewing public. Greek radio plays a wide range of music in large cities, but in the remote locales, you'll only be able to tune in that loud Greek-pop that bus drivers insist on playing at full blast during long trips.

■ Sports

Sports fanatics may be quick to associate Greek sports lore with the country's ancient "sound mind, sound body" fascination with athletics; present-day Greece is still governed by its fascination with sport. Although everything from handball to water polo is popular, soccer and basketball are the country's games of choice. Of the several Greek A-League **soccer** teams, three stand out in the hearts and apparel of Greek sports fans: *Olympiakos* (red), *Panathinaikos* (green), and AEK (yellow). Even the least devout of sports fans wear their favorite team's colors that, for some, are revered on a level well beyond religion. Although British hoodlums don't frequent soccer matches in Greece, the experience is significantly more rowdy than an afternoon at an American baseball game. **Basketball** is the country's newfound passion. The primary teams are the same as in soccer, but unlike the soccer league, Greek basketball is one of the premier European leagues. It has featured such foreign NBA stars as Roy Tarpley, Dino Radja and Walter Berry. During this upcoming season, Dominique Wilkins will be playing for the Greek team *Panathinaikos*, which has reached Europe's version of the Final Four each of the past two years. *Olimpiakos* is another basketball powerhouse. For **golfing,** there are 18-hole courses in Athens, Rhodes, Corfu, and Porto Carras on Halkidiki. Call the Glyfada Golf Course and Club in Athens, near the airport. **Tennis** has also gained great popularity among Greeks, especially with the success of native son Pete Sampras. There are public tennis clubs throughout the country. **Watersports** are what most sports enthusiasts who visit Greece dream about. Windsurfing, water skiing, sailing, and other sea sports can be found at most popular beaches. **Scuba diving** is forbidden in all Greek waters. It is allowed only under supervised conditions in Chalkidiki, Mykonos, Corfu, Cephalonia, and Zakynthos. Surprisingly, **skiing** has become popular among Greeks, and ski resorts can be found throughout the country.

Athens ΑΘΗΝΑ

A city of a little over four million, Athens sits unsettled in the sundrenched shadow of its history beneath the Acropolis, the most poignant reminder of its former greatness. Although its bright destiny has been thwarted by war and then expansion, Athens perseveres. Visitors harboring mental images of togas and philosophers may be disappointed because Athens is a 20th-century city in every sense of the word—it is crowded, modern, and polluted. The Neoclassical mansions that graced the city's streets only thirty years ago have been replaced by white monolith towers that can accommodate Athens' growing population. Aside from the odd restored Neoclassical building nestled among concrete high-rises, the Plaka neighborhood, in the city center, remains the only reminder of Athens' recent grandeur.

Column-bound temples stand as proud reminders of the faith of the ancient Athenians, but modernity cannot rest on teetering ruins—the city needs a comprehensive subway system, a manageable telephone system, and efficient living. In recent years Greece has begun to drag itself towards the Age of Efficiency, but Athens cannot help but be reminded of its history.

In the city center, Byzantine churches, situated beside ancient ruins, stand amid Neoclassical cafés and modern vendors. The incessant roar and exhaust of engines from buses, cars, and motorcycles stifles the air. Recently, the government has taken steps to revitalize the city and reduce the amount of traffic in the city's center in hopes of kindling memories of Athens' more ethereal past. The Acropolis and the area around it, including Plaka and Monastiraki, are majestic, and the city offers countless other pleasant neighborhoods.

HISTORY

A competition between **Poseidon** and **Athena** determined how Athens (*Athena* in Greek) would be named. The gods of Olympus decreed that whoever gave the city the most useful gift would become its patron deity. Poseidon struck the rock of the Acropolis with his trident and salt water came gushing forth. The populace was awestruck, but Athena's wiser gift, an olive tree, won her the right to rule.

Historically, Athens became a town of note in the 16th century BCE. Around the 8th century BCE, the city became the artistic center of Greece, conspicuous for its Geometric style pottery. It unified with Attica at about the same time, but the best was yet to come. After dramatic victories over the Persians at Marathon and Salamis in the 5th century BCE, Athens enjoyed a 70-year **Golden Age,** reaching its apogee under the patronage of Pericles. Iktinos and Kallikrates designed the Parthenon; Aeschylus, Sophocles, and Euripides wrote tragic masterpieces; and Aristophanes penned ribald comedies. Early historians, Herodotus in particular, challenged the assumption that gods, not human beings, govern history. Hippocrates, with a similar confidence in human autonomy (and anatomy), developed the study of medicine.

The bloody and drawn-out campaigns of the **Peloponnesian War** (431-404 BCE) between Athens and Sparta heralded the demise of Periclean Athens. Political power in Greece then shifted north to the court of Philip of Macedon and his son **Alexander the Great.** Through the late 5th and 4th centuries BCE, however, Athens remained important as a cultural center, producing three of the most influential western philosophers, Socrates, Plato, and Aristotle, as well as the great orator Demosthenes. But by the 2nd century BCE, the ravenous Roman Empire had feasted on Athens and drained the city of its zest. By the time the **Byzantine Empire** split off from the foundering remains of the Roman Empire (285 CE), Athens was no more than an overtaxed backwater specializing in Neoplatonism. The city remained the center of Greek education with elaborate institutes of learning, but the city's status (as well as its buildings) lapsed into ruin when Justinian banned the teaching of philosophy in 529 CE.

Around 1000, **Basil II,** the Holy Roman Emperor of Byzantium, visited Athens. After praying to the Virgin Mary in the Parthenon, Basil ordered craftsmen to restore Athens to its former glory. Under successive conquerors—the Franks in 1205, the Catalans in 1311, and the Accajioli merchant family in 1387—Athens underwent a resurgence. Although many hailed **Muslim Ottoman rule** in 1456 as a great deliverance, Athens remained in cultural hibernation until 1834, when it was proclaimed the capital of the new, independent Greece. Modern Athens, with its *plateias* (squares), wide boulevards, and tranquil National Garden, embodies plans drawn up by German architects under the direction of the Bavarian **King Otho,** who was awarded the newly created kingdom of Greece in the late 19th century.

In the 20th century, Athens has grown exponentially in population and industry, for two reasons. First, in 1923, the establishment of the **Republic of Turkey** led to a Turkish-Greek exchange of populations, which produced a mighty burden for the burgeoning city. Second, as with all industrial cities, Athens attracted workers from destitute regions of Greece. The past century has seen the population explode from 169 families to almost half the population of Greece—four million people. In an attempt to counteract noise and pollution, the transit authority now bans cars from a number of streets in the historic Plaka district and limits driver access downtown on alternate days. The **subway,** still under construction, should also eliminate much of the traffic, noise, and smog, but for now, it only adds to the confusion. Zeus' thunderbolt now shakes down acid rain, and longtime residents rue the infamous *nephos* (smog cloud) that settles in a most sinister fashion over Athens in summer.

ORIENTATION AND PRACTICAL INFORMATION

Coming from either airport, the bus stops at **Syntagma (Constitution) Square.** The center of modern Athens, this bustling plaza is packed with overpriced outdoor cafés (including a Hellenic McDonald's), luxury hotels, and flashy banks. A pale yellow Neoclassical building, formerly the royal palace and now home to the Greek Parliament, gazes over the toe-nipping traffic of Syntagma. The square is a good spot to begin your tour of the city. The **Greek National Tourist Office (EOT),** the **post office,** the **American Express office, transportation terminals,** and a number of **travel agencies** and **banks** surround the square. **Filellinon Street** and **Nikis Street,** parallel thoroughfares which head out from Syntagma towards Plaka, contain many of the city's budget travel offices, cheap hotels, and dance clubs. Unfortunately, Syntagma is currently being torn up for subway construction; cranes and dirt will detract from the square's charm for at least several years.

In front of the Parliament, facing Syntagma Sq., is the **Tomb of the Unknown Warrior.** The **Zappeion,** an exhibition hall, rests in the tranquil **National Garden,** bordering the south side of the Parliament. Continue east to the heavily guarded **President's House** and **Athens Stadium** constructed in 1896 for the first modern Olympiad. **Hadrian's Arch** and the **Olympeion** stand just south of the Garden in full view of the city's crowning glory, the **Acropolis.** On the north side of Syntagma, the city's embassies, consulates, and premier hospital (Evangelismos) congregate on broad **Vasilissis Sofias.** The Benaki, Byzantine, and War Museums, and the National Gallery cluster on this avenue. The affluent and chic **Kolonaki** district is bordered by Vasilissis Sofias, in the shadow of Lycabettos Hill.

Northwest of Syntagma, **Omonia Square,** actually a circle, is the site of the city's operational central subway station from which trains run to Kifissia (40min.), Monastiraki (3min.), and Peiraias (20min.), among other destinations. Inexpensive shops for food, clothing, and jewelry abound, but with the influx of refugees in recent years, this Times Square-esque area has become increasingly unsafe; there are, however, many cheap lodgings here. Mind your own business and try to be inconspicuous. Don't travel alone at night. Two parallel avenues connect Syntagma Sq. to Omonia Sq. (Panepistimiou and Stadiou). The **university** and **library** are on Panepistimiou St., halfway between Syntagma and Omonia. North on Patission St., which intersects the two avenues just before Omonia, is the **National Archaeologi-**

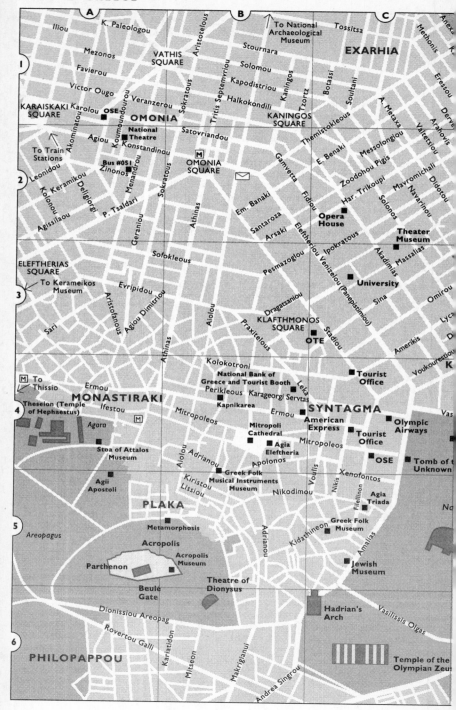

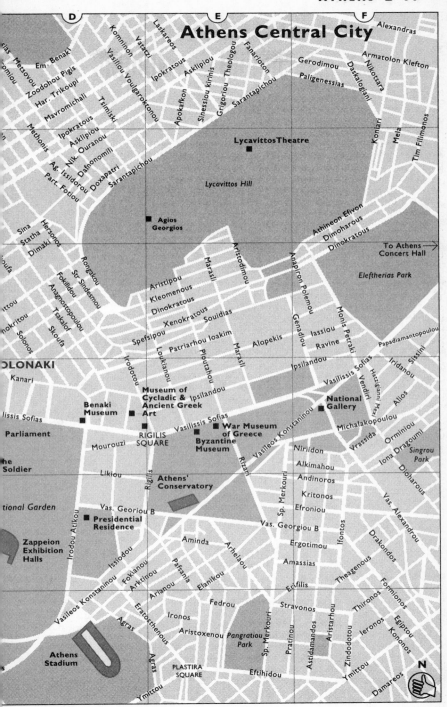

Athens Central City

D · E · F

Alexandras

Laskareos
Kominhon
Vatatzi
Vasiliou Voulgarokonou
Ipokratous
Apokafkon
Asklipiou
Sinessiou kirinis
Grigoriou Theologou
Fanarioton
Sarantapichou

Gerodimou
Paligenessias

Armatolon Kleton
Nikotsara
Daskologani
Koniari
Melia
Tim Filimonos

Em. Benaki
Metsovou
Zoodohou Pigis
Har. Trikoupi
Mavromichali
Ipokratous
Asklipiou
Nik. Ouranou
Ag. Issidorou
Dafnonomili
Part. Fotiou
Doxapatri
Sarantapichou

■ LycavittosTheatre

Lycavittos Hill

Sina
Statha
Hersonos
Dimaki

■ Agios
Georgios

Athineon Efivon
Dimoharous
Dinokratous

To Athens →
Concert Hall

Rongakou
Stir Sindemou
Fokilidou
Anagnostopoulou
Tsakalof
Skoufa

Aristipou
Kleomenous
Dinokratous
Xenokratous
Souidias
Spefsipou
Patriarhou Ioakim
Marasli
Aristodimou
Anapiron Polemou
Genadiou
Iassiou
Ravine
Monis Petraki

Eleftherias Park

Papadiamantopoulou

ittou
nokritou
Solonos

Loukianou
Ploutarhou
Marasli
Alopekis
Ipsilandou

Vasilissis Sofias
Vendiri
Hatzigianni Meksi
Alios
Iridanou
Sissini

Irodotou

OLONAKI

Kanari

Museum of
Cycladic &
Ancient Greek
Art ■
Ipsilandou

Michalakopoulou
Vrassida
Orminiou
Iona Dragoumi

■ **Benaki
Museum**

■ **National
Gallery**

lissis Sofias

Parliament

Mourouzi

RIGILIS
SQUARE

Vasilissis Sofias

■ **War Museum
of Greece**

■ **Byzantine
Museum**

Rizari

Vasileos Konstaninou

Niriidon

Alkimahou

Andinoros

Kritonos

Efroniou

Vas. Georgiou B

Ifontos

Singrou
Park

Dioharous
Vas. Alexandrou

he
Soldier

Likiou

**Athens'
Conservatory**

Rigilis

tional Garden

Vas. Georiou B

■ **Presidential
Residence**

Irodou Atikou

Issiodou

Fokianou

Arktinou

**Zappeion
Exhibition
Halls**

Aminda

Arhelaou

Pafsania
Elanikou

Ergotimou

Amassias

Erifilis

Theagenous

Drakondos

Formionos

Arianou

Eratosthenous

Agras

Fedrou

Stravonos

Pratinou

Astidamandos

Aristarhou

Zindodotou

Ieronos

Egiprou
Kononos

Ironos

Aristoxenou

*Pangratiou
Park*

Sp. Merkouri

Ymittou

Damareos

**Athens
Stadium**

PLASTIRA
SQUARE

Eftihidou

Ymittou

N

ORIENTATION AND PRACTICAL INFORMATION

cal Museum. Both train stations, **Larissis** and **Peloponnese,** are on Konstantinoupo-leos St. northeast of **Karaiskaki Square** and can be reached along Deligiani St.

Just west of Syntagma (follow Ermou St. or Metropoleos St.), **Aiolou Street** and **Athinas Street,** running between Omonia and the Acropolis, are lined with shops and department stores where wares spill out onto the sidewalk. Along Athinas St., midway between Omonia and **Monastiraki** (Athens' garment district), between Evripidou and Sofokleous St., is the **food market.** Here, the **Athens Flea Market,** the city's "new *agora*" (marketplace) surrounds the old one. South of here towards the Acropolis lies **Plaka,** the oldest section of the city, now brimming with shops, restaurants, and hotels. South of the Acropolis and neighboring **Philopappou Hill** (towards Athens' port, Peiraias) is the **Koukaki** section, a relatively calm residential area, and **Koukaki Square,** which contains an open produce market as well as the Olympic Airways headquarters. **Singrou** divides this area from **Kinossargous.** To get to Koukaki from Syntagma, walk down Amalias (which becomes Singrou beyond Hadrian's Arch) and turn right; for Kinossargous, turn left at Singrou. Singrou contin-ues straight down to the water, where it meets **Possidonis,** which contains numer-ous beaches and good clubs, and provides access to the airports. **Vouliagmenis** also heads south from below Plaka, leading to Glyfada and more nightlife.

Make use of the free quality **maps** available at the tourist office. The city one is clear and includes bus and trolley routes, while a more detailed street plan graces the pages of *Greece-Athens-Attica* magazine. Athenian geography mystifies new-comers and natives alike; if you lose your bearings, ask for directions back to the well lit Syntagma or look for a cab. The **Acropolis** provides a useful reference point. In contests between pedestrians and motorists, Athenian drivers always take the right of way; be alert when crossing the street, as drivers rarely pause for pedestri-ans. Be aware that Athenian streets often have multiple spellings or names. Lysikra-teus is also known as Lisicratous or Lissi Kratous; Aiolou as Eolou and Eolu; Victoriou Ougo as Victor Hugo. Panepistimiou St. is commonly called Eleftheriou Venizelou; Peiraias is Tsaldari. Many streets also change names along the way—Amerikis, for example, becomes Lykavittou.

Several publications list general information about Athens. Pick up a copy of the tourist office's *This Week in Athens* (free), which gives addresses, hours, and phone numbers for nightclubs, theaters, sights, museums, libraries, restaurants, airlines, churches, and more. News, movie, restaurant, and exhibit listings appear daily in Athens' English-language newspaper, the *Athens News* (300dr). The *Weekly Greek News* (300dr) and *Greece's Weekly* focus more on Greek politics and some interna-tional news. The monthly *Athenian* magazine features stories about Greek culture.

In summer, businesses are generally open Monday and Wednesday from 8:30am to 3pm; Tuesday, Thursday, and Friday from 8am to 2pm and from 5:30 to 8:30pm, and Saturday from 8am to 3pm. High season officially runs from mid-June to mid-September; however, be aware that each Greek may have his or her own version of "high season" (i.e. May-August, July-August, when you're there, etc.).

Tourist Office: Information window at the **National Bank of Greece,** 2 Karageorgi Servias, Syntagma Sq. (C5; tel. 322 2545). Bus, train, and ferry schedules and prices; lists of museums, embassies, and banks; colorful brochures on travel throughout Greece. Ask for the detailed Athens map if you plan to stay. Open Mon.-Fri. 9am-6:30pm, Sat. 9am-2pm. There is also an office in the **East Terminal** of the airport (tel. 969 4500), open same hours as above. The **central office,** 2 Amerikis St. (C3; tel. 322 4128), off Stadiou St., is only for very specific inquires. Open summer Mon.-Fri. 11am-2pm; winter Mon.-Fri. 11:30am-2:30pm.

Tourist Police: 77 Dimitrakopoulou St. (tel. 171). English spoken. Open 24hr.

Tourist Agencies: For **ISIC/FIYTO** purchases, see Identification on (p. 9).. In Ath-ens, the ISIC can be bought for 2500dr at either **USIT Youth Student Travel,** 3 Filellinon St. (tel. 324 1884; fax 322 5974; open Mon.-Fri. 9am-5pm, Sat. 10am-2pm), or **I.S.Y.T.S.L.T.D.,** 11 Nikis St., 2nd floor (tel. 322 1267; fax 322 1531; open Mon.-Fri. 9am-5pm, Sat. 9am-1pm). The latter sells FIYTO cards as well. Travel agencies along Nikis and Filellinon St. off Syntagma Sq. offer student discounts on international plane and train travel. There are *no* discounts for foreign students on domestic travel in Greece. **Magic Travel Agency** (formerly **Magic Bus**), 20 Filellinon St. (tel. 323 7471, -4; fax 322 0219), stands out. Extremely competent, English-speaking staff. Open Mon.-Fri. 9am-7pm, Sat. 9am-2:30pm. **Consolas Travel,** 100 Aiolou St. (tel. 325 4931; fax 321 0907), next to the post office. They have a second office on 18 Filellinon St (tel. 323 2812). Generally, it is best to shop around and look for specials at the agencies.

Greek Youth Hostel Association, 4 Dragatsaniou St., 7th floor (B3; tel. 323 4107; fax 323 7590), elevators on right as you enter the arcade. Lists hostels in Greece. Open Mon.-Fri. 9am-3pm.

The Hellenic Chamber of Hotels: In the National Bank of Greece next to the tourist office (tel. 323 7193; fax 322 5449). Provides information and reservations for A-, B-, C-, D-, and E-class hotels throughout Greece and some less expensive ones in Athens. All reservations require a cash deposit in trusty *drachmae*. Open Mon.-Fri. 8:30am-2pm, Sat. 9am-12:30pm.

Embassies: Australia, 37 D. Soutsou St. (tel. 644 7303). Open Mon.-Fri. 8:30am-12:30pm. **Canada,** 4 Ioannou Genadiou St. (tel. 725 4011). Open Mon.-Fri. 8:30am-12:30pm. **German,** 3 Karaoli Dimitriou St. (tel. 728 5111). Open 9am-noon. **Great Britain,** 1 Ploutarchou St. (tel. 723 6211), at Ypsilantou St. Open for visas Mon.-Fri. 8:30am-1pm. Visas granted for some Commonwealth countries; call in advance to inquire. **Ireland,** 7 Vas. Konstantinou Ave. (tel. 723 2771). Open Mon.-Fri. 9am-3pm. **South Africa,** 60 Kifissias St. (tel. 680 6645). Open Mon.-Fri. 8am-1pm. **Turkey,** 8 Vas. Georgiou B. St. (tel. 724 5915). Comprehensive listing of embassies available at the tourist office. **U.S.,** 91 Vasilissis Sofias (tel. 721 2951; fax 645 6282). Open Mon.-Fri. 8:30am-5pm. Call in advance to inquire about hours of specific department you need. Visas can be obtained 8-11am.

Banks: National Bank of Greece, 2 Karageorgi Servias St., Syntagma Sq. (tel. 322 2738, -7). Open Mon.-Thurs. 8am-2pm and 3:30-6:30pm, Fri. 8am-1:30pm and 3-6:30pm, Sat. 9am-3pm, Sun. 9am-1pm only for currency exchange. American Express, the post office, some hotels, and other banks (list available at tourist office) **exchange currency.** Expect commissions of 5% on average. Most banks close at 2pm on weekdays and are closed on weekends. Currency exchange at the airport is available 24hr., but the fee is high.

American Express: 2 Ermou St., P.O. Box 3325 (tel. 324 4975, -9), above McDonald's in Syntagma Sq. Air-conditioned and filled with Americans, the office cashes traveler's checks with no commission, runs a travel agency, holds mail for one month, and provides special services for cardholders. Open Mon.-Fri. 8:30am-4pm, Sat. 8:30am-1:30pm (only travel and mail services on Sat.).

OTE: 15 Stadiou St. (C4; 24hr.). Offices at **65 Stadiou St.** (tel. 324 5399), Omonia Sq., and **50 Athinas St.** Both open Mon.-Fri. 7am-10pm. The Omonia office doesn't cater to tourist needs; try 15 Stadiou St. to converse in English. Make overseas collect calls from any of these offices. Offices provide recent phonebooks—yellow and white pages—for most European countries, Australia, South Africa, and New Zealand. The office located at 15 Stadiou St. is open for telephone and telegraph services 24hr., and for currency exchange until 3pm (reasonable commission rates). For information on **overseas calls,** dial 161; for **directory assistance** in Athens, call 131; outside Athens, 132. Most **phone booths** in the city operate by convenient **telephone cards** that can be purchased for 1300, 6000, or 11,5000dr at OTE offices, kiosks, and tourist shops. Push the "i" button on the phones for English instructions. For **telephone information** call 134; for **complaints** 135; for a **domestic operator** speaking English 151 or 152.

Flights: East Terminal, foreign airlines and some charters; **West Terminal,** Olympic Airways domestic and international service; **New Charter Terminal,** most charters. From Athens, take the Express bus #090 and 091 from either Syntagma Sq., in front of McDonald's, or Stadiou St. near Omonia Sq. (#090 serves all three terminals, while 091 only goes to East and West). Buses run roughly every 30min., 6am-9pm, 160dr; every 40min., 9pm-11:30pm, 160dr; and every hour on the half-hour, 11:30pm-5:30am, 200dr. From the airport to Athens, look to your left after exiting customs for the blue and yellow express buses (160-200dr). A taxi costs 1500-2000dr, with an extra 55dr charge for each piece of luggage. Beware of drivers who rig the meters; watch them very carefully. Drivers may be unwilling to pick up travelers laden with luggage and might also make you share a cab. Express buses and cabs may be your most reliable travel option.

Trains: Larissis Train Station serves northern Greece (Thessaloniki 3720dr) and several European destinations (primarily Eastern Europe). Take trolley bus #1 from El. Venizelou (also called Panepistimiou St.) in Syntagma (every 10min., 5am-midnight, 75dr). **Peloponnese Railroad Station** (tel. 513 1601) is in a Victorian building with a silver roof. From Larissis, exit to your right and go over the foot-bridge, or take blue bus #057 from El. Venizelou (every 15min., 5:30am-11:30pm, 75dr). Serves Patras (1580dr) and major towns in the Peloponnese. Also has OSE buses to Bulgaria, Albania, and Turkey. For more information, call **Hellenic Railways (OSE)** (tel. 524 0601, -45). Call 145, 146, or 147 for timetables.

Buses: Please note that, unlike just about anything else in Greece, the KTEL buses are punctual, so be there and be square. For Athens and its suburbs, buses are blue and are designated by 3-digit numbers. Fare 75dr. Good for travel across the city, they are also ideal for daytrips to places like Daphni and Kesariani. For longer trips, take the orange or green buses. There are two main blue bus terminals, **Terminal A,** 100 Kifissou St. (tel. 514 8856), and **Terminal B,** 260 Liossion St. (tel. 831 7059). These buses are called KTEL (KTEA). Terminal A serves most of Greece, including the Peloponnese and northern Greece, and can be reached by blue bus #051, caught at the corner of Zinonos and Menandrou near Omonia Sq. (every 10min., 5am-11:30pm, 75dr). Be forewarned: the "information" booth at Terminal A is a privately-run agency; don't let them dissuade you from visiting the hotel you're interested in and don't get duped into buying useless "vouchers." Terminal B (Mavromateon stop, at one corner of Areos park) serving some destinations in central Greece (north of Athens, and Evia including Delphi, Meteora, Kimi, and Thessaloniki), can be reached by blue bus #024, caught at El. Venizelou (Panepistimiou St.; every 25min., 5am-midnight, 75dr). Note that the bus number may be displayed either above the windshield or on a sticker in the windshield near the front door. Bus stops list the numbers of the buses they serve. Buy a ticket at a kiosk from a station vendor and stamp it yourself at the orange machine on board. Kiosks only sell tickets for Athens and its suburbs; it is a good idea to buy several tickets at once if you intend to use the buses and trolleys frequently during your stay in Athens. Beware—bus strikes are frequent, but not all companies strike at once. Note that if you don't stamp your bus, trolley, or subway ticket (even when it seems nobody is there to make you pay) and hold onto it, you may get caught by police in a spot-check and fined 1500dr for not paying for the 75dr ticket. Some friendly advice—hold on tight as the buses lurch through the city.

Subway: One-line system running from Peiraias harbor to Kifissia in north Athens with stops at Monastiraki, Omonia, and Victoria, among others. Every 10min., 5am-midnight, 75dr in A and B zones; 100dr in C (Γ) zone. Buy tickets in stations, at booths or machines. Be forewarned, however, that the ticket machines do *not* give change. Ticket successfully procured, just punch it with the orange machine before entering, and hang on to stub until exiting. Inspectors randomly check trains, and passengers without tickets are fined 1500dr. Athens remains in the process of constructing a more extensive subway system. The project has been moving slowly, hampered by financial difficulties and archaeological finds; don't expect completion until at least 1999.

Trolleys: Yellow, crowded, and sporting 1- or 2-digit numbers. Fare 75dr. Trolleys no longer accept money. Buy a ticket (same as bus ticket) ahead of time at a kiosk. Frequent service; convenient for short hops within the city. Tourist office map of Athens shows most trolley routes.

Ferries: Most dock at **Peiraias** and go to all Greek island groups except the Sporades (which leave from Ag. Konstantinos or Volos) and the Ionian Islands (which leave from Patras in the Peloponnese). Some popular destinations from Peiraias (all fares one way) are Santorini (9hr., 4610dr); Mykonos (6hr., 3895dr); Ios (8hr., 4610dr); Aegina (1¼hr., 1040dr); Paros (5hr., 3275); and Rhodes (15hr., 7130dr). Departures to Haifa, Alexandria, and Limassol also leave from Peiraias. (Contact **Port Authority of Peiraias** at tel. 422 6000.) From Athens to Peiraias, take the subway to the last stop, or take green bus #40 from Filellinon and Mitropoleos St.

(every 10min., 75dr). To reach Syntagma Sq. (in Athens) from Peiraias, walk left (facing inland) along the waterfront to Roosevelt St., take the subway to Monastiraki (75dr), turn right up Ermou St., and walk 5min. Boats also leave from **Rafina,** a port suburb east of Athens, to Andros, Tinos, and Mykonos. To Kea or Kithnos, take a ferry (1650-2300dr) from **Lavrio**. The orange bus to Lavrio leaves from Mavromateon St. near Areos Park (take bus or taxi from Syntagma) for 700dr. Always check schedules at the tourist office, in the *Athens News* prior to departure, or with the Port Authority of Peiraias (tel. 422 6000) or any travel agency. Schedules change frequently without notice. Buy tickets at travel agencies in Athens or Peiraias. Ferry information is in any Greek newspaper or dial 143 for a Greek-recorded timetable (call day before or morning of departure).

Flying Dolphins: Hydrofoils speed above water between islands and from some ports, serving the Argosaronic, Sporades, and Cyclades groups. **Ceres' Flying Dolphins** (tel. 428 0001) and **Ilios Lines' Dolphins** (tel. 322 5139) are the two main companies. Hydrofoils, roughly twice as expensive and twice as fast, leave from **Zea Port** near Peiraias, Agios Konstantinos, and Volos. The tourist office and travel agencies can also provide guidance and information.

Taxis: The meter starts ticking at 200dr, with an additional 58dr per km within city limits (be forewarned—the rates double between midnight and 5am). 113dr per km in the suburbs. For trips from the airport, there is a 300dr surcharge, and from ports, bus and railway terminals 160dr (plus another 55dr for each piece of luggage over 10kg). Hail your taxi, shouting your destination—not the street address, but the area (i.e., "Kolonaki"). The driver may or may not pick you up, depending on whether he is or is not inclined to head in that direction. Get in the cab and *then* tell the driver the exact address or site. Most drivers don't speak English so have your destination written down (in Greek if possible) and include area of the city; i.e., Kolonaki, Peiraias, etc. (keep in mind that some streets in different parts of the city have the same name). Empty taxis are rare. It is common to ride with other passengers going in the same direction. For an extra 400dr, call a radio taxi (Ikaros, tel. 513 2316; Hermes, tel. 411 5200; and Kosmos, tel. 420 0042). A full list of radio taxis appears in the *Athens News*. Pay what the meter shows, rounded up to the next 50dr, but be wary of drivers who tinker with their meters.

Car Rental: Places abound on **Singrou Ave.,** all charging 8,000-13,500dr for a small car with 100km free mileage (prices include tax and insurance). Credit cards accepted and international drivers license is not necessary. Most require drivers to be 23 or older and to have driven for at least a year.

Luggage Storage: At the airport 100m outside on your right as you exit baggage claim and customs; look for the yellow "lockers" sign. Keep your ticket stub to reclaim; pay when you collect. 700dr per piece per day. After midnight you pay for an extra day. Open 24hr. Several offices on Nikis and Filellinon St., including **Pacific Ltd.,** 26 Nikis St. (tel. 324 1007; fax 323 3685). Per piece: 300dr per day, 600dr per week, 1800dr per month. Open Mon.-Sat. 7am-8pm, Sun. 7am-2pm. Many hotels have free, or at least inexpensive, luggage storage; ask the manager.

International Bookstores: Eleftheroudakis Book Store, 4 Nikis St. (tel. 322 9388). This bookstore is a pleasure. Greek, English, French, and German books, classical and recent literature, and many travel guides, including *Let's Go*. Open Mon.-Fri. 9am-8:30pm, Sat. 9am-3pm. **Pantelides Books,** 11 Amerikis St. (tel. 362 3673). Overflows with a huge variety of books; best philosophy/critical theory selection in town. Open Mon., Wed. 8am-4pm, Tues., Thurs.-Fri. 9am-2:30pm and 5-8:30pm, Sat. 9am-3pm. **Compendium Bookshop,** 28 Nikis St. (tel. 322 1248). Popular, large used book selection. Best selection of *Let's Go* around. Open Mon., Wed. 8:30am-3:30pm, Tues., Thurs.-Fri. 8:30am-8:30pm, Sat. 9am-3pm. Also houses new children's book room—a taste of a bookshop with a touch of a library. Open Mon., Wed. 9am-5pm, Tues., Thurs.-Fri. 9am-8pm, Sat. 9am-3pm.

Libraries: In the **Hellenic American Union,** 22 Massalias St., behind the university (tel. 362 9886; fax 363 3174), there is an **American Library** (tel. 363 7740), on the 4th floor. Open Mon., Thurs. 3-7pm, Tues., Wed., Fri. 11am-3pm. The Union also houses a **Greek Library** with English books on Greece, nestled on the 7th floor. Open Mon.-Thurs. 9am-8pm, Fri. 9am-5pm; closed in August. The **British Council Library,** Kolonaki Sq. (tel. 363 3215), has English reading material.

Open Tues.-Fri. 9:30am-1:30pm. The **Goethe Institut,** 14-16 Omirou St. (tel. 360 8111), off of Venizelou houses a German Library. Open Mon., Thurs. 11am-7pm, Tues., Wed., Fri. 11am-3pm. All sponsor cultural events as well.

Laundromats: The Greek word for laundry is *plinitirio,* but most places have signs reading "Laundry." Locations of self-serve laundromats include **10 Angelou Geronta St.** in Plaka, **9 Psaron St.** (tel. 522 2856), and **41 Kolokinthous and Leonidou St.** (tel. 522 6233), near the train stations. Expect to pay roughly 2000dr per load for wash, dry, and detergent.

Red Cross First Aid Center: #21, 3 Septemvriou St. (tel. 150 or 522 5555), three blocks north of Omonia Sq., on the left. English spoken. Open 24hr.

Pharmacies: Identifiable by a Byzantine-style red or green cross hanging into the street. The daily *Athens News* (300dr) lists each day's emergency pharmacies and their hours in its Useful Information section. One is always open 24hr. (refered to as *efimerevon* in Greek). They alternate. To find out which pharmacies are open after hours, dial 107 or 102.

Hospitals: Geniko Kratiko Nosokomio (Public State Hospital), 154 Mesogion (tel. 777 8901; fax 770 5980). **Hegia,** 4 Erithrou Stavrou (tel. 682 7904; fax 684 5089), is a top-notch private hospital in Marousi. Closer to the center of Athens, try the **Aeginitio** state hospital at 72 Vas. Sofias (tel. 722 0811, -2), and at 80 Vas. Sofias (tel. 777 0501; fax 777 6321). Near Kolonaki is a **public hospital** at 45-47 Evangelismou (tel. 722 0101; fax 729 1808). In Greek, "hospital" is *nosokomio.*

Emergencies: For **doctors** (2pm-7am), call 105; for an **ambulance** call 166; for **poison control,** dial 779 3777. The **AIDS Help Line,** dial 722 2222. The daily emergency hospitals are listed in the *Athens News.* Tourists can receive free emergency health care.

Medical Emergency: Dial 166.

Police: (tel. 100). Broken English spoken.

Main Post Office: 100 Aiolou St. (B2; tel. 321 6023), Omonia Sq. **Postal Code:** 10200. **Syntagma Sq.,** (tel. 322 6253), on the corner of Mitropolis. **Postal Code:** 10300. **60 Mitropoleos,** (tel. 321 8143), a few blocks from Syntagma Sq. All open Mon.-Fri. 7:30am-8pm, Sat. 7:30am-2pm, Sun. 9am-1:30pm. **Parcel post** for sending packages abroad at **29 Koumoundourou** (A1-A2; tel. 524 9359; open Mon.-Fri. 7:30am-8pm), and **4 Stadiou,** (tel. 322 8940). Open Mon.-Fri. 7:30am-2pm.

Telephone Code: 01.

ACCOMMODATIONS

Since most budget hotels are located in crowded and noisy sections of the city, be sure to ask for a room that faces away from the street. If you are planning to stay (and presumably sleep) in the orally toxic heart of Athens, you may want to bring ear plugs from home. Some balconies, however, offer vague compensation in their stunning views of Athens. If you are planning to stay fewer than three nights, a hotel owner can legally add a 10% surcharge to your bill. Hotel owners used to allow guests to sleep on the roof for a small fee when the rooms are full. Although the practice is still in effect at some hotels, it is *illegal* and should be actively avoided.

Many hotel hawkers meet trains at the station. Most distribute pamphlets with maps for decent places near the station, some of which are listed here. Others, however, have been known to lure tourists into fleabags miles from anywhere and then charge exorbitant rates. Some have even caused harm to the unsuspecting traveler when led back to the agreed upon "establishment." As always, please exercise extreme caution when choosing an accommodation. Try to call ahead to reserve a room or search out your own. If you do decide to follow a hawker, it is safest only when you are traveling in a group. Have the hawker point out the place on a large map of the city and set a firm price, in writing if possible, *before* leaving the station. Men arriving by bus from the airport should be aware of "friendly barkeepers" who may direct you to brothels rather than budget hotels. Do not sleep in the parks, even as a last resort. Camping anywhere in Athens is illegal, and extremely unsafe besides. Some hotels offer breakfast for roughly 1000dr. While this is convenient, you can visit a bakery and buy milk or juice for significantly less.

ACCOMMODATIONS

Note that the prices quoted below are from mid-1996 and are expected to increase in the next year. In 1997, expect a 10-20% rise from the prices in these listings. Prices are 20-40% less in off season (September through May).

Plaka-Syntagma Area

Most of the city's cheap hotels cluster in this central and busy part of town, and this really is the best place to stay—safest, quietest, most convenient, and best for people-watching. You may want to make a reservation—it's worth it.

Student-Travelers Inn, 16 Kidathineon (tel. 324 4808; fax 321 0065), in the heart of Plaka. With its convenient locale, friendly owner, great staff, garden café, and hardwood floors, this hotel is more than worthwhile. 24-hr. hot showers. Breakfast 800-1000dr, served 5:30am-noon. Singles 6000dr. Doubles 7000dr. Triples 9000dr. Quads 10,800dr. 10% discount with student ID or Youth Card.

Hotel Dioskouros, 6 Pitakou (tel. 324 8165), across the street from Hadrian's Arch, Pitakou branches off Amalias in the direction of the city center. Clean and summery. 9am check-out. Dorm beds 4500dr. Doubles 9000dr. Quads 18,000dr.

Thisseos Inn, 10 Thisseos St. (tel. 324 5960), from Syntagma Sq., take Karageorgi Servias (which becomes Perikleous); Thisseos St. is on the right. This home-turned-hostel is popular with students who want to stay near Syntagma's sights but far from its noise. Very quiet at night. TV in reception area, kitchen, common showers (24hr., hot). Curfew 2am. Dorm beds 2400dr. Doubles 5000dr.

Hotel Phaedra, 16 Herefondos St. (tel. 322 7795), from Hadrian's Arch on Amalias, walk 1 block up Lysikrateous St. to the intersection with Herefondos. Phaedra is next to a small park and Byzantine Church. Many rooms have balconies with Acropolis views. Check-out noon. Breakfast 1500dr. Singles 6500dr. Doubles 8000dr. Triples 10,000dr. Quads 12,000dr. Bargain. Prices slashed in winter.

Hotel Festos, 18 Filellinon St. (tel. 323 2455). Although the facilities are a bit run-down, this is a festive place; reservations often needed. Bar with daily happy hour and nightly movies. Wide range of food served (vegetarian menu available). CNN and MTV available in bar. Luggage storage 200dr per day. Hires travelers. Hot showers morning and evening only. Check-out 9am. Dorm bed 2000dr. Doubles 6000dr. Triples 9000dr. Quads 10,000dr.

Hotel Economy, 5 Klisthenous St. (tel. 522 0520; fax 522 0640), from Omonia Sq., go up Athinas and turn left after the town hall onto Kratinou St., which leads to the hotel's front door. Central location, 24-hr. bar, and clean, peaceful rooms. Breakfast 1000dr, served 6:30-9am. Singles 7000dr. Doubles 8000dr. Bargain.

Monastiraki-Thission Area

Near the central food market and the central tourist market, this neighborhood has an ever-increasing, never-ceasing noise problem. But it's also near the Acropolis and the subway, practically on top of the Agora site, and home to some bargains.

Hotel Tempi, 29 Aiolou St. (tel. 321 3175; fax 325 4179), from Syntagma Sq., follow Ermou St. and take a right on Aiolou (also spelled Eolu and Eolou); in Monastiraki. 24-hr. hot water. Laundry service 1000dr. Singles 4500dr, with bath 6500dr. Doubles 7500dr, with bath 8500dr. Triples 9000dr.

Pella Inn, 104 Ermou St. (tel. 325 0598, 321 2229; fax 325 0598), a 10-min. walk down Ermou from Syntagma Sq., 2 blocks from the Monastiraki subway station (entrance on Karaiskaki St.). Lounge and snack bar with eye-opening yellow and red furniture. Breakfast 1000dr. Free luggage storage. Singles 5000-7000dr, with bath 9000dr. Doubles 7000-9000dr, with bath 9000dr.

Railway Station Area

This overcrowded business and residential center is too far away from Syntagma for week-long stays, but ideal for a stopover because of its proximity to trains, buses, and (via the Victoria or Omonia subway stop) Peiraias. Be careful getting around the Omonia Sq. area: carry your wallet in your front pocket and try to move in groups.

Athens International Hostel (HI), 16 Victor Hugo St. (tel. 523 4170; fax 523 4015). From Omonia Sq., walk down Third September St., take a left on Veranze-rou; it will become Victor Hugo after crossing Marni St. The only HI-affiliated youth hostel in Greece. HI membership required (3000dr at hostel; get photo from nearby booth), although you can buy nightly passes for 500dr. All beds 2000-2200dr per person per night, including sheets. Reservations recommended.

Hostel Aphrodite, 12 Einardou St. (tel. 881 0589 or 883 9249; fax 881 6574), from the subway stop at Victoria Sq., follow Heiden for 2 blocks, and 2 more on Paion-iou. Take a right on Michail Voda, and a left 2 blocks later onto Einardou. From the train station, follow Filadelfias until Michail Voda. Easy access to both the train station and Victoria Sq. Friendly basement bar, travel services (ask about the 20-day island pass for 9000dr). Breakfast 900-1200dr. Dorm beds 1800dr. Doubles 6000dr. Triples 7500dr. Quads 9000dr. 10% discount with student ID.

Hostel Argo, 25 Victor Hugo St. (tel. 522 5939; fax 864 1693), down the street from the official hostel. Check-out noon. No curfew. Breakfast 600dr. Laundry 1500dr. Free luggage storage. Singles 4000dr. Doubles 6000dr, with bath 6600dr. Triples 7000dr with bath. Quads 8000dr. *Let's Goers* get a 10% discount.

Hotel Appia, 21 Menandrou St. (tel. 524 5155, -4561; fax 524 3552). From Omonia Sq., follow Tsaldari St. to Menandrou St. This modern hotel caters more to fami-lies than to backpackers. Telephones, ceiling fans, and radios in all rooms. Check-out noon. Breakfast 900dr. 24-hr. hot water. Reserve for July-Sept. Singles 3000dr, with bath 4500dr. Doubles 5500dr, with bath 7600dr. Triples 6500dr.

Hotel Arta, 12 Nikitara St. (tel. 362 7753). From Syntagma or Omonia, take Stadiou to Benaki, turn left, and take the third left on Nikitara. Modern hotel in a quiet part of the city center. Endearing non-English speaking reception. Immaculate rooms with desks and phones. Free luggage storage. Reception always open. Room for bargaining. Breakfast 1500dr. Singles 6000dr, with bath 7500dr. Dou-bles 7500dr, with bath 10,000dr. Triples 9000dr, with bath 13,000dr.

South of the Acropolis

These rooms are in relatively quiet residential areas. To the west, Koukaki and Veikou present 15-20-minute uphill hikes to the Acropolis or Syntagma Sq. To the east, Pangrati, a one-hour walk from Syntagma, can be easily reached by trolley.

Youth Hostel #5 Pangrati, 75 Damareos St., Pangrati (tel. 751 9530; fax 751 0616). Take trolley #2 or 11 from Syntagma Sq. to Filolaou or walk through the National Garden, down Eratosthenous St. to Plastira Sq., 3 blocks on Efthidiou to Frinis, and down Frinis St. until Damareos on the right (40-min. walk). No sign for the hostel on the street, just the number "75" and a black/gray door. Curfew mid-night. Hot shower 50dr. Sheets 100dr. Pillowcases 100dr. Blankets 50dr. Laundry 700dr. Key deposit 300dr. Dorm beds 1500dr. Singles 3500dr. Doubles 5000dr.

Marble House Pension, 35 Zin, Koukaki (tel. 923 4058 or 922 6461). From the southern side of Acropolis, follow Erechthiou St. until it ends and turn right onto Veikou, which will intersect Zin. 10am check-out. Breakfast 750dr. Singles 5000dr, with bath 6000dr. Doubles 7000dr, with bath 8000dr. Triples 8000dr.

Art Gallery Hotel, 5 Erechthiou St., Veikou (tel. 923 8376/923 1933; fax 923 3025). From the southern side of the Acropolis, Erechthiou stretches directly towards this pension. This welcoming family business is a 5-min. walk from the Acropolis (uphill) and a 20-min. walk from Syntagma Sq. Check-out before noon. No credit cards. Call a month in advance to reserve a room during high season. English, French, and Italian spoken. Singles 10,000dr. Doubles 12,000dr. Triples 13,000dr. Quads 15,700dr. Off-season rates are 2000-3000dr lower.

Hotel Greca, 48 Singrou St., Veikou (tel. 921 5262 or 923 3229; fax 360 1438). Rooms akin to hospital rooms—Greek hospital rooms. VISA accepted. English and French spoken. Check-out 11am. Luggage storage 300dr per piece per day. Doubles 8000dr, with bath 10,000dr. Triples 12,000dr, with bath 18,000dr.

FOOD

Athens offers a melange of stands, open-air cafés, outdoor side street *tavernas,* and intriguing dim restaurants frequented by grizzled Greek men. Athens' culinary claim to fame is cheap and plentiful *souvlaki* (250-400dr), either on a *kalamaki* (skewer) or wrapped in *pita,* is the Greek version of fast food. A *tost,* a grilled sandwich of variable ingredients (normally ham and cheese) for 250-500dr is another option. Locally brewed beer (Amstel and Heineken, also known as "Green Beer," for its green bottle) runs roughly 200dr per bottle. *Tiropita* (hot cheese pie) and *spanako-pita* (hot spinach pie) go for around 300dr. Ice cream is sold at almost every kiosk. A *koulouri,* a donut-shaped, sesame-coated roll, makes breakfast for 50-100dr.

The most popular place for tourists to eat is Plaka. You'll find many interesting places up and down Adrianou and Kidatheneon St. Once seated at the joint of your choice, relax: Greek restaurants are not known for their speedy service. Women should know that Plaka is a popular spot for *kamakia* (literally "octopus spears," or pick–up men) who enjoy making catcalls at women as they walk by. Sometimes they may even follow you, but keep walking and ignore them; in most cases, harassment is only verbal. Most places in Plaka serve early or all day, but outside these touristed quarters few restaurants open before 8pm. Restaurants tend to be deserted at 6pm, near-empty before 10pm, and crowded from 11pm to 1am.

Plaka-Syntagma

For do-it-yourself meals, various **minimarkets** on Nikis St. and in Plaka sell basic groceries. The Thisseos Inn in particular offers noteworthy kitchen facilities.

To Gerani, 14 Tripodon St. (tel. 324 7605), from Kidatheneon, one of Plaka's busiest strips, Tripodon is a side street. In a quiet niche with a wonderful balcony, To Gerani is cheaper than most, but be warned—they don't make many dishes each night. 2 or 3 small entrees make a good meal (500-900dr each).

Possidon Restaurant, 39 Kapnikareas St. (tel. 322 3822), at the corner of Adrianou. Very large and popular. Full exposition of traditional Greek cuisine. Specially cooked lamb (2200dr), *melitzanosalata* (eggplant dip; 800dr), yogurt and honey (850dr), and many other dishes. Visa and MasterCard accepted.

Eden Vegetarian Restaurant, 12 Lissiou St. (tel. 324 8858), on the corner of Minissikleous on the west side of Plaka. Airy and secluded. Popular with both herbivores and omnivores. Soy-meat in dishes like *moussaka* (1250dr). Entrees 1250-1600dr.

Zorbas, 15 Lissiou (tel. 322 6188), right across the street from Eden, is one of the cheapest places around. Entrees 1100-3000dr, most around 1500dr. Try the lamb Zorbas (1700dr) or the pumpkin balls (650dr). Ask for gum before leaving.

Orpheas, 6 Arsakiou (tel. 322 7103). Enter the Neoclassical arcade with the glass roof after Pezmezoglou St., coming down Stadiou St. Serves a wide array of light meals and desserts, each with a special twist. Have a creamy *frappé* for 730dr or a rich baguette sandwich for 1100dr. Open Mon.-Sat.

To Souvlaki tis Loxantras, 2 Ermou St. (tel. 331 2212). Greek alternative to McDonald's, right next door. Clever. Luscious chicken or pork *kalamaki* sandwich for under 500dr. You can enjoy it in the colorful little loft upstairs.

Diodos, 16 Ifaistou St. (tel. 324 5827). Traditional Greek coffee shop in Monastiraki. Homemade *glyko koutaliou* (fruit cooked in syrup) 300dr. Play a round of backgammon on the marble-top tables (games available at bar; no charge).

Blue Velvet, 3 Nikis St. (tel. 323 4971). A groovy café with Mexican food run by a Californian. Take-out and delivery available. Burritos and tacos 950dr.

T. Stamatopoulos, 26 Lissiou St. (tel. 322 8722), near the Eden Restaurant. Featuring live music in the summer. Entrees 1750-3200dr. Veal special 1950dr.

Golden Flower, 30 Nikis St. (tel. 323 0113). Tired of Greek food? A well maintained Chinese place. Vegetable dishes 1400-1650dr, chow mein 2050-2500dr.

For better (and cheaper) food, wander outside Plaka.

Restaurant of Konstantinos Athanasias Velly, Varnava Sq., Plastira. Take trolley #2, 4, 11, or 12 to Plastira Sq., walk 3 blocks up Proklou St. to Varnava Sq. At the square's far right corner, in a small white house with flowers in front.No English spoken, but your stomach can growl and you can point. Tomato salad 500dr, *keftedes* (Greek meatballs) with potatoes 900dr, and *fasolia* (bean soup) 400dr. Kosta and Nitsa have been cooking and serving here for over 30 years. Their *keftedes* would bring a Greek Betty Crockeropoulous to tears of joy.

To Meltemi, 26 Zinni St. (tel. 924 7606), Koukaki, near the Marble House Pension. Menu changes daily at this authentic *taverna*. Medium-sized variety plate 1300dr. Pork in the oven 1200dr and *gemista* (stuffed peppers and tomatoes) 900dr.

For an after-dinner treat, there are tons of **sweetshops** in Plaka, many virtually indistinguishable from their neighbors. *Baklava* tends to go for 250-400dr, ice cream 150-300dr per scoop. **Lalaggis,** 13 Speusippou St. in Kolonaki, is an above average sweetshop in the heart of the city (*baklava* 250dr). Check out their branch in Pagrati, at 29 Empedokleous St. **Artos & Zoe,** 73 Ermou St., has lots of yummy cookies and breads (*tiropita* 200dr). **Floca** is a chain, but tends to be better than average.

ENTERTAINMENT

Visitors to Athens often restrict themselves to the familiar Plaka and Monastiraki neighborhoods. Nights in Athens, however, can best be enjoyed by venturing beyond the heavily touristed areas to one of the city's clubs, theaters, or bars. Don't be fooled into thinking that nights here are full of hokey Greek dancing and dish-throwing. On the contrary, Athenian nightlife is varied and diverse enough to please highbrow, chic sophisticates; down and dirty backpackers; and members of the elite who have not gotten their fill of intellectual stimulation during the day. Nightlife is very different in off season when many outdoor spots close, but there should be plenty to do throughout the year.

During the summer months, young and hip Athenians head to the seaside clubs in **Glyfada** (past the airport) and on **Poseidonos Ave.** The most beautiful of these are right on the beach, with calming ocean views to help cool off the frenzied interiors. Dance-oriented and mill-around discoes play American or British tunes from 11pm or midnight until 2 or 3am until either Greek music is played, or a Greek singer takes the stage amid clouds of hurled flowers. Put on your best Euro-suave outfit because many of these clubs will not admit anyone in shorts. Covers range 2000-3000dr, and drinks are often ridiculously priced (beers run 1000-2000dr, cocktails 1500-3000dr).

Nearby, off the water, on Vouliagmenis St. in Glyfada, the best bars are all conveniently lined up. Some good hotspots include **La Namounia at La Playa** and **Amphitheatro** for dance beat, **Wild Rose** for rock, **Blue Jeans** as the dance spot of the year, and **Prinz** and **Prive** to run into trendy Athenians. Cover charge for these places is roughly 3000dr. Since you probably won't want to head out to any of these until after the buses have stopped running, expect to pay 1500-2500dr each way for a taxi from Plaka. Just get in and tell them what club you're going to; they'll know where to go. Be careful of cabbies trying to rip you off.

To quiet hungry stomachs, ask your taxi driver to take you to the **meat market** (no, this is not another club) on Athinas St., between Syntagma and Omonias, where popular early-morning restaurants replace the meat market (3-7am). Simply go into the kitchens and point away; *patsa* soup is an especially stomach-calming favorite.

If you're determined to stay around **Plaka,** there are several forgettable bars and clubs near Nikis and Filellinon. Be prepared to rub shoulders with other tourists or Athenians trying to pick up foreigners. Needless to say, plenty of other parts of town have good clubs. The posh **Kolonaki** district, on the way to Lycabettos sports Gucci shoes in chic shop windows which cost more than your whole vacation; however, a coffee or beer at any of the outdoor *tavernas* will not break the bank. While in the area, dig **Jazz Club 1920,** 10 Ploutarchou St. (tel. 721 0533), just up from the British Embassy (open nightly 10:15pm-1:15am for jazz, blues, latin, and rock). In **Kifissia,** a hip residential area north of Athens, there are many slick *tavernas* and discoes.

Greek Shadow Puppet Theater

As children gather earnestly around the screen of fine white material stretched across a frame, a bell rings and the shadow puppet theater begins. *Karaghiozis*, a poor, long-armed, balding hunchback appears dressed in rags, often without shoes. Always hungry and lacking money, he survives by his cunning: impersonating Turkish *hodjas*, politicians, or Hercules during his journey to the underworld. Shadow puppet theater first appeared in Java, China, and India, from which it spread to Turkey. The Turkish version, *Karagöz* (Black Eye), was popularized in Greece following the exchange of populations. The tales, which were passed down orally, often involve *Karaghiozis* trying to get rich and are peppered with slapstick humor. In its finest form, performances are accompanied by a small band and conducted by one or two puppeteers, who often mimic ten different voices and interject poignant social commentary and contemporary satire that is sophisticated enough for adults. Despite the rise of cinema and television, *Karaghiozis* remains popular among the young and the young at heart. Performances are rare and staged in Greek, but worthwhile.

Here you'll find the **Divina,** 2 Argiropoulou (tel. 801 5884), where you can boogie in air-conditioned comfort, and the **Follie Café,** known for its acid jazz, though it may be closed in summer. For **gay (primarily male) clubs,** try **Lembessi St.** off Singrou. Many of the clubs here tend not to be too friendly to itinerant heterosexuals.

Back in Plaka, **Cinema Paris,** at 22 Kidatheneon, shows recent (Greek "recent") films at an outdoor theater (2 shows per evening, 1700dr). Try to attend the late show since traffic noise and lingering dusk tend to mar the early one. Sit near the front to hear the already hushed film over intruding *bouzouki* music. Check the *Athens News* or a Greek paper for full movie listings. Most cost 1000-1700dr and are concentrated on Stadiou, Panepistimiou, and Patission St.

The **Athens Festival** runs annually from June until September, featuring classical theater groups performing in the **Odeon of Herodes Atticus.** Performances are also staged in **Lycabettos Theater** at the top of Lycabettos Hill, and in Epidavros (p. 127). The Greek Orchestra performs during this festival, as do visiting groups, which have ranged from the Bolshoi to B.B. King; from the Alvin Ailey Dance Company to classical Greek dramas; and from Pavarotti to the Talking Heads. The **Festival Office** (tel. 322 1459, -3111; ext. 240) is in the arcade at 4 Stadiou St. Student tickets are generally affordable (3000-5000dr; open Mon.-Fri. 8:30am-2pm and 5-7pm, Sat. 8:30am-1pm, Sun. 10am-1pm). The **Athens Box Office of the National Theater** (tel. 522 3242), at the corner of Agiou Konstandinou and Menandrou St. (Tickets cost 3000-4500dr, students 2000dr; closed in summer.)

If you've had enough to drink, the hokey **Sound and Light Show** (which depicts the Parthenon over the centuries) on Pnyx Hill (opposite the Acropolis) can be quite entertaining, though you'll leave unsure whether the title refers to the program or the click and flash of cameras saving tourists thousands of words (tel. 322 1459; after 2pm, tel. 922 6210; April-Oct. shows daily in English at 9pm; in French Wed.-Thurs. and Sat.-Mon. 10:10pm; in German Thurs.-Fri. 10pm; admission 1200dr, students 600dr.) Nearby in Dora Stratou Theatre on Philopappou Hill, **Greek dancers** kick and holler to live music on an open-air stage, celebrating traditions from all regions of the country. (For information, call 324 4395 between 9am and 3pm; from 7:30pm on, call 921 4650. Shows May-Sept. nightly 10:15pm, with an additional show Wed. and Sun. 8:15pm; tickets 2500-3000dr.)

Athens' two principal markets attract everyone from bargain-hunters to inveterate browsers. The **Athens Flea Market,** adjacent to Monastiraki Sq., has a festive, bazaar-like atmosphere and offers a potpourri of second-hand junk, costly antiques, and everything in between. Although parts of it have become overtouristed, there is still the occasional treasure to be found and lots of neo-hippies to watch. (Market open Mon., Wed., and Sat.-Sun. 8am-3pm, and Tues., Thurs.-Fri. 8am-8pm.) Sunday is the grand bazaar when the flea market overflows the square and Fillis Athinas St.

A huge indoor-outdoor **food market** lines the sides of Athinas St. between Evripidou and Sofokleous St. A sight, to be sure, the **meat market** is huge, but not for vegetarians or the faint of heart (open Mon.-Sat. 8am-2pm). Livers, kidneys, and skinned rabbits with cottontails still on hang throughout. There are also less visually challenging foods, such as fruits, vegetables, breads, and cheeses. It's open the same hours as regular food stores, but Athenian restauranteurs go early and purchase the choice meat and fish. Restaurants in the meat market are open at night.

SIGHTS

Acropolis

The **Acropolis**, or "high city," with its strategic position overlooking the Aegean Sea and Attic Plains, has served as both a military fortress and religious center. The heights afford an expansive view of Athens and the Aegean. Without a doubt, the Acropolis, particularly the Parthenon, is Athens' highlight. Today, the hilltop's remarkable ruins grace otherwise rubble-strewn grounds. Ongoing renovations require that steel scaffolding cling to the ancient marble columns.

In the 13th century BCE, wealthy landowners overthrew the monarchy in Athens who had ruled the city safely from their fortress in the Acropolis. The new rulers, the *Aristoi* (excellent ones), shifted the center of their government away from the Acropolis, ruling the *polis* (city-state) from the lower foothills of the city. The Acropolis, far from being abandoned, was then used as a shrine devoted to two aspects of the goddess **Athena:** Athena Polias, goddess of crops and fertility, and Athena Pallas, military guardian of the city. The original shrine was constructed out of wood. Following the Greek custom of putting money under the protection of a deity, the Acropolis also housed the city treasury.

In 507 BCE, the tyrannical *Aristoi* were overthrown and Athens began its successful experiment with **democracy.** In 490 BCE, Athenians began constructing a temple on the Acropolis—this time, out of marble. When the Persians sacked the temple ten years later, the Greeks threw the violated religious objects off the side of the Acropolis and buried the litter (now displayed in the Acropolis Museum).

In response to the Persian threat, Aegean rulers formed the Delian League. **Pericles** appropriated part of the taxes paid by the league to beautify Athens. Among his projects were the temples of the Acropolis, the Temple of Hephaestus in the *agora,* and the Temple of Poseidon at Sounion. These developments slowed during the **Peloponnesian War** (431-404 BCE), but by then the Athenians were committed to Pericles' plans, and construction sputtered along throughout the war and after his death in 429 BCE. Four of the buildings erected at that time still stand today: the Parthenon, the Propylaea, the Temple of Athena Nike, and the Erechtheum. They were designed and sculpted by Iktinos, Kallikrates, and a slew of eager-beaver apprentices all trying to outdo each others' artistry. Their construction has had an unrivaled influence on Western architecture.

Through the Hellenistic and Roman periods, the function of the Acropolis altered as often as it changed hands. The **Byzantines** converted it into a Christian place of worship. In a typical example of Christianity appropriating older "pagan" symbols, the Parthenon became the Church of St. Sophia ("Sophia," like "Athena," means wisdom). In 1205 CE, when Athens was liberated from the Byzantines by **Frankish crusaders,** the Acropolis once again became a fortress, serving as palace and headquarters for the Dukes de la Roche. The political situation settled down, and the Parthenon was then transformed into a Catholic church (Notre Dame d'Athènes). In the 15th century, **Turks** turned the Parthenon into a mosque and the Erechtheum into the Turkish commander's harem.

Tragedy befell the Acropolis during the **Venetian siege** in 1687, when a **Turkish supply of gunpowder** stored in the Parthenon was hit by a shell and exploded, destroying many sculptures. The Parthenon, which had stood steadfastly for hundreds of years came tumbling down. But the resourceful Greeks, unlike Humpty-Dumpty's horses and men, put it together again. The reconstructed temple is what you see before you. In 1822, the **Greeks** finally regained the Acropolis. Apart from a six-year occupation by the **Ottoman Turks** from 1827 to 1833 and a brief **Nazi occupation** in WWII, the Acropolis has been in Greek hands ever since.

The ramp that led to the Acropolis in classical times no longer exists. Today's visitors make the five-minute climb to the ticket window, enter through the crumbling **Beulé Gate** (added by the Romans and named after the French archaeologist who unearthed it), and continue through the **Propylaea,** the ancient entrance. Unfortunately, the site is not wheelchair-accessible. The marble can be slippery, so be careful if you are wearing shoes that have seen better days. Don't wear heels.

The Propylaea became famous for its ambitious multi-level design, although the entrance itself, begun by Mnesicles between 437 and 432 BCE, was never completed. In Roman times, the structure extended as far as 80m below the Beulé Gate. At the cliff's edge, the tiny **Temple of Athena Nike** was built during a respite from the Peloponnesian War, the so-called Peace of Nikias (421-415 BCE). Known as the "jewel of Greek architecture," this temple with eight miniature Ionic columns once housed a winged statue of the goddess Nike (not yet a brand-name label). One day, in a paranoid frenzy, the Athenians feared that their deity (and peace) would flee the city, so they clipped Athena's wings. Below the temple are the remains of the 5m-thick **Cyclopean wall** (so named for its one-eyed architects), which once surrounded the whole of the Acropolis.

The **Erechtheum,** to the left of the Parthenon as you face it, was completed in 406 BCE, just prior to Athens' defeat by Sparta. Lighter than the Parthenon, the Erechtheum is a unique two-level structure that housed a number of cults, including those of Athena, Poseidon, and the snake-bodied hero Erechtheus. The east porch, with its six Ionic columns, was dedicated to Athena Polias and sheltered an olive wood statue of her. On the south side of the Erechtheum, facing the Parthenon, are the **Caryatids,** six columns sculpted in the shape of women. Their artful tunics, which seem to flow into fluted columns towards the base, are plaster replicas—the originals were moved to the Acropolis Museum to protect them from air pollution.

Looming over the hillside, the **Parthenon,** or Virgin's Apartment," keeps vigil over Athens and its world. Designed by the architects Iktinos and Kallikrates, the Parthenon was the first building completed under Pericles' plan to revive the city. It once housed the legendary gold and ivory (*krysalphantine*) statue of Athena Parthena (Virgin Athena) sculpted by Phidias. The temple intentionally features many almost imperceptible irregularities; the Doric columns bulge in the middle and the stylobate (pedestal) of the building bows slightly upward in order to compensate for the optical illusion in which straight lines, viewed from a distance, appear to bend. Originally made entirely of marble except for a long-since-vanished wooden roof, the building's stone ruins attest to both the durability of the structure and the elegance of the **Classical Age.**

Metopes around the sides of the Parthenon portray victories of the forces of order over disorder. On the far right of the south side, the only side which has not been defaced, the Lapiths battle the Centaurs (Centauromachy); on the east the Olympian gods triumph over the giants (Gigantomachy); the north depicts a faintly visible victory of the Greeks over the Trojans; and on the west, one can make out the triumph of the Greeks over the Amazons (Amazonomachy). A better-preserved frieze in bas-relief around the interior walls shows the Panathenaic procession in Athena's honor. The **East Pediment,** the formerly triangular area that the columns propped up, once depicted the birth of Athena, who according to legend, sprang from the head of Zeus. The **West Pediment,** on the opposite façade, formerly documented the contest between Athena and Poseidon for Athens's eternal devotion. Various fragments of the originals are now housed in the Acropolis and British Museums.

To avoid massive crowds and the broiling midday sun, visit early in the morning. Cold drinks are hard to come by; bring bottled water to avoid the overpriced refreshment stand at the entrance (soda 600dr). You can reach the entrance, which is on the west side of the Acropolis (tel. 321 0219), from Areopagitou St. south of the Acropolis, or by walking uphill from Plaka. Follow the spray-painted signs at intervals in the narrow passageway (open in summer Mon.-Fri. 8am-6:30pm, Sat.-Sun. and holidays 8:30am-2:30pm; in winter 8:30am-4:30pm; admission 2000dr, students 1000dr, free on Sun. and holidays, 1000dr per video camera).

The **Acropolis Museum** (tel. 323 6665), footsteps away from the Parthenon, contains a superb collection of sculptures, including five of the Caryatids of the Erechtheum (the sixth now resides in the British Museum). Most of the treasures housed here date from the transition period from Archaic to Classical Greek art (550-400 BCE). You can trace this development in the faces of the statues, from the stylized, entranced faces and static poses of Archaic sculpture—seen in the famous *Moschophoros* (calf-bearer)—to the more familiar, naturalistic (though idealized) figures of Classical Art. Only a few pieces from the Parthenon are here—**Lord Elgin,** with the heartwrenching aid of rope lassoes, helped himself to the rest, which are now in the British Museum—but the collection is nonetheless impressive. (Museum open Mon. 11am-6:30pm, Tues.-Fri. 8am-6:30pm, Sat.-Sun. 8:30am-2:30pm; admission included in Acropolis ticket. Cameras without flash allowed, but no posing next to the objects, heathen tourist.) From the southwest corner of the Acropolis, you can look down on the reconstructed **Odeon of Herodes Atticus,** a still-functioning theater dating from the Roman Period, c. 160 CE. Nearby are the ruins of the Classical Greek **Theater of Dionysus** (tel. 322 4625; entrance on Dionissiou Areopagitou St.), the **Asclepion,** and the **Stoa of Eumenes II.** The Theater of Dionysus dates from the 4th century BCE (open daily 8:30am-2:30pm; admission to all three 500dr, students free with ID).

Near the Acropolis

The **Athenian Agora,** at the foot of the Acropolis, was the administrative center and marketplace of Athens from the 6th century BCE through the late Roman Period (5th-6th centuries CE). However, Prehistoric habitation and cemeteries have been evidenced here as well. The decline of the Agora paralleled the decline of Athens, as barbarian attacks buffeted both the city and the square from 267 BCE to 580 CE. It was in the Agora and on the **Pnyx** (the low hill and meeting place of the assembly, 1km to the south) that Athenian democracy was born and flourished. Socrates frequented the Agora, as did Aristotle, Demosthenes, Xenophon, and St. Paul. According to Plato, Socrates' preliminary hearing was held at the **Stoa Basileios** (Royal Promenade), which has been recently excavated and lies to the left as you cross the subway tracks upon leaving the Agora.

The sprawling archaeological site features three remarkable constructions. The **Temple of Hephaestus,** on a hill in the northwest corner, is the best-preserved Classical temple in Greece. Built around 440 BCE, it is especially notable for its friezes which depict the labors of Hercules and the adventures of Thisseos. The ruins of the **Odeon of Agrippa** (concert hall), built for the son-in-law of the Emperor Augustus, stand in the center of the Agora. In 150 CE the roof collapsed, and the Odeon was rebuilt as a lecture hall at half its former size. The actors' dressing room was made into a porch supported by colossal statues (the ruins of three of these statues remain to guard the site). To the south, the elongated **Stoa of Attalos,** a multi-purpose building for shops, shelter, and informal gatherings, was rebuilt between 1953 and 1956 and now houses the **Agora Museum** (tel. 321 0185). The original structure, built in the second century BCE, was given to Athens by Attalos II, King of Pergamon, in gratitude for the education he had received in the city. The museum contains a number of relics from the site and offers a cool sanctuary from the sweltering summer sun (agora and museum open Tues.-Sun. 8:30am-3pm; admission to both 1200dr, students with ID 600dr, seniors 900dr). There are several entrances to the Agora, including one at the edge of Monastiraki, one on Thission Sq., and one on Adrianou St. You can reach the Acropolis from here by exiting the south side of the Agora (follow the path uphill) and then turning right. The most commonly used gate is the one near the Acropolis entrance (turn right as you leave the Acropolis).

Northwest of the Agora, on the other side of the tracks at Thission Station, 148 Ermou St., is **Kerameikos.** This is the site of the 40m-wide boulevard that ran from the Agora, through the Diplyon gate, and 1½km to the sanctuary of Akademos, where Plato founded his Academy in the 4th century BCE. Public tombs for state leaders, famous authors, and battle victims were constructed along this road. Worshipers began the annual Panathenaean procession to the Acropolis at the Diplyon Gate, one of the two gates excavated at this site. The sacred road to Eleusis, traversed during the annual Eleusian processions, ran through the Sacred Gate, the second gate on the site. Family tombs adorn either side of the Sacred Road outside the gate. A **museum** on the site (tel. 346 3552), exhibits finds from recent digs as well as an excellent pottery collection. (Site and museum open Tues.-Sun. 8:30am-3pm; admission to both 400dr, students 200dr.)

The **Temple of Olympian Zeus** (Vas. Olgas and Amalias Ave.; tel. 922 6330) also deserves a visit. Fifteen majestic columns are all that remain of the largest temple ever built in Greece. Started in the 6th century BCE, the temple was completed 600 years later by the Roman emperor Hadrian. Nowadays, the Corinthian columns stand in the middle of downtown Athens, below the National Garden. The remains of a Roman bath, tiles and all, can also be seen here (open Tues.-Sun. 8:30am-3pm; admission 500dr, students 300dr). Next to the Temple is **Hadrian's Arch,** which was built in the 2nd century BCE to mark the boundary between the ancient city of Thisseos and the new city built by Hadrian.

MUSEUMS

The **National Archaeological Museum,** 44 Patission St., 128 Oktovriou next to Metsovion Polytechnion. A 20-minute walk from Syntagma down Stadiou until Aiolou and then onto 28 Oktovriou (tel. 821 7717) is well worth delaying your jaunt to the islands. Take trolley #2, 4, 5, 9, 11, 15, or 18 from the uphill side of Syntagma or trolley #3 or 13 on the north side of Vasilissis Sofias. Pieces that would be the prizes of lesser collections seem almost unremarkable amid the general magnificence. Expect to spend a long time here.

After checking your bags at the cloakroom (mandatory; no charge), go straight ahead into the **Mycenae exhibit** of Heinrich Schliemann's digs at Mycenae, including the golden "Mask of Agamemnon" (which is really the death mask of a king who lived at least three centuries earlier than the legendary Agamemnon). Also displayed are samples of Bronze Age jewelry and pottery from Mycenae, other sites in the Peloponnese, and various Prehistoric sites in Greece. This primary exhibit is skirted by findings from other tombs found in different parts of Greece and displayed in side rooms. In the red room is the bronze statue, **Artemisian Jockey** (140 BCE).

Don't leave without viewing the **kouroi,** or standing males (in the left wing of the museum). They are displayed chronologically and in the buff, allowing you to see the evolution of this "form." The **wall paintings from Akrotiri,** Santorini (1 flight up) are intriguing. These painted architectural and artistic treasures were buried during a volcanic eruption believed to have occurred around 1500 BCE and present a unique glimpse of life in the Bronze Age. The bronze statue of **Poseidon,** also in the left wing, is eerily life-like. With its hollowed-out eye sockets, it is impressive, as are the bronze sculptures in general. The **mask of a slave from Diplyon** (2nd century BCE) adds irony to the exhibits—with a wide, toothless grin and crazy eyes, the face seems amused by the starkly stoic statues which surround it. The right wing of the museum hosts a beautifully preserved **Aphrodite-Panas-Eros** from the Hellenistic Era. Look for the statue of the **Sleeping Maenad.** Also worth viewing is the extensive **vase collection** (on the same floor as the wall paintings)—Red and Black Ware, Narrative, and Geometric styles (museum open Mon. 12:30-7pm, Tues.-Fri. 8am-7pm, Sat.-Sun. and holidays 8:30am-3pm; admission 2000dr, students 1000dr, seniors 1500dr, free Sun. and holidays, no flash photography).

Opened in 1986, the **Goulandris Museum of Cycladic and Ancient Greek Art,** 4 Neophytou Douka St. (tel. 722 8321), near Kolonaki, is accessible by trolleys #3 and 13 (75dr). It has a stunning collection in a modern building with air-conditioning. Cycladic art is famous for its sleek, marble, angular, schematic, Picasso-esque, 90% female figurines. Some even exhibited painted details, possibly representing tattoos.

Many figurines were either looted from archaeological sites at the turn of the century or found buried with the dead in graves on the Cycladic Islands. Their actual, precise use in antiquity is still an enigma; however, plenty of theories have arisen and range from representations of goddesses to *psychopompoi* (tour guides to the Underworld) to ancient sex toys like the Egyptians had. The bronze jewelry from Skyros, as well as to the collection of Greek vases and statues from 2000 BCE to the 4th century CE, are also impressive. The new wing of the museum, on the corner of Vas. Sofias and Herodotou, is an extension of the Cycladic collection (open Mon. and Wed.-Fri. 10am-4pm, Sat. 10am-3pm; admission 400dr, students 200dr).

The **Benaki Museum,** at the corner of Koumbari and Vasilissis Sofias (tel. 361 1617), houses a diverse collection of treasures in a beautiful Neoclassical building which was once the residence of philanthropist Anthony Benaki. The museum displays Greek Bronze Age relics, Byzantine icons, gold jewelry of the 5th century BCE, textiles and costumes from the islands, and relics from the War of Independence. It also explores the influence of neighboring cultures on Greece by juxtaposing Islamic, Arabic, and Coptic artwork with Greek. Unfortunately, the Benaki is closed indefinitely for renovation.

Inside an elegant Florentine building with serene courtyards, the **Byzantine Museum,** 22 Vasilissis Sofias (tel. 723 1570), has an excellent and extensive collection of Christian art from the 4th-19th centuries. The collection includes early Byzantine sculptures, an icon collection containing works from the entire Byzantine period, and a reconstructed early Christian basilica, attesting to Greece's rich history even after the Golden Age. There are also a number of superb reliefs done in bronze, silver, and gold. One wing of the building features an array of well preserved frescoes and mosaics. The exhibits are poorly labeled, however—consider buying a book (2500dr) before you visit (open Tues.-Sun. 8:30am-3pm; admission 500dr).

Next door to the Byzantine Museum is the **War Museum** (tel. 729 0543). This museum traces the history of Greek armaments from Neolithic eras, through the 5th-century BCE Persian invasion and the expeditions of Alexander the Great, to the submachine guns of the modern era. The primary emphasis, however, is on the modern Greek arsenal (open Tues.-Sun. 9am-2pm; free).

The **National Gallery** (Alexander Soutzos Museum) is set back from Vasilissis Sofias at 50 Vasileos Konstandinou (tel. 721 7643). The museum exhibits Greek artists' works, supplemented by periodic international displays. The permanent collection includes some outstanding works by El Greco. The drawings, photographs, and sculpture gardens are also impressive. Consult *This Week in Athens* or call the museum for information on current exhibits (open Mon. and Wed.-Sat. 9am-3pm, Sun. 10am-2pm; free). At the **Theater Museum,** 50 Akadimis St. (tel. 362 9430), behind the university, you can see costumes, models, photographic paraphernalia, and dressing rooms (open Mon.-Fri. 9am-2:30pm; admission 300dr). In Plaka, the **Greek Folk Art Museum,** 17 Kidatheneon St. (tel. 322 9031), exhibits *laiki techni* (popular art) from all over Greece, including embroidered textiles, costumes, and puppets. Ornamental ecclesiastical silverwork and household pottery are also on exhibit. Don't miss the wall paintings by folk artist Theophilos Hadzimichail (open Tues.-Sun. 10am-2pm; admission 500dr, students and seniors 300dr; cameras with flash not permitted, without flash free). The **Greek Popular Musical Instruments Museum,** 1-2 Diogenous St., Plaka (tel. 325 0198), has an exquisite, interactive display of an array of musical instruments used in the 18th, 19th and 20th centuries (open Tues. and Thurs.-Sun. 10am-2pm, Wed. noon-6pm, closed Mon.; free).

On the south side of the Acropolis, just off Dionysiou Areopagiotou St., you can satiate your lust for gold at the **Ilias Lalounis Jewelry Museum** (tel. 922 1044). This private museum houses over 3000 designs created by Lalounis, as well as collections displaying the history of jewelry in Greece from ancient to modern times, including a workshop where visitors can observe different jewelry-making techniques (open Mon. and Wed. 9am-9pm, Thurs.-Sat. 9am-3pm, closed Tuesdays; admission 800dr, students and seniors 500dr, free after 3pm on Wednesdays).

The **Jewish Museum,** 36 Leoforos Amalias, third floor (tel. 323 1577), is in a 19th-century building with a United Nations flag. An impressive collection of textiles, religious artifacts, and documents traces the roots of the Greek Jewish communities dating from the Hellenistic period. The museum also contains the reconstructed Synagogue of Patras (open Sun.-Fri. 9am-1pm; free). The **Children's Museum,** 14 Kidathineon St. (tel. 331 2995, -6), is a colorful, friendly, hands-on experience in the heart of Plaka. The museum's philosophy is "I hear and I forget; I see and I remember; I do and I understand." Go to the attic to play dress-up in a quaint bedroom from times past. (Open Mon., Fri. 9:30am-1:30pm, Wed. 10am-7pm, Sat.-Sun. 10am-2pm. Hours can be a bit erratic so call in advance to check. Free.)

Byzantine sanctuaries, like their Classical counterparts, have been incorporated into the urban landscape. Traffic on Ermou St. must go around **Kapnikaria Church,** which has been stranded in the middle of the street, one block beyond Aiolou St. Walking down Mitropoleos from Syntagma, you may also notice a tiny church on the corner of Pentelis St., around which a modern building has been constructed. Other Byzantine churches in Athens include the **Agia Apostoli,** at the east edge of the Agora; **Metamorphosis,** in Plaka near Pritaniou St.; **Agia Triada,** on Filellinon St., a few blocks from Syntagma; and **Agios Eleftherios,** next to the **Mitropoli Cathedral,** on Mitropoleos St. Peek in for a respite from the day's heat. Most of these churches are open in the morning and for services, and require proper dress: skirts for women, long pants for men, and long-sleeved shirts for everyone.

The **Chapel of St. George,** on top of rocky **Lycabettos Hill,** offers a beautiful view of the city. Burn off dinner by walking up, or take the funicular (500dr one way 500dr, 1000dr roundtrip, children 500dr) to the top—the station is a healthy hike at the end of Ploutarchou St. The funicular leaves every 10-15 minutes for its dark but somewhat exciting two-minute uphill journey (chapel open Mon.-Wed., Fri.-Sun. 8:45am-12:15am, Thurs. 10:30am-12:15am). The cool, pleasant **National Garden,** adjacent to Syntagma Square, is an escape from the noise, heat, and frantic pace of Athens. Walk along its tranquil paths and visit the duck pond and poor excuse for a zoo. Women should avoid strolling alone here (open sunrise to sunset).

When you're passing through Syntagma Sq., don't miss the changing of the guard in front of the **Parliament** building. Every hour on the hour, two sets of enormously tall *evzones* (guards) slowly wind up like toy soldiers, kick their heels about, and fall backwards into symmetrical little guardhouses on either side of the **Tomb of the Unknown Warrior.** Unlike their British equivalents, *evzones* occasionally wink and even smile at tourists. Their jovial manner is as delightful as their attire—pom-pom-laden clogs, short pleated skirts *(foustanela),* and pony tail-tasseled hats. Every Sunday at 10:45am, the ceremony occurs with the full troop of guards and a band.

NEAR ATHENS

■ Kesariani and Daphni

If you're worn down by Athens's insane congestion, visit the **Monastery of Kesariani** (tel. 723 6619) for serenity and salvation. Located near the top of **Mt. Hymettus,** the site was originally a temple to Dimitra, goddess of agriculture and nature. In the Roman period (200-300 CE), another temple was erected in its place, employing the architectural techniques of the day. The structure's stones were used in the 14th century to build the existing monastery. The 17th-century frescoes (painted by Ioannis Ypatios) and the sacred atmosphere are splendid. Come alone or with a spiritual friend; tour buses are likely to whirl you through too quickly.

To reach Kesariani take blue **bus** #224 from the ΚΗΠΙΟΣ stop two blocks up Vas. Sofias from Syntagma Sq. (every 15min., 20min., 75dr). Get off at the last stop, follow the left-hand road uphill and, when you reach the overpass, bear right under it, staying to the right through two forks. A bit farther up the road, it splits, the right going up the mountain, the left coming down from it. Once again, stick to the right. Roughly a five-minute jaunt farther uphill, just as the road bends left, two branches spring from the right side. Ignore the barred one on the right, and take the stone path right up to the monastery. The entire walk takes 40-50 minutes, so be sure to bring lots of water. If you drain your water bottles, a 15-minute walk up the main road leads to a small store and a drinkable fountain. For a fabulous view overlooking Athens all the way to the sea, keep walking for 15 more minutes past the store. Many hiking trails meander away from the road throughout the area. The Monastery makes a wonderful spot for a picnic (monastery open Tues.-Sun. 8:30am-3pm; admission 800dr, seniors 600dr, students with ID 400dr, EU students free).

Built on the site of the ancient Temple of Daphnios Apollo and surrounded by a high fortified wall is the **Monastery of Daphni** (tel. 581 1558), a peaceful retreat 10km west of Athens, along the Ancient Sacred Way. Cool breezes sweep the area, and the 11th-century structure is pock-marked with birds' nests. The monastery has served as both an army camp and a lunatic asylum, which may explain the pronounced scowl on Christ's face as he stares down from the masterful mosaic dome. Even though the mosaics were seriously damaged when the Turks burnt the church during the fall of the Byzantine Empire, they still do have an enchanting aura (open daily 8:30am-2:45pm; admission 800dr, seniors 600dr, students 400dr, no charge for video, no flash cameras allowed). **Camping Daphni** (tel. 581 1563), right next to the monastery. (Reception open 7am-11pm. Check-out 2pm. 1100dr per person. 900dr per small tent. 1300dr per large tent. Prices include shower.)

To reach Daphni (pronounced daph-NI) from Athens, take bus #A16 from **Pl. Eleftherias** (from Omonoia Sq., go up Peiraias St./Tsaldari St.) for 75dr. From Peiraias Port, take #804 or #845 (every 15min., 6am-11:30pm, 35min., 75dr). From the final stop, go to the highway and cross it to get to the monastery.

■ Peiraias ΠΕΙΡΑΙΑΣ

The natural harbor of Peiraias has been Athens's port since the early 5th century BCE, when Themistokles began fortifying Peiraias, then an island, as a base for the growing Athenian fleet. In approximately 450 BCE, Pericles added the Long Walls from Athens to Peiraias, bridging the land masses. Though the opening scenes of both Kazantzakis' *Zorba the Greek* and Plato's *Republic* depict Peiraias as a charming port town, these days Peiraias has lost that loving feeling—it's dirty and smoggy, with endless stores vending cheap tourist trinkets and "aged" pastries glistening with grease. Use Peiraias only as the point of departure to most of the Greek isles. To get here, take the subway (75dr) from Monastiraki, Omonia, or any other station, to the last stop in the Peiraias direction, or take blue bus #049 on Athinas St. just off Omonoia Sq. (75dr). From Syntagma Sq., take green bus #040 on Filellinon St. (75dr) and get off at the Public Theater (Demotikon Theatron) and head down the hill, toward the port. The subway takes roughly 20 minutes, while the bus is a 40-minute ride. Long-distance trains for Patras and the Peloponnese leave daily from the station on Akti Kalimassioti. Long-distance trains for northern Greece (Larissis) leave daily from the station on Ag. Dimitriou across the harbor.

Orientation and Practical Information
Ferries ply the waters from Peiraias to nearly all Greek islands except the Sporades and Ionian groups. There is a small but invaluable map of Peiraias on the back of the Athens map available at the tourist office in Syntagma Sq. Most of the boats and ticket agencies are on two streets, **Akti Poseidonos** and **Akti Miaouli.** The subway deposits you at the top of Akti Poseidonos; facing the water, head left. It merges with Akti Miaouli at **Themistokleous Square,** where you arrive if you walk down **Vas. Georgiou** (from the bus stop at **Korai Square**). Themistokleos Sq. is also the departure point for boats to the Saronic Gulf Islands and **hydrofoils** to Aegina (every 2hr. 8am-8pm, 40min.; 25,500dr; students 21,700dr). There are no student discounts on domestic travel in Greece, but discounts on international fares can be found. The larger ferries dock at

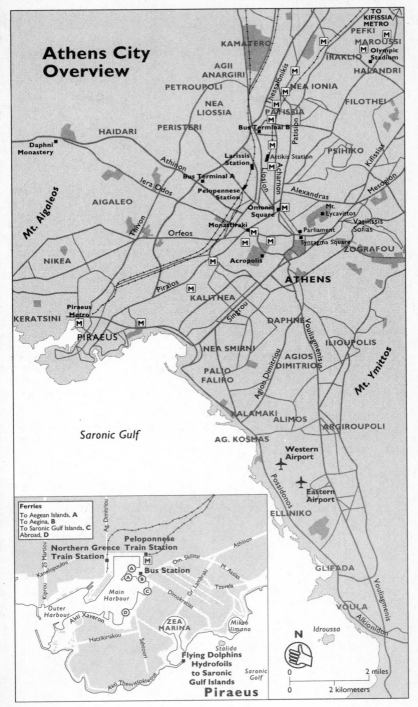

PEIRAIAS

TO KIFISSIA METRO
PEFKI
KAMATERO
MAROUSSI
Olympic Stadium
IRAKLIO
AGII ANARGIRI
HALANDRI
PETROUPOLI
NEA IONIA
NEA LIOSSIA
FILOTHEI
Tsessalonikis
PERISTERI
PATISSIA
PSIHIKO
HAIDARI
Bus Terminal B
Patision
Daphni Monastery
Athinon
Larissis Station
Attikis Station
Kifissias
Bus Terminal A
Acharnon
Iera Odos
Peloponnese Station
Liosion
Mesogion
Alexandras
AIGALEO
Omonia Square
Mt. Lycavittos
Vasilissis Sofias
Tthinon
Monastiraki
Parliament
Orfeos
Syntagma Square
ZOGRAFOU
NIKEA
Acropolis
ATHENS
Piraios
ATHENS
Piraios
KALITHEA
Singrou
KERATSINI
Piraeus Metro
DAPHNE
Voullagmenis
ILIOUPOLIS
PIRAEUS
NEA SMIRNI
AGIOS DIMITRIOS
Agiou Dimitriou
PALIO FALIRO
ARGIROUPOLI
Mt. Ymittos
KALAMAKI
ALIMOS
Saronic Gulf
AG. KOSMAS
Western Airport
Possidonos
Eastern Airport
ELLINIKO
GLIFADA
Voullagmenis
VOULA
Alkionidon
Idroussa

Athens City Overview

Mt. Aigaleos

Ferries
To Aegean Islands, A
To Aegina, B
To Saronic Gulf Islands, C
Abroad, D

Ag. Dimitriou
Kanelopoulou
25 Martiou
Kiprou
Peloponnese Train Station
Northern Greece Train Station
Athinon
Om. Skilitsi
Bus Station
M. Assas
Gr. Lambraki
Tzavela
Main Harbour
Dimokratias
Outer Harbour
Akti Xaveron
ZEA MARINA
Mikro Limano
Hatzikiriakou
Saltourt
Stalida
Flying Dolphins Hydrofoils to Saronic Gulf Islands
Saronic Gulf
Akti Themistokleous

N

0   2 miles
0   2 kilometers

Piraeus

Akti Miaouli; international ferries are at the end toward the Customs House. Small ferries depart from Akti Poseidonos. **Kentriko** (tel. 412 1181 or 412 1172; fax 413 3193), in the subway station, with a large, blue-lettered sign, offers extremely helpful advice on where to find your boat in the glut of vessels in the port and luggage storage (300dr). Inquire about their special 20-day unlimited island-hopping packages, available after June 15 (9500dr). Open daily 5:30am-10pm. It is harder to avoid **banks** than to find them in this town—most are located on the waterfront. The **National Bank of Greece,** 3 Antistasseos St. (tel. 417 4101), is one block up from Themistokleous Sq. Open Mon.-Thurs. 8am-2pm, Fri. 8am-1:30pm. There is a **Citibank** with **ATMs** at 47-49 Akti Miaouli (tel. 417 2153). All banks **change currency,** as does the **Thomas Cook,** one block down Akti Poseidonos from the subway, and the numerous other agencies which **exchange currency** litter the port. **OTE** is at 14-16 Akti Poseidonos (open daily 7:15am-1pm). **Telstar Booksellers,** 57 Akti Miaouli (tel. 429 3618), offers an impressive array of magazines in English, French, and Arabic, and a small selection of paperbacks and some stationery supplies (open Mon.-Fri. 7am-8pm, Sat. 8am-4pm). **Port Police:** tel. 422 6000. **Post Office:** Tsamadou St. (tel. 412 4202), on the right off Antistasseos St., one block inland from Themistokleous Sq. The subway station offers travelers a smaller **post office,** to the right of the Akti Poseidonos doors (open Mon.-Fri. 7:30am-8pm, Sat. 8am-2pm, Sun. 9am-1:30pm). **Postal code:** 18503. **Telephone Code:** 01.

On the opposite side of the peninsula is the port of **Zea.** Hydrofoils depart from here to the other Saronic Gulf islands and to Kea and Kithnos. Along the water and under the sidewalk (to the right if you are coming from inland) at Zea are a **port police** office (tel. 459 3145), a **post office** (open Mon.-Fri. 7:30am-2pm), and a **tourist office** upstairs (tel. 413 5716; open Mon.-Fri. 8am-2:30pm), look for the EOT sign. Private boats dock in the harbor on the left (facing the water); hydrofoils await on the right. To get to Zea, walk away from the water on any of the roads off Akti Miaouli; it takes roughly 10 minutes to get there.

Accommodations, Food, and Sights For those unfortunate enough to be marooned by ferry schedules, your best bet is to head away from the water, where the hotels will at least be safe. **Hotel Phidias,** 189 Koundouriotou St. (tel. 429 6480; fax 429 6251), is close to Zea on a side street off Boumboulinas, which itself springs from Akti Miaouli. (Singles 11,000dr. Doubles 14,000dr. Triples 16,800dr. All with bath.) **Hotel Glaros,** 4 Char. Trikoupi St. (tel. 451 5421 or 453 7887; fax 453 7889), on a street which runs away from the lower part of Akti Miaouli, offers cheap rates. (Singles 4800dr, with bath 6500dr. Doubles 7000dr, with bath 8500dr.) Don't sleep in the dirty and dangerous park at Themistokleos Sq.

Inexpensive fast food restaurants line the dock, offering mediocre fare at uniform prices. To find a good, cheap meal, the best approach is to do it yourself at the **Peiraikon Supermarket** (tel. 417 6495). Go one block up Antistasseos St., and turn left right at the National Bank of Greece; the supermarket is at the end of that block (open Mon.-Thurs. 8am-8pm, Fri. 8am-9pm, Sat. 8am-3pm). The bakery **Europa,** 166-168 Koundouriotou (tel. 412 2597), near Hotel Phidias, offers cheap, mouth watering treats (*baklava* 250dr). Try the juicy *souvlaki* sandwich (350dr) at **Drosopigi,** 24 Akti Moustopoulou (tel. 428 0645), right along the Zea boardwalk.

The prize possession of the **Archaeological Museum,** 31 Char. Trikoupi St. (tel. 452 1598), is the ancient "Peiraias Kouros," a large hollow bronze statue with outstretched arms. The bronze statues of "Artemis" and "Athena" are also well worth your time (open Tues.-Sun. 8:30am-3pm; admission 500dr, students 400dr, European students free, seniors 400dr; no charge for video; no flash allowed). Near the museum is the 2nd-century BCE **Hellenistic theater.** Farther south at Zea, facing the harbor and underneath the sidewalk on Akti Themistokleous, is the **Maritime Museum** (tel. 451 6822), which traces the history of the Greek navy using detailed ship models. The courtyard is home port to torpedo tubes, naval weapons, and anchors (open Tues.-Fri. 8:30am-2:30pm, Sat.-Sun. 9am-1pm; admission 400dr).

■ The Petalion Gulf Coast

CAPE SOUNION

Local legend has it that off the coast of Cape Sounion lie the remains of fabled **Atlantis,** which sank into the sea millennia ago. A strikingly similar local legend exists at Akrotiri, Santorini. Take your pick. The **Temple of Poseidon** (tel. 39 363) still stands on a promontory high above the coast. Stand at the foot of the temple, overlooking the endless azure of the Aegean, in the path of the strong winds, and you will sense the mystical powers that led the Greeks to dedicate a temple to Poseidon here. The original temple was constructed around 600 BCE, destroyed by the Persians in a 480 BCE temper-tantrum, and rebuilt by Pericles in 440 BCE. The 16 remaining Doric columns still suggest the graceful symmetry of the original temple. Scattered remains of the **Temple of Athena Sounias,** the patron goddess of Athens, litter the lower hill. Sunrise is the ideal time to view the temples. If you sleep in, try to visit before early afternoon (when the tour buses funnel in) or around sunset (after they've drained out). Pack a lunch and bypass the pricey cafeteria (temples open daily 9am-sunset; admission 800dr, students 400dr, EU students free). Last bus to Athens departs according to the hour of the sunset (usually between 8:30 and 9pm in summer); check the schedule at the bus station upon arrival.

To reach the ocean, follow one of the many paths from the inland side of the temple. The agile and adventurous can negotiate the cliff on the ocean side. Swarmed with vacationing families, the **beaches** along the 70km Apollo Coast between Peiraias and Cape Sounion have a crowded carnival atmosphere, especially on summer weekends. Some are owned by hotels, which charge a 150dr admission fee, but towns usually have free public beaches as well, and some seaside stretches along the bus route remain almost empty. The driver will let you off almost anywhere.

Two orange-striped KTEL buses travel the 65km road to Cape Sounion. One goes along the coast and stops at all points on the **Apollo Coast,** leaving every hour on the half hour (6:30am-6:30pm) from the 14 Mavromateon St. stop in the square just below Areos Park in Athens. You can meet the bus 10 minutes later on Filellinon St. at Xenofontos St., but all the seats will probably be filled (2hr., 1050dr). The other bus leaves from Areos Park (every hr. on the hr., 6am-6pm, 2¼hr., 1050dr). The bus leaving on the half hour is a beautiful, pleasant ride with crystal blue water in sight the whole time (catch a seat on the right side of the bus to enjoy the scenery). The bus that leaves on the hour follows a slightly less scenic inland route. Every hour, on the half hour, buses head from Cape Sounion to the port of **Lavrio** (20min., 200dr). Buses depart from Athens to Lavrio to catch the ferries (every 30min. 5:50am-7pm, 8:15pm, 9:30pm, 1½hr., 800dr). **Ferries** go from Lavrio to Kea (1¼hr, 1610dr) and Kithnos (2½hr., 2300dr). For tickets call 2677.

If you want to spend the night to see the temples or if you miss the last bus to the ferry at Lavrio, accommodations can be found at **Aegaeon Hotel** (tel. 39 200; fax 39 234), located five minutes from the bus stop toward the temples (if you plan to stay, get off the bus at the main stop rather than up at the temples). It is hard to miss the large yellow building down by the beach on the right. (Singles 12,000dr. Doubles 16,000dr. All with bath.) The **Belle Epoque Hotel,** 33 Klioni St. (tel. 27 130 or 26 059), at Lavrio, has reasonably priced rooms. (Singles 5000dr. Doubles 9000dr. Triples 15,000dr. Full breakfast 1500dr.) To find it, walk a very short distance from the bus stop away from both the port and the center of town. **Telephone Code:** 0292.

RAFINA

For the purposes of most travelers in Greece, Rafina might as well be named "Little Peiraias." Situated across from its larger twin on the Attic Peninsula, Rafina is more pleasant on the eyes, ears, and lungs than its counterpart. Uphill from the port, life is pretty much centered around the white-paved town square.

THE PETALION GULF COAST

Following the ramp up from the waterfront will bring you to Plastira Sq. The **Commercial Bank** (tel. 25 182) is located on the far left corner of the square (open Mon.-Thurs. 8am-2pm, Fri. 8am-1:30pm) and the **Ionian Bank** (tel. 24 152), which is equipped with an **ATM** as well, is two blocks farther inland (open Mon.-Thurs. 7:45am-2pm, Fri. 7:45am-1:30pm). Both banks offer **currency exchange**. The **OTE** (tel. 25 182) is across the street from the post office on the far side of the square (open Mon.-Fri. 7:30am-2:30pm). For information and ferry tickets, try one of the English-speaking offices along the waterfront. The offices clearly display which tickets they sell. **Strintzis Lines, Gatsos Lines, Agoudimos Lines,** and **Ventouris Ferries** operate various ferries, while **Ilios Lines** and **Hermes Lines** operate hydrofoils. **Taxis** line up right in front of the square. There is a **pharmacy** one block down Kyprion St. off the left side of the square. Look for the green cross (open Mon., Wed. 8:30am-2pm, Tues., Thurs. 8:30am-2pm and 5:30-9pm). With the water at your back, the **post office** (tel. 23 315) stands two streets to the right on Eleftheriou Venizelou (open Mon.-Fri. 8am-1:30pm). **Postal Code:** 19009. **Telephone Code:** 0294.

Rafina is accessible by frequent **buses** from 29 Mavromateon St., two blocks up along Areos Park in Athens (every 30min., 5:45am-10:30pm, 1hr., 400dr). **Ferries** sail to Karystos in Evia (2-3 per day, 1¾hr., 1550dr); Marmari in Evia (4-6 per day, 1¼hr., 914dr); Andros (2-3 per day, 2hr., 2096dr); Tinos (2-3 per day, 4hr., 2998dr); Mykonos (2 per day, 5hr., 3474dr); Paros (1 per week, 8hr., 3306dr); and to Naxos (6hr., 3407dr). **Hydrofoils** sail to Andros (2 per day, 1hr., 4121dr), Tinos (2 per day, 2hr., 6168dr), and Mykonos (2 per day, 2½hr., 7333dr). There is a daily hydrofoil to Tinos, Mykonos, Paros, Naxos, Ios, and Santorini and a daily **super-Catamaran** to the Cyclades in summer. Mr. Rigos at **Auromar tourist office** (tel. 28 666), along the port, can help. For more information, call the **port authority** (tel. 22 300).

Be prepared to pay heartily for the dubious pleasure of spending a night in Rafina. **Hotel Korali** (tel. 22 477), in Plastira Sq., offers cramped but clean rooms with shared baths. (Singles 5500dr. Doubles 8000dr. Triples 12,000dr.) **Hotel Avra's** (tel. 22 780, -3; fax 23 320) similar rooms are immeasurably enhanced by ocean views. Visible from the port, this enormous brown concrete building can be reached by heading left at the top of the ramp leading away from the boats. (Singles 15,000dr. Doubles 17,000dr.) Those who wish to **camp** can head to the beach of **Kokkino Limanaki** (tel. 31 604 or 78 780; fax 31 603), 1½km from the port; there is a blue and white sign at the top of the ramp. (1250dr per person. 1100dr per small tent. 1250dr per large tent. Shower included with 24-hr. hot water.)

MARATHON

In 490 BCE, when the Athenians defeated the Persians at the bloody battle of Marathon, the messenger Pheidippides ran 42km to Athens to announce the victory and then collapsed dead from exhaustion. Today, international marathons (*sans* fatal collapse) commemorate this act. Runners trace Pheidippides' route twice annually.

Beautiful **Lake Marathon**, with its huge marble dam, rests 8km past the otherwise uninspiring town. Until WWII, the lake was Athens's sole source of water. At **Ramnous,** 15km to the northeast, lie the ruins of the Temples of Nemesis, goddess of retribution, and Themtis, goddess of custom, law, and justice.

On the coast near Marathon, **Schinias** to the north and **Timvos Marathonas** to the south are popular beaches. Many people camp at Schinias since the trees offer protection, but the mosquitoes are thirsty and mean, and freelance camping is illegal.

The **bus** for Marathon leaves from 29 Mavromateon St. by Areos Park in Athens (every hr., 5:30am-10:30pm, 1hr., 650dr). To get to the **Archaeological Museum of Marathonas** (tel. 55 155), ask the driver to let you off at the sign for the museum ("Mouseion and Marathonas"). Follow the signs and don't despair; the museum is 2km farther (roughly a 30-min. walk) at the end of the paved road (open Tues.-Sun. 8:30am-3pm; admission 500dr, students 300dr, seniors 400dr). To reach the Marathon Tomb or the nearby beach, walk 1½km back toward Athens. Lake Marathon, Amphiareion, and Ramnous are accessible by automobile only.

■ Delphi ΔΕΛΦΟΙ

Zeus sent forth two eagles from opposite ends of the earth in hopes of discovering the world's center. The birds impaled each other with their beaks above Delphi and fell to the ground where the *omphalos* (navel stone) still marks the spot of their ill-fated rendezvous. The birds' landing also marked the sight of the Oracle of Apollo, where troubled denizens of the ancient world flocked in the 2nd millennium BCE to seek *Pythia's* profound, if cryptic, advice.

Orientation and Practical Information   The municipality **tourist office** (tel. 82 900), housed in the town hall on with entrances on both Pavlou and Apollonos St., is run by friendly and tetra-lingual Mrs. Efi. Come here to get tips on just about anything under the Delphic sun, including bus schedules and hotel and camping rates (open Mon.-Fri. 7:30am-2:30pm). If the office is closed, check the front window for posted museum, site, and bus schedules. On the second floor of 40 Apollonos St. are the **tourist police** (tel. 82 220; open daily 9am-2pm, but someone's there 24hr.) and the **police station** (tel. 82 222). The **National Bank** (tel. 82 622; open Mon.-Thurs. 8am-2pm, Fri. 7:30am-3pm) is on Pavlou St. and has an **ATM** which accepts MasterCard. Farther down Pavlou St. is the **OTE** (open Mon.-Fri. 7:30am-3pm). The post office, banks, and OTE may be open longer hours in July and August depending on decisions made at headquarters in Athens. At the foot of Pavlou St. across from Hotel Pythia are free **public toilets** and the **taxi stand** (tel. 52 000). The **post office** (tel. 82 376; open Mon.-Fri. 7:30am-2pm, Sun. 9am-12:30pm) is on Pavlou St. **Postal Code:** 33054. **Telephone Code:** 0265.

   Buses leave Athens from the station at 260 Liossion St. for Delphi (tel. (01) 831 7096; 5 per day, 3½hr., 2600dr). Take blue bus #024 from Amalias Ave. at the entrance to the National Garden or El. Venizelou (Panepistimiou) by Syntagma Sq. to get to the station (30min., 75dr). Buy your ticket at the booth labeled ΔελΦοι (Delphi). Try to arrive early to avoid long lines. With a railpass, take a train to Levadia; from there, buses head to Delphi (700dr). From Delphi buses leave for Thessaloniki via Volos, Larissa, and Katerini (7 per week, 5½hr., 5500dr); Patras (1-2 per day, 3hr., 2150dr); Lamia (3 per day, 2hr., 1500dr); Nafpaktos (4 per day, 2½hr., 1900dr); Amphissa (7 per day, 30min., 340dr); Itea (7 per day, 30min., 320dr); and Galaxidi (4 per day with a switch in Itea, 50min., 600dr). At the bus station/café **Castri**, 14 Frangon St. (tel. 82 317), most of the staff speak English and will help decipher intricate bus schedules (open daily 8am-10pm).

Accommodations   There are more hotels in Delphi than you can shake a stick at. Closest to the bus station is the immaculate **Hotel Athina,** 55 Pavlou St. (tel. 82 239), with balconied rooms and marvelous views of the gulf of Corinth. Check-out is 11am. (Singles 5000dr. Doubles 6000dr, with bath 7000dr. Triples 8000dr, with bath 9000dr.) If you don't mind sharing a bathroom, head over to **Pension Odysseus** (tel. 82 235) on Filellinon, parallel to and below Pavlou, where Mrs. Toula will show you to one of her clean and breezy rooms. (Singles 4900dr. Doubles 6300dr.) **The Sun View Rooms,** at 84 Apollonos St. (tel. 82 815), are new and in pristine condition. Look for the last house on Apollonos before the European center and ring the bell at the brown door under a "Rooms to Let" sign. Mrs. Loula says there's room for bargaining. (Doubles 7500dr. Triples 9500dr) The nearest campsite is **Apollo Camping** (tel. 82 762, -50; fax 82 639), 1½km down from the bus station. (1100dr per person. 650dr per tent. 600dr per car.) **Delphi Camping** (tel. 82 363; 1200dr per person. 800dr per tent. 700dr per car) is 4km down the road and **Chrissa Camping** (tel. 82 050) is 10km out of town. (1300dr per person. 900dr per tent.) Ask the bus to drop you off at either of these campsites.

Food And Entertainment   Delphi's *tavernas* have terraces that overlook the mountains and the Gulf of Corinth. **Taverna Vakchos,** 29 Apollonos St. (tel. 82 448), is cheap and popular. The Greek salad (700dr) is reminiscent of just how good

DELPHI

olive oil can taste, while the speedy, polite service may make you forget that you're in Greece (fixed menu 1400-2200dr). If your stomach grumbles later in the evening, head over to **Thimios,** 51 Pavlou St. (tel. 83 130), for a deliciously cheap *souvlaki* (250dr; open daily 7:30pm-midnight). **Markets** can be found along Apollonos and Pavlou St. For great fresh breads and pastries, go uphill off Apollonos St. and follow signs to the **Artotechniki bakery** (tel. 82 045), on the right (open daily 5am-10pm).

The only places to shake a leg after dark are **Club No Name,** 31 Pavlou St., and **Katoi** (tel. 82 655), across the street from the bus station, where you can mingle with Delphi's youth for a 500dr cover, sipping 500dr beers or 1000dr cocktails. Better yet, if your timing is lucky, there is a **Festival of Ancient Greek Drama** put on by the **European Cultural Center of Delphi** (tel. 82 731, -92; fax 82 733). The Center, open daily 9am-2pm, also has temporary international art exhibitions. To find it, walk down the Amphissa/Itea road and follow the signs back uphill. Delphi is home to several other summer festivals, so ask around and keep a sharp eye out for posters when you arrive. Also, from April to October, you can get food, drink, and Greek folk dances at **Villa Symposio** every night. Call **Delphi Consultants** (tel. 82 086) for information on prices and transportation.

SIGHTS

The ancient Greek gods expressed their wishes to humans through oracles. Politically, **Delphi's oracle** was supreme—leaders throughout the Mediterranean sought its infallible advice. Whenever a Greek city won a battle, its leader would erect a dedicatory offering to the oracle. As a result, the entrance to the sanctuary was cluttered with tributes from all over Greece.

To the ancients, a temple was only complete with striking natural surroundings. Resting near the foot of Mt. Parnassos, the Oracle's site is flanked by a towering cliff on one side and the ominous 600m-deep Pleistos ravine on the other. Legend claims that Apollo slew the monster Python, which had presided over Delphi. But the snake, an earth-spirit, continued to speak to postulants through an intermediary, an elderly woman known as the *Pythia,* who could be seen only by specially elected priests. Sitting directly over the *omphalos,* the *Pythia* inhaled the vapors wafting up from the chasm below, got high, and then chanted deliriously. Her incoherent mutterings were "versified" by the priests, who would announce her prophecies to the waiting public. Often the *Pythia* would say things with double meanings: "You will win not lose" or "you will have a boy not girl." Depending on which side of the "not" you paused on, you got a different answer to your urgent inquiry. The Delphic Oracle remained important among Greeks from the 7th century BCE until after the Christianization of the Roman Empire.

The main body of structures, known as the **Sanctuary of Apollo,** lies 300m east of town on the road to Athens (follow the highway and take the paved path on your left to the ruins and museum, a 5-min. downhill walk out of town). **Maps** of a 1st-century BCE reconstruction of the site are available in the shops in town or at the kiosk across from the bus station for 300dr. The *Delphi* brochure, free at the tourist information office, has a smaller map. The **guidebooks** available at the museum (1500-2500dr) are far from indispensable for the ruins, where most signs are in English, but they're useful in the museum, where Greek and French are *de rigeur*.

Now as then, the **Temple of Apollo** is the prime attraction. The building burned in 548 BCE and the 373 BCE reconstruction was shattered by an earthquake. What stands today are the remains of a second united effort at reconstruction. This is where oracular priests would announce the *Pythia's* verdicts. The huge walls were once inscribed with famous maxims of Greek philosophers. The theater and the stadium are also worth a look. Scamper up the hills past tour groups to the stadium, sit and relax, then meander down the mountain at your leisure, pitying the tour groups huffing and puffing their way up (site open in summer Mon.-Fri. 7:30am-7:15pm, Sat.-Sun. 8:30am-2:45pm; in off season Mon.-Fri. 7:30am-5:15pm, Sat.-Sun. 8:30am-2:45pm; admission 1200dr, students and seniors 600dr, European students free). Be sure to visit Delphi's **Archaeological Museum** (tel. 82 312), located just before the

Pythian Sanctuary along the path from town contains the frieze of the Siphnian Treasury and the Charioteer of Delphi (open Mon. noon-6:30pm, Tues.-Fri. 7:30am-7:30pm, Sat.-Sun. 8:30am-3pm; admission 1200dr, students 600dr).

The unfenced ruins of the **Temple of Pronaia Athena** are roughly 200m past the main set of ruins heading away from town (the entrance is just past the "exit" sign). On your way, you'll pass the **Castelian Spring,** where pilgrims cleansed themselves both physically and spiritually before calling upon the oracle. Drinking from the spring is said to give you the gift of eloquence. To your right is the millennia-old **Gymnasium.** The three remaining Doric columns of the circular 4th-century **Tholos** at Athena's sanctuary are the most photographed of Delphi's ruins. Although scholars have inferred from ancient texts that the *Tholos* was an important part of the Delphic complex, no one now knows exactly what function it served. Next to the *Tholos* lies the **Treasury of Marseilles;** this gift from the citizens of ancient France attests to the extent of the oracle's prestige (ruins open 24hr.; free).

■ Near Delphi

LEVADIA

For die-hard oracle fans who want a second opinion, the **Oracle of Trophonios** is on a cliff which overlooks Levadia (ancient Lebadea). The site once attracted pilgrims on their way to Delphi. In the 14th century, Frankish Crusaders built a castle over the site of the oracle, now a 15-minute walk from town. It is the best preserved castle in the area. From the bus station, turn right, walk uphill to the square, and go right again onto Venizelou St. At the end of the street take a right, then a left at the church. The oracle once stood at the stream; the castle ruins are 200m farther.

Buses to Athens (2hr.) via Thebes (45min.) leave every hour from 6am to 8pm (2050dr). Levadia is also accessible by train from Athens, but the station is 5km from town. Buses in town tend to wait for more than one train and then drop travelers off 10 minutes away from the bus stop to Delphi and Osios Loukas (with no directions in sight, of course). If the scarcity of bus connections compels you to spend the night in Levadia, the **Hotel Levadia** (tel. (0201) 23 611; fax 28 266) is at the top of the town square. All rooms have bathrooms. (Singles 10,000dr. Doubles 14,000dr.) High season here is in winter since the slopes of Mt. Parnassos lie only 65km away.

OSIOS LOUKAS

Although it is toilsome to reach, **Osios Loukas** is worth the trouble. This pastoral and inspiring spot may instill in you pangs of longing for the monkhood. More than 1700m above sea-level, the stone monastery complex contains magnificent mosaics and affords tremendous views. Dress modestly (no shorts or bare shoulders, no pants for women); makeshift coverings are available at the gate.

To allow for transportation difficulties, give Osios Loukas a full day. There's one daily **bus** which climbs up the mountain to Osios Loukas and it leaves Levadia at 1:40pm (45min., 480dr); make sure you tell the driver you are headed for the monastery or he might just skip the mountain route altogether and go directly to Distomo. From Athens, take blue bus #024 from Amalias St. or El. Venizelou to the Liossion St. bus station (every 20min., 30min., 75dr) and buy a ticket to Levadia (every hr., 5:50am-8:30pm, 2hr., 2050dr). Six buses per day leave from Delphi (700dr). In the unfortunate event that you miss the sole bus directly to Osios Loukas, head over to Distomo. Take the Distomo bus from Levadia (30min., 190dr) or, if you get one of the Delphi-Athens buses, get off at the cross road for Distomo (tell the driver well in advance so that he doesn't miss the turn-off; 400dr) and walk 3km to Distomo. From there, take a taxi up to the monastery (9km, 1000-2000dr).

Getting out of Osios Loukas may also be problematic. Travelers used to mooch lifts from commercial tour **buses,** but they're increasingly wary of police and thus reluctant to let people bum rides. The bus station in Distomo is a joke—buses, when they come, only go to Levadia. The best bet to anywhere else is to share yet another **taxi** (4000dr). All this means that your afternoon of birds, breezes, and mosaics may wind up being rather pricey, but a taxi can save you grief. The **post office,** where you can change money, is down the hill near the bus stop (open Mon.-Fri. 7:30am-2pm). The **OTE** is a few buildings down the road (open Mon.-Fri. 7:30am-3pm). For **medical emergency** dial (0267) 22 791.

If you're stranded in Distomo, there are two hotels up the hill to the right of the main intersection. The first you'll come to is **Hotel America** (tel. (0267) 22 079, -82). (Singles 4000dr. Doubles 7000dr.) **Koutiaris Hotel** (tel. (0267) 22 268), near Hotel America, offers slightly larger rooms. (Singles 4750dr. Doubles 6000dr.) Eating options are sparse; a *souvlaki* joint, **Corner,** is up the main road on the left. **Odysseus** (tel. 22 616) is on 10th Iouniou 1944 St., 400m past the bus stop (open daily 8:30am-midnight). There are several **supermarkets** and **pharmacies** in town.

Kill some time (you'll need to) at the **archaeological museum,** up the road to Osios Loukas (open Mon.-Fri. 8am-6pm, Sat.-Sun. 9:30am-3pm). Ask to be let into the locked half in order to see a few cool mosaics. The main building in the Osios Loukas complex, the arresting **Church of St. Luke** is dedicated to a local hermit, known for his powers of healing and prophecy. According to locals, when Luke died in his cell in 953 CE, a myrrh tree sprouted from the cold floor. The entrance to the 10th-century church is adorned with Byzantine **mosaics,** most notably a faceless Doubting Thomas inserting his finger in Christ's wound. The more beautiful mosaics, the Nativity, Presentation at the Temple, and Baptism, are tucked into the squinches that support the dome. Although not as famous as the ones in the upper church, the 11th-century **frescoes** that cover most of the **crypt's** interior are every bit as gorgeous; a flashlight is needed for best viewing. Don't miss the saintly frescoes removed from their original homes and now displayed in a building at the very back of the complex, off the courtyard behind the churches. The oldest part of the monastery is the 10th-century **Church of St. Mary** adjoining the larger church. Despite Osios Loukas' indoor attractions, the flowers, birds, and encompassing mountains outside the monastery (tel. (0267) 22 797) are most enthralling (open daily 7:30am-2pm and 4:30-7pm; admission 800dr, students 400dr, seniors 600dr).

ARACHOVA

Stacked onto the slopes below Mt. Parnassos, the village of Arachova, 10km east of Delphi, revels in its own relaxed atmosphere in summer and caters to skiers in winter. This is a perfect place to collapse after you've spent the day fighting the crowds at Delphi. It's a charming mountain town with narrow streets and little shops. Even though it is in the winter that Arachova lives the intensity of a bustling ski resort, a breezy summer afternoon amid the town's trendy youth can be a delight. The area's culinary distinctions are its amber honey and tasty *saganaki* (fried cheese). The main street oozes with *souvlaki* and souvenirs. The sweaters, woven rugs, and coonskin-type hats that you'll find here befit the town's popularity in winter.

The **Cooperative Office Kiparissos** (tel. 31 519) serves as a **tourist office** with information on the town and accommodations. To find it, continue on the main road in the direction of Athens. You'll soon see a stone building with a red painted entrance; this is the school. The cooperative office is right next door (look for the red and yellow sign). In the first of the town's three squares you'll find the **post office** (open Mon.-Fri. 7:30am-2pm), which exchanges money. Across from the post office is the **OTE** (open Mon.-Fri. 7:30am-3:10pm). Stay on the main road and head further into town to find the **National Bank** on your left (open Mon.-Thurs. 8:30am-2pm, Fri. 8:30am-1pm). If it's closed, don't pout—it has an **ATM.** The **police** are across from the bus station, on the second floor (tel. (0267) 31 133). Farther east, past the third square, is a **pharmacy** (tel. (0267) 31 186). **Postal Code:** 32004.

Roughly five **buses** per day run between Athens and Delphi, stopping in Arachova, while an additional 8 make the run from Arachova to Delphi (20min., 160dr). All buses to Delphi go to Itea (1hr., 500dr) and two make connections from Itea to Galaxidi (15min., 150dr). A brown and yellow "Celena" sign identifies the bus station (tel. (0267) 31 790), which doubles as a café and winter restaurant.

Near the first square (coming from Delphi) are several hotels, pensions, and "Rooms to Let," including **The Apollon** (tel. 31 540) and **Pension Nostas** (tel. 31 385), with a cozy mountain lodge feel to it. Each offers doubles for 10,000-15,000dr (off season 5000-8000dr). Ask at the "Celena" bus station café for rooms around town. The closest **campground** is west of Delphi (see p. 99). Moderately priced *tavernas* include **Liakoura** (tel. 31 783), next to the OTE (*saganaki* 800dr, *souvlaki* 1250dr), and **Lakka** below the police station (salad 700-1000dr, *saganaki* 500dr). The more daring, non-vegetarians can head over to **Dasargiri** (tel. 31 291) for *kokoretsi* (1500dr) and *kontosouvli* (1800dr)—animal viscera cooked delightfully.

Apollo and the Muses now share their abode with ski buffs on **Mt. Parnassos.** The mountain (2700m) is one of the most accessible. If you're interested in hiking up in summer, take a taxi to the **Mt. Parnassos Ski Center,** 27km northwest of Arachova. From the ski center, it's a steep 2km climb up to the summit, where vultures glower overhead. The ski season on Mt. Parnassos runs roughly from November-May. There are 14 lifts and tickets average 5000dr per day; rentals are 1500-3500dr per day. To stay in the area, try Delphi or Arachova, but you'll have to pay 7000-8000dr for the roundtrip cab, since the taxi lobby won't allow public buses to run to the ski center (**taxi** tel. (0267) 31 566). Alternately, make a daytrip from Athens (**bus** leaves 6am, 3hr., 2500dr roundtrip). For information on skiing, find Mr. Kostas Koutras at his **ski shop** (tel. 31 841, -767) on the first left coming from Delphi.

ITEA

A quiet escape from Delphi, this semi-industrial town offers only a rocky beach and the long waterfront boardwalk lined with cafés and *tavernas.* Enjoy the view in the afternoon when the construction has silenced and the sun glints on the water. The beach east of town is equipped with outdoor showers. A cleaner and more solitary beach is **Kira Beach,** 2km from town. The **post office** is along the beach near the bus stop (open Mon.-Fri. 7:30am-8pm, Sat. 7:30am-2pm). A **bank** is across the street (open Mon.-Thurs. 8am-2pm, Fri. 8am-1:30pm). Itea has the only **motorbike rental** shop in the Delphi area; inquire at the **tourist shop** Tsonos (tel. (0267) 33 317), past the post office 100m to the left of the bus station (small motorbikes 2500-4000dr per day). Frequent **buses** run from Delphi to Itea (11 per day, 6:30am-8:20pm, 1hr., 300dr). The last bus back to Delphi from Itea is at 5:45pm; a **taxi** (tel. (0267) 32 200) is a good option for late returns (1200-2500dr according to the number of passengers). It's a five- to six-hour walk uphill to Delphi. If you want to stay here, try the **Hotel Galini** (tel. (0267) 32 278; fax 32 323) on the waterfront street Akti Poseidonos. (Singles 6500dr. Doubles 9000dr. All rooms have bath.) Or continue to walk, with the water on your right, down the street to **Hotel Akti** (tel. 32 015, -257), which is cheaper but not quite as clean. (Singles 4000dr. Doubles 6000dr, with bath 7500. Triples 7000dr.) Moderate cuisine for moderate prices can be found along the waterfront. The **Dolphin II Restaurant,** on the water as you walk away from town, has superb seafood, as do most of the *tavernas* on Akti Poseidonos and the beach.

GALAXIDI

Seventeen kilometers from Itea, Galaxidi, across the harbor, is home to better beaches. Local legend has it that the mermaid Galaxa rose from the sea and set the boundaries of the town. Some say that the name of this seafaring town is a coagulation of *gala* (milk) and *xidhi* (vinegar) and reflects the bittersweet experiences of a seaman's wife. These days in Galaxidi, there's no need for wives to wring their hands—they can find their husbands floating their boats at one of the town's cafés.

The bus drops off at one end of **Nik. Mama,** the main street in the town center that leads down to the waterfront and harbor. Though Galaxidi is pretty sleepy most of the year, things get hectic here just before Easter. If you happen to be here on Mardi Gras, be sure that you're not wearing your Sunday best—food fights break out, with pies being the weapon of choice. There are also more sedate pleasures, such as watching the town's children dance in traditional garb. The **OTE** is down

THEBES (THIVA)

the first right from the bus stop off Nik. Mama (open Mon.-Fri. 7:30am-3:10pm). For indigestion and other mild post-party traumas, head to the **pharmacy** (tel. (0265) 41 122), one block to the right of the bus station on Nik. Mama. Galaxidi's **post office** is at the end of Nik. Mama (open Mon.-Fri. 7:30am-2pm). **Postal Code:** 33052.

From the bus stop, turn right and head down Nik. Mama St. to find **Hotel Poseidon** (tel. 41 246), a breezy old home turned hotel blessed with a friendly manager. (Singles 4000dr. Doubles 8000dr.) **Pension Votsalo** (tel. (0265) 41 788, -542) is pricier but near the waterfront. Cross the square from the bus stop and go down Novorhou Ageli St. at the right side of the square until you see the pension on your left. Don't be put off by the twists and turns of the street; you'll see the place soon enough. (Doubles 10,000dr. Longer stays get better deals.) At the other end of town, several blocks down the last right off Nik. Mama before the water, **Hotel Galaxidi** (tel. 41 850; fax 41 026) has nice rooms with A/C. (Singles 6000dr. Doubles 10,000dr. Triples 12,000dr.) In August or any summer weekend, expect the prices to be roughly 20% higher than listed. There are also a few "Rooms to Let"; ask at the bus station/*taverna* or other restaurants, or keep your eyes peeled for signs.

It doesn't take much to figure out that fish is the local specialty. The main waterfront (turn left at the end of Nik. Mama) is lined with *tavernas*, most of which serve a variety of fish for 3000-10,000dr per kg. If fish isn't your cup of tea, try the flowery patio of **Restaurant Dervenis** (tel. 41 177), a block down the first right off Nik. Mama from the bus stop (*moussaka* 1200dr). But perhaps the best deal is a trip to either of the supermarkets on Nik. Mama, followed by a swing through **To Konaki** (tel. 42 258), an excellent **sweet shop** next to the supermarket closest to the bus stop (scoop of ice cream 150dr, special soupy almond concoction 1800dr per kg).

For wonderful swimming, head to the forest side of the harbor (over the "bridge" as you walk down Nik. Mama past Restaurant Steki and walk all the way around). Small islands float offshore and flooded caves overhang scant beaches. Rouse yourself from the beach to visit the nautical **Museum of Galaxidi** (tel. 41 558). Make a left off Nik. Mama opposite the Galaxidi Supermarket, walk a few blocks, and then turn right as you see the small church on your left (open daily 8:30am-1:30pm; admission 300dr). The **Church of St. Nicholas,** near the museum, houses many fine mosaics. The 13th-century **Monastery of Transfiguration,** with sublime 1000-year-old wood carvings and a great view of town, is 500m from Galaxidi on the uphill road outside of town. Coming from Itea, make a right before the gas station.

Many travelers continue from Galaxidi to **Nafpaktos,** close to the mouth of the Gulf and to the ferry crossing for the Peloponnese at **Antirion.** The **bus** to Nafpaktos runs out of Delphi and stops in Galaxidi (2½hr. from Delphi, 2hr. from Galaxidi). If you stay, try the **Aegli** (tel. (0634) 27 271; singles 4000dr, doubles 7000dr).

■ Thebes (Thiva) ΘHBA

Thebes once ranked among the most powerful cities of ancient Greece. Its location gave it control over the strategic routes connecting the Peloponnese and Attica with northern Greece, and its fertile soil cinched the town's prosperity. But the town is most famous as the setting for the story of Oedipus. The sphinx that guarded the gates of Thebes was a plight to the town's trade and prosperity until Oedipus came along and did away with the dreadful monster by solving its reputed riddle: "What animal walks on four legs in the morning, two in the afternoon, and three in the evening?" (Answer: Man). Modern Thebes can't compete with its racy past. Razed by Alexander the Great in the 4th century BCE, it has never recovered.

The **National Bank of Greece,** 94 Pindarou (tel. (0262) 27 782), one street over from Eparminon also has an **ATM** (open Mon.-Thurs. 8am-2pm, Fri. 8am-1:30pm). The **OTE** at 2 Vousouba (tel. (0262) 27 799) is in the center of town (open Mon.-Fri. 7:30am-3pm). Thebes' new **bus station** is on Kiprou St., which meets Epaminon near the top of the hill. Street signs are rare but people are more than willing to give directions. Bus service is frequent to the Liossion St. terminal in Athens (every hr., 1½hr., 1400dr). To travel to Chalkis, take the frequent Athens bus to the Skimatari stop (30min., 400dr). Across the street, the Athens-Chalkis bus runs every 30 minutes (10min., 300dr). For a **taxi,** call 27 077. The town's **hospital,** 2 Tseva (tel. (0262) 28 101), is located directly across the street from the museum and the **post office,** 17 Drakou St. (tel. (0262) 27 810) is near the top of Epaminon St. (open Mon.-Fri. 7:30am-2pm). **Postal Code:** 32200.

If you are obliged to spend the night here, the **Hotel Niovi,** 63 Epaminon St. (tel. (0262) 29 888), may be your best bet. (Doubles 7560dr, with bath 9180dr.) In the evening, the many *tavernas* that line Epaminon and Pindari streets provide lively R&R for the neighboring military base.

Follow Epaminon St. downhill, take a right past the ruins, and on your left will be the **Archaeological Museum** (tel. 27 913). Be sure to see the **Mycenaean larnakes,** clay coffins adorned with paintings of funerary rites, mosaics, and reliefs. The guidebook is particularly informative (open Tues.-Sun. 8:30am-3pm; admission 500dr, students 300dr, senior citizens 400dr). The scanty remains of the **House of Kadmos,** a Mycenaean palace dating from the 14th century BCE, are visible from Pindarou St. Underneath the modern town of Thebes are an extensive **Mycenaean palace and acropolis.** Historians and archaeologists begrudge Thebes' every new building, fearing construction may endanger what little remains of the Mycenaean civilization.

■ Evia (Euboea) EYβOIA

Wrenched from the mainland by an ancient earthquake (or perhaps by Poseidon's trident), Evia grazes the coastline north of Athens. The second largest island in Greece (after Crete), Evia was, in ancient times, a major trading center and maritime power. Although nowadays the local tourist committee likes to highlight Evia as a Greek island with frequent bus service from the mainland, it seems more like a part of Central Greece. Travelers may pass over the short wooden swingbridge at Chalkis and barely notice it. What *is* noticeable about Evia is its central mountain range choked with chestnuts and pines—paradise for hikers. Though several beaches are sprinkled around the coast of Evia, it has yet to be infested with too many resorts.

CHALKIDA (CHALKIS)

Bus travelers through Evia will almost inevitably encounter the suffocating port town of Chalkida. But spending time here may be not be as uneventful as you think. Aristotle was desperate because of his inability to comprehend what still may be the most interesting thing about Chalkida—the bizarre tidal flow through the straits between Evia and the mainland. Aristotle threw himself in the nearby Evia strait in a fit of anguish; please refrain from following in his footsplashes. Contemporary scientists can't fully explain why the water changes direction at the narrowest point between the land masses—up to six times daily during full and near moons (1-4 times per day for the rest of the month).

The English-speaking **tourist police,** 32 El. Venizelou (tel. 22 100), are located two flights above the police station and can help with bus schedules (open Mon.-Fri. 7am-2:30pm; someone's there 24hr). You can **change money** closer to the water at the **National Bank** (open Mon.-Thurs. 8am-2pm, Fri. 8am-1:30pm). The **OTE** is located on Papiadaiou St.; walk up El. Venizelou four full blocks from the water (2 blocks after the park with the fountain), then make a left on Papiadaiou, continuing for one block (open Mon.-Fri. 7am-10pm) and the **bus station** is in the center of town. A **bus** from Liossion Station in Athens goes to Chalkida (every 30min., on Sun. every 45min., 1½hr., 1200dr); the **train** runs nearly as frequently from the Larissa station (18 per day, 2hr., 880dr). Arrival by train leaves you on the mainland; just cross the bridge to the island and the busier section of Chalkida. Roughly five blocks to the left of the bridge is El. Venizelou St., running uphill. If you get off at the bus depot, look for Papanastasiou, and turn right; walk down one block to El. Venizelou St. **Flying dolphins** now leave from the dock to the right of the bridge as you face the mainland. Purchase tickets to Limni, Aedipsos, and the Sporades at the shack on the waterfront just in line with the dock (tel. 21 521, -621). For **taxis,** dial 24 411. To get to a **pharmacy** (tel. 24 646), head down El. Venizelou and make a left on A. Gobiou St. just before the waterfront. The **post office** is on Karamourzouni St., the second left off El. Venizelou as you walk uphill from the water (open Mon.-Fri. 7:30am-8pm). **Postal Code:** 34100. **Telephone Code:** 0221.

If you must spend the night, try **Hotel Kentrikon** (tel. 22 375), the pink building on Ageli Gobiou St., the last left off El. Venizelou just before the waterfront. (Singles 7230dr. Doubles 8000dr, with bath 10,000-12,000dr.) The rooms at **Hotel Kymata** (tel. 21 317) on the waterfront street on the left side of the square (facing the water) have high ceilings. (Singles 3135dr. Doubles 4180dr.) The **Archaeological Museum** (tel. 76 131), on El. Venizelou across from the police station, is a roomful of findings from the Classical and Roman eras (open Tues.-Sun. 8:30am-3pm; admission 500dr, students 300dr, senior citizens 400dr). Facing the big pink building, and heading down that street, turn right on the little downhill road and look for the **Folklore Museum** on your left at 4 Skalkola St. (tel. 21 817; open Wed. 10am-1pm and 6-8pm, Thurs.-Sun. 10am-1pm; free).

ERETRIA

Modern-day Eretria rests languidly on the coast, still free from an overabundance of tourists. First inhabited between the 15th and 17th centuries BCE, permanent occupation began in the 8th or 9th century BCE. The town rivalled ancient Chalkis as the most important city on the island, its importance stemming from its convenient location for trade between Greece (and later Italy) and the Near East. In the 3rd century BCE, Menedimos, the town's most famous son and a disciple of Plato's, founded a school of philosophy here. The Roman era saw a decline in Eretria's fortunes and the town was only sporadically occupied from the 1st century CE onwards. More recently, the town's easy access from Chalkida (30min. by bus) and from Oropos on the mainland (30min. by ferry) has led to a moderate resurgence.

Orientation and Practical Information The first, and more convenient, of the two bus stops, is at the lower end of the main commercial street, Menedimos. A little farther along, the same road leads to the **National Bank,** which **changes money** and has an **ATM** (open Mon.-Thurs. 9:15am-1:30pm, Fri. 9:15am-1pm). A right at the main intersection leads to the **OTE** (open Mon.-Fri. 7:30am-3:10pm), a few blocks down on the right, and then to a small square where the town's past and future meet—fenced ruins are overlooked by the bright lights and whizzing bumper cars of an amusement park. Continuing straight ahead, you'll find one wing of the town's waterfront, lined with *tavernas* and, eventually, the town's few hotels. A right down the other waterfront road yields more *tavernas* and the ferry dock for boats to Oropos. Eretria is accessible by **bus** from Chalkida because everything heading south to Karystos, Kimi, or Amarinthos swings through here (roughly every 30min., 30min., 340dr). There is also a **ferry** from Oropos on the mainland (every 30min. 5am-9pm and every hr. until 11:45pm, 30min., 280dr). **Taxis** can be found by the water or by calling 62 500. Two blocks up from the bank is the intersection with the town's other main road, Archaiou Theatrou. There is a map of town here, helpfully labeled in English and Greek. A left turn here brings you to the **post office** (open Mon.-Fri. 7:30am-8pm, Sat. 8:30am-2pm), which also changes money. At the end of the street are the Archaeological Museum, an extensive area of low-lying ruins, and the scant remains of the ancient theater. **Postal Code:** 34008. **Telephone Code:** 0229.

Accommodations **Pension Diamanto** (tel. 62 214), along the waterfront stretch of Archaiou Theatrou St., has rooms with bath, fridge, and A/C above the Babylon Café. (Doubles 9000dr. Triples 11,000dr.) Farther down the street, turn left at the sign and walk 200m inland for the modern apartments (all with kitchen, fridge, A/C, and bath) of the **Eretria Sun Rise Hotel** (tel. 60 004; fax 60 648). Sadly enough for the budget traveler, this hotel is one of the better deals in town. (Doubles 12,000dr. Triples 14,000dr. Quads 16,000dr.) Ask at *tavernas* for rooms.

Food, Entertainment, and Sights If all the fresh air whets your appetite, look for **La Cubana** (tel. 61 665), on Archaiou Theatrou near the waterfront and try the *dolmadakia* (900dr) or a plate of *moussaka* (1100dr). On the other waterfront stretch across the dock is **Dionisos** (tel. 61 728), which prides in its *kolokythakia* (fried zucchini 600dr) and fresh fried squid (1200dr). For dessert, **Stamatoukos** (tel. 60 909), the large sweet shop on Archaiou Theatrou, serves fresh homemade ice cream in delicious flavors (200-250dr per scoop). For some nightlife, pick the crowd and ambience you like best; most places serve beer for 500dr, cocktails for 1000dr.

The **Archaeological Museum** (tel. 62 206) is at the inland end of Archaiou Theatrou St. It's not the biggest collection around, but there are some quality pieces, such as a gorgeous terra cotta Gorgon's head from the 4th century BCE, and the mysteriously six-fingered Centaur of Lefkandi, which dates from 750-900 BCE (open Tues.-Sun. 8:30am-3pm; admission 500dr, students and senior citizens 300dr, EU students free). Exhibits are in Greek and French, but you can get the red guidebook in English (2000dr). Beyond the museum is a large excavated area of the old city. Although there is nothing particularly spectacular here, simply wander in (there is no gate to the fence which surrounds the site) and let your imagination roam. The ancient theater is behind the excavations, but it is less well preserved and the entrance is barred by a fence. Far more amazing than either of these is the creatively named **House with the Mosaics.** You must find someone at the museum to bring you to the site (300m away) and unlock it, but it's definitely worth it. The four mosaics in two separate rooms are among the best preserved and most ancient (4th century BCE) of all Greek mosaics. Because of their age and importance, they are enclosed in a room which visitors can't enter without special permission, but the glass walls afford a good view. The Swiss School of Archaeology in Greece has put out a brochure (in Greek, English, French, and German), which explains the history of the house (available from the museum for 1000dr). There are no set hours when the House is open or closed, but since the key must be obtained from the Archaeological Museum, it is *de facto* open Tuesday-Sunday 8:30am-3pm (free).

KARYSTOS

Surrounded by mountains and flanked by two long sandy beaches, Karystos, which takes its name from the son of the centaur Chiron, is easygoing despite being the largest town in South Evia. Pointed round straw umbrellas, like the mushrooms in *Fantasia,* dot the sands that extend in either direction from the port.

Orientation and Practical Information The bus stops one block above the main square, next to the **National Bank** (open Mon.-Thurs. 8am-2pm, Fri. 8am-1:30pm); look for the KTEL sign above a restaurant roasting chickens in the window. The **OTE** is on Amerikis, the next cross-street beyond the square, across from the Church of St. Nicholas (open daily 7:30am-3pm). **Buses** from Karystos travel twice daily to Chalkis (4hr,, 1700dr) and Stira (1¼hr., 500dr) and thrice daily to the slightly crowded resort town of Marmari (30min., 250dr). Three to four **ferries** per day head to Rafina (2hr., 1550dr) and Marmari (1½hr., 800dr). In Karystos, ferry tickets are sold across from where the boat docks. **South Evia Tours** (tel. (0224) 25 700; fax 22 461; open 8am-10pm), on the left of the square as you face the water, sells tickets for **flying dolphins** which go thrice weekly to the Cycladic islands of Andros (2256dr), Tinos (4436dr), and Mykonos (6019dr). **Taxis** (tel. 22 200) queue in the square. To find the **police station** (tel. (0224) 22 252), turn in to the small alley past the bank and climb the stairs. To reach the **post office** from the OTE, turn left on Amerikis and then take the first right past the playgrounds; you'll see the round yellow sign (open Mon.-Fri. 7:30am-2pm). **Postal Code:** 34001.

Accommodations The **tourist office,** on the left-hand side of the square (facing the waterfront), helps find rooms and decipher ferry schedules. Look for "Rooms to Let" signs at restaurants on the dock. **George and Bill Kolobaris,** 42 Sachtouri St. (tel. (0224) 22 071), offer cozy rooms and boundless hospitality. George may pick you up on his motorbike and sing to you on the way to his pension. (Doubles 8000dr. Triples 8000dr. Includes hot water and use of kitchen.) Carry on along the waterfront (200m) to the more luxurious rooms of **Hotel Karystion** (tel. (0224) 22 391; fax 22 727). The proprietor, the amiable Charis Mitros, is the president of the local Tourist Association and a good source of information about the area; he also speaks fluent English. (Singles 6500-7600dr. Doubles 9150-10,950dr. Triples 12,680-13,880dr. All with bath, TV, A/C, and breakfast.)

Food, Entertainment, and Sights The octopi (*oktopodia*) lined up and drying in the sun give fair warning of the town's favorite food. Find incomparable food and prices at **Kabontoros,** one block inland on Parodos Sachtouri St., in the alleyway a half block right of the main square (sautéed green beans in olive oil with a puréed garlic sauce, 800dr), or walk past the touristy crowds in the *tavernas* and pizzerias lining the waterfront to the very end of the strip (on the far right facing the water) until you come to the all-Greek crowd at **Kalamia** (tel. 22 223; stuffed tomatoes 650dr). If you're not stuffed after your meal, skip down the alleyway off Parodos Sachtouri St. to the water and find **Tsimis' sweet shop.**

Various seaside pubs and cafés are popular day and night. **Archipelagos,** on the beach at the right edge of town, offers beer for 500dr. The view and heady sea air here may tempt you to linger. For serious dancing, head to the **Barbados Disco** (tel. 24 119), 3km from town towards the mountains. The 1300dr cover includes your first drink. A cab will run 500dr, probably more after midnight.

To inspect the interior of the coastal **Fort of Bourtzi,** which dates from the Crusades, ask at the tourist office (fort open July-Aug. Mon., Wed.-Fri. for 2hr. in the morning). Otherwise, peek into one of the holes at the back of the fort (from which boiling oil was poured on attackers) to imagine life in the 1100s. If you're lucky, you may catch a summer student theatrical production inside. There is a **Folklore Museum** on Sachtouri St., the first street parallel to the waterfront, several blocks to the right of the main square, opposite the ruins of a **Temple of Apollo.** At the other end of town, past the fort, an **Archaeological Museum** (tel. 22 472) should be open by 1997, in the waterfront building which houses the library.

If you have a free morning, explore the villages north of Karystos. Follow Aiolou St., one block east of the square, out of town; continue straight at the crossroads toward **Palio Chora,** a village nestled among lemon and olive groves. For a more strenuous walk, turn right at the crossroads outside Karystos and go towards the village of **Mili.** The road ascends sharply and follows a clear stream to the village, where water flows from the mouths of three lions in a small roadside fountain. From Mili, a 20-minute hike up the hill on the left and across the stone bridge leads to **Kokkino Kastro** (the Red Castle), a 13th-century Venetian castle named for the blood that was spilled there during the war between the Greeks and the Turks. The village of **Agia Triada** is also worth a trek; take a left at the crossroads and walk to this shady valley that features two small, rustic churches under gnarled trees.

For more extensive hiking, climb Evia's second highest mountain, **Mt. Ochi** (1398m), where Zeus and Hera supposedly fell in love. It's located in the heart of the placid south area. The stone refuge hut on the mountain is a three- to four-hour hike from Karystos. Some claim that the refuge, made of unmortared stone blocks during the Pelasgian Period, was a temple to Hera; others believe it was a signal tower. The ruin is known as the "dragon's house" and is allegedly haunted.

KIMI

With an abundance of foliage and cool, tangy sea breezes, Kimi offers a refreshing respite from the parched Greek summer. Dubbed "the balcony of the Aegean" because of its perch 250m over the water, Kimi was once a major harbor renowned for its fishing, figs, and wine. Legend has it that, when cholera struck the town, the Virgin Mary opened her hands and pushed the disease away. But 30 years ago, a locust plague destroyed the vineyards and the population dropped from 30,000 to 10,000. Kimi has two main parts—Kimi Town, built atop a hill, overlooks its port Paralia Kimi, on the waterfront. Locals say that the contractor who designed the road between the two was an obsessed gambler. He twisted the road into 54 turns, 52 playing cards plus two jokers, thus paying tribute to his favorite pastime.

Orientation and Practical Information   To reach the main square of Kimi Town from the bus station, make a right as you exit the station and turn left up the steep hill. At the crest of the hill is the main drag; a right from here leads to a plaza around the town church. Across from the church is the **National Bank** with its **ATM** (open Mon.-Thurs. 8am-2pm, Fri. 8am-1:30pm). The **OTE** is one block below the church on the right (open Mon.-Fri. 7:30am-3:10pm). There is a bus to and from Paralia Kimi to three times daily (180dr). The 5km downhill walk affords glorious views, but keep an eye out for traffic. **Buses** run to Kimi directly from Chalkis (8 per day, 2¼hr., 1450dr) and from 260 Liossion St. in Athens (7 per day, 3½hr., 2600dr), some with a transfer in Chalkis. From Karystos, take the bus to Lepoura for a tour of the mountainside (2 per day, 2½hr., 1150dr) and transfer from Lepoura to Kimi (10 per day, 1hr., 600dr). Call Kimi's bus station at 22 257.

Two agents in Paralia Kimi sell **ferry** tickets. To the left of the road descending from Kimi Town, next to the Sosco gas station, is the agent for ferries (tel. 22 601), which run to Skopelos (4hr., 4102dr) and Alonissos (3hr., 3780dr). In July and August, the ferry runs twice a week. To the right of the road descending from Kimi Town, in the blue and white striped building 75m down, is the agent for **Likomedes** (tel. 22 020, -522; open daily 9am-1pm and 3-7pm). This vessel serves Skyros exclusively (2-3 per day, 2hr., 1875dr). For information on **flying dolphins** (tel. 23 722), go to the agent 20m up the road to Kimi. There is one weekly run to Skiathos (9330dr), Skopelos (8391dr), Alonissos (7797dr), Skyros (4002dr), and Ag. Ioannis on the mainland (9955dr). To get to the beach/port from town, you're best off getting a **taxi** (tel. 23 666 in Kimi Town, tel. 23 255 in Paralia Kimi) for 900-1100dr. The Georgios Papanicolaou **hospital/clinic** (tel. 22 332), which houses Kimi's **health center** (tel. 23 252, -3), is located 3km from the station. To get there, head north from the station, make a right on the first main road, and follow it uphill until you reach the hospital. The road leading down to Paralia Kimi begins at the corner, just before the post office, also where the bus stops. To find the **police** (tel. 22 555), go left down the road from the bus station, following it as it bends downhill and to the right. Entrance to the yellow building is on the downhill side (open 24hr.). One block above the town church is the **post office** (open Mon.-Fri. 7:30am-2pm). **Postal Code: 34003. Telephone Code: 0222.**

Accommodations, Food, and Sights   Because there is no public transportation to the north coast's beaches (and because the *meltems* wind batters it in July and Aug.), Kimi is more popular as a jumping off point to the Sporadic Islands than as a place to spend time. Hotel proprietors are aware of this, so prices are high. In Paralia Kimi, the hydrofoil agent (tel. 23 722), 20m up the road to Kimi Town, offers rooms. (Doubles with bath 6000dr.) **Hotel Beis** (tel. 22 604; fax 22 870), at the left of the waterfront facing the water, has doubles with bath for 8500dr.

Restaurants and cafés line the harbor at Paralia Kimi. On the south side of the waterfront, you'll find decent meals at **To Aigaio** (spaghetti with meat sauce 850dr). For a quick and inexpensive meal in Kimi Town, go past the post office to **Pikantiki Restaurant** (spaghetti 600dr). Otherwise, you'll have to find sustenance at *souvlaki* stands or the **supermarket** (which has a good deli counter), down the main road past the OTE. You'll find fresh produce on the street behind the church.

A small whitewashed seafarer's chapel and the ruins of a windmill are poised on the hill behind town. A climb to either affords tremendous views of Kimi or the sea. On the east side of the same mountain, 5km from Kimi, is the 700-year-old, majestically situated **Monastery of the Savior.** When pirates landed at Kimi in the late 18th and 19th centuries, signals calling for aid were sent from the **Venetian Castle** above the monastery and passed along to other castles. Voyeurs might enjoy the **Folklore Museum** (tel. 22 011), on the road descending to Paralia Kimi. They have a collection of women's traditional undergarments (you've come a long way, baby!) and an exhibit dedicated to Kimi's most famous son—**Georgios Papanicolaou,** inventor of the Pap smear (open daily 10am-1pm and 6-8:30pm; admission 400dr).

LIMNI

According to legend, Zeus married Hera in Limni. An infelicitous earthquake destroyed the wedding temple long ago, but today, Limni, a lively port town, nonetheless has much to offer. Activity centers on the long waterfront stretch overlooking rickety, bobbing rowboats and neon windsurfers. Adjacent to a rocky beach and connected by bus and hydrofoil to surrounding towns, Limni makes a pleasant base for exploring Northern Evia. As tourists are few and transient, there are only a few hotels, so call for reservations, especially on weekends.

To find the **OTE,** walk down to the far left of the waterfront, walk uphill two blocks, and look for the blue sign (open Mon.-Fri. 7:30am-3:10pm). **Buses** run from Chalkis to Limni (4 per day, 2hr., 1200dr). There is also bus service to Aedipsos (30min., 400dr) with connections to Istea (30min., 260dr) and Pefki (15min., 140dr). Buses drop off at the center of the waterfront, next to the **bank** (open Mon.-Thurs. 8am-2pm, Fri. 8am-1:30pm). The **post office** is in the little square just off the waterfront, up the street from the bank (open Mon.-Fri. 7:30am-2pm). **Postal Code:** 34005. **Telephone Code:** 0227.

The **Plaza Hotel's** (tel. 31 235) lovable rooms are filled with antiques. (Doubles 5800dr, with bath 6800dr.) **Hotel Limni's** (tel. 31 316) clean, spacious rooms have private baths. (Open March-Nov. and for special occasions in off season. Singles 4500dr. Doubles 7500dr. Breakfast 800dr.) Both are on the waterfront.

Nights are cool in Limni, but most people still choose to dine by the water. Go for a slow *volta* (stroll) before you munch on something in a waterfront *taverna, ouzerie,* or sweetshop. Kicklines of severed octopus legs and other exotic catches hanging on racks by the tables signal fresh seafood.

AEDIPSOS

The village of Aedipsos, 30km northwest of Limni, was praised by Herodotus, Aristotle, and Aristophanes for its healing sulphurous waters. Aedipsos is worth a day-trip for anyone who wishes to enjoy the hot springs' relaxing vibes. Locals advise that you swim no longer than 30 minutes, as hours of bathing will leave you in a therapeutic stupor. The bus drops off in a small square at Ermou St., from which you will be able to see the waterfront. The **hot springs** are in a large complex on a road heading inland from the left end of the waterfront (facing the water), 200m past the post office. For more information call the **tourist information office** (tel. 23 500). They are open all year but extend their hours in summer (daily May-Oct. 7:30am-1pm and 5-7pm). A variety of specialized pools and equipment is available.

The **tourist police,** on the first floor of 3 Oceanidon St. (tel. 22 456), might be of some help. Facing the water from the town square, take a right onto Ermou St., then your first left. The **OTE** is hidden behind a black gate and a garden in the square (open Mon.-Fri. 7:30am-3pm). **Buses** run between Athens and Aedipsos (3 per day, 3¼hr., 2200dr) and between Aedipsos and Limni (30min., 400dr). **Flying dolphins** connect Aedipsos with Limni, Chalkida, and the Sporades. The hydrofoil agent can be found in the center of the waterfront (tel. 23 760). To find the **post office,** 25th Martiou (tel. 22 252), make a left turn (facing the water) away from the water at the left end of the waterfront (open 6:30am-12:30pm and 5-6:30pm) and **exchanges money** (Mon.-Fri. 7:30am-2pm). **Postal Code:** 34300. **Telephone code:** 0226.

Peloponnese
ΠΕΛΟΠΟΝΝΗΣΟΣ

Separated from the rest of the mainland by the Corinth Canal, the Peloponnese is a fertile hand-shaped plain that unites human achievement and natural beauty. The ancient theater at Epidavros, the shell of a medieval city at Mystra, Agamemnon's palace at Mycenae, and Olympia, the site of the first Olympic games, are impressive architectural and artistic masterpieces. Beyond these massive ruins, however, the Peloponnese's rocky mountains conceal undeveloped sandy beaches and wondrous mountain villages, such as Dimitsana and Stemnitsa, waiting to be explored.

CORINTHIA AND ARGOLIS
ΚΟΡΙΝΘΙΑ ΚΑΙ ΑΡΓΟΛΙΔΑ

Argos, a grotesque beast covered with 100 unblinking eyes, once stalked vast stretches of the north Peloponnese, subduing unruly satyrs and burly bulls. Today's Argolis and Corinthia hold impressive monuments produced during the Peloponnese's 3,500-year history. In summer, try to visit the sites at Mycenae, Corinth, Tiryns, and Epidavros early in the day, before tour groups arrive and the heat soars. Nauplion is a good base for visiting the nearby ruins.

■ New Corinth ΚΟΡΙΝΘΟΣ

New Corinth sits across from the Gulf of Corinth just west of the Corinth Canal. Not to be confused with its ancient predecessor, Corinth's dusty, noisy, industrial façade manages to retain some charm. The waterfront opens the city to the sea. In 1858, 1928, and 1986, New Corinth was the victim of serious earthquakes that have since inspired sober city-planning. The city issues building permits for only the most shatter-proof structures, and as a consequence, it sits low, squatting, though it sits securely. Corinth sprawls southward in a near-perfect grid.

ORIENTATION AND PRACTICAL INFORMATION

The main drag, **Ethnikis Antistasis Street,** borders the park and runs to the sea. **Ermou Street** runs parallel to Ethnikis Antistasis and borders the park on the other side. **Kolokotroni Street** runs along the city's eastern side, parallel to Ethnikis Antistasis. The station for **buses to Athens** and the vicinity lies at the corner of Ermou and Koliatsou on the park. The other **bus station,** serving the rest of the Peloponnese, is one block past the park at Aratou and Ethnikis Antistasis. To reach the main park from the **train station,** walk half a block up Demokratias, turn right on Dimaskinou, then left on Ermou several blocks later. While the city is relatively safe, tourist police advise women not to walk alone in poorly lit areas after midnight.

> **Banks: National Bank,** 7 Ethnikis Anastisis St. (tel. 24 149), on the corner of the first block in from the water. Offers **currency exchange.** Open Mon.-Thurs. 8am-2pm, Fri. 8am-1:30pm. An **ATM** is located on the block before the park along Ethnikis Anastisis St. that's hooked up to both PLUS and Cirrus networks.
> **OTE:** 32 Kolokotroni St. (tel. 22 111). Sells phone cards, but easier to buy at kiosks near the harbor. Open daily 7am-10pm; collect calls Mon.-Fri. 7am-10pm.
> **Trains: Station** (tel. 22 522), on Demokratias St. Trains run to Athens (14 per day, 2hr., 800dr) via Isthmia. Two major train lines serve the Peloponnese: one along

the northern coast from Corinth to Pirgos and south to Kyparissia, the other south from Corinth to Tripolis and Kalamata. Almost all major coastal cities in the Peloponnese can be reached by train from Corinth. Trains go to Patras (8 per day, 8am-8pm, 2hr., 980dr); Pirgos (5 per day, 8am-7pm, 4hr., 1640dr); Olympia (4 per day, 5hr., 1780dr); Argos (7 per day, 1hr., 510dr); Tripolis (4 per day, 2hr., 900dr); Kalamata (5 per day, 5½hr., 1640dr); Lefktro (3 per day, 3hr., 1140dr); Kyparissia (4 per day, 5hr., 2050dr); and Kalavryta (6 per day, 1½hr., 900dr). Express trains can cost 400-1000dr extra. 25% off for roundtrips. **Luggage storage** costs 250dr per piece per day. Trains from Athens to Patras may be full.

Buses: Ermou and Koliatsou Station (tel. 25 645). Buses run until 10:10pm. To Ancient Corinth (every hr., 6am-9pm, 20min., 190dr); Athens (every 30min., 5:30am-9:30pm, 1¼hr., 1350dr); Loutraki (every 30min., 6am-10pm, 20min., 240dr), Isthmia (5 per day, 20min., 190dr); and Nemea (7 per day, 1hr., 700dr). **Ethnikis Antistasis and Aratou Station** (tel. 24 403) runs a bus to Mycenae (every hr., 1hr., 650dr); Argos (every hr., 1½hr., 800dr); and Nauplion (2hr., 1000dr); it leaves at 7:15am and every hr. 8:30am-9:30pm. Note that the bus to Mycenae drops passengers at Fichtia, a 1½-km walk from the site. To catch a bus to Sparta and other southern locations on the Peloponnese, take the Loutraki bus to the Corinth Canal and pick up buses coming from Athens to Sparta (7 per day), Kalamata (10 per day), Koroni, and Tripoli.

Taxis: (tel. 22 361 or 22 229), along the park side of Ethnikis Antistasis St.

Car Rental: Gregoris Lagos, 42 Ethnikis Antistasis St. (tel. 22 617), across the street from the moped rental. Prices start at 6500dr per day up to 100km, 50dr per additional km. Minimum age 21. Open daily 8am-1pm and 4:30-9pm.

Moped Rental: Liberopoulos, 27 Ethnikis St. (tel. 72 937 or 21 847), inland past the park. Mopeds 4000-5000dr per day. Open daily 8am-1:30pm and 5-9pm.

Laundromat: 49 Adimantou St. (tel. 22 247), across from OTE and 77 Koliatsou St. Through the park and toward water. Open Mon.-Sat. 7am-2:30pm and 5:30-10pm.

Public Toilets: Across from the park on Ethnikis Anastasis St. Avoid these like the plague. But if you've gotta go, they're free and open 24hr.

Pharmacy: 27 Ethnikis Anastasis St. (tel. 24 213). Open Mon., Wed. 8am-2pm, Tues., Thurs.-Fri. 8am-2pm and 5-9pm. Many others on Koliatsou St.

Hospital: (tel. 25 711), on Athinaion St., inland past the train station; bear left. Open 24hr.

Police: 51 Ermou St. (tel. 22 143), facing the park, near the bus station. Open 24hr., but travelers may be better off dealing with the English-speaking **tourist police** (tel. 23 282), housed in the same building. Open daily 7:30am-10pm.

Post Office: (tel. 22 015), on Adimantou St., which borders the park on the end farthest from the water. Open Mon.-Fri. 7:30am-2pm. **Postal Code:** 20100. **Telephone Code:** 0741.

ACCOMMODATIONS

Most hotels in Corinth are clustered near the waterfront and the railroad station.

Ephira Hotel, 52 Ethnikis Antistasis St. (tel. 24 021), two blocks inland from the park. Spacious rooms, ceiling fans, private baths, daily maid service. Singles 6500dr. Doubles 8000dr. Triples 9000dr. Continental breakfast 1000dr.

Hotel Acti, 3 Ethnikis Antistasis St. (tel. 23 337), near the waterfront. Tiny, tidy rooms. Singles 3000dr. Doubles 4500dr.

Blue Dolphin Campground (tel. 25 766) is 3km from Ancient Corinth, right on the beach. 1050dr per person. 750dr per small tent. 850dr per large tent. 600dr per car. Electricity 600dr.

Camping Korinth Beach (tel. 27 969 or 29 057), down the road from the Blue Dolphin Campground. To get to either campground, take the bus to Ancient Corinth and get out at the bottom of the hill. Signs will direct you to the campgrounds; they are right off the beach. 700dr per person. 500dr per tent.

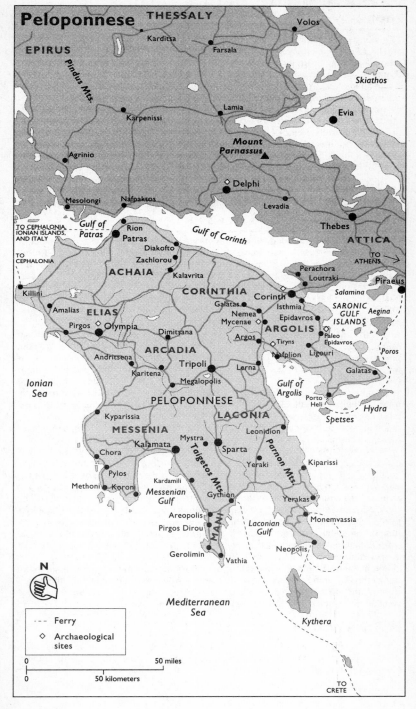

Peloponnese

CORINTHIA AND ARGOLIS

FOOD

The split personalities of the waterfront restaurants contrast with the city's *tavernas* and its affection for fast food. Greek and Italian cuisine, while perhaps not the most rational pairing, is the most frequent one. Expect to pay about 2000-2500dr for a dinner along the harbor. Restaurants almost invariably close when their customers leave, most often around 1 or 2am, opening at 10am. **Kentriko** (tel. 22 525), on Ethnikis Anistasis St., four blocks from the water, is popular with the locals, selling *gyros* and chicken (about 300dr and 800dr respectively). **Il Capolavoro** (tel. 22 449) offers Italian fare for a reasonable price (dinners around 1200dr). Vast outdoor, canopied dining area overlooks the port. **Fast Food** (tel. 85 335), on Ethnikis Anistasis St., serves fast food featuring hamburgers (500dr), fries, chicken (750dr), and fluorescent lights. This is not a place for atmosphere addicts (open 24hr.). **Kanita** (tel. 29 868) serves the old Greek standbys—*kalamari, souvlaki, moussaka* (around 1250dr)—along with linguine plates and spaghetti. Also serves fresh, local fish (2000dr). **Neon** (tel. 84 950) is a glorified coffee shop, with exemplary desserts (500dr), a refreshing a la carte layout, and cheap and easy sandwiches (500dr).

ENTERTAINMENT AND SIGHTS

Corinth should be included on the itinerary of anyone doing a videogame-parlor tour of Europe—they flourish here. Other forms of leisure can also easily be found, including beach-going and bar-hopping. Both are best done, in summer, in the **Kalamari Beach** area. West of the city, it can be reached by walking four blocks past the park along Ethnikis Anistasis St. Any right turn will take you there (about ten blocks). Beach bars breed here (three more under construction in 1996), along with outdoor seating and raucous music. The most formidable of the beach bars is **Montezuma,** and beware—after 11pm, in the summer season, the place is packed. Above the entrance to the bar stands a menacing ten-foot torso of a North American Indian chief, complete with head-dress. The music is heart-stopping techno, home-mixed in the back of the bar by the tribal DJ. Notable are **Gazibo,** which has a dance floor, and **La Plaza** (next door to Montezuma). The most popular time to frequent these places is July; they're closed in winter. They open around 10am and close when everyone leaves (two, three, four, five am…). **Caffé-Caffé** is a relatively quiet coffee bar two blocks from the behemoth, a nice alternative to its neighbors' rabble, offering coffee and iced coffee (450dr) and ice cream (600dr).

Kalamari Beach opens in May and closes after September. During the winter months, Corinthians successful at garrulous intoxication tend to go to a strip of bars off Ethnikis Antistasis St. These are sleek, overly marbled places off the harbor, down the tiny path (labeled" ΟΔΟΣ πυλαρινου ζωτραθου"). Certainly not indigenous to the region, they feel like airport bars that try for atmosphere—a little otherworldly. Still, they swell on weekend evenings with a young crowd. They open around 7am and close in summer at midnight or 1am; in winter at 2 or 3am. The most popular along the strip are **Aspetto, Retro** café and pub, and the **Half-Note** pub. Each caters to a slightly different crowd, so you may want to browse before settling on one. **Sivé** ΛΑΙΣ ΘΕΡΙΝο ("Lais Therino") a movie theater one block inland from Kalamari beach, shows a variety of largely American movies at 9 and 11pm. It is open air, very clean, and costs 1200dr.

If you spend the day in town rather than at the ruins, you may want to amble on out to the **Folklore Museum,** housed in a modern white building next to the waterfront at the end of Ermou St. (open daily 8am-1pm; free). The town **beaches** to the west are rocky and crowded, though the water is quite clean.

■ Ancient Corinth

Strategically based on both the Corinthian and Saronic Gulfs, the ancient city was a powerful commercial center and one of the most influential cities in ancient Greece. Corinth, allied with Sparta, reached the apex of its power in the 5th century

BCE, but the increase in Athenian naval power led to an inevitable clash. The conflict became the chief cause of the Peloponnesian War, from which the Corinthians, with the Spartans, emerged victorious. Nonetheless, Ancient Corinth was greatly weakened and Sparta alone became the leading Greek city. Eventually the city was conquered by the Romans, who exterminated the city's population in 146 BCE. Corinth remained deserted until Julius Caesar repopulated the city as a colony in 44 BCE. Much to the dismay of St. Paul, who preached here in 51 CE, this decadent band of Corinthians raged on, worshipping Aphrodite.

Orientation And Practical Information Enveloping ruins that have seen eons pass, the village of Ancient Corinth offers the peace and serenity that its modern counterpart lacks. The passage of time here slows to a trickle, and days languish endlessly. **Buses** travel from Modern Corinth to Ancient Corinth at the mountain's base every hour, returning every 30 minutes (30min., 190dr). **Taxis** will take you up for the steep price of 1200dr. The **post office,** along the road to Modern Corinth, offers **currency exchange** (open 7:30am-2pm). **Telephone Code:** 0741.

Accommodations Ancient Corinth's pensions are a great alternative to the bustling hotels in the new city. At **Rooms Marinos** (tel. 31 209 or 31 180), Papa Spiros and Mama Elisabeth run a peerless, extended-family-style establishment. They serve excellent home-cooked meals in enormous portions, complete with Mama's own desserts. Rooms have recently been renovated. To get here, go right at the fork behind the bus stop (away from the entrance to the ruins), walk along Sisyphos St., and turn right, uphill, at the sign for Argos. (Singles 5000dr. Doubles 8500dr. Triples 11,500dr. Breakfast included.) **Shadow Rooms** (tel. 31 481), complete with its downstairs *taverna,* near the end of the village towards the highway, is a wonderful place to spend the night. The new pale pink rooms are sparkling clean and have private bathrooms with shower. (Singles 4500dr. Doubles 7500dr. Triples 9000dr.)

Food The *taverna* beneath Shadow Rooms has breakfast for 1000dr. Lunch and dinner entrees cost 500-2500dr (sandwiches 500dr, fish 2000dr). At the site, you can eat at the **Acrocorinthos Restaurant** (tel. 31 503 or 31 099), ledged on top of the mountain. It serves, among other delicacies, *souvlaki* (1350dr) and *moussaka* (1000dr; open daily 9am-10pm). **O Tassos** (tel. 31 225) is a delightful *taverna* on the road to modern Corinth, after the post office (superb *moussaka* 900dr).

Sights The remains of the ancient city stand near the base of the Acrocorinth. This is where the **Ministry of Culture Archaeological Museum** (tel. 31 207) and **archaeological site** are located. Columns, metopes, and pediments, apparently spread by a whimsical Fury, lie in fascinating chaos in the museum's courtyard. Facing the museum, the Corinthian columns on your left are the façade of a Roman shrine. Pick up Nikos Papahatzis' guidebook, *Ancient Corinth,* at the museum entrance if you missed it at the ticket counter (1700dr). The museum, erected in memory of Ed Alonzo Small ("a scholar who delighted in the culture of Hellas"), houses a wonderful collection of statues, well preserved mosaics, and tiny clay figurines. Its collections of sarcophagi (one with a skeleton under glass) and headless statues in the green, open-air courtyard are impressive and eerie. The **Asclepion Room** off the inner courtyard displays a collection of votive offerings from the sick to the god of medicine: misshapen phalluses, sore ears, and wart-afflicted hands.

As you exit the museum, to your left stands the archaeological site including the remains of the 6th-century BCE **Temple of Apollo.** Behind the museum is the **Fountain of Glauke,** named after Jason's second wife who drowned herself while trying to douse the flames that sprouted from an enchanted shirt given to her by the vengeance-minded Medea, Jason's first wife. In the middle of the row of central shops, you'll see the **bema** on the right, a dais from which the Romans made announcements and official proclamations; it was later converted into a Greek, then Catholic church. Ahead is the **Julian Basilica.** To the left a broad stone stair descends into the

Peirene Fountain. This is where the Ancients say winged Pegasus was drinking when he was captured by Bellerophon. Crawl into the tunnels behind the fountain for a cool break. Just past the fountain is the **Perivolos of Apollo,** an open-air court surrounded by columns. Near the Perivolos is the **public latrine.** (Site and museum open Jul.-Aug. daily 8am-7pm; Sept.-June 8:45am-3pm; admission to both 1200dr, students 600dr, free for all on Sun.) **Tourist police** will answer any questions.

Built on the lower of the Acrocorinth's twin peaks, the **fortress** has foundations dating back to ancient times. The summit originally held a **Temple to Aphrodite,** which was served by "sacred courtesans" who initiated free-wheeling disciples into the "mysteries of love." The surprisingly intact remains are a medievalist's fantasy. Relatively empty, the fortress contains acres of towers, mosques, gates, and walls.

In early July, Ancient Corinth celebrates Agioi Anargyroi, its most important **summer festival,** commemorating the physicians Saint Kosmos and Saint Damian.

■ Near Corinth

LOUTRAKI

The name may seem familiar. Much of the bottled water (½liter, 80dr) you'll be clutching during your travels gushes from Loutraki's sweet wells, but Loutraki hardly springs to mind as an ideal Mediterranean vacation spot. A clean, little city, Loutraki rests across the crescent-shaped bay from Corinth (20min.-bus ride, 240dr). If you're visiting Corinth, you might want to stop and tap the source of the town's allure. Stroll along the stone boardwalk that flanks the body-blanketed beach, shadowed by the **Yerania Mountains**. The main street is El. Venizelou, which runs parallel to the water, curves at the port, and becomes Georgiou Lekka St.

Orientation and Practical Information To get to Loutraki from Isthmia, cross the canal bridge; the bus stop is next to a railroad station sign. Stay on the bus until the last stop, a triangular road island where El. Venizelou St. meets Periandou and Eth. Antistasis. English-speaking **tourist police** (tel. 65 678) respond to the needs of travelers (open daily 9am-9pm). Day boat excursions are available at the dock past the park. **Albona Cruises** goes to Lake Vouliagmeni—the "Blue Lake" (Tues.-Thurs., 2500dr). Cruises down the Corinth Canal leave Sundays at 10am and Thursdays at 5pm (3950dr). To get to the **National Bank,** 25 Martiou Square, bear left where the road forks (open Mon.-Thurs. 8:30am-2pm, Fri. 8:30am-1:30pm). At 10 El. Venizelou, you'll find the **OTE** (open Mon.-Fri. 7:30am-3:10pm). **Buses** (tel. 22 262) from Loutraki go to Athens (8 per day, 6am-7:30pm, 1300dr, roundtrip 2000dr); Corinth (every 30min. 5:30am-10:30pm, 20min., 240dr); Perachora (9 per day 6am-8pm, 20min., 190dr); and Vouliagmeni (July-Aug. only, departs 10am, returns 1pm, 45min., 700dr).

For **moped rentals,** make a right at the post office and turn at the second corner on the left to reach **Andreas** (tel. 23 812; Vespas 4000-5200dr, bikes 1000dr). Follow E. Venizelou St. (which changes to G. Lekka St.) toward the mountains. Periandrou St., the first side street on the right across from the bus station's road island, is home to **Laundry Self-Service** (tel. 63 854) which provides wash (1200dr), wash and dry (1600dr), and ironing (upon request; open Mon.-Tues. 8:30am-1:30pm, Wed.-Sat. 8:30am-1pm and 6-9pm). On the left, the densely congregated trees guard a **public fountain** that spouts Loutraki water; fill your bottle. For the **health center,** dial 63 444. The center itself is roughly 5km from the center of town. To reach it, walk 5 blocks up from El. Venizelou St., turn right, and continue along that road. There is a **pharmacy** at 21 El. Venizelou St. (tel. 21 787), and an outdoor movie theater opposite the tennis courts (operates in summer only). From the bus station, walk down **El. Venizelou Street** with the water to your left, and you'll reach the **post office** at 28th Octovriou St. #4, one block down to the right (open Mon.-Fri. 7:30am-2pm). **Police** (tel. 63 000 or 22 258) keep the peace across the street from the OTE on the 2nd floor. **Postal Code:** 20300. **Telephone Code:** 0744.

Accommodations There are only a few budget hotels in Loutraki. One of these, the **Hotel Brettagne**, 28 G. Lekka St. (tel. 22 349), has a kindly, semi-English-speaking manager. Rooms and baths sparkle, and every floor has a refrigerator. (Singles 4300dr. Doubles 6600dr. Triples 8000dr.) To find **Pension Marko** (tel. 63 542) go left from the bus station (facing the water) and take your second right onto L. Kalsoni St. Marko. All rooms with balcony and bath/shower. (Singles 6000dr. Doubles 8000dr.) **Camping** is at Lake Vouliagmeni, accessible by bus.

Food The formula for the best food may simply be what is closest at hand. If applied to Loutraki, such culinary logic says fish. And that's what you'll find strung along the 2km of white-tiled waterfront walkway. Avid beef-eaters will also adapt well, although vegetarians may have to work a little harder, in the back streets and markets of Loutraki, for their fare. **Horiatiki Taverna,** 70 El. Venizelos (tel. 22 228), has been serving fruits and stellar fish dishes for over 30 years. This *taverna's* staff (as its card suggests) are only "specialists in fish." An elegant garden seating area and the freshest seafood draw large French and German crowds. **Kazino's** (tel. 22 332), on the waterfront, has an English menu and inexpensive fare including Greek salads (700dr) and stuffed tomatoes (1000dr; opens at 7am, closes around 2am). **Canadian Steak House** (tel. 23 993) is on the waterfront next to Kazino's—cute place, unfortunate name. From schnitzel (2000dr) to *souvlaki* (1900dr), carnivores of all stripes make the trek to the Steak House for atmosphere and copious protein (open 10am-4pm and 6pm-2 or 3am). For a little class you may want to swing over to the **Hotel Agelidis Palace,** 19 G. Lekka St. (tel. 28231). Though you may not want to sleep here, (prices begin at 30,000dr), you may want to eat here.

Entertainment Nightlife consists of a ritual alteration between eating and dancing. Waterfront restaurants swell in summer until midnight and beyond. Taxis lorry anxious feet to the discoes on the fringe of the city. The flagship disco in Loutraki is undoubtedly **Baby-o**. Precariously placed between a vast and lonely looking bottling company and a shrub-covered wasteland, Baby-o caters to a weekend crowd of 1000 to 1500 people. Baby-o is the only disco open year-round in the Corinth-Loutraki area. Others include **Biblos** and **Club Bazaar,** both in town and both near the waterfront (open in summer).

Sights The majority of Greek tourists go to Loutraki for the healing waters. Whirlpool baths and hydromassage are offered at the **Hydrotherapy Thermal Spa,** 26 G. Lekka St. (tel. 22 215). These will cure "rheumoatoarthritic, spondycarthritic" and "chronic gynecological diseases," or so the bilingual sign printed on the door promises (open Mon.-Sat. 8am-1pm). The waterfalls, on the edge of town away from Corinth, merit a visit. They are theme-park-like in construction but less impressive, although as pleasant to listen to as their cousins in nature. The water funnels to the top from a series of fountains at the base of the cliff. Hike around the waterfalls. There are rows of tables along the side of the falls, as though the hill were terrace-farmed by the **café** that sits below (open daily 10am-3am). Garishly lit at night, these falls may seem less an imitation of nature than some obscure preternatural force.

ISTHMIA

Ancient Greek jocks used to gather in Isthmia and Nemea to compete in the Pan-Hellenic Games, drink beer, and slap each other's backsides. Take the bus from Corinth heading toward Isthmia, and ask to be let out at the **museum,** a green building up and on the right of the road from the bus stop. The carefully diagrammed exhibits display finds from the Temple of Poseidon and the sites of the Isthmian games. Of particular interest are the glass *opus sectile* (mosaic panels) discovered at nearby Kenchreai. which managed to survive the earthquake of 375 CE. The entrance to the ruins lies to the right of the museum. All that remains of the **Temple of Poseidon** is its despoiled foundation. The **theater** is below and farther to the right of the temple. **Cult caves,** where many people enjoyed dinner and entertainment during the Archaic Period, lie above the theater (museum and site open Tues.-Sat. 8:45am-7pm; off season 8:45am-3pm, Sun. 9:30am-2:30pm; closed holidays).

NEMEA

Pausanias wrote in the 2nd-century CE edition of *Let's Go: Nemea,* "Here is a temple of Nemean Zeus worth seeing although the roof has fallen in and the cult statue is missing." Were he to visit it today, he might be peeved that the temple has dwindled to three columns. The walkway takes you past a wall built around a glass-encased grave, complete with skeleton. Don't miss the well preserved **baths.** The **stadium** is 500m down the road to Corinth. The well organized **museum** on the site (tel. (0746) 22 739) has excellent explanatory notes in English, some artifacts, and several reconstructions of the site (museum and site open Tues.-Sun. 8:30am-7pm; off season Tues.-Sat. 8:30am-3pm; admission 500dr, students 300dr). The ruins of Ancient Nemea are 4km from Modern Nemea, so if you are coming by bus from Corinth, ask to be let off at the ancient site (1hr., 700dr).

■ Mycenae MYKHNAI

No city figured more prominently, or morbidly, in Greek mythology than Mycenae. The city was allegedly founded by Perseus, who slew Medusa, the snake-haired gorgon whose looks could kill. Eventually the Mycenaeans chose Atreus, whose family was immortalized by Aeschylus in the Oresteia trilogy, as their ruler. But out of hatred for his brother, Thyestes, Atreus murdered his nieces and nephews (Thyestes' sons and daughters) and served them to their father for dinner. This culinary *faux pas* provoked the wrath of the gods; they upheld the curse that Thyestes had pronounced on Atreus and his progeny. When Atreus' son Agamemnon returned after ten years at the Trojan War, he was met by his bitter wife Clytemnestra, her lover Aegisthus, and Aegisthus' lethal dagger. Agamemnon's son Orestes later avenged the murder of his father by slaying his mother, but was then haunted by the Furies, who tormented those who killed their family members. Athena finally pardoned Orestes and lifted the curse from the House of Atreus.

Mycenae's hazy origins, its interactions with other Near Eastern civilizations, and its subsequent decline have long beguiled historians. The site was settled as early as 2700 BCE by tribes from the Cyclades who were colonizing the mainland. Clay tablets written in Linear B, an early form of ancient Greek, were found at Pylos and Knossos and serve as a record of the Mycenaeans' well developed bureaucratic system of account-keeping. Mycenae flourished financially after the fall of Knossos around 1400 BCE and Mycenaean culture spread as far as Cyprus, Syria, and Sicily. Mycenae was probably destroyed by Dorian tribes from the north led by disgruntled rivals of the House of Atreus, imprisoning the Furies under faraway Athens.

The remarkable artifacts (among the most celebrated archaeological discoveries in modern history) from the well preserved ruins of ancient Mycenae, which include an extensive fortress, Grave Circles A and B, and *tholos* (beehive) tombs, are now on display in the National Museum in Athens. In summer, mobs stampede the famed Lion's Gate and Tomb of Agamemnon. Visit early in the morning or late in the afternoon to avoid becoming part of them. Although most travelers make Mycenae a daytrip from Athens, Argos, or Nauplion, you can spend the night in the adjacent modern village, where restauranteurs across the street from each other will vie for your attention in one of several languages.

ORIENTATION AND PRACTICAL INFORMATION

The only direct **buses** to Mycenae are from Nauplion (3 per day at 10am, noon, and 1:30pm, 40min., 450dr) and Argos (6 per day, 30min., 260dr). A bus from Athens (15 per day, 2½hr., 1750dr) stops at Fihtia, 1½km away. From Fihtia, the site is located on the Corinth-Argos road. Simply follow the sign to Mycenae. Three buses make the return trip from Nauplion at 11am, 1, and 3pm. They stop in the town of

Mycenae (up the street from the Iphigenia Restaurant) and at the site (a 20-min. walk from the town). Buses and **trains** (5 per day) run from Athens via Corinth to Fihtia. There is another bus stop by the intersection near the train station. Although the town has no banks, the **post office** at the site handles **currency exchange** (open Mon.-Fri. 8am-10pm, Sat. 8am-3pm). **Postal Code:** 21200. **Telephone Code:** 0751.

ACCOMMODATIONS

Mycenae has few inexpensive accommodations. If campgrounds aren't your thing, seek out private rooms; to find them simply look for the signs off the main road. You may want to browse, because prices vary considerably.

Belle Helene Hotel (tel. 66 225) serves as a bus stop on the main road. Clean, spacious rooms with carpeting, but there is some noise from the restaurant downstairs. Heinrich Schliemann stayed here, as did lyrical beatnik Allen Ginsberg, who came in 1961 lacking the money to eat. The register display on the wall also claims that Virginia Woolf and Claude Debussy slept here (but not in the same bed). Doubles 5000dr. Triples 7000dr.

Hotel Klitemnistra (tel. 76 451), also on the main road, is closer to the ruins. It features enormous rooms, 24-hr. hot water, and a restaurant. Singles 4000dr. Doubles 7000dr. Triples 8500dr. Breakfast included.

Camping Atreus (tel. 76 221), at the bottom of the hill on the side of town farther from the ruins. It is a 5-min. walk from the strip of restaurants and hotels. Atreus offers a TV room, kitchen, and a cafeteria/bar. 1000dr per person. 500dr per small tent. 1000dr per large tent. Hot showers and electricity included.

Camping Mycenae (tel. 76 121; fax 76 247), in the middle of town, closer to the ruins. The lemon groves lend the camp their wondrous fragrance. There is also a bar/restaurant and a kitchen, where the gracious owner prepares inexpensive homemade food. 990dr per person. 1700dr per tent. Hot showers included.

FOOD

Most of the restaurants in town prey on tourists willing to pay, but a few pleasant, cheap places survive. **Restaurant/Taverna Micinaiko** (tel. 76 245), next to the youth hostel, has nice folks and tasty food (and a 15-20% student discount). Prices are marked in high season; otherwise, ask (Greek salad 800dr, chicken 950dr, *moussaka* 900dr). **Menelaos** (tel. 66 311), next door to Taverna Micinaiko, has a shady porch to dine on and interesting wall murals, especially en route to the restroom (*retsina* 400dr per 500g, Greek salad 750dr, *moussaka* 1000dr). Students receive a 20% discount. **Aristidis O Dikeos** (tel. 76 258), across the street, has a pleasant proprietor whose *taverna* is distinguishable by its flower-filled porch. (Greek salads 800dr, *dolmadakia* 900dr.) All restaurants open at about 9am, closing when the customers leave, most often around midnight or 1am.

SIGHTS

The excavated site of Ancient Mycenae extends over a large tract of rough terrain tucked between Mt. Agios Elias to the north and Mt. Zara to the south. The site is enclosed by 13m-high, 10m-thick monstrous walls called "Cyclopean" by ancient Greeks. The ancients believed that Perseus and his descendant who founded the city could only have lifted the stones with the help of the Cyclopses, one-eyed giants with superhuman strength. Although modern historians scoff at monsters (and probably can't see Mr. Snuffleupagus either), they have no better explanations of how the stones were moved. The bulk of the ruins standing today date from 1280 BCE, when the city was the center of the far-flung Mycenaean civilization.

German businessperson, classics scholar, and amateur archaeologist **Heinrich Schliemann** uncovered Mycenae in 1874, having located the site by following clues in the writings of Homer and later Greek dramatists, who had placed the House of Atreus in the vicinity. Schliemann began digging just inside the citadel walls at the spot where several ancient authors indicated the royal graves would have been located. Discovering 15 skeletons, "literally covered with gold and jewels," Schliemann bedecked his new sixteen-year-old Greek wife with them and had her to pose for photographs. Schliemann believed he had unearthed the skeletons of Agamemnon and his followers. Wrenching some of the riches from his sweetie's wrists, neck, and earlobes, he sent a telegram to the Greek king that read: "Have gazed on face of Agamemnon." Moments after he removed the mask, the "face" underneath disintegrated. Modern archaeologists shudder at the thought. Less romantic archaeologists, however, have dated the tombs to four centuries before the Trojan War. One skull, sporting a golden death mask still referred to as "The Mask of Agamemnon," is now exhibited in the National Archaeological Museum in Athens.

Before visiting the site, consider obtaining a map and flashlight. The book by S. E. Iakovidis, covering both Mycenae and Epidavros, includes a map and is well worth the 2000dr. For a more scholarly approach, try the book by George E. Mylonas, director of the excavation (1700dr). If you want information on other ruins, buy the large guide, *The Peloponnese,* by E. Karpodini-Dimitriadi (2800dr). All are available at the entrance to the site in Greek, English, German, and French.

The bus will take you to the end of the asphalt road; the ruins are on your right. Down the hill in the lower parking lot area is the largest of the *tholos* (beehive) tombs, the so-called **Tomb of Agamemnon,** in the Treasury of Atreus. As you walk into the *tholos,* look up; the lintel stone weighs 120 tons. To the right on the walk up to the main site are pathways to two often overlooked *tholoi,* the **tomb of Aegistheus** and the more interesting **tomb of Clytemnestra.** Bring a flashlight; the *tholoi* are dark inside. The gate and the **Cyclopean Walls** of the upper citadel date from the 13th century BCE. The imposing **Lion's Gate,** with two lionesses carved in relief above the lintel, is the portal into ancient Mycenae. These lionesses were symbols of the house of Atreus and their heads (now missing) had eyes of precious gems. Schliemann found most of his artifacts (now on display in Athens) in **Grave Circle A.** These 16th-century BCE shaft graves were originally located outside the city walls, but the city grew and now they rest to the right of the entrance. The **barracks** are up the stairs to your left immediately after the gate.

The ruins on the hillside are the remnants of various homes, businesses, and shrines. The **palace** and the **royal apartments** are at the highest part of the citadel on the right. The open spaces here include guard rooms, private areas, and more extensive public rooms. Look for the **megaron,** or royal chamber; it has a round hearth surrounded by the bases of four pillars (note the pillar bases). To the left of the citadel sit the remaining stones of a Hellenistic **Temple of Athena.** At the far end of the city, between the palace and the **postern gate,** is the underground cistern used as refuge in times of siege. Be careful—the steps are worn and slippery.

Follow the asphalt road 150m back toward the town of Mycenae to the **Treasury of Atreus** (tel. 76 585), the largest and most impressive *tholos.* The tomb of Agamemnon can be reached through a 40m passage cut into the hillside. The famous tomb was found empty, but is believed to have held valuable goods that were spirited away by thieves. A new museum is being built on the site, with hopes of housing treasures currently in the National Gallery, by 1997. (Site open April-Sept. Mon.-Fri. 8am-7pm; Oct.-March Mon.-Fri. 8am-5pm. Admission to citadel and Tomb of Agamemnon 1500dr, students 800dr, free on Sun. Keep your ticket or you'll pay twice.) Note: a sign at the entrance declares "Visitors are prayed to enter decently dressed." So act accordingly.

■ Argos ΑΡΓΟΣ

The inconvenience of having ancient ruins beneath your city doesn't seem to have discouraged construction in Argos. Archaeologists need to inspect each building site before a permit is issued, but the city has grown rapidly in spite of the red tape. In summer, Argos is hot and feels far from the water, though the small park and the city's main square, home to the **Church of St. Peter,** will cede you some quiet shade. Every Wednesday and Saturday, the city hosts the largest **open-air market** in the Peloponnese in an otherwise cosmically empty square across from the **museum.** Evening festivals punctuate the summer months; the larger of these runs in mid-June. Music, food, and classical plays performed in the city's **theater** draw crowds from Athens and beyond (call (0751) 62 143 for program details).

ORIENTATION AND PRACTICAL INFORMATION

The four streets that form the sides of the central square in Argos correspond roughly to the four points of the compass. Surrounding the Church of Saint Peter, they are the principal avenues of the city. Visible from the square is **Larissa Hill,** topped by a **citadel** of the same name. Larissa borders the city on the west. **Vasilios Georgiou B** is parallel to the citadel. Opposite this street on the east side is **Danaou St.** The north edge is **Vasilios Konstantinou** and the south side is **Vas. Olgas St.**

Banks: National Bank (tel. 68 211), on the eastern side of the square, offers **currency exchange,** 1 block behind Danaou St. and the park. Also has a 24-hr. **ATM.** Open Mon.-Thurs. 8am-2pm, Fri. 8am-1:30pm.

OTE: 8 Nikitara St. (tel. 67 599), north of the park. Or, facing the park from the main square, take the street running the park's left side. Open daily 7am-10pm.

Trains: The **station** (tel. 67 212), is 1km south of the main square. To get to the main square, take a right on Nauplion St. and bear left on Vas. Sofias at the 5-way intersection. Five trains per day go to: Athens (3hr., 1400dr); Corinth (1hr., 510dr); Tripolis (1hr., 600dr); Kalamata (3½hr., 1300dr); Mycenae (10min., 105dr); and Nemea (45min., 200dr). Discounted roundtrip tickets.

Buses: There are two **stations.** The first is a few doors down from the **Athinon Station,** on Vas. Georgiou B., near the corner of Vas. Olgas St. (look for the Arcadia café). Buses go to Athens (every hr. 5:30am-8:30pm, 2½hr., 2040dr); Nauplion (every 30min. 5:30am-8:30pm, 30min., 220dr); Nemea (2 per day, 1hr., 500dr); Mycenae (4 per day, 25min., 200dr); and Prosimni (2 per day, 30min., 280dr). The **Arcadia-Laconia Station,** 24 Pheithonos St. (tel. (0752) 22 094). Follow Vas. Olgas St. 2 streets past the museum and turn left. Walk down several blocks, past the Agricultural Bank. Buses leave from here for Tripolis (8:30, 11:30am, 2:30, and 5pm, 1hr., 900dr). From Tripolis you can make connections to Sparta, Olympia, Andritsena, Gythion, and Monemvassia.

Hospital: (tel. 24 455 or -6), Corinth St., opposite St. Nicholas Church. Open 24hr.

Police: 10 Agelou Bobou St. (tel. 67 222). From the northeast corner of the square, follow Corinth St. and turn right on Agelou Bobou. English spoken. Open 24hr.

Post Office: 16 Danaou St. (tel. 68 066), past the southern end of the square. Open Mon.-Fri. 7:30am-2pm. **Postal Code:** 21200.

Telephone Code: 0751.

ACCOMMODATIONS

Argos has few accommodations. Since the sights can be seen in half a day, it's possible to make Argos a daytrip from Nauplion or, if you want to camp, from Mycenae.

Hotel Apollon, 13 Papaflessa St. (tel. 61 182 or 68 065). Take Nikitara off the square, turn left at the red and yellow café, then turn right into the nearby alley—it's on the left. Follow the signs. Large, tidy rooms. Singles 3800dr, with bath 4300dr. Doubles 5000dr, with bath 6000dr. Triples 7000dr, with bath 8000dr.

Hotel Telesilla, 2 Danan St. (tel. 68 317), just off Saint Peter's Sq., near the entrance to the park. A new, clean hotel. Singles 4000dr, with bath 6000dr. Doubles 6000dr, with bath 8000dr.

Hotel Mycenae (tel. 68 754 or 68 332), in the main square across from the church. Offers nice rooms in one of the prettiest parts of Argos. Singles 6000dr, students 4500dr. Doubles 12,000dr, students 8500dr. All rooms with private bath.

FOOD

The food is discouragingly bad in Argos, so you might want to eat something quick and get it over with. However, the cafés of Argos provide air-conditioning. Tough call. One nice place is **Restaurant Aglee** (tel. 67 266), in the northwest corner of the square (omelettes 700dr, pizza 1250dr). Another choice is **Retro Pub and Restaurant,** next to the Hotel Mycenae. They serve spaghetti (900dr), Greek salads (800dr), and pizzas (1300dr). The **Dixon** café, just off the square, has a quiet atmosphere where you can drink but starve—the only food cafés usually serve is ice cream. **Café Polon,** located behind the church, serves beverages and stays open until 1 or 2am. Frequented by a young crowd, Polon houses its own DJ at night.

SIGHTS

According to Homer, Argos was the kingdom of the hero Diomedes and claimed the allegiance of Mycenae's powerful king Agamemnon. Invading Dorians captured Argos in the 12th century BCE, around the same time as the fall of Mycenae, and then used it as their base for controlling the Argolid Peninsula. Through the 7th century BCE, Argos remained the most powerful state in the Peloponnese and even defeated its rival Sparta. By the 5th century BCE, however, it was no match for the invincible Spartan war machine. In the famous battle of 494 BCE, Kleomenes and the Spartans nearly defeated Argos but failed to penetrate the city walls.

In medieval times, Franks, Venetians, and Turks captured and ruled Argos in turn. They each had a hand in creating the **Fortress of Larissa,** a splendid architectural hodgepodge which includes Classical and Byzantine elements. Getting to the fortress is a hike. You can walk along Vas. Konstantinou St. for roughly one hour, or climb the foot path from the ruins of the ancient theater. The ruins, which lie among overgrown weeds, are mainly of interest to avid scholars of bees or architecture—particularly those endowed with cars. Archaeologists had hoped to uncover a large part of the ancient city of Argos, but most of it lies under the modern town. The principal **excavations** have occurred on the city's western fringe; digs are currently going on there and in different areas throughout the town. To get to the site, walk past the post office and turn right and walk to the end of Theatron St.

With a seating capacity of 20,000, the ancient **theater** was the largest in the Greek world when it was built in the 4th century BCE. Though not as well preserved as its famous counterpart in Epidavros, it is striking nonetheless. Next to the theater are the **Roman baths.** Segments of wall give a good impression of the original magnitude of these ancient social centers. The **Roman Odeon** (indoor theater) is here, as is the **agora,** with blue-and-white mosaics still in place. Past the Odeon are the remains of a smaller theater (all sites open Tues.-Sun. 8:30am-3pm; free).

Hera was the patron deity of the Argives, and the temple of her cult, the **Argive Heraion,** is a short bus ride north of Argos (take the Prosimni bus, 220dr). The complex contains, among other things, a pair of temples, a *stoa,* and baths. At **Prosimni,** several kilometers northeast of Argos and past the Heraion, archaeology aficionados will delight in a series of prehistoric graves. A few kilometers east of Agias Trias lie the remains of the city of **Dendra,** where tombs yielded the completely preserved suit of bronze armor now on exhibit in the Nauplion museum.

The small but superb **archaeological museum** (tel. 68 819), west off the main square on Vas. Olgas St., has a collection of Mycenaean and pre-Mycenaean pottery, some of which dates back as far as 3000 BCE (open Tues.-Sun. 8:30am-7pm; off season 8:30am-3pm; admission 500dr, students 300dr, EU students free).

■ Nauplion ΝΑΥΠΛΙΟ

The city of Old Nauplion is a soothing antidote to the hustle of Corinth and the hordes of sun-worshippers on the islands. Venetian architecture, shady squares, and hillside stairways that foil noisy mopeds make Old Nauplion a perfect base for daytrips into the Peloponnese and nearby ruins. In contrast, New Nauplion is unattractive, its design kindles thoughts of an on going construction site. Remnants of Nauplion's illustrious past include Palamidi, a Venetian fortress in which Turks imprisoned the national hero Kolokotronis before the Revolutionary War of 1821, and the Bourtzi, a floating Venetian stronghold that once housed retired executioners, but now caters to people of a more benign occupation—tourists.

Nauplion has suffered from chronic instability. Before the Venetians built it on swamp land in the 15th century, the city (named for Poseidon's son Nauplius) consisted entirely of the hilltop fortresses. It passed from the Venetians to the Turks and back again. In 1821, it served as headquarters for the revolutionary government, and as the capital of Greece (1829-1834). John Kapodistrias, the president of Greece, was assassinated in St. Spyridon Church. (The bullet hole is still visible in the church walls; the assassins hid behind the fountain across the street.) Recent years have held less calamity for the city, and, under the watchful eyes of its surrounding fortresses, Nauplion seems content to while away a few more centuries in serenity.

ORIENTATION AND PRACTICAL INFORMATION

The bus terminal, on **Singrou Street,** sits near the base of the Palamidi fortress, which caps the hill to the right facing inland. To reach **Bouboulinas Street,** the waterfront promenade, just walk right (facing the bus station) down Singrou to the harbor. The area behind Bouboulinas and Singrou is the old part of town, with many shops and *tavernas.* If you arrive by water, Bouboulinas St. will be directly before you, across the parking lot and parallel to the dock.

There are three other principal streets in the old town, all of which run off Singrou Street parallel to Bouboulinas. Moving inland, the first is **Amalias,** a chief shopping street. The second, **Vasileos Konstandinou,** ends in **Syntagma Square** (Platia Syntagmatos), which has *tavernas,* the bookstore, the bank, the museum, and at night, scores of aspiring soccer stars. The third street is **Plapouta,** which becomes **Staikopoulou** in the vicinity of Syntagma Sq. Here you'll find more good restaurants.

Across Singrou St., Plapouta becomes **25th Martiou,** the largest avenue in town. This side of Singrou St.—everything behind the statue of Kapodistrias—is the new part of town. The new section radiates outward from the 5-way intersection split by the road to Argos and the road to Tolo.

Tourist Office: (tel. 24 444), across the street from the OTE. English-speaking staff provides free pamphlets, maps, and changes money. Open daily 9am-9pm.

Tourist Police: (tel. 28 131), with your back to the old town, walk along 25 Martiou; 6 blocks past the turn-off for the road to Tolo. English-speaking police are very helpful and cheerfully provide pamphlets and information. Open 24hr.

Banks: The **National Bank** (tel. 28 355), Syntagma Sq. Open Mon.-Thurs. 8am-2pm, Fri. 8am-1:30pm. Other banks in Syngtama Sq. and on Amalias St. charge 500-700dr commission for **currency exchange.**

Town Hall: (tel. 24 444), near the hydrofoil landing. Changes money and offers information. Open daily 9am-1pm and 5-9pm.

OTE: 25th Martiou St. (tel. 22 139, 22 121 or 25 899), at Arvantias; in yet another yellow building across Kapodistrias Sq. Open daily 7am-10pm.

Buses: Station on Singrou St. (tel. 27 323), off Kapodistrias Square. Buses go daily to Athens (every hr. 5am-8pm, 3hr., 2150dr), stopping at Argos (30min., 220dr) and Corinth (2hr. 1000dr); Mycenae (3 per day, 40min., 480dr); Epidavros (4 per day, 1hr., 480dr); Tolo (every hr., 7am-8:30pm, 20min., 220dr); Kranidi (3 per day, 2hr., 1200dr); Galatas (5:45am and 2pm, 2hr., 1400dr); and Ligouri (every 2hr., 5:30am-7:30pm, 1hr., 480dr).

Ferries: There are no regular ferries out of Nauplion or Tolo. The Pegasus, an expensive cruise ship, offers day tours and leaves every Wed. and Fri. from Tolo. Cruise tickets to the Saronic Gulf islands range from 4000-7000dr. For tickets or reservations, consult **Staikos Tours,** 50 Bouboulinas St. (tel. 27 950 or 22 444), on the left of the waterfront. Open daily 8:30am-3:30pm and 6-10pm. More convenient is the **flying dolphin,** which operates in July and Aug. A dolphin leaves for Peiraias (Tues.-Sun. 7:15am, 4hr., 7000dr), stopping in Spetses (1hr., 2550dr); Ermione (1¼hr., 3050dr); Hydra (2hr., 3850dr); Poros (2½hr., 4700dr); and Aegina (3hr., 6600dr). Staikos also arranges for **plane** and **train** travel.

Taxis: (tel. 27 393 or 23 600), congregate on Singrou St. across from the bus station. The trick is to get drivers who operate out of the destination you desire; they charge less if they're returning. Taxi to Palamidi fortress 700dr.

Bike/Moped Rental: Motomania (tel. 21 407), on Navarino St.; take Konstantinou St. towards New Nauplion and Navrinou is on your left. Mopeds 3000dr per day. Open daily 8am-9pm.

English Bookstore: Odyssey (tel. 23 430), Syntagma Sq. Sells English language books. Open daily 8am-10pm; off season Mon.-Sat. 9am-1pm, Sun. 5-9pm.

Hospital: Call the tourist police or visit **Nauplion Hospital** (tel. 27 309 or 24 235). Walk down 25th Martiou St. and turn left onto Kolokotroni St., which eventually becomes Asklipiou St. (a 15-min. walk).

Police: (tel. 22 458), on Praitelous St., a 15-min. hike along 25th Martiou St. from the bus station—follow the signs. Open 24hr. for drug busts, murders, and other felonies; **security police** (tel. 27 776), in the same building, concern themselves with other less glamorous crimes. Both are a block from the tourist police.

Post Office: (tel. 24 230 or 24 231), the large yellow building on the corner of Sidiras Merarchias and Singrou St., one block from the bus station toward the harbor. Open Mon.-Fri. 7:30am-2pm. **Postal Code:** 21100.

Telephone Code: 0752.

ACCOMMODATIONS

Prices have risen in the old part of town, but it's still the cheapest, most pleasant district. Check the streets at the east end of town (below Dioscuri Hotel) for rooms. In the off season, prices are 20-40% less than those listed here.

Hotel Economou (tel. 23 955), on Argonafton, off the road to Argos. A 15-min. walk from the bus station, Hotel Economou offers swept rooms, pressed sheets, balconies, and pleasant company. 2000dr per person.

Eleni's Rooms (tel. 22 351), on the far right of Old Nauplion just below the Xenia hotel. Take the second to last street on your left; it's the first door on your right. Some rooms with full kitchen, some with verandas. Call the number to reserve, but specify Eleni's Rooms, and not Hotel Byron, since both establishments share the same number. Doubles 7000dr. Triples 7000dr.

Hotel Epidavros (tel. 27 541), on Ipsiladou St., 1 block below Amalias and 4 blocks up from Bouboulinas. Divided into two parts—hotel and pension. The hotel, described by the owner as a "family" kind of place, is clean and roomy. Singles 6000dr. Doubles 8000dr. All rooms have private bath.

Hotel Artemis (tel. 27 862), on the Argos road, 1500m from the bus station. Located in the noisy new town, but has lots of aqua and wood paneling—clean and at a good price. Singles 4000dr. Doubles 5000dr.

Hotel ERA (HPA in Greek), 9 Vas. Georgiou B St. (tel. 28 184), off Bouboulinas St. in the new part of town. Clean, airy rooms. Doubles 6000dr; off-season 2300dr. Triples 7500dr; off-season 3000dr.

FOOD AND ENTERTAINMENT

The food in Nauplion is excellent, though it is not often cheap. At times (about 8pm-midnight), the city may seem one *taverna*-packed back-alley after another, lit by soft flood lights and strewn with plants, balconies, and people. The waterfront is lined with fish restaurants, though these can charge as much as 5000-7000dr per entree. Better dining options occupy the street above Syntagma Sq., behind the National Bank, where proprietors will lure you with calls of, "Good food, good food here." **Taverna Basiles** (tel. 25 334), on Plapouta-Staikopoulou, one street above the square, serves wonderful fresh fish, and a rabbit in onions (1200dr) that will delight even the most avid Beatrix Potter fan. **Zorba's Tavern** (tel. 25 319), to the left of Basiles, caters to local tastes (*moussaka* 900dr) and offers some cheap starters (stuffed tomatoes 800dr). **Ellas** (tel. 27 278), in Syntagma, is the cheapest restaurant around (chicken and fish entrees 950-1250dr), and boasts an international clientele including Marcello Mastroianni (ask to see the pictures). **The Old Mansion** (tel. 22

449), on Ipsalidou St., is one of the treasures of Nauplion's back streets. Its specialty is veal in cream sauce (1350 dr), with vegetarian options like vine leaves (850dr). **Taverna Kauarapauns** (tel 25 371), on Vas. Olga St., parallel to the Old Mansion, serves only dinner. With crepes (1100dr) and stuffed vine leaves (800dr), this *taverna* is a secluded relief from the crowds surrounding Syntagma and the waterfront.

Nauplion's discoes have all relocated to **Tolo** (15min., 1400dr by taxi; see Tolo on (p. 126). Most of the action in town now happens at after-dinner ice cream joints. Dessert shops crawl with lascivious teenagers, but the **Igloo** (an ice cream chain), 100m out of the lower left corner of Syntagma Sq., is especially popular. If all play and no work has made you regress, head to the **Luna Park**, a permanent carnival, at the right end of the harbor and re-live your childhood under the neon lights. Or take a **minicruise** of the harbor (which run until 7pm), and tour around the Bourtzi. Small *caïques* leave from the end of the dock (500dr roundtrip).

SIGHTS

A stroll through the streets of Nauplion is more edifying than a slide show in Architecture 101. Everywhere you look there is impressive contrast from the building styles from various periods. An amazing example is the 18th-century **Palamidi fortress** (tel. 28 036), property first of Venice, then of Turkey, now of Greece. The 999 grueling steps that once provided the only access to the fort have been superseded by a 3km road. Taxis cost 700dr each way, or you can attack the road by foot. If you opt for the steps, bring water and climb in the morning. The views of the town, gulf, and much of the Argolid are spectacular. The steps begin on Arvanitias St., across the park from the bus station. A snack bar on the site opens at 9:30am and serves fresh juices, coffee, water, and snacks. The lion steles that adorn some of the lower citadel's walls are Venetian. Years ago, there were eight working cisterns at the site; today you can still tour the cool interiors of the two remaining underground reservoirs (open Mon.-Fri. 8am-6:30pm, Sat.-Sun. 8:30am-3pm; off season Mon.-Fri. 8:45am-2:30pm, Sun. 8:45am-2pm; admission 800dr, students 400dr).

The walls of the **Acronauplion** were fortified by three successive generations of conquerors: Greeks, Franks, and Venetians. Approach the fortress either by the tunnel that runs into the hill from Zigomala St., where you can take the Xenia Hotel elevator. The views of the Palimidi, the Gulf, and Old Nauplion are fantastic. Ludwig I, King of Bavaria, had the huge Bavarian Lion carved out of a monstrous rock as a memorial after seeing many of his men die in an epidemic in 1833-34. Today, a small park sits in front of it. Instead of turning right onto Praxitelous St. to go to the tourist police, make a left onto Mikh. Iatrou St. and walk 200m.

Nauplion's **Folk Art Museum** (tel. 28 379), winner of the 1981 European Museum of the Year Award, comprehensively displays the styles and weaving techniques of ancient, medieval, and 18th-century Greek clothing (enter on Ipsiladou St. off Sofroni). The exhibits here are superb and include explanations in English (open Wed.-Mon. 9am-2:30pm; closed in Feb; admission 400dr, students 200dr). The **Military Museum,** one block above the Folk Art Museum, has artifacts and high-quality black and white photographs from the burning of Smyrna (İzmir), the population exchanges of the 1920s, and WWII (open Wed.-Mon. 10am-1pm; free). The **archaeological museum** (tel. 27 502), in a Venetian mansion on Syntagma Sq., has a small but esteemed collection of pottery and sympathetic-looking idols, as well as Mycenaean suit of bronze armor (open Wed.-Mon. 8:30am-3pm; admission 400dr). Across from the bus station, near the statue of Kapodistrias, there's a playground in a large, peaceful park; the **carnival** is at the right end of the waterfront.

■ Near Nauplion

Several kilometers south of town, crowded **Tolo** and **Asini** have long, sandy beaches. Northwest from Asini are the remains of the 3rd millennium ancient Asini. The ruins include the walls of an acropolis and remains from several other buildings. **Karathona Beach** is accessible by foot; follow the road which curves around the left-hand side of the Palamidi. There's also a footpath from the parking lot between the Palamidi and the end of Polizoidou St. It runs along the water from the left. The 45-minute walk conceals three quiet, rocky coves. Karathona beach is nothing special, just a thin strip of sand in the middle of nowhere.

Four kilometers northwest of Nauplion on the road to Argos lie the Mycenaean ruins of **Tiryns** (or Tirintha), birthplace of Hercules. Perched atop a 25m-high hill, Tiryns (tel. 22 657), one of the finer prehistoric sites outside of Mycenae, was impregnable during ancient times—that is, until it was captured by the Argives and destroyed in the 5th century BCE. Parts of the stronghold date as far back as 2600 BCE, but most of what remains was built 1000 years later, in the Mycenaean era. The massive walls surrounding the site indicate the immensity of the original fortifications. Standing 8m in height and width, the walls were called "Cyclopean" by ancients who believed only a Cyclops could have lifted stones to build them. They reach a width of 20m on the eastern and southern slopes of ancient acropolis. Inside these structures lurk vaulted galleries. The palace's frescoes are on display in the National Archaeological Museum in Athens. One huge limestone block (the floor of the bathroom) remains (open daily 8am-6:30pm; admission 400dr, students 200dr). The site is easily reached by the Argos bus from Nauplion (every 30min., 175dr).

TOLO (ΤΟΛΟ)

Tolo exists mainly to provide what nearby Nauplion and the archaeological sites lack—a spectacular sandy beach and tons of discoes. That's it—no culture, art, or architecture; just beach, booze, and boogying. Party on.

Orientation and Practical Information   The town is long and thin, arranged around the main street, **Bouboulinas.** After roughly 700m (water on your left), the street curves sharply and becomes **Sekeri St.** Shortly after, the town peters out. There is a **Commercial Bank** on Sekeri St. past the curve (open Mon.-Fri. 8am-1pm). The **OTE** is farther down Sekeri St.; turn right at the blue OTE sign and walk up the hill (open Mon.-Sat. 7:30am-3:10pm).

Buses go from Nauplion every hour on the half-hour, passing through (and stopping in) Asini and Drepano (1:30am-9:30pm, 220dr). **Hydrofoils** run in July and August to Spetses (1½hr., 2550dr); Hydra (2hr., 3850dr); Aegina (3½hr., 6600dr); and Peiraias (4hr., 7000dr); with another line going to Monemvassia (3½hr., 3959dr), and Kythera (8203dr). An expensive **tour boat,** the Pegasus, leaves on Wednesday and Friday on a Poros-Hydra-Spetses cruise (4700dr, roundtrip 7000dr). For reservations or tickets, contact **Tolon Tours** (tel. 59 686), on Bouboulinas St. (open daily 9am-2pm and 5-10pm). They will also arrange for **bicycle rental** in Drepano at 2500dr per day. For **moped rental** try **Moto-Rent** (tel. 21 407), on the beach close to Nauplion (small moped 4000dr per day, large moped 5000dr per day). The **police station** (tel. 59 202), is at the end of town closest to Nauplion; right at the meat market and the first set of stairs on left. Near the bank is the **post office** (open Mon.-Sat. 7:30am-2pm). **Postal Code:** 21056. **Telephone Code:** 0752.

Accommodations   Most of Tolo's hotels are along Bouboulinas or Sekeri St., where rooms and campsites abound. **Hotel Christina** (tel. 59 001), at the edge of town, is close to Nauplion. Offers simple rooms, some with balconies and ocean-front views. (Doubles 8000dr. Triples 9500dr. Quads 11,500dr. Reservations recommended.) **Rooms Mari,** 31 Bouboulinas St. (tel. 59 006, -522) has snazzily decorated black and white rooms right above the beach. (Singles 67500dr. Doubles 8500dr.) **Arcadia Rooms** at 25 Bouboulinas St. (tel. 59 551) provides another option. (Singles 6500dr. Doubles 8000dr. Triples 9600dr.) To camp, try **Sunset Camping** (tel. 59 195). (1000dr per person. 600dr per small tent. 900dr per large tent. 600dr per car.) Or check out **Camping Xeni** (tel. 59 133), on a large stretch of beach (1000dr per person, 600-800dr per tent). To reach Xeni, continue along the road that rings the beach, past the turn-off for Nauplion. It will appear 2km from the center of Tolo.

Food and Entertainment   The food in Tolo is overpriced, and simply not as good as can be found in Nauplion. The beach is what draws people here, and with the frequency of the buses, it can be done in an afternoon. There are several *tavernas* along Bouboulinas and Sekeri St., with prices at the high end of reasonable. One of the cheaper places is **Restaurant Koronis** (spaghetti 800dr). **Taverna Marina** is a typical family-style *taverna* with entrees averaging 1250dr. Look for the hanging innertubes at the door. A large **supermarket** is on Sekeri St.

Tolo's discoes are legendary for miles around. There are three right after the curve in the road: **Gorilla** (cover 1000dr and first drink), **Rainbow** (cover 500dr), and the brand new **Europower** (no cover). For daytime entertainment, try the beach (the closer to Nauplion the better). There are umbrellas (500dr), jet skis (5000dr per hr.), pedal boats (1500dr per hr.), and windsurfing equipment (2000dr per hr.) for rent.

■ Epidavros ΕΠΙΔΑΥΡΟΣ

Henry Miller claimed that amid Epidavros' powerful serenity he heard the pounding "great heart of the world." It's easy to see why—the theater at Epidavros is acoustically impeccable. From the top of its graceful, perfectly preserved 55 tiers of seats, you can hear a *drachma* drop onstage. Even with the midday din of eager tourists and busloads of schoolchildren singing hymns and folk songs, Epidavros, surrounded by pine groves, is endowed with a sense of peacefulness that relaxes frenzied tourists. You'll leave with a serene feeling, in the site's healing tradition.

Try to visit Epidavros on a Friday or Saturday night from late June to mid-August when the **National Theater of Greece** and visiting companies perform plays from the classical Greek canon (Euripides, Sophocles, Aristophanes, etc.). Performances are at 9pm and tickets can be purchased at the theater four hours before showtime. Also buy tickets in advance in Athens at the **Athens Festival Box Office** (tel. (01) 322 14 59; see p. 86). In Nauplion, buy tickets at **Bourtzi Tours** on 9 Thessaloniki St., near the Atlantic Supermarket (tel. 21 249). For performances by the National Theater of Greece, tickets are also available at the **Athens Box Office of the National Theater** (tel. (01) 522 32 42; see p. 86). Tickets cost 3000-4500dr, 2000dr for students. The rule which prohibits children under six is strictly enforced. All performances are in Greek, so bring your favorite translation. **Telephone Code:** 0753.

Unless you're going to Epidavros for the theater, make the small town a daytrip from Nauplion, Athens, Corinth, or a Saronic Gulf Island, since it has few accommodations. Bypass the Xenia and head for cheap lodgings in touristy **Ligouri,** 4km from Epidavros. The **Hotel Alkion** (tel. 22 002; fax 22 552) is just past the turn-off for Epidavros and has A/C, hot water, and a restaurant open for all three meals. (Singles 4500dr. Doubles 7000dr. Triples 8000dr.) If you're in Ligouri for a meal, visit the **Restaurant Oasis** (tel. 22 062), the first place on the road from Nauplion. Here Greeks outnumber tourists, and the owners imbue the place with a festive spirit (pork chops 1200dr). To get to Ligouri, take a taxi (800dr). A **bus** from Nauplion leaves 3 times per day and drops off near two campgrounds at **Paleo Epidavros,** 15km from the site (480dr). On nights of performances, additional **KTEL** buses make a roundtrip to Epidavros, leaving Nauplion at 7:30pm (960dr).

The theater is a grand structure, built in the early 4th century BCE to accommodate 6000 people. In the 2nd century BCE, more tiers were added for a total capacity of 14,000. Despite severe earthquakes that destroyed much of the sanctuary in 522 and 551 CE, the theater was miraculously saved; it is quite well preserved for a Greek theater. Note the restored Corinthian columns which support the entrances. Performances were staged here until the 4th century CE and again in the 20th century. A pine grove surrounding the theater hides it from the entrance path.

While the other key sites in the Argolid (Mycenae, Nauplion, and Tiryns) were built as fortified cities, the small state of Epidavros was designed as a sanctuary for healing. Its ruins, the remains of hospital rooms and sick wards, attest to the blurred boundaries between medicine, magic, and religion common in antiquity. From its founding in the 6th century BCE, Epidavros was dedicated to gods of medicine—first Maleatas, then Apollo, and finally Apollo's son Asclepius.

The **museum** is on the way from the theater to the ruins. The first room includes painted decorations from the ruins and huge stones containing inscriptions of hymns to Apollo and Asclepius and accounts of repairs to the temple. (Theater, site, and museum open May-Oct. Tues.-Sat. 7:30am-7pm; Nov.-Apr. Tues.-Sat. 7:30am-5pm. Admission 1500dr, students 800dr; free (to the theater only) on Sun. Hold onto ticket stub for the museum. Tel. for all 22 009.)

The ruins of the Sanctuary of Asclepius are extensive and can be confusing. Walking from the museum, you will first come across the **Gymnaseum** on your right, which contains the remains of an **odeon** built by the Romans. On your left are the remains of the **stadium**. In front and to the left are the ruins of the **Temple to Asclepius** and the famous **tholos,** thought to have been designed by Polykleitos, the architect of the theater. The *tholos* contains a maze, the purpose of which is unknown. Farther from the theater lie the ruins of the extensive baths built by the Romans before Sulla destroyed and looted the site in 89 BCE.

ELIAS AND ACHAÏA ΗΛΕΙΑΣ ΚΑΙ ΑΧΑΙΑ

In the rural provinces of Elias and Achaïa, tomatoes ripen beneath a blazing sun as beachgoers redden to a similar hue. The area between Pyrgos and Patras, the capitals of Elias and Achaïa, is a vegetable farmer's dream. Corn fields, rimmed with golden-sand beaches, are studded with ancient, Frankish, and Venetian ruins. The locals call these regions of the Peloponnese "tame" as opposed to the "wild" landscape in other parts of Greece. The current tranquility of the Northwest Peloponnese hides centuries of diverse cultural influence. The Achaïans from the Argolid were the first settlers of Achaïa, and in 280 BCE the Achaïan Confederacy was created. In 146 BCE the region fell to the Romans, in 1205 CE it was captured by the Franks, in 1460 it became Turkish property, and from 1687 to 1715 it was a Venetian colony. Ruins from each of these periods stand to this day. In 1828 Achaïa was liberated and has been Greek ever since.

▓ Patras ΠΑΤΡΑΣ

Patras, Greece's third largest city, sprawls noisily along its harbor. It's a transportation center, so menacing semi-trailers crowd the harbor roads and molest pedestrians. New Patras is divided from the older section that encircles the **castle.**

Residents are committed to Patras; most tourists see it as a stopover (ferries run to Italy, the Ionian Islands, and northern Greece). Although to those passing through, it can seem a collection of tour agencies, bars, and women's shoe stores, Patras may convince you to stay. It provides a base to reach much of the Peloponnese, including Olympia, the northern coast, and a resort-free beach in Kalogria. The city itself relieves urban homesickness, has the second largest number of bars and pubs of any European city, and hosts Carnival. From mid-January to Ash Wednesday, Carnival features music, food, and an all-night fete in which the city's port becomes one vast dance floor where Greeks and tourists from all over are bumped and ground.

ORIENTATION AND PRACTICAL INFORMATION

If you're coming from Athens by car, choose between the **New National Road,** an expressway running inland along the Gulf of Corinth, and the slower, more scenic **Old National Road,** which hugs the coast. Those coming from the north can take a ferry from **Antirio** across to **Rio** on the Peloponnese (4 per hr., 7am-11pm, 30min., 270dr per person, 1720dr per car) and hop on bus #6 from Rio to the station, four blocks uphill from the main station, at Kanakari and Aratou St. (30min., 200dr).

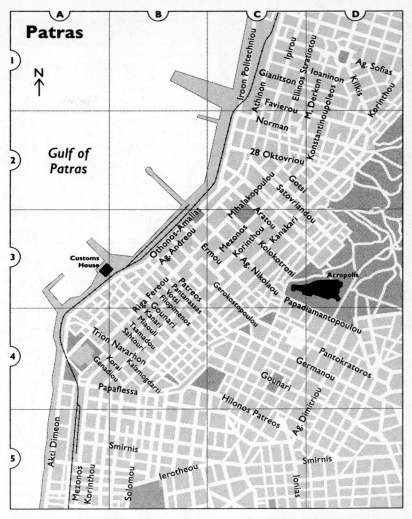

Patras

Gulf of Patras

If you're arriving by boat from Brindisi or any of the Ionian islands, turn right as you leave customs onto **Iroon Polytechniou Street** to get to the center of town. From the bus station to the train station, the road curves and its name changes to **Othonos Amalias Street.** Just past the train station is the large **Trion Simahon Square,** with palm trees, cafés, kiosks, and a large floral clock. **Ag. Nikolaou** runs from the square and intersects the major east-west streets of the city. From the corner of Ag. Nikolaou and Mezanos, three blocks from the water, turn right. You will see **Georgiou Square,** the city's largest and busiest square. Between Georgiou Sq. and Olgas Sq. (3 blocks to the west) is the heart of new Patras.

Tourist Office: (tel. 65 33 58), outside customs, on the waterfront just before Iroon Polytechniou. Multilingual staff gives free maps and bus and boat timetables; helps with accommodations. Open Mon.-Sat. 7:30am-9pm, Sun. 2:30-9pm.

Tourist Police: (tel. 65 18 93 or 65 25 12), in the new office at the customs pier, offers same services as tourist office. Lots of pamphlets. Open 7am-11pm.

Consulates: British, 2 Votsi St. (tel. 27 73 29), on the corner of Othonos Amalias St. Variable hours, though most often Mon.-Fri. 9:30am-1pm.

Banks: National Bank (tel. 22 56 56), Trion Simahon Sq., on the waterfront, just past the train station. Open Mon.-Thurs. 8am-2pm and 6-7:30pm, Fri. 8am-1:30pm and 6-8:30pm, Sat.-Sun. 11am-1pm and 6-8:30pm. Also at customs (open daily 7-10am and noon-8pm) and at the mobile post office just outside.

OTE: At customs. Open daily 7am-9pm. For collect international calls, go to the OTE at Trion Simahon Sq. Open Mon.-Fri. 7am-2:30pm, Sat.-Sun. 7:20am-1pm. Also at the corner of Kanakari and Gounari St., up from the waterfront.

Trains: Station (tel. 27 36 94), on Othonos Amalias St., 5 blocks to the right down the waterfront from customs. To Athens (8 per day, 2580dr) via Corinth (1470dr); Kalamata (2 per day, 6hr., 1500dr); and Pyrgos (8 per day until 8:30pm, 2hr., 820dr); transfer here for Olympia. Expect delays and a shortage of seats, especially on the trains to Athens. Even if you have a railpass, reserve a seat at the ticket window before taking a train.

Buses: KTEL (tel. 62 38 86, -7), 3½ blocks to the right, down the waterfront from customs, on Ag. Andreas. To Athens (every hr. until 9:30pm, 4hr., 3200dr); Killini (in summer only, 8am and 2:45pm, 1½hr., 1200dr); Kalamata (2 per day, 4hr., 3600dr); Pyrgos (11 per day, 1600dr); Tripolis (2 per day, 4hr., 2700dr); Ioannina (4 per day, 3650dr); Thessaloniki (3 per day, 7350dr); Kalavrita (3 per day, 1450dr); and Egion (every hr., 7am-10pm, 700dr). Buses to Lefkas leave from the intersection of Favierou and Konstantinoupoleos St., several blocks up from customs. **OSE** buses leave from the train station for Athens and Methoni. Some ferry companies also run their own buses with A/C to Athens (2500dr).

Ferries: From Patras, boats reach Cephalonia, Ithaka, and Corfu, in addition to Italy's Brindisi, Bari, and Ancona. Most boats depart at night; check-in is 2hr. before departure. For ferries to Brindisi or the Ionian Islands, show up at customs at the main terminal. Ferries to Bari and Ancona leave from a pier 1km to the west. Ticket prices fluctuate tremendously. In general, expect a discount if you are under 26 years old, a student, or on a railpass and going to Brindisi. In high season, it's a good idea to make telephone reservations with a travel agent. The waterfront is coated with travel agencies all selling **ferry tickets** for roughly the same prices: Cephalonia and Ithaka 2800dr (usually 1 boat per day), Brindisi (9000dr, 8250dr with a student card, roughly 5000dr with a railpass). Italy-bound ferries stop over at Corfu. For tickets to Italy, try **Mediterranean Star,** 34 Othonas Amalias St. (tel. 27 02 61, -18 28). Open daily 9am-9:30pm. For tickets to Cephalonia and Ithaka try **Strintzis Tours,** 14 Othonas Amalias St. (tel. 66 26 02). Open daily 9am-9pm.

Luggage Storage: 250dr per day. Ask at "Dafni" Travel, 5 Othonos Amalias St. (tel. 42 70 29), for InterRail information or at the tourist police.

International Bookstore: Lexis Bookstore (tel. 22 09 19), near the University on Mezonos (#3840). Provides a decent number of English, German, and French books from Dickens to Jackie Collins, but most of the store's titles are Greek.

Laundromat: Zaïmi and Korinthou (tel. 62 01 19), up 4 blocks from the waterfront. Wash and dry 1500dr. Open Mon.-Sat. 9am-9pm.

Hospital: Open on alternate days, **Ag. Andreas** (tel. 22 38 12) is 3-4km up Gounari and **Rio Hospital of Patras University** (tel. 99 91 11) is 5km away. The **Red Cross Emergency Station** (tel. 150), at Karoloua and Ag. Dionysiou St., several blocks from customs, dispenses first aid. For an **ambulance,** dial 166.

Post Office: (tel. 27 77 59, -46 42), Mezonos Enzieni St. Walk 2 blocks towards the bus station from customs and make a left onto Zaïmi—it's 3 blocks up on the left. Open Mon.-Fri. 8am-8pm. Also a **mobile post office** just outside customs. Open whenever the ferries come in. **Postal Code:** 26001.

Telephone Code: 061.

ACCOMMODATIONS

Cheap accommodations are threaded through the tangle of buildings on Ag. Andreas St., one block up and parallel to the waterfront. The tourist police has listings of hotels and pensions. C and D class listings are cheaper.

Youth Hostel, 68 Iroon Polytechniou St. (tel. 65 21 52). From the ferry, turn left and walk 1½km. This gorgeous turn-of-the-century mansion, now overrun by weeds, sat empty for 40 years after it was used as a German headquarters in WWII. It's a bit cramped (8 beds per room), but has a good location, an outdoor seating area, serves beer, and through the trees you can see the harbor. No curfew. Metered telephone for calls. Check-out 10:30am. Bed 1500dr. Sheets 100dr.

Pension Nikos, 3 Patreos St. (tel. 62 37 57), off the waterfront. Friendly owner, negotiable prices. Singles 3500dr. Doubles 5000dr, with bath 6000dr.

Hotel Hellas, 14 Ag. Nikolaou (tel. 27 33 52), has clean rooms and a huge hall bathtub in an ancient building. Singles 3000dr. Doubles 6000dr. Triples 7200dr.

Hotel Parthenon, 25 Ermou St. (tel. 27 34 21), off Ag. Andreas. Big rooms fill this old building. Singles 4300dr. Doubles 6200dr. Triples 7100dr.

Kavouri Camping (tel. 42 21 45), 2km east of town, next to the Patras swimming pool. Crowded, but cheap. Take bus #1 from in front of Ag. Dionysios Church; walk up Norman St. 1 block and turn left. 650dr per person. 480dr per car. 300dr per small tent. 700dr per large tent.

Camping: Rio Camping (tel. 99 15 85), 8km east of Patras. 1100dr per person. 900dr per tent. 600dr per car. **Rio Mare** (tel. 99 22 63), near Rio Camping. 1200dr per person. 800dr per small tent. 1100dr per large tent. 750dr per car.

FOOD

Food in Patras may sometimes feel far away from you and in between travel agencies. Restaurants along the harbor serve the obvious overpriced fish, so take to the side streets for your meals. If you look for white plastic chairs, you will doubtless be led to a cramped "fast-food" establishment selling cheap *gyros* (250dr) and *souvlaki*. These establishments are, for the most part, interchangeable, as are their *gyros*.

A great, nameless fish *taverna* lies past the hostel on the water. It's run by the local fishermen's club, so everything's fresh and their prices are the cheapest on the water (entrees 400-1100dr). There's live entertainment (if you can call it that) and the fried sardines, beer, and wine are all free, courtesy of the gracious fishermen.

A **fruit stand** is on the corner of Ermou and Ag. Andreas and another sits under a canopy at the corner of Aratou and Korinthou, up a few blocks from the water. **Bakeries** are most easily found around the intersection of Karolou and Ag. Dionysiou. The **Acropole Restaurant,** 39 Othonos-Amalia St. (tel. 27 98 09), on the harbor, is a favorite haunt of tourists who are not-so-fresh off the ferries. Acropole serves your Greek favorites cheaply. A vegetarian special runs 1900dr in the summer, including entree, feta cheese, bread, and drink. The new **Europa center** (tel. 43 48 01), at the corner of Othonos Amalias and Karolou, east past the KTEL bus station, is a bright pink establishment which caters to all the needs of a traveler: tickets to Italy, tourist information, a café and restaurant (*moussaka* 1200dr and baked zucchini 1500dr), and clean toilets (open daily 6:30am-3am). **Thelasses Restaurant** (tel. 33 99 26), past the ferry drop-off point, near the British consulate on Votsi St., has varied cuisine including mixed seafood (2000dr), squid (1000dr), and frog's legs (2000dr).

ENTERTAINMENT

It may not be the city of light, but Patras may be the city of light beer. Perhaps not immediately apparent, Patras' tiny side streets hide small but ubiquitous bars and cafés thinly populated in the summer months. From May to September, people drink in Rio. A number of outdoor cafés set up camp in the streets in summer, drawing decent crowds. Notable are **Caffé Luz,** off Olgas Square, on Aratoy St., and its neighbor **Napoli,** for beer, coffee, and backgammon (they supply the boards).

Blue Monday, along Radinou St., one street east of Olgas Sq., serves ordinary café fare, but play on average more Elvis Presley than any other bar on the Peloponnese. It takes its name from an old rockabilly song and silver-screen idols provide labels for each chair (try Charlie Chaplin, or Cary Grant and Katherine Hepburn—placed beside each other, of course—or browse). Look for its red Coke-bottle cap sign.

SIGHTS

The largest Orthodox cathedral in Greece, **Agios Andreas,** is dedicated to St. Andrew, who lived and died in Patras. As he felt himself unworthy to die on the same kind of cross as Jesus, St. Andrew was martyred by crucifixion on an X-shaped version. A little more than 10 years ago, the Catholic Church in Rome presented the Bishop of Patras with the saint's head. To the right of the cathedral is the old church of St. Andrew, which houses a small **well** said to have been built by the saint himself. It can be reached by a doorway to the right of the church, and legend has it that whoever drinks from this well will return to Patras again. Dress modestly; photography and videotaping are prohibited (open daily 9am-dusk). To get here, follow the water to the west end of town, roughly 1½km from the port (20min.).

The Venetian **castle** and surrounding park dominate the city. This 13th-century fortress was built on the ruins of the ancient acropolis, once the site of the temple of the Panachaïan Athena. Parts of the walls are still intact and the view from the surviving battlements is calming. To get here, follow Ag. Nikolaou St. inland from town; you'll see the daunting staircase up ahead (open Tues.-Sat. 8:30am-5pm, Sun. 8:30am-3pm). **Taxis** (tel. 22 28 29) also make the trek here. Up from Vas. Georgiou Sq. at the **Ancient Odeum** the Patras Festival holds a series of performances here during daylight hours (open Tues.-Sun.). Work out your aggressions at the local Luna Park carnival's **bumper-car rink,** Athinon and Ag. Sofias St., one block up and four blocks left from customs (open in evenings from 7pm onwards; 500dr for 15min.). The **Archaeological Museum,** 42 Mezonos (tel. 27 50 70), next to Olgas Sq. at the corner of Mezonos St. and Aratou, exhibits vases, statues, and other archaeological finds (open Tues.-Sun. 8:30am-3pm; free).

A traipse leads to **Achaïa Clauss winery,** 9km southeast of town. Its founder, Baron von Clauss, was dazed with lust for a woman named Daphne. Upon her death, he made a wine in her honor with his blackest grapes, called *Mavrodaphne,* "Black Daphne." Take bus #7 (20min., 185dr) from the intersection of Kolokotroni and Kanakari St. (tours daily 9am-7:30pm; off season daily 9am-5pm; free).

The **carnival season** in Patras begins around January 17 every year and lasts until Ash Wednesday. The locals describe *karnavali* as an indefinable energy that sweeps through town. With feasts every night, people of all ages dance in the streets, Patras's bash may be the best carnival in Greece. In 1995, the Gypsy Kings performed here, and on the last Sunday (before Easter) a 12-hour marathon parade takes over the streets. The Carnival's last night sees a ritual burning of King Carnival, an open party on the harbor lasting all night with habitual drinking. Call the Youth Hostel (tel. 65 21 52); they provide program details. For nearly a 100km radius, hotel rooms are booked for much of Carnival—advance reservations are a necessity.

■ Near Patras

To have fun, people in Patras seem to want to leave. As with many large coastal cities, a beach town satellite exists minutes away to give people a place to go. **Rio** is a small city, roughly 8km to the northeast of Patras. **Rion Beach,** however, can seem much father than that. It has no real services and most of its facilities consist of bar stools and mixing equipment. This stretch of beach bars, clubs, restaurants, and discoes is where Patras' nightlife transports itself in the summer months.

One of the more popular of the clubs is undoubtedly the **KU.** Famous in the area for the crowd it draws (for perhaps no other reason than to see each other being drawn), it opens at 11pm. Except for KU and a handful of others, most beach bars have small signs placed in out-of-the-way locations. A few others to try might be **O-**

9 (tel. 99 39 03), at the beginning of the strip, and the **Beer Society** (tel. 99 42 20), which opened in 1996 and has a vast outdoor garden drinking area. The Rion Beach area also hosts some of Patras' more popular restaurants. **Kallipso** (tel. 43 29 44) serves excellent fresh fish and octopus (1200dr), and there is a large glass tank outside where you can observe the last moments of the fish you may be eating soon.

To reach Rion, buses run until 10pm. You may have to take a cab home (2000dr). Take the #6 bus from the Kamakari and Araton St. (30min., 200dr). Once past the hospital, look for Hotel Apollo or the Castello Restaurant; this is the nearest bus stop and is located on Somerset St. Walk approximately 500m past the Deal with Taste restaurant. At the intersection, turn left and the strip will, in 200m, open to view and an imposingly large **castle** will face you. Vast, medieval-looking Rion Castle is free and open until 7pm. Since it's empty, it's an ideal haunt for a picnic or sun-bath.

Continuing past Rio, a one-hour train ride east from Patras leads to **Diakofto.** From here, take the tiny rack-railway train and marvel at the glorious landscape (480dr). Midway to Kalavrita the train stops in Zachlorou to allow hikers and donkey renters to climb to **Mega Spilaeou.** As the train ambles up the mountainous range, a waterfall bubbles through the rocks alongside the train tracks. If you arrive hours before the next train, catch the **bus** to Kalavrita on the sidewalk in front of the pharmacy and hotel (1020dr). The folks at the newspaper shop down the street have schedule information. The bus trip, which winds through cherry orchards and tiny mountain villages leads to **Kalavrita,** a popular **ski resort,** famous for its plane trees, charming homes, and tranquil atmosphere. A Venetian fortress, "the castle of Orea," stands outside town. There's a **bank** on 25th Martiou, which leads to the main square. From the train station, follow Ag. Alexiou St. up into the town—after four blocks the **OTE** is at the corner of Ag. Alexiou and Kommenou St. (open Mon.-Sat. 7:30am-10pm). **Buses** leave from the station at the end of Kallimani St. The **police** (tel. 23 333) are three blocks beyond the OTE, off Ag. Alexiou at 7 Fotina St. (open 24hr.). The main square is across from the large church a few blocks up from the train station. The **Hotel Paradissos** (tel. 22 210, -303), on Kallimani St., offers pleasant rooms with clean bath. (Singles 5000dr. Doubles 7000dr.) Down the street close to the main square, **Hotel Maria** (tel. 22 296), offers impressive rooms with bath. (Doubles 8500dr.) The **post office** is in the square (open Mon.-Fri. 7:30am-2pm). **Postal Code:** 25001. **Telephone Code:** 0692.

The famous monastery of **Mega Spilaeou** is 9km away. To get there, either take the bus from Diakofto (1km away) or a taxi (3800dr roundtrip; the driver will wait 30min.). A monk will greet you and give you a guided tour through the museum and church. The extensive museum collection includes an intricate 350-year-old cross and an icon of the Theotokos (Mother of God), said to have been made by St. Luke. Built in 362 CE, the monastery is 1000m above sea level.

Five **trains** per day leave Kalavrita, stopping at Zachlorou, close to the monastery, on their way to Diakofto. Trains leave from here for Patras (last train at 6:45pm, 280dr) and Athens (last train at 7:41pm, 950dr).

■ Killini ΚΥΛΛΗΝΗ

Most travelers come to Killini simply to catch the ferries to Zakinthos and Cephalonia. If you're stuck here for any length of time, hunker down at Killini's broad, sandy beach. The few tourists—mostly Greek, French, and Italian—who come here neither spoil the town's uncommercial air nor rush its leisurely tempo.

The path to town from the dock leads to the **police** (tel. (0623) 92 202; no English spoken). The **port police** (tel. (0623) 92 211) are on the dock (open 24hr.). From the police station, walk a few blocks along the water on your left to reach the **OTE,** inside a corner store (open in summer daily 8am-1pm and 5-10pm). The **post office** is a few blocks farther down, on a side street leading inland (**postal code:** 27068; open daily 7:30am-2pm). **Buses** travel to Killini from Pyrgos (3 per day until 2:35pm, 1hr., 1000dr) and Patras (2 per day, 1½hr., 1260dr). If you miss the bus from Patras, take the bus to Lehena (10 per day, 1½hr., 700dr); from there, buses go to Killini

(11:20am and 2:45pm, 20min., 120dr). **Taxis** (look for them by the port or on the road before the police station; open 24hr.) also go from Lehena to Killini (1500-1800dr). A daily bus to Athens leaves Killini at 9:30am. **Ferries** sail from Killini to Zakinthos (7 per day, 1½hr., 1400dr) and Cephalonia (2 per day, 3hr., 2800dr). Buy tickets on the dock.

The cheapest rooms in Killini are "Rooms to Let" along Glaretzas St., one block above the beach and parallel to the water. The **Glaretzas Hotel** (tel. (0623) 92 397) has well lit, fresh rooms with Scandinavian-revival decor. (Singles with bath 5000dr. Doubles with bath 8500dr.) The Frankish **Chlemoutsi Castle** and the mineral springs of **Loutra Killinis,** a well manicured resort with a long beach, are 20km from Killini. Getting to either is difficult unless you have your own transportation or are willing to pay for a taxi (1200dr to the castle, 3000dr to Loutra). From the square, buses leave for Loutra (6 per day, 140dr), and drop off at the turn-off to the castle, the mineral springs, and amid the camping area, **Camping Killinis** (tel. (0623) 96 259). The campgrounds are close to the sea, with a market and hot showers. (1200dr per person. 700dr per car. 720dr per small tent. 900dr per large tent. Electricity 490dr.) Three buses per day leave Loutra for the castle. Nearby is **Karitena,** the village pictured on the 5000dr bill. The birthplace of Kolokotronis, Karitena has ruins of a Frankish castle and a 13th-century church to St. Nicholas. Its beauty may entice you to stay. **Stamata Kondopoulos** (tel. (0623) 31 206) has rooms near the post office. (Singles 2500dr. Doubles 4200dr.)

■ Olympia ΟΛΥΜΠΙΑ

Were it not for the ruins of the site of the ancient Olympic games, modern Olympia would be a pleasant little town with absolutely no reason for tourists to set foot in it. As it stands, Olympia is as multicultural as the modern games that trace their heritage here. Walk the streets and hear English, Greek, French, German, Italian, and Japanese—and that's just from the restauranteurs.

ORIENTATION AND PRACTICAL INFORMATION

Modern Olympia essentially consists of a 1km main street, **Kondili Avenue.** The bus will drop you off across from tourist information. Head out of town and left for a five-minute walk to the ruins and the new museum. On the other side of town, towards Pirgos, sports enthusiasts will appreciate the **Museum of the Olympic Games** (tel. 22 544), which houses ancient sports paraphernalia. Located on Angerinou St., it's two blocks uphill from Kondili Ave. (open Mon.-Sat. 8am-3:30pm, Sun. 9am-4:30pm; admission 500dr, students free). In summer, the tourist shops all open late (10:30am) and close late (11pm). Since the town caters mainly to tourists, most restaurants open at 8am and close after 1am.

Tourist Office: (tel. 23 100), Kondili Ave., on the east side of town, towards the ruins. Open May-Sept. daily 9am-9pm; Oct.-April daily 11am-5pm.

Bank: National Bank, on Kondili Ave., offers **currency exchange.** Open Mon.-Thurs. 8am-2pm, Fri. 8am-1:30pm.

OTE: Kondili Ave., past the post office. Open Mon.-Fri. 7:30am-3:10pm.

Buses: The bus stops directly across from the tourist information shack, which has an up-to-date schedule posted outside. Buses go to Pirgos (15 per day, 6:30am-9:45pm, 40min., 340dr) and Tripolis (Mon.-Sat. 3 per day, Sun. 2 per day, 3½hr., 2050dr). Change at Pirgos for other points in the western Peloponnese.

English Bookstore: Galerie Orpheas, Kondili Ave., on the east end of town. Carries a pricey selection of guidebooks and classics. Compared to its French and German sections, the English-language bookcase is small. Open daily 8am-11pm.

Hospital: (tel. (0621) 22 222) in Pirgos, (tel. (0624) 22 222) in Olympia. Olympia uses Pirgos' hospital, but has a **health center** of its own. Walk away from the ruins down Kondili St. Before the church (on your left), turn left. Continue straight, and after the road winds right, then left, take a left. Open daily 7am-2pm.

Police: 1 Em. Kountsa St. (tel. 22 100). Open 9am-9pm, but someone's there 24hr.
Post Office: On a nameless, uphill side street just past the tourist information center. Open Mon.-Fri. 7:30am-2pm. **Postal Code:** 27065.
Telephone Code: 0624.

ACCOMMODATIONS

If all you want is a cheap place to crash, head for the youth hostel. Otherwise, choose from dozens of cheap hotels, most of which offer private baths, balconies, and modern rooms. Private rooms in Olympia are surprisingly uncrowded. Prices vary but hover around 5000dr per double. They are 20-40% less in off season.

Youth Hostel, 18 Kondili Ave. (tel. 22 580). Membership not needed for 1-night stay, no curfew. Check-out 10am. 1400dr per day. Breakfast 400dr.

Hotel Hermes (tel. 22 577), Kondili Ave. At the end of town, just before the entrance for Camping Olympia. Singles 4000dr. Doubles 5500dr. Show your *Let's Go* to receive prices quoted here.

Pension Possidon (tel. 22 567) offers clean rooms. Take a left at the National Bank and go uphill 2 blocks. Doubles 6000dr.

"Rooms to Let": Ask at the **Anesti Restaurant** (tel. 22 644), Avgerinou St., for new rooms with bath, hot water, and balconies. Doubles 5000dr. Or, inquire at the **Ambrosia Restaurant** (tel. 22 916), from which the Spiliopoulou family rents pleasant rooms. Doubles 5000dr. Mention *Let's Go* and get a 10% discount.

Camping Alfios (tel. 22 950, -1), 1km trek uphill from the western edge of town. Luxurious, with a pool, café, and minimarket. 1200dr per person. 700dr per car. 750dr per small tent. 900dr per large tent. Electricity 700dr. Student discounts.

Camping Diana (tel. 22 314), next to the sports museum. Offers a clean pool, hot water, and breakfast (700dr). 1300dr per person. 800dr per car. 900dr per small tent. 1200dr per large tent. Electricity 700dr. Ask about student discounts.

Camping Olympia (tel. 22 745), 1km west on the road to Pirgos, has a larger pool and shady sites. 1150dr per person. 630dr per car. 760dr per small tent. 880dr per large tent. Electricity 630dr. Free pool for guests. 20% student discount.

FOOD

Most restaurants on Kondili Ave. are cramped and overpriced. A walk toward the railroad station and away from the busloads of tours reveals some charming *tavernas*. **O Kladeus,** along the road to Olympia's train station (its sign is obvious), is the *taverna* you've been waiting for. The food varies—expect fish (900dr) and stuffed tomatoes (1100dr). The dirt floor, ramshackle canopy, ragged table settings, and the mysterious, potent "house wine" set the mood. Go early (7pm) so you can have it all to yourself. Just before O Kladeus, the management of **Ambrosia** (tel. 23 414) serves great food in a white building (entrees 800-1250dr). Along Kondili Ave., the **Aegean Restaurant** (tel. 22 904) offers *moussaka* (1350dr) and stuffed tomatoes (1100dr; open daily 8am-midnight). The **Strouka** pastry shop, on the road to the Museum of Olympic Games, serves yogurt with honey (400dr).

■ Ancient Olympia

This legendary site between the Kladeo and Alphios Rivers was not a city, but an event. Here, the leaders of rival city states shed their armor and congregated in peace to enjoy the Olympic games and make offerings to the gods. Only game officials were permitted in the sacred town of Olympia. The center of town was reserved for the **Altis,** a walled enclosure or sacred grove of Zeus. On the far east side were the **stadium** and the **echo stoa,** which was said to have had a seven-fold echo. Facilities for both administrators and participants comprised the remaining three sides of the Altis. Over the centuries, council houses and treasuries were added to the site. In addition, victors often built monuments to the gods here.

The site's dimensions remain impressive, although the ruins are not particularly well preserved. The setting is also striking for its natural beauty and tranquility. Few

ARCADIA

sections are cordoned off and you can walk or climb on the colossal remains of the Temple of Zeus. A guide and map are vital, as the ruins are poorly marked. Two thorough guides are available at the site—the red *Olympia* by Spiros Photinos (2000dr) and the blue *Guide to the Museum and Sanctuary* by A. and N. Yalouris (2500dr). The thigh-high remains of the **Gymnasium,** dating from the 2nd century BCE, lie inside the main gate. To the left as you enter is the **Prytaneion,** with its sacred hearth. Past the Gymnasium stand the re-erected columns of the **Palaestra.** This building was the wrestling school, a place for athletes to practice and dress and philosophers to ruminate. The next group of buildings includes the **workshop of Phidias,** the famous artist (supposedly the creator of the ivory and gold statue of Athena for the Parthenon), who was commissioned to produce a sculpture for the site. His tools, terra-cotta molds, and a cup bearing his name turned up during excavations. Farther on is the huge **Leonidaion,** the former lodgings of game officials.

The gigantic **Temple of Zeus** dominated the entire complex. Parts of the original mosaic floor can still be seen on the temple base. The nave of the temple once housed Phidias' 13m ivory and gold statue of Zeus on his throne, reckoned by the Greeks to be one of the **seven wonders of the ancient world.** Emperor Theodosius ordered that the gold and ivory statue be brought to Constantinople, where it was destroyed by fire in 475 CE. On the north edge of the Altis are the dignified remains of the **Temple of Hera.** Built in the 7th century BCE, it is the oldest and most well preserved building on the site, as well as the oldest Doric temple in Greece. Originally built for both Zeus and Hera, it was devoted solely to the goddess when Zeus moved to separate quarters in the south. The temple testifies to the ancient worship of female deities, fecundity, and mother earth. The **Olympic flame** is still lit here, then borne to the site of the modern games by the necessary vehicles, runners, school children, Hell's Angels, and anyone else wishing to join the panoply.

The archway on the east end of the Altis leads to the **stadium.** As originally constructed, the arena's artificial banks could accommodate 40,000 spectators. The **judges' stand** is still in place, as are the starting and finishing lines. Beyond the stadium flows the Alphios River, said to run underground all the way to Sicily, information which Hercules once found handy when he had to clean the Augean stables (tel. 22 517; site open daily 8am-7pm; admission 1200dr, students 600dr). **Free public bathrooms** and water fountains are inside the site.

The gleaming **New Museum** (tel. 22 742), across the street from the site, is set among marble pavilions and tree-lined avenues. It houses a large collection of well displayed statues, including the Baby Dionysus attributed to the 4th-century BCE sculptor Praxiteles, and a number of figurines including the **Little Man with the Big Erection** pictured on postcards throughout the country. It also contains two impressive constructions made of surviving pieces of the pediments of the Temple of Zeus and miniature reconstructions of the site as it might have appeared in antiquity (open Tues.-Sun. 8am-7pm; admission 1200dr, students 600dr; cameras with flash 500dr; video cameras 1000dr).

ARCADIA ΑΡΚΑΔΙΑ

Poets since Theocritus have fancied Arcadia as the archetypal scene of pastoral pleasure. Gods, too, appreciated the area—Pan and Dionysus chose this lush, mountain-ringed land as the site of their gleeful dances. Rural serenity can still be found in the hidden bays, deep green vegetation, dramatic mountains, and vast fir forests. Elsewhere, as in the bustling metropolis of Tripolis, the modern era has brought a rumble of buses and cargo to the fields where satyrs once cavorted.

■ Tripolis ΤΡΙΠΟΛΗ

Tripolis is the transportation hub of Arcadia. Its crowded sidewalks and perilous streets, negotiated by motorists who demonstrate their driving prowess by narrowly missing pedestrians, can initially be dismaying. Buses to the wonderful mountain villages are infrequent, and travelers may have to spend the night. If you stay, don't despair; Tripolis has pleasant squares with cafés, churches, trees, and a tourist-free atmosphere (simultaneously a compliment and indictment of this noisy, commercial city). Nightlife may be infrequent and the traffic appalling, but Tripolis's integrity rests in its unspoiled, modern concrete charm.

ORIENTATION AND PRACTICAL INFORMATION

Best to think of Tripolis as a cross. At its joint is **Agiou Vasiliou,** a large square marked by the Church of Agios Vasiliou. The square is the geographical center of the city. Four other squares form the ends of the cross along the four roads that radiate out from Ag. Vasiliou. Most buses arrive at Arcadia station in **Kolokotronis Square,** the square to the east of the center. Georgiou St. will take you from here to Ag. Vasiliou, with the OTE, tourist office, and post office located off side streets. Facing the Church of Ag. Vasiliou, take the street on your left (Ethnikis Antistasis St.) to reach **Petrinou Square,** home to the police and recognizable by the large Neoclassical Maliaropouli theater. This is the north part of the cross and, along with Kolokotronis Sq., sees most of the city's activity. Continue along Ethnikis Antistasis (the main shopping street), looking to your right to find the **park** (occupying about eight city blocks) and a vast open square with a 5-m-high statue of Kolokotrouis. The blocks around the park house most boutiques, cafés, clubs, and hotels, and provide the best outpost for people-watching and for the only vital signs of Tripolis' nightlife. If you don't have a map, try to get one—the tourist office usually has some.

The **tourist office** (tel. 23 18 44) is in the town hall down Ethnikis Antistasis St. (look for the Greek flag and colored windows). This new office provides maps, books, and information on Arcadia (open Mon.-Fri. 8am-12:30pm). The **National Bank** (tel. 22 54 89 or 24 29 53), on Ethnikis Antistasis, is one block from Ag. Vasiliou Sq. It offers **currency exchange** (open Mon.-Thurs. 8am-2pm, Fri. 8am-1:30pm). A 24-hour **ATM** is confusingly located 50m from the bank's entrance—look for the metal door on the left. There's also an **OTE,** #29 Octovriou 28th St. (tel. 22 63 99). From Ag. Vasiliou Sq., take Eth. Antistasis St. and bear left immediately on 28 Octovriou St.—you'll see its tower (open 24hr.). The **train station** (tel. 24 12 13) is 1km west of Kolokotronis Sq. Go through the bus station and turn right—the station is at the end of the street. Four trains per day go to Athens (4hr., 1500dr), Corinth (2½hr., 900dr), and Argos (1½hr., 590dr); three per day go to Kalamata (3hr., 860dr). **Arcadias Station** (tel. 22 25 60) sends **buses** to Athens (13 per day, 2hr., 2600dr); Dimitsana (8:30am and 6:15pm, 1½hr., 1100dr); Pirgos (8:30am and 6:15pm, 4hr., 2400dr); Andritsena (11:45am and 9:45pm, 1hr., 1300dr); and Megalopolis (9 per day, 4:45am-9:45pm, 30min., 550dr). **Blue buses** leave from the kiosk at Platia Areus for Tegea and Mantinea (every hr., 15min., 190dr). Buses go from the **KTEL Messinia and Laconia** bus depot (tel. 24 20 86), across from the train station, to Kalamata (3 per day, 1400dr); Pylos (2 per day, 2150dr); Sparta (12 per day, 6:30am-9pm, 1hr., 900dr); or Patras (6am and 2:30pm, 3½hr., 2700dr).

There's an **English bookstore** on Ag. Vasiliou Sq. that sells newspapers, magazines, and exclusively (English-language) pulp—Jackie Collins, Grisham, et. al. A **hospital** (tel. 238 542) is located on Panargadon Rd. (on the far western ring of the city). Walk due west from Ag. Vasiliou. The road becomes E. Stavrou, which intersects with Panargadon after 500m—at the intersection, turn left. After another 300m, look right. The **police** (tel. 22 24 11) are on Ethnikis Antistasis St., off the left-hand side of Petrinou Sq. (English spoken; open 24hr.). The **post office** (tel. 22 54 29) is on Plapouta St. With your back to the church in Ag. Vasiliou Sq., go straight on V. Pavlou St. (away from the church). Take the first right (Nikitara St.), and after one block, the post office is across the street (open Mon.-Fri. 7:30am-2pm). **Postal Code:** 22100. **Telephone Code:** 071.

Accommodations Tripolis is better suited for business conventions than for budget travelers, boasting numerous bloated and sub-par hotels with spotty lighting. Camping near Tripolis is non-existent, and impromptu camping illegal. But if you stay by the park, you do have some options. Your best bet is **Hotel Anactoricon** (tel. 22 25 45), along Ethnikis Antistasis two blocks before the park. It's disarmingly clean and almost elegant—note the brass and woodwork. (Singles 3000dr, with bath 6000dr. Doubles 6000dr, with bath 8000dr.) **Hotel Artemis** (tel. 22 52 21), right on the park, is a little pricey, but it offers large rooms with TVs. (Singles 7000dr. Doubles 10,000dr.) **Hotel Alex,** 26 Vas. Georgios St. (tel. 22 34 65), between Kolokotronis Sq. and Ag. Vasiliou Sq., offers standard rooms in varying shades of puce. Ask for a room at the back, because the noise from the nearby bus station can make Tripolis seem like the city that never sleeps. (Singles 4500dr, with bath 6000dr. Doubles 7000dr, with bath 8000dr.)

Food, Entertainment, and Sights The best food in Tripolis borders the park. The obvious choices stuff the square with chairs. Instead, look along the side streets for smaller enclaves and cheaper fare. **Kipos Sosoli Restaurant,** located in a cute garden-like backyard one block off Ethnikis Antistasis on Pavlou St., offers entrees under 1500dr. The menu is in Greek, but the staff will patiently translate for you. **Restaurant Lido** serves large portions of mostly European fare in a large outdoor dining area on the far west side of the park's square (spaghetti 900dr, pizza 1200dr). To the left of the mounted, bronze Kolokotronis statue, the **Park Chalet** restaurant offers ocean perch (1200dr), chicken with lemon (1300dr), and a "Greek country salad" (800dr). Overall, Tripolis lacks much culinary inspiration, and if you subscribe to the quick-fix theory of dining out, try **Brandy's** on Ethnikis Anistasis, one block past the theater. Eat with Bogart, James Dean, Elvis, and Marilyn Monroe movie posters (*souvlaki* 250dr, hamburgers 400dr; open daily noon-midnight).

Summer entertainment in Tripolis is provided by cultural events 400m from Ag. Vasiliou Sq. and at nearby villages. Posters advertise dance groups, theatrical performances, and choirs. Also, keep an eye out for "ΙΕΡΑ ΠΑΝΗΓΥΡΙΣ" (Iera Panigyris) signs, advertising festivals in villages. The most excitement is in the squares, where residents hang out and cultural groups perform. During Easter the town's bishop roasts a lamb in one of the squares, and all attendants eat for free. Other impromptu events of a more secular nature (dancing, drinking, and debauchery) take place nightly. Traveling companies and local performance groups stage shows in the attractive **Maliaropoulio Theater,** which dominates Petrinou Sq. All are in Greek. If you're interested, ask at the tourist office (tickets 1000-4000dr).

The new **Archaeological Museum** (tel. 24 21 48) is on Evangelistrias St., in a yellow flower-bedecked building. From Kolokotronis Sq. to Ag. Vasiliou Sq., take the first left and turn left again. It's full of pottery from the Paleokastro tombs—look for a giant amphora flanking the entrance (open Tues.-Sun. 8:30am-3pm; admission 500dr, students 400dr). The large blue **Church of Agios Vasilios** is in the square of the same name (open to visitors 9am-dusk except during services). Check out the shops underneath the church—they're great places to buy religious art.

■ Andritsena ΑΝΔΡΙΤΣΑΙΝΑ

Andritsena is falling apart, but that's what makes it lovable. A haphazard tumble of red-roofed old houses and shops with faded, speckled façades sprawls endearingly along a mountainside. Tourists are rare, despite the nearby temple at Vassae. Andritsena is a good base from which to visit Vassae; otherwise, there are more picturesque villages that are easier to reach and have more amenities.

In town, the **police** (tel. 22 209) are near the Shell station (open 24hr.; no English spoken). The **post office** (open Mon.-Fri. 7:30am-2pm) and the **National Bank** (open Mon.-Thurs. 8am-2pm, Fri. 8am-1:30pm) are next to the Shell station in the square. The **OTE** is off the main street, near the church (open Mon.-Fri. 7:30am-3pm). For the **clinic,** dial 22 210, -1. **Postal Code:** 27061. **Telephone Code:** 0626.

Andritsena is 1½hours west of **Megalopolis** and the same distance east of Pirgos. **Buses** leave from the **Café Apollon** in the main square (Greek coffee 150dr). In one direction, **buses** passing through Karitena (30min., 420dr), Tripolis (1½hr., 1300dr), and Argos (3hr., 2300dr) on their way to Athens (5hr., 2950dr) run twice daily, at 8:30am and 2pm. In the other direction, buses run to Pirgos (8am and 2pm, 1000dr), where connections can be made for the rest of the Western Peloponnese.

One option for slumber in town is the modern **Hotel Theoxenia** (tel. 22 219), at the end of town. (Singles 7500dr. Doubles 10,000dr.) If you passionately yearn for touristy activity, visit the **folk museum,** with its bizarre collection of bric-a-brac and well displayed costumes (open daily 11am-1pm; admission 300dr, students 200dr).

■ Near Andritsena: Vassae

Rising on the slopes of Mt. Kotilion, the **Temple of Epicurus Apollo** was built in tribute to Apollo for saving the people of Phygalia from a plague. Iktinos, the architect who built the monument in 420 BCE, later earned a fat fee by designing the Parthenon. The extant **columns** are thought to be the first of the Corinthian design.

Vassae remains sacred and solitary. The approach from Andritsena slithers up along cliffs for 14km, snaking between smooth rock pinnacles. At last the temple appears, pillar fragments littering its ancient **agora.** Though grand, the temple is now veiled by a canopy and entombed by scaffolding to protect it from acid rain. Those who hitchhike get to Vassae (there is no bus) by waiting at the turn-off just outside Andritsena on the road to Pirgos. You can share a **taxi** from Andritsena (roughly 3000dr roundtrip) to get here. Make it clear from the start that this is a group rate; some drivers may charge per person. Alternatively, you could walk back to town (3½hr. over the hills).

■ Dimitsana and Stemnitsa
ΔΗΜΗΤΣΑΝΑ ΚΑΙ ΣΤΕΜΝΙΤΣΑ

West of Tripolis, the little villages of Dimitsana and Stemnitsa make good bases for hiking, walking, or just slowing down to enjoy the villages' natural beauty. This area is known as the "Switzerland of Greece" for its green mountains and chalet-like houses. The atmosphere, however, is far from Swiss. In Dimitsana and Stemnitsa, travelers can still discover the charms of traditional Greek village life. The Erimanthos, Menalo, and Oligirtos mountain ranges, upon which the villages are perilously perched, separate the old settlements of the west from the beach resorts of the east. The timeless mountains are ancient and gnarled, and lush vegetation clings to all but the highest summits. When making treks into the mountains, don't be fooled by Greece's daytime heat—mountain towns get unbelievably chilly after twilight.

In **Dimitsana,** the bus deposits you on Labardopoulou St. next to the **post office** (tel. (0795) 31 234; code 22007; open Mon.-Fri. 7:30am-2pm) and a café which doubles as a **taxi stand.** Uphill from the café is **Pesonton Sq.** The **police** (tel. (0795) 31 205) are up around the corner from the post office (no English spoken; open 24hr.). To get to the **museum and library** (tel. (0795) 31 219; open daily 8am-1pm), follow the main street from the bus station and ascend the stairs before the main square (marked by a yellow sign). The town has been an educational center for more than 300 years—these two institutions commemorate its scholarly achievements. The **icon museum** (tel. (0795) 31 465), in the alley to the right of the *souvlaki* café, also merits a look (open Sat.-Tues. and Thurs. 9:30am-1:30pm). Continuing on, you'll reach the **OTE,** 402 Labardopoulou St. (tel. (0795) 31 599; open Mon.-Fri. 8:20am-2pm). The **National Bank** (tel. (0795) 31 210, -503) is at #406 just past the OTE (open Mon.-Thurs. 8am-2pm, Fri. 8am-1:30pm).

Buses run from Tripolis to Dimitsana (daily 8:30am and 6:15pm, 1½hr., 1100dr), and from Dimitsana to Tripolis (daily 6 and 11am). There are also buses leaving for Tripolis, Pirgos, and Olympia from nearby **Karkalou,** on the main highway, a 20-minute (800-1000dr) taxi ride away. Remember to leave time for connections, as there are only two taxis in town. Ask the police or in the cafés for details.

There's one hotel in town, the pretty but pricey **Hotel Dimitsana** (tel. (0795) 31 518, -9), on the road to Stemnitsa. (Singles 7500dr. Doubles 12,000dr. Breakfast included.) Another option is a delightful, appliance-filled room at **O Tholos Restaurant,** with bath and television (7000dr, with kitchenette 8000dr).

From Dimitsana, hike 11km along the road through perfumed wildflowers (or shell out 1000dr for a cab) to **Stemnitsa,** a perfect honeymoon location with beautiful homes, sun-dappled squares, and lovely restaurants. Completing the fantasy is a gorgeous hotel on the main road, **Hotel Triokolonion** (tel. (0795) 81 297). (Singles 6000dr. Doubles 8000dr. Bath and breakfast included.) The **post office** (tel. 81 280) is behind the church in the square (code 22024; open daily 7:30am-2pm), which hosts a telephone kiosk, outdoor cafés, and *tavernas.* Try **Café Psigoporio** for sumptuous Greek salad (600dr) and their special lamb chops.

Off the road from Dimitsana to Stemnitsa are several monasteries, some built right into the mountain face. One of these is the **Monastery of Ag. on Ioannis Prodromos,** 12km from Dimitsana. The road goes from asphalt to dirt, and finally becomes a footpath on the mountain. Here you can see the icons painted on the bare stone walls and monastic cells almost defying gravity as they hang off the mountain. Inhabited by only twelve monks (open dawn-dusk to modestly dressed visitors; free, though a small donation is expected).

MESSENIA ΜΕΣΣΗΝΙΑ

Messenia refreshes travelers, as an oasis of abundance in the arid Peloponnese. Olives, figs, and grapes spring from the rich soil on the region's rocky coastline, which remains largely tourist-free. Most Messenians live at the head of the gulf, around sprawling Kalamata, a convenient town from which to tour Mani's west coast. More alluring is the somnolent port town of Pylos, strategically located for bus, moped, and car travel to Koroni, Methoni, and the beaches of the south.

■ Kalamata ΚΑΛΑΜΑΤΑ

Kalamata, the second largest city in the Peloponnese after Patras, flourishes as a port and beach resort. Although Kalamata's past is not immediately evident, it was here that the Greek War of Independence of 1821 began. On March 23, two days before the official start of the war, a group of Kalamatans, impatient for the end of Turkish rule, overtook the sleeping Turks in a massacre that is commemorated each year with a reenactment of the Greek victory, parades, and traditional dancing.

ORIENTATION AND PRACTICAL INFORMATION

Kalamata's busiest areas form an "L," with the bus station and outdoor market at the top of the "L." The vertical stem is formed by the main thoroughfare, **Aristomenous Street,** which runs through **Georgiou Square,** site of most of the city's amenities, before it becomes **Fillelinon Street.** At the corner of the "L" is the Levi's factory and the port. **Navarinou Street** runs along the waterfront to form the horizontal leg.

Kalamata is large and spread-out—the bus station is 3km from the beach—but has an efficient public transportation system. **Bus #1** takes you anywhere you want to go; catch them buses at one of the blue *stasis* signs (150dr anywhere along the line; every hr. 8am-10pm). Buses begin their route at **23rd Martiou Square.** To get there, follow Artemidos St., three bridges from the bus station and three blocks to the left.

Then, cross the third bridge off Artemidos and turn right onto Aristomenous St. **Taxis** (tel. 21 112; 24hr.) from the bus station to the waterfront cost 550dr.

Tourist Police: (tel. 23 187), located on the port, at the end of Aristomenous St., 3rd floor of the same building as the regular police (look for the large Greek flag and sign with "i" as you approach the port). Open daily 7:30am-9:30pm, but the regular **police** (tel. 100) will help 24hr. **Port police** (tel. 22 218), on the harbor past the Levi's factory.

Banks: National Bank, 1 branch on Aristomenous St., off the north end of Georgiou Sq. and another on Akrita St. Both offer **currency exchange.** Open Mon.-Thurs. 8am-2pm, Fri. 8am-1:30pm. 24-hr. **ATM** at both locations.

OTE: Georgiou Sq., opposite the National Bank. Open daily 7:30am-10pm.

Flights: To Athens daily at 7:15pm (45min., 12,900dr, under 12, 5000dr). **Olympic Airways,** 17 Sideromikou Stathmou St. (tel. 22 376), just before train station. Open daily 8am-3:30pm. Taxis to the airport (6km from town, near Messini) cost 1500dr. Inquire at the KTEL station for airport-bound buses.

Trains: (tel. 23 904), station at the end of Sideromikou Stathmou St. Turn right on Frantzi St. at the end of Georgiou Sq., and walk a few blocks. Cheap and slow. Head to Athens (4 per day, 5:30am-3:40pm, 7hr., 2200dr) via Tripolis (2½hr., 840dr). To Argos (4hr., 1300dr); Corinth (5¼hr., 1650dr); Kyparissia (2hr., 600dr); Pirgos (3¼hr., 900dr); Patras (5½hr., 1500dr); and Olympia (900dr).

Buses: (tel. 22 851), information daily 7am-2pm. To Athens (8 per day, 5hr., 3750dr) via Megalopolis (1hr., 900dr); Tripolis (2hr., 1350dr); and Corinth (4hr., 2650dr). To Patras (2 per day, 4hr., 3600dr) via Pirgos (2hr., 2050dr). To Sparta (2 per day, 1hr., 800dr) via Artemisia (30min., 400dr). Also buses to Mavromati (2 per day, 1hr., 460dr) and Koroni (5-7 per day, 1½hr., 800dr). Some continue to Methoni (2 per day, 1½hr., 1150dr) and Finikountas (2 per day, 2hr., 1150dr). For Areopolis and Gythion, go via Itilo (3 per day, 2hr., 1100dr); change buses immediately. From Itilo, go to Areopolis (15min., 220dr) and Gythion (1½hr., 400dr).

City Buses: Depart from the bus depot near 23 Martiou Sq. Take the #1, which goes down Aristomenous Sq., then turns to run along the water, winding up at the waterfront or camping areas (150dr). Open daily 8am-10pm.

Moped Rental: Bastakos Motorbikes, 190 Faron St. (tel. 26 638). Mopeds 3200dr per day. Bicycles 1600dr per day. **Alpha Rental** (tel. 93 423), Vironos St. Mopeds 3500dr per day. Bicycles 1500dr per day. Both near waterfront and open daily 8:30am-8:30pm.

Taxi Service: (tel. 21 112), to the campsites from the city costs roughly 500dr.

Road Help: (tel. 104), to reach the auto club ΕΛΠΑ (Greece's AAA). Open 24hr.

Pharmacies: 40 Aristomeneous St. (tel. 21 819)—outside is a condom machine (300dr). Open Mon.-Fri. 8am-2pm and 6-9pm. Most open daily 8am-2pm, Tues. and Thurs.-Fri. also 5:30-9pm. For 24-hr. pharmacy information, dial 100.

Hospital: Athinou St. (tel. 85 203).

Medical Emergency: Call 25 555.

Post Office: 4 Iatropolou St. (tel. 22 810), near the south end of Georgiou Sq. Another branch on the waterfront at the port past the Levi's factory. Both are open Mon.-Fri. 7:30am-2pm. **Postal Code:** 24100.

Telephone Code: 0721.

ACCOMMODATIONS

Most of Kalamata's hotels are on the waterfront. Accommodations abound but "Rooms to Let" are uncommon here. Cheaper hotels are by the train station.

Hotel Nevada, 9 Santa Rosa (tel. 82 429), take bus #1 and get off as soon as it turns left along the water. The walls of these clean rooms are layered with a bizarre hodgepodge of posters. Tons, and we mean *tons,* of potted plants—you'll spot them a block away. Singles 3400dr. Doubles 4900dr. Triples 6790dr.

Avra, 10 Santa Rosa (tel. 82 759), across the street. Clean and comfortable rooms. Chirping birds in the lobby. Singles 5000dr. Doubles 6000dr. Triples 9000dr.

Hotel Plaza (tel. 82 590), on Navarinou St. The place for anyone determined to stay on the waterfront. Stay on bus #1 until you see the sign. Doubles have gorgeous seaside view. Singles 6500dr. Doubles 9100dr. Triples 10,800dr.

Hotel George (tel. 27 225), right near the train station. Clean and unassuming, convenient and cute. Singles 5000dr. Doubles 6000dr.

Camping Patista (tel. 29 525), 2km east along the water. Take bus #1 to the waterfront Mobil gas station and walk 100m. It's on the left, off a driveway. The hotel here rents rooms of varying size and quality (starting at 3000dr for singles, 4000dr for doubles). Maintenance and fruit-picking work for campers. 950dr per person. 530dr per car. 650dr per small tent. 750dr per large tent. Electricity 500dr.

Camping Maria's Sea and Sun (tel. 41 060). Luxurious as far as campsites go, and farther east. Take bus #1. Hot showers included. 1150dr per person. 650dr per car. 790dr per small tent. 915dr per large tent. Electricity 350dr.

FOOD AND ENTERTAINMENT

Before leaving town, sample the famous Kalamata olives and figs. Stop by the collection of edibles at the immense **New Market,** just across the bridge from the bus station. The best sit-down meals can be found along the waterfront. **Taverna Tzamaika** (tel. 18 926) is the most fabulous of the waterfront *tavernas,* but also the farthest away. Tzamaika is located 2km from the harbor, between two discoes (one is named GLOK and it looks like a Desert Storm bunker). This *taverna* has its own outdoor oven, a large collection of farm implements that appear to have lingered since the Agricultural Revolution, and a horse; simply good food (salads 400dr, spaghetti 1100dr, stuffed tomatoes 800dr). **Tampaki Restaurant** (tel. 23 225) is closer to town than Tzamaika, and serves good food at reasonable prices (*moussaka* 1000dr, stuffed vine leaves with rice 1200dr, and octopus 1500dr; open for dinner around 7pm). **Exociko Kentro** (tel. 22 016), with a seating area over the beach, serves a good lamb and potatoes (1200dr), veal (1400dr), and Greek salad (800dr).

Nightlife in Kalamata is extensive and a mild eyesore. Head to Georgiou Square or to the livelier waterfront. One kilometer past the harbor, the road is one overlapping, continuous techno beat. Kalamata's newest disco, **Palladium,** costs a fortune (cover 1200dr, includes one drink), and is not to be confused with its sister institution, **The Million Dollars Club,** housed in the same building (it hosts international strippers). Palladium attracts great crowds, but more soothing and moderately priced clubs surround it. Closer to the harbor is **Biraria** (tel. 82 186), enticing a mixed bag of drinkers from under-30s to over-60s.

SIGHTS

Only a few sights remain in Kalamata. The **Castle of the Villehardouins,** which crowns a hill above the old city, has proven remarkably indestructible. Built by the Franks in 1208, it was blown up by the Turks in 1685 and restored by the Venetians a decade later. It even remained relatively unscathed by the 1986 earthquake. Today the castle houses an open-air theater, which hosts "Cultural Summer of Kalamata" in July and August with everything from jazz and rock to classical Greek drama (ticket prices depend on the event, and start at 500dr). To get to the gates from 23 Martiou Sq., walk up Ipapandis St. past the church on the right side, and take your first left. At the foot of the castle is the **Convent of St. Constantine and Helen,** where nuns sell their linen and lacework at bargain prices. At the far end of the site is the **Byzantine Church** where a doe-eyed Virgin Mary icon was found, giving the city its name, which means "good eyes" (open daily 8am-dusk; free). There are also remains of a Byzantine church molder at the far edge of the site—scramble up for a sublime view (open daily 8am-dusk; free). At 221 Faron St., off the waterfront, Kalamata's **School of Fine Arts** exhibits work by Greek artists (open daily 9am-1pm and 6-10pm). Kalamata also supports two professional theaters and cinemas. Ask the **tourist police** for information on events in the **Pantazopoulion Cultural Center** on Aristomenon St. Local archaeological finds are exhibited in the nearby **Benaki Museum,** while folk art, crafts, and icons are on display at the **Folk Art Museum.**

Kalamata has been trying, with considerable success, to clean up its beaches. They are less crowded and less spoiled as you proceed eastward. With large shady trees, cafés, a performance area, and a duck pond, the **Train Park** (at the end of Aristomenous St., on the waterfront) extends several blocks towards Georgiou Sq. The main attraction is a simulated train station, life-size and open for exploration.

■ Near Kalamata

For more antiquities, take the bus from Kalamata to **Mavromati** (2 per day Mon.-Sat.; 460dr) to the well preserved remains of **ancient Messene** (not to be confused with modern Messini) on Mt. Ithomi. The striking 4th-century BCE wall epitomizes the period's defensive architecture. An **agora, theater,** and **Temple to Artemis** also remain. Up the road is the fallen doorpost of the colossal **Arcadian Gate,** designed by Epaminondas, the architect of Megalopolis. Also nearby is the 16th-century **Monastery of the Vourkano,** with some great frescoes. The only difficulty with this trip is the timing. If you want more than 15 minutes at the site, catch the morning bus and return on the post-Petralona leg of the evening bus, or take a taxi (4500dr).

The road from Koroni to Kalamata hugs the east coast of the Messenian peninsula. Between Harokopi and the coastal town of **Petalidio** is a chain of beaches. **Koroni** is a pleasant fishing village with a long sand beach and a castle of its very own. Unfortunately, it connects by bus only to Kalamata, making it difficult to reach. Pleasant **Koroni Camping** (tel. (0725) 22 119) is an option. (1000dr per person. 500dr per car. 650dr per small tent. 950dr per large tent. 10% discount for longer stays.)

■ Taygetus Mountains

South of Kalamata, the bus to Areopolis winds through the Taygetus mountains, which soar to 2630m at their highest point. The alluring grey peaks of Mani loom behind olive-covered hillsides. The first major bus stop comes at the coastal village of **Kardamili.** The town is a popular beach resort, so there are many "Rooms to Let," but call ahead in the summer (expect to pay 3000-5000dr for doubles). In the center of town hospitable **Joanna Stefania** (tel. 73 242) rents spotless doubles with balconies and a communal kitchen. (Doubles with bath 7000dr.) Look for the sign above **Gelateria,** which serves delicious exotic ice cream (2 scoops 300dr). On the Kalamata side of town, rooms are near a gorgeous white pebble beach. Follow the blue signs to **Camping Melitsina** (tel. 73 461; 1050dr per person, 650dr per car, 990dr per small tent, 1050dr per large tent, electricity 600dr). On the other end of town, follow the red and white "Rooms to Let" signs right after the post office and a cobblestone path. Here you'll find **Olivia Koumanakou's** tidy pension (tel. 73 326) with a communal kitchen. (Singles 5000dr. Doubles 6000dr.) For inspired food, try the family-run **Taverna Kiki,** on the waterfront below the village. There is a **supermarket** and **bakery** near the square. Kardamili's **police station** (tel. 73 209) is on the main road across from the church (open 24hr.). Farther towards Itilo is the **post office** (open Mon.-Fri. 7:30am-2:30pm). Following the road from Kardamili to Itilo, you will find several coves with pebble **beaches. Telephone Code:** 0721.

If you're bound for Areopolis, change buses in the village of **Itilo** immediately upon arrival—the bus leaves promptly. The frescoed **Monastery of Dekoulo** and the 17th-century Turkish fortress are poised on a nearby hill. The entertainment consists of two cafés off the small square and a reasonably priced restaurant. The bus continues 3km down to the magnificent **Neo Itilo.** At the heart of an enormous natural bay encircled by monumental barren mountains, the white pebble beach is ideal for swimming. From Neo Itilo, the road winds uphill, affording a view of **Limani,** the old harbor of Areopolis, with its sprinkling of fishing boats. The tiny port is home to the Mavromichaeli **Castle of Potrombei.** From here, buses continue to Areopolis. Bad roads and reckless drivers make this ride as much fun as putting your stomach through the spin cycle.

MESSENIA

■ Pylos ΠΥΛΟΣ

Pylos' shady square and tile houses framed by bobbing flowers are typical enough for a port town. In addition to a protected harbor, the sharp rock face of Sfakteria Island is a peculiarity that gives Pylos a defiant appearance. The town, also known as Navarino, is renowned for the 1827 sea battle which gave Greece its independence. As Turkish forces, reinforced by the Egyptian fleet, battered the coast, the English, French, and Russian fleets arrived at Navarino and saved the beleaguered Greeks. Pylos now espouses a warm, carefree attitude. A glance at its waterfront's inviting turquoise waters, filled by dozens of sunbathers, is enough to convince anyone that this is a place of endless summer daze.

Orientation and Practical Information   The **police** (tel. 22 316) are located on the second floor of a building on the left side of the waterfront (English spoken; open 24hr.). Continue around that turn to reach the **port police** (tel. 22 225). The **tourist police** (tel. 23 733) are in the same building as the police (open daily 7:30am-2:30am). The **post office** (tel. 22 247) is on Nileos St., uphill to the left (facing the water) from the bus station (open Mon.-Fri. 7:30am-2pm). To get to the **OTE,** pass the post office and take your first left; it is uphill on the right of the square (open Mon.-Fri. 7:30am-3:10pm). A **National Bank** is also on the waterfront (open Mon.-Thurs. 8am-2pm, Fri. 8am-1:30pm). To get to the **hospital** (tel. 22 315), take the road on the right of the square (back to the water; open 24hr).

Buses (tel. 22 230) leave regularly for Kalamata (9 per day, Mon.-Sat. 6:35am-9pm, Sun. 6 per day, 9am-9pm, 1¼hr., 800dr); Athens (daily at 9am, 7hr., 4550dr); and Finikountas (Mon.-Sat. 4 per day, Sun. 2 per day, 45min., 380dr), via Methoni (15min., 190dr). No buses travel directly to Koroni, but you can go to Finikountas and take the 5pm bus from there to Koroni. Buses also leave for Kyparissia (Mon.-Sat. at 7, 9, 11am, and 1:35pm; Sun. at 11am; 2hr., 950dr), all stopping at Nestor's Palace (30min., 350dr) and Chora (35min., 350dr). For moped rental, try **Venus Rent-A-Car** (tel. 22 393, -12; open daily 8:30am-1pm and 6-9pm; mopeds 2500-4800dr per day). **Postal Code:** 24001. **Telephone Code:** 0723.

Accommodations   There are several "Rooms to Let" signs as the bus descends the hill. In general, expect to pay 3500-5000dr for singles, 4500-7000dr for doubles, and 5000-8000dr for triples. Try the clean and simple rooms of **Anna Panoskalsi** (tel. 22 935), up the hill from the far right of the harbor. Go up a flight of stairs just past the new Hotel Koralis, and follow the sign for rooms. (Singles 4000dr. Doubles 6000dr.) **Navarino Beach Camping** (tel. 22 761) lies 6km north at Yialova Beach. (1250dr per person. 750dr per small tent. 950dr per large tent. Electricity 600dr.) In town, another good option is the **Pension** (tel. 22 748), located just before the OTE, offering singles and doubles for varying prices (depending on the length of stay), but within the above price range.

Sights   **Fortresses** guard both sides of Pylos' harbor. **Neokastro,** to the south, is easily accessible from the town; walk up the road to Methoni and turn right at the sign. The well preserved walls enclose a church (originally a mosque), a citadel, and a collection of remains from the Greek Revolution of 1827 named for Rene Puaux (open Tues.-Sun. 8am-7pm; admission 800dr, students 400dr, EU students free). The **archaeological museum,** located just before the castle on the road to Methoni, houses finds from Hellenistic and Mycenaean tombs (tel. 22 448 for both castle and museum; open Tues.-Sun. 8:30am-3pm; admission 400dr, students 200dr, EU students free). The **Paleokastro,** north of Pylos, is harder to reach. Drive to Petrochori and proceed south with caution—the road is poor, but clearly marked. Be careful, the weeds around the castle are home to hundreds of snakes and lizards.

To see **Sfakteria** up close, you can take a **boat tour** from the port. The hour jaunt around the island stops at various monuments to the allied sailors of the Battle of Navarino and shows off a sunken Turkish ship. Boat captains try to organize groups for tours (roughly 10 people). Inquire at the small booth on the waterfront or at the neighboring coffee bar under the police station, where the captains often rest. For ten people, the cost is 10,000dr, while for four people it is proportionally higher though still reasonable (7000dr). The ride takes one hour and twenty minutes.

■ Near Pylos

In the Mycenaean world, Pylos was second only to Mycenae in economic prosperity and cultural breadth. The **palace** at Pylos, where Nestor met Telemachus in Homer's *Odyssey*, was built by Neleus (Nestor's father and founder of the Neleid dynasty) in the 13th century BCE. The site is still being excavated and consists of three buildings. The main building, possibly the king's residence, originally had a second floor (and walls) with official and residential quarters and storerooms. To the southwest, archaeologists think that an older, smaller palace stood; to the north-east lie the ruins of a large complex of isolated workshops and more storerooms.

Important finds from Nestor's palace are **Linear B tablets** explaining some of its administrative operations, jewelry, bronze objects, and ivory knickknacks. Most are on display in the National Archaeological Museum in Athens. If you like to drink hornets with your water, there's a free hose. Otherwise, bring water. The site is covered, providing ample shade, but not enough to fill all the time between buses. Bring a book, or read the University of Cincinnati's scholarly *Guide to Nestor's Palace* (500dr), available at the entrance (tel. (0763) 31 437, -358; open Mon.-Sat. 8:45am-3pm, Sun. 9:30am-2:30pm; admission 400dr, students 200dr).

KYPARISSIA

Kyparissia, guarded by a mountain fortress, is a a place that looks like a city but has the friendliness of a quiet mountain town. It serves mainly as a transportation hub. At this point the train tracks end and buses continue north or south. On the square is a **National Bank** (open Mon.-Thurs. 8am-2pm, Fri. 8am-1:30pm) and **post office** (open Mon.-Fri. 7:30am-2pm). The **OTE** is just off the uphill right corner (open Mon.-Fri. 7:30am-10pm, Sat.-Sun. 9am-2pm and 5-10pm). The **police** (tel. 22 333 or 500) are up the street. For the **port police,** dial 22 128.

Trains go to Kalamata (4 per day, 2hr., 590dr) and Athens (5 per day, 8hr., 2560dr); four of these go via Tripolis (2½hr., 860dr), and five go via Pirgos (1½hr., 540dr) and Patras (3½hr., 1140dr). To get to Kyparissia's fortress, walk one block from the train station; at the five-way intersection take the second sharpest right. **Buses** leave for Athens (daily 8:45, 11am, 3, and 9:15pm; 5hr.; 3700dr) via Tripolis (1450dr) and Corinth (2550dr); Patras (daily 9am and 3pm, 2½hr., 2350dr); Chora (3 per day, 600dr); Pirgos (4 per day, 1½hr., 900dr); and Pylos (3 per day, 2hr., 900dr). **Postal Code:** 24500. **Telephone Code:** 0761.

Hotel Vassilikon, 7 Alexopoulou St. (tel. 22 655), has singles for 6000dr and doubles for 7000dr. **Inn Trifilia,** 25th Martiou St. (tel. 22 066), has humble, clean doubles with shared balconies (4800dr). The purple and white **Hotel Tsolaridis Beach** (tel. 22 145, -389), near the beach, is a conspicuous treasure. Rooms are large and so clean they're sanitary. (Singles 7000dr. Doubles 11,000dr. Breakfast included. Family rates available.) Posh **Camping Kyparissia** (tel. 23 491), at the far right of the waterfront, has ping pong, a restaurant/bar/minimarket, and a washing machine (900dr per load. 1100dr per person. 600dr per car. 750dr per small tent. 1200dr per large tent. Electricity 500dr.) It's located near **Sunset Bar** for late-night debauchery.

▓ Methoni ΜΕΘΩΝΗ

With its hibiscus-lined streets, Methoni is a refreshing reprieve for the weary traveler. Peer through the flowering trees at the spectacular 13th-century fortress along the beach. Forever "the Camelot of Greece," Methoni was once offered by Agamemnon to Achilles to cheer the sulking warrior. Cervantes was so taken with the place that he churned out romances even while imprisoned under Turkish guard.

The town's two main streets form a "Y" at the billiard hall where the Pylos-Finikountas buses stop. Shops are on the upper fork, the beach and fortress are at the end of the lower street, down to the left. The **police** (tel. (0723) 31 203; open 24hr.) are on a side street off the left fork near the beach. Past the sign on the left fork is the **post office** (open Mon.-Fri. 7:30am-2pm). The **OTE** is on the next parallel street to the left (open Mon.-Fri. 7:30am-3:10pm). The **National Bank** is 40m down the right fork (open Mon.-Thurs. 8am-2pm, Fri. 8am-1:30pm). **Buses** go to Kalamata (4 per day, 1½hr., 900dr) via Pylos (15min., 190dr), and to Finikountas (4 per day, 30min., 200dr). Two doors from the OTE, buses leave for Athens via Pylos, Kyparissia, Pirgos, and Patras. The police can provide more information. **Postal Code:** 24006.

Hotel Alex and **Hotel Giota** (tel. (0723) 31 290, -1), both behind the OTE and run by the Pavlogiannis family, offer rooms in the town's beachside square. (Singles 8000dr. Doubles 10,000dr. 1000dr less at Hotel Alex. Breakfast included.) **Camping Methoni** (tel. (0723) 31 228) is crowded but on the sea. (700dr per person. 500dr per car. 590dr per small tent. 640dr per large tent.) Rooms are cheaper farther from the beach. **Hotel Finikas** (tel. (0723 31 390), near the post office, offers recently renovated, homey rooms. (Singles 4000dr. Doubles 6000dr. Triples 7000dr.)

A visit to the southwest Peloponnese should include a trip to Methoni's **Venetian fortress,** a 13th-century mini-city. The **Bourzi,** a tower built by the Turks to fortify the shore, sits around the wall over the sea. Venture into the fortified walls, cisterns, parapets, and vaulted passages (open daily 8:30am-7pm, Sun. 9am-7pm; free).

■ Near Methoni: Finikountas ΦΟΙΝΙΚΟΥΝΤΑΣ

Halfway between Methoni and Koroni, Finikountas, a colorful fishing village, coaxes visitors to bask in sunshine and watch colorful *caïques* glide across the surface. For swimming, take the time to go to **Paradise Beach,** the cove beyond the rock jetty to the east. If you stay, change money in advance; Finikountas has neither a bank nor a post office. The **Supermarket Phoenix** sells stamps and houses an **OTE** (open daily 7am-1pm and 5-9pm). **Buses** stop across from the Hotel Finikounta and head to Kalamata (3 per day Mon.-Sat., Sun. 3pm; 2hr.; 1000dr) via Methoni (30min., 200dr) and Pylos (45min., 240dr). Buses also go to Kalamata via Harokopio (at 7:30am and 4:30pm, 1½hr., 1000dr).

Look for "Rooms to Let" signs along the waterfront or on the road from Koroni as you enter town. Most restaurateurs either rent rooms or know people who do. **Moudakis Restaurant** (tel. (0723) 71 224), to the right of the KMoil gas station (facing the water), has singles (3700dr) and doubles (7000dr). Finikountas has two campgrounds. **Camping Ammos** (tel. (0723) 71 262) is 2km east of town. (1100dr per person. 660dr per car. 660dr per small tent. 800dr per large tent. Electricity 540dr.) **Camping Anemomylos** (tel. (0723) 71 360) is 1km to the west. (950dr per person. 750dr per car. 650dr per small tent. 810dr per large tent. Electricity 600dr.)

LACONIA ΛΑΚΩΝΙΑ

In the 10th century BCE, a tribe of Doric warriors from the north invaded the southwest Peloponnese, drove out its Mycenaean inhabitants, and executed stragglers unlucky enough to get in their way. Famed for slaughtering their enemies, the region's new masters also distinguished themselves by their curt speech. While their northern counterparts argued in flowery rhetoric, Laconians often dispatched their opponents with a single, witty phrase. Thus, the reticent became "laconic." The Ancient Laconian qualities are still manifest throughout the area, especially in the barren peninsula. Although Laconia boasts three of the Peloponnese's most popular sites—Mani's Pirgos Dirou caves, Sparta's nearby Byzantine ruins of Mystra, and Monemvassia's "rock"—the region remains low key. Laconia's friendly villages are a welcome break from the urban atmosphere of other, more touristed areas.

■ Sparta ΣΠΑΡΤΗ

The Spartans are portrayed as the bad guys of the classical world—totalitarian war-mongers who insisted on pestering the civilized Athenian democrats. These stereotypes, however simplistic, hold true. Sparta's reputation for brutal, no-nonsense militarism is well deserved. Around 700 BCE, after Sparta barely subdued a revolt of the Messenians, the leader Lycurgus instituted reforms that transformed Sparta into a war machine. For the next 350 years, it dominated the entire central Peloponnese with its invincible armies and austere discipline. Outside of war, Sparta contributed little to Greek history—no philosophy, art, or architecture flourished here. Weary of further Athenian expansion, Sparta attacked its rival, beginning the 28-year-long Peloponnesian War. After triumphing in 404 BCE, it emerged as the supreme military power in the Hellenic world. The Spartans reveled in their power, not even bothering to build walls around their city. Only the combined effects of earthquakes, depopulation, and the resistance of its neighbors broke Sparta's hegemony.

A young Spartan's training for a life of war began early, even before conception. Lycurgus believed two fit parents produced stronger offspring, so he ordered all Spartan women to undergo the same rigorous training endured by men. Furthermore, newlyweds were permitted only an occasional tryst on the theory that the heightened desire of the parents would produce more robust children. If they weren't winnowed out as weak or deformed, boys began a severe regimen of training under the auspices of an adult Spartan. The young were forced to walk barefoot to toughen their feet and wore only a simple piece of clothing in both summer and winter to expose them to drastic weather changes. The Spartan creed dictated that young men be guarded against temptations of any kind—strict laws forbidding everything from drinking to pederasty governed Spartans' actions. Moreover, young Spartans were given the plainest and simplest foods for fear that rich delicacies would stunt their growth. (One visitor to Sparta, upon sampling the fare, allegedly quipped, "Now I know why they do not fear death.")

Fortunately, modern Sparta hardly resembles a boot camp. With its nightly roar of mopeds and its monotonous, modern architecture, the city is, ironically, culturally similar to Athens (though it's much smaller and quieter). The fruit trees that line the city's busiest streets lend it an almost endearing quirkiness, but Sparta is very much a city that goes about its own business—little effort is taken to win people over to this town's charms. Still, Sparta is the best and most convenient base from which to explore the Byzantine ruins of Mystra, only 6km away.

ORIENTATION AND PRACTICAL INFORMATION

Sparta's two main streets, **Paleologou** and **Lykourgou,** laced with trees, intersect in the center of town. To get to the center from the bus station, walk left on Paleologou for two blocks. The town square is one block to the right of the intersection on Lykourgou, and all of the necessary amenities are on these two streets. The ruins are on the north edge of town. Sparta is laid out in an appropriately no-frills grid.

Tourist Office: (tel. 24 852). To the left of the town hall in the square. English spoken. Bus schedules, hotels, and information. Map 400dr. Open daily 8am-2pm.
Banks: National Bank (tel. 22 997), on the corner of Dioskouron and Paleologou, 3 blocks down from the intersection, offers **currency exchange.** Open Mon.-Thurs. 8am-2pm, Fri. 8am-1:30pm. Other banks line Paleologou.
OTE: 11 Kleombrotou St. (tel. 23 799). Open daily 7am-9:40pm.
Buses: (tel. 26 441), walk down Lykourgou, museum-side away from the square. Continue past the fire station until the road peters out—it's on your right, 1500m from the center of town. Buses go to Athens (9 per day, 5hr., 3300dr), via Corinth (4hr., 2050dr) and sometimes Tripolis (3 per day, 1¼hr., 900dr). Buses also head to Neapolis (2-4 per day, 4hr., 2250dr); Monemvassia (2-3 per day, 2½hr., 1700dr; change buses in Molai); Pirgos Dirou and the caves (1 per day, 2¼ hr., 1250dr) via Areopolis (2hr., 1100dr; change buses in Gythion); Kalamata (2 per day, 2hr.,

950dr); Tripolis (3 per day, 1¼hr., 900dr); Gerolimenas (daily, 3hr., 1650dr); and Gythion (5 per day, 1hr., 700dr). For buses to Mystra, the station is at the corner of Leonidou and Kythonigou 2 blocks past the town hall (every 1½hr., 6:50am-8:20pm, 190dr). The schedule varies—call the tourist office to check.

Pharmacies: 117 Paleologou St. (tel. 27 212). Open daily 8am-2pm and 5:30-9pm. Three other pharmacies on Paleologou St. and many more throughout the city.

Hospital: (tel. 28 671, -5), Nosokomeio St. (Hospital St.). Open 24hr.

Police: 8 Hilonos St. (tel. 26 229). From the intersection, turn left on Lykourgou St. away from the square. The police are on a side street to the right, past the museum. Open 24hr. Helpful, earnest, English-speaking **tourist police** (tel. 20 492) are housed in the same building. Open daily 8am-3pm and 7-9pm.

Police Emergency: Dial 100.

Post Office: (tel. 26 565), past the OTE on Kleombrotou St., 1 block up from the intersection off Paleologou St. Open Mon.-Fri. 7:30am-2pm. **Postal Code:** 23100.

Telephone Code: 0731.

ACCOMMODATIONS

Something of Ancient Sparta must still linger in the modern city, for a stay at one of the town's more inexpensive hotels is certainly a character-building experience. Rooms are sparse and small. In these Spartan rooms, luxury is for the weak. The cheapest place to stay is the **Hotel Panellinion** (tel. 28 031), just past the Lykourgou intersection, with minimalist rooms and balconies. (Singles 4000dr. Doubles 6000dr.) Or try **Hotel Cecil** (tel. 24 980), five blocks north on the corner of Paleologou St. and Thermopilion St. The traffic roars audibly, but the rooms are unsullied. They'll give you free maps, Sparta information, and hot showers. (Singles 5000dr. Doubles 6000dr.) A more luxurious place is the **Hotel Laconia** (tel. 28 951, -2), on Paleologou St. between the bus station and the center of town. (Singles 6000dr. Doubles 9000dr.) Near Mystra is the new **Camping Castle View** (tel. 83 303), with pool, modern showers and toilets, and a mini-market. (1100dr per person. 700dr per car. 700dr per small tent. 900dr per large tent. Electricity 600dr.) To get to the campground, take the regular Mystra bus and ask the driver to let you off at the site.

FOOD AND ENTERTAINMENT

Sparta's few restaurants serve expensive fast food. For a reasonably priced meal under the fluorescent lights of **Dhiethnes** (tel. 28 636), head to the far right of the main square. Also called Restaurant in the Garden, it offers good vegetarian food (700dr per plate). A good grill called **O Finikas** (tel. 27 350) is across from the Hotel Cecil on Paleologou St. (entrees 900dr). At night, bop 2½km down the road towards Gythion to the **Aithrio Disco.** The **Imago,** a hip, artsy bar, is in the alley behind the town hall and offers a gay-friendly atmosphere (open daily 10pm-3am).

SIGHTS

There is almost nothing left of Ancient Sparta to clue us in to the people who lived there. Then again, maybe this lack of ruins is the most telling clue of all. At the north end of Paleologou St. stands an enormous **statue of Leonidas,** the famous warrior king of the Spartans. The Spartans built a large pseudo-tomb for their leader, who fell at the Battle of Thermopylae in 480 BCE, in hopeful anticipation of his remains, which were never found. The tomb lies in the middle of a grove that is now a public park, to the left of the ancient ruins. The ruins themselves lie to the north of the modern city (facing the statue of Leonidas; bear left). The ruins (1km from the main square at the north edge of the modern city) consist of the outlines of one of the larger theaters of ancient Greece and some fragments of the acropolis. Three miles away are three remaining platforms of the **shrine to Menelaus and Helen,** history's most sought-after beauty. The remains of the Spartans' **shrine to Apollo** are on the road to Gythion. A short walk east on the banks of the Eurotas River leads to the **sanctuary of Artemis Orthia.** Spartan youths had to prove their courage here by unflinchingly enduring public floggings. Headless statues beckon you to enter the

archaeological museum (tel. 28 575), through its beautiful, well kept park on Lykourgou St. (on the opposite side of Paleologou from the square). The collection includes spooky votive masks used in ritual dances at the sanctuary of Artemis Orthia, and a bronze boar which bristles in the room to the left of the entrance (open Tues.-Sat. 8:30am-3pm, Sun. 9:30am-2:30pm; closed weekends Oct.-May; admission 500dr, students 300dr; free on Sun). For modern art, visit the **Coumantarios Art Gallery,** 123 Paleologou St. (tel. 26 557; English not spoken). The permanent collection of 19th-century French and Dutch paintings is impressive. On the second floor are temporary exhibits of works by modern Greek artists (open Tues.-Sat. 9am-3pm, Sun. 10am-2pm; free).

For an evening excursion from Sparta, share a cab to the village of **Parolis,** 2km from Mystra. There you can sit in a *taverna* and watch the nearby waterfalls. Two kilometers farther is the village of **Tripi,** which has larger waterfalls, some of which run right under the excellent and affordable grill-restaurant **Exochiko Kentro** (tel. 98 314). Down the road past the restaurant is the **cave of Kiades,** where ancient Spartans tossed their sickly or deformed babies.

■ Near Sparta: Mystra ΜΥΣΤΡΑΣ

The extraordinary medieval ruins of Mystra (tel. (0731) 83 377) stand 6km west of Sparta. Overflowing with Byzantine churches and castle ruins, this site reveals the splendor of Byzantium's final flourish. In the late 14th century, Mystra, prospering from a lucrative silk industry, became an intellectual center. Many free thinkers, unhappy under the control of repressive feudal lords and clergy, surged into town and set up schools, tying Mystra to the Florentine humanist movement. Philosophers and students wandered the intricate network of paths that weaves the city together and that today renders sightseeing a complex affair. Try tracing a path around several key sites on the three tiers that correspond to the sectors for the commoners, the nobility, and the royalty (in ascending order, naturally). Fortunately, Mystra is one of the better-labeled sites in Greece. Enter through the main gate—the complexity will be easier to handle.

Don't miss the **Metropolis of St. Demetrios** in the lower tier, with its sanctuary and museum of architectural fragments. Wander on to the two churches of the monastery of **Vrontochion, St. Theodori,** and the frescoes of the **Aphentiko** (or Hodegetria). On the same tier is the **Pantanassa,** a convent with a beautifully ornamented façade and a multitude of frescoes, not to mention a miracle-working Virgin Mary icon. Finally, at the extreme left of the lower tier, the **Church of Perivleptos** is perhaps Mystra's most stunning relic; every inch of the church is bathed in exquisitely detailed paintings of religious scenes and figures, most of which had their eyes gouged out by invading Turks (you can still see the holes). Climb up to the **castle,** the fortress that was Mystra's first building (the town developed downward), built by the crusader Guillaume de Villehardouin in 1249 CE. The castle is closer than it looks; you can get there in roughly an hour walking from the main gate.

There are water taps inside the entrance through the main gate, at the Metropolis and at Pantanassa, but it's a good idea to bring your own water to combat Mystra's heat. Also, wear tough shoes—many of the paths are rocky and slippery. You'll enjoy Mystra more with a guidebook. You can buy one with a map at the entrance kiosk (700-2500dr); Manolis Chatzidakis' *Mystras* is the best (2000dr). Even a cursory inspection of the site requires at least three hours, including the long climb to the top. Be warned: it's been years since bathrooms at the site were in working condition. In summer, try to be at the site by 8am, since the sun becomes unbearable as early as 10am. If you arrive by bus from Sparta, get off at the sign for the Xenis restaurant, with the ruins on your left. Continue up the road, past the bend to the main gate. The site is 1500m beyond the town of Mystra. Aside from campsites, digs at Mystra are pricey—visit from Sparta (site open daily 8:30am-3pm).

LACONIA

■ Gythion ΓΥΘΕΙΟ

Situated on the east coast of Mani and connected by ferry with Kythera and Crete, Gythion, a lively port town, is an ideal place to station oneself while touring the bleakly dramatic territory of Mani. A 30-minute bus trip will bring you to Areopolis, the haunting fortified town which historically served as Mani's center. A concrete causeway connects Gythion to the tiny island of **Marathonisi,** where Paris and Helen consummated their ill-fated love. Modern Gythion boasts beautiful sand and stone beaches, picturesque houses, and friendly people.

ORIENTATION AND PRACTICAL INFORMATION

The bus stop is on the north side of the waterfront, near the town's amenities and cheaper stores. Small **Mavromichali Square** is in the middle of the waterfront near the quay. The harbor road continues to the right and south, where it eventually meets the causeway to Marathonisi. The **police** (tel. 22 271, -100) are on the waterfront, 500m before the bus station (English spoken; open 24hr.). Before the causeway, past Mavromichali Sq., you'll find the **port police** (tel. 22 262). The **post office** is on Ermou St. (open Mon.-Fri. 7:30am-2pm), and the **OTE** is at the corner of Herakles and Kapsali St. (open Mon.-Fri. 7:30am-3:10pm). **Theodore V. Rozakis** (tel. 22 650, -207), the travel agency on the waterfront near the square, provides information and tickets (open daily 7am-11pm). The **National Bank,** just beyond the bus stop towards the water, offers **currency exchange** (open Mon.-Thurs. 8am-2pm, Fri. 8am-1:30pm). There are other banks in the same area.

The **bus station** (tel. 22 228) is on the north end of the waterfront. Buses head to Athens (6 per day, 7:30am-3:45pm, 3950dr) via Sparta (1hr., 700dr); Kalamata via Sparta (2 per day, 700dr) or via Itilo (2 per day, 650dr); Monemvassia (daily, 2hr., 1250dr); Gerolimenas (2 per day, 2hr., 950dr) via Areopolis (30min., 420dr), Pirgos Dirou, and the caves (600dr). Buses also go to the campgrounds (including Meltemi, Gythion Beach, and Mani) south of town (6am, 10:15am, 1pm, and 7pm; 190dr). **Ferries** depart from the quay to the right of Mavromichali Sq. and run to Kythera (daily, 1200dr) and Crete (Wed., Sat., 4000dr). For **taxis,** call 23 400 (open 24hr.). **Moto Mani** (tel. 22 853), on the waterfront near the causeway, rents mopeds for 3500dr per day with reduced prices for longer rentals and free 100km allowance per day (open daily 9am-9pm). The **health clinic** (tel. 22 001, -2, or -3) is along the right side of the waterfront. **Postal Code:** 23200. **Telephone Code:** 0733.

ACCOMMODATIONS

Bypass Gythion's expensive hotels by staying in "Rooms to Let" or at one of the four nearby campgrounds. **Xenia Karlafti's** (tel. 22 719) rooms are in a house enclosed by a black railing, near the port police. The rooms are spacious and the gracious manager provides a breakfast area, washing machine, and clothesline for her guests. (Doubles 5000dr. Triples 6000dr.) Just behind the OTE at **Herakli #22** (tel. 22 915), you'll find spacious rooms with large balconies and international magazines. The owner, a Greek Canadian, is only around to rent rooms June through August. (Doubles 4000dr.) From Mavromichali Square, go up Tzanaki Gregoraki, turn right at the clock tower, **Koutsouri Rooms** (tel. 22 321) are just past the bakery on your left. (Singles 4000dr. Doubles 5000dr. Triples 6000dr. Suites with kitchen 7000dr.) The most luxurious campgrounds are **Meltemi** (tel. 22 833; 1000dr per person, 600dr per car, 900dr per tent, electricity 550dr) and **Gytheio Bay Campgrounds** (tel. 22 522; 1200dr per person, 700dr per car, small tent 800dr, large tent 900dr, electricity 700dr). Also try **Mani Beach** (tel. 23 450; 1020dr per person, 620dr per car, small tent 600dr, large tent 900dr, electricity 500dr). The campgrounds are south of town and accessible by bus. Ask at the station for the bus to the campgrounds.

FOOD AND ENTERTAINMENT

For a reprieve from the restaurants along the waterfront and the grocery stores around the main square which charge exorbitant prices, head to **Kosta's,** a non-touristy eatery across from the public beach near the bus station (chicken in sauce 900dr). The **Cork Room** (tel. 22 122), also on the waterfront, serves cheap, delicious food (lemon roast pork 1000dr, spaghetti 550dr). A decently priced place two blocks from the square, along the water, is **Poulikakis** (chicken and spaghetti 950dr). For a nice meal set closer to the islet, try **Tonisi Restaurant** (tel. 23 830) for delicious *moussaka* (1100dr), steak (1000dr), or salad (800dr). **Supermarkets** are along Vas. Georgiou St. As you walk along the waterfront towards the bus station, bear left at the fork for Vas. Georgiou. There is a fruit and produce **open-air market** every Tuesday and Friday morning (4:30am-noon), between Herakles and Archaia Theatrou St. The **bakery** up from Super Cycle Moto to the right has delightful cheese pie (200dr). This area also offers some cheap *souvlaki* joints (200-280dr). The small parks near the bus station or on the island are a short walk away and are perfect, cool spots for picnics. On the island itself, the museum has a pleasant outdoor café, set amid a coniferous park and along the sea. From this vantage, all of Gythion opens to view for 300dr (the price of coffee or lemonade). If you're drained from the sun, revitalize at **Disco Ferrari** on Selinitsa beach (1500dr cover with first drink), or **Spider Disco,** 3km down the road to the Acropolis.

SIGHTS

The ancient **theater** of Gythion, tucked away in a corner, has endured the centuries remarkably well. Note the differences between the seats for dignitaries in front and the simpler seats farther back. To get there, walk down Herakles St. from the bus station, go to Ermou St. and then right onto Archaiou Theatrou St. to its end. If you arrive in the early evening, join the soldiers getting their nightly pep talk here. **Pali-atzoures Antique Shop,** #25 Vas. Pavlou (tel. 22 944, -806), is the last of its kind in the entire Peloponnese, selling Greek farming and household tools and some trade tools from the Orthodox Church (open daily 10:30am-2pm and 6-11:30pm).

There is a **public beach** just north of the bus station, but the best beaches are north and south of town. Three kilometers to the south is the long, sandy beach of **Mavrovouni,** with a high surf and a number of surfer bars (mixed drinks 900-1000dr, beer 500dr). Three kilometers north is rocky **Selinitsa,** which has earned accolades from the European Union for its clean water. This beach is at its prettiest beneath the Lakonis bungalows. Neither beach is accessible by bus—ride a moped or take a taxi (500dr). Farther north than Selinitsa (500m past the bungalows) is a sandy beach which houses the remains of an abandoned drug-runner's ship.

For daytime entertainment, across the causeway on **Marathonisi Island,** is the newly opened **Maniot Museum,** housed in the island's Tzanetaki tower (named after the family who owned the island before donating it to the national tourist board). The museum, which houses Maniot crafts, is near the site of Helen and Paris' ill-received tryst (open daily 9am-1pm and 6-9pm; admission 600dr, students 300dr). When traveling from Gythion to Areopolis, keep your eyes peeled for the Frankish **Castle of Pasava** on the right (roughly 10km down the road); you can tour the ruin. Farther along, the **Castle of Kelefa** looks out to sea.

MANI ΜΑΝΗ

Mani is a minimalist's dream. The sparsely settled territory stoically circles the cinnamon-brown Taygetus Mountains, set off by the neighboring sea. Towering buildings add muted greys and greens to the stark landscape. Mani's residents broke off from Sparta during the Roman Period and founded the League of Laconians. They resisted foreign rule ferociously, thereby gaining the name "Maniotes" (from the Greek *mania* or fury). Old Mani is best characterized as the Greek version of *The Godfather's* Sicily—vendettas, organized crime, the works. Ultimately, the Maniotes' obstinacy paid off, as even today Maniotes boast that not a single Turk has set foot on Mani soil. In the Revolution of 1821, Maniot women joined in the struggle for independence by driving Turkish forces back to sea. Today, Maniot culture has softened considerably, and although they revel in their historical ferocity, the inhabitants make excellent hosts to wandering tourists seeking beautiful beaches and views.

■ Areopolis ΑΡΕΟΠΟΛΗ

In spring and autumn, this cliff-top village attracts artists seeking inspiration from its austere scenery. Summer brings tourists in search of respite from Gython or a place to stay the night *en route* to the Glyfatha Lake Caves to the south. In Areopolis, sit under the stars in contented reverie and listen to the occasional snorts of farm animals, or join the locals in the central plaza, which feels a lot like home.

Orientation and Practical Information   The **police** (tel. 51 209), down a little street off the square and opposite the bus station, speak English (open 24hr.). Kapetan Matapan St., off the square, is home to the **post office** (open Mon.-Fri. 8am-1:30pm). To get to the **National Bank** (Mon.-Fri. 9am-noon; only open Tues. and Thurs. in off season), walk down Kapetan Matapan St., turn right at the first small church, and continue up the street—it is before the Hotel Mani. The bus station and the post office will **exchange currency** and traveler's checks for a hefty fee. In case of emergency, call the **hospital** at 51 259 (to reach it, take the road to your right as you face Nicola's Restaurant in the main square). It will lead you past Hotel Kouris, and after you cross the main road, it will run past the hospital 500m from the square.

The **bus stop** (tel. 51 229) is on one side of the square, located in the restaurant Nicola's Corner. Three buses per day make the trip from Kalamata to Itilo (2hr., 1200dr), with connections to Areopolis. Buses from Areopolis go to Kalamata (3 per day, 1600dr) via Itilo (30min., 450dr) and Sparta (4 per day, 1½hr., 800dr), stopping in Gythion (4 per day, 30min., 220dr). Two buses per day go to the Glyfatha Lake Caves near Pirgos Dirou (11am, return at 12:45pm; 1pm, return 2:45pm; 190dr), stopping in the town (175dr), where connections can be made to Vathia (700dr) and Gerolimenas (660dr). Hitching to the caves is easy and encouraged by locals, who might help you find a ride. *Let's Go* does not recommend hitchhiking. **Postal code:** 23062. **Telephone Code:** 0733.

Accommodations   If you spend the night here, try to find a room in the old town, which best evokes Mani's intriguing, turbulent past. Rooms in a traditional Maniot tower are available at **Tsimova** (tel. 51 301), off Kapetan Matapan St., to the left behind the church. Supposedly, Kolokotronis slept here. (Singles 5000dr. Doubles 8000dr. Breakfast 500dr.) If you don't mind a bleaker room (snazzed up by leopard-pattern furniture), George will rent you lodgings across the street (4000dr for 2-3 people). The cheapest rooms in town are off Kapetan Matapan St. above the **Xanthi Restaurant** (tel. 51 205; 2500dr per person). The Xanthi is also called "Ο Μπαρμπαπετροσ." Call ahead, as these often fill up. Another traditional guest house, or tower house, is run by **Pierros Bozagregos** (tel. 51 354), near Tsimova, renting fabulous doubles with bath (10,000dr).

Food   For dinner, try either of the restaurants on the right side of the town square. **Tsimova** serves mostly grilled food (*kalamari* 900dr). Both are good places to sip Greek coffee (150dr). For something cheap and easy, try **Fistera Oalepis** (tel. 51 436), on the main road, serving good *souvlaki*, chicken, and other grill items cheap (400-1200dr). **Nicola's Corner** (tel. 51 366), in the square, serves traditional dishes such as Greek salads (1000dr) and "boiled goat" (800dr). For swimming, locals leave town and head to the port town of Limeni, a short but steep walk away.

Mani's Honey Makes Money

Peddlers at roadside honey stands take their business, one of the region's most revered traditions, seriously. Honey-making is so serious, in fact, that an off-the-cuff statement that the honey for sale is not *natural* may be taken as a personal affront. The bees that produce Maniot honey, you will no doubt be told, only pollinate wildflowers, giving the honey a pleasantly light, *natural* taste and odor. Persistence in challenging the honey's source will meet with a passionate diatribe about honey-making: the honey is collected in beehive cubes which contain small honeycomb boards. The boards are collected by well protected, but nonetheless fearless, bee collectors who place ten boards at a time into a large, metal centrifuge. The liquid honey is separated from the semi-solid wax and, after sitting in a vat for days to let the oils rise to the top, *pure* honey is siphoned out of the bottom. Of course, you could skip the lecture and just buy the sweet, thick, *natural* Maniot honey (2000-2200dr per kilo).

■ Pirgos Dirou and Glyfatha Lake Cave

With its subterranean river, the **Glyfatha Cave** (also known as Spilia Dirou or Pirgos Dirou) is one of Greece's most splendid natural attractions. The boat ride through the cave is 1200m and lasts roughly 30 minutes. Originally discovered at the end of the 19th century and opened to the public in 1971 (a new section was found in 1983), the cave is believed to be 70km long and may extend all the way to Sparta. Vermilion stalagmites slice through the water, which is 30m deep in places—squiggling with eels. Bats fly around the maroon stalactites. Don't miss **Poseidon's Foot,** a striking formation that looks like a giant foot hanging in the air. Since some guides speak only Greek, you may want to buy the small book *Caverns of Mani,* from the store near the entrance (1500dr). After the boat trip, walk through more of the caves. The caves are 4km from town, accessible by bus, and an easy trip from Gythion by moped (open June-Sept. 8am-5:30pm; Oct.-May 8am-2:45pm; admission 3500dr). There's a beach (free) and a cafeteria. For information, call 52 222, -3.

PIRGOS DIROU

South along the road from Areopolis is **Pirgos Dirou.** Although far less interesting than Areopolis, the village is closer to the cave. It's possible to walk here from Areopolis (follow the signs at the other end of town from the road, 5km). Roughly 500m before Pirgos Dirou town, **Yiannis Kolokouris** (tel. (0733) 52 204, -40) rents petite, clean rooms above his restaurant. (Doubles 5000dr. Triples 7000dr.) **Panorama** (tel. (0733) 52 280) offers rooms 1km from the caves (doubles 7000dr). "Rooms to Let" signs dot the road from town to the grottoes. In town, the **Hotel Diros** (tel. (0733) 52 306, -440) has clean rooms. (Singles 8000dr. Doubles 9000dr.) At the town turn-off to the caves, there is a **post office** (tel. (0733) 52 249; open Mon.-Fri. 7:30am-2pm), and **Baker's Supermarket** (tel. (0733) 52 255) lies farther along the road toward the caves (open 7am-10pm). A particularly good option is **Greek Kitchen and Bar,** near the south end of town, which has free camping space.

Near Pirgos Dirou

South of the caves, **Mani** sheds its tourist-brochure gloss. Here lies the Mani of bandits and blood feuds, where camouflaged tower houses peer wearily from the rocky terrain and Byzantine barrel-vaulted churches complement the landscape. There are no gas stations in the south or east of Mani—be sure to ask about locations ahead of time. Just 2km from Pirgos Dirou is a turn-off for **Harouda** and the church of **Taxiarchis** (another 2km away). This church, decorated with blue and green ceramic plates and intricately patterned masonry, is situated in a mesmerizingly calm olive grove; climb to the church terrace for the view (open until sunset). Parallel to the main road, a side street passes a series of hillside villages, including **Vamvaka** and

Mina, each with tower houses and small churches. To rejoin the main road, turn downhill at any of the rocky junctures. Two swimming coves are off the main road near **Mezapos,** which also has a 12th-century church. Continuing south, you'll eventually touch water at the craggy port of **Gerolimenas** (Old Port), once called home by bloodthirsty pirates. A few nice **beaches** lie beyond town, to the southeast. Two **buses** leave daily for Athens via Areopolis and Gythion.

On Monday, Wednesday, and Friday, buses go to Vathia from Gerolimenas. About 20 people live year-round in **Vathia,** a medley of mountains, crumbling fortresses, and deserted towers. The government is trying to revive the town by enticing travelers to stay in one of 14 restored tower houses. Call (0733) 54 229 for information.

■ Monemvassia MONEMBAΣIA

The ancient Byzantine city of Monemvassia juts out from a rocky island. Seen from the west, the island appears uninhabited, and from the mainland only a small *taverna* and gas station are perceptible. A short walk east along the sea, however, reveals sloping fortified walls and a staircase that climbs the sheer 350m promontory. At the mountain's summit is the **citadel,** fortified by the Venetians in the 16th century. The town, equally reinforced, rests below. Monemvassia was first conquered in 1248 CE by Guillaume de Villehardouin, and in the hands of the Franks it functioned as a stopover for crusaders headed east. In later years it was captured by the Turks, the Pope, and finally the Venetians.

Today, one must pass through a covered gateway to enter Monemvassia's town (hence the name, meaning one way). Entering old Monemvassia gives visitors an eerie Twilight Zone feeling of having crossed into another time. The narrow streets are a medieval delight to explore, full of stairways and jasmine-filled courtyards. Visible immediately, a sinuous path lined with staircases serves as the main street and leads to shops and restaurants. Continue past the small strip of tourist traps to reach the **town square.** Facing the ocean, the **Christos Elkomenos** (Christ in Chains) church is on the left. On your right is a church that has been made into a mosque. Follow the labyrinthine walkways and stairs to visit the island's churches. The **Agia Sofia,** a Byzantine church modeled after the monastery at Daphni, presides on the edge of the ruins. Some of the original frescoes were restored 30 years ago.

Orientation and Practical Information In modern Monemvassia, **23rd Iouliou Street,** the principal thoroughfare, runs along the waterfront straight up to the causeway that leads to the island. Across from the bus station is the **National Bank** (tel. 61 201; open June-Sept. Mon.-Fri. 9am-1pm; Oct.-May only Tues. and Thurs.), and next door, the **post office** (tel. 61 231; open Mon.-Fri. 7:30am-2pm). On 28th Octovriou St., which runs off 23rd Iouliou St., just past the bus station, is the **police station** (tel. 61 210), in a house with a brown wooden door (open 24hr.). The police have some rooms listings. The **OTE** (tel. 61 399)is uphill bearing left from the bus station (open Mon.-Fri. 7:30am-3pm). Helpful **Malvasia Travel** (tel. 61 752) is near the bus station and opposite the post office (open daily 7am-2:15pm and 5:30-9:30pm). Ask the manager about currency exchange and **moped rental** (4000dr per day, plus gas). **English language books** and newspapers are available at **Lekakis Supermarket** (bear left at the fork past the post office; open daily 7am-11pm), and at the small tourist shop right before the Minos Hotel.

The **bus station** (tel. 61 752) is on 23rd Iouliou St., in the Malvasia travel agency opposite the post office. Buses for all destinations either connect or stop in Molai. The only exception is the direct express to Athens (daily, 5hr., 3550dr). Buses leave (2-4 per day) for Sparta (2½hr., 1600dr); Tripolis (3½hr., 2400dr); Corinth (4½hr., 3580dr); and Athens (6½-7hr., 4500dr) via Molai (30min., 400dr). Daily buses connect from Molai to Gythion, leaving Monemvassia at 11:15am (1½hr., 1300dr). **Ferries** leave twice a week for Kyparissa (1½hr., 900dr); Peiraias (6hr., 3600dr); Neapolis (1469dr); Kythera (2280dr); and Crete (3350dr). In the summer, **flying dolphins** go to Kythera (1hr., 4700dr) and Neapolis (Mon.-Thurs. at 12:55pm, Sat. at

11:45am, 4700dr). The hydrofoil leaves daily at 5pm for Peiraias (4hr., 7000dr) with stops on the islands (including Spetses, Hydra, and Kythera). An express leaves for Peiraias (6 per week, 3hr., 7000dr), stopping only at Spetses and Portoheli. Check at the ticket office (tel. 61 219) for schedules (next to the Mobil station on the island side of the causeway). **Postal Code:** 23070. **Telephone Code:** 0732.

Accommodations and Food   The **Hotel Aktaion**, 23rd Iouliou St. (tel. 61 234), near the causeway, is more expensive but has clean, modern rooms with balconies, bug screens, and reading lamps. (Singles 6000dr. Doubles 7000dr.) Prices are 20-40% less in the off season. **Hotel Minos** (tel. 61 224), along the main road, has clean, balconied rooms with showers. (Singles 6000dr. Doubles 8000dr.) The medieval village on the island has some rooms, but lodgings here are scarce and costly. Still, it's an amazing place to stay—for a treat, call **Malavasia Hotel** (tel. 61 323; singles 10,000dr, doubles 12,000dr). A more affordable choice is to pitch a tent at **Camping Paradise** (tel. 61 123), 3½km along the water on the mainland. (1100dr per person. 700dr per car. 850 per small tent. 1000dr per large tent. Prices lower in off season. 20% discount for longer stays.)

For fairly priced grub, try **Matoula** (tel. 61 660) and eat under the gnarled fig tree in the pleasant garden (entrees average 1300dr). Cheapest of all is *souvlaki* or *gyros* (both 270dr) at **Fotis Souvlaki,** a small strip of tables all decked out in red along the waterfront, or other *souvlaki/gyros* joints in town. Some of the best Greek food is along the road to Camping Paradise. One to try is **Pipinellis Taverna** (tel. 61 004), 2km from Monemvassia. For the past 25 years, the restaurant has featured home-grown produce (stuffed tomatoes 1000dr, veal 1300dr).

■ Near Monemvassia

NEAPOLIS

Neapolis is a good starting point for trips to Kythera or Crete. Quiet and friendly, this town is also a nice place to linger. The **police** (tel. 22 111), which double as **tourist police,** are on Ag. Triados St., to the right of the square. Turn the corner from the police station and, at the next corner, you'll come to the **post office** (open Mon.-Fri. 7:30am-2pm). The **OTE** is 200m up Spartis St., at the end of town ((open Mon.-Fri. 7:30am-3:10pm)). The **National Bank,** 160 Akti Boion St. (open Mon.-Thurs. 8am-2pm, Fri. 8am-1:30pm), offers **currency exchange. Telephone Code:** 0734.

Four **buses** per day travel to Athens (7hr., 5350dr), stopping *en route* at Molai (1¼hr., 1100dr); Sparta (3hr., 2250dr); Tripolis (4½hr., 3000dr); and Corinth (6hr., 4200dr). Tickets can be purchased from the tiny **KTEL office** (tel. 23 222), just past the upper right-hand corner of the square (facing inland) in the center of town. **Ferries** leave daily for Kythera, Crete, and Elafonisos. The **Miras Ferries** office, #154 Akti Boion St., sells ferry and **flying dolphin tickets.** "Rooms to Let" in town are 3000-5000dr for a single and 4000-7000dr for a double.

KYTHERA ΚΥΘΗΡΑ

Myth holds that Zeus threw Chronus' severed genitalia into the ocean where Kythera came to be, and later Aphrodite sprang from the surrounding waters. Kythera, reclining just to the south of the Peloponnesian cities of Monemvassia, Neapolis, and Gythion, is an isolated and lovely spot. The land's tranquil mountainous landscape harbors a collection of evergreens and flowering shrubs, secluded villages, and sandy beaches. The government has attempted to promote tourism by putting up new road signs, but this is not a destination set up for budget travelers, who struggle with 2am ferry drop-offs, infrequent or non-existent bus connections, and a scarcity of budget accommodations. But whatever your means of travel, Kythera rewards travelers with serenity and azure water.

Ferries dock in Kythera at either the west port, **Agia Pelagia,** or the newer port of **Diakofti,** designed to eventually take the role of Kythera's main port. The island's main road runs between Agia Pelagia and **Kapsali,** lively port towns whose harbor is frequented by yachtsmen, with smaller villages connected by subsidiary roads. Besides the port towns, this road passes through **Potamos, Livadi,** and **Kythera** (Chora), Kythera's larger inland towns. It's best to station yourself on the southern half of the island, closer to the moped rentals, "Rooms to Let," restaurants, and shops. Kapsali has hopping nightlife, Chora has fabulous views and some of life's necessities (such as a bank), and the inland town of Livadi has the cheapest rooms.

Orientation and Practical Information   Agia Pelagia's **tourist office** (tel. 33 815) is open to greet all who anchor at their port (except for those unfortunate folks arriving on the 2am ferry). They provide maps and help find rooms. **Post offices** exist in Chora (tel. 31 274) and Potamos (tel. 31 228). Each is located in its respective town square (open Mon.-Fri. 7:30am-2pm, Sun. 8am-2pm). **Police** are located in Chora (tel. 31 206), past the road leading out of town to the castle, and in Potamos (tel. 33 222; both open 24hr.). To get to the **OTE** in Chora (tel. 31 212), go up the stairs next to the square's travel agent (look for the sign) and follow the path to the street behind the square (open Mon.-Fri. 7:30am-3:10pm). There are **National Banks** in Chora (tel. 31 209, -218) and Potamos (33 209, -350), each in its town's main square. The **hospital** is in Potamos (tel. 33 325, -203; open 24hr.). All of the doctors speak English. **Postal Code:** 80200. **Telephone Code:** 0735.

Olympic Airways (tel. 33 297) offers **flights** to Athens (3 flights per day in summer, 1 flight per day in winter, 13,400dr). Cost conscious travelers should opt for one of the two **ferries** that leave from Agia Pelagia on the northeast tip of the island. The "Martha" heads 5 times per week to Neapolis (1hr., 1500dr) and Gythion (3hr., 1000dr), while the "Theseus" leaves 3 times per week for Crete (4hr., 3350dr) and Peiraias (9hr., 4700dr). Ferry schedules are posted all over the island but are subject to change. Check with any **Miras Ferries** office. In Agia Pelagia, consult **Conomas Travel** (tel. 33 490, -890), and in Kapsali, **Pateros Nikitas** (tel. 31 301). The **port police** (tel. 31 222 in Kapsali, 33 280 in Agia Pelagia) can give you complete information about all sailings. **Flying Dolphins** whisk you from Peiraias to Kythera in midafternoon (the ferry arrives at 2 or 3am). Hydrofoils leave 5 times per week for Peiraias (5hr., 9000dr); Aegina (4½hr., 10,000dr); Poros (10,000dr); Hydra (9000dr); Neapolis (2700dr); Monemvassia (4700dr); Spetses (3hr., 8200dr); and Portoheli (8200dr). Contact Kythera Travel (tel. 31 390) in the main square for complete details. **Taxis** can be found in Livadia (tel. 31 160, -860), Chora (tel. 31 320, -196), and Potamos (tel. 31 480). In Kapsali, look outside Panayopolis Moto-Rent for Antonis Stathis' blue Datsun (tel. 31 640). A taxi from Chora or Kapsali to the airport costs 2800-3000dr and from Agia Pelagia to Chora or Kapsali, roughly 3500dr. The taxis have meters, but bargain for a flat rate beforehand. **Buses** are unfortunately lacking. One shuttles between Agia Pelagia and Kapsali in July and August (4 per day), stopping at villages on request. Locals and tourist agencies know the schedule.

Accommodations   Chora Town has few budget accommodations, and most are booked weeks in advance, especially in August. **Pension Ketty** (tel. 31 318) lets tastefully furnished rooms. Look for the signs near the phone booth across from the bank. (Doubles 8000dr; less in off season.) Near the bakery, **Mr. Lourandou** (tel. 31 106) rents clean rooms. (Singles 5500dr. Doubles 7000dr. Triples 9600dr.)

Mr. and Mrs. Megaloudi (tel. 31 340) have pleasant doubles in Kapsali on the waterfront (9500dr with bath and fridge). Sheltered in a conifer forest, a beautiful **campground** (tel. 31 580) lies 300m from Kapsali up the road to Kythera. (700dr per person. 700dr per small tent. 950dr per large tent. Open June 15-Sept. 15.)

Food and Entertainment   Most waterfront restaurants in Kapsali and Agia Pelagia are overpriced, but **Artema** (tel. 31 342), on the water in Kapsali, is fair (spaghetti 750dr, vegetables in oil 650dr). For inexpensive Greek food with a twist, head inland and try **Toxotis Restaurant** in Livadi, one of the best on the island. In Kythera, try **Zorba's,** located on the main street, downhill from the square (chicken 700dr, open for dinner only). **Papos-Favos,** close to the ferry drop-off in Ag. Pelagia, serves great Greek salads (900dr), grilled items (800-1300dr), and vegetarian dishes.

The nightlife in Kythera seems the domain exclusively of Kapsali. The principal road is cluttered with outdoor cafés and clubs. The most popular is the new **Barba-rosa Music Bar** (tel. 31 831). Drinks are a little expensive, but the music is home-mixed. Also popular is the **Yachting Club** (tel. 31 909), which plays up its nautical theme with maps, charts, and drunken sailors.

Sights Kythera is selective in exposing its secrets. Start your brave exploration with a climb to the **castle** in Chora. The summit, dappled with the ruins of old churches and buildings, offers an intoxicating view of Kapsali's double harbor. The **Archaeological Museum,** with Mycenaean and Venetian finds, is just out of town, past the turn-off into Chora on the road to Livadi (open Tues.-Fri. 8:30am-2pm, Sun. 9:30am-1pm; free). A visit to the cave of **Agia Sofia Milopotamou** takes an after-noon and would make Indiana Jones envious. You'll have to bike down treacherous rocky roads, hike up a cliff, and crawl around in small clammy spaces. Wear sturdy shoes—the passage is dark and slippery. A few feet from the entrance to the grotto are several beautiful frescoes (open July-Sept. Mon., Wed., Sat. 4-8pm; admission with tour 500dr; double-check times with the police; hours change). If you go to the square in Milopotamou at 4pm, the guide will lead you to the cave on the partially paved road in your car or motorbike. If you arrive later, follow the signs out of town.

Central and Northern Greece ΚΕΝΤΡΙΚΗ ΚΑΙ ΒΟΡΕΙΑ ΕΛΛΑΔΑ

Northern and Central Greece may seldom find their way onto postcards, but it's not for a lack of beauty. Robust and pretension-free, the region waits to be discovered by adventurous travelers seeking refuge from swarming hotel owners and glitzy overpriced hotels. Greece's somewhat forgotten sections are graced with goat paths on pine-filled mountains that lead to some of the country's more precious Byzantine treasures, graceful springs, and breathtaking mountaintop vistas. Swaying green trees, lush vegetation, and endless farmland in intricate patchworks of cultivated fields characterize this gorgeous region of hidden treasures.

THESSALY ΘΕΣΣΑΛΙΑ

Outside its charmless industrialized urban centers, Thessaly's villages conceal some of the better nature trails in Greece. To the west of the cultivated Thessalian plain, the monasteries of Meteora cling to towering gray pinnacles. The rocky crags of Mt. Olympus, throne of the pantheon of Greek gods, watch over Aegean beaches with stark majesty. To the southeast, traditional mountain hamlets on Mt. Pelion lie scattered among forests, apple orchards, and grapevines that reach out to the sea.

■ Volos ΒΟΛΟΣ

Volos isn't much of a small town anymore. A few large thoroughfares cross the city with paths of poorly muffled engines and stinking exhaust, continuing without relief through the night. Nevertheless, its centrality makes it a good regional base, and away from the thoroughfares, some charm remains. The city has some surprising architecture and quiet, tiny alleys. Alongside the waterfront, the resort-like east part of town affords a venue for pleasant nighttime strolls.

ORIENTATION AND PRACTICAL INFORMATION

The **bus station** is located at the end of **Gr. Lambraki Street,** an easy 10-minute walk away from town and the waterfront. The **main road,** leading from the bus station to town, runs past the train station and the tourist office and onto **Dimitriados Street,** from which intersecting roads lead to various hotels.

Tourist Office: (tel. 23 500 or 36 233), on the waterfront in Riga Fereou Sq. Open July-Aug. daily 7am-2:30pm and 5-7pm; Sept.-June daily Mon.-Fri. 7am-2:30pm.

Tourist Police: #179 18th Octovriou St. (tel. 27 094). The street was recently renamed; locals still call it "Alexandras St." Help in English provided when the tourist office is closed. Open daily 7am-2:30pm, but available anytime.

OTE: Corner of Eleftheriou Venizelou and Sokratous St., across from the fruit and vegetable market. Open 24hr. **Information:** 131.

Trains: The **station** (tel. 28 555 or 24 056) is 1 block west of the tourist office. From town, turn right at the kiosk past the tourist office and walk 2-3min. down the parking lot parallel to the tracks in the trainyard. You must change in Larissa (16 per day, 1hr., 560dr) for Athens or Thessaloniki, unless you catch the daily super-express train to Athens (2 per day, 5hr., 5410dr). Otherwise, to Athens (7

per day, 6-7hr., 1780dr), Thessaloniki (1 per day, 4hr., 1780dr), and Kalambaka (4 per day, 3½hr., 1140dr). Only the express train has A/C.

Buses: Bus station (tel. 33 254), at the end of Gr. Lambraki St. In summer Mon.-Fri., buses travel to Athens (10 per day, 5hr., 4650dr); Thessaloniki (5 per day, 3¼hr., 3150dr); Larissa (14 per day, 1hr., 950dr); Portaria (10 per day, 45min., 200dr); Makrinitsa (10 per day, 50min., 300dr); Zagoria (4 per day, 2hr., 600dr); Horefto (3 per day, 2¼hr., 800dr); Afissos (5 per day, 45min., 400dr); Platania (3 per day, 2hr., 1000dr); Drakia (3 per day, 50min., 280dr); and Ag. Ioannis (2 per day, 2½hr., 1150dr).

Ferries: 3-4 boats per day to Skiathos (3hr., 2303dr), Skopelos (4½hr., 2800dr), and Alonissos (5hr., 3200dr). Fewer on weekends and in off season. Tickets are sold at an agency on the waterfront, and on the pier itself.

Flying Dolphins: Hydrofoils run with equal frequency at twice the price to Skiathos (1hr., 4630dr); Skopelos (2hr., 6006dr); Alonissos (2½hr., 6711dr); and Glossa (1½ hr., 5660dr). Inquire at the agencies next to where the ferry tickets are sold.

Car Rental: Theofanidis Hellas, 79 Iasonos St. (tel. 36 238), the block parallel to the waterfront. 10,000dr per day for a Fiat Panda; motorbikes not available.

English Bookstore: Bookstop, 163 Alexandrias St. (tel. 22 924), behind Ag. Nikolaos church. Offers instructional language material. Open Wed.-Fri., Sun. 8:30am-1:30pm and 5:30-9pm, Mon.-Tues., Sat. 8:30am-1:30pm.

Police: (tel. 26 121). Open 24hr.

Post Office: On P. Mela St., off 18th Octovriou St. Open Mon.-Fri. 7:30am-8pm. **Postal Code:** 38001.

Telephone Code: 0421.

ACCOMMODATIONS

The amount of *drachmae* you may have to shell out for a room in Volos could also be used as a down-payment for a mighty fine goat. Saying that you're a student and that you want only a simple room *(aplo domatio)* may procure a small discount.

Hotel Avra (tel. 25 370), 1 block up the street from Hotel Iasson. Rents clean, basic rooms at what is one of the better deals in town. Singles 3000dr.

Hotel Galaxy, 3 Ag. Nikolav (tel. 20 750). Pleasant, clean rooms, A/C, private baths, and a phone booth in the lobby. Singles 10,000dr. Doubles 14,000dr. Triples 16,800dr. Breakfast 1200dr.

Hotel Iolkos, 37 Dimitriados St. (tel. 23 416). Perversely, not located between 36 and 38 Dimitriados; rather, many blocks away at the end of the street, intersected by Metamorfoseos. Singles and doubles 5000dr.

Hotel Iasson (Jason), 1 P. Melo St. (tel. 26 075). Well scrubbed rooms with private phones, showers, and TV. Singles 6000dr. Doubles 8000dr. Triples 9000dr.

Hotel Philippos, 9 Solones St. (tel. 37 607). Comfortable rooms with fans, showers, TV, and a telephone. Singles 7000dr. Doubles 10,000dr. Triples 12,000dr.

FOOD, SIGHTS, AND ENTERTAINMENT

Cafés and *tavernas* drench the waterfront like oil on a Greek salad. Between midnight and sunrise, the *tavernas* and *ouzeries* along the waterfront overflow with people slouched in chairs, absorbing alcohol. In late July and August, Volos hosts a **festival** in Riga Fereou Park, featuring concerts, dances, and special exhibits.

Volos' **Archaeological Museum,** 1 Athonassaki (tel. 25 285), displays finds from the latter part of the Paleolithic Era to the Roman period. The museum is set in a verdant floral garden in the east part of town and is well worth the 30-minute walk from the waterfront. Inquire here or at the tourist office for information on the nearby archaeological sites at **Dimini** and **Sesklo.**

■ Mount Pelion Peninsula ΟΡΟΣ ΠΗΛΙΟ

In mythology, the rugged Pelion Peninsula was home to centaurs—half-man, half-horse creatures—and to Chiron, their mentor. Legend proclaims that Chiron, a physician, chose Pelion as a stomping ground because it contained more than 1700 medicinal herbs. The diversity of plant life in the region stems from a cool, moist climate, a feature appreciated today by sun-weary tourists. Pelion's tortuous terrain once helped protect it from invasion and fanned Greek nationalism while the rest of Greece strained under Turkish rule. Steep slopes now form a barrier to hypertourism, resulting in fewer visitors than it deserves.

MAKRINITSA

Winding up the twisting road from Volos to beautiful Makrinitsa, you'll transcend noise and smog but not souvenir stands. The stone houses and cobblestone streets of this ancient village clutch the hillside overlooking Volos and the Aegean. Hiking trails weave past mountain springs, goat-begotten hills, and age-old monasteries. From the bus stop, passing the souvenir shops and a small waterfall on the right, the road leads to the town square, presided over by the tiny one-room church of **Agios Yiannis the Beheaded,** where he can be seen inside cradling his lost noggin with an air of wistful unconcern. All of the eleven nearby churches and monasteries are around 200 years old, but the hollowed tree in the square grandfathers them all at a cool 1050 years. From the square, follow the clock tower opposite Agios Yannis, taking the stairs as you go, to reach the building it belongs to, the austere **Xamiseos Theotokou,** the functioning church of Makrinitsa. The church houses the *krifto skolo,* a hidden school which secretly taught the Greek language and culture during the Turkish occupation. The roof visible directly below the edge of the terrace of the square belongs to the **Museum of Makrinitsa** (tel. (0421) 99 505), which displays authentic clothes, scabbards, and various other typical Makrinitsalia of two centuries past. Free tours are given by the museum's curator, who is glad to answer all questions about the exhibitions. The roof directly below the museum's covers the **Metamorphosi,** another of the more interesting churches. In the square, in the pit on the way to the museum, there is a very rudimentary **map** showing the way to other sites, including **Agios Georgios.** (All open daily 8am-7pm, sometimes with a midday break. Some require trousers or dresses for women, pants for men.)

Makrinitsa has been designated a traditional settlement by the Greek National Tourist Organization, so staying here will cost an arm and a leg. Budgeteers either splurge on one of the town's posh pensions, or make the town a daytrip. **Pension**

Archontiko Diomides (tel. (0421) 99 430), uphill from the Galini Restaurant (look for the sign along an uneven stone path), has beautiful rooms with whitewashed interiors, traditional furnishings, wood carvings, patios, and cozy communal living rooms on each floor. (Singles and doubles with bath 8000dr. Triples 9500dr. Quads 10,000dr.) The **Hotel Achilles** (tel. (0421) 99 177), just before the square, offers bright, modern rooms with sea views. Have breakfast (1200dr) in the taxidermist's-heaven-decor café. We're talking birds, ducks, foxes, and cowskins on the walls. (Doubles 7500dr.) **O Theophilos** (tel. (90421) 99 435), on the path through the square, offers wooden beds and fireplaces. Breaking the usual rule, the winter prices are in fact higher than the summer prices, due to the cost of heating these high-altitude rooms. (Singles 8000dr. Doubles 12,000dr.) The **Pantheon** (tel. (0421) 99 143), a *taverna* in the square, serves local specialties on a cliffhanging terrace (open daily 9am-midnight). Makrinitsa has paltry practical conveniences. Nearby **Portaria** offers **currency exchange.** There's no post office (only a mailbox) and the kiosk sells stamps.

■ Meteora ΜΕΤΕΩΡΑ

The mysterious black rock formations of Meteora rise majestically above the surrounding Thessalian plain. According to one theory, the rocks are large salt deposits from a primordial sea. Whatever their origin, the spectacle of the formations would be worth visiting even if they didn't hold 24 Byzantine monasteries with beautiful frescoes and astonishing views. Six of the 24 are still inhabited by religious orders and are open to the public. Although the site is one of the more popular in Northern Greece, the monasteries themselves offer an experience both quieting and serene.

In the 9th century CE, hermits and ascetics began occupying the pinnacles and crevices of Meteora, where they built a church dedicated to the Virgin. As religious persecution at the hands of Serbian invaders increased in the 12th century, Christians flocked to take refuge on the summits of these impenetrable columns of rock. In 1356, the region's first official monastic community was founded. In the late Byzantine Period, when the Turks ruled Greece, Meteora became a bastion of Christian faith, eventually growing into a powerful community of 24 monasteries, each embellished by fine artists. The communities' wealth, however, turned out to be their downfall. Quarrels over riches led to neglect and deterioration during the 16th century. But all was not lost; some of the monasteries (**Grand Meteoron, Varlaam, Agia Triada,** and **Agios Nikolaos**) are active to this day, while **Agios Stephanos** and **Agia Barbara** (Roussanou) now serve as convents.

ORIENTATION AND PRACTICAL INFORMATION

Buses travel from the main square in Kalambaka to the **Grand Meteoron** (2 per day, 20min., 190dr). Flag down the bus at any of the blue *stasis* signs along its route or go to the bus station. The bus may stop at the different monasteries along the way to Grand Meteoron. It's a good idea to begin your walking tour from the Grand Meteoron, the uppermost monastery, and then to visit the others as you make your way back to town. Five kilometers from Kalambaka lies the scenic hamlet of **Kastraki,** which is more restful, less crowded, and closer to Meteora than Kalambaka.

At least a full day is needed to see the monasteries, although it may be rewarding to spend more time visiting only a few in order to get a feeling for monastic life. Grand Meteoron and **Varlaam** are the largest, and cater to tourists; the others are more intimate. Modest dress (pants for men, skirts for women) is strictly enforced. Visitors should cover their shoulders and men with long hair may be asked to wrap it in a bun (as do the monks). Don't fret—women aren't asked to do the Princess Leia Star Wars thing. Unflattering cover-ups are available for rental at monastery entrances. Photography and filming inside the monasteries are forbidden—illicit attempts have been known to provoke the monks into less-than-divine fits of anger. The monasteries have staggered closing days, but all are open Saturday, Sunday, and

Wednesday from April until the end of September (open 9am-1pm and 3:20-6pm, but most stay open until visitors have left; admission to each 400dr).

ACCOMMODATIONS

Meteora offers several options for both avid campers and hotel goers. You may want to begin your campground search on the Ioannia-Kalambaka highway which leads out of Meteora, but inquire with locals before beginning your trek. An alternative is to check out the conveniently located, mostly clean hotels and pensions in town.

THE MONASTERIES

The Monastery of the Transfiguration (Metamorphosis), known as the **Grand Meteoron** (tel. 22 278), is the oldest and largest. Built on the most massive of the occupied stone columns, the complex looms 500m above the Thessalian plain. Founded by Athanasius, a monk from Mt. Athos, the monastery rose in the hagio-hierarchy when John Uresis, grandson of the Serbian prince Stephen, retired here in 1388.

The Grand Meteoron's central feature is the 16th-century **Church of the Transfiguration,** with brilliant frescoes of the Roman persecution of the Christians in its narthex. Directly across lies a chamber filled with carefully stacked skulls and bones—the remains of past monks (Grand Meteoron open Wed.-Mon.).

Three hundred kilometers from the Grand Meteoron stands the **Varlaam Monastery** (tel. 22 277), the second largest monastery on Meteora. Built in 1517, the monastery's crowning glory is its chapel's 16th-century frescoes, including a particularly disturbing depiction of the Apocalypse. Varlaam also has an extensive net and pulley system, which shows how earlier visitors were hoisted (open Sat.-Thurs.).

Visible from most of the valley, **Agia Barbara** (also called Roussanou; tel. 22 649) is a spectacularly situated and frequently photographed monastery. Originally founded in the 14th century, Agia Barbara was only recently abandoned in the early 1980s due to deterioration of its walls, which were built directly into the rock formation. Seven years ago, a small group of nuns moved in and began a restoration that is still underway. Smaller and less visited than Varlaam and Grand Meteoron, it features a lovely church covered in frescoes. Nun-made lace is available for sale (open in summer daily; in winter Thurs.-Tues.).

Versatile **Agios Stephanos,** at the road's end, was founded as a hermitage, became a monastery in the 14th century, and is now a convent. Stephanos is cleaner, lighter, and more spacious than Grand Meteoron and Varlaam. Of its two churches, only the more modern **Agios Charalambos,** built in 1798, is open. Although small, the museum displays artifacts of intricate detail (open Tues.-Sun.).

The Monastery of **Agia Triada** (Holy Trinity; tel. 22 220) lies 3km down the road towards the main intersection. Movie buffs will recognize it from the James Bond flick *For Your Eyes Only.* Looming above Kalambaka, the peak of Agia Triada gives a soul-searing view of the town and the distant, snow-capped **Pindos Mountains.** The monk Dometius built the monastery in 1476, but the wall paintings were added

Highway to Heaven (Sort of)

The first ascetics scaled the sheer cliff faces by wedging timbers into the rock crevices, thereby constructing small platforms, traces of which can still be seen. After the monasteries were completed, visitors usually arrived by means of extremely long rope ladders, but when these were pulled up, the summit became virtually inaccessible. Visitors who were either too weak or too timid to climb with the ladders were hoisted up in free-swinging rope nets. The half-hour ascent, during which the rope could be heard slowly unwinding, no doubt fostered profound faith in God. Motorized winches have since replaced monk-powered, rope-spool cranes, and today only provisions, not pilgrims, are elevated. In 1922, steps were carved into the rocks and bridges built between the pillars, so even the vertigo-prone would feel secure.

200 years later. A 3km footpath to the right of the entrance to Agia Triada leads to Kalambaka (open Fri.-Wed.).

Back down the road, past the main intersection and only 2.5km before Kastraki, rests the Monastery of **Agios Nikolaos** (also called Anapafsa; tel. 22 375). Built in 1388 and expanded in 1628, its highlight is the fresco work painted by the 16th-century Cretan master **Theophanes.** Visitors are admitted only in small groups, so wait in the entrance at the top of the steps for the door to open (open daily).

■ Near Meteora: Kalambaka ΚΑΛΑΜΠΑΚΑ

Once famous for its architecture, Kalambaka lost most buildings of importance to the occupying Nazis' brand of urban renewal. Today, the town caters to international tourists visiting Meteora. Kalambaka has two main squares. The first, two blocks up from the **bus station,** is the town's **central transit hub,** where **taxis** (tel. (0432) 22 310) congregate at a small kiosk (open daily 6:30am-midnight), from which all major thoroughfares radiate. The second, a few blocks to the right facing Meteora, has mostly **shops and restaurants.** The non-English-speaking but amiable **police,** 11 Hagipetrou St. (tel. (0432) 22 109), will not only enforce the law, but also help travelers find rooms (open daily 9am-9pm; officer on duty 24hr.). To get there from the bus station, walk one block uphill and take your first right. Facing the square is an **Ionian Bank,** with an **ATM** that accepts Visa (open Mon.-Thurs. 8am-2pm, Fri. 8am-1:30pm). Down Ioanninon St. (look for the traffic signs for Ioannina and Grevena, located at the top of the street), are the **OTE** and the **post office** diagonally across from each other. By way of Trikalon St. (Road to Trikala), you'll come to **Riga Fereou Square,** which, according to locals, is the town's "real" square because it boasts a pleasant, leafy park. Facing the park is a **National Bank.** Beyond the park, Trikalon St. transforms into an all-out nightlife scene—bars, discoes, neon signs, and a hopping crowd. There are **international bookstores** on both of the town's main squares, a **pharmacy** at the top of the square, and a **health center** (tel. (0432) 24 111; open 24hr.) 1km from town.

Trains depart from the **station** (tel. (0432) 22 451) on the main "highway" behind the bus station and off to the left (coming downhill from the bus station). They go to Athens (8 per day, 6½hr., 2700dr); Thessaloniki (6 per day, 5hr., 2200dr); Alexandroupolis (2 per day, 12 hr., 5390dr); Livadia (6 per day, 5hr., 2190dr); and Volos (4 per day, 4hr., 1140dr). Air-conditioned express trains cost 2200dr extra for Athens (2 per day) and 1100dr extra for Thessaloniki (1 per day). Be sure to change trains in Paleofrasis en route to Athens. From the **bus station** (tel. 22 432), buses go from Kalambaka to Meteora (2 per day, 9am and 1:20pm, 20min., 190dr). The early bus ensures you time to hike around visiting the **monasteries,** which are open daily 9am-1pm and 3:30-5pm. Most walk (6km downhill) back to Kalambaka, visiting monasteries along the way. Buses also go to Volos (4 per day, 2600dr) and Thessaloniki (3500dr).

Private rooms abound, but it's illegal for owners to solicit at the bus or railway stations, and those who do have been known to lure travelers with the promise of good prices and then add surcharges for supplementary services. Cozy, traditional, and utterly delightful, **Koka Roka** (tel. (0432) 24 554) warrants the 550m or so walk up from the bus station. (Singles 3000dr, with bath 4000dr. Doubles 6000dr, with bath 7000dr. Triples 7500dr. Prices negotiable for longer stays.) There are also **campgrounds** near Kalambaka.

For a hearty meat dish (manly grunt here—the region is known for its meat), head to **Nikos Tavern** (tel. (0432) 22 138), across from the bookstore (entrees 1500dr). **Restaurant Panellinio,** in the central square, has tasty and satisfying vegetarian entrees (800dr) and opens early for breakfast. **Restaurant Aitineio,** on Trikalon St. just before the park, provides a pleasant terrace amid traditional *bouzouki* music and a broad range of traditional dishes graces the menu (entrees 1200dr). The *taverna* at **Koka Roka** rewards wayfarers from the monasteries with delicious homemade specialties (entrees 1000dr). **Droutkas,** a sweet shop and bar on Trikalon St., beyond the park and opposite the Shell station, is one of Kalambaka's more popular hangouts. The largest of several **markets** is uphill past Hotel Astoria (open daily 7am-2:30pm and 5-9pm). In late July the town honors its patron saint with a **glendi** (celebration). Kalambaka holds a three-day **wine festival** with traditional dancing and **free wine** in late August.

Kalambaka's foremost sight is the Byzantine **Church of the Dormition of the Virgin.** Follow the signs, ubiquitous around the central square, and after several blocks you'll spy the graceful bell tower of the old church, haloed by a stork's nest. Built in the 11th century on the ruins of a 5th-century basilica, the main structure was remodeled in 1573. Unfortunately, the interior frescoes, painted by the Cretan monk **Neophytos,** have been badly blackened by centuries of candle flames, incense, and midnight seances. George Dailianas is the church tour guide (when he's not planting trees) and is fond of practicing his English with visitors. Modest dress is preferred (open daily 9am-2pm; admission 300dr).

■ Metsovo ΜΕΤΣΟΒΟ

Metsovo has been officially designated a "traditional settlement" by the Greek National Tourist Organization. Consequently, uniformly overpriced restaurants and dozens of geegan and junk shops fill the town's main square. Worn old traditional buildings have been spruced up to look like newly constructed old traditional buildings, and a booming trade in postcards and handmade wooden trinkets profitably romanticizes the economy of subsistence agriculture and petty commerce which it has replaced. Genuine charm remains, and Metsovo's lopsided mixture of local color and pre-packaged comfort may just strike a soothing balance. This snug little mountain hamlet, perched just below the 1850m Katara Pass, can be a relief. Native Metsovans are descendants of the **Vlachi,** a people once believed to have emigrated from Romania, but now surmised to have been Greeks trained by the Romans to guard the Equatia Highway connecting Constantinople and the Adriatic. The Vlachi language is closer to Latin than to Greek, and was used to communicate with the Italians during WWII. Today, it survives only on Metsovo's cobblestone streets.

Orientation and Practical Information Against the side of the patio of an outdoor café in the square is a large map of the town, which lists (in English) all hotels, sights, monasteries, restaurants, the town's two discoes, and the town's "sanitary station" for **medical emergencies** (tel. 41 111). There is a **National Bank** (tel. 41 203) in the square (open Mon.-Thurs. 8am-2pm, Fri. 8am-1:30pm), and the bank to the right of the newsstand has a 24-hour **ATM.** To reach the **OTE** (tel. 42 199), cut through the courtyard in front of the bank, then turn left and wind around to the right (open daily 7:30am-3:10pm). The municipal **police** (tel. 41 233) are on the right past the courtyard, and the police chief speaks English (office open daily 8am-2pm and 4-6pm, but available 24hr.). The **post office** (tel. 41 245) is up the main road from the square (open Mon.-Fri. 7:30am-2pm).

From the little shed in the square, **buses** depart for Ioannina (5 per day, 950dr) and Trikala via Kalambaka (3 per day, 1500dr). Buses to Thessaloniki stop at the main highway above town (9 per day, about 3000dr). For **schedule information,** go to the café across the main street from the bus stop shed. **Telephone Code:** 0656.

Accommodations Unblemished, inviting rooms fill **Hotel Athens** (tel. 41 725), down the hill from the main square. Sample the homemade specialties from their peaceful, parkside restaurant (vegetarians rejoice!). Hikers and campers are also welcome to store their gear (free of charge) at Hotel Athens during visits to Pindos Mountain, for which the owners can often suggest good routes. (Singles 5000dr. Doubles 6000dr.) If Hotel Athens is full, owners may direct you to nearby **Hotel Filoxenia** (tel. 41 011). (Doubles 8000dr.) The **Duros family** (tel. 42 415) offers traditional rooms on the downward path away from the square, below the post office. (Singles 5000dr.) The **Tsanaka family** offers traditional, clean rooms on

EVRITANIA

the street past the newsstand and the OTE. (Doubles with TV, kitchen, and bath 8000dr. Triples 9000dr.) The **Hotel Acropolis** (tel. 41 672) is up near the highway. (Doubles 9300dr. Triples 10,500dr.)

Food, Entertainment, and Sights   Just below the Hotel Athens, a peaceful **parkside restaurant** (tel. 41 725) serves tasty homemade specialties at a price and quality generally superior to the restaurants in the square. Of those in the square, locals favor the **Krifi Folia** (tel. 41 628) for its good deals (chicken 1100dr).

After dinner, the popular bar **Ianoi** will give you something you can dance to, spinning both Greek and foreign music. Look for the woodshed on the road leading to the post office (no cover; beer 500dr, cocktails 800dr; open in winter daily 9pm-3:30am; later in summer). A few buildings down, the bar **Mast** affords a similar scene at a similar price (beer 400dr, cocktails 700dr).

A wonderful example of Metsovite living during earlier decades is the **Tossizza Museum,** housed in a stone and timber Epirot mansion on the left up the main road (look for the sign opposite the Shell station). It's full of *Vlachi* furniture and clothing, suggestive of how Metsovite families spent long winters cooped up in their homes. The upper floor was **Vangeli Averof's** apartment when he was a diplomat. Visitors wait at the door until the guide magically appears (roughly every 30min.; open Fri.-Wed. 8:30am-1pm and 4-6pm; admission 300dr). The **folk art gallery** (tel. 41 210) off the main square is a treat (open in summer Wed.-Fri. 9am-1:30pm and 5-7:30pm; in winter 9am-1:30pm and 4-6pm; admission 300dr, students 200dr).

Gracing the central square is a statue of **Michalis Tossizza,** a native who found fame and fortune in Romania and shared his luck (Romanian *lei*) with Athens and Metsovo by building stadiums and museums (including the Tossizza museum). Signs near the square lead to **Ag. Nikolaos Monastery** and its 14th-century chapel.

EVRITANIA ΕΥΡΥΤΑΝΙΑ

At the end of every goat path in Evritania's pine-capped mountains lies a fragrant feast, the kind of place adventuresome nature lovers adore. Rare, first-time visitors to this region discover untouched mountainsides and serene villages that still mirror life as it was 40 years ago. Only recently, with the establishment of a **ski resort,** has the region turned its attention to tourism, but the fledgling industry has not yet affected the culture or prices. Not surprisingly, in a region where chickens outnumber cars, Evritania is considered to have the purest environment in all of Europe, the fourth cleanest in the world—as your body will tell you. Close your eyes. Breathe in.

Karpenisi ΚΑΡΠΕΝΗΣΙ

Karpenisi, the capital of Evritania, attracts its fair share of visitors each year—nature lovers, who explore the mountains and rivers, and skiers, who take advantage of the city's proximity to the Velouchi ski center, 12km away. For this reason, Karpenisi is a comfortable destination, with numerous hotels, cozy *tavernas,* and honest-to-goodness hospitality that is wholesomely refreshing.

Karpenisi confers almost inexplicable invigoration upon unsuspecting visitors. Established in Byzantine times during the mid-11th century CE, the city is set along the northwest slope of Mt. Velouchi, highest of the Timfristos Mountains, within a panoply of crisp forests of fir and chestnut, and ethereal blue-green lakes sweetened by the cool mountain climate. Despite its tranquil setting, Karpenisi has weathered a history of devastations—by Turks, Albanians, and Germans—and today, small and uncluttered, bearing modern façades, the city is not much to look at. But it's a fine place to look from, with an understatedness that helps you appreciate the surroundings all the more.

EPIRUS

Orientation and Practical Information   Since Karpenisi is spread along a slope, you can find almost everything within a five-minute walk from the square. The main road leading down from the bus station forks at the square. The **OTE** and the **police station** (tel. 25 100; open 24hr.) are in close succession along the road forking off to the right. Edging the square is a **National Bank** and the local **taxi stand** (tel. 22 666). The **bus station** is uphill from the square on the main road. **Buses** run to Athens (3 per day, 5hr., 4250dr); Lamia (4 per day, 2hr., 1200dr); Agrinio (2 per day, 3hr., 1800dr); and the villages of Proussou (3 per day, 1¼hr., 550dr); Mikro Horio (2 per day, 30min., 240dr); and Megalo Horio (2 per day, 30min., 240dr). One to two buses per day also run to surrounding villages for 500-1000dr. In the square fronting the cafés is the **town hall,** with tourist information. Diagonally across the street from the Agricultural Bank, after Maxim's Café, is the Karpenisi chapter of the **Greek Mountaineering Club (EOS),** 2 Georgiou Tsitsara, which can field your questions concerning mountaineering in the Timfristos Mountains. For the **hospital,** call 22 315. **Postal Code:** 36100. **Telephone Code:** 0237.

Accommodations   Karpenisi has no shortage of quality hotels, mainly because people flock here in winter for the nearby **Velouchi Ski Center,** which can only accommodate 50 people. The ski season runs from November through March. Expect to pay less in summer, when many of the hotels sit almost empty. **Hotel Galini,** 3 R. Ferou (tel. 22 930; make your first right after the Agricultural Bank), has cozy pleasant rooms with baths. (Singles 4406dr. Doubles 8812dr.) The rustic **Anessis Hotel,** 50 Zinopoulou (tel. 22 840), is nestled on the outskirts of town but within walking distance of the square. Follow the road that forks left from the top of the square, past Hotel Elvetia; Anessis will be on your right. English-speaking staff has ski information. (Singles 5000dr. Doubles 8000dr.) **Hotel Mt. Blanc** (tel. 22 322), just past the OTE on the way to the police station, is a spacious hotel with an outdoor terrace. (Singles 6000dr. Doubles 8800dr. 3-person family suites 15,800dr.)

Food and Entertainment   The **Taverna Klymataria** (tel. 22 230) on Kosma Aitolou radiates a light and cheerful atmosphere, with a cozy fireplace and a small bar. It offers seasonal specialties, classic grill, vegetarian options, special home wine, and live traditional Greek music Friday and Saturday nights (entrees 1500dr). Klymataria is located a few blocks down from the Agricultural Bank, named after the tree growing out front (open in summer and for festivals daily "all day"; in winter "evenings only"). **Taverna Panorama** (tel. 25 976), down the street from Hotel Galini, doesn't exactly have a panoramic view, but offers a broad (relatively panoramic) menu and outdoor dining. The menu, also in English, includes vegetarian options. The **sweetshop of Georgos Kitsios and Co.,** 13 Zinopoulou (tel. 24 082), just opposite the square (look for the pink-and-white sign), has probably the best selection of sweets in Karpenisi, and some of the better *baklava* you may ever taste (loads of walnuts and not too sweet). While in town, ask around about the **local fairs,** held throughout the summer, that feature live Greek music and tasty lamb.

EPIRUS ΗΠΕΙΡΟΣ

Epirus is among the lesser touristed and more beautiful regions in Greece, featuring stark mountains, gorgeous wildflowers, and lush forests. It is in Epirus that traditional mountain villages, inhabited by black-clad women and staff-holding shepherds, can still be found. The region spent 482 years under Ottoman rule and holds ancient ruins, Roman artifacts, and Turkish mosques in close proximity to one another. Epirus is also home to stellar mountain climbing, hunting, and hiking. The picturesque town and resplendent beaches of Parga see their share of visitors, but the mountains and timeless villages of Zagoria near the Vikos-Aoos National Park remain undisturbed.

■ Igoumenitsa ΗΓΟΥΜΕΝΙΤΣΑ

Igoumenitsa may be your first stop on the Greek mainland (boats from Brindisi and Corfu stop here), and if you begin exploring the country here, you'll be in good company—that's what Lord Byron did in 1809. Igoumenitsa is the consummate transportation hub, linking Central and Northern Greece, the Ionian Islands, and foreign destinations. There are no you-haven't-lived-until-you've-seen-them sights or sprawling beaches, but you may stroll along what is actually a lovely waterfront.

Orientation and Practical Information Buses depart from the station (tel. 22 309) to Ioannina (10 per day, 2hr., 1600dr); Thessaloniki (1 per day, 8hr., 6900dr); Athens (4 per day, 8hr., 7350dr); Parga (4 per day, 1hr., 1000dr); and Pereza (2 per day, 2hr., 1800dr). To reach the **OTE** (tel. 22 399), go left from the station, and turn left at the first corner (open daily 7am-10pm). The **post office** (tel. 22 209) is in the same building as the OTE (open Mon.-Fri. 7:30am-2pm).

Igoumenitsa has three main ports, which you'll come to in rapid succession. The **old port** mostly sends boats to Italy and houses the multilingual **EOT tourist office** (tel. 22 227), which has timetables and brochures, a list of hotels and their prices, and a helpful **map** (open daily 7am-2pm and 5-10pm). Across the road from the old port is a string of banks, including the **National Bank** (tel. 22 415) with an **ATM** (open Mon.-Thurs. 8am-2pm, Fri. 8am-1:30pm). Near the National Bank is an **American Express** office (tel. 22 406 or 24 333), which will change money, issue traveler's checks, and give you cash from your AmEx card (open Mon.-Sat. 7:30am-2pm and 4-11pm, Sun. 7:30-11am and 5-9:30pm). **Ferry tickets** to Corfu can be purchased at the **Corfu Port**, 100m farther, in the yellow kiosk in the parking lot. Across from the Corfu Port are the **police** (tel. 22 100) and the **tourist police** (tel. 22 222), who speak little English. Beyond the Corfu Port is the **New Port**, which sends boats to Italy and Corfu. The new port also houses a new **OTE**, which **exchanges currency,** sells telephone cards, and provides fax and telephone services, and a second **EOT office** (tel. 27 757). **Ferries** go to Corfu (every hr., 4:30am-10pm, 2hr., 836dr). For tickets to Italy or the former Yugoslav Republic of Macedonia, shop around at the waterfront agencies. "Budget" carriers vary from year to year, and some have student rates. Igoumenitsa's primary ferry agencies sell tickets for most shipping lines. **Minoan-Strintzis** (tel. (01) 689 83 40), **ANEK** (tel. 22 104), **Marlines** (tel. 23 301), **Adriatica** (tel. 26 410), **A.K. Ventouris** (tel. 22 001), and **Hellenic Mediterranean** (HML; tel. 22 780) are omnipopular options, although Adriatica and HML are the only two that accept Eurail and Inter-Rail passes. Destinations include Brindisi (9 per day, 10hr., 8600dr); Ancona (1 per day, 22hr., 17,600dr); Venice (4 per week, 30hr., 18,800dr); and Bari (4 per day, 12hr., 8000dr). Prices do not include port dues (1500dr in Greece, 4000 lira in Italy). Most boats depart before noon; arrive early or plan to spend the night. In Igoumenitsa, there is a **medical center** (tel. 24 420) that handles most health problems. If you need to go to a hospital, they will help you get to the one 15 minutes away. **Postal Code:** 46100. **Telephone Code:** 0665.

Accommodations and Food To find **Hotel Crossroads** (tel. 22 343), follow the street to the left of the park uphill for two blocks. The hotel offers pleasant rooms in slightly imperfect repair, away from the traffic. (Singles 4000dr. Doubles 6000dr. Triples 10000dr.) **Hotel Rex** (tel. 22 255; look for the sign on the door, on the opposite side of the block to the right of the bus stop) provides small but adequate rooms. (Singles 2000dr. Doubles 4000dr. Triples 6000dr.) **Hotel Equatia** (tel. 23 648), whose large sign is at the park's far right corner, has upscale rooms with private bath, TV, and phone. (Singles 6000dr. Doubles 9000dr. Triples 11500dr.)

The **Bakery Alexiou Spiridon** (tel. 24 617) is just off the waterfront at 7 El. Venizelou St. on your way to the ports; look for the Ionian Bank at the waterfront corner or try to catch the subtle white "Bakery" placard hanging a few storefronts inland. It offers a pleasing, family-style array of baked goods and sweets, including nutritious

EPIRUS

and hard-to-find whole grain and special diet sugar-free breads (open daily 6am-6pm). After dinner, you can dance and drink at the **Metropole** or **Traffic,** or another of the clubs and bars in town, all of which charge 1000dr to enter and buy your first beer. The nearby **Drepanon Beach** will also give you a place to dance, at **Billy's Club, Click,** or another hot spot.

■ Parga ΠΑΡΓΑ

Parga is invigoratingly different from Preveza and Igoumenitsa, its larger coastal neighbors. Snug within an arc of green mountains, the town is sheltered from the sea by a row of rocky islets and rests in coves of stunning, sand-and-turquoise beaches. It has not, however, been sheltered from tourism. Much like many of the Sporades, Parga presents old-style whitewashed buildings housing high-class jewelry shops, and stone alleyways lined with t-shirted vendors. The beaches and waterfront *tavernas* draw a fun-loving, sun-loving crowd (especially in July, when the streets ooze with Italians), who partake in the effervescent nightlife. The narrow streets, Neoclassical houses, and harbor views create a romantic mood that seems to have infected even the pink pastel supermarket.

Orientation and Practical Information   To reach the bus stop from the port, head to the northwest corner of the waterfront (with the ocean behind you), and walk uphill and inland. You'll find the **National Bank** (tel. 31 719) one block down the way (open Mon.-Thurs. 8am-2pm, Fri. 8am-1:30pm). Proceed uphill to pass the **OTE** (tel. 31 699), sporting a maroon façade (open in summer Mon.-Sat. 7:30am-10:00pm, Sun. 9am-2pm and 5-10pm). Farther up, the **bus stop** is the intersection with the church on its corner; the **post office** (tel. 31 295) is farther up still (open Mon.-Fri. 7:30am-2pm). Next door is the **police station** (tel. 31 222) and the **tourist police** (both available 24hr.). The **port police** can be reached at 31 227, the **fire station** at 31 199, and the **medical center** at 31 100. **Kanaris Travel** (tel. 31 490; fax 31 977), **Charitos Travel** (tel. 31 900), **Parga Holiday** (tel. 31 650; on the waterfront), and **Synthesis Travel** (tel. 31 700; fax 31 203; a half-block inland) help find rooms, rents mopeds, and arranges daytrips (all open Mon.-Sat. 9am-2pm and 5:30-10pm). They also sell **ferry tickets** to Paros and Antiparos (daily, 4500dr roundtrip for both, 3500dr roundtrip for just Paros), and Corfu Town (Fri., 8000dr). **Buses** connect Parga with Preveza (5-6 per day, fewer on weekends, 2hr., 1200dr); Igoumenitsa (3-4 per day, 1hr., 1000dr); Athens (4 per day, 9½hr., 6800dr); and Thessaloniki (1 per day, 7950dr). **Postal Code:** 48060. **Telephone Code:** 0684.

Accommodations, Food, and Entertainment   The number of vacationers in Parga increases each year, but the rooms more than keep up. Hotels in Parga are expensive—check out the rooms extolled by folks who greet incoming buses, or try off the beaten track, at the south end of the town and the top of the hill. Better yet, head to one of the tourist offices.

As for food, pick your *taverna* by its tablecloth colors; the *tavernas* are all the same. Head 500m inland from the entrance to the Venetian fortress to find the **Restaurant Panorama** (tel. 32 447); try the *moussaka* (1200dr) while enjoying the view of the bay and beaches. The restaurant will pay for your taxi to their establishment (open daily 9am-midnight). On the waterfront, **Christos Giakis** (tel. 31 711), with red and white checked tablecloths, gives a better value than usual, with spaghetti for 900dr.

One floor up at the start of the waterfront, the **Caribou Bar** gives thirty-somethings a place to boogie to flashing colored lights and earnestly modern, synthesized music. On the waterfront, **Billy's Bar** plays more conventionally hip music. Youth frequent the **Camares Disco Club,** whose neon sign above a waterfront alleyway leads the way to some sexy nocturnal gyrations, while **Factory,** in an alleyway to the left, plays to a more mixed set. At all places, 1000dr admits you and buys you a beer; once inside, another brewski is 500dr and cocktails are 1000dr each.

Sights The **Venetian fortress,** the largest in the area, dominates the town. Constructed by the Normans, the Venetians controlled it from 1401 to 1797. Today, the structure seems a mere shell beneath the shade of majestic pines. But in the afternoon heat, it's a luscious spot for a picnic or a snooze. Follow the steps from the harbor up the hill, only five minutes from the water (open daily 7am-10pm; free). Subdued green floodlighting creates a tasteful backdrop for a waterfront dinner or walks on the pier. Three minutes down and behind the castle is **Valtos Beach,** a voluptuous crescent of fine pebbles and clear water. **Golfo Beach,** five minutes to the left of the town beach, is more secluded but has rocks the size of golf balls. The town beach pales in comparison to Valtos, but is clean and relaxing. The islets 100m offshore, home to a small, postcard-worthy church, can be reached by a short swim or pedalboat. The travel offices book a variety of excursions, including the **Styx** (Acheron), the mythical pathway to the underworld, as well as the sites of the Oracle of the Dead. The kiosk on the pier sells tickets to Valtos Beach (every 20min., 9am-11:30pm, 250dr one way, 400dr roundtrip), and excursion tickets to the outlying smaller beaches (1200dr). Near Parga, accessible only by car or taxi (3500-4500dr), is **Necromonteion,** the Oracle of the Dead. The Necromonteion's main subterranean chamber, cool and dimly lit, seems convincing as a threshold to another world. On rare occasions travel agencies organize trips—ask around (open daily 8am-3pm; admission 400dr).

■ Ioannina ΙΩΑΝΝΙΝΑ

With its Eastern flavor, staid castle walls, idyllic lake island, and racy, if troubled, past, Ioannina is much more than a mere transportation hub. It is Epirus' largest city, the capital of the region, and, curiously, the town with the most marked Turkish influence in all of Greece. Founded by Emperor Justinian in 527 CE, Ioannina has suffered under a colorful succession of petty autocrats. The town was invaded by Normans in 1082, conquered by Turks in 1430, and finally taken by Greek armies in 1913. Ioannina's most notorious foreign ruler, however, was Ali Pasha, the Turkish governor of Epirus just before the Greek Revolution. Ali attempted to secede from the Ottoman Empire and create an independent kingdom. His exploits became infamous as he combed the region, amassing a harem of hundreds of young women (and men) to serve as concubines. Those who resisted, like virtuous Kiria Efrosini, were thrown into the lake. Efrosini, her faithful maid, dove in after her.

Today, Ioannina is more than just the inheritor of an exotic history. Although it boasts more than its share of sites and museums, and of course the obligatory string of waterfront *tavernas,* it has not been shaped by the desire to attract tourists.

ORIENTATION AND PRACTICAL INFORMATION

All the main thoroughfares in Ioannina change names, and many posted street signs are obsolete. The main bus station is between **Sina** and **Zossimadon Streets.** Zossimadon continues south, changing its name twice, to merge with **28 Octovriou Street** at the post office. The merged street crosses **Averof Street,** at the town's largest intersection, and changes to **Vizeniou Street** as it continues to the town's second bus station. Averof St., running northeast, points to the Old Town, the castle, and the harbor before it narrows, turns left, and becomes **Anexartissis Street,** which merges with Zassimadon going north from the main bus station. The city of Ioannina is built around a large lake with an island in the middle. To reach the dock, walk straight down Averof St., past the bank to the left of the walls.

> **Tourist Office:** The **EOT office** (tel. 25 086), across the street from the grid-faced building on your left; turn right from Octovriou into Dodonis St. Open in summer daily 7:30am-2:30pm and 4-8pm; in winter daily 7:30am-2:30pm.
> **Tourist Police:** (tel. 25 673). From the main bus station, follow Zassimadon to the post office, then double back on 28 Octovriou until you reach the police station, where they are located. Open daily 8am-10:30pm.

OTE: (tel. 28 849 and 72 148), opposite the police. Open daily 7:15am-11:45pm.

Hellenic Mountaineering Club: 2 Despotatou Ipirou (tel. 22 138). Information on mountain trips for the outlying region. Open Mon.-Fri. 7:30-9pm.

Banks: National Bank on Averof, toward the waterfront. Open Mon.-Thurs. 8am-2pm, Fri. 8am-1:30pm.

Flights: To Athens (1 per day, more on Fri., 17,000dr) and Thessaloniki (1 per day except Tues., 10,700dr). The **Olympic Airways** office (tel. 23 120; **airport branch** 39 131) sits across from the tourist police. Open Mon.-Fri. 8am-3:45pm.

Buses: Leave from the **main terminal** (tel. 26 404) for Athens (9 per day, 8hr., 6450dr); Igoumenitsa (up to 9 per day, 2½hr., 1500dr); Metsovo (3 per day, 3hr., 950dr); and Thessaloniki via Larissa (5 per day, 7hr., 5000dr) and Konitsa (1 per day, 1000dr). Check the schedule; changes are common, and they may run more frequently in high season. Buses leave from the **other station** (tel. 25 014) for Preveza (8 per day, 2hr., 1500dr) and Dodoni (2 per day on Tues., Wed., Fri., and Sat., 1 on Sun., 30min., 3420dr).

Rental: Budget Rent a Car (tel. 43 901), on Dodonis St. 8900dr per car per day.

Laundromat: 86 Napoleon Zerva St. (tel. 70 493). Wash 900dr. Dry 100dr per 10min. Open Mon.-Fri. 8:30am-2pm and 6:30-9pm, Sat. 8:30am-2:30pm.

Hospital: There are 2 hospitals, each about 5km from the center of town, which handle emergencies on alternating days of the week, one (tel. 80 111) for even dates, another (tel. 99 111) for odd days.

Police: (tel. 26 226, -326), with the tourist police. Open 24hr.

Post Office: (tel. 25 498), at the intersection of 28 Octovriou St. and Zossimadon. Open Mon.-Fri. 7:30am-8pm, Sat. 7:30am-2pm. **Postal Codes:** 45221 and 45444.

Telephone Code: 0651.

ACCOMMODATIONS, FOOD, AND ENTERTAINMENT

Hotel Egnatia (tel. 25 667 or 24 886), at the first corner on your left walking away from the bus station down Zossimadon. Rooms with private bath, TV, and phone. Singles 8000dr. Doubles 11,000dr. Breakfast 900dr.

Hotel Tourist 18 Koletti St. (tel. 26 443 or 25 070), next to Hotel Metropolis. Singles 5000dr, with bath and TV 7000dr. Doubles 8000dr, with bath 11000dr. Triples 9000dr, with bath 13,000dr. Prices about 1000dr less in off season.

Hotel Metropolis (tel. 25 507 or 26 207). Take Anezartissos in the direction of the old town, turn right as it becomes Averof St.; the sign will be on your right. Singles 3500dr. Doubles 6000dr. Triples 7500dr.

Several unpretentious, reasonably priced *tavernas* are on Georgiou St. in the Old Town. Across the street, the **Restaurant Pantheon** (tel. 26 414), run by affable Elias Saras, has quick service and a varied menu (open daily 7am-midnight). For a hearty meal at a low, low price, try **Nick's Grill** on Averof (*gyros* 280dr, fries 250dr). In the evenings, teens frolic along Averof and cruise the harborfront.

SIGHTS

Ali Pasha fans get their fix at the island's **Ali Pasha Museum** on the site of Ag. Nikolaos monastery, where Ali Pasha once sought refuge (to no avail) from the assailing Sultan's forces. The diminutive museum displays his costumes and those of his mistress, and shows how he lived and where he died. He was shot through the floorboards of his apartment and was posthumously beheaded on the stone steps (open daily 9am-10pm; admission 100dr). Chickens wander among whitewashed houses, elaborate gardens, small shops, and winding paths that lead to the gates of curiously silent **monasteries. Boats** (tel. 25 885) leave for an unnamed **scenic island** (in summer every 30min., 7am-midnight, 15min., 180dr; in winter every hr., 7am-10pm), which is home to tasty *tavernas* and the cheapest silver in Greece.

There's plenty to see on the mainland. Just above the harbor are the massive stone walls of the **Castle of Ioannina,** built near the time of the city's founding and reinforced in the 11th and 14th centuries. Today, they divide the old and modern parts of the city. Among the old buildings, the streets of the old city hold a **synagogue** built in 1790, a testament to its once-large Jewish population. At the north tip of the walls reposes **Ali Pasha's tomb.** To see skateboarding, motorbike stunts, and lots of commemorative statues, head to the city **park** on your right (facing the harbor past a large café halfway down Averof St.).

The **Archaeological Museum** (tel. 33 357) has a collection featuring minute stone tablets etched with political, romantic, and cosmological questions that Roman emperors asked of the oracle at Dodoni from the 6th to the 3rd century BCE, translated for your convenience. The museum also houses paintings by 19th-century Greeks, mostly portraits, though you'll also find a few funky fish paintings. The museum is in a park off Averof St., below the clock tower (open Mon. 12:30-5pm, Tues.-Fri. 8am-6pm, Sat.-Sun. 8:30am-3pm; admission 5400dr, free on Sun. and holidays). The **Municipal Museum** (tel. 26 356) resides in the **Asian Aga Mosque,** called the *Tzami* by natives, a splendid 18th-century reminder of Turkey's 500-year ascendancy in the province. Once the home of Ali Pasha, it relates the history of Ioannina's old Jewish and Muslim inhabitants. The mosque sits at the edge of the old town, reflected in the lake next to Skilosofou St. (open Mon.-Fri. 8am-8pm; admission 500dr, students 300dr). Nearby is the **Archaeological Site of the Inner Acropolis,** which, in addition to its fine views of lake and city, has particularly interesting broad stone tunnels that are fun to explore (off to the right when you enter the site; open Tues.-Sun. 7am-10pm). Also on-site is a **Byzantine Museum** (tel. 25 989), featuring some large, wood-carved iconostases and a **Silverworks Museum,** with beautiful and delicate examples of silvercraft (both museums open Tues.-Sun. 8:30am-3pm; admission 500dr, students 300dr, seniors 400dr). The **Folklore Museum** (tel. 20 515), off Pargis Sq. (follow the signs), concerns itself mainly with beautiful Asian-inspired costumes and old tools (open Mon. 5:30-8pm, Wed. 10am-1pm).

The cave at **Perama** is not to be missed. Its caverns are cool (a refreshing 17°C year-round), enchanting, and accessible. Discovered in 1940 by villagers seeking shelter from Italian bombardment, the cave is roughly 5km northeast of Ioannina on the Metsovo highway; local bus #8, which you can catch behind the park across from 28 Octovriou will take you there (every 20min., 280dr roundtrip). The 45-minute guided tour of the grottoes takes you past backlit stalagmite and stalactite formations with imaginative names (open daily 8am-8pm; admission 1000dr, students 500dr). Wax figure and Classics buffs will enjoy the **Vrelli Wax Museum** (tel. 22 414 and 92 128), which has the world's only **full-body wax statue of Socrates** (unique but unimpressive). The museum is 13km from Ioannina towards the unenthralling village of **Bizani.** This larger museum is not to be confused with the smaller Vrelli museum in the city, run by the other Vrelli brother (open daily 8:30am-7:30pm; free). Take bus #2 (8 per day, 30min., 250dr); it stays at the site for 20-25 minutes while you watch the statues come to life before your very eyes.

Off the highway between Ioannina and Igoumenitsa, and accessible by bus, is the village of **Lia,** immortalized by Nicholas Gage's 1983 book *Eleni.* An immediately appealing place, Lia is filled with historical buildings, gorgeous wildflowers, black-clad shepherds, and renegade goats. Buses serve Lisa twice weekly from Ioannina, daily from Igoumenitsa, and twice weekly from Athens.

■ Vikos Gorge and Zagoria
ΒΙΚΟΣ ΚΑΙ ΖΑΓΟΡΙΑ

This spectacular combination of dramatic scenery, Dali-esque rock formations, and gray-stone villages inexplicably fails to attract more than a handful of adventurous travelers. From the 15th to the 17th centuries, the mountain villages of the Vikos area, northeast of Ioannina, formed a political and economic confederation recognized by the ruling Turks. Unique architecture and fierce regional pride emerged from the confederation's prosperity. In 1973, the Vikos Gorge and the intersecting Aoos River and canyon were declared a national park. More recently, the GNTO labeled the majestic stone villages "traditional settlements."

Monodendri may not seem like it has much to offer—a sole monastery, **Agia Paraskevi,** built in 1412, and the handmade embroidery of Greek-Albanian refugees at the **Rizarios handiwork school** are its main attractions. It serves, however, as a terrific base for exploring the nearby Vikos Gorge and Zagoria village. Another good base is the slightly more developed town of **Konitsa.** For more information on the area, consult your local **GNTO.**

■ Dodoni ΔΩΔΩΝΗ

Ancient Dodoni rests at the foot of a mountain 21km south of Ioannina. Though the oracle at Delphi is better known, Dodoni is mentioned by name in the *Iliad,* the *Odyssey,* and in Herodotus' writing. It is here that Odysseus came for absolution after killing Penelope's suitors. The site has been a **religious center** for almost 4000 years, playing host to successive waves of mother-earth worshippers, tree worshippers, Zeus worshippers, garden-variety Christians, and most recently the occasional rock concert. Around 800 BCE, the site became an **oracle dedicated to Zeus,** who, while courting a nearby cypress tree, was believed to have resided here as the roots of a giant oak. The Helloi interpreted the rustling of the huge oak's leaves as Zeus' advice, and the Argonauts, according to legend, had wood from the tree made into a ship keel, endowing the vessel with the ability to speak in times of need. A **temple** was built sometime around 500 BCE, then destroyed along with the oak tree by the Romans in 167 BCE. The last vestiges of the old religion were further subverted by the Christians, who built a basilica on the site in an attempt to diminish pagan influences by incorporating them into Christianity (its remains are still visible).

The central attraction at Dodoni is a classical **amphitheater** last restored in the 3rd century BCE. Originally designed to seat 18,000, it was reconstructed by the Romans for **gladiator games,** and still dominates the surrounding landscape. Bring your imagination, and you can walk in the footsteps of wily Odysseus or join the audience of an opening-night Sophocles; in the first week of August the **theater** (tel. 82 287 and 82 296) hosts a festival of classical drama. Left of the theater await the remains of the oracle and foundations of several buildings, including a Christian basilica, a temple to Hercules, and a temple to Aphrodite, where now there is not much action to be found, only stones, weeds, and echoes. A small oak has been thoughtfully replanted in the middle of the ruins of Zeus' sanctuary (open Mon.-Fri. 8am-7pm, Sat.-Sun. 8:30am-7pm; admission 500dr, students 400dr).

The peaceful village of Dodoni, next to the ruins, is reached by **buses** from the second of Ioannina's two bus stations (2 per day, Tue.-Wed. and Fri.-Sat., 1 per day, Sun., 30min., 340dr). The buses return almost immediately after reaching Dodoni, but you may be able to sweet-talk your way onto a tour bus heading back to Ioannina. Groups may opt for **taxis** (3000-3500dr), which will usually wait 30 minutes.

MACEDONIA ΜΑΚΕΔΟΝΙΑ

Once the stomping ground of Alexander the Great, Macedonia, now the largest Greek province, retains its proud tradition. Thessaloniki, the focal point of Northern Greece, has emerged as a worthy competitor to Athens in fashion and nightlife. The countryside conceals the Lake District's natural splendor and the excavations at Pella, Dion, and Vergina pay homage to the region's past. Macedonian pride is visible throughout this region of deep green foliage and red-roofed houses similar to those found in Eastern Europe. Men may find a trip to the monastic community of Mt. Athos the highlight of their trip—the peninsula is closed to women.

▓ Kastoria and the Lake District

ΚΑΣΤΟΡΙΑ ΚΑΙ ΠΕΡΙΦΕΡΕΙΑ ΤΗΣ ΛΙΜΝΗΣ

MACEDONIA

Kastoria, Florina, and Pella, tucked against the borders of Albania and the former Yugoslav Republic of Macedonia, are rarely visited by tourists. The natural setting is stunning, the villages attractive and unassuming, and the absence of sputtering buses refreshing. English-speaking residents are about as scarce as goats' wings, but you can immerse yourself in your surroundings by trying out your Greek.

The city of **Kastoria** (named after Kastor, one of Zeus' sons) originally rested securely on an island in Lake Kastoria. Around the 10th century CE, the townspeople began dumping garbage into the lake to build a causeway to the shore. Today, the bulk of the city is squeezed onto this narrow isthmus, and the island proper is nearly deserted. Kastoria, reminiscent of Switzerland, rests on the edge of a group of mountains separated by a lake. Savor the beauty of the lake all you want, but don't even think about taking a dip—the town recently stopped dumping raw sewage into the water, but the biological clean-up process is still years from completion.

Orientation and Practical Information The first floor of the town hall, room #3 (tel. 22 312), will provide **tourist services** (open Mon.-Fri. 7am-5pm, Sat. 10am-3pm). There are no tourist police, but the kindly **municipal police** (tel. 83 333), located behind the bus station on Gramou St., are somewhat familiar with English (open 24hr.). The **National Bank** (tel. 22 350) is on the mainland at 11 Noembriou St., which you can turn onto from Gramou, bearing left as you head northeast uphill. They have a 24-hour **ATM** which accepts MasterCard or Cirrus (open Mon.-Thurs. 8am-2pm, Fri. 8am-1:30pm). The **post office** (tel. 22 991) is along the lakefront road, Megalou Alexandrou Ave., around the bend from the bus station. They also **exchange currency** (open daily 7:30am-2pm). The **OTE** is uphill, midway between Davaki Sq. and Dexamenis Sq., at 33 Ag. Athanasiou St. (open daily 7am-10pm). The **Olympic Airways** office (tel. 22 275 or 23 125) is on the waterfront (open Mon.-Fri. 8:30am-4pm). A taxi travels to the airport (12km away) in Argos for 1500dr. **Flights** go to Athens (Fri.-Wed., 17,900dr). Kastoria's main **bus terminal** (tel. 83 455) is on 3 Septemvriou, one block from the lake. **Buses** run to Thessaloniki (6 per day, 3½hr., 3300dr); Edessa (4 per day, 2hr., 1850dr); Athens (2 per day, 9hr., 8600dr); Kozani (5 per day, 1¾hr., 1550dr); and Veria (2 per day, 2½hr., 2250dr). To reach Florina or Kalambaka, multiple bus connections are required. **Taxis** (tel. 82 100, -200) converge near the bus station (available 24hr.). To contact the **hospital,** call 28 341, -2, or -3. **Postal Code:** 52100. **Telephone Code:** 0467.

Accommodations **Hotel Acropolis** (tel. 83 587), located one block behind the bus station at 14 Gramou St., is one of the better bargains in Kastoria. Opt for a higher floor to secure a view of the lake. (Singles 4850dr, with bath 5500dr. Doubles with bath 7300dr.) Neighboring **Hotel Anesis,** 10 Gramou St. (tel. 83 908, -9; fax 83 768), is a slightly fancier option. (All rooms with bath and TV. Singles 7800dr. Doubles 10,500dr. Triples 12,600dr.) **Hotel Kastoria** (tel. 85 508) is 1km to the right (facing the water) of the bus station on the waterfront road. Spacious, neat rooms are free of tacky decoration. (Singles and doubles 7000dr. Triples 8000dr. Breakfast 1000dr.) Professional, English-speaking **Europa Hotel,** 12 Ag. Athanasiou St. (tel. 23 826, -7; fax 25 154), on the main road out of Davaki Sq., running towards Dexamenis Sq., offers spacious rooms with bath and TV. (Singles 8400dr. Doubles 10,400dr. Triples 13,100dr. Breakfast 1100dr.) You can **camp** (tel. 22 714) by Mavriotissa for roughly 1000dr per person if you get permission from the priest.

Sights Along with its voluminous fur production (some 5000 garments per day and God knows how many little furry creatures), Kastoria is renowned for its churches—40 Byzantine and 36 post-Byzantine edifices scattered throughout the city—with elaborate masonry and exquisite decoration. In most churches, though,

the saints's eyes have been gouged out. Greeks explain that occupying Turkish soldiers desecrated the images, while Turks claim that faithful pilgrims collected the
eyes as talismans. Regardless, the tiny Byzantine **Panagia Koumblelidhiki,** in the
center of town (open Tues.-Sun. 8am-6pm), and the **Church Mavriotissa** (open
daily 9am-8pm), 3km out of town, house particularly spectacular frescoes which,
unfortunately, are marred by modern graffiti. To visit Mavriotissa, stroll out of town
past the hospital and towards the island. The priest who lives there conducts a tour
(in Greek or German) and opens the churches sometime between 9am and 10pm.
To be certain of getting in, however, and to facilitate your visit to any other church,
make your first stop the **Byzantine Museum** (tel. 26 781), off Mitropoleos St. in Dexamenis Sq., at Kastoria's center. At the museum, arrange for a guide to open the
churches for you (open Tues.-Sun., 8am-6pm; free).

AROUND THE LAKE DISTRICT

One kilometer out of town stands **Mount Psalida,** where, legend has it, Alexander
the Average resolved to become Alexander the Great by conquering the world.
Bound by the borders of Yugoslavia, Albania, and Kastoria, the tranquil **Lake District** is an area of dense wilderness and swimming lakes. **Florina,** accessible from
Edessa and Thessaloniki, makes a good base from which to explore the area. **Trains**
run to the Florina **train station** (tel. (0385) 36 239) from Thessaloniki (7 per day,
4hr., 1340dr) and Edessa (7 per day, 2hr., 650dr). **Buses** jostle from Thessaloniki (6
per day, 3½hr., 2650dr) and also to Edessa (6 per day, 2hr., 1350dr). For the Florina
bus station, call (0385) 22 430. Florina has little to offer tourists apart from its location, a fragrant market area, and the **Hotel Ellenis** (tel. (0385) 22 671) in the town
center. (Singles 7000dr. Doubles 8500dr. Triples 10,500dr.) The **Alpine Club** runs a
large refuge near the village of **Pissoderi** on Mt. Verna.

■ Edessa ΕΔΕΣΣΑ

Greek vacationers love Edessa because it contains the country's only waterfalls.
Perched securely on top of a steep, formerly fortified butte on the foothills of Mt.
Vermion, the city was named "Edessa" (meaning "the waters") by the occupying
Bulgarian army. The town ends on the brink of a ravine, where numerous streams
flowing under Edessa's arched stone bridges cascade into an abyss, plummeting
more than 25m to the verdant valley floor. It's not quite as magnificent as it sounds;
concrete viewing balconies, overgrown weeds, and danger signs along the water's
edge detract from the experience. But, if Edessa's main attraction is not as spectacular as it tries to be, the town's temperate climate, aromatic flowers, petite parks, and
water-bound walkways give the town an easy-going feel that is its own attraction.

Orientation and Practical Information Hotels and the town center
await at the top of **Pavlou Mela,** where the road intersects **Egnatia** and **Democratias Street** as they merge. Farther along, out from Democratias St., **18th Octovriou
Street** branches out and terminates at the railroad tracks at the end of town. For
tourist information, call 24 330 (open daily 7am-2:30pm). If you're in dire need of
information, turn right at 20 Democratias (walking away from the bus station) and
look for the **police station** (tel. 23 333), at the corner of Filippou and Iroon Polytechniou (open 24hr.). Edessa's **post office** (tel. 23 332), on Democratias St., one
block from the *agora,* exchanges money for a commission (open Mon.-Fri. 7:30am-
2pm). The **OTE** is a blue and white building facing the Byzantine clock tower on
Ag. Dimitrios. The **National Bank,** 1 Demikratou St., is surrounded by an iron fence
on the corner of 2 Arch. Penteleiminos and has an **ATM** which takes MasterCard
and Cirrus (open Mon.-Thurs. 8am-2pm, Fri. 8am-1:30pm). The main **bus station**
(tel. 23 511) is at the corner of Pavlou Mela and Filippou St. **Buses** run to Athens (3
per day, 8hr., 7850dr), Thessaloniki (7 per day, 1hr.40min., 1400dr), and Veria (6
per day, 1hr., 800dr). A second depot, marked by a bus sign, is located at a family-

run sandwich shop and grill just up the block at Pavlou Mela and Egnatia (look for "KTEL" painted on the window). Buses go to Kastoria (4 per day, 2hr.10min., 1800dr) and Florina (6 per day, 1½hr., 1250dr). The **train station** (tel. 23 510) is at the end of 18th Octovriou St., a 10-minute walk from the post office. **Trains** run to Florina (7 per day, 2hr., 720dr); Thessaloniki via Veria and Naoussa (9 per day, 2hr., 840dr); Kozani (8 per day, 820dr); and Athens (1 per day), either directly (7540dr) or via Plati (3940dr). **Taxis** (tel. 23 392 or 22 904) congregate on 18th Octovriou St., near the bank. **Telephone Code:** 0381.

Accommodations, Food, and Entertainment The **Hotel Alfa** (tel. 22 221), two blocks up from the bus depot and across the square, has clean rooms with TV and bath. (Singles 7500dr. Doubles 10,000dr.) Next door, the **Hotel Pella**, 30 Egnatia St. (tel. 23 541), has rooms with bath. (Singles 6000dr. Doubles 8000dr.)

Edessa has no shortage of cheese pies and rotisserie chicken. The fish *taverna* **Boulgouri,** near 18th Octovriou on the way to the train station, provides a pleasant atmosphere for a fish dinner (1200dr). A good way to appreciate the town is to walk west up Monasteriou St. (behind Egnatia and to the right of the **Byzantine Clock Tower**) to the **Byzantine Bridge,** under which flows the main rivulet that eventually splits off to form the many streams flowing through town. Many unpretentious cafés reside here. In the direction of the waterfalls, a few restaurants offer seats with a magnificent view of the mountains and the valley beneath, including the ruins of the ancient city, visible in the distance on marble columns. The **Public Waterfall Center Restaurant** (tel. 26 718), right at the top of the falls, has many seats and decent prices (goulash 1350dr). Near the post office, a side street on the left of Democratias leads into a cluster of **bars,** which offer beers for around 500dr, cocktails for around 1000dr, and pleasant outdoor seats facing quiet parks.

Sights To reach Edessa's largest waterfall, **Katarrakton,** keep to the stream farthest to your left (with your back to the bridge). As the stream forks, pursue the branch to your left. Alternately, walk down Democratios St. and watch for the large and clear waterfall signs. The roar of surging cascades and the vision of bustling souvenir stands will herald your arrival. Enthusiasts should continue down the path at the bottom of Katarrakton into the valley to see the three larger falls near the hydroelectric plant or stroll into the waterfall's none too impressive cave (50dr). Almost all the cliffside terraces spanning the east rim of town offer beautiful panoramic vistas of the agricultural plain below. You will be able to spot a large, red-tiled building complex, a convent, and the adjacent pillared ruins of the ancient town. Below the town to the east lie the 4th-century BCE **ruins** of the ancient city which were unearthed in 1968; follow the signpost on the road to Thessaloniki. Until the discovery of the ruins at Vergina, Edessa was thought to be ancient **Aigai,** the capital of Macedonia. Except for a few churches, the only other attraction is a small **Archaeological Museum** in the mosque on Stratou St. at the edge of town.

■ Vergina ΒΕΡΓΙΝΑ

The discovery of the ancient ruins of Vergina, 13km southeast of Veria, was an archaeological watershed. In 1977 and 1978, **Manolis Andronikos** discovered the remains of **royal tombs** and a large **palace,** dating from 350 to 325 BCE. The tombs display such superb artistry (and skeletal remains) that scholars believe that these could only have belonged only to the royal Macedonian family of **King Philip II,** father of Alexander the Great. The dig turned up some fabulous treasures, now on display in Thessaloniki's Archaeological Museum (p. 181). The remains suggest that Vergina, and not Edessa, was the site of the ancient Macedonian capital of **Aigai,** where members of the royal family were buried.

A superb, modern complex encloses the tombs, but the scattered rubble, unfortunately, is poorly labeled and makes little sense to a dilettante. A good selection of books on Vergina, as well as other sites, is available at the café/souvenir stand across

MACEDONIA

the street from the tombs. The site office farther up the hill, at the entrance to the palace ruins, also sells books but has a limited selection.

There is a bus stop at the block next to the one housing **The Royal Tombs** (tel. 92 347). Inside, archaeologists found a golden *osteothike* (bone box) that contained the cremated remains of some royal personage. A little farther uphill are the open ruins of the 3rd-century BCE **Palace of Palatitsa** (tel. (0331) 92 394). There's an exquisite mosaic floor on the south wing of the ruins. (Tombs and palace both open late June to early Oct. Tues.-Sun. 8:30am-7pm; late Oct. to Early June 8:30am-3pm. Admission to tombs 1200dr, students 900dr, seniors 600dr. Admission to palace 500dr, students 300dr, seniors 400dr.) **Buses** run from Thessaloniki to Veria, 74km away (every 30min., 2hr., 1150dr), and from Edessa to Veria (6 per day, 800dr). From Veria, take the "Alexandria" bus and get off at Vergina (12 per day, 15min., 240dr).

■ Thessaloniki ΘΕΣΣΑΛΟΝΙΚΗ

Cosmopolitan Thessaloniki encircles its harbor and waterfront promenade with assurance. Wealthy, energetic, and proudly displaying sophisticated shops, cafés, and myriad tree-lined avenues, modern Thessaloniki will reward visitors with a rich experience. The city is at its best at the close-cornered markets that fringe popular squares, heralding thick-walled ruins and Roman monuments. Its well trafficked thoroughfares, lined with modern high rises, continue to accommodate splendid mansions. The old city's quiet, winding, castlebound streets surprise the wayfarer with their residential charms and panoramic views. Few foreigners make it this far north, but those who do discover a pleasant anomaly—a Greek urban center that shows off its history without being overshadowed by it.

The capital of Macedonia and the second largest city in Greece, Thessaloniki is teeming with Byzantine churches and Roman ruins and offers one of the better archaeological museums in Greece. On the crossroads of important trade routes, the city has flourished since its founding in 315 BCE by Cassander, brother-in-law of Alexander the Great. Named for Cassander's wife, ancient Salonika prospered after the Roman conquest of Greece. Being the only port on the Via Egnatia (the ancient east-west highway) no doubt helped, and the city's cultural influence led Paul the Apostle, in the 1st century CE, to write two epistles to disciples of the churches he founded here (I and II Thessalonians). While Athens was in the throes of a cultural slump, Thessaloniki usurped its position as the most important Greek city in the Byzantine Empire. After the 10th century, missionary followers of the brothers Methodius and Cyril (inventors of the Cyrillic alphabet) exerted their wide-ranging influence from headquarters here. In the early 20th century, the city's population, which included Slavs, Albanians, and a vast Jewish community, was more characteristically Balkan than Hellenic. More homogeneously Hellenic today, the city nonetheless continues to project cultural vigor.

ORIENTATION AND PRACTICAL INFORMATION

In 1917, a raging fire burned down the entire city center and, in the restoration that followed, a French architect laid out a gridded street plan which today greatly simplifies transit. Running parallel to the water, the main streets are **Nikis, Mitropoleos, Tsimiski, Ermou,** and **Egnatia.** Intersecting all these streets and leading from the water into town are **Aristotelous** and **Ag. Sophias.** The main shopping streets are Tsimiski, Mitropoleos, and Ag. Sophias. Aristotelous forms Aristotelous Sq. as it reaches the waterfront, which is lined by the tourist office, train office, airport bus terminal, and a string of overpriced cafés. The cheaper hotels are on Egnatia, banks and post office on Tsimiski, and waterfront bars and cafés on Nikis. The railway station is west of the square along Monastiriou St.; the main park, fairgrounds, and university are east of the downtown area. The **Lefkos Pirgos** (White Tower), the symbol of Thessaloniki, stages a solitary game of chess over the harborfront.

Navarinou Square, whose centerpiece of Roman ruins is intriguing in itself, incorporates old and new in a captivating meeting ground for Thessaloniki's youth. If you head left, facing inland, on Mitropoleos, about four blocks past Aristotelous, is the **Ladadika** district. This ex-red-light neighborhood has been restored into a charming pocket of turn-of-the-century buildings that houses authentic Greek *tavernas*. Roughly 15 blocks inland, north of **Athinas Street** and flanked by ancient castle walls, wind the streets of the **old town.** A marvelous place for morning or evening strolls, here you'll find a welcome degree of tranquility, panoramic views, and inexpensive *tavernas*.

Tourist Office: (tel. 27 18 88 or 22 29 35), off Aristotelous Sq. at #8, 1 block from the water. Take any tram on Egnatia to Aristotelous Sq. Has free city maps, hotel listings, transportation schedules, and information on the **International Trade Fair, Film and Song Festival,** held annually in Sept., and the **Dimitria Cultural Festival,** held in Oct. Open Mon.-Fri. 8am-8pm, Sat. 8:30am-2pm. **United Travel System,** 28 Mitropoleos St., 7th floor (tel. 28 67 56; fax 28 31 56), near Aristotelous Sq. Ask for English-speaking Liza and make sure you're carrying *Let's Go*. Open Mon.-Fri. 9:30am-5pm. Other offices at the **port** (tel. 59 35 78), near the Olympic Airways office, and the **airport** (tel. 42 50 11, ext. 215).

Tourist Police: 4 Dodekanissou St., 5th floor (tel. 55 48 71; fax 55 48 70). Offers free maps and brochures; English spoken. Open 24hr., or so they say.

OTE: 27 Karolou Diehl St., at the corner of Ermou, 1 block east of Aristotelous. Open Mon.-Sat. 24hr.

Banks: National Bank, 11 Tsimiski St. (tel. 53 86 21). Open for **currency exchange** Mon.-Fri. 8am-2pm and 6-8pm, Sat. 9am-1pm, Sun. 9:30am-12:15pm. A 24-hr. **ATM** takes MasterCard and Cirrus; many Visa-accepting **ATMs** elsewhere. Smaller banks charge slightly higher commission. **Citibank,** 21 Tsimiski St. (tel. 26 60 21), handles sophisticated international banking needs and has more reliable **ATMs.** Open Mon.-Thurs. 8am-2pm, Fri. 8am-1:30pm.

American Express: Northern Greece representative at **Memphis Travel,** 23 Nikis St. (tel. 22 27 96), on the waterfront. Open Mon.-Fri. 9am-1pm.

Consulates: U.S., 59 Nikis St. (tel. 26 11 21), on the waterfront west of the White Tower. Men can pick up a form letter here requesting permission to enter Mt. Athos. Women are forbidden there; see Mt. Athos (p. 187). Open Tues.-Thurs. 9am-noon. **Britain,** 8 Venizelou St. (tel. 27 80 06) and other EU countries. Open Mon.-Fri. 8am-3pm. **France,** 8 Mikenzi St. (tel. 24 40 30), across from the church of Ag. Sofia (open daily 9am-1pm). **Bulgaria** (tel. 82 92 10); **Cyprus** (tel. 26 06 11); **Italy** (tel. 83 00 55); and **Turkey** (tel. 20 99 64).

Ministry of Northern Greece: (tel. 25 70 10), on the corner of Ag. Dimitiriou St. and Venizelou. After obtaining form letters from the U.S. consulate, men wishing to visit Mt. Athos must obtain permits here, room 222. Open Mon.-Fri. 10am-2pm.

Flights: Airport (tel. 47 39 77), 16km from town. Take bus #78 (110dr) or a taxi (1800dr). **Olympic Airways Office,** 3 Koundouriotou St. (tel. 23 02 40). Open Mon.-Sat. 8am-4pm. Call 281 880 for reservations between Mon.-Sat. 7am-9pm. Flights to Athens (9-10 per day, 20,000dr); Limnos (1 per day, 5:45am, 14,000dr); Lesvos (1 per day, 5:45am, 20,000dr); Crete (4 per week, 27,000dr); Rhodes (2 per week, 30,000dr); and Ioannina (1 per day, 11,000dr). Flights also connect Thessaloniki with European cities and Larnaka in Cyprus.

Trains: Main Terminal (tel. 51 75 17), on Monastiriou St., in the western part of the city. Take any bus down Egnatia St. (75dr). Trains to Athens via Larissa (10 per day, 8hr., 3800dr); Kalambaka (5 per day, 3hr., 2300dr); Volos (13 per day, 3½hr., 2000dr); Edessa (7 per day, 2½hr., 900dr); Florina (5 per day, 4hr., 1400dr); Alexandroupolis (5 per day, 7hr., 3000dr); İstanbul (1 per day, 22hr., 9500dr); and Sofia (1 per day, 7hr., 5300dr). You can also catch trains from Athens headed for Budapest (1 per day, 20hr., 38,000dr) and Germany (1 per day, 30hr., 45,000dr).

Buses: The privately run **KTEL** bus company operates out of dozens of stations scattered throughout the city, each generally servicing a district of Greece named for its largest city. While printed timetables and price lists are virtually nonexistent, departure times are posted above ticket counters. The depots servicing the seven largest districts are distributed in three clusters: the depot for Athens (tel.

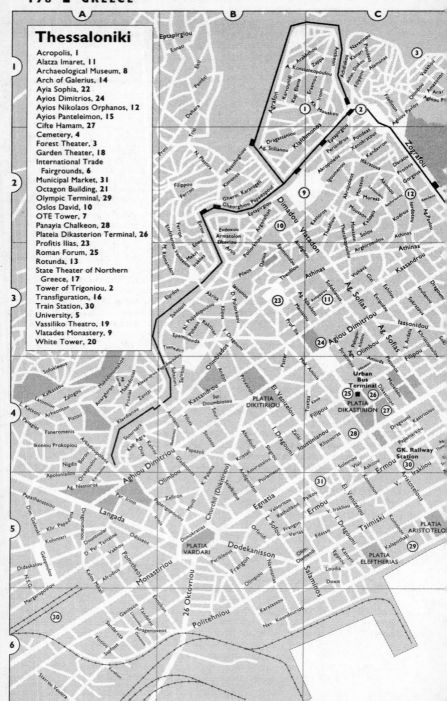

Thessaloniki

Acropolis, 1
Alatza Imaret, 11
Archaeological Museum, 8
Arch of Galerius, 14
Ayia Sophia, 22
Ayios Dimitrios, 24
Ayios Nikolaos Orphanos, 12
Ayios Panteleimon, 15
Cifte Hamam, 27
Cemetery, 4
Forest Theater, 3
Garden Theater, 18
International Trade
    Fairgrounds, 6
Municipal Market, 31
Octagon Building, 21
Olympic Terminal, 29
Oslos David, 10
OTE Tower, 7
Panayia Chalkeon, 28
Plateia Dikasterion Terminal, 26
Profitis Ilias, 23
Roman Forum, 25
Rotunda, 13
State Theater of Northern
    Greece, 17
Tower of Trigoniou, 2
Transfiguration, 16
Train Station, 30
University, 5
Vassiliko Theatro, 19
Vlatades Monastery, 9
White Tower, 20

Gulf of Thessaloniki

MACEDONIA

51 08 34) is across from the train station (9-10 per day, 6¼hr., 7300dr); the depots for Katerini (tel. 51 91 01; 30 per day, 1hr., 1100dr); Kozoni (tel. 52 15 18; 15 per day, 2½hr., 2050dr); Veria (tel. 52 21 60; every 30min., 1½hr., 1150dr); and Volos (tel. 54 30 87; 5 per day, 3hr., 3150dr) are all within two blocks of the corner of Essopou and Promitheos, one street south of Monasteriou. The depots for Alexandropolis (tel. 51 41 11; 5 per day, 5hr., 5000dr) and Kovala (tel. 52 55 30; every hr., 6am-10pm, 2½hr., 2500dr) are both near the corner of Ivanof and Galonaki, a street southwest of Largada. Call 142 for Greek language information on the telephone numbers and street addresses of all depots.

City Buses: An office across from the train station provides scheduling information. 75dr, 150dr to the beaches (bus #69 departs every 15min., 45min.).

Ferries: 2 departures per week in summer for Lesvos (13hr., 7000dr), Limnos (7hr., 4400dr), and Chios (18hr., 7200dr). To Paros (1 per day, Mon.-Wed., Fri.-Sat., 82080dr); Santorini (1 per day, Mon.-Sat. 8200dr); Skiathos (3700dr), and Iraklion (1 per day, Mon.-Sat. 9500dr). Buy tickets at **Nomikos Lines,** 8 Kountourioti St. (tel. 52 45 44 or 51 30 05); take your first left after Nikis becomes Kountourioti St. along the waterfront. Open Mon.-Fri. 9am-8:30pm, Sat. 9am-2:30pm.

Flying Dolphins: Hydrofoils travel daily (Sept.-June 4 per week) to Skiathos (1 per day, 3½hr., 10,000dr), Skopelos (1 per day, 4½hr., 11,200), and Alonissos (1 per day, 5hr., 11,200dr). Fares average roughly 10,000dr. **Crete Air Travel,** 1 Dragoumi St. (tel. 54 74 07 or 53 43 76), directly across from the main port, sells hydrofoil tickets. Open Mon.-Fri. 9am-3pm and 5-9pm, Sat. 9am-3pm.

International Bookstore: Molcho Books, 10 Tsimiski St. (tel. 27 52 71), across from the National Bank. International newspapers available daily. Open Mon., Wed., and Sat. 8:40am-2:50pm, Tues., Thurs.-Fri. 8:40am-2:20pm and 5-8pm.

Laundromats: Bianca, 3 L. Antoniadou St. (tel. 20 96 02). From the Arch of Galerius, go inland up the median boulevard, and turn right at the KousKous Café. It's directly across from the small church. 1400dr per load includes wash, dry, and soap. Open Mon.-Fri. 8am-2:30pm.

Hospital: Ippokration Public Hospital, 49 Konstantinoupoleos (tel. 83 79 20), supposedly the best in Thessaloniki; some doctors speak English.

Medical Emergency: Red Cross First Aid Hospital, 6 Kountourioti St. (tel. 53 05 30), located at the entrance to the main port. Provides minor medical care in a no-frills fashion. Bring a Greek-English dictionary. Services are free.

Post Office: 45 Tsimiski St., midway between Agia Sophias St. and Aristotelous St. Open Mon.-Sat. 7:30am-8pm. **Postal Code:** 54101.

Telephone Code: 031.

ACCOMMODATIONS

Many hotels await along the western end of Egnatia St., between Vardari Sq. (500m east of the train station) and Dikastirion Sq. Prices rise 20% in September during the international fair. Single women should avoid offers for cheap rooms touted by English-speaking tourist information impersonators at the train station.

Hotel Argo, 11 Egnatia St. (tel. 51 97 70). Old rooms, good bargains, and classical music. Singles 4000dr, with bath 5500dr. Doubles 5000dr, with bath 7000dr.

Hotel Atlas, 40 Egnatia St. (tel. 53 70 46 or 51 00 38; fax 54 35 07). Singles 5000dr. Doubles 7000dr, with bath, TV, and A/C 10,000dr. Add 20% per extra bed.

Hotel Aegean, 19 Egnatia St. (tel. 52 29 21). Blandly Mike Brady-designed hotel from the 70s, but bright and cheery. Singles 5000dr, with bath 8000dr. Doubles 8000dr, with bath 10,000dr.

Hotel Kastoria (tel. 53 62 80), at the intersection of Egnatia St. and L. Sofou St. Tidy, dark rooms with clean baths. Singles 5000dr. Doubles 5500dr.

Hotel Tourist, 21 Mitropoleos (tel. 27 63 35), 1 block from Aristotelous Sq., on a pleasant, tree-lined street near the waterfront. This generically named hotel has an interesting ambience, with 4.5m high ceilings, cavernous hallways, and an old-fashioned salon and elevator. Singles 7500dr, with bath 9000dr. Doubles 10,000dr, with bath 13,000dr. Triples with bath 16,200dr.

Youth Hostel, 44 Alex. Svolou St. (also called Nikolaou St.; tel. 22 59 46). Take tram #8, 10, 11, or 31 on Egnatia and get off at the Arch of Galerius. Go towards the water and turn left 2 blocks later onto Svolou. Free showers 6-10pm only. Doors close 11pm-7am; exact hours vary. Check-out 11am. Singles 2000dr.

Camping: Take city bus #72 to **Agia Triada** for **Thermaikos Beach Campground** (tel. (0392) 51 352). Supermarket, showers, and beach. 340dr per sleeping bag. 2400dr per tent. **Asprovalta** (tel. (0397) 22 249), 80m outside of the city towards Kavala, has similar facilities. 1100dr per person. 650dr per tent.

FOOD

Don't go to Thessaloniki for your standard *moussaka* and Greek salad; this town is known and loved throughout Greece for its excellent, carefully prepared *mezedes*. The food is prepared for locals, so it's almost sure to be cooked right and priced fairly. Thessaloniki's downtown is flecked by inexpensive self-service foodlets and shops. Lively and full of bargains, the *agora* (marketplace) is bounded on four sides by Irakliou, Egnatia, Aristotelous, and Venizelou St. To stock up on fruits, vegetables, bread, and groceries, visit the open-air markets of Vati Kioutou St. just off Aristotelous. The restaurants along the seaside serve standard fare at near-identical prices. Explore the old town for inexpensive, family-oriented *tavernas*.

The Brothers (tel. 26 64 32), in Navarino Sq., offers traditional Greek meals and an exceptional potato salad. Full meal 1500dr. Open daily noon-midnight.

Ta Spata, 28 Aristotelous (tel. 27 74 12), offers a wide selection of tasty, inexpensive, moderately sized entrees (1500dr). Open daily 11am-midnight.

New Ilyssia, 17 Leontos Sofou St. (tel. 53 69 96), a neighborhood restaurant and grill located off Egnatia St. Serves large helpings of traditional Greek food in an unpretentious setting. Entrees around 1200dr. Open daily 8:30am-2am.

Chopsticks (tel. 27 66 65), on Vyros St. off Navarinou Sq., fronting the ruins. Chinese chef flames up fresh, tasty meals to order (vegetable chop suey 1100dr). Open Mon.-Thurs. 6pm-1am, Fri.-Sun. 6pm-1:30am.

Sweet Shops: Poxani, 7 Venizelou St. (tel. 22 35 25), just inland from the corner of Venizelou and Tsimiski St., a few blocks west of Aristotelous Sq. Fanciful treats and even sweeter staff. Open daily 7am-10pm. Also try **Titania,** 22 Karolou Dienl St. (tel. 27 98 79), just inland from Tsimiski and a half block down from the OTE. Surprising array of sweet-scented cookies inside.

ENTERTAINMENT

Thessaloniki's nightlife used to be centered around bars, but has lately become café-centric. Cafés abound—try the **Journal** across from the Agia Sophia. The king of all café-hangouts for bohemian locals, however, is **Milos.** On weekend evenings, mingle with Greeks along **Plaza Dhimitrio Gounari.** Fashion-conscious couples promenade from the waterfront to the Arch of Galerius. A trendily more guttery crowd mellows out with a cup of coffee in the park and at **Navarinou Square,** one block west of D. Gounari. Lesbian and gay revelers head to **Taboo** on Kastritsiou St., one block from Egnatia. Turn toward the water on Mitropolitou Genadiou and take your first left. Ladadika district has some clubs and live Greek music. All the big, noisy nightclubs that boom to the beat of techno and other dance music are near the airport. You can only get there by taxi (about 1500dr). Thessaloniki's favorite is **Ab Fab** (as in Absolutely Fabulous), past the turn-off for the airport. Most clubs have a cover of about 1500-2000dr that includes the first drink.

At Thessaloniki's **movie theaters** you can see vaguely recent American releases—both art-house and Hollywood—in the company of hip young Salonicans. **Natali Cinema,** 3 Vassilissis Olgas (tel. 82 94 57), on the waterfront, five minutes past the White Tower heading away from the city center, shows open-air movies in summer.

SIGHTS

If you have time for only one stop in the city, the superlative **Archaeological Museum** (tel. 83 05 38 or 83 10 37) spotlights a collection of Macedonian treasures, like gold *larnakes* (burial caskets) that once contained the cremated royal family of

MACEDONIA

Vergina. The museum's most prized exhibition displays the artifacts of Vergina. When this unpillaged tomb was first discovered, archaeologists assumed that it belonged to a king. After putting together the skeleton of this king from the bones in the tomb, they noticed two idiosyncracies: one leg was shorter than the other and the skull had a disfigured eye socket. Ancient historians had documented that Kings Philip the Great, father of Alexander, had been born with one leg shorter than the other and had suffered an eye injury caused by a spear thrown at him in an assassination attempt while watching an athletic tournament. These historical references confirmed that this tomb was indeed King Philip's. Notice in the exhibit his special shin guards (one shorter than the other) and the solid gold case that held his bones and crown. There is also a piece of ancient purple silk occasionally on display. Take bus #3 from the railway station to Hanth Sq. (open in summer Mon. 12:30-7pm, Tues.-Fri. 8am-7pm, Sat. 8:30am-3pm; in winter Mon. 10:30am-5pm, Tues.-Fri. 8am-5pm, Sat.-Sun. 8:30am-3pm; admission 1500dr, students 800dr, EU students free, seniors 1100dr). The **International Fairgrounds,** next to the museum, hold a variety of festivals in September and October (for information, call 23 92 21).

On the other side of the park on the waterfront looms the **Lefkos Pirgos** (tel. 26 78 32), all that remains of a Venetian seawall. Formerly known as the Bloody Tower because an elite corps of soldiers was massacred within it, the structure was painted white to obliterate the gruesome memories. The tower, which houses a fascinating museum of early Christian and Byzantine art, presents a slide show every hour (same hours as archaeological museum; admission 800dr). The extensive ruins of the **Eptapirgion Walls,** erected during the reign of Theodosius the Great, stretch along the north edge of the old city. Take bus #22 or 23 from Eleftherias Sq. on the waterfront. Eleftherias Sq. is also where buses #5, 33, and 39 leave for the **Ethnology and Popular Art (Folklore) Museum,** 68 Vas. Olgas St. (tel. 83 05 91), which houses traditional costumes (open Fri.-Wed. 9:30am-2pm; free).

The celebrated **Arch of Galerius** stands at the end of Egnatia St., at the corner of Gounari St. (under renovation and covered with scaffolding). Next to it and closed for reconstruction is the **Rotunda,** which started out as an emperor's mausoleum, but was renamed **Agios Georgios** by Constantine the Great. For further historical pursuits, head north of Dikastirion Sq. to the Roman ruins between Filippou and Olibou St. The ruins, which include a somewhat hyper-restored theater, are still being excavated. The crux of the remains of the **Palace of Galerius,** near Navarino Sq., is the well preserved **octagonal hall.**

Over the centuries, most of the churches in this region were damaged or destroyed by recurring earthquakes. The few lucky survivors, such as **Agios Dimitrios** (tel. 27 00 08), **Panagia Halkeon** (tel. 27 29 10; on the corner of Egnatia and Aristotelous St.), and **Agios Nikolaos Orfanos** (tel. 21 44 97; 20 Iradotou St.) all feature brilliant mosaic work and frescoes from the late Byzantine era.

Another noteworthy example of Byzantine art is the splendid 9th-century mosaic of the Ascension in the dome of the **Agia Sophia** (tel. 27 05 23), in the park of the same name. The church, modeled after the Ayasofya in İstanbul, has extraordinary iconography with a particularly stunning dome. More mosaics decorate the **Panagia Ahiropitos** (tel. 27 28 20), two blocks farther north at 56 Agia Sophias St. (churches open approximately 7:30am-noon and 5-10:30pm; closed for morning services Sun. and holidays). You can also visit the beautiful **Old Synagogue** at 35 Sigrou St. (tel. 52 49 68). The temple is no longer in use, but the caretaker at the **Jewish Community Center,** 24 Tsimiski St., will let you in.

■ Near Thessaloniki

PANORAMA

Atop Mt. Hortiatis, this site has a name that says it all. Unfortunately, most of the sheds for viewing the valley and the city of Thessaloniki have been usurped by private residences. Because of the cool, soothing weather at the summit, the suburban village is a popular destination for summer excursions, and it's possible to find cafés that offer impressive views out to the Aegean nestled among pines. Buses #57 and 58 make the 10km trip from Dikastirion Sq. (every 30min., 20min., 75dr) at the corner of Mitropolitou Genadou and Ioustinianou St.

Perea, Agia Triada, and **Nea Mihaniona** are as full of bikinied urbanites as you'd expect for beaches accessible by bus from Greece's second-largest population center. From Dikastirion Sq., bus #72 goes to Perea, Agia Triada, and to Nea Mihaniona (every 10min., 45min., 150dr). Agia Triada has **Epanomis** (tel. 41 378), one of the better campgrounds in Northern Greece. The water is somewhat fetid; for less bacterial swimming, head to the Halkidiki peninsula (p. 186).

PELLA

The ruins of ancient Pella, discovered by a farmer in 1957, prove a rewarding daytrip. Pella, 38km west of Thessaloniki, served as a port in ancient times, when the surrounding plain was covered with water from the Thermaïko Gulf. Around 400 BCE, King Archelaus opted to build his palace there, and Pella became the largest city in Macedonia. Pella was the **first capital of a united Greece** during Philip II's reign; his son, Alexander the Great, used the city as the starting point for his lifelong mission to unify the world under Macedonian rule. On the other side of the highway, the small **Pella Museum** (tel. (0382) 31 278 or 31 160) contains the exquisite mosaics "Dionysus Riding a Panther" and "The Lion Hunt." With their skillful use of *chiaroscuro* and foreshortening, these are the earliest-known mosaics that attempt to convey three-dimensionality (museum and ruins both open Mon. 12:30-7pm, Tues., Thurs., Sat. 8am-7pm, Wed. 8am-8pm, Sun. 8:30am-5pm; admission 500dr).

Buses to Pella depart from the 22 Anagenniseos depot near the train station in Thessaloniki (every 30min., 550dr). Walk down Octovriou St. past the courthouse and turn right onto Anagenniseos St. The KTEL is on the corner of Damonos St. Pella takes roughly one hour to see and two and a half hours total with roundtrip transportation; the museums alone make the trip worthwhile. Buses to Thessaloniki (2-3 per hr.) pass the site, which is right on the main highway. To go between Pella and Vergina, change buses at the *taverna* in **Halkidona,** 3km east of Pella.

■ Mount Olympus ΟΛΥΜΠΟΣ

The charm of Olympus does not lie in its natural beauty; nor its physical magnitude; the beauty of Olympus is spiritual, it is divine. . .
—Boissonade

Rising from the coastal plain 90km southwest of Thessaloniki, Mt. Olympus so impressed the seafaring ancient Greeks that they exalted it as a suitable home for the gods. First climbed in 1913, Olympus has been harnessed by a network of well maintained hiking trails that make the summit accessible to anyone with sturdy legs. The zenith rewards visitors with incomparable views and ethereal blue skies, particularly in June and September, when the air is clearest. Mt. Olympus is buried in six or more feet of snow each winter, so the unofficial climbing season lasts only from May to October; you may meet snow until late July. If you make the ascent between May and September, you'll need no special equipment besides sturdy shoes (hiking in sandals is discouraged), sunglasses, serious sunscreen, a hat, and water. If you plan on climbing the upper regions, you may need a waterproof windbreaker, an extra shirt, and gloves. You can rush through the climb in one day, but plan on a two- or three-day trip to fully enjoy the wilderness. Consider staying overnight in one of the refuges or camping on the mountain. In either case, bring warm clothes and leave your pack in Litohoro.

LITOHORO

The gateway to Olympus is the small village of **Litohoro**. Surprisingly, given its proximity to the mountain, the friendly town is relatively free of souvenirs and other tourist accoutrements. Near the **bus station,** on the main street, is an information booth which acts as the town's **tourist office** (tel. (0352) 83 100) and offers free maps of the area (open mid-June to Sept. daily 9am-2:30pm and 3:30-9pm). Litohoro's **National Bank** (tel. (0352) 81 025) resides in the main square (open Mon.-Thurs. 8am-2pm, Fri. 8am-1:30pm) with the **post office** (**Postal Code:** 60200; open Mon.-Fri. 7:30am-2pm). The **OTE** is across from pieces of a playground undergoing construction, on the main street (open in high season Mon.-Sat. 7:30am-3:10pm; in off season Mon.-Fri. 7:30am-3:10pm).

Trains (tel. (0352) 61 211) stop at Litohoro, between Thessaloniki and Larissa, and sometimes on the line between Thessaloniki and Athens (7 per day, 1hr.40min. from Thessaloniki, 900dr), but the station is 1km from the bus stop (by the BP station, left facing the water). The Katerini-Litohoro bus will take travelers the remaining 5km into town (every 30min., 190dr). **Buses** (tel. (0352) 81 271) from the KTEL station, opposite the church in the main square, travel from Litohoro to Thessaloniki and back, via Katerini (15 per day, 1½hr., 1500dr); Katerini (16 per day, 2½hr., 380dr); Larissa via Katerini (16 per day, 2½hr., 1680dr); and to Athens (3 per day, 6½hr., 6400dr).

Near the bus station in Litohoro, down the main street on the right, are the offices of Greece's two alpine clubs—the **EOS Greek Mountaineering Club** (tel. (0352) 81 944), which offers a free map and brochure (open June-Aug., Mon.-Fri. 9am-12:30pm and 6:30-8:30pm, Sat.-Sun. 9am-noon) and the **SEO Mountaineering Club.**

SEO's Main Refuge is the highest in the Balkans and offers a glorious view of the mountain, the valley, and Thessaloniki (2760m; open July-Aug.), but **EOS's Refuge A** (open June-Sept.) is closer to the end of the road and more accessible by car. Both refuges have running water and cost 1700dr per night; less for club members. The refuges fill up Friday and Saturday nights. Try to make reservations through the club offices. EOS owns three other refuges on Mt. Olympus that are locked on weekdays; keys are available at the EOS office. Both clubs provide maps and information about the mountain, maintain the trails, and organize emergency rescues. Litohoro has a **health center** (tel. (0352) 22 222) with emergency facilities.

The pleasant **Hotel Aphroditi** (tel. (0352) 81 415; fax 22 123) is located on the road to the youth hostel. Many of the comfortable rooms offer stunning views of the mountain, and the friendly management can offer suggestions about other places to stay. They will hold baggage for 500dr. (Singles 8000dr. Doubles 12000dr. Triples 16000dr. Prices may be as much as 4000dr lower in off season.) Four **campgrounds** squeeze between the railroad and the beach, 5km out of town across the highway. **Do not freelance camp** on the north side of the road connecting the town and the highway: this is a training ground for the armored units of the Greek army.

THE PEAKS

Mount Olympus has eight peaks: **Kalogeros** (2701m), **Toumba** (2785m), **Profitis Ilias** (2786m), and **Antonius** (2815m) are dwarfed by the thrones of **Skala** (2866m), **Skolio** (2911m), **Stefani** (also called the Throne of Zeus, 2909m), and **Mytikas** (or the Pantheon, 2917m). There are two approaches to the peaks from Litohoro, and they can be accomplished as a cycle, taking two nights in the mountains, instead of one. To reach the beginning of both trails, take the road that winds upward just before the square in Litohoro. There is no bus service between the trails and the village, so it's best to find a group at the hostel to share a taxi with (5000dr to Prionia). Those who hitch usually start early, since most climbers drive up in the morning; *Let's Go* does not recommend hitching. For the first approach, hiking alongside the Enipeas River from Litohoro to Prionia is an option; the 18km trail is good but difficult. It begins past the town cemetery and Restaurant Mili in the upper part of Litohoro. At the fork in the trail, follow the yellow diamond marker uphill on the left

MACEDONIA

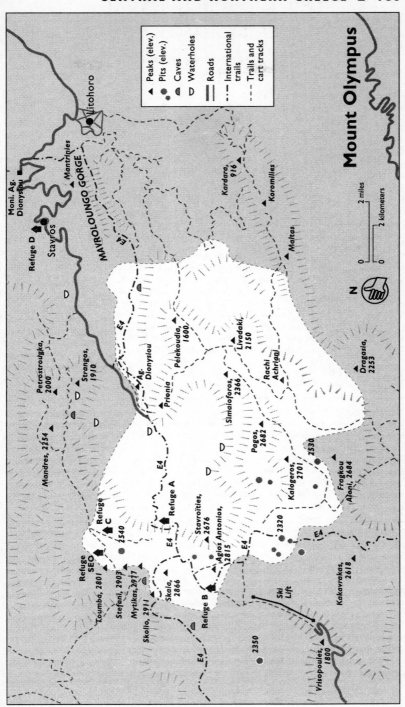

Mount Olympus

Legend:
- ▲ Peaks (elev.)
- ● Pits (elev.)
- Caves
- Waterholes
- — Roads
- —·—· International trails
- ----- Trails and cart tracks

Litohoro

Moni. Ag. Dionysiou

Mantinies

MAVROLOUNGO GORGE

Refuge D

Stayrós

Kardara, 916

Koromilies

Maltas

2 miles

2 kilometers

N

Petrostrougka, 2000

Strangos, 1910

E4

Ag. Dionysiou

Pelekoudia, 1600

Livadaki, 2150

Rachi Achrigai

Dragasia, 2253

Mandres, 2254

Prionia

Simaioforos, 2366

Pagos, 2682

2530

E4

Refuge A

Kalogeros, 2701

Fragkou Aloni, 2664

Refuge C

2540

E4

Stavroities, 2676

Agios Antonios, 2815

2320

Refuge SEO

Koumba, 2801

Stefani, 2903

Mytikas, 2917

Skala, 2866

Refuge B

2350

Skolio, 2911

Ski Lift

Kakavrakas, 2618

Vrisopoules, 1800

side of the **Mavrolungo Gorge.** This path takes you up and down hills for four hours, but traverses astonishing scenery. You will also pass the charred shell of a monastery that gave refuge to Greek partisans during WWII until the Nazis burned it. If you decide not to hike through the gorge, walk to Prionia along the asphalt road (which becomes an unpaved path).

At **Diastavrosi,** just 14km from Litohoro, the first trail slopes up to the right of the road, being the second approach to the peaks. This route offers views of the Aegean, the Macedonian plain, and the smog layer over Thessaloniki far below. You can find water in two places along this trail: at the turn-off between Barba and Spilia (1½hr. from the trail head), marked on the trail, and at the spring at Strangos. It's a long haul (5-6hr.) from the start of the trail to the **SEO refuge,** "Giosos Apostolides," where you can seek shelter (1700dr). Ample blankets are provided and hot meals served throughout the day. At 2760m (only 157m from the summit of Olympus), this shelter is less frequented than its counterpart Refuge A, below, and offers a magnificent view of the Stefani peak at sunrise. Just as exhilarating is the lunar landscape overlooking the **Plateau of the Muses,** named after the mythical sisters who inspired creativity. From here, the summit is a painless 1½ hours away.

Mytikas is the highest (2917m) and most climbed peak of Olympus. From Refuge A, take the path uphill and follow the red marks along mountain meadows strewn with indigo wildflowers. The last leg of the ascent to Mytikas is usually made by one of two routes. If you take the fork in the path at Refuge A, you'll see the peak **Skala** (2866m) to your left and the SEO Refuge to your right. From Skala, there is a sinuous descent a bit before the ascent to Mytikas. This trail to Mytikas, prone to rock slides and avalanches, is considered dangerous; it's not a good idea to lug a large pack along this route. Many trails are appropriate only for experienced hikers in excellent physical condition, particularly the rockslide-plagued **Locki.** If you return to Skala, it's a relatively easy walk to **Skolio,** the second highest peak (2911m) and the best point for viewing the sheer western face of Olympus. From Refuge A, you can go directly to Skolio, taking the path left from that to Skala.

HALKIDIKI ΧΑΛΚΙΔΙΚΗ

Three-pronged like Poseidon's trident, the Halkidiki peninsula advances southward into the Aegean, yielding spectacular scenery and some of the finer sandy beaches in Greece. On the eastern prong is **Mount Athos,** the largest enduring monastic community in Western society, which earns the region its title, the Monastic Republic of Mt. Athos (*athos* means holy). **Kassandra** on the western leg contains ritzy resort towns for the upper crust. Sandwiched between them is **Sithonia,** whose largely unspoiled interior is ringed with gorgeous (if crowded) beaches. Attempting to use public transportation on Halkidiki can be quite a challenge. Frequent buses run between the 68 Karakassi St. station in Thessaloniki (tel. (031) 92 44 44) and the three peninsulas, but bus service does not accommodate travelers wishing to hop from peninsula to peninsula; you may have to return to Thessaloniki in order to catch a bus to another peninsula.

■ Sithonia ΣΙΘΩΝΙΑ

Although it withstood the barrage longer than its western neighbor, Sithonia has recently been seduced by visitors sporting BMWs and fistfuls of *drachmae.* The area has since plunged into the sordid world of beachside villas and plastic souvenirs. On the more isolated beaches to the south, a measure of tranquility persists. Sithonia is popular as a beach and nature retreat from Thessaloniki. There are two back road routes through Sithonia—west via Nea Marmaris and east via Vourvourou.

Nea Marmaras' police (tel. (0375) 71 111), on a side street left of the main street, away from the church, and its **tourist police** (tel. (0371) 23 496) are on the first street parallel to the highway (open daily 8:30am-2:30pm and 8:30-10pm; no English spoken). The town **post office (Postal Code:** 61381; tel. (0375) 71 334) is in the second square, near the Café Metro (open Mon.-Fri. 7:30am-2pm). To reach the **OTE** from the bus stop, walk to the bottom left corner of the square, then hike up the street for about two minutes (open daily 7:30am-midnight). The **National Bank** (tel. (0375) 72 666) is on the main street (open Mon.-Thurs. 8am-2pm, Fri. 8am-1:30pm, and for **currency exchange** only Sat. 9am-1pm).

Before arriving at Nea Marmaras (also called Marmaras), you'll pass the beach at **Agios Ioannis,** where some people stake tents. Numerous signs for official campgrounds line the roads. Nea Marmaras is a small upscale vacation spot with jewelry stores and stylish bars. Rooms here are expensive (singles from 6000dr, doubles from 10000dr). The English-speaking staff at **Doucas Tours** (tel. (0375) 71 959), near the bus stop, recommends rooms, sells **flying dolphin** tickets for Volos (1 per day, 2hr., 5700dr) and Skiathos (1 per day, 2½hr., 5700dr), **exchanges currency,** and books excursions (open daily 8am-3pm and 5-10pm). **Bus timetables** are posted outside of Dionysus's next door. They run to Thessaloniki (2-3 per day, 2hr., 2200dr) and smaller nearby towns. **Albatros "Rooms To Let"** (tel. (0375) 71 003, -738), on Themistokli St., has spacious, modern, clean rooms with kitchenettes, and large balconies. (Singles 8000. Doubles with bath, kitchen, and TV 12,000dr.) On the beach, **Camping Marmaras** (tel. (0375) 71 901) is 1km back and clearly marked by road signs. (Open June to early Oct. 1300dr per person. 1200dr per tent.)

Nea Marmaras enjoys its existence largely due to the **Porto Carras** hotel complex situated just across the bay. This amusement park contains restaurants, boutiques, beaches, an open-air cinema, and a new casino, **Casino Magic.** Although doubles start at 30,000dr, all rooms are fully booked in summer. Ferries shuttle between the second square and Propondis in Marmaras to Porto Carras (every 30min., 15min., 400dr). The 20-minute walk around the coast is free.

Dionysios Tavern (tel. (0375) 71 201) serves good seafood (fried mussels 1200dr; open daily 8am-2am). The **Cool Bar** (tel. (0375) 71 829) on the waterfront in the town's second square is, surprisingly enough, just that. Chic young Greeks converge here (open daily 9pm-2:30am). The **bus** around the peninsula to Sarti (4 per day, 1hr., 580dr) passes by the most deserted, desirable turf on Sithonia. After climbing the road 5km south of Porto Carras, you'll see a beach near **Agia Kiriaki,** with a small reef and an outlying island. It's a long, hard climb down from here.

■ Mount Athos ΑΘΩΣ–ΑΓΙΟΝ ΟΡΟΣ

The monasteries on *Agion Oros* (Mt. Athos) have been the standard bearers of asceticism for more than a millennium. Today, the easternmost peninsula of Halkidiki is an autonomous state comprised of 20 Eastern Orthodox monasteries and countless *skites* (hamlets), with some 1400 monks. The absence of development has helped to preserve the peninsula's luxuriant foliage. Only the jagged marble peak of Mt. Athos itself, soaring 2033m above the encircling waves of the Aegean, is exposed. Against the background of this lush turf, the monks of Mount Athos isolate themselves from the outside world in an attempt to transcend material pleasures and live a truly spiritual life. The community on Mount Athos has been structured to varying degrees since 883 CE, when Basil I issued an imperial charter to Athos preventing local military officials from interfering with the monks. An edict of the Emperor Constantine from 1060, enforced to this day, forbids women—and female animals—from setting foot on the peninsula. How it remains populated is a mystery to us. *Let's Go* does not recommend illegal freelance procreating on Mount Athos.

HISTORY

According to legend, the Christian history of Mt. Athos began when the **Virgin Mary,** on a sea trip from Ephesus to visit Lazarus in Kitium on Cyprus, was thrown off course by a tempest and led by divine sign to the Athonite coast. The peninsula, known then as **Akte,** was a notorious center of paganism, but the moment Mary's foot graced its soil, the false idols all smashed to bits in proclamation of their own worthlessness. Mary then declared Athos her **holy garden,** forbidden to all other women for eternity, and blessed the land before sailing back to Jaffa.

Following centuries of occupation by Christian hermits and ascetics, the oldest monastery, **Megisti Lavra,** was established in 963 CE by **Athanasius.** Under the protection of Byzantine emperors, the building of monasteries flourished until, at its zenith in the 15th century, Mt. Athos harbored 40 monasteries and some 20,000 monks. When Constantinople fell to Turkish armies in 1453, the monastic community prudently surrendered, thus remaining unplundered and relatively autonomous. In 1926, a decree of the Greek government made Mt. Athos officially part of Greece while allowing it to retain an **autonomous theocratic government.** Due to gradual attrition and the diminishing influx of young novices, Mt. Athos' eminence slowly declined until the 1950s, when it became a prime target of greedy real estate developers. In recent decades, however, *Agion Oros* has been miraculously rejuvenated, and hundreds of young men, inspired to take their vows, have donned the black robes and hat of **Orthodox monasticism.** Now more than 1400 monks live alone in *skites* or inhabit the 20 monasteries.

Athos contains unsurpassed wealth in Paleologian and Late Byzantine art, manuscripts, treasure, and architecture. Each monastery also houses *lipsana,* remains of dead saints which only Orthodox Christian men are allowed to see. Especially impressive is the **hand of Mary Magdalene,** who bathed Jesus, which remains (skin intact) in **Simonos Petra** as warm as a living hand.

The most impressive part of the Athos experience, however, is not the material treasure, but the **monks** themselves, who offer their stories and advice along with complimentary *loukoumi* and coffee or *raki.* Most visitors to Athos, both Greek and foreign, find the brotherhood comforting and discover astounding internal peace of mind, regardless of their religion. A trip to Athos is not merely a visit to monasteries, and should not be approached as such, but is an attempt to understand the ascetic way of life. Pilgrims who plan to rush through too many monasteries too quickly usually change their minds once on the mountain. Most of the visitors to the mountains are indeed pilgrims. Orthodox visitors, who compose the great majority, are expected to attend morning and evening services, which may last over three hours, and to join the silent contemplative meals with the monks immediately afterward. The non-Orthodox eat separately and may be forbidden from entering the monastery's church. Nevertheless, the monks have an old tradition of hospitality and are generally welcoming.

Any visit to Athos will be greatly enhanced by reading beforehand about the art, history, and legends of the individual monasteries. *Athos the Holy Mountain,* by Sydney Loch, a book with the same title by Philip Sherrard (1985), and *Mount Athos,* by Norwich, Sitwell, and Costa, are highly informative.

ORIENTATION AND PRACTICAL INFORMATION

When visiting Mt. Athos, keep in mind that guests from "the outside world" inherently conflict with the spiritual goals of the monastic life. Hone your discretion and sensitivity. Rules vary from monastery to monastery, and generally include no photographing icons or wall paintings and no swimming.

Those without a permit can view the monasteries by boat. A **day cruise** from Thessaloniki costs 10,500dr. From Ouranoupolis, tours (roughly 3½hr.) cost 3000dr. Contact Doucas Travel, 8 Venizelou St., Thessaloniki (tel. (031) 26 99 84) or try Avdimiotis Theophilos in Ouranoupolis (tel. (0377) 51 207, -244).

Permits

A special entrance pass, issued **only to adult males,** is required in order to visit Mt. Athos. These passes are issued at **Ouranopolis,** the main gateway to Athos, upon presentation of a special permit. To get this permit, first get a letter of recommendation from your embassy or consulate (tell them you are a student interested in theol-

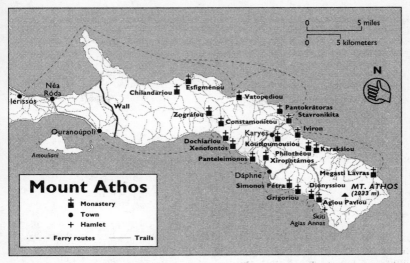

Mount Athos

0   5 miles
0   5 kilometers

N

Néa Róda
Ierissós
Chilandaríou
Esfigménou
Vatopedíou
Wall
Pantokrátoras
Zográfou
Stavronikíta
Constamonítou
Ouranoúpoli
Karyés
Ivíron
Dochiaríou
Xenofóntos
Koutloumousíou
Karakálou
Amouliáni
Panteleímonos
Philothéou
Xiropotámos
Dáphne
Megísti Lávras
Simonos Pétra
Dionyssíou
MT. ATHOS
(2033 m)
Grigoríou
Agíou Pavlou
Skíti
Agías Annas

Mount Athos

✝ Monastery
● Town
✚ Hamlet

- - - - Ferry routes   Trails

ogy, history, architecture, or Byzantine art); a letter from your university stating your academic interest in Mt. Athos could also be helpful. Deliver this letter to the **Ministry of Northern Greece,** room 222 Pl. Dikitirou, Thessaloniki (tel. 25 70 10), a minimum of 15 days before the intended date of your visit (open daily 10am-2pm). A **separate permit** is required for photographing the art in the monasteries. The U.S. and British consulates can give you the form letter in very little time. If you rush from there to the Ministry, you might be given your permit on the same day. They might insist that under-age visitors be accompanied by someone older than 18, though the Ministry can waive this restriction. Because only **10 visitors per day** are admitted to Mt. Athos, the summer months are always booked well in advance. The minimum 15 days will probably not be enough, so either wait for a cancellation or write a letter to the Ministry of Northern Greece at least a month in advance to secure a reservation. If you can show proof that you are Orthodox (baptism papers, a letter from your bishop, etc.), you may be allowed to be the day's eleventh visitor. Since most Greeks visit in the summer, it may be necessary to place reservations with the particular monasteries you plan to stay at; the Ministry will give you telephone numbers. The permit can be gotten from Athens; call the Ministry for details.

In Ouranopoli, bring your permit and your passport to the **Athos office,** just downhill from the bus stop by the gas station, by at least 9:30am of the day your visit begins. Passes cost 5000dr for foreigners, 3000dr for Greeks (who are allowed to stay for seven days), 3000dr for students with ISIC, 1000dr for Greek students. A non-Greek pass is good for four days. Getting it extended means going to Karges, where the official request will almost certainly be rejected; individual monasteries, however, might let you stay longer unofficially if they feel you show a genuine interest in their way of life. You must strictly observe the **date of arrival** on your permit. If you arrive a day late, you will be turned away. Without your **passport,** you will not be admitted. The **tourist office** in Thessaloniki has more information.

Getting There

Permit in hand, arrive in Halkidiki the night before your entry date into Athos, or catch the 6am bus leaving Thessaloniki for Ouranopoli the day of your visit. The standard approach to Athos is via Ouranoupoli, by boat to Daphni, then by bus to the capital city of Karyes. **Buses** for Ouranoupoli leave from Thessaloniki's Halkidiki station (tel. 92 44 44), located at 68 Karakassi St. (4 per day, 3hr., 2800dr). A bus for Thessaloniki will be waiting immediately after your arrival from the mountain.

Ouranoupoli is a beach resort favored by Germans, quiet in the off season. From here, a ferry leaves for the three closest monasteries and Daphni, the port city of the holy mountain. **Tickets** may be purchased across from the tourist agencies.

Since you'll be doing a lot of hiking on Mt. Athos, arrange to leave your belongings behind in Ouranoupoli (preferably at the place you've stayed), and carry just a day-pack and a water bottle. Be sure to bring long pants, as the monks forbid visitors to wear shorts. Meals at monastery refectories are hearty—bread and cheese, beans, and sometimes fish or noodles. The meals are eaten in silence while a priest reads from the Bible. As no lunch is served, it doesn't hurt to stock up on snacks. During fasting periods, guests are fed normal rations.

Arrive at the port at roughly 9am and look for the stand where officials will issue your **final permit.** From Daphni you can take Athos's one **bus line** (1 per day, 30min., free) bus to the capital city of Karyes, which has an **OTE** to the right of the Athonite Holy Council building, a **post office** (**Postal Code: 63086**), and two inexpensive hotels (1500dr per person). You may also take a smaller boat to the monasteries or *skites* on the west side of the peninsula (150-350dr). **Boats** generally leave soon after arrival, and operate on a whimsical, non-specific schedule. They are supposed to go to Levra, but often stop short (roughly 3hr.). Some monks may approach you in Daphni and say that the boat to Levra will not leave. They may offer to make the trip on a *caïque* for 20,000dr. Don't get swindled; even monks can lie.

Remember that walking is an integral part of the Athos experience. Before you leave Karyes, pick up the brown *Mount Athos Touristic Map,* which includes a pamphlet offering general information (500dr). For more details about Mt. Athos, pick up one of the well illustrated guidebooks (2500dr).

Accommodations and **food** in the monasteries are free, but you are entitled to a one-night stay only, unless you receive permission for an extension from the *archontari* (guest-master). The gates close at sunset—you *must* reach the monastery before this time or you won't be able to enter, so leave plenty of time to get to the monastery. Paths are narrow, overgrown with vegetation, and poorly marked; furthermore, the ones on the map might unexpectedly fork in four different directions, or not exist at all. It's a good idea to keep to the roads or seaside paths and to travel in groups. Another good strategy is to follow the telephone poles that run between monasteries. Even if you are turned down for lodging at a monastery, you will be offered a cup of Greek coffee and *loukoumi* for your efforts.

MONASTERIES OF THE MOUNTAIN

Each of the 20 monasteries has a distinct character. **Megisti Lavra,** the largest, is imposing and fortress-like; the monks tend to be old and conservative. **Iviron** is delightfully dilapidated, full of relics and icons. The gas lighting gives the guest house an air of mystery. Along with moated-and-turreted **Vatopedi,** these two are the most frequently visited of the cloisters. While beautiful and well worth seeing, they are aptly referred to as the "museum monasteries"; try to visit some of the smaller and more remote spots as well.

At one time, there were nearly equal numbers of Greek and Slavic monks at Athos, but the Russian Revolution cut off the supply of funds and novices at its source, and today only three Slavic monasteries remain. The Russian **Panteleimonous,** the Bulgarian **Zografou,** and the Serbian **Xilandariou** contrast with the monasteries on the rest of the peninsula. Recently, the collapse of Communism has reopened Russian hearts and wallets to the favorite opiate of the masses, and swelling church coffers have financed a restoration of Panteleimonous. Five thousand Russians seek entry to this large monastery, but its population is forbidden to outnumber that of its nearest Greek neighbor, home to a booming community of about 50. Elsewhere on Mt. Athos, **Ag. Dionisiou** has foreboding, dark iconography. **Philoteou,** embedded in a plush forest, is the only monastery with a grassy courtyard and is known for being relatively liberal.

The most complete experience at Mt. Athos involves developing an understanding and appreciation of the monastic way of life. Always address monks by their title, *Patera,* and instead of goodbye, say *evlogite* (Bless us, Father). Although most monks are Greek, the Athos renaissance has drawn neophytes from the U.S., Canada, Germany, France, England, and elsewhere. Many young monks are university-educated, and some speak English reasonably well. When you arrive at a monastery, ask the *Archontari* if it's possible to speak with someone in your native tongue.

Life on Mt. Athos befuddles the outsider. Meatless meals are eaten in silence. Men cover their bodies completely at all times, and male animals are castrated. Novices learn to repeat the Prayer of the Heart with each breath—inhaling they recite, "Lord Jesus Christ," and, exhaling, "Have mercy on me, a sinner," until prayer becomes reflex, uniting mind and heart. All monasteries follow their own time system—midnight is marked by the setting of the sun, placing the island ahead of secular time.

Climb Mt. Athos for a day or two of invigorating hiking crowned by an august view. The approach is by path from the skitic community of **Agia Anna.** A five-hour climb will take you to the **Church of the Panagia,** dedicated to the Virgin Mary, which has beds for an overnight stay. The summit is another hour away. You might want to stay overnight at Panagia to watch the sun rise.

▓ Kavala ΚΑΒΑΛΑ

The modern port city of Kavala, a tobacco town and a bastion of communism in the 1930s, reversed both its preferred commodity and political orientation after the end of WWII. Today, having born the brunt of Greco-Turkish conflict and Bulgarian occupation, Kavala remains a trading center. A bustling city with tree-lined avenues, stretching from the seaside up the slopes of Mt. Simvolo, Kavala is well organized and relatively smog-free. Buried beneath the new city is the 3000 BCE city of Neapolis, later dubbed the city of Christoupolis, where Paul the Apostle later came to preach. Although modernized, Kavala retains something of a traditional appeal, as congested avenues give way to fruit vendors and flower markets, particularly around Kavala's old section, the **Panagia District** (District of the Virgin Mary).

ORIENTATION AND PRACTICAL INFORMATION

The city's main draw, the Panagia District sits east of the port on its own peninsula, hemmed in by ancient walls and under the shadow of the dominating **Byzantine fortress.** Just outside these walls is the main square, **Eleftherias Square,** from which Kavala's two major commercial streets, **Eleftheriou Venizelou** and **Erithrou Stavrou,** extend westward. **Vassileos Pavlou** runs along the waterfront near the Thassos ferry dock. Parallel to it, one block inland, is Erithrou Stavrou, two blocks inland Eleftheriou Venizelou. The Panagia District is directly behind the Aegean ferry dock. The entrance is near **Doxis Square.**

Tourist Office: (tel. 22 24 25, -87 62, or 23 16 53), on its own little traffic island at the corner of Eleftherias Sq., 1 block inland from the main port. Has city maps and a list of hotels, and plans international travel. Open Mon.-Fri. 7am-2:30pm.

Tourist Police: (tel. 22 29 05), on the ground floor of the police station. Open daily 7:30am-2:30pm.

Banks: The **National Bank** (tel. 22 21 63), on the corner of Onomias and Paulo Mela St., 1 block north of the GNTO. Has a 24-hr. **ATM** for MasterCard and Cirrus. Bank open Mon.-Thurs. 8am-2pm, Fri. 8am-1:30pm. The **Commercial Bank,** 17 Eleftherias Venizelou (tel. 22 33 54), across from the tourist office, is open the same hours and has a 24-hr. **ATM** that accepts Visa.

OTE: (tel. 22 30 99), west of the main port at the corner of Ethnikis Andistassis and Averof St. Open in summer daily 6am-midnight; in winter 6am-11pm.

Flights: Olympic Airways (tel. 22 36 22), across from Thassos ferry dock, on the corner of Ethnikis Aristasis and Kavalas Hris. Open Mon.-Fri. 8am-3pm. Tickets to Athens (1 per day, 8:10pm; Tues., Thurs., and Sat. 8:10am; 1hr., 16,800dr). Public buses to airport run 2hr. before scheduled airplane departures (30min., 500dr), and from airport to Kavala center immediately following flight arrivals.

Trains: There is no train station in Kavala, but catch a **bus** (every 20min., 40min., 680dr) to the **train station in Drama** (tel. (0521) 32 444), and from there the 5pm daily to İstanbul (10hr., 9450dr), or one of 6 daily trains to Alexandroupolis. Or, take a bus to Xanthi (every 30min., 1hr.) and hop on the 8pm train to İstanbul (12hr.). For further information on transportation and international bus service to İstanbul (Fri.-Wed., leaves at 5am) and Sofia, Bulgaria (Thurs. and Sat., leaves at 8am), contact **Alkion Tourist Office,** 24 Venizelou (tel. 23 10 96; fax 83 62 51). Open in summer Mon.-Fri. 8:30am-2pm and 5-8pm, Sat. 8:30am-1pm; in winter Mon.-Fri. 8:30am-2pm, Tues.-Thurs. and Fri. 8:30am-2pm and 5:30-8pm.

Buses: (tel. 22 35 93), at the corner of Filkis Eterias and K. Mitropolitou St., a block from Vassileos Pavlou St. and the waterfront, around the corner from the OTE. Buses to Thessaloniki (every hr., 6am-8:15pm, 2½hr., 2500dr); Drama (every 30min., 55min., 650dr); beaches to the west (take bus to Iraklitsa, every 20-30min., 20 min., 250dr); and Athens (3 per day, 10hr., 9850dr, A/C). Contact the **KTEL Office** (tel. 22 33 22) near the post office (open daily 5am-8:30pm) or the **Alkion Agency.** For bus service to Alexandroupolis (5 per day, 2½hr., 2600dr), go to the **Dore Café,** on Erithrou Stavrou St., beyond the Oceanis Hotel, where tickets are sold, departure times are posted, and the bus stops.

Ferries: Nikos Milades (tel. 22 64 17), on the corner of the main port beneath the castle; provides ferry information. Open daily 8:30am-1:30pm and 5:30-8:30pm. Ferries go to Limnos, Lesvos, Samos, Chios, Patmos, Sigri, Ag. Efstraitos, and Peiraias. July-Aug., ferries shuttle to Samothraki. Contact **Arsinoi Travel,** 16 K. Dimitriou (tel. 83 56 71), for more information. Open daily 8am-9pm.

Flying Dolphins: Hydrofoils connect Kavala with nearby Thassos, Alexandroupolis, Lesvos, and Limnos. For tickets and schedule information, head for the well marked booths near the hydrofoil dock, opposite the OTE.

Taxis: (tel. 22 70 80) congregate in 28 Octovriou Sq. Available 24hr.

Hospital: 113 Amerikanikou Erithrou Stavrou (tel. 22 85 17 or 22 45 55). Open 24hr. Call 166 in case of **emergency.**

Port Police: (tel. 22 37 16), on the second floor of the OTE building. Open 24hr.

Police Station: 119 Omonias St. (tel. 22 29 05), 4 blocks north of the port. Open 24hr. **Emergency** tel. 100.

Post Office: (tel. 83 33 30). Main branch at K. Mitropoliteou St., on the corner of Erithrou Stavrou, 1 block north of the bus station. **Exchanges currency.** Open Mon.-Fri. 7:30am-7:30pm. **Postal Code:** 65110.

Telephone Code: 051.

ACCOMMODATIONS

Rooms that are simultaneously attractive, clean, *and* inexpensive are tough to find in Kavala. There are several pensions and budget hotels clustered around Eleftherias Sq. Rooms come easier on weekends, when crowds flock to Thassos.

George Alvanos, 35 Anthemiou St. (tel. 22 84 12, -17 81), a 10-15min. walk from the center. Follow Poulidou St. into Old Town, bear left at Mehmet Ali St., then left onto Anthemiou. A homey establishment with spotless shared bathrooms. Proprietors speak only Greek, though their English-speaking children may be around. Call ahead. Kitchen 800dr. Singles 3000dr. Doubles 5000dr.

Hotel Akropolis, 29 E. Venizelou St. (tel. 22 35 43). Clean rooms with a view of the bay. Singles 4000dr, with bath 5000dr. Doubles 7000dr, with bath 9000dr.

Camping Irini (tel. 22 97 85, -76). Take the #2 or 3 bus east or walk 2km along the coast from the port (130dr). The campground closest to town. Electricity 500dr. 1000dr per person. 1300dr per person with tent.

FOOD, SIGHTS, AND ENTERTAINMENT

Dining in Kavala may not be like savoring a crepe on the French Riviera—or in Athens for that matter—but it offers quality Greek food at reasonable prices. **Mihalakis,** 1 Kassanarou St. (tel. 22 11 85), three blocks inland from the post office, is in a quiet courtyard away from waterfront pedestrian traffic (open daily for lunch and dinner). **Panos Zafeira,** 20 K. Dimitriou St. (tel. 22 79 78), is situated on the waterfront (open daily 9am-midnight). **Verona Pizza Grill** (tel. 83 54 00), at the Thassos ferry dock and around the corner from the OTE, has a pleasant place to sit while waiting for your ferry (open daily 10am-1am). In summer, **bars** in the center of Kavala empty out at 11pm, when locals head to beachside discoes.

The sprawling, 13th-century **Byzantine Castle's** turreted walls dominate the city; saunter atop them for a city view (a guard often gives tours; tipping is polite). A small **amphitheater** is set up for occasional evening music and cultural performances. For scheduled events, ask the guard or at the refreshment stand. During the **Eleftheria Festival** (freedom festival) in June, students celebrate Kavala's liberation from the Turks by performing dances at the castle. Visitors are welcome to join in.

The 400-year-long Ottoman domination of Northern Greece left its mark on the city. The **İmaret** (Ottoman soup kitchen for the poor), the largest Muslim building in western Europe, is now a trendy bistro. On the corner of Pavlidou and Mehmet Ali St. stands the **House of Muhammad Ali.** Born here in 1769, Ali was the self-appointed ruler of Egypt who reportedly floated like a butterfly but could sting like a bee (ring for the caretaker; tip 100dr).

You just can't overlook the colossal 16th-century **Kamares Aqueduct** at the north edge of the old town, near Nikotsara Sq. Süleyman the Magnificent had the graceful, double-tiered structure built to transport water from mountain springs above the city. On the other side of town, overlooking the water, the **Archaeological Museum** (tel. 22 23 35) on Erithrou Stavrou St. contains such treasures as polychrome busts of goddesses from Amphipolis and a Hellenistic dolphin mosaic from Abdera (museum open Tues.-Sun. 8:30am-6pm; admission 500dr). Kavala has a small **folk art museum** (tel. 22 27 06) for you to explore (open daily 8am-2pm, Sat. 9am-1pm; free, but a donation is tacitly requested).

■ Near Kavala

Several sandy **beaches** west of Kavala are accessible by intercity bus. The closest is just outside the city of **Kalamitsa.** At **Batis,** 3km outside of Kavala, is a **GNTO campground** (tel. 24 30 51), which you might mistake for a parking lot. (1200dr per person. 1500dr per large tent. 900dr per small tent. 750dr per child. 1800dr per mobile home. 500dr to swim.) There's a supermarket and snack bar. Every 30min., Blue bus #8 treks to Batis from Kavala. Every hour, buses to Iraklitsa stop at Batis (120dr). For car rentals, **Budget Rent-a-Car** (tel. 22 87 82) is at 35 Venizelou (cars 12,000dr per day; open Mon.-Fri. 8am-1pm). **Philippi,** roughly 15km north of Kavala, lies in ruins. Philip II of Macedonia founded the city to protect Thassian gold miners from Thracian attacks. Modestly, he named the city after himself—his son later followed suit in Egypt. Crucial battles of the Roman civil war dogged the city in 42 BCE, when Marc Antony's soldiers defeated the army of Brutus and Cassius.

In 50 CE, missionaries Paul and Silas arrived from Anatolia to preach Christianity, and the first European Christian, **Lydia,** was baptized here. The **Cell of Paul** is the apostle's own budget accommodation. Shut the door and peek at the Roman **latrines;** most of the 42 marble seats are intact, but the lids have all been left up (site open daily 7am-7pm; admission 800dr; call 51 64 70 for more information).

The entrance on the other side of the highway leads up to the **acropolis.** On summer weekends, classical drama is performed; it's worth attending even if it's all Greek to you. Ask at the theater or the Kavala GNTO for details. (Tickets 2000-2500dr. Site open daily sunrise-sunset. Admission 200dr, students 100dr.) There's a **museum** (tel. 51 62 51) nearby, closed during summer 1996 for renovations but expected to be open by 1997 (open Tues.-Sun. 9am-3pm; admission 800dr, students free). A **bus** to Philippi leaves every 20 minutes (50min., 300dr). Tell the driver you're going to the archaeological site, not the village. Otherwise, you'll end up in the boonies. The bus back to Kavala stops down the road from the site.

THRACE ΘΡΑΚΗ

For centuries, Thrace has served as the meeting place for the diverse cultures of Turkey and Greece. Separated from Turkish Thrace by the Evros River, Thrace, which is Greece's northernmost province, serves as both a political and cultural gateway between the two countries. Ruled by the Ottomans until 1922, the region still bears evidence of Turkish influence in the small Turkish and Armenian communities scattered throughout it. In general, however, Thrace is now as Greek as the blue and white gate at its border. Its complex political history is mirrored in its chaotic landscape—a tangle of rivers, arable land, swamps, and lonely rolling hills.

■ Alexandroupolis ΑΛΕΞΑΝΔΡΟΥΠΟΛΗ

Traveling through Thrace inevitably means a stop at the modern city of Alexandroupolis, which lies on the main west-to-east highway and is accessible by **rail**. This mellow, if somewhat seedy, port city is packed in the summer with overland travelers and Greek vacationers. Accommodations in July and August are scarce; visitors usually coordinate boat and train arrivals to avoid overnight layovers.

Especially in summer, Alexandroupolis is not the ideal departure point for Turkey. Trains are hot, slow, and crowded; most buses to Turkey originate in Thessaloniki and become tourist-laden by the time they reach Alexandroupolis. A last resort to get to **Turkey** is to take a train (1 per day, 8hr., 2380dr) or bus (1 per day, 6hr., 4000dr) to **İstanbul**. Both depart from the train station, where tickets are sold. People who hitch across make a trilingual sign asking for a ride across the border; *Let's Go* does not recommend hitching. It is illegal, however, to cross on foot. Count on a one-hour delay in Turkish customs.

ORIENTATION AND PRACTICAL INFORMATION

The **ferry dock** and **train station** are virtually neighbors along the waterfront, south of Eleftherias. The **bus station** is five blocks inland and slightly west. Facing the water, turn right from the train station to the active center of the waterfront.

Tourist Police: In the same building as the police. Open Mon.-Fri. 8am-2pm.

Banks: The **National Bank** (tel. 23 162) is on L. Demokratous St., east of the buses. Has a 24-hr. MasterCard- and Cirrus-friendly **ATM**. The **Commercial Bank** (tel. 24 720), 1 block east (left facing the water), gives advances on your Visa card during banking hours. Both banks open Mon.-Thurs. 8am-2pm, Fri. 8am-1:30pm.

OTE: (tel. 28 099), corner of I. Kaviri and Venizelou St. Open daily 6am-11pm.

Flights: Olympic Airways, 4 Ellis St. (tel. 26 361, -207), offers flights to Athens (2 per day, 45min., 17,100dr). There are no buses to the airport, and taxis cost roughly 1000dr. Office open Mon.-Sat. 8am-4pm.

Trains: From the **station** (tel. 27 906), trains run to Thessaloniki (5 per day, 7hr., 3000dr) and İstanbul (1 per day, 8hr., 2380dr). Station open daily 6:30am-11:30pm.

Buses: From the **station** (tel. 26 479), buses head for Kavala (6 per day, 2½hr., 2600dr), and continue to Thessaloniki, Komotini (12 per day, 1hr., 1000dr), and Xanthi (6 per day, 1½hr., 1850dr).

Ferries: There is no direct ferry to Kavala. Ferries run to Samothraki (3 per day, 2½hr., 2100dr) and Limnos (1 per day, 6hr., 3000dr). **Saos Tours** (tel. 26 721) has tickets and information on Kyprou St., a small street just off the waterfront, opposite the dock entrances. Open daily 8am-2:30pm and 5-8pm. **Flying Dolphins** are also handled by Saos. Hydrofoils run to Lesvos, Kavala, and Limnos.

Laundromat: (tel. 21 229) 1 block left (facing inland) from the police station. Open Mon.-Sat. 9am-2pm and 6-9pm.

Taxis: (tel. 22 000, 27 700) run 24hr.

Hospital: 19 Dimitras St. (tel. 25 772). Open 24hr.

Police: 6 Karaiskaki (tel. 37 424), just before the lighthouse. Open 24hr.

Port police (tel. 26 468), on the waterfront, 2 blocks before the lighthouse, at the corner of Botsari. Open 24hr.

Post Office: (tel. 23 122), along the waterfront, past Karaiskaki St. Open Mon.-Sat. 7:30am-2pm. **Postal Code:** 68100.

Telephone Code: 0551.

ACCOMMODATIONS

Hotel Majestic (tel. 26 444), in Eleftherias Sq., visible from the train station. Rooms are old, but clean. Singles 4500dr. Doubles 6000dr. Prices vary.

Hotel Mitropolis (tel. 26 443 or 33 808), on the corner of Emporiou and Athan. From Platia Eleftherias, turn left onto Emporiou and walk down several blocks (to the left facing inland). The rooms are immaculate, with bath, radio, and phone. Singles 8500dr. Doubles 12,000dr. Triples 14,000dr. Prices lower in off season.

Hotel Erika (tel. 34 115), near the Hotel Majestic, on the waterfront. Rooms with TV, fridge, kitchen, and bath. Singles 10,000dr. Doubles 12,500dr.

Camping Alexandroupolis (tel. 28 735), conveniently located 3km northwest of Alexandroupolis, off L. Demokratias St. A bus runs hourly to Hili or Makri. The campground is on the beach and has clean facilities. 950dr per person. 450dr per youth. 800dr per tent. Discounts for longer stays.

FOOD, SIGHTS, AND ENTERTAINMENT

On Kyprou St. (200m left of the rail station facing inland) are restaurants and *ouzeries* with decent, cheap food. Fish *tavernas* cluster 100m left of the rails, facing inland. The **Ouzerie Mynos,** opposite the post office on the waterfront, is unmistakable for its Hollandesque windmill and unforgettable for its sweet, permeating scent of olive oil and freshly baked bread. The 18th-century icon of a limber Christ, whose legs form a heart, is displayed at the Neoclassical **Ecclesiastic Art Museum,** next to the Cathedral of St. Nicholas, two blocks inland from the bank. Priests at the nearby church of Ag. Nikolas let visitors in (open daily 10am-midnight; 200dr donation).

Crete ΚΡΗΤΗ

In middle of the sable sea there lies An isle call'd Crete, a ravisher of eyes, Fruitful, and mann'd with many an infinite store; Where ninety cities crown the famous shore, Mix'd with all-languag'd men.
—Homer, *Odyssey*

There's a Greek saying that the Cretan's first loyalty is to the island and second to the country. Indeed, some of Crete's rugged individualism (that treats even Greeks as foreigners) still exists; simply look to the long-mustached men who sit by the harbor polishing their high black boots. Like the island, they are hospitable, but prefer to keep their distance—staid and stoic.

Crete's history combines trauma, glory, and mediocrity. Inhabited as far back as 6000 BCE (Neolithic Period), Crete was supposedly both the birthplace of Zeus and the home of the man-eating Minotaur, who dwelled at Knossos. The Neolithic Cretans dwelled in open settlements and worshipped their deities by placing terra-cotta statuettes on the tops of mountains, now referred to as peak sanctuaries. Crete's glory, however, began when settlers arrived from Asia Minor around 3000 BCE.

These inhabitants, throughout the span of a few thousand years, created intriguingly sophisticated "palaces," or architecturally well planned, multi-story buildings. Among the artifacts found from this time are artistically-flared pottery sherds, wall frescoes, golden jewelry, horns of consecration, renditions of bull's heads, stone libation vessels, Linear A and B tablets, and anthropomorphic figurines. This period lasted from 2800 to 1100 BCE and is known as the renowned **Minoan Civilization.**

The Minoans not only survived three waves of destruction—an earthquake, a series of tidal waves following the eruption of the volcano on Santorini, and (probably) a Mycenaean invasion—but also rebuilt their civilization after each setback. These periods are now referred to as the Early, Middle and Late Minoan Periods, based on pottery styles. Crete's most glorious days were spent during the Middle Minoan Period, when the Palace at Knossos functioned as the center of an Aegean marine empire. Newly established trade routes beckoned prosperity and sophistication, and Minoan artistry reached its climax. This period is also famous because it was believed to have been the one and only time in human history when men and women lived together in pure peace, harmony, and equality. Unfortunately, archaeological discoveries in recent years (weaponry and evidence for human sacrifice) suggest that the state of Minoan affairs *may* not have been so hunky-dory after all.

Nevertheless, in the 8th century BCE Dorians occupied the island, and jewelry-making, sculpture, and pottery thrived. The Roman conquest in 67 BCE found the island increasingly unstable, with aristocratic families dominant and intercity warfare frequent. In the Medieval and Modern periods, Crete was ruled in succession by the Byzantine, Arab, Genoese, Venetian, and Turkish empires, and in 1898, the island became an English protectorate. Finally, after the Balkan War of 1913, Crete joined the Republic of Greece. For more background on Crete's glorious past, read Adam Hopkins's witty anecdotal history, *Crete: Its Past, Present, and People;* Oliver Dickinson's archaeologically inclined, *Aegean Bronze Age;* Sinclair Hood's artistically insightful, *Arts of Prehistoric Greece;* or Michael Herzfeld's anthropological account of the Cretans, *History of the Past: A Cretan Town.*

GETTING THERE

Olympic Airways has cheap, fast, domestic **flights** from Athens to Sitia on the east, Iraklion in the center, and Chania on the west. Air Greece also has flights to Crete, and often their prices are cheaper, but they service fewer destinations than Olympic Airways. Most flights take less than an hour. Check out the practical information listings in your destination city.

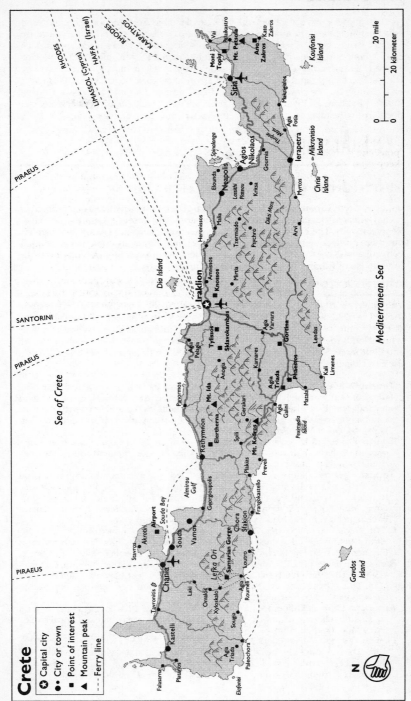

Crete

- ✪ Capital city
- ● City or town
- ■ Point of interest
- ▲ Mountain peak
- --- Ferry line

RHODES

KARPATHOS

LIMASSOL (Cyprus)

HAIFA (Israel)

RHODES

Vai
Palaikastro
Moni
Toplu
Mt. Petsofa
Ano
Zakros
Kato
Zakros

Koufonisi
Island

PIRAEUS

Sitia

Havgas

Agia
Fotia

Ierapetra

Thripti Mtns.

Agios
Nikolaos
Spinalonga
Elounda
Gournia

Neapolis
Lasithi Plateau
Kritsa
Dikti Mtns
Myrtos

Dia Island

Heronissos
Malia
Tzermiado
Psychro
Arvi

Chris
Island

Mikronisio
Island

SANTORINI

Iraklion
Amnissos
Knossos
Mirtia

PIRAEUS

Tylissos
Skavokambos
Agia
Pelagia

Agia
Varvara
Gortina

Mediterranean Sea

Sea of Crete

Panormos
Anogia
Kamares
Mt. Ida
Gerakari
Phaistos
Kali
Limenes

Agia
Triada

Lendas

Matala

Eleftherna
Rethymnon
Spili
Mt. Kedros
Agia
Galini

Paximadia
Island

Plakas
Preveli

Airport
Akrotiri
Souda Bay

Almirou
Gulf

Georgioupolis

Frangokastello

Chora
Sfakion

Savros
Souda
Vamos
Chora

Gavdos
Island

PIRAEUS

Chania

Lefka Ori

Samarian Gorge

Laki
Omalos
Xyloskalo
Agia
Roumeli
Loutro

Souga
Kastelli

Agia
Triada

Falasarna
Plakias
Paleochora

Elafonisi

N

20 mile

20 kilometer

Most travelers arrive in Crete by **ferry**. The island has frequent connections during summer, but boats often fall behind schedule. The larger the boat, the more frequently it runs, and the more dependable its schedule. All prices listed are for deck-class accommodations. Boats run to Iraklion, Chania, Kastelli, and Agios Nikolaos. There are **international ferry** connections to Ancona in Italy, Çeşme in Turkey, Limassol on Cyprus, and Haifa, Israel. For Egypt, change boats in Cyprus. From April to October, the *Vergina* leaves Haifa, Israel on Sundays and travels to Cyprus, Rhodes, Iraklion, and Peiraias; deck-class costs roughly 20,000dr between any two ports. Those heading to Italy must go to Peiraias and change boats.

CENTRAL CRETE

■ Iraklion (Heraklion) ΗΡΑΚΛΕΙΟ

Iraklion, Crete's metropolis and the fifth largest city in Greece, has stumbled in recent years as developers have crammed concrete hotels within the old city's Venetian walls. The city has many of the vices and few of the virtues of urban life, but there are worse things than being stranded here for a day. Take in the magnificent ruins at Knossos, the impressive archaeological museum, perhaps even the tomb of Nikos Kazantzakis—but then take the first bus out.

ORIENTATION AND PRACTICAL INFORMATION

Though Iraklion spreads for miles, almost everything important lies within the circle formed by Dikeosinis Ave., Handakos St., Doukos Bofor Ave., and the waterfront. The city centers are **Venizelou Square,** known to tourists as **Lion Fountain Square,** where Handakos St. meets Dikeosinis and 25th Augustou Ave. in the center of town, and **Eleftherias Square,** at the intersection of Doukos Bofor and Dikeosinis Ave. on the east side of the old city.

Tourist Office: 1 Xanthoudidou St. (tel. 22 82 03 or 24 46 62), opposite the Archaeological Museum in Eleftherias Sq. Free city maps, lists of hotels, message board for travelers, bus schedules, and some boat schedules (check times with the boat company). English-speaking staff is helpful but overworked. Information on harvest jobs. Open Mon.-Fri. 8am-2:30pm.

Tourist Police: 10 Dikeosinis St. (tel. 28 31 90 or 28 96 14), one block from intersection of 25th Augustou Ave. and Dikeosinis. Provides general tourist information. Open daily 7am-11pm.

Tourist Agencies: Shop around among the hordes of agencies on 25th Augustou Ave. **Prince Travel,** #30 25th Augustou Ave. (tel. 28 27 03, -6). Provides information on air, bus, and boat tickets. Holds luggage for 300dr per piece per day. Open Mon.-Fri. 9am-2:30pm and 5-7:30pm, Sat. 9am-2pm. Many tourist agencies exchange currency at bank rates and remain open until 9pm.

OTE: 10 Minotavrou St. (tel. 282 399); follow signs on Minotavrou near El Greco Park. Telephones, telegrams, and telex. Open daily 7am-11pm. **Branch office** in Eleftherias Sq. Open March-Oct. Mon.-Fri. 8am-11pm; Nov.-Feb. Mon.-Fri. 1-9pm.

Banks: The banks on 25th Augustou Ave. are open Mon.-Thurs. 8am-2pm, Fri. 8am-1:30pm. The **National Bank,** 25th Augustou Ave., is just beyond CaRavel. Open Mon.-Thurs. 8am-2pm, Fri. 8am-1:30pm. Gift shops in Venizelou Sq. **exchange currency** after hours at slightly lower rates.

American Express Office: 13 Arkoleontos St. (tel. 34 25 01, -2), near Lion Fountain Sq. Handles client mail and arranges for cardholders to cash checks at local banks. Open Mon.-Fri. 8am-5pm, Sat. 8am-2pm, Sun. 10am-1pm.

Flights: Olympic Airways, 42 Eleftherias Sq. (tel. 22 91 91). Open Mon.-Fri. 8am-3pm. The Stratones city bus #1 goes from Eleftherias Sq. to within 50m of the airport (every 10min., 6am-11pm, 200dr). Flights leave for Athens (6 per day, 45min., 19,200dr); Mykonos (1 per week, 30min., 17,300dr); Rhodes (4 per

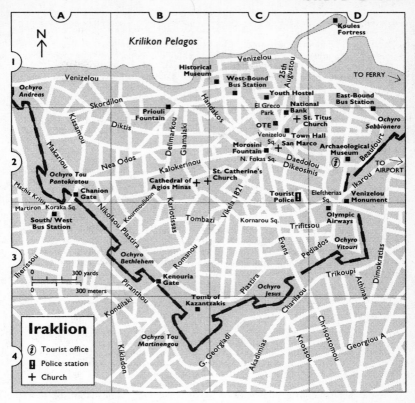

Iraklion

(i) Tourist office

[] Police station

+ Church

week, 30min., 19,000dr); Thessaloniki (5 per week, 1hr., 25,600dr); Santorini (3 per week, 30min., 13,900dr); and Corfu via Athens (3 per day, 2hr., 36,600dr). **Air Greece** offers less frequent but less expensive service to Iraklion; for information, call their office in Athens, 20 Syntagma (tel. (01) 325 5011).

Buses: There are several **KTEL** bus terminals, so match the station to your destination. **Terminal A** (tel. 24 50 17, -9), between the old city walls and the harbor near the waterfront, serves Ag. Nikolaos (22-24 per day until 9pm, 1½hr., 1200dr); Lassithi (1-2 per day, 2hr., 1150dr); Hersonissos (every 30min., 45min., 500dr); Malia (every 30min., 6:30am-10pm, 1hr., 650dr); Sitia (5 per day until 4pm, 3¼hr., 2350dr); Ierapetra (7 per day until 5:30pm, 2½hr., 1850dr); Archanes (13 per day Mon.-Sat., 6 per day Sun., 30min., 300dr); and Ag. Pelagia (5 per day, 45min., 530dr). **Terminal B** (tel. 25 59 65), outside the Chania Gate of the old city walls, runs buses to Phaistos (9-10 per day, 1½hr., 1100dr); Ag. Galini (6-7 per day, 2¼hr., 1350dr); Matala (5-7 per day, 2hr., 1350dr); Lentas (1 per day Mon.-Fri., 3hr., 1400dr); Anogia (5 per day, 2 on Sun., 1hr., 650dr); and Fodele (2 per day, Mon.-Fri., 1hr., 550dr). The **Chania/Rethymnon Terminal** (tel. 22 17 65) is near the waterfront. Walk down 25th Augustou Ave. to the waterfront, turn right, and walk about 500m. The station will be on your right about 200m before the ferry landing. It serves the same destinations as Terminal A, plus service to Chania (14 per day, 2300dr) and Rethymnon (17 per day, 1½hr., 1350dr). Bus company publishes schedules subject to change.

Ferries: Boat offices on 25th Augustou Ave. Most open daily 9am-9pm. Boats leave for Athens (2 per day, 12hr., 5880dr); Santorini (5 per week, 4hr., 2955dr); Paros (9 per week, 8½hr., 4500dr); Naxos (3 per week, 7hr., 4500dr); Mykonos (2 per week, 9hr., 5255dr); Rhodes (2 per week, 12hr., 5745dr); and Thessaloniki (6 per week, 11hr., 9750dr).

Taxis: Tariff Taxi of Iraklion (tel. 21 01 02). Take a taxi from Iraklion to Ag. Pelagia or Hersonissos (4000dr). Farther destinations will cost you (Rethymnon 10,500dr, Ierapetra 13,000dr, Chania 17,500dr, or Knossos 1100dr). Open 24hr.

Car Rental: Rental car companies are scattered along 25th Augustou Ave. Shop around. Make the owners compete for your business by quoting prices from their neighbors. For advance reservations, call **Budget Rent-a-Car,** #34 25th Augustou Ave. (tel. (01) 922 4444), at their central office in Athens. **CaRavel** at #16 and #39 25th Augustou Ave. (tel. 24 53 45, -50; fax 22 03 62) will rent cars to anyone more than 19 years old. Prices average 9000dr per day. A copy of *Let's Go* will get you free insurance or a 40% discount on any car. Car delivered free from airport. Open daily 7am-10pm.

Moped Rental: Iraklion's rates are among the higher in Crete. Cheap rentals line Handakos St., El Greco Park, and 25th Augustou Ave., but prices fluctuate significantly. Check if the quoted price includes the 20% tax and insurance. 50cc bikes 3500dr per day; tax and third-party liability insurance included. **Nikos Rent-a-Vespa,** 16 Doukos Bofor St. (tel. 22 64 25), across from Marin Hotel. Open daily 8am-8:30pm.

Luggage Storage: Prince Travel, #30 25th Augusta Ave. (tel. 28 2703). For 300dr per piece per day. Open Mon.-Fri. 9am-2:30pm and 5-7:30pm, Sat 9am-2pm.

Laundromat: Washsalon, 18 Handakos St. (tel. 28 08 58; fax 28 44 42). 200dr for wash and dry; soap included. Self-service. Provides luggage storage (250dr, with locker 300dr). Open daily 8:30am-9pm.

Public Toilets: El Greco Park. Open daily 7am-9pm. 30dr per use. Also in public gardens near Eleftherias Sq.

Library: Vikelaia Municipal Library (tel. 24 65 50, -2), in Venizelou Sq. Limited number of books in English on the second floor. Open Mon.-Fri. 8am-3pm.

Bookstores: Kouvidis and Manouras International Bookstore, 6 Dedalous St. (tel. 220135), has a decent selection of English and German paperbacks. Open daily March-Nov. 8am-10pm, reduced winter hours. **Newsstands** in Eleftherias Sq. sell foreign newspapers like the *International Herald Tribune* as well as paperbacks. Open daily 8am-10pm. The **bookstore** (tel. 28 96 05) at the base of Chandakos St. near the water has a huge selection of Penguin classics and is run by the English-language book wholesaler who also runs **Planet Bookstore** (tel. 28 15 58), a 5-floor megastore on the corner of Hortatson and Kidonias St. Open Mon.-Fri. 8:30am-2pm and 5:30-8:30pm, Sat. 8:30am-noon.

Pharmacy: (tel. 22 46 08), on Agiou Titou St. off 25th Augustou Ave. Open Mon.-Fri. 9am-10pm. One open 24hr. by rotation—its name and address is posted on the door of every pharmacy. All are marked by a red cross.

Hospital: (tel. 23 95 02 or 26 93 73), Venizelou St., on the road to Knossos. Take bus #2 (20min.). Also **Panepistimiako Hospital** (tel. 26 91 11 or 26 94 62). One open 24hr. each day; schedule rotates.

Police: Same location as the tourist police. Open 24hr. One station services the east side of town (tel. 28 45 89 or 24 34 66); another station in the same building takes care of the west (tel. 28 26 77 or 28 22 43). **Port Police** (tel. 22 60 73).

Post Office: Main office (tel.24 38 96 or 28 99 95), off Gianani St. Open Mon.-Fri. 7:30am-8pm. **Branch office** in El Greco Park. Open Mon.-Fri. 8:30am-3pm. **Postal Code:** 71001.

Telephone Code: 081.

ACCOMMODATIONS

Iraklion has a bunch of cheap hotels and hostels, most near Handakos St., at the center of town. Others are on Evans and 1866 St., near the market. If you arrive late at night and take a taxi, be aware that some taxi drivers get commissions from hotels.

The **"Rooms to Let" Association** (ΦΙΛΟΞΕΝΙΑ; tel. 22 92 52), run by a conglomerate of hotel owners, is not a great resource for places to stay in Iraklion, but is a godsend for advance bookings in Hersonissos, Malia, and resorts in eastern Crete.

Good luck finding the small office at Kornarou Sq. Phone calls often suffice—some English spoken (open daily 9:30am-1pm).

Youth Hostel, 5 Cyronos St. (tel. 28 62 81 or 22 29 47), off 25th Augustou Ave. Standard hostel rooms; cool and quiet. Curfew midnight. Luggage storage 300dr. 24-hr. hot water. Check-out 10am. Open for late arrivals. Larger rooms for families and couples. You get what you pay for. Café/bar breakfast 350dr, beer 350dr. 1400dr per person. Doubles 3800-4000dr.

Hotel Paladion, 16 Handakos St. (tel 28 25 63). Centrally located, this hotel's marble stairs lead to clean rooms with sink, closet, small desk, and chair. Some rooms off garden patio in rear; upstairs rooms have balconies. All share bathrooms, but they are large and clean. Hot showers 24hr. Singles 3500dr. Doubles 5200dr. Triples 700dr. Quads 8600dr.

Hotel Rea, Kalimeraki St. (tel. 24 21 89). Walking toward the harbor, turn right off Handakos St.—2 blocks above the waterfront. Clean, airy rooms, with pleasing pastel trim. Hot showers included. Luggage storage free. Reduced rate on rent-a-car services. Manager speaks English. Doubles 5000dr, with bath 6000dr. Triples 7000dr, with bath 8000dr. Dorm-like quads 8000dr. Breakfast 850dr.

Rent a Room Vergina, 32 Chortason St. (tel. 24 27 39). Walking toward the harbor, turn right off Handakos onto Kidonias, take your first left on Hortason, and walk down 2 blocks—it's on the right. Clean, homey rooms. Washtubs and clotheslines. High ceilings, new furniture. Free luggage storage. Check-out noon. Deposit necessary with advance reservations. Doubles 5000dr. Triples 7000dr.

FOOD AND ENTERTAINMENT

Around the Morosini Fountain, near El Greco Park, and in Eleftherias Sq. are ritzy cafés perfect for lounging. Take a left off 1866 St., one block from Venizelou Sq., to reach tiny Theodosaki St. Though not the most upscale place in town to dine, it's certainly colorful, with 10 *tavernas* serving Greek fare jammed side by side. The cheaper dishes go for roughly 650dr and the portions are impressive. If there's no menu, fix the price before you sit. For more elegant dining, try any of the *tavernas* on shop-and-boutique-lined Daedolou St. *Souvlaki* joints abound on 25th Augustou Ave. **Thraka,** 14 Platokallergon (4 Lions Square), is the most fun thanks to its 30-year tradition of only grilled ham meat gyros and *souvlaki*. No electricity is used here, only charcoal, and the friendly *gyro*-makers behind the counter will remind you loudly and often. Try the *souvlaki* with bread crust (350dr, gyros 400dr). The manager of the **Minos Restaurant,** on Daedalou St., will personally guide you to have a look in the kitchen (swordfish 2000dr) and choose the dish that looks tastiest. The same owner for 26 years has served a delicious special of lamb with yogurt (lamb "Elvasan" yogurt 2500dr; open daily 11am-3pm and 6-10pm).

During the day, the best show in town is the **open-air market** on 1866 St., which starts near Venizelou Sq. Both sides of the boisterous, aromatic, narrow street are lined with stalls piled high with sweets, spices, fresh fruits, vegetables, cheeses, and meat in glass cases. The huge cauldrons of yogurt sold here far eclipse the filtered, pasteurized brands found elsewhere. For delicious yogurt try **Amalthia** (tel. 28 50 84), in the market. Named after the goat of Zeus, they serve traditional sheep's milk yogurt (600dr per kg), as well as local cheeses like the special Cretan Gruyere (2000dr per kg; market open Mon-Sat. 8:30am-2:30pm, Tues., Thurs., Fri. 8:30am-2:30pm and 5:30-9pm). The two **sweet shops** in Lion Fountain Sq. sell *bougatsa,* a cheese or cream-filled phyllo pastry (open daily 6am-11pm).

Antonios Nerantzoulis, 16 Ag. Titoy St. (tel. 24 62 36), behind the St. Titus Church. This bakery has been run by the same family since 1900. Their selection of biscuits and bread may leave you indecisive. They are famous for *oktasporo* (8 grain leaves; 800dr) and *Kaltsounia,* little moist cheese biscuits (1200-1800dr per kg; open Tues., Thurs., Fri. 7am-3pm and 5-8pm, Mon., Wed., Sat. 7am-3pm).

Iraklion natives are the first to point out that the "in" places change rapidly, so ask around. Cafés are often fun places to check out the Iraklion nightlife. One very popular, always crowded one is **Aktarika Café** (tel. 34 12 25), across from the Lion

CENTRAL CRETE

Fountain Square. All day and all night this huge atrium-like cafe teems with hip twenty- to thirty-something Iraklionites clad in black and the people who watch them (*frappés* 600dr, cocktails 1500dr; open daily 9am-2:30am; DJ on duty 11am-4pm and 7pm-2:30am). If you're feeling energized after your archaeological excursions, you could head to **Factory,** formerly Athina, which plays rave and disco on Thursday to Saturday nights. For Greek music, head to **Café Aman. Disco Trapeza** sports a young crowd. Schedules for Iraklion's **movie theaters** are posted near the tourist police office. The **Galaxia** (tel. 23 42 72) and the **Cine Romantic** (tel. 22 52 82) are outdoor cinemas (open June-Sept.; daily show times usually 9 and 11pm; admission 1500dr). For an evening of free sociological entertainment, join Greeks and tourists at Venizelou Sq., where Iraklion's annual **summer festival** combines cultural events such as concerts, theater, ballet, and folk dancing, and has some shows at the lovely outdoor Kazandzakis Theater. Most shows begin at 9:30pm and cost up to 300dr. Students usually pay at the most 150dr. Pick up a schedule of events booklet from the tourist police or tourist information office. Call 24 29 77 for information (mid-June to mid-Sept.).

SIGHTS

Iraklion's capital attraction is its superb **Archaeological Museum** (tel. 22 60 92), off Eleftherias Sq. Exhibits are organized chronologically from the Neolithic period to Roman times. The museum's most outstanding feature is the **Hall of the Minoan Frescoes.** An illustrated guide available at the Museum's gift stand is well worth the 1500dr—otherwise you'll have to see the frescoes *sans* historical insights. The frescoes depict ancient Minoan life: ladies in blue offering libations, blue monkeys frolicking in the palatial gardens, and costumed Minoans forming a ritualized procession against an impressionistic mountain landscape (open Mon. 12:30-7pm, Tues.-Sun. 8am-7pm; admission 1500dr, students 800dr, free for those under 18, students from the EU, and students of classical studies and fine arts not from the EU). Iraklion also has a **Historical Museum** (tel. 28 32 19), on the corner of Grevenon and Kalokerianou, two blocks from the Xenia Hotel. Unlike the crowded Archaeological Museum, this museum is undervisited. Its eclectic collection includes both a byzantine and Medieval Collection, folk collection, frescoes, Turkish gravestones, finely woven tapestries, photographs from the WWII German invasion, and the only **El Greco** on Crete—strange, considering that El Greco, or Theotokopoulos, was a native Cretan. The museum also features a reconstruction of Kazantzakis' library including manuscripts from his desk in Aegina (open Mon.-Fri. 9am-5pm, Sat. 9am-2pm; admission 1000dr, students 750dr, children under 12 free).

The austere **Tomb of Kazantzakis** has views of Iraklion, the sea, and the Mountain of Zeus to the east and offers a peaceful and green respite from the crowded

---

It's El Greco to Me

Though he made his name at the Spanish court, Domenikos Theotocopoulos (1541-1614) clung to his Greek heritage throughout his artistic career. Born at Iraklion (then under Venetian rule), the Cretan artist incorporated his early Byzantine training with the teachings of the Venetian and Roman schools, where he trained with masters like Titian, Raphael, and Michelangelo. El Greco, as he came to be known, was a master of Mannerism, a style of painting that places internal emotions above nature and the ancients. El Greco's reputation was built on his portraits and religious imagery that featured rigid figures filled with surprising emotion. His best-known work, *The Burial of the Count Orgaz,* staged a historical event in the contemporary world, a tradition in Western painting that echoes throughout the history of art. Although El Greco moved to Toledo, Spain, in 1576, the Spanish subjects and contexts of his work never eclipsed his feeling that he was a stranger in that land—and throughout his career, El Greco would continue to sign his paintings in Greek.

city of Iraklion. To get there, either walk along the top of the Venetian walls to Martinengo Bastion at the south corner of the city, or go down Evans St. until you reach the walls and the bastion. Because of his heterodox beliefs, Kazantzakis, the author of *The Last Temptation of Christ,* was denied a place in a Christian cemetery and was buried here without the full rites of the Orthodox Church. True aficionados can visit the **Kazantzakis Museum** (tel. 742451) in the nearby village of Varvari. The carefully presented exhibit includes many of the author's original manuscripts, as well as photographs of his theatrical productions. A slide show (in English) provides historical background. A bus from Station A takes you to Mirtia (22km from Iraklion), only a short walk from the museum. For schedules, inquire at the station or call 24 50 17, -9. (Open March 1-Oct. 31 Mon., Wed., Sat.-Sun. 9am-1pm and 4-8pm, Tues. and Fri. 9am-1pm; Nov. 1-Feb. 28 also open Sun. 10am-3pm; 500dr.)

Several interesting churches hide in the modern maze of city streets. Built in 1735 in Agia Ekaterinis Sq., the **Cathedral of Agios Minas** (tel. 28 24 02) piously graces the area (open daily 7am-8pm). **St. Catherine's Church of Sinai** (tel. 288825), in the square, served as the first Greek university after the fall of Constantinople in 1453. The church features six icons by the Cretan master Damaskinos as well as other icons from monasteries and churches around Crete (open Mon., Wed., and Sat. 9am-1:30pm, Tues., Thurs.-Fri. 5-8pm; admission 400dr). **St. Titus Church,** 25th Augustou Ave., is a Turkish mosque converted into a Christian church. The **Armenian Church** (tel. 24 43 37), constructed in 1666, can be reached by heading away from the town center on Kalokerianou St. Take a right on the street just after the fruit market at 174 Kalokerianou St. and *oriste*—you're there. The priest gives free tours of the grounds. **Agios Mattheos,** a 10-minute walk on Markopoulou St. from Agia Ekaterinis Sq., has excellent icons. Ask the priest behind the church for the key.

As you scamper around, take note of the various monuments built during the Venetian occupation of Iraklion. Omnipopular is the 17th-century **Morosini Fountain** in Lion Fountain Sq., graced with marble lions. The reconstructed **Venetian Loggia,** Lion Fountain Sq.; the 13th-century **Basilica of St. Mark,** 25th Augustou Ave., now an exhibition hall; the **Venetian Arsenal,** off Kountouriotou Sq., near the waterfront; and the **Koules Fortress** (tel. 24 62 11), which guards the old harbor (open Mon.-Fri. 8am-6pm, Sat.-Sun. 10am-5pm; admission 500dr, students 300dr) deserve peeks, as do the impressive 15th-century **Venetian walls** around the city.

■ Near Iraklion

Iraklion is an ideal base for exploring Central Crete. Many archaeological sites, including the great Minoan complex at Knossos and lesser Minoan finds at Malia, Tylissos, and Arhanes, are within a half-day's excursion from the city.

KNOSSOS

Knossos is undoubtedly the most famous archaeological site in Crete; few visitors escape the island without at least a token visit. Myth claims that when **King Minos** of Crete refused to sacrifice a fine white bull to Poseidon, the sea-god drove both **Pasiphaë,** Minos' queen, and the bull mad with lust. Their passion spawned the **Minotaur,** who stalked through the labyrinth and required 14 well cooked Athenian youths per year. Finally **Theseus,** Prince of Athens, entered the maze and slew the monster with the aid of **Ariadne,** Minos' daughter, and **Daedalus,** the master architect who designed the labyrinth. Theseus had intended to take Ariadne back to Athens to marry her (or so he said—the cad), but at the bidding of Dionysus, he abandoned her on the island of Naxos. When Minos discovered that Daedalus had helped Theseus escape, he imprisoned both the architect and his son, **Icarus.** Daedalus built them both wings of feathers and wax and off they flew. Hubristic Icarus, however, soared too close to the sun, melting his waxen wings and fell into the Aegean near the modern island Ikaria. Ovid's *Metamorphoses* is a compelling account of the story, as is Mary Renault's novel *The King Must Die.*

During the first millennium BCE, Cretans were ridiculed for imagining that they sprang from such illustrious forebears as the **Minoans.** Time, however, has proven the Cretans right. **Sir Arthur Evans,** one of Heinrich "Troy" Schliemann's British cronies, purchased the hill and spent the next 43 years and his entire fortune excavating it. His thorough work showed that from 1700 BCE to 1400 BCE, Knossos was indeed either an important temple complex, or a distribution center, that stood at the center of the first great European civilization.

Dr. Evans creatively, though in many instances inaccurately, restored large portions of the palace to what he believed were their original configurations, based on evidence unearthed during the excavations. Walls, window casements, stairways, and columns were reconstructed in reinforced concrete, and copies of the magnificent frescoes were mounted in place of their original counterparts (now in Iraklion's Archaeological Museum). In some cases, restorations prevented the walls from falling down as the excavations continued, but Evans' reconstruction crossed the boundaries of preservation and reflected his own interpretation. While purists feel that the complex at Knossos is an outrage, it is impressive nonetheless.

The extended series of magazines (storage rooms with large clay jars) give the palace its labyrinthine architecture and are its claim to fame. The large open space in the middle of the site, imaginatively named the Central Court, was quite possibly an arena for bull-leaping (a Minoan rite of passage ceremony). The **Throne Room,** to the left of the Central Court, enshrines the original throne. A wooden replica is in an adjacent room for your very own Kodak moment. Although Evans really wanted the throne to have belonged to King Minos, it was more likely the perch of a "Queen Mina." Iconographically throughout antiquity, a seated figure surrounded by palm fronds (strikingly similar to those that Evans blatantly changed in his reconstruction) was always a woman (i.e. a goddess). The throne faces a frustratingly enigmatic structure known as a lustral basin (a deep square area possibly used for religious purposes). Note the elaborate drainage system, occasional mason's marks on the shiny, cut-stone architecture, and the I-shaped cement bumps on the ground where doors ingeniously slid into the walls and let in, or kept out, the sunlight. The areas painted red around each window and door were actually constructed out of wood in antiquity; they cushioned the walls from frequent seismic shock. Don't miss the **Queen's Bathroom**—over 3000 years ago, that lucky girl could flush her own toilet. Finally, gaze upon the **Royal Road** in the complex's northwest sector— it served not only as an entryway, but also as a reception area for important guests.

For general reference, check out *Knossos and the Iraklion Museum,* by Costis Davaris (1500dr), *Knossos: The Minoan Civilization,* by Sosso Logadiou-Platonos (1200dr), and a new one—*Knossos: A complete Guide to the Palace of Mines,* by Anna Michailidou (2000dr), all on sale at the site. Even more helpful and enlightening is an English-speaking tour guide (the price varies depending on a particular group's size, 1000-2000dr for a 1-hr. tour). Make sure that the guide is official and has the required papers, or he could be spouting nonsense. The ruins (tel. 23 19 40) are open daily 8am-7pm (admission 1500dr, students 800dr; free on Sun.). Take bus #2, which stops along 25th Augustou Ave.—look for the signposts on the west side of the street (every 20min., daily, 7am-10:30pm, 200dr).

TYLISSOS, FODELE, AND GORTINIA

Although Knossos is secure in its status as the most popular site on Crete, it cannot lay claim to being the oldest. At **Tylissos,** 14km southwest of Iraklion, archaeologists have unearthed a Minoan city dating back to 2000 BCE. Unlike Knossos, the ruins at Tylissos remain relatively unaltered. Halfway between Tylissos and Anogia are the remains of the Minoan villas at **Sklavokambos.**

Also accessible from Iraklion is **Fodele,** a village full of orange trees and famous as the home of **El Greco** (see box on page 202.) For information on buses to Anogia and Fodele, see page 199.The first stop of historical interest on the road south, **Gortina** contains the ruins of the Greco-Roman city, Gortyn. In 67 BCE, when ancient

Gortyn fell to the Romans, the city was designated the capital of the island. Most of the remaining ruins here are from the Roman occupation, including the **Roman Odeon** (music hall). One of the few remains from the Hellenistic city, the Law Code tablets, are the most important extant source of information regarding pre-Hellenistic Greek law. They are written in a Dorian dialect of Greek and date from roughly 450 BCE when the city thrived under Greek control. The stones were so handsomely cut that the Romans used them as building materials for the odeon.

The site of ancient **Gortyn,** en route to Phaistos, is on your right as you come from Iraklion. The first thing you'll see is the bird-inhabited 7th-century **Basilica of Saint Titus.** The odeon is behind the church. The site also has a hall with 14 sculpted figures and a mammoth statue of a soldier. To get to Gortyn, take one of the many **buses** that go to Matala or Phaistos. See those towns for schedule details.

PHAISTOS

Imperiously situated on a plateau with a magnificent view of the surrounding mountains, the palace at Phaistos (tel. (0892) 91 315) housed powerful Minoan royalty. At the turn of the century, Halbherr began excavations here and unearthed two palaces. The first was destroyed by the earthquake that decimated Crete around 1700 BC; the second was probably leveled in a mysterious catastrophe in 1450 BC. Surprisingly enough, a final excavation in 1952 came upon traces of two even older palaces. Since the excavations, minor reconstruction work has been done on the walls, chambers, and cisterns. Built according to the standard Minoan blueprint, the complex included a great central court, from which extended the private royal quarters, servants' quarters, storerooms, and chambers for state occasions. The grand staircase is still intact. Phaistos may be a disappointment to those not well-versed in Minoan archaeology because it's difficult to visualize what the palace looked like in its heyday. The incredible artifacts from Phaistos in the Iraklion museum alone make a visit to the site worthwhile (open daily 8am-7pm; admission 1200dr). **Buses** from Phaistos go to Iraklion (5-7 per day, 1½hr., 1100dr), Matala (3-5 per day, 20min., 200dr), and Agia Galini (3-5 per day, 25min., 200dr).

■ Matala ΜΑΤΑΛΑ

LSD, psychedelic colors, and groovy music once filled the caves strewn along Matala's seaside cliffs. Anyone who visited Matala 20 years ago is likely to muster only intoxicated memories of a more hallucinogenic trip. Before you pack your rolling papers, be aware that hardly anything of these hedonistic fiestas remains, and Matala is now a resort town for families. Along the beach are huge, pale cliffs with tiers of caves that have been inhabited since Neolithic times.

Orientation and Practical Information Matala has **three main streets:** one on the water, one behind it, and one that intersects both. On the first you'll find cafés, restaurants, souvenir stands, and a covered market; on the second, the bus station, motorbike rental agencies, and stores. At Matala's square, these two join the hotel-and-pension-lined road to Phaistos. Several motorbike rental places, all in the main square, handle **currency exchange** at similar to bank rates. **Monza Bikes** (tel. 45 732) serves as an informal tourist office and provides information on hotels and beaches. Monza rents **mopeds** for 2000-9000dr per day (depending on size and kind), with reduced prices for longer rentals (open daily 9am-11pm). The **OTE,** in the beach parking lot, resembles a small prison (open Mon.-Sat. 8am-11pm, Sun. 9am-2pm and 5-10pm). The **laundromat,** across from the campground, up a small asphalt road, in an unmarked white building, charges 1000dr per wash and 400dr for drying (open daily 9am-1pm and 3-7pm). The **post office** is near the entrance to the beach parking lot (open Mon.-Fri. 8:30am-2pm) and in summer, **buses** go to Iraklion (3-6 per day, 2hr., 1350dr), Phaistos (5 per day, 20min., 450dr), and Agia Galini (3-5 per day change at Phaistos, 45min., 600dr). The town's **police station**

CENTRAL CRETE

(tel. 45 168) is behind the bakery on the second inland road. The **hospital** and **pharmacy** are in Mires, 17km northeast. In an **emergency,** call 23 312 and a doctor or dentist will drive to Matala (open 24hr.). **Public toilets** are located in the main square next to Monza Bikes. **Postal Code:** 70200. **Telephone Code:** 0892.

Accommodations Matala has more than a dozen hotels and pensions, but bargains are scarce. Singles cost as much as doubles and rarely drop below 3000dr in summer. German and British developers often pack the town with tour groups, but there are lots of "Rooms to Let" on the road forking off the main road 750m out of town. It may be a good idea to make Matala a daytrip. Cheaper accommodations are available in Matala's surrounding villages, but don't try to sleep on the main beach or in the nearby caves—it's illegal and police occasionally raid them. Your best bet in town is **Rent Rooms Dimitri's** (tel./fax 45 740 or (093) 32 07 37). From the town center, walk out of town 200m, turn right onto the winding road at the blue Dimitri's Villa sign, then follow the path around, or call from the bus stop and one of the owners may come pick you up by motorbike. Dimitri has immaculate, shiny rooms with private bath, balconies, and hot water. He also offers *Let's Go* users a plethora of advantages (don't leave home without it). *Let's Goers* receive **currency exchange without commission,** 600dr breakfasts, a 25% discount on bike rentals, and a free ride from Mires to Matala to stay in his rooms. (Singles 2500dr. Doubles 3300dr. Triples 4000dr.) Another fine option is **Pension Matala View** (tel. 45 114), on the right opposite the Zafira Hotel, near the main square. They have tidy, good-sized bedrooms with baths and balconies. (Singles 3500dr. Doubles 5000dr. Triples 6000dr.) **Pension Jannis** (tel. 42 784), a 10-minute walk past Tsirterakis on the road to Phaistos (ask at the Xenophon Hotel), has doubles for 4000dr. Spacious **Matala Camping** (tel. 45 720), on your right in the town center, has showers. (950dr per person. 650dr per tent. 600dr per car. 1100dr per RV.)

Food and Entertainment Better food, as usual, is farther from the mainstream hangouts. **Nassos** (tel. 45 250), near the waterfront, offers good *souvlaki* (250dr) and *gyros* (400dr; open daily 9am-1 or 2am). Tucked away near the end of the stream of bars that face the caves is **Skala** (tel. 45 489), a family-run restaurant known by its simpler nickname, the Fish *Taverna.* Try the special Cretan salad, a sampler of all the *tzatziki*-related dishes Crete has to offer (1800dr; open daily 8am-midnight). **Antonio's Taverna** (tel. 45 552), near the turn-off for Dimitri's Rooms, has tasty charcoal roasted chicken (1200dr; open in summer daily 10am-2am). The **bakery** (tel. 45 450), in front of the police station, is a small room offering a large array of standard Greek pastries, biscuits, and loaves of fresh bread (open daily 7am-11pm). **Sirtaki** (tel. 45 001), one of the many restaurants right on the beach, is a little less commercial (no photos of food on boards outside). All meat and fish is fresh and cooked on the grill over hot coals. Mixed fish platter, including shrimp as well as chips, vegetables, and salad (1500dr; open daily 8am-midnight or later). Nightlife in Matala means drinking, dancing, and gazing at the ocean until dawn. At the **Seahorse Bar** (tel. 45 724), dig the reggae, hear the waves, sip the Metaxa, and gaze across to the caves from this porch-turned-bar with tropical plants and a water wall (open daily 9am-7am or whenever). **Kahlua** (tel. 45 253) is a more mellow nighttime spot. Sip coffee or brandy among patrons who are out to converse rather than carouse (open daily 5pm-late). **Yorgos** (tel. 45 722), the energetic bartender and owner of this lively bar is bound to make you happy with his spunky dancing, chit-chat, and ice-cold beers (open daily 6pm-late).

Sights Matala's main attraction is its three tiers of **caves** next to the beach. Hike along them to find a private spot. Sit in its cool, dim interior and spy on the beach action below while reflecting on the cave's possible previous occupants—flower children, Nazis searching for British submarines, and long ago, Roman corpses.

Matala has more than its share of great **beaches.** Past the crashing waves rises the dim outline of Paximadia Island; the view of which is slightly marred by the hordes of other tourists enjoying it with you. For an equally good shore and more secluded caves, bikini- and speedo-clad sun worshipers join nude bathers on **Red Beach,** 20 minutes down the path behind the church. Comparatively shut off, with a small community of freelance summer residents and a lone *taverna,* **Kommos Beach** is a 5km walk from Matala. Archaeologists are currently excavating a Minoan site that overlooks the sea, arguably the bluest in Crete. The presence of the site guarantees that the coast will remain undeveloped. The bus from Iraklion will let you off roughly 500m from the beach (bus schedule posted by the station in Matala). Bring water; the hike down is long and dusty.

■ Near Matala: Agia Galini (ΑΓΙΑ ΓΑΛΗΝΗ)

Agia Galini, a once-tranquil fishing village west of Matala on the southwest coast, has become a pleasant resort town with glitzy hotels, discoes, and bars. Friendly locals make up for the busloads of people you could have met at home.

Orientation and Practical Information Agia Galini is perched on a hill—no matter where you are in town, just head down to reach the sea. The **post office** is below the bus station on the left (open Mon.-Fri. 8am-2pm). **Cretan Holidays** provides essential services, such as **currency exchange,** tourist information, and car rental (13,000-16,000dr per day, insurance included; open April-Oct. daily 8:30am-9pm). **Public toilets** (100dr) are down towards the water on the right hand side of the same street as the bus stop. The **police** (tel. 91 210) and the **port police** (tel. 91 206) are next door to the toilets (both open 24hr.). Several agents rent bikes. Try **Biggis Bikes** (tel. 91 142), near the post office (automatic 80cc mopeds 3500dr, 150cc Vespa scooters 4000dr; open daily 8:30am-11:30pm). Farther down from the post office, there is a **pharmacy** (tel. 91 168), toward the harbor and on the left (open daily 9am-2pm and 5-9pm). A **doctor** (tel. 91 091) is located a few doors down from the OPSIS office, toward the harbor (open Mon.-Fri. 10am-1:30pm and 7-8pm, Sat. noon-1pm and 7-8pm, Sun. 7-8pm). Facing the harbor, turn left at Biggis and then turn right onto **Vas. Ioannis Street,** Agia Galini's main drag. **Candia Tours** (tel. 91 278; fax 91 174; open in summer daily 9am-1pm and 5-9pm) and a **bookstore** called "Book Shop/Leather" (open daily 9am-11pm) are both on this street. The **health center** (tel. 91 111) is in the police station. A doctor visits the health center two days per week; the exact schedule varies. When the doctor is out, it is essentially a first aid station (open in summer Mon.-Fri. 9am-2pm and 5:30-8:30pm; in winter 9:30am-1:30pm). **Postal Code:** 74056. **Telephone Code:** 0832.

Accommodations The pensions along the upper tier of Agia Galini are cheaper than the hotels in the center of town. **Hotel Manos** (tel. 91 394), 25m from the bus stop, has attractively furnished rooms with wide, comfortable beds and grapevine-entwined shared balconies. (Doubles with bath 3000-5000dr.) About half-way up the main road or up the steps from the harbor (take a right on the tier before the Hotel Daedalus) is **Hotel Acteon** (tel. 91 208), which has decent, large rooms. Ask for the middle floor—it's high enough for a view of the water, but too low for the glorious panorama of the parking lot. (Doubles 4000-5000dr. Triples 6000dr. Prices negotiable in early high season; reserve 2 weeks in advance.) Next door is the **Hotel Mirago** (tel. 91 140, -494), with clean, bright rooms. (Doubles 4000dr. Triples 5000dr.) **Camping Agia Galini** (tel. 91 386) is at the turn-off 3km before town on the road from Iraklion. From the harbor, follow the beachfront 500m and look for the sign. Walk across the tilted footbridge to the end of the beach, then walk another 150m. The grounds have gravel tent sites shaded by olive and carob trees. Beware of the dogs (1000dr per person. 400dr per tent.)

Food and Entertainment Agia Galini is smothered by restaurants, bars, and discoes, which have similar prices. Although you'll find it on the main street that is cluttered with *tavernas* that all look the same, **Taverna Kosmas** (tel. 91 222) is something else. Traditional Cretan cuisine is happily served under the unusual upside-down tree trunk lights made by Kosmas himself (the tree is called the "never die" tree by Greeks). Enjoy all the traditional specialties of Crete as well as home-made wine (500dr per 500mL) and organic vegetables. The tasty *dolmades* are stuffed organic vine leaves (750dr; open daily 11am-3pm and 6pm-whenever). Be sure to ask for any seasonal specialties not on the menu. **Charlie's Place** (tel. 91 065), still known by locals as Horiarti's, recently underwent a facelift but still serves good *taverna* fare at reasonably prices. Try the *tava* (oven roasted lamb ribs, 1000dr) or the rabbit (1400dr; open daily 6pm-1am). For a quick meal, head to **Mr. Karamouzos** (tel. 91 023) for a huge *gyro* (400dr; open Feb.-Nov. daily 10am-1am).

Nightlife in Agia Galini is dominated by roof garden bars and loud discoes. **Parad-iso** is a fun roof garden bar and the **Juke Box Disco** fills with jukers and jivers. Meet other dancin' travelers at the nightly happy hour, when all cocktails are 700dr (daily 10pm-midnight). For a mellower scene and a calm escape and respite from the bar and disco crowds, **Incognito** (tel. 91 414) offers live guitar music and singing in a cozy as well as air-conditioned atmosphere. Couples and families come to enjoy cof-fees (*frappés* 350dr) as well as cocktails (900-1200dr) and cider (700dr). Tasty breakfasts like mushroom omelettes (750dr) are served too (open daily 8am-late).

WESTERN CRETE

While Crete's eastern half has been home to burgeoning tourism for years, Western Crete has remained quieter and more rustic. In the west, beaches are less populated and much of the scenery remains undisturbed. Chania's café-lined yet tranquil port, the stunning Samaria Gorge, and the sandy beaches of Paleochora all encourage travelers to heed the prophetic words of the Village People and "Go West."

■ Rethymnon ΡΕΘΥΜΝΟ

The Turkish and Venetian influences pervading the cities of northern Crete are best appreciated in Rethymnon's harbor. Arabic inscriptions lace the walls of its narrow, arched streets, minarets highlight the old city's skyline, and a Venetian fortress guards the harbor's west end. On any given day, even the most energetic travelers may inexplicably find themselves waking up just in time for the afternoon *siesta* and lounging until the wee hours of the next morning in a café by the ocean.

ORIENTATION AND PRACTICAL INFORMATION

To get to **Arkadiou Street** and the waterfront from the bus station, turn right down Demokratias St. to the Venizelou monument, cross **Kountouriotou Street,** and walk down **Varda Kallergi Street.** You'll find everything you need in the rough tri-angle formed by Arkadiou, **Antistassios,** and **Gerakari Street,** but get the tourist office's free map anyway.

Tourist Office: (tel. 29 148), down by the waterfront, west of the Old City. Effi-cient staff provides free maps, bus and ferry schedules, museum hours, and a list of all-night pharmacies. They also suggest daytrips and publicize local events. Open Mon.-Fri. 8am-5:30pm, Sat. 9am-2pm.

Tourist Police: Iroon Polytechniou St. (tel. 28 156; fax 53 450), 3 blocks from the fortress. Provides services similar to the tourist office. Open Mon.-Fri. 7am-10pm.

OTE: 28 Kountouriotou St. Open May-Oct. Mon.-Sat. 7am-midnight, Sun. 8am-11pm; Nov.-April daily 7am-10pm.

Banks: Bank of Crete, at the intersection of Kountouriotou and Varda Kallergi, near the bus station, offers **currency exchange.** Open Mon.-Thurs. 8am-2pm, Fri. 8am-1:30pm. Many banks are marked on the tourist office map. The **National Bank** is on Kountouriotou St. Open Mon.-Thurs. 8am-2pm, Fri. 8am-1:30pm.

Flights: Olympic Airways, 5 Koundouriotou St. (tel. 24 333 or 22 257), opposite the public gardens. Open Mon.-Fri. 8am-7:30pm, Sat. 8am-3:30pm.

Buses: KTEL station (tel. 22 212, -659), south of the fortress on the water at Igoum Gavril St. To Iraklion (22 per day, 1½hr., 1250dr); Chania (23 per day, 1hr., 1200dr); Agia Galini (4 per day, 2hr., 1000dr); and Plakias (6 per day, 1hr., 800dr).

Taxis: (tel. 22 316, 24 316, or 28 316). Available 24hr.

Moped Rental: Motor Stavros, 14 Paleologou St. (tel. 22 858). 80cc motorcycles 4500dr, insurance and taxes included. Bikes 1000dr. Prices negotiable. Open daily 8:30am-9pm. **Fahrrad Rent-a-Vespa,** 15 Kountouriotou St. (tel. 29 331), across from the OTE. Mountain bikes 2000dr. Open daily 8am-2pm and 5-9pm.

International Bookstore: International Press, 15 Petichaki St. (tel. 51 673 or 24 111), near the water. Sells books and magazines. Open daily 9am-11pm. **Spontidaki Toula,** 43 Souliou St. (tel. 54307), buys and sells used books.

Laundromat: 45 Tombasi St. (tel. 56 196), next to the youth hostel. Wash and dry 2000dr. Open Mon., Wed., and Sat. 8:30am-2pm and 4-8:30pm, Tues., Thurs., and Fri. 8:30am-2pm and 4-7pm. Drop off service.

Hospital: Trantalidou St. (tel. 27 814), in the southwest corner of town. From Igoum Gavril St. at the bus station, take Kriari St. to G. Trandalidor St., and bear left; it's on the left. Open 24hr.

Police: (tel. 25 247), located in Iroon Square. Open 24hr.

Post Office: Main branch on Moatsou St., near the public gardens. Open Mon.-Fri. 7:30am-8pm, Sat. 7:30am-2pm. **Caravan office,** on the beach, open same hours. **Postal Code:** 74100.

Telephone Code: 0831.

ACCOMMODATIONS

Arkadiou St. and the harbor, near the fortress and the Venetian port, are lined with hotels and "Rooms to Let." Most are spacious and expensive. The **Association of Rooms to Let,** 2 Petichaki St. (tel. 29 503), a block from the harbor, will tell you what's available. High season prices are listed here; prices are 20-40% less in off season. **Buses** run from the Rethymnon station to both campsites listed (150dr). If you're arriving from Iraklion, ask the driver to let you off at one of the sites.

Youth Hostel, 41-45 Tombasi St. (tel. 22 848), at the center of the old town. Rooms as well as outside bunk beds on the veranda or roof are available. Teeming in the summer with international youngsters who enjoy the pleasant garden areas and bar. Spontaneous parties are known to form. Hot showers in summer 8-10am and 5-8pm. Reception open in summer daily 8am-noon and 5-10pm; in winter 8am-noon and 5-9:30pm. 1200dr per person in summer. Breakfast 400dr.

Olga's Pension, 57 Souliou St. (tel. 29 851), on a nicely restored street off Ethnikis Antistaseos. Cheery decor in comfortable rooms, all with bath. Note the trippy mosaic made of coins on your way up the front stairs. Homemade *raki* at the terrarium. Singles 4500dr. Doubles 5000dr. Quads 9000dr.

Hotel Paradisos, 35 Igoum Gavril St. (tel. 22 419). From the bus station, walk down Igoum Gavril; the hotel is on the left, across from the public garden. Clean, quiet, nondescript rooms and a spacious shower and bath. Singles 2900dr. Doubles 3850dr. Triples 4500dr. Hot showers 500dr.

Elizabeth Camping (tel. 28 694), 3km east of town at the beginning of the old road to Iraklion. Tent pitches on shaded grass. Free parking next to reception. The staff lends camping and kitchen supplies. Self-service *taverna* open daily 9am-11pm. Open May-Oct. 3600dr for 2 people and a tent.

Arkadia Camping (tel. 28 825, 29 927), 500m beyond Elizabeth. Gravel pitches. Offers currency exchange and moped rentals. Self-serve *taverna* open daily 7am-11pm; store open daily 8am-9pm. 800dr per person. 400dr per tent. 200dr per small car. 600dr per large car.

FOOD AND ENTERTAINMENT

Rethymnon has plenty of *souvlaki* (150dr) stands scattered throughout the city. There's also an **open-air market** on Thursdays next to the park, between Moatsou

WESTERN CRETE

and Kountouriotou St. The market opens very early (6 or 7am) and closes by midday (1 or 2pm). To get the best, freshest vegetables, arrive early; by 9 or 10am the selection is drastically diminished. For a thriving nighttime dining scene, tourists and locals head to Petichaki Sq. and fill the *tavernas*.

Dimitris, 35 Ag. Varvaras St. (tel. 28 933). There is no menu in this *raki* bar, but the food is tasty. If you order alcohol made by the owner (150dr), you'll receive a plate of snacks, usually olives, cheese, and meat. Their specialty (besides *raki*) is oven-roasted potatoes (200dr). Open daily 8am-2pm and 5-11pm or midnight.

Taverna Kyria Maria, 20 Moskovitou St. (tel. 29 078). Rabbit (1300dr), lamb with potatoes (1300dr), and octopus in wine sauce (1100dr). Large vegetarian plate (1100dr) with loads of veggies, rice, and spaghetti. Free hot cheese pies drenched in honey after dinner. Open mid-March to Oct. daily 10am-11pm.

Montios, 34 Melissinou St. (tel. 57 024). Homemade Greek specialties. Fresh, delicious stuffed *kalamari* (1300dr), Greek salad (500dr), *moussaka* (800dr), and *souvlaki* with pita (300dr). The street closes every day at 3pm, making these outdoor tables beneath the Fortezza a pleasant place to dine. Open daily 8am-midnight.

Mona Liza, 36 K. Paleologou St. (tel. 23 082), is the place to find delicious pastries. The *baklava* (300dr) is dense with nuts. Fresh homemade sheep's milk ice cream in 4 flavors (250dr per scoop). Open daily 8:30am-3pm and 5:30-11pm.

The bar scene at Rethymnon centers around Petichaki St. and Nearchou St. near the west end of the harbor. The happening **Rockafé Bar,** on Petichaki St., and the **Fortezza Disco Bar,** 14 Nearchou St. (tel. 21 493), book-end several Greek *bouzouki* places. Both have pricey beers (1000dr). On the other side of the beach, the outdoor **Delphini Disco** sports a pool (beer 600dr).

SIGHTS

Rethymnon has been occupied nearly continuously since the late Minoan period. At its apex in the 4th century BCE, it was overrun by Mycenaeans. During the Fourth Crusade, the Franks sold the island to the Venetians for 520 pounds of silver. The Venetians fortified Rethymnon, which was crucial to their chain of trading outposts. The Ottomans took the city in 1646, enlarging it and incorporating Turkish designs into the buildings. For an enlightening background, *Rethymnon: A Guide to the Town,* by A. Malagari and H. Stratidakis is sold for 800dr.

Rethymnon's **Archaeological Museum** (tel. 54 668) is in a former Turkish prison, adjacent to the fortress. Once inside, you'll feel like you've wandered into the storeroom of an absent-minded archaeologist—headless statues lean on walls behind rows of figurines, and Minoan sarcophagi lie next to Roman coins (open Tues.-Sun. 8:30am-3pm; admission 500dr, students 300dr). The **Historical and Folkore Museum,** 28-30 Vernerdov St. (tel. 23 398), primarily showcases traditional national and regional arts and a collection of traditional farming tools (open Mon.-Sat. 9am-1pm and 6-8pm; admission 400dr, students 300dr).

New to Rethymnon is the **L. Kanakakis Center of Contemporary Art,** 2 Himaras St., at the corner of Salaminus St. Works by Rethymnon's Kanakakis are part of a larger collection of modern Greek paintings. The center also hosts temporary exhibitions (open Tues.-Sat. 10am-2pm and 6-9pm, Sun. 10am-3pm; admission 300dr).

At some point during your visit you should make a pilgrimage to the **Venetian Fortezza** (tel. 28 101), dating from around 1580. The walls of the citadel are in excellent condition, but most of the buildings inside the fortress were destroyed by Turks in the 17th century, and even more bit the dust three centuries later during WWII (open daily 8am-8pm; admission 500dr). The city's **Renaissance Festival,** featuring theater, concerts, and exhibitions, is held in the fortress in July and August.

Rethymnon's Turkish legacy is evident in the city's structures—the **Neratzes Minaret,** on Antistassios St.; the **Nerdjes Mosque,** a block farther, which was formerly a Franciscan church; the **Kara Pasha Mosque,** on Arkadiou St., near Iroon Sq.;

and the **Valides Minaret,** which presides over **Porta Megali** gate at the beginning of Antistassios St. in 3 Martiou Sq. Cretans who sought refuge in the Early Byzantine **Arkadi monastery** in 1866, 23km from Rethymnon, blew themselves up rather than surrender to the Turks. The monastery also has a **museum** (admission 200dr).

Rethymnon's annual **Wine Festival,** during the first week in August, is a crowded all-you-can-drink fest which costs only 700dr and begins at 8:30pm. (Souvenir glasses are expensive—bringing a carafe will be cheaper.) A local dance troupe performs early in the evening; later on, it's a free-for-all. Every odd year, an exhibition of Cretan handicrafts coincides with the wine festival. The work is worth a look, but you can usually find better prices at local artisans' shops in each major town. Rethymnon's own craft shops cluster around Arkadiou, Antistassios, and Gerakari St. The **Herb Shop,** 58 Souliou St. (tel. 29 664), stocks folk remedies and herbs exclusive to Crete for emergency aromatherapy. For 50 years, this shop has sold dried Cretan herbs for cooking and healing. *Senes* helps heal stomach ailments (300dr for a small bag), and oregano tastes good on salad (500dr per bag; open Mon.-Sat. 10am-2pm and 6-11pm, Sun. 6-11pm).

▓ Chania XANIA

Chania survived an attack from Germany's best paratroopers during WWII and, earlier, endured occupation by the Minoans, Turks, Venetians, and Egyptians. Nonetheless, Chania (pop. 70,000) today is a vibrant town of skinny, four-story Venetian structures. Chania was the capital of Crete until 1971, when the title was passed to Iraklion. With its thriving nightlife and chaotic history, however, Chania is still regarded by many islanders as the spiritual capital of the island. Visitors meander through the winding streets (an architectural pastiche of styles), absorb the folk music from streetside cafés, or while the day away gazing at the old Venetian Harbor. No matter how tourist-oriented the waterfront cafés become, they don't mar the beauty of the harbor, silhouetted at sunset by Turkish domes.

ORIENTATION AND PRACTICAL INFORMATION

From the bus station, walk right on Kidonias St. for two blocks and turn left onto Platia 1866; going north, the road becomes Halidon St. and leads to the old **harbor,** the setting for much of Chania's nightlife. To lighten the load while looking for a room, you may leave your bags at the bus station (storage open 6am-8pm; 100dr per bag). Ferries dock in the nearby port, **Souda.** A bus from Souda drops you off at Chania's Municipal Market (10min., 240dr). Facing the market, turn left and walk two blocks on Gianari St., then right onto Halidon. Even with maps from the tourist office, finding your way around is no cinch. Luckily, Chania isn't too large so you can't stay lost for long. Chania's business district is mostly contained within the area across from the market, around the intersection of **Gianari Street** and **Tzanakaki Street.**

Tourist Office: (tel./fax 92 624), 1st floor of the Megaro Pantheon, Platia 1866, behind the Greek Agricultural Bank. Information on flights, ferries, buses, hotels, and package tours; free maps. Open Mon.-Fri. 7:30am-2:30pm, Sat-Sun. 8am-3pm.
Tourist Police: 60 Karaiskaki St. (tel. 73 333), by the central bus station. In an **emergency,** call 100. Open daily 7:30am-8pm. **Port Police:** (tel. 98 888).
OTE: 5 Tzanakaki St. Exceptionally efficient. Open in summer daily 6am-midnight; in off season daily 7am-11pm. Telex and telegram Mon.-Fri. only.
Banks: Credit Bank, 106 Halidon St., near Platia 1866. Open Mon.-Thurs. 8am-2pm, Fri. 8am-1:30pm for **currency exchange.** The **National Bank** is on the corner of Nikiforou and Foka St. Open Mon.-Thurs. 8am-2pm, Fri. 8am-1:30pm.
Flights: Olympic Airways, 88 Tzanakaki St. (tel. 57 701 or 57 213), near the public garden. Buses for the airport leave from the main office on Tzanakaki 1½hr. before each flight. Ticket issuance Mon.-Fri. 8am-3:15pm. Phone reservations Mon.-Fri. 7am-10pm, Sat. 8am-3pm. Flights to Athens (3 per week, 18,600dr).

Buses: Central bus station (tel. 93 052, -306), on the corner of Kidonias and Kelaidi St. Bus schedules change often; go to the tourist office for an updated schedule. To Paleochora (5 per day, 1250dr); Chora Sfakion (3 per day, 1200dr); Kastelli (14 per day, 760dr); Samaria (4 per day, 1000dr there, 1200dr return); and Iraklion (24 per day, every 30min., 2400dr).

Ferries: ANEK Office (tel. 53 636), in Venizelou Sq., near National Bank. *Kriti* and *Aptera* go to Peiraias (8pm, 11hr., tourist-class 8800dr, deck-class 5100dr).

Moped Rental: Cluster on Halidon St. Automatic mopeds at 4500dr per day, 90cc models at 5000dr, and 250cc at 7000dr. **Olympic Rent-a-Car,** 74 Halidon St. (tel. 94 915; fax 88 025), rents **cars.** Fiat Panda 8000dr per day. 25% discount for *Let's Go* users. Open daily 8am-10pm.

Laundromat: (tel. 52 494), next to Hotel Fidias. Wash 800dr, dry 700dr. Soap free. Open daily 7am-11pm.

Hospital: (tel. 27 000), corner of Dragoumi and Kapodistriou St., 5 blocks east of the harbor center. Out-patient clinic open Mon.-Sat. 12:30-2pm and 6-9pm, Sun. 8am-9pm. For **emergencies,** call 22 222. Available 24hr.

Post Office: 3 Tzanakaki St. Open Mon.-Fri. 7:30am-8pm. **Postal Code:** 73100. **Telephone Code:** 0821.

ACCOMMODATIONS

In the old town, most of the inexpensive pensions overlook the harbor, a convenient but noisy area. Small hotels sprout from the beaches on the west coast, but expect to lay out the cash for the brown sand of **Nea Kydonia** and **Agia Marina. Association of Rooms to Let: Unikreta Travel Agency,** 20 Dor. Episkopou (tel. 43 601; fax 46 277), a block left of harbor center, can help find rooms (open Mon.-Fri. 9am-2pm). Some people freelance camp on the east side. Be wary of the eclectic bunch of locals at the bus station who illegally try to entice newcomers to stay in their private rooms. It is dangerous, and they are often dishonest about prices and intentions. A much better choice is the **Association of Rooms to Let.** If you provide them with specifics, they'll give you a list of addresses and phone numbers.

Meltemi Pension, 2 Agelou St. (tel. 92 802), at end of west side of harbor, next to the Naval Museum. Rooms have elegantly worn, wooden floors painted deep maroon, marble-topped desks, and high ceilings. Some with beautiful views of the harbor. The Meltemi Café downstairs serves delicious *frappés* (500dr), breakfast, and drinks. Doubles 4000-7000dr. Triples 8000dr with private shower.

Hotel Fidias, 6 Sarpaki St. (tel. 52 494). From Halidon St., turn right at the cathedral on Athinagora St., which becomes Sarpaki St. With poster-coated walls and linoleum floors, the lodgings look like clean dorm rooms. Run by a Greek actor-turned-hotel-owner. Hot showers, TV, international calls. Reception open daily 7am-11pm. Singles 3000-3500dr. Doubles 3800-4000dr. Dorm triples 5000dr.

Ifigenia Rooms (tel. 99 184; mobil phone (094) 501 319). Several buildings all in the old town close to the harbor, with a variety of rooms available. Most rooms have private bath, fridges, and some studios have kitchenettes. Prices for doubles range from 5000-9000dr, depending on the season and the size of the room. Head to Ifigenia III at 15 Theotokopolou St. at the Café Orio to find the manager. To get there, walk up Angelou St. from the Naval Museum, take a left on Theotokopolou St., and the Café and Pension is on the right.

FOOD AND ENTERTAINMENT

The **public market,** at the south end of the old town at the intersection of Tzanakaki St. and Hatzi Michali Gianari St., is in an old beautiful building built for the market in about 1912. Produce, cheese, herb, and meat shops mix with leather shops and tiny seafood restaurants to make for a bustling market scene (open Mon-Sat. 8am-2pm, Tues. and Fri. 8am-2pm and 6-9pm). Tiny restaurants serve fresh fried seafoods and delicious stews from huge pots for pretty good prices.

Many cafés cater to a non-touristy crowd. Locals head to inconspicuous **Yordanni's,** 18 N. Plastira (tel. 44 710), the insider's place for *bougatsa,* a phyllo pie filled with white, salty Cretan cheese (350dr). Yordanni's is Yorgasmic. For an intimate dinner, try **Tamam,** Zabeliou 49 (tel. 96 080), which features super veal with mushrooms (900dr), as well as vegetarian alternatives (open daily 7-11pm or 1am). One block off the waterfront is **Sultana's Home Cuisine,** 2 Moshon (tel. 97 128), housed in a Venetian palace and former harem built in the 15th century (spaghetti with octopus 1700dr, *moussaka* 1100dr, baklava 600dr; open March-Nov. daily noon-1 or 2am). **Dinos** (tel. 41 865) is famed all over Crete for its outstanding seafood. To try a plateful of fresh local seafood, splurge on the mixed fish plate for two (6500dr). Garlic fans should request the special Greek sauce. Scenes from the film *Zorba the Greek* were filmed in the café next door (open daily noon-1 or 2am).

Late at night, Chania's normally sluggish bloodstream heats up considerably. The **Plaza Disco** (52 254), right on the harbor, is definitely the place to be. The pricey 1500dr cover includes your first drink. After that, beers are 1000dr (shots 500dr; open nightly 11pm-4 or 6am). Tiny **Fagotto Bar,** 16 Agelou (tel. 71 877), plays hot jazz and rhythm and blues from their huge collection (cocktails 1200dr; open daily 10pm-3am). The **Praxis Café,** 3 Skufon St. (off Zambeliou on the west side of the harbor), is a grotto-like bar with tables outside. Around 1am, the crowds move to the discoes (open daily 10pm-2 or 3am). Pedestrians groove at the club **Street** (tel. 74 960), next to the Amphora Restaurant on the harbor (shots 600dr, beer 700-800dr; café open daily 10am-10pm, bar open daily 10pm-dawn). **Kirki Club** (tel. 92 883), on the west waterfront, is a good place to drown your sorrows (no cover, beer 500-600dr; café open daily 9:30am-10pm; club 10pm-late).

SIGHTS

Kastelli Hill, the area north of Kanevaro St., is studded with reminders of Chania's past. Remnants of Ancient Kydonia's Bronze Age prosperity are evident at the **Late Minoan House** (circa 1450 BCE), on the corner of Kandanoleu and Kanevaro St. Unfortunately, the site is fenced off. In the Middle Ages, Venetian occupiers enriched the city's architecture, but much of their artistry was destroyed in WWII. Chania has many empty frames of Venetian houses open to the sky and intermingled with modern structures. With their melange of Turkish and Venetian buildings, the waterfront alleys reflect the city's varied history. Pass through several archways on Moshon St. to reach the **Venetian Chapel,** decorated with Latin inscriptions and Turkish graffiti. Young Greeks mellow out in the **Municipal Gardens,** once the property of a Turkish *muezzin* (prayer caller). The leafy grounds also harbor a small zoo. **Sfakianaki,** a 19th-century neighborhood with tree lined streets, is beyond the gardens to the east, as is the **Historical Museum and Archives,** 20 Sfakianaki St. (tel. 52 606), which contains Cretan weaponry, photos of 19th century generals, clothing, and a tattered flag of Cretan independence (open Mon.-Fri. 8am-1:30pm).

The **Venetian Inner Harbor** is a thriving social scene and an architectural relic that has retained its original breakwater and Venetian arsenal. The Venetian **lighthouse** was restored by the Egyptians during their occupation of Crete in the late 1830s (enter at the east end of the harbor). On the opposite side of the main harbor, the **Naval Museum** (tel. 91 875) exhibits nautical pictures and pieces of boats (open in summer daily 10am-4pm; in winter 10am-2pm; admission 400dr, students 250dr). The **Archaeological Museum** (tel. 80 334), on Halidon St. opposite the cathedral, displays Cretan artifacts. Once a Venetian monastery, it also served as the mosque of Yusuf Pasha (open Mon. 12:30-7pm, Tues.-Fri. 8am-7pm, Sat.-Sun. 8:30am-3pm; admission 500dr, students 300dr, free for EU members and visitors over 65).

■ Near Chania: Samaria Gorge

The most popular excursion from Chania is the five-hour hike down the formidable 16km Samaria Gorge, Europe's longest. Worn away by millions of years of river runoff, the White Mountains' pass retains its allure despite being mobbed by visitors and spotted with litter. Bird watchers can glimpse the rare bearded vulture; horticulturists can admire the wildflowers and shrubs which peek out from sheer rock walls; and goat lovers can spot the nimble *agrimi,* a wild Cretan species in one of its few remaining natural habitats. The Samaria Gorge is an exceedingly beautiful hike. Please follow Chania Forest Protection Service's rules to keep it that way.

The 44km, one-and-a-half-hour bus ride from Chania to **Xyloskalo,** at the start of the trail, offers spectacular scenery. Passing between cliff walls up to 300m high, the path, only 3m wide at some points, winds down along a riverbed that runs nearly dry in the summer. Parts of the hike are shaded by clumps of pine trees, goats, and the towering walls of the gorge itself. The hike ends in Agia Roumeli on the south coast. From there a boat sails to Loutro and Chora Sfakion, where buses run back to Chania. Experienced hikers and masochists can hike from Agia Roumeli to Chora Sfakion (10hr.) along one of the more outstanding coastlines in the country; see the Southwest Coast (p. 216). The bus to Chania from Chora Sfakion passes through the village of **Vrises,** where there are doubles to let (4000dr). The downhill hike favored by most people (from Xyloskalo in the Omalos Plain to Agia Roumeli) takes four to six hours. A less traveled path ascends Mt. Gingilos to the west.

Whichever route you choose, bring plenty of water and trail snacks, and wear good walking shoes. The Gorge is dry and dusty in summer, and the stones on the path become slippery. Furthermore, the altitude often makes the top of the gorge cold and rainy. If you get tired on the hike, don't worry; you can always take the donkey taxis which patrol the trail. If all you want to see is the dramatic tail of the gorge, Agia Roumeli is a great place to start the journey. The path to the trail begins just behind Rooms Livikon. From the quay, walk straight to the rear of the village. Known as "Samaria the Lazy Way," the two-hour climb to the north takes you to the gorge's dramatic and narrow pass, the "Iron Gates." The gorge is open May 1 to October 15; during the winter and spring, the river goes back to work cutting its trail through the rock. Flash floods in the winter have claimed many lives. During the open months, passage is officially allowed through the gorge between 6am and 4pm (admission 1200dr). For gorge information, call the **Chania Forest Service** (tel. 92 287) or pick up information at the tourist office.

Pricey accommodations for the night before the hike are available at the **Tourist Pavilion** (tel. 63 269) in Xyloskalo. Reservations can be placed with the Chania tourist office. Five kilometers north of Xyloskalo, **Omalos** has food at **Drakoulaki's Restaurant** (tel. (0821) 67 269) with rooms to let. (Doubles 5000dr. Triples 7000dr.) On the plain of Omalos, take a left onto a dirt road for the one-and-a-half-hour trek to the Spartan **Kallergis refuge huts.** From there, hikers can make a day's climb to the summit of **Pakhnes** or **Mount Ida** (2456m), where Zeus was raised as a child.

Buses for Omalos and Xyloskalo leave Chania four times per day. When you ask to buy a ticket to Omalos, the ticket office at the bus station will sell you a roundtrip ticket from Chania to Omalos and from Chora Sfakion to Chania (1200dr); if you don't want the return ticket, you can ask for a one-way ticket (1000dr one way to Omalos). Since Agia Roumeli is connected by boat to Chora Sfakion, you can make the complete roundtrip from Chania in one day, leaving on either of the morning buses. Taking the earliest bus will ensure cooler weather and less company for the hike. An alternative is to plan a leisurely hike and spend the night in a coastal town.

A hot and dusty hike beyond the official exit from the gorge leads to **Agia Roumeli,** a seedy oasis for tired and thirsty hikers. Those 3km aren't entirely terrible, though—it's a great photo-op. Finally, you'll arrive in Agia Roumeli proper, a town with little to show but its beach. The black pebbles are unbearably hot, but the water is refreshing. The town itself exists mainly to sell food, souvenirs, and lodgings for tired, susceptible hikers. If you do stay, you can sleep at **Hotel Livikon** (tel. 91 363), on the inland end of town. (Doubles 4500dr. Triples 5500dr.)

■ Paleochora ΠΑΛΕΟΧΩΡΑ

Once a refuge for the embattled rear guard of the 1960s counterculture, Paleochora is the stop for diehard devotees. Just 77km from Chania, Paleochora is a pleasant retreat, with a wide, sandy beach with a shady grove and a stunning backdrop of

Cretan mountains, one main street with necessities and *tavernas,* and a harbor lined with reasonably priced pensions.

Orientation and Practical Information   Paleochora is on a small peninsula. Running north-south through the town center is **Venizelou Street,** the main thoroughfare. It crosses **Kentekaki Street,** which leads west to the beach and east to the harbor. **Buses** to Chania (5 per day, 2hr., 1250dr) stop at this intersection.

The **tourist office** (tel. 41 507) is on Venizelou St. (open Wed.-Mon. 10am-1pm and 6-9pm), as is a **bank** (open Mon.-Thurs. 8am-2pm, Fri. 8am-1:30pm) and the **OTE** (open Mon.-Sat. 7:30am-11pm, Sun. 9am-2pm and 6-11pm). The **police station** (tel. 41 111) is on Kentekaki, near the quay; **port police** can be reached at 41 214. **Econoline Travel** (tel. 41 529; fax 41 745) is helpful for ferry information, tickets, car rental (6000dr per day for a Fiat Panda), motorbike rental (2000-8000dr per day depending on type), and bicycle rental (1000dr per day), as well as basic information about the region. From Paleochora, one to two **ferries** per day leave for Sougia (30min., 850dr); Ag. Roumeli (1hr., 1900dr); Ch. Sfakion (3hr., 3200dr); and Loutro (2¾hr., 2600dr). One boat a day departs Paleochora at 10am and leaves from Elafonisi at 4pm (1hr., one way 1200dr). A post boat goes to **Gavdos** every Tuesday and Friday (4hr., 2800dr), and a regular ferry goes to Gavdos every Thursday, Saturday, and Sunday (2½hr., 2800dr). A bus departs for Samaria daily at 6am, and returns to Paleochora by boat from Agia Roumeli at 4pm (3150dr roundtrip). Entrance to Samaria costs 1200dr. A boat goes to Anidri Beach Monday and Wednesday at 10:30am (1000dr). For a taxi, call **Paleochora Taxi Office** (tel. 41 128, -061). The **medical center** sits down the road from Interkreta Travel (from the office, make a right onto the cross street). Look for the sign with the blue cross (open Mon.-Fri. mornings until 2pm). The **pharmacy** (tel. 41 498) is on Venizelou St. (open Mon.-Sat. 9am-1:30pm and 6-10pm). The **post office** is on the beach next to the Galaxy Café (open Mon.-Fri. 7:30am-2pm). **Postal Code: 73001. Telephone Code:** 0823.

Accommodations   A walk along the road closest to the harbor will bring you to the small hotels. One you can trust at the center of the harbor (it's the tallest white building marked "Rooms for Rent") is run by **Nikos Bubalis** (tel. 41 112). A kindly older couple has clean doubles and triples off a staircased area. All rooms have access to the balconies which look out on the picturesque harbor and gorgeous mountains that descend to the sea. (Doubles 4000-6000dr. Triples 7000dr.) The **Café Alaloom,** adjacent to the OTE, books rooms at **Savas Rooms** (tel. 41 075) for reasonable prices. (Doubles 5000dr.) Another good option, **Rooms Oriental Bay** (tel. 41 322) is right on Rocky Beach as you enter town. (Doubles 5000dr. Triples 8000dr.) **Christos Restaurant** (tel. 41 359), along the harbor, has clean rooms with private baths. (Doubles 5000dr. Triples 6000dr.) **Camping Paleochora** (tel. 41 120) rests 1500m east of town. To reach the campground, walk north on Venizelou (away from the harbor), turn right opposite the gas station, and take the second left on the last paved road before the beach—1km to the site. It's also convenient to Paleochora Club—the town's popular open disco that hosts some pretty wild parties. (Open March-Oct. 800dr per person. 600dr per tent. Moped rental 200.)

Food and Entertainment   The waterfront sports a row of restaurants serving traditional Greek food from traditional tourist menus at traditional mid-range prices (*tzatziki* 400-600dr, *moussaka* 850-1000dr, *baklava* 500-700dr). There are several markets in the center of the town and on Venizelou St. More *tavernas* line the road and have similar menus. Vegetarians and carnivores alike should appreciate the fresh homemade Greek, Asian, and European vegetarian dishes prepared by the family at the **Third Eye Vegetarian Restaurant** (tel. 41 234). Everything is delicious, but you might hope to catch the vegetarian paella (700dr) or the vegetable curry (850dr). Nothing on the menu costs more than 850dr, unless, of course, you order something from the grill—yes, they've kept a grill for meat lovers who just can't live without their *souvlaki* (open April-Oct. daily 8am-3pm and 5pm-midnight).

For inexpensive Greek baked goods, **George Vakakis'** bakery (tel. 41 069), close to the ferry dock (follow the signs), sells generously sized cheese, spinach, or sausage pies (200dr), chocolate croissants (150dr), and traditional biscuits (1000dr per kg). Cretan *kalitsinia* are fresh and tasty (1700dr per kg). They also bake fresh Cretan sweet bread served on special occasions like weddings and christenings (600dr per kg; open in summer daily 7:30am-3pm and 4-11pm; in winter 8am-2:30pm and 4:30-10pm). **Paleochora Club,** near Camping Paleochora, is the town's open-air disco (beer 600-700dr; open daily noon-4am).

AROUND THE AREA

Six kilometers above Paleochora lies the peaceful town of **Azogizes,** which affords a lovely view of the promontory and the sea. Here you'll find the 13th-century caves of the 99 Holy Fathers and a museum featuring relics of the Turkish occupation dating from 1770. Farther inland, the frescoed churches of Kakodiki date back to the 14th century. These mountain villages can be reached by taking the bus toward Chania. Boats run five times per week (one takes 2½hr., the other 4hr.; 2800dr) to the nearly deserted island of **Gavdos,** the southernmost point of Europe.

The satisfying journey to miraculous **Elafonissi,** a small uninhabited island at the southwest corner of Crete, must be made on foot. Like nowhere else on earth, this place will leave you speechless and astounded. Boats can't make the crossing, but at low tide the ocean is so shallow that you can wade out to the island. A recent influx of tourists has left this retreat strewn with litter, but the authorities are increasing their efforts to keep it clean. There are several small cantinas serving snacks and drinks, but you may want to pack a picnic to avoid high prices. The residents of nearby **Moni Chrisoskalitissis** can provide water and lodgings. **Buses** run daily from Kastelli as far as Chrisoskalitissis (9:30am and 2:30pm, 900dr). From there, a 5km hike leads to a pinkish-white beach. You can also hook up with excursions leaving from Paleochora or Chania. Boats go from Paleochora to the beach across from Elaforisi daily (1200dr one way, 1hr.). The boat ride along the coast is astounding, and the cliffs diving into the deep sapphire blue sea at the extreme southwestern tip of Crete are inspiring. Even closer to Paleochora is beautiful **Anidri Beach.** Just a 30-minute walk west out of Paleochora brings you to one of the lovelier beaches in Crete (according to some locals). Alternately, the boat from Paleochora also goes to the beach (Mon. and Wed. at 10:30am, 1000dr).

■ Southwest Coast

Between Agia Roumeli and Chora Sfakion, Loutro reclines in a tiny cove which yawns into the Libyan Sea. Loutro holds the distinction of being the only town in Crete where topless sunbathing is prohibited. Surrounded by the ocean on one side and austere mountains on the other, the prawn-sized village can be reached only by boat. Because of the logistical difficulties, Loutro is a quiet respite from the south coast and worth seeing for its sheer seclusion. The beach here is rocky, but not entirely uncomfortable. **Ferry** service connects Loutro with Chora Sfakion (4 per day, 600dr) and Ag. Roumeli (3 per day, 700dr).

There are rooms to rent along the cove and, since it takes roughly four minutes to see all of Loutro, it's easy to check them out. Singles are rare but you may be able to bargain with a proprietor. On the west end of the cove, **Vangeli and Giorgo's** rents doubles. Next door is Loutro's nameless **Hotel,** which also has rooms. East of the kiosk, **Manousos** has similar offerings.

CHORA SFAKION

The scenic town of Chora Sfakion lacks the intimacy of Loutro or Paleochora, but serves as the transportation hub of the south coast. The town's pebbly cove and fishing fleet look tempting from afar, but up close you see that the beach is littered with trash. Chora Sfakion's one strong point, but also its downfall, is that it has frequent bus connections. Since Chora Sfakion lacks the dusty heat that pervades Agia Roumeli, it's an adequate resting spot after the Samaria Gorge hike. The **post office** is next to Sfakia Tours on the waterfront (open Mon.-Sat. 7:30am-2pm). The **OTE** is on the road leading away from town, near where buses leave (open Mon.-Fri. 7:30am-3:15pm). The **supermarket** is also on the street behind the harbor—a good place to stock up if you plan a tour of more remote beaches. The **police station** (tel. (0825) 91 205) and **port police** (tel. (0825) 91 292) are on the corner of the waterfront near the **bus station**, which is usually staffed the hour before a bus departure (police station open 24hr.). A travel office, **Sfakia Tours** (tel./fax (0825) 91 130), is also located here (mopeds 4500dr per day; open daily 8am-10pm).

Buses from Chora Sfakion go to Plakias (2 per day, 1¼hr., 800dr) and then to Rethymnon (4 per day, 1½hr., 1200dr) to meet the ferry. At the same time, a bus leaves for Agia Galini (2 per day, 2hr., 1850dr) or Anapolis (4 per day, 30min., 250dr). To get to Iraklion from Chora Sfakion, change buses at Rethymnon. Four buses per day go to Chania (2hr., 1200dr), but be sure to ask the exact time of departure at the station. If your ferry is late, don't worry—the buses wait for the boats to arrive. **Boats** from Chora Sfakion travel to Ag. Roumeli (5 per day, 1¼hr.). Most of these routes stop in Loutro. These run only from April to October; in winter, travelers go to Loutro by foot or fishing boat. It's a good idea to check boat schedules with the **ticket office** (tel. (0825) 91 221). Boats run from Chora Sfakion to Gavdos every Saturday through Sunday (at 9am, returning 5pm). **Caïques** to Sweetwater Beach run twice daily.

There are plenty of inexpensive accommodations here. The cool, grotto-like **Hotel Xenia** (tel. (0825) 91 202) has spacious, immaculate rooms. (Singles 5000dr. Doubles 6000-8000dr. Triples 10,000dr.) **Lefka Ori** (tel. (0825) 91 209), on the waterfront, rents singles for 5000dr and doubles with small, dark bathrooms for 6000-10,000dr. **Rooms Samaria** (tel. (0825) 91 261), on the east end of the back street, is large and cool, with wrought-iron balconies, but they can get buggy. (Open March-Nov. Doubles with terrace and bath 6000dr. Triples 8000dr.)

EASTERN CRETE

The road east from Malia and Hersonissos leads to less frequented, more rewarding territories. The endlessly winding main highway joining Malia and Hersonissos to Agios Nikolaos, Ierapetra, and Sitia is spectacular: it grips the side of the mountains, ascending and descending deep valleys. Its destinations are equally worthwhile: white villages with small green gardens, olive plains, and an astonishingly blue sea. The area is well served by buses, making it cheap to exploration.

■ Hersonissos ΧΕΡΣΟΝΗΣΟΣ

This port town, 26km east of Iraklion, is free of ancient sites, monasteries, or Cretan village culture. More than 40 bars, discoes, and nightclubs cluster in a 500m radius, and the beach is never far away. If you're bored with Iraklion's nightlife, just hop on the bus; you probably don't have to know the Greek words for vodka and orange juice here—it's about as Greek as Las Vegas.

ORIENTATION AND PRACTICAL INFORMATION

There is one main road in Hersonissos, **Eleftheriou Venizelou,** with offices, markets, and discoes. Perpendicular streets lead to the beach and other parts of town.

Tourist Police: 8 Minoas St. (tel. 21 000), toward the beach in the police station. Fairly unhelpful office provides information on Hersonissos. Offers **currency exchange.** Open daily 7am-11pm.

EASTERN CRETE

Tourist Agencies: Zakros Tours, 46 El. Venizelou (tel./fax 24 715). Open daily 8am-10pm. **Mareland Travel** has three branches, one conveniently at 12 Minoas St. (tel. 24 424), across from the police station. Both rent cars, sell boat tickets, exchange currency, and have maps. Open daily 8am-1am.

Banks: Several on El. Venizelou that exchange currency. **National Bank** is on the east end of the road. Open Mon.-Thurs. 8:30am-2pm, Fri. 8am-1:30pm.

OTE: Behind the town hall on Eleftherias St., down El. Venizelou from the post office. Open Mon.-Sat. 7:30am-10pm, Sun. 9am-2pm and 5-10pm.

Buses: Several bus stops in Hersonissos; there's no central bus station. Buses run east and west every 30min. Service to Iraklion (45min., 500dr), and from Iraklion via Hersonissos to Malia (20min., 200dr); Agios Nikolaos (45min., 850dr); Sitia (2½hr., 2150dr); and Ierapetra (2hr., 1500dr).

Taxi: Station (tel. 23 723, -722 -193) on the west end of El. Venizelou near the Hard Rock Café. Open 24hr.

Car and Motorbike Rental: Several agencies on El. Venizelou.**Odyssey,** 51 El. Venizelou (tel.24649), rents bicycles (100-1500 per day) and motorbikes (400-6000 per day). Open daily 9am-10pm

Laundromat: Wash Saloon Ilios, 3 Margaraki St. (tel.22 749), just up the street from Selena Pension and restaurant. Does your laundry in 3hr. 1500dr per 6 kg load includes soap price. Open daily 9am-10pm.

Public Toilets: Across from Zakros tour office on El. Venizelou St. Free.

Pharmacies: Several on El. Venizelou. Get off the bus at the first stop in Hersonissos from Iraklion, cross the street, and after 2 or 3 blocks (or 30m), **Lambraki's Pharmacy** (tel. 22 473) will be on your left. Open Mon.-Fri. 9am-11pm. Consult the signs on the doors of any to find one open after hours and on Sunday.

Medical Services: Dr. Babis Kokodrulis (tel. 22 063; fax 21 987) has a medical office on El. Venizelou St., opposite the bus stop from Iraklion, before the pharmacy. Open daily 9am-10pm, but call ahead, he also works at the medical center, and could be there. For emergencies, call him at home (22 836) or on his mobile phone ((094) 51 71 70). **Hersonissos Health Center,** 19 El. Venizelou (tel. 25 141), near the Hard Rock Café. Open 24hr.

Post Office: 122 El. Venizelou. Follow the signs. Open Mon.-Fri. 8am-2pm. **Postal Code:** 70014.

Telephone Code: 0897.

ACCOMMODATIONS

Hersonissos' digs can be pricey and hard to come by. Tour companies book a majority of the rooms for the entire season. Before arriving, consult Iraklion's **"Rooms to Let Association"** (see Iraklion, p. 200).

Youth Hostel, Plaka-Drapanos (tel. 23 282). Cheap beds and pleasant owners. No curfew. Roughly 1.4km from town toward Malia—get directions or ask the bus driver to let you off there. 1500dr per person.

Selena Pension, 13 Marogaki St. (tel. 22 412), just off Main St., toward the waterfront. All immaculate rooms have private bath. Doubles 6000-7000dr.

Camping Hersonissos, Anisara (tel. 22 902). Take a bus or walk 3km toward Iraklion—it's on the right. Restaurant, minimarket, bar, and hot water. 950dr per person. 640dr per tent.

Camping Caravan, Limenas (tel. 22 025). Walk or take bus 2km east toward Agios Nikolaos until Nora Hotel, then another 300m. English spoken. Open March-Oct. 1100dr per person. 800dr per tent.

FOOD AND ENTERTAINMENT

The Hersonissos waterfront sports the usual assortment of restaurants serving "traditional Greek food." For less commotion try **Selena Restaurant** (tel. 22 412), beneath Selena Pension. A family-run restaurant, Selena serves house wine from their own vineyard and fresh rabbit (1500dr) from their farm (not on the menu—ask for it grilled or stewed in wine; open daily 8am-11:30pm; greek salad 450dr, *tzatziki* 400dr). **Taverna Kavouri** (tel. 21 161) is a thoroughly enjoyable escape from the commercialized waterfront (walk toward Iraklion, turn right onto Irinis Kai Filias St. near the Hard Rock Café, and walk around the bend). Fifteen tables rest under grapevines and among hanging fishing equipment from more physically industrious days. No menu—just go into kitchen and point at whatever looks appealing (such as the chicken for 1500dr). Opens daily at 6pm.

Nightlife in Heronissos is "jammin'" as Greeks like to say. The bars and discoes that line Main St. and the Paraliakos offer every kind of atmosphere, music, and drink imaginable. Try the **Black Cactus Bar,** 72 E. Venizelou (tel. 23 590), on Main St. (open daily 9am-6am). As the night progresses, hit the bars on Paraliakos and on the waterfront (beer 300dr). The dance floors of **Disco 99** (open daily 9pm-4:30am) or **La Luna** (tel. 22 014) are large and crowded by English tourists (La Luna open daily 10:30pm-5am). The hottest club in town is the **Camelot Dancing Club** (tel. 22734), where both locals and tourists crowd in to dance to international rave and house (open daily 10pm-5:30am). **Aria,** across from the Hard Rock Café, is the largest club in Crete. The **Cine Creta Maris** is an outdoor summer cinema showing English-language (usually American) films nightly at 9:45pm.

The open-air museum **Lychnostatis** (tel. 23 660), located roughly 1km toward Agios Nikolaos, exhibits Cretan houses and offers windmill, ceramic, and weaving workshops as well as the opportunity to tread grapes or bake pumpkin pie (open Tues.-Sun. 9:30am-2pm for visit and 3 daily guided tours at 10:30, 11:30am, and 12:30pm for 2250dr; admission 1000dr, 500dr for kids under 12).

▓ Malia ΜΑΛΙΑ

Once hospitable, Malia has been increasingly encroached upon by self-aggrandizing hotels whose neon signs welcome guests in five tongues. The number of advertisements in languages other than Greek is matched only by the number of sandwich boards displaying kitschy photographs of food. Nonetheless, the palatial Minoan site at Malia merits a visit. Malia's best as a daytrip or, if you must stay, the old village is peacefully away from the bustling waterfront. It's worth searching out the few remaining quiet rooms in this mostly unremarkable beach resort.

Orientation and Practical Information   The main road from Iraklion (Eleftheriou Venizelou) should satisfy most practical needs, while the path down to the beach, with the discoes and watering holes, panders to the primal. The **post office** is off the main street toward Iraklion (look for the sign), behind the church (open Mon.-Fri. 7:30am-2pm). The **National Bank** is just off the main road. Bear left at the first street past the road to the beach (open Mon.-Thurs. 8am-2pm, Fri. 8am-1:30pm). The **OTE** is in the old village—follow signs from 25th Martiou, at the Bimbo Café (open Mon.-Fri. 7:30am-3pm). **Buses** connect Malia with Iraklion (1hr., 650dr) via Hersonissos (every 30min. until 11pm, 20min., 200dr), Agios Nikolaos (25 per day, 30min., 650dr), and Lassithi (8:45am, returning at 2pm, 1½hr., 1050dr). **Taxis** (tel. 31 777) idle at the intersection of the main road and the beach path (open 24hr.). There's a **laundromat** (tel. 31 709, -61) next to the Malia Holidays Hotel (open Mon.-Sat. 9am-8pm; wash and dry 2300dr). If you require medical assistance, Dr. Tsagari Georgia (tel. 31 529) has a **medical office** on the main road, next to the bus stop, above the market. In case of **emergency,** call her at home (tel. 31 880), or on her mobile phone (tel. (094) 52 51 42). The **pharmacy** (tel. 31 332) is next to her office (open Mon.-Sat. 9am-10pm, Sun. on rotation). **Postal Code:** 70002. **Telephone Code:** 0897.

Accommodations   Finding reasonably priced rooms in Malia is a challenge. Otherwise, look for the cluster of pensions and "Rooms to Let" in the old village. You can vaguely wander off into 25th Martiou St. and look around for a place that suits your fancy. Walking away from town, after the point where the bus drops you off on the main road, make a right onto 25th Martiou St. to reach **Pension Aspasia** (tel. 31 290), with large, clean, balconied rooms and common baths. (Doubles 4000-

5000dr. Triples 6000-7000dr.) Or, try **Pension Menios,** #2 25th Martiou St. (tel. 31 361), near the corner of the main road. It has new, immaculate rooms, wood furnishings, small balconies, and private baths. (Doubles 5000dr, 6000dr with bath. Triples 6000dr.) **Tsigari Manolis,** 11 Oplarhigon (tel. 31 880), offers clean double rooms, all with private bath (6000dr).

Food and Entertainment   Eating in Malia is cheap compared with the rest of Crete. Places on the waterfront road usually serve an English breakfast for 600dr. Many restaurants offer special combination dinners: salad, a main course (typically *moussaka,* lasagna, or chicken), and coffee or *metaxa* brandy, all for 1500dr. Head to the old village where you are more likely to find smaller *tavernas* and bakeries with more authentic food. On the way to the archaeological site, down the beach road, is **Kipouli** (tel. 32 847), a family-run *taverna* where you can get a Greek plate with a little of a lot of dishes (1290dr; open daily 9am-1am). Also on the main road, **banana vendors** have bunches of small, ripe bananas for sale (4000dr per kg).

There are two areas to head to for Malia's thriving nightlife. The waterfront road is home to many of Malia's (and Crete's) more popular dance clubs. For a lively club scene, check out **Highway** and **Nitro** across the street from each other on the beach road. House, international, rave, and dance music also blare at **Zoo, Zig Zag,** and **Corkers,** while **Terma's** is the place for authentic Greek tunes. Clubs open around 9pm, get really packed by 1am, and stay that way until 3:30 or 4am during the week. Most of them rock all night (until 6am) Thursday through Saturday. For a quieter, but still exciting night, head for the narrow, cobbled streets of the old town. Due to the presence of many Irish, English, and Scottish vacationers, there are many pubs at which you can imbibe. Ireland meets the Mediterranean at **The Temple Bar** (tel. 31 272), where huge tropical plants grow out of the bar tables, and Greeks and Celts lap up pints of Guinness on tap (1100dr per pint). Every hour is happy hour at this open-air pub, cocktails are always 700dr (next to St. Dimitrios Sq.; open daily 9am-3 or 4am). **Kipouli** (tel. 31 138), also in the old village, serves strong brews to English, Irish, Scots, and Greeks who do a mean karaoke. It's the only bar open 24 hours in Malia (though if the police come, they'll close). The **Stone House Pub** (tel. 32 268) serves good drinks in an open-air vine-covered bar area, as well as inside the cozy old stone house. Cool tones waft through the mellow crowd on nights when there is no Greek dancing. There's a pool table and dart board inside. Most drinks are around 1000dr (open April-Oct. daily 7pm-morning).

Sights   The **Minoan Palace** (tel. 31 597) at Malia, one of the three great cities of Minoan Crete, lacks the labyrinthine architecture and magnificent interior decoration of Knossos and Phaistos, but is still imposing. First built around 1900 BCE, the palace was destroyed in 1650 BCE, rebuilt on an even more impressive scale, but then destroyed again around 1450 BCE. Notice the **Hall of Columns** on the north side of the large central courtyard, incomprehensibly named for the six columns supporting the roof. The *loggia,* the raised chamber on the west side, was used for state ceremonies. West of the *loggia* are the palace's living quarters and archives. Northwest of the *loggia* and main site slumbers the **Hypostyle Crypt** that may have been a social center for Malia's intelligentsia. Follow the road to Agios Nikolaos 3km to the east and turn left toward the sea, or walk along the beach and then 1km through the fields (open Tues.-Sun. 8:30am-4pm; admission 800dr, Sun. free).

■ Agios Nikolaos ΑΓ. ΝΙΚΟΛΑΟΣ

Overgrown Agios Nikolaos is an appealing mix of humility and pretension. Good ol' St. Nick has moved closer to the naughty mood of a nouveau chic resort town, but still retains some nice facets of a low-key fishing village. The town's visitors include beach-obsessed patrons, one-stop holiday-makers, and hikers on their way to more obscure destinations. There are few bargains in Agios Nikolaos or in its satellite beach towns, but the town's intense nightlife, its diverse selection of intriguingly glamourous tourists, and its remnants of indigenous Cretan culture make Agios Nikolaos a lively concoction—a place that's fun without the sense of having been used up and spit out by tourists.

ORIENTATION AND PRACTICAL INFORMATION

It's easy to get around Ag. Nikolaos—the center of town is actually a small peninsula, with beaches on three sides and most services, hotels, restaurants, and discoes in the center. If you've just gotten off the bus, walk to the end of the block (with the terminal on your right), and take the first right. Follow **Venizelou Street** to the monument, where it leads into **Roussou Koundourou,** which heads downhill to the harbor. The tourist office is to the left, across the bridge. Don't confuse the nepotistic street names: R. Koundourou, I. Koundourou, and S. Koundourou St.

Tourist Office: 21A S. Koundourou St. (tel. 22 357), at the bridge between the lake and the port. Assists with accommodations, **exchanges currency,** provides bus and boat schedules, and distributes a free brochure with a town map and practical information. Open Apr.-Oct. daily 8:30am-9:45pm.

OTE: (tel. 82 880), on the corner of 25th Martiou and K. Sfakianaki St. Open Mon.-Sat. 7am-midnight, Sun. 7am-10pm.

Banks: National Bank (tel. 28 735), at the top of R. Koundourou St., near Venizelou Sq. Open for **currency exchange** Mon.-Thurs. 8am-2pm, Fri. 8am-1:30pm.

Flights: Olympic Airways (tel. 22 033), on Plastira St. overlooking the lake. Open Mon.-Fri. 9am-4pm. The closest airport is in Sitia.

Buses: (tel. 22 234), Atlandithos Sq., the opposite side of town from the harbor. To Iraklion via Malia (24 per day, 1½hr., 1200dr); Lassithi (2 per day, 2½hr., 950dr); Ierapetra (8 per day, 1hr., 650dr); Sitia (6 per day, 1½hr., 1200dr); and Kritsa (12 per day, 15min., 200dr). Buses to Elounda (15 per day, 20min., 200dr) and Plaka (6 per day, 40min., 300dr) leave from the stop opposite the tourist office.

Ferries: Globe Travel, 29 R. Koundourou St. (tel. 22 267). Air and ferry tickets for departures from Ag. Nikolaos and other Cretan ports. Open daily 9am-11pm. For ferries to Peiraias, the Greek islands, Cyprus, and Israel, cross the street to **Nostos Tours,** 30 Koundourou St. (tel. 22 819). Open daily 8am-2pm and 5-9pm.

Car and Motorbike Rental: Economy Car Hire, 15 S. Koundourou St. (tel. 28 988); also an office at 5 K. Sfakianaki St. Fiat Panda 24,000dr for 3 days. 50cc mopeds for 3000dr, 100cc for 4000dr. Open daily 8am-10pm.

International Bookstores: Anna Karteri, 5 R. Koundourou St. (tel. 22 272). Books in English, German, and French. Open Mon.-Fri. 8am-10pm, Sat. 8am-2pm.

Pharmacies: Dr. Theodore Furakis (tel. 24 011), at the top of R. Koundourou St. Open Mon.-Tues., Thurs.-Fri. 8am-2pm and 5:30-9pm, Wed. 8am-2pm.

Hospital: Paleologou St. (tel. 25 221), at the north end of town. From the lake, walk up Paleologou St., 1 block past the museum.

Police: (tel. 22 321) share the **Tourist Police** building (tel. 26 900). Follow 28th Octovriou St. past Venizelou Sq. until it becomes G. Kontoghianni St. After a good 10-min. walk, it will be on the right-hand side of the street.

Post Office: #9 28th Octovriou St. (tel. 22 062). Open Mon.-Fri. 7:30am-8pm, Sat. 7:30am-2pm. **Postal Code:** 72100.

Telephone Code: 0841.

ACCOMMODATIONS

As a result of Agios Nikolaos' popularity, many of the better hotels are booked months in advance by European tour groups. There are many pensions in town that offer clean, cheap rooms. They do fill up quickly, so it may be wise to call ahead and make a reservation. The tourist office has a bulletin board with many of Ag. Nikolaos' pensions and their prices. Prices listed are 20-40% less in off season.

Argiro Pension, 1 Solonos St. (tel. 28 707). From the tourist office, walk up 25th Martiou and turn left onto Manousogianaki. After 4 blocks, go right onto Solonos.

Unsullied, cool rooms in a huge, stately old house with a serene, jasmine-scented garden. Quiet, yet close to town. Doubles 4500-4700dr.

Pension Perla, 4 Salaminos St. (tel. 23 379). Big clean rooms, some with balconies and ocean views. Comfortable TV lounge. All but 2 rooms have private bath. Singles 3000-3500dr. Doubles 3500dr-4000dr. Triples 5000dr.

The Green House, 15 Modatsou St. (tel. 22 025). From the tourist office, turn left onto R. Koundourou, left again onto Iroon Polytechniou, and right onto Modatsou. Relax in the shady, tangled garden. If you're lucky, you'll get homemade Italian ice from the multilingual proprietors. Singles 3500dr. Doubles 5000dr.

Christodoulakis Pension, 7 Stratigou Koraka St. (tel. 22 525). Spotless rooms, kitchen facilities, and friendly proprietors. Singles 3000dr. Doubles 5000dr.

FOOD AND ENTERTAINMENT

Agios Nikolaos is overrun by overpriced, touristy, bland to mediocre to terrible restaurants claiming to serve "traditional Greek food." Many of these places are recognizable by their brightly colored menus with photographs of their food out front, along with pushy waiters who try to pull you in. Generally, the restaurants that are open all year (rather than just in the summer tourist season) cater to the native Greek clientele and serve more authentic food. Head to the central square at the top of R. Koundourou St. to **Hellinikon** (tel. 82 767), which serves traditional mountain village dishes healthfully prepared casserole-style. The menu changes daily, depending on what the owner decides to prepare (most entrees under 1500dr; open daily 10am-midnight or 2am). **Itanos** (tel. 25 340) serves large portions of fresh Greek salads (600dr), homemade barreled wine (800dr per 1L), vegetarian entrees (a plate of stuffed vegetables 700dr), and meat (entrees 600-1400dr; open daily 10am-11pm). If you don't mind relaxed service, go to **Stelio's,** at the bridge, for a dazzling harborside view and excellent *tzatziki* (500dr; open Apr.-Oct. daily 8am-midnight). Next door, at the **Actaion** (tel. 22 289), fish dishes start at 1200dr (open Apr.-Oct. daily 9am-midnight). The **New Kow Loon Chinese Restaurant,** 1 Pasifais St. (tel. 23 891), serves surprisingly decent Chinese cuisine. Pretty standard egg rolls (850dr), mixed veggies (1150dr), and lemon chicken (1500dr) are an interesting surprise in Greece (open daily noon-3pm and 7pm-1am). **Xenakis Family Bakery,** 9 M. Sfakianaki St. (tel. 23 051), several blocks from the port on the street leading to Kitroplatia Beach, sells delicious loaves of freshly baked bread (150-300dr). Try their *tyropitas* (200dr) or their equally delicious raisin rolls (100dr; open Mon.-Sat. 7am-4pm).

For nocturnal pursuits, stroll around the harbor on I. Koundourou St., or walk up 25th Martiou St. The **Mediterraneo Terrace Bar,** near the building with the huge "Lipstick Bar" sign indulges your most sophisticated desires, offering dinner (at a Greek prime minister's ransom) and alcoholic beverages; nurse a drink and blend into the atmosphere. The **Sorrento Bar** on the waterfront is a good place to warm up before hitting the dance floors (beer 500dr). **Charlie Chan's** nightclub is farther down on the waterfront (beer 500dr and mixed drinks 700dr during happy hour; daily 11pm-2am). **Sixties,** 40 R. Koundourou (tel. 82 451), serves a multigenerational crowd grooving to nostalgic tunes (the DJ takes requests) and smooth cocktails (1200dr). Alcohol-free drinks like the Temperance (lemon juice, egg yoke, and grenadine 900dr) are also served (open daily 9am-late). **Lipstick Night Club** (tel. 22 377), close to the Mediterraneo on the waterfront, attracts a touristy crowd looking for fun (specials on drinks like 2 cocktails for 1000dr; open 10pm-late). Each summer from mid-July to mid-September, the town celebrates with the **Lato Festival.**

SIGHTS

According to legend, Artemis and Athena bathed at the "bottomless" lake, **Xepatomeni,** near the tourist office (it is actually 64m deep). In 1867, the regional governor dug a canal linking the lake with the sea, creating a perpetual flushing mechanism. Three beaches are within walking distance of the main harbor. With minimal effort, you can sunbathe on the concrete piers that jut out from S. Koundourou St. To reach a better spot, catch the bus, which departs every hour, headed to Ierapetra or Sitia and get off at **Almiros Beach,** 2km east of Agios Nikolaos. The sandy beach at **Kalo Chorio,** 10km farther along the same road, is less crowded. Get off the bus headed for either Sitia or Ierapetra at the Kavos Taverna (tell the driver to stop). Another beautiful beach on the road to Elounda is the **Harania Beach.** A winner of the European Blue Flag award for 1996, it is clean and secluded. Take the bus towards Elounda and get off at Harania.

For more cerebral pursuits, visit one of Ag. Nikolaos' two museums, or see if anything's playing at the theater on M. Sfakianaki St. The **Archaeological Museum** (tel. 24 943), just outside the center of town, a few blocks down the road from Iraklion, houses a modest collection of Minoan artifacts (open Tues.-Sun. 8:30am-3pm; admission 500dr). The **Folk Art Museum,** in the tourist office's building, displays tapestries, embroidered clothes, furniture, icons, 16th-century manuscripts of contracts, and stamps for the holy bread at church (open Sun.-Fri. 9:30am-1:30pm and 6-930pm; admission 250dr; free on Sun.). To shop for inexpensive clothes, visit the weekly **market** on Ethnikis Antistassios St., next to the lake (open Wed. 7am-noon).

The archaeological site of **Gournia** is located 1.9km from Agios Nikolaos. Take the bus heading to Ierapetra or Sitia—ask the driver to stop there (open Tues.-Sun. 9am-3pm; admission 800dr). One kilometer before Kritsa on the road from Agios Nikolaos, Crete's Byzantine treasure, the **Panagia Kera** (tel. 51 525), honors the Dormition of the Virgin. The interior is adorned with a patchwork of smoky 14th-century paintings in the central nave and 15th-century Byzantine frescoes in the wings (open Mon.-Sat. 9am-3pm, Sun. 9am-2pm; admission 800dr; free on Sun.).

▓ Ierapetra ΙΕΡΑΠΕΤΡΑ

Ierapetra aims for the glitz and the neon glamour of resort towns, but it hasn't quite mastered the technique. Instead, Ierapetra sits in tourism's rare *purgatorio*—it teeters between the cosmopolitan and the rural. Ierapetra's star attraction is its remote island, **Chrisi,** eight nautical miles from the mainland. Several small ferries depart every day at 10:30am and return at 5 or 5:30pm. The trip to Chrisi takes one hour. Free from stores and crowds, Chrisi is completely flat, adorned by green pine, and surrounded by transparent green sea. Pack a lunch and bring water; you won't even find a small market, though there are two *tavernas* open all day near the dock.

Orientation and Practical Information Most of Ierapetra's services are on the streets parallel to the waterfront. The **police station** also houses the **tourist police** (tel. 22 560) on the waterfront, a few blocks before Eleftherias Sq. (open 24hr.) The **port police,** 29 Kyvra St. (tel. 22 294), are near the excursion boat port. The **National Bank,** in Eleftherias Sq., is across the street from Ierapetra Express (open Mon.-Thurs. 8am-2pm, Fri. 8am-1:30pm). In Kanoupaki Sq., five blocks south of the bus station toward the port, is the **post office,** 3 Stilianou Hota St. (open Mon.-Fri. 7:30am-2pm). The **OTE** is at 25 Koraka St., three blocks from the water (open Mon.-Fri. 7:30am-1pm). **Tourist agencies** on the street parallel to the water distribute free city maps. The **Ierapetra Express office,** 24 Eleftherias Sq. (tel. 28 673 or 22 411), is helpful (open daily 8am-1:30pm and 4-9pm). **Olympic Airways,** 26 Losthenous St. (tel. 22 444), has flight information and sells tickets (open Mon.-Tues., Thurs.-Fri. 9am-1:30pm and 6-8pm, Wed. and Sat. 9am-1:30pm). Across the street is the **bus station,** 41 Lasthenous St. (tel. 28 237). To get to the waterfront from there, head past the palm tree and you'll see signs for the beach. There are two fleets of **taxis** in Ierapetra. **Radio Taxi** (tel. 26 600) lines up cars in Kanoupaki Sq., and another fleet lines up taxis in Eleftherias Venizelou Sq. (tel. 25 512). Rentals in Ierapetra are expensive; try **Galaxie Moto** (tel. 25 374), 18 Metaxaki St. (50cc bikes 3000dr per day, 80cc 6000dr; open daily 9am-1pm and 5-8pm). **Europlan,** 39 M. Kothri St. (tel. 26 771), rents cars (30,000dr per 3 days, unlimited km; open daily 8:30am-2:30pm and 7-10pm). The **hospital** (tel. 22 488) is north of the bus station left off Losthenous Sq. at 6 Kalimerake St. (open daily 8:30am-1:30pm, open 24hr. for emergencies). The town has several **pharmacies,** including one (tel. 22 231) in

Eleftherias Sq. (open Mon.-Fri. 8am-2pm and 5:30-9pm). **Postal Code:** 72200. **Telephone Code:** 0842.

Accommodations   There's a sign at the bus station that leads visitors to the charming **Cretan Villa,** 16 Lakerda St. (tel. 28 522). The 200-year-old building hides a garden surrounded by beautiful, white stucco-walled, brick-floored, high-ceilinged rooms. The owner, a University of Missouri alum, speaks fluent English. All rooms have private bath. (Singles 5000dr. Doubles 6000dr. Triples 8000dr. Prices rise by 1000dr in high season.) **Pension Diagoras,** 1 Kyvra St. (tel. 23 898, -218), above café-bar Diagoras on the waterfront, offers immaculate rooms with balconies. (Doubles 5000dr.) For your camping pleasure, **Ierapetra** (tel. 61 351) and, 7km from Ierapetra, the new **Koutsounari** (tel. 61 213), 9km away on the coastal road to Sitia, provide the ground, a restaurant, a bar, and a beach. Take the bus to Sitia via Makri Gialo (7 per day) and ask to be let off at the campgrounds. The bus costs 200dr and the 7km trip takes about 10 minutes. (1100dr per person. 850dr per tent.)

Food and Entertainment   Nearly all of Ierapetra's restaurants lie on the waterfront and feature identical prices (*moussaka* 800-1000dr). Among the touristy *tavernas,* **O Calles** near the Venetian Fortress offers traditional Greek fare (*moussaka* 800dr, *tzatziki* 500dr), as well as delicious grilled fresh seafood (octopus 1250dr) and friendly service (open in summer daily 5am-3am; in winter 5am-midnight). At **Veterano** (tel. 23 175), in Eleftherias Venizelou Sq., you can peek in the gigantic kitchen where you may see old men alongside young boys shelling almonds, mixing frostings, and layering cakes. Sit in the shade with a large piece of fresh *baklava* (400dr) or Ierapetra's own *kalitsenia,* an individual-sized sweet cheese tart like pie (200dr each; open daily 7:30am-midnight). **Hrisofakis Stelios** (tel. 25 328) also runs a popular sweet shop in the old town at the square at the mosque and sells traditional biscuits and tortes. *Kalitsenia* (2200dr per kg) can be bought by the piece (open late Aug. to July daily 8am-10pm). The **public market,** two blocks up Konaki St. from Kanoupaki Sq. on the left, has fruit and vegetable stands as well as bakeries which sell cheap, fresh loaves (250-300dr; market open Mon.-Tues., Thurs.-Fri. 7:30am-2pm and 5-8 or 8:30pm, Wed. and Sat. 7:30am-2pm). On Saturdays there is also a **street fruit market** on the corner of Panagou and Kalimerake St. (open daily 7am-1:30 or 2pm).

Nightlife in Ierapetra is low key. The bars at the south end of the waterfront (closer to the Fortress) are frequented by locals and play mostly Greek music. **Bar Alexander** is packed with locals who come to groove to the DJ'd Greek tunes. (cocktails 1200dr; open daily 9pm-3:30am). The bars on the other end of the harbor are busy with primarily German tourists. **Acropolis** (tel. 23 659) has a beautiful view from the center of the waterfront; inside, tourists enjoy mostly oldies and jazz mixed by the DJ with rock, rave, and even some Greek music (open daily 9am-8am—it gets real crazy from about midnight until 4am).

Sights   There are loads of historical sights in Ierapetra; unfortunately, most are closed. Locals laud **Napoleon's House,** in the old town, where the French commander supposedly spent the night on June 26, 1798, en route to Egypt to battle the Mamluks. The restored **Venetian fortress** *(Kales),* at the extreme south end of the old harbor, was begun in the early 13th century and is open daily for visiting (admission 100dr). The **Kervea festival** each summer in July and August sometimes holds some of its music, dance, and theater performances at the fortress. Call the **town hall** (tel. 24 115) for information (open Mon.-Fri. 7:30am-2:30pm). Also in the old town are a **mosque** and an **Ottoman fountain,** built near the end of the 19th century. Ierapetra's **Archaeological Museum,** at the beginning of Adrianou St. at Kanoupaki Sq. on the waterfront, has a small collection of Minoan and Classical artifacts from the south coast (open Tues.-Sat. 9am-3pm; free).

■ Sitia ΣΗΤΕΙΑ

A scenic drive on coastal and mountain roads from Agios Nikolaos leads to Sitia, a sleepy fishing and port town. The wave of tourism that has engulfed the coast from Iraklion to Agios Nikolaos slows to a trickle before Sitia. Use Sitia as your base for exploring Crete's east coast, including Vai, the Toplou Monastery, and Kato Zakros.

ORIENTATION AND PRACTICAL INFORMATION

To get to the center of the waterfront from the bus station, head for the sign for Vai and Kato Zakros, then bear left. **Dimokritou** and **Venizelou Street** intersect with the waterfront at the square where you will find a small palm-treed traffic island, Sitia's restaurant strip, and several kiosks.

Tourist Police: 62 Therissou St. (tel. 24 200). From the square walk up Kapetan Sifi St. 2 blocks to Mysonos St. Take a left on Mysnos and continue until it turns into Therissou St.; it's several blocks up on the right. Open daily 7:30am-9pm.

OTE: 22 Capitan Sifis St. (tel. 28 099), from the main square, turn inland at the National Bank, and walk uphill 2 blocks. Open Mon.-Sat. 7:30am-10pm.

Banks: National Bank (tel. 24 990), in Venizelou Sq., offers **currency exchange.** Open Mon.-Thurs. 8am-2pm, Fri. 8am-1:30pm.

Flights: Olympic Airways, 56 Eleftheriou Venizelou St. (tel. 22 270), off the main square to the east. Open Mon.-Sat. 8am-2pm and 5-9pm. To Karpathos (1½hr., 8400dr) and Kassos (1hr., 8400dr). There are also flights to Athens (3 per week, 22,800dr). No buses to airport. Taxis cost 300-400dr for the 1km uphill ride.

Buses: 4 Karamo St. (tel. 22 272), on the east end of the waterfront. To Agios Nikolaos (6 per day, 1½hr., 1300dr); Iraklion (5 per day, 3¼hr., 2500dr); Ierapetra (5 per day, 1½hr., 1050dr); Vai (3-4 per day, 1hr., 500dr); and Kato Zakros (2 per day, 1hr., 900dr).

Ferries: The *Kornaros* travels once per week to Kassos (4hr., 2460dr) and Karpathos (5hr., 2682dr) and thrice weekly to Peiraias (16-17hr., 6655dr) via Agios Nikolaos (1½hr., 1446dr) and Milos (7-8hr., 4021dr). **Porto Belis Travel,** 3 Karamanli St. (tel. 22 370), near the bus station, provides ferry information, rents rooms, sells airplane tickets, rents cars and mopeds, and **exchanges currency.** Open in summer daily 8:30am-9pm; in winter 8:30am-8pm.

Taxis: (tel. 23 810, 23 298, or 28 591) lounge in Venizelou Sq. Sometimes they run all night, sometimes they don't; weekends there are usually cabs available 24hr.

Car Rental: Sitia Rent-a-Car, 4-6 Itanou (tel. 23 770, -030), first left walking towards town from bus station. Fiat Panda 8500dr per day, 30dr per km over 100km. Open daily 9am-1pm and 3-9pm.

Moped Rental: Knossos (tel. 22 057) on Ithanou St. up the block from Sitia Rent-a-Car. Knossos rents cars and bikes and can help you find a room. Vespas 3000dr per day. Open daily 8am-8pm.

Pharmacies: Many on streets behind the waterfront. One is straight from the square up 1½ blocks, on the left. Open Mon. and Wed. 8am-1:30pm, Tues. and Thurs.-Fri. 8am-1:30pm and 5:30-8:30pm.

Hospital: (tel. 24 311), off Therissou St. just past the Youth Hostel, away from town. Follow the signs from the main square. Open 24hr.

Police: (tel. 22 266, -59), in the same building as the tourist police. Open 24hr.

Post Office: Main branch, 2 Ethnikis Antistasis St. (tel. 22 283). From the bus station, walk south and follow the road around to the right. Open Mon.-Fri. 7:30am-2pm. **Postal Code:** 72300.

Telephone Code: 0843.

ACCOMMODATIONS

It is difficult to find rooms in July and August, and during mid-August, when the Sultana Festival is held, it is nearly impossible. Off season prices are 20-40% less. The youth hostel is friendly and informal, but for more privacy, head to the main road which leads up to the hostel, and to the back streets at the west end of the waterfront, especially Kornarou and Kondilaki St.

Youth Hostel, 4 Therissou St. (tel. 22 693). From the bus station, take a left on Ithanou (after road bends it becomes Papanastasiou), follow until the BP gas station, where road becomes Therissou, and uphill another 100m on the left. Only 50 beds, but you may be able to sleep on the veranda or the floor. Reception open in summer daily 8:30am-10pm; in winter evenings, but if no one is around, feel free to find a bed, settle in, and register later. Hot water all day. Open year-round. 1300dr per person. Private doubles 3000dr. Breakfast 600dr.

Porto-Belis, 34 Karamanli Ave. (tel. 22 370). Apartments, studios, and rooms above the Porto-Belis Travel Agency. The bright, sunny rooms in this new building are spacious and clean. Some of the rooms's balconies look on to the sea. All rooms have large private baths, white tiled floors, balconies, and fridges. Doubles 4500-5300dr. Triples 5500-6300dr. Studio for 2-3 people with kitchenette 5200-5800dr. 2-room apartment with kitchenette for 3-4 people 7500-8500dr.

Venus "Rooms to Let," 60 Kondilaki St. (tel. 24 307). Walk uphill from the OTE and take your first right. Green courtyard, sunny rooms with balconies, and kitchen facilities. Clean shared baths. Doubles upstairs have private bath, couch, and sea view balcony for 7000dr. Doubles 5500dr. Triples 8000dr.

"Rooms to Let" Apostolis, 27 Kazantazis St. (tel. 22 993 or 28 172). Pleasant rooms with private baths. Wash basin and lines. Doubles 6500dr. Triples 8500dr.

FOOD, ENTERTAINMENT, AND SIGHTS

Sitia's restaurants specialize in fresh fish and lobster. **Zorba's** (tel. 22 689), on the west side of the harbor, has a variety of good, moderately priced entrees (*moussaka* 950dr). Set menus of meat or fish, salad, wine, and dessert are sometimes a good, if touristy, bargain (1500-3000dr). For fresh fruits and veggies, you can visit one of the many produce markets on Fountalidou St. Bakeries are also a good place to find fresh, delicious nourishment. One of the better in town is **Ailmakis,** 27 Mysonos St. (tel. 25 098). Huge loaves of round bread with ornately stamped tops are 150dr (open Mon.-Tues. and Thurs.-Fri. 7am-2pm and 6-8pm, Wed. and Sat. 7am-2pm). Tucked away and removed from the touristy waterfront, locals claim **Taverna Michos,** 117 V. Kornarou (tel. 22 416), to be one of Sitia's best restaurants. Swordfish-prawn *souvlaki* is served with rice and delicious Cretan vegetables (1400dr; open daily noon-3pm and 6pm-1 or 2am). **Taverna Panorama** (tel. 25 160) in neighboring Agia Fotia on the road to Palaikastro and Vai, serves home-cooked traditional Cretan dishes. The menu varies daily, but specialties include octopus cooked in red wine and tomato sauce, fresh fish, and grape leaves. It is usually only open for dinner, but call ahead. **Paradosiaka Glyka** (tel. 28 466), one block from the main square, specializes in traditional Cretan biscuits and pastries. *Kserotigano* are a special wedding pastry (they're round, sticky, and covered with sesame seeds 2400dr per kg). *Kalitsenia* come in two varieties—an open tartlike pie and a small, soft roll-like biscuit—both are filled with cinnamon-spiced delicious Cretan cheese (950dr per kg; open daily 8:30am-2pm and 5-9 or 9:30pm). **Kalampokis,** 95 El Venizelou (tel. 22 287), just across and in back of the taxi stand in the main square, sells some of the more delicious pastries around (*baklava* 270dr, black forest cake with chunky cherries 300dr; open daily 9am-11pm). Fountalidou St., off N. Katzanakis St., has numerous fruit shops and small markets.

During the middle of August, Sitia hosts the **Sultana Festival,** which features unlimited wine, dancing, and music for roughly 2000dr. Nightlife is not Sitia's strong point, but one exception is the **Planetarium Disco,** 2km west of the second pier on a sweeping balcony. The 1500dr cover includes first drink (open daily 1am-sunrise). **De Sitia Peris** is a "garden bar" in Sitia, past all of the *tavernas* on the harbor, is near the end (no cover; beer 700dr; cocktails 1200-1500dr; open daily 10pm-4am).

The **fortress** at the hilltop provides a view of the town and the city's bay. The distant end of the town's **beach,** extending 3km east of Sitia toward Petra, is usually empty. The **Archaeological Museum** (tel. 23 917) houses a small collection from nearby sights. Take a left on Ithanou; when you come to the sign for Iraklion, take another left on the road to Ierapetra. Be sure to note the Late Minoan **Palaikastro Kouros** statuette, perhaps one of the very first representations of Zeus (open Tues.-Sun. 8:30am-3pm; admission 500dr, students free).

■ Near Sitia

Toplou's monks, under siege by pirates and Turks for centuries, carefully armed their **monastery.** Their efforts went for naught in 1471, when the entire complex fell to the Turks who destroyed it. The rebuilt structure now contains a number of relics, including the 2nd-century BCE inscription of a treaty between the Cretan cities of Itanos and Ierapetra and the province of Magnesia in Asia Minor, and elaborate icons by the 18th-century master Ioannis Kournaros. Dress appropriately (pants for men, long skirts for women). The monks lend clothes if need be. **Buses** do not go to the monastery; get off the Vai bus 12km outside Sitia at the Moni Toplou turnoff, and walk the last 3km. Drivers follow the road east from Sitia along the coast and turn at the junction (open daily 9am-1pm and 2-6pm; admission 500dr).

Not long ago, tourists headed east to the sylvan palm beach at **Vai** for refuge from Sitia's crowds. Today, several buses roll into this outpost every day, depositing tourists eager to ponder Europe's only indigenous palm tree forest. Legend has it that the forest is the legacy of the Arabs who conquered Crete in the 9th century (park open daily 8am-9pm; free). Most visit Vai via the crowded public bus from Sitia. Buses leave Sitia and stop at Palaikastro en route to Vai (4 per day, 1hr., Sitia-Vai 500dr, Palaikastro-Vai 200dr). Camping is forbidden in the park itself, but many unfurl sleeping bags in the cove to the south of the palm beach. If sandy pajamas and the possibility of arrest don't appeal to you, rent a room in quiet Palaikastro, a town 8km back toward Sitia. A **tourist office** and **currency exchange center** are located in the parking lot (open Apr.-Oct. daily 11am-5:40pm). The *au naturel* method of beaching is Greek-kosher on the *other* side of the tempting hill to your right. When those places on which the sun don't usually shine start burning, slap on some more cocoa butter (and clothes) and check out the **watersports** on the far end of the beach. There is also a **scuba diving center** (tel. (0843) 71 548; call ahead since it opens seasonally). At the Vai tourist shop, inquire about the nearby **Open Air Banana Plantations and Sub-Tropical Cultivations** (tel. (0843) 61 353). An old, retired sea captain gives tours in German, English, French, and Greek. A free banana awaits you at the tour's end—have you had your banana today? (open Apr.-Oct. daily 8am-8pm; admission 800dr, group rate 600dr). Beyond Vai sprawls the mellow and secluded **Itanos Beach.** Do the Minoan-*thang* and explore the beachside archaeological site.

PALAIKASTRO

This lazy, dreamy village is the perfect place to use as a base for exploring eastern Crete. Its majestic beaches and serene landscape make up for the virtual lack of anything else to do. If you're into olive trees, bring a camera.

Orientation and Practical Information Palaikastro's *plateia* contains all necessities in just a few buildings. The **police** (tel. 61 222) stand guard, ready for action, above the tourist souvenir shop. Unexpectedly, the village's most brilliant resource is the **OTE** (tel. 61 225). The diligent staff **exchanges currency,** sells stamps, hands out free maps, suggests area excursions, and helps tourists find rooms. They also have two metered phones and sell phone cards (open Apr.-Oct. daily 9am-10pm; Nov.-Mar. 9am-1pm and 5-8:30pm). One phone card machine is located in the square behind the fountain, the other is across the street from Kastri Pizza, where the only road in town forks off to the left. **Buses** run from Sitia to Palaikastro (30min., 360dr) and go on to Vai (15min., 200dr). Direct from Sitia to Vai (45min.-1hr., 500dr). A taxi from Sitia costs 2500dr. The **Hotel Hellas** (tel. 61 240) rents **motorbikes,** and, not surprisingly, **Lion Cars** (tel. 61 482) rents cars. A cheese

To Have Tattooed or Not Have Tattooed

Archaeologists and scholars alike have largely overlooked the available evidence for the use of paint and tattoos used to adorn the human body during the Aegean Bronze Age. Perhaps the thought of Artemis, with a red heart bearing the inscription "Aphrodite 4-Ever" emblazoned on his arm, is somewhat unappealing to Classics scholars. It has been argued that body painting and tattooing may have been more popular forms of artistic and cultural expression on the Cycladic Islands, Minoan Crete, and mainland Greece than anyone had previously realized. Body art was already a fad by Biblical times, when God finally put His foot down and proclaimed, "You shall not make any cuttings in your flesh on account of the dead or tattoo any marks on you: I am the LORD" (Holy Bible, Leviticus 19:28). "Paint ghosts" and remnants of blue and red pigments on Cycladic marble figurines suggest that the islanders tattooed their faces and upper torsos with lines and dots. The wall paintings of Akrotiri (Santorini) seem to show that women wore "make-up" (i.e., eye-, lip-, and nail-pigment) and that both men and women dyed their skulls blue after they shaved them. Wall paintings and terra-cotta figurines from Minoan Crete hint at possible abstract tattoo patterns. And the Sphynx from Mycenae shouts, "I put dots on my face, and they're not pimples!" Although no "ancient tattoo parlors" have been excavated yet, archaeological evidence for "body art" (needles, pigments, applicators) is strong. Rumor has it, in areas where the Poppy goddess was popular, it hurt a little less.

and meat shop, two small fruit and food stores, and a bakery are behind the Hotel Hellas, near the church. **Postal Code:** 72300. **Telephone Code:** 0843.

Accommodations   **Yiannis Perrakis,** a kind-hearted Greek and German-speaking villager, and his wife run one of the lovelier pensions (tel. 61 310) in town. When you get off the bus, follow the road which forks to the right. Look for green-house-enclosed banana trees on your right; the pension is up the gravel path on the left. Lemon trees and magenta flowers invite you to immaculate, bright, beautiful rooms. (Singles 2500dr. Doubles 4000dr. Triples 5000dr. Prices lower in off season.) Alternatively, the **Thalia Hotel** (tel. 61 448, -217) is equally clean and pleasant. From the square, go past the church and *gyro* stand. The pension will be on your right. (Open all year, though rates vary with the season. All rooms have private baths. Doubles 5500-6000dr. Triples 6500-7000dr. Breakfast 1000dr.)

Food and Entertainment   A handful of *tavernas* cluster in Palaikastro's tiny square. The **Hotel Hellas** (tel. 61 455) serves standard Greek food (Greek salad 590dr, stuffed eggplant 950dr). A **sweet shop** is next to the bus stop, near the Hotel Itanos. Locals know that the best music and atmosphere can be found at the **Enigma Bar** (open daily 10pm-late). From the square, follow the left fork of the road on the way to Vai. A young, wanna-be-chic Euro-crowd frequents the **Design Bar,** a glittery disco replete with pink exterior, strobe lights, and shimmery fountain (open daily 9 or 9:30pm until late). Palaikastro, and neighboring Agathia, are divine places to try *raki* (i.e. wreck me), the indigenous moonshine of Crete. Sip it slowly; it comes in thimble-sized glasses for a reason.

Sights   If you've got a beach fetish, you've come to the right place. For sizzling and swimming in the immediate area, orient yourself around **Kastri Hill** (the mysteriously sloping land mass by the sea). A 25-minute walk (although only enchanting for the first 5min.) through a labyrinthine path of silvery olive groves leads to either **Kouremenos Beach** (on the left side of Kastri) or **Chiona Beach** (on the right). Kouremenos is the site of the **Nathalie Simon (French) Windsurfing Club.** Eastern Crete kicks up quite a wind at times, and conditions are said to be great during the summer. Inquire at the OTE. Chiona Beach has its advantages as well—two stellar *tavernas* await you after a long hard day at the beach.

Alas, when that twinge of cerebral guilt strikes, stop by the archaeological site of **Roussolakos,** near Chiona Beach. Three series of excavations, begun in 1902, continue to this day. Follow the well marked signs posted throughout the "seven buildings" of the site, which date to 3000-2000 BCE. Make sure to notice the **Minoan Hall** (Polytheon), the well planned architecture, and the site of the discovery of the Paliokastro Kouros and sealstone in the sandy hughes of the red soil. If you're lucky, you may even catch a glimpse of the site's real-life **archaeologists.** Rumor has it, they're the biggest thing to have hit Crete since the tidal waves caused by the eruption of the Thera volcano. If you just can't get enough of this stuff, hike to the top of **Petsofas** and commune with the gods of the **Minoan peak sanctuary.**

Cyclades ΚΥΚΛΑΔΕΣ

"Happy is the man, I thought, who, before dying, has the good fortune to sail the Aegean Sea."

—Nikos Kazantzakis

Chances are, when people speak longingly of the Greek islands, they're talking about the Cyclades. Whatever your idea of the Aegean—winding cobblestone streets and whitewashed houses, *ouzo* sipped seaside during warm sunsets, inebriated revelry—you can find it here. In classical antiquity, the islands received their name from the shape of their layout. The ancient Greeks saw the other Cycladic islands forming a circular, or "cyclical" pattern, spiraling around their sanctified Delos. Today, somewhat less romantically, the islands can be grouped into three broad categories. Although each has quiet villages and untouched spots, Santorini, Mykonos and Ios are known to all as the party islands and are the most heavily touristed. Of these three, Santorini is the most chic and the most expensive and offers an impressive history and some of the most spectacular views in all of Greece. Mykonos runs a close second in sophistication (and price), but also provides some of Greece's most sizzling nightlife. Ios can be summed up in four words: American frat party run amok (all right, that was five words, but after a week on Ios you won't be able to count either). Paros, Naxos, and Amorgos are also popular, but are less frantic and more pristine. Syros, Tinos, Andros, Kea, Kithnos, Serifos, Sifnos, and Milos get few foreign visitors and are primarily dependent on Greeks tourists. If you visit during the winter, you may be the only foreigner on some of these islands. (Be forewarned that tourist amenities on many of these islands, especially accommodations, are only open April through October).

MYKONOS ΜΥΚΟΝΟΣ

Mykonos has been an object of envy and desire ever since the 18th century, when pirates vied for the right to lounge on the island's long, blonde beaches. Mykonos today is chic and sleek, playing host to sophisticated revelers who retain a strong sense of history and culture. The word Greeks use to describe this island is invariably *kosmopolitikos*, and that it certainly is. You'll find that the wealthy and well dressed abound on Mykonos and one too many sun-tanned goddesses will be peering at you from behind Versace sunglasses that cost more than your entire vacation. After several years of decline, Mykonos' gay scene has begun to regain the acclaim which made it the hottest spot for gays in the Mediterranean. A word of caution: don't pester Petros the Pelican, the island's mascot. According to one popular tale, Petros was killed several years ago when a couple of tourists tried to procreate with him. The story isn't true, and Petros has since been provided with a new pink mate.

■ Mykonos Town

If you stay in Mykonos long enough, chances are you will spend at least one drunken evening lost in Mykonos Town's maze of endless, winding alleys lined with indistinguishable whitewashed buildings. These labyrinthine streets, closed to motor traffic, were created to disconcert and disorient pirates. Apparently, they never bothered to straighten them out because they seemed to work just as well for tourists. Despite the influx of visitors, the town has resisted large hotel complexes. Fishing boats in the harbor, basket-laden donkeys, drag queens, high-fashion models, and Petros the Pelican help preserve the town's authentic charm. Nonetheless, Mykonos is unmistakably a tourist town. Depending on your degree of homesickness, you will either exult or grieve over the availability of cheeseburgers, milk-

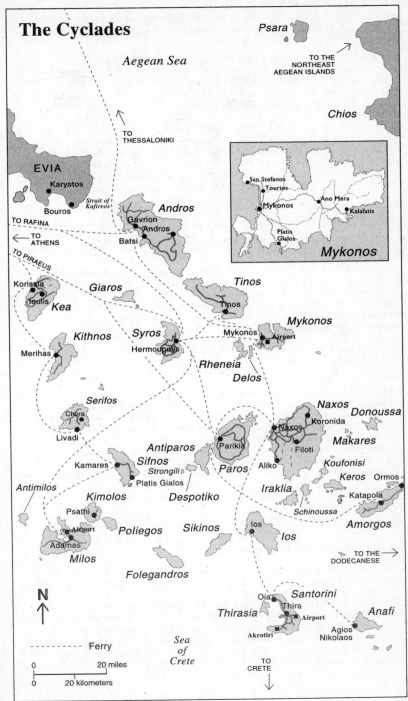

The Cyclades

Aegean Sea

Psara

TO THE
NORTHEAST
AEGEAN ISLANDS

Chios

TO
THESSALONIKI

EVIA

Karystos

Bouros

Strait of
Kafireos

Andros

Gavrion
Andros

Batsi

TO RAFINA

TO
ATHENS

TO PIRAEUS

Korissia
Ioulis

Kea

Giaros

Tinos

Tinos

Mykonos

Mykonos   Airport

San Stefanos
Tourlos

Mykonos

Ano Mera

Kalafatis

Platis
Gialos

Mykonos

Kithnos

Merihas

Syros

Hermoupolis

Rheneia

Delos

Naxos   Donoussa

Serifos

Chora

Livadi

Antiparos

Sifnos

Kamares

Strongili

Platis Gialos

Paros

Parikia

Koronida

Filoti

Naxos

Aliko

Makares

Koufonisi

Keros   Ormos

Iraklia

Katapola

Schinoussa

Amorgos

Antimilos

Kimolos

Psathi

Airport

Adamas

Milos

Poliegos

Despotiko

Sikinos

Ios

Ios

Folegandros

TO THE
DODECANESE

N

Oia

Thira   Airport

Santorini

Thirasia

Akrotiri

Agios
Nikolaos

Anafi

Sea
of
Crete

TO
CRETE

--- --- Ferry

0   20 miles

0   20 kilometers

shakes, fish and chips, Chinese food, and "English breakfasts." Don't come to Mykonos to experience unadulterated Greek culture; come instead to witness an unstoppable world of Dionysian delight.

ORIENTATION AND PRACTICAL INFORMATION

Boats dock at a pier on the far left of the waterfront (facing inland). One road leads along the water past the town beach to **Taxi Square** and the center of town. Another road heads uphill to the **North Station** bus depot, then wraps around Mykonos Town to the **South Station** on the opposite side. Everything you need or want is near the waterfront—banks, travel agencies, shops, cafés, *tavernas*, bars, and discoes—but much of the real shopping, fine dining, and partying goes on in the infamous narrow, winding back streets (especially Matogianni, Kalogera, Mitropoleas, and Enoplon Dinameon). On the right side is another pier for excursion boats. Past the pier is a series of churches, the lovely part of town called **Little Venice,** and a small hill with a line of five windmills.

Tourist Police: (tel. 22 482), in an office at the ferry landing. Very helpful English speakers. Open daily 8am-10pm.

Banks: National Bank of Greece (tel. 22 234), in the center of the waterfront, offers **currency exchange** and has an **ATM.** Open June-Sept. Mon.-Thurs. 8am-2pm and 6-8pm, Fri. 8am-1:30pm, Sat.-Sun. 10am-1pm; Oct.-May. Mon.-Thurs. 8am-2pm, Fri. 8am-1:30pm.

American Express: (tel. 22 422), left of the bank inside **Delia Travel Ltd.** Full AmEx travel services for cardholders. Open Mon.-Fri. 9am-9pm, Sat.-Sun. 9am-3pm and 6-9pm.

OTE: (tel. 22 699), at the left end of the waterfront in a big white building, uphill and to the right of the dock. Open Mon.-Sat. 7:30am-11pm, Sun. 8am-11pm.

Flights: Olympic Airways (tel. 22 490, -95 in town, 22 321 at airport). Flights to Athens (4-10 per day, 40min., 17,300dr); Thessaloniki (25,500dr); Santorini (7 per week, not daily, 30min., 13,800dr); Iraklion (1 per week, 1hr., 23,400dr); and Rhodes (1 per week, 1hr., 23,400dr). The main Olympic Airways office is perched uphill from the South Station. There are no buses to the airport; a taxi from Mykonos Town costs 1000dr.

Buses: Two stations. **North Station,** uphill from the ferry dock, serves Ag. Stefanos beach (17 per day), Ano Mera and Kalafatis (8 per day), Elia Beach (8 per day), and Kalo Livadi beach (2 per day). **South Station,** uphill from the windmills at the opposite edge of town, serves Plati Yalos beach (every 30 min.), Paradise Beach (every 30min.), Ornos Beach (21 per day), and Ag. Ioannis (20 per day). All fares 190dr. Detailed schedules are posted at each station. The last buses to and from the beaches (in July and Aug. only) are around 3-4am.

Ferries: Boats sail to Tinos (3-5 per day, 45min., 1335dr); Paros (2-3 per day, 2hr., 1640dr); Naxos (1-2 per day, 3hr., 1570dr); Syros (1-3 per day, 2½hr., 1410dr); Andros (1-3 per day, 3½hr., 2490dr); Santorini (1-3 per day, 6½hr., 2980dr); Ios (1-2 per day, 4hr., 2805dr); Peiraias (1-4 per day, 6hr., 4115dr); Iraklion (2 per week, 5035dr); Thessaloniki (2 per week, 7605dr); Samos (4 per week, 3540dr); Ikaria (4 per week, 2180dr); and Rafina (1-3 per day, 3535dr). The **Port Authority** (tel. 22 218) is above the National Bank along the waterfront.

Flying Dolphins: Hydrofoils are faster but more expensive and less reliable. Daily they serve Paros (3150dr), Santorini (6300dr), Naxos (2730dr), Ios (5920dr), as well as Amorgos (2 per week, 5920dr) and Sikinos (1 per week, 4675dr). There is also a **SeaJet** service to Tinos (2 per day, 2515dr), Syros (2665dr), Andros (2 per day, 5485dr) and Rafina (1-2 per day, 7400dr).

Taxi: (tel. 22 400, -700), available at Taxi Sq., along the waterfront.

Moped Rentals: Agencies surround both bus stops. 1500-5000dr (depending on model) per day. Some rent jeeps as well (10,000-16,000dr per day).

International Bookstore: International Press (tel. 23 316), in the small square opposite Pierro's, follow signs from the waterfront. Eclectic books, magazines, and newspapers in English, French, and German. Open daily 8am-midnight.

MYKONOS

Laundry: Quite a few around, especially near North Station. Go down the road (from the cluster of churches at Paraportiani) into Little Venke. Across from the linen shop, Venetia, there is a store that says "Laundry" (tel. 24 982). Wash 1800dr. Dry 1200dr. Open daily 9:30am-10:30pm.

Pharmacy: (tel. 23 250). From Sea and Sky travel agency on the waterfront, go up 1 block on Matogianni St. Look for it on your right across from Pierro's. Open Mon.-Sat. 8:30am-1:30pm and 5-10pm.

Hospital: (tel. 23 994, -6), 1km east of Mykonos Town. Take the bus to Ano Mera (8 per day, 160dr) or a taxi (600dr). For an emergency, call an **ambulance** at 166.

Police: (tel. 22 716, -215), in Laka past the South Station. Open 24hr.

Post Office: (tel. 22 238), around the corner from the police in Laka, behind the South Station. Ask for directions persistently until you discover it—it's a tough one. Provides **currency exchange.** Office open Mon.-Fri. 7:30am-2pm. **Postal Code:** 84600.

Telephone Code: 0289.

ACCOMMODATIONS

Hotels on Mykonos are *expensive;* however, accommodations-hawking here is a full-blown industry. Pension owners stake out the port in Mykonos, armed with slick photo-montages and shuttle vans with the engines running. You may see the competition lower prices before your eyes. Alas, beware of hotel owners who say their rooms are "on the beach"—they are often miles away from town. Alternatively, bear right coming off the boat and look for the line of numbered offices—1 for hotels (tel. 24 540; open daily 9am-midnight), 2 for "Rooms to Let" (tel. 24 860; open daily 9am-11pm), and 3 for camping (tel. 23 567). These provide information on availability, location, and prices, and will telephone proprietors on your behalf. Keep in mind that freelance camping is illegal. Prices are 20-40% less in off season.

Chez Maria Pension, 30 N. Kalogera St. (tel. 22 480). From the waterfront, turn inland next to Sea & Sky Travel Agency onto Matogianni St., then, after a few blocks, turn right onto Kalogera at the yellow building across from the Credit Bank. There are signs leading you there. Doubles 12,000dr. Triples 15,000dr.

Hotel Apollon (tel. 23 271 or 22 223), on the waterfront. The oldest hotel in town, in an old, antique-laden house with many rooms overlooking the harbor. Common baths. Singles 10,000dr. Doubles 12,500dr. Triples 15,000dr.

Hotel Karboni/Matogianni (tel. 22 217), on Matogianni St., inland from the waterfront. Pleasant and spotless. Ask about cheaper back rooms. Doubles 15,000dr. Triples 18,000dr. Breakfast 1500dr.

Hotel Phillippi, 32 N. Kalogera St. (tel. 22 294), next to Chez Maria. Friendly owners, gorgeous gardens, and clean rooms. Doubles 13,000dr. Triples 18,000dr.

Hotel Maria, 18 Kalogera St. (tel. 24 212), in an alley off Kalogera. Don't confuse it with Chez Maria or the nearby Marios Hotel. A/C and private bath. Run by Petros, a former soccer star. Doubles 17,000dr. Triples 20,000dr.

Paradise Beach Camping (tel. 22 852, -129; fax 24 350), located on a beach 6km from the village. You can take a bus here (380dr roundtrip). Situated directly on one of the island's more popular beaches. Even though it's quite large, it often feels crowded, is something of a design nightmare, and there are random nude people walking around. Free shuttle service from port and airport. 1500dr per person. 800dr per small tent. 900dr per large tent.

Mykonos Camping (tel. 25 915, -916; fax 24 578), near Paradise Beach, is smaller, quieter and cleaner. 1500dr per person. 800dr per tent. 1500dr per tent rental.

FOOD

On Mykonos, overpriced, self-consciously trendy food is the rule, but several cheap, good places can be found nonetheless.

Klimataria (tel. 24 051), on Florov Zouganeli St., up past Taxi Sq.—look for the blue tables. Good prices compared with other places, and a 5-language menu. *Moussaka* 1000dr, *soukoukia* (spicy meatballs) 1000dr. Open daily 9am-1am.

MYKONOS

Taverna Antonini (tel. 22 319), in Taxi Sq. *Moussaka* 1200dr, *kabab* 1500dr.

Alexi's (tel. 26 904), at the back of Taxi Sq., below the Piano Bar. Since 1970—the oldest greasy spoon in Mykonos. Alexi puts on a show as he cooks up your *gyro-pita* (350dr) or hamburger (450-650dr). Open daily 24hr.

Niko's Taverna (tel. 24 320), in a cluster of restaurants inland from the excursion boat docks. A hoppin' place for traditional Greek cuisine. Baked *kalamari* and cheese 1600dr, mussels with tomato and cheese 1200dr. Open daily noon-2am.

La Mexicana (tel. 24 194), at the end of Kalogera St. Food cooked up by Joe, of San Antonio, Texas. Cheese enchiladas 1950dr. Happy hour daily 6:30-8:30pm.

The Donut Factory (tel. 22 672), at the intersection of Mitropoleos, Ipirou, and Enoplon Dinameon St., roughly 3 blocks down from South Station. Delightful doughnuts (300-450dr) and fresh fruit juices (500-600dr). Open daily 24hr.

ENTERTAINMENT

There are too many bars and discoes to list in full, so here are some favorites. Few have cover charges, but drinks are so expensive that you'll forget you got in free.

Skandinavian Bar, near Niko's Taverna and the waterfront. This perennially packed party complex sprawls over 2 buildings and a patio. Evening mellowness becomes madness 'round midnight. *Everyone* will pass through this place. Beer 500-700dr. Cocktails 1100dr. Open Sun.-Fri. 7:30pm-3am, Sat. 7:30pm-4am.

Windmill Disco, near Skandinavian Bar. Very popular spot in a refurbished wind-mill. Go crazy by the indoor palm tree. Greek music nightly 9-11pm, then jam to the wild sounds of disco. Beer 500dr, cocktails 1000dr. No cover.

Pierro's, on Matogianni St., reputedly the most happening place on Mykonos. Pierro's was the first gay bar in Greece. Best dancing around the island and loud music—the crowd spills out into the square. Shares building with the not-so **Irish Bar Stavros.** Beer 1000dr. Cocktails 2000dr. Stavros open 11pm-morning.

Nepheli-Blue Bar, upstairs from Pierro's. A popular gay hangout. Beer 1000dr, cocktails 1400-1600dr. Next door, **Icaros** has a similar atmosphere.

Montparnasse (tel. 23 719), on Agion Anargyron St., in the Little Venice district. Step into a Toulouse-Lautrec and have a cocktail by the bay window overlooking the water while being serenaded by the cabaret tunes of a live piano. Groovy and sophisticated. Wine 800dr. Cocktails 900-2000dr. Open daily 7pm-3am.

Caprice Bar, on the water in Little Venice. Popular and crowded, with a fruit motif befitting a waterfront bar—beware the sea spray, matey. Open daily 4:30pm-4am.

Watermania, in Elia. A cross between a waterpark and a raging disco. This is the place to catch the Greek supermodel scene and the men who go to catch the Greek supermodel scene. There are 8 buses per day to Elia per day (450dr).

SIGHTS

The prime daytime activities on Mykonos are shopping and perfecting that tan. **Galatis,** left of Taxi Sq. (facing town), has lovely handwoven sweaters (from 10,000dr). Note the list of signatures of famous people, like Jackie O., who shopped here (open April-Oct. daily 9am-10pm). **O Liondis,** 55 Matogianni St., sells individu-ally crafted leather sandals from 2000dr. Look for **Benetia** on the main shopping street in **Little Venice,** just down from Paraportiani, which sells beautiful white linen embroidered by hand (small table cloth starting at 10,000dr). Mykonos is also famous for gold, silver, ceramics, and watercolors.

To pretend that people come here to experience cultural enrichment or indige-nous Greek life verges on the ridiculous. Nevertheless, the **Archaeological Museum** (tel. 22 325), on the uphill paved road between the ferry dock and the center of town, has a 7th-century BCE *pithos* (large terra-cotta storage jar) with relief scenes from the Trojan War, and a bronze *kouros* (open Tues.-Sun. 8:30am-3pm, get there early if you plan to be let in; admission 500dr, students 300dr, European students free, seniors 400dr). The **Aegean Maritime Museum** (tel. 22 700), around the cor-ner from the inland end of Matogiannis, contains ship models, rare ancient coins with nautical subjects, and navigational instruments (open daily April-Oct. 10:30am-

1pm and 6:30-9pm; admission 200dr, students 100dr). Next door is **Lena's House,** an intact 300-year-old home with traditional furniture from the 19th century. The home is part of the folklore museum and remains exactly as its owner left it. Take a step back in time (open Mon.-Sat. 6-9pm, Sun. 7-9pm; free). The **Folklore Museum** (tel. 22 591) is in the nearly 300-year-old house of a former sea-captain, at the south edge of town, inland from the excursion boat docks. The lovely collection is open at convenient hours for beach-goers (open April-Oct. Mon.-Sat. 5:30-8:30pm, Sun. 6:30-8:30pm; free). Next door is the **Paraportiani,** a cluster of white churches, probably the most famous of Mykonos' sights and on every other postcard of Greece.

You will inevitably find yourself on the beach. Nearest to town, after the unexceptional town beach, is **Megali Ammos,** a 1km walk past the windmills on the southwest corner of the harbor. **St. Stefanos Beach** is not spectacular, but very convenient (16 buses run from North Station inland from the ferry dock daily 8:15am-2am, 10min., 140dr). Crowded **Psarou Beach** is a hop, skip, and jump from town. The **nudist beaches,** full of gay men (although anyone is welcome), are unquestionably the best on the island and can be reached by catching a bus (175dr) to **Plati Yialos** (which is not bad in its own right), and taking a *caïque* from there. **Buses** leave every 30 minutes 9am-midnight from South Station roughly 250m up the hill along the street that runs behind the windmills. (Look for painted signs pointing to "buses for Plati Yialos.") From Plati Yialos, *caïques* go to **Paradise Beach** (270dr), officially called Kalamopodi and virtually packed with the beach towels of the semi-clothed and to **Super Paradise Beach** (340dr). Paradise Beach can also be reached by the 7km strip of road connecting it to town. A large, more secluded **nude beach** is **Elia** (430dr). From the same bus stop, buses also run hourly to the beach at Ormos.

If you can bear to abandon the beaches, visit **Ano Mera,** the island's only other village, 7km away. The main item of interest is the 18th-century Tourliani monastery, featuring an ornate, 16th-century marble tower covered with folk carvings. Buses travel from North Station eight times per day.

DELOS ΔΗΛΟΣ

The sacred heart of the Cyclades, Delos holds the famous **Temple of Apollo,** built to commemorate the birthplace of Apollo and his twin sister, Artemis. After Zeus impregnated Leto, he cast her out, fearing his wife Hera's wrath. Leto searched desperately for a place to give birth and at last came across this rocky island bobbing in the sea. She declared that the child would stay forever at his birthplace, casting light upon the riches all around. At her word, the island stopped drifting, and Leto, reassured, decided to stay. Upon her son's birth, the island was bathed in radiance; its name, A-delos (meaning invisible) was changed to Delos because it could now be clearly seen. Immensely grateful, Leto promised to make the island the seat of Apollo's worship. The presence of the sanctuary made Delos a religious center.

The mortal history of the island has not been as charmed. Delos had long been a religious and commercial focus for the Cyclades when the Ionians dedicated it to the **cult of Leto** in the 10th century BCE. By the 7th century BCE, Delos had become the political and trade center of the Aegean League of Islands. Three centuries of struggle for hegemony between the Delians and the Athenians ensued. During these years, the Athenians ordered at least two "purifications" of the island, the latter, in 426 BCE, decreeing that no one should give birth or die on its sacred grounds. Delians who violated the edict were banished to nearby Rheneia. The Athenians later instituted the quadrennial **Delian Games,** which they always dominated.

After Sparta's defeat of Athens in the Peloponnesian War (403 BCE), Delos enjoyed independence and wealth. Sweet prosperity soured, however, during the Roman occupation in the 2nd century BCE. The island subsequently became the slave-trading center of Greece, where the transfers of as many as 10,000 slaves occurred daily. By the 2nd century CE, after successive sackings, the island was left virtually uninhabited apart from a few odd pirates. Today, its only residents are legions of leaping lizards and members of the French School of Archaeology, which has been excavating ruins here since 1873.

A map to the extensive site is highly recommended, whether you choose to follow the tour detailed below, tag along with a guided tour, or improvise. For more background information, a readable source is *Delos: Monuments and Museum,* by Photini Zaphiropoulou, which includes a map (1500dr, available at the entrance and at the museum or at tourist shops in Mykonos).

Occupying almost an entire square mile of this very small island, the archaeological site is neatly sectioned off into the central part of the city, including the Temple of Apollo and the Agora, the outlying parts of the ancient city, Mt. Kythnos, and the theater quarter. While it takes several days to explore the ruins completely, you can see the highlights in three hours or less. Most of your fellow ferry passengers will follow a similar route when they disembark; reverse the route if you want some privacy. Bring a water bottle; the cafeteria on site is pretty expensive.

From the dock, head straight to the **Agora of the Competaliasts,** where Roman guilds built their shrines. Nearby are several parallel **stoas,** the most impressive of which were built by Philip of Macedon. This line of altars, pillars, and statue bases (you can still see the statues' prints) forms the western border of the **Sacred Way.** Follow this road to the **Temple of Apollo,** with its immense, partly hollow hexagonal pedestal that once sustained the weight of the 8m-tall marble statue of the god of light. The famous, skinny **Delian Lions,** a gift of the people of Naxos to the holy island, lie 50m to the north. In the 7th century BCE, nine marble lions were placed in a row on a terrace facing the sacred lake; only five remain here—a sixth, pirated by the Venetians, guards the entrance to the arsenal in Venice.

Proceed up the small crest left of the lions, to the creatively named **House of the Hill.** Because the building was dug deep into the earth, this archetypal Roman house is still substantially intact. Downhill lies the **House of the Lake,** with a well preserved mosaic decorating its atrium and the desecrated **Sacred Lake.** A lone palm tree keeps watch over the surrounding shrubbery. Next to the cafeteria, the **museum** contains an assortment of archaeological finds from the island; unfortunately, the best sculpture from the site is in Athens (Delos museum open Tues.-Sun. 9am-2:30pm). From there, you can hike up the path on **Mt. Kythnos** (where Zeus watched the birth of Apollo) and you'll pass several temples dedicated to the Egyptian gods. The elegant bust in the **Temple of Isis** depicts the sun. The 120m-tall hill affords a marvelous view of the ruins and islands. The **Grotto of Hercules** is on the way down. Its immense building blocks seem to date it to Mycenaean times, though some experts suggest it is a Hellenistic imitation of Mycenaean architecture.

At the base of the hill, go towards the water to the **House of the Dolphins** and the **House of the Masks,** which contains the mosaic *Dionysus Riding a Panther.* Continue on to the **ancient theater,** which has a rather sophisticated cistern (as cisterns go), **Dexamene,** with nine arched compartments. Also try to explore the **House of the Trident,** graced by a mosaic of a dolphin twisted around a trident; the **House of Dionysus,** containing another mosaic of Dionysus and a panther pal; and the **House of Cleopatra.** The famous statue of Cleopatra and Dioscourides is sequestered in the museum; a plaster copy takes its place on the site (ruins open Tues.-Sun. 9am-2:30pm; admission 1200dr, students 600dr, European students free).

GETTING THERE

Delos is most accessible as a daytrip from Mykonos. **Boats** leave from the dock on the waterfront near town (not the dock for large ferries) Tuesday-Sunday every 30-45 minutes 8:30am-11:30am and return between 11am-3pm (25min., 1600dr roundtrip). Most will let you explore the site for three hours. Each boat line has several return trips in the afternoon, so you have some flexibility about how much time you spend exploring. Tickets are available at many tourist offices along the waterfront and in town, or can be bought at the dock. Other nearby islands (especially

Tinos, Naxos, and Paros) offer joint trips to Mykonos and Delos, but often allow less time to explore the ruins.

IOS ΙΟΣ

If you're not drunk by the time you get here, you will be by the time you leave. On Ios, beers go down and clothes come off faster than you can say, *"Opa."* Think spring break in Florida with a backdrop of whitewashed buildings and people speaking English with European accents. It has everything your mother warned you about—people swilling wine from the bottle at 3pm, wishing you slobbery "good evenings;" drinking games all day along the beach; condoms scattered on dirt roads; men and women dancing naked in bars (of which Ios had 113 at last count); and more. Drink here is cheap and plentiful; Ios imports one and a half mega-truckloads of beer a day—and exports the equivalent of empty bottles each morning. Though the island has settled down a tad in the past few years, it's still about ready to sink under the weight of well built, sun-tanned 20-year-olds. There is zilch to do in Ios but sleep late, sunbathe in the afternoon, and join the drunken cavorting by night. Make the pilgrimage to this mecca of the young and the restless only if you're prepared for hangovers, the occasional groping hand, and the lustful stares of the inebriated. Men, women, dogs, and cats alike often come to Ios looking for sex, so be prepared for some rather crude propositions. In the spirit of *Spinal Tap's* musical genius Nigel Tufnell, this place goes to eleven.

ORIENTATION AND PRACTICAL INFORMATION

Ios is simple. The good life centers around three locations, each 20 minutes apart along the island's paved road. The **port** is at one end of the road; the **village,** the focus of nocturnal activity, sits above it on the hill; and crowded **Mylopotas beach** rests over the hill on the other side of the village. Frequent buses shuttle from port to village to beach and back roughly every 10-20 minutes (8am-2am, 190dr).

Ferries from Ios go to Peiraias (4-5 per day, 7-8hr., 4758dr); Naxos (7-8 per day, 80min., 2159dr); Santorini (6 per day, 1¼hr., 1588dr); Paros (7-8 per day, 2½hr., 2464dr); Mykonos (2 per day, 4-5hr., 2922dr); Syros (2-3 per week, 5hr., 3304dr); Crete (3 per week, 5hr., 3478dr); Folegandros (3-4per week, 1hr., 1625dr); Sikinos (3-4 per week, ½hr., 1132dr); and less frequently to smaller Cycladic islands. **Flying Dolphins** serve Rafina (daily, 4-5hr., 7787dr); Santorini (3 per day, 35min., 2857dr); Paros (3 per day, 1hr.20min., 4971dr); Naxos (2 per day, 45min., 4304dr); Mykonos (2 per day, 2hr., 6032dr); Syros (1 per day, 2½hr., 6787dr); Andros (1 per day, 3½hr., 7788dr); and Tinos (1 per day, 2½hr., 6652dr). There are 4 roundtrip excursions per week to Sikinos (2000dr) and Folegandros (3000dr). The **port authority** (tel. 91 264; open 24hr.), is at the far end of the harbor next to Camping Ios.

The port where the boat lets you off is not the heart of the Dionysian oblivion, but a colorful, breezy harbor with cheesy yet pleasant restaurants, an abundance of ferry agents, and an overtaxed beach. **Acteon Travel** (tel. 91 343, -318, or -002; fax 91 088) has offices all over the island, an English-speaking staff, free luggage storage, excursions around the island, stamps, maps, foreign press, travel services, and a full-service **American Express** office. The main office is by the bus stop in the port (open 8am-midnight). To find serious drinking, climb the infamous "donkey steps" to the right of the paved road, which lead to the village; the strenuous ascent assures that the rooms along the stairs are the last to fill up. Otherwise, join the rest of the visitors who cram themselves into the bus that shuffles between the ferry landing and the village (190dr). Bus service stops for the night at 2am. When ferries dock after buses have stopped, you can always crash portside at the cute 'n' crowded **Camping Ios** (tel. 91 329; 1200dr per person, 1000dr per tent rental).

IOS

■ Ios Village

Miraculously, Ios Village has not become as trashed as its visitors. If you arrive in the morning, you'll peer skeptically at the cluster of whitewashed houses that look too innocuous to be Party Central. As you approach, however, the sheer density of bars with storefront advertising gimmicks, the occasional dried sidewalk vomit, and the odd comatose carouser will be assurance enough that you got off at the right port.

ORIENTATION AND PRACTICAL INFORMATION

You can do most of your "serious" business within five minutes, by foot, from the village bus stop on the paved road opposite the large, blue-domed church. The **Tourist Information Center** (tel. 91 135), immediately adjacent to the bus stop, is a private travel agency that sells ferry and hydrofoil tickets, provides currency exchange, helps with accommodations, and offers free luggage storage and safety deposit boxes (open daily 8am-11pm). Behind the helpful tourist office is the English-speaking **police** (tel. 92 222; open 24hr.); look for the building with the Greek flag. The **OTE** (tel. 91 399), is a few minutes out of the village along a path starting from the main paved road after Sweet Irish Dream. Look for signs (open Mon.-Fri. 8am-3pm). Next to the main church, the **National Bank** has an **ATM** (open Mon.-Thurs. 8am-2pm, Fri. 8am-1:30pm). The village branch of **Acteon Travel** (tel. 91 004, -5) is just up the road from the bus stop. Funky cartoon maps and English information booklets are available free at most travel agencies in the village and port (open daily 8am-midnight). If you aspire to see more than the beach and village, you can rent a moped or a jeep at **Trohokinisi** (tel. 91 166), past the parking lot between the church and the main road (moped 3000-5000dr per day; jeep 10,000-14,000dr per day). Motor travel is prohibited on bad roads marked on the island map. Otherwise, public transport suffices. Two streets up in the densely packed village is the town square, off which you can find those oh-so-needed **public toilets**. The **Medical Center** (tel. 91 227), full of travelers patching up wounds from drunken mishaps, is next to the bus stop at the back of the big yellow building (open daily 10am-1pm and 6-7pm). For **emergencies**, call 91 727, -827, or (093) 400 423, (093) 423 207 (open 24hr.). A **pharmacy** (tel. 91 562) is on the bar-infested street in the old village (open Mon.-Sat. 9am-2pm and 5-10pm). There is a **supermarket** in the complex on the main road. The **post office** (tel. 91 235) is buried in the old village between the main road and the road with many bars; look for signs (open Mon.-Fri. 7:30am-2pm). **Postal Code: 84001. Telephone Code: 0286.**

ACCOMMODATIONS

Ios is yet another case of hawks at the docks. Make sure you are in a bargaining mood when you disembark because this is one island where market forces rule. Depending on how the season is going, prices fluctuate between 2000-6000dr for singles, with bath 3000-7000dr; 2500-7000dr for doubles, with bath 3000-10,000dr; and 4500-9000 for triples, with bath 5000-12,000dr.

Francesco's (tel./fax 91 223). From the top of the "donkey steps," walk up the path to the square next to the church, take the uphill steps in the left corner of the square, and then your first left. Rooms with a spectacular view of the harbor sit atop the hotel's terrace bar. Reservations encouraged. Doubles 5000dr, with bath 8000dr. Triples 6000dr, with bath 9000dr.

Pension Markos (tel. 91 059; fax 91 060). From the bus stop, take the right (uphill) just before the supermarket. It's on another side street to the left, with a sign visible from the street uphill. Friendly, clean, popular, with a happening pool. Bar serves breakfast (800dr) all day, plus pizza (900dr). Make a reservation a few days in advance. All rooms with bath. Doubles 8000dr. Triples 10,000dr.

Hotel Petradi (tel. 91 510), equidistant from the village and the beach on the main road. Every room has a balcony with a romantic ocean view. Large, pleasant patio. Quiet at night. Restaurant/bar downstairs. Doubles 8000dr. Triples 9000dr.

Kolitsani View (tel. 91 061). Follow the path past the OTE and look for the white archway. Approximately 10min. from the village's action, a quieter collection of spotless rooms with a family atmosphere. Expansive view of beaches and Santorini (on a clear day). Free pick-up from port. Doubles 7000dr, with bath 9000dr. Triples 9000dr, with bath 13,000dr.

Pension Panorama (tel. 91 592, -186), a bit of a hike uphill on a path below the village, next door to Francesco's. The view makes up for the hike. Doubles 9000dr. Triples 12,000dr. Continental breakfast 600dr.

Pension Irini-Vicky (tel. 91 882), next to the new medical center at the port, set back 3min. from the beach near the dock. A far quieter option for those attempting to escape the island's buzz; rooms have embroidered island curtains. Watch out for the mosquitoes. All rooms with bath. Doubles 10,000dr. Triples 16,000dr.

Far Out Camping (tel. 92 301, -2; fax 92 303), at the far end of Mylopotas beach, is the hippest, most luxurious choice. Club Med at 1000dr per night, with a restaurant, bar, minimarket, basketball, volleyball, swimming pool, scuba diving (lessons open to public), showers, launderette, live music, and "happenings" with live bands and parties during summer. Open April-Sept. 1000dr per person. Doubles 6000dr. Triples 9000dr. Tent rental 400dr.

Camping Stars (tel. 91 612; fax 91 611), on Mylopotas beach. Quieter and less crowded than Far Out. Open June-Sept. 1200dr per person. 500dr per tent rental. Doubles 8000dr. Triples 12,000dr. Quads 16,000dr.

Camping Ios (tel. 91 329), at the port, is ideal for late-night arrivals. Open June-Sept. 1000dr per person.

FOOD

Interspersed among the omnipresent bars and discoes in Ios village are several good, reasonably priced restaurants. You can't beat **Pithari,** near the National Bank, for Greek specialties (veal with tomato sauce and potatoes 1200dr, *souvlaki* 1500dr). For exquisite Greek cuisine, forgotten Greek recipes, and even Ancient Greek delicacies, look for **Lordos Vyron** (tel. 92 125), uphill from the National Bank on the tiny street below the main drag (*strapatsada* (special Greek omelette) 1000dr, *fava* bean dip 900dr). There are cheap, greasy *gyro* joints near the bars just waiting to serve starving revelers (350dr). Ready for some variety after having eaten at Far Out Camping for the past week? Mylopotas Beach actually offers two quality international restaurants. **Harmony** (tel. 91 615), on the right at the bottom of the footpath leading to the beach from the village, offers Mexican food and has a large number of daytime activities (burritos 1600dr). Just down the slope is **Delfini,** with an enormous menu of Thai food (stir-fried vegetables with basil and garlic 1400dr). True gourmands might want to make their ways to **Polydoros** (tel. 91 132), 2km north of the port on Koubara Beach, for what's reputed to be the island's best food.

ENTERTAINMENT

Of Ios' alleged 113 bars, at least 90% are packed into the initially unassuming old village area. Some of the larger and louder hang-outs can be found along the main paved road. Smaller bars line the main pedestrian street in the village, which could be intimate if it weren't for the loud music and continuous traffic of increasingly wasted amusement seekers passing in (and out). Some bars offer happy hours early in the evening, but the real drinking doesn't begin until at least 11pm. From then on, the drunken mob shuffles to the ever-popular Irish pubs ('cause, you know, IOS means Irish Over Seas) and rattling discoes. By the end of the night (or beginning of the next day), people are passed out on the street or dragging themselves to bed (not necessarily their own).

Sweet Irish Dream (tel. 91 141), a large building down towards the "donkey steps." Everyone ends up here, but the cheaper option is to loosen up elsewhere before hitting here after 2am to dance on tables. Beer 500-600dr. Cocktails 700-800dr. 1000dr cover charge includes first drink after 2am; before 2am, no cover.

The Slammer Bar (tel. 92 119), just uphill from the Main Square/Meeting Place in the Village. Its specialty—tequila slammers, a shot glass filled with tequila, Tia Maria, and Sprite, slammed on the bar (600dr). Always packed.

Kalimera, lower down off the main strip. Perhaps the classiest bar, playing jazz, acid jazz, and reggae. Beer 500-800dr. Cocktails 1000-1200dr.

Dubliner (tel. 92 072), across the street from Sweet Irish Dream, with a pub-like wooden section and a jamming disco section. Heats up later, but also a nice place to sit earlier in the evening. Beer 400-500dr. Cocktails 600dr.

Scorpion Disco, outside of town on the way to the beach. A dance emporium. 800dr cover includes first drink.

Sports Bar, close to the main square. Popular among the big, burly crowd. Live satellite feeds for international sporting events. Often live music as well. Beer 450-700dr. Cocktails 700-1000dr.

Pegasus, also on the main drag a couple of doors down form Kalimera—loud rock. Beer 500-600dr. Cocktails 600-1000dr.

Blue Note, popular with Americans, Scandinavians, and those staying at Francesco's. Beer 400-500dr.

BEACHES

With the exception of a solitary monastery, some castle ruins, a modest pile of rubble at the north tip of the island reputed to be **Homer's tomb,** and the ancient town on the hill to the left of Ios town, the **beaches** are the place to be on Ios. Most head for **Mylopotas Beach** on foot (roughly 20min. downhill from Ios town) or by bus service from the port or village (daily 8am-1am, 190dr). The beach, like the town, is a bastion of bacchanalia with loudspeakers blasting everywhere. The outer reaches offer a modicum of privacy. The farther you go, the fewer clothes you'll see (or wear). **Watersports** are available: windsurf (2000dr per hour), waterski (3000dr per hour), or snorkel (800dr per hour), but for Pete's sake, put some clothes on first.

Of course, there are prettier and less crowded beaches on Ios. If you continue uphill from OTE, look for the path that leads down to the secluded beach and crystal pool of water at little **Kolitsani** bay (15-minute walk from Chora). Excursions leave daily for the **nude beach** at beautiful **Manganari Bay,** stopping at the monastery (11am, return 6pm; 2000dr). Nudist, secluded **Psathi** on the eastern coast is a 7km walk along donkey tracks. Several times per week, an excursion goes to Psathi, stopping at the castle ruins (11am, return 6pm; 2000dr). Other nudist beaches include **Koubara** (2km walk north from the port) and **Ag. Theodoti** near Psathi.

SANTORINI (THIRA) ΣΑΝΤΟΡΗΝΗ, ΘΗΡΑ

Santorini is a diamond at the end of a string of Cycladic pearls. Plunging cliffs, burning black sand beaches, and deeply scarred hills make its landscape as dramatic as the cataclysm that created it. Even those with no interest in Santorini's intriguing past will find ample delights in its present—long stretches of beach, tiny cliffside towns, and spectacular landscapes forged by centuries of volcanic activity. Santorini's whitewashed homes are strewn against a cliffside, its ridges rising sharply out of the Aegean. The black beaches, stark against cobalt waters, and the boiling fields of pumice are unique in their beauty among the Greek islands.

HISTORY OF THE ISLAND

From approximately 2000 BCE to 1628 BCE, one of the more advanced societies in ancient Greece flourished on this isle (then called Thira). Then, in 1628 BCE, a massive volcanic eruption buried every sign of civilization beneath tons of lava and pumice. In the centuries since, fact and fiction have mingled, leading some to identify Santorini as Plato's lost continent of Atlantis. More serious historical speculation has convinced many scholars that the eruption on Santorini triggered a tidal wave large enough to account for the destruction of several Minoan sites in Crete.

SANTORINI (THIRA)

In 1967, Professor Spyridon Marinatos, an advocate of the latter theory, resumed excavations on the Akrotiri site. The Greek School later unearthed a town, preserved virtually intact, like Pompeii in Italy, beneath layers of volcanic pumice. Its paved streets are lined with multi-story houses, with wooden doors and windows.

Modern Santorini is really only the eastern crescent of what was once a circular island, originally called "Strongili," or round. The explosion in 1628 BCE left a crust of volcanic ash overstretching the hollow center of the island. When the crust caved in, water filled the resulting *caldera* (basin) that is now Santorini's harbor. The two islands to the west, **Thirasia** and **Aspronisi,** appear to be separate, but are in fact a continuation of the rim of the original island.

ORIENTATION AND PRACTICAL INFORMATION

As the final stop for many **ferries** in the Cyclades, and frequently a stop for some Crete-bound ferries, Santorini is easily accessible but incredibly crowded. Boats dock at one of the ports: **Athinios** is the most important and has frequent buses (at least 20 per day, 30min., 300dr) to Thira (the main town) and to Perissa Beach. Hostel-bound travelers can board the free shuttle bus to either Thira Youth Hostel or Perissa Youth Hostel. It is also possible to get free rides from the pension proprietors at the port. At the old port of **Thira,** you'll be confronted by a 587-step footpath leading up the cliff to the town above (a difficult 20-min. climb). The cable car o departs every 20 minutes from 6:40am-midnight and costs 700dr; or, for the same price, you can hire a mule. Boats dock at **Oia,** on the northern cape of the island.

Ferries depart for Peirais (3-6 per day, 10hr., 4998dr); Ios (6-10 per day, 1½hr., 1588dr); Paros (8-10 per day, 5hr., 2805dr); Naxos (6-8 per day, 4hr., 2592dr); Mykonos (3-5 per day, 7hr., 3092dr); Iraklion (1-3 per day, 8hr., 2957dr); Syros (1-2 per day, 6hr., 3581dr); Rhodes (2 per week, 16hr., 5669dr); Sikinos (6 per week, 1795dr); Folegandros (5 per week, 1790dr); Anafi (3 per week, 1801dr); and Milos (3 per week, 2650dr). Three ferries per week go to Sifnos (2785dr), Serifos (2948dr); and Kithos (3074dr); two per week to Kassos (3573dr); Karpathos (4199dr); and Thessaloniki (8348dr); and one per week to Skiathos (7150dr); Skyros (6417dr); and Amorgos (4434dr). **Flying Dolphins** serve Rafina (9216dr); Ios (2857dr); Paros (5716dr); Naxos (4867dr); Mykonos (6398dr); Syros (7168dr); Tinos (7122dr); and Amorgos (4434dr). **Olympic Airways** has **flights** from Santorini to Athens (6-8 per day, 20,200dr); one per day to Mykonos (13,900dr), Iraklion (13,900dr), and Rhodes (20,400dr); and Thessaloniki (3 per week, 27,300dr).

Renting a moped may be the ideal way to travel around the island, especially since the roads are well paved. During the summer, however, Santorini becomes densely crowded and moped dealers rent bikes to just about anyone. Inexperienced riders, poor bikes, and carefree drivers create a dangerous combination. If you choose to ride, make sure you're satisfied with the bike's quality, and be cautious. Travel by foot or bus (Santorini's service is excellent) may be a better option. The least painful choice is a half- (3000dr) or full-day (4500dr) bus tour. **Kamari Tours** (tel. 31 390 or 31 455), with offices all over, including 20m south of the bus station, is reputable. Other agencies may offer student discounts. There is a severe **water shortage** on Santorini; fresh water accounts for most of the price of rooms on the island.

■ Thira Town

The center of activity on the island is the capital city, **Thira** (Fira), which in Greek means "wild island." Some say that the harbor below the town plunges into a bottomless abyss which leads to the door between heaven and hell. Stepping off the bus from the port, you may conclude that hell is actually on this side of the door. First-time visitors have been known to wonder aloud if they have disembarked on the wrong island when confronted with the mess of glitzy shops, whizzing mopeds, and hordes of tourists. Fortunately, the ugly roadside strip is only one aspect of this multi-faceted town. Thira is perched on a cliff and the short walk to the town's west-

SANTORINI (THIRA)

ern edge, the *caldera*, reveals a stunning view of the harbor, Santorini's coastline, and the neighboring islands and volcano, making it a popular site for weddings and honeymoons. T Although the town is overrun with tourists in summer, nothing can destroy the pleasure of wandering among the narrow cobbled streets, inspecting the craft shops, and arriving at the western edge of town in time to watch the sun bathe the harbor in a magenta glow.

ORIENTATION AND PRACTICAL INFORMATION

It's easiest to navigate about Thira if you envision the city divided into three parts, each running north-south. Facing the street with the bus station behind you, a walk left and uphill will lead you to **Theotokopoulou Square,** which is full of travel agencies, banks, and restaurants galore. At the fork in the road, the street on the right is **25th Martiou Street,** the main paved road leading from the square north towards Oia. It is home to both of Thira's youth hostels (look for signs), as well as other accommodations. The second part houses Thira's back streets that are lined with jewelry stores, sweet shops and, by night, many of the best bars and discoes. To get here, head up from the left branch north of the bus stop to 25th Martiou and turn on to any westbound street. Farther west is the third part, the *caldera*, where expensive restaurants and art galleries are overshadowed only by the spectacular view.

Tourist Police: (tel. 22 649), on the main road south of the bus depot. Open 24hr. They share a building with the **police.**

Port Police: (tel. 22 239), on the main road, north of Theotokopoulou Sq.

Tourist Agencies: Dozens surround Theotokopoulou Sq. **Pelikan Travel** (tel. 22 220 or 23 667), on the northwestern corner of the square, has particularly efficient service. **Luggage storage** 300dr per day. Open daily 8am-11pm, or later.

OTE: (tel. 22 399), 100m north of square on road to Oia. Open daily 8am-10:30pm.

Banks: National Bank, on the avenue that branches off from the main road south from the square. Offers **currency exchange.** Open Mon.-Thurs. 8am-2pm, Fri. 8am-1:30pm. The **Agricultural Bank** and **Commercial Bank** also **exchange currency.** Both open Mon.-Thurs. 8am-2pm, Fri. 8am-1:30pm.

American Express: (tel. 22 624), in the office of **X-Ray Kilo Travel and Shipping Agency,** in the square. All AmEx services. Open daily 8am-11pm.

Flights: Olympic Airways (tel. 22 493). From the bus depot, go downhill on the main road, take your first left, then a right. Reserve 1-2 weeks in advance. Standby tickets possible (arrive 2hr. before take-off). Office open Mon.-Fri. 8:30am-4pm.

Buses: To Perissa (25 per day, 30min., 350dr); Kamari (40 per day, 20min., 200dr); Akrotiri (15 per day, 30min., 330dr); Athinios (10 per day, 15min., 300dr); Oia (25 per day, 30min., 240dr); and the airport (12 per day, 30min., 220dr).

Taxis: Call 22 555.

Moped and Car Rental: Try **Zeus Rent-A-Car** (tel. 24 013), next to Penguine laundry. Fiat Panda 12,000dr per day. Car prices in Santorini are high July-Aug. but often 25% less in off season. For mopeds, try **Marcos Rental** (tel. 23 877), 50m north of the square. Prices range from 3000dr for a 50cc to 3500dr for an 80cc moped. Free helmets included with every rental. Open daily 8:30pm-7pm.

International Bookstore: International Press (tel. 22 942), at the top of the plaza between Theotokopoulou Sq. and the cliff. Open daily 8:30am-10pm.

Laundromat: Penguine (tel. 22 168), north of the square on the left. For 5kg, wash 950dr, dry 900dr. Soap 200dr. Open daily 8:30am-3pm and 5-9pm.

Public Toilets: 25th Martiou St., down and across the street from the bus depot.

Pharmacy: (tel. 23 444), 20m north of bus station. Open daily 8:30am-10:30pm.

Medical Center: (tel. 22 237), first left off the main road down from the bus depot. Routine cases and free physicals daily 9am-2pm. Open for **emergencies** 24hr.

Post Office: (tel. 22 238; fax 22698), on 25th Martiou St., between the square and the bus stop. Open Mon.-Fri. 8am-2pm. **Postal Code:** 84700.

Telephone Code: 0286.

ACCOMMODATIONS

Santorini does not lack accommodations, but in summer the pensions and hotels are almost all booked by noon. The cheapest options, and your best bet if you arrive late, are the (non-HI) youth hostels in Thira—two at Perissa Beach and one at Oia; see Southern Santorini (p. 245) and Northern Santorini (p. 246). You can start hunting early the next morning for other lodgings. There are good accommodations in private homes all over the island, so don't hesitate to branch out. The settlement of **Karterados,** 2km south of Thira, provides many options. Private doubles in outlying towns run as low as 2500dr. Head for **Karterados, Messaria, Pyrgos, Emborio,** or any of the small inland towns along the main bus routes. Some hawkers at the port misrepresent their rooms, so be clear about where you are going and what you are getting. In Thira, doubles run roughly 10,000-12,000dr in high season. Prices listed below are for peak season; rates decrease by as much as 50% in off season.

Thira Youth Hostel (tel. 22 387), on the left roughly 300m north of the squares, set back 25m from the road to Oia. Clean, quiet, and livable dorm rooms, a few even quieter "small dormitories," and pension-quality private rooms with baths. Dorm rooms either mixed gender or women-only. Hot showers 24hr., but bring your own toilet paper. Free transportation to Perissa and Athinios. Reception open 24hr. Owner enforces quiet after 11pm. Open April-Oct. No smoking in dorm rooms. Check-out noon. Dorm beds 1700dr. Doubles 8000-9000dr.

Kontohori Youth Hostel (tel. 22 722, also 22 577 in summer only), down a slope roughly 400m north of the square; look for signs. Popular among the crowd working or staying for long spells on Santorini. Single-sex dorm beds. Reception open 24hr. Check-out noon. Hot showers 4-9pm only. Dorms 1500dr. Doubles 7500dr. Special rate for people staying in the hostel more than a week.

Kamares Youth Hostel (tel. 24 472), north of the square with a turn-off before Kontohori hostel; just above Thira Hostel. Single-sex dorm rooms. The beds available on the canopied roof are a good option. Reception open 8am-1pm and 5-9pm. Check-out noon. Hot showers 5-9pm only. Dorm beds 1300dr. Roof 1200dr.

Pension Andreas (tel. 22 587 or 23 562), one of a line of new, clean, and nearly identical pensions lining road to Santorini Camping. Prices jump high during July and Aug., but are affordable in off season. Doubles 12,000dr. Triples 15,000dr.

Villa Litsa (tel. 22 267), on 25th Martiou St.; north of the square on a noisy street. Go up the green astroturf stairs. Large, slightly ornate rooms with baths. Every 3 rooms share a kitchen. Open June-Sept. Doubles 9800dr. Triples 12,800dr.

Santorini Camping (tel. 22 944, 25 062 or 25 064; fax 25 065). Follow the blue signs leading east of the square inland. Lively atmosphere and shady campsites make this a great option for those who don't mind sleeping on the ground. Washing machine 1200dr (soap included). Swimming pool free for campers, 500dr for guests. Hot showers 5-9pm. Café, bar, and minimarket. Reception open 7am-midnight. Open April-Oct. 1300dr per person. 800dr per tent. 200dr per tent rental. 600dr per car. 400dr per motorbike.

FOOD AND ENTERTAINMENT

Escape from the bustle at **Nikolas Taverna** (tel. 24 550), on a side street a few blocks above Pelikan Travel (take a right at the Hotel Τατάκη). This traditional *taverna,* with a posted menu only in Greek serves delectable beef stew with noodles (1400dr) and stuffed tomatoes (800dr; open Mon.-Sat. noon-3pm and 6-11pm, Sun. 6-11pm). Overlooking the water, **Restaurant Niki (NIKH)** is one of the older restaurants on the caldera and serves relatively inexpensive food (*kalamari* 1100dr, 450dr, tuna *souvlaki* 1600dr; open daily 11am-1am). For a touch of elegance, try **Meridiana** (tel. 23 427), which features perhaps the best view in Thira. Diners watch the sunset from the highest spot on the caldera and chat and sip drinks. Entrees range in price from 1900-4800dr and include Thai specialties l (1600dr; open daily noon-3pm and 6pm-midnight; music and drinks until 3am). Or try **Alexandria's** (tel. 22 510), at the far left of the *caldera* below Hotel Atlantis (meal-sized appetizers around 2000dr). The cuisine is best described as Nouveau Greek—it's grandma's old recipes with creative new touches. Slightly higher on the main road is **The Roosters** (tel. 23 311), a good cheap restaurant with a special appeal for vegetarians (daily vegetarian plate 800dr, *dolmades* 580dr; open daily noon-3pm and 5:30pm-12:30am). The **Blue Note** bar is home to **Mama's Breakfast Café** (tel. 24 211), where the ebullient owner serves American-style breakfasts (pancakes with homemade syrup 700dr, yogurt with fruit 700dr; open daily 7am-1pm).

Close to both the Thira and the Kamares Youth Hostels is **Naoussa** (tel. 24 869), a simple open-air family restaurant serving standard Greek fare cooked by a kind family and recommended by locals (Naoussa special house potato salad 750dr, dolmades 500dr, stuffed vegetables 850dr; open daily noon-1am). **Sweet shops** litter the windy streets between the main road and the *caldera*, but tend to have uniform fare at uniformly high prices (*baklava* 350-400dr). Those with a real sweet tooth may want to check out the candy store **Popori** (tel. 24 184), near Restaurant Niki (350dr per 100g; open daily 9am-5pm). For the cheapest water around, head down the hill past the bus station until you spot the sign touting **Santo Wines/Supermarket/Coop,** which sells inexpensive water (90dr for a 1.5L bottle), cheap food (canned tuna 380dr), and various household products (open Mon.-Sat. 8am-9pm).

Thira's nightlife is deservedly well known, ranging from hot, packed clubs that rival Ios, to mellow jazz bars. **Tropical** (tel. 23 089), high up on the *caldera*, is usually hopping, and is run by a sweet California girl who knows how to mix drinks (beer 700dr). "Sunset coffees," like the Bob Marley Frappé—dark rum, kahlua, iced coffee, and cream, go well with the gorgeous sunset views over the *caldera* and the heavy bass that beats the night away (open daily noon-3 or 4am). The **Blue Note** (tel. 24 211) tends to be packed and has a free pool table (beer 400-700dr, pitchers 2100dr, cocktail specials 800dr). **Tithora Club** is built into a 14th-century cave on the east side of the road to Oia and is great for those who prefer hard, loud rock (beer 600-800dr). The watering-hole atmosphere of **Two Brothers** parties and drinkers often dance to what might be the bar's theme song—*Freedom*. Take a left at Hotel Tataki (beer 500-700dr; both open up at 10pm and stay open until 3, 4, 5, or 6am). The **Kira Thira Jazz Club** (tel. 22 770), a bohemian refuge with live jazz (beer or *sangria* 800dr, cover for live jazz 1000dr, includes first drink) is on the same street as Nikolas Tavern (open daily 11pm-3am). Later at night, discoes take over for some of the most intense, slickest dancing in Greece. Two of the more popular are the **Koo Club** (tel. 22 025) and **Enigma.** Most crank on into the wee hours and charge ridiculously high covers (1000-3000dr, with drinks priced to match). Across the road from the Thira Youth Hostel (and directly across from Mama's) is the **Backpacker's Bar** (tel. 22 853). The budget traveling community gathers here to enjoy the good prices and atmosphere. A large beer (16oz.) costs 500dr, and from 10pm to midnight is accompanied by a free shot (spirits 800-1000dr; open daily 5pm-late). Foreigners put pins on the large world map to show where they're from.

SIGHTS

Thira's **Archaeological Museum** (tel. 22 217), near the cable cars, holds an impressive collection of vases, mostly from the site of ancient Thira. Keep climbing upward in the alleys and follow the signs to the cable cars (open Tues.-Sun. 8am-3pm; admission 800dr, students 400dr). The private **Museum Megaro Gyzi** (tel. 23 077), housed in a restored Santorinian family's mansion, near Kamares Hostel, has an engrossing collection of old maps, engravings, and photographs of Santorini and other islands. In July and August, the museum hosts several classical music concerts and temporary art exhibitions (open May-Oct. Mon.-Sat. 10:30am-1:30pm and 5-8pm, Sun. 10:30am-4:30pm; admission 400dr, students 200dr, free on Sun.).

■ Southern Santorini

AKROTIRI

The archaeological site of **Akrotiri,** where extensive excavations are still underway, bewilders novices. With the aid of a helpful guide book (1200dr), it's easy to breeze through on your own; the less adventuresome folks tag along with the guided tours. Bus tours (4000-4500dr through any travel agency like Kamari Tours or Pelikan) are coupled with a visit to **Profitias Ilias Monastery** and a local wine-tasting. Professor Marinatos found the paved streets of Akrotiri lined with houses connected by a sophisticated central drainage system. Each house had at least one room lined with wall paintings, some among the most magnificent in Greece. Since only heavy objects, and no valuables, were found, a common theory is that everyone escaped before the eruption (site open Tues.-Sun. 8am-3pm; admission 1000dr, students 500dr, free on Sun.). Fifteen buses per day run here (280dr).

BEACHES

Santorini's two most frequented black sand **beaches** are **Perissa** and **Kamari** on the southeast coast. Perissa, the farther of the pair, is more popular with students and offers two youth hostels, camping, and a casual nightlife. The black sand sizzles in the sun—a straw mat and sandals would be welcome accessories. The water here, as elsewhere on the island, is brisk and clear with a slippery rock and seaweed bottom. Five minutes from Akrotiri is **Red Beach,** named for the reddish rock formations on the coast. Akrotiri is not a convenient place to stay (and it's really dusty).

Perissa

The **Perissa Youth Hostel** (tel. 81 639; fax 286 82 668), 400m along the road leading out of town, has a swimming pool, 24-hour hot salt water showers, and kitchen facilities. Reception is open 7am-11pm. (Dorm beds 1500dr. Compartment beds 1700dr. Room beds 2500dr. Private rooms 3500dr. Sheets 200dr. Pillow and case 500dr. Continental breakfast 500dr.) Up and across the street, **Youth Hostel Anna** (tel. 82 182) provides new, clean women's and mixed dorms and a connected restaurant (Dave's Place). Reception is open 24 hours. (Hot showers 11am-5pm. Checkout 11:30am. Dorm beds 1800dr.) Enormous **Perissa Camping** (tel. 81 343) is adjacent to the beach. (Check-out 1pm. 1300dr per person. 800dr per tent.) Rooms in private homes (you'll meet the proprietors at the dock) offer more privacy. (Doubles range 6000-8000dr.) The delicious calzones, pizza, and pasta at **Bella Italiana,** near the end of the main road, make taste buds hot for more (hot pepper and onion calzone 1150dr; open daily 11am-1 or 2am). **Dave's Place** (tel. 82 182) serves simple food, but diners get a free glass of wine with every meal (Amstel 100dr, cocktails 500dr; open daily 9am-2 or 3am). The open-air bar at **Beer Garden** (beer 300dr and up, cocktails 600dr) is an affordable choice near the hostels. Roughly 25 buses per day travel from Thira to Perissa, stopping in Pyrgos.

Kamari

Kamari Beach is closer to Thira and more popular with well-to-do tourists. Forty buses per day (175dr) travel from Thira, and a rocky **shuttle boat** scoots between Kamari and Perissa as well (every 30min., 9am-5pm, 800dr). The long beach is covered in umbrellas and lined with pricey hotels, cafés, and travel agencies. Double rooms range from 8000-24,000dr. Contact **Kamari Tours** (tel. 31 390), or stop in the office on the waterfront. The **Pension Golden Star** is on the road that goes inland from the beach at the Yellow Donkey Disco. It has clean double rooms with balconies (8000dr). To pick up an inexpensive snack along the waterfront you can head to **Ariston** (tel. 32 603). Betwixt the touristy restaurants and *souvlaki* shops, this bakery and small grocery sells fresh loaves of bread baked on the premises (0.5kg loaf 50dr) and raisin bread twists (200dr; open daily 6:30am-11pm). The **Yellow Donkey Disco** (tel. 31 462) is one of the busier clubs along the waterfront of

SANTORINI (THIRA)

Kamari Beach. The club is often crowded with people who come from all over the island to enjoy the 1000dr cocktails that come with a free shot (open daily 9pm-late). **Kamari Camping** (tel. 31 453), 1km inland along the main road out of town, is open June through September. (1200dr per person. 1000dr per tent.) The winery **Canava Roussos** (tel. 31 954, -278), 1km from the campsite, will wine and dine you (100dr per glass; open daily 10am-8pm).

Monolithos

Those who prefer sandier beaches might want to check out **Monolithos Beach.** More popular with locals than with tourists, this smallish beach is easily accessible due to its proximity to the airport (15 buses per day, 190dr). If you want a bite to eat, the fish *taverna* **Skaramagas** (tel. 31 750) is the least expensive on the strip. Fresh seafood is caught by the father of the family who owns the business; they keep what they need for the restaurant, and sell the rest to other establishments in the area. Many locals come here for lunch several times per week to enjoy the famed *kakavia* (special fish soup 1500dr), *kalamari* (1200dr), or a great Greek salad (700dr; restaurant open May-Oct. daily 11am-11pm or midnight).

PYRGOS AND ANCIENT THIRA

Buses to Perissa stop in lofty **Pyrgos,** which is surrounded by medieval walls. Once a Venetian fortress, the town then came under Turkish rule until 1828. The village's 25 blue- and green-domed churches dot the horizon. The **Profitis Ilias Monastery,** a 20-minute hike up the mountain from Pyrgos, lugubriously shares its site with a radar station. On July 20, the monastery hosts the **Festival of Profitis Ilias.** From Profitias Ilias, it's approximately a one-hour hike to the ruins of ancient **Thira.** The ancient theater, church, and forum of the island's old capital are still visible, though less spectacular than the Akrotiri excavations (open Tues.-Sun. 8am-3:30pm; free). Cheerful, whitewashed **Emborio,** some 3km inland from Perissa, has frequent bus connections to the beach and to Thira.

▓ Northern Santorini

OIA

Oia (pronounced EE-ah), an intricate cliffside town on the northwestern tip of the island, famous for its dazzling sunsets, is a fascinating mixture of devastation and renewal. The 1956 earthquake leveled this small town on the island's rocky north point. Its present 600 inhabitants have carved new dwellings into the cliffside among the shattered ruins of the old. Although the budget traveler will not thrive long in Oia, an afternoon visit affords enough time to wander the cobbled streets; window-shop at exquisite jewelry, craft, and embroidery shops; and glance at the menus of elegant, expensive restaurants before the riveting descent of the sun. A 20-minute climb down 252 stone stairs at the end of the main road brings you to rocky **Ammoudi** beach, with a few boats moored in a startlingly deep swimming lagoon. **Buses** run from Thira to Oia (25 per day, 15-30min., 240dr), and a few **ferries** dock at Oia before continuing to Thira or Athinios—check when you buy your ticket.

After a relaxing few hours spent lying around on and among the rocks, and another few swimming in the beautiful, deep blue water, climbing back up the cliff may seem like no small task. You can hire a **donkey** to carry you to the top; with surprising speed, it'll sprint up the stairs as its trainer follows on his own donkey yelling a Greek version of "Giddy Up!" (700dr per person).

If you opt to stay in Oia, you'll probably cross paths with Manolis or Markos Karvounis. Their family runs Youth Hostel Oia, the Karvounis Tours travel agency, and the Neptune restaurant. **Karvounis Tours** (tel. 71 290, -2; fax 71-291) can give you information about the Youth Hotel, traditional cave house rental, Oia itself, Santorini, and other general travel information, including ferry and airline tickets. The

Youth Hotel Oia (tel. 71 465; fax 71 291) is the classiest of Santorini's youth hostels. Painted bright white with bold blue trim and decorated by gorgeous pink flowers, it has a superb view from the roof terrace and a bar open for breakfast or evening drinks. When it's full below, the roof is available. (1500-3200dr per person. Hot water 24hr. Breakfast included. Wheelchair accessible.) Oia prides itself on being an escape from the rest of the world and is a popular site for honeymoons and weddings. This atmosphere makes it difficult to find short-term accommodations—most proprietors expect a stay of at least five days.

Likewise, dining will cost you a bit more than in Thira, but some restaurants serve exceptional food. At the end of the **main road** in Oia, overlooking the *caldera,* is the oldest restaurant in Oia, **Petros** (tel. 71 009), opened in 1948. Petros' son, Petros, continues the family tradition of making homemade wines and catching much of the seafood served in the restaurant. His Santorinian tomato balls are especially delicious in June and July, when Santorini's special fresh cherry tomatoes are available (800dr). Fresh, savory seafood is grilled to absolute perfection (*kalamari* 1200dr; open April-Oct. daily 5pm-midnight).

Melissa's Vegetarian and Prano Café (tel. 71 305) serves vegetarian brunch, lunch, and dinner. From 9pm until late, it has live jazz piano music that wafts up to the beautiful rooftop terrace. Among the items for sale are yogurt with dried fruit, nuts, honey, and cinnamon (1500dr); cappuccino (800dr); banana splits (2500dr); and a variety of cocktails (1200-1500dr). They also have English books in the café (open daily 11:30am-3pm and 6pm-late). The Karvounis' **Neptune** (tel. 71 294) offers stuffed tomatoes (1200dr) and a special *moussaka* (1400dr). **Restaurant Lotza** (tel. 71 357) is ideal for lunch with a view, serving up curried chicken (1600dr), eggplant with yogurt (1500dr), and (for breakfast) yogurt with walnuts and fruit (900dr; open daily 9am-midnight). **Café Greco** (tel. 71 014) has *gyros* in pita for 400dr or vegetables with cheese and pita (400dr; open daily 11am-1am). There is a small but inexpensive and complete **grocery/bakery** (tel. 71 121) close to the square in which the buses stop. Either follow the signs for the bakery or the crowds of hungry customers who come for fresh loaves (150dr) and creative croissants and pies (170-350dr; open Mon.-Sat. 7am-9pm, Sun. 7am-2pm).

The bus route between Thira and Oia passes through the tiny town of **Imerovigli.** Ask the driver to let you off if you want to explore. Imerovigli's sunset is said to rival that of Oia and Thira, and the town hosts fewer members of the camera-toting set.

■ Thirasia and Surrounding Islands

Santorini's unspoiled junior partner, Thirasia (pop. 300), is worthy of a detour. Built along the island's upper ridge, the villages of **Manolas** and **Potamos** have spine-tingling views of Santorini's western coast. Thirasia offers a refreshing change from the Cycladic crowds. The only way to reach Manolas is to climb the steep road (30min.) or take a donkey (about 1000dr). You'll be better off if you walk when the sun is low—chances are it'll be pretty steamy. As you reach the top, you'll find a *taverna* on your left and a minimarket on the right. Farther down on the right is another *taverna,* with a breezy roof terrace. Manolas has no hotels, but you can ask a donkey owner at the dock to direct you to private "Rooms to Let."

Excursions to Thirasia are often coupled with trips to the **volcanic crater** and **hot springs** and sometimes Oia as well. Tours can be found at the various travel agencies (1500-5000dr). Trips to the volcano and hot springs, as inexpensive as 1500dr roundtrip, can be wonderfully convivial. Be forewarned that to get to the hot sulphur springs, you'll have to swim through cold water first; to get to the volcano's crater, you'll have to hike uphill for 30 minutes. **Theoskepasti agency** in the main square in Thira has trustworthy daily trips to the volcano for 1500dr, on a boat by the same name (Theoskepasti) that leaves from the old port of Thira at 3pm. As with most trips and excursions, reservations should be made a day in advance.

PAROS

PAROS ΠΑΡΟΣ

The geographical center of the islands and third largest of the Cyclades, Paros seems to gracefully absorb the hordes of tourists that arrive each summer. Its historical claim to fame is its pure white marble, slabs of which have been sculpted into the renowned Venus de Milo as well as parts of Napoleon's mausoleum in Paris. Paros is a favorite destination for many travelers because of its golden beaches and tangled whitewashed villages. More importantly, Paros has the necessary means to accommodate tourists without fully relinquishing its idyllic Cycladic aura. Paros is also a convenient base for excursions to other islands.

■ Paroikia

Behind Paroikia's shallow commercial façade, flower-filled streets wind beneath archways, past two-story whitewashed houses, historic basilica, and windmills.

ORIENTATION AND PRACTICAL INFORMATION

From the ferry, most restaurants, hotels, and offices lie to the left (facing inland). Straight ahead, past the windmill and the tourist offices, is the main square, behind which a whitewashed labyrinth brims with shops and cafés. To the far right around the bend, a host of bars, the island's party district, await. Starting around September 10, foreigners can earn measly wages during the two-week grape harvest.

Tourist Office: (tel. 24 528), to the right of the windmill, facing inland. **Exchanges currency.** Information on buses, sights, and beaches, and free maps of the island. Open daily 8:30am-12:30am.

Tourist Agency: The **General Travel Agency** (tel. 22 092; fax 21 983), next door to the OTE. Has up-to-the-minute ferry, hydrofoil, and airplane schedules. Open daily 8am-1am.

Banks: National Bank (tel. 21 298). From the windmill, head to the main square inland and to the right—it's at the far corner past the playground in the fortress-like building. **ATM** and **currency exchange** machine available 24hr. Bank open Mon.-Thurs. 8am-2pm, Fri. 8am-1:30pm.

OTE: (tel. 22 139), one block to the right of the windmill (its back borders the main square). Open Mon.-Fri. 7:30am-11pm, Sat.-Sun. 8am-11pm.

Flights: Olympic Airways (tel. 21 900, 22 511), in the main square to the far right of the National Bank. Open Mon.-Fri. 8am-3pm. 6 flights per day to Athens (17,100dr). Take a taxi to the airport (2000dr), or catch the bus to Aliki (270dr).

Buses: (tel. 21 395, -133). Complete schedule posted in the shack a few blocks to the left of the windmill (facing inland). Buses run to Naoussa (20-30 per day, 15min., 220dr); Lefkes (10 per day, 25min., 240dr); Pounda (19 per day, 15min., 190dr); Aliki and the airport (10 per day, 30min., 270dr); Piso Livadi (17 per day, 40min., 380dr); Chrisi Akti (17 per day, 50min., 500dr); Drios (17 per day, 1hr., 500dr); Marpissa (17 per day, 35min., 380dr); Kamares (2 per day, 20min., 190dr); and the Valley of the Butterflies (8 per day, 10min., 190dr).

Ferries: Sail to Peiraias (5-8 per day, 5-6hr., 3890dr); Naxos (6-10 per day, 1hr., 1330dr); Ios (4-9 per day, 2½hr., 2315dr); Santorini (6-9 per day, 3½hr., 2655dr); Mykonos (1-3 per day, 2hr., 1600dr); Syros (1-7 per day, 1½hr., 1445dr); Amorgos (6 per week, 3hr., 2480dr); Rhodes (6 per week, 16hr., 5930dr); Crete (8 per week, 8hr., 4300dr); Thessaloniki (5 per week, 10hr., 7590dr); Sifnos (1 per week, 2hr., 2480dr); Samos (6 per week, 6hr., 3700dr); Ikaria (6 per week, 4hr., 2600dr); Tinos (4 per week, 1585dr); Kos (4 per week, 3675dr); Anafi (3 per week, 3100dr); Sikinos (7 per week, 1710dr); Astypalea (3 per week, 3705dr); Coufonisia (3 per week, 2315dr); Folegandros (6 per week, 1710dr); Volos (1 per week, 5835dr); and Rafina (1 per week, 3306dr).

Flying Dolphins: Catamarans and hydrofoils speed to Santorini (2-3 per day, 5565dr); Mykonos (3-5 per day, 3100dr); Ios (2-3 per day, 4821dr); Naxos (2-3 per day, 2530dr); Syros (4 per week, 2630dr); Rafina (9 per week, 7370dr); Tinos (2-4 per day, 3100dr); Amorgos (1 per week, 5356dr); Coufonisia (2 per week, 4300dr); and Sifnos (1 per week, 3985dr).

Taxis: (tel. 21 500). Look for them inland and to the right of the windmill.

Luggage Storage: (tel. 23 582). Look for blue and yellow Left Luggage signs across the windmill in the first shop area. 300-500dr per day. Open daily 8am-1am.

Laundromat: For full- or self-service, go past the bus station and look for **Top** (tel. 23 424), on your right just after the ancient ruins. Wash, dry, soap, and folding (optional) for 1800dr. Open daily 8am-11pm.

Public Toilets: Beside the small blue and white church to the left of the windmill.

International Bookstore: M.K. Bizas (International Press; tel. 21 247), past the National Bank; head straight and it's on your right. Large selection of English books (2500dr) and newspapers (350-400dr). Open daily 8am-11pm.

Pharmacies: (tel. 22 223), next to the self-service laundromat. Open daily 8:30am-1:30pm and 5:30-8:30pm. Others abound, particularly in the old town.

Medical Clinic: (tel. 22 500), across the street from the toilets. Free physicals. Open Mon.- Fri. 7am-2:30pm. Open for emergencies 24hr.

Police: (tel. 23 333), across the square behind the OTE, on the 2nd floor above the photo shops. Open 24hr. **Tourist police** (tel. 21 673), in the same building. Open 9am-3:30pm. **Port Police** (tel. 21 240), off the waterfront, past the bus station. Information about all sailings. Open 24hr.

Post Office: On the left side of the waterfront, 2 blocks past the bus stop. Open Mon.-Fri. 7:30am-2pm. **Postal Code:** 84400.

Telephone Code: 0284.

ACCOMMODATIONS

Many hotels and "Rooms to Let" are near the waterfront and in the old town, but a slew of new, fairly cheap pensions and boarding houses have opened up behind the town beach. The dock hawks often offer good deals and many represent better options in Naoussa, Piso Livadi, and Antiparos. Just make sure it's not too far from where you want to be. In off season, rooms are 20-40% less than the prices listed.

Festos Pension (tel. 21 635; fax 24 193), turn right on the street before the waterfront church. Sister to its swinging namesake in Athens. 2500-4000dr per person. Laundry 1000dr. Luggage storage 300dr. Check-out 10am. Reserve early.

Parasporos Camping (tel. 22 268 or 21 100), 1500m south of the port with shuttle service. Showers, laundry, and kitchen. 900dr per person. 500dr per tent.

Koula Camping (tel. 22 081, -082), 400m north of town on the beach. Amenities include market, laundry, and kitchen. 1000dr per person. 500dr per tent.

FOOD

As usual, the more authentic places tend to be away from the water. Inland, many *tavernas* have pleasant gardens.

L'Italiano, left of the waterfront. Sick of Italian food cooked by Greeks? Head here for the real stuff. Excellent *gnocchi* with bleu cheese and zucchini 1300dr.

Happy Green Cow (tel. 24 691), a block farther inland off the main square behind the National Bank. Good vegetarian food in a psychedelic setting. *Falafel* 800dr, *soya gyros* 500dr. Open daily noon-1am.

To Tamarisko, near Mimikos Rooms—follow the signs. Lush flower garden, romantic setting. Meatballs 1200dr, pork "Tamarisko" 1600dr.

Levantes (tel. 23 613), near Hotel Dina on the "Market" street beyond the National Bank. Middle Eastern and Greek delicacies. Tabouli 700dr, hummus 700dr.

Nick's Hamburgers, next to Corfo Leon. Paros' first hamburger joint, established 1977. 100% beef. Nikburger 430dr. Nikfeast (2 burgers, chips, and salad) 890dr.

PAROS

ENTERTAINMENT

Almost all of Paros' nightspots are along the waterfront, left of the windmill. On any given night, throngs of foreigners congregate on the strip, sit in circles around *ouzo* bottles, and sing drunken songs. On the far end of the ferry dock, just before the small white bridge, are hangouts for English-speakers. **Irish Bar Stavros** has a rambunctious crowd which periodically dances on the bar bathed in Irish memorabilia. There's also an incongruously sedate garden (beer 500dr, cocktails 1000dr). **The Slammer Bar/7 Muses Disco,** specializes in tequila slammers for 400dr—there are posted instructions for the uninitiated. **The Paros Experience** consists of two mind-boggling party complexes which round out any night out on Paros. The larger of the two, at the far end of the strip of bars, contains under one roof **The Dubliner, Down Under, Cactus Shots Bar,** and the **Hard Rock Club.** Sit around or dance to any of the four tunes blaring simultaneously (beer 600-700dr, cocktails 1000dr). A little closer to town is the other boozing megaplex, containing **The Londoner, Tequila Bar,** and **Sodoma Dance Club** (beer 600-700dr, cocktails 1000dr). **Aroma's Café** is there for you when you're hungry and everything has closed (open 24hr.).

SIGHTS

Anyone with a fondness for Byzantine architecture will be enraptured by the **Panagia Ekatontapiliani** (The Church of Our Lady of 100 Gates), an imposing 6th-century edifice that houses three separate adjacent churches, cloisters, and a large peaceful courtyard resplendent with pear and orange trees. Only 10 of the 100 doors are immediately obvious—don't waste your time counting. The main structure is the mammoth **Church of the Assumption,** with three tremendous chandeliers. **Church of St. Nikolas** (the oldest of the three) flanks this central structure to the north as does the **baptistry** to the south. To reach the church, walk inland from the public garden (tel. 21 243; open daily 8am-9pm). In the courtyard there are two tiny museums, the **Church Museum** on the right (open Mon., Wed., and Fri.-Sun. 9am-1pm and 5:30-9pm; admission 500dr) and the **Byzantine Museum,** next to the entrance (open daily 9am-1pm and 5-9pm; admission 500dr). Behind the church, next to the schoolyard, is the **Archaeological Museum** (tel. 21 231), which includes a 5th-century BCE statue of Wingless Nike and a piece of the Parian Chronicle (open Tues.-Sun. 8:30am-2:30pm; admission 500dr, students 300dr, Sun. free).

Just 10km south of town is the cool, spring-fed **Valley of the Butterflies** (Petaloudes), home to an enormous spawning swarm of brown-and-white-striped butterflies. These amazing creatures cover the foliage, blending into their surroundings until they expose their bright red underwings in flight. In June, the butterflies converge on this lepidopterous metropolis to mate. You can visit by taking the bus from Paroikia that goes to Aliki (15 per day, 10min., 190dr). Ask to be let off at the butterflies (*petaloudes*). From there, follow the signs up the steep winding road 2km to the entrance. You can also take a tour from one of the various travel agents (2500dr), although it would be a shame to be whisked through here too quickly (open Mon.-Sat. 9am-8pm, Sun. 9am-1pm and 4-8pm; admission 230dr).

If you're wandering through Paroikia's old town, look for the **Frankish Castle,** whose walls were built with marble removed from the ancient **Temple of Athena.** You can actually spot the temple's columns in the Venetian structure. To get there, take a right after the international bookstore and look for it near the top of the hill. At the top of the same hill is the charming, yet eerie, Byzantine **Church of Agios Konstantinos,** and to the right of the church, overlooking the archipelago, are the foundations of Athena's Temple, set there in 525 BCE.

■ Naoussa

Naoussa is a pleasant alternative to Paroikia. It is a natural harbor and a popular port, cradled on both sides by long, sandy arms in the shape of crab claws. Ancient Persians, Greeks, Romans, medieval Venetians, Saracens, Turks, and Russians have all anchored in the harbor. The tradition continues today as visitors the world over converge on Naoussa's magnificent beaches and dizzying array of accommodations, restaurants, and shops. Although much of the town has been usurped by this current influx, a stroll along the harbor proves that beneath its tourist-friendly exterior, Naoussa remains, at heart, a traditional Greek fishing village.

Orientation and Practical Information   Naoussa's layout is not very complicated. From the bus stop facing the water, the road heading left past the little bridge leads to the beaches of **Kolimbithies** and **Monastiri.** On the right is Naoussa's commercial strip flanking the town. If you walk along the waterfront, you'll see how the harbor wraps around the town. On the road to Kolimbithies is the **OTE** (tel. 51 499), on the left (open Mon.-Sat. 7:30am-10pm, Sun. 9am-2pm and 4-9pm) and farther down the **police** (tel. 51 202), on the steps after OTE on the right (open 24hr.). On the commercial strip, directly across from the bus stop, is the **medical center** (tel. 51 216), on the second floor (open Mon.-Fri. 9am-1:30pm). Further down, on the left, is the **General Bookstore** (tel. 51 121), which sells English books from Shakespeare to Danielle Steele. On the same road, 400m down (passing by the blue-domed church), you'll find the **post office** (tel. 51 495), just past the Santa Maria turn-off (open Mon.-Fri. 7:30am-2pm). On the waterfront, just to the right of the little bridge, is the **pharmacy** (tel. 51 550; for emergencies 51 004; open Mon.-Sat. 8:30am-2:30pm and 5:30-11pm, Sun. 10am-2:30pm and 5:30-11pm). Along the marina, as it curves right and then left, is the **National Bank** (open Mon.-Thurs. 8:30am-2pm, Fri. 8:45am-1:30pm). **Postal Code:** 84401. **Telephone Code:** 0284.

   Buses head from Paroikia to Naoussa roughly every 30 minutes and every hour during *siesta* (30 per day, 15min., 220dr). From Naoussa, there are also bus connections to Santa Maria (4 per day); Ampelas (2 per day); Piso Livadi (7 per day); Drios (7 per day); and back to Paroikia (40 per day). Consult the detailed schedule at the bus stop booth. **Taxi boats** also leave Naoussa for nearby beaches. The little blue booth on the waterfront across from the first stretch of cafés sells roundtrip tickets to Kolimbithies (12min., 500dr), Monastiri (15min., 600dr), Laggeri (20min., 750dr), and Santa Maria (50min., 1500dr). If you're looking for the true Greek fishing experience, it'll cost you 2500dr. A fishing boat takes curious tourists along every Thursday morning at 7am, to help drop the nets, and brings them back at 10am.

Accommodations   For a small town, Naoussa offers many hotels and "Rooms to Let." In off season, prices decrease by 20-40%. **Pension Hara** (tel. 51 011), at the top of the stairs just past the OTE, has clean rooms with balconies and refrigerators. (Doubles 11,500-15,000dr.) Right next to the bus stop, **Hotel Aliprantis** (tel. 51 571, -648) is convenient. (Doubles 11,500dr and up.) English-speaking Katerina at **Simitzi Tours** (tel. 51 113; fax 51 761), opposite the bus stop, rents studios with kitchens. (Open 8:30am-11pm in high season. Doubles 7000-11,000dr. Quads 12,000-17,000dr. Rates depend on season.) "Rooms to Let" cost roughly 5000-11,000dr for doubles and 6000-13,000dr for triples. There are two campsites near Naoussa. **Camping Naoussa** (tel. 51 595) awaits on the road to Kolimbithies. (1300dr per person. 800dr per tent.) **Camping Surfing Beach** (tel. 51 013 or 51 491; fax 51 937), 4km towards Santa Maria, hosts waterskiing, windsurfing, and other summer fun stuff. (1300dr per person. 800dr per tent.)

Food and Entertainment   Naoussa kitchens are famed for cooking up superb seafood. If you follow the waterfront as it bends rightward, you'll come to a crowded cluster of *tavernas.* **To Ouzeri ton Naftikon** in this square is the embodiment of the traditional, unpretentious Greek *taverna* with excellent and cheap fresh fish. **Diamantis,** behind the church, is an excellent choice for Greek fare (swordfish *souvlaki* 1100dr, stuffed tomatoes 850dr). **Zorba's,** with eye-catching pink tablecloths and blue chairs, is in front of the church (4-cheese tortellini 1350dr, *pastitsio* 950dr; open 24hr.; Visa accepted). For dessert, **To Paradosiako** (tel. 52 240) is unbeatable for its mouthwatering *loucoumodes* (donut holes in syrup,

500dr) and traditional island sweets. From the commercial street, turn left at the Naoussa pastry shop and continue past the little white church. Look for a brown wooden sign and a pan of *loucoumodes* in the window (open daily 5:30pm-1am). There are quite a few low-key cafés and bars mixed in with the *tavernas*—look for dimmed lights and groovy music. All the noise in Naoussa comes from **Amemoesa** (tel. 51 108), a bar/disco on the main road near the post office (open daily 2-8am). If you can't stay up that late, try your luck swatting mosquitoes at the **outdoor movie theater** next to Diamantis (shows nightly at 10pm). On the first Sunday in July, cruise around Naoussa's harbor and feast on free fish and wine as you watch traditional dancing at the **Wine and Fish Festival.** On August 23, festivities commemorate a naval victory over the Turks.

■ Around Paros Island

Cutting through the center of the island towards the east coast, you'll reach **Marathi,** 5km from Paroikia. The marble quarries that made Paros famous in ancient times are nearby. Still considered to be among the finest in the world, Parian marble is translucent up to 3mm thick, one-third the opacity of most other marble. The quarries are now idle (they're also difficult to find).

Lefkes, 5km from Marathi, was the largest village on the island in the 19th century when Parians moved inland to escape the pirates swashbuckling off the coast. Now a quiet village of 400 inhabitants, its classic Cycladic architecture makes it the prettiest town in Paros' interior. Road meets sea at **Piso Livadi,** 11km from Lefkes. If you're not into Paroikia's nightlife, Piso Livadi can be a fine place to while away your hours on Paros. **Perantinos Travel & Tourism** (tel./fax 41 135), across from the bus stop, provides information on rooms around town as well as an international phone (open daily 9am-10pm). Doubles range from 6000-8000dr, depending on season and quality. Up the street from the bus stop toward Paroikia are two straightforward, clean, hotels. **Hotel Piso Livadi** (tel. 41 309) offers doubles with bath for 10,000dr. (Triples with bath 12,500dr.) The **Londos Hotel** (tel. 41 218) offers the same prices. Serene **Camping Captain Kafkis** (tel. 41 479) is roughly 1km back along the same road. (820dr per person. 500dr per small tent. 650dr per large tent.)

Buses run from Paroikia to **Pounda** (25 per day, 15min., 170dr) and **Aliki** (15 per day, 40min., 250dr) on Paros' west coast, home of pleasant, remote beaches. From Pounda, 30 boats per day cross to **Antiparos** (10min., 150dr). There are also boats from Paroikia's harbor to **Krios, Martselo,** and **Kaminia** beaches (every 15min., 9:30am-7pm, 15min., 340dr), all of which are relatively calm and secluded.

■ Near Paros: Antiparos

Like Piso Livadi on mainland Paros, Antiparos is a quiet, easygoing alternative to Paroikia and Naoussa. Those uninterested, or unable, to find rooms on Paros take refuge here. Literally "opposite Paros," Antiparos is so close to its neighbor that, according to local lore, travelers once signaled the ferryman on Paros by opening the door of a chapel on Antiparos. Its proximity and unique underground caves also make Antiparos a popular daytrip. From Paroikia, take a direct boat (14 per day, 45min., 410dr one way), or one of the 25 daily buses to Pounda (15min., 200dr) followed by one of 30 daily boats to Antiparos (10min., 150dr one way).

Orientation and Practical Information   Most of this small island is undeveloped—virtually all of its 700 inhabitants live in the town at which the ferry docks, and there's no bus service (except to the stalactite caves). At the harbor you'll find a few waterfront restaurants and several hotels and pensions. Tourist shops, *tavernas,* and bakeries line the street leading from the dock to the center of town, where a cluster of funky pubs and bars have opened up. The center has a wide-open plaza with cafés under shady trees. Go through the stone archway to the right of the square to reach the **Castle of Antiparos,** a village built in the 1440s.

Oliaros Tours (tel. 61 231; fax 61 496), on the waterfront next to the National Bank, assists with finding rooms (doubles with bath and refrigerator 8000dr) and has boat and bus schedules. It also has an international telephone and currency exchange. The **National Bank** next door is open only in high season (Mon.-Fri. 9am-1pm). The **post office** is on the left side of the street leading from the waterfront to the square (open Mon.-Fri. 8am-1pm). Past the post office the road bends left and passes the diminutive **OTE,** which will be on your right just before the road opens into the main square (open Mon.-Fri. 8:30am-12:30pm and 5-10:30pm). Closer to the water on the same street are the self-service **laundry** (wash, dry, and soap 2000dr; open daily 10am-2pm and 5-8pm) and an **English bookstore** (tel. 61 255). Behind the unobtrusive wooden sign hides a stupendous collection of new and used books, both meaty and cheesy, in English (500-1500dr; open daily 10am-4pm and 7pm-midnight). The number for the **police** is 61 202, for a **doctor** 61 219. **Postal Code:** 84007. **Telephone Code:** 0284.

Accommodations   The **Mantalena Hotel** (tel. 61 206), to the right of the dock (facing inland), has clean rooms with private baths and balconies. (Doubles 8000dr, with bath 12,000dr. Triples with bath 14,000dr.) On the road to Camping Antiparos, the **Theologos Hotel** (tel. 61 244) offers sunny rooms with gleaming bathrooms. (Doubles 6000-8000dr.) Pleasant, cheap (6000dr) rooms lie inland to the left of the harbor (facing town). **Camping Antiparos** (tel. 61 221) is 800m northwest of town on Ag. Yiannis Theologos Beach. (900dr per person. 200dr per tent.)

Food, Entertainment, and Sights   Some excellent restaurants include **Taverna Klimataria** (take a left down the alley next to the bookstore), under blazing pink azalea bushes (*kalamari* 1000dr, Greek salad 800dr), and **O Spyros** next to the National Bank on the waterfront (*kalamari* with pasta 800dr). The inland main square is jam-packed with rock 'n' roll bars and watering holes, as Antiparos follows the lead of its neighbors. Choose your favorite ambience from among **Time Pub, Clown Pub, The Doors,** and many more. Beers run 400-700dr.

Antiparos' main attraction is its cool, wet stalactite caves at the south end of the island. Names of the caves' famous visitors are written on the walls with their years of entry (alongside some of their less famous 20th-century counterparts who took it upon themselves to leave a mark). Some of the stalactites were broken off by Russian naval officers in the 18th century and "donated" to a St. Petersburg museum while still more were destroyed by Italians during WWII. Despite the graffiti and history of theft, the caves, plunging 100m down into the earth, retain their beauty. Ask a ticket taker about the various stories associated with the caves—how Queen Amalia lost her earrings in 1840 or how a team of French archaeologists spent Christmas, 1673, inside. **Excursion buses** run from Antiparos' port every morning hour (20min., roundtrip 1000dr; caves open 10:15am-4:45pm; 400dr).

NAXOS ΝΑΞΟΣ

Alluring interior villages and tranquil beaches draw a crowd of old and young alike to the Cyclades' largest and most fertile island. Naxos' rocky promontories, squat windmills, and demure villages tucked between rolling hills are still illuminated by one of the sky's brighter stars. Natural wealth has made the island one of the richer of the Cyclades, a fact which becomes apparent on a short walk through town of Naxos. The island's independence of foreign money is a refreshing change.

Naxos has one of the more colorful Cycladic histories: Parians, Cretans, Ionians, Athenians, Macedonians, Egyptians, Rhodians, Romans, Byzantines, Venetians, Turks, and Russians all ruled the island in succession. The island's strongest historical link, however, is shrouded in myth. After Ariadne, the daughter of King Minos of Crete, saved Theseus from her father's labyrinth, the young prince fled with her to

Naxos. After they had spent the night there, Theseus, who said he was going to wash his hair, abandoned her. Even mythical princes are only after one thing. Ariadne wept at finding herself alone on the shore, but her despair was soon remedied. Along came Dionysus who, on his way, had quite an adventure. Captured by pirates, he immobilized the ship's sails with spontaneously growing vines and turned the malevolent buccaneers into serpents and himself into a lion. Arriving on Naxos, Dionysus married Ariadne. When she died, the god put her bridal wreath among the stars where the Corona Borealis shines today.

■ Naxos Town

As you drift into the harbor, you can't help but notice Portara, the entrance to an unfinished ancient temple to Apollo. Naxos Town can be roughly divided into two sections: the old, historic, mesmerizing half and the practical, altogether uninteresting newer half. The latter includes the buildings on the far side of town near Agios Georgios beach and the whole waterfront façade. Old Naxos lies behind the waterfront shops, on the hill leading up to Venetian castle. As you wander through the tangled streets of old Naxos Town, you may feel as though you jumped into a painting. The ancient wooden porticoes and glimpses of the brilliant blue sea enhance the charm. Low stone archways, flowers, and trellised plants engulf the old homes of the castle, and colorful markets whirl with activity.

ORIENTATION AND PRACTICAL INFORMATION

All ferries dock in Naxos Town. Maps can only get you so far; streets are poorly labeled and tend to zig and zag. The dock is at the left end of town. Along the waterfront, you will find offices, stores, and agencies that can meet all your traveler's needs, ranging from suntan lotion to ferry tickets. At the right end of the waterfront is the main road out of town. Between this road and the shop-lined waterfront is the old town. The easiest entrance into this maze is from behind the **Promponos** local goods shop on the waterfront. There is a sign at the rear of that little square that reads "Welcome to the Old Market."

Tourist Office: (tel. 24 358 or 25 201; fax 25 200). There is a privately run tourist agency sitting directly on the dock, but the *real* tourist office, farther along, has more of what you're looking for—advice on hotels and rooms-to-let; booking service for Naxos and all of Greece; bus, ferry, and hydrofoil schedules; currency exchange; international telephone; luggage storage (400dr); safety deposit boxes (400dr); and laundry service (2000dr). Sells guides on island walking tours (4000dr) and lends *Let's Go* guides. Despina (home phone after hours 24 525) speaks English. Open daily 8am-midnight.

Port Police: (tel. 22 300) Nikodemos St., above the old Zas Travel, near the bus depot, on the waterfront. Entrance around back. Open 24hr.

OTE: Next to the Hotel Hermes at the right end of the harbor. Open July-Aug. Mon.-Sat. 7:30am-10pm, Sun. 9am-10pm; Sept.-June Mon.-Fri. 8am-11pm.

Bank: The **National Bank** (tel. 23 053) offers **currency exchange.** Walk down the waterfront with the water on your right; the bank is roughly in the middle of the waterfront stretch in a yellow Neoclassical building. **ATM.** Open Mon.-Thurs. 8am-2pm, Fri. 8am-1:30pm. Several other banks line the waterfront.

Tourist Agency: Zas Travel (tel. 23 330; fax 23 416). Two offices along the waterfront and one in Agia Anna (tel. 24 023). Telephone, **currency exchange,** accommodations, car rental, and ferry/hydrofoil tickets. Open daily 8am-11pm.

Flights: An **Olympic Airways** desk is housed in **Naxos Tours** (tel. 22 095), at the right end of the waterfront. There are 2 flights per day to Athens (18,000dr).

Buses: The depot is directly in front of the ferry dock. Schedules are posted both at the Tourist Information Center and the bus station across the street and a little to the left (facing inland) from the depot. Arrive 10min. early; buses tend to be packed, especially the ones to Filoti (6 per day, 320dr) and Apollonas (4 per day, 2hr., 900dr). Buses also run to Agia Anna beach (21 per day, 15min., 220dr) via

Agios Prokopios beach, Chalki (6 per day, 30min., 280dr), Apiranthos (5 per day, 1hr., 480dr), and Pyrgaki beach (3 per day, 1hr., 300dr).

Ferries: Travel to Peiraias (4-6 per day, 7hr., 4027dr); Paros (6-9 per day, 1hr., 1300dr); Ios (4-7 per day, 1½hr., 1976dr); Santorini (4-7 per day, 3hr., 2408dr); Mykonos (2-4 per day, 2hr., 1329dr); Syros (1-3 per day, 2½hr., 1889dr); Amorgos (1-3 per day, 3½hr., 2102dr); and Crete (1 per week, 7hr., 4270dr). Ferries also sail to smaller Cycladic islands, and occasionally to the Dodecanese. Ferries to Iraklia, Schinoussa, Koufonisi, and Donoussa (1-2 per day, 1½hr., 1347dr).

Flying Dolphins: There are hydrofoils and catamarans daily to Rafina (7113dr), Mykonos (2974dr), Ios (4230dr), Santorini (4782dr), Paros (2608dr), Andros (5460dr), Iraklion (2490dr), and Amorgos (4354dr).

Taxis: (tel. 22 444), on the waterfront, next to the bus depot.

Motorbike Rental: Ciao (tel. 23 498), one block inland on the paved road to the right of the bus depot. Bikes start at 2500dr per day. Be very cautious driving on the somewhat "primitive" island roads. Open daily 8am-midnight.

Public Toilets and Showers: Behind Toast Time on the street parallel to the waterfront. Turn left after the old Zas Travel and then make a right. Toilets 100dr, showers 600dr (men and women separate). Open daily 8am-2pm and 5-11pm.

English Bookstore: Vrakas (tel. 23 039). Look for signs reading "gold-silver used books." In the back of a jewelry shop, Vrakas buys and sells used books (buys at half the original price, sells 200-1800dr).

Pharmacies: (tel. 22 241), next to the inland road, across the bus depot and to the right along the waterfront. Open Mon.-Tues. and Thurs.-Fri. 8am-2pm and 6-9:30pm, Wed. and Sat. 8am-2pm. For after-hours emergencies inquire at the store-front window for the phone number of the stand-by pharmacy (*efimerevon*).

Health Center: (tel. 23 333 or 22 661), turn right past Hotel Hermes and continue along that road for about 500m; you will see it on your left. Has 14 doctors (some English-speaking) and can access helicopter service to Athens in emergencies. A taxi there costs 700-1000dr. Open daily 9am-9pm.

Police: (tel. 22 100 or 23 280), turn onto paved inland street, just past the bus depot, bear right; the police station is on the left. Open 24hr.

Post Office: Walk down the waterfront (water on your right), left after Hotel Hermes, and take your first right. Open Mon.-Fri. 7:30am-2pm. **Postal Code:** 84300. **Telephone Code:** 0285.

ACCOMMODATIONS

In late July and August on Naxos, most hotels fill to capacity. At other times of the year, expect to pay 40-50% less. People who meet the boat charge roughly 3000-4500dr for singles, 4000-8000dr for doubles, 7000-10,000dr for triples, and 5000-10,000dr for studios (doubles with kitchenette and bath). At the dock, put on your bargaining shoes and watch prices drop to your feet and crawl. A plethora of inexpensive rooms can be found by pursuing the trail of "Rooms-to-Let" signs in old Naxos Town, among the more pleasant settings.

Anna Legaki's Rooms (tel. 22 837). Take the first left before the post office and look for the sign on the right. Doubles 4000dr, with bath 5000dr. Triples with bath 7000dr. Breakfast included.

Hotel Panorama (tel. 24 404), in Old Naxos near Hotel Dionysos (follow red-hand signs pointing the way). Clean and welcoming, especially suited for families. Very proud of the—you guessed it—panoramic view of the harbor and town. Singles 8000dr. Doubles with bath 10,000dr. Triples 11,000dr. Breakfast 800dr.

Hotel Anixis (tel. 22 112), also next to Hotel Dionysos. Sparkling and verdant. All rooms with bath. Doubles 10,000dr. Triples 12,000dr. Breakfast 1500dr.

Hotel Chateau Zevgoli (tel. 22 993). Follow the light blue signs in old Naxos. Bedside dried flowers, potpourri in the bathrooms, nurturing owners. Doubles 15,000dr. Triples 18,000dr.

Hotel Dionysos (tel. 22 331), in old Naxos—follow the signs. Essentially a youth hostel and accordingly cheap; a bit run down (lots o' mosquitoes and other beasties), but social. Stay if you're desperate for lodging. Check-out noon. Dorm beds 1500dr. Doubles with bath 5000dr. Illegal roof space 1500dr.

Naxos Camping (tel. 23 500, -501), the closest to town. 1500m by foot along St. George's beach. Swimming pool. 1000dr per person. 300dr per tent. 10% discount to *Let's Go* readers.

Maragas Camping (tel. 24 552 or 25 204; fax 24 552), farthest away but also the nicest and virtually on the beach. Shuttle bus service waits at the ferry-docks, or take the frequent buses to Ag. Anna beach (26 per day, 250dr). 800-1000dr per person. Doubles with bath 3000-6000. 0-300dr per tent.

FOOD AND ENTERTAINMENT

Christo's Grill, one street back from the waterfront near the dock, is a meat eater's heaven (chicken 800dr). **Koutouki,** high up in the old city, is one of the hungry traveler's best pitstops in town. All portions are big and entrees come with mixed vegetables, french fries, and rice (*souvlaki* 1300dr, stuffed peppers 1300dr). **Lucullus,** around since 1908, has excellent service (all waiters have taken their be-friendly-to-customers course) and a scrumptious, yet pricey, menu (*moussaka* 1850dr, veal in lemon sauce 1950dr, octopus salad 1150dr). The best-kept secret in Naxos is the fish *taverna* **Galini,** 500m down the inland road past Hotel Hermes; look for it on your left just before the medical center. Cheap, fresh fish in an unassuming environment. **Apolafsi** (Delight; tel. 22 178), on the second floor on the water, has good quality Greek *apolafsi* (veal, smoked pork, 1300dr; veal with pasta 1000dr). **Rendez-Vous** (PANTEBOυ) on the waterfront prides itself on hot, delicious, gooey *loukoumades* (honey pastries) for 500dr. Farther down, **Aktaion** competes for the sweet-toothed crowd (chocolate pastry 450dr).

Naxos' nightlife isn't as frenetic as that of some of the other islands. Many people stroll the main promenade before heading to a bar. Bars offer happy hours in the earlier part of the evening (8-11pm) with drinks at half-price. For those who must boogie, there are a few nearby discoes as well (usually open at 11pm). Popular bars include: **The Jam,** behind the OTE, with loud music and (allegedly) 2002 different cocktails (1000-1500dr each), **Mike's Bar,** across the street, decorated with Dali posters (draft beer 300-700dr), and **Musique Café,** a popular hangout on the waterfront (beer 600-800dr, cocktails 1000-1200dr). Two lively discoes are the **Ocean Club** (tel. 24 323), behind the National Bank with Euro dance music (beer 800-1000dr), and **Asteria Disco** (tel. 22 173), five minutes from town on Ag. Georgios beach with music ranging from Guns 'n' Roses to the Village People (beer 700dr). For a more low-key adventure, there is a 9 and 11pm showing at **Cine Astra,** the open cinema on the road to Agia Anna just outside town (15-minute walk; 1000dr).

SIGHTS

While in Naxos Town, walk around the old **Venetian Castle,** a series of mansions inhabited by descendants of the original Frankish and Venetian nobility. Up from the Hotel Pantheon, The Castle and The Loom merit a visit for folk art merchandise. The engrossing **Archaeological Museum** is in a house where Nikos Kazantzakis, author of *Last Temptation of Christ* and *Zorba the Greek,* once studied. The museum contains beautiful Cycladic artifacts, as well as vases, sculpture, jewels, and implements found in Mycenaean and Geometric chamber tombs (open Tues.-Sun. 8:30am-3pm; admission 500dr, students 300dr, free on Sun. and holidays).

From the waterfront, you can see the white chapel of **Myrditiotissa** floating serenely in the harbor on its man-made islet. Nearby is the **Portara,** an intriguing marble archway on the hilltop near the port. According to myth, this was where Ariadne lost Theseus and found Dionysus; later, it was the site of Ariadne's palace. Excavation has debunked this romantic reasoning—in fact, the archway, along with the platform and some columns, is merely detritus from yet another temple to Apollo, this one unfinished. This is one of the few archaeological sights in Greece where you can actually climb all over the ruins. No admission, open 24 hours, no guards, and thus recommended for romantic sunsets or midnight star-watching.

■ Around Naxos Island

Mopeds can be ideal for reaching the popular beaches south of town and some nearby inland sites and villages. Much of the island, however, is mountainous and roads are not in the best condition; several people die each year on Naxos' more rocky, tortuous roads. Many travelers opt instead to take a morning bus to **Apollonas** (Apollon; 2hr., 900dr), a small fishing village on the northern tip of the island. From Apollonas, you can slowly make your way back to Naxos alternating between bus and foot, stopping in towns like Korouida, Koronos, Apiranthos, Filoti, and Chalki. On the initial bus trip to Apollonas, examine the exhilarating scenery and note which areas you may want to investigate further on the way back.

The first hour of the ride from Naxos Town to Chalki takes you through cultivated mountainsides rich with olive trees, churches, and wildflowers that sprout each spring and summer. Before Chalki, there's a turn-off for **Ano Sangri,** an isolated town of winding flagstone streets 1km west of the road. You can get off the bus at the turn-off and walk or trek the entire way from Naxos Town (roughly 1½hr.).

Chalki, a placid village surrounded by Venetian towers, marks the beginning of the magnificent **Tragea**—an enormous, tremendously still Arcadian olive grove. Stop in at the **Panagia Protothonis,** the parish church of Chalki, right across from the bus stop. Restoration work there has uncovered wall paintings from the 11th through 13th centuries. If the church is closed, the priest can let you in.

If you have a motorbike or car, an alternate route takes you from Naxos Town through Melanes to **Flerio,** where one of the magnificent **kouroi** of Naxos sleeps in a woman's garden. *Kouroi,* larger-than-life, Egyptian-influenced sculptures of male figures, were first made in Greece in the 7th century BCE. This one was probably abandoned in its marble quarry because it broke before completion. Its owner runs a small *kafeneion* in the garden. From Flerio, backtrack and follow a road which passes through a trio of charming villages built in a river valley—**Kato Potamia, Mesi Potamia,** and **Ano Potamia**—before reaching Chalki. A map is essential.

Soon after leaving Chalki you'll reach **Filoti,** a village where the Tragea ends and the road climbs the flanks of Mt. Zas. These slopes offer superb views extending all the way to Poros and the sea beyond. Serious hikers might want to check out the **Cave of Zeus,** most easily accessible from Filoti. Legend has it that this is the spot where the king of gods was raised by an eagle (from which he received the power of hurling thunderbolts). This 150m deep cave is a good 1½-hour trek uphill from Filoti. Determined mythologists, or those simply looking for a good hike with some excellent views, should wear sturdy footwear, bring water and a flashlight, and should not come alone (last year it took a helicopter search crew a week to find a man who fell and injured himself here). If this excursion sounds appealing, head up the road to Apiranthos for roughly 20-30 minutes until a dirt road branches off on the right. Follow this road to its end (passing through a gate on the way), just before a clearing with a drinkable **spring water fountain.** From there, keep going on, staying on the left (uphill) whenever possible. Look for red marks on stones, but don't expect any signs. Forty-five minutes more should bring you past some rather difficult terrain to a second potable fountain, just below the mouth of the cave. The grotto itself is large, cool, and rather slimy, but quite interesting to explore.

A 15-minute bus ride from Filoti brings you to the small town of **Apiranthos,** which houses the **Michael Bardani Museum** in a white building on the right side of the main street. The museum contains many remnants of Cycladic artifacts. Also in Apiranthos are a modest **folk art museum** and a **Geology Museum.** All three are "officially" open early in the day (daily 8am-2pm). The museums lack posted hours, and the villagers won't necessarily open the doors for you. Many homes in Apiranthos are 300-400 years old, and lie in the shadows of the two castles that dominate the town (closed to the public). The mountain views from the edges of the town are stunning, and locals are cordial to the few tourists who come this way. From Apiranthos through **Koronos** and **Koronida,** a one-hour drive away, the road snakes through interior mountain ranges. The terraced landscape, laden with fruit and olive trees, plunges dramatically into the valleys below.

One of the more famous *kouroi* of Naxos lies a short walk from the harbor at **Apollonas.** At 10½m long, this *kouros* is more massive, if less finely sculpted, than the one in Flerio, and is also incomplete. From the Apollonas bus stop, walk back along the main road uphill until you come to the fork in the road. Take a sharp right (onto the fork the bus did not take coming into town) and walk up until you see the stairs at the "προσ κουρο" ("Pros Kouro") sign. It's roughly a 20-minute walk.

On your return trip from Apollonas to Chalki, you might want to get off the bus at Filoti (roughly 2km away) and walk through the **Tragea.** Footpaths off the main road will lead you into the dense grove. It is easy to get delightfully lost wandering among the scattered churches and tranquil scenery of the Tragea. Head west to return to the main road. A map is more than helpful here. Would-be hikers might pick up a copy of *Walking Tours on Naxos* by Christian Ucke, an exceedingly informative book available from the Tourist Office in both English and German (4000dr).

The most remote, uncrowded **beaches** and clearest waters are the farthest from town. Near town, the long sandy stretches of **Agios Georgios, Agios Prokopios, Agia Anna,** and **Plaka** border crystal blue water but may be crammed with sunbathers and unsightly modern buildings. All traces of authentic Greek culture are obliterated along these beaches, which are lined with hotels, Rooms-to-Let, bars, *tavernas,* discoes, and *creperies.* As you move away from town, younger, more beautiful, and less clothed bathers begin to take over. By Agia Anna, you'll encounter nude sunbathers. The beaches at **Mikri Vigla, Kastraki, Aliko,** and **Pyrgaki** are also accessible by bus from Naxos Town. Here desert meets sea; scrub pines, prickly pear, and century plants grow on the dunes behind you, shooing you towards the water.

AMORGOS ΑΜΟΡΓΟΣ

Amorgos' stunning cliffside monastery, idyllic Chora, scattered churches, and assorted beaches offer a welcome respite from the throngs of tourists on other islands. Although the island's popularity has increased since the filming of *Le Grand Bleu* here in 1988, Amorgos is still the place to come for a restful few days. Ferry connections are relatively infrequent and generally stop at Amorgos' two ports in succession—**Aegiali** in the northeast and the larger **Katapola** in the southwest. Be sure to disembark at your desired port; transportation between the two is sporadic.

▓ Katapola

Katapola, the island's central port, is a welcoming village with windmills, whitewashed houses, and narrow streets in the shadow of the remnants of a Venetian castle. It is small, quiet, and free of the bustle of many other port towns in the Cyclades.

Orientation and Practical Information   Across from the ferry dock is a **tourist agency** (ΠΡΑΚΤΟΡΕΙΟ; tel. 71 201 or 71 748; fax 71 278). This is one of the few establishments on the island that takes credit cards, and it offers helpful information, currency exchange, an international telephone, and some ferry and hydrofoil tickets. If they don't sell the ticket you want, they'll tell you where to buy it. Since there's no post office or OTE in Katapola, go there to take care of all that business (phone cards and stamps on sale; registered mail handled; open daily 8:30am-2pm and 5-11pm; longer in high season). The **port police** (tel. 71 259; open 24hr.), are on the right along the small street near the **pharmacy** (tel. 71 400; open Sun.-Fri. 9am-2pm and 6:30-9:30pm, Sat. 10:30am-1pm and 6:30-9pm); both are on a side street heading inland from the main square. The **medical center** (tel. 71 257) is along the waterfront as it bends around the harbor in the white building behind the two statues (next to the playground). For **medical emergencies,** call 71 805.

Buses frequently connect most desired destinations in Amorgos in summer. Buses run from Katapola to Chora every hour on the hour 8am-midnight (10min., 200dr). Between 8am-7pm, the same bus continues on to Monastiri (from Kapapola 20min., 250dr; from Chora 10min., 200dr) and Agia Anna (from Katapola 25min., 250dr, from Chora 15min., 200dr). There is also a bus from Katapola to Aegiali roughly every two hours from 9:30am-10pm (45min., 400dr). From Amorgos (both ports), **ferries** sail to Peiraias (1 per day, 8-13hr., 4000dr); Naxos (2-3 per day, 2½-4hr., 2100dr); Paros (2-3 per day, 2357dr); Mykonos (2 per week, 2700dr); Tinos (2 per week, 2700dr); Syros (5 per week, 2910dr); Andros (1 per week, 6hr., 2900dr); and Astypalea (2-3 per week, 3hr., 2400dr). Once a week, there is also a ferry going to Kalymnos, Kos, and Rhodes. **Hydrofoils** head to Rafina (4 per week, 8000dr); Naxos (1 per day, 4244); Paros (1 per day, 5300dr); Santorini (1 per day, 4250dr); Ios (1 per day, 4004dr); Mykonos (1 per day, 5800dr); Tinos (1 per day, 5800dr); Syros (4 per week, 7370dr); and Andros (3 per week, 5683dr). Ferry and hydrofoil schedules are subject to sudden change. Ask a travel agent for help. **Public toilets** are at the beginning of the rocky town beach across the street from **Rent-A-Bike Thomas** (tel. 71 007), where a helpful English-speaker charges 2500-3000dr per day for a moped. Call a **taxi** at 71 255. **Postal Code:** 84008. **Telephone Code:** 0285.

Accommodations   It's probably wise to firmly walk past the dock hawks and look for one of the amiable pensions or "Rooms to Let." As is standard practice, prices in off season are 20-40% lower. In a tiny olive grove, with a soothing view and free kitchen facilities, is **Dimitri's Place** (tel. 71 309). Walk along the harbor with the water on your left and take a right just before the small bridge. From there, look for the adorable "Dimitri's P(a)lace" sign. Dimitri welcomes you with a cup of Greek coffee and offers a range of rooms for a range of prices all flexible and subject to market forces. (Doubles with bath 6000dr.) Also in a ravishing garden setting is **Pension Anna** (tel. 71 218); follow the signs on the inland road behind the small square with Pension Amorgos. It's a big white house with red shutters up behind the OTE shack. (Doubles 6000dr. Triples 8000dr. Studios with kitchens and baths 10,000dr.) Closer to the water is **Pension Amorgos** (tel. 71 013, -814), with blue trimmed rooms and an open roof-top veranda with a view. (Doubles and triples 4000-8000dr, with bath and kitchen 5000-9000dr.) **Katapola "Rooms to Let"** (tel. 71 007) on the waterfront has simple but cheap rooms. (Doubles and triples with bath 5000dr.) Cheapest, the pleasant **Community Campsite** (tel. 71 802) is a short walk from town. Cross the small bridge on the quay, and follow the signs.

Food and Entertainment   Even though the waterfront is lined with *tavernas* and cafés, Katapola is not home to superb food. **The Corner** (tel. 71 191), on the waterfront past most of the *tavernas,* has moderate prices for well cooked food (*pastitsio, moussaka, dolmades,* and *papoutsakia* all 900dr each). A scrumptious exception to the town's otherwise unexciting cuisine is the small, sweet, and trendy creperie **To Kalderimi** (tel. 71 722). Look for it past the pharmacy (chocolate crepe 900dr; cheese, ham, and tomato crepe 1100dr). Nighttime entertainment is subdued in Amorgos, but if you head to the other side of the bay to Katapola's other settlement, look for the waterfront bar **Le Grand Bleu** (blue and white sign with dolphins). Here, cokes and beers cost 500dr but the showing of the movie *Le Grand Bleu* in English with Scandanavian subtitles is free.

■ Around the Island

Katapola literally means "below the town." In this case, the town above is **Chora,** also known as Amorgos, 6km from the harbor along the island's only significant paved road. Less convenient as a base for your stay, Chora is nonetheless a restful and ravishing option. Sights include a 14th-century Venetian **fortress,** a row of retired windmills precariously perched on the mountain ledge above town, simple churches, 45 Byzantine churches, and the first ever high school in Greece, built in

1829 (look for it on your left on your way up to OTE). Roughly 16 buses per day travel from Katapola to Chora (10min., 200dr), and 10 continue on to the monastery and Agia Anna (250dr). Chora is home to Amorgos' only **post office** (tel. 71 250), past the small square with the snack bar on the uphill end of town (open Mon.-Fri. 7:30am-2pm), and its main **OTE** (tel. 71 339), on the right at the very top of town (open Mon.-Fri. 7:30am-3pm). There is a **police station** (tel. 71 210) in the main square with the big church, next to Café Loza (open 24hr.; after hours knock loudly). The **medical center** (tel. 71 207) is on the main road into Chora from Katapola (open 24hr.). A branch of the **Agricultural Bank** operates in the small square with the snack bar (open Mon.-Thurs. 8am-2pm, Fri. 8am-1:30pm). If you decide to spend the night, look for "Rooms to Let" signs throughout the town's narrow streets. Below the bus stop is **Pension Panorama,** and on the road from Chora to Monastiri, toward the lower end of Chora, is **Pension Ilias** (tel. 71 277). Both offer clean, stark rooms. (Doubles with bath 5000-9000dr.) Several *tavernas* and cafés are tucked in the meandering streets. Wander until you find **Kastanis** for hearty fare and occasional live Greek music (*moussaka* 950dr). **Liotrivi,** below the bus station, offers *kalamari* and stuffed tomatoes for 900dr each. In front of the main church in Katapola is a sign for the ancient town of **Minoa** (40-min. hike). This settlement was inhabited between the 10th and 4th centuries BCE. Look for the base of the temple among the ruins with the bust of a statue still rising from within.

A trip to Amorgos is incomplete without a visit to the **Chozoviotissa** monastery (tel. 71 274). From Katapola, you can catch a bus that goes through Chora. If you're in Chora, you may choose to go down the steps that begin at the top of Chora, past the OTE antenna. Both options take you to the beginning of the 350-step staircase that climbs up to the 11th-century whitewashed edifice (a 15-min. hike). Wear comfortable shoes and take a hat to tackle this hike. The monastery is built so flawlessly onto the sheer face of a cliff that it appears to have grown there. Legend has it that attempts to build the monastery on the shore were twice thwarted by divine intervention before the workers discovered their bag of tools mysteriously hanging from the cliff, causing them to interpret the omen as advice on where to recommence construction. The monastery is undoubtedly one of the more exhilarating visual spectacles in all of Greece. If you complete the hike up between 8am and 1pm (also 5-7pm in the summer), the monks may reward you with cold water, Greek liqueur, and *loukoumi* (Greek sweets). Before leaving, ask the monks to show you the downstairs exhibit, which includes writings, relics, and church items dating to the founding of the monastery. Wander through the chambers farther below to get a sense of the serenity and solitude this hamlet secures. Contrary to the sign posted at the base of the climb, spare clothing is available at the entrance, but it is more respectful for men to wear long pants, women dresses or long skirts—no bare shoulders. The downhill road from the turnoff for the monastery takes you to the lone and crystal waters of **Agia Anna.** From the bus stop at the end of the road, there is one path at the upper left end of the clearing (facing inland) that leads to one beach and another path at the bottom of the central steps leading to the other beach. Though Greece has many beautiful beaches, this may be one of the more enchanting. Other spots on Amorgos are **Plakes** and **Agios Panteleimonas,** a mere 10-minute walk from Katapola around the left end of the harbor and over the hill, and **Paradisia** in the south. A bus leaves Katapola for the latter at 10am daily and returns at 3pm (45min., 400dr). If you make it to this beautiful lone beach, ask the locals to direct you to the **Olympia shipwreck** *(navagio).*

TINOS ΤΗΝΟΣ

Tinos has been a place of religious significance for Greeks since the War of Independence, when a nun named Pelagia, guided by a vision, found a miracle-working icon of the Virgin and Christ buried in an underground church. The **Icon of the Annun-**

ciation, also known as the *Megalochari* (Great Joy) or *Panagia Evangelistria,* is one of the most sacred relics of the Orthodox church. Each year on the Feasts of the Annunciation (March 25th) and the Assumption (August 15th), thousands of pilgrims crowd the island to pray at the icon.

Although the icon is its primary attraction, Tinos has played home to some of Greece's most prominent artists and offers 100 other churches, 15 natural beaches, 10 museums, a rustic interior, and a more authentic view of Greece than most Cycladic isles. Much of the island's beauty lies in Tinos' countryside, punctuated by beautiful **dovecote towers** that play home to countless pigeons.

■ Tinos Town

Tinos Town is unmistakably a place of religious worship. Even sellers of tacky Greek souvenirs sell plastic vials of *agiasmos* (holy water) and cheap, imitation icons here. The town is clean and generally calm except for the yearly fortnight when it overflows with pilgrims. This port rose to prominence on August 15, 1940, when an Italian submarine torpedoed the Greek cruiser "Elli," which was docked in the harbor for the holiday. The attack came two months before Mussolini declared war.

Orientation and Practical Information   From the main dock next to the bus depot, walk left to the center of town where **Leoforos Megalochares,** a wide avenue leading uphill to the Neoclassical façade of the **Panayia Evangelistria** church, will sprawl. Parallel to Leoforos Megalochares up to the church, **Evangelistrias Street** (nicknamed Bazaar St. by the locals) overflows with religious trinkets. The **police station** (tel. 22 100, -255), which also houses the **tourist police,** is located five minutes out of town on the road to Kionia. The **port authority** (tel. 22 348) lies along the waterfront, across the taxi stand and on the second floor. Facing inland, the **post office** is on the far right end of the waterfront, behind the small square (open Mon.-Fri. 7:30am-2pm). A few blocks up Leforos Megalochares on the right is the **OTE** (open Mon.-Fri. 7:30am-3:10pm). The **National Bank,** on the waterfront across from the bus depot, has an **ATM** (open Mon.-Thurs. 8am-2pm, Fri. 8am-1:30pm). To get to a **pharmacy** (tel. 22 272; fax 22 740), look for a green cross across the dock and to the left along the waterfront (open Mon.-Tues. and Thurs.-Fri. 8am-2pm and 6-9pm, Wed. and Sat. 8am-2pm). **Public toilets** are at the left end of the waterfront near Dolphin Sq., behind the Hotel Lito.

Buses (tel. 22 440) leave from the station a few storefronts left of the National Bank. They depart two to seven times daily for the villages of Pyrgos (600dr), Panormos (650dr), Kalloni (470dr), Steni (250dr), Skalados (320dr), Kionia (170dr), and Porto (170dr). A schedule is posted in the KTEL bus station/ferry ticket agency across the depot. For a **taxi,** dial 22 470 or inquire at the blue booth to the right of the waterfront (available daily 6am-2am). Renting a **moped** is probably the best way to see Tinos, but take special care on the narrow, gravel mountain roads. If you look at a new map of the island, the red roads are all paved but the yellow ones are still pretty bad. Try **Vidalis,** 16 Zanaki Alavanou St. (tel. 23 400), which is on the main road leading out of town off the right side of the waterfront. The staff offers free information on the island to those using *Let's Go* (open daily 8am-10pm). Or try **Jason's** (tel. 22 583, 24 283), just before Alavanou St., on the waterfront (open daily 8am-10pm). Prices are 2500-3000dr per day at both.

Tinos can be reached by frequent ferries and hydrofoils from both Peiraias and Rafina near Athens, as well as Mykonos, Syros, and Andros. **Ferries** from Tinos travel to Mykonos (4-5 per day, 30min., 1200dr); Andros (2-4 per day, 2hr., 1700dr); Syros (2 per day, 40min., 900dr); Peiraias (2 per day, 5½hr., 3885dr); and Rafina (2-4 per day, 4hr., 3000dr). In high season, there is weekly service to Paros (1590dr) and Naxos (1780dr). A **catamaran** departs daily for Mykonos (30min., 2500dr); Paros (1¼hr., 3000dr); Naxos (1¾hr., 3500dr); Ios (3hr., 6500dr); Santorini (4hr., 6500dr); Amorgos (6¼hr., 5800dr); Folegandros (6¾hr., 4600dr); and Sikinos (7¼hr., 4600dr). The agents at the ticket agency (tel. 22 470) answers queries (open daily

7am-11pm). **Mariner** (tel. 23 193), next to the pharmacy, handles **flying dolphins,** which leave daily for Mykonos (2450dr), Andros (3420dr), Rafina (6190dr), Paros (3065dr), Naxos (3570dr), Santorini (6570dr), and three times per week for Amorgos (5850dr). There is also an **excursion boat** to Mykonos and Delos (Tues.-Sun. depart 9am, return 6pm, 4000dr). **Postal Code:** 84200. **Telephone Code:** 0283.

Accommodations

Tinos has plenty of accommodations, except at festival time (Eastern Orthodox Easter week and occasionally on July and August weekends, when Athenians flock here). Most hotels are expensive, so try your bargaining skills with the crowd of smiling faces holding "Rooms to Let" signs when you disembark. If the hustlers are too much, head to **Loukas Apergis'** fine rooms (tel. 23 964, -231). Take a left onto Zanaki Alavanou St. just before the post office, then the second left onto 25 Martiou at the second little park (the one with the little boy fountain) and look for signs along that street. (Doubles 5000dr. Triples 6000dr. Both with bath.) In the same neighborhood, **Mrs. Plyte** (tel. 23228) has her rooms with common baths and kitchens. Make your left at the first little park and at the top of the road look for a white house with blue shutters above a woodshop on your right. You can inquire about the rooms in the woodshop downstairs. (Doubles 5000-7000dr. Triples 7000-10,000dr.) The braver of the budget travelers may choose **Giannis** (tel. 22 515), at the far right end of the waterfront for his simple but airy rooms in a traditional house with green shutters. The package includes challenging common baths, a kitchen, laundry facilities, and a lovely flower garden sitting area. (Doubles 6000dr. Triples with private bath and kitchen 12,000dr.) A clearly marked 10-minute walk to the right-hand side of town, well kept **Tinos Camping** (tel. 22 344, -548) has kitchen and laundry facilities, showers, bungalows, a bar/restaurant/café, and animals wandering the tents. (1000-1200dr per person. 700-800dr per tent.)

Food and Entertainment

The most reasonably priced food in Tinos Town is not found in the restaurants in the main square. Take the first right off Evangelistras St. and pass the other restaurants until you come to **Pigada** (tel. 24 240). Don't shy away from the exterior; the food is excellent (true Greek *moussaka* 900dr, *dolmades* 1200dr). The second left off Megalochores leads to **Peristeriones** (tel. 23 425); try the house specialty, vegetable fritters (600dr). **Mesklies** (tel. 22151, -373) is a pastry shop, and two doors farther to the left, a restaurant/pizzeria. After having pizza made in a traditional oven (1600-2800dr), spaghetti (1000-1700dr), or a calzone, top off your meal with a sweet cheese cake (330dr). There is a branch of the sweet shop at the base of Evangelistras St., across from a *gyros* joint. Most of the town's bars are on the water to the left of the harbor, behind Hotel Lito. **Sivylla** (tel. 22511), close to the port but one block inland, plays Greek and American dance music and becomes jam-packed on weekends (beer 800dr, cocktails 1200dr). The blue building behind Hotel Lito is home to a happening disco, **Kala Kathoumena** (featuring A/C), but in general, wander the strip until the music strikes your fancy. Prices are pretty similar (beer 500-800dr, cocktails 1000-1500dr).

Sights

In 1822, Sister Pelagia, a Tiniote nun, had a vision in which the Virgin Mary instructed her to find an icon buried at the site of an ancient church, destroyed in the 10th century by pirates. A year later, the icon was housed, amid great rejoicing, in the **Panagia Evangelistria,** where it resides to this day. To the faithful, the find is evidence of the power and presence of the Holy Virgin. The relic reputedly has curing powers and is almost entirely covered with gold, diamonds, and jewels left at the church by people wishing to thank the Holy Mother for their good health. Countless *tamata*—beautifully crafted plaques praising the Virgin for healing the body part depicted—have won the Panayia the title of "Lourdes of the Aegean."

The most devout pilgrims make the journey up Leoforos Megalochares (the wide road rising from the sea to the church) on their knees to show their reverence. Others light offertory candles (100-1000dr donation depending on candle size). In a chapel below the marble entrance stairs flows the **Well of Sanctification,** a natural spring discovered during excavations, from which the faithful fill their jugs for drinking or carrying as talismans. The spring was said to have been dry until the icon was unearthed; since then, it has flowed continuously. On March 25 and August 15, flocks of devout pilgrims arrive at the church. To the right of the Well is the mausoleum of the Greek warship Elli, which was sunk by an Italian torpedo in 1940. The ship had docked in observance of the religious holiday. To the left of the well, in an adjoining chamber, the spot where the mysterious icon was found is marked by a marble plaque and wooden icon.

There are lodgings and facilities, but on August 15, Tinos Town is so crowded that the nearly 30,000 visitors sleep *everywhere*—along the dock, on the sidewalks, and even in the church itself, almost sinking the island under their weight. The next day, after making the 10km walk to the convent of Kechrovouni in a procession led by the icon, the masses depart on dozens of ferries specially chartered for the fête. No one will stop you here, but try to come modestly attired (long sleeves and pants or skirts, no bare shoulders) and be respectful of the Orthodox worshipers—remember you are sightseeing a serious and moving religious event. Don't miss the oil painting of a weeping Mary Magdalene contemplating the crown of thorns in the gallery opposite the church entrance. A free English information booklet full of history, colorful reports of miracles, and explanations of holidays is available at the second floor to the right of the sanctum (tel. 22 256; open daily 7am-8pm; free). Tinos is also famed for its art. After you visit the Panayia, drop by the church complex's art and archaeological museums, featuring works by native Tiniotes (open 8:30am-3pm, hours are variably extended in the summer; free).

Tinos' **Archaeological Museum,** on Leoforos Megalochares across and uphill from the OTE, contains artifacts from Poseidon's sanctuary at Kionia, a 1st-century BCE sundial, and a few vases from Xombourgo (open Tues.-Sun. 8:30am-3pm; admission 500dr, students 300dr). At **Kionia,** explore the ruins of the 4th-century BCE temple of Poseidon and Amphitrite, then sit by the sea at the steadily touristed **Tinos** or **Stavros Beaches,** both near town. If you stay late at Stavros, enjoy the locally acclaimed **Chroma Bar/Homa Club. Agios Fokas,** a closer and equally crowded beach, is a short walk east (on the opposite side) of Tinos Town.

■ Around the Island

To get to spectacular **Kardianis** beach, take the Pyrgos bus to Kardiani and travel down the winding street from the main road. Rustic Tinos will reward adventurers with secluded beaches and wonderful views of the fecund Tinos countryside. The 1000 **dovecots** dotting the landscape have become the island's symbol. Built in medieval times, these small white buildings have intricate lattice-work where birds roost. Stop by the picturesque town of **Pyrgos,** 33km northwest of Tinos Town (buses 3-5 times per day, 1hr., 650dr). With a marble quarry, Pyrgos has always been home to Tinos' artists and sculptors, including Giannouli Chalepas, whose *Sleeping Daughter* graces Athens' central graveyard. Two kilometers northeast of Pyrgos, Panormos Bay has a small beach and three *tavernas*. Be careful not to get stranded in the village—there are no night buses on Tinos and taxis are hard to find.

If you have wheels, investigate the delightful villages that encircle **Mount Exobourgo,** 14km north of Tinos Town, and the precipitous site of the Venetian Fortress, **Xombourgo.** After withstanding 11 assaults, this 13th-century citadel, then the island's capital, fell to the Turks in 1715. It was the very last territorial gain of the Ottoman Empire. Climb the mountain from the east foothill (near the village of Xinara or Loutra), and indulge in the resplendent panorama.

SYROS

SYROS ΣΥΡΟΣ

Syros's rise as a commercial power began when the Phoenicians used the island as a major sea port. Venetian control of the island, which began in the 13th century, solidified Syros's title as the trading capital of the Cyclades. The large Catholic population here has its origins in this era, and the privileges accorded Catholics under the subsequent Turkish rule guaranteed that Syros would keep its high status. Many of the grand buildings in Hermoupolis date from this period, when rich merchants built mansions and erected monuments. But all good things must come to an end, and the advent of steam-powered ships coupled with the rise of Peiraias sent Syros into a nose dive. During the last twenty years Syros has managed to recover, primarily thanks to a ship-building industry which now keeps the island "afloat" year-round and assures that it will not have to prostrate itself before the God of Tourism.

■ Hermoupolis ΕΡΜΟΥΠΟΛΙΣ

With a Greek Orthodox church on one hill and a Catholic church on the other, Hermoupolis, the spiritual city of Hermes (god of commerce), rests serenely on its natural harbor. Despite its decline as a major port, the city remains the shipping center of the Cyclades. Elegant Miaouli Sq. and the 19th-century mansions in Dellagrazia let us peek at Hermoupolis's opulent past and explain its former nicknames—the "Manchester of Greece" and "little Milan."

Orientation and Practical Information   The center of activity in Hermoupolis is **Miaouli Sq.,** two blocks up El. Venizelou St. from the center of the harbor where the winged statue stands. You can't miss the palatial town hall and large marble plaza. In Syros, **Gaviotis Tours** (tel. 86 606; fax 83 445), near the ferry dock and across from the bus depot, provides posted schedules and prices and sells tickets for ferries, hydrofoils, and flights (open daily 9am-10pm). The **National Bank** (tel. 82 451) on Kosti Kalomenopoulou St., in an elegant building at the end of the street the post office is on, offers **currency exchange** (open Mon.-Thurs. 8am-2pm, Fri. 8am-1:30pm). If you need an **ATM,** try the **Credit Bank,** just off Venizelou St. near the post office. The **OTE** (tel. 22 799) is on the right side of the square as you face the town hall (open daily 6am-midnight, 24hr. for emergencies).

Flights head to Athens (2-3 daily, 13,800dr). **Buses** (tel. 82 575), leave from the depot near the ferry dock and travel regularly to Galissas and nearby beaches (18 per day), Kini (6 per day), and Ano Syros (3 per day). A current schedule is posted next to the buses. From Syros, **ferries** head from the right of the harbor (facing the water) to Peiraias (1-4 per day, 4½hr., 3660dr); Tinos (2-3 per day, 40min., 900dr); Mykonos (2-3 per day, 1½hr., 1400dr); Andros (2 per week, 1800dr); Paros (1-2 per day, 1½hr., 1400dr); Naxos (1-2 per day, 2½hr., 1850dr); Ios (4 per week, 4hr., 3100dr); Santorini (daily, 5hr., 3350dr); Rhodes (2 per week, 5300dr); Kos (2 per week, 5050dr); and several of the smaller Cycladic islands. **Flying Dolphins,** departing from across the ferry docks (on the left, facing the water), speed to Tinos (2200dr), Mykonos (2650dr), Paros (2700dr), Naxos (3800dr), Santorini (7000dr), and Ios (6600dr). **Sea Jets** can get you daily to Rafina (1½hr., 6200dr), Tinos (15min., 2250dr), and Mykonos (35min., 2650dr).

Taxis (tel. 86 222) can be caught in front of town hall. There is a **pharmacy** (tel. 82 248), on El. Venizelou St. (open Mon., Wed. 8am-2:30pm, Tues., Thurs.-Sat. 8am-1:30pm, 5:30-9pm; look for red cross). In case of medical emergency, the **hospital** (tel. 86 666) is at the left end of the waterfront (facing inland) at Platia Iroon (20min. walk from Miaculi St.). The **port authority** (tel. 82 690) is housed in the yellow dock complex. The **police** (tel. 82 620) are opposite town hall on A. Singrou, a small, alley-like street and there is a **tourist police** officer on duty in the mornings. The post office (tel. 82 596) is roughly 40m down the second right off El. Venizelou (open Mon.-Fri. 7:30am-2pm). **Postal Code:** 84100. **Telephone Code:** 0281.

Accommodations Hermoupolis has plenty of cheap rooms. Off-season prices are generally cheaper by roughly 20-40%. At the ferry dock is a large map with names and phone numbers of hotels. For clean and amiable rooms with high ceilings, try the old house turned brand new **Hotel Nefeli,** 2 Parou St. (tel. 87 076), along the waterfront and left on Hiou St., just before Venizelou, into the open market. Parou is the first left off Hiou. Check out the roof garden bar with full view of the harbor. (Doubles 5000dr, with bath 7000dr. Triples with bath 8000dr.) For a dose of luxury, head to **Ariadni "Rooms to Let"** (tel. 81 307 or 80 245), on Nik. Fylini St. near the ferry dock (look for signs). Ariadni prides itself on a class "A" rating, and deservedly so—the rooms are spotless and radiant. (Show your *Let's Go* for a discount. Doubles 6000-7000dr, with kitchen 11,000dr. Triples 7200-8400dr. Apartments 10,000-15,000dr.) Another option is **Kastro Rooms,** 12 Kalomnopoulou St. (tel. 28 064), on the same street as the National Bank. Rooms are borderline luxurious and feature some of the few shower curtains you'll find in Greece. (Doubles 7500-9000dr. Triples 12,000dr.) For the full-on common bath experience, go to **Pension Venetiko,** 2 Em. Roidi (tel. 81 686), roughly two blocks from the lower right corner of the main square (facing inland). (Doubles 5000dr, with bath 7000dr.)

Food, Entertainment, and Sights For a traditional Greek dinner, hike to the **Tempelis** *taverna,* just below the Orthodox church. From Miaouli, climb up the long staircase behind the town hall just to the left of the clock tower until you come to Athan. Diakou, a paved road going downhill to the left. Turn left on this street, then right on Anastaseos; the restaurant is on the left. The owner doesn't speak English, but the menu is bilingual and you can always point and smile. Another true *taverna* experience awaits at **Folia,** which can be reached by heading up the main road leading from the top right corner of the main square. Stay to the left of St. Nicholas and keep going up, even after the road turns to stairs. Look for the sign on the left and take this street (Xenofontos). After roughly 50m, take a right and head uphill to the restaurant (chicken *souvlaki* 1100dr, pigeon 1050dr; they also have great *baklava*). If your ferry arrives in Syros late at night and you're famished, try **Elysee,** on the far right-hand edge of the harbor (chicken *souvlaki* 1200dr). **Mavrikaki** on the left side of the harbor (facing inland), has friendly service and good food (Greek salad 800dr, *gyro* to go 240dr). To sate that sugar craving, try **Melissa** on the first right of El. Venizelou, or **Kechaglas** on the waterfront corner of the same street (*baklava* 300dr). At night, the waterfront and Miaouli Sq. buzz with activity—you can hear loud techno at **Corto Bar** on the waterfront, the Violent Femmes at **Café Palladium** next to town hall, Tracy Chapman at **Cotton Club** on the waterfront, and Top-40 pop at **Highway Bar** on the waterfront. At these places and the boisterous **Pyramidia** in Miaouli Sq., beer costs 500dr, drinks 1000-1200dr.

Interesting sights and sounds abound at Syros's small **open market** between the lower left of Miaouli Sq. and the waterfront. Get your fresh, cheap fruit there. Make the ascent to **Ano Syros,** a medieval Venetian settlement that is still home to Syros' Catholics. To get there, go up the steps behind Miaouli Sq. or take the bus from the waterfront. The **Archaeological Museum,** the entrance to which is at the upper left corner of the Town Hall building, has a small collection of Cycladic Art (open Tues.-Sun. 8:30am-3pm; free). At the **Church of the Assumption** *(Kimisis Theotokou),* on St. Proiou St., view a painting created in 1562 at age 20 by famed Greek artist **El Greco.** This painting's discovery on Syros helped confirm the painter's Greek origin, dispelling inaccurate theories that he was Spanish.

■ Around the Island

Galissas, a village to the west of Hermoupolis, has a busy beach. Climb past the chapel of Agia Pakou on the left side (facing the water) to discover **Armeos**

ANDROS

Beach—tiny, beautiful, and **nudist.** Be forewarned that there are those who make the hike merely to ogle at the tiny, beautiful nude people. Women sunbathing alone may feel uncomfortable; bring a friend. There is a dizzying collection of "Rooms to Let" signs at the bus stop. The rooms at **George's Restaurant** (tel. 42 066), up the main inland street from the bus stop, are decorated with hand-woven tapestries. (Doubles 6500-9000dr. Triples 10,000dr.) **Angela's "Rooms to Let"** (tel. 42 855, -9), behind the mini-golf, has large, immaculate rooms surrounded by a spacious outdoor garden. Private bath and refrigerator included. (Doubles 7000-10,000dr. Triples 9000-13,000dr.) Angela also has fully stocked apartments which are suitable for up to four people (15,000-18,000dr). Also try **Tony's "Rooms to Let"** (tel. 42 482), at the end of the same street in the village. (Doubles 5000dr. Triples 6000dr.) Near Galissas beach are two **campgrounds, Yianna** (tel. 42 418) and **Two Hearts** (tel. 42 052), representatives from which may greet you at the dock with shuttle buses. Yianna is more secluded and offers a *taverna,* minimarket, hot showers, kitchen, laundry, safe-deposit boxes, and a nightly disco from 9pm to 2am with a cover including first drink 500dr. (1200dr per person. 300dr per small tent. 500dr per large tent.) Follow the signs from the bus stop. Two Hearts has two red hearts on its signs and advertises itself as a romantic campsite. It offers a restaurant and minimarket, but alas, no tunnel of love. (1300dr per person. 640dr per tent. 5000dr per two-person cabin.)

Galissas beach has most amenities imaginable—a moderately priced *taverna* on the beach affiliated with the Dolphin Bay Hotel, a less expensive self-service restaurant next door, mini-golf (next to Galissas Tours; open daily 7pm-1am), a few English language books at the Golden Corner, and even video games in the café/bar next to Galissas Tours. Although Americans laugh at the name, the **Green Dollars Bar** contributes to the playful scene with not only darts and backgammon, but also a life-size chessboard in a small courtyard (draft and bottled beer 300-400dr, drinks 900dr). If you exhaust the offerings at Galissas beach, **Galissas Tours** (tel. 42 801; fax 42 802) lets you make phone calls, change money, buy ferry tickets, rent mopeds (3000dr) or cars (9000-14,500dr), or take excursions around the island by boat (mid-July to August 2000dr to St. Stephanos Fisherman's Grotto; open Sept.-June daily 9:30am-2:30pm and 5-9pm; July-Aug. 9:30am-11pm).

From Hermoupolis, 18 buses per day travel to Galissas, alternating between a direct 15-minute route and a 45-minute route that stops in other villages first (200dr). In Hermoupolis, buses leave from the depot near the ferry dock and a current schedule is posted near the buses. Farther south along the coast are the beaches at **Poseidonia, Finikas, Angathopes,** and **Komito,** all connected by bus to Hermoupolis. The beach resort of **Vari** is most popular with families and package tour groups. North of Galissas is the tiny fishing village of **Kini.**

ANDROS ΑΝΔΡΟΣ

Tiers of straw fields and stretches of low-lying green and purple growth are partitioned by a network of streams and stone walls, lying like a spider's web fallen on the face of Andros' hillside. Winding above splendid scattered beaches, the hour drive from the ferry landing at **Gavrio** to **Andros Town** is magnificent. The ruins sprinkled across the Andrian hills memorialize the island's checkered history of Ionian, Spartan, Venetian, and Turkish occupation. Despite this tumultuous past, Andros today is one of the most peaceful of the Cyclades. It is the perfect place for family holidays, yet, at the same time, offers exciting outlets for those seeking sun and fun. Islanders claim Andros has 300 beaches; come and find out for yourself.

■ Gavrio

Crowned by the three-domed Church of Saint Nikolas, the dusty port town of Gavrio has little else to offer tourists. Most visitors stay overnight to catch an early ferry, but you can also use Gavrio as a base to explore some of the best stretches of smooth sand between the port and the popular tourist beach town of Batsi.

Good **maps** are available at tourist shops (350dr). Facing inland, the **police** (tel. 71 220) are to the right on a road parallel to the waterfront, up the steps opposite the bus stop. The building is unmarked, so look for the Greek flag (open 24hr.). The **port authority** (tel. 71 213) is the building with the glass façade and the Greek flag (again) to the right of the dock along the waterfront. The **OTE** stands one block to the left of Hotel Galaxy, on a side street in a building with green shutters (open Sept.-June Mon.-Sat. 7:30am-3pm; July-Aug. Mon.-Sat. 7:30am-10pm, Sun. 8am-2pm and 5-10pm). The **post office** (tel. 71 254) is two blocks farther on the waterfront (open Mon.-Fri. 7:30am-2pm). The **Agricultural Bank** (tel. 71 478) is on the corner at the right-hand end of the waterfront façade. (Open for **currency exchange** Mon.-Thurs. 9am-2pm, Fri. 9am-1:30pm.) A **pharmacy** is located in the left-center of the waterfront (tel. 71 329; open daily 9am-1:30pm and 6-10pm). For medical emergencies call the **hospital** at 22 222. **Postal Code:** 84501. **Telephone Code:** 0282.

To get to Andros Town, take one of the **buses** from the depot next to the ferry dock (5-7 per day, 1hr., 630dr). The same bus passes through Batsi (from Gavrio 15min., 190dr; from Andros Town 45min., 500dr). Check the bus schedules as early as you can. They tend to be erratic and structured around the ferry arrivals and departures of the day. From Andros, **ferries** sail to Athens' minor port, Rafina (2-5 per day, 2hr., 2096dr). They also head to Tinos (2-3 per day, 2hr., 1680dr); Mykonos (2-3 per day, 2½hr., 2400dr); Syros (2 per week, 2-3hr., 1600dr); Paros (1 per week, 2180dr); and Naxos (2 per week, 3½hr., 2370dr). Ferries run weekly to Thessaloniki (6360dr), Crete (5380dr), and Skyros (3090dr). There is daily **SeaJet** service to Rafina (1hr., 4120dr) and Tinos (50min., 3420dr). **Flying Dolphins** from Batsi zip to Tinos (1 per day, 3419dr); Mykonos (1 per day, 5418dr); Paros (4 per week, 4618dr); Naxos (4 per week, 5347dr); Ios (2 per week, 7038dr); and Santorini (2 per week, 7038dr). A **taxi** to Batsi costs 1200-1500dr and to Andros Town costs 3500-4000dr. You can rent a **moped** at **Andros Moto Rental** (tel. 71 605), behind the port authority (from 3500dr per day; open daily 8am-9pm).

Most accommodations are designed for longer term visits and family groups, but simple rooming arrangements and camping are also available. **Camping Andros** (tel. 71 444) has its own restaurant, minimarket, showers, and pool. From the OTE, there are signs to guide your five to 10-minute walk (1100dr per person, 800dr per tent). At the center of the waterfront, **Hotel Galaxias** (tel. 71 005, -228) has rather standard, somewhat boring rooms. (Singles 6000dr. Doubles 7500dr. Triples 9000dr. All with bath.) Look for "Rooms to Let" signs.

Fix your own meals with goodies from the **Andrios Supermarket** (tel. 71 341), on the right end of the waterfront (open daily 6:30am-11pm). **Galaxias** (tel. 71 005), in the same building as the hotel, has traditional Greek dishes (stuffed tomatoes 900-1000dr, depending on local tomato prices). Get a pizza at **San Remo** (tel. 71 150), next to the post office (1200-1600dr). For breakfast, try the bakery **Gavrio** (tel. 71 126), next to the pharmacy (ham and cheese pita 300dr).

■ Near Gavrio: Batsi

Batsi is undisputed as the tourist capital of Andros. With its long stretch of golden sand, crystal-blue water and old town climbing up the hill, Batsi has all the necessary means to make tourism run smoothly and the beauties of Andros accessible. If you take a bus to Batsi, sit on the right side of the bus to enjoy the gorgeous scenery rolling past. Between Gavroi and Batsi, there are numerous small coves with pools of clear water as well as the larger beaches of **Agios Petros, Psili Ammos,** and **Kipri**.

Orientation and Practical Information If you manage to resist and stay on the bus until Batsi, the main bus stop is at the end of the beach at a small square. The **taxi** stand is also there. There is a branch of the **National Bank** (tel. 41 400), to the right, continuing on the road to Andros Town (open Mon.-Fri. 8am-1:30pm). If you need an **ATM,** the **Ionian Bank** on the waterfront has one. The **mobile post office,** conveniently located for beachgoers writing postcards, is down the road along the beach, inland at the sign for Hotel Karanassos; the **post office** is across the dirt road from the hotel (open Mon.-Fri. 7:30am-2pm). On a street parallel to the main road, accessible from the stairs just past the National Bank, is **Dolphin Hellas Travel** (tel. 41 185; fax 41 719), which offers **currency exchange,** information on accommodations and ferries, and walking excursions throughout the island. There are **taxi boats** that leave Batsi for other beaches around the island (up to 1000dr roundtrip; open 9:30am-1:30pm and 6-9pm).

Accommodations It is easier to find accommodations here than in either Gavrio or Andros Town. Although accommodations may be more plentiful here, they also tend to be pricey. Expect to pay 8000-10,000dr for a double at one of the beachfront hotels. Look for "Rooms to Let" signs or inquire at souvenir or tourist shops (6000-10,000dr). **Mrs. Tzoumoni** (tel. 41 211) has large, clean rooms with fully equipped kitchenettes in a white house with blue shutters along the water-front (not even a hop, skip, and a jump from the beach), next to Supermarket Batis. (Doubles 7000-9000dr.) **Hotel Karanassos** (tel. 41 480, -1), one block from the beachfront, is breezy and comfortable. (Doubles 7000-11,000dr. Triples 9000-15,000dr. Quads 11,000-17,000dr. All with bath. Breakfast 1000dr.)

Entertainment To the left of the square, in a vine-covered setting along the waterfront, is the café/bar **Skala** (tel. 41 656). Get your fill of trendy music there all day and choose from a vast variety of beers to drown your beach sorrows (600-3000dr). If you want music with faster beat, head over to **Placebo** (tel. 71 800), half-way to Gavrio on the main road. The night club has a 1500dr cover including the first drink, but you can skip the cover and go into the bar (beer 800dr, cocktails 1200-1500dr). For daytime partying, take a taxi boat to the **Green Beach Club** (tel. 41 656), at the **Prasini Ammo beach** with water polo, canoeing, windsurfing, and other beach fun around a beach bar (beer 500dr) to the beat of beach music all day. You can ask Argiris when he's planning his next beach party and go there at night, too. On a quieter and more sophisticated note, check out the ruins of the ancient capital **Paleopolis** on the road to Andros Town, where remains of a theater and a sta-dium still stand. Roughly 2km southeast of Palaeokastro is the **Bay of Korthion,** with some of the finest swimming spots on Andros. North of Korthion are the rem-nants of the **Castle of the Old Woman.**

■ Andros Town (Chora)

A sophisticated village with striking Neoclassical architecture, **Andros Town** makes a worthwhile destination for island-hopping travelers. Built on a narrow peninsula, this town begins high above the water and gently slopes downhill to meet the sea on a windswept promontory. The benefice of the wealthy local Goulandris (i.e., "Cycladic marble") family has built two amazing museums in town.

Orientation and Practical Information At the far inland end of the main street, next to a playground, is the **police station** (tel. 22 300; open 24hr.). The **post office** (tel. 22 260), where you can **exchange currency** (open Mon.-Fri. 7:30am-2pm), resides next to an open, airy square where **taxis** (tel. 22 171) queue. The **OTE** (tel. 22 099) is across from the central square on the left (open Mon.-Fri. 7:30am-3pm). The **National Bank** is on the left farther down, on the way to the water (open Mon.-Thurs. 8am-2pm, Fri. 8am-1:30pm) along with **Pharmacies.** The **bus station** is coupled with a friendly restaurant, just to the right of the section of the town's main street which is closed off to traffic. A full schedule is posted in the outdoor waiting area. Walk down the stairs next to the high blue domes of the church to find the town's center. **Postal Code:** 84500. **Telephone Code:** 0282.

Accommodations   Rooms tend to be both hard to find and expensive. **Hotel Egli** (tel. 22 303) fills up quickly; reservations are a good idea. (Singles 7500dr. Doubles 10,000-14,000dr. Triples 12,000-17,000dr. Breakfast included.) The expansive, expensive **Hotel Xenia** (tel. 22 270) abides down to the left (facing the water) from the main street, where the beach meets the upward slope. (Singles 6700dr. Doubles 9200dr. Triples 11,500dr.) The numerous places on the beach get cheaper farther from the main drag. In high season, expect doubles to go for 5000-10,000dr.

Sights   Following the main street downhill leads to a small square with outdoor cafés and a marble fountain. On the left is the **Archaeological Museum** (tel. 23 664), which has an excellent display on the Geometric village of Zagora and many later (through Byzantine) marble relics, including a deservedly famous 2m-high statue of the messenger god Hermes (open Tues.-Sun. 9am-3pm; admission 400dr, students 200dr, European students free). Down the steps to the left of the square is the **Museum of Modern Art** (tel. 22 650), which prominently displays works by 20th-century Greek sculptor Michael Tombros. The weird, vibrating noises from downstairs are not a mechanical failure but the clatter of the electromagnetic "pieces" of the artist Takis. Don't miss the enormous temporary exhibition space across the street a little farther downhill. Visiting exhibitions arrive every summer (open Wed.-Mon. from when the proprietor opens the doors until 2pm; admission 600dr). Continuing straight through the square, through the white archway, you'll find the free **Maritime Museum of Andros** (open Mon. and Wed.-Sat. 10am-1pm and 6-8pm, Sun. 10am-1pm) which is somewhat of a let down after the splendor of the first two museums. Proceed farther for a view of the walls of an off-island Venetian turret. After trekking around town, down the steps to the right of the square, is a golden, sandy beach. Take a dip and wash those cares away. If the museum is not open according to the schedule, the guard next door will provide keys to the museum.

MILOS ΜΗΛΟΣ

For an island associated with such celebrated artistic achievements as the Venus de Milo, Thucydides's *Melian Dialogue,* and the *film-bête Milo & Otis,* Milos leaves a lot to be desired. It retains its small-town atmosphere, unequipped for mass tourism. However, the amazing postcard-blue water, the alleys of Plaka and the waterfront of Klima and the warmth and hospitality of the Melians amply reward the patient and adventurous visitor. The mineral-rich island has always prospered from the production of obsidian, sulphur, and porcelain, but after Milos refused to join the Athenian League during the Peloponnesian War, Athens executed the men and enslaved the women and children. Milos eventually recovered and reached the height of its artistic achievement in Roman and Early Christian times. Since then, Milos has flourished as a cosmopolitan mining center.

ADAMAS

This bustling port town is not the island's most attractive locale, but it serves as a convenient place to base yourself. Most of the island's nightlife and amenities are on **Adamas's** waterfront, and frequent buses can carry you to other parts of Milos.

Orientation and Practical Information   Across from the dock, extremely competent and multilingual Manos runs the **tourist information office** (tel. 22 445). Ask for brochures, maps, ferry and bus timetables, and a complete list of the island's rooms and hotels (open daily 10am-midnight). One good travel agency is **Milos Travel** (tel. 22 000, -200; fax 22 688), on the waterfront. The English-speaking staff sells most ferry tickets (open daily 9am-10pm). The **National Bank** is near the post office along the waterfront (open Mon.-Thurs. 8am-2pm, Fri. 8am-1:30pm). The **Olympic Airways** office (tel. 22 380; 22 381 at the airport) is on 25th Martiou St. (open Mon.-Fri. 8am-3:30pm). There are two to three daily Olympic Airways **flights** between Milos and Athens (12,700dr). The **bus stop** and **taxi stand** (tel. for both 22 219) are in a busy area on the waterfront. Taxis are available 24 hours. A complete bus schedule (180dr) and a list of fixed taxi fares are posted.

From Milos, **ferries** follow a twisted and complex, yet well posted, schedule. The destinations are Peiraias (1-3 per day, 8hr., 4100dr); Sifnos (1-3 per day, 1½hr., 1440dr); Serifos (1-3 per day, 3hr., 1510dr); Kithnos (1-3 per day, 2280dr); Kimolos (3 per week, 1380dr, and from Pollonia daily 700dr); Folegandros (3 per week, 1470dr); Sikinos (3 per week, 2530dr); Santorini (4 per week, 2500dr); Ios (2 per week, 2500dr); Kassos (1 per week, 9hr., 4820dr); Karpathos (10hr., 5980dr). Ferries also head to the Cretan ports of Agios Nikolaos (1 per week, 6hr., 3950dr) and Sitia (1 per week, 6½hr., 4080dr). You can rent a **moped** at **Speed** (tel. 22 440), the shack next to the tourist office (4000-6000dr per day). The **pharmacy** is one block from the bus stop on 25th Martiou St. (tel./fax 22 178, 22 011 after hours; open Mon.-Sat. 9am-2pm and 6-9:30pm). Along the waterfront you'll find the **post office** (tel. 22 288; open Mon.-Fri. 7:30am-2pm), two doors down and on the second floor of the **port authority** (tel. 22 100; open 24hr.). **Postal Code:** 84801 in Adamas, 84800 elsewhere on the island. **Telephone Code:** 0287.

Accommodations   The prices of even the cheaper accommodations in Adamas will appall the frugal traveler. Your best bet is to roam the streets and ask at *tavernas* for private rooms. Trekking down the beach away from the dock and exploring side streets away from the waterfront are most likely to yield satisfying results, although it may be necessary to venture to Plaka or Pollonia to find a vacancy in the peak summer months. With persistence and tough bargaining, doubles can be found for 7000-10,000dr and triples for 9000-12,000dr, slightly lower off season. It is possible to camp on a secluded beach, although camping is illegal, and there are no campsites on Milos. *Let's Go* does not recommend freelance camping on Milos. For clean and welcoming rooms, a vine-colored garden bar, and a quiet setting, stay at the **Semiramis** (tel. 22 118), off 25th Martiou, two blocks from the waterfront. Reserve two weeks in advance; prices lower in off season. (Doubles 12,000dr. Triples 14,000dr. Breakfast 1000dr.)

Food   The waiters at the two neighboring restaurants on the corner of the waterfront are understandably brusque with English-speaking customers in summer, but the food is superb. Try the veal with spaghetti (1100dr) or the broad beans (700dr) at **Kinigos** (tel. 22 349), around the first bend on the waterfront. **Floisvos** (tel. 22 275), before the bend in the waterfront, doesn't look like much, but offers superb, cheap food (chicken and potatoes 850dr). For an elegant dinner, ask for a table on the water at **Trapatseli's Restaurant,** a five-minute walk on the road to Achivado-limni Beach (octopus in vinegar and olive oil 1100dr). If you wake up hungry, head over to **Yangos** for breakfast, farther along the waterfront on the right-hand side.

AROUND THE ISLAND

Six winding kilometers from Adamas, the timeworn town of **Plaka** rests upon the mountaintops. A **post office** lounges at the bus stop—follow the path leading left (open Mon-Fri. 7:30am-2pm). On the main road going through Plaka are **OTE** (tel. 22 135; open 7:30am-3pm Mon.-Fri.), and farther down is the **medical center** (tel. 22 700, -01; ask the bus driver to let you off there). The Milos **police** (tel. 21 378) are in the square off the bus stop (open 24hr.). The terrace of the **Church of Panagia the Korfiatissa** leans into a view of verdant countryside, blue ocean, and red islets a god's arm's length away. Next door, the town's **Folk Museum** (tel. 21 292) has an eerie display of mannequins (open Tues.-Sat. 10am-2pm and 5-7pm, Sun. 10am-

SIFNOS

2pm; admission 400dr, students 200dr). Near the bus stop, on the road to Tripiti, the **Archaeological Museum** (tel. 21 620) houses artifacts unearthed at Fylakopi, including the mesmerizing "Lady of Fylakopi" (open Tues.-Sun. 8:30am-3pm; admission 500dr, students 300dr, EU students free, seniors 400dr). For a truly spectacular view, head upwards until you reach the monastery **Panagia Thalassitra** at the top of the old castle. The 15-minute walk from the bus stop is more than worth it—from the summit, the island is visible, spread out far below like a child's board game.

South of Plaka, outside the small town of **Tripiti**, the **catacombs** (tel. 21 625), hewn into the cliff face, are the oldest site of Christian worship in Greece (open Mon.-Tues., Thurs.-Sat. 8:45am-2pm; free). Archaeological finds in the ancient city on the hillside above the catacombs represent three periods of Greek history. You can still see part of the stone wall built by the Dorians between 1100 and 800 BCE. A plaque marks the spot where the **Venus de Milo** was buried around 320 BCE; she now resides in the Louvre. The well preserved theater dating from the Roman occupation offers a riveting ocean view. A 20-minute downhill walk from Plaka on the road that goes through Tripiti will get you to the seaside village of **Klima.** This tiny fishing village, loyal to its traditions with its white-washed houses looming over the waves, remains a beautiful expression of the Greek fishing community.

Pollonia is also a quiet fishing town with a pleasant beach. Boats run between Pollonia and the tiny island of **Kimolos** (2-3 per day). Kimolos Town and the port of Psathi are perfect places to unwind; few tourists venture there. Archaeology buffs will want to scramble among the ruins of **Filakopi,** 3km from Pollonia toward Adamas, where British excavations unearthed 3500-year-old frescoes of flying fish and lilies (now exhibited in the National Museum in Athens). There is a bus (every 45min., 15min., 220dr) from Pollonia to **Papafragas,** where gangling rock formations surround a pool of clear blue water. Take the bus from Adamas; ask the driver to stop at Papafragas. Buses run frequently from Adamas to Plaka and Tripiti (every 30min., 15min., 220dr) and Pollonia (every 45min., 20min., 220dr).

There are several **beaches** with exceptional seascapes on Milos. Most are on the eastern half of the island, inaccessible by bus. Beaches of renown cling to the southeast coast: **Paleochori** (6 buses per day, 25min., 300dr), and, northwest of Plaka, secluded **Plathiena.** Seven daily buses from Adamas jaunt to the more densely populated **Achivadolimni Beach** (15min., 300dr). On the southern coast, **Provatas** (8km from Adamas) is an ideal spot for a swim. Ask at **Milos Travel** (tel. 22 000), about the excursion boat—an excellent way to see all of the beaches, slivers of fishing villages, the lava formations of **Glaronissia,** enchanting blue waters of **Kleftiko,** and the weathered charm of **Klima.** You'll find swimming holes and a lunch break in **Kimolos** (boat departs 9am, returns 6:30pm, 300dr per person).

SIFNOS ΣΙΦΝΟΣ

In ancient times, Sifnos was renowned for the plethora of gold, silver, and copper in its mines. Legend has it that each year the islanders, in order to placate Apollo, would send a solid-gold dancer to Delphi. One year, the locals decided to substitute a gold-plated egg. As a result of this insult, Apollo sank the Sifnian mines under the sea and cursed the land with infertility. Barrenness claims most of Sifnos's western half, where boats dock. A short bus ride brings you to whitewashed villages sprinkled across the terraced walls of Sifnos's eastern, better half. This side of Sifnos is affluent, with olive grove-gorged hillsides plunging down to rock caves and calm beaches. Tourism is more easygoing here than on most islands, but accommodations are limited and simply not available in July and August. During high season your best bets are private rooms from affable residents, camping, or reservations made several months in advance.

SIFNOS

■ Kamares

Boats dock at Kamares, a magnificent harbor fortified by formidable brown cliffs which stand in fierce contrast to the gentle emerald sea. Here you can secure a room, swim, dine, and meander into the shops featuring ornate **pottery** molded by local craftspeople; look for κεραμικο (ceramic) signs throughout the village.

Orientation and Practical Information   Just opposite the ferry dock, the **Community Information Office** (tel. 31 977) helps find rooms and decipher boat and bus schedules (200dr; open Mon. 2-9pm, Fri. 5-11pm, Sat. 1-8pm, Sun. 10am-5pm; hours extended in high season). The **port authority** (tel. 31 617) next door has sea travel information (open 24 hr.). A visit to the **Aegean Thesaurus Travel Agency** (tel./fax 31 727), located along the waterfront as you walk from the dock to town, almost always pays off. The friendly, English-speaking staff **exchanges currency,** finds accommodations, stores luggage (300dr for 6hr., 1000dr for a day), and sells maps (250dr; open daily 9:30am-10pm, or until the last ferry arrives).

From Sifnos, **ferries** head to Peiraias (1-2 per day, 6hr., 3500dr); Milos (1-2 per day, 1½hr., 1400dr); Kimolos (1 per day except Sun., 1½hr., 1300dr); Serifos (1-2 per day except Fri., 1hr., 1000dr); Kithnos (1-2 per day except Fri., 2½hr., 1800dr); Folegandros (1-3 per week, 45min., 1100dr); Sikinos (1-3 per week, 2½hr., 1700dr); Santorini (1-3 per week, 4hr., 2600dr); and Syros (1 per week, 4½hr., 1800dr). There is **hydrofoil** service weekly to Paros (1hr., 4000dr); Mykonos (1½hr., 4524dr); Tinos (2hr., 4524dr); and Rafina (6hr., 6704dr). Prices rise during high season. From Kamares, buses go to Apollonia at least every hour from 7:30am10:30pm (250dr).

Accommodations   During high season, you are unlikely to find a budget hotel room; try private rooms, either by following "Room to Let" signs or by asking at one of the many waterfront *taverna*. Off-season prices are roughly 1000-2000dr lower. (Doubles 6500-8500dr. Triples 8000-11,000dr.) In Kamares, **Hotel Stavros** (tel. 32 383 or 31 641; fax 31 709) has clean, pleasant rooms with baths, many with panoramic views of the harbor's beach. Stavros and his English wife also offer travel services and car rental. (Doubles 10,000dr. Triples 12,000dr in high season.) For tighter budgets, there are also rear rooms with shared baths (3000dr). Freelance camping on Sifnos is illegal, but **Maki's Camping** (tel. 32 366) lies across the road from the beach in Kamares (open May-Oct.; 1000dr per person. 200-300dr per tent.). Other campsites in more secluded parts of the island include calm, clean **Platis Yialos Camping** (tel. 31 786), set amid olive trees and stone walls, a 10-minute walk inland from the Yialos Sq. bus stop (open July-mid-Sept.; 1000dr per person.)

Food and Entertainment   Each *taverna* offers food of roughly the same quality and price, but many have seaside seating. For Greek food with a charming twist, try **Kamares Ouzeri** (tel. 32 398), along the waterfront. Among the specialties prepared with care by the English-speaking chef and staff are the stuffed chicken (1200dr), the shrimp *saganaki* (1500dr), and *tzatziki* (400dr). Chick peas are a local specialty found in fried balls in a soup called *revithada* (700dr; served only on Sundays). It gets polished off early, so try it for lunch to be sure to get some. There are also several **groceries** and **bakeries,** which sell the local almond cookie delicacy, *amigdaloto*. Nightlife options in Kamares are **Collage,** along the waterfront on the second floor (listen for the music), and **Mobilize** past the little park.

APOLLONIA

Apollonia, the island's capital, serves as the central hub for travel around the island. Buses to Kamares (10min., 190dr) stop in the square in front of the post office, while those heading to outlying villages and beaches like **Kastro** (190dr) and **Plati Yialos** (230dr) stop around the corner near the Hotel Anthousa. Buses run to all three locales at least once every hour.

Just about anything you need to conduct your important business stands in a row along the main square. **Aegean Thesaurus** (tel. 32 190 or 31 145), near the post office (open daily 9:30am-10pm), is your source for **currency exchange,** luggage storage (300dr up to 6hr., 900dr thereafter), room finding, bus and ferry schedules, and island information packs (500dr). The neighboring **National Bank** (tel. 31 237) has an **ATM** (open Mon.-Thurs. 8am-2pm, Fri. 8am-1:30pm). **OTE** (tel. 31 215 or 33 399) is a few doors down on the road back to Kamares (open Mon.-Sat. 7:30am-10pm, Sun. 9am-2pm and 5-8pm). From the other bus stop near hotel Anthoussa, head up the road to Artemonas to find the **medical center** (tel. 31 315) on your left and the **police station** (tel. 31 210), in a small white building on your right. The bus from Kamares drops you off at the main square; at the top is the **pharmacy** (tel. 31 833; open Mon.-Fri. 8:30am-1pm, 5:30-8pm; Sat. 10am-1pm). Next door is the **post office** (open Mon.-Fri. 7:30am-2pm). **Postal Code:** 84003. **Telephone Code:** 0284.

During the summer, vacancies in Apollonia are rare. Prices are generally lower in off season. The **Hotel Sofia** (tel. 31 238) is just off the square; head up the wide paved road from the main square until you see it on your left above supermarket Sofia. Reservations should be made a month in advance. (Singles 6500dr. Doubles 9000dr. Triples 10,500dr. All rooms with private bath.) The **Hotel Anthoussa** (tel. 31 431 or 32 207), framed by flowered trees and located above the pastry shop, has more luxurious accommodations with daily cleaning service. Reservations needed several months in advance. (Doubles 12,000dr. Triples 15,000dr.)

Restaurants are excellent and not as expensive as their beautiful exteriors might suggest. The better *tavernas* are along the path across from the police. The restaurant at the Sifnos hotel is good (meatballs 1100dr). *Revithia* are served here with olive oil and lemon, cooked over a low fire all night in special ovens at Artemonos (800dr at your friendly *taverna;* go early—it's gone by dinner). The main drag behind the museum is where the island seeks its nighttime fun. No raging parties but the bars here do offer a pleasant evening ambience.

The **Museum of Popular Art** in the square features hand-woven laces, traditional dress, local pottery (still a primary industry), and several unusual paintings. (Call 31 341 to set up an appointment with the museum guide; admission 200dr.)

AROUND THE ISLAND

Travel in Sifnos is easy with the map available at any kiosk (300dr). Pack some picnic treats in Apollonia to nibble as you go through adjacent hillside Cycladic villages. The quiet but expansive white village of **Artemonas,** a 10-minute walk from Apollonia, has many fine mansions built by refugees from Alexandria and boasts a magnificent view. The enchanting village of **Kastro** is 3km east of Apollonia; take the bus from Apollonia (15min., 190dr). This cluster of beautiful white-washed houses and narrow streets is fitted on a mountaintop and overlooks the sea. Climbing to the top of the island's fortified former capital through its twisted whitewashed streets, you'll find a tiny **archaeological museum** (open Tues.-Sun. 11am-2:30pm; free). The solitary seaside chapel is arresting. There are no hotels, but ask around for rooms. Walk left at the base of the hill for the monastery of **Panagia Poulati.** The smooth rock alcove below reputedly offers the best swimming on the island.

Casual **Faros,** to the south, has several popular beaches. Farther east, **Fasolou,** the island's only **nude beach,** is tucked away beneath promontories. Continue west along the rocky hillside path past a dilapidated mine to reach a better beach at **Apokofto.** You can also reach Apokofto by getting off the bus to Platis Yialos at the Chrysopigi stop. At the far end of this bay, you'll see the striking **Panagia Chrysopigi.** A bridge connects this 17th-century monastery's rocky islet to the mainland. People swim from the flat rocks at the end of the islet. The monastery (tel. 31 482) has rooms to let; make reservations about two months in advance. (Doubles 4000dr.) Forty days after Easter, the two-day festival of Analipsos is celebrated at Chrysopigi. Up the path from Chrysopigi, **Vassilis Restaurant** offers food with a view—roast chicken (1000dr) or veal in a clay bowl (1100dr). To go to Chrysopigi, take the bus to Platis Yialos and ask the driver to let you off; it's a 20-minute walk.

Platis Yialos, the longest, most popular beach on the island, is accessible by bus from Apollonia every hour from 9am to 10pm. Buses also go to **Vathi** (7 per day), a beautiful fishing village with a beach. The village gets only intermittent electricity and has a single telephone for the entire community (phone calls are announced on a village megaphone). **Excursion boats** go to **Hersonissos** for beaches and fishing (Mon.-Tues. and Thurs.-Sat.; 1200dr roundtrip). To admire icons and an awe-inspiring view, ask to be let off 3km before the normal stop at **Panagia tou Vounou.** (Monastery accommodations. Doubles 4000dr. Triples with bath 8000dr.)

SERIFOS ΣΕΡΙΦΟΣ

As the daytime boat docks in the port town of Livadia, your first vision of Serifos is of the chocolate-brown hills and the ghostly white capital (Chora) gripping a mountain peak. Mythology claims that on this rocky isle, Perseus, the son of Zeus and Danae (who was immortalized by Harry Hamlin in the seminal cinematic tour-de-force *Clash of the Titans*), turned King Polydictes and his servants into stone by showing them Medusa's head; hence the stark, still, barren terrain. Even the main waterfront strip is a dirt road. With bus service running only between its port and capital, this mysterious island challenges the adventurer. Serifos takes pride in its hospitality and in its delicious fresh spring water which is a rarity in the Cyclades.

LIVADI

All boats dock in friendly, albeit non-descript Livadi. Most residents of Chora come down to this seaside town for the summer. Old couples sit on balconies and smile down at vacationers while Livadi welcomes its guests.

Orientation and Practical Information An island map which lists useful telephone numbers is available at kiosks (300dr). **Serifos Travel Agency** (tel. 51 241), behind the market, offers hydrofoil and ferry tickets and schedules in English (open daily 10am-1pm, 6pm-midnight). As you walk from the dock, the **port authority** (tel. 51 470) is in a big white complex (open 24hr.). The **police and tourist police** (tel. 51 300), both housed in the same building, are up the narrow steps to the right of the OTE shack (look for the Greek flag in the courtyard). The **Ionian Bank** is hard to miss along the waterfront and also has an **ATM** (open Mon.-Thurs. 8am-2pm, Fri. 8am-1:30pm). Serifos can be reached by regular **ferries** from Peiraias and other Western Cyclades as well as occasional boats from Paros, Syros, Ios, and Santorini. From Serifos, ferries travel to Peiraias (1-3 per day, 4½hr., 3200dr); Kithnos (4 per week, 1½hr., 1750dr); Sifnos (1-3 per day, 45min., 1340dr); Milos (daily, 2hr., 1550dr); Kimolos (3 per week, 2hr., 1550dr); Folegrandros (3 per week, 3hr., 1400dr); Sikinos (3 per week, 5hr., 2490dr); Ios (2 per week, 5½hr., 2800dr); and Santorini (1 per week, 6½hr., 2500dr). High-speed flying dolphins connect weekly to Rafina (3½hr., 7380dr), Paros (1hr., 4000dr), and Mykonos (1½hr., 5800dr). Farther along the waterfront, look for the green cross to locate the **pharmacy** (tel. 51 482, -205; open Mon.-Fri. 9:30am-2pm, 6-9:30pm; Sat. 10am-2pm). For **taxis,** call 51 245 or 51 435. **Telephone Code:** 0281. **Postal Code:** 84005

Accommodations On Serifos, don't expect people to aggressively offer rooms at the port. Instead look for pensions on the waterfront, on the street parallel to the waterfront road, and on the road that bears left from the Milos Express office heading toward the campgrounds. (Doubles 5000-9000dr, depending on season and amenities.) Arrive early or call the tourist police for information about reservations. Freelance camping on the beaches is illegal. Prices are 2000-4000dr less in winter. **Hotel Serifos Beach** (tel. 51 209, -468) is set back a block from the beach, but easy to find by virtue of its large blue sign on the main waterfront road. (Doubles 10,000-12,000dr. Triples 12,000-14,400dr. Breakfast 1000dr.) **Coralli Camping** (tel. 51 500;

LET'S GO® TRAVEL

1997

CATALOG

WE GIVE YOU THE WORLD...AT A DISCOUNT

1-800-5-LETSGO

TRAVEL GEAR

Let's Go carries a full line of Eagle Creek packs, accessories, and security items.

A. World Journey

Equipped with Eagle Creek Comfort Zone Carry System which includes Hydrofil nylon knit on backpanel and shoulder straps, molded torso adjustments, and spinal and lumbar pads. Parallel internal frame. Easy packing panel load design with internal cinch straps. Lockable zippers. Black, Evergreen, or Blue. The perfect Eurailing pack. $20 off with rail pass. $195

B. Continental Journey

Carry-on sized pack with internal frame suspension. Detachable front pack. Comfort zone padded shoulder straps and hip belt. Leather hand grip. Easy packing panel load design with internal cinch straps. Lockable zippers. Black, Evergreen, or Blue. Perfect for backpacking through Europe. $10 off with rail pass. $150

ACCESSORIES

C. Padded Toiletry Kit

Large padded main compartment to protect contents. Mesh lid pocket with metal hook to hang kit on a towel rod or bathroom hook. Features two separate small outside pockets and detachable mirror. 9" x 4¾" x 4¼". Black, Evergreen, or Blue. *As seen on cover in Blue.* $20

D. Padded Travel Pouch

Main zipper compartment is padded to protect a compact camera or mini binoculars. Carries as a belt pouch, or use 1" strap to convert into waist or shoulder pack. Front flap is secured by a quick release closure. 6" x 9" x 3". Black, Evergreen, or Blue. *As seen on cover in Evergreen.* $26

E. Departure Pouch

Great for travel or everyday use. Features a multitude of inside pockets to store passport, tickets, and monies. Includes see-thru mesh pocket, pen slots, and gusseted compartment. Can be worn over shoulder, around neck, or cinched around waist. 6" x 12". Black, Evergreen, or Blue. *As seen on cover in Black.* $16

SECURITY ITEMS

F. Undercover Neckpouch

Ripstop nylon with a soft Cambrelle back. Three pockets. 5¼" x 6½". Lifetime guarantee. Black or Tan. $9.95

G. Undercover Waistpouch

Ripstop nylon with a soft Cambrelle back. Two pockets. 4¾" x 12" with adjustable waistband. Lifetime guarantee. Black or Tan. $9.95

H. Travel Lock

Great for locking up your Continental or World Journey. Anodized copper two-key lock. $5

CLEARANCE

Call for clearance specials on a limited stock of travel packs, gear, and accessories from the 1996 season.

Prices and availability of products are subject to change.

1-800-5-LETS GO

EURAIL PASSES

**Let's Go is one of the largest Eurail pass distributors in the nation.
Benefit from our extensive knowledge of the European rail network.
Free UPS standard shipping.**

Eurail Pass (First Class)
Unlimited train travel in 17 European nations.

5 days	.... $522
1 days	.... $678
month	.... $838
months	.... $1148
months	.... $1468

Eurail Youthpass (Second Class)
All the benefits of a Eurail pass for passengers under 26 on their first day of travel.

5 days	.... $418
month	.... $598
months	.... $798

Eurail Flexipass (First Class)
Individual travel days to be used at your convenience during a two month period.

10 days in 2 months	.... $616
15 days in 2 months	.... $812

Eurail Youthpass Flexipass (Second Class)
All the benefits of a Flexipass for passengers under 26 on their first day of travel.

10 days in 2 months	.... $438
15 days in 2 months	.... $588

Europass
Purchase anywhere from 5 to 15 train days within a two month period for train travel in 3, 4, or 5 of the following countries: France, Germany, Italy, Spain, and Switzerland. Associate countries can be added. Call for details.

Pass Protection
For an additional $10, insure any railpass against theft or loss.

Call for details on Europasses, individual country passes, and reservations for the Chunnel train linking London to Paris, Brussels, and Calais. Rail prices are subject to change. Please call to verify price before ordering.

DISCOUNTED AIRFARES
Discounted international and domestic fares for students, teachers, and travelers under 26.
Purchase your 1997 International ID card and call 1-800-5-LETSGO for price quotes and reservations.

1997 INTERNATIONAL ID CARDS
Provides discounts on airfares, tourist attractions and more. Includes basic accident and medical insurance.

International Student ID Card (ISIC)	.... $19
International Teacher ID Card (ITIC)	.... $20
International Youth ID Card (GO25)	.... $19

See order form for details.

HOSTELLING ESSENTIALS

1997-8 Hostelling Membership
Cardholders receive priority and discounts at most international hostels.

Adult (ages 18-55)	.... $25.00
Youth (under 18)	.... $10.00

Call for details on Senior and Family memberships.

Sleepsack
Required at many hostels. Washable polyester/cotton.
Durable and compact. $13.95

International Youth Hostel Guide
IYHG offers essential information concerning over 4000 European hostels. $10.95

TRAVEL GUIDES
Let's Go Travel Guides
The Bible of the Budget Traveler
Regional & Country Guides (please specify)

USA $19.99
Eastern Europe, Europe, India & Nepal,
Southeast Asia $16.99
Alaska & The Pacific Northwest, Britain & Ireland, California, France, Germany, Greece & Turkey, Israel & Egypt, Italy, Mexico, Spain & Portugal, Switzerland & Austria $17.99
Central America, Ecuador & The Galapagos Islands, Ireland $16.99
City Guides (please specify) $11.99
London, New York, Paris, Rome, Washington, D.C.

Let's Go Map Guides
Fold out maps and up to 40 pages of text
Map Guides (please specify) $7.95
Berlin, Boston, Chicago, London, Los Angeles, Madrid, New Orleans, New York, Paris, Rome, San Francisco, Washington, D.C.

1-800-5-LETS GO

ORDER FORM

International Student/Teacher Identity Card (ISIC/ITIC) (ages 12 and up) enclose:

1. Proof of student/teacher status (letter from registrar or administrator, proof of tuition payment, or copy of student/faculty ID card. FULL-TIME only.)
2. One picture (1 ½" x 2") signed on the reverse side.
3. Proof of birthdate (copy of passport, birth certificate, or driver's license).

GO25 card (ages 12-25) enclose:

1. Proof of birthdate (copy of passport, birth certificate, or driver's license).
2. One picture (1 ½" x 2") signed on the reverse side.

Last Name   First Name   Date of Birth

Street   *We do not ship to P.O. Boxes.*

City   State   Zip Code

Phone (very important!)   Citizenship (Country)

School/College   Date of Travel

Description, Size	Color	Quantity	Unit Price	Total Price

SHIPPING & HANDLING

Eurail pass does not factor into merchandise value

Domestic 2-3 Weeks
Merchandise value under $30 .... $4
Merchandise value $30-100 .... $6
Merchandise value over $100 .... $8

Domestic 2-3 Days
Merchandise value under $30 .... $14
Merchandise value $30-100 .... $16
Merchandise value over $100 .... $18

Domestic Overnight
Merchandise value under $30 .... $24
Merchandise value $30-100 .... $26
Merchandise value over $100 .... $28

All International Shipping $30

Total Purchase Price	
Shipping and Handling (See box at left)	
MA Residents (Add 5% sales tax on gear & books)	
TOTAL	

From which Let's Go Guide are you ordering?   ☐ Europe   ☐ USA

MASTERCARD ☐   **VISA** ☐   ☐ Other _____

Cardholder Name:

Card Number:

Expiration Date:

Make check or money order payable to:

Let's Go Travel

http://hsa.net/travel

67 Mt. Auburn Street • Cambridge, MA 02138 • USA • (617) 495-9649

1-800-5-LETS GO

fax 51 073), at the far end of the beach, is a 10-minute jaunt from the harbor. The campsite has a bar, restaurant, and minimarket. (Doubles 12,000dr. Triples with bath 14,000dr. Quad 16,000dr. Breakfast 1200dr. Camping is open May-Oct. 1200dr per person. 640dr per small tent. 1000dr per large tent.)

Food and Entertainment One of the islander's favorites for a delicious, well prepared meal is **Mokkos** (tel. 51 242), one of the first *taverna* along the waterfront. You can go for the excellent *moussaka* (1100dr) in a clay bowl and *tzatziki* (400dr), or try the catch of the day. Either way, you'll be licking your fingers at the end. To find **Sklavani's**, saunter to the very end of the town beach (all the way to the right facing inland) and look left for scattered tables, mismatched chairs, loose chickens, ducks, donkeys, sheep, inchworms, and other representatives of the animal kingdom. Preparations take time, but you'll be rewarded with fresh vegetables and fish at incredibly low prices (eggplant 350dr, fish 600dr). For a pleasant meal along the waterfront, try **Stamadis.** You can get fresh fruit at the **Marinos** (tel. 51 279) market on the waterfront, past the main stretch of *tavernas* and shops (open daily 8am-2pm and 4:30-10pm). If you feel like unwinding after a hard day at the beach, the places to be are **Praxis,** in the middle of the waterfront frenzy, and **Metalio** at the start of the road to Chora (beer 1000dr).

■ Around the Island

Not surprisingly, the beaches here are a prime attraction. Closest to Livadi is the relatively crowded beach of **Livadika** (a 10-minute walk on the inland road to the right of the dock; there's a sign). A two-hour walk past Livadakia Beach leads one to the adjoining sandy havens of **Koutalas, Ganema,** and **Vaya Beach. Psili Ammos,** perhaps the island's best, is a 45-minute walk past Livadakia Beach in the other direction. **Karavi,** over the hill from Livadakia Beach, away from Livadi Harbor, is a popular **nudist beach,** although not everyone on it is nude. Let's think about that.

The northern part of the island promises small traditional villages, scattered churches, several monasteries, and traces of ruins. The rest of the island is fairly inaccessible without a car or moped, a map, and excellent driving skills. For **moped rental,** call **Blue Bird** (tel. 51 511; 3000dr per day). By car or moped, visit the **Monastery of the Taxiarchs,** 10km beyond Chora towards the village of Galini. Built in 1400 CE on a site where a Cypriot icon mysteriously appeared (and returns whenever removed), the monastery houses an Egyptian lantern and several Russian relics in addition to the enigmatic icon. Try to visit close to sunset in order to meet the lone monk who has lived there for 20 years. Lucky visitors may be treated to coffee and cherries. Call 51 027 in the morning or afternoon to arrange a visit.

CHORA

Chora, the island's capital, is perched 5km above Livadi on a mountaintop. It was built so far up from the shore to be safe from frequent pirate ambushes that ravaged the Cyclades. Upon attack, the islanders would climb up to the town's **fort,** or *kastro,* and stay there until the coast was again clear. Today, Chora spills over onto two sides of the mountain in an intricate yet charming fabric of whitewashed streets and homes. Pick your way through alleys and underpasses up to the church of Agios Konstantinos, which crowns the remains of the old fort walls.

To get to Chora from Livadi, you can climb the narrow steps linking the two (you actually may prefer this route on the way down; 20min.) or take the **bus** from the center of the waterfront (10 per day, no service during *siesta,* 190dr). Schedules are posted at the Livadi bus stop. In Chora, the bus makes two stops. The first is near the **post office** (tel. 51 239), where you can change money (open Mon.-Fri. 7:30am-3pm). Continuing up the main road from the first bus stop, you will find the island's **medical center** (tel. 51 788), on your left. The friendly doctor is usually there 9am-noon. The second bus stop is at the top of the hill in one of the town's squares. Walk

K
E
A

back out of the square onto the main road again and make a right to get to the **OTE** (tel. 51 399) building, set back from the road (open Mon.-Fri. 7:30am-3pm).

To find rooms to let in Chora, follow the high paved road from the bus stop away from town, past the windmills. On the right, you'll spot **Anatoli's** palatial rooms with startling views (tel. 51 510); look for red "Rooms To Let" signs. (Doubles 8500dr.) Or head into town until you come to **Apanemia** (tel. 51 717), on the second highest road, 200m on the right past the "Rooms to Let" sign. (Doubles 8500dr. Triples 7800dr.) Both have nice rooms with gorgeous views, and reservations for both pensions should be made a month in advance. Most *tavernas* and all discoes are in Livadi; buses stop running at 11pm, and stays in Chora are only for those seeking seclusion. If you do get hungry while in Chora, look for **Petros'** (tel. 51 302) *taverna* right before the first windmill on the high road up from the second bus stop.

The **Archaeological Museum** lurks inside the beautiful, incongruous, faded orange Neoclassical town hall in the central *platia,* up the stairs to the right of the Upper Chora bus stop (allegedly open Tues.-Sun. 8:30am-1pm; free). The easily missed entrance is through a green door on the right side of the building.

KEA TZIA (KEA)

Kea is criss-crossed with gray stone fences that snake through the island's plentiful fruit orchards, archaeological remains, windmills, and rocky coves. The ruins of a Neolithic city at Agia Erini, the base of a classical temple at Karthaia, and the Byzantine monastery of Panagia Kastriani all attest to Kea's strong historical presence. Kea is the birthplace of the 5th- and 6th-century BCE poets Bacchylides and Simonides, the latter of whom is renowned for his epigram praising Athenian bravery in the Battle of Marathon. Kea is also infamous for its classical counterpart to the Kevorkian suicide machine—citizens toasted their 70th birthdays with a cup of hemlock. Although many bars have long since stopped serving hemlock, visitors may still exalt in the pleasure of feasting on *pasteli,* a confection made with sesame seeds, and the golden thyme honey that pours forth from the hills.

ORIENTATION AND PRACTICAL INFORMATION

Boats dock in the relatively quiet but congenial harbor of **Korissia.** From the left of the dock, a strip of gift shops and cafeterias stretches along the waterfront. One of the first shops you will see is Mr. Stefanos's **Stegadi** shop, which doubles as a hydrofoil agency and **tourist information office** (tel. 21 435; open daily 8am-11pm). The **police station** (tel. 21 100), which also houses the **tourist police,** is the large white building with blue shutters on the street directly above Stegadi.

Nestled 5km uphill is the island's capital, **Chora,** or ancient **Ioulis.** If you continue on the path past the town square, you will reach the convenience store which serves as the island's **bank** (tel. 22 350), on your right (open Mon.-Thurs. 8am-2pm, Fri. 8am-1:30pm). To get to **OTE** (tel. 22 099), go under the archway and turn right up the path into town. You will see OTE on your right just past the Archaeological Museum (open Mon.-Fri. 7:30am-3:10pm). To the right of the bus stop is the **pharmacy** (tel. 22 277; open Mon.-Tues., Thurs.-Fri. 9am-1:30pm and 6-9pm, Wed., Sat.-Sun. 9am-1:30pm). For a medical emergency you can contact the **medical center** in Ioulis (tel. 22 200), or Korissia (tel. 21 208) or, after hours, a **doctor** at his home (tel. 22 292, -131). The **post office** (tel. 22 325) is to the left of the bus stop (open Mon.-Fri. 8:30am-2pm). **Postal Code:** 84002. **Telephone Code:** 0288.

To reach Kea from Athens, take the **ferry** from Lavrion (2-5 per day, 1½hr., 1600dr) or from Kithnos (3 per week, 1¾hr., 1570dr). Hydrofoils go from Zea in Peiraias (1 per day in high season, 4400dr) and Kithnos (4 per week, 2520dr). A ferry departure from Lavrion is the cheaper option, but getting there entails a 1½-hour bus ride: take the bus from 14 Mavromateon St. (800dr). For more information on ferries and dolphins call the **port authority** (tel. 21 344).

Ask at Stegadi or at the police station for the season's bus schedule. **Buses** run to Voukari and Otzias from Korissia (80dr), and from Chora (250dr). They also go to Poisses (220dr from Korissia, 160dr from Chora). It's worth traveling from Chora to Poisses just for the spectacular view. You may opt to rent a moped at Korissia (roughly 5000-6000dr per day). You might need to get hold of a **taxi** if the bus system frustrates you (tel. 21 021, -228 or 22 217). The fare from Korissia to Chora is 800-1500dr, depending on how many passengers the driver can cram into his cab.

ACCOMMODATIONS

Rooms to rent in Korissia lie along the waterfront, where the boats dock, and behind the town beach, but they fill quickly, especially in summer—not surprising given the wonderful views. **Hotel Korissia** (tel. 21 484; fax 21 355), has pleasant rooms with balconies and a helpful owner, Mr. Takis Andronikos. (Sept.-June: Singles 6000dr. Doubles 8000dr. July-Aug.: Singles 8000dr. Doubles 10,000dr.) **Hotel Karthea** (tel. 21 204; fax 21 417), the only hotel open year-round, has spotless rooms. (Singles 7100dr. Doubles 9700dr. Breakfast 1200dr.) Try **Hotel Ioulis Kea** (tel. 22 177), for good rates. (Singles 6500dr. Doubles 8395dr, with bath 8970dr.)

SIGHTS

Beaches with clear emerald waters lie north of Korissia; a single road follows the shore, along which many homes double as private rooms. **Yialiskari,** 1km past Korissia on the way to Vourkari (a 10-minute walk), is a small, clean, sandy beach. **Vourkari,** 2km away, is a fishing town with colorful sailboats in its harbor. There are several picturesque but generally expensive fish restaurants on the waterfront. The capital houses a small **Archaeological Museum** (tel. 22 079; open Tues.-Sun. 8:30am-3pm; free), but ancient Ioulis's glory is best evoked by the enormous **Lion of Kea,** embedded in stone 1km east of Chora. The **Kea Kouros,** a life-sized statue of a young male sculpted in Pre-Classical Archaic style, was discovered at the nearby site of ancient Korissia in 1930, but now resides at the National Archaeological Museum in Athens. The peninsula of **Ayia Irini,** across the bay from Korissia, contains remnants of settlements that seem modest to the layperson, but actually constitute one of the more important archaeological sites in the Cyclades. Excavated by American archaeologists since the 1960s, Ayia Irini is a 2500 BCE settlement that traded with the Minoan and Mycenaean civilizations. The city reached its zenith between 1600 and 1450 BCE but was sparsely settled thereafter. The site is closed off. If you wish to visit it, make arrangements with the museum guard. Admission is free.

The road cuts inland at a highway sign and continues 3km to the quiet bay of **Otzias.** If the 10 or 15 people on the beach are too many for you, rent a paddle boat (1000dr per hr.) and find your own sandy shore in the bay. For other **sea adventures,** try waterskiing (3500dr per hr.) or a banana-shaped vessel tugged by a power boat that may land you fortuitously in Kea's waters (1000dr per hr.). The 5½km uphill country path after Otzias leads to the **Monastery of Panagia Kastriani** (tel. 31 348). An icon of the Virgin Mary mysteriously appeared on the site and inspired two monks to build a monastery dedicated to the Panagia. After they built it, however, they decided that they did not like living there and deserted it. Today the monastery welcomes pious guests for the night at nominal fees. A popular beach lies south of Korissia at the site of another ancient city, **Poisses,** whose name, which means "green" in ancient Greek, appropriately describes the ubiquitous cherry and orange *perivolia* (orchards). Freelance camping on most beaches is prohibited. In mid-August, Kea celebrates a festival called **Simoneidia** in honor of its great ancient poet. The four-day celebration features dancing, theater, sports, and a bazaar.

KYTHNOS

KYTHNOS ΚΥΘΝΟΣ

Travelers rarely make it to Kythnos, lending the island a curiously quiet air even in mid-summer. Secluded beaches and gorgeous views from chalky mountaintops are disturbed only by Athenians enjoying their vacation homes for summer weekends.

■ Merichas and Loura

Boats dock in the small port of **Merichas**. The **tourist office** (tel. 32 250), practically on the dock, provides maps, information on the island, and boat schedules, but has limited hours (open July-Aug. 11am-1pm and 5-8pm). The best time to find ferry lines open is up to an hour before departure. The **port police** (tel. 32 290) can be contacted for information on all sailings during other hours. Just off the dock area behind the information shack is the **Milos Express** ferry office (tel. 32 104, -248), another source for information on ferry schedules and rooms to let as well as **motorbike** rental (4000dr; open 9am-1pm and 5-9pm, although there is often someone here all day long). Farther along the waterfront are the **Ventouris Sea Lines** office (tel. 32 242), with more ferry tickets (open 9am-2pm and 5-9pm, sometimes open all day), and the representative of the **National Bank** (tel. 32 345), in a store that doubles as a minimarket and hydrofoil agent (open 8am-3pm and 6-10pm).

There are three taxis and two buses on the island. To get a **taxi,** either look for one near the square, or call 31 272 or 31 280. Most island taxis do not have meters so it is a good idea to fix a price before you get in just to avoid any unpleasant surprises. Fares are high (Merichas-Chora 100-1500dr). In Kythos timetables, price lists, and schedules have little meaning and consistency; this is especially true for **buses.** When they do come, they take you either to Driopida and Kanala or Chora and Loutra. Inquire at one of the shops about the season's schedule. From Kythnos, **ferries** voyage to Peiraias (1-3 per day, 3hr. tour, 2600dr); Serifos (1-3 per day, 1½hr., 1750dr); Sifnos (1-3 per day, 2½hr., 1840dr); Milos (1-3 per day, 4½hr., 2280dr); Kimolos (1-2 per day except Sunday, 4½, 2250dr); Santorini (3 per week, 6hr., 2430dr); Syros (weekly, 1900dr); Kea (2-3 per week, 1½hr., 1620dr); and Lavrio near Athens (2-3 per week, 2½hr., 2250dr). There are also two to three **flying dolphins** weekly to Kea (45min., 2530dr) and Zea port in Peirais (2hr., 2740dr). Look for the green cross a few doors down from the ferry office to find the **pharmacy** (tel. 32 240; open Mon.-Fri. 8:30am-1:30pm and 6-8:30pm, Sat. 10am-1pm).

Private rooms are readily available in Merichas; you're likely to be approached upon arrival and "rooms to let" signs are practically ubiquitous. Prices range from 6000-9000dr and are often negotiable. If you are traveling in July and August, call in advance and arrange your rooms. **Kythos Hotel** (tel. 82 247; fax 32 092), up the road from the pharmacy and Milos Express, has clean and comfortable rooms. (Doubles 8000dr. Triples 9000dr.) **Panorama** (tel. 32 184), located to the left of the Milos Express office, has palatial rooms overlooking the harbor, all with kitchenette and bath. (Doubles 9000dr. Triples 10,000dr.) You can also call Mrs. Panagiota (tel. 32 268) or look for her at her nameless *taverna* a couple of doors down from Sailor's Restaurant on the waterfront. Her rooms are set back from the main road but are simple and comfortable. (Doubles 8000dr. Triples 9000dr, if not bargained down.)

There are several *tavernas* along the waterfront but one that stands out for excellent cuisine and friendly service is **Sailor's** (tel. 32 056). Sit at one of the tables on the beach and feast on *sfougato* (traditional fried cheese of Kythnos, 600dr) or *kakavia* (fish soup, 2000dr depending on the price of the fish).

Loura, the village inlet resting down winding roads from Chora, is named for its hot springs, which reputedly can cure rheumatism, dermatitis, and gynecological problems. King Othon and Queen Amalia of Greece had a castle there, where Queen Amalia soaked in the warm waters so she could finally conceive.

Dodecanese
ΔΩΔΕΚΑΝΗΣΑ

The Dodecanese (literally, Twelve Islands, although there are more) have managed through their unique past to amass one of the more unusual and more compelling collections of culture and architecture in the Mediterranean basin. After Dorians settled there in ancient times, the region was captured in 1309 by the Knights of the Order of St. John, who remained there until the island fell to the Turks in 1512. During the Ottoman occupation, locals formed schools to preserve the indigenous culture. Although they played a key role in organizing the 1821 Greek revolution, the Dodecanese would not join the new nation for a century. In that time, the island group was subject to Italian control and then, during WWII, German occupation. The effects of history are clearly seen in this motley collection of islands, where landscapes are dotted with classical ruins, Italian buildings, and restored medieval homes. Today, the Dodecanese, and Rhodes in particular, endure tourism of frenzied proportions, which is checked only by the islands' distance from the mainland.

RHODES (RODOS) ΡΟΔΟΣ

Rhodes is the undisputed tourist capital of the Dodecanese. While the resort towns suffer from the maladies of commercialism, most of the island remains uncrowded and serene. Sandy beaches stretch along the east coast, jagged cliffs skirt the west, and green mountains fill the interior, where villagers continue their centuries-old traditions. Kamiros, Ialyssos, and Lindos show the clearest evidence of the island's classical past, while medieval fortresses rivaling those of France and Spain slumber in Rhodes and Monolithos. Although modern hotels dominate city skylines and the major shopping streets and New Town beaches are crowded, soothing strolls are still possible in smaller villages and along the cobblestone streets of the Old Town.

■ City of Rhodes ΡΟΔΟΣ

Led by the prosperous cities Ialyssos, Lindos, and Kamiros during the 7th century BCE, the island of Rhodes began flourishing as a major trading center. In 408 BCE, near the end of the Peloponnesian Wars, three city-states united and founded the city of Rhodes to serve as the island's capital. Determined to create a city which would reflect the prestige and prosperity of the new state, civic leaders hired **Hippodamos** from Miletus, the I.M. Pei of BCE. Rhodes' exceptional harbor and fine architecture made it one of the ancient world's most beautiful cities.

Always putting commerce ahead of politics, Hellenistic culture flourished in Rhodes during the next centuries. Alliances with Rome during the Carthaginian Wars helped secure Rhodes' independence until **Cassius** plundered the city as punishment for its residents' having backed his rivals in 42 BCE. The island fell to the **Goths** in 269 CE, but 28 years later, the **Byzantine Empire** consummated its political and cultural control over the island. Over the centuries, Crusaders, Ottoman Turks, and Italians ruled in succession, until Greece finally wrested control of the island from the Germans after WWII.

Although Lindos is the one city on the island which has been continuously populated since ancient times, the City of Rhodes has always been the source of the island's vitality. Though dominated by the legacy of the **Knights of St. John** and reminded of this by a vast impregnable fortress, Rhodes retains vestiges from each period of occupation, including Turkish mosques and Italian restaurants.

R H O D E S

ORIENTATION AND PRACTICAL INFORMATION

The city is divided into two districts: the **New Town,** stretching to the north and west, and the **Old Town,** below it, encapsulated within the medieval fortress walls. There are three adjacent harbors. Most boat traffic uses the **Mandraki,** the New Town's waterfront. Private yachts, hydrofoils, and excursion boats dock here. International and most domestic ferries use the **Commercial Harbor** outside the Old Town; **Acandia,** the harbor below it, provides a port for cargo ships. Beaches are located north beyond the Mandraki and along the city's west coast. **Rimini Square,** beneath the fortress turrets at the junction between the Old and New Towns, has the city's tourist office, both bus stations, and a taxi stand. To get here from the Mandraki, walk to the base of the vase-shaped Mandraki and head one block inland along the park on the New Town side. Follow the city wall on the side of the park opposite Rimini Sq. back towards to the water to **Eleftherias Gate** into the Old Town. **Symi Square** is on the other side of the gate, and just past the archway at the upper right end of the square is **Museum Square. Sokratous Street,** the major thoroughfare in the Old Town, runs east-west a few blocks south of Museum Sq. and is your yellow brick road when searching for lodgings.

Tourist Office: (tel. 35 945), tiny yellow building in Rimini Sq. Bus, boat, and excursion schedules, accommodations, **currency exchange,** and free city maps. Open Mon.-Sat. 8am-9pm, Sun. 8am-3pm.

Greek National Tourist Office (EOT): (tel. 23 255, -655), at the corner of Makariou and Papagou St. in the New Town. Walk up Papagou several blocks from Rimini Sq. Open Mon.-Fri. 7:30am-3pm.

Budget Travel: Castellania Travel Service (tel. 75 860, -2; fax 75 861), in Hippocrates Sq. at the intersection of Sokratous and Aristotelous in the Old Town. Low prices on **international travel, USIT** ticketing, **ISIC** and **GO25 cards** issued (2600dr), international telephones, free luggage storage, the works. Open in summer daily 8:30am-11:30pm; in off season daily 8am-1pm and 4-8pm. **Triton Holidays,** 9 Plastira St. (tel. 21 690), in the New Town, is also well regarded.

Consulates: The Voice of America (tel. 24 731), southeast of the city, just past Sigourou St. Handles consular matters, especially emergencies. Open Mon.-Fri. 8am-4:30pm. A **British** Vice-Consul is available Mon.-Sat. 8am-2pm through **Lloyd's Travel Bureau,** #23 25th Martiou St. (tel. 27 306, -247). **Turkish Consulate,** 10 Iroon Polytechniou St. (tel. 23 362 or 24 603). Open Mon.-Fri. 8am-1pm.

Banks: Ionian and **Popular Banks,** 4 Symi Sq. (tel. 27 434), offer **currency exchange.** Open Mon.-Thurs. 8am-2pm, Fri. 8am-1:30pm, Sat. 8:30am-1pm. The **National Bank** has an office in Museum Sq. with an **ATM** outside. Open Mon.-Thurs. 8am-2pm, Fri. 8am-1:30pm. In the New Town, the **National Bank** (tel. 27 031), in Kyprou Sq., also has **currency exchange** and an **ATM.** Open Mon.-Thurs. 8am-2pm, Fri. 8am-1:30pm, Sat. 9am-1pm. For exchange only Mon.-Fri. 3-8pm, Sat. 9am-1pm, Sun. 9am-noon. Many banks in New Town; few in Old Town.

American Express: c/o Rhodos Tours Ltd., 23 Ammohostou St., P.O. Box 252 (tel. 24 022). Open Mon.-Fri. 9am-1:30pm and 5-8:30pm, Sat. 7:30am-3pm.

OTE: 91 Amerikis St. (tel. 24 599), at the corner of 25th Martiou St. in the New Town. Open daily 6am-11pm.

Flights: Olympic Airways, 9 Ierou Lohou St. (tel. 24 571), near the central OTE. Open Mon.-Fri. 7:30am-9pm. Call 24 555 for reservations or 92 839 for the airport counter. The **airport** (tel. 91 771) is on the west coast, 17km from town, near Paradisi. Public buses run almost every hr. (7am-midnight; 270dr). Arrive at least 1hr. before scheduled departure. **Domestic flights** to Rhodes are usually booked at least 2 weeks in advance. Flights soar to Athens (3-4 per day, 23,000dr); Kos (5 per week, 13,100dr); Karpathos (1-3 per day, 12,000dr); Kassos (1 per day, 12,000dr); Kastellorizo (1 per day, 10,500dr); Thessaloniki (2 per week, 29,800dr); Crete (4 per week, 10,200dr); Santorini (4 per week starting in April, 20,300dr); and Mykonos (3 per week starting in June, 20,300dr). Off-season departures are less frequent and subject to change. All prices include taxes. There are **international flights** to Rome and Larnaka.

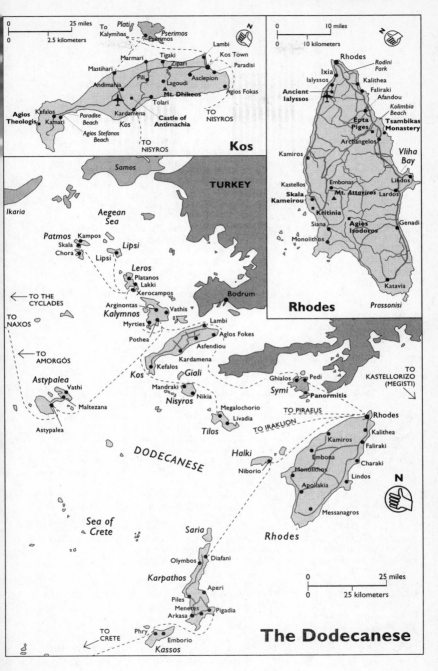

Kos

Rhodes

The Dodecanese

Ferries: Daily ferries to Peiraias (2-4 per day, 14hr., 7500dr), Kos (2-3 per day, 3072dr), and Kalymnos (1-2 per day, 3762dr). Also, ferries to Leros (7 per week, 4180dr); Patmos (6 per week, 4770dr); Symi (4 per week, 1418dr); Tilos (4 per week, 2407dr); Nisyros (4 per week, 2514dr); Kastellorizo (3 per week, 3464dr); Thessaloniki (1 per week, 11,498dr); Chalkis (1 per week, 1756dr); and Astypalea (2 per week, 4093dr). Two ferries per week sail to Peiraias via Karpathos (3375dr), Kassos (4252dr), Crete (5523dr), Santorini (5485dr), Ios (4588dr), and Paros (5856dr). There are **excursions** to Kos (10,000dr roundtrip) and Symi (2500dr roundtrip) that also stop at the monastery of Panormitis. **International ferries** head to Limassol, Cyprus (2 per week, 17hr., 18,700dr in low season) and Haifa, Israel (2 per week, 36hr., 26,400dr in low season). There are daily ferries and hydrofoils to Marmaris, Turkey. Roundtrips may be cheaper than one-way tickets (roughly 10,000dr one way, 12,000dr roundtrip; hydrofoil prices similar).

Flying Dolphins: Hydrofoil service connects Rhodes with the Northeast Aegean islands, Turkey, and the Dodecanese. To Symi (2675dr), Tilos (4585dr), Nisyros (5327dr), Kos (6665dr), Kalymnos (8055dr), Astypalea (8550dr), Samos (12,036dr), Patmos (10,338dr), Leros (9076dr), Chalki (3532dr), Ikaria (11,105dr), and Fourni (11,105dr). Check travel agencies for current schedules.

Buses: East served by KTEL. Lindos (12 per day, 850dr); Faliraki (16 per day, 270dr); Archangelos (14 per day, 500dr); Kolimbia Beach (9 per day, 500dr); Afandou (13 per day, 320dr); and others—schedules vary, so call 27 706 or 24 268 for current details. **West** served by RODA. To Paradissi Airport (24 per day, 270dr); Ancient Kamiros (2-3 per day, 800dr); Monolithos (1 per day, 1200dr); Petaloudes (2 per day, 800dr); and others. For information, call 26 300. Stations lie on opposite sides of Papagou St. at Rimini Sq.

Taxis: (tel. 27 666), in Rimini Sq. Radio taxis also available (tel. 64 712, -34, -56, -78, -90). Check the price list posted for destinations outside town. Open 24hr.

Road Emergencies: Dial 104.

Moped Rental: Mandar Moto, 2 Dimosthenous (tel. 34 576), in the Old Town. Take Sokratous to Hippocratous Sq. and continue on Aristotelous until Evraion Martiron Sq. Rentals 2500-4000dr per day. Open daily 8am-11pm.

Bike Rental: Mike's Motor Club, 23 I. Kazouli St. in the New Town (tel. 37 420). Mountain bikes 1000dr. Cobblestones in the Old Town and maniacal drivers in the New Town make roads here generally unsafe. Open daily 8am-8pm.

English Bookstore: Kostas Tomaras Bookstore, 5-7 Soph. Venizelou St. (tel. 32 055), in the New Town. Open Mon.-Fri. 8am-1pm and 5-9pm, Sat. 8am-2pm.

Libraries: Catholic Academy Library, 7 Dragoumi St. (tel. 20 254), off Diakou in the New Town. English books on the island's history and a few novels. Open Mon.-Tues., Thurs.-Fri. 9am-2:30pm, Wed. 9am-2:30pm and 5:30-8pm. The library in the **Municipal Cultural Centre,** Rodiaki Epavli-King's Garden (tel. 37 144), has an English section. Open Mon.-Fri. 7:30am-2:30pm and 6-9pm, Sat. 8am-noon. **Municipal Library,** 1 Aristotelous St. (tel. 24 448), in the Old Town. Open Mon.-Tues., Thurs.-Fri. 9am-2pm, Wed. 9am-2pm and 5-7:30pm.

Laundromat: Lavromatik, #32 28th Octovriou St. (tel. 24 161), between Dragoumi and Fanouraki in the New Town. Self-service. Wash, dry, and soap 1500dr. Open Mon.-Fri. 9am-1:30pm and 4:30-8pm.

Public Toilets: Strategic locations in the New Town include Rimini Sq. next to the tourist office and the new market. In the Old Town, search out facilities at Orfeos St. and Sokratous St. Free, but bring your own toilet paper.

Public Baths: Hamam (Turkish Baths; tel. 27 739), Arionos Sq. in the Old Town. Not your typical shower, but a good way to get clean. Single sex. Wed., Sat. 300dr, Tues., Thurs.-Fri. 500dr. Open Tues. 1-7pm, Wed.-Sat. 11am-7pm.

Hospital: (tel. 22 222 or 25 555), Erithrou Stavrou St. off El. Venizelou. Open for emergencies 24hr. **Visitor's clinic** open daily 5-9pm.

Medical Emergencies: Dial 100.

Police: (tel. 23 294), Ethelondon Dodekanission St., 1 block behind the post office. Open 24hr. **Lost and found** open Mon.-Fri. 8am-2pm. The **tourist police** (tel. 27 423 or 23 329), in the GNTO building, speak English. The **port authority** (tel. 22 220 or 28 888), or Central Harbor Master, on Mandraki just left of the post office. Complete boat schedules. Open 24hr.

Post Office: Main branch (tel. 22 212 or 34 873), on Mandraki St. Open Mon.-Fri. 7am-8pm, Sat. 7:30am-3pm, Sun. 9am-2pm. **Parcel service** 7:30am-2pm. **Poste Restante** window takes a lunch hour. Also a **mobile branch** (on wheels), in the Old Town on Orfeos, near the Palace of the Grand Masters. From Museum Sq., head down Ipoton. Open Mon.-Fri. 7:30am-2pm. **Postal Code:** 85100.

Telephone Code: 0241 (for the northern half of the island), 0244 (below Kolymbia on the east), and 0246 (below Kalavarda on the west).

ACCOMMODATIONS

Old Town

Pensions are scattered about the narrow pebbled paths of the Old Town, the preferred resting place for most travelers. Low prices here inevitably mean low luxury, so prepare yourself. Winding streets are inconsistently named—bite the bullet and buy a map. Off-season prices run roughly 20-40% cheaper than in summer.

Hotel Andreas, 28 Omirou St. (tel. 34 156; fax 74 285). Many rooms have loftbeds. Doubles 7000dr, with bath 8000dr. Triples 9000dr, with bath 10,000dr. Quads with bath 10,000dr. Breakfast 1000dr. Laundry 1200dr.

Pension Apollo, 28C Omirou St. (tel. 32 003 or 63 398), next to Hotel Andreas. One of the more affordable, yet still clean, choices around. Common baths and kitchen facilities. Doubles 3500dr. Triples 5000dr.

Rooms above Mango Bar, 3 Dorieos Sq. (tel. 24 877 or 28 324). From Sokratous, take Ag. Fonouriou up to Dorleos Sq. to reach sparkling rooms above a bar with the cheapest draft beer in town (450dr per pint). All rooms with private bath. Singles 3000dr. Doubles 5000dr. Triples 7000dr. Breakfast 800dr.

Minos Pension, 5 Omirou St. (tel. 31 813). Immaculate rooms with clean common baths. Doubles 8000dr. Triples 10,000dr. Breakfast 900dr.

Hotel Spot, 21 Perikleous St. (tel. 34 737). Newly renovated rooms with bathrooms that gleam like polished teeth. Doubles 8500dr.

Pension Sofia, 27 Aristofanous St. (tel. 36 181 or 30 990), in Harritou Sq. From Sokratous St., turn onto Apellou St. south, pass the Sydney Hotel and Kavo D'Oro restaurant, and cross the parking lot to the right—look for a sign. Rooms have private baths. Doubles 6000dr. Triples 7000dr.

Sydney Hotel, 41 Apellou St. (tel. 25 965). Across from Kavo D'Oro. Wood-paneled rooms with bath. Doubles 9000dr. Triples 11,000dr.

Hotel Stathis (Steve Kefalas' Pension), 60 Omirou St. (tel. 24 357). French and English spoken. Nightly folk music from nearby theater. Noon check-out. Breakfast 500dr. Laundry 950dr. Dorm beds 2500dr. Singles 5000dr. Doubles 7000dr.

Rodos Hostel, 12 Ergiou St. (tel. 30 491). From Sokratous, turn right onto Ag. Fanouriou and right again on Ergiou St. A bit run-down, but beds are cheap, and guests get deals at Castellania Travel. Check-out 10am, luggage storage, common fridge, laundry (1000dr with soap). Dorm beds 1400-1500dr. Doubles 3000dr.

New Town

The New Town, with its large apartment buildings and commercialized atmosphere, seems rather charmless; however, it is near the closest swimmable beach and has ample nightlife. Expensive hotels overshadow the coast, but affordable pensions can be found along the narrow streets of Rodiou, Dilberaki, Kathopouli, and Amarandou. Information about New Town pensions is available at the City Tourist Office. **Hotel Capitol,** 65-67 Dilberaki St. (tel. 62 016 or 74 154), has quiet, spacious rooms with private showers in a house once inhabited by Rhodes' mayor. (Singles 7000dr. Doubles 8000dr. Triples 12,000dr. Quads 14,000dr. Breakfast included.)

FOOD AND ENTERTAINMENT

The Old Town's crowded thoroughfares are lined with *tavernas,* but the food there tends to be mediocre, the waiters aggressive, and the prices high. Unfortunately, good food is hard to find; if you do find it, it'll be on back streets. A delicious exception is **Yiannis,** 41 Apellou St. (tel. 36 535), just off Sokratous. The food is prepared with care and the portions are challenging (*dolmades* 800dr, *moussaka* 950dr, Greek salad 600dr). From Hippocrates Sq., go south on Pithagora, turn right at Platonos, and left at a small square into a larger one to find **Aigaion** (tel. 36 228), which is quiet, new, and serves tasty food (grilled octopus 1200dr, *saganaki* shrimp 1700dr). Fruit vendors cluster in the New Market. **Paneri Health Foods,** 1 L. Fanouraki (tel. 35 877), has grains, herbs, pasta, vitamins, skin care products—even Birkenstocks (open Mon.-Fri. 9am-2pm and 5-9pm, Sat. 9am-2pm). For dessert, grab a crepe (600dr) at **La Cave de la Crepe,** 6 Sokratous St. (tel. 21 698).

The **Folk Dance Theater** (tel. 29 085), on Andronikou St. in the Old Town, stages hokey performances featuring dances and songs from all over Greece (shows May-Oct. Mon., Wed., Fri. at 9:10pm; admission 2800dr, students 1500dr). Evening **Sound and Light Shows** (tel. 36 795) at the palace give an account of the Turkish siege of the city during the Crusader occupation. It sounds enthralling, but don't expect much. The entrance is on Papagou St. in Rimini Sq. (English shows Mon.-Tues. 9:15pm, Wed., Fri.-Sat. 10:15pm, Thurs. 11:15pm. Admission 1000dr, students 600dr.) **St. Francis Church** (tel. 23 605), at the intersection of Dimokratias and Filellinon St., echoes with organ recitals Wednesday nights at 9pm. Check with the tourist office for performances in the **ancient theater** near Monte Smith. The **National Theatre** (tel. 29 678), off the Mandraki next to the town hall, stages occasional winter productions. **Rodon,** near the National Theatre, shows both new flicks and subtitled classics (daily shows at 8:30 and 10:30pm; admission 800dr).

According to the effusive *Rodos News,* Rhodes has more discoes per capita than London, Paris, New York, or Berlin. The piasters party in the New Town—most places start shaking around 11pm and don't fizzle out until 3am. Crowds flock to the clubs near the intersection of Diakou and Venizelou and along Orfanidou. Popular places have expensive drinks, while empty bars will cut deals. The cheapest draft beer on the island is at the **Mango Bar,** 3 Dorieos in the Old Town (tel. 24 877; 350-450dr per pint). In the New Town, the **1960s Bar, Luka's,** and the **Underground** line Diakou, while the **Down Under Aussie Bar** and **Flanagan's Irish Bar** are popular international watering holes on Orfanidou St. **Bar Berlin** (tel. 32 250), on Orfanidou, and **Valentino's** (tel 34 070), off Apellou St. in the Old Town, are two **gay bars.** Shake your booty at **Amazon (La Scala),** a hoppin' disco with fountains, tropical waterfalls and a light show. **La Scala** is one of a cluster of discoes near the beach to the west outside of town (just after the intersection with Kennedy St.). Closer discoes include **Zig Zag** and **Zoo Club** on Diakou. For true class, try Rhodes' tribute to Elvis, **Presley's** on Dragoumi St. in the New Town, or **Grand Master's Inn,** 64 Sokratous St. in the Old Town, where two knights in armor greet guests from the balcony.

SIGHTS

Rhodes' most famous sight, the **Colossus of Rhodes,** can no longer be seen. The 35m bronze statue of Helios, the island's patron deity, was one of the **seven wonders of the ancient world. Chares of Lindos** began work on it in 302 BCE. According to legend, *Kirios* Colossus stood astride the harbor—highly improbable, though various pictures insist the contrary. An earthquake toppled it just 65 years after it was built. Bronze deer mark the spot in the harbor where it allegedly stood.

The Old Town: The Castello

Replacing Hellenistic structures, most of which had survived intact for centuries until the knights' arrival, with their own array of castles and fortresses, medieval knights left an enduring mark on the city. The best place to begin exploring the Old Town is **Symi Square,** inside **Eleftherias Gate** at the base of the Mandraki, the main passages between the Old and New Towns and the waterfront. To the right, with your back to the arch, is the **Municipal Art Gallery,** with paintings by local artists (open Tues.-Sat. 8am-2pm; admission 500dr). Behind the **Temple of Aphrodite** in the middle of the square (3rd century BCE) stands the 16th-century **Inn of Auvergne,** with an Aegean-style staircase attached to the façade.

Past Symi Sq. is **Argykastron Square,** with a relocated Byzantine fountain in the center. On the right side is the 14th-century **Palace of Armeria,** now the **Archaeological Institute.** With its small windows and lumbering Gothic architecture, it resembles a fortress. Connected to the palace is the **Museum of Decorative Arts,** with Dodecanese costumes, carved sea chests, and ceramic plates (open Tues.-Sun. 8:30am-3pm; admission 600dr, students 300dr). **Museum Square** is after the low archway; to its left is the **Church of St. Mary** (Church of the Virgin of the Castle). The Knights of St. John transformed this 11th-century Byzantine work into a Gothic cathedral. Most of the rich interior frescoes were obliterated by the Turks as they remodeled the building into the Enderoum Mosque. The Italians made the mosque into a church, which has since retired to a quiet existence as an icon museum (open Tues.-Sun. 8:30am-3pm; admission 500dr, students 300dr). Nearby, the **Inn of the Tongue of England,** built in 1919, is a copy of the original 1493 structure. Dominating the other side of the square with its beautiful halls and courtyards, the former **Hospital of the Knights** is now the **Archaeological Museum** (tel. 27 674). Its treasures include the small but exquisite *Aphrodite Bathing* from the first century BCE, the 4th-century Apollo (open Tues.-Fri. 8am-7pm, Sat.-Sun. 8:30am-3pm; admission 800dr, students 400dr, EU students free, seniors 400dr).

The **Avenue of the Knights** (Ipoton St.) sloping uphill near the museum, was the main boulevard of the inner city 500 years ago. The Order of the Knights of St. John of Jerusalem consisted of seven different religious orders, called "tongues" since each spoke a different language. Their inns, now government offices, are not open to tourists. Because each tongue was responsible for guarding one segment of the city wall, parts of the wall are labeled "England" or "France" on the map.

At the top of the street, a second archway leads to Kleovoulou Sq. To the right sits the pride of the city, the **Palace of the Knights of St. John** (Palace of the Grand Master), with 300 rooms, moats, drawbridges, huge watch towers, and colossal battlements. The palace survived the long Turkish siege of 1522 only to be devastated in 1856 by the explosion of 300-year-old ammunition left forgotten in a depot across the street. The Italians began rebuilding the castle at the beginning of this century. Determined to outdo even the industrious Knights, they restored the citadel and embellished many of its floors with mosaics taken from the island of Kos. However, the interior decoration was completed only a few months before the start of WWII, so the Italians had little chance to savor the fruits (coins, illuminated manuscripts, icons, and sculptures) of their megalomaniacal effort (open Tues.-Fri. 8am-7pm, Sat.-Sun. 8:30am-3pm; admission 1200dr, students 600dr). You can walk on the city walls (Tues., Sat. 2:45-3pm; admission 1200dr, students 600dr).

Several blocks west of the south end of the Old Town off Diagoridon, a **stadium,** a small **theater,** and a **Temple of Apollo** have been partially reconstructed on the hill near Monte Smith. The stadium and theater are quite well preserved, but the temple, to put it graciously, is an irreparable ruin. The few standing columns can be seen from the ferry—they're just before the last stretch of hotels (open 24hr.; free). The only other pre-Roman site is the ruined 3rd-century BCE **Temple of Aphrodite.**

The Old Town: The Chora

To experience a different era of the city's history, turn right into Kleovoulou Sq. after the palace. After passing under several arches, turn left onto Orfeos St., better known as the **Plane Tree Walk.** The large **clock tower** on the left marked the edges of the wall separating the knights' quarters from the rest of the city. The setup was identical during the Ottoman Era, but the boundaries changed; the Old Town became a ghetto of Turks and Jews, while the Christian Greeks lived outside its walls. For 600dr, you can climb the tower; they'll give you a free drink for your trouble (open daily 9am-11pm). The **Mosque of Süleyman,** one block from the clock tower, dates from the early 19th-century with red-painted plaster walls, a garden, and a stone minaret. The original mosque on this site was built immediately after Sultan Süleyman the Magnificent captured Rhodes in 1522. Its location makes it a good landmark in the Old Town (closed to the public).

The **Turkish library,** built in 1793, opposite the mosque, is full of 15th- and 16th-century Persian and Arabic manuscripts (open daily 10am-1pm and 4-7pm; free, but a donation is nice). The other Turkish buildings and monuments in the Old Town are in various states of decay. One worth your time is the 250-year-old **Hamam** (Turkish Bath; tel. 27 739) in Arionos Sq. Notice the dome above with little stars carved out of it letting the sunlight pour through (open Tues. 1-7pm, Wed.-Sat. 11am-7pm; Wed., Sat. 300dr; Tues., Thurs.-Fri. 500dr).

Leading downhill from the Mosque of Süleyman is the main shopping strip, **Sokratous Street.** Continuing east along Aristotelous St., you'll reach **Martyron Evreon Square** (Square of the Jewish Martyrs) in the heart of the old Jewish Quarter. In 1943, 2000 Jews were taken from this square to Nazi concentration camps; only 50 survived. A little way down Dossiadou St., where it becomes Simiou St., the **synagogue,** restored by the survivors after the war, has Oriental rugs covering the stone mosaic floor and hanging "eternal lamps." To see the synagogue's interior, ask Lucia, who lives above, to contact the caretaker, Mr. Soviano, at 16 Polytechniou St. (tel. 27 344). Services are held Friday at 5pm; modest dress is required.

At the threshold between the Old Town and the New Town at Eleftherias Gate near Symi Sq., you'll find a small herd of **deer** in the moat. Eight hundred years ago, deer were imported to alleviate a serious snake problem. Apparently, the deer loved to impale the snakes with their hooves and antlers, and Rhodians have been grateful ever since. Now indicative of a more general sense of protection, the deer statues in Mandraki's harbor have become the city's symbol.

The New Town and Mandraki

Italian architecture dominates this modern business district. Mussolini-inspired stone buildings preside over wide Eleftherias St. The bank, the town hall, the post office, and the National Theater are the more imposing structures on the far side of the street. Directly opposite, along the waterfront, is the majestic **Governor's Palace** and a cathedral built by the Italians in 1925. The cathedral replicates St. John's Church, which was leveled in an 1856 explosion.

Named after Süleyman's admiral who died trying to capture Rhodes from the Knights of St. John in 1522, the **Mosque of Mourad Reis** is an important remnant of the Turkish presence. The small, domed building inside is his mausoleum.

Three defunct **windmills** stand halfway along the harbor's pier. The **Fortress of St. Nicholas** at the end of the pier, built in 1464, guarded the harbor until the end of WWII. (Generally closed to the public.) Greece's only **aquarium** (tel. 27 308 or 78 320), also a vital marine research center in the Dodecanese, is at the northern tip of the island. Various creatures of the Aegean depths are exhibited (open April-Oct. daily 9am-9pm; Nov.-March daily 9am-4:30pm; admission 600dr, students 400dr).

■ Eastern Rhodes

Excursion boats, tracing the beach-filled coast from Rhodes to Lindos, leave in the morning and return in the afternoon, making several stops, including Faliraki. Schedules and prices are posted at the dock along the lower end of the Mandraki; most cost 3500dr roundtrip. **Waterhoppers** (tel. 38 146) offers **scuba diving** lessons and trips to Kalithea (lessons 11,000dr; non-diving passengers 5500dr; kids under 6 free; snorkeling free). Certificates are available (5-day course 65,000dr).

Beyond the city, the landscape subsides into countryside. **Rodini Park** is a forested area with streams, trails, a restaurant, and some animals left from the time when Rodini was a zoo. **Kalithea,** 10km south of town, features a deserted spa that once bathed rich Europeans. For food there is only the meager snack bar at the beach cove, nearby Koskinou (2km inland), Faliraki, or the city of Rhodes. **Buses** run 15 times per day to Faliraki (270dr) and Lindos (850dr).

RHODES

FALIRAKI

With its sandy beach and rocking nightlife, the popular resort Faliraki, 5km south of Kalithea, resembles a New Jersey boardwalk more than a Greek town. There are two main bus stops, one on the Rhodes-Lindos road and one on the waterfront. Directly opposite the waterfront bus stop, to the right of the main road connecting the beach with the Rhodes-Lindos highway (facing inland), is the **first aid station** (tel. 85 555). Dr. Zanettullis can be reached 24 hours at (094) 582 747 if he's not at the station (open daily 8am-6pm). The **pharmacy** (tel. 85 998) is on the main road up to the highway; look for the green cross (open daily 9am-10:30pm). There is a **taxi stand** next to the waterfront bus stop. **Buses** run between Rhodes City and Faliraki (15 per day, 270dr). The bus from Faliraki to Lindos leaves the waterfront bus stop (10 per day, 550dr). Faliraki is also a base for boat trips to Lindos (4000dr), Kos (11,000dr), and Symi (3000dr). There is also a bus tour originating in Faliraki (3 per week, 8000dr). **Travel Center** (tel. 85 520 or 86 312), across from Ideal Hotel on the main road up to the highway, offers **currency exchange,** international telephone, and safe-deposit boxes (open daily 9am-10:45pm).

There's a **campsite** (tel. 85 516, -358) off the main road 1500m before Faliraki; ask the bus driver to let you off. Facilities include TV, disco/bar, market, hot showers, and a pool. (1150dr per person. 500dr per tent.) Otherwise, lodgings in Faliraki are hard to find during the peak season because most places rent their rooms to British package tour companies. Faliraki is best seen as a daytrip from Rhodes.

During the day, the beach teems with sunbathers. On the north side of the beach, you'll find **Mike's Windsurfing.** As night falls, the volume rises at all bars on the main street where uniformly priced beer (500-600dr) makes for a jubilant drinkfest. **Chaplin's** (tel. 85 662), on the beach at the base of the main road, is noisy with Friday afternoon karaoke competitions (shots 500dr). **Bianco,** on the main road, offers pool and pinball (beer 450dr). Nearby **Jimmy's Pub** is relatively unspectacular but, for some reason, always seems to be full (draft beer 550dr per pint). **Incas,** next to the Commercial Bank, has the cheapest beer in town (400dr for a large beer, 450dr for a pint of draft). Disco names and locations change frequently, but it's more trouble avoiding Faliraki's nightlife than finding it.

Eleven kilometers farther south, just before Kolymbia, a road to the right leads to a dirt road 3km away, which continues to **Epta Piges** (Seven Springs). The nature walks in this area are wonderful, but most people trek no farther than the inexpensive restaurant next to the main stream. The tunnel behind the restaurant leads to a beautiful hidden lake (springs open 24hr.; free). There's no direct bus service—ask any Lindos/Archangelos bus driver to let you off there. Continue inland past Epta Piges to visit the Byzantine **Church of Agios Nikolaos Fountoucli,** 3km past Eleousa, which has 13th- and 15th-century frescoes. **Buses** stop at Eleousa (3 per day) on the way to Rhodes. Villagers in **Arthipoli,** 4km away, rent rooms.

A worthwhile stop if you have wheels is the **Tsambikas Monastery,** a Byzantine cloister atop Mt. Tsambikas. The asphalt ends at the Tsambikas Beach turn-off, but the road ahead takes you pretty far. You'll have to walk the last kilometer. **Kolymbia** and **Tsambikas** beaches are sandy and peaceful. **Buses** run from Rhodes to Kolymbia (9 per day) and return 11 times per day (500dr one way). From Lindos to Kolymbia, two buses run daily and one returns the next morning (550dr one way). A bus leaves Rhodes for Tsambikas daily at 9am and returns at 4pm (550dr one way).

Roughly 10km farther down the road from Tsambikas (15km north of Lindos), take the turn-off to **Charaki,** where you can swim next to a hill topped by the crumbling **Castle of Feracios,** built by the Knights of St. John. Rooms and restaurants line the beach. **Buses** to Charaki leave from Rhodes (Rimini Sq.) three times per day.

LINDOS

With whitewashed houses clustered beneath a soaring castle-capped acropolis, Lindos is the most picturesque member of the Rhodes family. Vines and flowers line narrow streets, and pebble mosaics carpet courtyards. The town's charms, however, are no secret. In summer, Lindos' packed streets make the City of Rhodes resemble a ghost town, and tourists pay dearly for the privilege of being one of the crowd. Lindos is also notoriously hot and short of rooms in the summer, making it a place to visit outside of high season, if possible. **Buses** run to Lindos leave from Rimini Sq. in Rhodes—arrive early, as they get packed. **Excursion boats** from Rhodes depart at 9am and return at 5pm, stopping elsewhere on the coast.

Orientation and Practical Information

Lindos is a pedestrian-only city. All traffic stops at **Eleftherias Square** where the bus and taxi stations are. From there, **Acropolis Street,** the main avenue, leads through the eastern part of town and up to the acropolis. **Apostolous Pavlou,** the other main street, runs perpendicular to Acropolis St., just past the Church of the Assumption of Madonna, whose stone belfry rises above the middle of town. No other streets are named. Houses are distinguished only by numbers which change periodically.

The rather unhelpful **tourist office** (tel. 31 288 or 900), in Eleftherias Sq., offers **currency exchange** and sells decent maps (the best is the watercolored "Lindos-Illustrated Map" for 500dr; open daily 7:30am-10pm). **Pallas Travel** (tel. 31 494; fax 31 595), on Acropolis St., has an even better (free) map of Lindos, offers currency exchange, and can plan various excursions (open Mon.-Sat. 8am-10pm, Sun. 9am-1pm and 5-9pm). Other travel offices line Apostolous Pavlou St. The **National Bank** is on Apostolous Pavlou (open Mon.-Thurs. 9am-2pm, Fri. 9am-1:30pm, Sat. 9am-1pm). The **post office** (tel. 31 314) is up the hill to the right of the donkey stand (open Mon.-Fri. 8am-2pm). The **pharmacy** (tel. 31 294) is also on Apostolou Pavlou past Yiannis Bar (open Mon.-Sat. 9am-10:30pm, Sun. 9am-3pm). Most of the town's services are near Acropolis St. Sheila Markiou, an expatriate Bostonian, runs a superb **lending library** (tel. 31 443) of 7000 English, Italian, German, French, and Greek books (100dr per day with 1500dr deposit; used books 300-1200dr). Walk to Pallas Travel and bear right where the road forks; the library is up and to the left (open Mon.-Sat. 9am-8pm, Sun. 9am-4pm). Borrow a used book to read while doing **laundry** at **Sheila's service** (1200dr wash, 1800dr wash and dry, soap included). The **medical clinic** (tel. 31 224) is to the left before the church (open Mon.-Sat. 9am-1:30pm and 6-8pm). The doctor is always there for **medical emergencies.** There are **public toilets** across from the information office near the taxi/bus station (100dr). The **police** (tel. 31 223) are at 521 Vas. Pavlou (open Mon.-Fri. 8am-3pm; for emergencies open 24hr.). **Postal Code: 85107. Telephone Code: 0244.**

Accommodations

In July and August, Lindos is best seen as a daytrip; lodgings, even in the tiniest spots, are hogged by European package tours. Off-season rooms are easier to find and cost a fraction of summer prices. In summer, arrive in the morning before the tour buses rumble in, and ask the tour companies' offices if they have any empty rooms. The few free agents rent doubles for 5000-7000dr in high season—singles are difficult to find. For a good place to start looking, take the first left downhill after the donkey stand. This road leads down to the beach and is packed with pensions and private rooms. **Pension Electra** (tel. 31 266), at #66, offers a garden, terrace, and clean rooms. (Doubles 8000dr, with bath, A/C, and fridge 12,000dr. Triples 10,000dr, with bath, A/C, and fridge 14,000dr.) Less expensive rooms await in more remote corners. Inquire at Restaurant Stefany's on 230 Acropolis St. about rooms in **Pension Venus,** which has simple doubles (10,000dr).

Food and Entertainment

Eating on a budget in Lindos poses a challenge—restaurant prices range from expensive to exorbitant. The only cheap alternatives are *souvlaki-pita* bars, *creperies* (crepes start at 600dr), and grocery stores on the two main streets. "Snack bar" shops serve the best option in Lindos (a bowl of yogurt with honey and fresh fruit 500-700dr). **Cyprus Taverna** (tel. 31 539) has rooftop tables below the acropolis where you can dine on Greek food with a Cypriot twist (*kleftiko* 1350dr, *hummus* 450dr). **Gelo Blu,** just past Sheila's library/laundrette on the right, boasts delicious homemade ice cream (300dr per scoop).

Lindos' nightlife is loud and fervent. Most people visit the town's bars until the music ends at midnight, then head to the discoes on the other side of the main square. Indulge in cheap booze below the acropolis at **Lindos By Night** (tel. 31 463; open daily 7pm-3am; beer 500dr, cocktails 700dr). **Jody's Flat** on Apostolou Pavlou shows a film daily at 6pm (400dr for a pint 5-10pm). **Pantheon** is Lindos' Greek myth extravaganza; an air-conditioned palace houses the 12 gods of Olympus near the end of Apostolou Pavlou on the left (open daily 10am-3pm and 6-10pm).

Sights Lindos' premier attraction, the ancient **acropolis,** stands amid scaffolding at the top of sheer cliffs 125m above town. The impenetrable walls of a Crusader fortress further enclose the caged structure. Excavations by the Danish Archaeological School between 1902 and 1912 yielded everything from 5000-year-old Neolithic tools to a plaque, inscribed by a priest of Athena in 99 BCE, listing the dignitaries who visited Athena's Temple—Hercules, Helen of Troy, Menelaus, Alexander the Great, and the King of Persia. The winding path up to the acropolis is veiled in lace tablecloths sold by local women; the cobwebbed pall makes for a surreal ascent. Right before the final incline, don't miss the fabulous ancient Greek warship *(trireme),* carved into the cliffside as a symbol of Lindos' inextricable ties with the sea. The 13th-century **crusader castle** looms over the entrance to the site. As you leave the castle, make a U-turn to your left to reach the imposing **Doric Stoa** (arcade) whose 13 restored columns dominate the entire level. The arcade, built in approximately 200 BCE at the height of Rhodes's glory, originally consisted of 42 columns laid out in the shape of the Greek letter "Π." The large stone blocks arranged against the back wall originally served as bases for bronze statues which have long since been melted down. At the top of the steps, the **Temple of the Lindian Athena** comes into view. According to myth, a temple was built here as early as 1510 BCE. All that remains today are parts of the temple built by the tyrant Cleoboulos in the 6th century BCE. Once a tremendously important religious site, it's now one of the few ancient temples with inner walls still fairly intact; colonnades flank both sides. Donkey rides to the acropolis are a rip-off (1000dr one way)—the 10-minute walk isn't too strenuous (acropolis open Mon. 12:30-6:45pm, Tues.-Fri. 8am-6:45pm, Sat.-Sun. 8:30am-2:45pm; admission 1200dr, students 600dr).

The graceful stone bell tower projecting from the middle of town belongs to the **Church of the Assumption of Madonna,** rebuilt by the Knights of St. John circa 1489. Brightly colored 18th-century frescoes, retouched by the Italians in 1927, illuminate the interior (open daily 9am-1pm and 3-5pm; modest dress required). At the southwest foot of the acropolis are the remains of the **ancient theater.** The **Voukopion** is on the north side of the rock face, visible from the donkey path. This cave, which the Dorians transformed into a sanctuary for Athena, is believed to date from the 9th century BCE and was supposedly used for special sacrifices that could be performed only outside the acropolis.

■ Western and Southern Rhodes

A string of high-rise hotels abuts the 8km stretch of sand west of Rhodes. The west end of this luxury hotel district is the town of modern **Ialyssos** (Trianda). The hotels were built in the late 60s and early 70s under Greece's military dictatorship. Along with Lindos and Kamiros, Ancient Ialyssos, 5km inland near the town of **Filerimos,** was once one of the three great cities on the island. The ruins are rather meager. Most impressive are the 4th-century BCE **Doric fountain** ornamented with four lion heads, the adjacent monastery, and the **Church of Our Lady of Filerimos** (actually four conjoined chapels). The church and monastery occupy the site of a 3rd-century BCE **temple to Athena and Zeus Polias.** On the stone floor just inside the doorway of the room to the left rests a remnant of the original Byzantine structure—a fish (the symbol of Christ) carved into one of the red stones. The path past the chapel leads to the ruins of a Byzantine castle (site open Tues.-Fri. 8:30am-2pm, Sat.-Mon. 8:30am-3pm; admission 800dr, students 400dr). Unfortunately, there is no easily

KOS

negotiable road to Filerimos. Taxis from Rimini Sq. will make the trek (3000dr roundtrip). Aside from a moped, the only other alternative is the bus from Rhodes to modern Ialyssos (6 per day, last bus at 10:55pm, 220dr), but the bus stops 5km before the town. Taxis cost 1500dr. **Monolithos** (single rock), on the island's southwest tip, is tiny—a collection of scattered houses. The **Castle of Monolithos,** 2km west, is well worth the trip. In ruins, the fortress sits at the summit of a 160-m-high rock pillar, and visitors can walk inside (open 24hr.; free). To get here, follow the only western road out of town. Despite its uninspired name, the **Restaurant/Bar Greek Food** has decent entrees. Two buses leave Rhodes daily for Monolithos via Embona and Ag. Isidoros (depart at 1:15pm, return at 6:15am, 2½hr., 1100dr).

In the south, the island assumes an entirely different character. Here, in farm and goat-herding country, grassy yellow flatlands slope gradually into hills studded with low-lying shrubs. **Buses** run to Lardos (3 per day, 800dr) and Tuesday, Thursday, and Saturday to Asklipio (900dr), Katavia (1200dr), and Messanagros (1100dr).

KOS ΚΩΣ

While it is not commonly recognized for its contributions, Kos' past is as varied and rich as that of other notable Greek islands. Its residents have dabbled in the fields of medicine, literature, religion, and politics, and Kos is known as the home of **Hippocrates,** father of medicine, whose 2400-year-old oath is still taken by doctors. In ancient times, the island was both a major trading power and the sacred land of Asclepius, god of healing. The home of poets **Theocritus** and **Philetas,** it reached its prime as a literary center under the Ptolemies, when its population neared 160,000 (compared to today's 20,000). Several hundred years later, Kos served as an episcopal seat for the **Byzantine Empire.** It was also occupied by various predatory naval forces. The Knights of St. John took Kos in 1315, turning it into one of their outposts. Since then, its history has been like that of the other Dodecanese—the Turks took over Kos, and then, in the 20th century, the Italians, Germans, and British.

Belying its complex and intriguing past, Kos today drowns in a flood of package tours and, in many places, poses as a full-fledged resort. The ancient ruins of Kos Town are surrounded by loud bars, and lengths of sandy beaches in the south hold mammoth hotels, but if you look carefully, you'll find some gems.

■ Kos Town

In Kos Town, minarets from Turkish mosques stand alongside grand Italian mansions and the massive walls of a Crusader's fortress. The town is an archaeological repository of archaic, classical, Hellenistic, and Roman ruins. Unfortunately, it's also one of the more expensive places in the Dodecanese. Package tour agents have made contracts with many of the cheaper pensions, leaving very few rooms for independent travelers. Despite this, the remarkable combination of ancient, medieval, and modern styles make Kos a very pleasant city in which to wander, especially early in the morning, before the tours and the heat set in.

ORIENTATION AND PRACTICAL INFORMATION

As your ferry pulls into the harbor of Kos Town, you'll see only the colossal walls of the Castle of the Knights of St. John. If you walk left from the harbor (facing inland), the stately trees framing the **Avenue of Palms** (also called Finikon Street) will assure you that you're not in Alcatraz. Continuing along the waterfront past the Palms leads to **Vas. Georgios** and the rocky beach alongside it. Turn right onto the Palms and follow it to the next corner of the fortress and you'll come upon **Akti Kountouriotou,** another waterfront street that wraps around the lightbulb-shaped harbor. The city bus station, boats to Turkey, travel agencies, restaurants, and Kos' thriving nightlife can all be found here. Branching off Akti Koundouriotou inland are the town's main arteries—**Venizelou Street** leads through a row of travel agencies directly into the shopping district. **Megalou Alexandrou,** a few blocks down, heads to **Palaiologou Square,** the ruins of ancient Kos Town, and eventually the inland villages. The town's other sandy beach originates near the end of Akti Koundauriotou.

Tourist Office: (tel. 28 724 or 24 460), at the crux of Akri Miaouli, Hippokratous St., and Vas. Georgiou. Free maps. Kiosks sell the same map for 250-300dr. Information on excursions, events, lodgings, and ferry and hydrofoil schedules. Open Mon.-Fri. 7:30am-8:30pm, Sat. 7:30am-3pm.

Tourist Agencies: No one agency in Kos has comprehensive boat information. Two large ferry companies (DANE and GA) and two hydrofoil lines (Ilio and Dodecanese) serve Kos and its neighbors. **Travel Agency Koulias** (tel. 27 311, -7; fax 21 517), on the ground floor of the waterfront building with the DANE SEA LINE sign. Sells DANE and Dodecanese hydrofoil tickets and offers printed schedules. Open daily 8am-10:30pm. **GA Office** (tel. 28 917; fax 22 156), near the City Bus depot on the waterfront, plans excursions. Open daily 8am-2pm and 5-9pm.

Banks: National Bank (tel. 28 517), in back of the Archaeological Museum, 1 block inland from the water on A.P. Ioannidi. 24-hr. **ATM** accepts MasterCard and Cirrus. Open Mon.-Thurs. 8am-2pm, Fri. 8am-1:45pm. **Commercial Bank,** 7 Vas. Pavlou (tel. 28 825), inland from the City Bus station, advances money on Visa. Open Mon.-Thurs. 8am-2pm, Fri. 8am-1:30pm. After hours, **exchange currency** at the travel agencies along the waterfront.

American Express: (tel. 26 732), follow Akti Koundouriotou to the dolphin fountain and look for it at the corner of Boubouliras St. Full AmEx services for cardholders. Open Mon.-Sat. 9am-2pm and 5-9pm.

OTE: (tel. 22 499), around the corner from the post office, at the corner of L. Virona and Xanthou. Open Mon.-Sat. 7:30am-10pm, Sun. 8am-10pm.

Flights: To Athens (2-3 per day, 19,800dr) and Rhodes (2 per week, 9000dr). **Olympic Airways,** 22 Vas. Pavlou St. (tel. 28 331, -2). Open Mon.-Fri. 8am-3:30pm. On Sat.-Sun., call 51 567 for information. Olympic runs a **bus** from Kos Town to the airport 2-4 times per day. Schedule posted in front window. Arrive 2hr. before departure (1000dr). Kardamena or Kefalos buses can let you off near the airport. Taxis from Kos Town to the airport cost 5000-5500dr.

Buses: (tel. 22 292). Leave from Kleopatras St. near the inland end of Pavlou St. behind the Olympic Airways office. To Tigaki (11 per day, 30min., 250dr); Marmari (10 per day, 35min., 250dr); Asfendiou-Zia (4 per day, 40min., 250dr); Pyli (5 per day, 30min., 250dr); Mastihari (4 per day, 45min., 410dr); Antimachia (6 per day, 40min., 330dr); Kardamena (6 per day, 45min., 430dr); and Kefalos (6 per day, 600dr). Full schedule posted by the stop.

City Buses: (tel. 26 276). Leave from 7 Akti Kountouriotou on the water. Cheap tickets in front of the town hall. Fares 180-200dr, to Agios Fokas (57 per day, 15min.), Nea Halicarnassus (34 per day), Marmaroto (8 per day), Therma (9 per day, 20min.), and Asclepion (16 per day, 15min.). Schedules at the station.

Ferries: Sail to Peiraias (1-4 per day, 11-15hr., 6400dr); Rhodes (2-3 per day, 4hr., 3000dr); Kalymnos (1-2 per day except Sun., 1¼hr., 1400dr); Leros (1-2 per day, 2½hr., 2000dr); Patmos (1-2 per day., 4hr., 2400dr); and Astypalea (3 per week, 2400dr). Ferries travel weekly to Thessaloniki (17hr., 10,500dr); Paros (3500dr); Naxos (3500dr); Syros (2800dr); and Sarnos (3400dr). Also, 2-3 boats per week set sail for Nisyros (1400dr); Tilos (1500dr); Symi (2300dr); and Kastelorizo (2800dr). One ferry per week to Cyprus (14-15hr., 14,500dr). **Greek boats** to Bodrum, Turkey (near ancient Halicarnassus), every morning (12,000dr roundtrip). **Turkish boats** leave in the afternoon and return the next morning (12,000dr one way). Since travel is international, it's not regulated by the Greek government—shop around and ask for student discounts.

Flying Dolphins: One per day to Kalymnos (2800dr), Leros (4100dr), Patmos (5400dr), and Samos (5900dr). One per week to Tilos (2900dr), Agathonisi (5600dr), and Astypalea (5400dr). Also to Symi (4 per week, 5600dr); Lipsi (6 per week, 3000dr); Nisyros (3 per week, 2800dr); Fourni (2 per week, 6800dr); and Rhodes (1-2 per day, 6665dr).

Taxis: (tel. 22 777), congregate near the inland end of the Avenue of Palms.

Moped/Bike rentals: Sernikos, 21 Herodotou St. (tel. 23 670), take first right off Megalou Alexandrou—2 blocks down. Mopeds from 2500dr. Bikes 500-1000dr.

Laundromat: 124 Alikarnassou St., turn off Megalou Alexandrou on either Pindou or Kyprou St. and walk 2 blocks. Wash, dry, and soap 1400dr. Open Mon.-Fri. 8:30am-1:30pm and 5-9:30pm, Sat. 8:30am-4pm.

Public Toilets: On the Avenue of the Palms, almost directly below the bridge from the Plane Tree to the Castle. Free.

Pharmacies: 5 Va. Pavlou St. (tel. 22 346), next to the Comercial Bank. Open Mon.-Tues., Thurs.-Fri. 8:30am-2pm and 5-9:30pm, Wed., Sat. 8:30am-2pm. After hours, check the door for the phone number and address of the on-call pharmacy.

Hospital: (tel. 28 050), on Mitropoleas St., between El. Venizelou and Hippocrates (or Ippokratous). **Emergency** tel. 22 300 (open 24hr.); **information** tel. 28 013.

Police: (tel. 22 222), on Akti Miaouli St. in the large yellow Italian building next to the castle. Some English spoken. Open 24hr. **Tourist Police** (tel. 25 462), in the same building. Open daily 7:30am-2pm.

Port Authority (tel. 26 594), at the corner of Negalou Alexandrou and Akti Kountouriotou. Open 24hr.

Post Office: 14 Venizelou St. (tel. 22 250). Follow the signs from Vas. Pavlou, which lead past Eleftherias Sq. and the fruit market and make a left onto Venizelou St. Open Mon.-Fri. 7:30am-2pm. **Postal Code:** 85300.

Telephone Code: 0242.

ACCOMMODATIONS

During July and August, hotel vacancies are rare, so start your room search early. Inexpensive places are mostly on the right side of town (facing inland). It's best to seek out your own room (the dock hawks in Kos are notorious), but if your boat docks in the middle of the night, you may have no choice. Camping on the beach or in the park along the Avenue of Palms is illegal. Prices are generally 20-40% lower during the off season.

Pension Alexis, 9 Herodotou St. (tel. 28 798 or 25 594), first right off Meg. Alexandrou, on the back left corner of the first intersection. International ambience and a jasmine-vined patio. If rooms are full, the proprietor will put you up with a mattress and sheets on the patio (1200dr) or cut you a deal at his elegant **Hotel Afendoulis** in the ritzier part of town. Balconied, wood-floored rooms, common baths, and a guest book dating back to 1979. Prices flexible, especially if you're carrying *Let's Go*. Doubles 5000-6000dr. Triples 7000dr. Breakfast 700dr.

Hotel Afendoulis 1 Evrilpilou St. (tel. 25 321 or 25 797), down Vas. Georgiou. Evripolou is on the right. Smart, well kept rooms in a quiet part of town near the beach. All rooms with private bath. Doubles 7000-8000dr. Breakfast 700dr.

"Rooms to Let" Nitsa, 47 Averof St. (tel. 25 810), near the beach north of town. Super-clean rooms with baths and kitchenettes. Doubles 6000dr. Triples 7500dr.

Hotel Hara (tel. 22 500 or 23 198), at the corner of Chalkonos and Arseniou St., 1 block inland from the water. Private phones, baths, and towels provided. Singles 6600dr. Doubles 8500dr. Triples 9800dr. Show your *Let's Go* for a discount.

FOOD AND ENTERTAINMENT

As a rule, try to avoid the waterfront cafés and restaurants—any hope of finding good, cheap food lies farther inland. **Ampavris** (tel. 23 612), a true diamond in the rough, is one of the few places on Kos you will find authentic cuisine (stuffed flower buds 800dr, Greek salad 600dr). Take the road to Ampavri past the Casa Romana; it's about 10 minutes from town. In town, your best option is **Hellas** (tel. 24 790) for immense portions of touristy, yet superbly prepared, Greek dishes. Make the first right off Meg. Alexandrou and look for it on your left after a few blocks (*moussaka* 1100dr, octopus 950dr, chicken salad 900dr; vegetarian menu available). **Taverna Theodoros,** 22 Pindou St., the fourth right off Meg. Alexandrou, has delicious dishes (stuffed tomatoes 800dr). If you want Chinese, try **Far East** (tel. 20 469), on Bouboulinas St., parallel to Meg. Alexandrou (cashew chicken 1400dr, sweet 'n sour spare ribs 1400dr). Those looking for sweets should head to **To Epe-kial,** one block from the museum (*baklava* 300dr). The fruit and vegetable **market** in Eleftherias Sq. on Vas. Pavlou St. is inside a large yellow building with a picture of grapes over the doors (open Mon.-Fri. 7am-9pm, Sat. 7am-6pm, Sun. 10am-2pm).

The nightlife in Kos can be heard pounding all over the Dodecanese; there are pubs and bars all over town. Most are in two districts; the first includes the streets of **Exarhia** between Akti Koundouriotou and the Ancient Agora and around Vas. Pavlou, which feature **Aman, Hamam,** and **Nova Vita** blasting music. The second is **Porfiriou St.** in the north near the beach, where drinks are cheaper and the atmosphere more subdued. Beers at **Pub Cuckoo's Nest** and **Crazy Horse Saloon** are often accompanied by free shots (beer 500dr). The "in" discoes of Kos are **Heaven** and **Kahlua** on the beach (2000dr cover charge, which includes the first drink).

SIGHTS

The 15th-century **Castle of the Knights of St. John** was reinforced with elaborate double walls and inner moats during the 16th century in response to Turkish raids. Cross a bridge from the Plane Tree to enter the castle. The Order of St. John on Kos was originally dedicated to healing the sick, but you'd never know it from the size of the fortifications (open Tues.-Sun. 8am-2:30pm; admission 800dr, students 400dr).

Before crossing the bridge, between the Palms and the ruins of the agora, you'll see the gigantic **Plane Tree of Hippocrates,** allegedly planted by the great physician 2400 years ago. (The tree, with a 12m diameter, is actually 500 years old.) Nonetheless, Hippocrates is said to have taught pupils and written books under its foliage. A spring next to the tree leads to an ancient sarcophagus that the Turks used as a cistern for the nearby **Hadji Hassan Mosque.** Behind the tree, the monumental former **Town Hall,** originally the Italian Governor's Palace, now houses police, justice, and governmental offices. The most impressive Turkish structure is the **Defterdar Mosque** in Eleftherias Sq. Nearby, on Diakou St., is the abandoned **Synagogue of Kos,** in use until WWII. The city's Byzantine **Greek Orthodox Cathedral** is on the corner of Korai and Agios Nikolaou St.

The **Archaeological Museum** (tel. 28 326), down Nafklirou St. alongside the ruins of the ancient agora to Eleftherias Sq., features the celebrated statue of Hippocrates found at the Odeon of Kos. A magnificent 2nd-century CE Roman mosaic in the central courtyard depicts Hippocrates and a colleague entertaining the god Asclepios (open Tues.-Sun. 8am-2:30pm; admission 800dr, students 400dr).

The field of ruins bounded by Nafklirou St., Hippocrates St., and the waterfront is the **agora,** now ruled by a thriving cat colony sunning itself among the ruins, where you'll find a **Temple of Aphrodite** and the 2nd-century CE **Temple of Hercules** (agora open 24hr.; free). The second site, dating from the 3rd century CE, is more impressive. Two short stairways descend to the ruins from Grigoriou St., which runs along the south edge of town—the main roads intersect it 1km from the sea. The site itself is bordered by two Roman roads—the **Cardo** (axis), perpendicular to Grigoriou St., and the **Decumana** (broadest), parallel to Grigoriou and intersecting Cardo. An ancient gymnasium, a swimming pool from the Roman era, and an early Christian basilica built over a Roman bath all loll nearby. At the end of the Decumana, the 3rd-century CE **House of Europa,** protected under a modern wooden shelter, has a mosaic floor depicting Europa's abduction by a bullish Zeus (open 24hr.; free).

Across the street is the old **odeum,** an ancient Roman theater, preserved in excellent condition (open 24hr.; free). The 3rd-century CE **Casa Romana,** down Grigorious St., uncovered by an Italian archaeologist in 1933, concealed the ruins of an even more striking Hellenistic mansion two centuries older (open Tues.-Sun. 8:30am-3pm; admission 500dr, students 200dr, seniors 300dr). Opposite the Casa Romana are the meager ruins of a **Temple of Dionysus.**

A lot of the northern part of the island is flat and many roads have bike lanes, so slap on the sunscreen and ride your bike to any number of beaches. If you take the main road east of town, you will pedal past a sandy, crowded, stretch to get to **Ther-**

K
O
S

mae and its hot springs near the road's end. **Lampi Beach** is at the northernmost tip of the island. Going west from there will take you all the way to the shady and busy **Tigaki** (10km west of Kos). The waterfront road is interrupted at **Aliki Lake,** so turn inland and cycle on the road parallel to the highway past fields with grazing livestock. **Marmari** and **Mastinari** are pleasant, longer rides. A hat and map are essential. If cycling isn't your thing, buses run to Thermae (9 per day), Lampi (34 per day), Marmari (10 per day), and Mastinari (4 per day), but prepare for snug rides.

■ Asclepion

The Asclepion, an ancient sanctuary dedicated to the god of healing, lies 4km west of Kos Town. In the 5th century BCE, Hippocrates opened the world's first medical school and encouraged the development of a precise science of medicine. Combining early priestly techniques with his own, Hippocrates made Kos the foremost medical center in ancient Greece. This past year, the Asclepion was named "peace capital of the world," and many doctors-to-be still travel here to take their oaths.

Most of the ruins at the Asclepion actually date from the 3rd century BCE. The complex was built on five levels terraced into a hill overlooking Kos Town and the Aegean. Remains of the ancient buildings are plentiful, and if you can ignore the swarms of tourists, it's easy to envision the structures as they once stood. A forest of cypress and pine trees, sacred in ancient times, adjoins the site, and inside are 2nd-century CE Roman baths. Stroll past the *natatio* (pool), the *tepidarium* (room of intermediate temperature), and finally the *caldarium* (sauna).

The most interesting remains at Asclepion are in the three central terraced planes, called **andirons.** These contain the **School of Medicine,** statues of deities, and a figure of the god Pan, the mythical half-goat, half-human. Climb the 30 steps to the second andiron to see the best preserved remains of the Asclepion, the elegant white columns of the **Temple of Apollo** from the 2nd century BCE, and the 4th-century BCE **Minor Temple of Asclepios.** The 60-step climb to the third andiron leads to the forested remains of the **Main Temple of Asclepios** and affords a view of the whole site, Kos Town, and the Turkish coast.

Buses go to the Asclepion in summer (16 per day, 15min.), and it is easy to reach by bike or moped. (Follow the sign off the main road west and continue as straight as possible.) Taxis to the site should cost 500dr, or you can ride a bike up; it's a shady and pleasant 4km route (site open June-Sept. Tues.-Sun. 8:30am-3pm; admission 800dr, students 400dr).

■ Central Kos

The impact of package tours seeking "traditional Greek villages" is beginning to wear on the villages south of Kos Town. Where fertile fields once yielded quantities of tomatoes and olives, tourism is now the main crop. Nevertheless, this area makes wonderful terrain for short trips by bike or moped, especially because the island has many paved roads. It is possible to go from Kos to Mastihari and then up to Pyli and Zia entirely on back roads. For those who prefer the bus, the main road leads first to the modern village of **Zipari,** which includes the ruins of the early **Christian Basilica of St. Paul,** 11km southwest of Kos Town. From there, a twisting road slowly winds through the green foothills of the Dikeos Mountains to **Asfendiou,** consisting of five small settlements, of which **Lagoudi** is the prettiest. It's easy to hike for hours and not encounter a soul. Buses from Kos go to Asfendiou-Zia (4 per day, 40min., 250dr). South of Lagoudi, the road narrows to a mule path and the hills become even less cultivated. A mere 8km farther (although a good spell of it is uphill), you'll come to the compact ruins of old Pyli—14th-century frescoes in a Byzantine church built within the walls of a castle. Buses go to Pyli from Kos (5 per day, 30min., 250dr). From Pyli, a twisting, pothole-plagued paved road climbs over the hills and descends into Kardamena.

One kilometer before Antimachia on the main road, to the left, is the turn-off for the **Castle of Antimachia.** Yet another legacy of the Knights of St. John, the fortress sits majestically on an isolated hilltop. Antimachia is a relatively uninteresting town but it does happen to house the island's only operating **windmill,** which you can see to the left of the main road. About 2500m out of Antimachia on the road to Kefalos is the turn-off for Plaka, a small forest, home to friendly peacocks, perfect for picnics. Mastihari and Kardamena are the two resorts of central Kos. Both offer grand beaches, streets with few cars, and places to eat fresh food. **Mastihari,** north of Antimachia, is quiet, cozy, and popular among families. If you wish to make this more than a daytrip, try **Hotel Arant** (tel. 51 167; fax 51 168), equidistant from the bus stop and the beach (doubles 7000dr). Or try any of the many pensions and rooms available along the beach (doubles 8000dr). **For You Tourist Services** (tel. 51 149, -520), a block from the bus, helps find rooms. **Boats** go to Kalymnos from Mastihari (3 per day, 810dr). Four **buses** per day leave Kos for Mastihari (45min., 410dr).

■ Southern Kos

Rolling hills, ravines, and occasional cow pastures cover southern Kos. **Kefalos,** Kos's capital in ancient times and the only town of any real substance on the south half of the island, is neither crowded nor terribly interesting. North of Kefalos is the picturesque little harbor of **Limionas** (tel. (0934) 22 002). The fish is cheap and freshly plucked from the store owner's fishing nets (*barbounia* 6500dr per kg, octopus 700dr, Greek salad 600dr). The beach that stretches from Limionas to Mastihari is gorgeous and deserted. Just west of Kefalos, a 4km hike from town, is one of the island's most special shores, **Agios Theologos.** Because it's so hard to get to, you'll probably have it all to yourself. On the southeast shore of the island along the main road before Kefalos, you'll find the best beach in all of Kos. Closer to Kefalos, where the road dips to sea level, **Ag. Stefanos** beach has been appropriated by Club Med. On the beach, on a tiny peninsula, are the ruins of a Byzantine church meeting the waves (go down the dirt road that turns off the main road from Kefalos just before Club Med) and the tiny island of **Kastri** is just a short swim from the shore. On the stretch up to Kardamene, **Camel** is a beautiful, mildly busy beach; **Paradise** has its own bus stop and is popular and more crowded; **Magic,** with a Hawaii-ish look to it, farther north is empty and temptingly blue. Ask the driver to let you out at any of the beaches on the way.

KALYMNOS ΚΑΛΥΜΝΟΣ

Kalymnos has always been famous for its sponge-diving industry. In years past, most men would depart for five or six months to dive for sponges in the southern waters of the Libyan Sea, off the coast of North Africa—a solution to the problem of earning a living while living on a large, barren rock. Today, the squishy amorphous yellow lumps lurk everywhere (warehouses, tourist kiosks, restaurant display-cases), harkening back to the island's glory days as the sponge capital of the world.

Unfortunately, the sponges are dying off, and Kalymnos' former staple industry is now in decline. The island's economy has been partially resuscitated by an influx of tourists on its western beaches. But perhaps because it refuses to give in to tourism, Kalymnos feels more traditionally Greek than most of its neighbors. Most of the island's development clings to the coast, leaving the interior mysteriously barren. The rugged mountains, cascading into wide beaches and blue-green water, more than compensate for this island's lack of ruins. Unlike more popular destinations in Greece, in Kalymnos the people treat tourists like the human beings they are; locals will stop you in the street to whole-heartedly say hello.

KALYMNOS

■ Pothia ΠΟΘΙΑ

During the Italian occupation at the turn of the century, many locals painted their houses blue, Greece's national color, to antagonize the Italians. Pink and green buildings have since infiltrated Pothia's neighborhoods and, although slightly grayed, this relatively large town (population 10,000) remains more variegated than its white Aegean counterparts. Pothia is not made to accommodate tourists; there are few rooms, few agencies, few attractions. Before heading for the beach towns on the west coast, though, enjoy its rainbow architecture and the pride, authenticity, and genuine hospitality of the locals.

ORIENTATION AND PRACTICAL INFORMATION

Ferries unload at the far left end of the port (facing inland). The road leading from the dock bends around the waterfront until it runs into the large, cream-colored, Italian municipal building and then a church and town hall. A narrow shop-lined street, **Eleftherias** heads one way inland at this point, leading to **Kyprou Square,** which is home to the post office, OTE, police, and taxis. The waterfront road continues past Town Hall, but there is little of interest besides several fruit stands. The second most important avenue, **Venizelou** intersects Eleftherias at the end of the harbor near the Agios Christos church. Continue on this road to reach the west part of the island. Follow the harbor promenade past the police station to join up with the road leading to Vathis. Most streets in Pothea remain unnamed, but it's easy enough to trace the landmarks.

Tourist Office: (tel. 28 583), along the waterfront, in a small shack in the shadow of the Olympic Hotel. It's a little white house behind the kiosk and statue of Poseidon. English-speaking help with rooms, transportation, and sights. Bus schedules, xeroxed maps of island and town. Open daily 8am-7pm.

Port Authority: (tel. 24 444), in the yellow building across from the customs house, at the end of the dock. Updated ferry information (in Greek). Open 24hr.

OTE: (tel 29 599). From the taxi square up Eleftherias St., take the inland road on the right. Open Mon.-Fri. 7:30am-1pm.

Bank: National Bank (tel. 29 794), on the waterfront, has an **ATM,** advances cash on MasterCard and Visa, and offers **currency exchange.** Open Mon.-Thurs. 8am-2pm, Fri. 8am-1:30pm.

Tourist Agencies: Sadly, there's no one agency to satisfy all your tourist needs—especially if you're looking at boat schedules. **Magos Travel** (tel. 28 777, -652), on the waterfront near the port police, sells hydrofoil tickets and some ferry tickets. Open daily 8:30am-9pm. The **Kamiros Office** (tel. 28 651), near the Olympic Hotel, sells more ferry tickets, but between Magos and Kamiros, you still can't find all tickets. Open daily 9am-1pm and 5:30-9pm.

Flights: Olympic Airways (tel. 29 265; fax 28 903). Take the first left past the National Bank; it's 50m on the left, around bends. There's no airport, but the office is open for reservations. Open Mon.-Tues., and Thurs.-Fri. 8am-1:30pm and 5-8:30pm, Wed. and Sat. 8am-1:30pm.

Buses: Every hr. on the hr. 7am-10pm, buses leave for Kastelli (50min.) via Chora (10min.), Panormos (15min.), Myrties (20min.), and Massouri (25min.). Fares 100-250dr. Six buses go to Vilhadia, 2 to Emborio, 4 to Vathis, 3 to Argos, and 3 to Plati Gialos. Buses to towns in the west leave from the town hall in the center of the harbor. Buses to Vathis from the northeast corner of the waterfront.

Ferries: Sail to Peiraias (1-2 per day, 13hr., 5824dr); Leros (1-3 per day, 1hr., 1616dr); Patmos (1-3 per day, 3hr., 2145dr); Kos (1-3 per day, 1½hr., 1500dr); Rhodes (1-3 per day, 6hr., 3762dr); Astypalea (2 per week, 3hr., 2000dr); Lipsos (3 per week, 1900dr); Tilos (3 per week, 1900dr); Symi (3 per week, 2500dr); Nisyros (3 per week, 1400dr); Mykonos (1 per week, 3100dr); Thessaloniki (1 per week, 10,500dr); and Tinos (1 per week, 4068dr). There is also service to Mastihari in Kos near the **airport** (3 per day, 800dr). Kalymnos also sends daily

excursions to the small island of Pserimos between Kalymnos and Kos (1800dr roundtrip), home to superior beaches and a few *tavernas*.

Flying Dolphins: Fast but more expensive and severely contingent on weather conditions. Daily to Kos (2740dr), Leros (3040dr), Patmos (4077dr), Lipsos (3358dr), Ikaria (5410dr), Fourni (6216dr), Agathonisi (4658dr), Samos (5588dr), Tilos (3678dr), Nisyros (2742dr), Symi (5948dr), and Rhodes (8055dr).

Taxis: (tel. 24 222 or 29 555) congregate in Kyprou Sq. up Eleftherias St. Between 7am and 9pm, taxis also operate as taxi buses; i.e., if there's a bunch of people going in one direction, the driver will take them altogether.

Car/Moped Rental: Cars from 9000dr, mopeds from 2000dr per day.

Pharmacies: One is near the intersection of Eleftherias and Venizelou (tel. 29 338). Open Mon.-Tues. and Thurs.-Fri. 9am-1pm and 5:30-8:30pm, Wed. 9am-2pm.

Hospital: (tel. 28 851), on the main road to Chora, 1.5km from Pothea.Open 24hr.

Police: (tel. 22 100). Go up Eleftherias St. and take the left inland road from the taxi square. In a blue and yellow Neoclassical building on your right. Open 24hr.

Post Office: (tel. 28 340), on your right, just past the police station. Open Mon.-Fri. 7:30am-2pm; also has **currency exchange. Postal Code:** 85200.

Telephone Code: 0243.

ACCOMMODATIONS

Securing a room in Pothea is hassle-free; pension owners await even late-night ferries and the tourist office shack is helpful. For true hospitality, head inland from the waterfront at the National Bank, take the first left, follow the bends, and look for signs to the Panorama Hotel. When the road splits at the embankment wall, go right: the first white house on the right is **"Rooms for Rent" Katerina** (tel. 22 186). Katerina rents large, spotless rooms with tile floors, communal bath and kitchen facilities. Family members or guests can help you communicate. (Doubles 4000dr. Triples 5000dr.) On the way to Katerina's, turn right instead of left at the Astor Sponge Factory, to find the hospitable **Pension Greek House** (tel. 29 559), which has pristine rooms with bath and refrigerator. (Doubles 5000dr. Triples 7000dr.)

FOOD AND ENTERTAINMENT

Clustered tightly on Pothea's harbor is the typical array of café/bars and modest *tavernas*. Try the **Navtikos Omilos Restaurant** (tel. 29 239), isolated at the end of the harbor (facing inland, all the way on the left). Depending on the season, you'll be treated to either front row seats to the lights and crowds of the town's amusement park (open June-July) or you'll enjoy a quiet meal looking out on the water. In any event, the food is inexpensive (spaghetti *neapolitana* 490dr, Greek salad 500dr). If you're on a quest for the best doughnuts in the Aegean, you've come to the right island; they're hiding out at **MacDonuts** (tel. 48 165) on Eleftherias St., on the right-hand side in a storefront with 1899 carved on the edifice (open daily 7:30am-midnight; 150-250dr). Nightlife in Pothia is far from hoppin', but you can mellow out in the evening at the **Muses Reading Room.** It's a cultural library/café located on the waterfront before the big church (open daily 7am-12:30pm and 3:30-10pm).

SIGHTS

Learn first-hand about the island's historic **sponge industry.** On the waterfront near the port police is the sponge shop of **Nikolas Gourlas.** Mr. Gourlas speaks English and will be happy to show you around the factory where sponges are cleaned and chemically treated (sponge mementos from 500dr). From Venizelou St., follow the blue signs to the **Archeological Museum of Kalymnos** (tel. 23 113), housed in the former mansion of Catherine and Nikolaos Vouvalis, a turn-of-the-century sponge baron from Kalymnos (open Tues.-Sun. 10am-2pm; free). The new **Marine and Folklore Museum** (tel. 24 862), housing traditional island wares and clothing and exploring the life and work of the island's sponge divers, is a few doors down from the town hall, on the second floor (open Tues.-Sun 10am-2pm; admission 500dr, students 250dr). The hilltop **Monastery of Agion Pantes and Agios Savvas** overlooks the town. Visitors can enter at the gate on the right side; the first chapel on your left contains the bones of a canonized Saint Savvas in a sarcophagus. The nuns there may welcome you with water and the occasional sweet. The monastery is always open, but its best not to disturb the nuns during their afternoon chores (free).

From the customs house, take the roads to the left to reach the beach at **Therma,** 2km away. Arthritic patients make pilgrimages to the sanitarium here to wade in its **sulphur mineral baths.** (Doctor's permission required to bathe. Those without medical problems won't want to con a prescription; the baths have a strong phosphorous odor.) The main beach is crowded. A short walk around the bend leads to a quiet swimming spot. Farther west from Therma (backtrack towards Pothia and then slightly north) is the tranquil beach at **Vlichadia** (6km from Pothia), the island's only **scuba-diving** site. Ask about it at travel agencies or at the *tavernas* in Vlichadia.

■ Western Coast

Kalymnos has two main roads: one runs northwest out of Pothea, the other northeast. A few kilometers along the northwest road a side road to the left leads up to a fortress of the Knights of St. John, also called **Chrissocherias Castle.** Hidden in its remains are a number of little chapels. Painted sections of wall indicate where privateers dug holes to search for treasure. The **Pera Castle,** a fortress from the Byzantine epoch, looms north of Chrissocherias across the valley. This structure, originally Byzantine, was enlarged and fortified by the Knights. Nine tiny white churches are scattered throughout the ruins and maintained by elderly Chorian women. Directly opposite lies the small village of **Argos**—once the ancient city of Argiens, now a suburb of Pothea. Both the Pera Kastro and Argos overlook the town of **Chora,** once Kalymnos' capital but now little more than another of Pothea's tentacles.

One kilometer or so beyond Chora, just after the road begins to descend into Panormos, a few white steps by the side of the road lead to the shell of the **Church of Christ of Jerusalem,** a Byzantine church built by the Emperor Arcadius to thank God for sparing him in a storm at sea. The stone blocks with carved inscriptions are from a 4th-century BCE temple to Apollo that stood on the same site. By incorporating and subordinating these architectural elements, the church came to be viewed as a symbolic victory over paganism (open 24hr.; free). At Panormos, the road branches. One offshoot goes to **Kantouni,** which the locals protect from overcrowding. **Kantouni Beach Hotel/Pool Bar** is a relaxed pool bar on the waterfront that's open to the public. Also on the waterfront, the **Domus Bar/Restaurant** serves excellent food (Greek salad 800dr) and then bumps and grinds into the night. Don't miss the rooftop sunset. Another road from Panormos leads, after about 2km, to the sandy and less crowded beach of **Plati Gialos.** Stay at **Pension Plati Gialos** (tel. 22 014), perched on the cliff with a memorable view of the coastline. (Doubles 6000dr.) Both the gray-sand beach at **Myrties,** 7km up the coast, and the pebbly one at **Massouri,** the next town up, can be alarmingly full. Massouri, the center of the island's nightlife, entertains with the great pubs **Flamingo, No Name,** and **Smile.**

Myrties' finest attraction, a short boat ride out of town (every 30min., 15min., 200dr), is the tiny, rocky islet of **Telendos,** severed from Kalymnos by an earthquake in 554 CE. A city occupied the faultline where the island cracked—traces of it have been found on the ocean floor, but the rift is invisible on the surface. The Roman ruins on Telendos are modest at best, but a few small, secluded beaches fringe the island. (Turn right from the ferry dock for the best beaches.) Past the beaches to the right is the **Byzantine Monastery of St. Constantine** (open only for liturgy). Accommodations in Telendos fill only for a couple of weeks in August. Most pensions charge 3000-5000dr for a double—prices are generally lower in off season. **Uncle George's Pension** (tel. 47 502), near the docks, has an excellent restaurant and clean rooms. (Doubles with bath 4000dr. Studios with kitchenette and bath 5000dr.) Inquire at the restaurant **Ailena** for similar rooms a little closer to the beaches. (Doubles 3000dr.) Farther along toward the beaches is another option, **Galanomatis** (tel. 47 401; doubles 4000dr). Before leaving Myrties, look back at

Telendos to see a woman's profile along the left-hand side of the mountain. According to residents, she's mourning her lost husband as she looks forlornly out to sea.

Back on Kalymnos, the emptiest beach stretches out at **Arginontas,** at the end of a long, narrow inlet. Both roads to the beach rise dramatically along cliffs that plunge into turquoise water. Though not the cleanest place on the island, **Vanzanelis'** (tel. 47 389), at Arginontas Beach, has a *taverna* and rooms with bath and refrigerator. (Doubles 7000dr. Triples 8000dr.) Two buses from Pothea venture this far (250dr). The last village on the west side, **Emborio,** is unruffled and remote. **Harry's Restaurant** (tel. 47 434), 20m from the beach, provides good food and beds. (Doubles 8000dr. Triples 9000dr. All with bath and kitchenette.) The **Restaurant Themis** (tel. 47 277), the white building with blue trim facing the beach, has nice rooms, stately balconies and private baths. (Doubles 4000dr.) A small boat makes an **excursion** from Myrties to Emborio daily at 10am (1500dr).

Although most of Kalymnos supports only grass and wildflowers, the valley at Vathis (6km northeast of Pothea) is a rich potpourri of mandarins, limes, and grapevines. The valley starts at the village of **Rina.** There's no beach here (swim off the pier), but the exquisite scenery and lack of tourists compensate for the lack of sand. On the north side of the inlet is **Daskaleios,** a stalagmite cave you can swim to. In Rina, the **Hotel Galini** (tel. 31 241) has decent rooms. (Doubles with bath and balcony 6000dr.) The three *tavernas* on the tiny waterfront also rent rooms.

PATMOS ΠΑΤΜΟΣ

Declared the "Holy Island" by ministerial decree—signs at the port warn that nudism and other "indecent" behavior will not be tolerated—Patmos' historical and religious significance is evident. In ancient times, the people of Patmos worshiped Artemis, goddess of the hunt, who was said to have raised the island from the sea. Orestes built a grand temple to Artemis after seeking refuge on Patmos from the Furies who were pursuing him for murdering his mother, Clytemnestra.

While he was in exile from Ephesus, St. John established a Christian colony here and purportedly wrote *The Book of Revelations* in a grotto overlooking the main town. In the 4th century CE, when the Christian faith spread with the Byzantine Empire, a basilica replaced the razed Temple of Artemis. In the 11th century, the fortified Monastery of St. John was built on a hill that surveys the entire island. Until recent centuries, only monks inhabited the island, but news of its austere rocky mountains and serene beaches eventually spread. Patmos today is lively and sophisticated, and thus far has managed to successfully strike a delicate balance between today's popularity and a solemn past. The yellow flag with the black two-headed eagle is the age-old banner of the Byzantine Empire and Greek Orthodox Church.

■ Skala

Built along a graceful arc of coastline, Skala is a neat and colorful port that gives only a hint of the diversity of the island's terrain. Patmos' port, Skala was not developed until the 19th century, when fear of pirates subsided and people could live safely by the water. The main administrative buildings, which now house the post office and customs house, were constructed during Italian occupation (1912-1943). Today, whitewashed churches are camouflaged among the village buildings, but Skala also offers more secular features of the island: lively cafés, bars, *tavernas,* and shops.

ORIENTATION AND PRACTICAL INFORMATION

Skala's amenities are all within a block or two of the waterfront. Small ferries dock opposite the line of cafés and restaurants, while larger vessels park in front of the interloping Italian building that houses the police and post office. The building bor-

PATMOS

ders the main square, where banks are located. Skala is on a narrow part of the island; if you walk away from the water, you'll be on the other side in 10 minutes.

Tourist Office: (tel. 31 666), in the big Italian building across the dock. Maps, brochures, bus schedules, information on all ferries, and help with accommodations. Ask for the free and chipper *Patmos Summertime* guide, which includes maps of Skala and the island. Open Mon.-Fri. 8:30am-2:30pm and 4-10pm, Sat. 9am-noon.

Port Authority: (tel. 31 231), to the left of the ferry dock, facing inland; next to the snack bar. Information on ferries. Open 24hr., but knock forcefully if it's late.

OTE: Follow the signs in the main square. Open Mon.-Fri. 7:30am-9:45pm. The café-bar at the boat dock has an international telephone.

Banks: National Bank (tel. 31 123, -774, or -591), in the far end of the square. Cash advances on MasterCard and **currency exchange.** Open Mon.-Thurs. 8am-2pm, Fri. 8am-1:30pm. There is also an **ATM** next to the post office. Exchange at the **post office** and **Apollon Agency** as well.

Tourist Agencies: All over the waterfront, but each offers information only on those ferry lines for which they sell tickets. Consult the tourist office or the port police for complete schedules and then ask where to buy your particular ticket. **Apollon Tourist and Shipping Agency** (tel. 31 356, -4; fax 31 819) is the not-so-helpful local agent for **Olympic Airways.** Open daily 8:30am-8:30pm.

Buses: The bus stop is across the little park, to the left of the police station. From Skala, 10 per day go to Chora (10min.), 7 of which continue on to Grikou (10min.), and 4 to Kampos (15min.). All fares 190dr (children free). Consult schedule posted at bus stop or tourist office.

Ferries: Daily service to Peiraias (10hr., 5339dr); Leros (1½hr., 1330dr); Kalymnos (2½hr., 1938dr); Kos (4hr., 2382dr); and Rhodes (10hr., 4639dr). Boats also run to Lipsi (4 per week, 1040dr) and Samos (6 per week, 2130dr). Ferries run twice weekly to Agathonisi (1515dr), and 1 per week to Lesvos (4004dr), Limnos (5810dr), Mykonos (2600dr), Syros (2820dr), Nisyros (2463dr), Tilos (2755dr), Naxos (2426dr) and Paros (2600dr). Private **excursion boats** go to Lipsi (daily, 1500dr one way, 2500dr roundtrip), and different beaches around the island (round trip 1000dr.). Check out the deals posted along the waterfront.

Flying Dolphins: Two per day to Leros (30min., 2740dr), Kalymnos (1hr., 1938dr), and Kos (2hr., 5374dr). Two per week to Agathonisi (40min., 3225dr), and 4 per week to Lipsos (20min., 2500dr) and Rhodes (4hr., 10,338dr). Also to Samos (2-3 per day, 1hr., 3345dr), Ikaria (daily, 50 min., 3350dr) and Fourni (3 per week, 1hr.10 min., 2790dr).

Taxis: (tel. 31 225) congregate in the main square 24hr. in summer, but difficult to catch in the *après*-disco flurry, and from 3-6:30am. Taxis to Chora 700-1000dr.

Car Rental: Patmos Rent-a-Car (tel. 32 203), take a left after the post office and look for it on your right (2nd floor). 9000dr and up. Open daily 8am-11pm.

Moped Rental: Express Moto (tel. 32 088). Turn left after the tourist office and make your first right. New models 1500-5000 per day. Open daily 8am-8pm.

Laundromat: Just Like Home, 5min. from the dock on the waterfront road towards Meloi and Kampos. 2000dr per 5kg load (wash, dry, and soap). Open Mon.-Fri. 9am-1pm and 5-8pm.

International Bookstore: International Press (tel. 31 427), behind the Pantelis Restaurant—look for the signs. Open daily 8am-9:30pm.

Pharmacy: (tel. 31 500), behind Apollon Travel, on the first street parallel to the waterfront. Open Mon.-Tues. and Thurs.-Fri. 8:30am-1:30pm and 5:30-9pm, Wed. and Sat. 8:30am-1:30pm and 7-9pm, Sun. 11am-12:30pm and 6:30-9pm. Call 31 083 for after-hours emergencies.

Hospital: (tel. 31 211), on the main road to Chora, across from the monastery Apokalipsi (2km out of Skala). Open daily 8am-2pm. In an emergency, call the **police,** who know doctors' schedules and will contact them (tel. 31 087, 31 571). One doctor has his practice in town, on the road that leads out of Skala to Chora (Vas. Georgiou St.). Look for his red cross before Pizza Zacharo. Open Mon.-Sat. 9:30am-1:30pm and 6:30-8:30pm.

Police: (tel. 31 303), upstairs from the Tourist office, in the Italian building. (open 24hr.). **Tourist Police** (tel. 31 303) also housed there.

Post Office: (tel. 31 316), on the main square, next to the police. Open Mon.-Fri.
7:30am-2pm. **Postal Code:** 85500.
Telephone Code: 0247.

ACCOMMODATIONS

In summer, Skala's hotels are often full, but finding a room in a pension or private home is usually easy. Even boats arriving at 1am are greeted by a battalion of locals offering rooms. (Average prices: singles 4000dr, doubles 6000dr.) Off-season prices are generally lower by 20-40%. To find a room, walk left from the ferry dock and right onto Vas. Georgiou St. Roughly 50m on the left, after Pizza Zacharo, across from the basketball court, is a "Rooms to Let" sign. **Maria Paschalidis** (tel. 32 152 or 31 347) runs a jubilant pension with spotless rooms, permeated by the fragrance of jasmine. (Doubles 6000dr, with bath 8000dr. Triples 8000dr, with bath 10,000dr.) Between Maria's rooms and Pizza Zacharo, above a Tae Kwon Do school, is **Pension Sofia** (tel. 31 501, -876). Knock on the second floor or ask next door on the right for the immaculate rooms. (Doubles with bath 7000dr. Triples and quads with common bath 5000dr. Breakfast 500-1000dr.) Closer to town is **Hotel Rodon** (tel. 31 371; follow the side street next to Pantelis past the international press), which has simple rooms. (Doubles 6000dr, with bath 8000dr.) Many rooms can be found on Vas. Georgiou St. and on the street that leads to the OTE. Two kilometers northeast of Skala, the excellent **Flower Camping at Meloi** (tel. 31 821) has a minimarket and a popular café/restaurant. Follow the waterfront road all the way to the right, facing inland; look for signs. (1200dr per person. 650dr per tent. 650dr per tent rental.)

FOOD AND ENTERTAINMENT

Several seafood restaurants with pricey fish entrees line the waterfront. For better and more reasonably priced fare, head for the locally acclaimed **Grigoris** (tel. 31 515), across from the bus stop, at the corner of the road to Chora (swordfish *souvlaki* 1400dr). The **Old Harbor Restaurant,** with its woodwork balcony on the waterfront road to Meloi, serves the island's best seafood. The prices may bite a bit but the fish—straight from the owner's fish market though they are—certainly won't. **Pantelis** (tel. 31 230) has inexpensive, delicious vegetable dishes (*gigantes*—baked white beans—800dr; omelette with potatoes and feta cheese 800dr). It is behind the central strip of cafés, on the street parallel to the waterfront. **Augerinos,** on the road to the OTE, has excellent take-out *souvlaki-pita* (350dr). There are several **groceries** clustered around the main square, as well as numerous **sweet shops,** where you can try the Patmian dessert *pouggia,* a ball of honey and nuts (almonds, walnuts, or peanuts) covered in dough and sometimes smothered in powdered sugar (220-300dr). As befits such a sacred island, the nightlife here tends to be rather tame, more centered on promenading or casually sipping drinks than on rowdy carousing. One of the more popular hang-outs is **Arion,** (tel. 31 595), a café next to Apollon Travel (beers 500-850dr, cocktails 1200dr). Sit outside or dance inside **Meltemi Bar** at the far left of the harbor facing the water. (Beer 500dr, cocktails 1500dr.) After dinner start walking to Meloi and look for **Cine Meloi** (tel. 31 579), on your left. A 15-minute walk from the dock will get you to the 9 or 11pm showings of Hollywood hits under a starlit sky.

■ Chora

From almost any part of Patmos, you can see the white houses of Chora and the majestic, gray walls of the nearby Monastery of St. John the Theologian above. Roam Chora's labyrinthine streets, hiding gardens behind grand doors, all snug in the shelter of the monastery, and view the Patmos shoreline and the outlying archipelago.

Orientation and Practical Information Because of the convoluted layout of the town it's impossible to give precise directions. The map of Patmos available at kiosks and tourist shops comes with a sketchy illustration of town. Take care of business before arriving; a few phonecard telephones and a mailbox at the bottom of the hill are the only links between Chora and the outside world. **Buses** travel to Chora from Skala (10 per day, 10min., 190dr). The bus drops off at the top of the hill outside the town; this is also the point of departure for buses from Chora to Grikou. A taxi here from Skala costs roughly 1000dr. If you decide to walk (4km and steep), the steps to Chora will be quicker and safer than the main road.

Food and Entertainment **Vangelis** (tel. 31 967), home to traditional Greek cuisine cooked by his wife, is the talk of the town. The journalist, who featured it in his *LA Times* article, thought the *tzatziki* (600dr) was called *tsitsitsitsi*. Make sure you peek into the pots and pans—this is what good Greek food looks like (*moussaka* 900dr). To get there, head towards the monastery and follow the signs. **To Pantheon** (tel. 31 226), near the bus stop, has less ambience, but offers fried zucchini with garlic sauce for 750dr (opens for dinner at 9pm). A few doors down, **To Balkoni** offers a view of the harbor for free along with salad (700dr) and *dolmades* (600dr). Near Vangelis, **Café Stoa** (tel. 32 226) knows its drinks (beer 500dr).

Sights The turreted walls and imposing gateway of the **Monastery of St. John the Theologian** make it look more like a fortress than a place of worship. St. Christodoulos founded the monastery in 1088, nearly 1000 years after St. John's celebrated stay on the island. Pragmatic considerations proved more important than aesthetics, as the proximity of Muslim Turkey made the monastery a constant target of pirate raids. The memorial to St. John was transformed into a citadel with battlements and watchtowers. As you enter the courtyard, notice the 17th-century frescoes to the left that portray stories from *The Miracles and Travels of St. John the Evangelist,* written by John's disciple Prochoros. To the upper right, a fresco portrays St. John's duel with a local priest of Apollo named Kynops. When the saint threw Kynops into the water at Skala, the heathen was turned into stone. The rock is still in the harbor—ask any local to point out the unfortunate heretic's corpse.

Continue to the **Chapel of the Virgin Mary,** covered with original 12th-century frescoes. In 1956, tremors revealed these frescoes beneath the ones currently exhibited. The **treasury** guards icons, ornamented stoles, some of which were donated by Catherine the Great of Russia, a copy of St. Mark's Gospel, and an 8th-century Book of Job. Look for **Helkomenos,** an icon painted by El Greco near the end of the exhibit (admission 1000dr). The **Chapel of the Holy Christodoulos** holds the remains of the monastery's illustrious founder. Shortly after Christodoulos' death, many visitors attempted to appropriate his saintliness by carrying away his remains, so the monks built a marble sarcophagus and covered it with a silver reliquary.

In summer, try not to visit the monastery at midday, when it becomes crammed with tourists and hollering tour guides. If you come in off season, one of the monastery's 20 monks (there were once 1700) may volunteer to show you around. In summer, you'll have to tag along with a guided group. (Tel. 31 398; monastery and treasure museum open Mon. 8am-1pm, Tues. 8am-1pm and 4-6pm, Wed. 8am-1:30pm, Thurs. 8am-1pm and 4-8pm, Fri.-Sat. 8am-1:30pm, Sun. 10am-noon and 4-6pm. Dress appropriately—no shorts or bare shoulders. If necessary, wrap a towel or shawl around legs or shoulders. Free.)

Half-way uphill on the winding road that connects Chora and Skala (2km from each) is a turn-off for another monastery, the **Apocalypsis,** a large, white complex of interconnected buildings. Most people come here to see the **Sacred Grotto of the Revelation** (tel. 31 234), adjacent to the Church of St. Anne. In this cave, St. John dictated the *Book of Revelation,* the last book of the New Testament, after hearing the voice of God proclaim "Now write what you see, what is to take place hereafter." (Rev. 1:19). According to legend, when God spoke to St. John, he cleft the ceiling of the cave with a three-pronged crack representing the Holy Trinity. Silver plating marks the spot where St. John presumably slept (Apocalypsis open same hours as Monastery of St. John; dress appropriately; free).

■ Around Patmos Island

Grikou has a somewhat touristy beach with watersport rentals (paddleboats 1500dr per hr.), a few hotels, and a couple of restaurants. Only 5km southwest of Skala, and 5km west of Chora, the town is visited by several buses daily from both (170dr). At the south, quiet end of the beach, **O Flisvos** (tel. 31 380, -961) rents studios for up to three people (10,000dr. with bath) above a shaded *taverna* overlooking the bay. At the north end (left, facing the water) is a smaller cove not visible from the bay (watch the thistles). Mopeds can continue 2km south to the secluded Plaki beach, where the road degenerates. Only 3km west from Plaki is **Psili Ammos,** the best beach on the island. Try hiking to it, but get directions first. An easier route is by **excursion** boat from Skala (1 per day 10am, returning at 4pm, 1200dr). **Kambos** has stretches with variations of sand (4 buses per day, 15min, 190dr) and the tiny cove of **Lambi** in the north is famed for its multicolored round pebbles.

ASTYPALEA ΑΣΤΥΠΑΛΑΙΑ

Few travelers venture to butterfly-shaped Astypalea, the westernmost of the Dode-canese islands, and everyone else doesn't know what they're missing. This quiet, placid island with vaguely Cycladic architecture and a colorful port retains the con-veniences of its larger neighbors. Inland, the jagged hills and secluded orange and lemon groves merit leisurely exploration.

Orientation and Practical Information   Ferries land at the town of **Astypalea.** Surrounded by tawny hills, the town itself is a hillside conglomeration of cubical dwellings. Just before the town's small beach, the **police** (tel. 61 207) and **port police** (tel. 61 208) share a building (both open daily 8am-7pm). The **OTE** (tel. 61 212, -5) is at the foot of the Paradissos Hotel (open Mon.-Fri. 7:30am-2pm). **M. Karakosta,** in the store under the Aegean hotel, is an agent of the **National Bank** (open Mon.-Thurs. 8am-2pm, Fri. 8am-1:30pm). For transportation questions, try the **travel agency** (tel. 61 224; open Mon.-Fri. 9am-1pm). The **post office/currency exchange** (tel. 61 223; code 85900; open Mon.-Fri. 7:30am-2pm) and several **super-markets** (open daily 9am-1pm and 5-9pm) are all in this older section of town. In case of **medical emergency,** call the clinic at 61 222. **Ferries** arrive in Astypalea spo-radically. Boats travel to Peiraias (3 per week, 12-18hr., 5117dr); Kalymnos (3 per week, 3hr., 2200dr); Kos (1 per week, 3½hr., 4500dr); Rhodes (2 per week, 5hr., 3826dr); Paros (2 per week, 7hr., 3000dr); Naxos (2 per week, 5½hr., 2900dr); San-torini (1 per week, 4hr., 2500dr); and Amorgos (2 per week, 2-3hr., 2500dr). As always, ferry schedules change frequently. Ferries do not leave Astypalea every day, so you may be stuck here for a few days. Excursion boats also leave daily for the island's beaches. **Postal Code:** 85900. **Telephone Code:** 0243.

Accommodations   Rooms on the island fill up fast in July and August, but the available ones are cheap (singles 5000dr, doubles 7000dr, triples 8000dr). Ask the **travel agency** for help. The **Hotel Aegean** (tel. 61 236) has rooms with baths. (Sin-gles 3000dr. Doubles 4000dr. Triples 5000dr.) **Camping Astypalea** (tel. 61 338) is 2½km east of town near Marmari; follow signs or take a bus towards Maltezana. (950dr per person. 650dr per tent.)

Sights   At the top of the hill, a striking row of windmills leads to the **castle,** a ram-shackle Byzantine structure shedding segments of walls and windows. From here there is a clear view of the island and its flock of tributary islets. A 20-minute walk west (over the hill) from town will bring you to the sandy beach of **Livadia.** The beach is crammed with tents and kids in July and August, but on the beach of **Tza-**

naki, a 20-minute hike along the coast to the southwest, nude bathers do their thing.
Ag. Konstantinos beach is reachable by a dirt road (1½-hr. hike from Livadia).

In the other direction from Astypalea Town, the quiet fishing villages of **Malte-zana** and **Analipsi** occupy the narrow isthmus. Home to some largely intact Roman mosaics, Maltezana is accessible by bus (2 per day, 120dr). The narrow natural harbor at **Vathi** is subdivided into **Exo** Vathi (outside) and **Esa** Vathi (inside). In winter, when the winds are too strong for boats to dock at Astypalea, the ferries go to the bay at **Ag. Andreas.** The lovely beach here is accessible by road. Another rocky road leads to the **Ag. Ioannis Monastery,** majestically balanced atop a hill.

KARPATHOS ΚΑΡΠΑΘΟΣ

Karpathians embody Greece's famed hospitality; cheerful greetings from strangers are common. In the mountains, residents preserve tradition, but Karpathos Town straddles the line between quaint and cosmopolitan.

War and conquest mark Karpathos' history. Karpathians fought with Sparta in the Peloponnesian War in 431 BCE and lost their independence to Rhodes in 400 BCE. In 42 BCE the island fell to Rome and in 395 CE was annexed by Byzantium. A few centuries later, Karpathos was ruled in turn by the Arabs, the Genovese pirate Moresco, the Venetians, and the Ottoman Turks. Turkish rule ended only when the Italians conquered the island during WWI. The Germans relieved them in WWII. In 1948, after 654 years of foreign conquest, Karpathos finally became part of Greece.

■ Karpathos Town

Karpathos Town used to be referred to as Ta Pigadia, meaning "the wells." Before that, the town was called Possi, for "Poseidon Polis," but many objected to this name, which also meant "drinking about." Today, Karpathos Town is the island's administrative and transportation center.

ORIENTATION AND PRACTICAL INFORMATION

The best way to orient yourself in Karpathos Town is to bear in mind the Greek free spirit. The streets and square are not named, but don't fret. There are only two main roads. One, running along the water, is lined with *tavernas,* cafés, pharmacies, and the National Bank; the other, one block inland, runs parallel to the first and contains the post office, bakery, and signs for various guest houses. If you still insist on buying a map, make sure it's up to date. The best places to purchase accurate town maps are **Karpathos** and **Possi Travel Agencies** (400-500dr). Maps of the area in tourist shops are often old and will confuse rather than assist you.

Travel Offices: Karpathos Travel (tel. 22 148; fax 22 754), Dimokratia St., between the bus station and waterfront. Complete bus information and most boat schedules. Arranges accommodations, rents cars (32,000dr for 3 days, insurance and tax included), and exchanges currency. Sells tickets for excursions to Lefkos, Diafani, and Olymbos. Open Mon.-Sat. 8:30am-1pm and 5:30-9pm, Sun. 9-11am and 6-8pm. Both Karpathos and **Possi Travel** (tel. 22 235; fax 22 252), around the corner on Apodimon Karpathion St., sell maps for 500dr. Open Mon.-Sat. 8:30am-1pm and 5:30-8:30pm, Sun. 5:30-8:30pm. Possi offers all travel services.
Banks: National Bank, opposite Possi Travel, offers **currency exchange.** Open Mon.-Thurs. 8am-2pm, Fri. 8am-1:30pm. Visa and MasterCard **ATM** outside.
OTE: Past the post office, then left uphill. Open Mon.-Fri. 7:30am-3pm.
Flights: Olympic Airways office (tel. 22 150, -057) is on the street parallel to the water, 1 block back. Open Mon.-Fri. 8am-3pm. **Nonstop flights** to Athens (3 per week, 24,700dr), and **indirectly** via Rhodes (4 per day, 24,600dr). Flights to Kassos (4 per week, 5800dr) and to Sitia, Crete (2 per week, 11,500dr).

Ferries: Boats travel to Peiraias (5 per week, 21hr., 6067dr); Iraklion (6 per week, 6hr., 2500dr); Kassos (3 per week, 1½hr., 927dr); Paros (4 per week, 17hr., 4290dr); Rhodes (2 per week, 5hr., 2696dr); and Santorini (4 per week, 12hr., 3210dr).

Buses: 1 block up Dimokratia St. from town center. Serve most villages (300-1000dr); check the schedule at Karpathos Travel or call Manolis at 22 192.

Taxis: (tel. 22 705; 24 hr.), go to all the villages (2000dr to nearby villages). Taxi prices, regulated by the government, are posted in Karpathos Travel and at the taxi station on Dimokratia St.

Moped/Car Rental: Gatoulis Motorbikes (tel. 22 747), same street as the post office, but farther down the road leading out of town. 50cc bikes 3500dr per day. Cars 12,000dr per day plus tax. Open daily 8am-3pm and 5-8pm.

International Bookstore: John Pavlakos (tel. 22 389), next to Possi Travel, has writing supplies and guidebooks. Open Mon.-Sat. 9am-2pm and 5:30-11pm.

Pharmacies: There are three **pharmacies** in town, all near the water. All open Mon.-Fri. 8am-1pm and 5:30-8:30pm.

Medical Assistance: Contact the **Health Center** (tel. 22 228), a large white building 100m past Platia 5 October, on N.K. Matheou St. After 2pm, go directly to the center and ring the bell for emergency. No English spoken. Open 9am-2:30pm.

Police: (tel. 22 222), at the corner of Ethn. Anistassis St., next to the post office. They don't speak much English but try valiantly to help you. Open 24hr.

Port Authority: (tel. 22 227), on the ferry dock.

Post Office: Take the uphill road right of the bus station. Open Mon.-Fri. 8am-1:30pm. **Postal Code:** 85700.

Telephone Code: 0245.

ACCOMMODATIONS

Freelance camping, though illegal, transpires mostly undisturbed on the town beach to the north. *Let's Go* does not recommend illegal freelance camping. Room prices are roughly 1000-2000dr less in off season.

Mertonas Studios (tel. 22 622 or 23 079), 2 blocks to the left and uphill of the bus station, facing inland. Eva Angelos rents gorgeous, furnished studios with private baths and maid service that would make Mr. Clean weep with joy. Telling fortunes from coffee grounds is her specialty. Doubles with bath 5000-7000dr. Studios in winter 50,000dr per month for doubles without utilities.

Harry's Rooms to Rent (tel. 22 188), just up the hill and to the left from the Avra. Modern, clean rooms with balcony and common bath. Singles 3200dr. Doubles 4800dr. Triples 5000dr.

FOOD AND ENTERTAINMENT

Land and Sea (tel. 22 007) grills tasty chicken breasts with rice, peas, and potatoes (1600dr). **Café Anapsyktirion** (tel. 22 309), behind the church and opposite the fruit stands, is frequented by a young, hip crowd. The town's sweetshop, **Bee-Hive** (tel. 22 530), is near Karpathos Travel. Most of the town's several **minimarkets** are on the same road as Karpathos Travel. **Minas Vlahos,** the most acclaimed artist on Karpathos, displays his works at his **Art Center** near the mayor's office; follow the tranquil vibes of Enya radiating from his studio. (Hand-made cards 500dr; open Mon.-Sat. 9am-1pm and 5-9pm.) **Nightlife** converges around the waterfront's north end. **La Mirage,** a romantic spot hovering high above the harbor, plays live Greek music. Along the waterfront, the popular **Eros Bar** provides a scenic balcony and cozy tables on which to drink your *drachmae* away.

■ Southern Karpathos

The rest of southern Karpathos is known for its stone farmhouses, tiny isolated chapels, and tendon-tearing views over terraced hillsides to the sea. On August 6, the towns of Menetes, Aperi, and Othos hold lively church festivals.

On a branch of the road south out of Karpathos Town are the hillside towns of **Menetes** and **Arkasa.** Menetes's huge church sprouts from the terraced houses below. Its marble pillars were salvaged from the ruins of an early Christian basilica. In the house in front of the church there should be a woman with the key. Ask at **Manolis Kafeneion** (tel. 81 356) for a key to the tiny **folk art museum** (free). In Arkasa, the remains of five parallel Cyclopean walls divide the peninsula southwest of town. **Buses** from Ta Pigadia leave for Arkasa (1-2 per day, 20min., 600dr); check the schedule for afternoon return times. **Taxis** from Ta Pigadia cost 2000dr.

The island's only other paved road leads north and then west out of Karpathos Town into lush hiking country. Freelance campers can be found on a small beach cove close to the sandy shore of Agios Nikolaos; follow the road from Arkasa to Agios Nikolaos, a five-minute walk from Anna's boarding house. **Aperi** became the island's capital in medieval times when Arab raids forced the Karpathians to abandon their coastal town. Today, it remains the island's spiritual capital. The church here holds the *Panagia* (Virgin Mary) icon revered throughout Karpathos. Legend has it that long ago a monk was chopping wood when blood suddenly spurted from one of the logs. The perplexed monk recognized the log as an icon of the Virgin Mary, and although the object disappeared several times, it always reappeared in an old church in Aperi. The monk understood that the *Panagia* wished to stay in that spot, and in 1886 a bishop's church was built (church open to visitors daily 8-11am, when overseer is present). Buses go to Aperi (600dr).

Amopi Beach, 8km south of Karpathos Town towards the airport, has clean golden sand and is the most crowded beach on the island. Two **buses** per day travel to the beach from Karpathos Town (20min., 700dr). For the illusion of seclusion, check out the several kilometers of relatively unpopulated beach that stretch south below Amopi. If the fierce wind kicks up an infamous Amopi dust storm, move one cove south to the pebbly beach and enjoy the breeze.

■ Northern Karpathos

There are no good roads connecting the rural north and commercial south of Karpathos. Whatever modernization might have infested this beautiful, arid region was stalled by a 1983 fire which devastated most of the Aleppo Pine Forests between Spoa and Olympos. Daily **excursion boats** from Karpathos Town are the most reliable and scenic means of transport. Karpathos Travel offers boat-and-bus trips to Diafani (2hr. one way; 4500dr includes roundtrip bus to Olympos). Twice per week a boat journeys to the dazzling white beach of **Apela** and to the island of **Saria** north of Karpathos (from Diafani 1hr., roundtrip 2000dr). Here you can visit **Palatia,** a deserted village halfway up the east coast with peculiar, cone-roofed houses built by Syrian pirates in the 7th-9th centuries. Don't get stranded here—the village has few inhabitants and no water.

DIAFANI

Staying in languorous Diafani (Transparent) allows you to stick close to the beaches and the harbor of North Karpathos, but it has nothing more to offer than overpriced *tavernas* and a sleepy port. If exploring Olymbos is your goal, however, take the first bus out of Diafani and absorb Olymbos at your leisure (2 per day, 350dr). **Orphanos Travel and Shipping Agents** (tel. 51 410; fax 51 316), on the dock to the right of the *tavernas,* offers **exchange services,** room information, and ferry and excursion tickets. Ask about free boat trips to local beaches (open daily 8am-1pm and 2:30-10pm). There's no bank in Diafani. A telecard **phone** is in front of the travel agency. The **police station** (tel. 51 213) is in the center of town (open 24hr.). There's a **post box,** but the postman only rings three times per week. "Rooms to Let" abound; expect to pay 3000-4500dr per single and 5000-7500dr per double. A **campsite** (tel. 51 288) offers shaded pitches starting at 700dr per person.

OLYMBOS

Olymbos is traditional, though no single word can convey the thoroughness of its isolation and insularity. Ethnologists and linguists have lauded the region's preservation of its centuries-old customs. Several words in the local dialect date to 1000 BCE. The radiant long-sleeved white shirts and flowered aprons worn by women—a striking contrast to their weathered skin—vivify the gray, windswept village. From the flat base of the village, tireless women carry sacks of produce on their heads step by step to *their* houses, which, according to the village's **matriarchal tradition,** their *daughters* will inherit. Plaster-sculpted nymphs, angels, eagles, and Venetian lions decorate the exteriors of traditional homes. Two **working windmills** overlook the cliffs on the west side of the village—here the women of Olymbos grind flour for bread, which they bake in huge stone ovens smoldering under the hillside. Meanwhile, the men either idly play backgammon or musical instruments in the coffeehouses, or oh-so-strenuously lead the overworked donkeys in the right direction. The **folk museum,** next to one of the windmills (pick your way up the narrow village path), offers a free glimpse of a 19th-century Karpathian home, with tools, adornments, and overpriced souvenirs outside. While you're there, check out the windmills. If someone is present, you can brave the tiny ladder inside and watch one whirl behind the scenes. If you're willing to bound over stone walls, visit the oldest chapel on Karpathos, **Agia Triada,** one of two adjacent stone chapels easily visible from the town above (look down to the right of the bus stop for earthy red arched roofs). The frescoes inside are 13th- or 14th-century "aniconic" geometric paintings of birds and fish.One of the few men you'll see laboring in Olymbos is the cobbler **Nichokis Kanakis,** who makes the red and tan leather boots that are standard footwear in the village. At 45,000dr per pair, though, these boots are not made for walking. **Pension Olymbos** (tel. 51 252), around to the left of the bus stop near the start of the village, rents old-style rooms with hand-carved beds. (Singles 2000dr. Doubles 2500dr, with bath 5000dr.) Anna and Michalis also serve home-cooked food in the adjacent *taverna; pastitsio* and *moussaka,* both 1800dr, are worth every *drachma.* To travel between Olymbos and Diafani, you can take a taxi or the small bus that leaves Diafani daily (when the boat from Karpathos Town arrives) and Olymbos daily. The dusty two- to three-hour hike along a valley floor is another alternative, if you've got the time and energy.

SYMI ΣΥΜΗ

The mountainous island of Symi is a small but dramatic showpiece of the Dodecanese. The famous Panormitis Monastery rests in a remote spot at the island's south end, while the historic port of Ghialos adorns the northern tip. Monasteries were the only dwellings on these steep, barren shores until commercial growth in the 19th century led to the construction of the port. During this period, shipbuilding, sponge diving, fishing, and trade flourished, while Symi became the capital of the Dodecanese and received concessions from the Sultans. Ships made in Symi still have a reputation for being easily handled and quick. Ghialos is one of the lovelier ports in Greece: islands dot the ocean corridor to the town, and pastel houses ring the waterfront. Despite Symi's charms, backpackers may meet with a cool reception. The island's livelihood depends on the whims of wealthy Italian visitors, and if you're not prepared to spend lots of money, you may have to beg for attention.

The Greek government declared the port of Symi an historic site in 1971. Many Neoclassical houses here date from the 19th century. Around town, the abandoned buildings attest to the depletion of the island's population from 30,000, at the peak of its sponge-fishing industry, to 3000 today. Symi is fighting its way back from this recession but remains comparatively poor. The entire island seems to anticipate the docking of excursion boats. The waterfront, unbearably hot in summer, can also be unbearably frenetic when boats arrive. The evenings are more peaceful, as island residents linger in the *tavernas* and drink; few tourists stay here overnight. The island's interior is calm and fragrant—Symi still cultivates its own spices.

Orientation and Practical Information   As you disembark at the Ghialos clock tower (on the right side of town facing inland), the **police** (tel. 71 111) are right next door. The **post office** (tel. 71 315) is in the same building, on the left, up the other steps and offers currency exchange and stamps (open Mon.-Fri. 7:30am-2pm). The **port authority** (tel. 71 205) is in the big white building along the uphill steps to the left of the post office. Go to the second floor for help with ferries in rough English (open 24hr.). You can exchange money at the **National Bank** (tel. 72 294), straight ahead and to the right after the footbridge where the harbor bends left, or the **Ionian Bank** (tel. 71 122), closer to the water (both open Mon.-Thurs. 8am-2pm, Fri. 8am-1:30pm). If you need an **ATM**, you'll find it there, too. Head inland along the left-hand side of the park in the middle of the harbor and follow signs from the Naraida restaurant to the **OTE** (open Mon.-Fri. 8am-2pm). Behind the Ionian Bank, **Symi Tours** (tel. 71 307) sells ferry, hydrofoil, and plane tickets, handles currency exchange, and helps with lodgings (open daily 9am-2pm and 6-10pm). The **medical center** (tel. 71 290) is next to the church, inland directly opposite Hotel Kokona (open Mon.-Fri. 9am-1pm; after hours call the police). There is a **pharmacy** (tel. 71 888) on the waterfront at the left side of the harbor past the Ionian Bank (open Mon.-Sat. 9am-2pm and 5-9pm, Sun. 9am-2:30pm).

A small **international bookstore** (tel. 71 690; fax 71 773) sits on the waterfront near the pharmacy and sells newspapers, magazines, and novels in English. **Fax services** are also available (open daily 8:30am-midnight). **Taxis** (tel. 72 666) congregate on the east waterfront past the Ionian Bank. The **Symi Bus,** actually a green van, leaves from a stop a short distance farther up along the waterfront (every hr., 150dr). Free **public toilets** are located to the left of O Meraklis Restaurant down an alleyway. Most of Symi's visitors come on daily **excursion boats** from Rhodes, which visit the Panormitis Monastery and Ghialos (2500-3000dr roundtrip), and if you're trying to do anything else, be prepared for confusing schedules and sporadic departures. Almost everything leaving Symi goes through Rhodes anyway, so in case of extreme trouble, you can always hop on an excursion boat heading back there (1750dr one way). Twice a week, **ferries** pass through Symi on the way to Peiraias (6020dr), Kos (1916dr), and Kalymnos (2400dr), stopping once a week at Tilos (1417dr) and Nisyros (1900dr). Also twice per week, **flying dolphins** head to Rhodes (2736dr), Kos (4675dr), and Kalymnos (6901dr), and once a week to Samos (10,600dr). **Postal Code:** 85600. **Telephone Code:** 0241.

Accommodations   Although most travelers don't spend the night, enough do that the usual herd of dock hawks await ferries and hydrofoils. **Hotel Kokona** (tel. 72 620 or 71 451), to the left of the old church tower, at the back of a small plaza off to the right past Neraklis, has pristine welcoming rooms with baths that actually smell clean. (Doubles 7500-9000dr. Triples 9000-10,800dr. Quads 12,000dr. Breakfast 800dr.) **Helena "Rooms to Let"** (tel. 72 931), a few storefronts past the Ionian bank, has comfortable rooms with private baths. (Doubles 7000dr.)

Food and Entertainment   Despite the influx of excursion boats, restaurant prices have not yet gone sky high. For good, authentic food, steer away from the waterfront and make the hike up to Chora. **George's Restaurant** (tel. 71 984), at the top of the steps, reputedly serves the best food on the island in a luscious garden setting (Greek salad 800dr, *kalamari* 1400dr, octopus 1400dr). Locals get their *souvlaki* at **Mylos** (tel. 71 604), a renovated mill (the only one with a roof) at the top of the hill at the bus stop (*souvlaki* 300dr, *mezedes* 500dr, wine 500dr). Waterfront restaurants are expensive, so the farther you walk from the ferry landing, the better. Check out the plaque above **Les Caterinettes Restaurant:** this is where the Italians signed the agreement surrendering the Dodecanese to the Allies on May 8, 1945 (stuffed eggplant 950dr). **Meraklis,** a block from Symi Tours, specializes in luscious stuffed tomatoes (900dr). Another excellent dinner option is **Restaurant Panorama,** near George's Restaurant. Sit on a veranda overlooking the harbor below (Greek salad 600dr, *kalamari* 1000dr).

For 700dr cocktails between 8 and 9pm or friendly conversation all night long, visit the **Jean and Tonic Pub** (tel. 71 819), up the hill from George's. Jean, a British vacationer who loved Symi so much that she never went home, can help with accommodations. **Pat's Bar** (tel. 71 945), in the harbor, satisfies your alcohol cravings (cocktails 650dr 7:30-8:30pm). To cool off in the port, try **Igloo** ice cream, inland and before the footbridge (one scoop 300dr, 3 scoops 600dr).

SIGHTS

Panormitis Monastery, the grand Monastery of the Archangel Michael, friend of travelers, looms at the center of a remarkable horseshoe-shaped harbor in the south part of the island and greets you with its chiming bells. The monastery was founded at the spot where a local woman chanced upon an icon of Michael. Although it was brought to Ghialos, the icon kept returning to Panormitis. The palatial white buildings of the monastery, dominated by an elegant bell tower in the center contains two small museums, one with ecclesiastical relics and worshipers' gifts to the monastery and one with folkloric exhibits (both open daily 10am-12:30pm and when excursion boats visit; admission 200dr for both). The small monastery church houses an exceptional wooden altar screen. The icon is famous throughout the Dodecanese for its wish-granting powers, and tokens in the museum represent supplicants' requests. No regular buses run to the monastery, but tour buses from Ghialos run four times per week (1hr.), and a boat from Ghialos heads here as well. All excursion boats from Rhodes stop here. There are free toilets to the left of the complex. If you get hungry, the bakery under the archway to the left has fresh goodies.

At Ghialos, the **Naval Museum,** housed in a yellow Neoclassical building at the back of the main waterfront strip, is worth a visit (open daily 10:30am-3pm; admission 200dr). A steep 20-30-minute hike ends at Chorio, the section of town fortified against pirate raids. Several sets of stairs lead up from the east side of the waterfront. The shadiest and most straightforward is the one farthest along the water, quite close to the road bending upwards. Follow the road at the top of the stairs and you'll see signs for the **archaeological museum** (tel. 71 114), housing classical and Byzantine pieces as well as island costumes and utensils (open Tues.-Sun. 10am-2pm; admission 500dr, students 300dr, seniors 400dr, children under 18 200dr). Signs will lead you through a maze of streets to the ruins of the old **castle.**

Nos Beach, a 10-minute walk from Ghialos (head north along the waterfront, past the shipyard), is tiny but close to the port; a small *taverna*/disco lingers nearby. The beach at **Nimborio,** 45 minutes on foot past Nos, is mediocre, but the views make the walk worthwhile. You can also take a taxi boat for 800dr roundtrip. **Pedi,** a short distance by bus, boasts radiant sands and water. Symi's tiny coves shelter a few excellent beaches accessible only by boat (daily, 1000dr roundtrip) at **Ag. Marina, Nanou,** and **Marathounda** on the east side of the island. Boats also go to **Seskila Island** south of Symi (roundtrip 3000dr). Excursion boats follow no set schedule. They all line up with destinations and prices posted in the morning.

NISYROS ΝΙΣΥΡΟΣ

Greece's *other* volcanic island, Nisyros is not quite as popular and dramatic as Santorini, but Nisyros has unspoiled island beauty, virgin landscape, and a community not yet infiltrated by the vices of tourism. With its volcano, clifftop monastery, and picturesque ghost town, Nisyros is a latent treasure of the Aegean. Small and unfrequented by travelers, rowdy backpackers come here to detox between parties in Kos and Rhodes.

Orientation and Practical Information Ferries dock in the tiny white-washed port of **Mandraki**. The **port authority** (tel. 31 222; open 24hr.), the **police** (tel. 31 201; open 24hr.), and **post office** (tel. 31 249; open Mon.-Fri. 7:30am-2pm), which also offers **currency exchange,** are all housed in the white building on the dock with the Greek flag. The road continuing left around the bend (facing the water) leads into the town. **Enetikon Travel** (tel. 31 180; fax 31 168) is on that road on the right side in a tiny building on the rocks. A multilingual staff helps with boats, flying dolphins, accommodations, excursions, and faxes (open daily 9:30am-1:30pm and 6-9pm). Along the same road, parallel to the waterfront, you'll find **Alfa Rent** (tel. 31 438), in the first waterfront square, which has moped rentals (open daily 8:30am-9:30pm). Farther along the same path is the representative of the **National Bank** (tel. 31 459; open Mon.-Thurs. 8am-2pm, Fri. 8am-1:30pm) in **Diakomitalis Tours.** If you take the first left off the road from the dock into town, you'll reach the uptown square. The red cross on the left marks the **pharmacy,** which is usually open evenings. In a little office behind the town hall, Eleni Kendri sells tickets for ferries to the island and for **Olympic Airways** flights (tel. 31 230; open daily 7-9pm).

Two **ferries** per week serve Nisyros on their way to Rhodes (2200dr), Kalymnos (1300dr), Tilos (1200dr), Symi (2000dr), Kos (1300dr), and Peiraias (6057dr). **Flying dolphins** speed twice per week to Rhodes (5327dr), Tilos (2518dr), and Kos (2713dr). **Buses** on Nisyros run on their own time, but when they do turn on the engine, two per day head to Loutrs (5min.), Paloi (10min.), Emborio (20min.), and Nikeia (30min.). There are many private buses heading to the crater of the volcano, Stefanos. Ask around when you dock—most wait to meet incoming boats. There are two **taxis** on the island: **Babis'** (tel. 31 460) and **Irini's** (tel. 31 474). **Postal Code:** 85303. **Telephone Code:** 0242.

Accommodations In high season, doubles range from 4000-7000dr; in off season rates may fall by up to 50%. Rooms are scarce but generally available except in mid-August, during the island's big festival for the Virgin Mary—prices shoot up with demand. On the road leading left from the dock (facing inland), **Hotel Romantzo** (tel. 31 340) has clean rooms with bath at negotiable prices. (Singles 3000dr. Doubles 4000dr. Triples 6000dr.) If you head to town, ask at **Taverna Nisyros** (tel. 31 460) for a double with bath and kitchenette. (Doubles 4000dr.)

Food It is generally a good idea to wander away from the cafés and *tavernas* that attract most excursion visitors. A small sign points to **Fabrika** (tel. 31 552) on one of the little streets leading from the town hall square to the water. Go down the steps for books, music, and superb Greek *mezedes* at this cozy and friendly *ouzeri* (octopus 1000dr, *raki* 200dr, beer 400-500dr). Look a sign on the road parallel to the waterfront, pointing to **Tavernas Nisyros** (tel. 31 460), where Polyxeni cooks up a storm (Greek salad 450dr, *moussaka* 300dr, lamb chops 900dr). **Captain's** (tel. 31 225), at the water's edge, sells delicious *soumada* (almond juice), the island's specialty (1100dr per bottle), and cheap fish (swordfish filet 1500dr).

Sights As soon as you dock, it's obvious that the **volcano** is the island's main attraction. Tour guides and travel agents toting volcano signs crowd the dock—there's even a model of the island glorifying the volcano on the quay. Trips up to the **Stefanos crater** are often pre-booked, but you can join a group for 1000-1500dr. The bus ride is 20 minutes and you have 45 minutes to wander around in the crater. Another option is renting a moped, but drive carefully—the roads are narrow. There is no admission fee to the crater. The café on the site charges 350dr for a soda (open daily 8am-8pm). The toilet is behind the café. Inside the crater, you'll see piles of sulphur and jets of scalding steam against the island's gorgeous landscape. In some parts of the crater, you can hear the rumbling below. On the cliff at the end of the Mandraki is the **Panagia Spiliani Monastery.** The sacred icon of this monastery used to reside in a small cave just above Mandraki's port. It would mysteriously disappear from the sanctuary only to be found on the site of today's monastery. After several disappearing acts, the monks took it as a sign and built a new home for the icon, making a large replica of it in 1798 to display in the new church. The tender looks of Christ and the Virgin Mary have been known to grant relief from pain. The church also has relics of Agios Charlambos in its antechamber. Recently, on the rear face of the icon of the Virgin Mary, an altarboy discovered the iconographer's hidden portrait of Agios Nikolaos, which he had covered with an old cloth for over two centuries. Pictures of the back of this two-faced icon are displayed in the church as well. To get up to the monastery, climb the narrow uphill steps across from the church with the pink bell tower (monastery open daily 10am-3pm; free).

On those same steps up to the monastery is the tiny **Historical and Popular Museum** with folkloric exhibits on life on Nisyros (open Fri.-Wed. 10:30am-2:30pm and 6-8pm; free). The Cyclopean walls, built by the Venetians, are perched at the edge of Mandraki and extend to the monastery (open 24hr.; free).

On the road past the dock, a 10-minute walk from Mandraki, are the **thermal springs** of Loutra. Because of their therapeutic qualities, these springs are open only to visitors bearing a doctor's prescription. A 45-minute walk down the same road takes you to the charming fishing village of **Paloi.** The waves roll into a sandy beach and *tavernas* await at the water's edge. **Emporis,** surveying the volcano's crater and breathtaking surrounding landscape, used to bustle with life until an earthquake 30 years ago scared people away. Now, the town is inhabited by ten lonely souls. **Nikeia,** on the other side of the island, is another ghost town with only 50 residents.

Nisyros has few pleasant beaches, thanks to the steaming black volcanic rocks and sand, which torment the feet. Behind the monastery's cliff, along a waterfront path, is a small secluded beach (five-min. walk from Mandraki). On the road to Paloi is the island's best beach, **White Beach** (2km from Mandraki). Depending on demand, Enetikon Travel organizes trips to the nearby island of **Giali** for its better beaches (1900dr roundtrip).

Ionian Islands
ΝΗΣΙΑ ΤΟΥ ΙΟΝΙΟΥ

The Ionian Islands have shared an historic fate apart from the rest of Greece. Situated on the country's western edge, the islands escaped Turkish occupation, and were instead overrun by the Venetians, the British, the French, and the Russians. The Ionians' uninvited visitors, milder and more concerned with development than the Turks, left a lasting cultural, commercial, and architectural imprint. Despite being governed as a British protectorate until 1864 and occupied by Italian forces during WWII, the islands are comparatively wealthy. They also retain an international flavor; where else in Greece can you find pick-up games of cricket? Historical ties make the islands a favorite among Brits and Italians, and they also see the usual ferry-hopping backpackers who make the short trip over from Italy.

CORFU (KERKYRA) ΚΕΡΚΥΡΑ

Corfu has been renowned for its lush beauty ever since its first visitor, Odysseus, washed ashore. At various times the property of Franks, Venetians, and the French, Corfu's most noticeable foreign influence comes from the British. Traditionally a favorite haunt of European royalty and aristocrats, Corfu is the most eclectically international Ionian island. Only here do British palaces sit on an esplanade modeled after the rue de Rivoli in Paris next to the shuttered alleyways of an ersatz Venice—not to mention the international cricket matches and Asiatic Museum of Art.

■ Corfu Town

Corfu Town is the logical base for touring the island; all ferries and most buses originate here. At the New Port, a barrage of tourist officers proffering scooters, ferry tickets, and rooms greets arrivals. Apart from this melee, Corfu's two fortresses hulk over the waterfront, still guarding the Old Town. Quieter and more dignified, the narrow lanes near the Spianada (esplanade) and near Sanrocco Sq. present a charming mix of Byzantine, Venetian, and Greek architecture. Despite the numerous souvenir shops and the preponderance of English-speakers, the Old Town retains much of Corfu's traditional character, with its narrow streets, pastel and white Neoclassical buildings, brilliant pink flowers, and stray cats.

ORIENTATION AND PRACTICAL INFORMATION

Familiarize yourself with the Theotokos family. Four of Corfu's main streets are named after members of this clan; you may pass from **N. Theotoki Street** to **M. Theotoki Street** to **G. Theotoki Street** to **I. Theotoki Street** without even realizing it. Use a map (available at kiosks and the Lyroudis bookstore for roughly 300dr; keep in mind that the tourist office has moved 2 blocks west since the map was issued), and you'll be fine. Better yet, get lost in the **historic center** and bask in Neoclassical splendor. On the north coast of town are the **New Port,** which serves boats to Patras and the international ferries, and the **Old Port,** where boats leave for Paxos and Igoumenitsa. The New Fortress, behind which sits Corfu's long-distance **bus station,** separates the two ports. The Old Town, at the center of historic Corfu, is a beautiful, befuddling maze of alleyways, dignified despite its occupation by leather stores, jewelry dealers, and the like. It is contained by the **Spianada,** an esplanade littered with chic cafés and the New Fortress. To reach the Spianada from Old Port, simply follow the waterfront road (water on your left); you will see an arch and

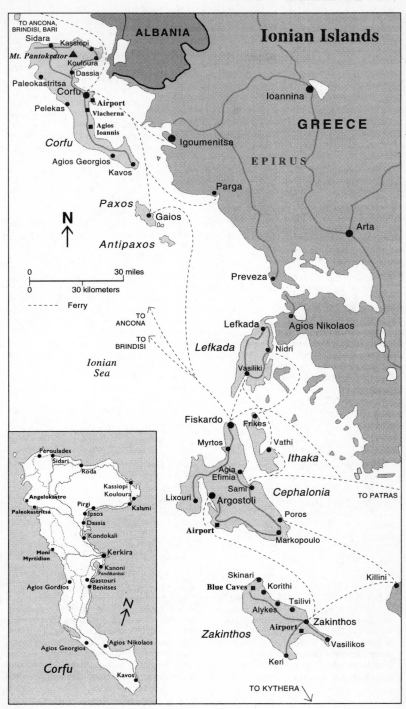

CORFU

once through it, you'll find the long set of cafés straight ahead and the park to the left. From there, any right will take you into the maze. From New Port, follow the same strategy, or turn inland onto Napoleotos St., which turns into I. Theotaki. This leads you past **Sanrocco Square,** where there is the city bus terminal, fewer tourists, and a more citified sensibility. Turn left along G. Theotaki, and you will be led into Old Town. Any progress reasonably straight will bring you to the Spianada, the Old Fortress, and eventually the water.

National Tourist Office: (tel. 37 520), at Rizospaston Voulefton and Iak. Folila. The building is marked, but climb upstairs to the 2nd floor to find the office. Open Mon.-Fri. 8:30am-1:30pm. The **municipal office** holds complementary hours. Open Mon.-Sat. 9am-9pm, Sun. 9am-3pm. A tourist office kiosk in Sanrocco Sq. provides similar services. Open daily 9am-9pm.

Municipal Tourist Offices: (tel. 58 509 or 42 601), on the Spianada, one office across from Customs, and another inside Customs (at the port). Office on the Spianada has a multilingual electronic information screen attachment on it; look for green "i" symbol. Open April-Oct. Mon.-Sat. 9am-9pm, Sun. 9am-3pm.

Tourist Police: (tel. 30 265 or 39 503), in the direction of Sanrocco Sq., with the Old Town at your back, walk along G. Theotaki. Turn right on I. Theotaki and take the first right. The tourist police is on the 4th floor. Open daily 7am-2:30pm. For an **emergency,** you can contact the **police** (same building) at tel. 39 509.

British Vice Consul: 1 Menekratous (tel. 30 055 or 37 995), down the street from the post office. Open Mon.-Fri. 8am-2pm. Call 39 211 in an emergency.

Banks: 4 banks on G. Theotoki St., near where it narrows and becomes Voulgareos, including the **National Bank (24-hr. ATM).** Most open Mon.-Thurs. 8am-2pm, Fri. 8am-1:30pm. Some have additional hours July-Aug. 4-6pm or 5:30-7:30pm and Sat. 8:30am-1pm. Try the currency exchange window at the **airport** (open when planes arrive or depart). Most hotels and tourist agencies near the Old Port charge 20% commission. The tourist offices change money at the National Bank rate.

American Express: Greek Skies Travel, 20a Kapodistriou St., P.O. Box 24 (tel. 30 883 or 32 469), at the south end of the Spianada. Holds mail and cashes AmEx traveler's checks. Open Mon.-Fri. 8am-noon and 5:30-8:30pm, Sat. 8am-noon.

Room-Finding Services: Tourist agencies along Arseniou St. Stratigou St. by the New Port find rooms in pensions. Many operate without commission and have information on cheap lodgings. Most open daily 8:30am-1:30pm and 5:30-9pm. Singles from 3000dr, doubles from 4000dr, triples from 5000dr; add 1000-1500dr for private bath. Prices negotiable for longer stays. Ask at the tourist police for rooms or call "the Association of Owners of Private Rooms and Apts. in Corfu" (tel. 26 133; fax 72 560), in the heart of the Old Town.

OTE: Main office, 9 Mantzarou St., off A. Theotaki St. Open daily 8am-midnight. Smaller offices at Kapodistriou St., on the Esplanade, and in mobile white buildings at both Old and New ports. Open daily 7:15am-1pm.

Flights: 20 Kapodistriou St. (tel. 38 694, -5, or -6; airport 30 180), on the Spianada. Free buses from the airport. A taxi ride takes only 5min. and is the only way to get to the airport unless your hotel or tour group has buses. (Before getting in, agree on a fare of roughly 1500dr.) To Athens (3-4 per day, 50min., 19,200dr including 1100dr tax) and Thessaloniki (3 per week, 19,200dr). A relatively new airline, **Air Greece** (see Greek Skies Travel for information), is starting up service between Corfu and Athens. Only 4 flights per week (Mon.-Tues. and Fri.-Sat.), but they offer 3000dr student and senior discounts for flights to Athens. Contact **Chalikipoulos Travel,** 5 Arseniou St. (tel. 24 023 or 30 626; fax 37 079 or call Air Greece at 33 410). In summer, book 2-3 days ahead; 1 day ahead in off season.

Buses: KTEL (long-distance), behind the New Port on Avraniou St. (tel. 30 627 or 39 985). Pick up a handy timetable available at the station or from tourist agencies. Schedules for the main KTEL line are also posted on a billboard outside the new office behind Corfu Town's New Fortress, from which the green KTEL buses leave. Other (blue) buses, including those to Kontokali (the youth hostel), leave from Sanrocco Sq.—schedules are printed on the signs. To Paleokastritsa (10 per day, 45min., 380dr); Glyfada Beach (9 per day, 45min., 280dr); Kavos (11 per day, 700dr); Kassiopi (7 per day, 550dr); Sidari (11 per day, 550dr); Ag. Gordios (7 per day, 240dr); Athens (2 per day, 7250dr); and Thessaloniki (2 per day, 7100dr). Buses run less frequently on Sun. Buy tickets for Corfu destinations on the bus; all others in the office. Open daily 5:30am-8pm.

City Buses: #10 to Achilleon from Sanrocco Sq. and the Old Town in front of the Hotel Constantinoupolis (6 per day), #6 to Benitses (13 per day), #7 to Dassia (every 30min., 7am-10pm), #8 to Triklino (10 per day), #11 to Pelekas (9 per day). Schedule distributed at the information booths and the hostel. Fares for city buses average 110-155dr. Less frequent service on Sun. For information call 31 595.

Ferries: Book a day early in high season, especially to Italy—even deck class sells out. Agents for the various shipping companies line Xen. Stratigou St., opposite the New Port. Try **Fragline** to Brindisi (Mon.-Fri. 9am, 8hr., 5000dr) and Patras (2 per day, 10-11hr., 4800dr). **Adriatica** and **Hellenic Mediterranean** recognize Eurail and Inter-rail passes. Ferries sail for Ancona (1 per day, 22hr., 13,600dr), Bari (3-4 per week, 6000dr), and other Italian ports of call. Ferries to Igoumenitsa run every hr. (990dr). To Paxos, you have a choice of ferry (1 per day, Mon.-Tues. and Thurs.-Sat., 1900dr) or catamaran (1 per day, 3200dr). When traveling to foreign ports find out if the port tax is included in the price of your ticket. Ferry agencies, open all day in high season, follow regular store hours off-season (Mon., Wed., and Sat. 8am-2pm; Tues., Thurs., and Fri. 8am-1:30pm and 5-8pm); always open at ferry departures. **Corfu Mare** (tel. 32 467), at New Port, located beneath Ionian Hotel, sells tickets. For changes and updates on ferry schedules, contact the **port police** (tel. 38 425), in the customs house along the port, or the **port authority** (tel. 32 655 or 40 002).

Taxis: At the Old Port, the Spianada, Sanrocco Square, and G. Theotoki St. For **Radio Taxis,** call 33 811 or 41 333. Available 24hr.

Car Rental: A Fiat Panda goes for 10,000-12,000dr, plus 10-20dr per additional km, with 100km free. Make sure quoted prices include the 20% tax. Third-party insurance is usually included. You must have a current driver's license or international permit to rent cars. Agencies along Xen. Stratigou all rent for roughly 10,000dr per day. **Hertz** and **Interrent/Europcar** are more expensive. International car rental at **Greek Skies,** 20 Kapodistriou St. (tel. 33 410). Pandas go for 10,000dr per day. Min. age 21-23; for more expensive cars, min. age 25 with credit card. Full payment in advance or major credit card required. Open Mon.-Fri. 8:30am-1:30pm and 5:30-8:30pm, Sat. 8:30am-1:30pm.

Moped Rental: The most popular way to see the island is by moped. Rental places abound; you shouldn't pay more than 3000-4000dr per day. Make sure the brakes work. You're responsible for any damage to the vehicle, but the rental fee should include third-party liability and property damage insurance. **Spiros Pagratis' shop,** on 14 El. Venizelou along the waterfront (tel. 32 031). Mopeds for 3500dr per day, bicycles for 1000dr per day.

Luggage Storage: Several places on Avrami St., directly across from the New Port. 250dr per day. Check access times before leaving your bags. Try the bank on your right as you first enter Avrami. On the first floor, big, white, and clean, though it keeps banker's hours.

Laundromat: 42 I. Theotoki St. (tel. 35 304), just past Sanrocco Sq. Wash and dry 2000dr. Open Mon.-Fri. 9am-2:30pm and 5:30-8:30pm, Sat. 9am-2:30pm.

Public Toilets: On the harbor at the Old Port, on the Spianada near the bandstand, and in Sanrocco Sq. Those on the Spianada are clean and wheelchair accessible.

Hospital: Corfu General Hospital (tel. 45 811, -2, or -3; emergency room 25 400), walk down G. Theotoki, turn right at I. Theotoki and as the road splits into 3 after one block, choose the middle course (Poluchroniou Koustanta St.). After 3 blocks this road forks; bear right onto Iulias Andreadi St. and look right. For a list of foreign language-speaking doctors, call the Medical Association of Corfu at 39 615 or 46 023 or the tourist office. For an **ambulance,** call 39 403 or 166.

Post Office: (tel. 25 544), on the corner of Alexandrius St. and Rizospaston. Walk down G. Theotaki, at Sanrocco Sq., turn left. After 2 blocks, post office is on your right. Open Mon.-Fri. 8am-8pm for stamps and Poste Restante, for all else Mon.-Fri. 7:30am-2:30pm. **Postal Code:** 49100.

Telephone Code: 0661 Corfu Town; 0662 South Corfu; 0663 North Corfu.

CORFU

ACCOMMODATIONS

Decent, reasonably priced rooms are available in Corfu. Some hotel managers fill their rooms with camp beds, which they then offer as dorms for the price of singles. True singles are nearly impossible to find. Hotels near the water fill up first, and the effectiveness of bargaining diminishes later in the day. Fortunately, prices drop roughly 1000dr per person in off season, and longer stays are often discounted at small pensions. Consider finding a room in a base town and taking advantage of Corfu's extensive bus service for daytrips around the island. Freelance camping is practically impossible and indubitably illegal.

Youth Hostel Kontokali (tel. 91 202), 4½km north on the main road from the port on the edge of Kontokali Village. Take the #7 Dassia bus from Sanrocco Sq. (every 30min. until 10pm, 20min., 155dr). Taxi will cost roughly 1500dr. Location not central, but bus service is accessible. Near a mediocre beach and a not-so-groovin' disco. Supermarket nearby, restaurant and pool in hostel. Reception open 8am-12:30pm and 5-8pm. 1500dr per person.

Hotel Acropolis, 3 Zavitsanou St. (tel. 23 936 or 39 569; fax 23 937), fronting the old port and fairgrounds. Big old building with clean rooms; management is friendly. 4000dr per person.

Hotel Evropi (tel. 39 304). From the New Port where the boats to Italy dock, look across the street for the fork in the road and bear left, looking for the red signs. Conveniently located, liveable rooms. Singles 4500dr. Doubles 5500dr, with bath 7000dr. Triples 7500dr, with bath 9000dr.

Camping: Close to Corfu Town is **Kondolaki Camping** (tel. 91 202), next to the hostel. 950dr per person. 630 per small tent. 750 per large tent. 530 per car.

FOOD

The premier restaurant areas are at the two ends of N. Theotoki St., near the Spianada and by the Old Port. Lunch is served outdoors until 3pm, dinner until 11pm. Because nearly all the restaurants in town are strictly regulated by the tourist police, the prices are fair but the cuisine monotonous. For cheap, go to the daily open air **market** on Dessila St., near the base of the New Fortress. Some stalls stay open all afternoon, but arrive around 7:30am for the best selection of goodies. Cheap *gyro* places abound; look in alleyways and in the small streets of Old Town where they tend to materialize (typically 300dr per pita). The **Supermarket Spilias,** 13 Solomou St., near the bus station (open Mon., Wed., and Sat. 8:30am-1:45pm, Tues. and Thurs.-Fri. 8am-1:30pm and 5:30-8:30pm), and the **Supermarket Koskinas,** in Sanrocco Sq. (open Mon.-Fri. 8am-2pm), have a supply of materials to fix a snack.

Nautikon, 150 N. Theotoki (tel. 30 009), near the Old Port. Natuikon is large and friendly, with appetizing food, some English spoken, and 50 years of experience. The delicious *moussaka* (1100dr) will impress even palates tired of this Greek standard. (Most entrees 1300-1500dr.) Open April-Oct. daily noon-midnight.

Pizza Pete, 19 Arseniou St. (tel. 22 301), on the waterfront halfway between the Spianada and the Old Port, is very popular with both tourists and locals. Great grub (entrees 1300-1900dr). Try the "Pete special" pizza (1400dr). Open April-Oct. daily 10am-3am.

Restaurant Bellissimo, 2 Kyriaki (tel. 41 112), off of N. Theotoki. Coming from the Spianada, turn left onto the narrow alleyway to Kyriaki. In a charming gardened enclave of its own. Nicely priced (*kalamari* 800dr, *sofrita* 1100dr).

Averof Restaurant, behind the Acropolis Hotel, offers great food in a family setting. Grilled items start at 1500dr *(souvlaki),* with great service and multiple smiles. Spaghetti (950dr) and *gyro* (350dr).

Cavalieri Hotel (tel. 39 041), Roof Garden Restaurant, on I. Kapodistriou at the top of the hill from the Espianada. The view is everything, so go at night. Pricey but fun (espresso 600dr, spaghetti with shellfish sauce 1500dr). Open daily 6:30pm-1am.

Sweet Shops: Bakery-hopping can best be done along Philarmonikis, as most sweet shops in the old town are along this road which runs parallel to the Spianada, one block inland. To get you started, try **Bella Piazza,** 8 Philarmonikis, which offers an enticing array of sweets. From N. Theotoki heading inland and turn right onto Philarmonikis. Open daily 7:30am-9pm.

ENTERTAINMENT

In the evening, parade up and down the Spianada and its adjacent park—it's perky until early morning. The demographics of a weekend evening lean heavily on young girls and middle-aged tourists. Cafés charge double what those in less popular locations do, but (after all) being seen has its price. Wander off the main catwalk into the streets of the Old Town. You might catch the dulcet tones of Corfu's seven music schools practicing simultaneously. The **Pallas Cinema,** on A. Theotoki St. near Sanrocco Sq., and the open-air cinema on Marasli St. often screen English language films (1200dr). The annual **Corfu Festival** in August and September features an international selection of ballet and music. The best times to visit Corfu, however, are during Carnival and Easter week, when Corfu's inhabitants practice the local tradition of smashing pottery to celebrate the Resurrection. The tourist office has details.

The east coast of Corfu is awash with **nightclubs,** which cater mainly to British package tours. To the south, in Benitses and Kavos, the dancing can sometimes turn to fighting. There's less trouble in the resort towns of Gouvia, Dassia, and Ipsos north of Corfu Town, but you might find yourself forgetting you are in Greece. For bars and clubs that are both safe and authentically Greek, head north of Corfu town past the Old Port along the port road. **Eidolo** plays only Greek music, while **Sax,** a favorite with the locals, is a classy, somewhat costly bar in a converted stable.

SIGHTS

Built by the Venetians in the late 14th century, the **Palio Frourio** (Old Fortress), east of the Spianada, was thought to be impregnable. In 1864, however, the British blew it up before leaving Corfu to the Greeks. It was renovated for the European Socialist Party Leaders' Conference in 1993 and is now open to the public. On the grounds is the **Church of St. George,** harmoniously adapted to accommodate museum displays, including absolutely exquisite mosaics (tel. 27 370; site open Tues.-Fri. 8am-7pm, Sat.-Sun., and holidays 8:30am-3pm; admission 800dr, students 400dr).

At the north end of the Spianada stands the **Palace of St. Michael and St. George** (tel. 30 443; open daily 8:30am-3pm). Unmistakably British, the palace was built as the residence of the Lord High Commissioner. The **Archaeological Museum,** 1 Vraila St. (tel. 30 680), on the waterfront south of the Spianada, contains relics of the island's Mycenaean and Classical past. An intimidating—but smiling—Gorgon sculpture glowers over the collection, which includes a horde of ancient coins from different regions. (Open Tues.-Sat. and holidays 8:30am-3pm, Sun. 9:30am-2:30pm; admission 800dr, seniors 600dr, children and students with ID free; Sun. free.)

Corfu's two most famous churches are the **Church of St. Jason and Sosipater** and the **Church of St. Spyridon.** The former is a 12th-century Byzantine stone structure located in a fishing neighborhood on the way to Mon Repos Beach (continue past the Archaeological Museum along the waterfront), with a dazzling array of silver and gold ornaments, medieval paintings, an impressive ceiling mural, and gorgeous Byzantine icons. The church was once covered entirely by murals of saints, but the islanders painted over them to prevent their decimation by the Turks. The Church of St. Spyridon, named for the island's patron saint, was built in 1590 (take Ag. Spyridon off the Spianada and the church is on your left; another entrance on the other side). Although St. Spyridon had been dead since the 4th century CE, he is said to have appeared in 1716 and shattered the morale of the invading Turks. Following outbreaks of plague in the 17th century, residents of Corfu began parading the silver reliquary containing the remains of the saint around town every Palm Sunday and on the first Sunday of November. Each year he is given a new pair of slippers to

CORFU

replace the old pair he wears out wandering the island doing good deeds. In the right light, if you lift the gold cover, you can still see his oddly disconcerting grin beneath a black shroud behind the glass. St. Spyridon holds a traditional **Greek Festival,** with music and dancing on July 13. Both churches are open until 7pm.

North of N. Theotoki, near the Spianada, is the Ionian Bank Building, which houses a **museum of paper currency** (tel. 41 552). It advertises itself as "one of the most interesting museums of its kind in the world," and it is home to the first bank note printed in Greece. Recommended for fanatical finance capitalists (open Mon.-Sat. 9am-1pm; free). Behind the Old Port lies the old **Jewish Quarter** of town. The **synagogue,** on Velissariou St., served a growing Jewish community from its construction in 1537 until 1940, when 5000 Jews were gathered on the Spianada to be sent to Auschwitz. For fans of Cousteau-like exploration, the confused **shell museum,** 7 Solomou St. (tel. 42 900), in the old town, has a biological lab-style collection of fetuses, stuffed birds, and snakes (open 9:30am-7pm; admission 400dr, students 200dr). The 375-year-old **New Fortress** (tel. 27 477), above the ferry ports, affords panoramic views of Corfu Town for sun-drenched picnics. The fortress houses a small gallery of etchings, maps, and watercolors with nautical motifs, and contains an additional museum exhibit of reproductions and noteworthy items from other museums around Greece (open daily 9am-9pm; admission 400dr).

Corfu's most recently opened sight (and its most recently closed sight) is the **Mon Repos Estate,** which the British government gave to the Greek royal family in 1864. Since the royals' exile in 1967, the lovely Neoclassical palace has fallen into disrepair, and large gardens filled with rare trees have become overgrown. In 1992, the mayor of Corfu opened the grounds to the public, stating that since a temple to Artemis rests on the area, the land, like any site of archaeological significance, belongs to the Greek people. Mon Repos was closed in summer 1996, but check with the tourist office, as it may open intermittently pending the lawsuit brought forth by former King Constantine, who is in exile in London and suing for possession. Just before the large, gated entrance to the Estate is the entrance to the **monastery of St. Efthimeaus** (open daily 8am-1pm and 5-8pm). On the opposite side of the road is the **Archaeological Site of Paleopolis Roman Baths,** closed to the public but visible through the fence. Be careful crossing the street. Before Pizza Pete's, along the waterfront between the Spianada and the New Port, is the **Byzantine Museum,** housing a vast collection of icons. Look for the sign or the collection of steps leading up to the building. (Open Tues.-Sun. 8:30am-3pm; admission 500dr, but free for EU students; all other students and seniors, 300dr).

■ Southern Corfu

Some 6km south of Corfu Town, the islet of **Vlacherna,** home to a tiny white **church** and parallel to the famous postcard island of Pondikonissi, connects to the main island via a causeway: take bus #2 (Kanoni) from the Spianada and ask the driver to let you off near Vlacherna (every 30min. until 10pm, 230dr).

Nearby stands **Achillion Palace,** 9km south of the port of Corfu in the village of **Gastouri.** Eccentric and ostentatious (but incredibly lovely), it was commissioned by Empress Elizabeth of Austria as a summer residence in honor of Achilles and Thetis. The Empress' Achilles fetish may be due to the death of her favorite son, whom she felt resembled the god. Kaiser Wilhelm II of Germany whiled away his summers here until WWI diverted his attention. The gardens and view are especially cinematic: the 1981 James Bond flick *For Your Eyes Only* was filmed here (open daily 9am-4pm; admission 700dr, children 350dr). While in the area, do what most don't—leave the palace for long enough to explore the intriguing village of Gastouri. Take bus #10 from Sanrocco Sq. (6 per day, every 3hr., 30min., 155dr). The arriving buses also make return trips. Fewer buses run on weekends and holidays.

Farther south is the rowdy little tourist/fishing village of **Benitses,** where you can see the remains of a Roman bathhouse and a 3rd-century CE Roman villa. Bus #6 runs to Benitses from Sanrocco Sq. (every hr., 30min., 250dr). At the lively waterfront bars and discoes, shoot pool, watch videos, or cruise. At night, be forewarned that the brawling and dancing at some of the bars can get out of control. Most have happy hours and infamous all-you-can-drink specials. You might as well have stayed at home and gone to a frat party. The **Museum of the Sea** offers hung-over revelers a soothing way to pass the time (open Tues.-Sat. 10am-7pm).

Shallow but clear and pleasant, **Kavos Beach** lies at the southern tip of the island, 47km from Corfu Town. Buses leave from behind the New Fortress (roughly every hr. 5am-7:30pm, 650dr). On the southwest coast stretches the gorgeous, sandy beach at **Agios Georgios** (2 buses per day from behind the New Fortress, 1hr., 480dr). The nearby, attractive **Vitalades Beach** is one of Corfu's few deserted spots.

■ Northern Corfu

Tacky come-ons to tourists scar the first 20km of the coastline north of Corfu Town. The resort towns of **Dassia, Ipsos,** and **Pirgi** consist of a chain of hotels, discoes, and boutiques. Official campsites are plentiful in this area: Dassia has **Karda Camping** (tel. (0663) 93 595), Ipsos has **Ideal Camping** (tel. (0663) 93 243) and **Corfu Camping Ipsos** (tel. 93 579), while Pirgi has **Paradissos Camping** (tel. (0663) 93 558). These campsites cost 1000dr per person, 700dr per small tent, 850dr per large tent, and 850dr per car. All have markets on the premises and include hot showers. For nightlife, head to any of these towns; for less spoiled country, venture farther north.

The Kassiopi **bus** serves this coast. It leaves from the bus station and stops at every hamlet along the way (9 per day, Sun. 2 per day, 1¼hr., 550dr). Past Pirgi, the road begins to wind below steep cliffs. **Mt. Pantokrator,** on your left, towers 1000m above, and the cliffs on the right loom dramatic as Albania comes into view across the straits. After passing through Nissaki and Gimari, you'll reach **Kouloura,** 28km north of Corfu, with its Venetian manor-house, pebbled beach, marina, and matchless *taverna*. The right fork to **Kalami** meanders down to a sandier beach where there are "Rooms to Let" (July-Aug. doubles roughly 8000dr). In the 1930s, author Lawrence Durrell lived in Corfu with his family, including his wacky brother Gerald. His small white house can still be seen (from the outside, at least). Buy the brothers' Corfu-inspired books (Lawrence's *Prospero's Cell* and Gerald's *My Family and Other Animals*) in Lyroudi's bookstore. Rooms are available for rent in both towns. The walk to Kalami or Kouloura from the main road takes roughly 15 minutes.

Kassiopi, 36km north of Corfu and just 2km across the sea from the Albanian port of Sarande, is over-commercialized and caters mostly to English couples with young children. The white-rock beaches are clean but overcrowded. For salamanders, overgrown weeds, and barbed wire, trek over to the 9th-century **fortress** which the Venetians destroyed in 1836, overlooking the beach. The **Panagia Kassiotropi Church** is where the Virgin Mary reportedly emerged from an icon and restored a blinded boy's sight. Doubting town officials were convinced because the boy's new eyes were blue instead of their original brown. **Travel agencies** on the main street help find rooms. Expect to pay 8000dr for doubles and 10,000dr for triples. There are no singles in Kassiopi. The innkeepers here, accustomed to package tourists, deplore one-night stays and often charge a premium for them. The preponderance of English-speaking tourists makes it seem like Britain, only warmer.

Northwest from Kassiopi on the main road, the quieter beach resorts of **Roda Chanin** and **Sidari** provide excellent camping and beaches enveloped by cliffs. Sidari is particularly spectacular, especially the stretch of picture-perfect coves and sea caves along the shore towards Peroulades. A 5th-century BCE temple has been found here as well. Try **Roda Beach Camping** (tel. (0663) 63 209), or buy supplies at the market here. Catch a sunset at **Peroulades;** by road, the 3km walk there takes you past farms. The bus to Sidari leaves from behind the New Fortress (11 per day, 550dr). In Sidari, hire a motorboat for a daytrip to the islands of **Othoni, Erikoussa,** and **Mathraki** (1hr., roughly 1500dr), inhabited by fishers, farmers, and their crops. For more information, inquire at **Sellos Travel** (tel. 31 239). Each of these islands is picturesque and quiet. There are no hotels available, only a few rooms. Sidari has eight C-class hotels with "budget" prices. Affordable hotels in Roda include the **Milton** (tel. (0663) 93 295), and the **Silva Beach Hotel** (tel. (0663) 93 134).

To wander even farther off the main trail, explore the mountain villages in the north of the island, each with gorgeous views, a couple of *tavernas*, and a few foreign visitors. A bus from Kassiopi occasionally runs to the village of **Loutses**, passing the little hamlet of **Perithia**, near Mt. Pantokrator.

■ Western Corfu

Swimming on Corfu's west coast is like being trapped inside an all-blue kaleidoscope. The **Paleokastritsa (Old Castle) beach** rests among some of the lovelier scenery in Greece, with six small coves and sea caves casting shadows over shades of blue; this also makes Paleokastritsa's beautiful beach the coldest on the island. Renting a pedal boat is the best way to visit the caves (1500dr per hr.). The 13th-century fort of **Angelokastro** sits above the town, while a natural balcony, **Bella Vista**, rests halfway up. Jutting out over the sea is the bright white **Panagia Theotokos Monastery** with a collection of Byzantine icons, gorgeous views, and the skeleton of a sea monster (open daily April-Oct. 7am-1pm and 3-7pm). Come as early as possible; by mid-morning it is a mess of tour buses. **Buses** run to Paleokastritsa from behind the New Fortress (11 per day, 45min., 380dr). Travelers willing to hunt can find affordable lodgings. Just wander up the footpath to Lakones and comb the olive groves for inexpensive pensions (5000-7000dr), or check out **Hotel Apollon** (tel. (0663) 41 211), whose large rooms offer a splendid view of the beach. (Doubles 7000dr. Breakfast 1000dr.) There is a **market** on your right as you come into town.

The road to Paleokastritsa is a whirl of bright reds, whites, and the colors of tourism. Signs for hotels, campsites, car rental places, restaurants, and clubs abound. Before you reach the town, look to your left. You'll see **Paleokastritsa Camping** (tel. 41 204), a cute campground close to the beaches. (1070dr per person. 620dr per small tent. 850dr per large tent. 600dr per car. All prices in the high season).

South of Paleokastritsa is **Pelekas,** an excellent base town in the west with some of the island's best beaches. Kaiser Wilhelm II used to watch the sun set over the Ionian Sea from a small hill outside town. **Agatha's Travel Service** (tel. 94 283, -602), on the main street in town to the left of the church, rents mopeds (3000dr per day) and can help find rooms. Doubles start at 4000dr (open 8:30am-2am).

The western exposure and elevation of Pelekas make it ideal for watching sunsets over whitewashed villages in the hillsides. **Pelekas Beach,** a 30-minute downhill walk from town, attracts a large number of backpackers. The beach is popular with freelance campers, as accommodations are nonexistent. Although freelance camping is illegal, police don't generally hassle sleepers. Don't attempt to make the harrowing journey by moped. Bus #11 runs to Pelekas Town from Sanrocco Sq. (9 per day, 30min., 230dr). **Glyfada Beach,** 5km up the coast from Pelekas Town, is served directly by the Glyfada bus from behind the New Fortress (every hr., 30min., 280dr). It is far more touristed, but still picturesque. Both beaches, bracketed by scrubby cliffs, are remarkably shallow. Single women should watch out for smooth-talking Greek *kamakia* (octopus spears—i.e., men) who cruise Glyfada, occasionally making a move. *Kamakia* make their living getting foreigners to pick them up and support them for a few days. They even have a union. Just ignore them.

A little north of Glyfada and accessible via dirt path off the main Pelekas road lie the isolated beaches of **Moni Myrtidon** and **Myrtiotissa,** extolled by Lawrence Durrell as the most beautiful beaches in the world. A section of sand at Myrtiotissa is the island's unofficial nude beach. Everything here is very casual, although once in a while the local monks from the Monastery of Our Lady of the Myrtles complain to the police, who reluctantly bring offending nudists to court. Above these beaches is the small restaurant **Myrtiotissa.** You can camp here for free and use the bathroom if you buy breakfast (850dr) and clean your site when you're done camping.

Agios Gordios, accessible by bus (7 per day, 45min., 240dr), with its steep cliffs and impressive rock formations, is the setting for the **Pink Palace** (tel. (0661) 53

Daytrip to Albania

Improved relations between Greece and Albania have made Albania's Ionian coast accessible to tourists in Greece. One of the more popular and easily accessible spots for a daytrip is the Greek settlement of **Butrint,** Albania, one of archaeology's better kept secrets. Layer upon layer of civilization, from as early as the 6th century BCE to the 19th CE, has left its mark on the small site. Very little effort has been made to maintain Butrint, now overgrown and deserted, for today's visitors. Not every ruin is labeled, and the rest are described cursorily in Albanian. But this is part of Butrint's appeal. Wandering around, it is easy to imagine discovering these treasures for the first time. In Butrint, no one will tell you to climb out of that 2nd-century well when you feel like playing Indiana Jones. (Ruins open daily 8am-sunset. Admission 150 lekë, or US$2.)

The best way to reach Butrint is by **taxi** from Sarande (45min.). It costs roughly 1000 lekë (US$11) roundtrip, including the wait while you tour around the site. There may also be a morning bus. A one-minute ride in the ferry stationed across from the entrance to the ruins takes you to an **island.** There stands a 19th-century triangular **fortress** built by the Turks. Check it out before leaving. Two **ferries** per day leave from Corfu to Sarande (1½hr., 3000 lekë, or US$34).

024, -103, -104; fax 53 025). Run by Greek "Dr." George, his sister Magda, and an energetic crew of Aussies, Brits, Canadians, and Swedes, this resort has legendary status among English-speaking beach revelers and late-night-drinking-party-aficionados. An eternal pink *ouzo* circle for some, the Pink Palace also attracts substantial crowds of road-weary young travelers who celebrate their "vacation from vacation" by extending their stays (longer stays receive certain discounts) and taking advantage of opportunities to do everything from innertubing, jet skiing, and parasailing to cliff diving and bungee jumping. Many of these activities—particularly, oh, say, cliff diving—are unsafe. Also available to guests are basketball and volleyball courts (with organized tournaments), bus excursions, laundry services, long-distance AT&T service, money exchange, and free safety deposit. Oh, and don't forget the weekly toga parties. The Pink Palace spans from road to beachfront and includes 13 buildings which can house up to 700 people. They won't turn anyone away, but reservations are accepted and a call will get you a free ride from port to palace. Rooms vary in size, quality, and location (4300dr per person, 3300dr per terrace cot; price includes all-you-can-eat breakfast, dinner, towels, shower, and nightclub). And if heading back to Corfu Town along the Paleokastritsa road, be sure to stop at the fabulous **Koum Kouaf distillery.** Four kilometers from Paleokastritsa, the booze shop is home to over 35 different methods of intoxication, and the staff is friendly and more than willing to procure you some free refreshment (open Mon.-Fri. daylight hours). The Koum Kouaf, a shrunken orange-like fruit the size of a golf ball, is turned into a sweet and medium-sweet liquor, while the distillery also can serve some of the old favorites—*ouzo*, brandy, table wines, and whiskey. The stuff is made only rooms away, and there is more than enough to take a bottle home with you (for a price).

ZAKINTHOS ΖΑΚΥΝΘΟΣ

Most visitors to Zakinthos come to admire the island's gorgeous beaches. While the beaches in the east make the trip worthwhile, the less popular Vrachionas mountains on the west fringe and the flower-filled villages in the interior, conceal some deserted beaches and quiet towns. Sunbathers share sand at Gerakas Beach with the *Caretta caretta* turtles, who consider the coast to be prime real estate. If you tire of vying for elbow-room, however, seek solitude in the fragrant pink-blossomed interior or in the west.

ZAKINTHOS

■ Zakinthos Town

Tidy Zakinthos Town welcomes visitors to the east coast of the island with arcaded streets and whitewashed buildings. After an earthquake destroyed it in 1953, locals renovated the city to its former state, making an effort to stay true to the Venetian architecture in certain areas, like the spacious Solomou Sq. to the right of the boat landing. It's a pretty town, but with all the other opportunities available, you may want to blow this joint and head for the more remote beaches.

ORIENTATION AND PRACTICAL INFORMATION

As you disembark from the ferry, you'll see the stately **Solomou Square,** lined with palm trees and pastel buildings. Along the waterfront, **Lombardou Street** and the boardwalk beckon with *gelateria* and tourist gift stores. The first street parallel to Lombardou away from the water is **Filita Street,** home to the bus station. Behind it are **Foskolou, Alex. Roma** (the main shopping street), and **Tertseti,** in that order. Behind Solomou Sq., **Vasileos Georgiou B** leads quickly to **Agiou Markou Square.**

Banks: National Bank, El. Venizelou St., near Solomou Sq., by the town hall, has **currency exchange.** Open Mon.-Thurs. 8am-2pm, Fri. 8am-1:30pm.

OTE: 2 Vasileos Georgiou B, between the 2 squares. Open daily 7am-10pm.

Flights: The **airport** (tel. 28 322) is 6km south near Laganas. Flights to Athens (in summer 2 per day, off season 1 per day, 45min., 16,300dr; students under 24, 13,300dr). **Olympic Airways,** 16 Alex. Roma St. (tel. 28 611 or 42 617). Open Mon.-Fri. 8am-3:30pm.

Buses: 42 Filita St. (tel. 22 255), on the corner of Eleftheriou St.—6 blocks along the water from Solomou Sq., then 1 block back. Long-distance buses piggyback on the ferry to Patras (3 per day, 3hr., 2800dr including ferry ticket) and then to Athens (4 per day, 6hr., 4235dr). Schedules for local service posted outside the bus station. Complete list is available at the information window. Buses run to Volimes (3 per day, 440dr); Vasiliko (Porto Roma); Geraka (2 per day, 30min., 240dr); Alykes (4 per day, 30min., 190dr); Argasi (7 per day, 190dr); Tsilivi (9 per day, 190dr); and Laganas (12 per day, 190dr). Buses run less frequently Sat.-Sun., and the schedule changes often, so ask for the updated schedule at the desk.

Ferries: Arrive at Zakinthos Town port from Killini (4-6 per day, 1½hr., 1400dr). Also from Ag. Nikolaos to Pesado in Cephalonia (2 per day, 1½hr., 850dr). Tickets available at the **boat agencies** along the waterfront. For more information, call the **port police** (tel. 22 417). Some agencies run a bus to the north of the island for the Cephalonia ferry, departing from Skinari and Ag. Nikolaos.

Taxis: line Vasileos Georgiou B (tel. 28 655) and Solomou Sq. (tel. 23 628; 24hr.).

Car Rental: Hertz, 38 Lombardou St. (tel. 45 706), on the waterfront. Cars from 10,000dr per day and 72dr per km. Many moped places also rent cars. Must be over 21. Open daily 8am-1:30pm and 5:30-9pm.

Moped Rental: Try **Stamatis Rental,** near the customs building on Lombardou St. (tel. 23 673). Mopeds 2500dr per day. Bicycles 600dr. Open daily 8:30am-9pm.

Laundromat: At the corner of Foskolou and D. Stefanou St. 1 block below Alex Roma. Prices vary according to quantity of clothing, but expect to pay 2500dr for a load (wash and dry). Open daily 8am-2pm and 5:30-9pm.

Hospital: (tel. 22 515, -514), above the city center. Walk down Lombarou St. until Ag. Eleftheriou. Follow this road inland until Kokkini St., where the road jogs right and becomes Ag. Spiridona. At the end of this road is the hospital (roughly 1km from the water). Open 24hr.

Police: (tel. 22 200), Lombardou and Fra. Tzoulati St., 5 blocks along the waterfront from Solomou Sq. Open 24hr. Laid-back **tourist police** (tel. 27 367) speak English, answer questions, and can help find rooms. Open daily 8am-10pm.

Post Office: (tel. 42 418), on Tertseti and Skirou Gouskou St. Offers **currency exchange.** Open Mon.-Fri. 7:30am-8pm. **Postal Code:** 29100.

Telephone Code: 0695.

ACCOMMODATIONS

Rooms in Zakinthos Town are expensive and scarce in July and August. If you're stuck in town for a night try the **Ionion Hotel,** 18 Alex. Roma (tel. 42 511), which offers clean rooms with big balconies. (Singles 4000dr. Doubles 6000dr.) For "Rooms to Let" near town, call **Fotis Giatras** (tel. 23 392), located 2km from a popular beach. (No English spoken. Singles 5500dr. Doubles 8500d. Moped rental 2200dr per day.) Taxis from town to Giatras' place cost roughly 820dr.

FOOD

The restaurants clustered in Ag. Markou Sq. are a tad overpriced, but a *souvlaki-pita* or a *tiropita* will only set you back a mere 250dr. At the corner of Rizospaston and Ignatiou, **To Tavernaki** serves wonderful veal with potatoes (1100dr). There's a well stocked **market** on Lombardou St. between the gas stations (open daily 8am-2pm and 6-8pm), and another one block back on Filita. A good *gyro* joint popular with residents is **Fisteria,** one block from Solomon Sq. (pitas 350dr). If you've found yourself along the waterfront, stop by **Molos Restaurant** (tel. 27 309), a cute place serving great specials (*moussaka*, salad, and dessert 1800dr). Day or night, head to the café/bar **Platia San Marco,** which dominates the square, playing loud, groovy English disco music for a diverse clientele (mixed drinks 800-1200dr). On your way home from the Venetian castle, you can stop at the **House of Latas** (tel. 26 178), and listen to the quartet sing Greek folk songs and local *cantadas* (large swordfish with vegetables 1350dr; open daily 8pm-2am).

SIGHTS

Zakinthos is famous for its **Church of Agios Dionysios,** which is named not for the ancient Greek god, but in honor of St. Denis, the island's patron saint. Located roughly 10 blocks east on the waterfront, the church displays a silver chest which holds the saint's relics. Modest dress code is strictly enforced. In Solomou Sq., the **Byzantine Museum** (tel. 42 714) houses icons from the "Ionian School," a distinctive local hybrid of Byzantine, Renaissance styles, and other religious eras (open Tues.-Sun. 8:30am-2:30pm; admission 800dr, students 400dr, free on Sun.). Above the town is the **Venetian Castle** where Solomos wrote the words to the Greek national anthem. The castle affords a view of the town (open daily 8am-7pm; free).

■ Around the Island

The terrain and beaches on Zakinthos will easily lure you away from the otherwise pleasant port town. It's possible to see the entire island, including the inaccessible **western cliffs,** by boat (leave daily at 9am from Zakinthos Town, 8hr., 7500dr, lunch included). Local tourist offices also offer a **bus tour** of the entire island on Thursdays (3500dr). **Boats** make excursions to the blue caves, turtle beach, and "Smuggler's Wreck." Inquire at the tourist police or agencies. To explore independently, tour the island by **moped** (there's at least one rental place at each beach) or by bus. Because the island is developing rapidly, many new roads won't appear on maps, but the most recent map available is the yellow Zakinthos map found at kiosks (350dr; a different but free map is available from the tourist police).

The beaches at **Laganas,** 10km south, have been mangled by large hotels, souvenir stands, and tourists. If you must stay, try **Laganas Camping** (tel. 51 708, -585), which has a pool. (1300dr per person. 800dr per car. 800dr per small tent. 1100dr per large tent.) The white-sanded **Tsilivi Beach** remains one of the best beaches on the island, but unfortunately, many other people also realize this. **Tsilivi Camping** (tel. 44 754), also called Zante Camping, is Zakinthos' only campsite located on a beach 6km from town. It has a cafeteria and minimarket. (1200dr per person. 650dr per car. 850dr per small tent. 1080dr per large tent. 10% discount for *Let's Go* users.) From Zakinthos Town, walk to the beach along the asphalt road skirting the shore. **Planos,** just inland, has plenty of rooms. **Buses** run from Zakinthos Town to the beach (9 per day, 30min., 190dr).

Unscathed beaches carpet the peninsula extending out to the town of **Vasilikos,** 16km from Zakinthos Town, and are most plentiful near **Porto Roma.** Signs for "Rooms to Let" coat the road to Vasilikos, especially near **Agios Nikolaos Beach.** On the other side of Vasilikos, facing Laganas Bay, lies **Gerakas Beach.** Daily buses leave Zakinthos Town for Vasilikos (2 per day, 240dr).

It is a five-minute walk from Gerakas to **Turtle Bay.** For nine million years, the 100-150kg mothers-to-be of the *Caretta caretta* species of sea turtle have returned from Africa to these beaches to lay their eggs safely in the softest sand in Greece. The *Caretta caretta,* commonly known as a Loggerhead turtle, only lays her eggs at night, when no humans are allowed on the beach. But if you visit during the day, you might get lucky and see a pregnant 150-kg turtle splashing towards you. Concern for the turtles' environment may prompt you to swim elsewhere.

Alykes, 16km from Zakinthos Town, is more pleasant and less crowded than its counterparts in the south. Filled with romantic restaurants and fringed with soft, clean sand beaches, Alykes gets somewhat crowded, although less so than the other resort towns. For spacious, clean, balconied doubles with bath (5000dr), ask at **Montes Restaurant** (or Jimmy's Place; tel. 83 101, -2), off the main drag, which also serves excellent budget fare (large Greek salad 500dr, breakfast 600dr). Or, one block down from Montes, the **tourist shop** (tel. 83 138), beside the bakery, has big rooms with small kitchen. (Doubles only 6000dr.) The **Apollo Restaurant,** on the edge of town, has fantastic chicken *souvlaki* (850dr). For a post-feast party, head to **Disco Dream** (beer 450dr). Buses run to Alykis four times per day; the last bus returns at 7pm (200dr). Buses leave from Hotel Montreal at the far edge of town.

Buses go to the sprawling old village of **Volimes** (3 per day, 440dr), where the residents specialize in needlepoint and crochet. Bring cash because this is the perfect opportunity to get a cheap, colorful rug, or other non-tacky presents (no credit cards accepted). One kilometer east, up the hill in the upper part of the village (Ano Volimes), the **Women's Agricultural Tourist Cooperative,** in the main square, finds rooms with a local family. If the office is closed, inquire about "Rooms to Let" at the *pantopoleion* (grocery store) opposite, or the **police** (tel. 31 204), next door. Crumbling medieval bell towers and abandoned windmills dot the lower village.

At the extreme north tip of Zakinthos is the tiny village of **Korithi,** locally known as Agios Nikolaos, where the ferry to Cephalonia departs. Buses arrive twice per day (550dr), and special buses occasionally come out to meet the ferry (ask at the station in Zakinthos Town). Here you can visit the beautiful **blue caves,** seen only from the water. A one-hour motorboat excursion from the beach costs roughly 1000dr per person. You can also rent canoes and other small craft on the tiny beach.

LEFKADA (LEFKAS) ΛΕΥΚΑΔΑ

Separated from Greece by a 50m canal, Lefkada resembles mainland Greece shrunken and transmuted into a floating resort. Although Lefkada has some of the lesser spoiled beaches in Greece, the atmosphere in town is not obviously enthralling. The hospitality of Lefkada's inhabitants may swell the farther away from the congested northeast edge of the island you travel. According to Thucydides, Lefkada (Greek for white rock) was part of the mainland until 427 BCE, when inhabitants dug a canal. The modern bridge, which connects Lefkada to the mainland, has only recently replaced the archaic chain-operated ferry built by Emperor Augustus.

■ Lefkada Town

Lefkada Town, directly across from the mainland, is a thinly touristed, humid city next to a section of sea that may look more like a vast swamp. It can appear a poor copy of upscale Greek resort towns, but for that reason offers a break for those allergic to the commodities of heavy tourism—the gaudy signs, procreating leather and jewelry stores, and mess of buses. The city is punctuated by pleasant although dirty architecture and some squares unspoiled by traffic.

Orientation and Practical Information   There is no tourist office, but the **tourist police** (tel. 26 450), a few blocks to the right of Lefkada Town's bus station (facing the water), offer handy brochures, and will call around for rooms (open daily 7am-10pm). For budget travel, try **Lefkada Travel** (tel. 22 430), on Dörpfeld St., **Melas Travel** (tel. 22 538, -905), or **St. Maura Travel** (tel./fax 25 119). All travel agencies are open normal Greek business hours (daily 8am-2:30pm and 6-8pm), sometimes longer in high season. There is a **National Bank** along Dörpfeld St. (open 8am-2pm, but with a 24-hr. **ATM**), near the post office. Dörpfeld also leads to the main square, filled with cafés and an occasional traveling music act. (William Dörpfeld was the archaeologist who unsuccessfully tried to identify Lefkada as Homer's Ithaka.) For the **OTE,** turn right off Stratigou Melas to Pataneromenis St., head back towards the beginning of town, and look for the tower (open daily 7am-10pm).

From the bus station (tel. 22 364), on the waterfront, **buses** cross the canal to Athens (5 per day, 5½hr., 6000dr) and Aktion (3 per day, 320dr). To reach Preveza, take the ferry from Aktion across the mouth of Amvrakikos Bay (every 20min., 15min., 100dr). The 21km journey by taxi costs 2500-4000dr. The **local island buses** run to Nidri (16 per day, 30min., 260dr); Agios Nikitas (5 per day, 20min., 220dr); Poros (2 per day, 45min., 400dr); and Vasiliki (4 per day, 1hr., 660dr). Be sure to pick up a bus schedule at the station (or from tour offices) detailing additional transit routes and indicating return times. **Ferries** link Lefkada with Ithaka and Cephalonia to the south. From Vasiliki in Lefkada, ferries make the run to Fiskardo on Cephalonia (2-3 per day, 1hr., 1000dr), then to Ithaka (1¾hr., 1000dr) and on to Sami on Cephalonia (2½hr., 1700dr). From Nidri in Lefkada, ferries sail to Cephalonia and Frikes on Ithaka (3 per day, 1000dr). For Vasiliki ferry information, call 31 555; for Nidri 92 427. Travel offices have information and sell tickets. Lefkada may well be **excursion boat** paradise. Excursion boats **Nidri Star** and **Vasiliki Star,** bearing their home port namesakes, run daily day-long cruises to Cephalonia, Ithaka, and Skorpios (9am departure, roughly 3500dr). Excursion boats also shuttle beach devotees to Lefkada's numerous cloistered beaches, including the famously beautiful **Porto Katsiki,** which is inaccessible by bus. Some also stop at the cave of **Papanikoli.** Inquire at waterfront kiosks or travel offices, or try to read the hard-to-miss signs aboard the little boats. The **tourist police** are in the same building as the **police station,** 30 Iroon Politechniou (tel. 22 346; open 24hr.; English spoken). The **post office** is along the main market street, Dörpfeld St., lined with tourist services and the first pedestrian mall running inland (open Mon.-Fri. 7:30am-2pm). **Postal Code:** 31100. **Telephone Code:** 0645.

Accommodations   The charming and clean **Hotel Byzantion** (tel. 22 629) is at the end of Dörpfeld St. next to the harbor. To find it, walk along the harbor. When the cafés begin to appear, look left. (Singles 4000dr. Doubles 7600dr. Triples 9420dr.) Farther up the street in the corner of the main square, **Hotel Patras** (tel. 22 359) offers cozy, clean rooms overlooking the cafés. (Singles 6000dr. Doubles 8500dr. Triples 10,000dr.) Also try asking a travel company for rooms. (Doubles from 6500dr. Triples from 8000dr.)

Food and Entertainment   A jolly owner makes for a good time at the popular **Taverna Pyrofani** in a whitewashed building roughly two blocks from the water on Dörpfeld (entrees 900-1200dr; open daily noon-midnight). Also try **Regentos,** off the main square on Verrioti St.; follow the signs to the self-proclaimed cosmic tavern (*moussaka* 700dr, grilled meats 1000dr; open daily 7:30pm-2am). Or try the popular **Taverna of the Nine Islands.** It's off Dörpfeld St., near Pyrofani, and serves wonderful fish. (Open for dinner daily at 7pm.)

Frolic through the famous **Folklore Festival,** now in its 33rd year, in the first and third weeks of August. (Details from Lefkada Travel; tickets roughly 500dr.) Also look for the **folklore museum** signs to the right of the main square. The small museum offers a taste of old Lefkada (open Mon.-Fri. 10am-1pm and 7-10pm; admission 500dr). Groove over to the bizarre **Phonograph Museum,** past the square to the left; inquire at the meat market for access (open Mon.-Fri. 9am-1pm and 6-11pm). The **Archaeological Museum,** 1km down the road to Ag. Nikitas, is tiny and worthwhile for only the most dedicated, since the majority of Lefkada's treasures are in Athens or in Ioannina (open 9am-12:30pm and 6-8pm; admission 500dr).

■ Around the Island

While Lefkada Town has no sandy beaches, the north half of the west coast offers miles of deserted white pebbles and clear water. Rent a moped (3000dr per day) at **Santa's Rentals** (tel. (0645) 25 250), or one of the other places to the right of Dörpfeld St. on the water port. The best stretch lies north of **Agios Nikitas.** Buses leave from Lefkada Town for Ag. Nikitas (6 per day, 220dr). The road there leads to the monastery **Moni Faneromenis** (tel. (0645) 22 275), with a sweeping view of the ocean and one resident monk (monastery open daily 7am-10pm; free). Follow the footpath through the woods for a pick-up game of basketball with the students at the monastery school. Michael Jordan, look out.

Nidri, a strip of garish tourist agencies and tacky cafés, ensnares unwary travelers solely because it's the last stop of the otherwise delightful Frikes-Nidri ferry. The waterfront, flush with pleasure boats, boasts a handsome view of the dappled coves of numerous small islands. The **post office** (open Mon.-Fri. 7:30am-2pm) and **OTE** (open Mon.-Fri. 8:30am-12:30pm and 5:30-9:30pm) are on the main street, occasionally referred to as Center St. Many stores and tour offices display signs indicating telephone access for local and international calls on their premises. **Buses** from Nidri go to Lefkada (15 per day, 30min., 260dr), Vlino (16 per day, 150dr), and Vasiliki (5 per day, 320dr). "Rooms to Let" are scattered along the main (and virtually only) street, parallel to the waterfront. In July and August, when the entire island slumps under the burgeoning weight of tourists, rooms are always full, and prices are inevitably high (doubles from 7000dr). The self-explanatory **Beautiful View** pension (tel. (0645) 92 361), along the main street to the left from the ferry, offers doubles for 8000dr. On the road from Nidri to Lefkada rests **Camping Episkopos** (tel. (0645) 23 043 or 71 388; 1000dr per person, 700dr per small tent, 800dr per large tent, 600dr per car). To escape the pervasive manufactured appeal of Nidri, climb the 5km to **Neochori** at dusk. Three kilometers south is the tiny village of **Vliho,** accessible by bus from Lefkada (9 per day, 150dr), with a striking church (proper dress required) in an idyllic setting of wildflowers and cypress trees. **Thesimi Camping** (tel. (0645) 95 374), on the road from Nidri to Vliho, camps for campers (1100dr per person, 700dr per small tent, 1000dr per large tent, 600dr per car).

Vasiliki, at the south tip of Lefkada Island, with white pebbled beaches and cafés drawn straight up to the water's edge, bears charms both tranquil and invigorating. **Buses** run five times per day from Lefkada (550dr) and Nidri (300dr). Smaller and currently less touristed than Nidri, Vasiliki is becoming increasingly popular with the young international watersports crowd. Rated among the world's finest **windsurfing** resorts, "the 3rd best in Europe," Vasiliki is usually graced with consistent gentle winds in the morning, which rise to steady force-five gales in the afternoon, to tempt and tease novices and experts alike.

The main road running inland from the waterfront winds past the **post office** (**postal code:** 31082; open Mon.-Fri. 8am-2pm). Also along this road, before the post office, is **Samba Tours** (tel. (0645) 31 520, -555; fax 31 522), an all-purpose tour office willing to "help and advise by fax or phone" (open daily 8:30am-11pm). From Vasiliki, two **ferries** per day run to Fiskardo, Cephalonia (1hr., 1000dr), Ithaka (1¾hr., 1000dr), and Sami (2½hr., 1700dr). Inquire at the kiosk next to the pier. To contact the **health center,** call 31 065. The **police** (tel. (0645) 31 218; 24hr.) are a short distance inland along the road; ask for directions.

Rooms are plentiful and signs easy to spot, particularly along the road leading uphill from the bus stop (on the waterfront and along the main post road). The popular **Vasiliki Beach Camping** (tel. (0645) 31 308, -457; fax 31 458) boasts superlative amenities and rests a hop, skip, and a jump away from the beach. Head for the beach and make a right on the road running inland just before the Windsurfing Club (1550dr per person, 1000dr per child, free for kids under 4, 1100dr per small tent, 1100dr per car). The **Galaxy Market** (tel. (0645) 31 221), around the corner at the back side of the ferry dock, lets tidy, simple rooms. (Singles 6000dr. Doubles 7000dr.)

Full meals can be inexpensive and well prepared in Vasiliki, even in the waterfront cafés and eateries. Most have similar menus and prices, so choose your haunt according to what aspect of sun and sea seems most appealing. Give the **Alexander the Great Restaurant** a try; it is on the waterfront on the way to the beach (mixed salad with fresh parsley 500dr; fried *kalamari* with a touch of thyme 600dr). A haven for the high-spirited, **Zeus' Bar,** on the waterfront, serves up drinks to soothe the salt- and sun-weary (particularly refreshing is the orange juice and soda water 300dr; open daily morning to late night). For a morning treat or for bus journey snack provisions, try the **bakery** above the bus stop. Scoop into their big barrels of tasty sweet rolls (molasses and a taste of caraway 50dr).

At the southernmost tip of the island there's a **lighthouse** built on the site of the Temple of Lefkas Apollo. Worshippers exorcised evil with an annual sacrifice here. The victim, usually a criminal or a mentally ill person thought to be possessed, was thrown into the sea from the cliffs. Live birds were tied to the victim's arms and legs for amusement as well as aerodynamic advantages. It was from these 70m cliffs that the ancient poet Sappho leapt to her death when Phaon rejected her. The cliff, called **Sappho's Leap,** is known in Lefkada as *Kavos tis Kiras* (Cape of the Lady).

ITHAKA (ITHAKI) ΙΘΑΚΗ

What most tourists see of Ithaka is a hinge of harborfront that composes the island's largest city, Vathi. The port itself is a bulbous growth, the largest natural inlet of its kind in Greece. For those whose luck it's been to land here, the first sense of Ithaka may be the overpowering impression that nothing is going on. If you are patient, however, the island will endear itself to you as it has to many others.

It is the legendary home of Odysseus, hilly and forested. The only boats that arrive today seem to be yachts from Peiraias and underpopulated ferries. It is a lovely, rocky, riveting island coursed by walking trails and quiet roads. It doesn't brow-beat with its beauty, but rather suggests it on the breathe of a slight breeze.

■ Vathi

Vathi is the main port and largest town on the island. Ferries to Ithaka dock here or at **Piso Aetos,** a deserted harbor at the foot of a mountain that is a 10-minute ride to the left of Vathi (taxis cost 1500-2000dr). The casual town curves around the edge of a long, natural harbor and is almost completely circumscribed by mountains. In the evening, the town's cats, children, and scooters crowd around the right-hand side of the waterfront with equal disregard for passersby. Art galleries, craft stores, and souvenir shops control the waterfront, which sprawls at the far right-hand corner of the horseshoe as you face the town.

Orientation and Practical Information   One block in from the corner of the harbor near Polyctor Tours is the **National Bank** (open Mon.-Fri. 8am-2pm). The **OTE** sits on the water (open Mon.-Sat. 7:30am-3:10pm). The **Marlines** office,

ITHAKA

located opposite the ferry landing, keeps somewhat irregular hours, but is open when boats come in. Getting to Ithaka will be easier for you than it was for Odysseus (although with the capriciousness of Greek ferry schedules, you never know); the web of **ferries** around the Ionian islands enmeshes Ithaka. Boats run between Frikes on Ithaka to Nidri on Lefkada (2 per day, 2½hr., 1230dr). From Vathi, there are ferries to Agia Efimia on Cephalonia (4pm, 1hr., 1230dr), Sami on Cephalonia (7am, 1hr., 960dr), and Astakos on the mainland (11am, 2hr., 1500dr). There are also boats from Piso Aetos to Sami (7am, 2, and 8:30pm, 500dr) and to Brindisi in Italy (3-4 per week, 12-14hr., 15,500dr, no student discounts). Be sure to check boat schedules at your port of departure. For a **taxi,** call 33 030. Most **moped rental** places charge roughly 3000dr per day. Try your luck at **Moto-Rent** (tel. 32 035), near Lazarus Tours. You can also rent small motorboats (where the little boats dock) for 8000dr. The **bookstores** (tel. 33 204 for the one on the left, tel. 32 413 for the one on the right), on either side of the bank, sell English-language reading material ranging from Homer to *Beverly Hills 90210* fan magazines. The **hospital** can be reached at 32 222, or walk along the port until you see a sign reading "Hospital." It is roughly 1km. Along the way, you will see the **police** station where English is spoken (tel. 32 205; open 24hr.). The **port police** can be reached at 32 909, and the **pharmacy** at 32 251. The **post office** is in the main square (open Mon.-Fri. 8am-1:30pm). **Postal Code: 28300. Telephone Code: 0674.**

Accommodations   Helpful, friendly **Lazarus Tours** (tel. 32 587) rents the cheapest rooms. (Doubles with bath 6000dr. Open daily 9am-10pm.) Farther from the ferry landing, **Polyctor Tours** (tel. 33 120) also helps find rooms starting at 8000dr for a double with bath (50% student discount in June and Sept; open daily 8am-10pm). The chunky **Hotel Mentor** (tel. 32 433, -292) squats next to the OTE. This hotel's high prices are flexible, and, unfortunately, the lowest in town. (Singles 6000dr. Doubles 9000dr. Triples 11,000dr. Breakfast included.) Your best bet is a private room. Although it is impossible to predict the price you will be offered, even in July, if you are a student, you may find a room for 4000dr or sometimes 3000dr. **Camping** on the beach under the eucalyptus trees or any place else outside is generally tolerated, provided that campers clean up after themselves.

Food   Restaurants tend to be expensive. To save a few *drachmae* on food, try **Fast Food,** at the side of the harbor away from the ferry landing. The fare is better than the name suggests. In the center of town, one block back from the water and across from the scooter rental place, is **Taverna To Trexantiri** (tel. 33 066), popular among locals (entrees average 1100dr). Although there inevitably had to be the **Odysseus Restaurant,** the food is surprisingly good. And since it is located away from the center of town, it poses an alternative to the storming of the harbor-front fish *taverna*—a phenomenon easily documented on these islands (squid 1200dr, Greek salad 800dr, or fried potatoes 700dr). To get there, simply walk to your left, facing the water, and after 800m look left.

Sights   The **Vathi Archaeological Museum** is small but free (open Mon.-Fri. 9am-3:30pm). Those with poetic imaginations may want to make the 45-minute, 4km climb up to the **Cave of the Nymphs,** where Odysseus hid the treasure the Phoenicians bestowed upon him. To get here, walk around the harbor with the water on your right, and follow the signs. Peerless views of Vathi unfold during the climb. Bring a flashlight (admission 200dr). A 2-hour hike southeast up a well marked but rocky road leads to the Homeric **Arethousa Fountain,** along a steep mountain path through orchards. In summer, the fountain is dry. To find the path to the fountain, follow Evmeou St. up the hill until it turns to dirt, and look for signs. Spend an afternoon sifting through the multicolored stones of the beach at **Piso Aetos Bay,** 15km from town. Ask at Polyctor Tours about the **Greek Theater Festival** (late August) and the popular **Music Festival** (early July; Greek folk and modern music) which take place in Vathi. There is a **Wine Festival** in Perahori on the last Sunday of July.

■ Around Ithaka Island

An excursion from Vathi transports to scenic, remote villages scattered across Ithaka's rocky coast. The island's one **bus** runs north from Vathi, passing through the villages of Lefki, Stavros, Platrithiai, Frikes, and Kioni. Leaving Vathi at 6:30am and 10:40am, it arrives in Kioni one hour later (300dr). The stunning road skirts both sides of the isthmus, and offers superlative views of the strait of Ithaka and Cephalonia on the west and of the coastline on the east. Check the times of return buses before setting out; taxis from Kioni to Vathi cost roughly 3800dr.

Stavros, the highest point on the island, merits a visit for its mountaintop location and its lone sight. The schoolmaster's wife has a key to a small museum at the alleged site of **Odysseus' Palace,** recommended for fanatical Homerists; a small tip is expected. Homer described this site as the place from which three different waters could be seen. Still visible from this point are the Bays of Frikes, Aphales, and Polis.

CEPHALONIA ΚΕΦΑΛΛΟΝΙΑ

The east and west coasts of arid Cephalonia are generally steep and rocky and the inland areas are forbiddingly mountainous. In contrast to many of the other Ionian islands which have been home to vacationers since Roman times, Cephalonia, with its rugged countryside, has remained relatively tourist-free despite its beautiful, sandy beaches, easy bus connections, friendly people, and charming towns. In this century, Cephalonia has endured a plucky but troubled history. When the Germans invaded in 1943, 9000 Italian soldiers occupying the island mutinied and resisted their Nazi "allies" for seven days. Only 33 Italians survived. Ten years later, a disastrous earthquake forced the island to rebuild. Because of this, only Fiskardo, which was relatively undamaged, retains the pastel Neoclassical look associated with the Ionian islands. Nonetheless, Cephalonia's coasts and inland cities, which are home to unique flora, are the perfect place for a relaxed vacation.

■ Argostoli

The capital of Cephalonia, Argostoli is a busy, noisy town whose palm tree-lined streets are regularly jammed with traffic. Argostoli hosts an international **singing festival** in late August.

ORIENTATION AND PRACTICAL INFORMATION

Tourist Office: (tel. 22 248, -466), at the port. Gives free maps and offers candid advice on accommodations, restaurants, and beaches in the area. Also has a list of "Rooms to Let." Open Mon.-Fri. 8am-10pm.

Tourist Police: 52 Metaxa St. (tel. 22 200), right of the bus station. Little English spoken. Open 24hr.

Banks: Sprinkled along the waterfront and Konstantinou St. Note that the **National bank** does not have currency exchange. Open Mon.-Thurs. 8am-2pm, Fri. 8am-1:30pm.

OTE: Uphill edge of the square. Open 7am-11:30pm.

Flights: The **Olympic Airways** office occupies 7 R. Vergoti St. (tel. 28 808, -81). Olympic flies to Athens at least once per day (14,100dr). Office open Mon.-Fri. 8am-3:30pm. Office at the airport (tel. 41 511) is open daily 6am-6pm.

Buses: The bus station (tel. 22 281) is on the waterfront. Buses head to Skala (Mon.-Sat. 4 per day, Sun. 10am, 600dr); Poros (4 per day, 1¾hr., 700dr); Fiskardo (2 per day, 1½hr., 750dr); Sami (4 per day, 400dr); Assos (2 per day, 1¼hr., 550dr); Ag. Gerasimos (3 per day, 9:30am-2pm, 220dr); and Kourkoumelata (4 per day, 7:15am-1:45pm, 200dr). There are also buses which piggyback on the ferry to Athens (7:45am and 1:30pm). Buses to Argostoli meet most of the **ferries** arriving in Sami (5 per day, 45min., 400dr). The road winds around hairpin curves, treat-

CEPHALONIA

ing passengers to glorious mountain vistas, screaming engines, and high blood pressure. Bus station open 7am-8pm.

Ferries: Unlike most islands, Cephalonia has several ports for different destinations. Buses connect Argostoli to other ports. From **Sami,** boats sail to Ithaka (daily at 3pm, 1hr., 1230dr) and Patras (daily 8:30am, 2830dr). This is also the place to catch boats to Italy. To Brindisi (daily at 8:30am, 14,700dr) and Bari (daily at 3pm, 15,950dr). From **Agia Efimia,** service links Cephalonia with Astakos on the mainland (2 per day, 9:15am and 5:30pm, 3½hr., 1700dr) and Ithaka (daily at 9:15am, 2400dr). From **Argostoli** boats go to Killini on the mainland (daily at 8am, 24840dr), and several boats shuttle to nearby Lixouri.

Car and Moped Rental: Myrtos Rent-a-Car (tel. 24 230 or 25 023), on the waterfront. Rents cars starting at 12,500dr per day. Open 8:30am-1pm and 7-9:30pm. **Rent-a-Moto** (tel. 23 613); at the port authority, take a left. Rents mopeds for 2500dr per day.

International Bookstore: Petratos Bookstore (tel./fax 22 546), 2 blocks down from the post office, across from the church. Stuffed with foreign newspapers and magazines. Open Mon.-Sat. 8am-1pm and 5-9pm, Sun. 8am-noon; reduced hours in winter.

Post Office: (tel. 23 173); walk 2 blocks inland from the port to D. Konstantinou, the town's main street, and turn right. Open Mon.-Fri. 7:30am-2pm. **Postal Code:** 28100.

Telephone Code: 0671.

ACCOMMODATIONS

Cheap rooms are rather scarce in Argostoli. The **Hotel Parthenon** (tel. 22 246), a spiffy white building on a small side street left of the post office, offers sunny balconies and doubles at cheap prices. (Singles 3000dr. Doubles 5500dr.) The **Argostoli Beach Campground** (tel. 23 487), 1½km from town, is a convenient option. (Open April-Oct. 1400dr per person. 800dr per small tent. 1250dr per large tent. 935dr per car.) Another budget option is **Hotel Allegro** (tel. 28 684), two blocks to the right of the post office. Clean rooms, gracious owners. (Singles 4000dr. Doubles 6000dr.)

FOOD

Restaurants which line the water are expensive and average. They serve fish (2000-6000dr) and *moussaka* (200dr, on average), along with some Italian fare. A more economically sound option is to choose a small *gyro* going on one of the streets leading from the harbor to the town. Pitas (250dr) or *gyro* plates (600dr) are worth the price. Other noteworthy restaurants include **Restaurant Anonymous** (tel. 22 403), 100m left of the bus station. It serves cheap food without a lot of fuss over its name (entrees 800-1100dr). **Mister Grillo** (tel. 23 702) is near the port authority. This restaurant offers plenty of vegetarian options including black beans in oil (600dr) and stuffed peppers (700dr). **Restaurant Hellenic** (tel. 23 529) is on Ag. Gerasimos, one block from the port police. Excellent service brings you Greek salads for 800dr and most Greek entrees for under 1500dr.

SIGHTS

From Petratos Bookstore, go one block farther; you'll hit the square and the **Argostolian Archaeological Museum** (open Tues.-Sun. 8:30am-3:30pm; admission 400dr). From the museum, turn right onto R. Vergoti St. and continue two blocks to reach Corgialenios Library, which houses the **Historical and Folk Museum** (tel. 28 835). This museum is crammed with household belongings from the 19th century. Argostoli's French coffee cups, English top hats, and antique dolls all create a picture of confident luxury. Best of all are the photographs of Argostoli during the last century, including shots of the damage from the devastating 1953 earthquake and the ensuing reconstruction (open Mon.-Sat. 8:30am-2:30pm; admission 400dr).

■ Near Argostoli

The Venetian **Castle of St. George,** 9km southeast of Argostoli, rests on a hill over-looking the village of Travliata. Chug along the road to Skala and turn right when the road splits. **Buses** travel to the site (3 per day, 10min., 150dr). From the battlements, admire the panorama that inspired Lord Byron (open Tues.-Sun. 8:30am-3pm; free.) To swim at **Lassi,** one of the island's best sandy beaches, follow the road leading from the town to the airport. There are several options for exploring more of the island. Boats leave regularly for **Lixouri,** in the center of the west peninsula (every hr., 30min., 240dr). Once home to the satiric poet Lascaratos, Lixouri offers miles of practically tourist-free coastline. Rent **mopeds** at several places in Lixouri; **buses** run to several smaller villages in the area.

A few beaches and interesting towns dot the island south of Argostoli. One of the best beaches is at **Ormos Lourda,** in the middle of the south coast; closer to Argostoli is **Platis Gialos** (7 buses per day, 30min., 150dr). Here visit one of Byron's adopted towns (though his house no longer exists) at **Metaxata,** or see **Kourkoumelata,** a village completely restored by a Greek tycoon after the 1953 earthquake. If you decide to stay, check out the comfortable **Hotel Kourkoumi** (tel. 41 645). Doubles with bath and breakfast, 6000dr. A multi-layered *tholos* tomb found in the village of **Dargoti** is thought to be Odysseus' grave, supporting the theory that Homer's Ithaka was really modern-day Cephalonia. **Poros,** on the southeast coast, is a modern coastal town with a beach; "Rooms to Let" are everywhere. Buses run from Argostoli (4 per day, 1½hr., 700dr).

On the night of August 15, the nearby village of **Omala** hosts a festival and a vigil in the saint's church. East of Argostoli is the monastery **Agios Gerasimos,** in which a monk's preserved corpse lies; the town goes wild on the saint's namedays (Oct. 20 and Aug. 16). Contact the tourist office for more information. Omala has an excellent **Archaeological Museum** (tel. 28 300; open daily 8:30am-3:30pm).

By far the best beach on the island is the pebble and sand beach at **Scala.** The town itself is prohibitively expensive (7000dr for plain singles), but the beach to the right of the rocks is heavenly. Three buses per day arrive from Argostoli; the latest returns at 5pm. If you must stay, ask at **Scalini Tours** for rooms, and catch a bite at the **Sun Rise Restaurant** (beef stew 850dr).

■ Sami

A small town on a harbor surrounded by lush green hills, Sami stays quiet during the day, offering an ethereal small pebble beach. By night the town waxes romantic to the glimmer of lighted ships in the harbor. The blue and white Hotel Kyma, two blocks from the ferry landing, dominates Sami's main square. There is no official tourist office, but the police may be able to answer your questions, or visit **Sami Travel** (tel. (0674) 23 050), which offers rooms, tickets to Italy, excursion tickets, and general information. It is located off Akti Posidonos St. (the one that runs along the port), at the end opposite the main square. The **Marketou Travel/Strintzis Line Office** (tel. (0674) 22 055 or 23 021), on the waterfront just to the left of the ferry landing in Sami, is also very helpful. You can **exchange money** at the **bank** on Sami's waterfront (open Mon.-Fri. 8am-2pm) or at most of the travel agencies. The **OTE** (open Mon.-Fri. 7:30am-3:10pm), is opposite the cathedral, near the **police station** (tel. (0674) 22 100; open 24hr.). I. Metaxa St., which bears right as you face the hotel, leads to the **post office (postal code:** 28080; open Mon.-Fri. 7:30am-2:30pm).

Lodgings in Sami cost 20-40% less in off season. Try the **Hotel Kyma** (tel. (0674) 22 064) in the town square. Many of the clean rooms offer spectacular views and cool breezes. (Singles 4500dr. Doubles 8500dr.) The **Hotel Melissani** (tel. (0674) 22 464), several blocks back from the water on the left side of town as you face inland, offers lovely views of the harbor and surrounding hills. (Singles 7000dr. Doubles 9500dr.) The rooms above the **Riviera Restaurant** (tel. (0674) 22 246), on the waterfront, go quickly in summer. (Doubles with bath 6000dr.) **Karavomilos Beach**

Camping (tel. (0674) 22 480) is set on top of the beach, has a snack bar and small restaurant, and is clean and popular. The management also offers laundry services and a mini market. (1350dr per person. 850dr per small tent. 1350dr per large tent. 700dr per car.)

The caves of **Melissani** and **Drograti,** two sites near Sami, impress both troglodytes and surface-dwellers. Melissani, the more impressive of the two, can be reached by foot from Sami (30min.). Follow I. Metaxa and turn right at the sign for **Agia Efimia,** then follow the signs past the village of Karavomilos. At the lake, guides punt around the two large caverns flooded with sparkling water, studded with stalactites and squirming with eels. For best viewing, go when the sun is high (open until nightfall; admission 950dr; a polite 50dr tip is expected). To reach Drograti, 4km from Sami, head inland on the road to Argostoli and follow the signs (open until nightfall; admission 750dr). Just 10km north of Sami at the other end of the bay is the pretty harbor town of Ag. Efimia (10:15am and 4pm, 360-550dr).

■ Around Cephalonia

Cliffs plunge into the sea along the coastal road north from Argostoli or Sami to Fiskardo. The beaches of **Agia Kyriaki** and **Myrtos** on this road are generally serene. Signposts on the main road after the hamlet of Divarata advertise Myrtos, but swim cautiously there—the undertow can be powerful and sudden. Roughly 4km up the road are the fragrant gardens of **Assos,** joined by a narrow isthmus to an island with a Venetian fortress. A daily bus from Argostoli departs at 2pm, returning the next day at 6:45am (550dr); the 30-minute walk from the main road is challenging.

The road north ends at **Fiskardo,** the only town on the island left undamaged by the 1953 earthquake and thus the only remaining example of 18th- and 19th-century Cephalonian architecture. Once called Panoramos, Fiskardo was magnanimously renamed after Robert Guiscard, a Norman, who died here in 1085 while attempting to conquer the town. A ruined Norman church visible from the harbor is believed to predate Robert by some 800 years. Alongside the dilapidated old Venetian lighthouse, pine-sheltered campsites await. Rooms are expensive (doubles 7000-10,000dr), but the cheapest are on the road out of town past the bakery and left. The **Panoramos** (tel. 51 340) is Fiskardo's most accessible hotel. (Doubles with bath 13,000dr.) Restaurants line the harbor and are fairly expensive. The **Restaurant Fiskardo,** along the harbor, serves the tasty local specialty *kreatopita* (meat pie; open daily noon-midnight). Fiskardo's beach is unbeatable, lying 500m out of town on the road back to Argostoli and offering flat rocks for sunbathing. One **bus** per day arrives from Sami (1hr., 550dr). Two buses arrive daily from Argostoli (1½hr., 750dr) with a daily ferry connecting Sami and Fiskardo.

On August 15, an unusual and spooky festival in the village of **Markopoulo** in the southeast corner of the island celebrates the Assumption of the Blessed Virgin Mary. Celebrants hold an all-night church liturgy. According to legend, during the service hundreds of small harmless snakes with black crosses on their heads appear and slither over the icons.

Northeast Aegean Islands
ΒΟΡΕΙΟΑΝΑΤΟΛΙΚΑ ΝΗΣΙΑ ΤΟΥ ΑΙΓΑΙΟΥ

After centuries of resisting the Ottoman Empire, the Northeast Aegean Islands have learned how to stay closely guarded. Though pirates and Ottomans no longer pose a threat, many of the islands continue to isolate themselves from an influx of tourism in hopes of preserving their traditional Greek atmosphere. Intricate, rocky coastlines enclose the thickly wooded mountains and bland port towns that give way to unspoiled villages and secluded beaches. Located only a few miles off the Turkish border, the islands have a sizable military presence; the large numbers of young soldiers may cause women traveling alone to feel uncomfortable. Less trafficked than any others in the archipelago, these islands remain both tranquil and resplendent. Travelers seeking undiluted Greek culture without the complicating intrusion of foreign influence may well find it here.

CHIOS ΧΙΟΣ

When the mythical hunter Orion drove all the wild beasts off Chios, grand pine, cypress, and mastic trees sprouted on the vast mountainsides. Since antiquity, Chios has cultivated and exported *masticha* (mastic; a bitter-sweet, gummy resin used in varnishes, cosmetic creams, chewing gum, floor waxes, and color television sets). Long both a military base and a center of Greek shipping, Chios has only recently been opened to the tourist industry, and the island remains pleasantly indifferent to the vagaries of foreigners. Chios' striking volcanic beaches and medieval villages are not easily accessible from the more popular Cyclades. While Northern Europeans do visit the island, most of the tourists it attracts are Greeks and Greek-Americans visiting with their Chiotian families.

Sakız Adası (Mastic Island), as Chios is known in Turkish, has endured invasions and catastrophes brought on by its prime location. The reputed birthplace of both Homer and Christopher Columbus, Chios has been successively under Venetian, Genoese, Turkish, and Greek rule since 1204. In 1822, a failed Greek rebellion against the Turks, who had ruled since 1566, led to the slaughter of more than 25,000 Greeks. The massacre drew European attention and sympathy to the Greek fight for independence, inspiring Lord Byron to join the struggle in which he eventually died. In 1881, a major earthquake brought more destruction to Chios. Foreign rule continued until Chios was reunited with Greece in 1912 after the Balkan Wars.

■ Chios Town

Chios Town is home to many sailors (identifiable by their red license plates) and several wealthy ship owners (identifiable by their fancy cars). Ravaged by German troops during WWII, the unadorned waterfront, with its modern Athenian-style skyline, turns an indifferent face to the newcomer. Though it is packed with numerous restaurants, clubs, and cafés, as well as the requisite ferry offices and businesses, the waterfront, like the rest of Chios Town, endures tumultuous automotive frenzy.

CHIOS

ORIENTATION AND PRACTICAL INFORMATION

Most services, buses, and taxis are around **Vounakio Square,** the social center of town, which is located two blocks inland from the right side of the waterfront (facing inland). Walking left from Vounakio takes you to the **market street,** pleasantly bustling and shaded in the morning. Most points of interest around the island are accessible only from Chios Town, the source from which all transit routes radiate. Every night the waterfront closes to traffic, cafés pack, and the Greek *volta* (promenade) begins, offering pleasant respite from the clamor that roars after the midday shutdown. Between 9pm and 1am, this is the place to be.

Tourist Office: 18 Kanari St. (tel. 44 389). Turn off the waterfront onto Kanari St., towards the square. The office is almost immediately to your left (look for the "i" sign). Provides lists of accommodations and **currency exchange.**

Tourist Agencies: Hatzelenis (tel. 26 743). Facing the water, turn left and walk down to the white building at the northern elbow of the harbor. Makes travel arrangements, including daily trips to Turkey. Open daily 7am-1pm and 6-9pm, and usually when boats arrive (often late at night).

Banks: Several in the vicinity of the OTE. The **Ionian Bank,** 16 Kanari, is across from the tourist office. Open Mon.-Thurs. 8am-2pm, Fri 8am-1:30pm, Sat. 9am-1pm. The **National, Commercial,** and **Ionian Banks** have **ATMs.**

OTE: (tel. 23 599), across from the tourist office. Open Mon.-Fri. 7am-2:30pm.

Flights: Olympic Airways (tel. 23 998), on waterfront near corner of Psychari St. Open Mon.-Fri. 8am-4pm. Flights to Athens (5 per day, 40min., 14,600dr), Lesvos (2 per week, 7100dr), and Thessaloniki (2 per week, 1hr., 21,100dr).

Ferries: Travel to Samos (3 per week, 4½hr., 2475dr); Patmos (2 per week, 9hr., 4850dr); Thessaloniki (1 per week, 18hr., 8100dr); and Kavala (1 per week, 16hr.). Ferries reach Ikaria via Samos and Limnos via Kavala. There are also excursions to Çeşme on the Turkish coast (1 per day, 45min., 8000dr, 4000dr port tax). Compare prices at different agencies for the lowest fares. The largest is the **generic office** (tel. 23 971) with the blackboard schedules inside.

Buses: (tel. 27 507) leave from both sides of Vounakio Sq., right off the public gardens. **Blue buses** (tel. 22 079), on the right side of the square on Dimokratias St., are for travel within the immediate vicinity of Chios Town (9km). Blue buses make 5-6 trips per day to Karfas, Vrondados, and Karies. Consult tourist agencies for schedules and information on buses which service the rest of the island.

Taxis: (tel. 41 111) cluster in the main square. Open 24hr.

Hospital: (tel. 44 306 or 44 301), 2km north of Chios; open 24hr.

Pharmacies: Chios Town has more than 20. Notices on pharmacy doors indicate which are open on weekends.

Port Police: (tel. 44 434), in the white building at the far corner of the northern side of the harbor. Open 24hr.

Post Office: (tel. 23 407), after the Olympic Airways waterfront office. Follow Omirou St. Open Mon.-Fri. 7:30am-2pm. **Postal Code:** 82100.

Telephone Code: 0271.

ACCOMMODATIONS

Most of Chios Town's accommodations are located in converted Neoclassical mansions with creaky wooden staircases and high ceilings. In high season, when rooms are scarce, it's better to let a tourist agency call around for you. Expect to pay 4000dr and up. Most cheap pensions cluster at the south end of the waterfront. Freelance camping is prevalent but illegal.

Chios Rooms, on the waterfront, past the turn-off to Pension Giannis. Ask at **Hatzelenis tourist office.** Singles 3500dr. Doubles 5000dr, with bath 6000dr.

Artemis Rooms, 3 N. Vamva St. (tel. 25 011), 2 blocks up from the waterfront and down the road from the cathedral, offers homey, clean rooms and kitchen facilities on a noisy, but convenient street. Doubles 4000dr.

TO
KAVALA

Limenas

Neos
Prinos
Theologos

Thassos

TO
ALEXANDROUPOLIS

Kamariotisa
Samothrace
Alonia
Therma

Samothrace

Gökçeada

Çanakkale

Dardanelles

TO
THESSALONIKI

Sardar
Plaka
Panagia

Bozcaada

Myrina
Thanos
Moudros

Limnos

TURKEY

Aegean Sea

TO
KIMI

Molyvos
Mandamados
Ayvalik

Eressos

Mesotopos

Lesvos

Agiassos

Plomari

Mitilini Channel

Mitilini

Psara

Andipsara

Marmara

Limnos

Chios

Mesta
Pirgi

Chios
Town

Emborios

Chios Strait

Cesme

G R E E C E

Samos
Kokari Town

Karlovassi

Pythagorion

Samos

TO
PIRAEUS

Evdilos

Armenistis

Agios
Kirikas

Ikaria

Fourni

Northeast
Aegean Islands

N

0   50 miles

0   50 kilometers

Chios Camping (tel. 74 111), on the beach at Agios Isidoros, 14km north of Chios Town. Has its own rocky beach. Open July-Sept. 1200dr per person. 800dr per child. 680dr per car. 800dr per tent.

FOOD AND ENTERTAINMENT

Myriad vendors hawk their milk, cheese, meat, bread, and produce around Vounakio Sq. Good deals are harder to find, but you can get a nice light lunch of stuffed (vegetarian) grape leaves for 750dr at the **Dolphin Taverna** (tel. 22 607), on the waterfront. For a tasty, fresh meal, try **To Meltemi** (tel. 21 624), sandwiched among the numerous waterfront cafés. Look for the "homemade spesialities" sign out front (1300dr for a spesial meal). If you don't mind a long stroll, the **Hotzas Taverna** (tel. 23 117), in a traditional house on 74 Stef. Tsouris St., serves inexpensive fresh food. Follow Vamva St. inland from the waterfront to the Bank of Crete, turn left, bear right at the first fork, and keep walking. For 250dr, you can lunch on the fresh *spanakopita* (spinach pie) available early in the day in the numerous **pastry shops** around Vounakio Sq. and along Rodokanaki St. **Café Everest,** on Rodokanaki St. close to the cathedral, offers a pleasant retreat from the late afternoon uproar.

A popular **bar** in town is **Remezzo,** on the waterfront, where the restaurants begin. They play a tasteful selection of American rock and alternative. Here, as elsewhere, beer costs 800dr and cocktails 1200dr. Farther down the waterfront, **Metropolis** is also popular, with a similarly young crowd and similar prices. An 1100dr taxi ride will take you to a cluster of bars outside of town, in **Karfos.** Of these, **Stasi** is the hottest, drawing people in with cheap beer (500dr).

SIGHTS

The town has several relics of its past, as well as an active shopping district centered on Vounakio Sq. The walls of the **Byzantine Kastro,** a castle reconstructed by the Genoese, enclose the narrow streets of the **Old Town.** A tiny **Byzantine Exhibition** (tel. 22 819) is inside the main gate off the square, across from the taxis (open Tues.-Sun. 9am-3pm; free). The **Turkish Mosque,** on Vournakio Sq., has metamorphosed into a museum that displays various finds from the archaeological site at Emborio (open Tues.-Sun. 8am-1:30pm; free). The **Folklore Museum,** on the first floor of the **Korais Library** (open Mon.-Thurs. 8am-2pm, Fri. 8am-2pm and 5-7:30pm, Sat. 8am-12:30pm), is adjacent to the **Mitropolis.** The popular sandy beach of **Karfas,** victim of Chios' latest burst of development, is only 6km south of Chios Town. The rocky beaches of **Vrondados** and **Daskalopetra,** 9km north of town, are also nearby. Blue buses from Vounakio Sq. travel to both.

The impressive **Nea Moni** (New Monastery), built in the 11th century, is cradled by the pine-covered mountains 16km west of Chios Town. Long ago, an icon of the Virgin Mary miraculously appeared to three hermits who promptly founded the monastery with the aid of an exiled emperor. Over the centuries, the monastery complex was rebuilt and enlarged. Although rather run-down, it remains one of the world's most important Byzantine monuments. Though an earthquake in 1881 destroyed much of the complex itself, most of it has been carefully restored, and the interior is pleasantly chaotic. The 11th-century mosaics in the inner narthex are worth a look. Even their state of partial decrepitude can't hide the original artistry (open daily dawn-1pm and 4-8pm; free). Several kilometers past Nea Moni on the paved road is the **Monastery Of Trion Pateron** (Three Fathers), which commemorates the three ascetic hermits who founded Nea Moni. Fifteen kilometers west of Nea Moni is **Anavatos,** staggeringly beautiful but with a tragic past. The women and children of the village's 400 families threw themselves off the precipitous cliffs of this "Greek Masada" after their failed attempt to withstand the Turkish invasion in 1822. Check with the bus station (Green bus) for excursion packages to both sites (1-2 per week, roundtrip 1500dr). If you miss the bus, you can take one of the more frequent buses to Karies (10 per day, 15min., 220dr) and walk the remaining 6km up the steep hillside to Nea Moni. Taxi drivers may agree to drive you to the site, wait 30 minutes, and bring you back. From Karies, a **taxi-tour** of Nea Moni and Ana-vatos costs 6000dr (decide on a fare before leaving for the monastery). The road is hilly but well paved until Nea Moni, where it deteriorates into an uneven, rocky path, passable by car and motorcycle, but murderous on mopeds.

■ Southern Chios

PIRGI

The villages in the southern half of the island, called *Mastichochoria,* are home to Chios's famous resin, produced by squat mastic or lentisk trees. The main "mastic village" is Pirgi, high in the hills 25km from Chios. This unique town is a maze of alleys lined by traditional homes. Bear right at the fork in the road and walk into town past the first seven or eight houses. You'll see the English-speaking Chios headquarters of the **Women's Agricultural Tourist Collective** (tel. 72 496), which arranges rooms in private farmhouses in Armolia, Pirgi, Olymbi, and Mesta. The female farmers, symbolized by the *melissa* (bee), will show you around their farms, but it's best to make reservations a few weeks in advance or to call before arriving in Pirgi, especially in July and August. (Office open Mon.-Sat. 8am-2:30pm. Doubles 6500dr, some with bath. Triples 6000dr. Breakfast 1000dr. Afternoon meals 2000dr.) You can also make your own arrangements for "Rooms to Let" with village proprietors; look for "rooms-to-let" signs scattered about town. **Rent Rooms Nikos** (tel. 72 425) is through Platia Georgiou M. Theotoka, right past the police (100m down). Nikos has immaculate rooms, some with private baths, that include shared kitchen facilities. (Doubles 6000dr and up.) A mobile **National Bank** comes to Pirgi (Mon. and Thurs. noon-1:30pm), followed closely by the **Commercial Bank** (Wed. and Fri. 10-11am.) The **post office** is in the main square, Despoti Germ. Theotoka (open Mon.-Fri. 9am-12:30pm). Taking a left from this square onto Mich. Kolika St., you'll find the one room **OTE** (open daily 9:30am-1pm and 4-10pm). The **pharmacy** (tel. 72 444) is in Georgiou M. Theotoka Sq. (open Mon.-Fri. 9am-2pm and 5-8pm; call during off hours in an emergency). The **police** (tel. 72 222) are nearby (open 24hr.). **Marianne Rent Motor** (tel. 72 488) rents **mopeds** (2700dr), and runs a shop where you can snack, **change money,** and learn about the village (located just up the road from the bus stop; open daily 8am-9pm).

Just northeast of the square is the 14th-century **Agioi Apostoloi** church, a replica of the Nea Moni. Almost every inch is covered with 16th-century frescoes and paint-ings created by a Cretan iconography school. The caretaker must unlock the front gate for you; ask for Michalis Vassilis at 27 Mix. Kolika St., directly across from the OTE (open Mon.-Fri. 9am-3:30pm; 100dr donation is expected).

One km back along the road to Chios and 5km south is the beach of **Emborio**. Its light brown volcanic cliffs contrast strikingly with the black stones and deep blue water below. The bus from Chios Town or Pirgi drops passengers off at the harbor.

Craftsmen with a Fork and a Dream

Pirgi's charm is for romantics who would prefer goat-tending in a traditional vil-lage to life in the big city, but at the same time it blinds visitors with a dazzling spectacle. Although it is built in the twisting alleyways of a medieval castle, Pirgi is more recognizable for its *ksista,* the unique geometric patterns that coat walls of every house in the village. Instead of whitewashing homes as is common in the Cyclades, Pirgian craftsmen first coat each house with a paint made from the gray stone beach at Emborio. The houses are then whitewashed and, while the paint is still wet, the craftsmen form geometric patterns with a fork, creating the village's trademark design. After both coats of color have dried, artists paint col-orful designs on some parts of the wall, adding splendid color to the black-and-white geometric designs.

Up the only road to the right (facing the water), and up and down the hill you'll find the first beach. There's a smaller, less crowded shore up the stairs to your right. Good shoes will save you from cuts and bruises on the nasty sharp stones.

■ Northern Chios

The poorer (and less visited) region, the north half of Chios is the silent partner of the *Mastichochoria*. **Voriochora** (North Town) was left even more destitute by a 1981 fire, but its beaches and quaint villages remain tranquil and inviting. Since few foreigners visit, it may be difficult to find a place to stay. Roughly 5km outside Chios Town, just past Vrondados, the beach of **Daskalopetra** (Teaching Rock), is where Homer held class. After Daskalopetra, the main roads wind northwest along the coast past Marmaron to **Nagos** (30km away), which features a gray stone beach (a popular spot to cut Homer's classes). **Volissos** (40km west), Homer's legendary birthplace, is crowned by a Byzantine fort and girdled by stone houses. On July 22, the island gathers in Volissos for a festival honoring **St. Marcela** and **St. Isidore,** protectors of the island and the mastic trees, who proclaimed that the trees would only grow on Chios. St. Marcela was killed by her Turkish father, but when flowers sprouted from her grave she was recognized as a saint. Some say that during the festival the sea turns boiling red and miracles occur.

LESVOS (LESBOS) ΛΕΣΒΟΣ

It seems odd that Lesvos's seemingly barren, volcanic landscape has nurtured one of the richer cultural legacies in the Aegean. After all, Lesvos does not strike visitors as an island that was once home to the musician Terpander, the poet Arion, the writer Aesop, and most notably the 7th-century BCE poet Sappho. The main tourist haunts in particular seem to indicate that Lesvos' greatness remains firmly in its fabled past. Yet even in this century, Lesvos has given rise to the Nobel Prize winning poet Odysseus Elytis, the Neoprimitive artist Theophilos, art publisher Tériade, and the family of 1988 U.S. Presidential candidate Michael Dukakis.

Legend has it that the population of Lesvos, Greece's third largest island, was once entirely female. This notion may owe its origin to the Athenian assembly's 428 BCE decision to punish the recalcitrant residents of Mitilini by executing all adult males on the island. After some debate, however, the decision was repealed. For hundreds of years, Mitilini flourished as a cultural center. Its inhabitants would have been astonished to know that later generations would consider 5th-century Athens, not Mitilini, to be the zenith of Greek civilization. The Philosophical Academy, where Epicurus and Aristotle taught, brought the island well deserved fame.

Until recently, the island (often called Mitilini after its principal city) was relatively remote, cultivating its offbeat character (a blend of horse breeding, serious *ouzo* drinking, and leftist politics). Although Lesvos' major towns now host a growing number of foreign visitors, tourism has not reached Cycladean proportions. Most travelers to the sparsely populated island stay for months at a time, exploring the many historical sites and uncovering the island's truly variegated landscape—tall pines, cornfields, and taffy-trunked olive trees that rise from the scruffy hillsides.

■ Mitilini

Mitilini, the central port city and capital of Lesvos, can be picturesque from a distance. It is a yawning harbor adorned with yachts, colorful fishing boats, and an encircling weave of modern highrises and Neoclassical mansions standing in shoulder to shoulder ascent up the Amali mountains. The city sits under the shadow of the decaying Gattelusi castle, and is accented by the prominent dome of Agios Therapon, the city's hallmark. Yet a closer look proves Mitilini crowded and crumbling—her once grand mansions too expensive to restore, illegal to tear down, and in a regrettable state of decay.

ORIENTATION AND PRACTICAL INFORMATION

The city spreads chaotically along the waterfront; **Pavlou Koudoutrioti** and **Ermou Street** run parallel one block inland. The most interesting quadrant of town is the **old market,** which advances inland from the waterfront, below the castle and to the right of the church. It's easy to get lost among the market's knotted streets and cobbled ways. For those tired of pristine shops, the assortment of flea markets, produce stands, and neighborhood stores is a welcome change. Here you can shop free of tacky key chain peddlers and enjoy the aroma of the nearby fish market.

Tourist Police: (tel. 22 776). From the ferry, head left towards the interior harbor and main waterfront road. The official passport control building, at the corner of the pier, houses the tourist police. Enter by the back side, which doubles as a **tourist office.** They speak English, help find rooms, offer free brochures, and provide maps. Open in summer daily 8am-9pm; in winter 8am-2pm.

Banks: The **National Bank** (tel. 20 340), on the right side of the waterfront, facing inland. The **Commercial Bank,** near the center of the waterfront, has an inconspicuous **ATM.** Both open Mon.-Thurs. 8am-2pm, Fri. 8am-1:30pm.

OTE: (tel. 28 299), 2 doors up from the post office. Open daily 7am-10pm.

Flights: Olympic Airways main office, 44 Kavetsou Ave., or any ticket agent will have times and locations of flights. Book flights roughly a week in advance.

Buses: Green buses leave from the intercity bus station (tel. 28 873) and service destinations on the island. The **station** is behind Ag. Irinis park, diagonally 1½ blocks from the south edge of the harbor. In summer, buses from Mitilini go to Molyvos (4 per day, 1½hr., 1150dr); Sigri (2 per week, 2½hr., 1750dr); Vatera (2 per day, 1½hr., 1050dr); Agiassos (4 per day, 50min., 480dr); Skala Eressos (1 per day, 2½hr., 1750dr); and Plomari (3 per day, 1¼hr., 800dr). Fewer buses chug along on weekends. **City (Blue) buses** (tel. 28 725), based on the waterfront, service local routes around Mitilini.

Ferries: Connect Lesvos to the Northeast Aegean and beyond. **NEL Lines,** 47 Pavlou Koudoutrioti St. (tel. 22 220), along the waterfront 3 blocks from the pier, is the only place to buy tickets. Office open Mon.-Fri. 7am-9pm, Sat.-Sun. 7am-2pm. In summer, ferries travel to Peiraias (1 per day, 12hr., 5830dr); Limnos (4 per week, 5hr., 3450dr); Samos (3 per week, 4½hr., 2475dr); Patmos (2 per week, 9hr., 4850dr); Thessaloniki (2 per week, 12hr., 7100dr); Kavala (2 per week, 12hr., 5430dr); and Çeşme, Turkey (daily, 45min., 8000dr, 4000 port tax).

Moped/Car Rental: In general, **mopeds** run about 4000dr per day; **cars** 8500dr. Try **Just Rent a Car** (tel. 43 080), on the waterfront.

Hospital: (tel. 43 777), southwest of the city on E. Vostani. Open 24hr.

Emergency: Dial 166.

Port Police: 27 Votsani St. (tel. 28 888, -27). In the same building with the **police,** a few blocks south of the port on the waterfront.

Post Office: (tel. 28 836), on Vourhazon St. near the intercity bus station. Signs pointing the way to the post office are behind the park (which has free **public toilets**), near the taxi stand. Open Mon.-Sat. 7:30am-2pm. **Postal code:** 81100.

Telephone code: 0251.

ACCOMMODATIONS AND FOOD

Dhomatia IREN, 41 Komminaki St., (tel. 22 787), 1 block inland, on the left-hand corner of Imvrou and Komninaki St. From the ferry landing, walk along the first stretch of waterfront, past the Superfast Ferry offices, and down Imvrou. IREN, on a quiet street, has cool, commodious rooms. 24-hr. hot water. Doubles 8000dr.

Hotel Anna-Lena (tel. 21 494), along the tourist café-laden avenue on the south waterfront. Offers clean, simple rooms with baths. Inquire at their waterfront *taverna,* Fanari, prominently signposted near the corner of Pavlou Koudoutrioti and the string of waterfront cafés. Doubles 6000dr.

Cafés and *tavernas* abound along the waterfront. Locals tend to dine to the north, tourists usually congregate to the south. For a full-fledged fresh fried fish feast, you might consider the more touristed *tavernas* on the southern waterfront, if for no other reason than to enjoy your meal in a traffic- and congestion-free environment. Elsewhere, cheese pies, charmless croissants, and *gyro* abound. The **Averof,** in the center of the waterfront, has traditional food at a decent deal (Greek salad 800dr). For breakfast with the locals, saunter behind the local bus station onto Limnou St. and take the first right onto Thasou St. You'll see them, they'll see you—expect a few stares, and real Greek coffee.

SIGHTS

The ubiquitous signs in Mitilini helpfully egg on tourists to the various sights. The **Archaeological Museum,** 7 Argiri Eftalioti St. (tel. 28 032), has an impressive collection of the island's historical finds. All pieces are labeled and accompanied by thorough descriptions of the archaeological sites's roles in Lesvian history. The artifacts include Mycenaean, Protogeometric, and Archaic pottery; Classical and Hellenistic vases and sculpture; and remnants from the Temple at Fressos. Make sure to visit the second, smaller building hiding behind the main museum quarters—it contains ancient tablets of rare Aeolian type (open Tues.-Sun. 8:30am-3pm; admission 500dr, EU students free). If you have a spare hour in Mitilini, visit the enormous, late 19th-century **Church of St. Therapon,** on Ermou St., whose dome seems to betray Western influence. The church towers over the fish market's daily catch—sardines, octopi, and occasionally small sharks (open daily 9am-7pm; free). By the tall clock tower at the south end of the harbor is the impressive **Church of Ag. Theodoros.** The church contains the bones and skull of its patron saint. From the ferry dock, all roads leading uphill will take you to the **Gattelusi Castle** (tel. 27 970). Surrounded by redolent pines above the town, the *kastro* protects its panoramic view over Mitilini and across to Turkey. It was originally constructed by Emperor Justinian on the site of a Byzantine castle, but has since been repaired by the Genoese, the Turks, and the Greeks. The walls contain leftovers from each epoch, and are capped by a telephone cable, the 20th century's contribution. The castle is named for Francesco Gattelusi, who received Lesvos as dowry in 1355 after he married the daughter of the Byzantine Emperor. Subsequently, the castle was overrun by Turks and Greeks (open Tues.-Sun. 8:30am-3pm; admission 500dr, students 300dr). The highest point on the north side of Mitilini town is the 3rd-century BCE **ancient theater,** built during Hellenistic times. Here 15,000 spectators attended performances with acoustics as perfect as Epidavros's. In fact, the theater was so impressive that it inspired Pompey to build Rome's first stone theater (open Tues.-Sun. 8:30am-3pm; free).

■ Near Mitilini

The pleasant and pebbly GNTO **beach,** north of the main pier beneath the castle attracts hordes in summer (open daily 8am-8pm; admission 150dr). **Neapolis Beach,** a 5km bus ride south, is also jammed. For a peaceful, deserted stretch of sand, loners persevere and head 13km south of Mitilini to the beach at **Agios Ermogenis.** It's slightly more touristy, but there are also fewer people. A taxi costs 3000-4000dr if the driver agrees to go; most don't like to because the dirt road ruins their cars.

Only 4km south of Mitilini along the same route (El. Venizelou), the tiny, unassuming village of **Varia** surprises wayfarers with the **Theophilos Museum** (tel. 41 644), which features the work of the famous neoprimitivist Greek painter Theophilos Hadzimichali (open Tues.-Sun. 9am-1pm and 6:30-8pm; admission 500dr). Next door is the **Musée Tériade.** Tériade, a native of Lesvos whose real name is Stratis Eleftheriadis, rose to fame as the foremost publisher of graphic art in Paris during much of the 20th century. The museum displays an excellent collection of Picasso, Miró, Leger, Chagall, and Matisse lithographs (open Tues.-Sun. 9am-2pm and 5-8pm; admission 350dr). **Buses** to Varia depart from the waterfront depot (tel. 28 725; every 30min., 15min., 140dr). Follow **Naumahias Elis** (running along Mitilini's north port) 4km north, then head 2km west to a well preserved Roman aqueduct at **Moria. Buses** to Moria run every 30 minutes from the waterfront (230dr).

▓ Northern Lesvos

MOLYVOS (MITHIMNA)

On the island's northern tip, Molyvos is Lesvos's most visited spot after Mitilini. Also an artist colony, the town conveys an almost picture-perfect charm—stone houses, topped with red tiles and neatly cornered with multi-colored shutters, intricately stack up into a castle-peaked hill. Exploring the cobbled weave of alleys is a fine afternoon adventure, likely to reward with magnificent terraced vistas of the Aegean and Turkey. The **Genoese fortress** is striking in the evening light; walk up during the day for a view of the coastline and a closer look at the wildflowers growing in the ruins. Upon your descent, take your first left to enter the small **church.** The soul-penetrating eye above the altar doesn't wink. If the town beach is crowded, try the pebble beach of **Eftalou,** 5km north of Molyvos (bus 200dr).

Orientation and Practical Information   Just up from the bus stop (bear left at the fork) on Poseidonos St. is the municipal **tourist office** (tel. 71 347), which keeps sporadic hours but is usually open when buses arrive. They have free brochures and help find rooms. Next door is a **National Bank** (open Mon.-Thurs. 8am-2pm, Fri. 8am-1:30pm). At the top of the hill, the road forks; bear right and you will come to the **main post office** (tel. 71 246), which also **exchanges currency** (open Mon.-Fri. 7:30am-2pm). There is a **mobile post office** on the main traffic highway (open in summer Mon.-Fri. 8am-2pm). The steeply ascending cobbled road to the right of the tourist office is the town's main market thoroughfare. Nearby is **Akti Rentals** (tel. 71 997), which rents **motorbikes** (3000dr), **cars** (8500dr), and **jeeps** (14,000dr; open daily 9am-1:30pm and 5:30-9:30pm). Bear left from the fork to reach the local **laundry** (wash 1100dr, dry 600dr; open daily 9am-3pm and 5-10pm). On the first uphill stretch is a **pharmacy** (tel. 71 903) and an official **medical office** (tel. 71 903). Across from the main post office is a thickly shaded, cave-like café, the local haunt for morning coffee. At the corner, you'll find signs with arrows to the town hall and the public library. The signs will also direct you to the **archaeological museum** (tel. 71 059), which is not too far away (open Tues.-Sun. 8:30am-3pm), and the **police station** (tel. 71 222). Special **taxi phones** (pick one up and dial the number posted) are just about everywhere, especially along the "traffic route," as are regular **phone booths. Postal Code:** 81108. **Telephone Code:** 0253.

Accommodations and Food   Your stay will be much easier if you let the tourist office call around for you, or even help you sort through the offers made by locals greeting you at the bus stop. If the tourist office is closed, take heart—on nearly every turn in Molyvos' cobbled intricacy are "Rooms to Let" signs in traditional homes, at whatever altitude you decide to perch. During peak season, rooms tend to get expensive. **Eleni Vourgoutsi** (tel. 71 065) lets cool, high-ceilinged rooms. (Doubles with bath 5000dr.) Up the cobbled market street just past the tourist office, visible off a side street to the right, is **Nassos Guest House** (tel. 71 022), which offers eight rooms, some with bath. (Doubles from 5000dr.) Inquire at Nassos Restaurant. **Camping Mithyma** (tel. 71 169, -079) is 1km east of town; follow the road to the right of the bus station. The site is comfortable, with hot water and a refrigerator, but quite a hike from town. (800dr per person. 550dr per tent. 500dr per car. Electricity free.)

Numerous **beachfront cafés** exist, but the *tavernas* with decks cantilevered out above the main road are particularly inviting. **Taverna Sansibaba,** near the OTE, offers live Greek music Tuesday and Thursday nights, and has a pleasant terrace shaded by large plane trees, overlooking the Aegean. **Gato's** (tel. 71 661), farther up, also makes the farthest reach out from the cliffside, offering unparalleled views and fashionable fare (stuffed eggplant 800dr, Greek salad 600dr).

Sights   The rugged road north out of Molyvos heads to **Eftalou** (5km northeast), home to a long stretch of secluded **beaches,** many lying beneath towering rocky cliffs. To reach these beaches, walk through a small white building containing a thermal bath not much bigger than a jacuzzi (free). Walk 15 minutes to the south of Molyvos along the coastal road for tiny but breathtakingly beautiful Psalaria Beach, nestled in a secluded cove. Molyvos also has an **archaeological museum** and regular **exhibitions by local artists** in its town hall.

■ Southern Lesvos

PLOMARI

After arson demolished the village of Megalochori in 1841, people resettled in the Turkish-inhabited region 12km south, now modern **Plomari.** From its earliest days, this southern coastal town has manifested a split personality—it is at once a no-holds-barred resort town (with discoes, cheery *tavernas,* and all the other accoutrements for package tour groups) as well as a fishing village, full of fishermen nailing octopi to telephone poles to dry in the sun. The overall effect, aided and abetted by Plomari's large *ouzo* industry, is cheerful and relaxing. The local product is far better than the bottled industrial variety. Try a sample at the **Barbayanni Ouzo Factory** (tel. 32 741), roughly 2km east towards Ag. Isodoros on the way to Plomari (open Mon.-Fri. 8am-10pm, Sat. 8am-3pm). An annual week-long **Ouzo Festival** is held in late August and features song, dance, drunken tourists, and, of course, free *ouzo.* Large groups may receive a free tour. Throughout the summer, Plomari hosts several religious celebrations and cultural events. The **Festival of Benjamin** commemorates the revolutionary leader of the 1821 war against the Turks with dancing and theatrical presentations in Greek (1 week in late June).

Orientation and Practical Information   Manolis Stefanis at **Plomari Travel** (tel. 32 946) on Lesviou St. has information about everything from accommodations to excursions. To get to Plomari Travel from the **Commercial Bank** at the end of the square, turn right into **B. Lesviou Square,** and then take your first right up Lesviou St. The **bank** is also in the square (open Mon.-Thurs. 8am-2pm, Fri. 8am-1:30pm). The **OTE** (tel. 32 399) resides in the main square (open Mon.-Fri. 7:30am-10pm) and the **post office** (tel. 32 241) is nearby (open Mon.-Fri. 8am-2pm). **Buses** go to Plomari (3-5 per day, 750dr) and Agiassos (5 per day, 460dr). The road hugs the **Bay of Geras,** and passes through the charming villages of **Paleokipos** and **Pappados. Postal Code:** 81200. **Telephone Code:** 0252.

Sights   Beaches appear intermittently around Plomari. To reach rocky **Arnovdeli Beach,** turn onto Ag. Nikolaou Rd. and follow the signs; it's roughly a 15-minute walk south of town. If you continue straight on Ag. Nikolaou, you'll come to **Agios Nikolaos,** a church sparkling with icons spanning 400 years. If you aren't into stone-infested coasts, the best beaches for you (and loads of other people) are at **Agios Isodoros,** 3km east of town along the main road.

Fifteen kilometers north of Plomari, the village of **Agiassos,** on the slopes of Lesvos's Mt. Olympus, remains an active center for ceramic crafts. An **Orthodox church** here contains an icon of the Virgin Mary made by St. Lucas, originally destined for Constantinople in 330 CE. When the priest transporting it whispers of war, he feared for the icon's safety and deposited it in the church. Every year on August 15, Agiassos hosts *Panagia,* a grand celebration in honor of the Virgin Mary. The village also boasts an **Ecclesiastical Museum,** with Byzantine religious works (ask church officials and priests in town), a **Folk Museum** featuring traditional costumes, and a **library** with some English books.

■ Western Lesvos

SKALA ERESSOS

Determined sunbathers congregate at **Skala Eressos** (known as "Skala"), located at the opposite end of Lesvos from Mitilini. Skala's 1500m **beach** has won the EU's "Blue Banner" award for cleanliness. Its western half is one of the few legal **nude beaches** on the island. Skala's companion village of **Eressos**, 3½km inland, the poet **Sappho's birthplace,** is a gathering place for Lesvians and lesbians alike in summer.

Orientation and Practical Information   Eressos Travel (tel. 53 076, -7; fax 53 576), one block northwest of the main square, provides **currency exchange,** a kiosk for calls, excursion and accommodation information, and car and motorbike rentals (open daily 8:30am-1:30pm and 5:30-10pm; reduced hours in off season). **Post offices** post in Skala Eressos (off the main square; open daily 7:30am-2pm) and Eressos (tel. 53 227). The **OTE** (tel. 53 399) is in Eressos (open Mon.-Fri. 7:30am-2:30pm), along with the **police station** (tel. 53 222). **Snapi Travel** has information on rooms, car and moped rentals, and excursions (open Sat.-Thurs. 10am-noon and 6-10pm, Fri. 10am-noon). **Postal Code:** 81105. **Telephone Code:** 0253.

Accommodations   Ask at **Eressos Travel** about the **Eressos House,** which has sparkling double rooms with private bathrooms and shared refrigerators. (6000dr per person.) **Rooms to Let Maritsa Padermou** (tel. 53 267) has spotless, breezy doubles (5700dr) and triples (7000dr), all with private baths and shared refrigerators. **Pension Krinelos** (tel. 53 246) has new, beautifully furnished rooms with private baths and an airy terrace. (Singles 4000dr. Doubles 6000dr. Triples 7200dr.) Both Padermou and Krinelos are located in a quiet field 100m from the sea; facing the water, they are to the right and back of the beach parking lot. **Camping** is possible on the beach six blocks west of the town's center. Tassos Kokkas at **Exersis Travel** (tel. 53 044) provides help in finding rooms.

Food   Surrounded by new-fangled outdoor cafés and a serene view of the Aegean Sea, the stone-layered square of **Anthis and Evristhenous** is a hot spot for Skala's young international visitors. Restaurants with bamboo-covered wooden piers sit right at the beach and serve up elegant sunset views of **Sappho's Profile** along the western mountains. At the end of the walkway is the **Bennetts' International and Vegetarian Restaurant** (tel 53 624; open mid-April to mid-Oct. daily 9:30am-3pm and 6:30-11pm). Run by Max and Jackie Bennett, a British couple, the restaurant has lots of meatless options. Prices are reasonable, and you'll lick the platter clean.

Sights   The early Christian basilica of **Agios Andreas,** three blocks north of the beach, once housed 5th-century mosaics, which can now be found in Mitilini's Archaeological Museum. Greek Orthodox services are held here on Sundays (7-10am). Behind the church is the **Skala Museum,** with displays of 5th- and 6th-century vases, sculptured tombstones, inscriptions in the Aeolian dialect, and an anchor of a Turkish frigate from the Greek War of Independence in 1821. In the museum yard is the tomb of St. Andrew. The uphill road leading east is the pilgrimage route for travelers going to the remains of **Sappho's Home** in Eressos. At dusk, the view from the hill is transcendent. The river, just west of Skala's center, serves as a habitat for many rare and exotic birds. (Peak **birdwatching** season here is early April to mid-June.) Farther inland, at **Antissa,** are the **petrified trees** of Lesvos, preserved by volcanic activity at least 700,000 years ago in one of only two such forests in the world (the other is on the Arizona-New Mexico border in the U.S.). Roughly 200 plant and animal fossils make up the "forest" which requires a one and a half-hour walk. From Mitilini town, take the bus to Sigri and walk or ride the 8km to the forest. From Skala, rent a moped or car, or check at Eressos Travel about tours.

SAMOS ΣΑΜΟΣ

With its sultry landscape and engrossing architectural remains, Samos is perhaps the most beautiful and certainly the most touristed island in the Northeast Aegean. The island draws an older, more sedate crowd, and is quieter than the more popular spots in the Cyclades and the Dodecanese. The wealthiest of the Aegean islands, Samos was home to many notable Greek architects, sculptors, poets, philosophers, and scientists. Samos' illustrious citizenry has included Epicurus, the moral philosopher; Aesop, the author of fables; and Aristarchus, the astronomer who argued that the sun was the center of the universe nearly 1800 years before Copernicus. The island's most beloved native son, however, is the ancient philosopher Pythagoras, whose visage has been adopted as the symbol of Samos.

Present-day Samos enjoys a level of tourism in between its less-frequented northern neighbors and the roaring popularity of the Cyclades to the west. Many people come to Samos simply to make the short hop to **Kuşadası** for the ruins of **Ephesus** on the Turkish coast. The archaeological site is the most extensive and possibly the most evocative remnant of ancient Hellenic civilization. Founded around 1100 BCE, Ephesus rapidly bloomed into the largest metropolis in Asia Minor (see Ephesus, p. 492). Alternately, those who are archaeologically impaired teeter to Samos to unearth the sumptuous local **kokkino krasi** (red wine), which oozes from village-made barrels and gives the island its fifteen minutes of lush-ous fame.

■ Samos Town

With its wide white sidewalks, colorful fishing boats, and picturesque red-roofed houses nestled in the mountainside, Samos Town is among the Northeast Aegean's more attractive ports. While the waterfront is a snarl of tourist shops and cafés, the residential lanes farther inland offer a table of local lifestyles.

ORIENTATION AND PRACTICAL INFORMATION

Samos Town unfurls around a crescent-shaped waterfront. **Pythagoras Square,** easily identifiable by its four large palm trees, hosts banks, cafés, and taxis.

Tourist Office: (tel. 28 530, -82). Follow signs from the waterfront, on a side street 1 block before Pythagoras Sq. Open July-Aug. Mon.-Sat. 8:30am-2pm.

Tourist Agencies: Samos Tours (tel. 27 715), at the end of the ferry dock, provides information on everything from museum hours to accommodations. Free luggage storage. Open daily 6am-midnight and usually when boats arrive. **ITSA Travel** (tel. 23 605; fax 27 955), right next door, offers similar services and free luggage storage. Open daily 6am-2:30pm and 5pm-midnight.

OTE: Next to the post office. Open daily 7am-10pm.

Flights: Olympic Airways (tel. 27 237). Daily flights to Athens (4 per day, 50min., 16,100dr) and bi-weekly flights to Chios, Lesvos, Mykonos, and Kos. Open Mon.-Fri. 8am-4pm. Samos' airport (tel. 61 219) is 4km out of Pythagorion and can be reached only by taxi from Samos Town (4000dr).

Ferries: Run regularly between Samos Town and Peiraias in summer (daily, 12hr., 4824dr), stopping at Ikaria (2-3hr.). To Naxos and Paros (5 per week, 6hr., 3670dr); Chios (4 per week, 4½hr., 2475dr); Ikaria (4 per week, 3hr., 1800dr); Fourni (4 per week, 2hr., 1554dr); Lesvos (1 per week, 7hr., 3465dr); Kavala (1 per week, 12hr., 7295); and Patmos (2 per week, 2½hr., 2500dr). In summer, ferries also travel to the Cyclades, Syros, and Mykonos (1 per week, 3300dr). Ferries to Kuşadası, Turkey, leave from Samos Town (daily at 8am and 5pm) and Pythagorion (in high season 3 per week; in off season 1-2 per week). Boats to Kuşadası cost about 7000dr (with slight discount for a roundtrip ticket). You'll be charged a Turkish port tax of 3000dr (US$10) and a 4000dr Greek port tax upon return. If you are American or British, you'll also be charged a $20 fee for your entrance visa. It is preferable to pay the Turkish tax in dollars. If you stay overnight in Turkey and leave from Kuşadası, you'll have to pay the tax again.

Flying Dolphins: Zip from Samos Town to Patmos (daily, 4616dr), taking half as long (and twice the drachmae) as the ferries. Consult the waterfront agencies to learn about the most recent schedule—including lines added in high season.

Police: (tel. 27 980), on the far right of the waterfront (facing inland), also doubles as the **tourist police.** Some English spoken.

Taxi Stand: (tel. 28 404), in Pythagoras Sq.

Motorbike Rental: The only way to get around the more mountainous and remote western end. **Rent A Motor Bike Bicycle** (tel. 23 756) is on the left side of the waterfront. Mopeds 2500dr. Bikes 1000dr. 10% off for 3-4 days; 20% off for a week. Open daily 8am-9pm.

Laundromat: (tel. 28 833), near Georgiou's *Taverna*, 1 block to the left side of the waterfront. Wash 900dr. Dry 700dr. Soap 150dr. Open daily 8am-11pm.

Public Toilets: Lurk to the left of the entrance to the municipal gardens.

Buses: To get to the **station,** follow the waterfront past Pythagoras Sq., turn left at Europe Rent A Car onto Lekati St., and walk 1 block. The bus schedule is posted here, but you can also pick up a copy at most tour offices.

Hospital: (tel. 27 407 or 27 426), to the left of the ferry dock (facing inland).

Port Police: (tel. 27 318), at the end of the ferry dock. Open 24hr.

Post Office: (tel. 27 304), 1 block up from the waterfront behind the Hotel Xenia; turn at the immense palm tree and walk through the municipal gardens. Open Mon.-Fri. 7:30am-2pm. **Postal Code:** 83100.

Telephone Code: 0273.

ACCOMMODATIONS

There aren't nearly enough rooms to go around on Samos—finding one can be a chore. If the following are full, try the pensions around the Ionia.

Pension Ionia, 5 Manoli Kalomiri St. (tel. 28 782). Be skeptical of port-side room-hawkers who tell you it is full—they may be lying. To get there, turn right at the end of the ferry dock, left onto E. Stamatiadou St. before the Hotel Aiolis on the waterfront, and then take the second left onto Manoli Kalomiri St. 3 buildings of inexpensive, attractive rooms. Friendly Mr. Zavitsanou will give you a cot in the garden if his rooms are full. 24-hr. hot showers. Singles 2500dr. Doubles 3000dr.

Hotel Artemis (tel. 27 792), in Pythagoras Sq. Offers clean rooms and suggests restaurants. Doubles 4000dr, with bath 5000dr.

Pension Trova, 26 Kalomiris St. (tel. 27 759), up the road just to the left of Pension Ionia. Singles 2000dr. Doubles with bath 4000dr.

Pythagoras Hotel (tel. 28 601; fax 28 893), a 10-min. walk along the waterfront away from the town. Clean, well maintained rooms and a restaurant downstairs. 24-hr. hot water. Singles 3000dr. Doubles with bath 4000dr.

FOOD, ENTERTAINMENT, AND SIGHTS

Christos (tel. 24 792), two blocks inland from the library, offers tasty Greek cuisine (each dish 1000dr or less). A worthy local favorite is **Gregory's** (tel. 22 718), near the bus station at the right of the waterfront (fried squid 900dr). The **Chicken** (tel. 28 415) serves its namesake at 900dr a plate. Sweet, strong, and full of spirit, their local wine is everything it should be. **Sweet shops** abound in Samos, along the pedestrian road parallel to the waterfront, one block in. **Mascot** is an especially good choice, with outdoor seating along a cobbled walk. The **Golden Dragon,** on the way to Hotel Pythagoras, offers an all-you-can-eat buffet (Tues.-Wed. 3000dr).

On the waterfront in the afternoon, the café/bar **Traffic** is popular with locals and plays recent American hits. The most popular bar at night is **Escape,** a five-minute walk on the way to the Pythagoras Hotel. A patio stretches out over the bay below, a large screen displays a random mixture of sports and political clips, and the bar inside fills up as the drinks go down. By 3am, the party is underway at the discotheque **Totem,** a 100dr taxi ride from town.

SAMOS

Finds from local digs, including an impressive 5m tall Kouros from 575 BCE, have made their way to the **archaeological museum** (tel. 27 469), next to the post office. Half of the museum is now closed due to construction, but the entrance fee is fully functioning. At present, the only views are of pre-Classical torsos (open Tues.-Sun. 8:30am-3pm; admission 800dr, students 400dr); postmodern torsos are on display at the local beaches. Nearby, the lilliputian but lovely **municipal gardens** contain caged monkeys and birds, 200 varieties of flowers, and a little café (gardens free).

■ Pythagorion

Boats from Patmos and points south arrive in Pythagorion, the former capital of Samos. The town features numerous archaeological sites, quaint side streets, and proximity to some of the island's nicer beaches.

Fourteen kilometers south of Samos Town, Pythagorion is served by convenient, hourly buses (240dr, only 5 per day in off season). The **bus stop** is on the main street, which runs perpendicular to the waterfront. The **tourist office** (tel. 61 389) is in a pink building, halfway between the bus stop and the water (open April-Oct. Mon.-Fri. 8am-10pm, Sat.-Sun. 10am-2pm). On the same street is a **National bank** (open Mon.-Fri. 8:30am-2pm) and a **post office** (open Mon.-Fri. 7:30am-1:30pm). The **tourist police** (tel. 61 100) are nearby and the **OTE** is on the waterfront to the left of the intersection with the main street (open Mon.-Fri. 8am-1pm and 5-9pm). The **port police** (tel. 61 225) are at the other end of the waterfront. **Taxis** can be called at 61 450. Most **pensions** are on the main street and are packed and pricey in summer (doubles 5000-7000dr). **Hotels** line the waterfront and the main street.

The ancient city of Pythagorion, once the island's capital, thrived during the second half of the 6th century BCE under the reign of **Polykrates the Tyrant.** According to Herodotus, Polykrates undertook the three most daring engineering projects in the Hellenic world, all of them in and around Pythagorion. One of the more impressive is the **Tunnel of Eupalinos** (tel. 61 400), 1500m up the hill to the north of town, which diverted water from a natural spring to the city below. About 1.3km long, it is in remarkably good condition, though only about 200m are open to visitors (open Tues.-Sun. 9am-2pm; admission 500dr, students 300dr, seniors 400dr). Polykrates's second feat was the 40m deep **harbor mole** (rock pier), on which the modern pier now rests.

Polykrates's *magnum opus* stood 5km west of Pythagorion, toward Ireon. The goddess Hera had been worshipped on Samos for seven centuries when Polykrates decided to enlarge her temple. Supported by 134 columns, the **Temple of Hera** (tel. 95 277), erected in 530 BCE, was 118m long and 58m wide, and one of the **seven wonders of the ancient world.** Damaged by fire in 525 BCE, it was never completely reconstructed, perhaps because in 522 BCE Polykrates himself was damaged and never reconstructed. The map near the entrance shows how various incarnations of the temple were cantilevered atop one another (open Tues.-Sun. 8:30am-3pm; admission 800dr, students 400dr).

While there are three buses per day from Samos and Pythagorion to the site, a walk along the beach will bring you to the Ireon at your leisure—there's a back gate leading right onto the beach. If you can't enter through the gate, along the beach past two houses, there is a path that brings you inland to the main road and main entrance. This inland path runs close to the route of the ancient **Iera Odos** (Sacred Way) from Pythagorion to the temple. It may be a good idea to wear togas and bear libations in quirky jugs—it's local custom (or at least it *was*).

On the south side of town rest the ruins of the **Castle of Lycurgus,** built during the beginning of the last century by Lycurgus, a native of Samos and a leader in the Greek War of Independence. The **Church of the Transfiguration,** built within the ruined walls, is a pale blue variation on classical Orthodox architecture and interior decoration (free, but a small donation is appreciated).

Blocks of column, wall, and entablature are strewn throughout Pythagorion like Lincoln Logs after a floorquake, and the presentation in the small **Archaeological**

Museum (tel. 61 400) is no different. In fact, only a little over half of the collection fits into the building; assorted ruins are haphazardly scattered on the sidewalk in front (open Tues.-Thurs. 9am-2pm, Fri.-Sun noon-2pm; free).

■ Northern and Western Samos

Built on a peninsula 10km west of Samos Town, the northern village of **Kokkari** deserves a spot on your Samos itinerary. White pebble beaches and clear waters almost completely encompass the village. The **northern coast** of Samos, particularly the stretch between Kokkari and Karlovassi, has a few deserted pebble beaches tucked away in little coves occasionally whipped by strong winds. Most of the coast is easily accessible from the road to Karlovassi.

   Lemonakia Beach, 1km west of Kokkari and next to Tsamadou, and the wide white beach just west of **Avlakia** are both alluring. You can trek into the mountains from the village of **Platanakia,** near **Ag. Konstandinos,** in the "valley of the nightingales." The valley is famous for its lush greenery, tall trees, and the thousands of birds that wake up to chorus in the mountain valley after midnight. They'll lull you to sleep (or wake you up) at 3am. Hiking is best from May through June and especially during September, when the grapes from nearby vineyards are harvested and sweeten the air. The 16th-century monastery **Moni Vrontianis** rests near the village of **Vourliotes,** 5km south of Avlakia. **Karlovassi,** Samos's western port, is an unattractive city cluttered by empty modern buildings, but convenient for excursions to Western Samos via bus or ferry. **Marathokampos,** 7km southwest of Platanos, is uncrowded and probably the easiest place on the island to find rooms. A couple of kilometers west of this peaceful coastal hamlet stretches the spacious beach at **Votsalakia;** another kilometer farther is an even better beach at **Psili Ammos. Mount Kerkis** (1440m) winds around the island's western end in a harrowing passage.

IKARIA IKAPIA

Ikaria is associated with one of the better known Greek myths. Daedalus fashioned wings for his son Icarus to use when escaping from Crete. Intoxicated with his newly acquired power, Icarus soared too close to the sun, melted his waxen wings, and plunged to his death near Ikaria's coast. In spite of the island's mythological fame, however, Ikaria's tourist industry is decidedly low profile. The notoriously idiosyncratic Ikarians have successfully resisted development; now visitors, mostly Greek, come for the promise of healing offered by Ikaria's medicinal springs, renowned for their radioactivity and chemical composition. At one time, Ikaria was known for its thriving apricots, but locals got tired of "shaking the trees" to harvest the fruits. Now Turkey's got the Ikarian apricot trees and Ikaria's got none.

   Split by a rocky mountain chain, the deceptively rugged landscape boasts up to 2500 species of plants, mostly herbs, which give subtle color and fragrance to the island. Large patches of Ikarian forest, devastated by a 1993 fire, are slowly returning to life. Most villages cling to the winding, windy coastline. There is no bus service to speak of, and many roads are in poor repair, so rent something you're sure you can handle or expect to do a lot of walking. The two main port towns, the larger **Agios Kirikos** to the north and **Evdilos** to the south, are located on opposite faces of the island. The mountains are separated by long, treacherous distances, and locals maintain themselves in relative isolation. Some villages, notably **Agios Christos,** have built reputations for their nocturnal habits, drawing heat from the Greek government, which wishes to standardize business hours. Stores, including pharmacies, are open only in the mornings and evenings, often until 2am. Most of Ikaria appears subliminally affected by this—expect quiet, lazy days and lively, late nights.

■ Southern Ikaria

AGIOS KIRIKOS

Unassuming and congenial, Agios Kirikos is filled with white-washed houses; its **waterfront** is lined with small cafés where the locals congregate. As Ikaria's main port, Agios Kirikos is the most convenient place from which to coordinate travel. Although the town's pier is marked by a large sculpture of Icarus plummeting to the ground, getting here has become considerably easier and safer since Icarus's time. Coming off the ferry, a walk up the pier, onto the main waterfront road, and a right will take you to the **town square.**

Orientation and Practical Information On the way to the town square from the ferry dock, you will pass the **Sine Rex,** the town's presently defunct movie theater, and **Ikariada Travel** (tel. 23 322 or 22 277; fax 23 708), which offers friendly, English-speaking service and can arrange room or vehicle rental (open daily 8am-9:30pm). **Dolihi Tours** (tel. 23 230 or 71 240), on the corner of the waterfront road beyond the cafés, also sells tickets, distributes tourist information, and can help arrange lodging in Ag. Kirikos, Armenistis, and other towns (open in summer daily 8am-1pm and 6-10pm; in off season 8am-1pm). The **port police** (tel. 22 207) and **tourist police** (tel. 22 207) share a building; climb the steps to the left of Dolihi Tours and continue up the road (both open daily 8am-2pm). There is a **hospital** (tel. 22 330) nearby and Agios Kirkiros has two **pharmacies.** The island's only two **banks,** including the **National Bank** (tel. 22 553), are in Ag. Kirikos, in the square near the ferry offices (open Mon.-Fri. 8am-2pm). After hours, tourist offices and big hotels offer **currency exchange.** No credit cards are accepted on the island. About 100m up the street are the **post office** (tel. 22 222), to the right of the National Bank (open Mon.-Fri. 8am-2pm), and the **OTE** (tel. 22 399; open Mon.-Fri. 7:30am-3pm).

Ikaria's new **airport** offers service to Athens (4 per week, 40min., 16,000dr) and is located on the northeast tip of the island, near Fanari Beach. **Ferries** run to Athens (1-2 per day, 10hr., 4100dr); Samos Town (2-3 per day, 3hr., 1880dr); Patmos (4 per day, 1½hr., 2700dr); Paros (3-4 per day, 4hr., 2500dr); and Mykonos (3 per week, 4hr., 3300dr). Boats alternate stops at Evdilos in the north and Agios Kirikos, where taxis await to shuttle passengers to the other port for 2000-2500dr. It can be difficult to find a hotel your first night, so know your port of arrival and call if possible. **Flying Dolphins** leave for Samos (4 per week, 1½hr., 3800dr); Patmos (4 per week, 1hr., 3500dr); and Fourni (4 per week, 30min., 2500dr). Three **caïques** leave for Fourni every week (1000dr). **Postal Code:** 83300. **Telephone Code:** 0275.

Accommodations, Food, and Entertainment Climb the stairs to the left of Dolihi and take your first left, just before the police station, to reach the new **Hotel Kastro** (tel. 23 480). Comfortable, modern rooms overlook the harbor (8000dr with bath and TV). To reach **Hotel Akti** (tel. 22 694), climb the same stairs to the left of Dolihi, but take your first right into a tiny, short, seemingly private alley and climb the steps; follow the new signs. Hotel Akti has a decidedly Greek appeal, enhanced by a plant-filled courtyard overlooking the Aegean Sea. (Singles 4500dr. Doubles with bath 6500dr. Triples 7500dr.) On the way to Hotel Akti you'll pass the **Hotel O'Karras** (tel. 22 494), offering pink rooms and spacious baths. (Singles 2500dr, with bath 3500dr. Doubles 4000dr, with bath 4500dr.)

The **T'Adelfia Taverna,** the town's most established full-scale restaurant, offers summer "Greek nights" with some jivin' tunes (entrees from 700dr; open daily 9am-2am). At **Flik-Flak,** 1km out of town, get down to American favorites. Nearby **Aquarius** plays Greek music and hits from the age of *Hair.* There are some rocky **beaches** west of the ferry dock, but if you pass the tourist police to the east of town, you can clamber down to the sandy beaches and crystal blue water at the coves.

■ Northern Ikaria

EVDILOS

Heading north from Ag. Kirikos, the tiny road to Evdilos offers breathtaking views of the coast as it snakes along sheer cliffs through the florid hill country. From the island's eastern heights you can see Samos, Patmos, and the Fourni Archipelago; unfortunately, taking pictures near the military base is forbidden. On the way to Evdilos, the road passes a few tiny villages and beaches, many of which offer services and accommodations. **Bus** service is unreliable and tourist routes operate only in July and August. The schedule reported by the tourist police is often inaccurate. **Taxis** may be your best bet, so buddy up to cut costs (Ag. Kirikos to Evdilos 6000dr; Ag. Kirikos to Armenistis 8000dr; Armenistis to Evdilos 2000dr).

Evdilos, the island's minor port town, overlooking a sandy cove, features red-tiled roofs against a background of hills, trees, terraces, and grass. The **post office, OTE,** and **pharmacy** keep hours similar to the offices in Ag. Kirikos. The post office can be reached by the small set of white stairs leading out of the right of the central square (facing inland). Past the post office, across from the church, is the OTE. There is a **health clinic** (tel. 31 228), numerous restaurants, and rooms to let. Proprietors descend upon those stepping off the ferry from Peiraias. The **beaches** near Kampos, 500m west of town, induce euphoria.

ARMENISTIS

Armenistis, 58km from Ag. Kirikos, considered by some the "Greek Mexico" because of its relaxing environment, is the most touristed Ikarian haven. In off season, its population falls to 15. Life here, as elsewhere on Ikaria, sleeps away the day on the sandy beaches and dances away the night. **Ikaros Rooms,** up the steps from the small beach, offers comfy rooms. (Singles 3000dr. Doubles 4000dr.) **Hotel Pashala** (tel. 71 302) is comfortable, with cheap, clean rooms and a pleasant restaurant. (Doubles 3500dr.) **Livadi Camping** (tel. 41 349), on the beach roughly 300m before town, charges 500dr per person. **Restaurant Simbioso** offers numerous vegetarian options and mouth-watering homemade cakes for breakfast. The mountain villages of **Christos Rachon** (near the Monastery of Evangelistrias), **Frantato,** and **Dafni** provide calming alternatives to over-crowded Armenistis. **Marabou Travel** (tel. 71 460) can provide information about the outlying villages, local sites, rooms, and ferry schedules. The nearby village of **Nas** has remnants of a **Temple of Artemis,** down by a small beach heading into lush little gorge.

THASSOS ΘΑΣΟΣ

Thassos's imposing, dark green mountain side differs strikingly from the chalky dry cliffs on many Greek islands. Villages, archaeological sights, and beaches are all engulfed in plush foliage on Thassos, which is nicknamed "Green Island." Despite suffering devastating fires in 1985 and 1993, the once-charred forests are slowly reviving; with its still abundant vegetation, pine-forested coastal drives, and abundant bee-keeping and jam-making, Thassos remains an island of natural riches.

Since antiquity, the island has thrived on the gifts given to it by Hades, the god of wealth. Thassos cut loose from the Delian League of Athens in 411 BCE, only to be recaptured by the Athenians 22 years later. Nonetheless, the island maintained a veneer of wealth and independence. During Roman times, builders from all over the world sought Thassosian marble, and its gold mines made Thassos one of the richer members of the Delian League. The island was the birthplace of Timoxenos, an athlete credited with some 1400 victories, and the home of Hippocrates for three years. During medieval times, marauding pirates and Ottoman invaders prompted

THASSOS

the population to desert the city and hide out in the interior of the island. The Turks and then Egyptians controlled the island until it was retaken by the Greeks in 1912.

■ Limenas (Thassos Town)

Built atop the foundations of the ancient city of the same name, Limenas has become the island's capital and tourist center. Accordingly, this lively albeit dusty port is more crowded and more expensive than the rest of the island.

ORIENTATION AND PRACTICAL INFORMATION

The only street sign you'll ever see is **19th Octovriou Street,** the main way one block from and parallel to the waterfront. Street maps are available for 350dr at kiosks and tourist shops. The **large blue sign** across from the Mobil station lists the names and phone numbers of area hotels, pensions, and campgrounds.

Tourist Police: (tel. 23 111), on the waterfront. Open Mon.-Fri. 8am-7pm.

Tourist Agency: Thassos Tours (tel. 22 546 or 23 225; fax 23 005). Continue up the waterfront road from the port police toward the old port (now used only for small boats), until you see their blue awning. Rents motorbikes, suggests accommodations, and sells ferry tickets. Open daily 9am-10pm.

Bank: National Bank, near the main square, has an automated 24-hr. cash exchange machine and an **ATM** that accepts MasterCard and Cirrus. Open Mon.-Thurs. 8am-2pm, Fri. 8am-1:30pm.

OTE: Heading inland from Thassos Tours, turn right at the first corner. The building is on the left. Open Mon.-Fri. 7:30am-3:10pm.

Buses: Station (tel. 22 162), to the right of the ferry landing, next to the Mobil sign. Open daily 7:30am-8:15pm. Buses head west across the island to Limenaria, stopping at Skala Prinos (8 per day, 30min., 330dr); Panayia (11 per day, 15min., 190dr); and Skala Potamia (10 per day, 30min., 270dr). Others trek to Potos and Pefkari (8 per day, 1¼hr., 800dr); Aliki Beach (3 per day, 1hr., 650dr); and Theologos (5 per day, 1½hr., 1000dr). Ask at the tourist police or the bus office for schedules. Bus service is erratic—allow time to catch the last boat off the island. Contact **Theagenis Tours** (tel. 71 538; fax 71 888), directly up the street from the ferry landing, for information on buses between Kavala and Prinos.

Ferries: Run from Limenas to Keramoti (10 per day, 30min., 280dr) and Kavala (10 per day, 1¼hr., 550dr), and from Prinos to Kavala (8 per day, 1½hr., 550dr). Be sure to note from which port, Limenas or Prinos, your boat leaves. If it leaves from **Prinos,** you can easily get there from Kavala, as bus schedules between Prinos and Leminas are synchronized with the ferries. To go to other islands of the Northeast Aegean, you must first return to Kavala for ferry connections. Schedules posted at the grey port police building.

Flying Dolphins: Hydrofoils zip between Thassos's main port of Limenas and nearby Kavala (7 per day, 40min., 1400dr). Schedules are posted near the pier at the port police, and docked boats indicate upcoming departure times from signs on board. Tickets are bought on board.

Hospital: (in Prinos 71 100). Open 24hr.

Police (tel. 22 500), in the same building as the tourist police. **Port Police** (tel. 22 106), in a gray building at the waterfront's center. Open 24hr.

Post Office: Head inland from Thassos Tours and turn right at the fourth corner. Open Mon.-Fri. 7:30am-2pm. **Postal Code:** 64004.

Telephone Code: 0593.

ACCOMMODATIONS

Accommodations are a free-for-all on Thassos, especially on the weekends when Greeks flock to the island from nearby Kavala and Thessaloniki. Roughly 100m to the left of the Thassos-Kavala hydrofoil dock, behind the **Marina Restaurant,** sit several reasonably priced pensions. A listing of hotels, pensions, and campgrounds is posted in front of the bus stop, but since this only includes the pricier hotels, it's worthwhile to hunt around for substantially cheaper pensions.

Giorgos Raxos (tel. 22 778), on the right side of the waterfront (facing inland); look for the green-tiled house next to the barber shop. Rooms are spacious and clean. Doubles 4000dr. Triples 5000dr.

Theodorou Eva (tel. 22 665, 168). Look for the "Rooms to Rent/*Zimmer*" sign visible from the corner near the post office. Doubles 4000dr. Triples 5000dr.

Pension Philipus (tel. 23 076, -513). With the post office at your left, continue along the road, past the dry cleaners, and follow the bend. Philipus is on the left with a blue Philip sign. Doubles with bath and access to kitchen 4000-6000dr.

Villa Edem (tel. 23 096), a 5-10-min. walk from the center of town. Studios with fully equipped kitchens and balconies, or rooms with breakfast for 7000-8000dr.

FOOD

For a yummy snack head to the ever-popular **Appetitio,** near Gregory's Art, for a *bougatsa,* a cheese- or cream-filled pie(300dr). For a more filling meal, **Selinos taverna** (tel. 23 214), 800m inland past the port, serves *kolikomezedhes* (zucchini burgers 700dr) and *octopomezedhes* (octopus 800dr). For a hearty, traditional Greek meal, walk up to Prinos and at the crossing look past the supermarket for **Toxotis,** a local favorite (open daily 1pm-1am). **Platonakia,** on the waterfront near the old port, serves pricey but delicious meals (full meal 1800dr).

SIGHTS

In addition to impressive remains of buildings and walls dating from the 6th and 5th centuries BCE, the island flaunts a 4th-century BCE Greek **theater,** built on the remains of the acropolis of ancient Thassos. The ruins are easy to find; turn right behind the old port and continue to a three-pronged fork in the road beyond a recessed ruin—the middle path leads to the theater. Unfortunately, the classical dramas usually staged here in summer have been suspended due to renovations. The archaeological sites are free and always open. The **Thassos Museum** (tel. 22 180), near the old port, contains mosaic floors and sculptures found on the site, including a colossal 6th-century BCE marble statue of Apollo with a ram draped around his shoulders. Under repair in summer 1996, it should reopen in 1997 (open Tues.-Fri. 8am-7pm, Sat.-Sun. 8am-3pm; admission 500dr, EU students 200dr, seniors 400dr). Next to the museum is a large **agora** (same hours as museums; free).

■ East Coast

Buses travel from Limenas to Limenaria (10 per day, 750dr), stopping 10km south in the villages of **Panagia** and **Potamia** (1500-1550dr). Three kilometers apart, both villages overlook Ormos Potamias, a gorgeous, sandy cove. The aromas of grilled goat meat and syrup-saturated walnuts greet you as you approach Panayia, which retains its traditions despite a minor tourist influx. Potamia houses a small **Folk Museum,** tucked under the shadow of the town church, featuring traditional costumes and outdated agricultural tools (open Mon. and Wed.-Sun. 8:30am-3pm). Both villages have private rooms; Panayia also has an inexpensive hotel, the **Helvetia** (tel. 61 231), at the north entrance to town. (Doubles start at 6000dr.)

The golden beach of **Chrisi Ammoudia** stretches endlessly 6km east of Panayia. Farther south, Potamia's beach is capacious but less attractive. (Those who choose to camp may be able to use the water tap at the entrance to the olive grove, roughly 1km from the beach towards Potamia.) The twin coves of **Aliki** (11km south of Kinira) hide the more tranquil beaches on the island. The northernmost one, sheltered by foliage, is often isolated. The south beach cove, formed as sand shifted over a Roman marble quarry, shelters slabs of bleached white rock and crevices ideal for snorkeling. The main beach in between gets more crowded, but it's good for grab-

SAMOTHRAKI

bing a meal at one of the *tavernas*. After you towel off, trudge to the monastery of **Archaegelon,** a simple, whitewashed church with stone floors and colorful icons.

■ West Coast

No longer the capital of the island as it was in Turkish times, **Limenaria** has a small waterfront that is home to numerous cafés, *tavernas,* and shops. Even though daily buses haul in tourists from Limenas (700dr), finding a private room amid Limenaria's Turkish houses is not difficult (doubles start at 5000dr). Facing inland, the **post office** and **National Bank** are to the right of the harbor. The Greek-speaking **police** are on the waterfront. Exemplary beaches are at **Pefkari** and **Potos,** 4km away. Seven buses per day run from Limenas to Potos (750dr). **Pefkari Camping** (tel. 51 190), 1km north of Potos, runs an outstanding campground. (830dr per person. 650dr per tent. 930dr per car. Electricity 500dr per day.)

SAMOTHRAKI (SAMOTHRACE) ΣΑΜΟΘΡΑΚΗ

Samothraki first welcomed Greek colonists in the 7th century BCE. The island soon achieved fame as a religious center specializing in the worship of the *libiri,* twin gods who helped infertile women bear children. At the **Sanctuary of the Megaloi Theoi** (Great Gods), Philip of Macedon met his wife Olympius. After the requisite nine months, **Alexander** (a.k.a. "the Great") was born. The starkly beautiful island, now home to 999 churches but fewer than 3000 people, draws the occasional hardy adventurer. Fegari, the highest peak in the Aegean (1670m above sea level), rises out of this stony, oblong isle. According to Homer, it is from this summit that Poseidon rooted for the home team in the Trojan War.

■ Kamariotisa

The waterfront of Kamariotisa, Samothraki's port, is surrounded by houses, and though the town has ample tourist venues, these are pleasantly free of neon-lit restaurants blasting bad Euro-techno. Although **Chora** is nominally the island's capital, Kamariotisa is where people go to do anything or get anywhere else on the island.

Orientation and Practical Information   The **port police** (tel. 41 305) are on the waterfront facing inland two blocks left of the ferry dock; look for the Greek flag (open 24hr.). On the road stretching inland, just across from the **National Bank,** is the **pharmacy** (tel. 41 581; open Mon.-Fri. 9am-1:30pm and 6:30-8:30pm, Sat. 11am-1pm). Just up the road on the left from the pharmacy is a **mini-market** and **OTE.** A 10-minute jaunt up the quiet hillside's main street, characterized by red-tiled houses and chickens dodging the occasional passing automobile, brings you to another **OTE** and the **post office.**

Ferries connect Samothraki with Alexandroupolis (3 per day, 2½hr., 2600dr), Limnos (1 per week, 3½hr., 2350dr), and Kavala (1 per day, 4hr., 2810dr). In summer, **buses** run 8-10 times per day around the island's perimeter, leaving from the ferry dock to Loutra, Profitos Ilias, Therma, and Psira Potomos (370dr); Paleopolis, Alonia, and the Chora (200dr); Lacoma (250dr), Kariotis (570dr), and the campsites (400dr). All rides last less than 30minutes. Bus and ferry information as well as car rental (15,000dr per day) is available at **Saos Tours** (tel. 41 588), on the waterfront (open daily 8am-2pm and 6-9pm). **Taxis** await customers near the bus stop (tel. 41 341) between 8am and 1am. **Moped rentals** are available at the unnamed **garage** (tel. 41 511) opposite the ferry dock (5000dr per day; open daily 8:30am-9pm). **Postal Code:** 68002. **Telephone Code:** 0551.

Accommodations   The English-speaking Saos Tours, your all-purpose tourist agency, can brief you on the room situation. Doubles average 5500dr, with bath 8000dr, although in high season even without bath they can cost as much as 7000dr. Friendly, family-run **Vasiliki Karoyiannis** (tel. 41 165) has clean rooms with shared baths. Hang a right just past the National Bank at the "restaurant/rooms" sign to get there. (Doubles 5000dr. Triples 5500dr.) The restaurant below the hotel has delicious, fresh *loukoumades* (Greek honey doughnuts 500dr). Roughly 100m farther to the right (facing inland) are the well maintained rooms of **Maria Mamougiorti** (tel. 41 315), who speaks German. Look for the blue-and-white "rent rooms" sign high above the building. (Doubles 5600dr. Triples 6300dr.)

Food, Sights, and Entertainment   The restaurant beneath **Mrs. Karoyiannis' pension** (tel. 41 165) has delicious authentic Greek meals (Greek salad 800dr). The nightlife, which congregates in Kamariotisa, may not lastingly relieve your ennui, but you can try the several café-bars on the waterfront—**Bloody Mary, Diva, Big Blue,** and **Cocktail.** One kilometer west (left facing the water) are the dance clubs **Disco Rebel** and **Music Hall Apropto** (drinks 1200dr; no cover).

Just 7km east of Kamariotisa is **Paleopolis** (Old City), with the ruins of the **Megaloi Theoi.** Dedicated to Axieros (Demeter, goddess of the harvest and of fertility), and a hubbub of other deities as well, the Megaloi Theoi witnessed the initiations of both the Spartan King Lysander and the historian Herodotus. Ruins of the theater, *temenos,* and palace remain. The **Paleopolis Museum** (tel. 41 474), next to the ruins, houses artifacts including gargantuan entablatures from the Rotunda Arsinoe and the Hieron, and a cast of the Nike of Samothrace. Sign the guest book if you think the original Nike, now in the Louvre, should be returned to Samothraki (site and museum open Tues.-Sun. 9am-3pm; admission 450dr, students 250dr).

LIMNOS ΛΗΜΝΟΣ

It is said on Limnos that when one insensitive clod made a dirty joke about Aphrodite, the goddess put a curse on the island, causing the women to kill the men. Only the king, helped by his daughter, escaped. Upon arrival, the Argonauts found grieving widows; shortly thereafter, the repopulation of the island was underway.

Limnos' scruffy hills, filled with the bleating of goats, shoulder vast expanses of golden grassed meadows. Knuckled ridges of volcanic handiwork and fantastic rock formations fall away to long, unspoiled stretches of smooth, sandy beaches. Modern by most standards, this eighth largest of the Greek islands remains one of the Northeast Aegean's best-kept secrets.

■ Myrina

The island's capital and primary port, Myrina is a charming, well proportioned fishing village keenly aware of its beauty. The skyline, made strange by volcanic configurations, is dominated by an impressive Genoese-Turkish fortress which is illuminated at 10pm each night (along with the church across the harbor). Against the star-studded sky, its turreted tower achieves almost ethereal definition.

Orientation and Practical Information   Myrina has two main **waterfronts,** perpendicular to each other, each hosting numerous *tavernas.* The longer, prettier, and more popular one runs parallel to Kyda, about two blocks to the left (facing inland). The other, from whose left side the pier juts out, constitutes the main **harborfront.** The harborfront fashions a plaza around which are *tavernas,* ferry and tour agencies, and a few old hotels. **Kyda Street,** the main road leading inland, takes you past a variety of shops and into the town's **central square,** recognizable by its many **taxi stands** (tel. 23 033 or 22 348). The **OTE** (tel. 22 299) is in the square (open Mon.-Sat. 7:30am-10pm, Sun. 8am-1pm and 5-10pm), as is a **National Bank,** with an **ATM** (open Mon.-Thurs. 8am-2pm, Fri. 8am-1:30pm). The **post office** (tel. 22 462) is one block farther along Kyda St., which is Garofalidi St. (open Mon.-Fri. 7:30am-2pm). You can find a self-service **laundry** (tel. 24 392) here, too (1000dr per kg; open Mon.-Sat. 8:30am-2pm and 5-9:30pm). The **police** (tel. 22 200) are a few blocks past the post office and the **hospital** (tel. 22 222) is to the left of Garofalidi St., on the street farthest from the waterfront (open 24hr.). The **bus station** (tel. 22 464) is located in El Venizelou Sq., the second square you come across as you continue up Kyda St., past Garofalidi St. Buses are few and do not go to most towns (open Mon.-Fri. 8am-2:15pm, Sat. 8am-noon). Limnos can be seen by renting a **bicycle** (1000dr), **moped** (2500dr), **car** (8000dr), or **jeep** (9000dr); insurance is extra. **Express Rental office** (tel. 23 830; fax 23 494), at the far corner of the waterfront in Myrina, below the Kastro, rents all four (open daily 8am-2pm).

Praulis Travel (tel. 22 471 or 24 617; fax 22 471), located in Myrina's port square, can provide information for **Olympic Airways flights** (tel. 22 078) to Athens (3-4 per day, 40min., 13,900dr), Thessaloniki (1 per day, 30min., 14,100dr), or Mitilini (1 per day, 25min., 12,700dr). Buses to the **airport** (tel. 31 204) cost 1150dr. **Ferries** depart from the side of the port opposite the castle, a short hike from the port square. In high season, ferries run to Kavala (4 per week, 6hr., 3228dr); Lesvos (5 per week, 6hr., 3400dr); Thessaloniki (2 per week, 7hr., 4400dr); Chios (3 per week, 10hr., 4642dr); Rafina (3 per week, 9hr., 4647dr); Agios Efstratios (3 per week, 9hr., 1571dr); Peiraias (4 per week, 22hr., 6052dr); Samos (1 per week, 5789dr); and Patmos (1 per week, 5952dr). Contact **Nicos Vayakos' Tourist and Travel Agency** (tel. 22 900) in Mirina's port square for details. **Flying Dolphins** leave from the opposite side of the port, beneath the castle; they speed once per week to Alexandropolis (2hr., 300dr) and Samothraki (2hr., 3000dr). **Postal code:** 84100. **Telephone Code:** 0254.

Accommodations, Food, and Entertainment

Gerondoudi Suites (tel. 22 050), just above Kosmos pizzeria, has rooms with bath, TV, and kitchen. (Singles 4000dr. Doubles 5000dr.) **Hotel Aktaion** (tel. 22 258) is on the harborfront below the castle. The pristine rooms have sinks, refrigerators, and balconies overlooking the colorful fishing boats. (Singles 4500dr. Doubles 8000dr, with bath 9000dr. Triples 10,500dr.) The waterfront *tavernas* are uniform in their prices, and identical in their offerings. The two nighttime hotspots are **Karagiozis Bar** (beer 600dr, cocktails 1000dr), a bit past the waterfront *tavernas,* and the mellow **Patio Café,** left of the harborfront overlooking the pier, accessible by the road leading past the building of the port police.

Sporades ΣΠΟΡΑΔΕΣ

The jagged coasts and thickly forested interiors of the Sporades (Scattered Ones) were first colonized by Cretans, who cultivated olives and grapes on the scattered islands until Athenians took over in the 5th century BCE. The residue of ancient structures on these islands attests to the 2nd century BCE Roman presence, the Venetians' 13th century rule, and Turkish rule until 1821, when the Sporades became Greek. Lush islands of fragrant pines, luxurious beaches, and abundant fruit orchards, the Sporades of today offer travelers (mostly Germans, Norwegians, and Brits), a smorgasbord of earthly delights. Although word has gotten out about the Sporades, and the islands' fledgling tourist facilities are quickly maturing, there are spots on this small archipelago that remain relatively quiet and inexpensive.

SKIATHOS ΣΚΙΑΘΟΣ

Secondary to the other Sporades in natural beauty, Skiathos has tried to compensate by hosting the group's largest social scene. In terms of the number of visitors, the strategy has been a success, but most islanders agree that Skiathos is now too expensive. The traditional culture has been pretty much obliterated; your only recourse may be to read about it. Fortunately, Skiathos was home to writer Alexandros Papadiamantis (1851-1911), and this is one of the few places where his books can be found in English translation.

■ Skiathos Town

Skiathos Town has weathered the deluge of foreign tourists far better than much of the coastline. The cobblestone streets of the commercial section are packed with loitering tourists and expensive stores, but in the residential neighborhoods, balconies burst with white gardenia blossoms and magenta bougainvillea while grapevines overhang shady, undisturbed terraces. Skiathos Town is known as *the* place to party in the Sporades—the slew of nightclubs and discoes *opas* until 4am.

ORIENTATION AND PRACTICAL INFORMATION

The long waterfront, lined with travel agencies, *tavernas,* and various bike and car rental dealers, is intersected by **Papadiamanti Street,** the main drag. Traveling inland, Papadiamanti is intersected by **Pandra Street** at the National Bank, and by **Evangelistra Street,** farther inland at the post office. Parallel and to the left of Papadiamanti, but not appearing until Pandra, is **Politechniou Street,** home to a string of decent bars. On the far right of the waterfront, still facing inland, a road winds up to the airport and several beaches. On the far left, along a harbor perpendicular to the main waterfront, is a row of fishing boats that charter daily excursions. A mediocre map is available at all kiosks (300dr).

Tourist Police: (tel. 23 172), on the right side of Papadiamanti St. in a small white building, inland past the OTE. Their *Summer in Skiathos* brochure has a map. Open daily 8am-9pm. The **police** (tel. 21 111) are across the street. Open 24hr.

Banks: National Bank, midway up Papadiamanti St., on the left side, offers **currency exchange.** Open Mon. and Wed. 8am-2pm, Tues. and Thurs. 8am-2pm and 7-9pm, Fri. 8am-1:30pm, Sun. 9am-noon. Lines are long and slow July-Aug.

American Express: 21 Papadiamanti St. (tel. 21 463, -4), on the left before the post office, in the travel agency of Mare Nostrum Holidays. All tourist services, including excursions around the island (4900dr per day). Open Mon.-Sat. 8am-2pm and 5-10pm, Sun. 9:30am-1pm and 5-10pm.

SKIATHOS

OTE: (tel. 22 135), Papadiamanti St., 1 block inland from the post office. Open in summer Mon.-Fri. 7:30am-10pm; in winter Mon.-Fri. 7:30am-3pm.

Flights: 1-2 flights per day to Athens (50min., 12,900dr). **Olympic Airways Office** (tel. 22 229, -049), at the airport. Call 24hr. prior to take-off to confirm flight. Open Mon.-Fri. 8am-4pm. Taxis from the harbor to the airport cost 1000dr.

Buses: Depart from the bus stop shack at the far right end of the wharf (facing inland), along the island's main road, ending at Koukounaries beach (every 15-20min., 7:15am-1am, 270dr, less in off season).

Ferries: Nomikos/Goutos Lines (tel. 22 209), in the middle of the waterfront. Open daily 7am-11pm. Ferries travel to Skiathos most frequently from Agios Konstantinos, Volos, Skopelos, and Alonissos. From Athens, take the daily bus from the station at 260 Liossion St. (every hr., 6:15am-9:30pm, 2½hr., 2650dr) to Agios Konstantinos, and then the **ferry** from there at noon or 1pm (3½hr., 2975dr). From Volos, 3-5 boats sail daily (3hr., 2300dr) to Skopelos and continue on to Skopelos and Alonissos. Other ferries run from Skiathos to Skopelos (3-4 per day, 1½hr., 1300dr) and Alonissos (2-4 per day, 2hr., 1450dr). To get to the Pelion Peninsula, catch 1 of the **excursion boats** leaving Platania at either 8am or 9am, returning from Koukounaries Beach on Skiathos at 5pm (1500dr).

Flying Dolphins: (tel. 22 018), at the center of the waterfront. Open daily 7:30am-9:30pm. Hydrofoils travel to Agios Konstantinos (3-4 per day, 1¼hr., 5300dr); Skopelos (9-11 per day, 35min., 1815dr); Volos (5-6 per day, 1¼hr., 4650dr); Alonissos (8-9 per day, 1hr., 2346dr); Platania (1-2 per day, 25min., 2569dr); and Thessaloniki (1 per day, 3¼hr., 10,011dr).

Taxis: (tel. 21 460). Queue along the waterfront, next to the "Rooms to Let" kiosk; prices are posted on the shack. Open 24hr.

Moped Rental: Numerous places along the waterfront, including **Avis** (tel. 21 458), on the right of the waterfront. Open daily 8am-10pm. Bikes from 2500dr per day.

English Bookstore: Skalino (tel. 23 647). Make a left on Evangelista St. and it's on your right. Some English-language material, including Papadiamantis's books.

Laundromat: Miele (tel. 22 341), right off Papadiamanti at the National Bank. Wash 1800dr. Dry 600dr per 15min. Iron 600dr per 30min. Open daily 8am-2pm and 5-10pm. Detergent and required tokens available at the grocery store across the street. Store open daily 8am-2pm and 5-11pm.

Pharmacy: (tel. 21 230). On the left side of Papadiamanti St., near the bank with a red cross sign. Open daily 8:30am-2pm and 5-7pm.

Medical Emergency and Hospital: (tel. 22 040), on the "Acropolis" hill behind Skiathos Town. Open 24hr.; after 1pm, emergencies only.

Post Office: (tel. 22 011), at the intersection of Papadiamanti and Evangelistria St. Open Mon.-Fri. 7:30am-2pm. **Postal Code:** 37002.

Telephone Code: 0427.

ACCOMMODATIONS

Usually visitors make reservations for July and August before they arrive. Singles are almost impossible to come by in high season, while doubles often cost over 10,000dr. "Rooms to Let" are your best bet. Signs abound, but if you're stuck, try the **Office of "Rooms to Let"** (tel. 23 852 or 22 990), in the ducky yellow kiosk right on the dock where the metal fence meets the water (open daily 8:30am-midnight). Also, check out Evangelista St. or the streets parallel to it for cheap sleep.

Pension Danaos (tel. 22 834), on the left-hand side of the street off Papadiamanti; right across from the OTE. Doubles 10,000dr.

Camping Aselinos (tel. 49 312), located near one of the island's nicer beaches, offers a *taverna,* a palm canopy on the beach, and plenty of shady spots. Buses run frequently to the site (20min., 250dr); ask at either of the 2 waterfront information booths. 12,000dr per person, 14,000dr including tent. Free in off season.

Camping Koukounaries (tel. 49 250), on the bus route, between stops 19 and 20. Has a restaurant, minimarket, and wooded campground 1km from the beach. 1500dr per person. 1000dr per tent.

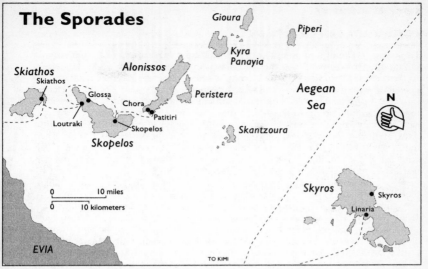

The Sporades

Skiathos
Skiathos
Glossa
Loutraki
Chora
Patitiri
Skopelos
Skopelos
Alonissos
Gioura
Kyra Panayia
Piperi
Peristera
Skantzoura
Aegean Sea
Skyros
Skyros
Linaria
EVIA
TO KIMI

0 — 10 miles
0 — 10 kilometers

N

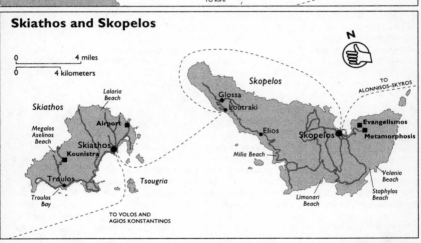

Skiathos and Skopelos

Skiathos
Lalaria Beach
Airport
Megalos Aselinos Beach
Skiathos
Kounistra
Traulos
Troulos Bay
Tsougria
Skopelos
Glossa
Loutraki
Elios
Skopelos
Evangelismos
Metamorphosis
Milia Beach
Yelanio Beach
Limonari Beach
Staphylos Beach

TO ALONNISOS–SKYROS
TO VOLOS AND AGIOS KONSTANTINOS

0 — 4 miles
0 — 4 kilometers

N

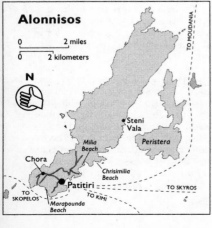

Alonnisos

Chora
Patitiri
Steni Vala
Milia Beach
Chrisimilia Beach
Peristera
Marapounda Beach

TO MOUDANIA
TO SKOPELOS
TO KIMI
TO SKYROS

0 — 2 miles
0 — 2 kilometers

N

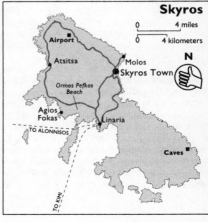

Skyros

Airport
Atsitsa
Molos
Skyros Town
Ormos Pefkos Beach
Agios Fokas
Linaria
Caves

TO ALONNISOS
TO KIMI

0 — 4 miles
0 — 4 kilometers

N

SKIATHOS

FOOD AND ENTERTAINMENT

The cheapest dining option in Skiathos is to hit the *gyro/souvlaki* (350dr) stands which line Papadiamanti and the waterfront or to forage in any of the numerous **supermarkets.** Turn left off Papadiamanti when you see the National Bank, follow its wall to your right, and you will find the **Mouria** (tel. 23 069). Seahorses etched into the supporting beams look down into this cozy restaurant, which serves a menu of carefully prepared traditional Greek cuisine (*kalamari* 1200dr). There are also many overpriced Greek *tavernas* around. **Dionissos,** on Pandra St., is a little cheaper than most and has an enormous menu (four-cheese risotto 1200dr, fixed menus 1900-3500dr). On the waterfront, **Kalypso** (tel. 23 051) offers upscale Italian fare (pastas 1400-2000dr). Uphill and slightly inland from the other end of the harbor (past Avra) sits a multinational duo. **Garden of the East** (tel. 21 627) has Chinese vegetarian dishes; **Le Bistrot** (tel. 21 627), across the street, does Italian, including snails in a spicy sauce (both open daily 6pm-1am).

Nightlife here runs the gamut from mellow waterfront *tavernas* to hellbent all-night discoes. Generally, Evangelistras and Polytechniou streets are home to most pubs and simple discoes. For larger dance havens with delusions of grandeur, walk along the waterfront east of town. Most close in off season. **Kalypso** (tel. 23 051), one of the classier places in town, is on the water above the restaurant of the same name; the door is on the street parallel to the waterfront road. Classical music grooves until midnight, when an eclectic mix of jazz, reggae, and New Age takes over in a gay-friendly atmosphere (beer 600dr, cocktails 1200-1400dr). The last of the waterfront discoes, **BBC,** has the best dancing and features rave and other fast-paced music (beer 1000dr, cocktails 1800dr). **Admiral Benbow** (tel. 22 311) may be Polytechniou's most eccentric pub. Brits Mick and Elaine play oldies, rock, blues, and soul, and serve imported beers for 500-700dr. The **Scorpio** (tel. 23 208) attracts a youngish crowd, which comes to dance along with the fast music and flashing lights (300dr cover). For more sedate entertainment there is the open-air **Cinema Paradiso** (tel. 23 975 or 21 463), playing recent Hollywood hits in English with Greek subtitles (1300dr). Programs are available in the National Bank.

■ Around Skiathos Island

The island's main paved road runs along the south coast from Skiathos Town to Koukounaries. Resort hotels dominate the beaches. A **bus** travels this route leaving the harbor in Skiathos Town (every 15-20min., 7:15am-1am, 270dr), with stops at many beaches, including **Megali Ammos, Nostos, Vromolimnos, Platanias,** and **Troulos.** The bus route and the road end at the pine grove beach of **Koukounaries,** where swaying branches shelter clear turquoise water and fine white sand. A short walk away is the curved yellow **Banana Beach,** slightly less populated than the others. From Koukounaries, take the paved road to the left of the bus stop, follow it to the bend, and make a right on the uphill dirt road. At the top, take the worn path through the gate on the left. A quick scamper over the next hill leads to **Little Banana Beach,** a nude beach full of unpeeled bathers. The beach is popular with (but not exclusively for) gay men.

Just east of Troulos a road turns off for **Asselinos,** a beach and campground on the north edge of Skiathos. From the main road, it is a 45- to 60-minute walk to **Megalos Asselinos** beach, home to a *tavernas,* campsite, and good snorkeling. You can reach it by car, troika, moped, rollerblades, inflatable armadillo, or a long walk from Troulos. Alternatively, take the high road which forks after 2km—the right branch leads uphill to **Panagia Kounistra,** a small monastery with a grape arbor and a *taverna* within its walls. To the right of Megalos Asselinos is **Micros Asselinos.** The latter is the more secluded of the two, though neither is crowded, except at lunchtime when excursion boats stop at Megalos Asselinos. Getting to Asselinos Town is a bit easier—buses leave until 10pm from **Asselinos Tours** (tel. 21 905 or 49 312) on the waterfront for the 20-minute trip. Inquire about **camping** at Asselinos Tours.

West along the coast past Lalaria Beach are the ruins of the medieval walled **castle** (a 2-hr. walk on a path from Skiathos Town). The Greeks built the castle during the 16th century to take refuge from marauding pirates. When independence dawned in the 19th century, they abandoned this headland and began work on what has blossomed into present-day Skiathos. Two churches are all that remains of the ancient community. The **Church of the Nativity** has fine icons and frescoes. Daily excursion boats leave from the long strip at the far left side (facing inland) of Skiathos' harbor for Lalaria, on a tour of the caves and castle (3000dr roundtrip). Departure is between 9 and 11am, return 4pm; buy a ticket on the boat. For a full day of swimming, hop on one of the boats that leave for the small island of **Tsougria** (every hr., 10am-5pm, 1200dr roundtrip). Boats also leave the harbor each morning for a full day excursion to Skopelos and Alonissos (3500dr). For details and other trips, call the American Express office and the small tourist office (tel. 21 763), off Papandrios St. on the waterfront (open daily 8am-noon and 6pm-10pm).

SKOPELOS ΣΚΟΠΕΛΟΣ

The looming cliffs rising from the coastline gave this island its name, "Steep Rock From the Sea." Tempering the mountains' starkness, acres of pine, olive, and plum trees blanket the hills. Originally a Cretan colony ruled by King Staphylos, strategic Skopelos has been occupied by Persians, Spartans, Athenians, Romans, Franks, Venetians, and Turks. It was conquered in 1538 by the illustrious Turkish admiral Khayr El-Din Barbarossa (Red Beard), who executed the entire population. Today, Skopelos' own culture dominates, and the island has managed to keep tourism within sane limits. Women practice their traditional occupations of weaving and embroidery and wear the distinctive Skopelan *morko*—a silk shirt, short velvet jacket with flowing sleeves, and a kerchief—all finely hand-embroidered.

■ Skopelos Town

Except for the front line of tourist offices and *tavernas* curving around the horseshoe waterfront, Skopelos Town is a complex and delightful cobblestone maze stacked against a hillside. Even the tourist shops are examples of true handiwork. The tightly packed architecture in Skopelos Town is a jumble of Venetian, Byzantine, Macedonian, and Neoclassical styles, visible in one third of the island's 360 churches. For a view of this vividly colored settlement, climb to the top of the castle walls on the north side of town.

ORIENTATION AND PRACTICAL INFORMATION

Boats dock at the concrete jetty on the left tip of the horseshoe as you look seaward, where tourist agencies and *tavernas* line the waterfront. Behind the crowded eateries, one block past the Commercial Bank, **Galatsaniou Street,** a fashionable path rich with trinkets and goodies, darts upward. Buses depart from the right edge of town, facing the water; directly inland from the stop there is a square (which is in fact a triangle) affectionately known to locals as "Souvlaki Square" for its cheap eats.

Tourist Office: (tel. 23 220), in a side door of the white building near the jetty. Offers a useful map and accommodation suggestions. Open daily 9am-10pm.

Tourist Agencies: Most exchange currency, rent mopeds and/or cars, and sell ferry and/or hydrofoil tickets. **Thalpos** (tel. 22 947, 23 466; fax 23 057), left of the Commercial Bank, is on the 2nd floor. Open daily 9am-3pm and 6-10:30pm.

Banks: National Bank (tel. 22 224, -0691; fax 23 206), on the left leg of the horseshoe waterfront. Open Mon.-Thurs. 8am-2pm, Fri. 8am-1:30pm. It has an automatic currency changer out front. The **Commercial Bank** (tel. 22 015) is at the

S
K
O
P
E
L
O
S

center of the waterfront. Open Mon.-Thurs. 8am-2pm, Fri. 8am-1:30pm. Both have **ATMs** which accept Visa and MasterCard.

OTE: (tel. 22 399). Take Galatsaniou St. from the waterfront for 50m. Open Mon.-Sat. 7:30am-10pm, Sun. 9am-2pm and 5-10pm.

Buses: At the parking lot area behind where the breakwater meets the beach and on the left edge of town facing inland. To: Stafilos (22 per day, 50min., 190dr one way) and Agnotas (22 per day, 65min., 190dr one way); Milia and Elios (16 per day, 35min., 440dr); and Glossa (8 per day, 1hr., 700dr).

Ferries: A bus runs from Athens to Volos and Ag. Konstantinos before ferries leave for Skopelos (2½hr. from Ag. Konstantinos). Ferries to Skopelos depart from Volos (4hr.) and Ag. Konstantinos (4hr.). Ferries from Skopelos leave for Skiathos (1hr.), Alonissos (30min.), and Kimi (3½hr.). The ferry to Alonissos leaves in the evening and returns in the morning. **Excursion boats** from Skopelos take 1hr.

Flying Dolphins: Zoom from Skopelos to Ag. Konstantinos (3-4 per day, 2hr., 7065dr); Volos (daily, 6005dr); Skiathos (7-11 per day, 45min., 1815dr); Alonissos (6-7 per day, 20min., 1464dr); and less frequently to Thessaloniki (11,205dr) and Kimi (8391dr). Most ferries and hydrofoils also stop at **Loutraki,** the port for the north town of **Glossa** on Skopelos.

Taxis: Rev up their engines at the center of the waterfront, amid the block of tavernas, and stick around in the square daily 7am-2am.

Moped Rental: Motorbike for Rent/Horizon (tel. 23 279). Make a left on the street heading diagonally away from the inland square and walk by the bars.

Laundromat: Several around town, including one near Greca's Crêperie and a second inland past the Commercial Bank; walk uphill following the bakery sign. Open Mon.-Tues., Thurs.-Fri. 8am-1pm and 4:30-8pm, Wed. and Sat. 8am-1pm.

Pharmacy: (tel. 22 252), across from the OTE. Open Mon.-Fri. 9am-2pm and 5:30-11pm. Also on the waterfront. Open Mon-Sat. 9am-2pm and 5pm-midnight, Sun. 10:30am-2pm and 6pm-midnight.

Medical Center: (tel. 22 222). Follow the left-hand road inland from Souvlaki Sq. until it dead-ends, then turn right and you'll shortly see it on the right. Open Mon.-Fri. 9am-2pm for free walk-ins; 24hr. for emergencies.

Police: (tel. 22 235), behind the National Bank. Open 24hr.

Post Office: At the top of the horseshoe where the block of *tavernas* ends and the bus stop area begins, take the first right inland, make a sharp left before you enter the small inland square (look for the sign to your left), then your first right, then your first left (then do the hokey-pokey as you shake it all about). Or just follow the clear signs. Open Mon.-Fri. 7:30am-2pm. **Postal Code:** 37003.

Telephone Code: 0424.

ACCOMMODATIONS AND FOOD

If you don't get scooped up by hustlers, the cheapest accommodations can be found by wandering through the narrow labyrinthine streets behind the waterfront and looking for "Rooms to Let" signs or asking locals. If you prefer a larger, more anonymous hotel, try **Hotel Georgios L.** (tel. 22 308), on the far right of the waterfront, facing inland (doubles 10,000dr). There are no official campgrounds on Skopelos; *Let's Go* does not recommend illegal freelance camping.

Skopelos is blessed with quite a few tasty dining options; as usual, the waterfront is not the place to find them. Locals praise **Greca's Crêperie.** A Parisienne artist, Greca came to Skopelos decades ago on a UNESCO project to help children. Ever since, she has run her crêperie for the love of it, offering delicious crêpes (800-1200dr) and her rare *joie de vivre* (open daily 6pm-midnight; also for breakfast in summer). The **Kimata** (tel. 22 381), at the far left of the waterfront, offers traditional Greek fare. A steep 2000dr will buy a delicious meal of bread, fish, and fish soup.

■ Around Skopelos Island

Mt. Palouki, which faces the town across the water, conceals three **monasteries.** Two paved roads leave the town from the bus depot on the right end of the waterfront. To get to the monasteries, follow the left road, which circles the harbor, ascends the mountain, and becomes a dirt road 600m past the Hotel Aegean. At the next fork, two signs will point the way to the monasteries (30min. by foot from town). **Evangelismos,** clinging to the rocks across from Skopelos Town, hails from the 18th century, but its enormous gold-plated altar screen from Constantinople is 400 years older. Take the left-hand fork up the hot and winding mountain road (a 45-min. walk). Start early in the morning before the heat and bugs intensify. If you are a dedicated monastophile or a masochistic hiker, descend back to the fork and climb to the **Monastery of Metamorphosis,** standing amid pines on a breezy knoll. The little chapel, set in a flowery courtyard, dates from the 16th century (a 1½-hr. walk from the fork). **Prodromou** is visible from Metamorphosis, on the next ridge. Once a monastery, this refuge is now a cloister dedicated to St. John the Baptist and inhabited by nuns (a 2-hr. walk from the fork).

Beaches line the coast south of Skopelos up to Loutraki. The main one, **Staphylos Beach,** is long, sandy, and crowded. Archaeologists discovered the tomb of the ancient Cretan general Staphylos on a hillside near here, as well as a gold-plated sword dating from the 15th century BCE (now in the Volos museum). A better option is **Velanio Beach,** accessible by the ridge at the east edge of Staphylos. Advertised as the only legal **nude beach** on Skopelos, it is considerably less crowded and less cluttered with plastic pails and their screaming, toddling owners. Farther along the paved road is **Agnotas,** a pleasant harbor perfect for a seaside picnic.

For a superb hike, take the bus to Glossa and walk the dirt track across the island to the **Monastery of Agios Ioannis,** clinging to a boulder above the ocean. (Take the main road east from Glossa and turn left on the first dirt road to Steki Taverna; after that it's clear sailing.) At the road's end a path drops to the sea, and stone steps, cut in the escarpment, lead up to the monastery. There is a cistern of potable water in the rock. Allow at least four hours for a roundtrip visit to Agios Ioannis, and bring at least a liter of water per person. Most of the road is navigable by motorbike.

ALONISSOS ΑΛΟΝΝΗΣΟΣ

Alonissos is the most isolated and, with only 1700 inhabitants, the least populated of the Sporades. Its story is also one of the sadder in the tumultuous post-war history of Greece. In 1950, Alonissos' once-lucrative vineyards were annihilated, and much of Alonissos' male population was forced to take up construction work in Athens. By 1965, just as the island had recovered some prosperity through farming and fishing, an earthquake struck, shaking down the harbor of Patitiri and the capital town of Alonissos on the hill above. The dictatorship then began a housing development in the port town of Patitiri and forced all but nine Alonissians to leave their town.

As a result of this devastation, Alonissos lacks polished beauty, but it is one of the friendlier and less touristed islands in Greece. The beaches are magnificent, and the mountains maintain a pristine, almost icy, emptiness. If the sedate, unruffled atmosphere here suits you, you may be tempted to stay a while, but come soon—architects and real estate agents are already setting up shop.

■ Patitiri

All boats dock at Patitiri, for all intents and purposes the only town on the island. As your boat glides toward the port, you'll see whitewashed Old Alonissos clutching the slopes of the hill. Patitiri, a city of concrete buildings and interchangeable restaurants, is neither the best nor the subtlest introduction to Alonissos. Unassuming during most of the year, Patitiri attracts the usual jumble of island-hoppers in summer, as well as an assortment of travelers using this city as a home base.

Orientation and Practical Information From the docks, there are two main parallel streets running inland, **Pelasgon** on the left and **Ikion Dolophon** on the right. On the left half of the stretch of waterfront between them, you'll find **Alonissas Travel** (tel. 65 188; fax 65 511), which can help find rooms, **exchange currency,** book excursions, and buy ferry tickets. **Ferries** come from Athens via Agios Konstantinos (5½hr., 3850dr) and Volos (5hr., 3180dr). They also travel here frequently from Skiathos (2hr., 1500dr); Skopelos (30min., 950dr); Kimi (2 per week, 3hr., 3780dr); and Thessaloniki (1 per week, 5730dr). To the right is **Ikos Travel,** where amiable, English-speaking Mr. and Mrs. Athamassiou provide similar services, in addition to handling the Flying Dolphin tickets. **Flying Dolphins** leave for Agios Konstantinos (3 per day, 2¾hr., 7415dr); Skiathos (6 per day, 1¼hr., 2350dr); Thessaloniki (1 per day, 4hr., 11,200dr); and less frequently for Skyros and Kimi. **Taxis** wait farther to the right (tel. 65 573, -425), and are available 24 hours in high season. Going up Pelagson, follow the "bakery" sign to your right to reach the English-speaking **police** (24hr.) and the red sign of the **laundromat.**

Going up Ikion Dolophon about 30m, the **National Bank** (tel. 65 477) is to the left (open Mon.-Thurs. 8am-2pm, Fri. 8am-1:30pm). The **pharmacy** (tel. 65 540) is farther up the street to the left (open daily 8:30am-2pm and 5-8pm) and the **post office** (tel. 65 560) is farther still to the right (open Mon.-Fri. 7:30am-2pm). Continuing, **Rent-a-Bike** (tel. 65 731) is on the left, and offers a wide selection of motorcycles (4000-6500dr per day in high season). The **hospital** (tel. 65 208) is even further up; the last major facility on the road. **Postal code:** 37005. **Telephone code:** 0424.

Accommodations Prices are negotiable and vary, according to season, from 1000 to 5000dr per person. The **Office of "Rooms to Let"** (tel. 65 577), in a brown, paper shack in the center of the waterfront, can help find digs for the night (open daily 9am-10pm). Also look for signs advertising rooms on the two inland streets perpendicular to the waterfront. **Dimakis Pension** (tel. 65 294) is 20m up Pelagson Ave.; inquire at Boutique Mary. (Singles and doubles with bath 6500dr.) **Café Pleiades** (tel. 65 235), uphill from the bakery near the police, rents rooms, cleaned daily, with bath and views of the village and the harbor. (Singles and doubles 8000dr. Guests are entitled to a 10% discount on breakfast at the café.) For camping, head to **Camping Rocks** (tel. 65 410), on Pelagson, a partially uphill, 1km hike following the signs. (1500dr per person with tent.) The disco stops blaring at 3:30am.

Food and Entertainment Just inland at the corner, you can find somewhat cheap prices at the unpretentious **Flesvos** (tel. 65 307), where a plate of spaghetti costs 900dr (open daily 8am-11pm). But if you must have a more expensive, waterfront view, then nothing will beat the **Argo** (tel. 65 141; fax 65 161). Saunter down to the far right, well past Ikion Dolophon, and follow the short footpath up to the Argo, perched atop the cliff face, where you can munch your grilled octopus (1400dr) while listening to Greek music. Alternatively, take the downward-looking branch of the footpath, debarking out onto the rocky beach, bring some bread and feta, and the same romance will cost less than half as much as Argo.

After dinner, double back onto the third branch of the footpath to reach the happening **Pub Nephali,** where locals and travelers alike dance and drink to the same commanding view of the sea. Upon request, the well schooled barkeep Yiannis will mix the club specialty, a *nephali*. On the left end of the waterfront, **Pub Dennis** provides a vaguely tropical atmosphere, with brightly colored furnishings, advertisements for exotic drinks, and an interior heavy on the bamboo. Just next door, **Pub En-Plo** aims for a less mellow variety of cool, playing recent Western music in a dark bar with room for dancing. All pubs offer beers for roughly 600dr, cocktails for 1200dr, and serve a variety of desserts. You might also dance the night away at **Disco 4x4,** just up Pelagson, perhaps most notable for a colorful array of weekend contests and games (beer 1000dr, cocktails 1500dr).

THE OLD TOWN (CHORA)

Set high on the hill to ward off pirate attacks, this rebuilt Chora (Old Town) stands out amid the craggy rocks. Exploring the little byways of the town is like discovering the ruins of a castle, as nearly every direction offers old stone buildings commanding a fabulous view of the bay, the mountains, and the city below. The town's **Christ Church,** run by Papa Gregorias, village priest and local legend, dates back to the 12th century. The island's only **bus** runs between Chora and Patitiri every hour from 9am-3pm and 7-11pm in summer (10min., 200dr). A schedule is posted on the sidewalk in front of Ikos Travel, where the bus picks up sojourners. A **taxi** will give up to four people a ride for roughly 2000dr roundtrip. A walk to the town, however, affords as glorious a view as the town itself. Start on Pelasgon and follow the main road uphill. At forks, either follow signs to Chora or take the uphill choice. **Maps** (500dr) can help. Bring at least a liter of water per person with you—the parching walk from Patitiri takes roughly one hour. On its hill, the town is quiet, breezy, and cool. The almond sweets at **Kaphereas** may be the best on the island.

■ Around Alonissos Island

Only the south end of the island is inhabited, leaving the mountainous central and northern sections cloaked by pristine pine forests. Since the island's roads are unpaved and there is little public transportation, your own two feet are the best means of transportation and exploration on Alonissos. The dirt roads are passable by motorbike as far north as Diasello, about three-fourths of the way to the north tip. The tourist agencies sell good maps (500dr).

A 30-minute downhill walk south leads to any of four beaches—**Marapouda, Vithizma, Megalo Mourta,** or **Mikro Mourta,** sheltered beneath steep pine-clad slopes on the tip of the island. Alternatively, take an **excursion boat** from Patitiri (boats leave in the morning as they fill, 1000dr roundtrip). In the other direction *caiques* (800dr) bring you up the coast to **Milia** and **Chrisinokastro**—considered by some to be the outstanding beaches of Alonissos—and also to **Xabkinokastro.** Here the acropolis of Alonissos, then called "Ikos," has been inundated by the sea. Wavy shards discovered on Alonissos are marked *Ikion*, "product of Ikos." For an additional several hundred *drachmae,* you can continue to **Steni Vala** or **Kalamakia,** or farther still to **Agios Dimitrios,** a long, sweeping, semi-circular beach.

A 7000dr full-day tour or a 3000-4000dr charter boat visits the various **neighboring islands. Gioura** was where the **cyclops Polyphemos** had his *kamaki* pad until he was so rudely interrupted by Odysseus and his crew. Several islands claim this distinction, but Gioura, with its large cavern (temporarily closed) complete with thousands of stalagmites, best fits the Homeric description. However, as we all know, plagiarist-Homer just wrote it all down. Gioura is also home to herds of brown **goats,** with black crosses covering their spines and shoulderblades, which have been a protected species in the national park of Gioura since 1930.

SKYROS ΣΚΥΡΟΣ

Rolling purple hills nibbled by goats, groves of fragrant pines, sandy beaches, and gnarled cliffs form the spectacular backdrop for daily life on Skyros. The island's idiosyncratic culture remains strong; throughout the entanglement of sidestreets, women embroider and weave rugs while men fashion sandals, ceramics, and intricately hand-carved wooden furniture. By far the quietest island of the Sporades, Skyros is the largest and most isolated as well.

■ Skyros Town

Crowned by a Venetian castle, Skyros Town spills down from this rocky summit away from the sea. The town's off beat architectural layout is the result of several pirate invasions. As a safety measure, houses were built on an inland cliffside. As you approach by bus, there is no sign of the town until you actually enter it. Skyros

SKYROS

Town's steep and narrow paths make for a *de facto* ban on cars. What confounded pirates then may confuse you now; get clear directions to wherever you're going.

ORIENTATION AND PRACTICAL INFORMATION

Boats to Skyros dock at quiet **Linaria,** where a bus for Skyros Town, and perhaps one for Molos (on the beach) will be waiting (180dr). Ask the drivers their destinations, as buses may be marked somewhat counterintuitively (e.g., "Topikon" (The Place), for the town and "Skyros" for the beach). A **taxi** ride to Skyros runs 1500dr. If you come in by plane, taxis are available at the airport. The bus drops off just outside this maze-like town. Continue along the bus's aborted path to the town's **central square** and you'll be on the main drag, **Agoras Street.** Again, like the town, this strip of restaurants, travel agencies, and tourist shops is completely hidden. Follow Agoras to its end on the opposite side of town and you will arrive at an **open square,** overlooking Molos and the sea, in the center of which stands the bronze statue of the uncharacteristically nude English poet Rupert Brooke. From this square a path leads down to Molos. Once downhill, the road leads to a little church. Turn right and you'll reach Molos Beach. Turn left and you'll have a long inland walk to several hotels. Ask for directions; Agoras St. twists and winds confusingly.

Police: (tel. 91 274). Follow the street across from Skyros Travel to the end, then take a right. It's the white building with light blue gates and trim.

Budget Travel Offices: Skyros Travel (tel. 91 123, -600), on Agoras St., is the agent for **Flying Dolphins** and **Olympic Airways.** Organizes boat trips to the south (6000dr) and bus trips (600-1000dr); helps with accommodations and sells quality island maps (400dr). Open daily 9:15am-2:15pm and 6:30-11pm. A few steps downhill on Agoras, the **Flying Dolphin Office** (tel. 92 152) has hydrofoil information and maps. Open daily 9am-2pm and 7-11pm.

Banks: National Bank (tel. 91 802), up from the bus stop, on the left before the central square. Open Mon.-Thurs. 8am-2pm, Fri. 8am-1:30pm.

OTE: (tel. 91 599). From the bus stop, turn around and walk back out of town—it stands 50m on the right. Open Mon.-Fri. 7:30am-1pm and 1:30-2:30pm.

Flights: (tel. 91 660), 10km from Skyros Town on the northern tip of the island; accessible by foot or taxi. One flight daily to Athens (45min., 15,000dr).

Buses: From Skyros Town to Linaria (6 per day, 10min., 250dr); Molos (6 per day, 5min., 200dr); and back. Check Skyros Travel for posted schedule.

Ferries: To Skyros, travel by bus from Athens to Kimi on Evia (2 per day, 3½hr., 2600dr). June 15-Sept. 15 ferries from Kimi's port area, Paralia Kimi, travel twice per day to Skyros (2hr., 1870dr). There is no ferry service to the other Sporades.

Flying Dolphins: To: Alonissos (7 per day, 1¼hr., 7327dr); Skopelos (7 per day, 30min., 7327dr); Skiathos (7 per week, 1¼hr., 7633dr); Volos (2 per week, 6hr., 12,318dr); Kimi (1 per week, 45min., 4134dr); Marmaris (3 per week, 5½hr., 8514dr); and Thessaloniki (2 per week, 6hr., 13,794dr).

Taxis: (tel. 91 666). Queue at central square, not to be confused with Rupert's square, which is at the far edge of town.

Medical Center: (tel. 92 222). Clinic with 2 doctors located at the edge of the village, 400m from the bus stop.

Post Office: (tel. 91 208), first right as you walk from the bus stop to the central square. **Exchanges currency** and cashes traveler's checks. Open Mon.-Fri. 7:30am-2pm. **Postal Code:** 34007.

Telephone Code: 0222.

ACCOMMODATIONS

There are "Rooms to Let" in tiny Linaria. For most of your stay, however, you will probably want to base yourself in Skyros Town because it has more creature comforts. One of the highlights of staying in Skyros is seeing the interior of a Skyrian house. Rooms are embellished with an assortment of family heirlooms—crockery, copperware, dolls, icons, portraits, and hand-carved furniture from all over the world. Initially, only aristocratic families possessed these precious items. By the late

19th century, though, as the upper class moved to Athens and began to sell off their possessions cheaply, members of the lower class began to decorate their homes as well. Reinforced with heavy cross-beams and thatched with local "bamboo," the ceilings of these homes are also artistic masterpieces. Unfortunately, you're not likely to see any of this if you're snatched up by someone whose business is renting rooms; you'll have better luck with the casual offer from a local. Try wandering through the back streets of Skyros Town or along the dirt roads by Molos beach.

Check out the beautiful, marble-floored **rooms** (tel. 91 459) below the National Bank of Greece in Skyros Town. Blooming plants surround the entrance, the lobby is clean and comfortably furnished, and showers are hot and have good water pressure. (Doubles 7000dr.) If your primary goal in visiting Skyros is to soak up the sun, you can stay a bit closer to the beach. At the end of the marble steps leading down from the naked poet statue awaits a house with blue railings and **rooms** (tel. 91 386) with balconies. (Doubles with bath 7500dr.) Next door is a **campground** (tel. 92 458) in a pleasant, if dry, field. There is a restaurant and a minimarket but few other amenities. (1000dr per person with tent.) On the road to the right past the campground, leading to the beach, is **Pension Galini** (tel. 91 379), which offers clean rooms. (Singles 7000dr. Doubles 9000dr.)

FOOD AND SIGHTS

As always, small, half-hidden *tavernas* may offer better deals and better food than their more flashy, better-situated counterparts. **Sisyfos** (tel. 91 505), on Agoras St. 50m past the bus stop, caters to both vegetarians and carnivores (vegetarian stuffed tomatoes 900dr, *moussaka* 990dr). **Kabanera** (tel. 91 240) lies tucked away in the maze of Skyros Town. Walk up Agoras St. until you come upon the first **"fish taverna"** sign and follow it and its successors (*kalamari* 1300dr). For quick, cheap eats, try the *souvlaki-pita/gyro* **stand** in the central square (*gyro* 250dr).

There is also a collection of *tavernas* on the beach, at the end of Molos away from Skyros Town. The very last in the row, **Milos** (tel. 91 378), reputedly has the best lobster with pasta, a specialty of the island. Skyros, like the rest of the Sporades, produces much of the pine resin that flavors *retsina* in the country's larger distilleries; its own brand of kegged *retsina* is among Greece's finest. Particularly good is *Kokkinelli* (rosé)—ask for it *apo to vareli* (from the barrel). The unnamed **sweet shop** (tel. 91 005) along Agoras St. has the makings of a good sugar fix, as well as a Skyrian specialty, *amigdolata* (sweet almond taffy covered in powdered sugar) for 300dr.

A variety of **myths** draw their inspiration from Skyros. Legend has it that the Athenian king **Theseus** met his end when he was unceremoniously dumped off this cliff by Skyros' King Lykomedes, with whom he had hoped to find asylum. The warrior **Achilles** spent much of his youth here. To prevent his enlistment to fight in the Trojan War, his mother dressed him up as a girl. But when Achilles couldn't resist buying a sword from Odysseus, the well worn traveler called his bluff. Skyros was also the home of **Atalanta,** the princess who refused to marry anyone who could not defeat her in a foot-race. Her suitor Melanion (or Hippomenes) slowed her down, winning the race by throwing three golden apples in her path.

Perched atop Skyros Town are the **Monastery of St. George** and the **Castle of Licomidus.** The monastery's 11th-century fresco of St. George is worth a peek. The castle, generally believed to be Venetian, may actually have been a stellar patch-up job on an earlier Byzantine fortification. The reclining marble lion set into the stone wall above the castle's entrance dates from the 4th century BCE, when Athenians taunted Skyrians with this symbol of Attic ascendancy. On the southeast side of the castle peak lie the remains of an aqueduct whose main shaft was once used as a prison. To get there, make the steep hike uphill from anywhere on Agoras St. As you climb to the fortress, you'll be surrounded by dancing doves, leaping lizards, and striking scenery. Do not stop short—you reach the top of the castle after passing through all of the doorways with plaques. The view at the top is spectacular (open March-Aug. daily 7am-10pm, Sept.-Feb. 7:30am-6pm; free).

Take Agoras St. to the tip of town; you'll find a plaza circumscribing the bronze statue of the English poet **Rupert Brooke,** who died of fever here en route to Galli-poli during the disastrous Dardanelles campaign of WWI. The poet's tomb, con-structed near a bay in south Skyros, is the island's only modern claim to fame. On the statue's right side, the **Archaeological Museum** (tel. 91 327) lies down the mar-ble stairs leading to the beach (open Tues.-Sun. 8:30am-3pm; admission 500dr, stu-dents 300dr). Down the steps and to the left of the Brooke statue, the **Faltaits Museum** (tel. 91 232) has a folk art collection. The museum has a superb collection of local embroidery, carved furniture, pottery, costumes, copperware, rare books, and relics from the island's annual carnival. It also runs a **theater** and **music festival** from the last week of July to the last week of August; inquire at the museum or the affiliated shop on Agoras St. (Museum open daily 10am-1pm and 5:30-8pm. Guided tour in English; free, but donations welcome.)

If you are on Skyros 40 days before Easter, you'll witness the **Skyrian Carnival,** a part religious, part folk satire festival. A *geros* (an old man dressed in a goat mask and costume clanging some 80 sheep bells attached to his waist) leads a *korela* (a young man dressed in Skyrian women's clothes but wearing a goat mask) and a *frangos* (a mocking figure dressed as a 17th-century European man with one large bell), on a wild, raucous dance through the town to the Monastery of St. George. The ritual, commemorating a legendary land-use dispute between shepherds and farmers, is unique to Skyros and the occasional adventurous fraternity.

The pleasant beach below the town stretches along the coast through the villages of Magazia and Molos, and continues around the point. Crowded and crawling with children in July and August, it's undeniably convenient—just a 15-minute walk down the stone steps from the Brooke statue. By car or moped, turn left coming into Skyros Town just after the bus stop at the sign for Magazia and Molos. There you'll find multiple water toys (waterskis, paddleboats, sailboards, etc.) for rent. Ten minutes south of the town beach is the local nude beach—ironically named *Tou papa to homa* (The Sands of the Priest)—which is cleaner and less crowded than the town beach, and naturally, has lots more naked people (not including bronze Brooke). The regular public buses which run from Linaria to Skyros Town also stop midway at the crowded **Ormos Mealos** beach.

■ Around Skyros Island

Skyros is roughly 5km wide at its narrowest point, and 35km long, but most of the island is inaccessible. You can explore it by car, motorbike, or by one of the orga-nized bus or boat trips. If you rent a motorbike, a map is essential. Several roads have been paved recently, so travel is now easier and safer. Once home to a com-pany of nymphs, **Nifi Beach,** on the south side of Skyros, is beautiful and deserted, with a natural spring. The rest of the south part of the island is scenically barren, with dirt paths leading to the beaches. The most interesting sites here are accessible only by boat. The sea caves at **Spiliés** were once a pirate grotto, and one of the larger pirate centers in the Aegean was **Despot's Island.** During the Turkish occupation, merchant and war ships used this natural port as a shelter from storms.

The north part of the island, optimistically named *Meroi* (tame), is hilly, covered with pine trees, and scarcely cultivated. Going north from Skyros Town, turn right for the beach at the little white chapel of **Agia Ekaterina.** If you continue straight and take a left on the road to the airport (marked with a highway sign), the road will take you high into the hills, and then dip down to cross a long valley. When you reach the top of the island, you'll come to a crossroad. Straight ahead lie two very pleasant beaches and the **airport.** The road continues around the west side of the island to the beach at **Kalogrias** and then the beautiful **Atsitsa Beach,** where rocks and pines are mirrored in the water. A *taverna* here lets rooms, and there's camp-ing on the beach. The **Atsitsa Center,** a holistic health and fitness joint, operates on the beach, so don't be surprised if mantras and a sense of peace emanate from the sands. Transcendental meditation isn't exactly a part of most Skyrians' lives. Yet.

Saronic Gulf Islands
ΤΑ ΝΗΣΙΑ ΤΟΥ ΣΑΡΩΝΙΚΟΥ

Diverse, captivating landscapes and proximity to Athens have made the Saronic Gulf Islands an enduringly popular destination. Narrow alleys and walkways barely separate houses that lead up to mountainous interiors decorated with ancient temples and tranquil monasteries. Many of the islands' beaches are pebbly, but the surrounding plush green hills make them some of Greece's most scenic swimming spots.

Despite geographic proximity, each island retains its own distinct character. Poros' magnificent lemon grove, Aegina's temple of Aphaia, Spetses' pine-filled forests and Hydra's fashionable waterfront attract countless Athenians seeking weekend getaways. The Saronic Gulf Islands' popularity also makes them among the most expensive in Greece, and freelance camping is illegal.

AEGINA ΑΙΓΙΝΑ

Aegina's whitewashed buildings, narrow streets, horses decorated with brightly-colored tassels, and aqua-hued water seem like they have been produced in a Disney studio. Unfortunately for those seeking solitude, Aegina is an easy daytrip for Athenians; on weekends half the city makes its way there. Try to avoid spending too much time in Aegina town, whose bustle is reminiscent of the traffic in Athens. Instead, you may want to head for the purple and white sands of Agia Marina and Marathon. In recent years even Agia Marina has begun to attract more tourists. Nevertheless, the beaches alone make Aegina worth the trip.

In ancient times, relations between Aegina and Athens were hardly chummy. The little island made up for its size with spunk and initiative, resisting Athenian encroachment. The island produced the first Greek coins—the silver "tortoises," which gained great financial leverage throughout the Greek world—and at pan-Hellenic games, Aegina's sprinters zoomed past the competition. With the onset of the Persian War in 491 BCE, the Aeginetans sided first with Xerxes' army, to the ire of the besieged Athenians. In 480 BCE at Salamis, the greatest of all Greek sea battles, they returned to the Greek side and won the praise of the Delphic Oracle as the swiftest navy on the seas. Island life flourished and Aegina's inhabitants built the magnificent Temple of Aphaia during the next 30 years. But they suffered the misfortunes of having taken the wrong side in the Athenian-Spartan clash and were thoroughly trounced by Athens in 459 BCE. By 431, Athens had displaced Aegina's population with Athenian colonists. Sparta restored the native population to the island in 405 BCE.

To get to Aegina from Athens, take green bus #40 from almost anywhere in Athens and get off at the Public Theater (*Demotikon Theatron*) in Peiraias (30min., 75dr). From there, you can see the pier where ferries leave for Aegina. Alternatively, take the subway (75dr) to the stop at Peiraias and walk the few blocks to the ferry, or from the Athens airport, take the #19 bus directly to Peiraias.

■ Aegina Town

Most likely you will disembark in the port of **Aegina Town,** the central point of departure for buses around the island. For the best beaches you will probably want to head elsewhere. Some ferries go directly to **Agia Marina** (on the opposite coast).

AEGINA

If the ferry drops you off there, walk uphill to the main road, turn left, and hop on the bus to Aegina Town (every 45min. from Agia Marina, 30min., 350dr).

ORIENTATION AND PRACTICAL INFORMATION

There are two main piers on the harbor. Hydrofoils leave from the smaller one, ferries from the larger one around the corner.

Tourist Office: (tel. 22 220), in the town hall. Offers general information about Aegina. Open Mon.-Fri. 8am-2:30pm and 7-9pm, Sat.-Sun. 10am-1pm and 7-9pm.

Tourist Police: (tel. 27 777), 2 blocks up Leonardou Lada St. English spoken. Open daily 8am-10pm.

Port Police: (tel. 22 328), on the pier. Provides updated ferry schedules. English spoken. Open daily 8am-2:30am.

Tourist Agency: Colona Toura (tel. 22 334), on the second floor at the corner of Leonardou Lada St.; decorated with "Tourist Office" signs. Sells maps (500dr) and books. May also help with finding rooms, but prices are better if you deal directly with pension owners. English spoken. Open daily 7am-midnight.

OTE: (tel. 22 599), up Aiakou St. to the right—keep trudging up Aiakou when the street narrows into a walkway; the building has a monstrous rooftop satellite dish. Sells telephone cards. Open Mon.-Fri. 7:30am-3:10pm.

Banks: National Bank (tel. 24 438 or 25 697 or 22 632), on the waterfront to the left of the quay at the corner of Peleos St. Cirrus, Plus, and Visa accepted. Open Mon.-Thurs. 8am-2pm, Fri. 8am-1:30pm.

Buses: (tel. 22 787). Bus schedules change seasonally, but run to Agia Marina (and to Aphaia Temple) beginning at 6:30am, running about every 45min. until 7:45pm (30min., 350dr). They run to Perdia every 1½hr. (20min., 190dr), and with same frequency to Souvala (30min., 250dr).

Ferries: Every hr. from Aegina Town to Peiraias (6am-8pm, 1½hr., 1100dr). Four boats also land at Agia Marina (1½hr., 1000dr). Four boats per day head to Methana (45min., 800dr) and Poros (1½hr., 1100dr). One boat per day to Hydra at 9:30am (2000dr). Spetses same boat as Hydra (2200dr). Tickets sold at **ticket stands** (tel. 28 311, 28 312) near the boat landing. Schedules change.

Flying Dolphin: Ticket stand (tel. 27 462) next to the port police. Sells hydrofoil tickets to Kythera, Nauplion, Peiraias (10 per day, 35min., 3400dr), Poros (2 per day, 40min., 3000dr) via Methana (25min., 2400dr), Ermione (1 per day, 30min., 2800dr), and Porto Heli (1 per day, 45min., 3400dr). Schedules are inconsistent and posted time tables are rarely in English.

English Bookstore: Giotis (tel 23 874). International books and magazines; large selection in English. Open daily 6am-midnight.

Pharmacy: 19 Irioti St. (tel. 25 317), second street inland parallel to the quay. Open Mon., Wed., Fri.-Sat. 7:30am-1:30pm, Tues.-Thurs. 7:30am-1:30pm and 5-8:30pm. Always at least 1 pharmacy open Sun. 8am-11pm by rotation.

Hospital: (tel. 22 251), on Nosokomiou St. above Aegina Town and beyond the OTE. English-speaking doctor available. Open 24hr.

Post Office: (tel. 22 398), to the left of the ferry landing on Ethnegersias Sq. Cashes traveler's checks. Open Mon.-Fri. 7:30am-2pm. **Postal Code:** 18010.

Telephone Code: 0297.

ACCOMMODATIONS

The island fills up fast with family vacationers, so you may have trouble finding a place to stay. The high season norm is 5000dr for singles and 7000dr for doubles. To find rooms, ask at hotels or look for "Rooms to Let" signs. Well priced pensions are sprinkled generously throughout the streets a few blocks inland from the port and tend to have the lowest prices.

Hotel Artemis (tel. 25 195), on Leonardou Lada St., up from the tourist police. Friendly management offers simple, spotless rooms, all with private bath. Some baths are outside of the bedroom itself. Rooms on roof have a spectacular view of

AEGINA

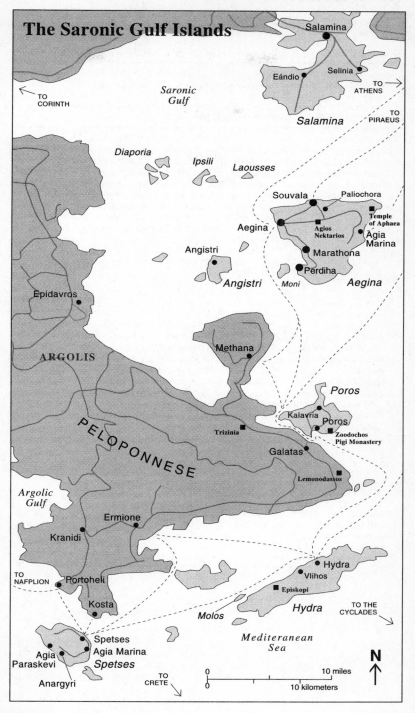

The Saronic Gulf Islands

Saronic Gulf

TO CORINTH →

Salamina

Eándio   Selinia

→ TO ATHENS

TO PIRAEUS

Salamina

Diaporia

Ipsili

Laousses

Souvala   Paliochora

Aegina   Agios Nektarios   Temple of Aphaea

Angistri   Agia Marina

Marathona

Angistri   Perdiha

Moni   *Aegina*

Epidavros

ARGOLIS

Methana

Poros

Kalavria   Poros

Trizinia   Zoodochos Pigi Monastery

PELOPONNESE   Galatas

Lemonodassos

Argolic Gulf

Ermione

Kranidi

Hydra

Vlihos

TO NAFPLION   Portoheli   Episkopi

Kosta   TO THE CYCLADES →

Molos   *Hydra*

Spetses   *Mediteranean Sea*

Agia Paraskevi   Agia Marina   N

Spetses   ↑

Anargyri   TO CRETE ↓

0 ——— 10 miles

0 ——— 10 kilometers

A
E
G
I
N
A

the island. Offers special deal with a motorbike rental place—ask about low prices. Singles 6000dr. Doubles 8000dr. Large quad 12000dr. Breakfast 1200dr.

Hotel Xenon Pavlou (tel. 22 795), behind the church on the far right of the quay. Owned by the same kind-hearted man for 25 years. Offers comfortable rooms with balconies. Singles 7-9000dr. Doubles 10-14000dr.

Mr. Kiriakow Togias, 8 Fidiou St. (tel. 22 710). Clean, simple, fairly spacious double rooms share a bath. One double has a kitchenette and all have access to a fridge. Doubles 4500dr.

FOOD, ENTERTAINMENT, AND SIGHTS

There are many no-frills *tavernas* along P. Irioti St., which runs parallel to the waterfront one block inland along the right side of the harbor. Menus and prices are somewhat standardized (octopus 800dr, *kalamari* 800dr) so stroll and choose. One popular restaurant is **Vostitsano's** (tel. 23 995 or 26 555), with entrees from 1000 to 2000dr. The portions are small, but the *retsina* (a potent Greek wine) is cheap enough that, eventually, meals look twice as large (500dr for 500mL). For tasty sweets after dinner, **Bessis** (tel. 24 587), on the waterfront, offers a delightful array of sweets and pastries (*kataifi* 350dr).

Nightspots are usually open nightly 8pm-3am and drinks average 900-1300dr. **Anissis,** the outdoor **cinema,** up Aiakou St., often shows American films (summers only; admission 1500dr). In winter, you can see a film indoors at **Titina.** Check the signs on the fence near the museum for more information about evening events. At night, Agia Marina falls under a haze of club lights and a dissonant refrain of bar music. Most nightclubs open around 11pm or midnight and stay open until 4, 5, or 6am. **Zorba's The Castle** (tel. 32 275), in Agia Marina, is one of the more popular clubs. Saturday nights bring crowds of up to 2000 clubbers from as far as Athens (open 11pm-dawn). Head past the tourist traps to the **Disco-Club LED,** downhill to the left off the main road, to watch Greek men show off their *mangia* (manliness) as they dance to the lustful strains of *rembetika* music.

Aegina Town's archaeological fame rests tenuously on the last half-column of the **Temple of Apollo.** The 8m-tall Doric column dates to 460 BCE and stands on *Kolona* hill, a short walk out of town to the north. A new archaeological museum has opened at the sight (sight and museum open Tues.-Sat. 8:30am-3pm; admission 500dr, 18 and under free with ID). The underground church of **Faneromeni,** a 15-minute walk inland just south of the town, houses a rare icon of the Virgin Mary. Locals say the night before construction was to begin on a site above Faneromeni, the architect had a vision in which he was instructed to dig instead. The man discovered the church and unearthed the icon (modest dress required; open daily 3-5:30pm; small donation recommended).

■ Around Aegina Island

On the road between Aegina and Agia Marina, in the middle of the island, is the village of **Paleochora,** where the islanders once took refuge from invasions. Paleochora was once "the town of 300 churches." Only 15 of these remain, some with inspiring frescoes. Modest dress is required.

Two km from Agia Marina, on a prominent peak, rest the magnificent 5th- century BCE remains of the **Temple of Aphaia.** Aphaia, daughter of Zeus, was a nymph-huntress worshipped solely on Aegina as a protector of women. Her temple, which is built on the foundation of an earlier 6th-century temple, boasts a rare and spectacular set of standing double-tiered columns (admission 800dr, 18 and under free with ID). The Agia Marina bus stops right at the temple. Determined and fit classicists can bicycle uphill to the temple from Aegina Town (11km, 14km via Souvala). The coastal route is much gentler and affords gorgeous views of rocky shores and other islands. To get to the temple from Agia Marina, walk to the end of town with the water on your right and then straight up Kolokotroni St. until it becomes a wooded trail—this is the footpath to the Temple of Aphaia. At night, peacocks roam the quiet hills by the temple (museum and temple sites both open Mon.-Fri. 8:15am-7pm., Sat.-Sun. 8:30am-3pm).

POROS ΠΟΡΟΣ

Only a sliver of water separates the sinewy hills of the mainland from this tiny isle. The approach by boat from the Peloponnese unveils the red-roofed town and the windmill-laden lemon groves that make Poros memorable. A mere three hours from Peiraias, Poros is actually two small, lush islands—Kalavria and Sphaeria—cut by a canal. Its name, meaning "passage," refers to the channel that forms its border.

The arcane Kalavrian League, a seven-city council, met in Poros to ward off hostile naval powers and order the building of the Temple of Poseidon in the sixth century BCE. Three hundred years later, the great orator Demosthenes, who improved his diction by speaking with marbles in his mouth, killed himself beside its columns. Poros was sparsely populated for most of modern history until Greeks arrived from Turkey in the population exchange of the 1920s.

■ Poros Town

Poros Town occupies most of tiny Sphaeria, while woods extend over rugged Kalavria. Less crowded than Aegina, Poros still overflows on the weekends. You can find serenity and spectacular views by climbing the narrow passageways that lead to the top of Poros Town and the hills beyond, away from the crowded waterfront. Recently the town of Poros has engaged in an aggressive campaign to attract "the young adventurous tourist." Not content with just a scuba school, they have built hang-gliding and ultralight facilities for the more thrill seeking visitor.

ORIENTATION AND PRACTICAL INFORMATION

Ferries (3hr., 1650dr) and **flying dolphins** (1hr., 3250dr) leave Peiraias for Poros several times per day. En route, the boats stop in **Methana,** on a volcanic peninsula of the Peloponnese, known since antiquity for its therapeutic springs. In Poros Town, **hydrofoils** dock at the main landing in the center of town, while car ferries dock either there or a dozen blocks to the left (facing inland) on the northwest side of town. The quay is the center of activity, with tourist agencies to the left, restaurants and souvenir shops in the center, and discoes and bars to the far right. The town plans call for a new kiosk by summer 1997 near the flying dolphins dock—complete with touch computer screens in several languages with ready tourist information.

Tourist Police: (tel. 22 462), on Agiou Nikolaou St., 500m to the right of the main ferry landing. Same office as the **regular police** (tel. 22 256). Helps find rooms. Open 24hr.

OTE: 30 Kalomiri, just around the big bend in the waterfront street to left of main landing. Open Mon.-Fri. 7:30am-3:10pm.

Bank: The **National Bank,** 68 Agiou Nikolaou St., 175m right of landing. Open Mon.-Thurs. 8am-2pm, Fri. 8am-1:30pm.

Tourist Agencies: Family Tours, 14 Iroon St. (tel. 22 549 or 24 281; fax 24 480). English-speaking staff. Provides general information, sells maps (300dr), offers **currency exchange,** and finds rooms. Open Mon.-Fri. 9am-10:30pm. **Lela Tour** (tel. 24 439 or 24 780) offers showers for 500dr. Open daily 8am-10pm.

Ferries: To Peiraias (5 per day, 3hr., 1650dr) stopping in Methana (45min., 800dr) and Aegina (1½hr., 900dr). Ferries also run to Spetses (2 per day, 2½hr., 1500dr). Small boat ferries to the far right of the quay go to the mainland (Galatas) every 10min. (daily 8am-8pm, 80dr). Inquire at the **port authority** (tel. 22 274), 2 doors down to right of post office. Offers updated and complete ferry schedules. Open 24hr. Tickets bought across from ferry when it docks.

POROS

Flying Dolphin: (tel. 23 423). To Peiraias (10 per day, 1½hr., 3250dr), Hydra (8 per day, 30min., 1250dr), and Spetses (6 per day, 1½hr., 1970dr). Office open daily 6:30am-10:30pm.

Bike/Moped Rental: Stelios's (tel. 23 026) and **Kosta's** (tel. 23 565) are on the waterfront to the left of main landing. Both open daily 9am-9pm.

English Bookstore: (tel. 25 205), along the waterfront near George's Café. Sells books and magazines in English and Spanish. Open daily 8:30am-midnight.

Laundromats: Suzi's Launderette Service, to right of the OTE (facing inland). Wash and dry 1800dr. Drop-off only; 1-day service. Open daily 9am-2pm.

Pharmacy: (tel. 24 793 or 22 241), in the open plaza on Iroon Square. 10m to the left of the post office. Open Mon.-Sat. 8am-10pm.

Post Office: (tel. 22 275; fax 23 451), occupies the first square to the right along the water. Open Mon.-Fri. 7:30am-2pm. **Postal Code:** 18020.

Telephone Code: 0298.

ACCOMMODATIONS

Most of the low-priced pensions and rooms for rent in Poros are clean, but private baths and singles are extremely rare. Travel agencies can often find rooms (singles with bath from 4000dr; doubles with bath from 6000dr). Most of the rooms are a 10-minute walk out of town by Askeli beach. Shop around for prices before agreeing to a room. Many pensions flank the Hotel Latsis, 12 blocks to the left of the main pier. In high season, call ahead to secure weekend accommodations. Rooms offered by **Nikos Douros** (tel. 24 721) are a safe bet. (Doubles 7700dr.) His brother **George Douros** (tel. 24 780), also has rooms with baths. (Singles 5000dr. Doubles 7000dr. Triples 9200dr.) During the week prices come down due to increased vacancies. For a nice room in the center of the waterfront, try the **Seven Brother Hotel** (tel. 23 412). Each room comes with private bath, balcony, and A/C for an additional 1500dr per day. (Singles 4000dr. Doubles 5000dr.)

FOOD AND ENTERTAINMENT

Poros Town has many of the best restaurants in the Saronic Gulf. For reasonably priced seafood and meats, try **Lagoudera** (tel. 22 389), on the wharf (open 8am-midnight; entrees 700-1500dr). In the square to the right of Takis, the atmospheric **Seven Brothers** (tel. 22 446) has large portions of well prepared food (from 900dr) and live music on occasion. The seafood specials (600dr) and the *giouvetse* (oven baked lamb 1500dr) are so good they may even distract you from ogling waiters' renditions of traditional Greek dances (open daily 9am-1pm and 6pm-1am). Another fraternal establishment, **Three Brothers** (tel. 23 972), offers a boisterously Greek atmosphere (entrees 900-2000dr; open daily 7am-midnight). **Zorba's** is conveniently located near the Askeli beach rooms (about 500m up the road to the left of the wharf facing inland). You can snarf down the *moussaka* (1000dr) or the stuffed grape leaves (1000dr) while enjoying their courtyard. **George's Cafe** (tel. 22 508) is located in the center of the quay. It opens at 6am for an early breakfast (1000dr for coffee and bread or pastry). Several **grocery stores** lie far to the right of the main landing; there is also one past Askeli Beach, which sells fresh bread and tasty cheese. Look for the "off-license" signs. You can find delectable goodies a short walk to the left of the harbor. The *baklava* (280dr) at **Spithouris** (tel. 25 844) is a local favorite (open daily 9am-11:30pm). **Vessala** (tel. 25 890) has home-made *kataifi* (300dr) to die for (open daily 9am-midnight).

Diana open-air cinema (tel. 25 204), to the left of Lela Tours, sheds light on a unique aspect of Greek movie culture. Sprawled out in a lawn chair, upon a roof and under the stars, cigarette and beverage in hand, you can view the American and British movies (subtitled in Greek) you missed six months ago (adults 1200dr, children 1000dr). If you're itching to groove, wiggle your tush, dancing "Greek" at **Kavos**, at the far right along the waterfront or **Corali**, a high-tech disco next door. Around the big bend, **Sirocco,** the most popular disco, boasts a wonderful view of the Gulf. Other popular clubs line the waterfront to the right of Iroon Square. The

Ship, Malibu, and the Karnaglis all attract crowds ready to live it up. Way up on a hill overlooking the town below sits the Posidonion (tel. 22 770), a hotel-resort-bar-disco that purportedly will reimburse parties for their taxi fare to the dance club. All nightclubs open around 10pm and go to around 4am. Covers vary irregularly but average 1500dr on the weekends; cocktails range from 1000-1500dr. The festivities of Nautical Week, an island-wide celebration of the sea, commence the first week in July. Events include folk dances and concerts of traditional music.

SIGHTS

In Poros Town itself, the archaeological museum (tel. 23 276), one block before the church along the water, has some interesting inscriptions and photographs of the ruins at Troizen (open Mon.-Sat. 9am-2pm; free).

The main sight is the18th-century Monastery of Zoodochos Pigis (Virgin of the Life-Giving Spring), which is nestled in an overgrown glade 6km from Poros Town. Since as early as 200 BCE, monks have been quaffing the monastery's blessed, cura-tive waters. Inside you'll find a spectacular gold-inlaid altarpiece depicting scenes from the lives of Jesus and the Apostles, as well as St. Barbara and St. Nikolas. Proper dress is required; men wearing shorts and women wearing pants are forbidden to enter. A few skirt-like coverings are available at the door (open daily 8am-4pm). It's a scenic bus ride from the stop next to the main port in town (every 20min. 7am-11pm, 20min., 150dr). Along the route to the monastery is Askeli, a secluded beach.

Unless you're a Greek history maven, the main incentive to visit the knee-deep rubble of the sixth-century BCE Temple of Poseidon is the panoramic view of the gulf. The Athenian statesman Demosthenes took sanctuary from his Macedonian enemies here in 322 BCE. Ignoring the temple's tradition of sanctuary, the Mace-donians gave him only a few moments reprieve to write a farewell letter to his fam-ily. His captors mocked his cowardice as he sat chewing his pen, but the crafty orator died as they waited, having dipped the end of his quill in poison.

■ Around Poros Island

Boats run between the Peloponnese and the harbor of Poros (5min., 70dr). Take the caïque across the channel to Galatas on the Peloponnese for the sunny beaches of Aliki (the nicer but farther of the two) and Plaka, both are quite a distance to the left as you walk along the shore. Aliki is a pleasant bike ride from Galatas town center. Riding east towards Plaka beach, a left on the dirt road 100m after Plaka will get you there. A 10-minute walk from both leads to the enormous lemon grove of Lemono-dassos; you can also take a taxi (5min., 600dr) to the bottom of the grove. Follow signs for another 20 minutes to the Karlassi Taverna for a cool glass of fresh lemon-ade (250dr) and a view of windmills and the 30,000 lemon trees that peer onto the sea. Tents crop up behind Plaka and Aliki Beaches, but camping is officially forbid-den and police are strict. Official camping can be found at Camping Kyrangelo (tel. 24 520), 2km northwest of Galatas. (1000dr per person.)

Most visitors to the island miss the surrounding Peloponnesian countryside and the best cycling routes around, which begin in Galatas going northwest away from the lemon groves. Bicycles can be rented along the quay. If you try Manos Pen-siones (tel. 22 100), about 700m left of the landing, you can count on the owner to bail you out of any kind of cycling tragedy within 20km of his shop (bicycles 1200dr per day, mopeds from 2500dr per day). The terrain is flat and the fields range from cultivated flowers to apricot groves. You won't ever be far from a cold drink, espe-cially if you pedal down the 3km turn-off by the carnation fields of Trizinia, the site of ancient Troizen. Buses run here from Galatas—schedules vary almost daily (call 22 480 for more information). Back on the main road, it's 10km from Galatas to the turn-off for Nauplion. Before the bakery in Kaloni is a sign for the long, tranquil Agios Georgios Beach. Neorion Beach is accessible by boat (150dr), foot, or bike. Take the road from the left of the pier about 3km and turn left at the Neorion sign

HYDRA (IDRA)

over the canal bridge. **Canali Beach** and its equally rocky neighbor lie just to the right of the bridge.

HYDRA (IDRA) ΥΔΡΑ

Hydra at first seems to be merely a snazzy version of the typical Greek port town, with its Neoclassical houses nestled quietly among steep, limestone hills and a bustling harbor. The uneasy knowledge that Hydra is unlike almost anywhere else you've been may come gradually, as the absence of rumbling cars, mopeds, and even bicycles sinks in. On the island you'll find donkeys, wild horses, boats bearing the sign "taxi," and steep roads and steps. The only automobiles are three lonely garbage trucks. Once famous for producing naval generals, Hydra "the well watered" is now the lush island home of many Greek artists, some of whom display their work along the water. Even more peaceful are the backstreets where the only disturbance is the occasional bray of a donkey. Inexpensive boats traverse the waves from Hydra's port to far-off peaceful beaches.

ORIENTATION AND PRACTICAL INFORMATION

Most tourist agencies and accommodations on Hydra are centered around the pleasant but chic waterfront area accentuated by the clock tower. The crescent-shaped main street wraps around the harbor, adjacent to smaller alleys.

Tourist Police: Miaouli St. (tel. 52 205), along the wharf and left after the clock tower. Open 24hr.

Port Police: (tel. 52 279), in the left-hand corner of the harbor. Open 24hr.

Tourist Agencies: Saitis Tours (tel. 52 184), on the quay 200m before the clock tower. Offers a free *Holidays in Hydra* guide. Open in summer daily 9am-9:30pm. **Greek Island Tours** (tel. 53 036), off quay on street before bank. Open daily 9am-1pm and 5-9pm. Sells ferry tickets.

OTE: (tel. 52 199), opposite the tourist police. Open Mon.-Fri. 7:30am-3:10pm.

Banks: National Bank overlooks the harbor between Tompazi St. and Miaouli St. Open Mon.-Thurs. 8am-2pm, Fri. 8am-1:30pm.

Ferries: Ticket office is located up the first alley to the right of the boat landing. Hydra is accessible by daytrips from Poros, Porto Heli, or Spetses. Ferries run once a day to Peiraias on weekdays (Mon.-Fri. 3:50pm) and twice on weekends (Sat. 12:30 and 3:50pm, Sun. 3:45 and 4:50pm). Ferry makes a stop in Poros (1½hrs., 823dr), Methana (2hr., 1248dr), Aegina (3hr., 1290dr), and Piraeus (4hr., 1870dr). Also a ferry to Spetses (11:30am, 1hr., 901dr). From Spetses you can take a small boat to Portoneli.

Flying Dolphins: Ticket office (tel. 53 969), 100m to the left before the clock tower—look for the blue sign. To Poros (7 per day, 30min., 1250dr), Methana (1 per day, 45min., 2440dr), Ermione (7 per day, 30min., 1564dr), and Porto Heli (10 per day, 45min., 1900dr). Open daily 6:30-7am and 8:30am-8pm.

Pharmacy: (tel. 53 260), opposite the Flying Dolphin ticket office. Open Mon.-Sat. 8:30am-1:30pm and 5:30-9:30pm. Call for emergency on Sun.

Hospital: (tel. 53 150 or 53 151), next to the town hall by the wharf. Open 24hr. for emergency care. Specialists come every Saturday morning on rotation basis.

Post Office: (tel. 52 262), in the alley to the left of the Bank of Greece—signs along the quay. Open Mon.-Fri. 7:30am-2pm. **Postal Code:** 18040.

Telephone Code: 0298.

ACCOMMODATIONS

Hydra has the most expensive accommodations in the Saronic Gulf. Singles are practically nonexistent and doubles cost at least 6500dr. Finding a place without reservation on summer weekends can be a near impossibility. **Greek Island Tours** (tel. 24 255 or 24 074), on the waterfront, books rooms on Spetses if Hydra is full. Or, try heading to the right corner of the harbor, down the alley to the left of the Pirate's Bar, to find **Sophia Hotel** (tel. 52 313), on the harbor. The center of the wharf for 62 years, Sophia's is one of the cheaper places in town. Some rooms overlook the busy wharf. The green iron-railed balconies will give the place away. Sophia has only six rooms, so reservations are recommended for weekends. (Open April-October. Singles 5500dr. Doubles 7150dr. Triples 9350dr.) **Pension Othon** (tel. 53 305) is 15 minutes up the street on which Sophia is located. Othon features immaculate doubles and a serene atmosphere. (Doubles 8000dr. Triples 10000dr.)

FOOD AND ENTERTAINMENT

Food prices on Hydra vary widely. *Souvlaki* (250dr) joints coexist alongside more posh establishments. The **Art Café** (tel. 52 236), in the westernmost corner of the harbor, is relatively affordable and serves enormous cheese toast. Ice cream (300dr), sandwiches (400-500dr), and round feta pastry pies stuffed with feta (300dr) are served with aplomb (open daily 7am-1am). **Restaurant Lulu** (tel. 52 018), straight up from the dock on the same road as Sophia's Hotel, is a bargain. Food is served in small but tasty portions (salads 500-900dr, *moussaka* 1000dr, veal dishes 1100dr). **The Garden** (tel. 52 329), up the street from the hydrofoil office, has a wide selection of reasonably priced food (entrees 1000-2800dr). The quiet garden is pleasantly removed from the waterfront (open 8pm-late). Up the street from the OTE, **Anemoni** (tel. 53 136) is a dream for an after-dinner treat of Greek pastries (300-350dr). Or, try the fresh homemade ice cream *(kaimaki)* made of lamb milk (220dr; open daily 7am-1am). **Gitoniko** (tel. 53 615), run by a husband and wife team, prepares fresh, homemade Greek-style food. The menu changes with the season, but they always serve fresh vegetables (800dr) and stuffed pork roll (1100dr), as well as both cheese and spinach pie (700dr each) and eggplant salad (500dr; open daily noon-3pm and 7pm-12:30am).

Hydra's clubs all have overpriced cocktails (1000dr), but die-hard dancers won't want to miss the scene. Most clubs are open nightly 8:30pm-6am. Check out **Karos Music Club** (tel. 52 416) or **Disco Heaven** (up the whitewashed stairs) on the western edge of the harbor for a more modern disco/dance club atmosphere. Lethargic souls sit outside at the **Pirate Bar** (tel. 52 711) on the water and watch the world, clad in sequined bra tops, go by (mixed drinks 1500-1700dr). **Lagoudera** (tel. 52 294) is open all day and offers an amazing view of the outdoor restaurant and bar on the easternmost side overlooking the harbor. The view may make the priciness worth it (entrees 1500-4100dr, *ouzo* 800dr). Greek music fans head to **Saronicos** (tel. 52 389), on the east side of the port. It stays open late into the night and is conducive to crazed Greek dancing on tables and the bar (open Mon.-Thurs. noon-8pm and 9pm-6am, Fri.-Sun. noon-8pm and 9pm-6am).

SIGHTS

Taxes were not levied on Hydra's arid land for most of the Turkish occupation. With few natural resources and a growing refugee population from the Peloponnese, Balkans, and Turkey, Hydra's inhabitants turned to managing other areas' exports, and its merchant princes became shipping magnates. Hydriots grew prosperous by dodging pirates and naval blockades during the late 18th and early 19th centuries and emerged in the 1820s as financial and naval leaders in the revolt against the Turks. **Koundouriotis,** whose house is on a hill to the west of the harbor, was one of the many Hydriot leaders in the War of Independence. To get to his house, walk up the narrow alley to the right of the Pirate Bar, which becomes Lignou St. Take the second alley on your right, turn right and go straight (and up) following the scenic path until you reach a small church in a shady pine grove. Koundouriotis's home is opposite the church. The view of the harbor is superb, but the house itself is usually locked. It may open during high season—check with the tourist police. The houses of **Votsis** and **Economou,** two Hydriots who contributed to the island's naval fame, are closer to the crest of the hill, right on Voulgari St. There are more houses and mansions, mostly locked, but fun to find. The home of Greek Admiral Iakovos Tom-bazis is now an **art school** (tel. 52 291) for Greek students (one block up from the harbor's right corner) that has exhibits (only open July-Aug.).

The **Ecclesiastical Church,** built in 1806, bears the clock tower that dominates the wharf. Its peaceful courtyard seems completely removed from the bustling waterfront, and the beautiful icons—lots of gold, silver, and dark wood—make this chapel a calming stopping place (150dr donation requested—free postcard in return). Also interesting are the frescoes at the **Church of St. John** in the Platia Kam-ina. (Modest dress required at both churches.) East of the harbor, set off by winding, anchor-flanked stairs, is the **Pilot School** of the Greek Merchant Marine, with paint-ings, models, and class pictures circa 1930 (open daily, variably 8am-10pm; free).

A short hike (1hr.) trudges up A. Miaouli St. from the waterfront (the road takes you out of town) uphill to the **monastery** of Prophitis Ilias and, on a lower peak overlooking the harbor, the **nunnery** of Efpraxia. While the nuns at Efpraxia do beautiful embroidery work, Ilias is the prettier of the two and the monk may be will-ing to show you around. (Both open 9am-5pm; modest dress, *bien sûr.*) To return to the harbor, climb down the monastery steps and follow the passageways down through town. Another hike is to **Episkopi,** a deserted monastery an hour's walk west from Ilias, along goat paths through beautiful uninhabited countryside. The Greek word for footpath is *monopati*—useful when asking for directions to return to town. Cut down to the north coast towards the right of the main harbor to get to the beach at **Vlihos,** reachable by a 40-minute walk from town along the coast or a small boat from the harbor (250dr).

These are long, hilly walks; it's best to bring water and leave early in the morning. If you feel too hot to walk up and down Hydra's hills or fight crowds on the water-front, a swim may be the thing to do. On the right of the harbor (facing inland) are three levels of flat rock perfect for sunbathing. Swimming to your right (facing inland) will lead you into purple caves—watch out for children jumping off rocks above. If you want to fit in with other sunbathers you should leave your top at home. The beaches on Hydra are rocky ledges a short walk west from town. When the water is calm, small *caïques* run regularly to pretty **Palamida** and neighboring beaches on the west side. For the munchies you should take food and drink with you; there's no place to buy it nearby. **Mira Mare Beach,** at Mandraki, is easier to reach, either by a beautiful 30-minute walk along the water from the east end of town or by 15-minute boat ride (300dr). This beach is less attractive and dirtier than others and is dominated by a new watersports center. Water taxis are convenient but expensive (1700dr to Vlinos, 1250dr to Mira Mare).

The **Historical Archives Museum of Hydra** (tel. 52 355) is on the western side of the harbor. This newly opened museum houses naval treasures such as tools, wood-carved ship decorations, guns, as well as a large collection of water colors of Hydriot sailing ships. Hydriot ship owners from 1750-1850 took pride in decorating their drawing rooms with these portraits of their own ships. Don't miss the heart of Admiral Andreas Miaovlis, embalmed and preserved in a silver and gold urn (open daily 10am-noon; free).

SPETSES ΣΠΕΤΣΕΣ

Ancient *Pitiusa*, or Pinetree Island, Spetses is a floating pine forest bordered by white and blue houses. The picturesque villages, tile mosaics, and rocky beaches have made the island a playground for wealthy Greeks. A favorite among British tourists, Spetses offers a variety of moods. Its café-,disco-, and tourist-filled water-front supplies excitement, while its quieter interior provides the same serenity that prompted John Fowles to write *The Magus* during his stay here. Spetses was settled just in time to make a significant contribution to the Greek War of Independence of 1821. It was the first island to take part in the revolution, an event commemorated annually by ceremonies held in the Panayia Armata chapel near Agia Marina. Spetses was also home to the fiery heroine Bouboulina, captain of her own ship during the war, who is immortalized in a statue on the waterfront of Spetses Town.

■ Spetses Town

The vast majority of Spetsiots live in Spetses Town, which is centered along the waterfront. Today, Spetses' population of 3500 is composed of locals, tourists (in season), hippies who came and never left, and wealthy Athenians who own vacation homes to the right of the main harbor. Jet-setters also dock their yachts in Spetses' Old Harbor to take advantage of the island's nightlife, proving that Spetses has charms to soothe the savage millionaire as well as the tame backpacker. One important detail—topless sunbathing is illegal on Spetses. Yet, this law is as well heeded as the law requiring helmets when riding mopeds; look around and don't offend.

ORIENTATION AND PRACTICAL INFORMATION

Restaurants and shops form a 2km line on either side of the port. Facing away from the water, the old harbor is a 20-minute walk left of the boat landing.

Port Police: (tel. 72 245), on waterfront 50m left of Remetzo on 2nd floor. Posts ferry and hydrofoil schedules. Open 24hr.

Tourist Agencies: Several around the corner on left side of boat landing. **Pine Island Tours** (tel. 72 314, 72 594), in front of the café on the right. English spoken. Open Easter-Sept. daily 9am-10:30pm. Offers free maps. Kiosks also stock maps (400dr). **Meledon Tourist and Travel Agency** opens daily in summer 9am-9pm; in winter 9-11am. Will return left messages ASAP in winter.

OTE: (tel. 72 199), on the right side of the Star Hotel. Open Mon.-Fri.7:30am-3pm.

Banks: National Bank (tel. 72 286), left of the OTE. Open Mon.-Thurs. 8am-2pm, Fri. 8am-1:30pm. Other banks open Mon.-Fri. 7:30am-2pm.

Ferries: Depart Spetses for Peiraias daily around 3pm, check with the agent (also Wed., Sat. 1:30pm, 4½hr., 2500dr). Two serve Hydra daily (1½hr., 790dr), Poros (2hr., 1400dr), Methana (2½hr., 1420dr), and Aegina (3hr., 1780dr). **Alasia Travel** (tel. 74 098 or 74 130) sells tickets (open 8am-9pm in high season; 10am-noon in off season). **Maledon Tours** (tel. 74 497 or 74 498) also sells tickets (open daily in summer 9am-9pm and winter mornings). Small ferries leave for **Kosta** from the front of **Remetzo's Cafe** (4 per day, 15min., 200dr). In rough weather they leave from the Posseidonion dock or from the old harbor.

Flying Dolphin: Ticket office (tel. 73 141), next to Pine Island Tours. **Hydrofoils** and **catamarans** go to Peiraias (in summer 5-7 per day, in winter 3 per day; 2hr.; 4830dr). They stop in Hydra (1650dr), Poros (1950dr), and Aegina (3500dr).

Bike Rental: Enolkiases (tel. 73 074), 50m to the right of the post office (when facing the post office). Bikes 1000-1500dr per day, scooters 2800dr per day, motorcycles 4000dr per day. Open Easter-Nov. daily 9:30am-1pm and 4-6pm.

Pharmacy: Mrs. Urati (tel. 72 480), at center of port near the boat landing. Open Mon.-Sat. 8:30am-1:30pm and 5:30-10:30pm, Sun. 10am-1:30pm and 6-10pm.

Hospital: (tel. 72 472). Open Mon.-Fri. 8:30am-1:30pm. Call police for doctor. **Emergency:** nurse 73 313, doctor's house 72 590, and his mobile phone 093275990.

Police: (tel. 73 100). Follow signs to the Spetses Museum; 150m before museum. Also houses **tourist police** (73 744) in basement. Supposedly open 24hr.

Post Office: (tel. 72 228), past the port police on the road parallel to waterfront behind Stelios Restaurant. Open Mon.-Fri. 7:30am-2pm. **Postal Code:** 18050. **Telephone Code:** 0298.

ACCOMMODATIONS

Often crowded, Spetses is a relatively expensive island to stay on. Hotels are plentiful and very visible, but the larger ones overflow with tour groups. Look for something smaller, like the rooms offered by travel agencies in town. **Pine Island Travel and Tourism** offers singles for around 5000dr and doubles with bathrooms for 5000-16000dr. On the waterfront to the left of the boat landing (facing inland), **Alasia Travel** (tel. 74 098) has singles (6000dr) and doubles (8000dr) to let (open daily in high season 8am-9:30pm). Next to it is **Meledon Tours** (tel 74 497 or 74 498), which has similar offerings and also sells ferry tickets. **Villa Christina** (tel. 72 218 or 74 228) has comfortable rooms off a flower-filled courtyard. Walk between the newsstand and Pine Island Tours, take the first right and follow it to the Palm Tree Café. Jog left and then right. A narrow walkway faces the church bell tower. Follow this to the top. The walk takes less than 10 minutes, but the manager will pick you up from the ferry if you call ahead. All have private bath shower. (Open April-October. In August, call ahead. Singles 8000dr, 6000dr in low season. Doubles 10000dr. Breakfast 1000dr or get a studio with kitchenette for 1000dr more per person.) **Hotel Dapia** (tel. 73 426 or 73 427) offers simple, small rooms centrally located near the harbor. (All with private shower. Doubles 6000dr. Triples 8000dr.)

FOOD AND ENTERTAINMENT

Restaurants, *tavernas,* and cafés abound in Spetses. Stop at **Stelios** (tel. 73 748), along the wharf past Takis, for traditional Greek fare (entrees 1100-2500dr). Owned for 20 years by the same family, specialties include veal with pasta cooked in a ceramic pot (11500dr; open daily March 20-Oct. 1 noon-4pm and 6-11:30pm). **Galera** (tel. 73 488), a bar and restaurant, serves old rock, disco, and quasi American food—the Tennessee Burger with cheese (1300dr) or a jacket potato (900dr). Cocktails (900dr) may help. (Food served until midnight.) A favorite restaurant among almost all Athenian visitors to Spetses is **Patralis Tavern,** which serves scrumptious fish at reasonable prices (fish in lime sauce with tomatoes 1500dr). Their homemade *retsina* is a must (400dr per mL). Catch it early in the season, before the barrels run dry (open Mon.-Fri. 10:30am-1:30pm and 6:30pm-2:30am, Sat.-Sun. 10:30am-3am). Also on the walk towards Patralis is **Spanos** (tel. 22 516), a small bakery selling fresh loaves (140dr) and crispies (like biscotti 750dr per kg) to locals. Come early—they sell out fast (open daily 6am-2pm). **Politis** (tel. 72 248), a coffee and pastry shop on the waterfront before the National Bank, serves full English breakfasts (1200dr) outside on tables by the water. Homemade pastries and biscuits baked by the same family for 36 years may leave you crying, "Sweet Jesus." Delicious *amigdaloto* (3000dr per kg; open daily 7am-midnight). **Argyris**, near the boat dock, has coffee (350dr) and *amigdaloto,* the island's signature almond cookie (2500dr per kg; open in summer 24hr.; daily in winter 6am-midnight). Most restaurants close from 4pm to 6pm, but many groceries and supermarkets are open then.

Spetses gathers for drinks at the **Socrates** bar (beers 500dr, drinks 900dr). Most bars open at 9pm. Devoted seekers of nightlife continue on to other bars in the new harbor, or pulsating **Club Fever** (tel. 73 718), which hosts popular all-you-can-drink orgies (3000dr at the door) every Wednesday, Friday, and Sunday night beginning at 11pm—all the beer, wine, *ouzo,* and Metaxa you can drink. Trendy young Athenians can be found in bars along the more sophisticated Old Harbor *(Palio Limani).* Try **Mouraio, Bracera,** or **Naos.** For traditional Greek music, head to **Atopia** (tel. 74 474), directly across the street from Patralis restaurant.

For a mellow evening, one of Spetses' two open-air cinemas may suit your fancy. **Ciné Marina,** near the mansion of Laskarina Bouboulina, often shows English language films (1500dr), as does **Ciné Titania** (tel. 72 090 to reserve), both near Bouboulina (1000dr). Marina is covered when it rains; Titania is always covered. Both have two showings nightly: one at 9pm, the other at 11pm.

SIGHTS

The **Anargyrios and Korgialenios College** (high school) is a 25-minute walk from town, to the right (facing inland), past the Posseidonian Hotel. John Fowles taught here from 1951-2 and immortalized both the institution and the island in his novel

The Magus (ask the guard if you can enter through the gate.) For a beautiful walk, especially at dusk, go left past Takis and continue along the stone path between the water and the high, whitewashed stone walls to the old harbor, which is quieter and has fewer tourist shops than the new port. *Spetsai,* by Andrew Thomas, is a helpful book that includes the island's history and walk suggestions.

A walk into the heart of the village takes you to the crumbling late 19th-century **mansion of Hadjiyanni Mexi,** Spetses' first governor. The imposing structure affords a great view of the island and houses coins, costumes, mastheads, folk art, religious artifacts and a casket containing the remains of Bouboulina. The building itself is worth seeing, with an old island fireplace, stained glass windows, and carved wooden doors. Follow signs to get there and beware of speeding mopeds (open Tues.-Sun. 8:30am-3pm; free). The **House of Lascarina Bouboulina** (tel. 72416) is next to the park near the Dapia. Mme. Bouboulina was a ship's captain in the Greek War of Independence. Her heroic exploits are celebrated on Spetses with a mock naval battle in which a small boat is blown up the first Saturday after September 8th (admission 700dr, 300dr children). The **monastery of Agios Nikolas** stands opposite a square of traditional Spetsiot mosaics in the Old Harbor. Among its treasures is a plaque commemorating Napoleon's nephew, who was pickled in a barrel of rum stored in a monastic cell at Agios Nikolas from 1827-32. You may want to rent a moped or car to get to the monastery—the walk is arduous. The nuns give free samples of their homemade yogurt. Modest dress is required.

The water in Spetses is clean and clear, but **Paradise** beach and some of the town beaches are crowded and litter-strewn. Check the town beaches on the waterfront heading towards Old Harbor; they are cleaner early in the season. Be careful of the **sea urchins** which plague Spetses' beaches and prick bare feet. The road past the tourist police leads to the island's main summit. The bumpy track takes you several kilometers into the hills through sweet-smelling pines to the panorama of the Peloponnese and its train of islands. There's a chapel on the way with picnic tables. From here, trails of similar length descend to the beaches of **Vrelos, Anargyri,** and **Agriopetres.** Vrelos is the nicest, with nude sunbathing to boot. A good plan is to take the bus to Anargyri (1-3 times per day from the bus stop by the town beach), or take the bus to Kaiki beach (a.k.a. College beach), Blueberry Hill Cove, and the Vrelos beach coves. This bus leaves from the Posseidonion Hotel (to the right of the New Harbor, behind the Bouboulina statue; every hr. 9:30am-1:30am; admission 240dr). It stops just before Zegoria beach, which has a *taverna*—the coves have no facilities. **Kaiki Beach,** opposite the Anargyrios and Korgialenios College of John Fowles fame, has a bar, a restaurant, and plenty of **watersports.** If you buy a return ticket keep your stub. **Motorboats** leave the harbor as soon as they are full (10am-noon, returning from the beaches at about 4pm, 1000dr). **Sea taxis** cost a fortune and only help save money for groups of eight or more (8000dr for Anargyri). Since only registered cars are allowed on the island, land transportation is provided by horse-drawn carriages, which usually won't go past Kastelli Beach or Agia Marina.

CYPRUS ΚΥΠΡΟΣ

US$1 = C£0.52	C£1 = US$1.93
CDN$1 = C£0.38	C£1 = CDN$2.65
UK£1 = C£0.81	C£1 = UK£1.24
IR£1 = C£0.82	C£1 = IR£1.20
AUS$1 = C£0.41	C£1 = AUS$2.49
NZ$1 = C£0.34	C£1 = NZ$2.82
SAR1 = C£0.12	C£1 = SAR8.69
100dr = C£.081	C£1 = 123.76dr
TL10,000 = C£0.23	C£1 = TL43,162

> Note: throughout this section, Cyprus pounds will be indicated by £.

ESSENTIALS

The Republic of Cyprus' history is preserved in the tangible remains of its complex past. History echoes in Aphrodite's birthplace; ancient temples, Roman mosaics, remote monasteries, crusader castles, magnificent mosques, and the Green Line resound with subtle pride. The land abounds in natural beauty from the sandy beaches of Agia Napa to the Kyrenia range to the cool, quasi-Alpine air of Platres. The island caters to diverse travelers and remains generally clean, pleasant, and grime-free even in its most industrial cities. The people of Cyprus are friendly and hospitable, even more so in recent years, when tourism, especially among Brits and Arabs, has become one of the island's more important industries. Almost all residents speak English, and most signs are in both English and Greek. Cyprus is more expensive than Greece, but does have some budget options. Please be aware that because of the whopping number of streets named "Leoforos Archbishop Makarios III" in Cyprus, we (like the Cypriots) have abbreviated it to "Makarios Ave."

■ Getting There

The third largest island in the Mediterranean after Sicily and Sardinia, Cyprus lies 64km from Turkey, 160km from Israel and Lebanon, and 480km from the nearest Greek island. The Republic of Cyprus is accessible by airplane or boat from Europe and the Middle East. Seemingly thousands of boat agencies connect Limassol to almost every imaginable place. Among your possible destinations/points of origin are Larnaka; Limassol; Rhodes; Peiraias; Iraklion, Crete; Haifa, Israel; and Port Said, Egypt. To reach the north, take a ferry from Mersin, Alanya, or Taşucu, Turkey.

Salamis Tours, 28th Octovriou Ave., P.O. Box 531, Limassol (tel. (05) 355555). In Peirais, inquire at **Afroessa Lines S.A.,** 1 Charilaou Trikoupi St. (tel. 418 3777); in Rhodes, **Red Sea Travel,** 11-13 Amerikis St. (tel. 22 460). Travel to Peirais and the Greek Islands. **Louis Shipping Ltd.,** 63B Gladstone St., Limassol (tel. (05) 363161). In Peirais, inquire at 11 Mavrokorstatou (tel. 429 1423, -4; fax 429 1445). To Peirais and the islands. **Vergina Lines,** 65A Gladstone St., Acropolis Center, Limassol (tel. (05) 343978). In Peirais, inquire at **Stability Line,** 11 Sachtouri St. (tel. 413 2392).

For a list of available tour agencies, ask for the Cyprus Tourist Organization's *Information Paper Unit 2*, at tourist offices in Nicosia, Larnaka, Limassol, and Paphos.

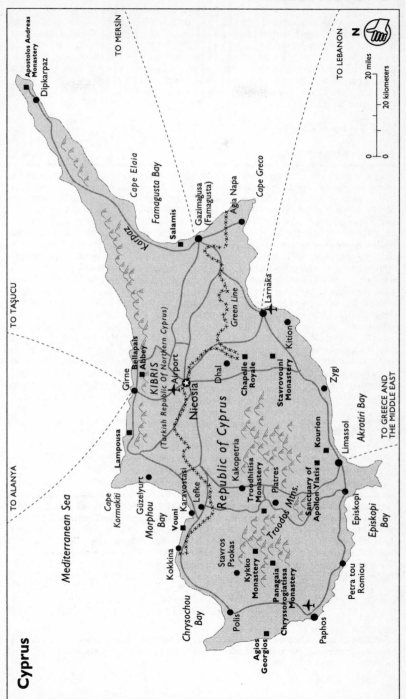

Cyprus

By air, Cyprus is accessible from Greece and other European and Middle Eastern countries on **Olympic Airlines** (U.S. tel. (800) 223-1226), **Egypt Air** (U.S. tel. (800) 334-6787), **Cyprus Airways** (U.S. tel. (212) 714-2310), and other commercial lines. Student fare from either Olympic (ages 12-28) or Cyprus Airways (ages 12-24) is US$190 roundtrip from Athens to Larnaka and back again; you will need to show a letter from your university or an ISIC. Otherwise, airfare from Athens to Cyprus is cheaper if purchased roundtrip, as one-way tickets are only available in business class. International airports are in Larnaka and Paphos.

■ Once There

TRANSPORTATION

A reliable highway system serves much of Cyprus, but use caution on the winding mountain roads. Cars drive on the left side of the road in the south and on the right in the north. Turks, however, may impound cars brought from the south. There are cars with steering wheels on the left and the right on both sides of the island. The south also has several British rotaries, which are particularly intimidating for American drivers. Transportation is widely nonexistent after 7pm. *Service* (shared) **taxis** run regularly Monday through Friday (until evening) between Limassol, Paphos, Larnaka, and Nicosia. *Service* taxis, most of which are converted Mercedes limousines, will pick you up and drop you off wherever you want in the city (£1.50-2 between the 4 major cities). *Service* taxis cost twice as much as the buses and are sometimes a harrowing ride, but their speed and frequency make them a good deal. If possible, choose the front passenger seat because drivers sometimes cram many people in the back. Hitching is not common, and neither locals nor tourists give rides.

Buses to the **Troodos Mountains** travel once daily from both Nicosia and Limassol. There is no direct bus connection from Paphos to Nicosia or Larnaka; you must pass through Limassol. Bus service throughout Cyprus is less frequent in the winter. There is one island-wide **bus schedule** available at tourist offices with all information and prices for buses and service and private taxis. It is accurate and well worth picking up—you're clearly not in Greece anymore. Cypriot law requires seatbelts in front seats. All Cypriot rental cars have manual transmission, and rates are standardized; the cheapest small cars should cost no more than £17 per day, small motorbikes £5, and larger motorcycles £7-8. To drive in Cyprus you need an international driver's license, or a national driver's license from your home country. You can obtain a temporary Cypriot driver's license, good for 6 months, from district police stations if you provide photographs and £1. Even though most dealers rent 50cc two-seaters, if two adults are riding a small bike, the police may stop and fine you.

TOURIST ORGANIZATIONS

Cyprus' extremely helpful and efficient **tourist offices** provide invaluable information. There are offices in Limassol, Nicosia, Larnaka, Paphos, Agia Napa, and Platres. The main office is the **Cyprus Tourism Organization,** P.O. Box 4535, 19 Limassol Ave., Nicosia CY 1390 (tel. (2) 337715); in the **U.S.,** 13 E. 40th St., New York, NY 10016 (tel. (212) 683-5280). In general, head for the C.T.O. offices immediately after you arrive in each town for excellent free maps, as well as information about buses, museums, and cultural activities, and a terrific publication called *The Cyprus Traveller's Handbook* (free). Tourist officials generally speak English, Greek, German, and French, among other languages. In the north, there are tourist offices in Famagusta, Girne, and Nicosia. The office in Nicosia is located just past the Ledra Palace.

GOVERNMENT

The government of the Republic of Cyprus is based on the Constitution of 1960 that was devised by conservative governments in London, Athens, and Ankara. The constitution was never intended to be a permanent document and it was not truly designed for the Cypriot people. Rather, it was meant as a compromise among the British, Greek, and Turkish governments over control of the island. Now in use for 35 years, the document's curious beginnings created a government that remains deeply divided between its two communities. For example, the president is always a Greek-Cypriot and the vice-president a Turkish-Cypriot. They govern their respective municipalities and are elected by separate elections, but both retain the right of veto. Civil service, police, and parliament posts were divided along a controversial 70:30 split meant to mirror the population. For a bill to pass in the 100-member parliament, it not only requires an overall majority, but also a majority within both communities. So, theoretically, 16 Turkish-Cypriot representatives could oppose a measure that was favored by the remainder and the bill would fail. This dysfunctional government, in case you were wondering, meets in Geneva.

Kıbrıs, the Turkish Republic of Northern Cyprus (TRNC), came into existence on November 15, 1983. The president is Rauf Denktaş, and his picture, like Atatürk's, graces the walls of many hotels and restaurants. Northern Cyprus has a parliamentary democracy based on the British system. The official language is Turkish and the official currency is the Turkish lira. The roughly 150,000 residents of Northern Cyprus are mostly Turkish Cypriot, but 40,000 of these are Turks who emigrated from the mainland. Several hundred British and German expatriates also reside in the north, but their presence is most noticeable during the summer, when a lot of Brits who own holiday homes come and stay for the season. Roughly half the population speaks English, and many older residents speak Greek.

■ Keeping In Touch

Post offices are open Monday through Friday from 7:30am to 1:30pm (1pm in the summer). Some have afternoon hours from 3:30-5:30pm (summer 4-6pm). *Poste Restante* is available only in Nicosia, Larnaka, Paphos, and Limassol (10¢ per piece). When sending a letter from the south, make sure your envelope or card is affixed with the 1¢ **refugee stamp**—mail will go nowhere without it.

Southern Cyprus has a fairly good **telephone company (CYTA).** Direct overseas calls can be made from nearly all public phones if you have enough change. For international calls, **telecards,** sold at banks and kiosks, are more convenient, they work in special phones and come in denominations of £2, 3, 5, and 10. To make a collect call, it is cheapest to directly dial an international operator in the destination country: you are charged only one unit. Otherwise, you must go to a CYTA office or a private phone, which in hotels may carry a 10% surcharge.

The **country codes** from the South and North are: **Australia** 0061, **Canada** 001, **Ireland** 00353, **New Zealand** 0064, **South Africa** 0027, **U.K.** 0044, and **U.S.** 001. For example, to call the U.S. from Cyprus, dial 001 before the number. To call the South from the U.S., dial 011, then 357, followed by the area code (without the zero) and finally the local number. For information on numbers in the South, dial 192. To reach an **international operator** in the U.S., dial 080-90-000 (MCI), 080-90-010 (AT&T), or 080-90-001 (SPRINT). For the U.K., dial 080-90-044 (BT). International operators are also available in Australia (080-90-061) and Canada (080-90-012). From the South **ambulance, fire,** or **police** dial 199.

■ Accommodations and Food

Cheap, clean hotels are rare. In general, prices for accommodations drop during off season to about 20% less than the rates quoted in this book. Nicosia, Troodos, Paphos, and Larnaka all have **HI youth hostels,** and Stavros tis Psokas has a loosely affiliated **forest station.** Although Cyprus has only a few formal campgrounds, you may sleep on beaches and in forests. Choose your site discreetly and leave it as clean as you found it. Be careful if you camp unofficially; women should be especially wary and never camp alone. In the Troodos area, try staying in the monasteries;

HISTORY

they're free, but you should leave a donation. Because of complaints from hotels, monasteries are starting to accept only Orthodox guests.

Cypriot food is similar to Greek and Middle Eastern cuisine. Try *meze,* a platter of about a dozen appetizers for two to four people, available in either meat or fish varieties. The exact composition varies between restaurants, but it can include olives, tomatoes, tahini, hummus, and small portions of *souvlaki* and octopus. *Kleftiko,* also popular, is lamb roasted in clay ovens over charcoal. Cypriot *kebab* is similar to Greek *souvlaki,* but the sandwich is larger, the meat less greasy, and it includes tomatoes, cucumbers, onions, and parsley. At £1 each, a *kebab* is probably the cheapest meal you can have. *Sheftalia* (ground meat with onions) is also served in pita pockets. At festivals and street fairs, Cypriots enjoy *soujoukko,* strips of jellied nuts dipped in hot grape juice that resemble a rubber hose. Vegetarians might have to subsist on traditional Greek salad, olives, *hallouni* (a type of cheese made only in Cyprus), or hummus and tahini. *Trahana,* a soup made with yogurt and wheat, is absolutely wonderful. *Lokurdas,* a sweet fried dough, is a popular dessert.

■ History

ANCIENT CYPRUS

The remains of round stone dwellings indicate settlement on Cyprus as early as Neolithic times, dating back to roughly 7000 BCE. The first settlers most likely originated from the nearby Syropalestinian coast. Cyprus first achieved local importance at the onset of the **Bronze Age** due to its wealth of copper ore. Linguists are unsure whether *Kypros,* from which the word "copper" is derived, first referred to the island or the metal itself. The Bronze Age witnessed an increase in Cyprus' trade and cultural exchange with neighboring countries.

The most dramatic change in island culture was fostered by the arrival of the Mycenaeans from the Peloponnese in the **Middle Bronze Age,** initiating a Hellenic tradition that has carried over to the present. The most obvious of these cultural influences can be seen in the pottery of the era, often depicting mythological scenes and bestiaries. From roughly 1400 to the mid-12th century BCE, **Mycenaean** traders visited the island regularly, spreading the use of the Greek language and introducing written notation for commerce. The arrival of **Phoenician** traders and colonists in the first millennium BCE introduced a fresh cultural impulse to the island. The Phoenicians shared political control with the Greeks until the arrival of the **Assyrians** in the 7th century BCE, who dominated the island for 100 years. After the waning of Assyrian power, the Egyptians briefly took hold of the island, but soon were overthrown by the Persian king. There was significant resistance to Persian rule by the native Cypriots, notably in the efforts of pro-Hellenic Evagoras I of Salamis, who forced Persians out of Salamis and fostered Greek culture within his kingdom.

As Persian expansion stagnated, **Alexander the Great** absorbed Cyprus into his growing empire. In 295 BCE, following Alexander's death, Ptolemy claimed Cyprus for Egypt. Under the succession of Ptolemies, Cyprus prospered; while cultural and religious institutions remained unchanged, the Greek alphabet came to replace the local syllabic script. Two centuries later, in 58 BCE, Rome took advantage of Ptolemy's declining fortunes by annexing Cyprus. Christianity was introduced to the island in 45 CE by the apostle Paul and the Cypriot apostle Barnabas. The spread of the Christian religion continued for three centuries thereafter, and, with the conversion of the Roman governor in 46 CE, Cyprus became the first country in the world to be ruled by a Christian.

BYZANTINE RULE TO THE OTTOMAN EMPIRE

When Constantinople was proclaimed the capital of the eastern half of the divided Roman empire, the stage was set for the synthesis of Roman civic thought, Greek philosophy, and the Greek Orthodox tradition. During these centuries, Cyprus passed through many dark periods—two devastating earthquakes in 332 and 342, a forty-year drought that severely scarred the island, and fierce Arab raids in the 7th century that once again proved the island's vulnerability to foreign attack. At the same time, however, many new towns were founded, and established towns expanded significantly. In 1191, **Richard the Lionheart,** en route to the Crusades in Jerusalem, quickly overran the island, which proved indispensable in provisioning the Christian armies. After robbing the island of its treasures, King Richard sold Cyprus to the **Knights Templar.** Soon after, when the Templars found they could not maintain the island, they passed responsibility on to Guy de Lusignan, a minor French noble who had been involved in the Crusades.

The **Lusignan Dynasty** (1192-1489) ruled through a feudalist system of class privileges and hierarchy that oppressed the lower classes and suppressed Cypriot culture and Greek Orthodox Christianity. Despite French subjugation of the locals, the Lusignan era left a legacy of impressive Gothic architecture in the form of churches, cathedrals, and castles. As setbacks in Palestine forced the Crusaders into full retreat, the Lusignans invited Crusader families to set up camp on the island. By the late 13th century, Cyprus had become the wealthiest island in the eastern Mediterranean. Yet in 1489 the **Venetians,** profiting from the Lusignans' dynastic intricacies, annexed the island. They remodeled and strengthened Cypriot military defenses, but were still no match for the Ottoman Empire. In 1570, following a two-month siege, Nicosia surrendered to the Turks. The fall of Famagusta one year later marked the beginning of the **Ottoman period** in Cyprus.

Cypriots welcomed the Ottoman abolition of feudalism, although the peasants who acquired land under this new system were taxed heavily. The Orthodox Church flourished in this period. Under the Ottomans, there was no separation of church and state, and the native Church of Cyprus served as a powerful administrative machine for the sultan. As the Empire weakened in the 19th century, Britain found itself defending Turkish territories in the face of Russian expansionism. In July of 1878, British forces landed peacefully at Larnaka and assumed control of Cyprus as a second military base. **Britain** entered into an arrangement with Turkey in which the island's excess revenue was used to pay off Turkish war loans. Although Cypriots did not enjoy political self-determination under the British, they benefited from the construction of many public works—roads, bridges, drinking and irrigation water supplies, a railway line, schools, and hospitals.

CYPRUS IN THE 20TH CENTURY

When Turkey joined the Central Powers at the start of WWI, Britain immediately annulled their previous agreement and annexed the island, and, in 1925, Cyprus formally became a British Crown Colony. Under British rule, cries for *enosis,* or union with Greece, grew increasingly strong, leading to the violent uprising in 1931 that avalanched into atrocities between ethnic Greeks and Turks. The British responded to the 1931 riot with stringent measures intended to repress nationalistic movements. During these years, the Pan-Cyprian Federation of Labor (PEO), encompassing both left-wing Greeks and Turks, continued to oppose colonial rule from the underground. When political meetings were once again allowed after 1941, the Progressive Party of the Working People (AKEL), a Communist organization that still strongly influences Cypriot life, was founded. In the municipal elections of 1943, AKEL gained control of two major cities, after which they began to support strikes and agitate for Cypriot rights under the British regime.

In 1954, **General George Grivas,** in conjunction with **Archbishop Makarios,** founded the EOKA (National Organization of Cypriot Fighters), an underground *enosist* movement. When the United Nations vetoed the Greeks' appeal to grant Cyprus self-government in 1955, General Grivas and the EOKA initiated a round of riots and guerilla warfare aimed at the British government. In response to increased EOKA activity, the underground, anti-Greek forces of Volkan (Volcano), under the leadership of **Rauf Denktaş,** founded the TMT (Turkish Resistance Organization). TMT was a paramilitary organization designed to fight the *enosists* and to push for

HISTORY

taksim, or partition of the island between Greece and Turkey. Weary of the perpetual violence but unconvinced by the viability of either *enosis* or *taksim,* Britain, along with the foreign ministers of Greece and Turkey, agreed in 1959 to establish an independent Cypriot republic. On August 16, 1960, Cyprus was granted independence and became a member of the U.N. and the British Commonwealth.

The new **constitution** stipulated that a Greek Cypriot president and a Turkish Cypriot vice-president were to be appointed through popular election and that the Greek to Turkish ratio in the House of Representatives would be 70:30. In 1959, Archbishop Makarios became the republic's first president, and **Fazıl Küçük,** leader of the Turkish Cypriot community, was elected to the vice presidency without opposition. In 1963, Makarios proposed thirteen amendments to the constitution, intended to facilitate bicommunal life, which included the abolition of the president's and vice-president's veto power and the introduction of majority rule. When the Turkish government threatened to use military force if these amendments were implemented, renewed violence broke out between the EOKA and TMT, resulting in the division of Nicosia along the Green Line. In February 1964, the U.N. dispatched UNFICYP (U.N. Forces in Cyprus), a "temporary" peace-keeping force that has been renewed indefinitely.

In 1968, Makarios and Küçük were both re-elected by an overwhelming majority, although in the years following they were subject to several coup plots, notably one by former ally General Grivas who returned to Cyprus in 1971 to found the militant EOKA-B and to revitalize the call for *enosis.* Intermittent violence suddenly exploded into an international affair in 1974 when the Greek Cypriot National Guard, assisted by the military **junta** in Greece, overthrew Archbishop Makarios and replaced him with **Nikos Sampson,** a notorious EOKA gunman who favored immediate *enosis.* Five days later, ostensibly moving to prevent the National Guard from attacking Turkish Cypriots, the Turkish army invaded Cyprus from the north, conquering 37% of the island. Early in 1975, the North declared itself the Turkish Federated State of Cyprus (TFSC), officially partitioning the island.

In November 1983, Turkish-occupied Cyprus proclaimed itself independent as the **Turkish Republic of Northern Cyprus (TRNC; Kıbrıs).** Though only Turkey has recognized the new state, the TRNC has established trading relations in Europe and with several Arab states. Led by Rauf Denktaş, the TRNC lags far behind the Republic of Cyprus economically but is generally supported by Turkish Cypriots who, in recent years, have been joined by thousands of settlers from mainland Turkey. In 1992, the decision was made to scale down UNFICYP significantly, leaving Cypriots to resolve their situation without much international intervention.

Through the latest presidential election (1993), **Glafkos Clerides,** former head of the conservative Democratic Rally (DISY), became head of the Republic of Cyprus. The re-election of Denktaş in the North aids the resumption of the negotiation process, and, in conjunction with the involvement of the U.S., resolution seems possible in the near future. After his election, Denktaş promised that 1995-96 would be years of "peace and settlement," although he is under pressure from Turkish nationalists not to compromise. Both Turkey and Greece are eager to win the favor of the U.S. and the E.U. Greek officials are hopeful that talks for the Republic of Cyprus' acceptance into the European Union, contingent on accord with Turkey, can begin by late 1998 or 1999.

CROSSING THE GREEN LINE

Crossing the infamous Green Line **from the south** is relatively easy, if you follow the strict regulations. Don't even try to get information about northern Nicosia on the Greek-Cypriot side. Greek-Cypriots have not crossed the line in more than 20 years. You will not be permitted to cross the line if you are a Greek citizen or if you are of Greek descent. Head for the **Ledra Palace Checkpoint** between the Greek-Cypriot and Turkish walls. This former hotel, its interior gutted and its exterior marred by bullet holes, stands on neutral territory and houses UN troops.

Before entering this area, you must show your passport and register on the Greek-Cypriot side. If you don't know exactly where to go, don't worry—they'll stop you. After checking in, you take a 5-minute walk through the UN wasteland. Ledra will be on your left, and unless you are specifically instructed to go there, there's no reason to stop. You will show your passport again on the Turkish side and fill out a general information form in order to receive a special visitor's visa (£1). They will not stamp your passport. *Do not let them stamp your passport.* If they stamp your passport, you will not be readmitted to Greek Cyprus. They will, however, give you a form to be stamped by someone at another window. Hold on to this form—you will need it to cross back at the end of your visit. If your travels originate from the north, and you have a Turkish stamp in your passport, you can never enter the south. Northern authorities may stamp a separate piece of paper if you ask.

Some reminders: (1) You may enter Northern Cyprus between 8am and 1pm, but must return by 5pm. No exceptions. (2) Cars are not allowed—you must cross by foot. (3) As in other areas of Nicosia and Cyprus, do *not* take pictures of anything that has to do with the military or police. (4) As you will be forewarned on the Greek side, you are not allowed to buy anything on the Turkish side. If you wish to buy food, you must exchange your Cypriot pounds for Turkish lira. Also, you cannot bring items from the south to the north—they will be confiscated. (5) Finally, if you have a problem, ask the UN soldiers with the blue berets for assistance.

Crossing the line **from the north** is impossible. The quickest way to get to South Nicosia, therefore, is to first fly to London, and then to the south. This trick will only work if you don't have a Northern Cyprus stamp on your passport. A cheaper, and much longer, way is to go by seabus (or ferry) to Taşucu in Turkey, take a bus from there to Marmaris, from there a ferry to Rhodes, and finally a ferry to Southern Cyprus. Travel time—about two days. To be safe, ask the Turkish authorities not to stamp your passport, as a Taşucu stamp gives away that you've been to Northern Cyprus (though this isn't always a problem).

■ Nicosia (Lefkosia) ΛΕΥΚΩΣΙΑ

Landlocked Nicosia, the capital of the Republic of Cyprus, sits astride the "Green Line," the border separating the Republic of Cyprus from Kıbrıs. The presence of Greek Cypriot and Turkish border patrols, as well as a significant number of United Nations troops, serves as a reminder of the bitterness that lies below the serene surface. Many tourists bypass Nicosia for the sun and sand in other regions of Cyprus, but a visit to this city is essential for anyone interested in Cyprus' political situation or in ethnic strife in general. Greek Cypriots call their city Lefkosia, but the use of Nicosia is common and inoffensive.

Built on the site of ancient Ledra during the Roman occupation, Nicosia prospered under the Lusignan dynasty. When Lusignan power waned, Venetians took over (1489), and, in 1567, built huge walls to ward off Turkish cannons. The fortifications were effective for a time, but three years later Turks concentrated their effort, gained victory in seven weeks, and ruled the city for several hundred years, until the British took over in 1878. When Cyprus gained independence in 1960, Nicosia became its capital.

The city has taken measures to restore the old *Laiki Yitonia,* the pedestrian shopping district, where the cobblestone streets are crammed with shops and restaurants, making a pleasant refuge from the hot, traffic-choked streets. The recent proliferation of museums and monuments reflects the town's eagerness to maintain its spirit and cultural heritage. Nicosia seems geared more towards bureaucrats than backpackers—Larnaka may be a better base from which to explore the east coast.

ORIENTATION AND PRACTICAL INFORMATION

The easiest way to orient yourself in Nicosia is to refer to the ominous Green Line running east-west at the north end of the city. The line splits the **Old City** within its circular Venetian walls. When you walk down the streets slashed in half by the border, you are confronted by sheet metal barriers or white and blue dividers. At several points throughout the city, signs forbid photography, and they mean it. The southern part of Nicosia within the Walls (as the Old City is officially known) contains most budget lodgings, museums, and sights. From **Eleftherias Square,** Evagoras St. heads southwest into the **New City.** Intersecting Evagoras are Makarios Ave., Diagoras St., and Th. Dervis St. (which leads away from the city to the youth hostel), where the banks, embassies, and travel agencies are located. The New City is much busier than the old and is the center of Nicosia's nightlife. Be sure to get a superb free **map** from the tourist office.

Tourist Office: 35 Aristokypros St. (tel. 444264), in the *Laiki Yitonia,* within the city walls. Entering Eleftherias Sq., turn right and follow signs from the post office. Route maps, a complete list of village buses, and free copies of *Nicosia: This Month.* A 2-hr. walking tour of Nicosia (Mon., Thurs. 10am) and a tour through the old suburb of Kaimakli leave from here (Mon. 10am). Tours are free and conducted in English. Open Mon.-Fri. 8:30am-4pm, Sat. 8:30am-2pm.

Embassies: Australian High Commission, 4 Annis Comninis St. (tel. 473001; fax 366486), 500m east of Elefthenias Sq. off Stassinou Ave. Open in summer Mon.-Fri. 7:30am-3:20pm. **Egypt,** 3 Egypt Ave. (tel. 465144; fax 462287). Open Mon.-Fri. 8am-2pm. **Greece,** 8 Lordou Vyronos (tel. 442880; fax 473990). Open Mon.-Fri. 9am-noon. **Israel,** 4 I. Grypari St. (tel. 445195). Open Mon.-Fri. 9am-noon. **Lebanon,** 1 Vas. Olgas (tel. 442216; fax 467662). Open Mon.-Fri. 9am-noon. **Syria,** 1 Androkleous St. (tel. 474481; fax 446963). Visas cost £25 and take 2 business days to process. Open Mon.-Fri. 8am-2:30pm. **U.K. High Commission,** Alexanderou Pauli St. (tel. 473131; fax 367198), west of the old city. Open Mon.-Fri. 8-11:30am. **U.S.,** Metochiou and Ploutarchou (tel. 476100; fax 465944). Open in summer 8am-4pm; in winter 8am-5pm.

Banks: Bank of Cyprus, 86-88-90 Phaneromeni St. (tel. 477774). **Currency exchange.** Open Mon.-Fri. 8:15am-12:30pm. Convenient branch in *Laiki Yitonia* (tel. 365959), on Drakos St. Open Mon.-Sat. 8:30am-noon.

American Express: A.L. Mantovani and Sons, 2D Agapinoras St. (tel. 443777), 1km south from Solomos Sq. down Makarios Ave. Issues traveler's checks. Open Mon.-Fri. 8am-12:45pm and 3:30-6:30pm.

CYTA: 14 Egypt Ave. (tel. 470200). Sells £3 telecards, worth about 30min. of local phonetime. Telecards work in pay phones in the lobby or anywhere on the island. Open Mon.-Fri. 7am-7pm. Dial 196 for **telegrams.**

Buses: Kemek, 34 Leonides St. south of Solonos Sq. (tel. 463989), and **Kolo Kassi** (tel. 347774), on Salaminos St. by the entrance to the Old City. To Limassol (3-4 per day, £1.25), Larnaka (4-7 per day, £1.30), and Platres (5 per week, £1.60). **EMAN** bus stop, down a flight of steps 50m east of the post office, runs similar routes. **City buses** (tel. 473414) run from Solonos Sq. daily 5:30am-7pm.

Service Taxis: Makris (tel. 466201), **Kyriakos** (tel. 444114), and **Karydas,** 8 Homer Ave. (tel. 462269) are all open daily 6am-6pm. **Akropolis** (tel. 472525) is open daily 6am-7pm. **Kypros** (tel. 464811) is open daily 6:30am-6pm. Makris, Kryriakos, Akropolis, and Kypros are on Stassinos Ave., a short distance east from Eleftherias Sq. Cabs leave every 30min.; lines form until departure. All run to Limassol (£2.15) and continue on to Paphos (additional £2); Makris, Akropolis, and Kyriakos travel to Larnaka (£2).

International Bookstores: Philippides & Son, 10 Paleologos Ave. (tel. 462984), opposite the post office. Well stocked, slightly pricey resource for reading matter of all kinds. English travel guides, literature, fiction, and mysteries, as well as Greek literature in translation. **The American Center,** 33B Homer Ave. (tel. 473145), around the corner from the museum. A/C library will remind you of high school. Extensive selection of periodicals and newspapers, including the *New York Times.* Open Sept.-July Mon.-Fri. 10am-12:30pm and 2-5pm.

Library: British Council, 3 Museum Ave. (tel. 442258; fax 477257), 2 doors down from the museum. Books, videos, and tapes. Open Sept.-June Mon., Thurs.-Fri. 9am-1pm, Tues.-Wed. 9am-1pm and 3-6pm.

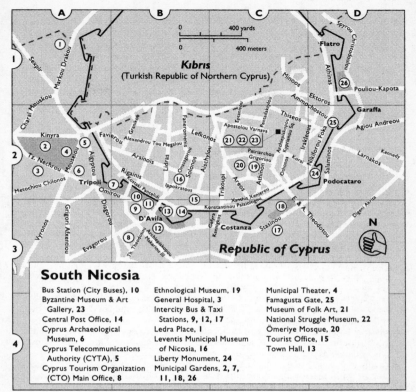

South Nicosia

Bus Station (City Buses), 10	Ethnological Museum, 19	Municipal Theater, 4
Byzantine Museum & Art	General Hospital, 3	Famagusta Gate, 25
Gallery, 23	Intercity Bus & Taxi	Museum of Folk Art, 21
Central Post Office, 14	Stations, 9, 12, 17	National Struggle Museum, 22
Cyprus Archaeological	Ledra Place, 1	Ömeriye Mosque, 20
Museum, 6	Leventis Municipal Museum	Tourist Office, 15
Cyprus Telecommunications	of Nicosia, 16	Town Hall, 13
Authority (CYTA), 5	Liberty Monument, 24	
Cyprus Tourism Organization	Municipal Gardens, 2, 7,	
(CTO) Main Office, 8	11, 18, 26	

Hospital: (tel. 451111), intersection of Omirou and Nechrou, 50m ahead on the left. Generous facility with modern technology. Don't be too frightened by the decrepit building—everyone swears it isn't a reflection of the quality of the medicine practiced here. Open 24hr.

Police: (tel. 30 3090), 150m east of Paphos Gate on Rigenis St., inside the Wall. Open 24hr.

Police Emergency: Dial 199. Open 24hr.

Post Office: Main Office (tel. 303231), on Constantinos Paleologos Ave., east of Elefthenias Sq. within the walls. Open in summer Mon.-Tues, Thurs.-Fri. 7:30am-1pm and 4-7pm, Wed. 7:30am-1pm; in winter Mon.-Tues., Thurs.-Fri. 7:30am-1pm and 3-6pm, Wed. 7:30am-1pm. Branch offices on Dhigenis St., Palace St., and Loukis Akitas Ave. (tel. 302531). **Postal Code:** 1903.

Telephone Code: 02.

ACCOMMODATIONS

Unfortunately, flats are not a sensible option in Nicosia. They are quite expensive and only offered by real estate agents to visitors who are planning a stay of at least a few weeks. Most of Nicosia's budget accommodations are within the city walls and are at least tolerably clean. If you don't like the room you're shown, ask to see another—the degree of cleanliness and comfort tends to vary widely at most places.

Youth Hostel (HI), 1 Hadjidaki St. (tel. 444808), a bit of a walk into the new city. Clean and popular with young people from around the globe. Communal kitchen and yard provide meeting spots for travelers. Clean showers included. £4 per person. Sheets £1.

Royal Hotel, 17 Euripides St. (tel. 463245), on a sidestreet off Ledra, at the corner of Euripides and Aeschylus, middle of Old Town. Clean rooms with fans. Most rooms with shower. A/C £2.15. Singles £8.25. Doubles £13.50.

Tony's Bed and Breakfast, 13 Solon St. (tel. 466752), at *Laiki Yitonia*. Rooms range widely in size, but all have TV, radio, phone, and fridge. A/C units, operated by special coin, £1 for 7hr. Canteen serves food and drink (25¢-¢1.50). Singles £11-15. Doubles £18-22. Triples £27. Quads £32. Full English breakfast included.

Sans Rival, 7C Solon St. (tel. 474383), a few doors down from Tony's. Nothing fancy, but a bed in the heart of the Old Town. All rooms with shower, sink, and fan. A/C £2.15. Singles £13-15. Doubles £12-14. Breakfast £2.

FOOD AND ENTERTAINMENT

As in most cities, there are many dining choices in Nicosia ranging from *tavernas* with live music to pubs, pizzerias, and full restaurants. The touristy joints around *Laiki Yitonia* serve Cypriot cuisine in clean, cool surroundings. The smaller restaurants in the Old Town cater more to locals.

Estiatorio, 40 Arsinoes St. (tel. 459945). May be hard to spot for those unfamiliar with the Greek alphabet. In the heart of the old city, near the Green Line. Rabbit *stifado* £3, boiled dandelions £1.75. Open daily 9am-10pm.

Mattheos (tel. 475846), behind the Phaneromeni Church (near a small mosque). Good food for low prices. Shaded tables outside. *Koupepia* (stuffed grape leaves) and *moussaka* £2.75 each. Open daily 5am-7pm.

Faros Barbeque Boss, 6 Tillirias St. (tel. 463326). Take away or have them deliver any kind of *kebab* you desire (£1.25-3.20) served with pita, fried potatoes, rice, and salad. Open daily noon-3pm and 7-10pm.

Berlin #2 Café (tel. 474935), corner of Lefkon St. Savor your *kebab,* salad, and pita (£2.50) in the shade of the blue and white Green Line. Open Mon.-Tues., Thurs.-Fri. 7:30am-6:30pm; closes early on Wed. and Sat.

Byzantine (tel. 477085). 1 block from the tourist office, this wooden beamed restaurant with a shady courtyard offers *meze* (£5), *moussaka* (£3.50), and salad (£2.25). Open Mon.-Sat. 8am-5pm.

Natural Choice, 11 Chytron St. (tel. 362674), in the new city, convenient to the youth hostel. All food is fresh and homemade at this pleasant natural foods eatery. Outdoor seating under huge cloth umbrellas, bright airy interior. Seasonal stuffed veggies £2.20, chicken curry £2.25. Huge slab of sugar-free apple pie 75¢. Open Mon.-Fri. 8am-midnight.

Most wines come from Cypriot wineries. The most inexpensive eating in Nicosia can be done at the **municipal market,** a huge warehouse is filled with a variety of food stands, on the corner of Digenis Akritas and Kallipolis Ave. You can buy fresh feta in blocks and make your own salad; hanging pigs will either make you ravenous or a vegetarian (open daily 6am-1pm and 4-6pm). A colorful streetside **produce market** sets up on Wednesdays near Eleftherias Sq. along Constantinos Paleologos Ave. (open Wed. 9am-1pm and 4-6pm).

SIGHTS

Sadly, many find the Green Line to be Nicosia's main attraction. The only spot on the border where photography is permitted is on Ledra St., where the military has erected a makeshift shrine to the north. Remember that this is a military zone and that taking pictures is a serious offense. The **Cyprus Museum** (tel. 302189) has a collection of life-size terra-cotta models of ancient Cypriots, complete with piles of bones, exquisite pottery, and thought provoking paraphernalia (open Mon.-Sat. 9am-5pm, Sun. 10am-1pm; admission £1.50). The colorful **botanical gardens,** whose aviaries showcase most of the island's indigenous species, are next to the archaeological museum and behind the Garden Café (open daily 8am-10pm; free).

The **Makarios Cultural Center** (tel. 43008) occupies the buildings of Archbishopric Kyprianos Sq., a former 15th-century Gothic monastery. Several very interesting museums are clustered here. The **Folk Art Museum** (tel. 463205) presents Cypriot masterpieces of woodcarving, embroidery, pottery, basketry, and metalwork from the 18th to 20th centuries. A guide to the collection costs 50¢ (open Mon.-Fri. 9am-5pm, Sat. 10am-1pm; admission £1). The neighboring **Greek Independence War Gallery** (tel. 302465), founded in 1961, contains photographs, documents, and other relics from the struggle for *enosis*, the union of Cyprus with Greece (open Mon.-Fri. 9am-4:30pm, Sat. 9am-1pm; admission 50¢). Also in the area is the **St. John Cathedral Church,** built in 1662 by Archbishop Nikiforos. Its 18th-century wall paintings depict incidents related to the discovery of the tomb of St. Barnabas (open Mon.-Fri. 8am-noon and 2-4pm, Sat. 9am-noon).

Near the Archbishopric is the **House of Hadjigeorgiakis Kornesios** (tel. 302447), known as **Konak Mansion** for short, at 18 Patriarch Gregory St., around the corner from the Archbishopric complex. A famous dragoman (an interpreter for Ottoman Turks and Greeks) lived in this luxurious, 18th-century structure (open Mon.-Fri. 8am-2pm, Sat. 9am-1pm; admission 75¢). Also close by is the **Ömeriye Mosque,** easily found by following the minaret. **Turkish Baths,** on 8 Tillirias St. (tel. 477588), are across from the mosque (open for women Wed., Fri. 8am-3pm; open for men Wed., Fri. 3-7pm, Tues., Thurs., Sat.-Sun. 8am-7pm; admission £2).

In the *Laiki Yitonia,* the **Leventis Municipal Museum** (tel. 451475), on Hippocratis St., won the European Museum of the Year award in 1991. The exhibit chronicles the history of Nicosia, beginning with the modern city, back through time to 3000 BCE (open Tues.-Sun. 10am-4:30pm; free). The **Cyprus Jewelers Museum,** 7-9 Odos Praxipou, is opposite the tourist office. It's miniscule but merits a look. The 18th- to 20th-century collection includes gold and silver plates, spoons, and jewelry handcrafted in the filigree and *skaleta* techniques. Note the traditional forks and spoons, made according to village customs and used for devouring sweetened fruits drowned in syrup (open Mon.-Fri. 10am-4:30pm; free).

Down Korais St. from the Archbishopric stands a marble monument depicting 14 Cypriots, each representing a period of the island's history, who are being released from jail by soldiers and overseen by a religious figure. Nearby, along the Venetian Walls at the end of Theseus St., is the recently restored **Famagusta Gate,** which served as the main entrance to the medieval city. Built in 1567, it now hosts plays, concerts, and lectures (open Mon.-Fri. 10am-1pm and 4-7pm; free). Free copies of *Nicosia: This Month* at the tourist office list event schedules.

■ Larnaka ΛΑΡΝΑΚΑ

The modern city of Larnaka (pop. 60,000) was built over the ruins of ancient **Kition,** making it one of the oldest continually inhabited cities in the world. In the north of town a segment of the ancient city walls and some Bronze Age temples remain, but Larnaka is curiously indifferent to its history, and instead it has become a tourist center offering visitors a long beach bordered by numerous cafés and restaurants. Quieter and cleaner than Limassol, sunny Larnaka charms visitors, and while it's a bit less expensive than neighboring Agia Napa, rooms are just as scarce in summer.

ORIENTATION AND PRACTICAL INFORMATION

Athinon Avenue, also known as the "Palm Tree Promenade," runs along the water and is Larnaka's most noticeable attraction. In summer, hordes of barefoot young Cypriots and sandal-clad foreigners fill its cafés, restaurants, pubs, and beach. Major renovations on the street are nearly completed, but the Promenade, adorned with tall, French-style lamp posts, already bursts with charm. **Plateia Vasileos Pavlou,** where you'll find most facilities, is one block west of the north end of Athinon Ave.

Cyprus Tourism Organization Office: (tel. 654322), Pl. Vasileos Pavlou. Open Mon., Thurs. 8:15am-2:30pm and 4-6pm, Tues.-Wed., Fri.-Sat. 8:15am-2:30pm. Hours tend to vary. Also an **Airport branch** (tel. 643000; open 24hr.).

American Express: (tel. 652024), Stassinou St., in the office of **A.L. Mantovani and Sons,** across from the C.T.O. No travelers' checks or currency exchange. Provides money check form for those drawing funds from AmEx cards. Guarantees personal checks so local banks will take them. Open Mon.-Fri. 8am-1pm and 2:30-5:30pm, Sat. 9am-noon; reduced hours in off season.

CYTA: 7-9 Z Pierides (tel. 132 or 640257), follow Lordou Vyronos toward the seafront. Office is on the right, before Zinonos Kitieos. **Telegram service. Phone cards** in £3, 5, or 10 amounts (available June-Aug. Mon.-Fri 7:30am-7pm, Sat. 7:30am-1pm; Sept.-May Mon.-Fri. 7:30am-6pm, Sat. 7:30am-noon). **Telecard phones** located throughout the city. Open Mon.-Fri. 7:30am-2:15pm.

Telegrams: Can be sent by phone Mon.-Sat. 7am-7pm, by dialing 196. Sun. and holidays, telegrams accepted only at the counter of the Cyprus Telecommunication Authority offices at Lord Byron St.

Airport: (tel. 692700). Most flights into Cyprus land at the Larnaka airport. Upon arrival, the #19 bus runs to town (in summer 14 per day, 6:20am-7pm; in winter until 5:45pm; 50¢). Taxis cost £2.50 to get to St. Lazarus Sq. in the center of town.

Buses: Leave from Athinon Ave., by the marina on the seafront. Look for a sandwich board on the sidewalk with the schedule. **Kallenos Buses** (tel. 654890, -50) go to Nicosia (7 per day, Mon.-Fri. 6:30am-4pm, 4 per day Sat. until 1pm; £1.30) and Limassol (4 per day, Mon.-Fri. until 4pm, 3 per day Sat. until 1pm; £1.50). No Kallenos buses on Sun. **EMAN** (tel. 721336) buses to Agia Napa leave from the same spot (Mon.-Sat. 8:30am-5:30pm, 4 per day Sun., 8:30am-4:30pm; £1.30). **P.E.A.L.** (tel. 650477; fax 654977) buses leave from St. Lazarus Sq. and stop at St. Helenis, Artemidos Ave., Meneou, Kiti, and Tersefanou (in summer 13-14 per day 6:20am-5:45pm and 7pm; in winter, same, but no 7pm bus; 60¢).

Service Taxis: Makris (tel. 652929 or 655333), King Paul St., opposite the Sun Hall Hotel. To Nicosia (£2), Limassol (£2.10), Paphos (£2 transfer from Limassol), Famagusta, Paralimni, Agia Napa. Runs Mon.-Sat. 6am-6pm; 24-hr. service for private taxi. **Akropolis** (tel. 655555), at the corner of Markarios Ave., opposite the police station, and **Kyriakos,** 2C Hermes (Ermou) St. (tel. 655100), also provide *service* taxi service. All run to Limassol (every 30min., Mon.-Fri. 6am-4:45pm, sometimes until 6pm, £2) and to Nicosia (£1.70). *Service* taxis also run from Nicosia to Limassol (£2.10). *Service* taxis will pick up and drop off anywhere in the city. Just call ahead. On Sun., the companies alternate, running until early afternoon. Prices may be higher (by roughly 50¢). **Private taxis** are shamelessly expensive.

Car Rental: Thaco Rent-A-Car, 1 Gladstonos St. (tel. 626871 or 632386; fax 657473). Prices from £15 per day. Unlimited mileage. Minimum age 25.

Hospital: (tel. 630300), off Leoforos Grigori Afxentiou, at the intersection of Agias Elenis and Konst. Zachariada St.

Police: (tel. 630200), on Makarios Ave., one block north of the tourist office. English spoken. Open 24hr. **Fire** tel. 199.

Post Office: Main branch (tel. 630180 or 630178), Pl. Vasileos Pavlou. Open Sept.-June Mon.-Tues., Thurs.-Fri. 7:30am-1:30pm and 3-6pm, Sat. 9-11am; July-Aug. Mon.-Fri. 7:30am-1:30pm and 4-7pm, Sat. 9-11am. **Postal code:** 6900. A branch is in **St. Lazarus Sq.** (tel. 630182). Open Sept.-June Mon.-Wed., Fri. 8am-1:30pm, Thurs. 8am-1:30pm and 3-6pm; July-Aug., Mon., Fri. 7:30am-1:30pm. **Postal code:** 6902. Each post office has a separate postal code.

Telephone code: 04.

ACCOMMODATIONS

The town's hotels and pensions tend to fall into three distinct categories—luxury hotels, flats, and dives. Cleaner and cooler than the dives, flats are hip alternatives to regular hotels in Larnaka. Prices tend to be £5-7 less in off season.

Youth Hostel (HI) (tel. 621188), Nikolaou Rossou St. in St. Lazarus Sq. Has three large rooms (all female, all male, and co-ed) with 10 beds in each. Open 24hr., but

LARNAKA

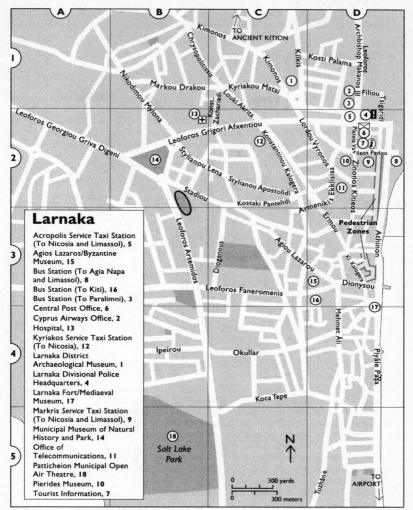

Larnaka

Acropolis *Service* Taxi Station
(To Nicosia and Limassol), **5**
Agios Lazaros/Byzantine
Museum, **15**
Bus Station (To Agia Napa
and Limassol), **8**
Bus Station (To Kiti), **16**
Bus Station (To Paralimni), **3**
Central Post Office, **6**
Cyprus Airways Office, **2**
Hospital, **13**
Kyriakos *Service* Taxi Station
(To Nicosia), **12**
Larnaka District
Archaeological Museum, **1**
Larnaka Divisional Police
Headquarters, **4**
Larnaka Fort/Mediaeval
Museum, **17**
Markris *Service* Taxi Station
(To Nicosia and Limassol), **9**
Municipal Museum of Natural
History and Park, **14**
Office of
Telecommunications, **11**
Patticheion Municipal Open
Air Theatre, **18**
Pierides Museum, **10**
Tourist Information, **7**

the front desk is not manned 24hr., so that guests can "sign themselves in" anytime. Bring sheets (or rent them for £1) and bug spray. £3.50 per person.

Petrou Bros. Holiday Apartments, 1 Armenikis Ekklisias St. (tel 650600, -1; fax 655122); head south from the C.T.O. and make a right at the Armenian Church. Call ahead. Front lobby moonlights as a bar and TV room. English spoken. Laundry service (£1.25 per kilo), currency exchange, and travel services. Access to nearby pool. Breakfast £1. Suites for 2-6 people. Immaculate rooms have phones and baths. Singles £10. Doubles £15. Quads £25. 6 person £30. Extra bed £2.

Harry's Hotel, 2 Thermopylon St. (tel. 654453), near Marina Pier, the second left inland from the tourist office. Common room upstairs with rag-tag couches, TV, fridge, and common bath/shower. Bar and arrangement of plants and sticks that may one day be a garden. Singles £8. Doubles £13. Breakfast £1.

Pavion Hotel, 11 Faneromeni St., St. Lazarus Sq. (tel. 656688), offers clean but musty rooms. Singles £11. Doubles £16. Breakfast included.

FOOD AND ENTERTAINMENT

Most of Larnaka's restaurants and bars are on the waterfront. Larnaka also offers an array of international cuisines—Chinese, Lebanese, Italian, French, and Indian.

Mauri Helona (the Black Turtle; tel. 650661), at the beginning of Mehmet Ali St., at St. Lazarus Sq. Offers *mezedes* and a cute logo—a turtle schlepping a jug of booze. On Wed., Fri. and Sat. nights, a small group of singers and musicians gathers until midnight. Fish £3.75-4.75. Chicken £2.75. Rabbit £4. Pork £2.75. House wines £3-4. Beer £1.25. Prices include 10% service charge and 8% V.A.T. Opens for dinner at 6pm.

Megalos Pefkos, at the southern end of the harbor by the fortress, has relatively inexpensive fish. Swordfish £3.75. *Meze* £4.50.

Midnight Sun (tel. 628885), on the south end of Athens Ave., is a popular fast-food café. Sandwiches £1.40. Hot dogs £1.30. Burgers £2.40. Beer 90¢-£1.50. Also cocktails and ice cream. Open 24hr.

The Hobo Pub and Restaurant (tel. 624993), near the north end of Leoforos Athinon. Pleasant rooftop restaurant and good chicken *kebab* (£3). Breakfast £1.30-2. Pizza £2-3.50. Pasta £2-2.50.

Nitro Café (tel. 664909), on the corner of Leoforos Grigori Afxentiou and Lordou Vyronos, specializes in coffee (£1) and desserts (£1.25-1.75). Sandwiches £1.20. Open daily 10am-6am, so their patrons will never lack a hip place to chat.

1900 Art Cafe, 6 Stasinou St. (tel. 653027). Run by a painter and journalist, the café aspires to the exchange of intellectual and artistic ideas over carafes of local wine (£2.50). Teas 90¢. Coffees 50¢-£1. The *milopita* (apple pie, £1.10) is their specialty. Bookshop, bar, fireplace, and display of local artists' works upstairs. Café open Mon.-Sat. 8:30am-2:30pm and 6pm-midnight, Sun. 6pm-midnight.

Elitor: The Patisserie, 35 Gr. Afxentiou Ave. (tel. 656929, -7097). Delectable *baklava*, pastries, and *kouriabiedes* (powdery almond cookies)—4¢ each or £3.50 per kilo. Ice cream cakes £3-4, birthday cakes £4. Open 7:30am-9pm.

Helioupolis Confectionery, 24 Z. Pierides St. (tel. 652573). Small but sweet collection of baked goods. Chocolates (35¢). *Baklava* (35¢). Cheese pie (35¢).

SIGHTS

The ancient city of **Kition** is the most historically significant spot in Larnaka, although most of it is now underground. Settled in the early 13th century BCE and abandoned soon after, Kition was rebuilt in 1200 BCE by refugees from the Peloponnese. The city was damaged in wars with the Phoenicians and Egyptians (4th century BCE) and leveled by earthquake and fire in 280 BCE. Ruins reveal part of an ancient Cyclopean wall, a big **Temple of Astarte,** goddess of fertility, and four small temples. To get there, follow Kimon St. to the Chryssopolitissa Church, cross in front of the church, and go straight on Sakellariou St. Take the first right to Loizou Filippou St., go left, then the first right again (open Sept.-June Mon.-Wed., Fri. 7:30am-2:30pm, Thurs. 7:30am-2:30pm and 3-6pm; July-Aug. Mon.-Wed., Fri. 7:70am-2:30pm, Thurs. 7:30am-2:30pm; admission 75¢).

The **Kition Archaeological Site** lies 500m northeast of the District Archaeological Museum. The small collection includes objects from Neolithic to Roman times. The newly renovated **Larnaka District Archaeological Museum** (tel. 630169) boasts Neolithic finds from the Larnaka District (museum and site both open Sept.-June Mon.-Wed., Fri. 7:30am-2:30pm, Thurs. 7:30am-2:30pm and 3-6pm; July-Aug. Mon.-Fri. 7:30am-2:30pm; admission 75¢). The private **Pierides Foundation Museum** (tel. 651345 or 652495), on Zinonos St., is the former home of Demetrios Pierides (1811-1895), a cultured man and collector of Cypriot artifacts. The museum is Larnaka's version of the Louvre. Prehistoric Cypriot idols are displayed in china chests. Pots take the place of end tables, and antique maps of Cyprus hang in lieu of wallpaper. Artifacts abound from 3000 years of Cypriot culture, including Byzantine and traditional art (open Mon.-Fri. 9am-1pm and 3-6pm, Sat. 9am-1pm; reduced hours in off season; admission £1, 75¢ per person for groups of more than 10).

At the north end of Athenon Ave. is **Larnaka's Marina,** upon which couples and families warm up for their *voltas* (nightly strolls) among the palm trees. A **Museum of Marine Life** should be open by the end of 1996. The **Municipal Museum of Natural History,** where 5000 Cypriot insects are individually labeled and pinned to styrofoam showcases, attracts those with an open mind. Three kinds of extinct snakes have been stuffed, and other dead, local animal species are arranged in panoramic displays. Outside there are live versions (so the kids don't have nightmares for the rest of their lives)—turkeys, buzzards, hamsters, canaries, seagulls, and a peacock. A park for all ages and a playground for children less than 10 surrounds this museum.

At the south end of the port, a small **medieval fortress** peers over the water's edge. Built by Venetians in the 15th century and rebuilt by Turks in 1625, the fort contains finds and photographs from Kition and other local excavations (open Mon.-Fri. 7:30am-7:30pm; reduced hours in off season; admission 75¢). The first left north of the fortress leads to the **Church of St. Lazarus,** built over the saint's tomb. Jesus Christ reportedly resurrected Lazarus, four days dead, in Israel. The resuscitated Lazarus came to Cyprus, became the island's first bishop, and lived in Kition another 30 years before dying again. Lazarus's remains were stolen from Constantinople, but appeared later in Marseilles. The church was built in the 9th century, but it has been burnt and rebuilt several times since then. You can visit St. Lazarus's tomb by descending steps near the iconostasis. The church's belfry was added in 1857. In the courtyard there's a small museum (tel. 652498) with ecclesiastical art. Modest dress is required. (Open in summer daily 8am-12:30pm and 3:30-6:30pm; in off season daily 8am-12:30pm and 2:30-5:30pm; free. Greek Orthodox services Sun. 6-9:30am. Museum open Mon.-Tues., Thurs.-Fri. 8:30am-1pm and 4-6:30pm, Wed., Sat. 8:30am-1pm; admission 50¢.)

For a brief encounter with Larnaka's artsy scene, visit the **Art Gallery of Maria Pyrgou,** 5 Stadiou St. (tel. 623993), behind the local market. Once a month (except August), Pyrgou exhibits works of well known Cypriot, Greek, and European artists in an enchanting 120-year-old traditional Cypriot building. For details on current exhibitions, inquire at the 1900 Art Café (tel. 653027; gallery open daily 5-8pm).

The **town beach** (a dismal mixture of packed dirt, cigarette butts, and ogling men) manages to satisfy the vacationers who bake there. The bustling beach also offers **watersports:** canoes (£3.50 per hr.), pedalboats (£5.50 per hr.), sailboards (£4.50 per hr.), waterskis (£5.50 per ride; £6 per lesson), jet skis (£10 per 15 min.), miniboats (£7 per 15 min., £12 per 30min.), or banana boats (£3.50 per person). Beautiful, less crowded beaches are farther northeast on the way to Agia Napa.

■ Near Larnaka

Built at the edge of a salt lake and surrounded by palm trees, the **Hala Sultan Tekke Mosque** is said to be the fourth (or so) holiest Muslim pilgrimage site after Mecca, Medina, and Jerusalem. Also called the Tekke of Umm Haram, the mosque was constructed during the Arab invasion of Cyprus (647 CE) and rebuilt in 1816, over the site where Umm Haram (Mohammed's maternal aunt) fell off a mule and broke her neck. Three gargantuan stones—reputed to have been quarried in Mecca—surround her grave in back of the mosque. The horizontal one supposedly hovered in the air for many centuries, until it lowered itself for fear of injuring the faithful. Bus #6, bound for Kiti, leaves St. Lazarus Sq. (in summer 12 per day, 8am-7pm; in winter last bus at 5:45pm, 15min., 50¢), and travels west to the Hala Sultan Tekke Mosque. Ask the driver to stop at the mosque, or you will end up in Kiti. To be dropped at the turnoff, tell the bus driver you're going to "Tekke." From there, walk along the paved road for 1km (open daily 7:30am-7:30pm, closes early in winter; free). The mosque is next to the **Larnaka Salt Lake.** In winter, the lake is covered with pink flamingos, but in summer, it dries up and the flamingos hop away. Legend claims that the lake was created one day when St. Lazarus turned an old woman's vineyard into a barren salt lake as punishment for her lack of hospitality.

The same bus that goes to the mosque goes on to the village of **Kiti** (25min. from Larnaka), where you can visit the church of **Panayia Angeloktisti** (literally, Built by the Angels). Again, ask the driver to stop there. This church was built in the 11th century, but it contains a section dating from several hundred years earlier. The mosaic in the central apse, representing the Virgin Mary with Christ surrounded by the Archangels Michael and Gabriel, is one of the more important works of art on the island. The narthex of the church was built in the 14th century by the Gibelet family—one of the most prominent Latin noble families of medieval Cyprus (open Mon.-Fri. 8am-4pm, Sat. 10am-4pm, Sun. 9am-noon and 2-4pm).

Forty kilometers from Larnaka and 9km off the main Nicosia-Limassol road is **Stavrovouni Monastery** (Mountain of the Cross). According to tradition, the monastery was constructed by order of St. Eleni in 327 BCE on a site called Olympus, where a pagan temple had stood. At the time, Eleni, mother of the Roman Emperor Constantine, was returning from Palestine, where she happened to find the Holy Cross. She presented a fragment to the monastery, where it is kept in the church's iconostasis. Although their founder was female, the monks do not allow women into the monastery. There are no buses to Stavrovouni, but you can go to Kornos and walk up to the peak. A taxi costs roughly £25 (open daily sunrise-noon and 3pm-sunset; closed for Green Monday Feb. 26 -27).

Thirty two kilometers from Larnaka is the Neolithic settlement of **Choirokoitia** (open Mon.-Fri. 7:30am-5pm, Sat.-Sun. 9am-5pm; admission 75¢). Forty kilometers from Larnaka is the **Traditional Museum of Embroidery and Silversmithing** (open Mon.-Sat. 10am-4pm; admission 75¢).

■ Agia Napa ΑΓΙΑ ΝΑΠΑ

Twenty years ago, Agia Napa was a quiet farming and fishing village. Most tourists went to Famagusta, 16km to the north, allowing Agia Napa's ruined monastery and white sandy beaches to lie peacefully vacant. But when Turkey occupied Famagusta in 1974, Agia Napa was gussied up almost overnight into a tourist center replete with marble and brass glitz, all the while absorbing a large refugee community from Northern Cyprus. Over the years, Agia Napa has developed a raucous nightlife popular among Cypriots and foreigners.

Orientation and Practical Information   Agia Napa's center is home to banks, restaurants, and tourist shops. The **C.T.O.** (tel. 721796) is now on Kyrou Nerou (open Tues.-Wed., Fri. 8:30am-2:30pm, Mon., Thurs. 8:30am-2:30pm and 3-6pm; reduced hours in off-season). The **bus station** and **Hellenic Bank** (tel. 721488; fax 722636) are on Markarios Ave. (open Mon.-Tues., Thurs.-Fri. 8:15am-12:30pm and 3:30-6:30pm, Wed. 8:15am-12:30pm; reduced hours in winter). A Cyprus Air representative, **AirTour-Cyprus**, 28 Makarios Ave. (tel. 721265; fax 721776), is nearby (open in summer Mon.-Tues., Thurs.-Sat. 8am-1pm and 4-6:30pm, Wed., Sat. 8am-1pm; reduced hours in winter). There are many places to rent bikes, including **Señor Frogis,** 6 Dionysiou Solomou St. (tel. 722344). Walk up Makarios Ave. and take a right. Rental fees range from £2.50-16 per day.

Buses make the 41km trip from Athens Ave. in Larnaka to the **EMAN station,** opposite the Leros Hotel in Agia Napa (9 per day, Mon.-Sat. 8:30am-5:30pm, 4 per day, Sun. 8:30am-4:30pm; returning to Larnaka 10 per day, Mon.-Sat. 6:30am-5pm, 4 per day, Sun. 9am-4pm; £1 one way). The **post office** is on D. Liperti St. (open Mon.-Fri. 7:30am-1:30pm, Sat. 9-11am). **Postal Code:** 5330. **Telephone Code:** 03.

Accommodations   Half of the buildings in town are luxury hotels full of European box-lunch tours, so inexpensive rooms are elusive and, in August, nearly non-existent. The **HI Youth Hostel,** 23 Dionysiou Solomou St. (tel. 723433), is converted from old tourist apartments so you and your buddies can have your own pad for the night, with communal kitchen, pay phone, and pool table. (6-12 beds and one bath per apartment. £5 per person. Check-out noon. English-language books, maps, and information about Cyprus in the open-air patio/lounge area. Currency exchange at bank rates. Self-service laundromat; wash £1 per pound, dry £1 per pound.) To get to **Xenis Rooms** (tel. 721086), go up the road to Paralimni until you have to turn. A left and then a right at the Four Seasons Supermarket will take you there—it's at the top of the hill. Rooms have fans and fridges. (Doubles £10.) The **campground** (tel. 721946) is 3km from town (£1.25 per person, £1.50 per tent) and near beautiful but crowded **Nissi Beach.**

Food and Entertainment Raven's Rook (tel. 721136), above the Hellenic Bank and near the tourist office, serves meals in a pleasant rooftop garden (tuna salad £2.60, *kebab* £3.65). **The Square Pub & Café,** in the central square, has inexpensive food and outdoor seating with a nice view of the square and monastery (Greek salad £1.60, *moussaka* with salad £2.40). The cheapest takeout in town can be found at **Cross Road,** 14 G. Pappoulis St. (tel. 721282), near Boyles Irish Bar. There is no menu here, but they'll offer what's fresh, and they always have good *kebab* (£1.50; open daily 7-11pm). The **Hard Rock Café** (tel. 722649), opposite the monastery, may or may not be a member of the American chain. You decide (burgers £1; open Mon.-Sat. 11am-2am, Sun. 5pm-2am). A **fruit market** (tel. 723372), on Pappoulis St. near Cross Road, sells fruits and veggies as well as fresh breads, olives, pastries, and drinks (open in summer Mon.-Sat. 7am-8pm, Sun. 8am-1pm; in winter Mon.-Tues., Thurs.-Fri. 7am-8pm, Wed., Sat. 7am-1am, Sun. 8am-1pm).

Agia Napa boasts the most intense nightlife in Cyprus. **Pizazz, Babylon,** and **Vip's** are huge places on the downswing which rarely fill but are still fairly popular. The really happening places to be from 1-5am are **String Fellows,** 9 Nissi Ave. (tel. 723566), a 60s, 70s, and 80s dance club, and the **Kool Club,** 3 Makarios Ave., up from the monastery square on the right. Agia Napa also has a thriving pub scene. **Minos Pub,** up from the monastery square, has a jukebox and music every night, but more important to its patrons are the draft beers (£1-1.60 per pint) and strong drinks (£1.50). The **Makedonia,** within one minute's stumbling distance of Minos, is where you can buy drinks for just £1 all night.

Sights Deserted beaches languish between Larnaka and Agia Napa, past the army base. Closer to Agia Napa, better beaches are north and south of **Protaras** (10km from Agia Napa). Opposite the tourist office is the 16th-century Venetian **Monastery of Agia Napa.** Within its walls you'll find a beautiful courtyard with flowers, plants, trees, and an octagonal, dome-covered, marble fountain. The huge sycamore outside the west entrance is famous in Cyprus. Every summer Sunday at 8pm, locals perform Cypriot **folk dances** in the square near the monastery. The monastery's small chapel is off the main courtyard (open daily 6:30am-8pm). You might hear the well which still supplies water to its cave. The well's appearance is connected to the Miracle of Panagiya. During pirate attacks, Christians would seek refuge in the chapel's cave. Once, when the pirates occupied the town for several days, the people in the cave were at risk of dehydration. Legend says that the Virgin appeared to the people and pointed to the fresh water coming from the corner of the cave; since then, the water has never run dry. Services are held every Saturday at 6pm. In the newer bigger church, outside the walls of the monastery, there are Orthodox services on Sundays beginning at 6:45am, followed by Divine Liturgy at 8am. English services are held every Sunday at 11am.

Close to Agia Anargyri and 8km east of Agia Napa is **Cape Greco.** You'll find no tourists here, no half built concrete hotels, no *tavernas,* and no sand—just rocky coves cascading into the magnificent blue sea. The cape has remained undeveloped because of a military radar installation, giving James Bond aspirants the chance to swim off the rocks beneath two realistic radar dishes. Two kilometers north of Paralimni, a stone's throw from the green line, is the small village of **Dherinia.** Several tourist viewpoints nearby look onto the "ghost" of occupied **Famagusta;** construction cranes stand exactly as they did a quarter of a century ago.

L
I
M
A
S
S
O
L

■ Limassol (Lemesos) ΛΕΜΕΣΟΣ

The island's second largest city and port of entry for most passenger ferries, Limassol is the industrial center of Cyprus, complete with a busy downtown area and merchant ships anchored offshore. The Cyprus Tourism Organization promises that "there's always a good reason" to "make Limassol your destination for any season," and this port town is a cordial introduction to a striking island. Rapid growth and a lack of urban planning have nurtured an endless row of hotels stretching east along the coast, and the city shuts down on weekends—in order to eat, you may have to head for the expensive seafront joints. Despite all of this, the old town is delightful, and the residents are extremely friendly. The city's palm-tree-lined waterfront promenade is attractive and, even at its worst, Limassol still retains some appeal.

ORIENTATION AND PRACTICAL INFORMATION

Centrally situated in Cyprus' south coast and equidistant from other major cities in Southern Cyprus (50-70km), Limassol is the hub for bus and taxi services. Passenger boats arrive at the **new port,** 5km southwest of the town center. As you enter the arrivals terminal, a **tourist desk** to your right has excellent free maps. Bus #1 runs to the port from the station near the Anexartisias St. market and bus #30 runs from the port to downtown Limassol (every 30min., Sat. every hr., 35¢). After ships arrive, buses wait near the customs building; otherwise, the stop is outside the port gates. A taxi to town costs £2.50. If you're headed for another major town, call the appropriate *service* taxi, and you'll be picked up at the port at no extra charge.

Cyprus Tourism Organization: 15 Spiro Araouzos St. (tel. 362756), on the waterfront 1 block east of the castle. Staff answers all questions, suggests daytrips, and provides maps and schedules. Open July-Aug. Mon., Thurs. 8:15am-2:15pm and 4-6:30pm, Tues.-Wed., Fri. 8:15am-2:15pm, Sat. 8:15am-1:15pm; Sept.-June Mon., Thurs. 8:15am-2:30pm and 3-6:30pm, Tues.-Wed., Fri. 8:15am-2:30pm, Sat. 8:15am-1:15pm. An office at the **port** (tel. 343868) is open immediately following arrivals. Another office is in **Dassoudi Beach,** 35 George I Potamos Yermassoyias (tel. 323211), opposite the Park Beach Hotel. Same hours as the Limassol office.

Tourist Agency: Amathous, 2 Syntagma Sq. (tel. 362145), near the tourist office. A chain selling plane and boat tickets. Open Mon.-Fri. 8am-1pm and 4-6:30pm.

American Express: 1 Archiepiskopou Kyprianou St. (tel. 362045), in the offices of **A. L. Mantovani and Sons.** Open for AmEx transactions Mon.-Tues., Thurs.-Fri. 9am-noon and 3:30-6:30pm.

CYTA: on the corner of Markos Botsaris and Athinon St. All phones in Limassol use telecards except a few in the port. Most guesthouses have international phones, but it's cheaper to use a telecard.

Buses: KEMEK terminal, corner of Irenis and Enosis St. To Nicosia (4 per day, Mon.-Fri., 3 per day, Sat. £1.25), Paphos (1 per day, Mon.-Sat. £1.25), and Larnaka (leaves from old port; 4 per day, Mon.-Fri., 2 per day, Sat. £1.50). **Kyriakos,** 21 Thessalonikis St. (tel. 364114). To Platres (1 per day, Mon.-Fri. £1.50).

City Buses: Andreas Themistokles St., near Anexartisias St. Bus #1 goes to the new port, buses #6 and #30 go east along the coast (most don't run on Sun.; 35¢).

Service Taxis: Karydas (tel. 362061) and **Kyriakos** (tel. 364114) share an office at 21 Thessalonikis St. **Kypros** (tel. 363979) and **Akropolis** (tel. 366766) share space at 49 Spiro Araouzos St. **Makris,** 166 Hellas St. (tel. 365550). Karydas, Kypros/Akropolis, and Kyriakos run taxis to Nicosia (£2.60). Akropolis and Makris run taxis to Larnaka (£2.25). All except Akropolis go to Paphos (every hr., £2.50). Less frequent service Sept.-May. Taxis run 6am-5:30pm. No shared taxis on holidays. One company operates on Sun. by rotation.

Bike and Moped Rentals: Agencies cluster on the shore road, near the luxury hotels. Motorcycle license required for rentals, but most agents will take you to the police station, where you can be issued a temporary Cypriot license (£1). Motorbikes £4.50 per day. For long term rentals, you'll find lower rates in Polis.

Limassol

English Bookstores: Bookworld, 156 St. Andrew St. (tel. 376448). Open Mon.-
Tues., Thurs.-Fri. 9am-1pm and 4-7pm; Wed., Sat. 9am-1pm. **Teveza's Book
Swap Shop,** 51 Kitoukyrianou. Open Mon.-Sat. 9am-1pm.

Laundromat: (tel. 368293), Kaningos St. off Markarios Ave., near the Archaeological Museum. Same-day service or do it yourself. Wash £1.80, dry 75¢. Open Mon.-
Tues., Thurs.-Fri. 7:30am-1pm and 3-6:30pm.

Pharmacy: Lakis Christodoulou, 8C Georgiou Gennadiou, near the central market (tel. 363350). Open Mon.-Tues., Thurs.-Fri. 8am-1pm and 4-7pm, Wed. 8am-
1pm., every other Sat. 8am-1pm. Other pharmacies all over town. Call 1402 for an
all night pharmacy.

Hospital: Government General Hospital, outside Limassol near the village Pole-
midia; take the #15 bus. There are many private doctors and clinics.

Police: (tel. 330411), Gladstone and Leondios St. next to the hospital.

Post Office: Main office (tel. 330190), Gladstone St., next to the central police station. Open May-Sept. Mon.-Tues., Thurs.-Fri. 7:30am-1:30pm and 4-6pm, Wed.
7:30am-1:30pm, Sat. 9-11am. **Postal Code:** 3900.

Telephone Code: 05.

ACCOMMODATIONS

In Limassol, you get what you pay for: budget rooms, clustered near the bus station,
are cheap but low quality, and prostitution is common. Solo travelers, especially
women, should stick to a starred hotel or one of the nicer guest houses listed below.

Guest House Luxor, 101 Agios Andreas St. (tel. 362265). Large, high-ceilinged rooms with wooden floors. Some with balconies overlooking the shopping street and fountain below. Fridge available. Reserve in advance in summer. Singles £5. Doubles £8, with bath £10.

Guest House Ikaros, 61 Eleftherias St. (tel. 354348). *Twin Peaks* comes to Limassol. Tapestries, fish tanks, animal skins, and chandeliers. Rooms are large and clean. Shared bath is off a lovely garden filled with large plants. Sinks are on the open-air patio. Each day, first shower free, second is 50¢. International phone. Call to reserve in high season. Singles £5. Doubles £10.

Continental Hotel, 137 Spiro Araouzos St. (tel. 362530). 2-star hotel. Some rooms have balconies with sea views. All rooms with bath, shower, and radio. Reduced rates for longer stays. A/C £2 per day. Singles £15. Doubles £25. Triples £35. Quads £30. Breakfast included.

Stalis Guest House, 59 Eleftharias St. (tel. 368197), next to the Ikaros. Rooms are clean enough with a bed, chair, and dresser. Toilet and shower off an outdoor veranda with hanging laundry. Most bring their own towels, but they have some if you need one. Singles £3. Doubles £5.80.

FOOD AND ENTERTAINMENT

There are a plethora of Cypriot *tavernas,* small *kebab* houses, and cafés lining the streets of Limassol. The best option for the health- and wealth-conscious traveler may be the **Central Market.** This huge warehouse spills onto the sidewalk outside and is filled with fresh produce, meat, seafood, and bread vendors (open Mon.-Tues., Thurs.-Fri. 6am-1pm and 4-6pm, Wed. 6am-1pm). You can put together a cheap, delicious lunch of grapes, a loaf of freshly baked bread, and locally made *halloumi* cheese for less than £1.

Makri Maria, 3 Ankara St. (tel. 357676). The owner of this endearingly unpretentious restaurant serves delicious Cypriot food cooked over hot coals. *Meze* consists of 20 standard dishes. The grilled *lountza* and *halloumi* is delicious, as is the refreshing *tzantziki.* Diners enjoy the streetside tables in summer and guitar playing inside in winter. Coffee 35¢. Open Mon.-Sat. 7pm-10:30 or 11pm.

Richard and Berengaria, 23 Irinis St. (tel. 363863), opposite the castle. This tiny *kebab* house serves inexpensive food to locals and tourists. Offers local specialties *shettalia* (£1) and *halloumi* sandwiches (75¢). Cypriot brandy sour (65¢).

Edo Lemosos, 111 Irinis St. (tel. 353378). Traditional Greek guitar music late into the evening at this lively *taverna.* Summer outdoor seating in a large tree-covered, candlelit courtyard. *Meze* (£7.75). Local brandies (½ bottle £3.75). Musicians indoors in the winter. Open daily 9:30pm-12:30am.

Café Artistiko, 1 Themidos St. (tel. 745711). If you want a bit of a Bohemian experience, this is the restaurant for you. 72 types of crepes, sandwiches, and salads. Special crepe made with Grand Marnier, orange marmalade, sugar, and butter £3, simpler ones £1-2.85. Backgammon sets on the tables and a nook crammed with current Greek periodicals. Open Mon.-Sat. 9am-2am, Sun. noon-2am.

Skoozi! (tel. 642549), St. Andrew St. at Salaminos, 1 block from the Guest House Luxor. Soups, salads, sandwiches, and pasta for a hip, local clientele. Youngish Cypriots enjoy jazz, trance, and opera music wafting over the stone floors and Byzantine arches. Delicious crepes (banana with ganache £2.60). Many kinds of fresh coffees 65¢.

In addition to the *tavernas,* there are many bars and nightclubs. Those along the coast near Dassoudi Beach are overrun by 16-year-old tourists who help create the wild pickup scene; **Whisper's, Temptations,** and **Basement Disco** can be fun if that's what you're in the mood for. According to locals, the hotter clubs are **La Bubu** and **Opu Opu** near Elias beach and Hawaii Beach. Close to Dassoudi Beach is **Sismos (Earthquake),** which is quite popular with local twenty- to thirty-somethings.

SIGHTS

The **Limassol Castle** is the only building of historical significance in Limassol proper. This 12th-century Frankish structure, where Richard married Queen Berengaria in 1191, was destroyed by earthquakes and Genoese assaults; the only traces of the old Byzantine fort are in the western wall of the building. In the early 14th century, the Knights Templar fortified the castle's walls and covered the Gothic windows. Later, the Knights of St. John converted the great Western Hall into a Gothic church and the chapel into a series of prison cells. The Turks claimed the castle in 1570, and the capacious West Hall was used as a prison under the British regime until 1940. The **Cyprus Medieval Museum** (tel. 330419) is the final incarnation of the castle (open Mon.-Fri. 7:30am-5pm, Sat. 9am-5pm; off season Mon.-Sat. 7:30am-5pm; admission 75¢). The **Archaeological Museum** (tel. 330132), on the corner of Kaningos and Vyronos, contains an assortment of funerary *stelae,* jewelry, statues, and terra-cotta figurines once used as stand-ins for Bronze Age Cypriots who were too hung over to do the temple thing on Sunday mornings (open Mon.-Fri. 7:30am-5pm, Sat. 9am-5pm, Sun. 10am-1pm; admission 75¢). On Byron St., closer to the sea, are the **public gardens** and town **zoo,** the largest in Cyprus (both open daily 9am-noon and 3-6pm; reduced hours in off season; admission 50¢). At summer's end, Limassol's gardens are transformed into a modern-day tribute to the ancient wine god, Dionysus. In the Limassol **wine festival,** participants are given a bottle to fill with as much of the local wine as they can handle. Between trips to the casks, digestion is aided by music, dance, and theater performances. A bottle of your favorite vintage makes a great souvenir at the evening's close (open late Aug. to early Sept. 6-11pm, admission £1.50). The **folk art museum,** 253 Agios Andreas St. (tel. 362303), one block east of the intersection of Zenon and Agios Andreas, houses 19th- and 20th-century embroidery and costumes (open Mon.-Wed., Fri. 8:30am-1:30pm and 3-5:30pm, Thurs. 8:30am-1:30pm; reduced hours in off season; admission 30¢).

Limassol's **Reptile House** (tel. 372770) at the Old Port showcases poisonous scaly critters from around the world (open daily 9am-5pm; admission £1, children 50¢). The city's long stone beach fails to inspire ecstasy, but a new breakwater has made the area more pleasant for swimming. **Dassoudi Beach,** 3km east of town, is far better. Take bus #6 from the market on Kanaris St. (every 15min., 40¢). The ebullient **Ladies Mile Beach** at the new port is also popular (take bus #1). At the end of June, actors from around the world trek to Limassol to take part in **Shakespeare Nights** (tel. 363015), when a Shakespearean drama is performed daily over a long weekend at the Kourion ancient theater. An **International Art Festival** is sponsored by the city of Limassol during the first two weeks in July. The theme and location change annually but always include performances of classical Greek dramas, exhibitions of Cypriot and international painters, and concerts (events usually begin at 8pm; some are free, some charge £3-5). The tourist office has brochures with the current festival's schedule. The **Wine-Fest** in early September promises divine euphoria. **Carnival,** 50 days before Orthodox Easter (usually in Feb.), is celebrated more intensely in Limassol than anywhere else in Cyprus, with various parades and balls. Details are available at the tourist office and in *This Month's Principal Events.*

■ Near Limassol: Akrotiri Peninsula

The **Kolossi Castle,** a square, three story structure 9km west of Limassol, played a crucial role during the Crusades. Both the Knights Templar and the Knights of the Order of St. John briefly made the castle their headquarters. When the latter knights moved to Rhodes in 1310, Kolossi, with the wealth of its vineyards, remained their richest overseas possession (open June-Sept. daily 7:30am-7:30pm, Oct.-May 7:30am-5pm; admission 50¢). To reach Kolossi, take bus #16 from the urban bus station in Limassol (every 20min., 40¢).

Outside the British sovereign base of Akrotiri, the small resort town of **Pissouri** frolics year-round with Her Majesty's military men. Built on a cliff with the standard enticing views, Pissouri has several bars and *tavernas*. The **Bunch of Grapes Inn** (tel. (052) 21275) has a restaurant and rooms. (Doubles £25. Breakfast included.)

The remarkably well preserved ruins of **Kourion** (Curium in Latin), 12km west of Limassol, are within the British Sovereign Base Area, which includes all of the Akrotiri Peninsula. First settled during the Neolithic Period, Kourion was colonized by Achaïans from Argos during the 14th and 13th centuries BCE. It became famous for its **sanctuary to Apollo** (8th century BCE) and its **stadium** (2nd century CE), both west of the main settlement. In the 4th century CE, Kourion was leveled by the same earthquake that destroyed several other Cypriot coastal cities. The city was rebuilt in the 5th century only to be burned in the 7th century during an Arab raid.

The impressive **amphitheater** is used for **Shakespeare Nights** in June, occasional summer concerts and theatrical productions, and weekend theater in September. The earliest structure on the site, a small theater built in the 2nd century BCE was enlarged in the first century CE. During Greek and Roman times, the theater was used for dramas, but by the 3rd century CE, civilization had progressed and the odeum became an arena for animal fights and professional wrestling.

Across the road from the basilica lie a group of ruins under excavation. In the north corner is a large Hellenistic building and a reservoir used until the 7th century. In the southwest corner a row of Corinthian columns is all that remains of the **Forum,** a marketplace dating from the end of the 2nd century CE.

Farther northwest are the remains of the **House of Gladiators** and its mosaic gladiator pinups. Try to avoid plummeting into the nearby cisterns. The **House of Achilles,** facing the highway at the end of the excavation site, is fenced off, but you can get the key at the ticket office, or climb in through the narrow path following the fence along the road (site open June-Sept. daily 7:30am-7:30pm; Oct.-May daily 7:30am-5pm; admission £1). The nearby **Museum of Kourion** in Episkopi village provides clear explanations of the artifacts (open Mon., Wed., Fri. 7:30am-2:30pm; Thurs. 7:30am-2:30pm and 3-6pm; admission £1).

Buses leave Limassol Castle bound for ancient Kourion and Kourion castle (every hr. on the hr., 9am-2pm, return from ancient Kourion 11:50am, 2:50, and 4:50pm, 60¢). Mopeders to Kourion usually go via Episkopi village. There are no signs for Kourion until you're within a couple of kilometers of the site, so a good map is essential. The highway lanes change and end abruptly, and traffic is heavy. Without a helmet, it's madness. Remember, Cypriots drive on the *left* side of the road; if you can't keep this in mind, don't bike.

■ Troodos Mountains ΤΡΟΟΔΟΣ

In this serene mountain range, isolated villages nestled amid cool, pine covered hills, halfway between Nicosia and Limassol, provide refuge from sun baked coastal cities. Tiny hamlets mingle with Byzantine churches while remote monasteries and pine forests ward off the summer heat. Hikers and campers in particular will find a small paradise here. What is usually a peaceful and rejuvenating natural experience in June and early July, however, can turn frustrating and costly in August when crowds descend, especially on weekends. From January to March, Mt. Olympus, the highest point in Cyprus (1951m), is host to hundreds of skiers.

Public transportation to the area and between the villages runs infrequently. One **bus** per day heads here from Nicosia and Limassol. The best way to get around is to rent some wheels or make a friend with a car. Some hitch, but *Let's Go* does not recommend it. It's difficult to maintain a rigid schedule here. In the mountains, only Platres has motorbike rentals, but you can easily rent mopeds or cars in Limassol, Paphos, Polis, or Nicosia. Mountain roads are tortuous, winding, bumpy, and sometimes steep.

PLATRES

Platres will most likely be your first stop in the Troodos region, as it is the most accessible by public transportation. **Zingas Bus** (tel. (02) 463154) in Nicosia runs to Platres at 12:15pm, returning at 6am (Mon.-Fri., £1.50 one way). From Limassol, **Kyriakos** (tel. 364114), a *service* taxi, leaves at 11:30am, returning at 7am (Mon.-Fri., £2 one way). A private **taxi** from either city costs £15-20. **Mountain bikes** can be rented from **Top Hill Souvenirs** (tel. 421729) on the main street, down the hill from the post office. There are some great bike routes in the Troodos, and the staff is happy to help you find them (4-gear bikes run £3-4 per day; open daily 10am-6pm).

Platres is divided into the **pano** (upper) and **kato** (lower) sections. Kato Platres, 20 minutes downhill from Pano Platres, remains unharried by tourism; all tourist facilities are in Pano Platres. The **tourist office** (tel. 421316) is left of the parking lot in the main square (open Mon.-Fri. 9am-3pm, Sat. 9am-2pm). The **post office** sits to the left of the tourist office (open in summer Mon.-Fri. 7am-noon and 3-5pm; in winter Mon.-Fri. 8-10am and 3-5pm). The **telephone office,** next to the post office, sells phone cards (open Mon.-Fri. 7:30am-1:30pm). The **Bank of Cyprus** is opposite the tourist office (open Mon.-Fri. 8:15am-12:30pm and 3-5:30pm). The **hospital** (tel. 421324) is below Pano Platres (open 24hr.). The nearest **pharmacy** (tel. 922020) is in Kakopetria (open Mon.-Fri. 8am-2pm, Sat. 8am-1:30pm). The **police** (tel. 421351) are opposite the tourist office in a converted military chapel. **Postal code:** 4815 in Kato and 4820 in Pano Platres. **Telephone Code:** 05.

The **Patsilypon Hotel** (tel. 421738) is over 100 years old, according to the current owner. The old wooden doors and the mountain views from large shuttered windows are lovely. (Singles £6. Doubles £12. Prices rise £1.50 per person July-Aug.) Two large **grocery stores** are just past the Patsilypon Hotel. **Soforla Supermarket** (tel. 421666) and **Cherryland** (tel. 421414) stock standard supplies and a huge selection of ice cream bars (Soforla open daily 7:30am-9pm; Cherryland open daily 7am-10pm). North of Platres on the road to Troodos, **Psilo Dentro** (Tall Tree; tel. 422050) serves sumptuous trout from its fish farm under a beautiful canopy of tall trees (whole trout £4.20; open daily 8am-5pm).

Near Platres is the cordial lace and wine village of **Omodos,** next to the famous **Monastery of the Holy Cross.** After a tour of the **folk museum** in the monastery and the restored **wine press** *(linos),* you can buy a bottle of local, dry wine (£1.70) or the fiery *tsipoura,* a Cypriot whiskey. As you return to Kato Platres, signposts lead to the red-tiled village of **Phini.** The **Pilavakion Museum** (tel. 421508) focuses on *pith-aria* (large, red, ceramic jars), wine-making equipment, and the "Pithari Sauna" used in traditional Cypriot obstetrics to avoid post-pregnancy stretch marks (if you call ahead, they'll open for you; admission £1). The family-run **Neraida Restaurant** (tel. 421680), serving fresh trout (£3.50), *meze* (£4), and *kleftiko* (£3.50), offers all *Let's Go* readers a free bottle of village wine (open Feb.-Nov. daily 8am-11pm.).

TROODOS

Though just 8km north of Platres, **Troodos** is only accessible by **bus** from **Clarios Bus Co.** (tel. 453234) in Nicosia (Mon.-Fri. at 11:30am, returns at 6:30am, £1.10). Private **taxi** from Nicosia costs £17. Taxi fare from Platres is £5 or you can hike it (at least 1hr.). Troodos village is an easily missed group of hotels, restaurants, and tourist facilities. The **police** (tel. 421623), just outside of town, offer **CYTA** information, but do not operate all year, and sometimes might not be there at all. For more reliable services, head to Platres or Limassol.

The **Troodos campground** (tel. 422249), 2km north of the main square in a pine forest (£1 per person), provides laundry facilities, a minimarket, a bar/restaurant, and a first aid station. The **Jubilee Hotel Bar** (tel. 421647), just outside of town, is a favorite of British expats. The sign for **horseback riding** is on the right driving into town from Platres. Trust the horse; he's going the right way (£5 per hr.).

Three self guided **nature trails** originate in the Troodos area. The first is 8½km long and goes from the Troodos post office to Chromion, passing by various villages. A 3km trail leaves from the coffee shop in Troodos Sq. and finishes at a divine lookout point. Shorter but even more captivating is the 2km path following a stream from the presidential palace in Troodos and finishing at beautiful Kaledonia Falls near Platres (45min.). Noteworthy trees and plants are labeled on the way. The tourist office has a pamphlet outlining the trails, and it's helpful to get a guidebook and map for starting points.

KAKOPETRIA AND ENVIRONS

Picturesque **Kakopetria,** literally "bad rock," on the main road from Troodos to Nicosia, is the most popular town in the northern part of the mountains. According to local legend, the large rock perched on the hillside was supposed to bring good luck to newlyweds. That is, until one day, the "bad rock" rolled over and crushed a couple. The government is preserving the oldest section of the village; the shady, cobblestone roads and mud brick houses overlook a river and soothing water mill. In the rest of the village, slick new pubs and "rustic" hotels cater to vacationers.

The **Bank of Cyprus** is in the main square (open Mon.-Fri. 8:15am-12:30pm), near the **post office** (open Mon.-Wed., Fri. 7:30am-1:30pm, Thurs. 7:30am-1:30pm and 3-6pm). The **police station** (tel. 922420, -255) is up the street from the bank. A **pharmacy** (tel. 2020) is below the Rialto Hotel (open 9:30am-9pm), and the **doctor** (tel. 3077) is a few doors down. The **Rialto Hotel** (tel. (02) 922438) charges £43 per double, breakfast included. The **Hekali** (tel. (02) 922501) offers clean rooms. (£18 per person. Breakfast included.) The **Kifissia Hotel** (tel. (02) 922421) has calming views of the small river. (£8 per person. English breakfast included.)

Kakopetria and its smaller neighbor **Galata** have five Byzantine churches between them; the most beautiful is **Agios Nikolaos tis Stegis,** 4km southwest of Kakopetria on a dirt road. The interior of this 14th-century church is painted with strikingly unique frescoes like the Virgin Mary breast-feeding Jesus. While more common among Roman Catholic scenes, such icons are very rare for Greek Orthodox Churches (open Tues.-Sat. 9am-4pm, Sun. 11am-4pm). **Buses** to Kakopetria travel from **Clarios Bus Co.** (tel. (02) 453234 in Nicosia; in summer 12-14 per day, Mon.-Sat., 2 per day, Sun., £1.10). A delicious dinner (lambchops £4.50) with a spectacular view of the Old Village can be had at **Maryland at the Mill** (tel. 922536), at the town's mill (open Mon.-Fri. noon-11pm, Sat.-Sun. noon-3:30pm and 7:30-11pm).

Sixteen kilometers northeast of Kakopetria, the teensy Byzantine church at **Asinou** *(Panayia Porviotissa)* contains some of the best mural paintings on the island. The church and original frescoes hail from the 12th century, but new frescoes were added and old ones restored after the church was tampered with by Turks in the 14th and 16th centuries. Today, the church is used for religious purposes only twice a year on feast days of the Virgin. To visit the church, find the priest in the nearby village of **Nikitare** (ask in the village cafés). The church of **Panagiatou Arakou,** 16km southeast of Kakopetria, is another repository of elaborate 12th-century frescoes, including Christ Pantokrator (on the inside of the dome). South of the church is the comely vineyard village of **Agros,** with the only rooms in the vicinity.

Eight monks and myriad animals make their home in the modern **Troodhitissa Monastery,** 5km from Platres on the Prodromos-Platres road. Dedicated to the Virgin Mary, the original monastery was built in 1250 to house one of her miracle-working icons. During the chaos of the iconoclastic movement of the 8th century, a monk hid an icon of the Virgin Mary in Troodos, where a miraculous pillar of fire protected it. More than 100 years later, a sign revealed the site of the monastery, which still stands today (open daily 6am-noon and 2-8pm).

Between Troodos and Prodromos soars **Mt. Olympus** (2100m), the highest peak on the island, now topped with radar stations and observation towers. From here you can get an amazing view of the entire island. From January through March, visitors sunbathe in Limassol and ski on the mountain's north face.

PRODROMOS

Approximately three buildings comprise Prodomos, which seems more a tribute to asceticism than to tourism. Ten kilometers northwest of the town of Troodos, **Prodromos** is the second-highest hill resort in the area (after Troodos). Relax at the nearby **Stephos Café** before heading on to **Pedoulas,** a small village to the north of Prodromos, featuring the Church of Archangel Michael, which has mural paintings dating from 1474. Up the street from the church is the **CYTA** and the **police,** who can answer most tourist questions. Across the street is the miniscule **post office. Postal Code** 4840. **Telephone Code:** 0295.

Kykko Monastery, in the northwest part of the mountains, 14km from Pedoulas and 33km from Troodos, enjoys more wealth and prestige than any other monastery on the island. Founded in the early 12th century when a hermit, after curing the Byzantine Emperor's daughter, was given the Apostle Luke's own Icon of the Virgin Mary. The monastery has burned down numerous times, but the celebrated icon has survived intact. As the icon is thought too holy to be viewed directly, it is completely ensconced in mother of pearl and silver casing. After entering the monastery's palatial courtyard, you may think you've wandered into a large luxury hotel; the monastery, whose present buildings date from the early 19th century, is somewhat unmonasteryish, with 400 beds for visitors, a tourist pavilion, and shops.

Kykko gained new fame this century as a communication and supply center during the Cypriot struggle and as the monastic home of Archbishop Makarios III. Only 1½km away were the headquarters of the first military leader of the struggle, " Dighenis" (General George Grivas). **Makarios' tomb** is just 2km farther in the high hills west of the monastery. The site, guarded at all times by two Greek Cypriot soldiers, is partially open to the east. Makarios requested the opening so that on the day Cyprus was reunited, sunlight would enter his tomb and he could celebrate with his people. Just above the tomb is a path leading up to an icon of the Virgin, called the *throni* (small throne). The bushes alongside the path are laden with scraps of clothing placed there by sick children hoping to be cured. A supermarket, an extortionistic tourist pavilion, and several sweet shops are nearer to the monastery.

■ Paphos ΠΑΦΟΣ

When the Ptolemies, Greek kings of Egypt, conquered Cyprus, they made Paphos their capital. The city grew fabulously wealthy and developed into a cosmopolitan, commercial center. Paphos maintained its exalted position under Cato and the Roman conquerors, but a 4th-century earthquake halted its supremacy. The Cypriot capital, with the accompanying political and social prestige, moved to Salamis (near modern Famagusta). Paphos remained a small village until the Turkish occupation rendered almost all of North Cyprus' tourist areas inaccessible to Southern Cypriots. Since 1974, Paphos has ballooned with luxury hotels and restaurants. Still, it remains a comfortable and manageable city, with all the standard-issue features of Cyprus at its best—archaeological discoveries, gorgeous mosaics, fabulous restaurants, and, in the surrounding countryside, sublime beaches and isolated villages.

ORIENTATION AND PRACTICAL INFORMATION

The city of Paphos is divided into two sections. The upper **Ktima Paphos** (referred to simply as "Paphos") is centered around Kennedy Sq., and the lower **Kato Paphos** lies roughly 1km to the south. Formed in the 8th century CE when the townspeople fled inland to evade Arab assaults from the sea, Ktima Paphos is now home to most of the city's shops, budget hotels, and services, while luxury hotels and holiday villas jam Kato Paphos, also the hub of Paphos's nightlife. Everything listed is in Ktima Paphos, unless otherwise noted.

Cyprus Tourist Organization, 3 Gladstone St. (tel. 232841), across from Iris Travel. Open Mon.-Tues., Thurs.-Fri. 8:15am-2:30pm and 3-6:15 pm, Wed.

8:15am-2:30pm, Sat. 8:15am-1:30pm; reduced hours in winter. **Airport C.T.O.** (tel. 422833) opens when flights arrive.

Budget Travel: Iris Travel, 10A Gladstone St. (tel. 237585), opposite the C.T.O. Ferry tickets to Rhodes, Crete, and Israel (student discounts up to 20%). Airline tickets to London and Greece available (student discounts up to 40% if between 24-28 years old and depending on airline). Rents cars (Suzuki 700 or Subaru Jeeps £13-22 per day, insurance £3, unlimited mileage; must be over 25) and apartments (from £5 per person). Open in summer Mon.-Fri. 8am-1pm and 4-7pm, Sat. 8am-1pm; in winter Mon.-Fri. 2:30-5:30pm.

Banks: Concentrated on Makarios Ave. **National Bank,** 108 Makarios Ave., with **ATM.** Open Mon. 8:30am-12:30pm and 3:15-4:45pm, Tues.-Fri. 8:30am-12:30pm. **Lombard Natwest National Bank,** 48 Makarios Ave. (tel. 250370), with **ATM.** Open Mon. 8:30am-12:30pm and 3-5pm, Tues.-Fri. 8:30am-12:30pm. **Bank of Cyprus,** Evagorou St., with **ATM.** Open Mon. 8:30am-12:30pm and 3:15-4:45pm, Tues.-Fri. 8:30am-12:30pm. **Hellenic Bank,** (tel. 233316), Kennedy Sq. at Oiogenis. Open Mon. 8:30am-12:30pm and 3:15-4:45pm, Tues., Thurs.-Fri. 8:30am-12:30pm and 4-7pm, Wed. 8:30am-12:30pm. Another branch is at 86 Makarios Ave. (tel. 235035). Open Mon.-Fri. 8:30am-12:30pm.

CYTA: (tel. 230228), Grivas Digenes Ave. Open daily 7:30am-7:30pm, or earlier.

Airport: C.T.O. (tel. 422641). Contrary to popular belief, there is a second international airport in Cyprus. Although most flights come into Larnaka, Paphos International Airport receives various European airlines and many chartered flights. Opens when flights arrive. Offers **currency exchange** and a C.T.O. branch. Private taxis from city center £4.25, from Kato Paphos £5. No bus service.

Buses: Nea Amoroza Co. (tel. 221114), 79 Pallikaridi St., across from the ESSO station. Minibuses run to Polis (10 per day, Mon.-Fri. 6:30am-7pm, £1). Some go as far as Pomes (£1.15 from Paphos). **KEMEK** (tel. 234255) runs buses to Limassol from the Mitropolis Bldg., off Thermopylon St. (2 per day, £1.25). Change buses in Limassol for Nicosia or Larnaka. **Excursion buses** make 2 roundtrips per day to Palaepaphos Museum and the birthplace of Aphrodite (£1.15). Bus #30 makes stops at most larger hotels.

City Buses: Municipal buses run between Ktima Paphos and Kato Paphos (Mon.-Sat. 31 per day, Sun. 14 per day, 30¢). Catch it in Ktima Paphos just up the road from the post office. In Kato Paphos, at any of the yellow benches on the road to town. Buses also go to Coral Bay (20 per day, 40¢). Schedules in the tourist office.

Service Taxis: Kyriakos/Karydas, 9 E. Pallikaridi St. (tel. 232459). **Kypros,** 134 Makarios Ave. (tel. 237722). **Makris,** 19 E. Pallikarides St. (tel. 232538), Kennedy Sq. To Limassol (every hr., 6am-6pm, £2.05); change there for Larnaka or Nicosia.

Moped Rental: Several shops in Kato or Ktima Paphos. Prices range £2.50-5.

International Bookstore: Axel Bookshop, 62-64 Makarios Ave. (tel. 232404). Books about Cyprus and novels in English. Open Mon.-Sat. 8am-1pm and 4-7pm. **Kiosks** in Kennedy Sq. sell international newspapers and *Cyprus Weekly.*

Pharmacies: Can be found on just about every corner in Paphos.

Hospital: Paphos General, Neophytos Nicolaides St. (tel. 240111). Free first aid. English spoken. Pretty far to walk; take a taxi. **St. George's Private Hospital,** 29 Eeleftherios Venizelos Ave. (tel. 247000, fax 241886), on the way to the youth hostel. Covers all medical cases, including accident and emergencies. Casualty and ambulance services. English spoken. Open 24hr.

Police: (tel. 240140), Grivas Digenes Ave. in Kennedy Sq., opposite the Coop Bank. English spoken. Open 24hr. For **emergencies,** dial #199.

Post Office: Main branch on Leoforos Eleftheriou Venizelou. Open Mon.-Tues., Thurs.-Fri. 7:30am-1:30pm and 3:30-5:30pm (afternoon hours for stamp purchase only), Wed. 7:30am-1:30pm, Sat. 9-11am. **Smaller office** (tel. 240223) on Nikodhimou Mylona St. Open Mon.-Fri. 7:30am-1:30pm, Sat. 9-11am. The post office in **Kato Paphos** is on Ag. Antoniou St. (tel. 240226).

Postal Code: 8900 (in Ktima Paphos); 8903 (in Kato Paphos).

Telephone Code: 06.

ACCOMMODATIONS

Finding inexpensive accommodations in Paphos is a chore. Solo travelers should stick to the youth hostel; groups might try renting an apartment. The following are in Ktima (upper) Paphos, unless otherwise noted. Prices are higher in Kato Paphos, but the nightlife is more high-powered.

Youth Hostel (HI), 37 Eleftheriou Venizelou Ave. (tel. 232588), on a residential street northeast of the town center. From the square, follow Pallikaridi to Venizelou; make a right onto Venizelou—a 10-min. walk from town. Hot showers. £3.50 per night. Sheets £1.

Hotel Trianon, 99 Makarios Ave. (tel. 232193). Toned-down exterior in keeping with the older interior. Rooms are reasonably clean, but common bathrooms leave much to be desired. Most comfortable for those (especially women) *not* traveling alone. Singles £5. Doubles £8.

Kiniras Hotel, 91 Makarios Ave. (tel. 241604). Costly, but classy and clean. All rooms with private bath and phone. Small, but aesthetically pleasing. Has restaurant and lovely patio. Guests receive a 20% discount on car rentals. A/C available at £2 per day. Singles £20. Doubles £30. Breakfast included.

Pyramos Hotel, 4 Agias Anastasias St. (tel. 235161), in Kato Paphos. Often booked with British tour groups. Singles £20. Doubles £24. Breakfast included.

Zenon Gardens Yeroskipou Camping (tel. 242277), east of the tourist beach on the sea, 3km from Paphos Harbor. Minimarket, restaurant, and kitchen. Open March-Oct. £2 per pitch. £2 per 3 people. £1 per small tent.

FOOD AND ENTERTAINMENT

While most restaurants in Kato Paphos are geared to pound-laden foreigners, there are some cheap options. **Hondros,** 96 Pavlou St. (tel. 234256), is one of the older restaurants in the area, founded long before the town's tourist boom. Sit under the bamboo-covered terrace beneath the grapevines and eat lamb *kleftiko* off the spit (£3.75; *moussaka* £2.50; open daily 11am-4pm and 7pm-midnight). One of the newer restaurants in the area, **Surfcafé,** 1 Gladstone St. (tel. 253125), across from the police, is classy and reasonably priced (sandwiches £1-1.50, crepes £1.50, coffee 40-80¢, beer 80¢). The café also boasts internet on two high tech computers (£1 per hr.). In Ktima Paphos, you can bask in the courtyard of **Trianon,** 100 Makarios Ave. (tel. 233010; stuffed vine leaves £2.50). **Peggy's Miranda Café** in Kennedy Sq. serves continental breakfast (£2) and hosts a book swap (open Mon.-Tues., Thurs.-Fri. 7am-6:30pm, Wed. morning, all day Sun.). Sugar-starved travelers may try the sweet shop **Athens,** 47 Evagora Pallekaride (tel. 232613).

The two most popular **beaches** stretch along **Yeroskipou** and **Coral Bay.** Yeroskipou is well touristed with showers and snack bars, while Coral Bay is sandier, a bit less crowded, and frequented mostly by locals. Bus #11 from Ktima Paphos goes to Yeroskipou (every 20-25min., 40¢), and bus #15 goes to Coral Bay from Yeroskipou (every 20min., 40¢).

SIGHTS

Kato Paphos

The mosaic floors of the **House of Dionysus,** the **House of Theseus,** and the **House of Aion** (tel. 240217) are the city's more dazzling ancient spots. Discovered accidentally in 1962 by a farmer plowing his fields and excavated by a Polish expedition, the largely intact mosaics covered 14 rooms of the expansive Roman House of Dionysus. The floors depict scenes from mythology and daily life with vibrance and a subtle use of the stones' natural hues. The villa's pervasive wine theme led some archaeologists to conclude that it belonged to a vineyard owner or wine merchant (or a drunkard). Even the abstract designs contain images of cups. Inscriptions exhort "In Vino Veritas." To get there, take Sophias Vembo St., off A. Pavlou Ave. (open daily 7:30am-7:30pm; reduced hours in off season; admission to all £1).

Farther towards the water rests the **House of Theseus** complex, dating from the 2nd to the 6th centuries CE. The ruins reveal a luxurious building complete with marble statues and columns, mosaic floors, and a bath complex. The two mosaics of Theseus and Achilles are accessible by walkways. To the north of the mosaics, you'll find the remnants of an *agora* beside the remains of a limestone Roman **odeon**—a small, roofed semi-circular theater. Built in the 2nd century CE, the odeon accommodates 3000 and is still used for performances (open in summer daily 7:30am-7pm; in winter 7:30am-5pm; free; ask the tourist office for performance schedules).

The musty **Catacombs of Agia Solomoni,** along the road between Ktima and Kato Paphos (opposite the Apollo Hotel), include a chapel with deteriorating Byzantine frescoes. Dedicated to St. Solomoni (Hannah), mother of seven children who were tortured to death for their faith during the persecution of Jews in Palestine (168 BCE), the chapel sits on the site of the old synagogue of Paphos. Part of the deepest chamber is filled with lucent water, which you may not notice until you're drenched in it. A tree with handkerchiefs draped from its branches marks the entrance to the catacombs on A. Pavlos Ave. The tree is said to cure the illnesses of those who tie a cloth to it (open 24hr.; free). St. Paul was allegedly whipped for preaching Christianity at **St. Paul's Pillar.** Built in the late 7th century on a hill overlooking the harbor, the **Byzantine Castle** (*Saranda Kolones* or 40 Columns) was intended to protect inhabitants from Arab pirates. To get there, take Sophia Vembo St. off A. Pavlou Ave. When an earthquake destroyed the castle in 1222, the Lusignans built the **Paphos Fort** at the end of the pier, which was used and rebuilt by Venetians and later by Turks (open Mon.-Fri. 7:30am-2:30pm, Thurs. 3-6pm, Sat.-Sun. 9am-5pm; admission 75¢).

Ktima Paphos

The **Archaeological Museum** (tel. 240215), on Grivas Digenes Ave., houses an array of Bronze Age pottery, tools, sculpture, statues, and artifacts from the House of Dionysus and the House of Theseus (open Mon.-Fri. 7:30am-2:30pm and 3-5pm, Thurs. 7:30am-2:30pm and 3-6pm., Sat-Sun. 10am-1pm; admission 75¢). Don't miss the **Ethnographic Museum,** 1 Exo Vrysi St. (tel. 232010), south of the town center in the century-old Eliades residence. The garden vaunts a 3rd-century BCE Hellenistic tomb, Christian catacombs, and *kleftiko* ovens (open Mon.-Sat. 9am-5:30pm, Sun. 10am-1pm; admission £1; guidebooks in English £3). The **Byzantine Museum,** #26 25th Martiou St. (tel. 232092), has icons and religious relics from local monasteries and churches (open Mon.-Fri. 9am-12:30pm and 4-7pm, Sat. 9am-12:30pm; reduced hours in winter; admission 50¢).

West of Ktima Paphos, a signposted road runs 1km to Paleokastra's **Tombs of the Kings** (tel. 240295)—a misnomer, since those interred in these stone tombs were merely upwardly mobile local aristocracy. The larger tombs consist of an open court encircled by burial chambers, with Doric columns carved out of the underground rock and stairways leading down to the interiors. The tombs, from the Hellenistic and Roman periods, were also used as hideouts by early Christians fleeing persecution. To the north of the tombs lies **Paleoeklisia** (literally old church) with fragments of Byzantine frescoes (both open June-Sept. Mon.-Fri. 7:30am-5pm, Sat.-Sun. 9am-5pm; Oct.-May 7:30am-sunset; admission 50¢).

■ Near Paphos

The area around Paphos conceals some of Cyprus's greater treasures. Adjacent to the modern village of **Kouklia,** 17km southeast of Paphos, lie the ruins of the great **Temple of Aphrodite** (tel. 432180) and **Paleopaphos** (Old Paphos), once the capital of a kingdom encompassing nearly half of Cyprus. The temple itself was the religious center of the island and a destination for pilgrims from all parts of the Roman world. Built in the 12th century BCE, it thrived until the 4th century CE, when the anti-pagan edicts of Emperor Theodosius and a series of earthquakes reduced it to rubble. The scant remains—merely piles of rocks—make little sense without a guide. *A Brief History and Description of Old Paphos,* published by the Cyprus Department of Antiquities, is available at most museums (sight open Mon.-Fri. 7:30am-5pm, Sat.-Sun. 9am-4pm; admission 45¢). The **Archaeological Museum** at the site houses pottery and inscriptions (holds same hours as site). The **Epigraphic Museum** next door has a variety of carved stones which represent aspects of life in the once-grand capital. The sites are most easily seen with the excursion buses (see Practical Information, p. 405). Another way to get to Kouklia is to take a shared taxi for Limassol and ask the driver to drop you off. Renting a moped is not advisable— there is heavy traffic on the road leading there (museums and temple open Mon.-Fri. 7:30am-5pm, Sat.-Sun. 9am-4pm; admission to ruins, city, and museums 50¢).

The **Monastery of Agios Neophytos,** with icons, Byzantine frescoes, and painted caves and buildings, lies 9km north of Paphos, near Coral Bay Beach. Roughly 100m from the monastery complex is a ravine with a winter stream and three rock caves carved out by Neophytos and covered with beautiful 12th-century frescoes. You can get here by taking the bus to Tala (6 per day Mon.-Fri., 4 per day Sat.-Sun.). and then walking to the monastery. Bring a flashlight (open daily 7:30am-noon and 3pm-dusk; admission 50¢).

Archbishop Makarios III, Cyprus's most revered figure, was born in the mountain village of **Pano Panayia,** 38km northeast of Paphos, where he lived until entering the Kykko Monastery. A monument to him stands in the town square, and the small house where he was born has been converted into a museum (open daily 9am-noon and 1-5pm; free). One kilometer southeast from Pano Panayia and 40km from Paphos is **Chryssorogiatissa Monastery,** the most picturesque monastery in Cyprus. According to legend, Ignatius found one of three icons of the Virgin Mary painted by St. Luke on the beach at Paphos. The Virgin told him to build a monastery in her honor, and he did. A fire destroyed much of the monastery in 1967, but its collection of 18th-century icons and frescoes is still intact. Four buses per day (until 4pm) run to Panayia from Pervola station, returning to Paphos the next morning (6 and 7:15am; 50¢).

■ Polis ΠΟΛΙΣ

Polis's minimalist name simply means "town," though Polis is far from pedestrian. Aphrodite, who came to Polis to bathe, was one of this coastal resort's first visitors. The goddess of beauty no longer bathes alone. Tourism has gained a foothold in Polis, which is smaller, cheaper, and more relaxed than Paphos, 37km to the south. Accessible by minibus and taxi, Polis is a popular Cypriot base for budget travel.

Orientation and Practical Information Polis boasts some stellar examples of traditional Cypriot architecture—large rounded wooden doors and stone masonry. At the end of the convoluted main street is the *platia,* where several **travel agencies** offer information (open 8am-1pm and sometimes 4-7pm). The **police** (tel. 321451; open 24hr.) roost one block from the square in the direction of the beach and speak some English. Around the *platia* you'll find three **banks** (all open Mon.-Fri. 8:30am-noon; reduced hours in off season). The **Popular Bank** and the **Bank of Cyprus** in the *platia* offer afternoon **currency exchange** (Mon. 3:15-4:45pm). The **post office** (tel. 321539; open Mon.-Fri. 7:30am-noon and 1-2pm) and **Spirides Taxi Service** (tel. 516161; private, not *service* taxis) are also on the *platia*. The **Lemon Garden** (tel. 321330) rents and sells **sports equipment** such as mountain bikes (£1.50-4 per day), fishing and diving equipment, and jet skis. **Pegasus** (tel. 321374 or 322156) in the *platia,* rents cars, mopeds (£4 per day, 4 day minimum), mountain bikes (£3 per day, 3 day minimum), and apartments. Two **pharmacies** (tel. 321253 and tel. 321167) are down the street from the post office. The **hospital** (tel. 321431) is on the way to the campsite, about a six-minute walk from the *platia* **Postal Code:** 8905. **Telephone Code:** 06.

POLIS

Accommodations   Freelance campers pitch tents on bluffs above the shore to the west, and along the road to the Baths of Aphrodite, and no one seems to care as long as the sites are kept clean. As always, *Let's Go* does not recommend illegal freelance camping. Several restaurants along this stretch provide free or almost-free camping and the use of facilities. **Campground** (tel. 321526), 1km from the town center in a fragrant eucalyptus grove by the sea, is open from March to October. (£1 per person. £1.50 per tent.) The **Akamas Hotel** (tel. 321330), at the beginning of the main street, has clean, tiny rooms with shared baths and a quiet courtyard. (Singles £5. Doubles £10.) The **Lemon Garden** (tel. 321443), past the *platia* to the right, is definitely worthwhile for its unique combination of quality rooms, food, and atmosphere. (All rooms with kitchenette, private bath, A/C, and view. Doubles £14-16. Larger rooms £16-20.) The Lemon Garden also has a **restaurant/bar** (meals £4-6, juice 80¢). Look for inexpensive rooms down the hill from the Bank of Cyprus, along the road to the beach, or inquire at a café. Rooms go for about £5-6 per person. On the right before the turn-off for the Vomos Taverna, **Mrs. Evlalia** (tel. 321580) rents bright, clean rooms, with kitchen access (£5 per bed). **Mrs. Charita Antoniou**, 7 Megalou Alexandrou (tel. 321989), away from the town center, next to the church, rents spacious rooms with access to a common bath and kitchen. Three front rooms open onto a porch. (£5 per bed. Private room negotiable.)

Food and Entertainment   Vomos Taverna (tel. 321143) serves snacks by the beach. In town, **Arsinoe** (tel. 321590), across from the church, is run by a fisherman's family and serves their daily catch (swordfish £3.50, fish *meze* £4.50; open daily 8am-1pm and 7pm-1am). Nearby, the **Kebab House** sells scrumptious *souvlaki* for £1.50. There's a beachside disco, but a more appealing option is to wander over to **Brunnen,** which is located just before the Akamas Hotel and down some steps. Marios has turned this dilapidated Turkish house into a sprawling **garden bar** (large beer £1, wine 75¢; breakfast served; open daily 9:30am-2pm and 5pm-2am).

Sights   The **Baths of Aphrodite,** a shady pool carved out of limestone by natural springs, are 10km west of Polis. Aphrodite supposedly came here to cleanse herself after her nocturnal exploits, and according to legend whoever bathes in the pool stays forever young. The pool of **Fontana Amorosa,** 8km away, can be reached by foot or a sturdy off-road vehicle through a narrow trail overlooking the sea. This pool is reportedly where Aphrodite married Akamas, the son of Theseus. (Buses run from Polis to Baths Mon.-Fri. 9:30, 10:30am, and 2:30pm; 50¢ one way. Baths free; bathing prohibited.)

AROUND POLIS REGION

The road from Polis to the Baths of Aphrodite leads past pristine **beaches** and some cheap lodgings. The friendly **Tamamouna** family (tel. 321269), 1km out of Polis, has excellent rooms. (Singles £5. Doubles £10.) The port of **Lachi,** 2km west of Polis, has a decent selection of coastline, hotels, and fish (tel. 321114 or 236740 for more information; bus from Polis 40¢). Below the **Baths of Aphrodite tourist pavilion,** 1km west, is a long sand beach; beyond it is **Ttakkas Bay,** a cove many consider the best beach on this part of the coast. **Ttakkas Bay Restaurant,** above the beach, has fresh fish and a terrace with a view (fish *meze* £4; open daily 9am-midnight).

The coastline and **beaches** east of Polis are just as lovely as those to the west. Between Polis and Kato Pirgos, roughly 65km to the east, there are no rooms to let, no seaside *tavernas,* and no freelance camping—only placid farming villages and deserted stretches of sand. Touring the area is difficult without wheels. **Minibuses** (tel. 236740 or 236822) from Paphos pass through Polis (10 per day Mon.-Fri., 6:30am-7pm, 5 per day Sat., 9am-4pm; £1). Two **buses** from Kato Pirgos also stop here. Some minibuses from Paphos continue on to Pomos (£1.15). Passing cars are rare, but those that come by usually stop. The second half of the journey is treacherous for mopeds—you may want to rent a car.

The coastline east of Polis is visible from the slender band of asphalt dubbed the "main road." Just find a beach that suits your tastes. Some of the beaches close to Polis are littered with garbage, so head 5-10km out of town before breaking out the cocoa butter. The road runs west along the coast, through banana plantations and tobacco fields, to **Pomos,** a quiet village with a few *tavernas* and a pebble beach. A few miles beyond Pomos is the village of **Pahiammos** (Thick Sand). Between Pahiammos and Kato Pirgos lies the village of **Kokkina** (Red), a small enclave occupied by the Turks. To prevent an entrance into Kıbrıs, the road to Kato Pirgos veers off into the mountains for a 25km detour (45min. by car). In **Kato Pirgos,** there are several places to stay—including hotels. Inquire in the coffee shop about renting rooms.

KIBRIS (TRNC)
NORTHERN CYPRUS

US$1 =83,003 Turkish Lira (TL)	10,000 Turkish Lira (TL) = US$0.12
CDN$1 = 60,431TL	10,000TL = CDN$0.17
UK£1 = 128,880TL	10,000TL = UK£0.08
IR£1 = 133,850TL	10,000TL = IR£0.07
AUS$1 = 62,500TL	10,000TL = AUS$0.16
NZ$1 = 55,555TL	10,000TL = NZ$0.18
SAR1 = 18,518TL	10,000TL = SAR0.54
100GRdr = 353,357TL	10,000TL = 2.83GRdr
C£1 = 43,840TL	10,000TL = C£0.23

> All prices are quoted in U.S. dollars because inflation in Kıbrıs tends to correspond roughly with the devaluation of the Turkish lira.

ESSENTIALS

Kıbrıs, the Turkish word for "Cyprus," refers to the northern 37% of the island—a mix of untouched beauty and Western influence. Not yet pinpointed by the usual hordes of tourists, many of the towns have been able to retain their charming native qualities while still incorporating many Western amenities into everyday existence. The beaches are some of the most beautiful in the Mediterranean and not as crowded as many of the Greek isles or Turkish coastal towns. Kıbrıs reveals layers of ancient Greek, Roman, and Ottoman history through the archaeological sites that spot the coastal and inland towns. The island is not a wild party region—you won't find drunken orgies on the beach or hip discoes that play wild throbbing music until the wee hours of the morning. In true British style, Kıbrıs is a serene haven for tourists who want to sit back, relax, and have a proper vacation without loud, obnoxious Euro-wannabes cruising around in true Valentino style. Since locals are trying to boost tourism, natives are accommodating to visitors. Although Kıbrıs is more pricey than Greece and Turkey, tourists are actually charged the same prices as the natives (so you probably won't get scammed).

GETTING THERE

Getting to Kıbrıs from the South is simultaneously possible and impossible. One-day passes are available from the "other side" of the Green Line, but the restrictions are stringent (see Crossing the Green Line, p. 386). The easiest way to get there is from Turkey, and ferries depart frequently from Mersin (İçel), Alanya, or Taşucu to Kıbrıs' main port-city, Girne. For those flying fanatics, you can take a plane from just about any major airport in Turkey that will drop you in Lefkoşa. Travelers who plan to go to the southern half of Cyprus should ask the customs officials in Kıbrıs to stamp a separate piece of paper. A stamp in your passport from Kıbrıs will deter you from entering the South. Crossing directly from the North to the South is strictly forbidden and is probably harder than breaking out of Alcatraz—don't try it.

ONCE THERE

> Driving in Kıbrıs can be dangerous. Tortuous roads, tortured drivers, and scores of tourists unfamiliar with driving on the left-hand side of the road in the right- (or left-) hand side of an uncomfortable sports utility vehicle provide less than optimal road conditions.

Renting a mule (simple, self-explanatory) is probably easier than taking the public transport buses in Kıbrıs (complex, hard). As bus schedules are erratic and unpredictable, your best bet is probably renting a car. Compared to Turkey, the buses in Kıbrıs are described as arthritic in terms of service. Be advised that many of Kıbrıs' most interesting attractions cannot be reached by public transport; you must either take a tour or rent a car. In order to drive in Kıbrıs, you need either an international driver's permit or a national driver's license from your home country. Several rental agencies are listed in each of the major towns. Alternatively, *dolmuş* are mini-vans that belong somewhere between buses and taxis. They don't keep to a regular schedule (what else is new?), but leave when they are full. You can find them in both Kıbrıs and mainland Turkey.

Kıbrıs has tourist offices in Famagusta, Girne, and Lefkoşa. The office in Lefkoşa is just past the **Ledra Palace**. Emergency treatment at hospitals is free for foreigners. *Beaches in North Cyprus do not typically staff lifeguards because there are no tides and no undertows.* The **emergency fire number** is 199, **emergency ambulance number** is 112, and the hospital and police numbers change from city to city; check the individual city listing.

GOVERNMENT

The Turkish Republic of Northern Cyprus (TRNC), or Kuzey Kıbrıs Türk Cümhurriyeti (KKTC), came into existence on November 15, 1983. It is not a part of Turkey, although Turkey is the only country that recognizes it as a separate state. The president is Rauf Denktaş, and his picture, like Atatürk's in Turkey, graces the walls of many hotels and restaurants. The TRNC has a parliamentary democracy based on the British system. The official language is Turkish and the official currency is the same as Turkey's—the Turkish lira. The roughly 150,000 residents of the TRNC are mostly Turkish Cypriot, but 40,000 of these are Turks who emigrated from the mainland. Several hundred British and German expatriates also reside in Kıbrıs, and their presence is most noticeable during the summer when they come out to enjoy the sun (a novelty for them). A good number of Brits also take up summer residence in their holiday homes for the season. Along with Turkish, roughly half the population speaks English, and many of the older residents speak Greek.

KEEPING IN TOUCH

Your best bet to send letters to Kıbrıs is via Turkey using the **postal code** Mersin 10, Turkey. A sample address is: Dome Hotel, Girne, Northern Cyprus, Mersin 10, Turkey. Kıbrıs has its own stamps which are accepted internationally.

For telephone calls, Kıbrıs functions as a part of Turkey. To call from abroad, dial 90 (Turkey) as the country code, followed by 392, the area code for Kıbrıs. Until the changeover to the mainland Turkish phone system, all numbers had five digits. Now they have seven—the same five as before, along with two more at the beginning of the number. All Girne numbers now start with 81, Lefkoşa 22, and Mağusa 36. The **country codes** from the South and North are the same: **Australia** 0061, **Canada** 001, **Ireland** 00353, **New Zealand** 0064, **South Africa** 0027, **U.K.** 0044, and **U.S.** 001. To call the U.S. from Kıbrıs, for example, dial 001 before the number.

■ Lefkoşa (North Nicosia)

The sounds of growth, construction, and urban traffic outside the old city cannot redress the silence one finds near the **Green Line**—the series of oil-drum, barbed-wire, and steel barricades separating the capital city of North Nicosia from the South. The violence of the conflict is not audible; it registers only the stale silence of intermittent peace. Lefkoşa teems with green-clad troops who pack together at street corners or around ATMs. They are youths instructed to be kind to tourists and who occasionally snap photos of each other in the desiccated grassy knolls that inlay the city's main square, **Atatürk Meydanı.** They are not the only ones there, though—occasionally, groups of Germans or Australians, and most commonly Brits, come to the square. While the Girne Gate and Atatürk Meydanı draw most tourists' regard, a stroll along the Green Line will reveal its array of rubble and ruin, curiously broken by elegant white and auburn-shuttered residences.

Budget travelers may not feel very welcome in Lefkoşa. The few hotels ask US$20-40 per person with Western amenities (fresh towel, air conditioning) but without charm. The many *pansiyon* generally cater to locals who can't afford apartments and live here instead. Nightlife is a contradiction in terms; the streets are dead at 10pm. It is probably best to do in a daytrip (buses from Girne are about US$1).

ORIENTATION AND PRACTICAL INFORMATION

Arriving by bus from other parts of Kıbrıs, you'll be dropped at the **bus station** (*otogar*), 1km from the old city. Take the street perpendicular to the Girne Rd., which runs beside the bus station to get to town—the **Hotel Lapathos Nicosia** should be on your right. The **Girne Gate** and the old city walls lie 1km farther. The tourist office is at the entrance to the gatehouse. From here, **Girne Caddesi,** the main street, runs to the main square, **Atatürk Meydanı,** and continues to the **Green Line.**

Arriving from the south at the **Ledra Palace** crossing, a roundabout (with a Turkish victory monument in the middle) is 500m up the street. The city walls will guide you to the Girne Gate. To reach the bus terminal, continue up this street (bearing left at the nearby fork); it is a 15-minute walk.

Tourist Office: At Girne gate. Open (theoretically) Mon. 7:30am-2pm and 3:30-6pm, Tues.-Fri. 7:30am-2pm.

Embassies: Only **Turkey** has a full embassy in Kıbrıs, at Bedrettin Demirel Cad. (tel. 227 2313). The following countries have "representative offices," which offer a degree of consular services: **Australia** (tel. 227 1115), in the Saray Hotel, open Tues. and Thurs. 9am-noon. **Germany,** #15 28 Kasım Sok. (tel. 227 5161). **U.K.,** 23 Mehmet Akif Cad. (tel. 227 1938). Open Mon., Wed., and Fri. 7:30am-1:30pm, Tues. and Thurs. 7:30am-1:30pm and 4:30pm-5pm. **U.S.,** 20 Güner Türkmen Sok. (tel. 227 2443), open Mon.-Fri. 8am-3:30pm.

Currency Exchange: Several offices along Girne Cad. Open Mon.-Fri. roughly 8am-1pm and 2-4pm. **Banks** close at noon. **ATMs** near Atatürk Meydanı.

Telephones: Pembe Telefon, 30m to the right of the post office, has metered booths and sells phonecards. Open Mon.-Fri. 7:30am-2pm and 3:30-5:30pm. **Government Telecommunications Dept.** is on Arif Salim Cad., one third of the way between Girne gate and the bus station.

Flights: Airport is 17km from town. Please be advised that only Turkish airlines deem this airport safe enough to fly here. Taxis roughly $15-20; no meters. Fix a fare in advance. **Cyprus Turkish Airlines** (owned by Turkish Airlines) has an office on Atatürk Meydanı. Flights to İstanbul, İzmir, and Ankara $60 one way, $100 roundtrip; London (daily) $225 one way, $400 roundtrip. Open Mon.-Sat. 7:30am-2pm and 3:30-6pm. **Akdeniz Air** (tel. 228 5827), Girne Cad., is a new local airline with slightly lower prices. Four flights per week to İstanbul and London; 1 per week to Ankara and İzmir. Open Mon.-Fri. 8am-6pm, Sat. 9am-2pm.

Buses: Buses leave from city station. With Girne gate . at your back, go right, bearing left at the fork. Hourly buses to Mağusa (Famagusta) ($1.25), Güzelyurt ($1.50), and Lefke ($2.25). Buses also run to numerous small villages, 1 per day in each direction, arriving in Lefkoşa by 7am and leaving in the mid-afternoon.

Dolmuş: Several departures from the bus station per hour to Girne ($1). You may also catch a *dolmuş* off the main street leading away from the Girne gate, which may be slightly cheaper. Services run from 7am-5pm; fewer on the weekends.

LEFKOŞA (NORTH NICOSIA)

Lefkoşa
(Northern Nicosia)

Büyük Hamam (Great Bath), **4**
Clinic (Poliklinik), **14**
Covered Bazaar, **2**
Cyprus Turkish Airlines Terminal, **20**
The Green Line, **13**
K. Kaymaklı Martyr's Memorial
(Şehitler Anıtı), **17**
Kyrenia Gate Tourism Information
(Girne Kapısı), **11**

Lapideri Museum, **5**
Main Post Office, **6**
Museum, **22**
Old City Walls, **1**
Parcel Post Office, **18**
Police Headquarters, **8**
Police Station, **19**
Post Office, **15**
Sultan Mahmut Library, **3**

Telecommunications Office, **16**
Tourism Information, **21**
T.R.T. Cyprus Office
(Kıbrıs Bürosu), **9**
Turkish Embassy, **12**
The Turkish Museum
(Türk Müzesi), **10**
The Venetian Column, **7**

International Language Bookshop: Rüstem Kitabevi, 26 Girne Cad. From Girne gate, it's 40m past Atatürk Meydanı, on the left. English-language fiction, books on Cyprus, textbooks, and Turkish-language items. Variable opening hours.

Hospital: (tel. 228 5441), on the road to Girne, roughly 700m from the Victory Monument. Look for the Hastane sign.

Police: (tel. 228 3311), Girne Cad., close to Atatürk Meydanı.

Post Office: (tel. 228 5982), Sarayönü Sok. From the Girne gate, take a right off Atatürk Meydanı. Open Mon. 7:30am-2pm and 3:30-6pm, Tues.-Fri. 7:30am-2pm and 4-6pm, Sat. 8:30am-12:30pm.

Telephone Code: 22

SIGHTS

Views of the **Green Line** provide tangible evidence of the tensions on the island. The sensitivity of the politics surrounding it is matched only by the coarseness of its construction. In places, the "line" is a barbed- or chicken-wire fence, sometimes screened with oil drums. Other places, it is a steel barrier or a wall blocking a road. Take a right off Atatürk Meydanı, walk alongside the old British courthouse for five minutes; any street to your left will drop you off at the Green Line.

In certain sections—especially near the Bedesten—and in the morning hours, the light seems to penetrate the stone and wood remains of the buildings that once linked the northern and southern halves of the city. Though the impression of waste may merit otherwise, photography is strictly prohibited. Try to restrain yourself.

The **Selimiye Mosque/St. Sophia Cathedral** is a bizarre sight; a seemingly ancient (1326) cathedral looms in the shadow of its more recent additions—two soaring

Islamic minarets. Despite the prayer rugs *(seccade)* and Islamic calligraphy all around, it still feels like a church. From Atatürk Meydanı, with Girne Gate at your back, continue down Girne Cad., looking left for its twin minarets. Beside it is the **Bedesten,** the Greek Orthodox cathedral of St. Nicholas, which dates from the 14th century. It was converted to a covered market and later a barn by the Ottomans. The city walls date from 1570. Formidable in appearance, they were a spectacular failure, as Turks poured into the city one year later and stayed for 300.

The **Museum of Barbarism** is situated in a suburban house where, in 1963, a woman and her children were murdered by Greek gunmen as they tried to take refuge in their bathroom. The museum is not for the faint of heart (open Mon. 7:30am-2pm and 3:30-6pm, Tues.-Fri. 7:30am-2pm; free). To reach it from Girne Gate, with Girne Cad. at your back, go left and follow the city walls (which should be on your left) to the first roundabout. Continue here for 700m and turn right at the second roundabout. The museum is 1.2km along this road and clearly marked. Go to the rooftop terrace of the **Saray Hotel** for a view of the whole city; if you entered via Kıbrıs, this is the closest you'll get to seeing the other side of the island.

Face the Green Line and follow it to your right (you will have to backtrack now and then due to blocked streets) to reach the **Derviş Paşa Museum.** The former mansion of a notable Turkish-Cypriot newspaper owner of the 20th century, it has been converted into a small museum housing a collection of clothing and household goods (open daily 9am-7pm, but usually closes around lunchtime; admission $2, with ISIC 50¢). Exit the museum, go right, and take the first right to reach **Arabahmet Mosque.** From this street you can see the spire of a 14th-century Armenian church, located behind the Green Line. The **Mevlevi Tekke,** near the tourist office, was once an Islamic monastery and is now a small museum, which houses life-size models of whirling dervishes and a collection of Islamic artifacts (open Mon. 9am-2pm, 3:30-7pm and Tues.-Fri. 7:30am-2pm; admission $2, with ISIC 50¢).

■ Near Lefkoşa

LEFKE

On the road stretching from Güzelyurt to Gemikonağı, on the far western rim of Kıbrıs, lies a patch of Mediterranean coastline given short-shrift by most tourists. A few gritty travelers—elderly British ones, for the most part—find their way here. The area around Lefke doesn't have the beaches or facilities of Girne, nor the vicissitudinal history of Lefkoşa, but it does have one precious characteristic: distance—distance from other tourists, distance from the low-rise, white-washed city scapes of most North Cypriot civilization, and distance from some of the last stubborn remainders of "modernity." Shepherds exist here, brandishing genuine crooked staffs, and locals are prone to wave to you more often than one might expect.

Two local objects draw the gaze of most tourists to this region. The first, and most worthy of your 95¢, is the **Soli Ruins.** The residue of 2000 years of practice at building cities (proving that city planning may, in fact, be the world's oldest profession), the Soli site first attracted Assyrians around 700 BCE. Later populated by Greeks, it derives its name from none other than Solon, the Athenian philosopher. Needless to say, the city changed hands, was razed, and was rebuilt as often as would suit the practitioners of the world's oldest trade. Today, it includes a gorgeous, semi-circular Roman amphitheater (currently being renovated), a few city ruins, and a basilica floor inlaid with still visible mosaics (admission 95¢, with ISIC 50¢). Simply follow the road from Güzelyurt (it is the main road from Lefkoşa heading west). Without turning off toward Lefke, continue straight and follow the signs that clearly mark the ruins. If traveling by bus, buy a ticket to Lefke and let the driver drop you off at the turn; from there, the hike is roughly 2-3km. Otherwise, take the bus into Lefke and find a taxi. Drivers will wait for you to examine the Soli site, but it will cost you more. Renting a car or jeep is the generally preferred option, though much more expensive ($30 per day, $5 for insurance, and $10-15 for gas). Car rental outfits abound in Girne, while Lefkoşa hosts two or three that rent for $10 less.

The second most popular destination near Lefke lies 10km west along the same road that leads to the Soli Ruins. The educational value of the **Vouni Palace** ruins is, however, eclipsed by the blind relief that you feel having survived the drive up the road that brought you there. The road to Vouni is a treacherous one. There are endless blind curves and thousand-foot drops. Even if you don't think you're scared of heights, you very well may be here. Delicate-stomached travelers should take a taxi and close their eyes. The Vouni site itself is not so impressive, but the view of the Mediterranean and Güzelyurt Bay is stunning.

Lefke is rather starved for accommodations, but if you choose to spend an evening near Lefke, you may want to try the **Soli Inn.** Just past Lefke and along the same road which extends to the Soli and Vouni ruins, the Soli Inn stands as perhaps the sole fruit of plucky development in an infrequently touristed area. Its main traffic seems to be made up of students from nearby **Lefke University.** Composed of thirteen bungalow-style rooms (all capable of housing 4-5 guests), the Soli Inn charges a modest $20-25 per person, including breakfast.

Finally, the **Liman Restaurant & CMC Bar** may provide the most compelling reason to visit Lefke. Look for its sign on the main road eastbound; it appears just after you have gone straight past the turnoff for Lefke proper. Located across from the monstrous copper slag-heaps and mining equipment left over from the Cyprus Mining Corporation (hence, CMC), the *liman* (port) encodes a small part of the island's history. The mine started up in 1917, after an American (dare we say "capitalist"?) geologist came to Cyprus on hearing it was an "island of copper." The entire operation was once run by steam and by Cypriots, though it shut down upon the Turkish invasion in 1974. Along the walls of the CMC Bar, masks, mining helmets, and WWII-era *curioso* fill, but do not clutter, the space. The Liman Restaurant serves a friendly plate of fish and chips for $5 from noon to 10pm. The CMC Bar opens at 8am and closes at 1am. Along with a drink at the bar (roughly $1-2), view ancient Roman wood-drift. Just ask the proprietor. Incidentally, the land on which the Liman Restaurant and CMC Bar stands is American soil, along with nearly a third of the town of Lefke (those greedy imperialist bastards).

GÜZELYURT

Güzelyurt is a large and none-too-interesting market town. Visit it to see **Agios Mamas,** a beautiful, perfectly preserved icon-filled Greek Orthodox church. Check out the **Tomb of Mamas,** an Orthodox saint, inside. It is believed that the moisture which occasionally oozes from the tomb is a cure-all for disease and a pacifier of storms. To visit the church you must first pay to enter the **Museum of Archaeology and Natural History** next door; the curator will admit you to the church. The museum itself contains a collection of stuffed animals and birds downstairs and ancient pottery upstairs; look for the two-headed lamb and the lamb with eight legs. Upstairs is the famed black-faced, multi-breasted statue of **Ephesian Artemis** from Salamis, which was recovered from the sea in the 1980s—you'll see this image on numerous postcards and books around Kıbrıs.

■ Girne (Kyrenia)

Broken by a thick wall 500m-long and running parallel to the coastline, the Mediterranean seems to sit affectionately near the city of Girne. The harbor created by the wall is rimmed by fish restaurants, pubs, and open-air cafés. A wide, grassy mall lines the coast from the harbor to the **Dome Hotel,** a rambling old colonial institution that seems to mark Girne's luxuriant center of gravity. This city is less a city than a chamber of light; it averages one day of rain each summer. Girne sprawls lazily (and polychromatically) along its coast. The **Kyrenia Mountain Range,** lodged right behind the city, seems to simultaneously contain the light and provide a barrier

GIRNE

from the heat and dust of Lefkoşa. Though the beauty here is of a rather obvious sort, i.e., combed beaches and old ruins, it is unabashedly beautiful. The city's charm leaves little to a traveler's imagination in Girne, which seems precisely why tourists come here in the first place. Miles of sand, European hotels, British expatriates (from before the war), and excellent seafood abound. Girne is a rich city; upscale markets stock beer from Germany and chocolates from England. But despite its ritzy image, budget travelers can survive and prosper here.

ORIENTATION AND PRACTICAL INFORMATION

Ferries from Turkey arrive at the **new harbor,** 1km as the crow flies from town, but 2km by road. *Dolmuş* will take you to the main square for 75¢; a taxi to most hotels costs $3.50. Arriving by boat at the new harbor, go out the port gates on your right and continue 500m down the road. Take a right at the main intersection. This is **Cumhuriyet Caddesi** (Republic St.). Walk for another 1500m. Just after the post office, you will hit a roundabout; this is the "main square." Beyond the roundabout is a dry, modern-art style fountain; behind it, to the left, runs **Hürriyet Caddesi** (Freedom St.). This is the main street in town, lined with shops and several cheap hotels. The streets to the right off Hürriyet Cad. lead to the seafront; the nearest ones, to the harbor.

Arriving overland, you'll be dropped at the **bus station.** Exit the station, turn right, and walk to the **International American University** (700m). Go left at this main intersection—the roundabout is 800m down the road. From the ferry terminal, you can take *dolmuş* to the roundabout. When available (usually in the afternoons), they cost 75¢, taxis $3.50. From the bus station, you'll probably have to walk.

Tourist Office: Walking out of Girne along the city's main road, the Hürriyet Cad., the office will appear on your left, 500m past the Dorana Hotel. Open Mon. 7:30am-1:30pm and 3:30-6pm, Tues.-Fri. 7am-1:30pm. Excellent free map of Kıbrıs, including city maps of Girne, Lefkoşa, and Gazimağusa.

Banks: Banking hours are Mon.-Fri. 8am-noon, with some variation between banks. There are **ATMs** at either end of this street. For fast over-the-counter cash advances on MasterCard or Visa, go to **Vakıfbank,** on the main square (English spoken). A hefty 8% commission is charged. Bring your passport.

Exchange offices: Cash only, open Mon.-Sat. roughly 9am-8pm. These are scattered along the street which leads from the Atatürk statue up to Hürriyet Cad.

Telephones: In the main square, beside Cumhuriyet Cad. They only accept phonecards. Although they are identical to Turkish phones, they do *not* accept Turkish phonecards (the logic escapes us). You may buy Kıbrıs phonecards in the **Telekomunikasyon Dairesi** opposite the post office, which is open until 2pm. The local phonecards are available in 30-, 60-, or 100-unit cards, and cost 95¢, $1.90, or $2.80, respectively. **Telephone Information:** (tel. 192).

Expatriates' Notice Board: In front of the post office. Provides information on local events, apartment rentals, etc. There is a community of several hundred British expatriates around Girne, mostly middle-aged to elderly.

Buses: Run hourly to Mağusa (Famagusta), Güzelyurt, and Lefke from the bus station. From the roundabout, walk up the Lefkoşa Rd. (beside Vakıfbank) for roughly 800m—you should pass Shell and Esso petrol stations on the way.

Dolmuş: To Lapta also run from here. To get to Lefkoşa (Nicosia), take a *dolmuş* ($1) from the little car park behind the main taxi stand beside the roundabout. Buses and *dolmuş* run, approximately, from 7:30am to 5pm, with restricted service during the weekends, though you can safely catch *dolmuş* until 7 or 8pm.

Ferries: Two daily **seabuses** to Taşucu (Turkey) are fast, cushy options. They depart daily at 11am and 2:30pm (2½hr., one way $16.25, roundtrip $29.50). Slower, tiny ferries also run to Taşucu—departures at 11am (6½hr., one way $14, roundtrip $23.25). The seabus returns from Taşucu at 11am and 4pm, and the ferry returns at midnight. From June-Sept. seabuses depart 3 times per week to Alanya (5hr., $46.50 one-way, $73 roundtrip). The schedule is highly subject to change. Tickets can be purchased from **Fergün Ferries** on the main square.

Taxis: Several firms have taxi stands around town. Unfortunately, none of them have meters; instead, all firms (should) have a printed list of fares. Trips within town, including the new port, officially cost $3.50, $6 for 3-8km outside, $8.25 for 8-11km outside, and $10.50 for 11-16km outside. These fares are high; try bargaining them down. Try to agree on a fare before accepting a ride.

Car Rental: Atlantic (tel. 815 3053), in the Dome Hotel, offers jeeps for $30 per day (insurance $5). Free pick-up from all points in Kıbrıs, including port and airport. For those without a driver's license from home, package tours are available from the affiliated agency **Kyrenia Tours.**

International Bookstore: The British owned **Green Jacket Bookshop,** 20 Temmuz St., roughly 1½km from town, offers a good selection of English-language fiction and books on Kıbrıs. Walk from the square to the end of Hürriyet Cad. and keep going along the coastal road for 700m—it's on the left. Open Mon.-Fri. 9am-1pm and 4-7pm, Sat. 9am-noon. **BBD** news agents on Hürriyet Cad., near the square, have a small selection of the major British and German newspapers.

Hospital: (tel. 815 2266), Cumhuriyet Cad., roughly 100m past the post office. There is a **doctor** (tel. 815 3528) at Hüseyin Cenkler.

Police: (tel. 815 2014, -125), just off the harbor, behind the **Harbor Club,** on the road immediately beside the Castle.

Post Office: Cumhuriyet Cad., off the main square (first left with your back to the sea). Open Mon.-Fri. 7:30am-2pm and 4-6pm, Sat. 8:30am-12:30pm. Parcel office open Mon., Wed., and Fri. 9:30am-12:30pm. **Postal Code:** 9900.

Telephone Code: 81.

ACCOMMODATIONS

You may have to spend some extra bucks for a harbor-front hotel (singles run about $20-22, doubles $35); however, your splurge will inevitably deliver an exponential increase of comfort and ambience. Hotel prices without breakfast are approximately $2.25 less than those listed. For diehard, fanatical budget travelers, there are several *pansiyon* around town aimed primarily at Turkish army privates and financially challenged Turks on holiday. A bed without breakfast can range from $6 for a single to $11.75 for a double. They're none too clean—and taking breakfast into account, your frugality in this case will save you little more than $3.

Finally, no guidebook would be complete without mentioning Girne's major landmark and meeting place, the **Dome Hotel** (tel. 815 2453). This grand old hotel, a colonial institution on the island, provides some of the prettiest promontories—bamboo umbrellas included—to linger over Mediterranean sunsets or sea-swollen vistas. Even if you don't stay, it will, at the very least, serve as your **public toilet** (singles $37.25, doubles $60.50, breakfast included).

New Bristol Hotel (tel. 815 2321), Hürriyet Cad. Every ex-Brit colony, from Gibraltar to Lagos, has, inexplicably, its own Bristol Hotel. Offers spacious, comfortable rooms with A/C. Singles $15. Doubles $22. Breakfast and bath included.

Bingöl Motel (tel. 815 2749), Hürriyet Cad., on the main square. Basic, comfortable *pansiyon*—rooms include private bath. The Bingöl is one of the budget traveler's most promising choices. Singles $11.75. Doubles $23.25.

Motel Elizel (tel. 815 4774). From Girne's main road heading towards the Dome Hotel, 1 block from the square, take a right (at the taxi stand) and follow the road until you see a sign for it. A clean room in a cheap but tasteful establishment. (It is not too much to ask for.) Singles $14. Doubles $20. Bath and breakfast included.

Sidelya Hotel (tel. 815 3951), Nasır Güneş Sok., second right off Hürriyet Cad., coming from the square. Clean, spacious rooms. Terrace has breathtaking views of the harbor. Singles $22. Doubles $35.

Hotel British (tel. 815 2240), overlooking the harbor, one street back. Enjoy its spacious balconied rooms and views of the harbor. A/C, TV, minibar, and private bath. Singles $22. Doubles $35. Excellent, English-style breakfast included.

The Ergenekon (tel. 815 4677), on the harbor—entrance at the back, opposite the Hotel British. Not as luxurious as the British, but it has plenty of character. Front

GIRNE

rooms have balconies overlooking the harbor; back rooms not really worth it. Singles $20. Doubles $35. Breakfast included.

FOOD

The harbor is the most obvious and pleasant place to find good food in Girne. You may pay more for tasteful settings—wicker chairs, harborside, and candlelight—than for tasteful cuisine, though the prices do remain moderate. In the angular, white-walled streets of Girne, bodacious, bargain food can be had, and it is in these streets that hardened budget travelers can reap their rewards. A handful of cafés and small restaurants serve tasty fare cheaply, and the dozen markets in the town provide the best prices of all. But perhaps the finest Cypriot food awaits the more adventurous travelers, those willing to venture out of the city of Girne and into some of the small villages which surround the city. Prices hover around $5-8.

Erol's (tel. 815 3657), in Ozanköy, a small village 1km from Bellapais; on the main road from Girne to Bellapais (well marked). Serves stellar Cypriot cuisine. Two dozen types of *meze* (snacks in saucers, from hummus and tabouli to grilled meats, beans, and vegetables). Try their fish *kebab* ($8) or lamb chops, but try to make a reservation first. Open for dinner.

Yama (tel. 822 2888), in Karaoğlanoğlu, a small beach town 3km along the main om Girne. Take a right at the "Güler's Fish" sign. Yama is at the end of the road on the right. It serves fantastic *meze*—it's 95% vegetarian. Also well regarded for their *mantı*—a ravioli stuffed with either cheese or chicken.

Niazis, established in Limassol opposite the Dome Hotel in 1949, this Cyprus institution moved to Girne in 1974, along with all of Limassol's Turks. For 46 years its specialty has been *kebab* ($9), *meze,* and a series of grilled meats.

Dedem, located in Girne's main square. Dedem serves typical Turkish *lokanta* fare, a delightful and inexpensive *döner kebab* ($3.50). Open for lunch; closes before "normal" dinner hours.

The Grapevine, on the Lefkoşa road beside the Esso station. It serves English food to Englishmen—largely octogenarian expatriates—including grilled liver and onions and fish and chips, along with a good *moussaka,* the only concession to local taste ($2.75-3.50). The price doubles between lunch and dinner. Eat fast.

Planter's, out on the coast road, 5km to the west, proves that *good* English food is not a contradiction in terms. Its Yorkshire puddings, steak, and kidney pies ($5 each) draw a (somewhat) younger crowd.

ENTERTAINMENT

Entertainment being the occupation of most tourists in Girne, it is, unsurprisingly, of a leisurely sort. Beach-going, street-walking, thing-buying, sun-avoiding, and nap-taking seem to be the stock activities, though more active leisure can be found.

Several local bars host large and young weekend crowds. **Café 34,** on the harbor, earns the highest marks for its tasteful indoor, and small, terraced outdoor, drinking areas. On a weekend night in high season, the place can be jammed. **Café Esquire** hosts a smaller (and select?) crowd (typically male) who come for the blaring American music, the pool tables, and video game rejects that may hearten a weary, Western traveler. It sits behind the taxi stand, off the harbor.

Sunset Beach comes equipped with an **outdoor disco** (tel. 821 83 30) teeming with local youth on summer weekends. Usually, five to six hundred natives swallow up the 15-20 tourists who make a Friday or Saturday night there. The club is open Monday through Saturday 11pm-3:30am, or perhaps until the last dance-drugged teenage disco queen staggers out into the night. Look under the listing for Sunset Beach for directions (p. 421).

SIGHTS

The preeminent sight in Girne is the huge medieval **castle** at the harbor's mouth. Built by the Byzantines with material plundered from the ruins of the now nonexistent Roman city, it was fortified by the Lusignans and refortified by the Venetians. Though these walls have fallen, the castle is in a good state of repair, and it now houses the Shipwreck Museum (see below). When you enter the castle after going through the tunnel, make a left through another tunnel to the small Byzantine chapel, the only remaining structure from the Byzantine period. Almost all of the present castle dates from the Lusignans, except for the outside walls and tower, which are Venetian. (Notice the Lusignan coat of arms above the doorway arch.)

Opposite the museum, or on the left side of the courtyard if you are facing the water, are dungeons with deep pits in the center. The scraps from the royal family's dinner were dumped from above as the prisoners attempted to grab at the flying food; their intended and cruel punishment came when they reached too far and fell into the pit. From the courtyard, notice the row of brown, locked doors on the upper level; these prison cells were last used by the British in the 1950s to house EOKA terrorists (see Cyprus in the 20th Century, p. 385).

The **Shipwreck Museum,** in the courtyard, contains the remains of a ship from the time of Alexander the Great, 2300 years ago. Also on display is some of the cargo, including 400 wine amphoras and 9000 blackened almonds, the crew's main staple (castle open daily 8am-7pm; admission $2, students 25¢). Walk along the pier afterwards to get an idea of its vastness. There is an interesting **Ikon Museum** in the **Archangelos Church,** behind the Hotel British (open 9am-1pm and 3-5pm; admission $1.75, students 25¢). A small **Fine Arts Museum** lies 1km from the Dome Hotel, but you can't reach it along that road—a militarized zone intervenes. You must walk along the main road, Hürriyet Cad., until you reach the Paşabahçe Sok.; from there, take a right. The museum is well marked but hardly spectacular. The charm of the exhibits—a handful of oil and oriental paintings, along with some European porcelain—is overshadowed by the charm of the house which displays them (open Mon.-Fri. 8am-7pm, Sat. 8am-3pm; admission $1, with ISIC 25¢).

The beaches strung along the north coast are some of the finest in Cyprus. Some are free, most are not, and above many of them rise monolithic, multi-storied resorts or "bungalow-style" condo developments. Nevertheless, for a small fee (usually around $3), one can storm these beaches as well. The **Kervon Saray** beach, the best of the area's free beaches, lies near the village of Karaoğlanoğlu, several kilometers to the west of Girne. Village buses run in this direction, but are infrequent, and their quirky schedules are unpredictable (check at the **otopark** (bus terminal) for details). A more reliable option may be to walk, but it will take close to an hour. Once in the village, look for the signs reading "Güler's Fish" or "Savarona"—they will appear on your right. Having turned here, you will find the beach at the end of the road.

To reach **Acapulco Beach,** perhaps the loveliest of the pay beaches, head down the coastal road eastbound on the Bellapais side of Girne. The beach is well marked, approximately 4km from the center of town, a walkable distance, though you may want to bring an umbrella, for there is little shade. Acapulco Beach rests before a yawning, bungalow-style resort called, not surprisingly, **Acapulco Resort.** The beach costs $3 for a day, and you can rent windsurfing equipment (about $5) or a bicycle (around $3). Of course, you may simply wrinkle under the sun for an afternoon, but be warned: on a good Sunday in summer season, over a thousand others will take to this beach, intent upon sharing your rays o' sun.

Sunset Beach is in the opposite direction from Acapulco, along the same road, 1km past the turn-off for Kervon Saray. It asks a little less than the Acapulco ($2), but has neither the equipment nor the glaring popularity. Still, it is a golden sandy beach with a couple of rocky islands one hundred meters into the sea on which you can turn your back to the shore.

■ East of Girne: Beylerbeyi (Bellapais)

Six kilometers from Girne is Beylerbeyi (also known as Bellapais), a tranquil hillside village that contains one of Kıbrıs' more notable sights, **Bellapais Abbey.** Founded by monks fleeing the Arab sacking of the city in the 13th century, it is a delicately arched Gothic structure. Huge, 30m-high Cypress trees tower above the cloisters. The **Kybele** restaurant, on the grounds of the abbey, frequently blasts classical music. (Restaurant open daily 11am-11pm; abbey open daily 8am-7pm; admission $2, students 25¢.)

Across from the abbey is the **Tree of Idleness**. Lawrence Durrell, a British writer, lived in Bellapais during 1953-56 and wrote *Bitter Lemons*. In the book he warns of the tree of idleness and the café lifestyle. A huge restaurant, the **Tree of Idleness Restaurant** has grown up around the tree and serves tasty food (Cyprus-Turkish night is Wednesday, when ten cold and ten hot *mezes* are served). You can take a break, relax, and then stroll over to the souvenir shop which sells "Tree of Idleness" baseball caps. If you walk uphill past the restaurant for 5 minutes you can see Durrell's house—marked by a yellow plaque. Three or four buses per day run from Girne to Bellapais. They're infrequent—you may have to walk back to Girne.

Ten kilometers from Girne, off the Lefkoşa road, is **St. Hilarion Castle.** Named for a local 8th-century holy man and built upon his grave, St. Hilarion was converted into a castle in the 10th century. The Venetians, who didn't need castles, tore St. Hilarion apart. Though damaged by a fire in the Kyrenia Range in 1995, it has reopened. Walking to the castle is prohibited—there's a military base on the way up. You may mistake it for the castle. Nevertheless, take a *dolmuş* or rent a car.

Together with the **Bufavento** and **Kautava** castles, St. Hilarion formed part of the Byzantine's early warning system in the Five Finger Mountain area. Bufavento, currently in a militarized zone, opens sporadically, most often on Wednesday and Sunday afternoons. Arrange for an escort who will accompany you to the site; the road is poor, and the castle closes at 5pm. Ask the tourist office for more information.

■ West of Girne: Karaman (Karmi)

A small hill village (180 houses lodged into the Kyrenia range), Karaman lies 10km southwest of Girne. Known as Karmi before 1974, it was abandoned by the Greeks during the war. Today, it is made up of 40% English, 40% Germans, and 20% mixed nationals (some Swiss, some French, some Swench). Literally propped on the side of a mountain, the village offers views of Girne, good hiking, a European atmosphere, and many walking trails. Its landscape is cut by ravines and is a spectacle best attended in the spring when anemones litter entire fields. No bus will take you here, but Karaman is popular among tourists, and rental cars fill the parking lot of the old **Orthodox Church.** Walking to Karaman is possible, though it's a long walk; the road leading up to the village is contorted and steep. To reach Karaman, head west along the coast road to Karaoğlanoğlu. Take a left—the sign is visible.

Once nameless, its streets have been given lush but similar-sounding names such as Geranium Way, Plum Road, and Azalea Alley. These "streets" may look like private steps. They are not, and in the summer months they are well planted and heavily fragrant. Numerous walking trails lead away from the village; **free maps** of the trails are available at Crow's Nest Pub. Diehard hikers may want to walk along the **Forestry Mountain Road.** It is 40 beautiful kilometers from St. Hilarion to the Lapta area. Not all hikes are so long. The Karaman **Steps** provide a panoramic stop, but wear good hiking shoes and pants, since they often seem less like steps and more like bramble-covered, minced rock. To reach them, simply follow the main village road past Karaman; when the road forks, go right up a steep hill, and 500m later you'll be at the road's end and the beginning of the steps.

A number of excellent restaurants can be found in the Karaman area. The **Crow's Nest Pub,** located behind the old Orthodox Church, serves good English pub food, lots of snacks, and a make-your-own dinner (choose the meat, sauce, chips or rice, and salad). An amiable bar, its proprietor is a mine of information. (open Mon.-Sat. noon-3pm and 7pm-midnight, and Sun. noon-3pm). The Orthodox church is only open on Sunday afternoons when the curator is available. The **Karaman Shop** is in front of the Crow's Nest, and is the only grocery in the village (open daily until 12:30pm and 6:30pm-8:30pm). The **Levant Restaurant** (tel. 822 25 94), along the main village road, offers Cypriot and Eastern Mediterranean fare. (Open Tues.-Sun., bar opens at 6pm; dinner service begins around 7pm. They have their priorities straight.) The **Treasure** (tel. 822 24 00), located farther along the village road toward Girne, offers English and Cypriot meals. Reservations are a good idea. The fish casserole ($8) and the *muluhiya*—a vegetable dish cooked with lamb, tomatoes, onions, and lemons—are both good bets. The Treasure's balcony rests over the precipice leading to Girne. (Open Thurs.-Tues., dinner service starts around 7pm.)

▓ Mağusa (Famagusta)

Mağusa is a hot and large coastal city, suffering from an obese port that sequesters the sea. It was once the world's richest city, *the* trading post between the Christian West and Muslim East. Stories are told of a local merchant who gave huge banquets; his tables were piled with precious stones, intended as gifts to departing guests. Shakespeare's *Othello* is believed to have been set here—the bard's descriptions of a "seaport in Cyprus" match the layout of Famagusta. Incidentally, the official name you'll see on maps and road signs is **Gazimağusa,** which means "Unconquered Mağusa." This appellate is shortened in local parlance, and on buses, business cards, etc., to **Mağusa** (occasionally printed G. Mağusa).

ORIENTATION AND PRACTICAL INFORMATION

Buses stop on the Lefkoşa road. Get out of the bus. Turn right along this road; after 250m you'll see the impressive **Victory Monument** in the center of a roundabout. Behind it are the old city walls. The **Rivettina Bastion** juts out from these walls; beside it is the **Land Gate,** a picturesque entry into the old city. Follow the road outside the city walls **(Fevzi Çakmak Blv.)** and after 500m you'll pass the **tourist office;** 400m more and you'll be at the sea. On the left is the **Canbulat Bastion** and Gate, and past it, the Port, where **ferries** from Turkey arrive.

Tourist Office: Fevzi Çakmak Blv., opposite city wall. Offers maps of Kıbrıs and its cities. Open Mon. 8am-1pm and 3:30-6pm, Tues.-Fri. 8am-1pm.

Telephones: 60 Polat Paşa Blv., the street to the right of the tourist office as you face it. Phonecards sold; two cardphones in the lobby. Open 7:30am-8pm.

Buses: To Lefkoşa (every hr. 7:30am-5pm, 1hr., $1.25). Rare village buses head to most points in the region, including Karpaz Peninsula. Buses arrive in Famagusta Mon.-Fri. by 7am, in time for the typical 7:30am start to the working day; return to villages from the station between 2 and 5pm. Only 1 bus per day in each direction; most villages have no accommodations.

Dolmuş: To Lefkoşa leave from the Victory Monument, at a point called İtimat on the left-hand side of the street (as your back is to the old city). *Dolmuş* depart once or twice per hour (7am-5pm or later, $1.75). *Dolmuş* to Girne leave hourly (7am-5pm, $2) from a point called Kombos, on the Lefkoşa Road, 100m past the roundabout on the left.

Ferries: Departures from the Port, between the city wall and the sea. To **Mersin,** Turkey. Departures Tues., Thurs., Fri. at 1pm (8hr., $25.75 one way, $42 roundtrip). Go to the harbor at least 1hr. before departure to allow for customs clearance. Tickets must be bought in advance from **Turkish Maritime Lines** (tel. 366 5786). From Canbulat Bastion, follow the sea to your right (as you face it). Past the roundabout, take the right fork; the *Feribot* office is 25m farther, on your left. The ferry, *Dolphin* of Mağusa, is tiny. Return from Mersin on Mon. and Thurs. at midnight. Faster, cheaper, more comfortable connections to Turkey are available from Girne.

Hospital: Polat Paşa Blv. (tel. 366 5328).

Police: İlker Karter Cad. (tel. 366 5310, -21).

Post Office: İlker Karter Cad., the street to the left of the tourist office as you face it; the post office is 300m along, on the left. Open 7:30am-12:30pm.

Telephone Code: 36

MAĞUSA

FOOD AND ACCOMMODATIONS

You're not exactly spoiled for choice of accommodations in this town because most people visit Mağusa on daytrips from Girne. There are a couple hotels that may not break your wallet, but your best bet is probably to stay in Girne. Restaurants here are more expensive than in other parts of Kıbrıs, but there are a few that may suit your needs. Better yet, search out the small cafés that spot the streets of the city.

SIGHTS

The **city walls,** surrounded by a huge moat, are quite a sight. The result of 20 years' labor by the Venetians in the 16th century, they are among the strongest fortifications ever built. Yet they failed in their task: after a vicious, year-long siege, the city fell to the Ottomans in 1571. Climb to the top of the **Canbulat Bastion** to get an idea of their thickness. **Othello's Tower** dates from the 13th century and is the city's oldest building. Formerly known as the **Citadel,** it was renamed by the British and the new name remains. At ground level, notice the old medieval hall and the dark passages and shafts. Peter Scaliger, the last of the Veronese ruling family, was imprisoned in one for 11 years by the Venetians (open approximately 8am-5pm daily; admission $1.50, students 75¢). The part of the tower which juts out into the port is still a military zone. **Canbulat Museum** is in the Bastion. Displays include the tomb of the commander of the Ottoman Empire and a 16th-century hand printed Kur'an (open Mon. 7:30am-2pm and 3:30-6pm, Tues.-Fri. 7:30am-2pm; admission $1).

Because Mağusa once nursed 365 churches, the city today displays a variety of withering, deserted, and crumbling medieval Christian architecture. **St. Nicholas Cathedral/Lala Mustafa Paşa Mosque** dominates the old city. Built in the 14th century, it was sacked by the Ottomans after the invasion and converted to a mosque, and a minaret was later added. It has been closed for restoration and is likely to remain so for a number of years—don't hold your breath. Built by a 14th-century merchant on the profits of one business transaction, the **Church of St. Peter and St. Paul/Sinan Paşa Mosque** is a stone church/mosque. Across the road is a car park, the site of the **Venetian Governor's Palace;** some bare walls still stand.

Back in the main square (Namık Kemal Meydanı), you can notice the **covered market** next to the Cathedral of St. Nicholas. If you are facing the Cathedral entrance, you can go right for a few blocks to reach the **Church of St. George of the Greeks.** Built in the 15th century, it combined Gothic and Byzantine styles. Its roof was destroyed in the Ottoman invasion; cannonball marks can still be seen on some walls. If you go farther right, you will find a pretty pair of tiny Orthodox churches. Opposite Othello's Tower, the **Church of St. George of the Latins** is merely an attractive shell. Continue away from Othello's Tower and the sea; you'll pass, on your left, the Twin Chapels of the **Knights Templar** and the **Knights of St. John of Jerusalem** which are usually locked. Continue straight to reach the **Nestorian Church,** or **Church of St. George the Exiler,** dating from the 14th century. There are a few more old churches near the city wall to your left as you face the sea, but this is now a military zone and cannot be entered. The beaches around Mağusa are generally the largest and most beautiful on the island. The bigger, the better. **Palm Beach,** located beneath a large hotel from which the beach takes its name, is the closest. From Canbulat bastion, simply follow the sea 1km. The beach snuggles up to the ghost city of **Varosha** (Maraş in Turkish). From the beach, one need only look up to see towering and deserted hotels, maimed by artillery. Larnaka rises in the distance. Varosha is a military area; you cannot enter it, and as always, photography is prohibited. **Glapsides Beach,** located 14km north of Mağusa, is a broad and wide hip of sand, popular with the city residents and university students from Mağusa's own 7500-student **Eastern Mediterranean University.** Other, quieter beaches can be found up the coast to the Karpaz peninsula.

■ Near Mağusa

MAĞUSA

SALAMIS

Salamis is one of the best preserved ancient cities of Cyprus (of which there were nine). Legend has it that it was founded in the 11th century BCE by **Teucer,** one of the heroes of Homer's *Iliad.* This metropolis became the richest city on the island. In 392 CE its name was changed to **Constantine.** It was destroyed by Arab invaders in the 7th century CE, after which Mağusa rose to prominence.

Close to the entrance, the two best-preserved buildings, the **Palaestra** and **Baths,** immediately on your left, give an idea of the city's former greatness. The Palaestra, surrounded by elegant columns, served as an open-air gymnasium. Beside it are the baths—look for the occasional mosaic (they were easier to spot back then...). Nearby is the **theater,** built in the Roman era. The lower seats are original; those higher up are a 1960s reconstruction. The remainder of the site is in a poor state of preservation; there is little to see. The ruins include a Roman villa, agora, temple of Zeus, and the old city walls. The **Kanpanopetra Basilica** has some interesting mosaics on its floor; from here there are excellent views of Famagusta and Varosha. Salamis is 18km from Mağusa. Infrequent buses will drop you at the signposted turn-off. Another choice is to catch the Salamis Hotel Bus, which lorries guests to and from the city. It waits along the Cafer Paşa Sokak. Watch for it around 1pm (though there are no set schedules). It will carry tourists, but not locals. The entrance to the site is 80m from the turn-off. Open daily during daylight hours (admission $2, students 50¢). Buses infrequently return to the city; you may have to walk back.

The **Monastery of St. Barnabas** was built in honor of a Cypriot Jew from Salamis, educated in Jerusalem, who returned to Cyprus to spread Christianity. He was, for a time, a companion of St. Paul. Four centuries after being put to death by Jews who regarded him as a traitor, St. Barnabas appeared to the Archbishop of Salamis, revealing the location of his grave and the existence of the Gospel. The Archbishop ordered the opening of the grave and found the perfectly preserved body of Barnabas and the handwritten Gospel. Hence the legend of St. Barnabas; this site marks the location of his tomb. There was an active monastery here until 1977, when the last monks abandoned it and went south (for the winter). The church is now an icon museum, and rooms near the church have been converted into the best **archaeological museum** in Kıbrıs, which houses exhibits of pottery and weapons. Finally, 150m from the monastery is the chapel tomb of St. Barnabas—get the key from the custodian. The actual body has since been moved to Jerusalem (open daily 8am-6pm; admission $2, students 50¢). In the **royal tombs,** (1km from monastery to Salamis) which date from the 8th century BCE, royalty were buried along with their possessions, including menservants and horses. There is a small museum, showing the site's excavations (open 8am-6pm daily; admission $2, students free).

KARPAZ PENINSULA

The Karpaz is Kıbrıs' most remote region. Brochures produced by the tourist office in Lefkoşa brandish color photos of Karpaz mules dragging wagons and slothful-looking sheep crowding a road. The captions read: "Moments of everyday life." Despite how dubiously touching scenes like these may seem to the urban concrete dweller, they are quite accurate. The Karpaz peninsula extends for roughly 70 to 80km, and at points is as wide as 20km (though more consistently 5 to10km wide). The peninsula itself is an arid, gently sloping land. At times it pitches up small mountains, covered with scrub and wildflowers. Along its main road—*the* paved road in the region—fields and occasional olive groves descend to the sea. The landscape is something like a cross between Israel and Los Angeles. Sociologically, the peninsula presents the last study of Greek and Turkish Cypriots cohabitating. In **Dipkarpaz,** the largest village in the peninsula, with a population of 3000, about 400 are Greek. The two cafés in the village are ethnically separated; the one with the signs in English is for Greeks. The two communities exist peacefully if not entirely harmoni-

MAĞUSA

ously. In 1991, however, the marriage of a Greek and Turk inspired angry demonstrations. There are few accommodations on the Karpaz. While several lonely looking hotels do appear near the Zafer Burnu, you'll have better luck farther inland. A few kilometers past Yenierenköy, the Karpaz's second largest village and site of the last petrol station, you can find the **Hotel Theresa** (tel. 374 4267, or after 5pm tel. 374 4368). This small but attractive hotel set above a bay offers electricity, a telephone, hot water, and plenty of beach (though not all of it sandy). You can rent fishing boats from the hotel, or walk along mountain trails. A medical doctor (the proprietor's wife) is often available. (Singles $15. Doubles $18. Breakfast included.) Another choice for a place to sleep lies near the tip of the peninsula. **Turtle Beach** offers camping equipment (tents for $3) or small bungalows ($10). Look for its sign along the road from Dipkarpaz to the Apostolos Andreas Monastery; it is about 2 to3km from the Zafer Burnu. The beach itself is massive and the sand is fine and white. Incidentally, it is among the last in the Mediterranean to be selected by turtles who lay their eggs during July and August. Two protected species, the Caretta-Caretta and the Green Turtle, frantically paddle sand in the summer to dig holes as deep as one meter in which they lay their eggs.

To orient yourself, turn right after the Atatürk statue in Dipkarpaz, and rattle down to the sea. This drive to the end of the peninsula, the **Zafer Burnu,** can yield 37km of meditation or else a landscape of psychosis (perhaps a bit of both). The land is thick with hills and along the inside seam of the peninsula, vast beaches stand unoccupied. Tortuous roads draw out every kilometer. Gas stations disappear. Three kilometers from the Hotel Theresa, in the village of Sipahi (follow the village road, keep looking to your right), lies a 6th-century **basilica.** An old Byzantine structure, the basilica is today in ruins, though some mosaics remain preserved. Entrance is free. At the base of the Karpaz peninsula, at over 600 meters in the Besparmak mountains, **Kantara Castle** was built by Richard the Lionheart in the 12th century, used by the Lusignans and Venetians, and abandoned in the 16th century. The castle is well marked; from Mağusa turn off at Boğaz. The views from that height alone justify the trip. The **Apostolos Andreas Monastery,** Greek Orthodox and set in a vast, empty square, lies approximately 25 poorly paved kilometers from Dipkarpaz. According to legend, St. Andres traveled to Palestine on a ship navigated by a half-blind captain. On the way, they sailed ashore to find drinking water. St. Andrew struck a rock where the monastery now stands, bashing open a spring—saltless and propitiously magical. Nonetheless, and after a little rubbing, the water restored the captain's sight. Today, transportation to the monastery is still difficult. Few cars pass, most of them rentals from Girne. Village buses run from Lefkoşa (11am) and Mağusa (noon), but only as far as Yenierenköy. That leaves about 40km, not to mention a ride back. Although the monastery has traditionally received Christian pilgrims on their way to Jerusalem, its only pilgrims today are the Greeks from Dipkarpaz who file down to the icon-filled church in a progression of rattle-trap, 1950s-era buses. The monastery is open daylight hours, and it is free.

TURKEY TÜRKIYE

US$1 =83,003 Turkish Lira (TL)	10,000 Turkish Lira (TL) = US$0.12
CDN$1 = 60,431TL	10,000TL = CDN$0.17
UK£1 = 128,880TL	10,000TL = UK£0.08
IR£1 = 133,850TL	10,000TL = IR£0.07
AUS$1 = 62,500TL	10,000TL = AUS$0.16
NZ$1 = 55,555TL	10,000TL = NZ$0.18
SAR1 = 18,518TL	10,000TL = SAR0.54
100GRdr = 353,357TL	10,000TL = 2.83GRdr
C£1 = 43,840TL	10,000TL = C£.23

> All prices are quoted in U.S. dollars because inflation in Turkey tends to correspond roughly with the devaluation of the lira.

Cultural contradictions, as much as majestic landscapes and archaeological treasures, fascinate visitors to Turkey. This same land reared Homer, Midas, St. Paul, and Santa Claus. Today there are actually two Turkeys—one sophisticated, the other rustic and parochial. It seems appropriate that Anatolia, the mountainous bridge between Europe and Asia, belongs to a secular state even though it contains the very first church in Christendom and has a Muslim population. Turkey's sophistication is manifested in the cosmopolitan resorts and cities that dot its coastline. Nude beaches, an outrageous nightlife, and promiscuous natives and tourists alike baffle visitors expecting a conservative country. Its rustic side encompasses the country's heartland, which remains virtually unaffected by tourism. All too many English-speaking residents of cities shamelessly swindle tourists; the obliging folk in the country, on the other hand, rarely speak English but still care to house and nourish the occasional wayfarer. Turkey is one of the ideal budget travel destinations in the world. Unfortunately, women traveling alone may feel uncomfortable in some of the more remote regions, although they probably won't have any problems in the more touristy coastal areas.

> Although the region of Eastern Turkey contains some of the more beautiful landscapes and sights in Turkey, single women and travelers who aren't fluent in Turkish may experience difficulties while traveling there. The areas surrounding Diyarbakır and the border with Armenia are not safe to travel through. Sporadic fighting with Kurdish populations and strained relations with Armenia have resulted in pocketed war zones barring safe travel. Please keep these warnings in mind as you plan your trip through Turkey.

ESSENTIALS

■ Once There

Government offices are open Monday-Friday 8:30am-12:30pm and 1:30-5:30pm and banks Monday-Friday 8:30am-noon and 1:30-5pm. Food stores, bazaars, and pharmacies have longer hours. During the summer, on the west and south coasts, government offices and other businesses close during the afternoons, but shops stay open until 10pm. Museums and archaeological sites in Turkey are open Tuesday-Sunday 9am-5pm. At all state-run museums, students with **ISIC** cards receive a 50% discount. Entrance to many museums is free with a **GO25** (FIYTO) youth card.

If you are in need of **medical care** in Turkey, an embassy or consulate can provide you with a list of English-speaking doctors, although they're common in most major hospitals. İstanbul has several foreign-run hospitals (see p. 454). Private hospitals generally provide a higher standard of care than public ones. Payment, with cash or a credit card, is expected at the time of treatment. For **emergency medical service** dial **112.** For the **police,** dial **155.** If your difficulties are not urgent, go to the nearest tourist office before trying the police; they can ease communication.

Be wary of English-speaking natives who approach you as friends. After befriending you, they'll offer to take you to a shop with "the best prices." Every time you spend a *lira,* your new best friend earns a commission (up to 50%). This scam is known as *hanut.* This also holds for people who approach you in bus stations offering accommodations. Have a hotel or *pansiyon* name in mind and tell the taxi driver that this is where you want to go. The taxi driver will more than likely be working on the same system and tell you that he knows of a better place. You may even be told that the place you want is full or has burned down. Stand firm.

Pensions that call themselves *aile* (family-style) try to maintain a wholesome atmosphere. Even if an establishment advertises 24-hour hot water, you may have to ask to have the hot water turned on in your room. Always carry toilet paper with you, since many places don't have any; other **toiletries**—including condoms, sanitary pads, and usually tampons—are cheap and readily available, though less so in the eastern part of Turkey.

If you have Visa or MasterCard (Access or Eurocard), or even an internationally networked ATM card from your home bank, use **ATMs:** plentiful in Turkey, they will give you the best exchange rate. American Express cardholders can use Akbank ATMs; Pamukbank ATMs, among others, are connected to the Cirrus network. Remember to keep your currency exchange receipts, as some banks will not change lira back into dollars even without a receipt.

■ Getting Around

Transport in Turkey can be both frustrating and time-consuming, but a little persistence will usually get you where you want to go. **Turkish Airlines** has direct flights once or twice weekly from İstanbul to Trabzon, Van, Diyarbakır, Erzurum, İzmir, and Ankara. Domestic flights average $80 one way, but passengers aged 12-24 may receive a discount. In some cities, an airport shuttle bus leaves from the downtown ticket office ½-1½ hours before flights (for an extra charge).

Frequent, modern, and cheap, **buses** run between all sizeable cities. Many lines provide a 10% discount to ISIC-carrying students who ask. You will need to go from booth to booth to piece together a complete schedule; one company may not divulge competitors' schedules. For long trips, try one of the more expensive bus lines. They usually offer larger seats, air conditioning, a toilet, and tea for only about 50% more than ordinary companies. Reputable companies include Varan Tours, Ulusoy, Kamıl Koç, Pamukkale, and Çanakkale Seyahat. Try to buy a seat in advance, but keep in mind that changing your ticket can be difficult. In rural parts of Turkey, it is customary when catching buses simply to flag them down from the roadside without reserving a seat in advance. Try to spot the bus's destination sign in the front window. Drivers, who keep an eye out for potential passengers, stop only if they have an empty seat. A steward hops off to stow your baggage while you board, and then collects your fare.

Extensive **shared taxi** *(dolmuş)* service follows fixed routes between small towns or within large ones. These are usually vans or minibuses, though occasionally cars are in service as well (in İstanbul they are usually an expanded 50s-make station wagon). They leave as soon as they fill up *(dolmuş* means stuffed), and are almost as cheap as municipal buses, which don't exist in some towns. Best of all, you can get on and off anywhere you like.

Despite low fares, **trains** within Turkey are no bargain. They are slow and follow circuitous routes. First-class gets you a slightly more padded seat and much more

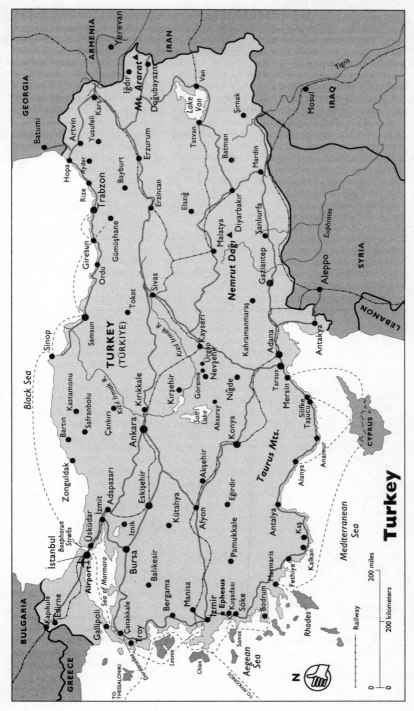

Turkey

room (most Turks travel second-class). Since couchettes are available, overnight train trips are preferable to overnight bus trips.

Turks drive on the right side of the road; the speed limit is 50kph (31mph) in cities, 90kph (55mph) on the highways, and 130kph (80mph) on *oto yolu* (toll roads). Road signs in English make **driving** somewhat easier. Archaeological and historical sites are indicated by yellow signposts with black writing; village signs have blue. Before taking your own car through Turkey, consider the likely effects poor roads will have on your vehicle. Official tourist literature warns against driving at night. If you get into an accident, you must file a report with the police. The **Turkish Touring and Automobile Association** (TTOK) can provide more information. Major offices include Maraşal Sevzi Çakmak Cad. 31/8 Beş Evler, Ankara (tel. (312) 222 8723), Antalya (tel. (242) 282 8140, -1, -2, -3), and İstanbul (tel. (212) 231 4631).

As in Greece, in contests between **pedestrians** and motorists, Turkish drivers take the right of way. They rarely pause for pedestrians, so be alert when crossing the street. Those who decide to **hitchhike** in Turkey generally offer to pay half of what the trip would cost by bus. Hitchers in Turkey signal with a waving hand. *Let's Go* does not recommend hitchhiking as a means of transportation, and urges readers to consider the risks inherent in hitching. Women should never hitch alone.

Ferries do not serve the west coast, but a **Turkish Maritime Lines** (TML) cruise ship sails between İstanbul and İzmir (1 per week, 21hr.). In summer, a weekly boat also connects İstanbul and Trabzon including intervening points on the Black Sea Coast. İstanbul has daily service to Bandırma. Larger ports have ship offices; otherwise, just get on the boat and find the purser.

TURKISH BUSES

Turkish drivers are notorious for recklessness. Anatolia's mountainous terrain and poorly maintained roads aggravate the problem. Even professional drivers for reputable bus lines are known for tearing over and around blind curves, dangerously risking passenger lives. Although road travel remains the most extensive, affordable, and modern way to get around Turkey, there are serious risks involved. You might consider safer options (such as by trains and ferries) despite the extra inconvenience. In Turkey, 22 people are killed in traffic accidents for every 100 million kilometers of vehicle travel; in the U.S., the comparable rate is 1.1 persons. (Source: *Association for Safe International Road Travel*)

For long trips there are always overnight buses; request a window seat in the middle of the bus, away from the driver's radio and behind the overhead window. Every so often a steward will come around spraying cologne; stretch out your palms to receive a squirt, then rub it over your face and neck. Every two to four hours or so, the bus will stop at a roadside rest complex where you can stretch your legs, use the toilets (10¢; paper extra), pray, and purchase overpriced cafeteria grub. The driver will announce the duration of the stop in Turkish before you get out, but it might vary by as much as 15 minutes either way, so keep an eye on your bus. Passengers who get left behind receive neither sympathy nor monetary compensation. If you get stranded, another bus going your way will probably visit the rest complex within a few hours; find the steward on board to buy a ticket for an empty seat. Nighttime travel is even more dangerous than daytime bus travel; beware of tourist bureau advice to travel at night in order to maximize touring time.

STREET ADDRESSES

As few Turkish cities follow a grid plan, maps can be difficult to use. To avoid confusion, a three-tiered addressing system is used. First comes the district, or *mahalle*. Then comes the nearest avenue (*cadde or bulvar*). Unless the address falls on this avenue, the side street off of it (*sokak, sokağı*) is specified next. Last comes the building's street number, prefixed by "No." A slash after the street number, or the word *kat*, introduces the number of the floor, if applicable. *Mahalle(si)* is abbreviated to **Mah.**, *Cadde(si)* to **Cad.**, *Bulvar(ı)* to **Blv.**, and *Sokak* (or *Sokağı*) to **Sok.** Thus, a complete street address in Turkey might look like *Çiğdem Mah. Atatürk Blv. Söğüt Sok. No. 6/2.* This book, which prints street numbers directly before the streets to which they refer, would list this address as *Çiğdem Mah. Atatürk Blv. 6/ 2 Söğüt Sok.* It means the second floor of 6 *Söğüt* St., off of *Atatürk* Ave., in the *Çiğdem* District. Few addresses will contain all of these parts. In towns and rural areas, the street names—rarely used by residents—may not appear on maps. Here you will receive nonstandard addresses specifying the desired building's position relative to some visible nearby edifice (e.g., *Süleymaniye Camii Önü*, "in front of Süleyman's Mosque"). In these situations, the following prepositions will come in handy: **önü** (in front of), **arkası** (behind), **üstü** (on top of), **altı** (beneath), **yanı** (beside), and **karşı** (across from).

■ Keeping In Touch

Mail to or from North America can take anywhere from one week to 17 days. **Post offices** (known as **PTT**) are easily recognized by their yellow signs. PTT stands for Post Office, Telegraph, and Telephone. Large post offices in major urban areas are open Monday through Saturday from 8am-midnight, Sunday from 9am-7pm. Major PTTs in İstanbul are open 24 hours. Smaller post offices share the same hours as government offices (Mon.-Fri. 8:30am-12:30pm and 1:30-5:30pm). To send mail Poste Restante, write the person's name, *Postrestant,* and *Merkez Postanesi* (Main Post Office), followed by the town's name; use the postal code if you have it. Picking up letters sometimes costs a small fee. Check under both your first and last name, and have a form of identification handy. Also, specify *Uçak İle* (airmail) when requesting stamps, and write it on your mail (or ask for aerograms). Tell the vendor the mail's destination: *Avustralya, Kanada, Büyük Bretanya* (Great Britain), *İrlanda, Yeni Zelanda* (New Zealand), *Güney Afrika* (South Africa), or *Amerika.*

Turkey has a surprisingly good **phone** system. With few exceptions, even the smallest village is accessible by phone. The numbering system was revised in 1994, so beware of out-of-date listings. Local numbers now all have seven digits, and all area codes have three. (In small towns, all numbers will start with the same three digits, so you may occasionally be given a four-digit phone number.)

When making a **long-distance** call within Turkey, first dial 0, wait for the tone to change to a lower pitch, then dial the area code and the number. Note that the area code and the number always have a total of ten digits. The number to dial for **information** is 118. To initiate an international call, first dial 0. When making a **direct international call,** dial 0, wait for the tone, then dial 0 again followed by the country code and the number, without pausing. There are four common phone tones: the dial tone, busy tone, and calling tone, as well as three short beeps followed by one repeated long beep, which means you need to dial again because your call is not going through properly for some reason. Phone cards *(telekart)* are very convenient and can be bought in denominations of 30, 60, or 100 units at PTTs; some kiosks also sell them. Most phones take *telekart;* some take *jeton,* little coin-like tokens also available at PTTs; regular coins are not accepted. *Telekart* are cheaper than *jeton* and easier to use, but villages often have a limited supply. Magnetic card public phones are abundant in big cities and resort areas; they have on-screen instructions in English, French, and German. To make calls using MCI (0080011177), AT&T (0080012277), SPRINT (0080014477), etc., a card or *jeton* must be deposited, but the call is free—no credit will be deducted from your card, and your *jeton* will be returned to you. Calling card calls usually terminate after three minutes if you are calling from a public phone.

The cheapest way to make international **collect** (reverse-charge) calls is to contact an operator in the destination country. From *any* (working) payphone, dial: U.S. 0080012277, U.K. 00800441177, Canada 00800331177, Ireland 008003531177, or Australia 0800611177.

Equally pleasant are *kontörlü telefon*. These are phones in the post office; the officer tells you how much you owe at the end of your call. Note that there may be long lines for these phones, especially during the day. Try to use one late at night at one of the 24-hour PTTs. The same kind of phone is available at some hotels and restaurants, but they may charge you 20-500% more.

LIFE AND TIMES

■ History

ANCIENT TURKEY

Civilization has flourished in what is now Central Turkey since the eighth millennium BCE, making it one of the oldest human settlements on earth. This geographical region (historically known as "Anatolia" or "Asia Minor") has long mixed Asian and Western cultures. During the 3rd millennium BCE (Bronze Age), an early Hittite nation settled in Central Anatolia. Besides developing techniques for forging iron weapons, the Hittites spoke an Indo-European language considered by scholars to be closely related to modern European languages. Following the massive migration of Greek islanders ("sea peoples") at the end of the 2nd millennium BCE, the Hittite empire collapsed. Cyrus extended the Persian empire along the coast of Asia Minor in the 6th century BCE, using the region as a base for forays into Greece.

Two centuries later Alexander the Great marched his army into Asia Minor and routed the Persians. Great metropolises emerged after the 2nd century BCE, when the coastline became the commercial and political core of the Roman province of Asia Minor. Following the creation of the Eastern Roman Empire in Byzantium (renamed Constantinople), Asia Minor prospered, became the center of Greek Orthodox Christian culture, and oversaw a renewed and vigorous empire stretching from the Balkans through Greece to the Levant and Egypt.

Turks began to migrate from their homeland in Central Asia in the second half of the 8th century CE, moving west and establishing independent states in eastern Iran, Afghanistan, and northern India. In the 11th century, Seljuk Turks, originally inhabitants of Mongolia, began the most significant Turkish migration, inhabiting the Muslim lands of Iran, Iraq, and Syria and settling on the plains of central Anatolia. Although Seljuk power was momentarily eclipsed by the pillaging Genghis Khan, the Seljuks were able to maintain their authority for a surprisingly long period. The Byzantine ports along the coast began to wane in economic importance as land routes to Asia were monopolized by the various Seljuk fiefdoms in the interior. When Seljuk rule broke down in the 14th century, separate Turkish emirates picked up the pieces. Osman claimed the northwest corner of Anatolia, and, in time, united several fiefdoms to challenge and defeat the Greeks. From such origins grew perhaps the greatest empire in the history of civilization: the *Osmanlı*, or Ottoman.

THE OTTOMAN EMPIRE

From the beginning of the 14th century to the middle of the 15th, Ottoman rulers gradually gnawed away at the Byzantine Empire. In 1453, Constantinople, an Ottoman target since the time of Osman, finally fell to Mehmet the Conqueror. Renamed İstanbul, the city became the heart of a youthful, vigorous Turkish Empire.

The Ottoman Empire incorporated Greece and soon Cyprus into the Muslim/Turkish state apparatus and penetrated the Balkans as far as Belgrade. Under Selim I (1512-1520), Ottoman armies conquered Syria, Palestine, Egypt, and Arabia. In a feat of military and religious grandeur, the sultan became guardian of the three holy places of Islam: Mecca, Medina, and Jerusalem. Although all power in the empire was vested in a sultan accountable only to God, a number of different individuals actually ruled the territories of the empire. Under the sultans, professional governors (often competing heirs to the sultanate) were sent out to the provinces. The sultans also gave *timar*, or land grants, to gain the support of Turkish military chiefs. In accordance with Islamic law, monotheistic communities paid the *cizye*, a special head tax, and were on the whole treated well. Orthodox Greek Christians, for example, fared far better under Muslim authority than they did under the crusading Franks. Many Jews, upon their expulsion from Spain in 1492, settled in parts of the empire and took up trade. Despite ruthless counters to occasional rebellions, the early days of the Ottoman Empire brought relative peace and prosperity.

As Ottoman expansion slowed, the military *timar* holders grew restless, missing the income they had gained from conquests. In order to reestablish military loyalty, Sultan Murad I created the first corps of **janissaries** (from *yeni çeri,* "new army") in the middle of the 14th century. Technically personal slaves of the sultan, these (mostly Christian) sons of subjects were forcibly taken from the provinces and converted to Islam. During their training they were given years of exams and drills and tracked into graduated echelons of the military. Those who made it to the top were assigned duties at the palace under the personal direction of the sultan. The great architect Sinan was a janissary.

When **Süleyman** became Sultan (1520-66), the Ottoman Empire was already considerable, but under him the expanse of the empire was doubled, stretching from the Balkans and Greece north to the Black Sea, west to Iraq, and southward into Africa. Court administration was centralized, and literature, architecture, and decorative arts flourished. Süleyman's military conquests and voluptuous court earned him the title of Magnificent among the Europeans. (It was Süleyman who knocked at the gates of Vienna in 1529.) Süleyman earned the title of *Kanuni* (the Lawgiver) for coalescing the *şeriat* (Islamic jurisprudence) with the *ferman* (court decrees).

Süleyman's most influential wife, **Roxelana,** convinced the Sultan to name his less-than-magnificent son **Selim** as his successor. In order to spend more time carousing in the well endowed imperial harem, Selim turned virtually all matters of the state over to the Grand Vizier. During the period that followed (a sozzled Selim had drowned in his tub in 1574), the palace was rife with infighting. Some scholars called this the "rule of the women," as the favorite wives or harem girls of the monomaniacal sultans vied for power. Mothers would order entire families strangled to ensure the throne for their own children. For example, Kösem, a concubine of Sultan Murad (1603-17), scarcely survived banishment to Beyazıt upon the sultan's untimely death, only to return triumphantly to the palace when her sons Murad IV and İbrahim became sultans in rapid succession. Kösem even lived to see her grandson become sultan, but in 1652 she was strangled by order of her daughter-in-law.

Weakness at the top only encouraged abuses by those nearer the bottom. Religious and ethnic minorities, such as the Armenians, Kurds, Greeks, and Jews, were sometimes treated quite harshly. Following a period of devastating inflation caused by the Spanish discovery of American silver, the Ottoman administration became continually weaker. After a series of disastrous military entanglements with Peter the Great and the Venetians, the Ottoman dynasty signed the **Treaty of Karlowitz** on January 26, 1699, consequently losing most of Transylvania and Hungary.

END OF AN EMPIRE

After the traumatic loss of Greece in 1832, life did not get any easier for the Ottoman Empire. **Muhammad Ali,** nominally the sultan's governor of Egypt, invaded the Levant. He would have captured İstanbul itself had it not been for the intervention of the European powers. In the mid-19th century, after crushing conservative opposition, the Ottomans instituted a series of administrative reforms collectively known as the *tanzimat.* Besides providing *de jure* religious equality to all, the *tanzimat* attempted to regulate taxation and government conscription and to establish the private ownership of land. Most peasants, however, were wary that the government's reforms were merely covers for more tax-raising schemes. So they registered their land in the name of wealthy *shaykhs* and landowners, whose great estates thus further accrued. As the Ottoman government became more and more indebted to British and French bankers, the once-fabulous Empire limped in such decrepitude that it was commonly referred to as "the sick man of Europe."

The British, after assuming a "protectorate" over Cyprus in 1878, began fearing that bondholders who had invested in Egypt would not be repaid, so they marched armies into the Nile. Meanwhile, as the self-proclaimed protectors of Greek Orthodox Christians everywhere, the Russians came forth with more extensive claims against the Ottomans, liberating territory in the Crimea. Foreign missionary schools sprang up in the Ottoman Middle East. Arabs, ruled by Turks for more than five centuries, began to blame the Ottomans for the corruption of Islam. Indeed, the Arabs had never recognized the Turks as legitimate protectors of the faith in the first place.

With the advent of the telegraph and steamship, the Ottoman central government was able to solidify its presence in the remote parts of the empire. As Britain and France vied with Russia for control of the strategic straits of the Bosphorus, the sultans had the opportunity to dive headfirst into the intrigues of European *realpolitik*. Although unrest in the early 1870s prompted the granting of a constitution complete with elected parliament, **Sultan Abdülhamid II** (who ruled 1876-1909) led a pan-Islamic counter-revolution and suspended all democratic reforms.

The 1908 coup of the **"Young Turks,"** a secret organization which had burst from the officer corps, ended Abdülhamid's hold on power. Welcomed at first by most of the ethnic populations, the triumvirate of military officials who controlled the empire soon began to implement a strident plan of Turkification. Traditionally, Islam had been the basis for Ottoman identity, and, in accordance with Islamic law, minorities had been allowed to open their own schools and keep their own customs. But now the central government decreed that Turkish was to be the national language of the empire for non-Turkish-speaking Muslims and non-Muslims alike.

The government of the Empire sided with the Axis powers in WWI. As British officers led an Arab revolt against the Turks (with a promise of independence), Turkish officials in the east began to "solve" their ethnic problems. A three-year period witnessed the death of more than 1½ million Armenian civilians after Armenian forces living in Turkey sided with the Russian army in an attempt to win their own independence. Officials in the German government expressed dismay at this plan, but no effort was made to interfere. Entire Armenian cities were disinhabited under the pretense of a relocation of their inhabitants to the safer environs of Mesopotamia. Although Turks take exception to this version of history, many of them are aware of the past government's mistakes, although it is never taught in public schools. Today, a strong group of Armenian lobbyists are fighting for the world to recognize the "Armenian Massacre" in hopes of gaining a larger homeland in Eastern Turkey.

THE TURKISH REPUBLIC

The Ottoman dynasty, however, had breathed its last by siding with the Germans in WWI. After the Allies won, Britain and France divided the Arab provinces, under the auspices of the League of Nations. Plans for the division of Anatolia were drawn up, and Greece invaded in order to capture disputed territory. These two undertakings were stifled by the rise of **Mustafa Kemal**, an Ottoman general who was able to reorganize his army in time to defeat the Greeks. On October 29, 1923, Mustafa Kemal, dubbed **Atatürk** (Father of the Turk), was elected the first president of the new Republic of Turkey. Atatürk turned his back on Ottoman tradition. Equating modernization with rapid Westernization and secularization, Atatürk abolished the Caliphate, outlawed Muslim courts and the veiling of women, decreed that Turkish be written in Latin rather than Arabic script, and, for a time, ordered that the *adhan* (call to prayer) be recited in Turkish rather than classical Arabic. He also gave women the right to vote. Needless to say, he was an enlightened man. These sweeping measures encountered extreme resistance from the religious establishment.

©1996 AT&T.

Someone back home *really* misses you.
Please call.

With **AT&T Direct**^{SM} Service it's easy to call back to the States from virtually anywhere your travels take you. Just dial the **AT&T Direct** Access Number for the country *you are in* from the chart below. You'll have English-language voice prompts or an AT&T Operator to guide your call. And our clearest,* fastest connections** will help you reach whoever it is that misses you most back home.

AUSTRIA●◇ 022-903-011	GREECE● 00-800-1311	NETHERLANDS● ...06-022-9111
BELGIUM● 0-800-100-10	INDIA✖ 000-117	RUSSIA●,▲,♪ (Moscow).755-5042
CZECH REP▲ 00-42-000-101	IRELAND 1-800-550-000	SPAIN◇ 900-99-00-11
DENMARK..................8001-0010	ISRAEL...................177-100-2727	SWEDEN................020-795-611
FRANCE.................0 800 99 0011	ITALY● 172-1011	SWITZERLAND● ..0-800-550011
GERMANY.................0130-0010	MEXICO▽ 95-800-462-4240	U.K.▲ 0800-89-0011

*Non-operator assisted calls to the U.S. only. **Based on customer preference testing. ●Public phones require coin or card deposit. Public phones require local coin payment through call duration. ◇From this country, AT&T Direct calls terminate to designated countries only. ▲May not be available from every phone/pay phone. ✖Not available from public phones. When calling from public phones, use phones marked "Ladatel." ♪Additional charges apply when calling outside of Moscow.

 **AT&T**

Can't find the Access Number for the country you're calling from?
Just ask any operator for AT&T Direct Service.

Greetings from LET'S GO

With pen and notebook in hand, a change of clothes in our backpack, and the tightest of budgets, we've spent our summer roaming the globe in search of travel bargains.

We've put the best of our research into the book that you're now holding. Our intrepid researcher-writers went on the road for months of exploration, from Anchorage to Angkor, Estonia to Ecuador, Iceland to India. Editors worked from spring to fall, massaging copy into witty and informative prose. A brand-new edition of each guide hits the shelves every fall, just months after it is researched, so you know you're getting the most reliable, up-to-date, and comprehensive information available.

We try to make this book an indispensable companion, but sometimes the best discoveries are the ones you make on your own. If you've got something to share, please drop us a line. We're Let's Go Publications, 67 Mount Auburn Street, Cambridge, MA 02138 USA (e-mail: fanmail@letsgo.com). Good luck and happy travels!

So You Want to Be a Dervish

Widely regarded as the "intellectuals" of mystical Islam, the Whirling Dervishes wielded great political power from the Seljuk period until 1923, when Atatürk dissolved the order. Their influence at court may partly account for the Ottoman policy of religious toleration toward conquered peoples, especially in the Balkans and Eastern Europe. Atatürk reportedly found the Dervishes's monarchist and politically conservative beliefs to be inconsistent with the reforms he sought to implement. Not long after his death, the government gave in, and now professional Dervishes are free to whirl once a year during a week-long festival held in Konya in mid-December (if that doesn't fit with your plans, you can see genuine dervish dances in İstanbul). The dances, in which the most adept Sufis sometimes make as many as 60 revolutions per minute, are pregnant with symbolism and result from years of constant training. In order to learn to spin in one place so fast without losing their balance, aspiring dervishes grip a spike in the ground between their biggest two toes, and whirl by walking their other foot around this post. One arm points down to Earth, the other upwards to Heaven, positioning the whirler as a channel unifying the energies from both.

Since the rise of Mustafa Kemal, Turks have been determined in their program to become a part of Europe. The **Republican People's Party** program of 1931 proclaimed the six principles of the modern Turkish state: republicanism, populism, nationalism, statism, secularism, and revolution. Changes were introduced to "reeducate" the public about Turkish achievement, and the government began a systematic campaign to purge foreign-derived words from the Turkish language. Turkification triumphed over the competing systems of Ottomanism and pan-Islamism, if only because it was the only option left.

Shortly before WWII, the increasingly autocratic Kemal died and was replaced by his associate **İsmet İnönü.** Though Nazi Germany's early successes resulted in a popular clamor to join the war on the side of Germany to avenge the humiliation of WWI, the government remained neutral. At the end of the war, with the impending defeat of Germany, Turkey joined the Allies, as the penetration of Soviet power into the south had become a pressing concern. When the Soviets demanded the sharing of control of the Straits and the ceding of large pieces of eastern Anatolia to Soviet Georgia, military and economic aid from the United States was shunted to Turkey. (Today Turkey is still one of the largest recipients of U.S. aid.)

WWII, however, led to the expansion of the Turkish military and fed its role in politics. When a growing professional class demanded increased political participation, the **Democrat Party** (DP) broke off from the old Kemalist Republican People's Party (RPP). Throughout the 50s, the government, dominated mostly by the DP, continually loosened censorship and expanded political rights. As the 50s progressed, however, economic conditions deteriorated almost as fast as relations between the RPP and the DP. When the DP threatened to outlaw the RPP, students participated in demonstrations and the army stepped in and took control.

After the eradication of the DP, the military's ruling **National Unity Committee** made a new constitution. Approved by voters in July, 1961, the constitution established a bicameral parliament that would elect the president jointly. Elections were held in October, and the army soon withdrew from politics. Many former DP members became influential in the new Justice Party (JP), which dominated elections after 1965. In 1970, after right-wing members of the JP split off and reconstituted the old Democratic Party, the army demanded the resignation of the government and assumed *de facto* control.

RECENT YEARS

During the 1970s, the government was controlled by a coalition that united the RPP with a new religious party. Tensions built as economic conditions worsened, and religious opposition to increased Westernization grew. Following the coup in

HISTORY

Cyprus which overthrew President Makarios, public opinion in Turkey led to the army's **invasion of northern Cyprus** in July, 1974, as fear that Cyprus would become part of mainland Greece increased. Economic and arms embargoes soon followed and Turkey responded by closing foreign military installations. By the end of the 70s, most normal foreign relations resumed.

The military took power again in September, 1980, as the government's control over the interior of the country dissipated. The military dissolved all opposition parties and punished and tortured thousands of opposition leaders. By 1983, the military relinquished most of its hold on power and martial law ceased; elections that year brought the centrist **True Path Party** of **Turgut Özal** to power. Turkish assistance during the Gulf War against Iraq in 1991 proved economically debilitating and led to terrorist attacks against government installations and foreigners. But by cooperating with the United States, Özal may well have claimed a new international role for Turkey, which had lost its traditional strategic position with the end of the Cold War. Boosted economic assistance from the West as well as the Gulf countries seems to have alleviated, for the moment, the threat of further crisis.

In May of 1993 the True Path Party voted **Tansu Çiller,** a woman, as its new leader. However progressive that victory may seem, the 1994 elections saw the emergence of Islamic fundamentalism as a political power at the state and local levels; fundamentalists captured the mayoral majorities of Ankara and İstanbul. In the wake of the Gulf War, **Kurdish separatists** stepped up their terrorist activity, prompting Çiller, in the spring of 1994, to turn the problem over to the military. Traditionally heavy-handed, the military began razing villages suspected of harboring rebels, and thousands of Kurdish villagers fled to the cities. The spring of 1995 has seen the Turkish military determined to destroy the **Kurdistan Workers' Party (PKK),** an unrepresentative Kurdish minority party suspected of using European drug trafficking to finance its terrorist activities. Thus, in an ironic turn of events, Turkey led a brief offensive into the power vacuum of northern Iraq left by the departure of the U.S. forces after the Gulf War. Strong threats of sanctions from the EU may have contributed to this campaign's speedy conclusion.

As the European Economic Community accelerated its drive toward unity, Turkey's role in the global economic arena stood undetermined. In 1987, Turkey applied for full membership, but was rejected in 1989 on the grounds that the completion of a previously defined European market was necessary before any expansion could be considered. Furthermore, the Commission of the European Communities noted Turkey's less than stellar human rights record, high rate of inflation, and control of Northern Cyprus as objections to granting Turkey's membership. (There is also fear that the existing 2 million Turkish workers in the rest of Europe will expand exponentially if visas are rendered unnecessary.) In early 1995, Turkey was finally accepted into the European Customs Union, on the condition that the Turkish parliament make hundreds of new laws and changes to the constitution by October. Some of the changes have yet to be made. Meanwhile, Turkey has sought economic opportunity in the East, namely in the Muslim former Soviet republics of Kazakhastan, Tajikistan, and Uzbekistan.

WHAT'S HAPPENING NOW

The biggest upset came in June 1996 when **Tansu Çiller** formed a coalition government with **Necmettin Erbakan,** the Fundamentalist Islam leader of the Welfare Party, to squelch an investigation of her misappropriation of government funds. Çiller had already formed a coalition government with **Mesut Yılmaz** (Motherland Party) after Erbakan won a majority of votes, but personality differences threatened the security of the nation and both Çiller and Yılmaz resigned as Prime Minister. In the second election, after the collapse of the government, Erbakan won another majority of votes but was unable to take control without the support of another party. Meanwhile, the Welfare Party was investigating Çiller for missing government funds, and she secretly agreed to form a coalition with Erbakan; in return, the investigation was dropped. It is unclear what the consequences of a Fundamentalist

Islamic leader will be in Turkey, but many in the Western world, especially Israel (Turkey is the only ally Israel has in the Middle East), are worried. This recent shift of national politics is not so much a return to fundamental religious beliefs as it is a reaction to the growing disparity between the rich and poor populations of the country. Pro-secular advocates claim that Erbakan bought his seat as Prime Minister by offering the poorer rural populations money and schooling for their children in return for votes. This is the first time since the reforms of Atatürk that Turkey's secularity is in question. The following year will demonstrate the role Erbakan, and the Fundamentalists, will play in Turkey's future.

On the Aegean front, Greece and Turkey had a few near-disasters over a rocky outcrop of land. A Turkish ship ran aground on a disputed Greek islet in the Aegean Sea and refused help from the Greeks. As tensions built, fueled by centuries of animosity, both countries deployed troops for a face-off over a piece of land inhabited solely by a herd of goats. Needless to say, U.S. President Bill Clinton was a little worried and stepped in to prevent a full-scale war from breaking out. Both countries sheepishly agreed to pull back. A few other altercations have broken out between the two countries since then, but nothing to cause serious concern.

■ Religion

Around 95% of Turks are Muslim. Orthodox Christians of Greek, Armenian, and Syrian backgrounds, and Jews (mainly in İstanbul) compose the remaining population. There's no official state religion, but religion matters enough that every Turkish citizen's national identification card includes a blank for it, filled out at birth by parents. While Atatürk set modern Turkey on a secular course, *İslam* (Islam) plays a key role in the country's history and culture.

The Arabic word *islam* means "submission," and Islam the religion is the faithful submission to God's will. Islam has its roots in the revelations received between 610 and 622 CE by **Muhammad,** who was informed of his prophetic calling by the Angel Gabriel. These revelations, received in Arabic, form the core of Islam and the **Kur'an.** Muslims believe the Arabic text to be immutable and untranslatable—the words of God embodied in human language. Consequently, the Kur'an appears in Turkey and throughout the Muslim world in Arabic. Muhammad is seen as the "seal of the prophets," the last of a chain of God's messengers which included Judeo-Christian figures such as Abraham, Moses, and Jesus.

Islam continued to grow after the Prophet's death (632), flourishing in the "Age of Conquest." The first four *halife* (caliphs), or successors to the Prophet, known as the Rightly Guided Caliphs, led wars against apostate nomadic tribes, and, by the year 642, the Muslims had defeated the Persian empire. By 672, they had reached the walls of Constantinople. The fourth Caliph, Muhammad's nephew and son-in-law Ali, was the catalyst for a major split in the Muslim world; for the first time Muslims fought Muslims. Ali lost power and in 661 was murdered. The *Shi'at Ali* (Partisans of Ali, or Shi'is) believe that Ali, as a blood relative of the Prophet, was the only legitimate successor to Muhammad, thus separating themselves from **Sunni** (orthodox) Islam. **Shi'ism** is not a creed of fundamentalism but is Islam with a focus on divinely chosen *imam* (leaders) who are descendants of the Prophet. **Sufism** is a mystical movement within Islam that stresses the goal of unity with God. Sufis are organized in orders, with a hierarchy from master to disciple. Most Turkish Muslims are Sunni.

PILLARS OF ISLAM

"Allahu akhbar. La ilaha il'Allah Muhammadun rasul Allah"—*"God is great. There is no god but God. And Muhammad is His prophet."* This beginning of the call to prayer (the *ezan*), sounding five times each day from the mosques, expresses some of Islam's most important tenets. The first line glorifies God *(Allah).* The next lines of the call form the *şahadet,* the profession of faith. The *şahadet,* the first of

the five pillars of Islam, reflects the unity of God *(tawhid)* and the special place of Muhammad as God's final Messenger. The second pillar is *namaz* (prayer), recited five times daily following the example of the practice of Muhammad. On Fridays, congregational prayer is encouraged; this is the only distinguishing feature of the Muslim "sabbath." The third pillar is *zekât* (charity). It is believed that Muhammad received the Kur'an during the month of Ramadan. Fasting during this holy month is the fourth pillar. Ramadan is a time of daylight fasting and meditation, while nights are filled with feasting. During Ramadan (January 11-February 9 in 1997), offices and businesses not catering to tourists may be closed or keep shorter hours. The last pillar, which is required only once in a lifetime, is the *hac* (pilgrimage). Every Muslim who can afford it and is physically able is supposed to journey to Mecca during the last month of the Muslim calendar.

MOSQUES

Any place where Muslims pray is a mosque *camii* (mosque). The direction facing Mecca, in which all prayer is spoken, is called the *kible*. It is marked by a niche, the *mihrab*. The *imam* (leader of prayer, not to be confused with the Shi'i leaders) gives a *hutbe* (sermon) at noon prayer on Friday from the *minbar* (pulpit). In larger cities, you may also see a *türbe* (mausoleum) or *medrese* (Kur'anic school).

There are no religious restrictions on non-Muslims entering mosques, but other restrictions may have been adopted for practical reasons in areas with many tourists. Prayer is not a spectator sport, and visitors should stay away during times of worship and always wear modest dress. Men in shorts may be particularly frowned upon. Shoes are usually removed before entering a mosque, and women should cover their heads as a courtesy even if it is not required (technically, men as well as women are supposed to cover their heads in the presence of God).

■ Architecture and Art

Sultan Süleyman introduced unprecedented imperial patronage of the arts, his empire's glory finding prolific expression in the mosques, textiles, painted miniatures, and calligraphy of the 16th century. Under Süleyman alone (1520-1566), over 80 major mosques and hundreds of other buildings were constructed in the empire. Almost every sultan built and was subsequently buried in a mosque, thereby creating a topographical line of succession along Divan Yolu, İstanbul's processional avenue. The master Sinan served Süleyman and his sons as Chief Court Architect from 1538 to 1588, during which time he created a unified style for all of İstanbul and for much of the empire. Trained first as a carpenter and then as an elite soldier who marched the length of the Empire, Sinan forged an architecture informed by early Islamic and Byzantine styles, but conforming to neither.

LITERATURE

To be Ottoman was, for many centuries, to be part of a palace culture that evolved separately from the cultures of the peoples the empire governed. Ottoman culture was designed to provide a common experience for a ruling class chosen from disparate ethnic, linguistic, and religious backgrounds. Perhaps the most obvious signifier of this cultural otherness was the use of Ottoman Turkish—an ornate combination of Persian, Turkish, and Arabic. Ottoman was the language of choice both for the administration and for literature. The creation of modern Turkish in the 1920s has meant that the literary traditions of the Ottoman administration are lost to all but specialists. Modern Turkish literature looks back not to the early modern period, as is so often the case in Western traditions, but earlier yet to the writings of Türkmen poets such as Celaleddin Rumi and Yunus Emre. Their verses survived the Ottoman centuries relatively unscathed, and interestingly, the Turkish these poets used remains intelligible to a speaker of modern Turkish in a way that Ottoman is not. The *türkü* (modern Turkish folk song), for example, uses language and form that would have been familiar to these late medieval poets.

The poems and songs of the frontier survived because of their vividness and because the society they portrayed, with its often utopian multiculturalism and lack of control, often seemed a more attractive alternative to the centralized policies and sometimes heavyhanded administration of the Ottoman Empire. *The Book of Dede Korkut,* a collection of stories set in the age of the Oghuz Turks, represents an earlier literary tradition yet, and provides the English-reader with a good introduction to a tradition that has been so prominent in Turkish literature. Many of these works were rediscovered during the nineteenth century when both pan-Ottomanism and pan-Islamism had lost out. Part of this renewed interest in folk literature was the propagation of the tales of Nasreddin Hoca, an amiable, sometimes bumbling, anti-authoritarian holy man, whose exploits every Turkish schoolchild knows about.

Contemporary Turkish writing could be said to have begun with Namık Kemal, whose writings satirized the failings of the Ottoman Empire. Satire has remained very important to Turkish literature, especially as serious critical writers have periodically been known to bring the government's displeasure upon them. Nazım Hikmet's lyrical yet hard edged poetry brought him literary fame, but he was exiled for his political views. In fact, the government was extremely fond of exiling literary figures of whom they disapproved. Aziz Nesin, a fervent republican and free speech advocate, is one of the foremost leaders of this movement of this genre, and some of his work, as well as an account of his life, is available in English. Perhaps the best known Turkish author is Yaşar Kemal who has been nominated several times for the Noble Prize for Literature. His writings have been consistently critical of Turkish society and the government in particular and was recently charged with having engaged in anti-Turkish activities for writing an article critical of the government's repressive treatment of Turkey's Kurdish minority. His most famous novel, *Memed, My Hawk,* is readily available in English. Other Turkish writers available in English include Orhan Pamuk whose allegories and historical pastiches often recall the works of Italo Calvino. *White Castle* and *Black Castle* are both relatively easy to obtain, and the new translation of *Black Castle* is highly acclaimed.

DECORATIVE AND PERFORMANCE ARTS

The Ottoman decorative arts amount to a wealth of nature motifs. (Ottoman artists did not always follow the Kur'an's injunction against portraying living beings.) While standard arabesques, inherited from earlier Islamic art, were common, court workshops developed distinctly Ottoman styles as well. The naturalistic ones included flowers and animals, while the *saz* (reed) style, thought to have been inspired by Chinese sketches on porcelain, featured long, self-piercing leaves wound around abstract lotus blossoms. Similar but unrelated was the *rumi* style, which originated in Iran and featured split leaves.

Until the mid-1800s, calligraphy, miniatures, and illuminations were the only formal examples of painting; İznik tiles and colorful *kilim* the most familiar Turkish handicrafts. Music, dance, and theater have become more institutionalized in the past 150 years. Turkish music runs the gamut from *halk müziği* (folk music) to *özgün* (protest music) to *arabesk* and *taverna* (popular music). The last decade has also seen the arrival of Turkish pop. Similar to the American 80s, new artists are popping up in every corner of Turkey. In 1971, concern over the integrity of Turkey prompted the government to establish the nation's Ministry of Culture to ensure the propagation of Turkish art. Today, several international arts and music festivals bring performers from all over the world to Ephesus, İstanbul, and other Turkish cities, while the handicrafts of Turkish culture (carpets, meerschaum pipes, knit stockings, and elaborately inlaid wood) continue to be prized.

Umm...

We've all heard the famous stories about foreign hosts who bungle their attempts to ingratiate themselves with English-speaking travelers abroad. Guests are cheerfully invited to take advantage of the washerwoman and cordially asked not to have children at the bar. An American who is a little shaky on her Turkish may experience the same kind of amusement when her hosts begin counting with *bir* (one), the very substance that may cause her to lose her *ability* to count later that evening. On the other hand, when it's her turn to speak, she may unfortunately miss the significance of the guffaws that her repeated *ums* elicit. On the lips of a Turk, this oft-repeated American stammer has a more *private* significance. The fluent and modest American, knowing better, will only discuss her *am* with her gynecologist.

■ Language

Once thought to be related to Finnish, Hungarian, and Mongolian, Turkish is today recognized as belonging to a distinct Turkic language group, spoken from Germany to China and comprising Azerbaijani, Kazakh, Khirgiz, Uyghur, and Uzbek. In his effort to forge a secular Turkish identity, in 1928 Atatürk ordered the language written in the Roman alphabet rather than the Arabic script. Furthermore, Atatürk purged Turkish of many of its Arabic and Persian borrowings. While these words continue to be replaced by new Turkish ones, this linguistic cleansing is not absolute; Islamic terminology notwithstanding, words as common as *merhaba* (hello) remain of Arabic and Persian origin.

Although you might never have heard anything like Turkish, it is not difficult to master the basics. Pronunciation is entirely phonetic: each letter of the alphabet represents a single sound. There are only six new letters to learn: ş (sh), ç (ch), ğ (silent), ı, ö, and ü, two of which are already familiar to speakers of German. Moreover, grammatical gender does not exist, and Turkish case endings are so regular that you can count the exceptions on your fingers (for more pronunciations and a brief glossary, see p. 575).

English is widely spoken wherever tourism is big business—mainly in the major coastal resorts. In the rest of Anatolia, only university students tend to know English. Buy a phrasebook, such as the *Penguin Turkish Phrasebook* or *Harrap's Turkish Phrasebook*. Langenscheidt has an excellent Turkish-English pocket dictionary (for a pronunciation guide and list of useful phrases, consult the Glossary, p. 575).

Body Vibes

Body language often matters as much as what is said. When a Turk raises his chin and clicks his tongue, he means *hayır* (no); sometimes a shutting or uplifting of the eyes accompanies this motion. Shaking your head sideways instead means *anlamadım* (I don't understand). More intuitively, *evet* (yes) may be abbreviated by a sharp downward nod. If a Turk waves a hand up and down at you, palm toward the ground, she is signaling you to come, not bidding you farewell. In Turkey the idle habit of snapping the fingers of one hand and then slapping the top of the other fist is considered obscene.

■ Leisure

Many popular Turkish pastimes still take place in all-male enclaves. A favorite is visiting the local *kıraathane* (coffeehouse), where customers sip coffee or tea over games of *tavla* (backgammon). Another popular game is OKEY which is basically the same as gin rummy played with tiles instead of cards. In İstanbul, you might still find men smoking *nargile* (hookahs, water pipes). If you purchase a *nargile* as a souvenir, make sure that customs officials do not mistake it for a bong. Traditional spectator sports include *yağlı güreş* (grease wrestling), *cirit oyunu* (tossing javelins at competitors on horseback), and *deve güreşi* (camel wrestling). These are mainly regional and not as popular as the everpresent game of soccer. Every man, woman, and child has a favorite Turkish *futbol* team, and games have been known to get absurdly out of control.

The Turkish Bath

It's worth your while to visit a *hamam* (Turkish bath) at least once while in Turkey. But, just as a caution, some Turkish hamams are also gay pick-up joints; you may want to be selective in the ones you choose to frequent. Also, many of the cheaper ones are dens for bacterial diseases. It is a good idea to check out the place before stripping down to your birthday suit. Because of the Islamic emphasis on cleanliness (pious Muslims perform ablutions before each of the day's five prayers), the baths have been a customary part of daily life since medieval times. Men and women use separate bath houses, or the same place on different days. Enter the bath house, deposit your clothes in a cubicle, don the provided *peştemal* (towel), and proceed to the sauna-like *göbek taşı* (large heated stone). As you sweat, an attendant will give you a rub-down. Following the massage, you can bathe yourself (bring your own shampoo, soap, and towel, or pay to use theirs, and take care not to douse your neighbors since they might have just finished a ritual cleansing) or be bathed. The *kese* (abrasive mitt) they use will strip you of excess skin cells. Men should never drop their *peştemal;* cleaning one's lower half is therefore tricky, but not impossible.

■ Food and Drink

It may come as a surprise that such popular Middle Eastern foods as hummus, falafel, and baba ghanoush are practically unknown in Turkey. Like other cuisines from the Balkans to the Persian Gulf, contemporary Turkish cuisine finds its roots in Ottoman kitchens. But Ottoman cooking draws from the nomadic traditions of the Central Asian tribes and from the many civilizations that swept Asia Minor for thousands of years. An Assyrian cookbook found during recent excavations showed that similar dishes have been served for thousands of years. *Kebap (kebab),* the most famous of these dishes, exemplifies today's simple and hearty Turkish cuisine. This land, which still produces a food surplus, is one of the few places left in the Mediterranean where eating cheaply still entitles you to sample a great variety of dishes.

HOW IT'S DONE

In many *lokantalar* (restaurants), guests are shown into the back kitchen and encouraged to order by pointing. The kitchen probably will not display such staples as shepherd's salad, lentil soup, rice pilaf, or yogurt; their availability is understood. Prices, where listed, are by the *porsiyon* (portion), and an excellent way to increase variety while saving money is to order *yarım* (half) or *çeyrek* (quarter) portions, for that fraction of the price. In this way, for example, one can cheaply and guiltlessly sample the sinfully wide variety of *baklava* in a Turkish *pastane* (pastry shop). The same tip applies to street vendors of *döner kebap* (gyros), who tend to be stingy with the meat in thick pocket-bread sandwiches, but who may give more than double the meat for double the price. Turkish restaurants nonetheless offer excellent value for money (filling meals often come to less than $6). Usually, you can't bargain in restaurants, except when ordering fish, because prices are fixed by municipalities. Restaurant food is the notable exception to the rule that the tourist in Turkey should bargain for everything she buys.

When choosing an authentic, out-of-the-way *lokanta,* beware eateries with cloudy water glasses on the table. Successive Turkish patrons of such establishments reuse these glasses without washing them: all they do is wipe off the rims with the colored sheets of paper provided. Although such places may serve safe and particularly cheap food, they probably will not have bottled spring water on hand. Moreover, restaurants that do serve bottled water tend to overprice it. Conse-

But Aren't There Any Bagels?

Hotels often overcharge for traditional Turkish breakfasts, which are heavier than Continental breakfasts but lighter than American ones. They consist of tea or coffee, *ekmek* (bread from a fresh oval loaf), *peynir* (cheese), *tereyağ* (butter), and *reçel* (preserves) or *bal* (honey). Sometimes fresh melon (*kavun*) or a hard-boiled egg (*yumurta*) is included as well. Or, you can purchase your breakfast *a la carte* from a pastry shop or open-air market. But Turks don't frequent pastry shops to feast on *baklava* or *kadayıf* for breakfast. *Börek*, a flaky layered pie filled with cheese or mincemeat, has the honor of satisfying Turks's early-morning hunger. Ubiquitous street vendors hawk *simit* (sesame-coated bread rings 10-25¢) that you may think of as the Turkish equivalent of a bagel.

quently, tourists who prefer water to soft drinks at meals should buy bottled spring water cheaply at a corner grocery store and bring it along into restaurants.

WHAT'S IN IT

An astonishing variety of simple meat dishes forms the heart of Turkish cuisine. Foremost among them, *kebap* means any food broiled or roasted in small pieces. Usually involving lamb or chicken, *kebap* cooking ranges from *şiş* (skewer) or *döner* (spit) broiling, to oven roasting. The result may be served on a plate or as a pocket-bread sandwich, and regional seasonings add personality. *Adana kebap* and *Urfa kebap* are spicy, the former as meatballs and the latter as stew. Originally from Bursa, the popular *İskender kebap* consists of *döner kebap* lamb strips on a mushy bed of yogurt-soaked bread pieces, topped with a tangy tomato sauce. *Kağıt* (paper) *kebap* describes a mixture of lamb and vegetables wrapped and cooked in paper, while *orman* (forest) *kebap* is a mutton and vegetable stew. Other variations on meat stew include *patlıcan kebap* (eggplant stew), *tas kebabı* (goulash), *güveç* (casserole), and *türlü* (generic, occasionally vegetarian stew). After *kebap*, the most pervasive meat form is the medallion-sized, grilled hamburger patty (*köfte*). Frequently mistranslated as "meatballs," these patties receive embellishments like embedded pine nuts (*içli köfte*). They come either skewered and roasted or served in a tomato broth with potatoes and vegetables. Rarer forms of meat include *bonfile* (sirloin steak), *pirzola* (lamb chop), and *pastırma* (pastrami-like smoked or sun-dried beef). For the brave there are even *kokoreç*—grilled intestines with spices. *Et* is the generic word for meat: lamb is *kuzu*, beef *sığır eti*, and veal *dana eti*. Chicken, usually known as *tavuk*, becomes *piliç* when roasted.

More than 8000km of coastline make Turkey's *balık* (fish) a specialty. The tastier, most expensive fish are *kılıç* (swordfish) and *kalkan* (turbot). From larger fish, one can make a steamed dish called *buğlama*. The tastiest fish are available in early fall. In winter, *hamsi* (anchovies) are made into over forty dishes, including one dessert. Turkey also offers *kalamar* (squid), *karides* (shrimp), and *midye* (mussels).

Vegetarians often choose to subsist on Turkey's wide variety of *meze* (appetizers). *İmambayıldı*, a cold concoction of split eggplant, tomatoes, onions, and olive oil, literally means "the priest fainted" (from its delicious taste). *Kabak kızartması* refers to sliced, fried squash in yogurt sauce, and *patlıcan kızartması* is the same dish with eggplant instead of squash. Easy-to-come-by rice is *pilav*. *Fasulye* means beans: (*zeytinyağlı*) *taze fasulye* is green beans, usually in a tomato sauce, and *kuru fasulye* refers to white beans. Unfortunately for vegetarians, the white beans often come stewed in bouillon. One cannot talk about Turkish food without mentioning *dolma*—yes, stuffed, like the taxis. They are sometimes filled with meat and rice and served hot; sometimes made without meat, cooked in olive oil, and served cold; and sometimes prepared using grape leaves rather than hollowed vegetables. *Pilaki* (a cold stew) and *piyaz* (a salad) look alike and share the cold ingredients of dried haricot beans, onions, parsley, and olive oil. *Cacık* consists of chopped cucumber in garlic-flavored yogurt. *Kısır*, a cracked wheat and vegetable salad, resembles tabouli. *Çoban salatası* (shepherd's salad), the quintessential Turkish salad, combines onions, juicy tomatoes, cucumbers, and spicy peppers. Hot sustenance for vegetarians is less plentiful but savory nevertheless. A delicious loose omelette with tomatoes and onions goes by the name of *menemen*. *Lahmacun* is Arab-style pizza; *pide* is a distant Turkish relative that is longer than *lahmacun*—flat bread served with your choice of eggs, meat, tomatoes, cheese, or spices. The Turkish version of nature burgers, *mercimek köfte*, are made of lentils. *Tost*, often found in fast food stands (*büfe*), can take the form of grilled cheese sandwiches. *Makarna* (pasta), is widely available in cafeterias, and is often served with a hot garlic-flavored yogurt or tomato sauce. One of Turkey's richest offerings is the bounty of the *çarşı* (fresh market): *kuru yemiş* (nuts), *meyve* (fruits), and *sebze* (vegetables) are cheap and plentiful. *Üzüm* (grape), *kavun* (honeydew melon), *karpuz* (watermelon), *şeftali* (peaches), *elma* (apple), *armut* (pear), *muz* (banana), *erik* (plum), *kayısı* (apricot), *kiraz* (cherry), and *incir* (fig) are all easy to find.

Turkish *çay* (tea) claims more drinkers than famous *Türk kahvesi* (Turkish coffee). The *çay*, also known as "rabbit's blood" for its deep reddish color, is served piping hot, along with sugar, in tiny, tulip-shaped glasses. The concave shape of the glasses allows fingers to grasp the rim without getting burned. Expect to be offered free *çay* at any shop you enter. The *kahve*, drunk widely throughout Greece and the Middle East, is served in demitasse cups. You must specify a level of sweetness: *sade* (unsweetened), *orta* (medium-sweet), or *şekerli* (sweet). Impress your friends by inverting the coffee cup on its saucer when finished: the drinker's fortune may be read from the way the grounds have oozed down the cup's interior walls. *Nescafé* (western-style decaffeinated coffee), cola, *limonada* (lemonade), and *süt* (milk) are also ubiquitous, as is *ayran*, a healthful mixture of yogurt and water, served ice-cold with a pinch of salt. Bottled drinks include *meyve suyu* (fruit drink; try cherry or peach nectar); *meyveli gazoz* (a sweet soda); *su* (Turkish designer water); and *maden suyu* (carbonated mineral water, also known as *soda*). Tap water in most larger cities is safe since it is heavily chlorinated, but since this adds nothing to the taste, you might want to buy the widely available bottled water. The water from roadside springs or fountains marked *içilmez* should not be drunk even if you are parched. Food is sometimes less than clean, but squeezing lemon juice over it aids digestion. If you develop a mild stomach ailment, yogurt may replenish your body's natural bacteria content. Or try the local remedy, thick Turkish coffee with very little sugar.

Alcohol, though widely available, is frowned upon in the more conservative parts of this Muslim country. Restaurants that post *içkisiz* in their windows have none, while those with *içkili* are taking special pains to announce alcohol's availability. *Bira* (beer) is popular: *Efes Pilsen* and *Tüborg* are the leading brands. The best domestic white wines are *Çankaya*, *Villa Doluca*, and *Kavaklıdere*. The best red wines are *Yakut* and *Kavaklıdere*. Ice-cold *rakı*, an anise seed liquor with the taste of licorice, is Turkey's national drink. Customarily mixed in equal parts with water, which clouds it, *rakı* has acquired the name "lion's milk." It's similar to Greek *ouzo*, but even stronger. İstanbul's local specialty is *balyoz* (sledge hammer, wrecking ball). Demolition is the appropriate concept here: *balyoz* consists of *rakı*, whiskey, vodka, and gin mixed with orange juice.

There's an endless array of sweet things—*baklava*, a flaky pastry jammed with nuts and soaked in honey; *kadayıf*, a shredded-wheat dough filled with nuts and sugar; and *helva*, a crumbly sesame and honey loaf. Of course, there's always *lokum* (Turkish Delight); and *acıbadem kurabiyesi* or *badem ezmesi* (Turkish marzipan) is perhaps the best in the world. Mail some home. Most restaurants serve some sort of fresh fruit or melon. *Tavuk göğsü* (chicken pudding), *sütlaç* (rice pudding), and *aşure* (fruit pudding) are all excellent. *Künefe* is a cheese dessert served hot.

İstanbul

Welcome to the only city in the world that stands on two continents: İstanbul, the home of some of the most splendid legacies of three great empires—Roman, Byzantine, and Ottoman. Here, contradictions surface. New is juxtaposed with old, east with west, and rich with poor—coexisting in a curious and irresistible harmony through architecture, art, culture, entertainment, and personal interaction. Opulent Ottoman architecture, built on an enormous scale, overlooks tiny, winding streets. Thousands of mosques sound the call to prayer five times daily (starting at 4:30am) as crowded, dusty markets filled with street merchants and peddlers sell gold, spices, aphrodisiacs, and more. Museums contain astonishing treasures—the hand of John the Baptist, the hair of the prophet Muhammad, and treasures of art, jewelry, and gold.

HISTORY

Scholars believe that the site of modern İstanbul was settled by **Mycenaeans** as early as the 13th century BCE. Evidence, however, is sparse and little more is known about the city's origins. By the 11th century BCE, settlers had established various fishing villages here, one of which occupied the exact site of today's **Topkapı Palace.** It was not until the Megarian colonists from Greece landed on the Asian shore of the Bosphorus around 700 BCE that the city's known history is recorded.

Byzas, before embarking on his adventure, consulted the infallible Oracle at Delphi, who told him to settle "opposite the Land of the Blind." As Byzas sailed the Bosphorus, they spotted the Megarian settlement on the Asian shore at Chalcedon (now Kadıköy, one of the centers of Asian İstanbul). A quick turn to the left, though, and they knew where their new colony would lie. Overcome by the glory of the harbor of the Golden Horn on the European shore, they reasoned that the people at Chalcedon must have been blind to ignore this site. This set of colonists settled here in 667 BCE, and Byzas' sister Ramona named the city **Byzantium.**

A power struggle within the Roman Empire at the beginning of the 4th century determined the city's fate for the next millennium. The abdication of Diocletian in 305 CE caused a struggle for power between **Constantine,** Emperor of the West, and his rival **Licinius,** of the East. Constantine pursued his nemesis to the city (then called Augusta Antonina) and across the Bosphorus to Chrysopolis (Üsküdar), where he defeated Licinius in 324 CE. Constantine consolidated his power here and declared Byzantium to be the "New Rome," capital of his empire in 330 CE. Following the emperor's inauguration, the city came to be known as **Constantinople.**

The spread of Christianity was in large part propagated by Constantine's rise to power. The culmination of this influence is evident in the edicts of the first and second Theodosiuses, who established Christianity as the state religion (380 CE) and forbade pagan practices throughout the Empire (435 CE). During the 5th century, **Theodosius II** supervised the construction of several significant edifices—a new, fortified set of walls around the city, and the **Ayasofya** (St. Sofia, or the Church of the Holy Wisdom).

Christianity's final defeat of paganism came in 529 CE when the emperor **Justinian** mandated the closing of all schools of pagan philosophy, including Platonic academies in Athens. Thus, the **Byzantine Empire** was ushered in. During this time, Christian and Greek influences joined Roman ones. A 532 CE insurrection (the **Nika Revolt**) by factions in the Hippodrome very nearly achieved its goals; but just as Justinian was on the verge of abdicating and fleeing, his wife convinced him that it was far nobler to stay and fight. Five days of bloodshed followed. Although victorious, Justinian faced a city in ruin. Justinian eventually restored the city to twice its former majesty, but frequent warring, a horrible plague, and hefty taxes devastated the population. When **Heraclius** gained power, the entire empire was in shambles.

Heraclius, unfazed, set out to rebuild in 610. His success marked the beginning of the **Byzantine period.** Thanks to Heraclius, the empire conquered Armenia, Syria, Egypt, Palestine, and Roman Mesopotamia. **Basil II,** who reigned from 976 to 1025, watched over a second renaissance for the empire and defended it against attacks by the Arabs and the Bulgars. For his treatment of the latter, Basil earned the sobriquet "Bulgaroctonus" (Bulgar-slayer). To celebrate his final victory, Basil blinded all but ten of 10,000 survivors, and these ten he left with one functioning eye. The Bulgars never again saw the need to challenge Basil.

Following Basil's death in 1025 the city was faced with numerous other troubles. The **Fourth Crusade** in 1204 resulted in yet another devastation of the city. The Crusaders, attacking from the sea walls in the Golden Horn, plundered the city and maintained control for sixty years. Venice was the lucky recipient of much of the pillaged art, and subsequently, the West began to take a fresh interest in Greek civilization. Following Latin rule, the Empire was seriously debilitated by internal crises of leadership and skirmishes with the Turks, who were steadily making territorial gains. The Byzantine decline was paired with the rise of a new power—the **Ottoman Empire**—in western Asia Minor at the beginning of the 14th century.

By 1451, when **Mehmet II,** known as "Fatih," or "the Conqueror," came to lead the Ottomans, the Byzantine emperor controlled little besides the coveted capital city—Anatolia and most of the Balkans were already in Ottoman hands. Mehmet immediately began to orchestrate the siege of the city. A victory would not only secure the glory of the Ottoman Empire, but would also cement Mehmet's control over the noble classes. Sparing no expense, his forces finished work on two fortresses on the Bosphorus in 1452 in anticipation of the conquest. Rumeli Hisarı and Anadolu Hisarı (the Castles of Europe and Asia) stood on their corresponding sides of the Bosphorus and enabled the Ottomans to control the strait. The Byzantine emperor tried to block the Golden Horn but could not foil Mehmet, who gathered all his boats at a cove and had them transported by slides to the other end of the Gilded Antler at night. He soon had the unprepared Byzantine defenders in submission. For his final bombardment of the Theodosian city walls, Mehmet insisted on purchasing the largest cannon yet invented. The city fell to the Ottomans in May 1453. The conqueror Mehmet took to rebuilding and repopulating the city, transforming İstanbul into the exalted administrative, cultural, and commercial center of his empire. The Ottoman Empire witnessed the development of this city into an architectural treasury, best known for its collection of imperial mosques. With the expansion of the Ottoman Empire to Eastern Europe, the Middle East, and North Africa, a motley assemblage of people from around the world came to the "Paris of the East." By the 19th century the city's glory was fading but still tangible.

Despite İstanbul's gloried past, it was Ankara that served as the base for Atatürk's campaign for independence. Atatürk felt the former capital was linked to too many imperial memories and vulnerable to attack by gunboats. On October 29, 1923, Ankara was officially declared capital of the Turkish Republic. Atatürk's modernization initiatives changed the color of the city, but İstanbul still exudes a confidence that is the product of 16 centuries of world prominence. In 1960, one million people inhabited the city. Today, more than fifteen million people live here.

ORIENTATION

Waterways divide İstanbul into three sections. The **Bosphorus Strait** (Boğaziçi) separates Asia from Europe, and divides İstanbul into European (west) and Asian (east) sections. Most directions in İstanbul are given by precinct or district (i.e. Kadiköy). The Asian side is mostly residential; historical sites, markets, mosques, and museums of the older quarters are situated on the south bank of the **Golden Horn** (Haliç), an estuary which splits the European half of the city. The modern north bank contains **İstiklâl Caddesi,** the main downtown shopping street, and **Cumhuriyet Caddesi,** lined with airline offices and hotels; both of these lead into **Taksim Square,** the center of the north bank. The **Sirkeci Train Station** lies just east of Eminönü, across

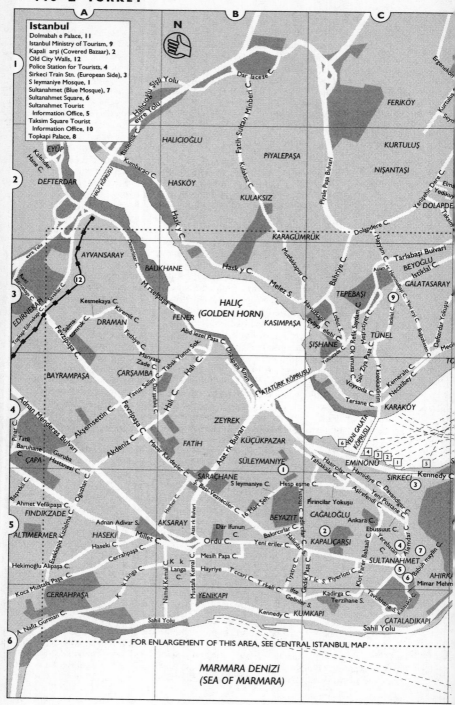

Istanbul
Dolmabah e Palace, 11
Istanbul Ministry of Tourism, 9
Kapali arşi (Covered Bazaar), 2
Old City Walls, 12
Police Station for Tourists, 4
Sirkeci Train Stn. (European Side), 3
S leymaniye Mosque, 1
Sultanahmet (Blue Mosque), 7
Sultanahmet Square, 6
Sultanahmet Tourist
  Information Office, 5
Taksim Square Tourist
  Information Office, 10
Topkapi Palace, 8

N

EYÜP

DEFTERDAR

HALICIOĞLU

HASKÖY

FERIKÖY

KURTULUŞ

NIŞANTAŞI

DOLAPDE

PIYALEPAŞA

KULAKSIZ

KARAGÜMRÜK

AYVANSARAY

BALIKHANE

HALIÇ
(GOLDEN HORN)

KASIMPAŞA

TEPEBAŞI

BEYOĞLU
GALATASARAY

FENER

DRAMAN

EDİRNEKAPI

KESMEKAYA C.

ŞIŞHANE

TÜNEL

BAYRAMPAŞA

ÇARŞAMBA

KARAKÖY

ZEYREK

KÜÇÜKPAZAR

FATIH

SÜLEYMANIYE

EMINÖNÜ

SIRKECI

ÇAPA

FINDIKZADE

ALTIMERMER

HASEKI

AKSARAY

BEYAZIT

CAĞALOĞLU

KAPALIÇARSI

SULTANAHMET

AHIRKA

CERRAHPAŞA

YENIKAPI

KUMKAPI

ÇATALADIKAPI

FOR ENLARGEMENT OF THIS AREA, SEE CENTRAL ISTANBUL MAP

MARMARA DENIZI
(SEA OF MARMARA)

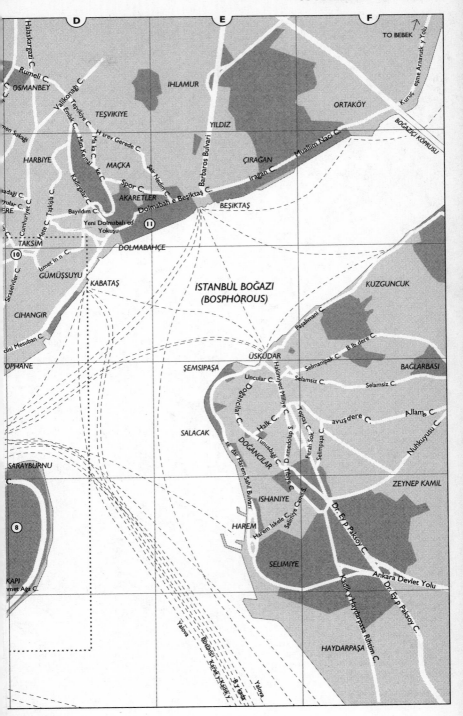

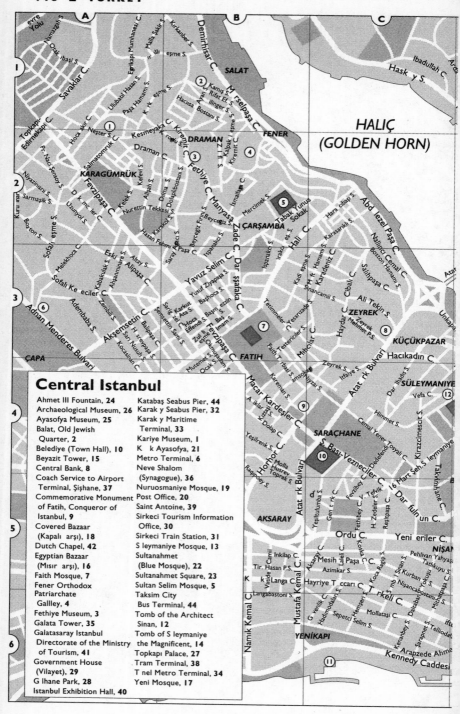

HALIÇ
(GOLDEN HORN)

Central Istanbul

Ahmet III Fountain, 24
Archaeological Museum, 26
Ayasofya Museum, 25
Balat, Old Jewish
 Quarter, 2
Belediye (Town Hall), 10
Beyazit Tower, 15
Central Bank, 8
Coach Service to Airport
 Terminal, Şişhane, 37
Commemorative Monument
 of Fatih, Conqueror of
 Istanbul, 9
Covered Bazaar
 (Kapalı arşı), 18
Dutch Chapel, 42
Egyptian Bazaar
 (Mısır arşı), 16
Faith Mosque, 7
Fener Orthodox
 Patriarchate
 Gallley, 4
Fethiye Museum, 3
Galata Tower, 35
Galatasaray Istanbul
 Directorate of the Ministry
 of Tourism, 41
Government House
 (Vilayet), 29
G lhane Park, 28
Istanbul Exhibition Hall, 40

Katabaş Seabus Pier, 44
Karak y Seabus Pier, 32
Karak y Maritime
 Terminal, 33
Kariye Museum, 1
K k Ayasofya, 21
Metro Terminal, 6
Neve Shalom
 (Synagogue), 36
Nuruosmaniye Mosque, 19
Post Office, 20
Saint Antoine, 39
Sirkeci Tourism Information
 Office, 30
Sirkeci Train Station, 31
S leymaniye Mosque, 13
Sultanahmet
 (Blue Mosque), 22
Sultanahmet Square, 23
Sultan Selim Mosque, 5
Taksim City
 Bus Terminal, 44
Tomb of the Architect
 Sinan, 12
Tomb of S leymaniye
 the Magnificent, 14
Topkapı Palace, 27
Tram Terminal, 38
T nel Metro Terminal, 34
Yeni Mosque, 17

> ### Kingdome Come
>
> The Byzantine **Ayasofya** offered inspiration to Sinan and the Ottoman architects who preceded him. Built by the Emperor Justinian between 532 and 537 CE as the Church of the Holy Wisdom, it was distinguished by a large dome buttressed by two half-domes, and was for 900 years Constantinople's cathedral. Upon the Ottoman conquest in 1453, Mehmet the Conqueror converted the building into a mosque. So ponderous were the height and girth of Ayasofya's central dome that, upon the cathedral's completion, Justinian supposedly proclaimed, "O Solomon, I have surpassed thee!" Sultan Süleyman, whose name meant "Solomon," was well aware of his empire's classical heritage and considered Justinian's gloating a personal challenge. Sinan made Süleyman's ambition a reality. It was Sinan who from 1568 to 1574 built the **Selimiye Mosque** in Edirne, which boasts a dome the size of Ayasofya's, supported by 8 columns, with 4 axial half-domes and a single half-dome in front. The size of the Selimiye's central dome surpassed even that of Ayasofya, and superior engineering ensured that it didn't collapse, as Ayasofya's original dome did. Thus Sinan surpassed Justinian, Süleyman surpassed Solomon, and Ottoman Classical architecture was born.

from the tram station. Budget travelers converge in **Sultanahmet,** the area around the Ayasofya mosque, south of and up the hill from Sirkeci. The main boulevard—leading west from Sultanahmet towards the university, the Grand Bazaar, and Aksaray—changes names from **Divan Yolu** to **Ordu Caddesi** as it nears Aksaray, right after the Çemberlitaş monument which resembles an antique version of the Washington Monument. Merchants crowd the district between the **Grand Bazaar,** east of the university, and the less touristy **Egyptian Bazaar,** just southeast of Eminönü. The **Kumkapı** district is south of the university and Yeniçeriler Caddesi. With help from a free map from the tourist office and landmarks, you can orient yourself through the winding tortuous maze of alleys that make up the city.

GETTING AROUND

If you come by plane, you'll arrive at either the international or the domestic terminal of **Atatürk Havaalanı** (Atatürk Airport); the two are connected by a free bus (theoretically every 20min., 6am-10pm). If arriving in the international terminal, take the "Havaş" bus to get into town (departs 10min. before the hour, every hour, 5:50am-10:50pm; $2.50). It stops at Aksaray and Şişhane. To get back, however, you can only catch the bus at Şişhane. There are a few campgrounds and one hotel nearby, see Londra Mocamp (p. 456). You could also take the bus which leaves from the Domestic Departures Building, stops in Aksaray and Bakırköy, and terminates its run at the THY Airlines Terminal in Şişhane. If you're going to Sultanahmet, get off at Aksaray and take the spiffy new tram five stops along Divan Yolu to the Ayasofya mosque in Sultanahmet. When you get off in Aksaray, you'll see two main streets in front of you. Follow the one that forks to the right for roughly five minutes until you reach the tram tracks. Veer right for another couple of minutes to reach the nearest station. You can buy a ticket at the little white booth across the road before boarding. Trams traveling to your right, in the direction "Sirkeci," go to Sultanahmet. Public bus #96 and *dolmuş* run to town from 8am until 10pm (30¢). The bus stop is on the highway in front of International Arrivals, beyond the parking lot. If you're new to İstanbul, you should use the bus unless you're a masochist who likes a complicated life. (You will see how the *dolmuş*—meaning "stuffed" in Turkish—got their name, and how the buses try to outdo them in cramming people in. You'll be deposited, well, God knows where… For the true diehard budget traveler only.) Be wary of occasional rip-offs with the airport taxi service. If you do take an airport taxi, the fare should be $8-12 during the day, 50% more from midnight to 8am. Every taxi has a meter—make sure the driver uses it.

To get to Sultanahmet from the **Sirkeci Train Station,** you can take the tram two stops to Sultanahmet Station and where the tram diverges from the main road, follow Babaîli Cad. uphill until it intersects Divan Yolu. Or, walk uphill for approximately 10 minutes, following the tracks. From the **Haydarpaşa Train Station,** take the ferry to Karaköy (6am-midnight, every 20min., 50¢); walk across the Galata Bridge (the only nearby bridge) to Eminönü, turn left, and walk for 5 minutes until you see the ornate Sirkeci railway station on your right. Take the tram (2 stops) from outside its entrance (on the right side of the station); buy a ticket (50¢) from the little booth before boarding, or follow the tram tracks uphill for 10 minutes.

The new intercity **bus terminal** in İstanbul, the **Esenler Otogar,** is several miles from the city. The **metro** (every 5min., 6am-midnight, 35¢) links it and Aksaray station. *Otogar* is the name of the bus terminal's metro stop. From Aksaray metro station, exit, cross the main road (Adnan Menderes Blv.), enter the nearest side street, and walk into its end; the Yusufpaşa train station will be in front of you. Catch the tram (direction *Sirkeci*) to Sultanahmet (6 stops, 35¢; buy ticket from the white booth before boarding). The old Topkapı bus station is closed, so beware of old maps.

Buses in İstanbul are plentiful and cheap, though confusing for the newcomer. Tickets (35¢) are sold at booths at the larger bus terminals (such as Eminönü and Taksim) at kiosks marked *Planktonluk*. At busy bus stops, they may be sold by street vendors at a market—for roughly 40¢. Stock up on tickets to avoid being stranded in the suburbs without a ticket seller for miles around. Short journeys cost one ticket, longer trips cost two, particularly ones requiring the crossing of a Europe-Asia bridge. Service begins at 6am and runs every 5 minutes or so on major routes. Buses are less frequent after dark and stop completely by midnight. Numbers and destinations are displayed at the front of the bus. For Sultanahmet, which has no bus station of its own, the nearest buses reach Beyazıt (from the north) and Eminönü (from the south and west); both are marked accordingly. One leaves from Sultanahmet: #210 departs from opposite the back of the tourist office and runs up the European side of the Bosphorus to **Emirgan,** the reputed home of superb teahouses. (Bus departs approximately every hour, Mon.-Fri. 7am-7pm, Sat.-Sun. 11am-6pm; schedule at the tourist office; two bus tickets each way.) Buses are inevitably slowed by İstanbul's considerable traffic, so if you're not going far, walk.

A **dolmuş** (shared taxi), either a minibus or a vintage Chevrolet or Buick with fins and buffed chrome (lots from 1956), is faster than the bus and generally costs around 40¢. *Dolmuş* run on fixed routes, usually between the main bus stops in each quarter (if you ask they'll let you off *en route*). The assumption here is that a *dolmuş* only slows down for pick-ups and drop-offs, and it never actually comes to a full stop; know what you're doing beforehand. Whereas regular public transportation is quite cheap and safe, the availability of drivers is very erratic.

SIDESTEPPING TOURIST PITFALLS

As in any "tourist trap" cosmopolitan city, the touristy parts of İstanbul have fast-talkers eager to unburden naïve travelers of their money. Most of those who approach you in a "friendly" manner want to sell you something—genuinely friendly Turks are much less brash. Realize, though, that many Turks familiar with these tourist sectors are highly eager and enthusiastic about offering advice, giving directions, inviting you to tea—any forum in which they may satisfy their curiosity about a foreigner's culture and meanwhile demonstrate their often minimal, but admirable, knowledge of MTV-imported English. Especially avoid people who offer to "help" you buy a carpet—they are helping *themselves* to a commission that can easily be as large as 30-50%. Also, do not exchange money with people on the street since fake bills are common. Please note that, via empirical evidence, it has been suggested that walking around with an exposed travel guide (even, let's say, an innocuous *yellow* one) is a plea: "I need help" or "I'm a sucker" are common interpretations.

Most areas of İstanbul are relatively safe even at night, but some districts to avoid after sunset are the **Galata tower; Beyazıt,** the neighborhood of İstanbul University; and the back streets of **Beyoğlu,** the area north of İstiklâl Cad., a fashionable shopping area by day, but a seething red-light district by night. Consider that you are in an unfamiliar neighborhood where you know no one, have no feel for the layout of streets, and can't find an address to save your life. Think about this feeling of discomfort and put it in a framework of İstanbul. While many regions of Turkey have been westernized, the culture is still undeniably a fusion of both east and west; in order to gauge which levels of comfort and security you should feel as an individual, it is imperative to defer to the culture at large sometimes. Most "catcalls" are not threats, though they are indeed unnecessary and annoying. However, in a situation in which you feel challenged or threatened, an alternative to ignoring the perpetrator is telling them in Turkish that you are uncomfortable. "Beni rahatzız ediyorsun" ("You're bothering me") or "Beni rahat bırakın, lütfen" (Leave me alone, please") have worked for women. Find and memorize your own expressions to suit your needs and wants; remember, these are hardly guaranteed-to-work formulas. Rather, these are options to employ when verbal communication with the harasser is difficult.

PRACTICAL INFORMATION

Tourist Office: In **Sultanahmet,** 3 Divan Yolu (tel./fax 518 1802; open daily 9am-5pm), north end of the **Hippodrome,** across from the Sultan Pub. In **Taksim,** in the Hilton Hotel Arcade (tel. 233 0592; open Mon.-Sat. 9am-5pm), and near the French Consulate (tel. 245 6876; open Mon.-Sat. 9am-5pm). In **Karaköy Maritime Station** (tel. 249 5776; daily 8:30am-5pm). In **Sirkeci Train Station** (tel. 511 5888; open daily 8:30am-5:30pm). In **Atatürk Airport** (tel. 663 0793; open 24hr.). Free country and city maps.

Tourist Police: In Sultanahmet, at the beginning of Yerebatan Cad., behind the obelisk in the park opposite the tourist office (24-hr. hotline tel. 527 4503 or 528 5369; fax 512 7676). Open 24hr.

Travel Offices: Gençtur, 15/3 Yerebatan Cad., 2nd floor (tel. 520 5274, -5; fax 519 0864), in the center of Sultanahmet. Sells ISIC ($8) and GO25 ($5), and provides a free Poste Restante service; soon moving to Prof. K. Ismail Gürkan Cad., Cağaloğlu Hamamı Sok., Kardeşler Iştlan, 4th floor. (same tel.). Organizes workcamps in villages. Open Mon.-Fri. 9:30am-noon and 1-5pm, Sat. 9:30am-1pm. **Seventur Travel Shop,** 2-C Alemdar Cad. (tel. 512 4183; fax 512 3641). Follow the Sirkeci tram tracks; 1-min. walk past Ayasofya, on the right. Sells ISIC and youth ID cards and provides free Poste Restante service. They issue reliable plane and bus tickets (some agencies have been known to sell bogus tickets). Seventur provides a shuttle to the airport (6am-midnight $4, midnight-6am $5). Check the schedule in the office. Open Mon.-Fri., Sat. 9am-1pm, Sun. 9am-6pm. **Indigo Tourism and Travel Agency,** 24 Akbıyık Cad. (tel. 517 7266; fax 518 5333), in the heart of the cluster of hotels in Sultanahmet. Open in summer daily 8:30am-7:30pm, in winter Mon.-Sat. 9:30am-6pm. Sells ISIC cards for $8 and GO25 for $5. Services include domestic and international bus, plane, and ferry tickets, airport shuttle service, and Poste Restante.

Consulates: All are open Mon.-Fri. **U.S.,** 104-108 Meşrutiyet Cad., Tepebaşı (tel. 251 3602); visas 8:30am-11am. **Canada,** 107/3 Büyükdere Cad., Gayrettepe (tel. 272 5174; fax 272 3427). **U.K.,** 34 Meşrutiyet Cad., Beyoğlu/Tepebaşı (tel. 293 7545); visas 8:30am-noon. **Ireland** (honorary), 26-a Cumhuriyet Cad., Mobil Altı, Elmadağ (tel. 246 6025); visas 9:30am-11:30am. **Australia,** 58 Tepecik Yolu, Etiler (tel. 257 7050, -1); visas 10am-noon. **New Zealand** nationals should get in touch with the embassy in Ankara, 24/1 Kız Kulesi Sok. (tel. (312) 445 0556). **South Africa,** 106 Büyükdere Cad., Esentepe (tel. 275 4793; fax 288 2504); visas 9am-noon. **Bulgaria,** 44 Zincirlikuyu Cad., Ulus/Etiler (tel. 269 2216). **Egypt,** 173 Cevatpaşa Cad., Bebek (tel. 263 6030). **Iran,** 1 Ankara Cad., Cağaloğlu (tel. 513 8230, -1; fax 513 5219); visas 8:30am-11:30am. **Jordan,** 119/2 Kalıpçı Sok., Daire 6, Teşvikiye (tel. 230 1221, -2; fax 241 4331); visas 9:30am-noon. **Pakistan,** 11 Abide-i Hürriyet Cad., Şişli (tel. 233 5800, -1; fax 233 5802); visas Mon.-Thurs. 10am-1pm, Fri. 10am-noon. **Syria,** Silâhhane Cad., Ralli Apt. #59, Teşvikiye (tel. 232 7110; fax 230 2215); visas 9:30-11am.

Banks: Currency exchange counters open Mon.-Fri. 8:30am-noon and 1:30-5pm. Most don't charge a commission. **ATMs** all over the city.

American Express: Headquarters at 57/4 Abdi İpekçi Cad., 4th floor, Teşvikiye (tel. 224 2610) is not open to individual card/checkholders, but they do field corporate inquiries and maintain a customer service hotline for lost or stolen cards/ traveler's checks (tel. 232 9556, -7 or -8). Individuals should deal directly with agents. **Türk Express,** 91 Cumhuriyet Cad., 2nd floor (tel. 230 1515), up the hill from Taksim Sq. They handle lost checks and cards as well as other related business. Open Mon.-Fri. 9am-6pm. Their office in the **Hilton Hotel lobby,** Cumhuriyet Cad. (tel. 241 0248), deals with lost cards only when Türk Express is closed. Open daily 8:30am-8pm. The above offices do not give cash advances or accept wired money; Turkish law requires that this be done through a bank. American Express's agent is **Koç Bank,** 233 Cumhuriyet Cad. (tel. 232 2600). Money is wired here without a fee if you accept Turkish *lira;* 1% fee for other currencies. To get a cash advance on your AmEx card, you must have a personal check or know your account number and the address of your bank. Open Mon.-Fri. 8:45am-12:30pm and 1:30-4:30pm; cardholder services until 4pm. Cardholders can use Akbank ATMs all over Turkey for cash advances.

Flights: Atatürk Airport, 30km from the city. It has a terminal for domestic flights and one for international flights, 800m apart, connected by bus (every 20min., 6am-10pm). Take a *Havaş* bus from either terminal to the city (10min. before the hr., 5:50am-10:50pm, 30min., $2.50). The bus stops at Aksaray, where you can catch the tram to Sultanahmet, and at Şişhane.

Trains: Haydarpaşa Station, on the Asian side (tel. (216) 336 0475, -2063). A convenient ferry connects the station to Karaköy pier 7, on the European side (every 20min. roughly 6am-midnight; schedule posted on the pier; 50¢). Pier is halfway between Galata Bridge and the Karaköy tourist office, where rail tickets for Anatolia can be purchased in advance at the **TCDD** (Turkish Republic State Railway) office upstairs. Office accepts couchette (*kuşet*) reservations for Ankara (2 days in advance if possible). Tickets also available at Sirkeci station. Trains to Edirne (2 per day, $3). Ticket office open 7:30am-11pm daily. Europe-bound trains leave from **Sirkeci Station** (tel. 527 0050, -1), in Eminönü (downhill toward the Golden Horn from Sultanahmet). To Sofia, Bulgaria (2 per day, $33), Athens (1 per day, $64), and Munich, Germany (1 per day, $221). Call ahead to verify schedules.

Buses: Intercity buses leave from the new **Esenler Otobüs Terminalı** in Esenler, several miles from downtown. To get there from Sultanahmet, take the tram 6 stops to **Yusufpaşa** (one stop beyond Aksaray). Before pulling in to Yusufpaşa station, you will pass an overhead motorway bridge; just past it, on your right, is the broad Adnan Menderes Blv., which contains **Aksaray Metro station** (roughly a 1min. walk from Yusufpaşa train station). Take the metro to the *Otogar* stop (15min., 35¢); you will be deposited in the middle of a huge hexagonal structure. Hundreds of buses leave here daily for virtually every point in Turkey and neighboring countries. All bus companies should have offices at the *otogar;* they may also have offices in Sultanahmet. **Varan Tours** (tel. 658 0277; fax 658 0280) is Turkey's most well known and is licensed to operate throughout Western Europe; **Ulusoy** (tel. 658 3000; fax 658 3010) serves Greece and domestic destinations; **Kamıl Koç** (tel. 658 2000; fax 658 2008), **Pamukkale** (tel./fax 658 2222), and **Çanakkale Seyahat** (tel. 658 3640, -1) are also recommended. Most bus companies are authorized to go to Eastern Europe. Unlicensed companies have been known to offer substantial discounts for Western European destinations and then abandon their passengers in Eastern Europe. Frequent buses to Ankara (8hr., $12.50), Bursa (4hr., $7.50), İzmir (9hr., $15), Bodrum (13hr., $21.25), and Trabzon (14hr., $24). European services include Athens (6 per week, 18hr., $25) and Vienna (1 per week, 36hr., $90). A station across the Bosphorus in **Harem**—accessible by ferry from **Karaköy**—serves Asia.

Ferries (National and International): Turkish Maritime Lines has offices near Pier 7 at Karaköy, just west of the Haydarpaşa ferry terminal. It is the building with the blue awning marked *Denizcilik İşletmeleri.* Sail to İzmir (1 per week, 5:30pm, 21hr., $11-26), Bandırma (4 per week at 9am, 5hr., $6), and Trabzon (1 per week, June-Sept. at 2pm, arrives Wed., $17-33). From Bandırma there are connecting trains to İzmir (11hr. total; buy combination boat-train ticket at Sirkeci station). Ferries to Trabzon (and intervening points on the Black Sea coast) depart from Sarayburnu; after exiting the Sirkeci station, turn right, and walk for roughly 5min. along the waterfront. These times, prices, and departure points change regularly; confirm at Turkish Maritime Lines. Although not from İstanbul, Turkish Maritime Lines also serves Venice and Kıbrıs (Northern Cyprus).

Ferries (Local): Ferries constitute a major part of İstanbul's public transport system. Some of the ferries to the north shore of the Golden Horn are commuter ferries. Since these leave in the morning and return in the evening, taking an evening ferry out could strand you. The following depart from the Sirkeci area; piers are clustered around Galata Bridge. Destinations written on each pier. Pier 1 serves Üsküdar (every 20min., 6:30am-11pm), Pier 2 serves Kadıköy (every 20min., 7:30am-9pm, 50¢), and Pier 3 sends out separate cruises along the Bosphorus ($4 roundtrip) and to the Princess Islands. From Pier 4, the seabus departs for Kadıköy (roughly every hr., 8am-7:25pm, 60¢). Pier 5 serves Adalar; Pier 6 Bağlat (past the Galata Bridge). Pier 7, in Kadıköy across the Galata Bridge, serves Haydarpaşa railway station (across the Galata Bridge; every 20min., 6am-midnight, 50¢). Timetables are posted at each terminal. Buy a *jeton* (token) and insert it in the turnstile to board. Numerous other ferries connect the various İstanbul suburbs. For details, buy the seasonal timetable *feribot tarifesi* (60¢), at each pier. The seabus timetable is not for sale but is posted at seabus terminals.

Taxis: Plentiful in İstanbul. Use of meters is imperative—make sure it's on and don't pay more than it says. *Gündüz Tarifesi*, or one light, on the meter indicates the day rate. Two lights indicate the night rate. The night rate, in effect from midnight to 8am, is 50% higher. The starting rate is 40¢ (55¢ after midnight), which rises by 10¢ (14¢) every 200m; waiting time costs 4¢ (6¢ per minute after the first 5min., which are free). Steer away from taxis from drivers who approach you in Sultanahmet. Avoid taxis waiting at the airport. Drivers seldom speak English; if you don't speak Turkish, have your destination written down.

International Bookstores: Aypa Bookstore, 19 Mimar Mehmet Ağa Cad., Sultanahmet (tel. 517 4492), behind the Blue Mosque. English and German spoken. Open daily 6:30am-8pm. **İstanbul Kitabığı,** 5 Kabusakal Cad. (tel. 517 6782; fax 517 6780), up the street from Aypa, has books on İstanbul and Turkey, magazines, and coffee table books. Open daily 9am-6pm. **Robinson Crusoe 389,** 389 İstiklâl Cad. (tel. 293 6968, -77; fax 251 1735), is tasteful and upscale, selling books in English, French, German, and Russian. Full reference section, fantastic art books, and *MAD* magazine. Open daily 9am-8pm. **Haşat** (tel. 249-1006; fax 249-1007), also on İstiklâl Cad., sells magazines and foreign newspapers, including the *New York Times* Sunday edition ($6.25) and spiffy coloring books. Open daily 7:45am-8:45pm. **Divan Book Exchange,** on a side street on Divan Yolu by the Sultanahmet tram stop. Open daily 9am-7pm.

Laundromats: Star Laundry, 18 Akbıyık Cad. (tel. 638 2302), below Star Pension, key location for those at Orient Youth Hostel. Wash and dry $1.25 per kg, minimum 2kg. English spoken. Open daily 8am-10pm. **Active Laundry,** at 14 Divan Yolu (tel. 513 7585), in the heart of Sultanahmet. Wash and dry for $2 per kg; ironing 65¢ extra. Open daily 8am-10pm. **Hobby Laundry,** 6/1 Caferiye Sok., part of Yücelt Hostel building. $2 per kg, minimum 2kg. Open daily 9am-6pm. The **Hotel Ema** does laundry for its guests, $2.50 per kg.

Hospitals: American Hospital, Admiral Bristol Hastanesi, 20 Güzelbahçe Sok., Nişantaşı (tel. 231 4050), is applauded by İstanbul natives and tourists and has many English-speaking doctors. The **German Hospital,** 119 Sıraselviler Cad., Taksim (tel. 293 2150), also hosts a multi-lingual staff and is more convenient to Sultanahmet. **International Hospital,** 82 İstanbul Cad., Yeşilköy (tel. 663 3000). All are private hospitals, which generally provide a higher standard of care than public ones. Payment with cash or a credit card is expected at time of treatment.

PTT: İstanbul has more than 100 post offices. The most convenient for those staying in Sultanahmet is the little booth opposite the entrance to Ayasofya, which sells stamps; English spoken. **Main branch,** 25 Büyük Postane Sok. Stamp, telegram, and currency exchange services open 8:30am-7pm. All PTTs accept packages; if a customs officer is not present, you will be directed to the **Kadıköy, Beyazıt,** or **Tophane** (on Rıhtım Cad.) offices. Packages more than 2kg can be mailed from the **packet service** on the back side of the main PTT. Open Mon.-Sat. 8:30am-12:30pm and 1:30-5pm. **Branch** off west end of Taksim Sq. on Cumhuriyet Cad. efficient for mailing packages or making calls. Open Mon.-Fri. 8am-

8pm, Sat. 8am-6pm. 24-hr. international telephone office in the building, but it does not arrange collect calls (see Keeping in Touch, p.431).

Telephone Codes: 212 (European side) and 216 (Asian side); you have to dial the code when calling from one side to the other. Pay phones are scattered in the city; **international calls** can be made from all, but usually cut off after 3min.

ACCOMMODATIONS

İstanbul's budget accommodations are concentrated in the **Sultanahmet** district, just steps away from the city's most awe-inspiring sights. Budget prices range from $4 for a cheap single or dorm bed to $20-30 at the middle price range. The side streets around **Sirkeci** railway station provide numerous singles and doubles in the $5-10 range; these are patronized mainly by working-class Turks. **Aksaray** offers dozens of hotels in every conceivable price range. Its streets are packed with Bulgarian and Romanian businesspeople, who often outnumber the Turks. The Aksaray area resembles an open-air bazaar—merchants, shoppers, and diners at open-air restaurants compete for space in a chaotic and fascinating scene. Prostitution is slowly on the rise here due to an influx of sex-workers (known as "Natashas") from Romania and the former Soviet republics. The **Taksim** district is home to many of the city's five-star hotels and a smattering of budget lodgings. All of *Let's Go's* recommendations are in Sultanahmet, due to its beauty and convenience. The following are short walks from the Sultanahmet tram stop. Rates rise by roughly 20% in July and August. Consider, too, that the ever-increasing inflation rates may distort the prices as well.

Hostels

Yücelt Hostel (HI), 6/1 Caferiye Cad. (tel. 513 6150, -1; fax 512 7628), in the little alley to the left of the Ayasofya mosque as you face the mosque's gate. To reach Ayasofya from the Sultanahmet tram stop, follow the tracks downhill toward Sirkeci for a couple of minutes; Ayasofya is the red-tinted mosque on your right. A great place to meet travelers. The attached self-service cafeteria has a loud stereo which is played at pre-announced parties. Yücelt is one of only 2 Turkish hostels accredited by HI. Free luggage deposit. Laundry $1.25 per kg. Transport to airport. Showers included (7:30-10am and 7:30-10pm). Reserve rooms two weeks in advance in summer. 6-8 person dorm room $4.40. 3-4 person dorm room $5.65. Doubles $7.50 per person. Roof $2.50 upon request.

Orient Youth Hostel, 13 Akbıyık Cad. (tel. 517 9493; fax 518 3894), near Topkapı Palace. International mix of hip teens and experienced travelers alike eager to hang out in the breezy roof-terrace cafeteria (open for most meals, offers a good selection and goodies for vegetarians). Hot water 7am-noon and 5pm-midnight. Benefits of luggage room, safe, and a travel agency right by the receptionist's desk. Popular for the weekly Friday night (free) bellydancing. Bring your own toilet paper and towel for communal bathroom use. Dorm beds $4.40. Doubles $6.25 per person. Quads $5.

Hanedan Hostel, Akbıyık Cad., 3 Adliye Sok. (tel. 516 4869; fax 517 4524). Pleasant view from terrace. Beautiful cafeteria. Currency exchange. 24-hr. airport transport available. 24-hr. hot water. Laundry $1.15 per kilo, sun-dried. Doubles $20, $26 with shower. Dorm beds $6. Breakfast included.

Hotels

Hotel Anadolu, Yerebatan Cad. 3 Salkım Söğüt Sok. (tel. 512 1035 or 513 8084; fax 527 7695). To get to Salkım Söğüt Sok. from the Sultanahmet tram, walk roughly 50m along the tram tracks towards Sirkeci; take a left at the major intersection (Yerebatan Cad.); Salkım Söğüt Sok. will be the first right, roughly 20m up the street. Rudimentary, well kept rooms, a few with tiny balconies. Small terrace outside the front door. Hot and cold showers. English spoken. Singles $13. Doubles $26. Triples $39. Roof beds $7.50 each.

Sultan Turist Otel, 3 Terbıyık Sok. (tel. 516 9260; fax 517 1626). Around the corner from the Orient Hostel. Turkish pensions don't get any better than the newly opened Sultan. Immaculate and highly professional. Great views of the Marmara

FOOD

from the roof restaurant/bar. Offers reasonably priced sandwiches and vegetarian omelettes. Happy hour 5-8pm (beer 90¢). TV and VCR in common room. Ping pong, in-house travel office, and international phone services. Singles $15. Doubles $18.75. Quads $6.90 per person.

Hotel Anadolu, Yerebatan Cad. 3 Salkım Sok. (tel. 512 1035 or 513 8084). To get to Salkım Söğüt Sok. from the Sultanahmet tram, walk 50m along the tram tracks toward Sirkeci; take a left at the major intersection (Yerebatan Cad.); Salkım Sok. will be the first right, 20m up the street. Rudimentary, well kept rooms; some with balcony. Small terrace outside where drinks are served. Hot and cold showers. Singles $13. Doubles $26. Triples $13 per person.

Hotel Pamphylia, Yerebatan Cad. 47 (tel. 526 8935 or 513 9548; fax 513 9549). Immaculate rooms, some with balconies and televisions. English and German spoken. Tiny terrace with a great view. Discount for *Let's Go* users. Singles $25. Doubles $35. Triples $50. Rates $5 less in winter. Breakfast included. V/MC accepted.

Near the tram stop park is a cluster of roughly 3 parallel streets and a dozen alleys. The following hotels are all located in this area:

Barut's Guest House, 8 Işakpaşa Cad. (tel. 516 0357, -5256; fax 516 2924). Hip little joint (owned by a painter). Lovely terrace overlooking one of İstanbul's oldest mosques and the Sea of Marmara. Immaculate rooms, private bathroom and showers, and big mirrors to help you monitor the progress of your tan. 10% student discount. Singles $35. Doubles $45. Triples $65. Breakfast included.

Alp Guesthouse, Akbıyık Cad. 4 Adliye Sok. (tel. 517 9570 or 518 5728), not just for mountaineers, this family-run guesthouse has spacious, spotless rooms, some with fine views. Mediterranean-style ambience. Superb views from the terrace; barbecues held here, and drinks served until 11pm. Alp's offers an airport transportation service, a safe, and a luggage room in the basement. All rooms with bath and shower. Singles $35. Doubles $45 (large) and $50 (really large). Breakfast $5.

Bauhaus Guesthouse, Akbıyık Cad. Bayram Fırın Sok. #11 (tel. 517 6697 or 638 6534). A three-floor, comfortable hotel of orderly rooms. 3rd floor has a sitting room with cable TV. Charming views. 10% discount for *Let's Go* readers. Singles $15. Doubles $25, with bath $30. Triples $35, with bath $40.

Hotel Side Pension, 20 Utangaç Sok. (tel./fax 517 6590). Basic little pension. 3rd floor walls are lined with beautiful, Ottoman-style tiles. Large, well kept rooms. Singles $15, tiny singles $6. Doubles $20, with bath $30. Breakfast included.

Ottoman Guest House, Cankurtaran Mah. 6 Tevkifhane Sok. (tel. 518 0790; fax 518 0792). Take Tevkifhane Sok. across the little park between Ayasofya and the Blue Mosque. Comfortable, with new furniture and an awesome terrace. Luggage room, safe, travel agency contact, phone in rooms, airport service ($3.75 per person). Doubles $30. Triples $50. Bath and breakfast included. V/MC accepted.

Hotel Park, Cankurtaran Mah. 26 Utangaç Sok. (tel. 517 6596 or 638 5077; fax 518 9603), in the heart of Sultanahmet. Friendly service, quiet environment, and spacious terrace with colorful flowers. Carpets sold in the foyer. Ask about a 10% discount for long stays (10+ days). Singles $20, with shower $35. Doubles $30, with shower $35. Breakfast included. Off season prices lower. V/MC/AmEx. accepted.

Star Pansiyon, 18 Akbıyık Cad. (tel. 638 2302), opposite Orient Youth Hostel. Spartan, no frills, but clean. 24-hr. hot water. All rooms have bath with shower. The word on the street is that this is the place for toilet paper and towels. Bonus for solo or small group travelers—no tour groups here. Doubles $20. Triples $25.

Camping

Londra Camping (tel. 560 4200), 1km from the airport, along the noisy and nerve-grating highway to İstanbul. No bus stop; take a taxi. Includes cafeteria, bar, and showers. $2.50 per person. $1.90 per tent. Two-person bungalows $12.50.

FOOD

İstanbul's budget dining options are superb. From the sandwich stands in the streets to the elegant seafood restaurants on the Bosphorus, you can expect high quality, kaleidoscopic variety, and reasonable prices. While Sultanahmet may be an optimal place to stay, it's not the premier eating locale—you'll fare much better in the **Kumkapı** district, south of the Grand Bazaar and justly famed for its seafood; or in **Beyoğlu**, where a wide variety of eating establishments await you around İstiklâl Cad. Besides these clusters, excellent restaurants are scattered all over the city. **Gengelköy** is known for its simple fish restaurants; **Kanlıca** is reputed to have the most delicious yogurt in İstanbul; **Ortaköy** has great restaurants with views of the Bosphorus. Some of İstanbul's top restaurants are scattered along the Bosphorus straits, on both the European and Asian sides. Bus #210, a double-decker (hourly 9am-6pm), runs along the European side of the Bosphorus and stops at Gengelköy and Kanlıca. For natural diets, two **open-air markets** are centrally located—a general one next to Çiçek Pasajı (Flower Passage), in Beyoğlu, and a fruit market next to the *Mısır Çarşısı* (Egyptian Spice Bazaar). The **Egyptian Spice Bazaar** sells an astonishing and mouthwatering collection of oriental sweets. For a quick stand-up lunch, the myriad *kebapçı* and *köfteci* will easily fill you up for less than $3. Stop at a *büfe* (snack shop) for *tost* and a soft drink, both for less than $1. Even a complete meal at a cheaper *lokanta* shouldn't run you more than $3.50.

Sultanahmet Area

Tourists fill the restaurants of Sultanahmet; however, many of these places serve bland, international-style food or relatively tasteless Turkish fare in a cafeteria setting. There are a few exceptions.

Cennet (Heaven), 90 Divan Yolu (tel. 513 1416), on the right as you walk along Divan Yolu from Sultanahmet towards Aksaray, 3min. from the Sultanahmet tram. Meat and veggie variations of its specialty—*gözleme* (Anatolian pancakes). You can gaze at the Turkish carpets and other wall-hangings while listening to typical Anatolian rhythms (performed nightly and throughout the weekend when fez hats are handed out), or you can pick up a few dance moves from one of the talented exhibitionist customers. Open daily 10am-midnight.

Türkistan Aşevi, 36 Tavukhane Sok. (tel. 638 6525, -6; fax 518 1344). A veritable feast for the eyes and taste buds, this three-part restaurant specializes in the cuisine of the Turkish-speaking former Soviet Republic of Turkistan. There are several variations of the seven-course lunch for $13 and the eight-course dinner for $16, all incredibly tasty. The Harput marriage feast soup (served hot) with meat, and the spicy *Saşlik* (Turkistani *şiş kebap*) are great. Vegetarian *kebap* $3.15. Eurocard/V/MC accepted. No alcohol served.

Pandeli Restaurant, 1 Egyptian Spice Bazaar (tel./fax 522 5534), a 15-min. walk from Sultanahmet. The Egyptian Spice Bazaar is the little 3-domed, 3-arched structure beside the Mosque, facing the Galata Bridge in Eminönü. Through the main archway, turn 180 degrees; entrance is on your right. Main courses are $5-7, starters $2.50. Tasty *yaprak dolması* (vine leaves stuffed with rice); the *hünkâ beğendi* (mushed eggplant with kebap) is superb. Open Mon.-Sat. noon-3pm.

Dârüzziyâfe, 6 Şifahane Cad. (tel. 511 8414, -5; fax 526 1891), in the Süleymaniye Mosque complex. Main courses $4.50-6. Tour groups abound. Mellow atmosphere and attentive service. The house specialty, *Sulemaniye Çorbası* (soup of vegetables and meat) is a must ($1.75), as is or *çilek* (strawberry) *keşkül* (pudding). On Sat. nights, classical Turkish musicians. No alcohol; it's part of a mosque. Beside it is the **İkram Bahçesi,** a Turkish tea garden. Come outside peak hours. Open daily noon-11pm.

House of Medusa Restaurant, Yerebatan Cad. 19 Muhteremefendi Sok. (tel. 511 4116 or 513 1428; fax 527 2822), on a main street intersecting with Divan Yolu, this four-floor, internationally renowned eatery is a must-see. Excellent Turkish cuisine can be tasted on the first floor garden (open in summer), the third floor divan area, or the fourth floor bar. Indeed, it's half restaurant, half museum. Every floor has its own unique, relaxed ambience. Delicious *piliç* (chicken stuffed with vegetables) for $3.75 and good vegetarian specialties; tasty pudding. Open daily 8am-midnight. Accepts major credit cards.

Pudding Shop, or Lale Restaurant, 6 Divan Yolu (tel. 522 2970; fax 512 4458), has been family-owned since 1957. A major pitstop on the Hippie Trail to the Far and

Middle East in 1970s. Affectionately nicknamed the Pudding Shop by hippies, it is now a lovely self-serve restaurant (meat dishes $2-2.50; veggie dishes $1.50) and super dessert stop. The creme caramel and *keşkül* (vanilla pudding) are sure to please, each for $1. The cappuccino rocks at only 65¢.

Backpacker's Underground Café, 14 Akbiyik Cad. A good-looking crowd can be found here often grabbing a beer during happy hour (daily 5-8pm; large beer 80¢), munching on the specialty sandwiches. Where fanny packs (or, bum bags) are a given, conversation is good, and the graffiti on the wall makes you think. Socially conscious music a plus. Open daily 7:30am-11:30pm.

Kumkapı Area

Kumkapı is a pleasant square with narrow cobblestone streets extending radially outward. The square and the streets are lined with fish restaurants—there is nothing else here—making the area look like one giant restaurant. Kumkapı is justifiably famous for its seafood. Prices are high by İstanbul standards (main courses $8-12), but it's worth coming here at least once. From the Grand Bazaar, cross Divan Yolu and walk for roughly 5 minutes down the narrow Tiyatro Cad. to the square. Restaurant staff will beckon you into their establishments. This annoying habit doesn't reflect the quality of the food—even the best restaurants do it. There is a map showing the location of all restaurants just before you enter the square. One commendable choice is the **Yengeç Restaurant,** 6 Telli Odalar Sok. (tel. 516 3227); turn right off the square, then right again. Open from noon to midnight, this establishment offers *bonfilet* ($7.50), catch-of-the-day ($9-15), attentive service, and festive live "gypsy" music nightly (8pm-midnight). One large fish is enough for two people.

İstiklâl Caddesi

To get to İstiklâl Cad. from Sultanahmet, follow the tram lines to Sirkeci, take a left and follow the water, cross the Galata Bridge (the first bridge you'll see), take a left onto the first major thoroughfare; the Tünel station is then on your immediate right. The Tünel is the world's oldest and shortest subway and will take you to İstiklâl Cad. (every 5min., 8am-9pm, 20¢). From the Tünel it is a 15-minute uphill hike via narrow, confusing streets. İstiklâl Caddesi is a narrow, European-style boulevard, a combination of Turkish and American fashion shops as well as more classic street vendors of *maraş* ice cream (smooth and irresistible) and *simit* (Turkish sesame pretzels). It is lined with smart boutiques, coffee shops, and foreign language bookstores, and crowded with wealthy shoppers, workers, and students—a kaleidoscope of İstanbul life. Several major consulates (i.e., French and Russian) are located here, as is the city's Catholic cathedral. A 1915 San Francisco-esque tram runs down the middle (from the underground Tünel station to Taksim Sq., every 10min., 30¢). This district is a favorite for eating out, and at night it metamorphoses into İstanbul's main nightlife (and red light) area—see safety warning (p. 459). About halfway between the Tünel and Taksim (on the left as you walk toward Taksim) is the famed **Çiçek Pasajı** (Flower Passage). It is here and in the many other side streets that one can find cheap but classy restaurants, bars, and cafés. The clientele is mostly Turkish—a good place to escape the tourist hordes.

Huzur Restaurant, (tel. 293 7129), at the back of the passage, offers main courses for roughly $2.50-3.75, salads for $1.25-1.90. Their lamb casserole is delicious. Daily fish special; large *rakı* (national drink) for $6.90. Open daily noon-11pm.

Cumhuriyet Meyhanesi (Republic Pub), (tel. 252 0886), at the far end of the fruit market. Where some of Turkey's top poets, artists, and journalists gather in the evenings to discuss politics, culture, and other intellectual matters. During the evenings, the second floor is the main eating attraction with its delectable items such as eggplant salad for $1.90. Open daily 10am-1am, possibly later.

Has Fırını, Kalyon Cukulluk Cad. #35, (when you step out of the end of the passage) for melt-in-your-mouth fresh *kurabiye* for $2.50 per kg, or, for the health-conscious, *anasonlu galete* ($1.75 per kg), made with no fat or salt.

Café Gramafon, 3 Tünel Meydanı (tel. 293 0786), to your left as you come out of the Tünel station, offers an international kitchen. Turkish coffee $1.90, cappuccino royal with amaretto, brandy, cacao, and espresso $3.75. The Gramafon filet and toast (sandwiches with veggies or meats) are divine. Live jazz (Thurs.-Sat., after 10:30pm; $6.25 cover) attracts mixed crowds. Open daily 11am-2am.

A major part of daily Turkish life is the *pastane* (pastry shop). Indeed, folks sit alone or with friends to enjoy pastries unique to the Turkish kitchen. A true gem is the **İnci (Pearl) Pastahanesi** at İskitlâl Cad. 124-2 (tel. 243 2412 or 244 9224). This shop has serviced the neighborhood for 52 years under the same owner, selling out stock (impressively large and varied, mind you) almost every night. The shop's specialty is *profitör*, a creme-filled cake smothered in chocolate sauce for a scandalously cheap $1.40 (open daily 7am-9pm).

ENTERTAINMENT

A large part of the nightlife in İstanbul consists of excellent restaurants or coffeehouses. Western European-style nightlife—bars and nightclubs—is concentrated in the Taksim district, where the action starts at midnight and rages until dawn.

Let's Go does not recommend club hopping in a haphazard manner here. Some clubs are reputable, but some are run by hustlers who have links with the nearby red light district. The hustlers will charge a lot—perhaps everything you've got—for a single drink. In one well known scam, a couple of girls sit at your table and order drinks. You get hit for an exorbitant bill even if you haven't ordered anything. The demand for payment is likely to be backed up with an impressive and frightening display of muscle. If you don't have enough money with you, they may even take you back to your hotel and take it from your room. As always, exercise good judgment and try to stay with a group of friends. Remember, safety in numbers.

The nightclubs are located on İstiklâl Cad., Sıraselviler Cad. (the other main street which runs from Taksim Sq. to the Bosphorus), and in the little side streets which run off them; and all are at the Taksim end. Be sure to try the local drink, **balyoz** (sledge hammer, wrecking ball). Demolition is the appropriate concept here— *balyoz* consists of *rakı*, whiskey, vodka, and gin mixed with orange juice. **Kemançı** (Violinist), on Sıraselviler Cad., on the left, roughly a one-minute walk from Taksim, is a wild and loud rock bar that hosts live bands. Long hair and tattoos rule ($4.75 cover charge on weekends includes one drink; *rakı* and beer $2.50). This is an excellent place to try *balyoz* ($4.75). It's on an alley off İstiklâl Cad., a two-minute walk from Taksim, to the right. **Bilçak,** Sıraselviler Cad., Soğana Sok. No 7 (tel. 293 2774), is the place for a more mellow scene. The fifth floor is the place to be for an intellectual, artsy crowd and an incredible view of the Bosphorus. The best drink is "Aysel's in the Ditch"—a shot of tequila (shot glass and all) in a glass of beer ($5).

The **Carnival Pub,** in the fruit market beside the Flower Passage, is a long, loud, cavernous bar where heavy metal and punk bands play. Live music every night— notice the vintage Judas Priest paraphernalia. **My Way Bar,** 14 Yerebatan Cad. Salkım Söğüt Sok, right under Hotel Elit, serves it up your way indeed. This wooden, trendy hangout has a funky interior and excellent drinks. (Open daily noon-2am.) **Leman Kültür,** on İmam Adman alley off İstiklâl Cad., is a spacious dimly lit bar with faded Turkish comic-strip wallpaper, earth-tone decor, and a funky spiral staircase. No live music, but billiard tables, good drinks, and a hip crowd listening to rock and jazz. Mellow your groove in the cozy alcove, **Asparagus Café and Bar,** on Büyükparmakkapıı Sok., another alley off İstiklâl Cad., where the name of the game is relaxing to Anadolu Pop. Live music starts at 9:30pm. Right across the alley is **Hayal Kahvesı,** a popular haven for artists—it's a little trendy. Live music (rock/blues/jazz) starts at 11pm. Keep an eye out for the awesome wooden menus and the sweet and satisfying house specialty, Hayal Cocktail ($3.75). The **Soldier Café and Bar,** 37 Ticarethane Sok, off Divan Yolu (tel. 511 3621), is filled with teens and twentysomethings relaxing here during the day. Foreign music and local live music make for a jumping groove, particularly with the help of the energetic crowd. Paintings of women in

SIGHTS

combat decorate the walls. (Open 11am-4am.) **Young Turks** also hang out in **Ortaköy** (ferry #22E, 22B, or 25 from Eminönü). With the exception of the Carnival Pub, you'll need to be pretty snazzy to get into many of the above places, so dress up. Usually, you'll be the only tourist there, but people are friendly.

For a truly authentic **Turkish bath** *(hamam)*, it's best to go to the nearby cities of Edirne and Bursa. İstanbul baths, however, can provide a reprieve for the down and dirty. The much-publicized **Cağaloğlu Hamamı** (tel. 522 2424), in Sultanahmet on Yerebatan Cad., is fancy, but avoid it if you are at all claustrophobic. It now charges between $10 and $20, depending on how much rubbing you want. (Open daily 8am-10pm.) Also try İstanbul's other famous *hamam*, the historical **Çemberlitaş Bath**, 8 Vezirhan Cad. (tel. 522 7974; fax 511 2535), which has stood since 1584, built under architect Mimar Sinan. With separate sections for men and women, it's one of the largest *hamam* in İstanbul and popular among Turks and tourists. A cathartic bath and massage costs $10; fresh orange juice $1. Before indulging in baths, female travelers should know that this Turkish tradition is male-oriented— most *hamams* have smaller facilities for women (open daily 6am-midnight).

Carpet and kilim (flat-woven mat) buying in İstanbul is truly a task for the expert bargainer. Merchandise is always overpriced, sometimes as much as 50%, but the quality here is the highest, if you know what you're looking for. "Shop around" is an understatement—you should seek out advice from any carpet/*kilim* vendor who speaks English (and most do). **Onur Carpets and Kilims** at 13/15 Mimar Mehmet Ağa Cad. (tel. 518 1880; fax 516 2251), beyond the Ayasofya and near the cluster of Sultanahmet hotels, has a vast selection and offers great advice on the production, history, and quality of carpet/*kilim* making. **Alser,** on Fetih İş Hane #27-31 (tel. 511 8055; fax 511 1089), off Divan Yolu, is also helpful. These are only suggestions— look around for yourself. Carpet shops are bountiful in İstanbul; the Grand Bazaar is the site of the most exorbitant prices, so beware. The name of the game is bargaining, so don't be afraid to stick by your bid if you know it's fair.

SIGHTS

İstanbul's incomparable array of world-famous churches, mosques, palaces, and museums can keep an ardent tourist busy for weeks, but five or six days of leg-work should be enough to acquaint you with the premier sights. A FIYTO card allows entry to most major museums for free; an ISIC card is usually good for half price.

The **Ayasofya Camii** was built by the Emperor Justinian between 532 and 537 CE. Upstart plebeians destroyed the original building during the Nika Revolt; Justinian built a new and improved church in order to cement imperial authority. Converted into a mosque after the Ottoman invasion in 1453, it was made a museum by Atatürk in 1935. An elaborate marble square in the floor by the altar marks the spot where Byzantine emperors were once crowned. You can walk up the stone ramp on the left to the upstairs gallery to observe the remains of the famous wall mosaics of Christ and the archangel Gabriel. (Museum open Tues.-Sun. 9:30am-4:30pm; gallery open Tues.-Sun. 9:30-11:30am and 1-4pm; admission $4.50, students $2.15.)

Sultan Ahmet I built the **Blue Mosque** *(Sultanahmet Camii,* or the Mosque of Sultan Ahmet) opposite Ayasofya in a bold, brazen attempt to one-up Justinian. The mosque's formidable silhouette is unforgettable, and the interior, with its blue İznik tiles, is stunning. In its day, the mosque was most famous for the controversy over its six minarets—religious leaders didn't want the sultan to match the number of minarets at Mecca. The ever-resourceful Ahmet averted the crisis by providing the money and workers necessary to build a seventh minaret at Mecca. Sultan Ahmet was the 6th sultan after the Turkish conquest of İstanbul—hence, the six minarets. The mosque has 16 balconies, symbolizing his role as the 16th sultan since the beginning of the Ottoman state. On the left side of the altar is the sultan's seal. Iron bars running across the domes indoors ensure that the whole structure bends in earthquakes—it has withstood 20 so far. An underground pool moderates the mosque's interior temperature—keeps it cool in the summer, warm in the winter.

You may visit the mosque outside of the five daily prayer times; modest dress and removal of shoes is required. Most mosques provide sarongs to cover your legs.

From the mid-15th century until the mid-19th century, the **Topkapı Sarayı** (Topkapı Palace) was the nerve center of the Ottoman Empire. It faces the Ayasofya Mosque, with the Archaeological Museum situated between them. This magnificent maze of buildings, built by Mehmet II, was originally the site of the Ottoman government and the Empire's most exclusive schools. It was also the home of the Sultan and his sizeable entourage of wives, eunuchs, and servants. Don't be overwhelmed by the seemingly endless attractions—you can punctuate your tours inside the palace by sunning on the terraces or reposing in the rose gardens. Not to be missed are the **First Court** and its huge East Asian porcelain collection, and the **Treasury,** which houses an inestimable wealth of diamonds, emeralds, gold, and jade. The latter also contains the spectacular Topkapı Dagger and some of St. John the Baptist's hand bones. Nearby, the **Pavilion of Holy Relics** contains remnants of the prophet Muhammad: his footprint, a lock of hair, a tooth, his original seal, and a letter written by his hand. The swords of the four caliphs are on display in an adjacent room. This is a sacred place to Muslims; men and women pray here. The Harem (the secluded quarters of the wives and concubines of the sultans), with its lush rooms and magnificent İznik-tiled walls, is worth the additional cost. To see it, take a tour (every 30min. 10am-4pm in English and Turkish; no tour at 12:30pm; admission $2.50). The **Circumcision Chamber,** near the patio throne overlooking the Bosphorus, is beautifully decorated with blue-green İznik tiles. According to Turkish tradition, males were not circumcised at birth (as prescribed by İslam), but after they had come of age. (Palace grounds open daily 9am-5pm; admission $6, with ISIC $3, with FIYTO free.) Other must-sees include the **Spoonmaker's Diamond,** an imperial treasure the size of a pear, bought for Sultan Mehmed IV (1648), and the display of royal robes and other Ottoman vestments. The **Gülhane Park** outside the palace is popular among locals. There's frequently live Turkish music at night: the best artists draw large, loud, adoring crowds. Most of the Gülhane consists of little plastic vending booths (admission 50¢, students 25¢).

There are several other sights in the nearby area. The enormous **Grand Bazaar** *(Kapalı Çarşı)* is a vast, arched, ornate, colorful, chaotic marketplace which specializes in leather and carpets. You will get lost, but you'll probably enjoy it. The old part of the Bazaar is a jumble of shops selling hookah pipes, bright baubles, copper filigree shovels, Byzantine-style icons on red velvet, ancient Turkish daggers (made in Taiwan), silver flintlock guns with mother-of-pearl handles, chess sets, and hand puppets, among other treasures. Unfortunately, several warnings are in order. Hawkers prey on tourists. Fake and faulty merchandise is ubiquitous. The summer tourist invasion inflates prices by as much as 300-400%. Beware of shiny, bright *kayseri*—these shoddy imitations of Persian carpets are worthless, though people have been known to pay as much as $1000 for them. The gold is mostly 14-karat, and contrary to rumor, is no more expensive elsewhere in Turkey. In short, it is better to look here than to buy. But if you know what you want, and know what price is reasonable, you may find a deal. To reach the bazaar from Sultanahmet, follow the tram tracks toward Aksaray for approximately 5 minutes until you see the large mosque on your right. Walk to the mosque, enter its side gate, and walk, with the park on your left, to the bazaar entrance (open Mon.-Sat. 9am-7pm). At the opposite entrance of the bazaar is the **Sahaflar Çarşısı** (used book market). A wide selection of books are sold here, along with Kur'anic inscriptions and university texts. The market opens onto a bustling square. Opposite stands the huge entrance gate of **İstanbul University,** which fronts a leafy, well-shaded campus, a haven from the bustle of the city. Its tranquility is spoiled somewhat by the constant presence of riot police, who rest languidly in the shade, helmets at their feet, ready for action. The University is a hotbed of political strife which, on occasion, turns violent. The campus contains **Beyazıt Camii,** the oldest mosque in İstanbul.

The university walls to the left reach the **Süleymaniye** mosque complex (completed 1557) is one of the three masterpieces of Sinan, who served as Chief Court

S I G H T S

Architect under Ottoman Sultans Süleyman the Magnificent and his son, Selim. The name "Sinan" remains venerated in Turkey today; Sinan almost single-handedly codified Ottoman Classical architecture, a style so influential that generations of architects began imitating it shortly after the master's death. The huge Süleymaniye complex—which includes a mosque, seven *medrese* (religious schools), an *imaret* (charitable soup kitchen), and the *türbe* (tombs) of Süleyman and his wife Haseki Hürrem—was intended as a center for Islamic higher education. It is said that there are buried treasures in the minarets. To the east of the mosque reposes a majestic courtyard; to the west a graveyard where Süleyman and Haseki Hürrem rest peacefully in opulent *türbe* drenched in İznik tile and diamonds. (Tombs open Tues.-Sun. 9am-4:30pm; 75¢ "donation" buys admission.)

A 20-minute walk northwest from the graveyard leads to the **Fatih (Conqueror) mosque,** the imperial mosque complex of Sultan Mehmet II, who appears notorious in European history books for seizing Constantinople in 1453, converting the Ayasofya into a mosque, and designing the Topkapı Palace. The Fatih Camii, nearly a century older than the Süleymaniye, remains impressive nonetheless. The people of Fatih have a reputation for Islamic fundamentalism (to match the 1996 election)— here you will see many women covered from head to toe in *chador* and bearded men in Islamic dress. The atmosphere differs markedly from the rest of İstanbul; some Turks liken it to Iran. The mosque itself is usually crowded, and the rest of the complex serves as a meeting and recreation area for the community. Back at the Süleymaniye, walk downhill toward Eminönü or Sirkeci. This 10-minute walk will lead you through the milling, heaving **market quarter**. About halfway down, there are numerous shops selling pistols and shotguns. We don't recommend any rash purchases. When you come within 200m of the Golden Horn, you will pass the **Rüstem Paşa mosque,** whose famous interior, almost entirely inlaid with İznik tiles, compensates for a humble exterior. Soon after is the 17th-century **Yeni Camii** (New Mosque), whose steps afford a shaded resting place. In front stretches the **Galata Bridge.** Beside Yeni Camii sits the **Egyptian Spice Bazaar.** Egyptians once dominated the spice trade in İstanbul and this is where they held shop. This feast for all the senses is much less touristy than the Grand Bazaar and does not sell leather or carpets. Instead, it is crammed with a mind-boggling array of sticky sweets (free samples); numerous varieties of Turkish delight, nuts, dates, honey cut straight from the hive; and aphrodisiacs, spices, and gold.

There are a few more sights back in the heart of Sultanahmet. The **Yerebatan Cistern** is a vast underground cavern where shallow water eerily reflects the 336 columns—one carved with Medusa's head. Wooden walkways allow you to wander among the columns, while atmospheric lighting and classical music in the background create an other-worldly effect. Underground waterways originally connected the cistern to the Topkapı Palace, but the passage was blocked to stop the traffic in stolen goods and abducted women (open daily 9am-5:30pm; admission $1.90, with ISIC $1.25, no FIYTO reduction). Two pleasant, candle-lit, albeit expensive subterranean coffee shops provide for your relaxation here (coffee $1.50). In the nearby **Sultanahmet** (Blue Mosque) complex, visit the tomb of Sultan Ahmet I, which, like other imperial *türbe* (tomb), houses the sarcophagi of the sultan and his immediate family (open Wed.-Sun. 9am-4:30pm; 75¢ "donation" buys entry). To your right as you leave the Blue Mosque are the **Carpet** and **Kilim Museums,** with carpets and woven *kilim* from all over the Muslim world (open Tues.-Sun. 9am-4pm). This is a worthy visit if you are interested in buying a carpet or *kilim* of your own, but keep in mind that the finer tapestries cost 50-100% more in İstanbul than in the Anatolian provinces. In any case, there are probably enough rugs to fray your cultural fiber along the road to the **Mosaic Museum.** In the gallery of shops below the mosque, the museum features mosaics dating from the 6th century, when the entire area was part of the Byzantine Imperial Palace. The collection is small and in poor repair (open Wed.-Mon. 8:30am-8pm; admission $1.25).

On the other side of the Blue Mosque is the ancient **Hippodrome,** a park erected in 32 days where Byzantine emperors once presided over chariot races and circuses. The tranquility of the park today is misleading—long ago it was the site of violent uprisings and demonstrations. In 532 CE, 30,000 people were massacred here as Justinian's troops put an end to the riots that had leveled much of Constantinople. In the Hippodrome stands the granite **Egyptian Obelisk,** the upper part of an obelisk from the 15th century BCE which was brought to Constantinople in 390 CE from Cairo. It was originally 25m high, but to move it they had to chop it to 18.5m. On the north side is a depiction of a joust race and the emperor holding a prize for the winner. The **Serpentine Column,** taken from the Temple of Apollo at Delphi, is a coarse column of unknown origin at the end of the Hippodrome. It was coated with bronze plates until members of the Fourth Crusade tore off the metal.

Across from the Hippodrome, next to İstanbul's legal administration buildings, stands the 16th-century **İbrahim Paşa Palace.** This magnificent building houses a museum of Turkish and Islamic art featuring tiles, Kur'ans, and a fine carpet collection. The courtyard houses a picturesque teahouse (open Tues.-Sun. 10am-5pm).

Walking back to Divan Yolu along Klodfarer Cad., you'll pass a small park opposite the Halı Hotel. Underneath lies the 5th-century **Binbirdirek Cistern.** Knock on the door of the shack to ask for a flashlight-guided tour (tip the guides roughly $2; don't let them charge you much more). You can experience huge carved columns, crumbling steps, and one or two shafts of light piercing the darkness. It's nice, but not as aesthetically spectacular as the **Yerebatan Cistern.**

A museum complex is through a gate marked "Archaeological Museum," downhill from the Topkapı Palace. The **Çinili Köşk** (Tiled Pavilion), once a petite pleasure retreat belonging to the Topkapı Palace, today houses the **Tile Museum.** Replete with yellows, blues, and greens, the building's own tiles constitute one of Turkey's best remaining examples of the Tabrizi Persian style, which the Ottomans increasingly avoided in favor of tiles with white backgrounds and naturalistic floral patterns (open May-Sept. Tues.-Thurs. and Sat.-Sun. 9am-4pm; admission $1.25). The **Museum of the Ancient Orient** (with English labels) has a buffet of Hittite, Babylonian, Sumerian, Assyrian, and Egyptian artifacts. Among them is a tablet on which part of the Hammurabi Code is inscribed, and another with a treaty between a Hittite ruler and the Egyptian Pharaoh Ramses II (open daily May-Sept. 9am-4pm; admission $1.25). The **Archaeological Museum** displays a prize-winning collection of early Greek, Hellenistic, and Roman marbles and bronzes, including a famous sarcophagus with carvings of Alexander the Great (open May-Sept. daily 9am-4pm; admission $1.25). The park on the ramparts of the Topkapı Palace overlooks the Bosphorus and Golden Horn and offers a respite from İstanbul's sweltering streets.

Across the Galata Bridge, the 62m-high **Galata Tower,** built by the Emperor Justinian in 528 CE and rebuilt in 1348 by the Genoese as a low-tech spy satellite for observing the old city, still serves its purpose today, allowing for a spectacular view of the Golden Horn and the Bosphorus. The tower was also the take-off site for the first intercontinental flight, executed in a Da Vinci-style hang glider. After hours, the tower degenerates into a pricey nightclub. To get to the Galata Tower, cross the Galata Bridge and walk 500m up the narrow, little alley. The tower is on your left, but it's easier to take the Tünel from here up to İstiklâl Cad. and walk down that same alley. Right along the Bosphorus, **Dolmabahçe Palace** was the home of sultans from 1856 until the demise of the Ottoman Empire after WWI. Soldiers guard the royal dock and the memory of Atatürk, who died in the palace on November 10, 1938, at 9:05am (all the clocks were stopped at that moment). Pseudo-French architecture reflects the sultan's pretensions of grandeur, even during the decline of the empire. Be sure to see the vast reception room, with 56 columns, and a huge crystal chandelier weighing 4.5 tons with 750 lights, and the Bird Pavilion, which housed birds from all over the world (open Tues.-Sun. 9:30am-4pm; admission $5). From Eminönü, take the ferry to Beşiktaş (50¢) or bus #58. The number of visitors per day is limited, so go early.

Round out your tour with other sights scattered around the city, including **Askeri Müze** (Soldiers' Museum; tel. 140 6255), in **Harbiye** on the European side. This is a 10-year-old child's paradise—swords and armor and other implements of war from the various cultures that have inhabited Asia Minor over the last few millennia garnish the walls (open 9am-5pm). **Beylerbeyi Sarayı** (tel. 321 9320), in Beylerbeyi, on the Asian side, was the rococo-style summer palace of the Ottoman sultans. Made of 19th-century white marble, it has a lovely garden teeming with magnolia trees (open daily 9am-4pm). **Rumeli Hisarı** (Thrace Castle), next to the second Bosphorus bridge on the European side, was an integral part of the Ottoman defense system. In wartime, a huge link chain was stretched from this fort to its mate, **Anadolu Hisarı** (Anatolia Castle), across the Bosphorus on the Asian side. One link is on exhibit in the Soldiers' Museum. The fortress is composed of towers around a central courtyard. The view of the Bosphorus from atop the walls is spectacular.

A mandatory stop for Byzantine art connoisseurs is the impeccably preserved **Kariye Camii,** a long way up Fevzipaşa Cad., near the Edirne Gate (accessible by *dolmuş,* bus #58 from Eminönü, or any bus in the direction *Edirnekapı*). Having undergone the transition from Byzantine church to mosque, and from mosque to museum, the building showcases superb 14th-century frescoes and mosaics. The realism and expressiveness of this strain of late Byzantine art influenced Giotto and other early Italian painters (open Wed.-Mon. 9:30am-4:30pm). From here you can see the ruined **Theodosian Land Walls,** which stretch from the Golden Horn to the Sea of Marmara. The only character to have ever surmounted these looming, 5th-century CE ramparts was Mehmet the Conqueror, in 1453.

Another İstanbul highlight is a **Bosphorus cruise.** Boats leave from Pier 3 beside the Galata Bridge in Eminönü. (In summer Mon.-Fri. 10:30am, 12:30pm, and 2:30pm, Sat.-Sun. 10am, 11am, noon, 1:30pm and 3pm; in spring and autumn daily 10:30am and 12:30pm; in winter 10:30am. All $4.) When the ferry makes its final stop on the Asian side, have some fish *kebap,* mussels, or fried *kalamari* for $2-5 from the street vendors. Then walk up the hill for beautiful views of the Black Sea. Double-decker bus #210 also runs hourly from behind the tourist office to points along the European side of the Bosphorus and costs two bus tickets each way.

The **TV tower** at Çamlıca Hill is İstanbul's highest point and offers views of the entire city and the Bosphorus straits. There is a beautifully decorated Turkish café here—classical Ottoman music is played, and waiters wear traditional 19th-century costumes. Especially at sunset, the best skyline views can be seen at **Salacak,** in the city of Üsküdar, another home of excellent cafés and tea shops. Take the bus from Üsküdar, then ferry to Çamlıca. The **Chamber of Florence Nightingale** in the Military Hospital in Haydarpaşa is open to the public. The **English Cemetery** in the Selimiye Barracks (one of the world's largest) is a beautifully maintained military cemetery for British soldiers who fell in the 1854 Crimean War against Russia.

Bağdat Cad. (Baghdad Ave.) in Kadıköy on the Asian side is a place of the Eurochic (ferry from Piers 3 and 7, every 20min., 50¢). **Ortaköy** is a liberal place, favored by artists and young people; a church, synagogue, and mosque here are representative of a secular Turkey (well, until recently). It is a bit avant-garde and bohemian. **Gengelköy** has excellent, cheap, and simple fish restaurants. **Anadoluhisarı** has small, waterside restaurants and cafés. **Kanlıca** is reputed to have the most delicious yogurt in all of Turkey. **Emirgan** is a peaceful village of old-style Turkish houses and excellent Turkish tea. An 1843 castle is nearby. Bus #210 heads to Kanlıca, Emirgan, and Anadoluhisan. İstiklâl Cad., the heart of modern İstanbul, is also worth a visit.

■ Near İstanbul

Eyüp, a popular Muslim pilgrimage site, houses the 15th-century tomb of Job, the eponymous companion of Muhammad who died during an Arab siege of the city in the 7th century. The Golden Horn ferries ride the waves twice hourly from pier 6 in Eminönü, above the Galata Bridge (35min., 45¢), or catch bus #55. You may see regally costumed young boys brought here by their families—the trip is customary for boys before circumcision. Once the refuge of the artists and the elite of the Ottoman Empire, today Eyüp is mostly a religious site, with Kur'an shops, the Eyüp Mosque, and lovely, spacious cemeteries.

■ Büyükada

The fourth stop on the ferry ride to the Princess Islands—the largest and most enjoyable of the isles. When you get off the ferry, you'll find yourself in the heart of the commercial district. Fish restaurants border the shore; delicious *kebap* restaurants and *pastane* (pastry shop) are abundant for a few blocks in any direction (except in that of the sea, of course). Primarily a popular summer retreat for natives of İstanbul, with many clubs, including the Anadolu and Su Spor, Büyükada offers lovely pinewood scenery, swimming, and peaceful walks farther behind the busy district and is excellent for a daytrip from İstanbul.

The **Tourist Police** is located on 2nd floor of its building (open Mon.-Fri. 9am-5pm). The **PTT**, 17 Balık Cad., is a left from the ferry's ticket office after the tiny passage; make the turn on your first right (where the fish restaurants begin). Walk the short block, then another left and walk for ½ block (open summer Mon.-Fri. 9am-9pm, Sat.-Sun. 9am-1pm; winter Mon.-Fri. 9am-6pm, Sat.-Sun. 9am-1pm). International phone service available. There are no cars or buses here. You'll deal—enjoy **walks** or a **horse-and-buggy** ride. Prices range from $2.50 for a short ride to $15 for a long, island tour (the tourists' favorite); you can also rent a bike for $1.90-2.50 per hr. **Ferries** depart from Eminönü or Kabataş on the north side; look for signs saying Sirkeci Adalar (from Eminönü, 6-7 per day, round-trip $2.50). A faster and slightly more expensive alternative is the *seabus,* which operates from Kabataş in the summer. Many **pharmacies** are on Çinar Cad., to the right of the busy dock district. They alternate the hours they are open, as is standard Turkish policy, to make 24-hr. service available. Check signs on the windows for details. The **Hospital** is Buyukada Hastanesi (tel. 382 6228), on 24 Lelahattun Cad. For **police,** go to 23 Nisan Cad. **Telephone Code:** 216.

Most of the hotels here are expensive and boast luxurious summer retreats with indoor everything (pool, disco, etc.). Büyükada is great for a day trip, but the **Ideal Aile Pansion,** 14 Kadıyoran Cad. (tel. 382 6857), is worth an overnight stay. The pension is large, looming, slightly Victorian, haunted house-style masterpiece, with large rooms that are more like apartments than hotel rooms. Communal showers and bathrooms. Doubles $18.75. Triples $9.40 per person.

On the ride back from Luna Park, one can find **Aşıklar Çay Bahçesi** (Lover's Teahouse), primarily for sweethearts, but a large, peaceful spot for a drink and a bite to eat. The following are among the miasma of restaurants in the central commercial area by the dock. **Yeni Bufé** (tel. 382 6357) has *lahmacun* (Turkish pizza on pita bread) for 65¢, *döner* $2.50, and *ayran* 38¢ (open daily 8am-11pm). A pastry shop recommended by locals of the island is **Dolci,** 23 Nisan Cad (tel. 382 6349), which has outdoor seating, cheap lemonade, *ay çiçeği* (moonflower: chocolate and nut cream in a pastry) for 32¢ (open daily 10am-1am).

Take a **horse and buggy ride** to Yöruk Ali and Dil Uzantisi for a day at the beach or a picnic. Another option is to take the buggy to Luna Park (ride should be no more than $7.50; 10-15min.) at the back of the island. **Donkey ride,** you plead? Rent one here for $6.25 for 30 minutes. Ask the locals about the path (along the right side of Luna Park) to the stone-covered **beach** with perhaps the cleanest swimming on the island at Adanın Arkası (literally "back of the island"). The most intriguing Greek relic is **St. George's Monastery,** the highest point on the island. Make sure to ask about the trails—hiking through the dense forest is forbidden in some places, and the guard in the watchtower overlooking the monastery may call the police.

NORTHWESTERN TURKEY

■ Safranbolu

Safranbolu is a hidden jewel in the dusty lands of northwestern Turkey. An old, atmospheric, perfectly preserved Turkish town, it contains some of the best examples of early Ottoman architecture in Anatolia. It is also famous for its unique brand of *lokum* (Turkish delight), and along with its rival, Afyon, it makes the best in Turkey. Still relatively untouristed, Safranbolu, with its narrow, winding streets and houses built of sun-dried brick, is arrestingly beautiful.

Orientation and Practical Information   Safranbolu has two distinct sections: the beautiful old town, and the dusty new one that consists of two long boulevards lined with five-story apartment buildings and little else of interest.

The heart of old Safranbolu, and its center of transportation, is the main square, **Mehmet Kurtulanı Meydanı.** Local and intercity **buses,** *dolmuş,* and taxis leave from here. Standing in the square, and looking toward the old baths, you will notice four streets. On the extreme left, the **Kastamonu road** leads to Hıdırlık Tepesi, a hill from which there is a superb view of the town. To the right of it is **Akın Sok.,** which leads to the old *kervansaray.* To the right of it is **Yukarı Çarşı Sok.,** which contains one of the tourist offices and the Arasna Café-Bar Pansiyon. To the extreme right, **Hasan Dede Sok.** leads past the Tahsinbey Konağı and Paşa Konağı hotels to the old government house, now in ruins. It was built on the site of the town's old castle. Safranbolu is small, and most points of interest are within a five-minute walk. Behind, to the left, **Hilmi Bayramgil Sok.** runs to the new town.

There are two rival tourist offices in Safranbolu. On the main square, the office of the privately owned **Safranbolu Culture and Tourism Association** (*Kültür ve Turizm Vakfım*), Çeşme Mah. 1 Arasta Sok. (tel. 712 1047), supplies maps and information on sights and accommodations (open daily 8am-4pm, variably open until 9pm). More helpful is the government-run **Tourism Information Office** (*Turizm Danışma Müdürlüğü*), 7 Arasta Çarşısı (tel. 712 3863), which provides similar services. Go down Yukarı Çarşı Sok., take the first left after the Aşiyan Otantik Café, then take an immediate right into the little shopping arcade; it's on the right.

There is a **telephone** in the main square of the old town, and another in the arcade opposite the tourist office. Both accept phonecards. In the new town, there are functional phones at the roundabout and on the main road, on the right as you go toward the new town. It is best not to use hotel reception phones, as they can be very expensive. Safranbolu is served by the Güven, Ulusoy, and Avrupa **bus companies,** which run to Ankara (5 per day, 3hr., $6); İstanbul (4 per day, 7hr., $9.50); İzmir (1 per day, 12hr., $16.25); Adana (1 per day, 13hr., $14); İskenderun (1 per day, 12hr., $16.25); Rize (1 per day, $19.75); Trabzon (1 per day, $17.50); and Samsun (1 per day, $11.75). Officially, all buses arrive at **Karabük,** the less-than-lovely steel manufacturing town 10km away. These companies continue into Safranbolu. Numerous other companies serve Karabük, from which you can catch a frequent minibus to Safranbolu. **City buses** also make the journey every hour Monday-Saturday, and every two hours on Sunday (25¢). A **taxi** from the bus station to old Safranbolu will cost $8-9; taxis are metered, and have the same rates as other Turkish cities. The **Ulusoy** office (tel. 725 4254, in Karabük 424 2111) is in the new town. Coming from the old town, turn right at the roundabout—it's roughly 15m down the street, on your right. The **Avrupa** office (tel. 712 4315) is 50m farther along, on your left. These companies offer a pick-up service in Safranbolu. Company employees are English impaired. Try to get tourist office personnel to make the call or to go to an office and buy a ticket. The tiny **PTT** office is at 26 Cincinam Sok., a few doors down from the *kervansaray* (open Mon.-Fri. 8:30am-12:30pm and 1:30-5:30pm, Sat. 8:30am-12:30pm). **Postal Code:** 78620. **Telephone Code:** 372.

Accommodations   Havuzlu Konak, 18 Beybağ Sok. (tel. 725 2883), is a luxurious, restored Ottoman villa. Rooms have delicate lace bedspreads, Ottoman couches, and brass tables. Bathrooms are larger than single rooms in most pensions. Reservations are recommended, and essential for Saturdays, when it fills with middle-class Turks on weekend trips. Stop in for a spot of *çay* even if you can't afford to stay—it's worth a look. (Singles $25. Doubles $35.) Also sharing the upper end are the **Paşa Konağı** and **Tahsin Bey Konağı**, 50 Hükümet Sok. (tel. 712 2014; tel./fax 712 6062). Run by the same owner, the two villas will indeed make a *paşa* out of you. Luxurious rooms with oriental rugs and a knockout view make these two worth the extra *lira*. (Singles $30. Doubles $42. Triples $65. Breakfast included. Weekday rates are $3 less.) The **Arasna Café-Bar Pansiyon** has four rooms similar to the Konaks but without the views. Some are restored originals—some less authentic. Nevertheless, this place is classy and comfortable and has an excellent bar. ($12.50-15 per person. Breakfast included.) It's hard to miss the signs for the **Çarşı Pansiyon**, 1 Bozkurt Sok., where you can choose between standard pension rooms with shared bath and floor-tossed mattresses in rooms with private bath. ($6.25 per person. Breakfast included.)

There are some pensions in the new town. You may want to stay in these if the ones in the old town are full. The **Konak Pansiyon**, 4 Sağlık Sok. (tel. 725 2485), on the main road between the old and new towns, is comfortable. (Singles $11.75. Doubles $18.75.) The **Hotel Ür** (tel. 712 1086, -2215), just off the roundabout in the new town, offers modern, comfortable rooms. (Singles $23. Doubles $30.)

Food   For food, don't miss **Kadıoğlu**, on the main square. Their specialty is *kuzu kebabı*, lamb baked in spices ($2). A three course meal will give you that six-months pregnant feel for just over $4. The friendly owner may reward such an effort with Turkish coffee *bizden* (on the house). The **Arasna Café/Bar** also features a full menu of similarly inexpensive Turkish cooking in a setting more "ethnic" than an EPCOT pavilion. **Konak restaurant,** in the middle of the shopping arcade, is a pleasant place for *çay* or *ayran*.

The local Turkish delight specialty is *fındıklı lokum*, a yellow delight with a hazelnut in the middle and covered with coconut sawdust. Many other varieties exist. An excellent shop is **İmren**, 1 Arasna Çarşısı, in the little shopping arcade, behind the Aşiyan Café and a couple of doors down from the government-run tourist office (open daily 8am-8pm). **Özkan Lokumlar,** on the street to the left of the private tourist office, roughly 10m down on the right, is an ancient shop with a mini-factory behind it. Stick your head in to see how Turkish delight is made—you'll be rewarded with odd looks and may be placated with a free sample. Turn right while facing the Çarşı Pansiyon, and after about 100m you'll come to an unnamed sweet shop on the corner (*baklava* for $3.25 per kg).

Sights   Any tour of Safranbolu should begin at the **Yemeniciler Arastası,** the shopping arcade which houses the useful Government Tourism Information Office. An oval-shaped complex, this was once home to Safranbolu's famous shoe industry. (Who doesn't own a pair of *Safranbolus?*) Now, candy stores and cafés, gift shops, and, yes, shoe stores crowd the intimate arcade. The Arasta gives one a unique glimpse into Turkey's past, albeit with more than a touch of touristy kitsch. The **Kaymakamlar Evi** (governor's residence), a restored house, is the local museum. Enter through the courtyard, where the animals were kept. Various tools and utensils are on display here, including wooden cone *frustums*. These were filled with yogurt and water to make *ayran*. On the next floor up are the winter living quarters—above them, the summer quarters, which have higher ceilings. From the market (at the back of the *kervansaray*), walk up the alley beside the T.C. Zakaat Bankası—the museum is the white building on the right (open Mon.-Fri. 8:30am-5:30pm; slipper charge 25¢). After wandering through the town's narrow streets, stroll up to **Hıdırlık Tepesi,** a lookout point at the town ramparts with excellent

BAĞLAR

views. Walk uphill along the snaking Kastamonu road for five to ten minutes, then take the paved path on your right to the official-looking building with the Turkish flag. You can find a shop and **public bathrooms** here.

■ Bağlar

When the hustle and bustle of Ankara and İstanbul get to be too much, head for Safranbolu. When Safranbolu gets to be too much, head for Bağlar. That's what the residents of old Safranbolu did for years. Two- and three-story houses, many bearing a seal proudly proclaiming their protection as historical sites, line cobblestone streets that are a joy to explore.

To reach Bağlar, take any bus, except those marked Karabük or Kayarlı, and get off at Bağlar's fountain square. The trip should take about 15 minutes. You will recognize the fountain by its large pile of stones, behind which the 3-dimensional, golden face of Atatürk stares out on the tiny **Cumhuriyet Parkası**—a set of four benches which face the Father of the Turks. Any last minute necessities can be taken care of in the square since the buildings which surround the fountain house a variety of stores, *çayhane*, *Kıraathane*, barbershops, and a Kontörlü telephone. Bus tickets, however, are not for sale, so be sure to purchase a roundtrip ticket in Safranbolu. From any pay phone you can call the **police** (tel. (372) 712 1224).

Visit one of Safranbolu's Tourist Bureaus for information on reservations for Bağlar—they are few and hard to come by. Better yet, stay in Safranbolu and make a daytrip to tiny Bağlar. Aside from the *çayhane* and *kıraathane*, most of Bağlar's restaurants are open only in the evening. The **Burhan Restaurant** (tel. (372) 712 4106) seats 400 in a beautiful indoor/outdoor plantation setting and offers an excellent traditional Turkish menu, a festive setting, and reasonable prices (full meal $2.15). Across the street from the Burhan, the **Safran Restaurant** (tel. (372) 725 1718; fax 712 1091) is marked by a large billboard. As the glyphs explain, the Safran offers delicious meals, a tea garden, a nighttime disco/bar, meeting rooms, and will host and plan your wedding banquet (and you were going to get married in Vegas!). Sharing the square, the immaculate, if unspectacular **Restaurant 78** (tel. (372) 725 4743) provides Turkish fare at reasonable prices. All three restaurants can be reached by heading out of the fountain square, down Anslar Sok. (facing Atatürk, it's the first street diagonally to your right, before the bottling plant). It's a 10-minute walk to the restaurants at the junction of Asanlar Sok., Adalet Sok., and Kavaklar Sok.

In the days when Safranbolu was a wealthy shoe-making city, the local people went to Bağlar for rest and relaxation. While there is little "to do," there is plenty to see and soak up. For a relaxing walk, go down Köyici Sok. next to the barbershop, which is over your right shoulder as you face Atatürk, at the end of the square. Follow the winding street to visit **Köyici Camii.** To the right and around the mosque are public bathrooms. After visiting the mosque you can continue into the neighborhood, marvelling at the large homes with their lush gardens. Between the houses, you can catch a glimpse of the magnificent views from this valley town. Leaving the fountain square down **Aslanlar Sok.,** you will soon come to a beautifully restored Bağlar mansion, now serving as the Bağlar branch of the **Safranbolu Kültür ve Turizm Vafkim.** Located in the historic **Kalri Ganioğlu Konuk Evi,** the Bağlar tourist bureau can make reservations, find you a room, and provide you with a map of Bağlar. Continuing down Aslanlar Sok., you will pass two mosques with minarets of corrugated steel, emphasizing function over form. Farther down, you come to Bağlar's restaurants and a fairly modern, if hokey, amusement park. You can ride the ferris wheel (15¢), or just enjoy the view.

■ Edirne

Edirne is a beautiful, peaceful medieval Islamic town that contains some of Turkey's best examples of Ottoman architecture. Located only a few kilometers from the

EDIRNE

Greek and Bulgarian borders, it remains quintessentially Turkish. Mind you, it's 227km from İstanbul, but it's worth visiting for the religious and cultural vestiges. The quiet city of today conceals an eventful past. Named Hadrianopolis after the Roman Emperor Hadrian in the second century CE, the city witnessed the catastrophic defeat of the Roman army by the Goths two centuries later. The Ottomans took control of the city and made it the capital of their empire from 1363 until soon after the fall of Constantinople in 1453. In the Empire's final days, the city was occupied no less than four times as Bulgaria, Greece, Russia, and Turkey struggled for control of the Balkans. Today, Edirne serves as a pleasant resting point for travelers *en route* to İstanbul and other points in the East. The city, situated near the junction of the Tunca and Meriç rivers, houses mosques and baths designed by the famous architect Sinan, including his masterpiece, the **Selimiye Camii.**

ORIENTATION AND PRACTICAL INFORMATION

Edirne is centered around the triangle-shaped **Hürriyet Meydanı** (Freedom Square), which is bounded by the **Eski Camii** (Old Mosque), Kervansaray Hotel, and a row of shops. *Dolmuş* from the bus station drop you here. Right behind the Old Mosque runs **Talat Paşa Cad.,** the main east-west thoroughfare. Walk from Hürriyet Meydanı to Talat Paşa Cad., take a left, and walk for roughly one minute; the first intersection, on your left, is **Saraçlar Cad.,** the town's main shopping street. Keep going to the next intersection; the tourist office is on the corner. This street (on the left), Maarif Cad., is home to a good selection of cheap hotels. On your right is the beautiful **Selimiye Mosque** overlooking a park. You can walk up the road to the left of the park and you will see on your left the main local bus and *dolmuş* terminal. To the left of the Selimiye Mosque is the **Üç Şerefeli Camii** (Mosque with Three Galleries). Keep walking for roughly five minutes along Talat Paşa Cad., past the tourist office, to the outskirts of town and the river.

Tourist Office: 17 Talat Paşa Cad. (tel. 213 9208), 200m west of the Eski Camii. Free maps. Open June-Aug. daily 9am-6pm; Sept.-May Mon.-Sat. 8:30am-5pm.

Bulgarian Consulate: 31 Talat Paşa Asfaldı (tel. 225 1069), 1km southeast of Eski Camii, on the road to İstanbul; it's on your left. Normally visas take a week to issue, and are priced: tourist $31.50, transit $21, double transit $42. Express visas—issued the same day—cost: tourist $46.50 and transit $31.50. Multiple entry: 3 months $42, 6 months $73.25, 1 year $105. Visas allow a 30-day stay. Foreigners should get express visas. Open Mon.-Fri. 9am-noon.

Trains: Two train stations serve Edirne, one on the road to **İstanbul** (tel. 225 1155 or 212 0914), and one in **Kapıkule** (tel. 238 2312), within walking distance of the Bulgarian border. To get to Kapıkule, take a *dolmuş* from in front of Rüstempaşa Kervansaray Otel (every 10min., $1), or a bus (hourly until 6pm) from the local bus station. Kapıkule is the last stop. There is one train per day to İstanbul (8am, 7hr., $2) and Thessaloniki (5:55am, 12hr., $9.50; board at the Kapıkule border station), two per day to Sofia (8hr., $19) and Budapest ($100), and one per day to Europe (arrives from Munich early in the morning and leaves late at night).

Buses: When you arrive at the *otogar,* walk across the street to take a *dolmuş* into Edirne. Buses depart for İstanbul (every 30min., 3hr., $6), and Keşan (5 per day, 1½hr., $4). Buses also run to Bursa (April-Dec. 2 per day $9.50, Nov.-March 1 per night, $9.50) and Ankara (2 per evening, 10hr., $20).

Dolmuş: Run regularly between the depot near mosques (7am-midnight) and **bus station** (*terminal*), a few km along the road to İstanbul (30¢).

Hospital: Edirne Devlet Hastanesi (tel. (284) 225 4603). Public.

PTT: 17 Saraçlar Cad. It has **telephones** and 24-hr. **currency exchange.** They cash traveler's checks Mon.-Fri. 8:30am-5pm, but it might be better to try a local bank (open 9am-noon and 3-5pm), as the PTT has been known to be unreliable about this service at times.

Telephone Code: 284.

EDIRNE

ACCOMMODATIONS

There are plenty of cheap options scattered along Maarif Cad., the little street to the right of the tourist office, 2 blocks from Hürriyet Meydanı.

Hotel Kervansaray (tel. 225 2195; fax 225 0462), runs the length of Hürriyet Meydanı, Eski Camii Altı. Built in the 1550s as an overnight resting place for camel caravans *en route* from Europe to the East. Recently renovated, rooms come with bath, toilet paper, TV, phone, and carpet. The call to prayer resonates through the corridors and rooms at 4:30am. You didn't want to be asleep then anyway. Singles $32. Doubles $50. Triples $69. Breakfast included. V/MC accepted.

Efe Hotel, 13 Maarif Cad. (tel. 213 6166, -466). Spotless rooms include modern bathrooms, telephone, and TV. Air-conditioned lobby and American bar. Singles $16. Doubles $22. Triples and quads $30. Breakfast included.

Hotel Aksaray (tel. 212 6035), a couple of doors down from Efe Hotel. Cheaper and much more basic than its counterparts. Small, plain rooms. Singles $5. Doubles $8.75. Triples $11.25. Rooms with bath (there are 2) cost considerably more.

Hotel Konak, 6 Maarif Cad. (tel. 225 1348). Two words: no frills. Communal TV room. Grim, cell-like singles cost only $3.25. Larger, brighter doubles cost $2.60 per person. Triples $2.40 per person. Quads $2.20 per person.

Fifi Camping (tel. 235 7908), on the main İstanbul road, 8km from the center of town. Has its own restaurant, bar, and pool. Hotels in town are just as cheap and more convenient. Camping fee $6 per person, tent rental $4, cars $3, caravans $6. 2 persons with car/caravan is $12. Single rooms $12. Double rooms $28. Triple rooms $38. All rooms have shower. Mastercard and Visa accepted.

FOOD AND ENTERTAINMENT

Do not leave Edirne without taking *çay* (tea) at **Sera** teahouse. No matter which way you turn, you'll have superb views. Look one way to see the glorious Selimiye Camii; turn around for the Eski Camii. These scenes, combined with the sound of the café's fountain and a glass of sweet Turkish *çay*, result in an experience which is quite sublime—drink it in at night, when the Selimiye Camii is floodlit. *Çay* comes in a small Turkish *çay* glass on a tiny steel tray, or in an ordinary cup (small 20¢, large 35¢, *Ayran* 35¢, *tost* 35¢). Sera is in the park between Selimiye Camii and Eski Camii, closer to the latter. Another excellent *çay bahçesi* (tea garden) is **Café Antik,** which takes up most of Hürriyet Meydanı. Prices and selections identical with Sera; however, Café Antik has a much wider selection of tasty snacks (*karışık sandviç* 45¢, cheeseburger 80¢, *tost* 35¢, ice cream 70¢).

For more substantial fare, head to **Gati Restaurant,** on Talat Paşa Cad. a few doors past the tourist office (if walking away from Eski Camii), has excellent mixed grill—*köfte* and grilled liver, the local specialty, with rice and fries ($2.50). Side dishes (60¢), *Efes* brand beer (65¢). **Vatan Restaurant,** on Kıyın Cad., is across the road from Selimiye Camii. Stand with Eski Camii to your back; then it's on the road that runs along the right-hand side of Selimiye Camii. This place is informal and packed with students—just grab a seat at one of the communal tables. (Tasty stew dishes, which change daily, cost 50¢ each; soup also 50¢; rice 20¢.) The **Park Hotel Restaurant** on Maarif Cad. serves excellent *köfte* and *kebap,* the house specialty ($2.50). The **Café M** is a student restaurant and a good place to go for a coffee. It's on Saraçlar Cad., on the upper floor of the Vakıf İş Hanı building.

For dessert, there are many **sweetshops** along Saraçlar Cad. One of the best for sweets (and worst for service) is **Roma Pastanesi,** at #99 (50m down from the PTT away from the mosques, on the opposite side), which offers treats to satisfy demanding sweet tooths ($3.50 per kg). A specialty is *badem ezmesi* (marzipan).

SIGHTS

Edirne will enchant you with its Islamic medieval architecture, primarily its mosques. The city's main sight is the **Selimiye Camii,** completed in 1579 by the Ottoman architect Sinan. This work of genius, which includes 71m minarets and

999 windows, is the town's symbol and can be seen towering above Edirne from several kilometers away. The exterior is impressive, but it's the interior that truly astounds you on first entry. It is vast and ornately decorated from dome to floor. The mosque is approached through an ancient shopping arcade; at the end of this, a small stone staircase (marked "Camii Giriş" and "Moschee Eingang") leads up to the courtyard. The nearby **Eski Camii,** completed 1415, is quite distinct from the others architecturally: instead of one large dome, it has a series of small ones. Its interior is undergoing restoration, but part of it is still in use and can be visited.

Edirne's other major sight is the **Beyazıt Complex,** a charitably endowed, spiritual and physical welfare facility a couple of kilometers from the center of town. The centerpiece is the **Beyazıt Camii,** a beautiful, single-domed mosque surrounded by multi-domed buildings which were designed to be schools, storehouses, and asylums. (No longer used, these buildings are locked; however, the mosque is usually open.) To get there, walk along Talat Paşa Cad. until you reach the river, but don't cross the bridge; turn right and walk along the dirt path that runs parallel to the river. After a 10-minute walk there is a bridge below on your left. Cross it, walk three to four minutes more, and you'll see the mosque. This is a beautiful walk through pleasant countryside. For the whole journey you'll see, on your right side, the domes and minarets of the Selimiye and Eski mosques rising out of the city, and on your left, the Beyazıt mosque, partly obscured by trees. On the way are two of Edirne's historic **stone bridges.** When you finally clear those trees and see the entire structure for the first time, the walk will seem worthwhile. (*Dolmuş* serve the mosque, but they are infrequent and confusing to use—the same old story.)

Back in the center of town, there are some other sights worth a quick look. The **Bedesten,** on Hürriyet Meydanı, is a half-millennium-old covered market. On the other side of Hürriyet Meydanı is the **Rüstem Paşa Kervansaray.** This multi-domed structure, designed in the style of the Eski Camii, was built as a resting place for medieval caravan trains. Two-thirds of it now serves as a university residence. The remainder is a hotel. Near the Selimiye Camii are two museums of minor interest. The **Ethnography Museum** exhibits clothing, carpets, and medieval armor (open Tues.-Sun. 10:30am-noon and 1-5pm; admission 60¢). The **Turkish and Islamic Art Museum,** which similarly exhibits examples of Ottoman architecture, Kur'ans, weapons, and glasswork, has the same hours and admission prices. The low prices and inspiring architecture may beckon you to sprawl out in reverie at one of Edirne's Turkish baths. Try Sinan's 16th-century **Sokollu Hamamı** (tel. 225 2193), beside the Üç Şerefeli Camii. You'll see the minarets from the tourist office. (Open daily 8am-10pm for men, 10am-5pm for women; admission $2.25, with massage $3.15.) Turkey's annual **grease wrestling** (*yağlı güreş*) tournament is in Edirne in the last week of June.

■ Yalova

Located on the southern shore of the Marmara Sea, Yalova has been a popular thermal resort since the days of the Romans, particularly for curing rheumatism. When you land in Yalova, you'll be in a busy commercial area, the "town" of Yalova. Here, budget-priced hotels and restaurants can be found. The main thermal center is in Termal and the beach is at Çinarcik. Yalova is really ideal for a daytrip from İstanbul or Bursa.

The most prominent reference point is the Atatürk statue, in which he is raising his right arm with a stern look on his face. The statue faces the water and is a convenient point of departure and arrival. Facing the statue, the **tourist office** (tel. (216) 814 2108; fax 812 3045) is right behind you on İskele Meydani. Free brochures (open in summer daily 8am-noon and 1pm-5pm; in winter Mon.-Fri. 8am-noon and 1-5pm). Banks, pharmacies, and exchange offices line **Cumhuriyet Cad.** which runs perpendicular to the back of the statue. Facing the statue, walk right 1½ blocks to find the *dolmuş* lot, with the names of the destinations written in the front window. Take the *dolmuş* marked "termal" to the thermal spring (15min., 38¢) or the one marked "Çinarcik" (20min., 38¢) to visit beaches, bufés, and discos. **Ferries** depart from İstanbul; you'll need to take *dolmuş* to Kabataş and buy a ticket from the booth along the shore marked "Yalova" ($5 roundtrip, 2½hr.). The **hospital,** Yalova Devlet Hastanesi (tel. (216) 814 1214), is at the intersection of Fatih Cad. and Koşu Yolu. Public. One block to the left (facing the statue) , you'll find the **police station** (tel. (216) 813 0377), marked "Jandarma." The **PTT** is at 40 Gazipaşa Cad. (open daily 8:30am-12:30pm and 1:30-5pm; 7am-11pm for mail, telegraph, and faxes).

There are several seaside and *kebap* restaurants, and Yalova has an abundance of delicious pastry shops. **Durak I Lokantası,** (tel. 813 3949), right next to the statue, serves up a good soup (65¢), vegetarian-friendly appetizers (65-75¢), and meat options. **Merkez 2,** near the *dolmuş* lot (tel. 814 3748), has clean, friendly service, and a pleasant but not overdone atmosphere (İskender *kebap* $3.75, lamb tandur and cola $4.40; open in summer daily 8am-midnight; in winter 8:30am-9pm). **Kent Pastanesi,** 10/1 Cumhuriyet Cad. (tel. 814 1909), offers sesame-glazed sweets 90¢, baklava $3.75 per kg, and pastries with nuts and/or cacao (15-30¢). Open daily 6am-6pm. **Yalova Pastanesi,** 4/1 Yali Cad. (tel. 814 1584), has finger-licking good tarts (chocolate cream with fruity top 40¢) and an excellent selection of cakes and chocolate (open daily 5:30am-1am).

To see and enjoy the **thermal springs** used by Emperors Constantine and Justinian to treat rheumatism, take a *dolmuş* to "Termal." From the *dolmuş* stop, walk uphill (in the opposite direction of the Termal police station) on the right-hand side of the main road for five minutes. Climb the winding stairs on your right and hang another right at the top. Walk uphill for two minutes. and the tourist *köy* (village) starts on your left. Pensions and eateries are sprinkled throughout both sides of the narrow street. Lowest prices include $4 per night for a single and $13 for a triple with bathroom and kitchen. Shop around, and use your discretion. If you plan to stay overnight, staying in one of the hotels in the town of Yalova may be a good idea. The hotels and restaurants along the thermal springs, which are located on the left before the winding stairs to the tourist *köy* (see above), are pricey. However, the **Turban Yalova Termal,** which regulates the springs, allow access for $3.15 per hour per person. You can use the outdoor pool, indoor pool, and sauna. For a stab at the sultan's bath, 1 person will pay $3.75, 2 people $6.25. Massages are extra. You are admitted into one of the sultan's cabins with 2 rooms—one with a bath, and another with a cooling-off room. The facilities are not luxurious, but relaxing and healing indeed. Take a walk through the thermal spring area of Yalova, a calming experience amid gardens, lush trees, and winding roads. If you really want nightlife here, locals suggest **Şilep** or **Amadeus** discoes which offer lively foreign music.

■ Bursa

Nestled in the shadow of the 2000m-high slopes of Mt. Uludağ (literally "Great Mountain," or Mt. Olympus), Bursa is a city of fascinating contrasts. Perhaps due to a tradition of gay singers from the city, some natives mockingly call it "Bursa the gay." But along with Konya, Bursa is one of Turkey's two holy cities of pilgrimage. While many of the 14th-century mosques and tombs are still frequented, Bursa has become an industrial center with a wealthy resort area. The vast gardens and parks, including Kültürpark which houses a zoo, and verdant plains at the center of a significant fruit production area contribute to the reputation of this city as "green." Furthermore, green is the symbolic color of Islam, and it is doubly appropriate here. Mt. Uludağ, which gives the city its traditional moniker "Green Bursa," is home to Turkey's leading ski resort. Bursa is famous for its silk trade, its local invention of İskender *kebap* (grilled meat in dish of bread, tomato sauce, melted butter and yogurt), towel production, thermal springs, and sweet candied chestnuts, sold in nearly every pastry shop.

Osman, the founder of the *Osmanı* (Ottoman) dynasty, besieged Bursa for nearly a decade; after his death in 1326, his son, Orhan Bey, came to power. Orhan made Bursa the capital of the blooming empire until Edirne usurped that distinction 75 years later. Despite the collapse of the Ottomans and the ascendancy of industry in Bursa, the well preserved monuments that are scattered throughout the city and the thermal baths in the **Çekirge** (Grasshopper) remain great attractions.

ORIENTATION AND PRACTICAL INFORMATION

To get to the center of town, take a *dolmuş* marked "Heykel" from the bus station (25¢) and get off at **Ulu Camii** (Great Mosque).

Tourist Office: To get to the **main tourist office** (tel./fax 221 2359), go to the Ulu Camii side of Atatürk Caddesi, walk towards the statue of Atatürk, pass the fountain, and go down the stairs on your left. Helpful staff; worthless map. Open June-Sept. Mon.-Sat. 8:30am-noon and 1-5:30pm; Oct.-May Mon.-Fri. 8:30am-noon and 1-5pm. On weekends, use the office on Atatürk Cad. As you walk away from the *heykel*, it lies about 100m before Ulu Camii. Open Sat.-Sun. 8am-5pm.

Buses: Depart for Bursa from İstanbul's Esenler Bus Station (every 30min., 4 hr., $7). **Kamıl Koç** is generally safe and reliable, as are **Ulusoy** and **Varan.** Routes connect Bursa to Ankara, İzmir, and other big cities (every 30min.). *Dolmuş* to the bus stations are marked "Garaj" and depart from Atatürk Cad.

Ferries: Bursa is accessible by ferry from Kabataş in İstanbul (Mon.-Fri. 8 per day, $2.50). On weekends the express ferry launches from Kartal on İstanbul's Asian coast. Early ferries (8:30 or 9am) beat the crowds. The ferries land in Yalova, where you can catch a *dolmuş* or bus to Bursa (every 30min., $2.50). The entire trip takes roughly 3½hr. There is also seabus service (5 times per day on weekdays, 8 per day on weekends) to Yalova and Bostancı.

Hospitals: Private Vatan Hastanesi (tel. 220 1040), on İnönü Cad. (left from clocktower). **State Devlet** (tel. 220 0020). Take a *dolmuş* from Atatürk Blv.

PTT: Across the street from Ulu Camii. **Currency exchange.** Cashes traveler's checks. Some English spoken. Open Mon.-Sat. 8:30am-noon and 1:30-5pm.

Postal code: 16300.

Telephone code: 224.

ACCOMMODATIONS

Otel Özendim, 135 Garaj Karşısı (tel. 254 9471), directly across from the depot. In the noisy and distant area around the bus station. Clean but utilitarian rooms. Singles $7.50 Doubles $12.50. Triples $15. Quads $16.25. Shower and bath included.

Otel Deniz, 19 Tahtakale Cad. (tel. 222 9238). More expensive, but also more comfortable—small, quiet rooms around a pleasant courtyard. Hot showers on demand. Free do-it-yourself laundry. Singles $7.50. Doubles $12.50.

Özen Şükran Otel, 39 İnönü Cad. (tel. 221 5453). A small hotel with old furniture, but charming nonetheless. Well kept and handy lamp tables in every room. Singles $7.50. Doubles $11.25. Triples $15. Student discount 20%.

Saray Öteli, İnönü Cad. Matbaa Çık No. 1 (tel. 221 2820). Spacious, well lit rooms. Communal bathrooms with sinks in every room. Safe and luggage room. Big singles $6.25. Doubles $12.50. Triples $18.75. Breakfast not included.

FOOD AND ENTERTAINMENT

Bursa is home to the mushy, tangy *İskender kebap,* a popular yogurt, tomato and lamb dish. Numerous restaurants named "*İskender kebap*" that specialize in the dish are clustered in the area between the Atatürk statue and the Green Mosque. **Kebapçı İskender** (tel. 221 4615), 7 Ünlü Cad., at the corner of Atatürk Blv. and İnönü Cad., claims to have invented the *İskender kebap* (one portion $3.15; open 11am-10pm). **Bursa Kebapçısı,** down the street from the tourist office, by the Orhan Gazi Mosque, is also well known but more expensive. Locals highly recommend **Gümüş Kebapçı** (tel. 220 3401), on Gümüşçeken Cad., a block down from Atatürk Blv. (*kebap* $3.50; open 9am-9pm). Also try the inconspicuous **Lalezar,** 14/c Ünlü Cad., farther up from Kebapçı İskender, which has tasty vegetarian appetizers

($1.25) and great desserts, including *kadayıf* in milk and nuts (75¢). Picnickers can stock up in the **market** on Tahtakale near the budget hotels.

Bursa's **Kültür Parkı** (take a *dolmuş* from Heykel, 30¢) has decent restaurants and is one of the few places to serve alcohol in this conservative city. Concerts, movies, or theater are occasional attractions. The **Arap Şükrü** district, near Altıparmak Cad., is next to the park and features fish restaurants, bars, and pubs. Try **Hanzade Bar/ Restaurant** (tel. 221 0052), Arap Şükrü Barlar Sok. No. 43. Catch the catch of the day here; prices range from $1.85-10. (*Şiş kebap* $2.50; open daily noon-1am). All of the restaurants in the district have tight outdoor seating. Try the pastry shop, **Kafkas** (tel. 221 5549), 35 Atatürk Cad. Kafkas offers delectable and reasonably priced chocolates, pastries, eclairs, and cakes, and, of course, candied chestnuts (open daily 7:30am-11:30pm).

SIGHTS

The city's layout was determined largely during its reign as capital of the Ottoman empire, and most of the mosques date back to the 14th and early 15th centuries. The famous **Yeşil Camii** (Green Mosque) and **Yeşil Türbe** (Green Mausoleum) in the east actually seem blue to many viewers. Spangled inside and out in rich turquoise, cobalt, and occasionally green İznik tiles, the structures are truly sights to behold. Before the capital was moved to Edirne in 1402, the mosque served both religious and administrative functions for the Empire, as well as occasionally housing the sultan and his family (open in summer 8:30am-5:30pm; in winter 8am-5pm; mausoleum expects 25¢ donation). Across the way, finely carved wooden doors and small stained glass windows accentuate Yeşil Türbe's handsome turquoise interior. The large postcard stand on the tomb of Mehmet I and his children is a more recent enhancement. To get there, walk along Atatürk Cad. past the clock to Namazgah Cad., then turn left onto Yeşil Cad. after the small bridge. The **Turkish and Islamic Art Museum,** including the **Ethnographic Museum,** is near the small bridge. It is located in the Green Medrese (Islamic school). The main loggia, or classroom, is now a display for traditional costumes. Many renowned scholars completed their education in this medrese, built by Hacılvaz Paşa in 1424 (open 8:30am-noon and 1-5:30pm; admission $1, students 50¢, free with ISIC).

The **Ulu Camii** (Great Mosque) diverges from the common architectural style found in İstanbul. Rectangular layout and numerous supporting columns are characteristic of the style, and scholars believe that the nearby intricately carved wooden *minbar* (pulpit) represents an astrological chart. The mosque was built by Beyazıt to commemorate his victory in Nikopolis in 1396. It is said that Beyazıt vowed to build 20 mosques if he won the war; but once victorious, he built just the Ulu Camii with 20 domes (a lousy trick to play on God). Walk west from Ulu Camii to Hisar (Fortress) for a classical view of Bursa. In this park along Cumhuriyet Cad. are the mausoleums of Osman, founder of the Ottoman Empire, and his son, Orhangazi, who was responsible for the capture of Bursa.

In June and September, you can witness the silk production for which Bursa is famous. The brilliantly dyed and patterned silk, *ipek,* can be purchased in the **Kapalı Çarşı (Bazaar)** or in **Koza Han,** by the tourist office, for $4-20 per square meter—you can also buy the silkworm cocoons themselves.

The **Eski Kaplıca (Old Springs) bathing complex** (tel. 233 9300), Çekirge Meydanı, Kervansaray-Termal, was built by Justinian in the 6th century. Take the Çekirge *dolmuş* and get off at the luxurious Kervansaray Hotel. Eski Kaplıca will be on the right when you face the hotel (open daily 7:30am-11pm; entrance to baths costs $6.25 for men and $3.75 for women, rubbing and massage $3.15 each). A short *dolmuş* ride just past the Kültürparkı and down the hill to the right will take you to **Yeni Kaplıca** (New Springs) (tel./fax 236 6968), 6 Yeni Kaplıca Cad., a bathing complex built for Süleyman the Magnificent in 1555. Three adjacent baths (one per sex and one for families), fed by natural thermal springs, feature cavernous bathing pools (open daily 7am-11pm; men $4.50 for first class bath, $3.25 for second class; women $2.25).

To reach the **Uludağ cable car** station, take a *dolmuş* marked "Televiewer" (25¢) from the Kafkas pastry shop on Atatürk Blv., two blocks past the statue. The cable car runs to the mid-station (every hour on the hr., 9am-9pm, roundtrip $3.75), and from the mid-station to a small, scenic town perched at the peak of the 2000m-high mountain (every hour on the half hr, 20min., $5). Be prepared for the cooler climate, sudden changes of weather, and high-priced hotels.

■ İznik

"The history of İznik," as the tourist office brochures aptly put it, "is very old." İznik was first constructed in 316 BCE by Antigonius, one of Alexander the Great's generals. In 310 BCE, another of these generals, Lysimachus, defeated Antigonius and renamed the city after his wife. The Romans later invaded and built walls, theaters, and laid out the city's Hellenistic grid plan. Under the Byzantine empire, Nicaea hosted the First Ecumenical Council in 325 CE. Pressured by the Emperor Constantine, the assembly of bishops accepted the Nicene Creed, which stated that God and Christ were one. Six more councils then convened to clear up debates. The last Council, called to resolve the issue of iconoclasm in 787 CE, returned to Nicaea and met in the Ayasofya church. After a short stint with the Crusaders and the Seljuks, İznik fell to the Ottomans in 1331. A porcelain industry developed and thus began the production of the renowned blue İznik tiles, like those which line the interior of the Blue Mosque in İstanbul. Today, İznik is a sleepy town, except for two months in the summer when vacationers fill the few lakeside motels and tea gardens.

İznik is calming, especially if you've been run down by the hustle and bustle of touristy İstanbul areas. Your best bet is to get a room with a terrace overlooking the serene İznik lake which presents an unforgettable indigo sunset. Nightfall signals the hypnotic rhapsody of the nocturnal frogs. Sit on a bench along the lake, stare at the interminable sky of twinkling stars, and chew on seeds (if you want to absorb all the local customs, that is!). The ruins here are in no way monumental, but the verdant hills and orchards and soothing waters of Lake İznik may engage you for a day or two. İznik makes a good daytrip from Bursa.

ORIENTATION AND PRACTICAL INFORMATION

Kılıçaslan Cad. and Atatürk Cad. separate İznik into quarters and meet in the center at the Ayasofya church. The lake is at the west end of town, and much of the city is enclosed by ancient walls.

Tourist Office: (tel. 757 1454; fax 757 1933). With your back to the bus station, walk 3 blocks to the right, turn left onto Kılıçaslan Cad., ascend stairs, and follow signs. Open in summer daily 8:30am-noon and 1-5:30pm; in winter officially Mon.-Fri. 8:30am-noon and 1-5:30pm.

Buses: *Dolmuş* and buses go to Bursa (every 30min. from 6:55am until dusk, 1½hr., $1.25). One daily bus each to Ankara and İstanbul. *Dolmuş* run to **Yalova** (every hr. through mid-afternoon, $1.90). Or hop off the bus to İstanbul at Yalova ($1).

Ferries: Leave from nearby Yalova (58km) for İstanbul—see Yalova, p. 471.

Police Station: 74 Kılıçaslan Cad., on the corner intersecting Atatürk Cad.

Hospital: Nearest hospital is in Yenişehir.

PTT: (tel. 757 1815), south of the tourist office on Kılıçaslan Cad. (With your back to the tourist office, turn left onto Kılıçaslan Cad.) Offers **currency exchange** and cashes traveler's checks. Open daily 8:30am-12:30pm and 1:30-5:30pm.

Telephone code: 224.

ACCOMMODATIONS

Burcum Motel, Kemalpaşa Mah., 20 Sahil Yolu (tel. 757 1011; fax 757 1202). Clean rooms and terraces facing the lake. All rooms have shower, toilet (even paper) and telephones. 24-hr. hot water when full, otherwise available 7:30pm-11am.

IZNIK

Singles $12.50. Doubles $18.75. Triples $21.15. Breakfast included. Forego breakfast and pay less. 10% discount for 20+ person groups. V/MC accepted.

Cem Pansiyon, 24 Göl Kenarı, (tel. 757 1687), along the lakeside near Murat Pension. Well kept rooms, some with terrace and superb views. Clean, huge communal bathroom and shower on every floor. Singles $6.25. Doubles $13.75. Triples $15.50. Breakfast included. 15% group discount for 10+ persons.

Murat Pension (tel. 757 3300), Spandau Blv. , farther up along the lake. Not as scenic as some other pensions, but cheaper, with 24-hr. hot water. Hall showers. Kitchen on each floor. Pool table in café. Caring, attentive family-run business. $10.75 per person in singles, doubles, triples, and quads. Breakfast $2.25.

FOOD AND ENTERTAINMENT

Restaurants by the lake offer inexpensive prices and a breathtaking location. Take a stroll along the lakeside and stop by one of these: enjoy a gelato after dinner at **Lambada Café** for a trifling 35¢. The **Kırık Çatal Restaurant,** next to the Burcum Motel, is a little more expensive, but the food is also a little better. Languish on the shady patio as you gaze at the lake, and enjoy the excellent service. Also, **Çamlık Restaurant,** adjacent to Çamlı Motel, offers tasty appetizers for $1.25 including *tarator* (garlic yogurt with spices). Grilled Yayin balık (catfish), a regional specialty, is worth the $3.75 (open 7am-1am). In town, locals suggest **Karadeniz Pide Salonu,** 130 Kılıçaslan Cad. (tel. 757 0143), a small but cheap restaurant with good food (*lahmacun* 40¢, *Kıymalı Sandviç* in pita with veggies, $1.10). A popular pastry shop is the **Ceren Pastanesi,** on Kılıçaslan Cad. (tel. 757 1379). Ceren serves *poğaça* (pastry with cheese) and tea for less than 30¢ (open daily 5am-midnight).

SIGHTS

The **Ayasofya Camii** (Saint Sophia or Church of the Holy Wisdom) at the town's central intersection was built as a church in the 4th century by the Byzantines. Osman, the founder of the Ottoman dynasty, converted the Ayasofya into a mosque in 1331. Chief Court Mimar (architect) Sinan renovated the building during the reign of Süleyman the Magnificent (1520-1566). Decrepit and surprisingly small, this is nevertheless an attractive site. The few pieces of religious art, including fading frescoes, are small and captivating (open daily 9am-noon, 1-5pm; admission $1, 50¢ with ISIC). The aging **Murat Hamamı** (Turkish bath) (tel. 757 1011), just south of the Ayasofya, still offers baths in the company of patrons who do not speak a word of English. (Open daily for men 6am-1pm and 6pm-midnight, for women 1-5pm only; bath 90¢, children 65¢. Massage 90¢.) The **Yeşil Camii** (Green Mosque), located near the tourist office in one of the quieter areas of town, was built by architect Hacı Musa in 1378. The shade and quiet there make the park a perfect place to have lunch and read in the afternoon sunlight (MOSQUE usually open 1:15-5pm).

Murat I built the **Nilüfer Hatun İmareti** (charitable foundation), across the street from the mosque, to honor his mother, the first Christian wife of an Ottoman sultan. The museum, established in 1960, now housed in this magnificent building, displays many artifacts excavated in İznik and briefly traces the history of İznik tile-making, including coins and medals from the Seljuks, who controlled İznık in 1078 (admission $1, students 50¢). In the winter, museum officials have the keys to all of the following: the Ayasofya; a 4th-century underground baptismal **spring;** and a **catacomb,** intricately decorated with Byzantine murals, 4km out of town (taxi to catacomb $5; $2 donation expected at the museum). The Roman Theater, the mosques around town, and the four major and 12 minor **gates** of the city walls are all worth a visit.

İznik's *faience* industry has not yet died. Shops along the main street sell earthenware tiles and plates decorated with opaque, colored glazes, starting at $10. Today's tilemakers occasionally let visitors watch the tilemaking process. Ask someone to show you the easy-to-find *fırın* (kiln), or follow the signs leading from the street that feeds into the bus station parking lot (no parking for tourists).

Aegean Coast

Fabulous classical ruins and a sinuous coastline that conceals sublime beaches have helped transform Turkey's once tranquil Aegean Coast into an increasingly popular destination. Cradled by 5000-year-old mythology and history, the culture veritably erupts here, offering an eye-full for the photographer, archaeologist, nature-lover, and hedonistic nomad. The Aegean Coast's natural beauty and five millennia of history are captivating, but you may have to search a bit to find traditional settlements.

The coast's first foreign visitors were the ancient Greeks, who established ports in the area. As Alexander the Great and subsequent Hellenic rulers pushed the Aegean empire eastward, the ports became the nerve centers of commerce along the major trade routes of the ancient world, growing even as Greek civilization declined. Today, Hellenistic ruins—especially extensive at Pergamon, Ephesus, Aphrodisias, and Heirapolis—stand as weathered testaments to the coast's classical heritage.

No legal barriers prevent tourists from traveling from the Greek islands to Turkey, though some travelers have reported complications and exorbitant port taxes.

■ Çanakkale

ORIENTATION AND PRACTICAL INFORMATION

Inexpensive accommodations and frequent bus connections to nearby sights and to other cities make **Çanakkale** an easy base from which to explore Gallipoli and Troy. Because of its proximity to the site of the disastrous WWI battle, Çanakkale is particularly hospitable to New Zealanders and Australians, many of whose troops were slaughtered at Gelibolu (Gallipoli). Turkish hotel and restaurant managers often mumble Australianisms like "G'day" and "No worries." Most hotels offer gimmicks and other "deals," but, for all intents and purposes, shop around and see for yourself if they practice what they preach.

Tourist Office: 67 İskele Meydanı (tel./fax 217 1187), from the bus station, take a left out the main doors, then take the next right onto Demircioğlu Cad. (following the "feribot" sign), and continue onto the docks. The **tourist office** will be on your left just before the shore. If you arrive by ferry, the office is straight ahead to your right. Open Mon.-Fri. 8:30am-noon and 1-5:30pm.

Tourist Agencies: Down Under Travel Agency, İsmetpaşa Mah., 14 Atatürk Cad., Eceabat 17900 (tel. 814 2431; fax 814 2430), based on the European side in nearby Eceabat, 7km from the Gelibolu battlegrounds, offers a bargain tour of Gallipoli for $6.90. The 30-year-old **Troyanzac Travel Agency** (tel. 217 5849; fax 217 0196), to the right of the clock tower, offers car rental, private guides, hotel reservations, and general information as well as half-day guided tours of Gallipoli (5hr., $16) and Troy (3hr., $15).

Buses: Arrive every 1½hr. from Bursa (5½hr., $8.15), Edirne (stops at Eceabat for ferry to Çanakkale, 5hr., $8.75), İstanbul (5hr., $10.65), Bergama (4hr., $8.15), Ayvalık (3½hr., $6.25), Ankara (12hr, $16.25), and İzmir (5hr., $8.75). Buses leave more often in the morning. *Dolmuş* run to Çanakkale (45min., $1.10).

Ferries: To Eceabat, 6am-midnight (every hr., in winter every 2hr., 50¢). Be careful not to take the smaller ferry to Kilitbahir. In Eceabat you can hire a taxi (officially $25, but drivers bargain) to tour the battlefields of Gelibolu.

Hospitals: Çanakkale Public Devlet Hospital (tel. 217 1098). **Özel Hastane Private Hospital** (tel. 217 7461).

Police Station: Off İnonu Cad. (tel. 217 1181), next to the post office.

Postal Code: 17100.

Telephone code: 286.

ÇANAKKALE

ACCOMMODATIONS

The tourist business here can be quite competitive, and while this situation can give the traveler a better bargaining position when settling on prices, it also lends itself to some cutthroat business practices. Use discretion when choosing accommodations and when dealing with pushy proprietors. Check out these places for yourself before you decide; it's an easy task, as they are located close to each other. Çanakkale hotels may test your strength of will and determination to find an accommodation suiting your needs and wallet size, but you may find many budget accommodations in the area surrounding the clock tower.

Yellow Rose Pension, 5 Yeni Sok. (tel./fax 217 3343), around a corner about 50m from the clock tower. Featuring an outdoor garden-café, wicked clean dorm rooms (single sex), generous laundry facilities, and large wall papered rooms. Ask about hot showers. The film "Gallipoli," with Mel Gibson (hubba hubba), is shown every night for those who plan to tour the site. Singles $6. Doubles $10. Triples $15. Roof $2.50. Breakfast $1.50.

Hotel Efes, Kemalpaşa Mah. Aralık Sok. (tel. 217 3256), one block from the clock tower behind the parking lot. Simple, colorful, and airy rooms with negotiable prices surrounded by a rose-filled garden with a duck-filled fountain. Obscure location allows for noiseless sleep (except for the calls to prayer, and there's no escaping those). Singles $5. Doubles $10. Triples $11.25. Breakfast $1.25.

Hotel Konak, 14 Fetvane Sok. (tel. 217 1150 or 217 1578), behind the clock tower to the left. The words "cheesy motel" may come to mind when you sink into the periwinkle chairs. Nonetheless, Konak offers spacious, albeit dark rooms. Speak up if the hot water runs out—you get a discount. Showers $1.25 for bathless rooms. Singles $5.63, with shower $6.25. Doubles $10, with shower $11.25. Triples $15. Quads $17.50. Breakfast $1.25.

Kervansaray Otel, 13 Fetvane Sok. (tel. 217 8192), across from Konak. A graceful timeworn structure with a fountain in the courtyard. Clean, sparse rooms with 4m-high ceilings. Kitchen access and laundry service available. Singles $5.65. Doubles $10, Triples $12.50, with shower $15. Breakfast $1.50.

FOOD AND ENTERTAINMENT

Lots of men drinking *rakı*, an acquired taste, is the staple scene at the restaurants along the quay—don't say we didn't warn you. But there's also fresh seafood that makes the trip worthwhile. Try **Yeni Entelektüel (New Intellectual) Restaurant** for fresh *lüfer* (bluefish), salad, and a beer ($5 per meal). A block or two inland, cheaper restaurants abound. **Yalova Liman Restaurant** is only a brief walk upstairs within 100m of the main pier. Dine on fried mussels and beer for only $2. Its atmosphere, while relaxed, is more formal than prices would suggest. The rooftop terrace affords an inspiring view of the Dardanelles (open daily noon-midnight). To stay away from more pricey harborside restaurants, waltz your Matilda over to the **Aussi/Kiwi Restaurant,** 32 Yalı Cad. (tel. 212 17 22). Take the street to the right of the clock tower and meet Kemal, the amiable manager. A mecca for backpackers of all nationalities, the A/K sells *şiş kebap*, vegetables, and a Coke for under $4 (open in summer 8-2am; in winter 8am-midnight). For a great meal at a reasonable price, also try **İntepe Seyir Yeri Aile Kır Lokantası** (Observation Point Family-Style Country Restaurant; tel. 223 3332), on İzmir Cad. halfway between Çanakkale and Troy (15min. by *dolmuş*). The view of the sunset over the Dardanelles is breathtaking.

SIGHTS

The town has only a smattering of sights. The **archaeological museum,** with artifacts from Troy, a fantastic statue of Hadrian, and busts of Augustus (open Tues.-Wed. and Fri.-Sun. 8:30am-5:30pm; admission $1, with ISIC 50¢). There's also a **fortress** with a vintage World War I cannon and warship to commemorate the Gallipoli battle. **Çimenlik Kalesi** (Grassy Castle), a castle-turned-naval museum, lies 200m past the clock tower (open Tues.-Wed. and Fri.-Sun. 9am-noon and 1:30-5pm; admis-

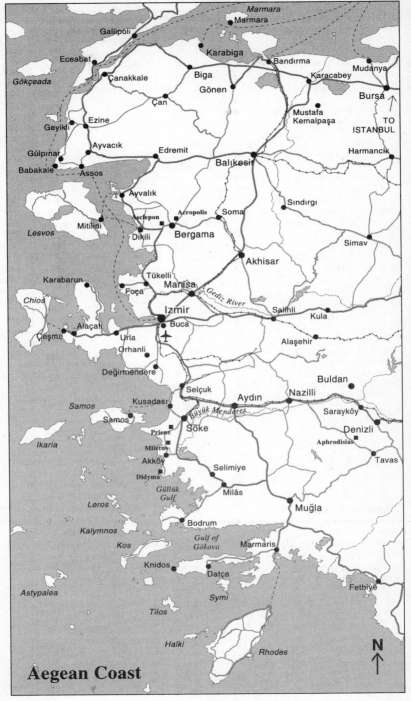

Aegean Coast

N

sion 38¢, students 13¢). As the coast's northernmost resort, Çanakkale faces the narrowest point of the Dardanelles, which in large part explains why the British chose to mount their disastrous WWI campaign here. About 55km southwest of Çanakkale lie the famed waters of the **Kestanbol thermal springs** (tel. 637 5223), reachable by *dolmuş* or taxi via Ezine (buses leave every 2-2½hr.). They boast of the minerals in the waters with special curative powers for people with skin, heart, and circulation problems (open daily 8am-midnight; men $3.75, women $2.50).

■ Near Çanakkale

GELİBOLU (GALLIPOLI)

Across the Dardanelles, on the European side, lies the battlefield of **Gallipoli,** known as Gelibolu in Turkey. In 1915-16, seeing an opportunity to secure the Balkan front, Winston Churchill proposed that Britain use its superior naval forces to launch an attack on the Dardanelles. The navy would then conquer Constantinople, drive Turkey out of the war, and open communications with Russia. The navy was bombarded at the narrowest part of the strait, so the British navy turned its forces to the peninsula. The British high command sent wave after wave of Australian, New Zealander, and British troops against the highly fortified Turkish positions here, with brutal losses. This battle launched its hero, **Atatürk,** on a rapid rise to his status as Turkey's founding father. Each year thousands of Australians and New Zealanders make pilgrimages to war cemeteries here, where 22,000 Allied dead lie buried. There is a special dawn ceremony at the cove.

To explore the battlefields systematically, you can take a guided tour. Relaxed and exceptionally affordable tours come from the newly established **Down Under Travel Agency,** based in nearby Eceabat. $6.90 covers transportation, lunch, and a showing of "Gallipoli." The tour guide T.J., affectionately nicknamed by tourists who likened him to Tom Jones, gives excellent Anglo-Australian language guidance. The **Troyanzac Travel Agency** (not to be confused with Yılmaz Tours) sends tours in summer 10am and 3pm (in winter 10am). If not enough people show up, the tour is sometimes cancelled. Bargain with Hüseyin, the theatrical guide. It is usually cheaper to take a tour than to shuttle around in taxis.

The **Kabatepe Museum** (tel. 814 1297) is accessible by *dolmuş* from Eceabat (open daily 8:30am-noon and 1-5:30pm; admission 63¢, tour groups 38¢) and located in the **National Park** (tel. 814 1128) which is free (open daily 8:30am-5:30pm). The tour path is undoubtedly a moving experience for those who are moved by the courage of the 500,000 soldiers who gave their lives on Gallipoli. From there it's a 4km walk to **Anzac Cove,** and a 7km hike uphill to the serene **Lone Pine Monument,** an Australian memorial. The primary memorial for New Zealanders is located at **Chisnik Bair,** at the highest point of the Gallipoli Peninsula. At this point, it is not accessible by *dolmuş,* but almost all tours stop there.

TROY (TRUVA)

Truva lies 32km south of Çanakkale. The site slept, forgotten, until **Heinrich Schliemann,** a German-born American millionaire-turned-amateur archaeologist, decided to prove that the Homeric myths were not pure fiction. Staking out the most promising site along the coast, he hired local workers and began excavating. To the astonishment of fellow archaeologists, Schliemann uncovered the ancient city.

People raised on stories of the **Trojan War** should not expect imposing ruins; the city Homer wrote about came tumbling down 3000 years ago. But the remaining Bronze Age fortifications, given their age, are remarkably well preserved. The tacky wooden horse that assures you that you've reached Troy is, however, a new addition. Nevertheless, if you are familiar with the Homeric stories of Hector, Paris, and the foxy Helen (whose beauty wreaked havoc), you will get the sensation that these immortalized characters did indeed play out the tragedy on this site. Nine distinct strata, each containing the remains of a city from a different period, have been identified and dubbed Troy I through Troy IX. An illustrated explanation of each stratum is available in the **Excavation House** (on your right after you enter and pass the horse). Troy I dates from 3200 BCE. The city of Homer's *Iliad* is now believed to be Troy VI, *not,* ironically, Troy II, the city Schliemann excavated. Look out for house foundations, city walls, a temple, and a theater, and bring a bottle of water (unless you have a camel-like capacity for water retention) because you'll need it (open daily 8am-7:30pm; off season daily 8am-5pm; admission $1.50, students 75¢).

Take a *dolmuş* (every 30min., 63¢) from the station in Çanakkale, and arrange for the *dolmuş* to wait for an hour or two while you explore the ruins. If you want more time to explore, other *dolmuş* are easy to find. If you must stay, the **Hotel Hisarlık** (tel. 283 1026 or 283 1992), right across the entrance to Troy, rents nice rooms with a hot shower, toilet paper, and a common balcony—but they aren't cheap. 24-hr. hot water. (Singles $15. Doubles with showers $25. Triples with showers $40. MasterCard and Visa accepted.) For some convenient good eating, try **Hisarlık Restaurant,** which covers all the bases in fast food and Turkish cuisine. Not as cheap as in Çanakkale, but when the tummy growls, look across the street from the entrance to Troy.

■ Ayvalık

"Ayva" means "quince" in Turkish, but this town is no haven for quince trees. Rather, Ayvalık's red rooftops and the turquoise waters of the Aegean form a pleasant juxtaposition that lends itself to the ineffable calm of the town. A wealthy Greek settlement until the 1923 exchange of populations, this small fishing village is reminiscent of a Greek town (don't break it to the natives) and it still makes its living from oil-production. A mere 30km from the Greek island of Lesvos, Ayvalık features pleasant beaches and varied seafood. The town is situated in the Gulf of Edremit, and surrounded by 25 outlying islands, pine woods, and olive groves.

ORIENTATION AND PRACTICAL INFORMATION

İnönü Cad., the main road, runs parallel to the coastline and turns into **Atatürk Cad.** after the bazaar area. The other main street is **Sefa Cad.,** which runs parallel to İnönü Cad. and Atatürk Cad. A bus from Çanakkale is $7.50; the ride takes 3½ hours.

Tourist Office: (tel. 312 2753), in Cumhuriyet Meydanı (Republic Square), on the docks, in the center of town. Open daily in summer 9am-1pm and 3-7:15pm.

Tours: Jade Tourism, formerly Ayvalık tours (tel. 312 2740; fax 312 2470), on Gümrük Cad. 41-A, near Kıyı Motel, offers tours of Lesvos (1½hr., $65), Bergama ($15), and nearby islands ($8). An agency of the same name is in Naci Bey Passage (along the seashore). Open in summer daily 8am-10pm; in winter daily 8am-6pm.

Currency Exchange: Günaydın Döviz (tel. 312 1918), across from the Ekonomi Hotel, exchanges currency and cashes traveler's checks. Open daily 9am-6pm.

Buses: *Dolmuş* pass along the highway every 30min. bound for the bus terminal, on İnönü Cad. next to the Türkiye İş Bankası. Easy service to Çanakkale (roughly every hr., 3½hr., $5) and İzmir (roughly every hr., 1½hr., $3.25). Minibuses run to **Sarımsaklı beach** (Garlicky) and **Altınova beach** (golden meadow) every 15min. (40¢), leaving from across the street from the tourist office.

Ferries: To Lesvos (3 per week; $40, not including a steep port tax of 4000dr).

Hospital: Ayvalık Devlet Hastanesı Public Hospital (tel. 312 1744). From PTT, 300m along İnönü Cad, to the left (with your back to the sea).

Police: İnönü Cad. (tel. 312 9500, -01).

PTT: İnönü Cad. (tel. 312 6041). Open 8:30am-11pm. **Traveler's checks** cashed 8:30am-5:30pm. **Postal Code:** 10400.

Telephone Code: 266.

ACCOMMODATIONS

Taksiyarhis Pansiyon, İsmetpaşa Mah., 71 Mareşal Kaçmak Cad.(tel. 312 1494), near Taksiyarhis Church. From Republic Sq., go up the second street across from the PTT. Or ask for directions to the church, about 500m off İnönü Cad. A jewel among Ayvalık's hotels, it's quiet and removed from the hectic tourist scene. 24-hr. hot water. Bike rental $6.25 per day and laundry service available. Singles $5. Doubles $10. Triples $15. Breakfast $2. Call in advance.

El Otel, 25 Talatpaşa Cad. (tel. 312 2217; fax 312 3332), off the main road. Spotless rooms decorated in blue and white for that soothing sensation. 24-hr. hot water, international phone, laundry, TV room, and cozy terrace. Singles $7. Doubles $14. Triples $21. 20% discount for students and groups in off season. Breakfast $2.

Yurtotel (tel. 312 2109), also near İnönü Cad., in Republic Square. Clean-ish rooms with shower. Second-floor terrace has a view of the water. Singles $3.75, with bath $5. Doubles $6.25, with bath $10. Triples with bath $15.

FOOD AND ENTERTAINMENT

Ayvalık may be quiet, but it is blessed with seaside restaurants and quality seafood. **Kardeşler (Brothers) Kebapçı** (tel. 312 18 57) has two branches. The first, 3 blocks inland at 42 İnönü Cad., sits across the street from the Emlak Bankası on İnönü Cad. and serves mainly *kebap* ($2.50) and *pide*. The second, well situated on the sea at 7 Sahil Boyu, offers delectable fish. (Both branches open daily 8am-2am). **Ağzımın Tadısın Sen** (You're the Taste of My Mouth), next to the Ayvalık Palas Hotel (tel. 312 8245) serves up döner, liver, and fried veggies. Tourists also rave about **Dayım Ocakbaşı,** across from the Ekonomi Hotel, which has *kebap* ($2.25-3.75), *pide* ($1.85-2.50), and salad ($1.25). For continental breakfast, pastries, or tea, visit the popular **Okad Cafeteria,** across from the Tourism office along the marina. Seafood lovers go to Alibey where there is a string of fish restaurants.

SIGHTS

Aya Nikola (Çınarlı Camii) boasts beautiful Old and New Testament frescoes (open daily 9am-noon and 1-11pm). Several 19th-century Byzantine churches, that have since been converted into mosques, house many of the city's treasures. The **Taksiyarhis Church** houses portraits painted on fish skins. Another church, on **Alibey Adası** (Sir Ali's Island, connected to Ayvalık via an artificial harbor), has remnants of frescoes on the walls. For a panoramic view of **Sarımsaklı** (one of Turkey's cleanest natural beaches and where some of Turkey's finest artists have summer homes) and of Alibey, visit **Şeytan Sofrası** (the Devil's Dinner Table), which is not a restaurant. From far away, this large rock does look like a table. The myth is that devils congregated here to dine. There is a monstrous footprint at the peak which is said to have been left by the hellraiser himself. Ordinarily, *dolmuş* (30¢) depart at sunset for the best viewing, wait 45 minutes, and then return. However they do not run if there are too few tourists. Sarımsaklı, 6km south of Ayvalık, is a growing, pricey resort town. Although hotels are expensive, the sandy beach is one of the finest in Turkey.

■ Pergamon (Bergama)

Pergamon had once been a dazzling center of cultural activity with one world's richest libraries; the ruins make it one of Turkey's finest archaeological sites. Bring your water bottle, skip the morning cigarette, and climb, climb, climb your way to the sights. Pergamon's archaeological sights, towering 330m above the city, are extensive and impressive, but don't let them distract you from the striking juxtaposition of 150-year-old Greek houses and thousand-year-old ruins in Bergama. The deep-bedded Caicus River flowing through the city adds to Bergama's quiet charm.

ORIENTATION AND PRACTICAL INFORMATION

The ruins of Pergamon are across the river at the pleasant, modern city of **Bergama**. The city's main road winds its way to the ancient ruins. The road, from the new bus station, in the direction of İzmir, is called **İzmir Cad.** From the PTT in the direction of İstiklal Meydanı, it is called **Uzun Çarşı Cad.**, but most people know that by İzmir Cad., you mean the main road.

Tourist Office: (tel. 632 1862), from the new main bus station, go right onto the main road and walk 1km. It's in Cumhuriyet Meydanı, on the left coming from the bus station. If you reach the bust of Atatürk, you've passed it. Open April-Sept. daily 8:30am-7pm; Oct.-March Mon.-Sat. 8:30am-5:30pm.

Buses: Two terminals (*garaj*) serve Bergama. The old terminal (tel. 633 1550), near the Basilica, runs buses to İzmir, İstanbul, Ankara, Bursa, and Soma. The new terminal (tel. 633 1545), across from the park on İzmir Cad., runs buses to the same major cities as well as minibuses to Ayvalık. Buses run to Bursa (2 per day, 5½hr., $10), İzmir (every 30min., $1.85), İstanbul (2 per day, 10hr., $15), and Ankara (1 per day running overnight, 10hr., $15). When arriving, try to take a bus that trundles directly into Bergama; most buses from İzmir to Çanakkale drop you at the turn-off 7km away. Frequent *dolmuş* service to town is available (50¢). If you arrive at night, you may have to spend up to $6.25 on a taxi into town. The center of town is to the right as you exit the station.

Hospital: Bergama Devlet Hastanesı (tel. 633 2490, -1099). Walk from the bus station toward the PTT; where the park ends, walk uphill for 2min. and turn right.

Police: (tel. 632 7001), across and up the street from the PTT.

PTT: İzmir Cad. (tel. 632 3996). No English spoken. Offers **currency exchange** during business hours. Open Mon.-Fri. 8:30am-12:30pm and 1:30-5:30pm.

Telephone code: 232.

ACCOMMODATIONS

Pension Athena (tel. 633 3420), in a restored Ottoman house. Their motto, "Not the best, but we're trying to get there," is a charming reflection of the quality of both rooms and ambience. Hidden in the winding road beyond İstiklal Meydanı, this peaceful pension offers 24-hr. hot water, living room cable TV, and a café. Dinner catering to vegetarians $2.50 in July-Sept. Generally $5 per person negotiable. Bathless singles $4.50, with shower $6.50.

Sayın Pension, Zafer Mah., 12 İzmir Cad. (tel. 633 2405 or 1209), near the bus station outside of town. Turn left as you leave the bus station; it's up on the right. Functional rooms but little ambience. Singles $5, with shower $6.25. Breakfast $1.90, dinner $5. Prices negotiable. 25% off for groups of 15 and up. MC/Visa.

Pension Nike, after İstiklal Meydanı walk on the left road and enter the turquoise-blue stone house. Lush flower garden, brightly colored, spacious rooms. Dinner menu available ($3-5). Kind owners offer self-made maps of archaeological sites. Singles $5. Doubles $9.25. Each additional person $4.25. Breakfast $1.90.

Berksoy camping (tel. 633 2595), and **Karavan camping** (tel. 633 3902), lie 2km beyond the tourist office on the main road. Guests have access to electricity, water, a kitchen, and a pool (non-guests may swim for $1).

FOOD AND ENTERTAINMENT

Relax under the shelter of luxuriant vines at **Meydan Restaurant** (tel. 633 1793), on the right side of the main street about 500m after Pergamon Pension as you walk from the station (full meal $4.50; open 7-2am; off season 7am-midnight). **Sağlam İşletmecilik,** 3 İstiklal Meydanı (tel. 633 20 46), off the main road as you veer left to follow the signs to Pension Athena, specializes in spicy southern Turkish food and has fantastic *kaşarlı kiremitte,* a hot dish of eggplant, tomatoes, peppers, onions, cheese, and bread ($2.50; open daily 7am-midnight). Diagonally across the street, **Sarmaşık (Ivy) Lokantası** (tel. 632 27 41), on İzmir Cad., serves great food at reasonable prices (full meal around $4; open 6am-10pm). **Sağlam 3,** near PTT, has delicious *kebap*. Request seating in one of the small authentic Turkish alcoves or the breezy garden. Sample the *baklava* at one of the many *pastane* in the area. Try **Hülya** (tel. 633 2183) or **Manolya** (tel. 633 2583) pastry shops, on Hükümet Cad. near the PTT. They're open until midnight and offer delicious cakes, puddings, and *kurupasta* (salty pastries) for $3-3.75 per kg.

SIGHTS

Pergamon's long history of fame began when Piletarus, a regional commander, seized the treasury he had been entrusted to keep and set himself up as king. Its ruins, loping over more than 30,000 acres, are located on two principal sites: the **Acropolis,** which looms above the town (open daily 8:30am-5:30pm), and the **Asclepion** (medical center) lying in the valley below (open in summer daily 8:30am-7pm, in winter daily 8:30am-5pm; admission 75¢, students 38¢, free with FIYTO). The theater, seating 3500 people, is also breathtaking. Under the direction of Galen, the most famous physician of the Roman Empire, Pergamon became the center of the cult of Asclepius, the Greek demi-god of healing and eponym of the Asclepion, which was both a temple and place of healing. Allegedly, no patient left here unhealed, though undoubtedly many were rushed out the back door in the throes of death. An impressive portion of the Asclepion remains, including a marble colonnade, a theater, and healing rooms. The ruins of a huge gymnasium, a Roman circus and the lavishly frescoed **House of Attalus** also lie scattered about. The most notable attraction is the mammoth **amphitheater,** capable of seating 10,000 spectators.

In ancient times, only the library in Alexandria surpassed Pergamon's, which contained more than 200,000 volumes. When the Alexandrians attempted to eclipse the Pergamon book bonanza by limiting the flow of papyrus from the Nile, Pergamon scholars invented parchment from goat hide. The plot thickened: when the library's Egyptian rival went up in flames, Marc Antony plundered Pergamon's shelves and presented the pilfered collection to Cleopatra. Most of the **Altar of Zeus,** consisting of the remains of a marble offering table, graces the Pergamon Museum—in Berlin. On your way up to the **Royal Palaces,** write down a wish and tie it onto a branch of the "wishing tree" on your left.

There are no buses to the ruins; walk, or, if too much *nargile* (water pipe) smoking has debilitated your lungs, take a taxi ($20 for full tour, $5 to the first site). If you take a taxi it's best to be dropped off at the **Acropolis,** and then to walk down through the rest of the ruins. To reach the Acropolis, follow the main road past the **Kızıl Avlu,** or Red Basilica, which was originally built as a second-century temple to the Egyptian God Serapis and converted into a basilica during the Byzantine Empire. Turn left off the road and walk towards the first ruins, the Lower Agora. Here you'll find a footpath that winds among the ruins to the summit. The hike to the top of the Acropolis can be exhausting, especially on hot days. The **Asclepion** is on the other side of town, 3km past the tourist office. (Do *not* take photos of the military base along the Asclepion; it is illegal, and armed soldiers take this law seriously.) The **Archaeological and Ethnographic Museum** displays artifacts such as earthenware statues (all arranged with full explanations) from Pergamon as well as a collection of traditional Turkish crafts (open daily 8:30am-5:30pm). (The Acropolis, Asclepion, and Basilica are all open May-Sept. daily 8am-7pm, Oct.-April 8:30am-5:30pm. The museum is open year-round 8:30am-5:30pm. Admission to Acropolis, Archaeological Museum, and Basilica $2 each, students $1; free with FIYTO.)

■ İzmir

Of the original Hellenistic city-states along the Aegean coast of Asia Minor, only **Smyrna,** now Turkish **İzmir,** survived the catastrophes that befell the region. From the rubble of Smyrna's past, İzmir (population 2 million) has risen to become Turkey's third largest city and second largest port. Now a western city with wide boulevards and plazas around an arc-shaped waterfront, İzmir is a sticky industrial

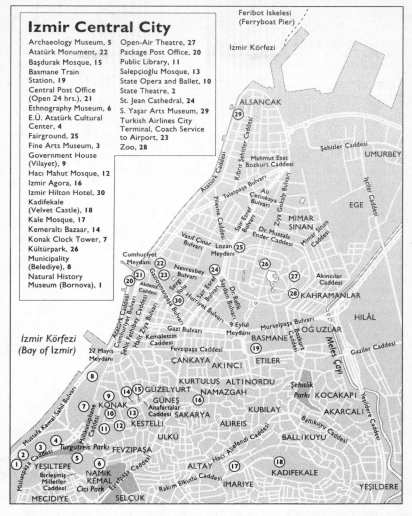

İzmir Central City

Archaeology Museum, 5
Atatürk Monument, 22
Başdurak Mosque, 15
Basmane Train
Station, 19
Central Post Office
(Open 24 hrs.), 21
Ethnography Museum, 6
E.Ü. Atatürk Cultural
Center, 4
Fairground, 25
Fine Arts Museum, 3
Government House
(Vilayet), 9
Hacı Mahut Mosque, 12
İzmir Agora, 16
İzmir Hilton Hotel, 30
Kadifekale
(Velvet Castle), 18
Kale Mosque, 17
Kemeraltı Bazaar, 14
Konak Clock Tower, 7
Kültürpark, 26
Municipality
(Belediye), 8
Natural History
Museum (Bornova), 1

Open-Air Theatre, 27
Package Post Office, 20
Public Library, 11
Salepçioğlu Mosque, 13
State Opera and Ballet, 10
State Theatre, 2
St. Jean Cathedral, 24
S. Yaşar Arts Museum, 29
Turkish Airlines City
Terminal, Coach Service
to Airport, 23
Zoo, 28

wasteland in some places and fascinatingly lush in others, earning the name "Beautiful İzmir" in Turkish. A stroll through the twisting alleyways in one of İzmir's residential districts may be enchanting, but the exhaust fumes on the major boulevards will surely put to rest any thoughts you may have of a Turkish wonderland.

Smyrna first came into its own in the 9th century BCE and thrived before Lydians from Sardis destroyed the town in 600 BCE. In 334 BCE, Alexander the Great conquered and then refounded Smyrna atop Mt. Pagus, now called the Kadifekale. During the Roman and Byzantine periods, the port of Smyrna grew prosperous and cosmopolitan. The diversion of the River Hermes prevented Smyrna's harbor from silting, thereby rescuing it from the landlocked fate of its neighbors. In 1535, Süleyman the Magnificent signed a treaty with France that brought trade to Smyrna. The constant influx of Christian and Jewish merchants during this time earned the city the moniker "Infidel Smyrna." After World War I, Greece, enticed by the vision of a born-again Byzantine Empire, attacked Turkey. Mustafa Kemal, soon to be Kemal

Atatürk, expelled the invaders with an impromptu army and regained the ashes of Smyrna in the final battle of the Turkish War of Independence on Sept. 9, 1922.

ORIENTATION AND PRACTICAL INFORMATION

İzmir's principal boulevards radiate from rotaries, called *meydan*. **Cumhuriyet Meydanı,** on the waterfront, is the city's financial center, home to several banks, travel agencies, and consulates. An astounding number of budget hotels and cheap restaurants, along with several bus company offices and the Alsançak **train station,** are located around **9 Eylül Meydanı,** the center of the Basmane district. From **Yeni Garaj,** the bus station, take municipal bus #50, 53, 56, 249, 250, or 260 to Basmane/Çankaya. Remember to buy your tickets (70¢) at the kiosk before you board. To get back to the bus station, take a bus from Basmane to **Konak Square** (3 stops, Konak being the last), from which you can take bus #50, 56, or 60 to Yeni Garaj. Konak, 10 blocks south of Cumhuriyet Meydanı along the coastal **Atatürk Cad.,** is the center for metropolitan buses and *dolmuş*. Finding your way can be difficult, and street signs are hard to come by, so it's best to make the tourist office your first stop.

Tourist Office: 1/1c Gaziosmanpaşa Blv. (tel. 484 2147; fax. 489 9278), near the Hilton Hotel. In early 1997, the tourism office is moving to Atatürk Cad. Eski Kolı Binası (same tel.). Take the 169 Alsancak or 211 Konak-Karşıyaka/Konak/Konak-Bornova bus to Balık Halı stop, and look across the street for your salvation. Open Mon.-Fri. 8:30am-7pm, Sat.-Sun. 9am-5pm; reduced hours in off season. Small tourist information in the **bus station.** Open daily 8am-noon and 12:30-8pm.
Tourist Police: Call 421 1476 or 422 3461.
Travel Agencies: There are so many travel agencies on Gaziosmanpaşa Blvd. that the signs will throw you for a loop. But have no fear: there are two agencies recommended by tourists and locals alike. **Ramtur,** 3/312 Gaziosmanpaşa Blvd. (tel. 425 2710; fax 483 3436; e-mail orale@cakabey.ege.edu.tr), Yenı Asır İşhani. Don't be intimidated by the signs you see in the entrance; you can go right up to the third floor. **Opal Travel Agency,** 1 Gazi Osmanpaşa Blvd. (tel. 445 67 67; fax 489 88 65). Both offer reliable daily tours to Efes, Bergama, and Pamukkale. Opal specializes in international tours. Both open daily 9am-6pm.
Consulates: Turkish-American Association, 23 Şehit Nevres Blv. (tel. 421 8873), open in summer Mon.-Fri. 9am-noon and 1-6pm, Sat. 9am-1:30pm; in winter Mon.-Fri. 9am-noon and 1-6pm. Performs duties of the **American and British Consulate,** #49 1442 Sok., Alsançak (tel. 463 5151), near the main train station.
American Express: Shares office space with **Pamfilya Turizm,** 270 Atatürk Cad. (tel. 422 4753). Open Mon.-Fri. 8:30am-5:30pm.
Buses: To İstanbul (every 30min., 9hr., $15), Bursa (5hr., $7.50), Çanakkale (5hr., $8.75), Bodrum (4hr., $6.25), Kuşadası (2hr., $2.50), Selçuk (1hr., $2.50), and Ankara (8hr., $15) to name a few. Buses to Sardis (Sart), 95km from İzmir, also depart from Yeni Garaj; take the bus to Salihli and ask to be let off at Sardis. **Pamukkale** (tel. 462 1011), which has the most frequent bus departures, has a central office in İzmir in the Otogar. For buses to Çeşme and other points west, go to the bus lot at **Üçkuyular,** southwest of the center. From Basmane, take a public bus to Konak, then take #4, 216, 217, 245, or 276. Ask where to get off (accomplished by saying *"Burası Üçkuyular mı?"* to the person next to you). From Yeni Garaj, take bus #249 or 250 directly to Üçkuyular. Buses run to Çeşme (every 30min. 6am-8pm). The bus companies and travel agencies near the tourist office often have shuttles to both bus stations.
Ferries: One ferry per week goes to İstanbul (Sun., 19hr., $15 and up).
Hospitals: Alsancak Devlet Hastanesı Public Hospital (tel. 463 64 65), on Talatpaşa Blvd., Alsancak. Also, **Yeşılyurt Devlet Hastanesı Public Hospital** (tel. 243 4343), Gazeteci Hasan Tahsin Cad., Yeşılyurt.
Medical Emergency: Call 112.
Police: Dial 155 (special "foreigners" department of the police at 482 2253, -1).

PTT: In Cumhuriyet Meydanı. Full phone facilities (open 24-hr.) and **traveler's check** and **currency exchange** services. Open 8:30am-5:30pm.
Postal code: 35
Telephone code: 232.

ACCOMMODATIONS

Look in the Basmane area—the small streets between Fevzipaşa Bulvarı and Anafartalar Caddesi are loaded with cheap hotels, but you should probably steer clear of the really cheap ones because most are located in unsafe areas. The cluster of hotels in Basmane are slightly more expensive, but the extra buck will probably be worth keeping your peace of mind and your wallet intact. Beware of taxi drivers in İzmir: some work on commission and insist on driving you to hotels of *their* choice. Hotels here exemplify the credo that "you get what you pay for."

Otel Divan, 61 1369 Sok (tel. 483 3675; fax 483 2243), most rooms, painted blue and white, have TV, bath, shower, a phone, and 24-hr. hot water, and comfy beds. Makeshift garden is quiet and breezy. Communal TV room, too. Singles, with access to communal bath, $5. Doubles $10. Triples $15.

Güzel İzmir Oteli, #8 1368 Sok. (tel. 483 5069), around the corner from Otel Divan. In the heart of the commercial district. Luggage room, TV salon, and (a rare find) a public phone in the lobby. Spotless bathrooms. Singles $5, with shower $8. Doubles $8, with shower $13. Triples with shower $18.

Bilen Palas Otel, #68 1369 Sok. (tel. 483 9246), right off 9 Eylül Meydanı. Spacious and clean, with decent views and helpful owners; unfortunately, it also has Turkish-style "pit" toilets, so stretch before you squat here. Large TV room, too. All rooms have showers. Singles $5. Doubles $8. Triples $12.

FOOD AND ENTERTAINMENT

Since you're in Basmane, you might as well try **Basmane Kebap Salonu,** 1571A Fevzipaşa Blv. (tel. 425 5019). Fevzipaşa Blv. is the street that dead-ends into the train station. A small, tidy place, the Salon serves full meals for about $5 (open daily 11am-midnight). The **9 Eylül Meydanı Restaurant** (tel. 445 0531) is jammed by locals at mealtime (mixed plate and Coke $2.50). Also, meat lovers can eat at the **Kardelen Et Lokantası,** of pink chairs and curtained fame, which serves up yummy *pide* and *şiş* dishes ($1.50-2). For a more upscale, trendy ambience, dine at the fantastic **Café Reci's,** 31/A 1382 Sokak, or Gül Sokak (tel. 463 8470), in the ritziest part of Alsancak. Amid a forum of high-fashion Eurostores, you'll find a classy decor and reasonably priced salads ($3) and omelettes ($3). Sample from their scrumptious desserts ($1.50) and just walk it off later (no regrets, baby). Chocolate lovers reach for the hot chocolate cake—it's heavenly (open daily until midnight). At night, **Alsancak** is İzmir's pumpin' place to be. **Club 33** has a humongous dance floor; admission is selective, so dress up (cover charge $10).

SIGHTS

İzmir's **agora,** or marketplace, was built in the 4th century BCE by Alexander, destroyed by an earthquake in 178CE, and rebuilt by Emperor Marcus Aurelius soon after. The uninspiring remains are accessible from Anafartalar Cad. Walk south along 941 Sok. from the Otel Saray (open daily 8:30am-5:30pm; admission $1, students 50¢, free with FIYTO/ISIC). Above the city at Mt. Pagus is the most enduring of Alexander's legacies, the **Kadifekale,** originally built in the 4th century BCE but repeatedly restored and altered by various conquerors (open 24hr.; free). The park within the walls of Kadifekale is at once vaguely unsavory and intriguing. The area may be unsafe after dark, so you might want to visit during the day. Bus #33 from Konak ascends the mountain and offers a thrilling panorama of the bay. If you stroll along Anafartalar Cad. from its beginning at the Basmane station, you'll pass remnants of a less industrialized Turkey—*çay salonu* (teahouses), men smoking *nargile* (water pipes), children and vendors filling the air with their cries, and colorful streets that eventually turn into İzmir's full-fledged **bazaar** (open Mon.-Sat. 8:30am-

ÇEŞME

7pm). İzmir's **archaeological museum,** near Konak Sq., displays the statues of Poseidon and Demeter among other antiquities (open Tues.-Sun. 8:30am-5:30pm; admission $2, students $1). Next door, there is an **Ethnographical Museum** which has folkloric items, including kilims and traditional costumes (open Tues.-Sun. 8:30am-5:30pm; admission $1, students 50¢, free with FIYTO/ISIC). İzmir's cosmopolitan character emerges most impressively in its cultural events. The annual highlight, the **international festival** in late June and early July, brings classical and folk music concerts to İzmir, Çeşme, and Ephesus (tickets $6-10, depending on the event).

■ Near İzmir: Sardis (Sart)

Sardis was the capital of the Lydian Empire, dominant over Aegean Ionia from 680-547 BCE. The Lydians embraced and embellished the existing Hellenic culture, providing the world with dice, balls, and coin minting. The expression "rich as Croesus" refers to the Lydian King Croesus, once the wealthiest man in the world. When he consulted the oracle at Delphi, it prophesied that if he crossed the River Halys, a powerful empire would be destroyed. Eager to fulfill the prophecy, Croesus promptly rushed his troops across the river, where the Persians trounced him.

Visit Sardis easily from İzmir, or make an ambitious daytrip from Kuşadası. Take one of the frequent **buses** to **Salihli** and ask to be let off at Sardis, or Sart in modern Turkish parlance (every 30min., 1½hr., $1.75). Buses leave from the eastern end of the İzmir train station (away from the bus company booths) and drop you off on the highway amid a few teahouses. Most of the ancient city occupies the left side of the highway, 100m from the bus stop. Trains between İzmir and Sart take three hours.

The entrance to the ruins leads to the **Marble Way,** lined by a row of **Byzantine shops.** From the end of the Marble Way, turn left to enter the **synagogue,** which houses splendid mosaic floors from the third century CE. The imposing columns of the **gymnasium**, which affirms the historic grandeur of this ancient city, shadow a **swimming pool** where fuming Lydians once cooled themselves. Go up the street that slips between two teahouses on the other side of the road, and follow it 1km uphill to the **Temple of Artemis.** Alexander the Great commissioned this temple, one of the largest in antiquity. Only a few columns remain, but their scrolled capitals are exquisite. Along the way to the temple, you'll pass an ancient Lydian gold refinery and a dome from a 12th-century Byzantine basilica built atop a 5th-century church (ruins open sunrise-sunset; admission $2).

■ Çeşme

Çeşme, a breezy seaside village, is centered around a 14th-century Genoese fortress, which was expanded and beautified by 16th-century Ottomans. Only one hour west of İzmir, Çeşme has deservedly gained popularity among tourists for its cool climate, peaceful beaches with crystal clear water, friendly locals, and proximity to the Greek island of Chios and to the Aegean. The nightlife in the discoes and café/bars along the marina is festive. Nearby Ilıca is popular for its fancy thermal centers, yachting opportunities, and friendly (although ritzy) natives.

Orientation and Practical Information From the bus stop, continue down the main road to the water for the main **tourist office,** 8 İskele Meydanı (tel./fax 712 6653; open Mon.-Fri. 8:30am-7:30pm, Sat.-Sun. 9am-5pm, reduced hours in off season). In Çeşme, the bus stops next to a private **accommodations service** (open in summer daily 8am-10pm), but the rooms they find are not necessarily the cheapest available. Continuing to the right along the shore you'll find the **PTT** (open daily June-Sept. 8am-midnight, Oct.-May 8am-8pm). For the **bus station,** walk 300m in the opposite direction from the tourist office and turn left before the small bridge. Buses, which are particularly crowded on weekends, leave roughly every half hour from the Üçkuyular bus lot in İzmir (see İzmir, p. 484). The last bus to İzmir is at 9pm (6pm in winter, $1.25), but late buses are often booked. You can reserve your seat at the bus station. A boat links Çeşme and Chios (1hr.). **Ertürk Fer-**

ryboat (tel. 712 6768), 6/7 Beyazıt Cad., near Kale, goes (July-Sept. daily; May-June 3-4 per week; one way $25, same-day return $30, open roundtrip $35). Port tax is 4000dr, not applicable to daily tours. Next door to the tourist office is the **police** station (tel. 712 6627). **Postal Code:** 35930. **Telephone Code:** 232.

Accommodations Çeşme abounds with pensions, most of which charge roughly $15 for doubles in high season. Several rooms cluster along Bağlar Sok., which runs diagonally inland south from the tourist office, and along Müftü Sok., which intersects it on the left. Ask at the tourist office for directions to rooms. The family-run **Adil Pansiyon** (tel. 712 7447), located in a quiet, beautiful area, offers spacious rooms with comfortable beds and new furniture. None of the management, however, speaks much English. All rooms have toilets, showers, and 24-hour hot water. ($10 per person, negotiable. Breakfast and laundry, each $1.50. Lodgers have access to the kitchen.) **Aras Pension** (tel. 712 7375), by the bus station, has been voted Çeşme's best pension three times and they're excited about this, judging from the display upon entry. But, it's still easy to see why—clean, light rooms with toilets, showers, and marble-like floors. It is a little out of the way, however, and the views are not spectacular. (Singles and doubles $19. Triples $25. Breakfast included.)

Closer to the castle and the tourist office, **Tarhan Pension,** Musalla Mah. 9 Çarşı Sok. (tel. 712 6599), is clean and even has marble floors. Each room has small table and chair, and the terrace seating is cozy. (Singles $9.35. Doubles $19. Triples $22.50. Breakfast included.) Next door is **Tani Pansiyon,** Musalla Mah., 5 Çarşı Sok. (tel. 712 6238), which is a small, sweet (like Turkish delight) family-run establishment. Communal bathrooms and sparkling kitchen; excellent view from the terrace. (Singles $7.50. Doubles $11.25. Triples $13.80. Breakfast $2.) Like most of the pensions in Çeşme, the nearby **Alim Pansiyon** (tel. 712 7828; fax 712 8319) is a bit pricey but very comfortable. Half the rooms have balconies that overlook a small orchard. All rooms have 2 beds as well as private bath, so singles may be unavailable in high season, but it's ideal for families. (Singles $10. Doubles $15. Triples $25. Breakfast included.) A few **campsites** dot the peninsula: the **V-Kamp** (tel. 727 2224), in Paşalimanı, for example. **Tursite Camping** (tel. 722 1221), near Altınkum in Başvuru, has a motel, bar, and private beach (camping $5 per person; caravans with electricity $8 a day for 2 people). Freelance camping is forbidden.

Food and Entertainment Numerous restaurants border the seaside at the center of town. Sample the delicious *İskender kebap* at **Sahil Café and Restaurant,** on the seashore about 300m towards the town center from the tourist office (*kebap*, salad, and cola $5). The **Körfez Restaurant, Bar, and Disco,** 12 Yalı Cad. (tel. 712 0191), on the shore about 400m toward the town center from the tourist office, is the pulse of the city's nightlife. During the day, Körfez serves pizza, hamburgers, and hot dogs, but at 10pm the eatery subsides to a pulsating disco that grooves until the wee hours of the morning ($1.50 cover charge; lunch about $5; cocktails $3.15-5). Closer to the tourism office, a few meters from the marina, is the colorful **Flamingo Café and Restaurant,** which offers a 10% discount for parties larger than 5, so make nicy-nice with fellow travelers and hop on over. Conveniently located across the street from Kaihan and Tanı Pensions, this joint has a breakfast menu and daily specials (full meal $6) and is cheaper than the seaside eateries.

Head to **Ilıca** (*dolmuş* from the tourist office in Çeşme are frequent) for some revelry. Located along the Çeşme-Ilıca highway (you can walk there from the bus stop, but it's safer to take a taxi at night), **Disco 10,** on Altınyunus Yol, is said to fill up most nights of the summer. **Club Biber** (Pepper Club), near Altınyunus, cards, so have your 18+ ID handy; they are selective, so it also helps to go with an "escort" or in a group. Cover charges range from $7-10, depending on club and night. Catch a *dolmuş* in front of the tourist office. If you left your dancing shoes at home, sip beer in the **cafés** lining Çeşme's harbor.

Sights The **castle** across from the tourist office was built in 1508 by Ottoman Sultan Beyazıt II for spying on Chios, 11km away. It now houses a tiny, one-room museum (open Tues.-Sun. 8:30am-noon and 1-5:30pm; admission $1.50, students 75¢). **Beaches** nearby include **Erythrai, Ildırı, Ilıca,** and **Altınkum.** Ilıca offers hot springs called Yıldız Burnu (where you can take surfing lessons), as does Sifne, where there is a resort. Alaçatı also has windsurfing schools. From the tourist office, a *dolmuş* runs to Ilıca and Alaçatı, another to Ildırı and the ancient Ionian village of Erythrai. In Çeşme, **Beyalık Plajı** (beach) is a 10-minute walk from the center, and the Kerman Hotel has a bantam beach to the far right of the waterfront. *Dolmuş* travel around the peninsula until 11pm with routes to Ilıca (6km, 50¢), Altınkum (until 8pm, 10km, 75¢), and south along the beach (5km). Trips to **Donkey Island** (Eşek Adası) cost $15 and up, including lunch.

■ Kuşadası

When luxury cruise liners and daytrippers from nearby Samos began adding Kuşadası to their Greek island itineraries, the resourceful fisherfolk and farmers of this formerly somnolent town found ways to bait better business and nurture profit. In summer, Kuşadası seems a bit out of control as its population quintuples. In the evenings, what seems like a thousand bars fuel a frenetic nightlife. Kuşadası may seem like tourism run amok, but its popularity is deserved; this coastal center is one of the best places from which to visit the Aegean Basin's most luminous classical sites—Ephesus, Priene, Miletus, and Didyma.

ORIENTATION AND PRACTICAL INFORMATION

Most visitors to Kuşadası arrive by boat in the harbor. It is best to pay the port tax ($10) in U.S. dollars to avoid station commissions and weak exchange rates. When disembarking, beware of the hustlers who will try to lure you to their "bargain" rooms and then present you with a much higher price.

The harbor master, the duty-free shop, the fish market, the passport police and the customs office are all in the port area. The bus station is about 2km east of the town center and frequent *dolmuş* connect it with İzmir (2hr.). *Dolmuş* also arrive from Selçuk and nearby smaller towns at a separate *dolmuş* stop about 1½km from the **Information Office** (tel. 614 1103) in the port on Iskele Meydanı. There's only one such official office; other booths marked "Information" provide information only about their own excursions. In the skyline, beyond the tourist office, are the turreted walls of an ancient Seljuk *kervansaray* (now a hotel) where itinerant merchants could once spend a night with their goods protected. The structure's turrets make a good orientation point. Facing the Kervansaray, **Yalı Cad.** runs right and uphill, passing through a covered bazaar. Continue up the hill to where **Aslanlar Cad.** intersects; in both directions, you'll find many cheap pensions. Left of the **Kervansaray Hotel** is the broad, pedestrian-only **Barbaros Hayrettin.** The **PTT, travel agencies,** and **banks** are also there. At the end of the street is a cubist medieval watchtower turned modern-day police station. Through the watchtower and along **Kahramanlar Cad.,** you'll reach the major artery out of town and, within a kilometer, the bus station. **Atatürk Blv.,** parallel to the coastline, exists so that the denizens of Kuşadası have a place to cruise their mopeds and build their luxury hotels. Perhaps the most practical information about Kuşadası is that if prices for anything are unlisted, you will most certainly be overcharged. Don't hesitate to bargain.

Tourist Office: (tel. 614 1103; fax 614 62 95), on İskele Meydanı in the port. The tourist office, 20m beyond the gangway, is conveniently positioned for those disembarking from a cruise liner. To get there from the bus station, it's best to take a taxi, but if you want to walk, direct your ox-strong legs out of the station to the right, staying on the left side of the street so that you can take the left fork on to **Kahramanlar Cad.** Follow this street to the water (it changes names to **Barbaros Blv.**). The tourist office, which offers listings of campgrounds, bus schedules, maps, and non-budget hotels, is around the corner to the left. Open Mon.-Fri. 8am-6pm, Sat.-Sun. 8am-noon and 1:30-5:30pm; reduced hours in off season.

Tourist Police: (tel. 614 1022), in the watchtower. English-speaking staff is helpful.

Budget Travel: Ekol Travel, with **WorldSpan,** Kibris Cad., Buyral Sok 9/1 (tel. 614 9255 or 614 5591; fax 614 2644). Cheap flights, ferry tickets, temporary baggage storage, room finding, message board, car rentals, and emergency help. Will bend over backwards to assist you; also to sell you *something*. English spoken. 15% discount on ferry tickets with *Let's Go*. Daily cruises (or "picnic boat tours") in 14m boat along the shore. Car rental, English-speaking doctors, and travel insurance available. Free legal advice. Open May-Nov. daily 8:30am-10pm; Dec.-April daily 8:30am-5:30pm.

Banks: Booths on the waterfront offer **currency exchange.** Open daily 8am-10pm. **ATM** access daily 9am-11pm.

Buses: Erbirlik Tourism (tel. 614 9570) to İzmir (every 30min., 2hr., $3.75, Denizli (4 per day, 3 in winter, $6.25); İstanbul (4 per day, $17.50); Pamukkale (4 per day, 4½hr., $7.50); Bodrum (5 per day, 3hr., $5); and Ankara (4 per day, $15). No connections to Pamukkale or Bodrum in off season. For Pamukkale, take the bus leaving from Denizli. For Bodrum, take the one departing from Söke. The bus line **Hakiki Koç** (tel. 614 5544) offers *Let's Go* readers a 20% discount.

Dolmuş: Depart from the corner of Adnan Menderes Cad. and Canadan Tehran Cad. to Ephesus, Selçuk, Söke, or Aydın (every 30min., 7am-8pm). Less frequent service to neighboring villages, including Davutlar and Güzelcamlı. *Dolmuş* run roughly every 15min. from the bus station through town and **Kadınlar Plajı** (Beach of Women). For Priene, Miletus, or Didyma, make connections in Söke.

Ferries: One way ferry fares to Samos, Greece, are fixed by the government at rates 25% higher on the Turkish side. ($32, same-day roundtrip $37, open roundtrip $60.) **Ekol Travel** undercuts the official rate. ($30, same-day round-trip $35, open round-trip $55.) Flash *Let's Go* and ask for your 15% discount. Port taxes ($10) are included in the price of the ticket for the country in which it was bought. Turkish boats leave daily in summer at 8:30am, returning at 5pm; off season, ferries run only when boats fill to capacity (roughly 2 per week). From Greece, you're permitted to take only a Greek boat. For the morning ferry, you must buy a ticket and show your passport at a travel agency at least 30min. before. (see page 344.)

Rentals: Toya-Sun Rent-A-Car, 60 Atatürk Blv. (tel. 614 6849). Scooters, cars, and sexy jeeps ($30, $65, and $90 per day, respectively, but prices vary in direct relationship with the sexiness of the vehicle). International driver's license required, plus 2-yr. experience with license for cars and jeeps. All-insured unlimited mileage. Must be 18 to rent scooter; no license required.

Bookstore: Kuydaş Kitabevi, 8/B İnönü Blv. (tel. 614 1828), sells newspapers, magazines, guidebooks, and pulp novels. Open daily 7am-midnight. For cheaper stuff, you can try **Art Kitabevi** 57 Sağlık Cad. (tel. 614 6454), near the PTT, which has a small but intriguing used book collection. Open until 12:30am.

Hospital: Kuşadası Devlet Hastanesi Public Hospital, Atatürk Blv. (tel. 614 1026 or 614 1614; fax 612 2438), on the waterfront at the northern edge of town.

Police: (tel. 614 5350), on Hükümet Cad. Finds translators in emergencies.

PTT: (tel. 614 1212 or 614 1034), next to the *kervansaray*, halfway up Barbaros Hayrettin. Services open daily 7am-midnight. **Telephones** available 24-hr.

Postal code: 09400

Telephone Code: 256.

ACCOMMODATIONS

Finding a room is rarely a problem, and pensions, like those which line smaller streets like Aslanlar Cad., are generally the cheapest. The high season rates listed here can often be haggled down. Women should avoid some of the cheaper places.

Hülya Pension, 39 İleri Sok. (tel. 614 2075), just up the street from Hotel Rose. Clean, well lit, and comfortable. Communal kitchen. Rooms are spartan, but enclose a lovely, breezy garden upstairs. Tickets to Pamukkale and Efes sold here. Doubles $8, with shower $10. Triples $12, with shower $15. Breakfast $1.50. Excellent more-than-you-can-eat Turkish dinner $3.

Hotel Rose (Salman's Pension), 7 Aslanlar Cad. (tel. 612 2588; fax 614 1113). Salman (a.k.a. Sammy) Kurt will offer you all sorts of deals on shopping and travel. Half-price Turkish baths. Comfortable rooms, sociable atmosphere, graffiti-decorated bar and lounge, international telephone, book exchange, 24-hr. hot water, laundry ($1.50 per kg), and roof terrace for dining. Popular with backpackers. *Let's Go* gets you a 15% discount. Roof $2.50. Dorm beds $4.25. Private rooms $5.75 per person (most with shower). Breakfast $1.50, dinner $4.25.

Park Pension, 17 Aslanlar Cad., before Hotel Ada, (tel. 614 3917, 612 6912). Colorful, unique rooms, some with spectacular space and furniture—superior comfort. Some smaller doubles: call in advance to snag a good room. Upstairs garden with sunbeds, and in-house restaurant. Friendly management. Bed and breakfast $5.

Camping: Önder (tel. 614 2413) and **Yat Camping** (tel. 614 1333), 2km north of town on Atatürk Blv. Take a Selçuk *dolmuş* or walk. Both have good facilities, including laundry ($2.50 per load) and swimming pools. Both campsites cost $2.50 per person and are open all year, but attached restaurants and rooms close during the winter. Tents are $1.50 (Önder) or $2 (Yat) extra, and neither rents them out. Both charge $2.50 for caravans, $1.25 for cars, and $1.25 for electricity.

FOOD AND ENTERTAINMENT

The countless small restaurants in Kuşadası differ only in the extent to which they overcharge tourists. A good way to gauge is by the price of the *şiş kebap:* anything more than $3.50 is a rip-off. There are many cheap, decent joints along Kahramanlar Cad. and its alley tributaries. If you want to meet backpackers, try Pub Lane, where the nectar rarely stops flowing. Sammy, the owner of Hotel Rose, owns a **kebap house** (tel. 612 6042), down the street from his hotel (*kebap* $1.50). Run by his wife, Hatiçe, it serves free tea and provides a 10% discount to *Let's Go* readers and to guests (open daily 8am-midnight). Waterfront eating is expensive, but the **Güvercinada Cafeteria** on **Pigeon Island** is a reasonable option. High on the rocks, it absorbs glorious sunsets and features hot *pide* ($2) and Italian pizza ($4), as well as *döner kebap* ($4) and other dishes. Lovely tea gardens flourish above (open 8am-midnight, sometimes until 3:30am). Breezy, pastel-colored environment and friendly, young service at **Café de Temple,** across from Kervansaray Hotel, offers pizza ($3.75), sandwiches ($2.50-3.75), and salads ($3.75) for reasonable prices. Next door is **Black and White,** a classy fast food joint with similar prices.

The **Grand Bazaar** and **Barbaros Hayrettin** are among the most expensive shopping infernos in the country. Nonetheless, it doesn't cost anything to browse. Connected by a slender causeway to Kuşadası, the picturesque Pigeon Island is a tiny fortified islet on which cooing tourists have replaced the birds. (Kuşadası literally means "bird island;" Güvercinada, "pigeon island.") Three kilometers beyond Pigeon Island (*dolmuş* 50¢), **Kadınlar Plajı** is a slightly better place to take in the sun than the meager beaches that line the coast in either direction, but it's usually crowded. Vastly superior are sandy **Karovaplajı** and **Yavansu Plajı;** take any *dolmuş* marked "Davutlar" for roughly 7km. Better yet, take a *dolmuş* marked "Güzelcamlı" and "Milli Park" to the National Park, just south of Kuşadası. The best **beach** is at the end of the *dolmuş* line. Meander down to the far end and scale some rocks to find a strip of sand all to yourself. Be careful; the rocks may be slippery.

Kuşadası is teeming with clubs, as new nightlife refuges open frequently to accommodate the exponentially increasing population of the island. Local and tourist favorites are **Club 33,** across from Güvercinada, with the word "discotheque" sprawled across it (another popular branch exists in İzmir) and the slightly larger, more eclectic **The Temple Club,** where concerts are occasionally held. Cover charge for both is $10.

■ Ephesus (Efes)

For a wholesale archaeological fix, search no farther than Ephesus. The findings here are not just your standard ancient heap, but the remains of one of the more important cities of the Roman Empire. The ruins from the Roman and early Christian era are so extensive and well preserved that one need not struggle to imagine the daily interaction of the 250,000 people who lived here nearly two millennia ago. As a strategic coastal gateway to the Eastern world, this Ionian refuge grew to be the second largest city in the Roman Empire, site of a Christian shrine, and one of the seven (or so) wonders of the ancient world.

HISTORY

The origins of Ephesus are shrouded in myth. Legend has it that the city was founded in a manner prescribed by the Delphic Oracle, which foretold that the appropriate site would be disclosed by a fish and a wild boar. The city's location had to be changed several times due to the continual recession of the harbor waters. Today, the ruins of the ancient port lie 10km inland from the coast.

Ephesians were reluctant to move, particularly because they sought to remain near the colossal city-protectress' shrine, the **Temple of Artemis**. The pioneer budget traveler Pausanias deemed this structure the "most wondrous of the seven ancient wonders" and "the most beautiful work ever created by humankind." The first major structure built entirely of marble and the largest edifice in the ancient Greek world, the Temple of Artemis was four times as big as the Parthenon in Athens. Remarkably, this massive monument was actually built twice. The temple was set afire during the reign of Mad King Hesostratos in 356 BCE on the night of Alexander the Great's birth. According to legend, the pyro Erostratus succeeded only because Artemis—watching over Alexander's birth at the time—was absent. Fittingly, Alexander himself restored the temple to its original dimensions and aura. Offerings by hundreds of thousands of pilgrims each year enabled the temple to grow so wealthy that it became the world's first bank. Today, little remains of the magnificent structure. Plundering Goths sacked the sanctuary in the 3rd century CE, followed by the Byzantines. You can see some of the original columns at the Ayasofya in İstanbul (see İstanbul, p. 444).

Ephesus reached its zenith after 129 BCE when the Romans established the province of Asia with Ephesus as the capital. It was second only to Alexandria in population, with more than 250,000 inhabitants. The ruins one sees today date primarily from this period. Saint Paul, recognizing the significance of the metropolis, arrived in 50 CE and converted a small group of Ephesians to the new religion. Some perceived this development of Christianity as a threat to the glory of Cybele (mother goddess of Anatolia) and Artemis, and forced Paul and his followers to depart. Ephesus, however, eventually became the center of Christianity in the Roman Empire.

Heraclitus of Ephesus, commenting on the ephemeral nature of life, remarked that one can never step into the same river twice. If you do, he said, you will drown in misfortune. This wisdom proved prescient. As the neighboring river Cayster emptied into the Aegean, it choked Ephesus's harbor with silt, transforming it into a marshy morass. By the 6th century CE, the recession of the sea had sealed the city's fate. The swamps became infested with malaria-carrying mosquitoes, which in turn triggered a tremendous epidemic that resulted in over 200,000 deaths.

ORIENTATION AND PRACTICAL INFORMATION

Disregard ominous signs at the travel agencies on Samos and in Kuşadası which insist that guided tours of Ephesus are "highly recommended." The tours are expensive (about $25 per day), and guides tend to rush you through the 2000-acre site (open daily 8am-6pm; admission to site $4.75, students with ISIC $2.40). The admission booth (tel. 892 6402) is helpful if you want to hire a guide beforehand. You can visit on your own with the aid of a good guidebook to Ephesus. One can be found for about $5 in Kuşadası's souvenir shops or at the entrance to the site. Bring a water bottle—it gets toasty, and the refreshment stands at the site shamelessly overcharge.

To get to Ephesus from the Kuşadası bus station, take a *dolmuş* to Selçuk, and tell the driver you want to get off at Ephesus. From the Selçuk train station, take any *dolmuş* towards Kuşadası. It should drop you at the Tusan Motel (the first Tusan, of which there are two). Walk 1km uphill along a narrow road to the main Ephesus gate, where you pay admission. Once inside, you can latch onto one of the many tours in your mother tongue. Next to the entrance are **toilets** (13¢), a **post office** with orphaned guidebooks, and several expensive restaurants with chewy Turkish ice cream (if it's authentic, you can stretch it close to a meter).

The *dolmuş* that return to Kuşadası are sometimes full—you can go to Selçuk first if you want to be sure to get a seat. You should stop in Selçuk anyway to supplement your exploration of Ephesus with a visit to the impressive **Ephesus Museum** (see Selçuk, p. 495). In the first or second week of May, the annual **Festival of Ephesus** presents drama, music, and folklore events in the new Selçuk amphitheater.

SIGHTS

If you don't take a guided tour, you'll probably approach the ruins from the road between Kuşadası and Selçuk, and your first glimpse of the site will be the outskirts of the ancient city. The most important of these remains is the **Vedius Gymnasium,** to the left as you proceed down the road to the main entrance. On the west end of the gymnasium courtyard (the main entrance is at the north end of the site) are **public lavatories** and a source of potable but warm **water.** Farther on unfold the contours of an enormous **stadium** (the seats were removed to build the Byzantine city walls). Just before the main entrance stand the ruins of the **Double Church** (Church of Councils) where the notorious Ecumenical Council of Churches met in 431 CE.

Once you pass through the main entrance, you probably won't be able to keep yourself from heading straight to the center of the site and marveling at **Arcadian Street,** a magnificent, colonnaded marble avenue. Like the present-day tourist drag in Kuşadası, Arcadian was lined with shops and extended to the harbor, where visitors disembarked and trading ships docked with cargo from the Far East. The street liquefies into a small marsh, but many of the original columns have survived.

Once at the far end of the avenue, turn around for a dazzling view of the **Grand Theater.** With seating for 25,000 and remarkable acoustics, the amphitheater dominates the entire site from an elevated setting, carved into the side of Mt. Pion. In ancient times, the Ephesians celebrated the Festival of Artemis every April. Singing and dancing, the denizens marched 89 golden idols of the goddess to the Grand Theater. St. Paul gave sermons here (open in summer daily 8:30am-6:30pm; in winter 8:30am-5:30pm; free). Today, the theater is the setting for the spectacular **International Efes Festival,** featuring artistic and folkloric exhibitions and shows, held annually in the spring (prices vary with events).

Running before the theater is the slightly elevated **Marble Road** (built by Nero, 54-68 CE), which once led all the way to the Temple of Artemis. Peek down one of the small holes in the road for a glimpse of the scented sewage system. The **Commercial Agora,** the main plaza of the city, stretches nearby. In the center of the colonnaded square stood a huge horologium, a combination sundial and water clock. Marble Rd. leads past the agora to the **Library of Celsus.** Almost entirely reconstructed by Viennese archaeologists, its elaborately carved marble façade suggests the luxury of ancient Ephesus.

Across from the library at the corner of Marble Rd. and Curetes St. are the vestiges of the **brothel** dedicated to the love-goddess Aphrodite. Romantic commerce took place by candlelight in the small, windowless side rooms. There is a secret passage from the library to the brothel. At the end of the brothel, farthest from the Grand Theater, is a sacred pump whose water supposedly made sterile women fertile. The statue of Priapus, the god of fertility, was found here and is now displayed in the Ephesus Museum in Selçuk. Just between the brothel and the library is the **world's first known advertisement**—a picture of a foot and a square containing an inscription. Supposedly, if cryptically, it was an ad for the brothel.

Uphill, the imposing ruins of the **Temple of Hadrian** dominate the left side of the road. Renovation shows off the intricately carved façade. The marble archway contains friezes depicting the mythical creation of the city of Ephesus, and a bust of the goddess Cybele adorns the keystone. Beyond the temple and adjoining the rear of the brothel are the **Baths of Scholastikia.** Across from the Temple of Hadrian burrow the yet unearthed **Terrace Houses,** containing handsome frescoes from the 2nd century CE, which extend up the hill. They once housed the wealthier and more prominent families of the city, who lavished the interiors with superbly preserved frescoes and mosaics. A visit here merits the extra entrance fee, though the attendant is not always there to collect it (open daily 8:30am-noon and 1:30-6pm; admission 90¢).

Farther up the hill lie the ruins of the exquisite **Fountain of Trajan.** Various fragments found here have been piled piecemeal to reconstruct the original structure. The statue of the Emperor Trajan that stood before the fountain has been completely destroyed—except for the base (whose fascination factor is abysmally low).

If you make a left after the hill of Trajan's fountain, before the main road, you'll come to the site of the **Grotto of the Seven Sleepers.** According to Christian tradition, seven men fleeing persecution in the 3rd century CE hid in these caves. When they awoke, one of them went to buy bread and discovered that he and the group had been sleeping for 209 years. The story is more interesting than the site.

■ Selçuk

The authentic "Turkishness" of Selçuk, for which the town has been deemed preferable to Kuşadası, has become aggressive and commodified. It is a tourist town. Although it is now encrusted with innumerable carpet shops, souvenir dens, and lame *kebapçı* with aggressive maîtres-d', flashes of the town's captivating history still glitter in places. Selçuk is smaller, less anonymous, and more beautiful than Kuşadası, and it is easy to escape the commercial fervor of the town center at the archaeological sights that lie in the breathtaking landscape that surrounds the town. On Saturdays in summer, locals as well as tourists flock to the huge **Open Air Market,** which features fresh fruit, cheeses, vegetables, tea, spices, and clothing. From Selçuk, the tranquil House of the Virgin Mary (Meryemana) can be reached by *dolmuş* or taxi (7km). Officially sanctified by the Vatican, this site on Bülbüdağı (Nightingale Mountain) is a Christian pitstop on holy treks.

ORIENTATION AND PRACTICAL INFORMATION

The main thoroughfare is the İzmir-Aydın road, yet another **Atatürk Cad.** The road from Kuşadası and Ephesus, **Sahabettindede Cad.,** intersects Atatürk Cad., forming the main crossroads of the town. The **Tourist Information Office,** Atatürk Mah. Agora Çarşısı, 35-6 Mirza Karşısı (tel. 892 6328), at the southwest corner, provides free maps (open in summer Mon.-Fri. 8:30am-5:30pm, Sat.-Sun. 9am-5pm; in winter Mon.-Fri. 8:30am-5:30pm). The **hospital** (tel. 892 7036) lies on the southeast corner of the intersection. With your back towards the tourist office, walk four blocks on Atatürk Cad. to the town center, a small square with a fountain facing the ruins. Behind it along **Cengiz Topal Cad.** are the **PTT** (open in summer 24hr., in winter 8:30am-midnight), the **police** (tel. 892 6016), **banks, restaurants, public baths,** and the **train station.** The **bus station** from which the Kuşadası *dolmuş* departs (until midnight, $1) is at the crossroads. Buses from İzmir also come here (1½hr., $1.50). Take a minibus back to İzmir (every 30min., $1.50) at the bus station, or a larger bus back to İzmir on the street in front of the bus station. Stand on the opposite side and signal the driver (buses every 30min., 1½hr., $1.50). **Pharmacies** are scattered around the town center. **Postal code:** 35920. **Telephone code:** 232.

ACCOMMODATIONS

One business practice that Selçuk's pension owners have adopted with increasing frequency over the past few years is to hire people on commission to either seduce or badger travelers into staying at their establishments. It is a good idea to have a specific pension in mind and stick to it. In some cases, hustlers pose as officials from the pension where you intend to stay, but lead you to their place instead. Take advice from the official tourist office and other travelers. Since the whole village goes into slumber mode after sunset, the main reason for staying in Selçuk is to arrive at the ruins early the next morning.

Tuncay Pension, İsabel Mah., 3 Ay Sok. (tel. 892 6260). Walking north from the bus stop, take the 4th left; then the first right, and right again. Large, carpeted, hygienic rooms; some with bathrooms. Clean hall baths. Free service to Ephesus, 24-hr. hot water, laundry ($2.63 per load), and common kitchen. Singles, doubles, triples, and quads available. $5 per person in high season. Breakfast $2.50.

Pansiyon Karahan (Smiley's Place), 9 I. Okul Sok. (tel. 892 2575), the 2nd right after the bus station heading north. Free service to Ephesus, beaches, and harbor. Immaculately clean, carpeted rooms, all with clean showers, balconies, secure locks, and comfortable beds. Management arranges boats to Samos (one way $30; roundtrip $35; open-return roundtrip $55. 10% student discount). Make summer reservations 1 week in advance. $6.25 per person negotiable. Breakfast $2.50.

Barim Pansiyon I, Müze Arkası Sok. (tel. 892 69 23), behind the museum off Turgutreis Cad. Barim is enriched with *kilim,* colorful artifacts, nesting storks, acid and trippy garden, and an art-deco fountain. Carpeted and quite clean, it offers outstanding decor—a bit like Tahiti, with grass mats on the floor and straw gazebos in the courtyard. Cool and quiet. 24-hr. hot water, and some rooms have bathrooms. Very little English spoken. $7.50 per person. Breakfast $3.

Australian New Zealand Pension, 7 Prof. Miltner Sok. (tel. 892 6050), behind the museum (follow the signs). Don your hiking boots and roll into the spacious, lively garden. Chill with experienced backpackers in the nomadic tent and roof lounge. Clientele mainly English-speaking, all ages. Grilled dinner every other night. Free service to Ephesus and the beach. Mountain camping packages and transport to Samos (one way $30, roundtrip $45, open-return roundtrip $55; 10% student discount). Discounts for trekking groups and groups larger than 7 (20%). Laundry $3.75 per load. $2.50 per dorm bed. $4 per person. Breakfast $1.50.

Pansiyon Kirhan (tel. 892 2257), behind the museum. An old Ottoman home with 4 comfortable, carpeted rooms to let. Garden, fireplaces, and 24-hr. hot water. Very stylish in its inconsistent decor. $5 per person. Breakfast $1.50.

Victoria Hotel, Atatürk Mah. 4 Cengiz Topel Cad. (tel. 892 3203; fax 892 3204), across from the PTT. Views of the town and the storks nesting in the Roman aqueduct. Lobby and separate TV room. 24-hr. hot water. All rooms come with marble-tiled bathroom, shower, towels, telephone, closet, and desk. This 2-star hotel offers 5 or more students a 20% discount. $12.50 per person.

International Guest House (Erol's Place), İsabey Mah., 21 Ak Sok. (tel./fax 892 2199), formerly known as Anzac and Artemis Pension. Walk on the right side of the Artemis statue in the square. Make the first left and walk 50m. This joint offers clean rooms, a sundrenched roof bar with a comfortable rug and cushioned corner, English books, and a common kitchen. Some rooms with balconies and/or private baths. $5 per person. All-you-can-eat breakfast $2.50.

FOOD AND ENTERTAINMENT

Restaurants are expensive in Selçuk. The **Özdamar Restaurant** (tel. 892 4097), on Cengiz Cad., has sidewalk tables steps away from the pretty fountain with a view of the pretty castle up the pretty hill, but it charges a pretty penny (*kebap* $1.25, vegetarian dishes $1; open 8am-midnight). The **Mine Restaurant** (tel. 545 3107), across from the Karahan Pension, is also good, if pricey (full meal $6; open until midnight). Bar-wise, check out the **Ekselans Bar and Café** 18/a 1. Okol Sok. (tel. 851 5266), which advertises that it's "sympathetic to Greenpeace"—the owner might sit you down to talk Turkish politics. Mellow is the scene in the dark upstairs room. **Petek Çöp Şiş** is an inexpensive joint with savory dishes (full meal $3.50). The mother's choice in Selçuk is the immaculate **Beget Sandwiches,** 5 Koçak (105) Sok. (tel. 892 8050), which has sandwiches and vegetarian options at a ridiculously low price. The ingredients are fresh and clean, and the owner will remind you of your mama.

SIGHTS

Selçuk's few fascinating archaeological sights have been overshadowed by the towering majesty of its neighbor, Ephesus. Taken alone, however, these sights represent a great reason to visit the town. The colossal and comparatively unadvertised **Basilica of Saint John** is a good place to escape the frenzied consumerism (that is, once you've slipped past the unctuous rug dealers and twinkly card stands near the basilica's entrance). The 6th-century church was constructed under the Byzantine emperor Justinian on the supposed site of St. John's grave. It was built on such an immense scale that, if reconstructed, it would remain the world's 7th-largest cathedral today. Its stately, if somewhat sparse, remains are characterized by a strange combination of Roman imperial grandeur and early Christian grace and weightiness (admission $3, students $1.50). The cathedral's idiosyncratic character is made even stranger by an 8th-century wall built around it by invading Arabs, who used materials taken from the 1st-century gymnasium of Ephesus, a stadium where the Romans gleefully watched lions tear Christians to bits.

The underwhelming and comparatively over-advertised **House of the Virgin Mary** lies 100m off the road from Ephesus to Bülbüldağı (Nightingale Mountain). About five years after the death of Christ, St. John is said to have accompanied the Virgin Mary to Ephesus, where they lived in a small house on the slopes of Mt. Bülbül. The site lay forgotten for centuries until 1892, when the archaeologist Katerina Emmerikin discovered a 7th-century church that was built over the original house. Later that year, Archbishop Timoni of İzmir accepted it as the site of the Virgin's home. A popular pilgrimage site today, both Christians and Muslims visit Mary's sanctimonious home, leaving bits of tissues tied around branches of dwarf trees, symbolizing their made wishes. Every August 15th, a morning commemoration celebration ceremony takes place here.

The stunning **İsa Bey mosque** lies at the foot of the hill on which the Basilica of St. John and the Ayasoluk castle stand. It was built in 1375 on the orders of Aydınoğlu İsa Bey, and features columns taken from Ephesus, which the Ephesians in turn had pilfered from Aswan, Egypt. The mosque represents a transition between Selçuk and Ottoman styles. Restored in 1975, the mosque has regained much of the august simplicity that 600 years of wear and tear had eroded. The **Temple of Artemis,** one of the **seven wonders of the ancient world,** used to be the largest temple on the planet; however, it is now as disappointing as it was once awesome. A lone reconstructed column now twists toward the heavens from a bog that roughly approximates the area of the temple's foundation. The ducks, geese, and lizards that caper among the sites's cracked marble blocks are as good a reason to visit the Artemision as the column (see Ephesus (Efes), p. 492). Selçuk's **Ephesus Museum** is the home of most of the archaeological finds unearthed in the region since WWII. Those discovered before then are in Vienna (open daily 8:30am-noon and 1-6pm; admission $3.10, students $1.55). The **statue of Priapus,** the randy little rascal that decorates postcards at nearly every stand in Turkey, is among the treasures you'll find here. The famous multi-breasted statue of Artemis, as well as exquisite busts of Eros, Athena, Socrates, the emperors Tiberius, Marcus Aurelius, and Hadrian make this one of the more important collections of ancient art in the world.

■ Near Selçuk

Priene, Miletus, and Didyma lie in a tidy row south of Kuşadası. Perch on the slopes of Mt. Mycale to view Priene, practice a soliloquy in the amphitheater of Miletus, and await a revelation from Apollo at Didyma. With an early start and a modicum of efficiency, you can reach all three sites in a daytrip. But you may prefer to explore the ruins in two leisurely days, as the largest site, Miletus, deserves extra time. Less well preserved but interesting to mystery cult buffs are the ruins at Priene, the Delphi of the Ionian cities. You'll only need an hour or so to visit the monumental temple at Didyma. It's possible to take an organized day tour of all three sites from Kuşadası (or more expensively from Bodrum) for roughly $25 per person. Check at the tourist office. You can try to catch an unguided tour from Selçuk ($9 for 1hr. at each site and 2hr. at Golden Beach), but these tours are often cancelled if not enough people show up by 9:30am. Otherwise, you can visit all the sites from Kuşadası through a series of *dolmuş* rides.

For a daytrip, a good strategy is to use **Söke** (reached by *dolmuş* from Kuşadası) as a base, and return there to make bus connections. This way is least confusing, and—since Söke functions as a hub for minibuses—guarantees a number of *dolmuş* to each site (every 20min., 50¢-$1.50). Another option is to go to Didyma first and then work your way back north. Go to Söke from Kuşadası, then pick up a second *dolmuş* to Didyma, where the temple of Didyma is located. To get to Miletus from Didyma, you can easily catch a *dolmuş* to **Akköy.** From there, you can hitch or take a taxi the 7km north to Miletus. To get to Priene, you can either continue hitching north from Miletus or go back to Akköy; from there take one *dolmuş* to Söke, and another to the small town of Güllübahçe at the foot of the Priene ruins. While in Güllübahçe, you may want to visit the **Şelâle Restaurant** (tel. 547 1009), where a waterfall from an ancient, moss-covered aqueduct cascades into a reflecting pool within splashing distance of the tables (entrees $3, *kebap* $4, beer 70¢; open in summer daily 8am-midnight; in winter daily 8am-10pm). Taxis usually wait at every site (all open daily 8:30am-7:30pm, off season 8:30am-5pm; Miletus and Priene ruins aren't fenced off; admission to each 75¢, students 40¢).

The tiny town of Didyma has only one monument, **The Temple of Apollo,** which was repeatedly looted and burned throughout history. Didyma has a spanking new **tourism office** (tel. 256) 813 3974), in the Belediye building in the center of town (open Mon.-Fri. 8am-noon, Sat.-Sun. 8am-noon and 1-5:30pm). Inexpensive pensions are the norm here. The **Orakle Pansiyon** (tel. (256) 813 1585), overlooking the temple, is the cheapest with a spectacular view. (Doubles $18.75. Triples $22.50.) There's not much to do in Didyma, but just 4km from the Temple of Apollo is the beautiful beach town of Altınkum with several sleeping options at lower prices. To the right, along the beach, you can stay at the **Saray Motel** (tel. (256) 813 1994), with balconies and a patio on the beach and clean rooms with baths. ($8.75 per person. Breakfast included.) **Aslan Tatilköyü,** 3rd Köy (tel. 813 4841), 200m from the *otogar,* is a family-run pension/campgrounds with an adjacent market. Decent rooms with bath and shower, balcony, and access to a kitchen. (Doubles $10. Triples $15. Breakfast $1.25. $1.15 for campers with car. $2.65 with tent. $3.90 with caravan (with electricity). 25¢ per person.) For **camping** closer to Didyma, try the **Orman Bakanlığı** (tel. 825 8921), the last campsite when going from Akköy to Didyma. There are a few more **campsites** ($3-4 per person), some with restaurants, at Lake Bafa, east of Akköy.

PRİENE (GÜLLÜBAHÇE)

Priene grew to prominence as a member of the Ionian Confederation of cities in the region of Smyrna (modern İzmir). The confederation controlled the Aegean coast after the decline of the Hittite empire, but Priene lingered in the shadow of its neighboring economic rival, Miletus. The city's population never exceeded 5000 and while its neighbors excelled in commerce, Priene devoted its resources to religion and sport. The city's ruins, on a plateau before the walls of Mt. Mycale, overlook the contortions of the River Meander. Keep an eye out for the unmistakable systems of geometric design introduced by Hippodamos of Miletus in the 4th century CE.

Dolmuş stop by a café. To reach the site from there, follow the road that struggles up the slope and forks off to the right of the road to Miletus and Didyma. First you'll encounter the massive ancient walls that circumscribe the ruined metropolis that was constructed upon the terraced slope of the mountain. From the main entrance, a path leads to what was once the main avenue of ancient Priene. The west side of the block (facing downhill) begins with the **Prytaneum,** the vaulted hearth of the city's sacred flame. Brought to Priene from Athens by the first settlers, the flame was extinguished only when the city was invaded and rekindled upon liberation. After the Prytaneum is the unmistakable **Bouleterion,** or Senate House, a well preserved, elegant square auditorium. The interior chamber was equipped with a huge marble altar on which sacrifices were offered both at the opening and closing of the sessions. Only the foundation of this altar remains.

More substantial congregations convened just up the hill at the handsome **theater.** The front row retains five **thrones** of honor with dignified bases carved in the shape of lions' paws. Farther along the upper terrace at the city's acme, the **Temple of Athena** transports you back to the heyday of Hellenistic architecture. Alexander the Great financed the project, and Pytheos, the architect whose *chef d'œuvre* is the Mausoleum of Halicarnassus (one of the seven wonders of the ancient world), designed the structure. The temple retains largely intact front steps and interior floors. Descend from the temple to visit the vast remains of the private houses of Priene, an unusual example of Ionian domestic architecture.

Heading back towards the entrance of the site, you'll pass through the spacious **agora.** Women were allowed here only if accompanied by a man, either husband or slave. At the center, a public temple once hosted official ceremonies and sacrifices. Beyond the agora is the 3rd-century BCE **Temple of Olympic Zeus.** Downhill on the lip of the plateau stand the **Stadium** and **Gymnasium,** with the names of many young athletes inscribed in the walls. On either side of the main hall were small rooms for bathing and exercise.

MiLETUS (MiLET)

Now surrounded by arid plains, Miletus once sat upon a thin strip of land surrounded by four separate harbors. Envied for its prosperity and its strategic coastal location, the city was destroyed and resettled more than once. Miletus suffered the same fate as its Ionian confederates—the silting of its harbor and waters by neighboring rivers caused its decline. For centuries, Miletus was a hotbed of commercial and cultural development. In the 5th century BCE, the Milesian alphabet was adopted as the standard Greek script. Miletus later became the headquarters of the Ionian school of philosophers, which included Thales, Anaximander, and Anaximenes. The city's leadership, however, eventually faltered in 499 BCE, when Miletus headed an unsuccessful Ionian revolt against the Persian army. The Persians retaliated by wiping out the entire population of the city, massacring the men and selling the women and children into slavery.

The site's main attraction is the **theater,** clearly visible from the Priene-Didyma highway. The strikingly well preserved structure dates from Hellenistic times, though most of the visible portion was constructed by Romans. The theater, which could seat 15,000, was originally positioned at the water's edge.

During all but the summer months, the remaining portions of Miletus are marshy. To the right of the theater as you enter the site is a Selçuk **Kervansaray** (perennially under restoration). Facing the theater, the footpath meandering to your right leads you to the mephistophelian **Faustina Baths** (behind the theater), erected by the wife of the Roman Emperor Marcus Aurelius. To the left of the baths are the **North** and **South Agoras.** Next to the baths is the **Delphinium,** or sanctuary of Apollo Delphinus. The temple was first constructed to honor Apollo, who transformed himself into a dolphin and led the Cretans to Miletus. All of the temple's priests were sailors. If nothing else, visit the abandoned 15th-century **Ilyas Bey Camii,** the peculiar dome-shaped structure just beyond the baths. Weeds sprouting atop its tiled dome make it look like a huge nest. The interior offers refuge from the heat as well as an exquisite *mihrab.* Roughly 500m before the main entrance stands a small **Archaeological Museum** (open daily 9am-6pm; admission 90¢, students 45¢).

DiDYMA (DiDiM)

Ancient Didyma was the site of a sacred sanctuary to Apollo and of an oracle that brought in most of the city's fame and wealth. The first Didyma oracles date from about 600 BCE. Roughly 100 years later, the sanctuary was destroyed by the Persians when they plundered Miletus. The temple lay deserted until Alexander the

Great's arrival, which inspired the arid sacred spring miraculously to flow anew. The present sanctuary was begun during the 2nd and 1st centuries BCE. Work continued until the 2nd century CE, but the original plans, like those for Alexander's empire, proved too ambitious and were never completed. Nevertheless, the awesome scale and elegance of the structure make it well worth visiting.

The **sanctuary** at Didyma ranked as the third-largest sacred structure in the ancient Hellenic world after its neighbors to the north, the Temple of Artemis at Ephesus and the Temple of Hera on Samos. Since virtually nothing remains of either of the latter two buildings, the sanctuary at Didyma stands alone as the best surviving example of such colossal temple architecture. It was built to last—many of its individual marble slabs weigh more than one ton. During the Roman period, the unfinished temple attracted pilgrims from all over ancient Greece. A church was constructed on the site in 385 CE after Emperor Theodosius I outlawed the solicitation of pagan oracles. The sacred road that ran from Miletus to Didyma ended at the temple gates. The statues which once lined the final stretch were relocated to the British Museum in 1858 and have been replaced by souvenir shops.

Inside the main gate rests a bas-relief of a giant **Medusa head,** once part of an ornate frieze that girded the temple's exterior and now star of countless brochures. The building's full magnitude is apparent only when you climb up the stairway to the main façade. Still, you are seeing only a fraction of the original—all that remains of the more than 100 magnificent columns are the bases and lower sections. To transport such immensely cumbersome chunks of marble, the Greeks constructed long shafts of stone leading to the temple site, lubricated them with soap, and then slid the building materials over the slippery surface.

In front of the temple trickles the spring that the priestesses supposedly tapped when receiving prophecies from Apollo. Climb the steps to enter the forecourt. Through the **Hall of Twelve Columns** is the **Hall of Two Columns,** where visitors waited to hear the pronouncements. From here, 22 steps lead down to the **audition.**

In the southeast corner of the courtyard are traces of another **sacred fountain,** as well as the foundations of a **naiskos,** a tiny temple that housed a venerated bronze statue of Apollo. The temple, which served as the site of the oracle, appears to have been erected in 300 BCE, before the larger edifice was begun.

■ Denizli

A blossoming agricultural and industrial center, Denizli, situated in the bosom of amazing mountains by the Büyük Menderes River, is an ideal pitstop before Pamukkale. A lush valley envelops the city, which has nourished multiple civilizations from its fertile plains, from the Luvians, its earliest inhabitants, to the Hittites, Persians, Macedonians, Romans, Byzantines, and Ottomans. Today, Denizli is a lovely mix of widely paved streets, markets, and picnic parks. In the Turkish mentality, natives of Denizli are a warm, hard-working breed, as evidenced by their friendliness and enthusiasm to help foreigners. Two large, imposing statues of chickens, the patron bird responsible for Denizli's economic success, one in the commercial district, and the other on the winding path to Pamukkale, will help you orient yourself.

ORIENTATION AND PRACTICAL INFORMATION

Visitors to Denizli will undoubtedly arrive at the hectic bus terminal *(otogar),* located at the intersection of İstasyon Caddesi and Cumhuriyet Caddesi. You may (okay, will) be accosted by various bus company flunkies who will either: ask you where you are going with such persistence that a tinge of admiration might surface in your otherwise strong hostility toward them; or, enumerate various locations (Pamukkale, Ephesus, Aphrodisias…) à la auctioneer speed until they are blue in the face. If you have an idea of where you are going next, enter the terminal building and talk to someone behind the desk at one of the bus company offices. They're more likely to be a little more chill, as well are more informed. The Denizli *otogar* is a major crossroads with buses departing frequently to several destinations. Hence, Denizli is an optimal stopover, considering that Pamukkale and Efes are traditionally daytrip sites, and that despite the costly accommodations, pensions in Pamukkale, in particular, are usually booked solid.

Tourist Office: (tel. 264 3971; fax 264 7621), on İzmir Blv. (across the street from the bus terminal), in the train station *(tren garı)*. Offers comprehensive maps and English service. Open daily 8am-noon and 1:30-5:30pm.

Budget Travel: None of the travel agencies in Denizli really organize daily tours to Pamukkale, Efes, etc.; these are usually dealt with in İzmir. However, for bus or plane tickets, you can call **Köeoğlu Turizm Seyahat,** Atatürk Blv. Denizciler Mah. (tel. 261 3746), next to İşbank. Or, **Kalamaki Turizm,** 20/24 Çaybaşı Mah. (tel. 264 5444), across from the central PTT, which also offers car rental services.

Banks: A large number of banks and exchange offices are located in Bayram Meydanı around the corner from the Ethnographic Museum.

Buses: To İzmir (every 30min., 4½hr., $6.25); Pamukkale (every 30min., 30min., 38¢ by Belediye bus or *dolmuş*); Efes (via İzmir, every 30min., 3hr., $5); Ankara (7hr., $10); Aphrodisias (via Pamukkale, buses run May-Sept., 2hr., $5); İstanbul (10hr., $15.65); Söke (via Kuşadası, 3hr., $4.40); Kuşadası (3½hr., $5); Marmaris (5hr., $6.25); Bodrum (4½hr., $7.50); and Fethiye (5hr., $7.50).

Pharmacies: Most of the pharmacies are clustered on Hastane (or Doktorlar) Cad., near the hospitals, one street behind the Ethnographic Museum.

Hospitals: Denizli Devlet Hastanesi (tel. 265 3430, -1,-2), directly ahead as you walk uphill on Hastane Cad. Public. **Özel Sağlık Hastanesi** (tel. 264 4311), located across from the Devlet Hospital. Private.

Police: (tel. 265 0034), located at the intersection of İstiklal Cad. and İnönü Cad. Also a a tiny police station next to the tourist office in the *otogar* (tel. 241 8920).

PTT: The main post office (tel. 263 5271) is located in the heart of the commercial district, where Mimar Sinan Cad. and Atatürk Cad meet (it's across from the big park near the police station). Open daily 8am-noon and 1-5:30pm. There's a dinky little PTT (tel. 261 1951) in the *otogar,* by the *otogar* police, as well.

Telephone Code: 258

ACCOMMODATIONS

Rooms in Denizli are cheaper than those in Pamukkale. The pensions, for the most part, are a refreshing break from the hustle and bustle of bigger tourist towns. Pensions are not abundant in Denizli, but the best ones are in Topraklı Mah., Deliktaş Mah., and on Atatürk Blv., behind the bus station.

Denizli Pansiyon, 14 1993 Sok. Deliktaş Mah. (tel. 261 8738; fax 264 4946), located about 1500m from the *otogar.* Tranquil ambience and clean, tasteful rooms with wood ceilings and carpeting. Young English speaking management offers car services to Aphrodisias and will pick you up from the *otogar.* Small, breezy garden with marble fountain; seating for sunbathers upstairs. Most rooms with bath and shower. This joint is popular, so you may want to call in advance in high season. MasterCard/Visa accepted. Doubles $15. Triples $21.25. Breakfast included.

Euro Pansiyon, 94 Atatürk Cad. (tel. 263 5536), across from the Gündoğdu Mosque. Spacious, carpeted rooms with new furniture. Communal bathrooms. Most rooms with balcony terraces upstairs. Groups of 10 or more get a 10% discount. Elevator available. $6.25 per person. Breakfast $1.90.

Güntaş Pansiyon, 3/5 Halk Cad. Topraklık Mah. (tel. 263 3579), located on the street parallel to İzmir Yolu, 200m behind the *otogar.* Entrance is through the basement into a large eating room/TV salon with marble floors. Rooms are understated and have phone, bathroom/shower, balcony, and tiny closet space. Singles $5.65. Doubles $10. Quads $4.60 per person. Breakfast and dinner $1.25 each.

FOOD AND ENTERTAINMENT

Since Denizli is not a popular tourist town (yet), there are countless *kebap* and *pide* restaurants that serve it up good at reasonable prices. Turkish-style pizza is available at **Pizza Plaza,** one of the cleaner joints in the Çinar district (behind the central police station, closer to Atatürk Cad.), a favorite hangout of the Denizli youth. For a change of pace, something a little snazzier (and more bourgeois), you can try the famous **Mantar (Mushroom) Restaurant** (tel. 266 0574), 5km outside of the commercial district, on Denizli Çıkış Acıpayım Yolu. Take a *dolmuş* or taxi in the opposite direction of Pamukkale to this feast of Turkish mushroom dishes (who knew fungi were so popular in fowl land?), seafood, and desserts. The oven-cooked mushroom with cheese and the mushroom sauté (served with salad and noodles) are superb. Dishes are a little pricey, but the taste is more than compensation.

Denizli also has some wonderful *pastaneler* (pastry shops). The local favorite is **Madlen Pastanesi** (tel. 264 3933), Delikliçinar Meydanı, past the rooster at 6/1 İstiklal Cad. Follow the sweet scents which waft from half a block away into the colorful shop with ample seating and some of the better cakes and pastries in town (open in summer daily 8:30am-1am).

SIGHTS

Denizli is not exactly brimming with touristic and historic sites, but the city is speckled with colorful mosques and lively markets. The **Atatürk Ethnographic Museum** (tel. 261 4029), located in the main city center (*merkez*), across from the Ulu Mosque on İstasyon Cad., has a small but impressive collection of folkloric clothing and traditional tools and *kilims* (open in summer Tues.-Sun. 8am-noon and 1:30-5:30pm; in winter Tues.-Fri. 8am-noon and 1:30-5pm; admission 40¢, students 20¢). Located 7km from Denizli is the **Akhan-Kervansaray,** the historic stopover site used by Seljuks and Ottomans on trade routes. You can get there by *dolmuş* or via the public buses that depart from the *otogar* (every 1-2hr., 25¢). Nearby is the **Myriokephalon,** a Roman, then Byzantine, settlement site which is still under archaeological excavation. Off the highway to Pamukkale is **Laodicea,** one of the seven churches of St. Jean, as elucidated in *Revelations.* To see Laodicea, 8km from Denizli, ask the Pamukkale-bound *dolmuş* driver to drop you off earlier at Laodicea, and then you'll be able to say that you saw the final abode of the great Cicero.

■ Pamukkale (Hierapolis)

Whether as Pamukkale (Cotton Castle) or ancient Hierapolis (Holy City), this village has been drawing the weary and the curious to its thermal springs for more than 23 centuries. The Turkish name refers to the extraordinary surface of the snow-white cliffs, shaped over millennia by the accumulation of calcium deposited by mineral springs. Legend has it that the formations are actually solidified cotton (the area's principal crop) that was left out to dry by giants. Dripping slowly down a vast mountainside, mineral-rich water foams and collects in bowls that terrace the decline, spilling over petrified cascades of stalactites into milky pools below. The site of ancient Hierapolis and the accompanying museums are overshadowed by the springs but are nevertheless fascinating.

Orientation and Practical Information   The bus stops in **Pamukkale Köyü,** the central square, or near the bus company offices up a curving street. The tourist complex, uphill from the train station, has a **PTT** (open daily 8:30am-5:30pm) and a **first aid center** behind the Roman Baths. A small **tourist office** (tel. 272 2077) is at the end of the row of shops and cafés near the main site entrance (open in summer daily 8am-7pm).

As you stand in the central square with your back to the tourist map/billboard, the road to the tourist complex starts off straight ahead and to the right, then curves around to the left past bus company offices and up the hill. Go up this hill to reach the tourist office and PTT. Technically, you've then entered the site, and you might be asked to pay the site fee just to get to the PTT. If you argue loudly in English, asking to see an official sign stating the entrance fees, they'll probably let you in free.

Most direct buses that run to Pamukkale leave from Selçuk or Kuşadası (5-6 per day, 4½hr., $4.50). Frequent *dolmuş* and minibuses run between Pamukkale and the regional capital, Denizli, which has extensive service to all major Turkish cities. Less expensive and less comfortable—unless you get an overnight couchette—are the trains that travel from İzmir and İstanbul to Denizli. *Dolmuş* and minibuses to Pamukkale leave from the Denizli bus station, roughly 100m south of the train station. Buses run twice hourly between İzmir and Denizli via Selçuk. From Pamukkale, there are **buses** to Bodrum (3 per day, 5hr., $6.25); İzmir (every hr., 4hr., $6.25); Selçuk and Kuşadası (2 per day, 4½hr., $7.50); Marmaris (5 per day, 4½hr., $7.50); Fethiye (6 per day, 5hr., $6.25); and Cappadocia (6hr.,$7.50). There are pharmacies in the village's central area, across from the Mustafa Motel. **Net Bookstore** (tel. 272 2266), next to the Mustafa Motel, carries travel guides and pop novels (open in summer 8am-midnight). **Postal Code: 20100. Telephone Code: 258.**

Accommodations   Logistically, Pamukkale presents travelers with a dilemma. Were it closer to the coast, it would make a great daytrip from Kuşadası or Marmaris. Unfortunately, it takes a good four hours to get there by bus, so most daytrippers end up spending almost twice as long in transit as they do at the site. The best solution is to spend the night and see the few sights thoroughly, rather than rush the trip and return to the coast exhausted. If you stay, beware of bus station hustlers who may tell you lies (i.e., "I'm so-and-so's brother. Let me take you there" Or, our favorite, "So-and-so dropped dead—may I suggest another place") to get you to another joint. You should ignore them and go straight to your pre-planned destination.

The motels in the tourist complex are all expensive, but relatively inexpensive pensions, often with small pools, crowd the village below. The **Kervansaray Pension** (tel. 272 2209; fax 272 2143) combines aesthetic appeal, professionalism, and friendliness to a degree rarely achieved by pensions. To get here from the map/billboard, turn right and take a left after roughly 90m (you'll see the pension from here). Pop out your *Let's Go* and watch a 10% discount materialize. ($8 per person. Breakfast $1.25. Regular and vegetarian dinners $7.) On the main road near the center of town, the **Mustafa Motel** (tel. 272 2240) has well kept rooms, many with shower/bath, quasi-vanity tables, and a two-tiered café with views of the springs. ($7.50 per person. Breakfast included.) **Halley Pension** (tel. 272 2204), in the center of town, is directly across from the map/billboard. Its quiet, sterile, recently renovated rooms have the same conditions as the manager's brother's place, **Özlem Pension** (tel. 272 2023), next door. (Laundry $4.25 per load. $6.50 per person. Breakfast $2.) On the road to the Pamukkale site, before the village (or *köy*) is a string of camping sites. Some are seedy, so you should probably check them out before you sign up. **Yalçın Pansion and Camping,** 16 Pamukkale Yol (tel. 272 2147), is one of the cheaper and cleaner ones. Communal kitchen and helpful management. You can walk (bring water) or take a *dolmuş,* if one passes by. Unfortunately, those are usually packed. Caravan and car prices are negotiable. ($2.50 per person.)

Food and Entertainment   Most of the pensions in town serve lunch and dinner, but locals recommend **Han Restaurant** (tel. 272 2792), next door to the Özlem Pension, which specializes in *kebap* dishes ($3-$5). **Gürsoy Aile Restaurant** (tel. 272 2267), around the corner, is a lovely, family establishment with tasty traditional entrees served with a Turkish touch (oven-baked Gürsoy house *kebap* $3.50). **Pamukkale Pizzeria and Restaurant,** down the hill from the Mustafa Motel, serves great pizzas (pizza $2-3, beer $1.25). In terms of night action, there isn't anything stellar. Nevertheless, off the main road, near the center of town, there are several small bars and discoes which get crowded if tourists are bored enough. You can try the **Sergi Bar and Restaurant, Atlas,** or the **Tiffany Bar.**

Sights The warm **baths** at Pamukkale bubble with oxygen. There are two series of terraces situated on either side of the main road down into the village. Elegant, shallow pools located in front of the Tusan Motel (nearest the highway) gradually become deeper farther down the slope. The deepest, most intricately shaped, and most popular terraces are directly behind the nameless restaurant/café facing the main parking lot. On weekends, locals flock to bathe in the flat, fan-like pools. Near the entrance to the tourist complex, you can seek out a place away from the zealots who crowd the pools and attempt to submerge their entire bodies in the six inches of available spring water (admission $3.75, students $1.90).

Between the motels soar the colossal vaulted archways of the **Hierapolis City Baths.** The visible portions of this 1st-century structure are all that remain of one of Asia Minor's greatest ancient tourist industries: hygienia. The springs of Hierapolis were particularly popular among vacationing Romans. After an earthquake leveled the spa in 17 CE, Hierapolis was promptly rebuilt, and it reached its heyday during the 2nd-3rd centuries CE. The city bath's glossy marble interior has now been converted into a mediocre **Archaeological Museum** (open Tues.-Sun. 9am-5pm; admission $1.75, students 70¢). Carved into the side of the mountain, the monstrous **Grand Theater** dominates the vista of Hierapolis. Almost all of the seating area for 25,000 is intact, and the various ornately sculpted decorative elements adorning the façade and stage area are well preserved. In front of the theater are the remains of the 3rd-century CE **Temple of Apollo.** Behind the temple stands the **Nymphaeum,** or Monumental Fountain. Nearby is the famous **Plutonium,** a pit that emits poisonous carbonic acid gas, a substance ancients believed could kill all living creatures except priests and pit-toilet-experienced backpackers. The Turks call it *Cin Deliği* (Devil's Hole). Farther to the right lies a hot-water spring. If you continue on the footpath, you'll reach the 6th-century **Christian basilica.**

Down the road to Karahayıt is the north **city gate** on the right, and the ruins of a 5th-century Christian basilica dedicated to St. Philip, who was martyred here in 80 CE. Outside the gate is the **Necropolis,** with more than 1200 tombs and sarcophagi. People who wished to be buried here believed that proximity to the hot springs and vapor-emitting cracks would ease their trip to the Underworld. Among the tombs lies the **Martyrium,** an octagonal 5th-century edifice believed to have been erected upon the site where St. Philip was martyred in 80 CE.

You shouldn't leave Pamukkale without a savory dip in the **sacred fountain** at the Pamukkale Motel (75m after the archaeological museum). Warm, fizzy waters bubble at the spring's source, now blocked off to prevent divers from disappearing into its depths. On the pool's floor rest remains of Roman columns, toppled by the earthquake that opened the source (open daily 9am-9pm; $3 per hour).

■ Aphrodisias

In antiquity, Greeks made pilgrimages here to pay respects to the goddess o' luv, Aphrodite, and ask for her blessing. The village evolved into a metropolis, however, only after King Attalos III bequeathed Pergamon to the Romans, spurring a massive exodus to this land of divine beauty and love. Aphrodisias was famed for its sculpture. Crafted from the white and bluish-gray marble of nearby quarries, the finer statues in the Roman Empire were often marked with an imprint from the Aphrodisian sculpting school. With the ascendancy of Christianity, temples were converted to churches, and the city's name became Stavropolis (City of the Cross).

While the stunning remnants of Aphrodisias have been scrutinized for decades, archaeologists believe that a great deal remains to be discovered. The ruins unearthed to date include a well preserved Roman stadium and *odeon,* as well as a temple, an *agora,* a palace, and some thermal baths. Although getting to Aphrodisias is a hassle, the site is less overwhelming (and less crowded) than Ephesus, and the carefully preserved ruins make it worthwhile. Optimistic archaeologists believe

Aphrodisias will outshine Ephesus in 50 years, and, already, the sensation of being transported back in time is palpable, standing in the midst of this sanctimonious site.

The highlight of a visit to Aphrodisias is the ancient **stadium,** the most well preserved ever excavated. Even the marble blocks that once marked the starting line for foot races are still in the central arena, whose seating capacity was 30,000. Roman gladiators shed blood here in the search of glory and prestige before a full house. The looming structure at the bottom of the hill is **Hadrian's Bath,** equipped with a sauna, frigidarium, and changing rooms. To the right, the **Temple of Aphrodite** marks the site of ancient venereal veneration. Although only a portion of its 40-column spiral-fluted Corinthian colonnade remains, the temple retains its elegance. Dating from the 1st century CE, the shrine originally housed a famous statue of Aphrodite, similar in appearance to the many-breasted Artemis of Ephesus. So far, only copies of the original have been unearthed. With its extraordinary blue marble stage, the **odeon,** just to the south, was the council chamber for the town's elected officials. The nine columns nearby were resurrected as part of a building christened the **Bishop's Palace** by archaeologists, owing to a large number of religious artifacts and statues unearthed on its premises. Some of the original marble floors remain intact. Among the highlights of the site's must-see museum are megastatues of Aphrodite and a satyr carrying the child Dionysus (museum and ruins open daily 10am-noon and 1:30-4pm; admission to ruins and museum each $1.65, students 85¢).

Getting to Aphrodisias is hard. The easiest way to see the ruins is to take a daytrip from Pamukkale. **Buses** leave daily at 10am and return at 5pm (2hr., roundtrip $10). Some travelers take a bus or *dolmuş* from Denizli, Nazilli, or Kuşadası/Selçuk to the small town of Karacasu, and hitch from there. Another option is to go to Aydın, accessible from Denizli, Selçuk, or İzmir by *dolmuş* or buses running at regular intervals. Buses on the Denizli-Muğla route pass through Tavas, 30km from Aphrodisias. Few hitch from Tavas since cars rarely pass along the road. **Aydın Tourism** (tel. 212 1489) offers an air-conditioned bus service to Aphrodisias (1½hr, $3.25).

Across the highway from the turn-off to Aphrodisias, 300m down the road, is **Chez Mestan** (tel. 448 8046, -132), très chic with comfortable rooms, free coffee and laundry. (Singles $6. Doubles with showers $11. 10% student discount. If all 14 beds are full, they may put you up in the adjacent carpet store for $2.50.) Or, the **Aphrodisias Hotel** (tel. 448 8132), in the teeny town of Karacasu, Aydın, offers well kept, spacious rooms with bath and toilet. (English and French spoken. Doubles $18.75. Triples $23.75. Breakfast included.)

The popular place to sit and chat with fellow tourists about how they managed to get to Aphrodisias is **Anatolia** (tel. 448 8138), at the Geyre Beldesı in Karacasu, Aydın (2km from Aphrodisias). This joint has four menus, with varied cuisine and prices. If you stick to the first (cheapest) menu, you can can enjoy a salad, cold appetizer, *şiş,* and fruit for roughly $5 and sit in the same lovely garden as those bourgeois fourth-menu types. Good vegetarian selection. 10% discount for student groups of more than five (open daily 9am-6pm). **Telephone Code:** 256.

■ Bodrum

Ensconced in the serpentine coastline of the Arcadian Peninsula, Bodrum is understandably the favorite retreat of many Turkish jet-setters, intellectuals, and artists. While Bodrum may not be an archaeologist's dream, it is certainly the place to be if you know how to sunbathe, shop, and dance semi-nude and semi-drunk. The nightlife here is unparalleled, as the ground vibrates to the beats echoing from the dozens of jam-packed nightclubs until the wee hours of the morning. Nearby are a bunch of beach towns where you can compete with locals and tourists for a faultless tan, and then hit the night scene by *dolmuş* (run until midnight from most towns and start up again by 6am). The only historically noteworthy sights are the remains of the mausoleum of **Halicarnassus,** one of the **seven wonders of the ancient world,** and the crusader *kale* (fortress) which guards the harbor. Still, Bodrum's beaches, rip-roaring nightlife, and deeply tanned tourists are entertaining.

HISTORY

Bodrum was built upon the ancient city of Halicarnassus, a powerful port town and capital of ancient Caria. (The Carians were an Anatolian people who lived in this area around 1200 BCE, prior to the Greek invasion.) Halicarnassus was known for its succession of **female rulers,** who succeeded their fathers, husbands, or brothers. One ruler, Artemesia I, led a fleet against the Athenians in their war with Persia in 480 BCE. Her story is related in the *Persian Wars* by Herodotus, another native of Halicarnassus. In 377 BCE, Mausolus of Cairo came to power and made Halicarnassus his capital. Work on his tomb began during his reign and was completed under his wife's direction following his death in 353 BCE. The tomb provided the inspiration for the modern word **"mausoleum."** Roughly 25 years later, Alexander the Great razed Halicarnassus, ending its period of prominence.

Until 1925, Bodrum was a small fishing village of less than 2000 people. Then, the British-educated **Cevat Şakir Kabaağaç** (known as "the Fisherman of Halicarnassus") settled here in political exile and began to write short stories about Bodrum and the surrounding area. A community of intellectuals flourished until tourists began to frequent Bodrum in the 1970s. A decade later, the town became one of the premier destinations for British and German package tours. Pensions and motels now cover the hillsides around the town. The Turkish intellectual and European package-tour communities lead separate lives in Bodrum, but the city has an atmosphere rare among resort towns combining sophistication and a thrilling nightlife.

ORIENTATION AND PRACTICAL INFORMATION

Streets in Bodrum are poorly marked. The city's most prominent and easily recognizable landmark is the centrally located *kale* (fortress), from which several streets emanate. Cheap pensions lie along the bank to the right of the *kale* as you face inland. Breakwaters almost completely enclose the other port, which forms the more picturesque half of town. Ferries and yacht cruises depart from this harbor.

The main thoroughfare along the waterfront starts from the castle and runs along the enclosed left harbor—it begins as **Karantina Caddesi,** becomes **Belediye Meydanı** after the mosque, and then changes to **Neyzen Tevfik Caddesi** along most of the harbor, and ends at the **yat limanı** (yacht harbor). Going right from the castle, Kasaphane Cad. becomes Kumbahçe Mahallesi, then changes to the main commercial drag of **Cumhuriyet Caddesi,** and ends by the Halikarnas Hotel as **Paşa Tarlası.** Extending inland from the castle towards the bus station, **Kale Caddesi** is Bodrum's main shopping strip lined with boat tour booths and sponge divers selling their precious finds. It eventually becomes **Cevat Şâkir Caddesi,** which runs past the post office and the bus station, from which all inter-city buses, taxis, and *dolmuş* depart.

Tourist Office: 12 Eylül Meydanı (tel. 316 1091; fax 316 7694), at the foot of the castle. Room listings and lousy maps, but helpful staff and bus information. Better maps available at the bookstore. Open April-Oct. daily 8am-7pm; Nov.-March Mon.-Fri. 8am-noon and 1-5pm.

Tourist Agencies: Karya Tours (tel. 316 1914), at the ferryboat landing. Coordinate ferries to Kos and the Datça Peninsula, and daily excursion to Pamukkale and Ephesus ($29). Open daily 8am-9:30pm. **Apak Tours** (tel. 316 5244; fax 316 3998), on Cevat Şâkir Cad., down the road from the bus station, towards the water on the left, also offers boat excursions and daytrips. **Noya Tourism,** 1 Hilmı Uran Meydanı (tel. 252 316), closer to the discoes. Similar deals with yachting, car rental, diving, and rafting options. **Botur,** 24/A Cevat Şakır Cad. (tel. 316 8815; fax 316 8208), offers tours and boat trips ($15 including lunch) and combined Efes and Pamukkale 2-day trips ($50).

Currency Exchange: Available at the PTT 24hr. There are many currency exchange booths by the harbor on Kale Cad., most of which do not charge commissions. Also in banks, which close at 5:30pm.

Buses: Cevat Şâkir Cad. Buses every hr. to Marmaris (3½hr., $5) and İzmir (4hr., $6.25). Buses to İstanbul (starting at noon, 5 per day, 14hr., $21.25), Ankara (3 per evening, 11hr., $17.50), and Pamukkale (3 per day, 5hr., $7.50). Frequent *dolmuş* and minibus service to Gümbet, Akyarlar, Bitez, Turgut Reis, Gümüşlük, and Gündoğan (in high season every 20min., 40-70¢).

Ferries: Tickets sold through any travel agent. **Bodrum Ferryboat Association** (tel. 316 0882; fax 313 0205) has offices in the bus station and near the castle. Boats to Kos leave at 9am and return at 5:30pm. (3-7 per week, 1hr., $13, same-day roundtrip $20, open roundtrip $22. Greek port tax $16 (4000dr), paid only on open ticket. Ferry to Datça Peninsula, 8km from Datça and 80km from Marmaris (2 per day, 2hr., $7.00, same day roundtrip $10.50).

International Bookstores: Bodrum International Bookstore, Cumhuriyet Cad. 4 Adliye Sok. (tel. 313 5242), before the disco lane on Cumhuriyet Cad. Tapes, English crosswords, and magazines. Open daily in summer 9am-2am, in winter daily 9am-10pm. English books at the bookstands on Cumhuriyet Cad. across from the 06 Lokantası (open in summer 24hr.).

Hospital: Bodrum Devlet Hastanesi (tel. 316 0880, -1 or -2), Kıbrıs Şehitler Cad., uphill from the amphitheater. Public.

Police: 12 Eylül Meydanı (tel. 316 1218), next to tourist office at the foot of the castle. **Main branch** (tel. 316 1004), left on the main highway up Cevat Şâkir Cad.

PTT: (tel. 316 1212, -560), on Cevat Şâkir Cad., 4 blocks from the bus station along the road to the harbor. Open in summer daily 9am-5pm; in winter Mon.-Fri. 9am-5pm. International phones next to the castle. Open 24hr. **Postal Code:** 48400.

Telephone Code: 252.

ACCOMMODATIONS

Rooms become scarce in summer—reservations are essential. Pensions are a better bet than hotels. There are hundreds of them and they're inexpensive—for Bodrum. Most rooms are $9-11 per person. Prices are 20-40% less in off season. If you're traveling solo, it may be a good idea to find a roommate, as pensions rarely have singles. Often rooms are available in private homes called *ev pansiyon*. Look for signs that read *Oda Var* or *Boş Oda Var* (vacancy). The pensions close to the discoes are affected by the nightlife (i.e., flashing lights, reverberating windows), but since you've chosen to come to Bodrum, you'll probably be out partying, too.

Uslu Pension (tel. 313 0665), on the very lively Cumhuriyet Cad., next to Şirin Büfe Döner. Rooms as clean as a hospital's, but more tastefully decorated. Communal bathrooms. Ask for a room in the back to minimize the shake-your-booty noise from the main street. The café next door will deliver breakfast if you ask in advance. Doubles, triples, and quads $12.50 per person; $6.25 in off season.

Yenilmez Pansiyon (tel. 316 2520), along Neyzen Tevfik Cad. (the road along the water to the right as you face the harbor), away from the tourist office. Turn right at the alley after Mola Bar (but before Sini Restaurant), and walk 1min. up the winding path. Spotless rooms, bathrooms, and showers. 24-hr. hot water. 10-min. walk to discoes and bars, but you're spared the noise. Access to fully equipped kitchen. Parking lot in back. $8.75 per person. Breakfast included. Group discount (15-20%) for packs of more than 15.

Albatros Otel and Pansiyon, 6 Neyzen Tevfik Cad. (tel. 316 7117), on the same street as Yenilmez, but earlier on the path. Stylish rooms with carpeting, mirror, nightlights, and bamboo-stick ceilings (for that tropical feel). Outdoor TV room. $12.50 per person in high season. $10 per person in off season. Breakfast $2.50.

Polyanna Pension (tel. 316 1528), on Ortanca Sok., a side street just before the Halicarnassis Disco end of Cumhuriyet Cad.—right at the center of Bodrum's nightlife. If coming from the tourist office, turn left off Cumhuriyet Cad. at the White House Restaurant. Clean rooms with showers arrayed around a soaring atrium. Terrace with view of the castle. $12.50 per person. Breakfast $3.15.

Camping: All the campsites in Bodrum have folded. Hopeful campers can take the very short *dolmuş* ride (from the bus station) to **Gümbet,** the next cove west.

BODRUM

FOOD AND ENTERTAINMENT

Bodrum is not bashful about being an expensive resort. But *lira* are well spent here—the port is famous throughout Turkey for its seafood, especially octopus and squid. For the cheapest provisions, stock up at the fruit and vegetable stands on Cevat Şâkir Cad. near the bus station, or at the big **market** that comes periodically on the other side of the station. Along Cumhuriyet Cad., before the harbor, there are a number of *kebap* salons, *dönerci* (purveyors of *döner*), stands that offer fried mussels, and the usual *pide* and *şiş*. One place to try is **06 Lokanta**, 156 Cumhuriyet Cad. (tel. 316 6863). It's the local tourist meeting place (*meze* $1-2; open 24hr.). **Hades Restaurant** (tel. 316 6542), the first among a string of restaurants along Çarşı Cad., boasts "Once visited. Never left." While their lamb with mushrooms may leave something to be desired, their vegetarian special in a deep tile dish will bring you to climax ($7.50). A favorite among locals is **Sini Restaurant** (tel. 316 3310), located 10 minutes from the bustling commercial artery at 90/A Neyzen Tevfik Cad. (around the corner from Yenilmez Pansiyon) which is famed for its *izgara* (grilled meat) dishes ($5-8.15). For cheap, non-pension breakfasts, you can pick up some fresh bread and morning pastries (to calm your hangover) at **Gürbüz Unlu Mamüller,** 34 Cevat Şakır Cad., directly across from the bus station. While our style-o-meter gauges zilch for this joint, it's take-out pastries are incredible. For something a little classier, try **Café Mavsoleion,** on Neyzen Tevfik Cad., Tepecik Camii Yanı (across from Sini Restaurant), popular for its desserts and milkshakes. The old-timers pastry shop in Bodrum is **Yunuslar Karadeniz,** 13 Cumhuriyet Cad. (tel. 316 1748), next to Uslu Pansiyon. Yunuslar is loved for its oven-fresh tarts and delicacies (open daily 7am-2am). Numerous pizza, Chinese food, and ice cream places abound.

For nightlife in Bodrum, the **Halicarnassus Disco,** Z. Müren Cad. at the end of Cumhuriyet Cad., 1500m from the center of town, should be your destination (it's marked on the tourist map). Perhaps the only chance in life you'll get to see elderly French women, bisexual Italian models, preppy American college students, and Turkish teenyboppers sharing the same dance floor. The $12.50 cover charge is allegedly necessary to recoup the $1.2 million plus poured into constructing this pseudo-Roman marble theater (the stage is the dance floor; open until 5am). One of the hotspots is the **Red Lion Bar,** on Cumhuriyet Cad. before Halicarnas Disco. Central location and lack of a cover charge attract multitudes of multicolored and polylingual thrill-seekers (open in summer daily noon-5am). Follow the cacophonous roar of the music from the Red Lion and the two adjacent bars. The **Hadi Gari,** Cumhuriyet Cad., is a Turkish bar with nominal dancing and the locals' hangout of choice. Pleasant pubs, like the **Meltan Bar,** two doors before the Red Lion Bar, suffice for relaxing and listening to music. Most bars are visible from the street and full of tourists. Others, frequented by Turks who make their summer residence in Bodrum, are more discreet. If you can shoulder the $4 first-drink charge (later drinks $1.75), visit the **Mavi Bar,** near the end of Cumhuriyet Cad, on the left before you get to Halicarnassus. This rather Turkish hangout features floor cushions, *kilim,* and musicians famous throughout the Turkish intellectual scene (open daily until 5am). **Fora Disco and Bar,** near the Uslu Passage, is open 24 hours in summer and has the rowdiest crowd. (No cover charge, but drinks are pricey.)

SIGHTS

Rising from the azure waters of the harbor, the **Kale** epitomizes a typical medieval fortress' squat austerity. It was built over the ruins of the ancient acropolis by the Knights of St. John during the 15th and 16th centuries CE. The castle towers, built by knights of different nations, have been unimaginatively dubbed the English, German, French, and Italian towers. Looming nearby are the stubby yet handsome **Harbor Tower** and the sinister-looking battlement, the **Snake Tower.** Be sure to visit the castle's torture chamber, whose entrance bears the inscription *Inde Deus Abest* (Where God Is Absent). A string of lurid red lights illuminates the passage to this ancient house of horrors, where canned moans and shrieks and anguished mannequins enhance the morbid atmosphere. Despite the castle's immense size and extensive fortifications, only 10 years after its completion in 1513, Sultan Süleyman the Magnificent overpowered the knights and forced them to retreat to Malta.

The castle houses Bodrum's **Museum of Underwater Archaeology,** a bizarre assortment of shipwreck flotsam from sites along the surrounding Turkish coastline. The museum itself, which consists mainly of some broken remnants back-lit for eerie effect, is the foremost of its kind in the world. A Byzantine courtyard in the central portion of the castle houses the **Bronze Age Hall,** which contains finds from a 1200 BCE shipwreck. Huge jars found on board date from 1600 BCE, and their artwork strongly suggests the existence of an ancient trade route between Crete and the Asia Minor coast. The museum also exhibits *cam* (glassware) recovered from a variety of ancient and medieval wrecks (castle open Tues.-Sun. 8am-5pm; admission $2.40, students $1.20; museum open Tues.-Fri. 10am-noon and 2-4pm; admission (including another museum exhibit) $1.55, students 80¢).

The ruins of ancient **Halicarnassus** are Bodrum's better known, if less picturesque, attraction. Most of the remains were either destroyed or buried underneath the modern town of Bodrum. The city walls are visible at points, as are the meager remains of the **theater** on Kıbrıs Schitler Cad., on the main road uphill from and parallel to the left harbor. The most famous of the ruins, the once wondrous **mausoleum,** consisted of a rectangular foundation and stone pedestal upon which the sepulchral chamber rested, supported by 36 Ionic columns. The 50m high mausoleum, covered with a pythonic pyramidal roof, was crowned by a statue of Mausolus driving a chariot drawn by four horses and is one of the seven wonders of the ancient world. To get to the mausoleum, turn onto Saray Sok. from Neyzen Tevfik Cad. It will be on your right at the end of the street (open Tues.-Sun. 8am-noon and 1:30-5:30pm; admission $1.55, students 80¢).

■ Near Bodrum

Bodrum's popularity among Turks stems largely from its location at the head of the enchanting **Bodrum Peninsula.** After a day of swimming and sunning, you can linger over dinner or partake of Bodrum's rousing nightlife. A few of the beaches on the south coast of the peninsula are accessible only by tour boats, which leave from the front of the castle (daily 9-11am, return 5-6pm). Known as *mavi yolculuk* (blue journeys), these tours are fine alternatives to all the archaic splendor of the ruins and to the Teutonic masses plaguing the beaches around the city. Itineraries for the tours vary widely (check the tour schedule at the dock). Some popular destinations are **Kara Island,** the village of **Akyarlar,** and the beaches at **Baradakçı, Çapa Tatil, Yahşi, Kargı Bay, Bağla,** and **Karaincir.** Boat tours cost $12 per person for the day, $18 with lunch. In summer, boats leave daily from the castle and head to tranquil **Orak Island** (same prices). These are some of the better swimming spots on the peninsula: pristine and uncrowded. There are no cheap accommodations at these places, so daytrips are your best bet. Locals strongly advise against drinking the tap water, so stock up on Hayat, Pınar, and SultanSu (Poland Spring a la Türkiye).

Three kilometers out of Bodrum is the colorful and enchanting **Gümbet Beach,** peppered with hotels, restaurants, and topless sunbathers galore. Most pensions are expensive, typical of a beachside resort. You may want to try **Şanlı Pansiyon,** 26 Adnan Menderes (tel. 316 2111), a two-minute walk from the sandy beach. All rooms are carpeted and spotless with large bathrooms, 24-hour hot water, and mosquito-netted windows. (Doubles $25. Triples $37.50. Breakfast $3.15.) The highly popular **Zetaş Camping** (tel. 316 1407; 316 2231 for reservations), right on the beach, falls within budget range. Zetaş has a market, an upscale beach restaurant, squeaky-clean bathrooms and showers, and a kitchen. If you arrive after midnight, enter through the beach—the gate near the *dolmuş* stop will be locked. ($3.75 per tent. 65¢ per car. $1.25 per caravan. $1.25 for electricity. $3.75 per person.) Farther up this road toward the main *dolmuş* stop is the **Gültekin Pansiyon,** 23 Adnan Menderes Cad. (tel. 316 4106), which offers carpeted rooms with bath, shower, and 24-hour hot water. ($9 per person. Breakfast $3.50.)

Less spoiled than the overpopulated south coast, the north end of the peninsula has rocky beaches and deep water. **Gölköy** and **Türkbükü**, once peaceful fishing villages, now host a large number of Turkish tourists and their yachts. Both offer affordable pensions. A few old windmills dot **Yalıkavak**, at the northwest end of the peninsula, where many even smaller villages, each with a few pensions, are scattered. The best way to find a place to stay is to walk the beach. You may consider camping in Yalıkavak at **Yalı Camping** (tel. 385 4142), across Belediye beach at the harbor. Facilities are clean and the owner is helpful. ($3.15 per person or caravan.)

A 20-minute *dolmuş* ride from the *otogar* is the gorgeous sand paradise of **Yahşi**, the longest beach in Bodrum. Flanked by surfers, sunbathers, and pensions, the turquoise waters gleam, offering a more serene (if not less crowded) warmth than other beaches in the area. Yahşi is a popular refuge for Turkish families and tourists alike, so call in advance to ensure your spot under the striped umbrella (brelly for the Brits). **Damla Pansiyon** (tel. 248 3056), sparkling white with an adjacent restaurant, is right on the beach (at the end of the path leading from the *dolmuş* stop). (Doubles $13.75. Breakfast included. Dinner $2.50.) **Yahşi Beach Pension** (Erkal Motel; tel. 348 3324), about 200m to the right of Damla if you're facing the water, has sterile rooms with blue-tiled baths. Upper rooms have balconies and charming furniture. Grassless camping site is also available. ($15 per person. Breakfast and dinner included. $2.50 per person on campsite. $6.25 per tent.) **Güzel Pansiyon** (tel. 348 3354), 300m to the left of Damla if you're facing the water, has quaint, clean rooms with colorful sheets, small bathrooms, and 24-hr. hot water. ($10 per person. Breakfast included.) Farther down on the road, by Kaktus Kamping, is the **Aras Pansiyon** (tel. 348 3140), whose owner can often be found in the adjacent market. Every room with balcony, shower, and 24-hour hot water. ($7.50 per person.) You can do your laundry and ironing at **Yahşi Laundry** (tel. 348 3595), across from the Damla Pansiyon (open only in summer 8am-9am; $4.10 per load).

On the sandy strip between the Damla and Yahşi Beach Pensions are many restaurants and bars. While most folks go to Bodrum for the evening, **Bacchus Restaurant** has incredible pasta dishes ($2.25-2.50) and grilled specialties ($3.15). **Olimpiyat Restaurant,** on Plaj Cad., on the corner of Dilek Pansiyon, has filling vegetarian dishes ($2.50-5). **La Villa Restaurant,** on the marina, specializes in both Turkish cuisine and pasta dishes ($4-6). **Greenbar,** on Abide Cad., 40m from the *otogar,* is the local favorite—it's a disco and a bar. **Jazz Bar,** on Plaj Cad., has a more beatnik following, with live music three times a week. **Tolga Bar,** near the *otogar,* is primarily a Turkish joint, but the drinks are cheap and the music won't put you to sleep.

Because the beach at **Bitez** is narrow, seaside bars have built pontooned docks over the water, where you can order drinks while you sunbathe. The beach around the next large cove from Gümbet is peaceful but has no cheap accommodations. *Dolmuş* from the Bodrum bus station travel to both beaches. The most accessible point on the west coast of the peninsula, **Turgut Reis** is 18km from Bodrum. We've given you the scoop on the longest beach—here's the widest. It's a one-dimensional beach-eat-sleep tourist town, and the stretch of coast is usually crowded, making it less appealing than villages to the north. There are a number of pensions in town, but they tend to fill up quickly in July and August. They line the street parallel to the beach to the right of the bus stop as you face the sea. **Ferah Pansiyon** (tel. 383 3030) offers clean, cool, eclectically decorated rooms with bath. There is a rooftop terrace with an amazing view and 24-hour hot water. There are few English-speakers here. (Singles $9.50. Doubles $12.50. Triples $15.) The recently renovated **Çeylen Pansiyon,** 39 Sevgi Yolu (tel. 382 2376), boasts beautiful views and clean rooms with showers. (Doubles $18.75. Triples $25. Breakfast $3.15.) From Turgut Reis, *dolmuş* run south along the coast to the crowded beaches at Akyarlar and Karaincir.

Words cannot do justice to the inspiring beauty of **Gümüşlük**, a tiny seaside paradise at the west tip of the Bodrum Peninsula. The Turkish name means "silvery," referring to ancient silver mines that were discovered in the area. Near the beach lie the ruins of ancient Mindos, a 4th-century BCE port impregnable even to Alexander the Great. The site consists of the impressive city wall, 3m thick, and a Roman basilica. Gümüşlük's sparkling vistas, cool sea breezes, and relaxed atmosphere make it a great place to escape the frenetic hedonism of Bodrum. **Telephone Code:** 252.

Rooms in Gümüşlük are scarce in high season, as groups usually reserve pensions and villas far in advance. The friendly **Anka Pansiyon** (tel. 394 3193), on the main road halfway between the village and the shore, is new and has pleasant rooms. The 10-minute walk from the beach is the drawback (go up the road towards the PTT), but it has a pool table, laundry, and a terrace. Rooms with bath and breakfast ($10 per person). A little closer to the water on this road, **Deniz Pension** (tel. 394 3149), is a converted village house with multilingual management. Some rooms have private bath ($10 per person).

Mediterranean Coast

During the first and second millennia BCE, the area around Fethiye and Kaş formed the Kingdom of Lycia. The Lycians, who reveled in fancy burial rites and funerary monuments, are not remembered for much else. Rock tombs are carved into cliffsides all along the coast, and Lycian sarcophagi litter the countryside—some are even perched on off-shore islands. The most significant of the Lycian cities that punctuate the coast are the ruins of Xanthos and Patara.

Extending from the edges of Greece to the Syrian border, Turkey's Mediterranean coast is alternately chic, garish, and remote—with pine forests, hidden coves, and sandy beaches dotting the stretch between Fethiye and Antalya. The swimming and sunbathing opportunities here are among the best in the world as thousands each year claim they've found "heaven on earth" in the Turkish coves and islands. Accommodations along the western segment of the Mediterranean coast are generally inexpensive, and excellent seafood abounds; farther east, broad swatches of sand and concrete speckled with castles and ruins mark the stretch of overcrowded shoreline that tourist propaganda calls the "Turquoise Coast."

The best boat connection between the Greek islands and Turkey's Mediterranean shores is the ferry between Rhodes and Marmaris. Allow enough time to explore farther east, and west to the enchanting Datça Peninsula. Distances on maps are deceiving: beyond Fethiye, the road winds through mountain terrain and becomes as slow as it is scenic. Boats run between Kıbrıs and the ports of Taşucu and Mersin. Travel from these ports to the Southern Republic of Cyprus is impossible.

MARMARİS COAST

■ Marmaris

Incongruously metropolitan for the region, Marmaris nonetheless displays palm trees and canopied side streets. Ignore the shops full of camera film and neon shorts, and enjoy the urbane cafés that line the harbor and the wooded mountains that form their backdrop. The town offers the pleasures of sun and sand without the rustic inconvenience that plagues many other resorts—the only danger is occasional overcrowding. Located at a hub of Turkey's Aegean minibus network, Marmaris is only a short ferry ride from Rhodes and makes a perfect point of departure.

ORIENTATION AND PRACTICAL INFORMATION

You're never more than three blocks from the sea in Marmaris—one flailing stretch of hotels, restaurants, and cafés hugs the shoreline. **Kordon Caddesi,** which becomes **Atatürk Caddesi** at the statue, runs along the waterfront. The tourist office, castle, and marina are at the east end of the waterfront (to the left facing the water). From the bus station, cross the bridge over a channel of water and then follow along the coast to reach the tourist office, a handy landmark. Sometimes buses deposit passengers at the dusty *dolmuş* stop. From this stop, head to the water, and turn left along the waterfront for 200m to find the tourist office.

Tourist Office: 2 İskele Meydanı (tel. 412 1035; fax 412 7277), on Kordon Cad. Open in summer daily 8am-7:30pm; in winter Mon.-Fri. 8am-7:30pm.
Buses: Follow the waterfront east (to the left facing the water), turn 1 block inland next to the marina, cross the bridge, and turn left. Buses to İzmir (every hr., 5hr., $8.75); Datça (4 per day, 2hr., $3.15); Fethiye (every hr., 3hr., $5); Bodrum (9 per day, 3½hr., $5); İstanbul (5 per day, 13hr., $21.25); and Ankara (4 per day, 10hr.,

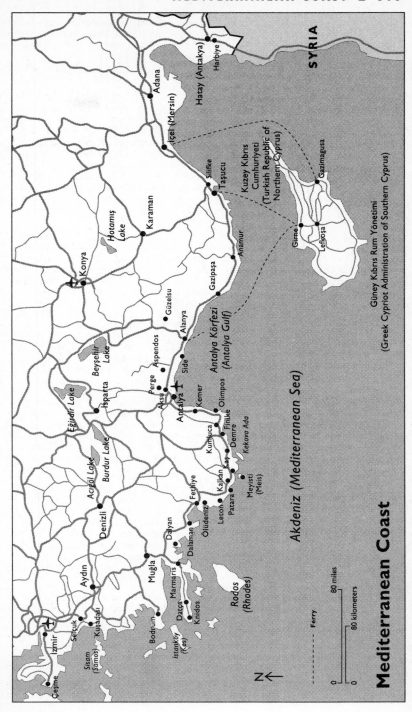

MARMARIS

SYRIA

Hatay (Antakya)
Harbiye
Adana
İçel (Mersin)
Silifke
Taşucu
Kuzey Kıbrıs
Cumhuriyeti
(Turkish Republic of
Northern Cyprus)
Gazimagusa
Anamur
Gazipaşa
Güzelsu
Karaman
Hotamış
Lake
Konya
Girne
Lefkoşa
Güney Kıbrıs Rum Yönetimi
(Greek Cypriot Administration of Southern Cyprus)

Antalya Körfezi
(Antalya Gulf)
Alanya
Aspendos
Side
Perge
Aksu
Antalya
Kemer
Kumluca
Olimpos
Finike
Demre
Kekova Ada
Kaş
Kalkan
Meyistİ
(Meis)
Letoon
Patara
Beyşehir
Lake
Isparta
Eğridir Lake
Acıgöl Lake
Burdur Lake
Denizli
Fethiye
Ölüdeniz
Dalaman
Dalyan
Muğla
Aydın
Marmaris
Datça
Knidos
Bodrum
İstanköy (Kos)
Sisam
(Samos)
Kuşadası
Selçuk
İzmir
Çeşme
Rodos
(Rhodes)

Akdeniz (Mediterranean Sea)

Mediterranean Coast

Ferry

N

80 miles
80 kilometers
0
0

MARMARIS

$17.50). Easiest to buy tickets at bus line offices across from town *dolmuş* stop (under the Pepsi sign). Shuttles run to the bus station 15min. before departure.

Ferries: To Rhodes (Mon.-Sat. 8:30 or 9am; $33, port tax $5 per port entered). Passports must be given to the agency the night before departure. There are many travel agencies along the waterfront that sell tickets. In winter, call 2 or 3 days before departure to ensure that the scheduled ferry is leaving. There is also a hydrofoil for roughly the same price (May-Sept. 9am, 50min.). The ferry dock is beyond the marina, away from the city center. It's a long walk—taxis run $2.

Hospital: Devlet Hastanesi, 167 Hatipirimi Sok. (tel. 412 1029), 5 blocks along the water away from the city center and the tourist office, then right onto İsmet Kamil Öner Sok., and up 2 blocks. Public.

Police: (main office tel. 412 1015; tel. 412 1494), at the corner of Kordon and Fevzipaşa Cad., 3 blocks along the waterfront from the tourist office. No English spoken. In case of **emergency,** call 155 or 156. The **passport police** (tel. 412 1696) are behind the new marina to the left of the tourist office as you face the water.

PTT: Fevzipaşa Cad. Three blocks along the waterfront towards the town center and 1 block inland from the tourist office. Open 24hr. **Currency exchange** daily 8:30am-11pm.

Telephone Code: 252.

ACCOMMODATIONS

Marmaris has quite a few reasonably priced pensions and hotels, most of which are booked in July and August. Arrive early in the day to secure a room.

Interyouth Hostel (HI): Tepe Mah. #45 42nd Sok. (tel. 412 3687, -7823; fax 412 7823), at the center of town. An impostor HI hostel lurks on the outskirts, at Kemeraltı Mah. 14 İyiliktaş Mevkii, complete with a huge "Interyouth Hostel" sign on it, but is in fact "Aşem Motel." To get to the *real* hostel from the city center, walk 1 block to the left facing the water, then turn left into the bazaar at the Garanti bank; it's on your right. MTV, book exchange, and boat excursions ($12 for hostel guests, $18 for others; lunch included). Breakfast in the terrace bar ($2.50), occasional barbecues ($2.75). English spoken. Ideal place to arrange *feribot* excursions to Rhodes. Dorm beds $4.25. Double-bedded singles/doubles $6. Laundry $5 per load. 10% discount for ISIC, IYH, and GO25 card-holders.

Kordon Pansiyon: Tepe Mah. 25 53 Sok. (tel. 412 4762). From the PTT, walk to the end of the block away from the water, turn left, and walk 1 more block. Tiny pension offers clean-enough carpeted rooms, half with balconies. Hall bathrooms with tubs. International phone and boat trips. Laundry $4.75. $6 per person.

Maltepe Pansiyon (tel. 412 1629), facing the water. Walk away from the centrum to the right, and turn right at the Disco and Cabaret. Follow this road around and cross the footbridge. Clean, airy rooms, shady garden, free laundry service for small loads, common kitchen. $6.50-7 per person. Roof $3.

Hotel Lahti, Tepe Mah. 9 Gül Sok. (tel. 412 1446; fax 412 1804). From the post office, follow Fevzipaşa Cad. for 5 blocks away from the water on a side street; ask for directions. Modern, clean, well lit, and cool. $11.75 per person. Breakfast $2. Ask for Ali, whip out your *Let's Go,* and get a 10% discount.

Camping: A few campsites around the west side of the bay. Every 5-10min., the "İçmeler" *dolmuş* drives around the bay, and will stop at the campgrounds if you ask. **Berk Camping** (tel. 412 4171), 4km from the center, is by the water.

FOOD AND ENTERTAINMENT

Resist the temptation to eat along the waterfront. Instead, investigate the inland streets. Cheap meals are scarce in Marmaris, but most places serve *kebap* ($3.50). At **Öz 49,** 200m inland from the PTT, a good full meal runs $3.50. If you're staying at the Tepe Mah. youth hostel, mention it to the waiter for a discount. Restaurants crowd the covered bazaar inland from the post office or the waterfront cafés. **Halil İbrahim Sofrası,** near the PTT in the bazaar, has a limited but tasty "Turkish Home Food." Its a bit pricey ($4 *kebap* and salad) but the dent in your *lira* will be ameliorated by the 10% discount offered to InterYouth Hostel guests (pick up a specially-stamped card at the hostel). **Mado Dondurma,** the Baskin Robbins of Turkish pastry shops, is on Fevzipaşa Cad., up from the PTT—a taste bud orgasm.

To meet other tourists, head to the Kuşadası-style row of pubs behind the tourist office. For dancing, the **Greenhouse** disco is is the most popular. Another tourist fave is the **B-52 Bar.** Sex on the B-52 drink is $4 and well worth it. Along the waterfront, on the other end of Marmaris, are the ritzier and more expensive clubs. To get to this string of bars, turn left at the Atatürk Monument (with your back to the water), and walk five minutes until you pass the open-air book vendors, the school, and the park. Try the **Metropol** outdoor bar with bedouin-style seating in the back. There's no cover charge, but you'll make it up after a couple of drinks.

SIGHTS

Marmaris itself has little to offer besides a large town beach and a **fortress,** built in 1522 by Süleyman as a military base for his successful campaign against the Crusaders of Rhodes (open Mon.-Fri. 8am-12:30pm and 1:30-5pm; admission $1, students 50¢). Only 1500m away, **Günnücek National Park** features a small beach and picnic tables set against a forest fragrant with frankincense trees. To reach the park, follow the coastal road past the marina across the small wooden footbridge.

While there is a **beach** in Marmaris proper, the better beaches and scenery around Marmaris are accessible only by boat (an exception is the pretty **İçmeler beach,** reachable by *dolmuş*). Serving the bay, *dolmuş moto* (*dolmuş* boats) depart from the harbor along Kordon Cad. every morning for a variety of destinations. Full-day tours cost roughly $8 per person. Most boats make a tour that stops at **Paradise Island Beach** and then the **Akvaryum,** a Turkish version of an aquarium. The tour also visits some phosphorous caves, and the popular **Turunç Beach,** across the bay from Marmaris. Flanking Turunç to the north and south, respectively, are the **Gölenye Springs,** whose waters reputedly cure intestinal ills, and the less crowded **Kumlu Buk Beach,** near the scanty remains of a fortress. Both are convenient to get to by boat. Most of the mouth of the Bay of Marmaris is sealed off by the heavily wooded **Nimara Peninsula.** Along the far end of the peninsula are the fluorescent phosphorous caves near **Alkoya Point,** another favorite stop for Marmaris' excursion boats. Between the peninsula and the mainland is the tiny uninhabited village of **Keçi,** which offers a good view of the surrounding coastline. The fine sand beaches of **Kleopatra's Island** are a good daytrip, which are not to be missed. Also known as Sedir Adası, Kleopatra's Island is laced with legend. Locals insist that Anthony imported this incredibly white sand from the Red Sea some 2100 years ago so his queen could enjoy afternoon rests. Others suspect that sand's purity is a function of its having mixed with fossilized plankton over the years. In any case, it is forbidden to take any of the sand out of the beach grounds. Sedir Island is reachable by daily tours (booked through any travel agency; $18.75). Or, you can do it yourself for roughly the same amount by taking a minibus or bus going to Muğla, to the fork in the road with the "Sedir Island" sign ($1.25), and walking 6km to the *dolmuş moto* dock. The boats cost $12 each with a $3 entrance fee to the island.

■ Around the Coast

DATÇA PENINSULA

Jutting out from the coastline at Marmaris, the slim Datça Peninsula extends 120km into the sea, only a short distance from the Greek island of Symi. Cleaved by indigo fjords, the land becomes increasingly appealing farther out. A picturesque, but at times terrifying, bus ride on winding roads leads through the peninsula's jagged landscape to drop you at the quiet town of **Datça,** a favorite vacation spot for Turks.

The English-speaking staff at the **tourist office** (tel. (252) 712 3163; fax 712 3546) has a pamphlet on the city and can help arrange a taxi to Knidos (open in summer daily 8am-7pm; in winter Mon.-Fri. 8am-5pm). To get there, exit the bus station heading toward the water, turn right, then make another right at the rotary to reach

Atatürk Blv. (a.k.a. Yalı Cad.). Within 1km you'll hit the PTT, the tourist office (behind a business complex), and the police. The tourist office also has a smaller office (open May-Oct. daily 8am-7pm) down the road on the left across from the Pamukkale Bus ticket office, where you can catch a shuttle to the bus station. To call the **police,** dial (252) 712 3792 or, in case of **emergency,** 155. On the other side of the tourist office stands the **PTT** (postal code 48900; open daily 8am-midnight). Banks **exchange currency** (open Mon.-Fri. 8am-5pm; exchange stops at 4:30pm). **Pir-Pak Laundry** (tel. (252) 712 2040) is at the end of Yalı Cad. past the taxi stand and offers service at $5 a load (wash and dry included; open daily 8am-10pm).

Buses travel to Marmaris every two hours (2½hr., $2.50). There is also a ferry from Bodrum which operates in summer only (1 per day, 2hr., $6.25 one way, $10 roundtrip, $11.25 open-ended ticket). Another returns to Bodrum from Datça at 9am ($7.75; a bus runs from the ticket office to the dock at 8:30am). Tickets are available at travel agencies in Bodrum. Buy them at the **Deniz Ticket Office,** or the Bodrum Ferryboat Association branch, behind the summer tourist office outpost on Yalı Cad (open daily 8am-midnight).

There are mosquitoes aplenty in Datça, so stock up on repellent or tablets. **Anta-lyalı Pension** (tel. (252) 712 3812) is centrally located and easy to find (on Yalı Cad., the main road). From the bus station, pass the PTT and take the left fork—the pension is on the right. Rooms are large and guests have access to the kitchen on the terrace. ($6.25 per person.) **Deniz Motel** (tel. (252) 712 3038) sits farther up the road. Take a left past the tourist office. All rooms have bath, balconies, and comfy beds. (Singles $7.50. Doubles $15. Triples $18.75. Breakfast included.) On the right side, farther down the road, the **Umut Pansiyon** (tel. (252) 712 3117), offers a great location, 24-hr. hot water, and a marvelous balcony. (Doubles $9.50.) Behind and above Umut, rooms in **Huzur Pansiyon** (tel. (252) 712 3364; fax 712 3052) are furnished balconies, sea views, and clean baths with toilet paper. ($9.40 per person. Breakfast included.) **Ilıca Camping** (tel. (252) 712 3400), on the beach beyond the harbor (turn right at the taxi station), has a restaurant and two-person bungalows with private baths ($5 per person. Camping $2.50 per person. Breakfast $2.)

Cheap food isn't easy to come by here, but good fare is. A dozen restaurants at the harbor specialize in fish with similar prices (*kalamar* $5, mussels $5). Across Umut Pansiyon is the **Akdeniz Restaurant** (tel. (252) 712 3884; fax 712 4051), which serves up ambrosia for mariners. Daily fish specials are the theme here; discount for sailors, naturally. A gorgeous terrace view enhances the house specialty, the oven-baked *Osmalı* ($7.50). Surprisingly wide vegetarian selection (open daily 8am-midnight; closed in winter). The **Yasu Restaurant and Bar** (tel. (252) 712 2860), across from the taxi stand and to the right, has a refreshingly diverse menu with daily vegetarian specials. Popular among German tourists, this joint hosts live music acts four times a week in summer. Above all, the ambience can't be beat—turquoise tables and chairs, idyllic location, and a great view (open daily 11am-2am). The **Kemal Restaurant** (tel. (252) 712 2044), halfway between Ziraat Bank and the Pamukkale bus station, is a true gem. Authentic home cooking, daily specials, and a modest decor. The **Eclipse Bar** (tel. (252) 712 4310), on Yat Limanı, has an outdoor bamboo-themed relaxing pit in the back. Cocktails and free advice on life (written on the walls) are available. The cream of 80s rock by day, livelier tunes blare by night (beer 70¢). The **Gallus Café and Bar,** under the taxi stand, is one step ahead of its competitors. The ambiance is oh-so-chic, with large striped beach chairs, a color TV, and a spanking new bar (cocktails $3-4). The only, and consequently favorite, disco is the **Disco New Castle,** past the taxi stand, and uphill 40m, which features light shows (admission $3). For fabulous Turkish pastries, try **Nokta Pastanesi,** up the hill from the taxi stand on Yalı Cad. (open daily 7am-3am).

Knidos, built in honor of Apollo, was once a wealthy port city, one of the original six cities of the Dorian League. A pair of **theaters** and **temples** dedicated to Dionysus and Demeter languish above the east harbor. Outside this area are two remote medieval fortresses surrounded by the ancient necropolis of Knidos. One of the artistic and intellectual centers of the ancient Hellenic world, it was the home of

Sostratos, designer of the Pharos lighthouse at Alexandria, and of the astronomer Eudoxos, who first calculated the earth's circumference. The city was renowned in antiquity for its **statue of Aphrodite.**

Because Knidos is a government-regulated archaeological zone, pensions and restaurants are forbidden to operate. **Boat tours** leave for Knidos from Bodrum and Marmaris during the summer (ask at the tourist offices). From Datça, take one of the boat tours that leave at 9:30am from the yacht harbor ($12.50 per person), or a taxi tour (roundtrip tour 3hr.; $37.50-43.75 per carload, negotiable).

CAUNOS AND DALYAN

The road from Marmaris to Fethiye passes by Lake Köyceğiz, connected to the sea by a river that outlines a stretch of lush marsh. Along this river are the ruins of the ancient Carian harbor city of Caunos, where archaeologists are turning up new structures as fast as they can dig. This settlement dates from 3000 BCE, and was established by Caunos, son of Miletos. The ruins are accessible only by boat from the nearby town of Dalyan. It's a 10-minute walk to the ruins. From the boat, look at the cliff above the river to glimpse at rock tombs dating from the 4th century BCE.

As you come up the hill in Caunos, the precariously perched **Kale** (castle) looms above. From the base of the mountain, climb (though not easily) the lofty **theater** for a panorama of the ruins and the distant beach. Facing the theater, the ruins of the **basilica** are on your left, and the ancient harbor of Caunos holds the remains of several **temples** and a recently excavated **fountain.** Many people come to Dalyan with quixotic hopes of seeing the endangered **Caretta Caretta** (Loggerhead Turtle) which lays its eggs on nearby İztuzu Beach, with untainted waters and crystal sands. It is *impossible* to see the turtle in Dalyan—the shy creatures appear only at night, when the beach is closed (open daily 8am-8pm). Environmentalists have struggled to prevent luxury hotels and tourist development from destroying the turtles' nesting ground. For the turtles' sake, please don't visit the beach at night, don't hire speedboats, and don't litter or stick an umbrella into the beach.

Stretched along the reedy river, the village of **Dalyan** stays cool in summer, but hosts the annual conventions of the Voracious Mosquitoes' Union. Make sure you've got bug repellent, or better yet, that your pension has electrified anti-mosquito tablets (most do), lest you wake up looking like a bad case of the mumps.

The **PTT** is the tall white building in the center of town (**postal code:** 48840; open daily 8am-midnight; currency exchange available 11am-11pm). To the left of the PTT as you face the river is the **tourist office** (tel. (252) 284 4235; open in summer daily 9am-noon and 1:30-8pm; reduced hours in winter). Next door is the **conservation information office** (open July-Sept. daily 9:30am-noon and 4-8:30pm). Stop in to say hello and see pictures of turtles. Between these two buildings, the **Dalyan Boat Cooperative** (tel. (252) 284 2094; fax 284 3255), operated by Gül Turizm, arranges public and private boat trips (10am public boat to beach, returns every hr. 1-6pm; $2.50 per person). *Dolmuş motoları* run to the baths, springs, ruins, and Turtle Beach ($4.50; departs 10:30am and returns 6pm; boat rental with customized itineraries $24). To get to Dalyan from Marmaris, take a *dolmuş* or **bus** to Ortaca (2hr., $2.50), then a *dolmuş* to Dalyan (15min., 65¢). A visit from Fethiye is shorter than the Ortaca-Dalyan *dolmuş,* making a daytrip possible (1¼hr., $2). Although the *dolmuş* runs from Dalyan back to Ortaca until 11pm, there is no service from 8 to 11pm (a taxi costs $9), so you should plan ahead so as not to get stranded. **Kaunos Moto** (tel. (252) 284 2816), across from the PTT, offers fully insured cars and scooters for your zooming pleasure. Daily cars ($50), scooters ($30), and bad-ass jeep safaris and river kayaking opportunities also at hand here.

If you like things quaint and quiet, you'll fall in love with **Dalyan,** and finding a room here should be as simple as finding one of 109 signs—there seem to be more pensions than inhabitants. Most of the pensions are to the left of the central plaza if you're facing the river. Coming from the center (with the *dolmuş* station, PTT, and tourist office), follow the main road so that the river is on your right. Three hundred meters ahead you'll hit an intersection. If you turn left and proceed roughly 50m, you'll reach the **Kristal Pansiyon** (tel. (252) 284 2263, -3153), on the left, embraced by a lush rose garden. Some cheaper rooms are available, with sinks in the rooms instead of full baths. (Doubles $12.50. Triples $18.75. "Cheap" double $10. Breakfast included.) Farther up the main street, **Yunus (Dolphin) Pansiyon** (tel. (252) 284 2102; fax 284 3906) has cool rooms with balconies and a terrace with a great view of the tombs. (Doubles $18.75. Breakfast included.) The **Albatross Pension** (tel. (252) 284 3287, -8), closer to the center of town, has a bar and clean rooms, all but two of which have private bath. (English spoken. $6.25 per person. Breakfast $3.75.) Campers should head along the main street out past Caretta-Caretta Restaurant to **Dalyan Camping** (tel. (252) 284 4157). Look for tents on the water ($2.15 per person. Caravans $7.50 for two people with electricity. Double bungalows with electricity $12.50. Breakfast $2.15). If you're trying to decide whether to camp out, think of the mosquitoes, and remember that pensions have screens.

The **Mediterranean Fruit Bar,** on the main road back toward town (with the river on your left), is an oasis. Enjoy fresh juices and shakes ($1.50-2), squeezed while you watch, from exotic fruits. Across the street is the newly opened **Korcan Café,** specializing in various *gözleme,* made right before your eyes ($1). Between Sahil Pansiyon and Dalyan Camping, **Caretta-Caretta Restaurant** (tel. (252) 284 3039) boasts menus in French, English, and German. New and on the water, its attentive staff serves steak, soup, *meze,* and beer for $5 (set menus for lunch: cold appetizer, salad, *ızgara* or fish, fruit or baklava $5; open daily 8:30am-midnight). There are innumerable small bars in the centrum (if you can call it that). Amist the abyss of clubs and bars, the **Crazy Bar,** across from the *ilkokul* (primary school), stands out with a cavernous interior that mercilessly abuses the color gray. The grill is open before 7pm, so come in the afternoon for a Bursa-style *ızgara,* and again in the evening for a walk on the wild side. There are two almost identical discoes close to one another at the end of the road, past Dalyan Camping. **Gel Gör** (Come See) is an enclosed building and the **Safari** is roofless. Toss a coin and have a ball.

FETHİYE COAST

■ Fethiye

Telmessos, the ancient Lycian city founded on Fethiye's site in the 4th century BCE, was known for its astrologists, mystagogues, palm readers, and oracles. Little of the old city's spirit is said to remain, but in 1958, when Fethiye was devastated by an earthquake, the Necropolis of Telmessos miraculously survived. Now Fethiye is a tumble of concrete buildings lining dusty streets—a small, quotidian port town that, aside from a few ruins, is of little interest. The town is near many interesting sights, however, and Ölüdeniz (14km away) is one of the Mediterranean's best beaches.

Orientation and Practical Information Buses drop off at the **station** 5km outside of town. Theoretically, the bus companies offer shuttles from there into town, but you may have to take a taxi. Head to the tourist office—they have listings of reputable accommodations divided by price range. If you arrive late at night and want to go directly to a hotel, tell the taxi your destination and ignore any "suggestions" he might have since this may be a commission scam. If you come by *dolmuş,* you'll be dropped off on **Çarşı Caddesi,** a street swamped by pension signs. The *dolmuş* to Ölüdeniz leaves from here. Çarşı Cad. veers right into **Atatürk Caddesi,** the main avenue running parallel to the harbor. **Banks, pharmacies, grocery stores,** and most of the town's shops can be found on this street. The **tourist office** (tel. 612 1975; fax 614 1527) , on the waterfront at the large pier where cruise ships dock, is to the left as you face the water from the intersections of Çarşı Cad. and Atatürk Cad. (open in summer daily 8am-noon and 1:30-5:30pm). You can **exchange currency** at the PTT, or at any of the local **banks** (open Mon.-Fri. 8am-noon; currency exchange stops at 4pm). Make a right onto Atatürk from Çarşı and walk a few blocks. The **police** (tel. 614 1040; emergency 155), **PTT** (open 24hr.; for letters 8am-noon and 1:30-5pm), and **hospital** (tel. 614 1499) are several blocks to the right of the tourist office as you face the water (10-minute walk). To get back to the **bus station,** your best bet is to go to a bus company office and catch a service bus. **Kamıl Koç** (tel. 614 1973) is here on this stretch of Atatürk Cad. **Pamukkale Turizm** (tel. 612 3767 or 614 1451) sits back around the corner on Çarşı Cad., on the left side as you head from Atatürk Cad. to the water. To get to the **bazaar,** turn right at the Atatürk-Çarşı junction, head along Atatürk (with the water on your left) 500m, then walk inland one block. Tuesday is market day. English-language tapes and a few books are sold at **Net Imagine,** 18 Atatürk Cad. (tel. 614 4846), left of the equestrian statue as you face the water, past the Garanti Bank. **Star Çamaşırhane** (tel. 614 5289), across the Turizm School, offers the only professional laundry in town. One load, wash and dry costs $5 (open daily 7:30am-11pm). **Postal Code:** 48300. **Telephone Code:** 252.

Accommodations   Several pensions line Çarşı Cad. between its *dolmuş* stop and the intersection with Atatürk Cad. Following the road around, you'll eventually reach a steep flight of stairs on the left, across from the Pamukkale bus office. At the top of the staircase is **Ulgen Pansiyon,** Çarşı Cad. Paspater. 3 Merdiven #8 (tel. 614 3491), with a refrigerator for guests and a pleasant vine-covered terrace with sea view. The management of this backpacker-oriented establishment is friendly and helpful, which makes up for the place's small inconveniences, like the cluttered hallways. (Singles $3.50, with shower $4.50. Doubles $6.75, with shower $9. Breakfast $1.75.) Closer to the *dolmuş* stop, down the street from the Yeni Mosque, is **Yakar Motel** (tel. 614 1557), at Sahil Yolu Yanı 14. The Yakar has tight but clean rooms and baths. Overlooking the bay, this motel has a vine-covered terrace, 24-hour hot water, and a friendly ex-colonel proprietor. (Singles $6.25. Doubles $12.50. Triples $18.75. Breakfast $1.25.) Around the corner is the luxurious **Pension Çetin** (tel. 614 6156; fax 614 7794), offering spacious, spotless rooms and baths. Most rooms have large balconies with views of the harbor. There's a café serving fast food downstairs. (Singles $6.25. Doubles $10, with balcony $12.50. Triples $18.75. Breakfast $1.90.)

Food and Entertainment   Gourmets should make their way to the upscale restaurants on the water and Atatürk Cad. There is less costly fare along Çarşı Cad. **Meğri Lokantası** (tel. 614 4047), a few doors from the Pamukkale office and across the street from Pizza Pepino, has A/C and a large, tasty selection of meat and veggie dishes (*döner* $3.50, chicken *şiş* $5.50, veggie casserole $4.50; open daily 8am-11pm). The **Sedir Restaurant** (tel. 614 1095), around the corner at 3 Tütün Sok., offers A/C, an English menu, and fast service. Turkish Pizza varieties are cheap (50¢-$1.50) and sauced skillet dishes ($5) are excellent (open daily 9am-11:30pm). Closer to the *dolmuş* stop, on Atatürk Cad. opposite the court, is **Birlik Lokantası** (tel. 612 2896), serving traditional Turkish meals at a fraction of the price of the coastal joints. *Izgara* dishes are a must ($2-3).

Several bars line Hamam Sok.; a tourist favorite is **Ceneviz Bar** (tel. 612 3778), with inviting bamboo outdoor seating. **Disco Marina** (tel. 614 9860), the local hotspot, has flashing lights, Eurotrash music, and scantily clad bodies—Mediterranean style. Follow Çarşı Cad. all the way to the *yat limanı* (harbor) to get there.

Sights   The road from the north into Fethiye ascends steep hillsides thick with pine trees, crickets, and sap. In ancient times, this region, isolated from the rest of Asia Minor, insulated Lycian culture. Believed to be the descendants of the pre-Hittite Anatolian peoples, the Lycians remained independent until their quixotic stand against Cyrus' Persian armies in 545 BCE. The city of tombs that remains, the **Necropolis of Telmessos,** is the most significant vestige of Lycian culture (admission $1.25). The façades of the cliff-hewn tombs resemble Greek temples down to the pediments, porticos, and cornices. The tombs themselves are thought to be replicas of Lycian homes. Connected to the road by several flights of steps just off Kaya Cad. (off Atatürk Cad.) is the **Tomb of Amyntas,** identifiable by a 4th-century BCE inscription on the left-hand column. Climb the 150 steps to the tomb to find a tiny chamber beyond the opening. You can enter the other tombs as well, though to reach them you must clamber around the rocks. From the necropolis, the remains of the **Fethiye Tower** and several islands sprinkled about the Bay of Fethiye are visible. The **Archaeological Museum,** one block down from the hospital towards the bus station, contains Lycian artifacts from neighboring digs (open June-Sept. Tues.-Sat. 8am-7:30pm; admission $1, students 50¢).

Fethiye's main beach, **Çalış,** 5km to the north, is a relatively uncrowded crescent of sand extending over several kilometers. *Dolmuş motoları* (*dolmuş* boats; every 20min., 20min., 95¢) depart from the harbor (look for the sign or call 613 2376). *Dolmuş* from the main *dolmuş* station (route goes around town; 30min., 20¢); or *dolmuş* from Atatürk Cad. near the water (route goes along the coast; roughly every 15min., 30min., 25¢) leave for the beach during high season. Boats run from the pier (near 12-island tour boats) to the beaches on the isle of **Sövalye** (every 30min., $1). Twelve kilometers farther to the north are the beaches of **Günlük Bay** and **Katrancı Bay,** which are less frequented than Çalış (minibuses every 10min. from the station behind the mosque, 30min., $1). Frequent minibuses run from the main *dolmuş* station to **Ölüdeniz** (every 10min., 30min., 50¢); **Saklıkent** (45min., 90¢); and **Kaya Köy** (30min., $1, departing from the *dolmuş* stop by the Yeni Mosque). For those who want to explore the region on their own, **Light Tours** (tel. 243 4061) rents cars for $80-140 per day with unlimited mileage. Another option is **First Rent-a-Car** (tel. 614 9312; fax 614 2593), up the street from the tourist office and opposite the marina.

■ Ölüdeniz

The highly romanticized Blue Lagoon is materialized in the serene, crystal clear lagoon of Ölüdeniz. While you've probably seen posters of this partially enclosed beach hanging on the walls of most Turkish hotels, no picture can convey the serenity of this legendary sight. Poised only 14km from Fethiye, this seaside town gets its share of visitors. Thankfully, the lagoon's breathtaking tranquility counters the bustle. Bring a lover, or a trashy romance novel—you'll have stars in your eyes by sunset and feel desperate for a vehicle to vent that sun-soaked "luv" energy.

Orientation and Practical Information   Even from the east, visitors go to Ölüdeniz via Fethiye. During the summer, *dolmuş* depart from the main minibus station (every 10-15min. 7:30am-11:30pm). The *dolmuş* to Ölüdeniz stop at a vast pebble beach. This is not Ölüdeniz—Ölüdeniz and most of its good (and cheap) hotels stand farther right, facing the water. To the left there is a string of bars, campgrounds, and restaurants. People who choose to hitch walk 2km to the main turn-off. There is no official tourist office, but the **Tourism Cooperative** (tel. 616 6950, -2), just up the Fethiye road from where it runs into the beach, helps with rooms and arranges boat trips and parasailing excursions (open daily 9am-midnight). The town, if it can be called that, has **grocery stores** and a **PTT** (open April-Oct. daily 9am-10pm) 50m to the right from the entrance to the lagoon. The phones in the PTT have been unreliable in the past—try the ones scattered around town. You can **exchange currency** at some of the larger campsites and at the grocery store to the right behind Derya Camping. **English-language newspapers** and magazines can be found at the newsstands along the beach. For **police,** call tel. 616 6005. **Postal Code:** 48300. **Telephone Code:** 252.

Accommodations   Up the hill from the beach (5-min. *dolmuş* ride, 35¢), the town of **Hisarönü** is growing in popularity because of its cheap pensions and hi-fi powered discoes (your *dolmuş* might stop there on the way to Ölüdeniz). Taxi drivers sometimes drive prospective customers into a campsite and deliver them to the proprietors—be forewarned. From the *dolmuş* stop, walk to the right (facing the water) 200m to the fork in the road. The national park is on your left, and on your right is the road to the campgrounds. **Ölüdeniz Camping** (tel. 616 6024) is roughly 300m north from the exit (to the right as you face the water), past the municipal beach; not to be confused with Ölüdeniz Pension on the exit road. The site is distant from the center of activity but set at the edge of the lagoon, with a small beach, market, café, and restaurant. They have information about paragliding. ($1.65 per person. $5 for 2-person caravans with electricity. $8.75 per double bungalow. Breakfast $1.65. $3.75 for other meals.) Near Ölüdeniz Camping, backpacker-oriented **Genç Camping** (formerly Asmali Camping; tel. 616 6176) offers campers some grass and shade as well as bungalows of two distinctly different quality levels. It also has a café/restaurant and a private (though less than spectacular) beach. (Laundry service available. $1.50 per person. Type A bungalows $6 per person. Type B $3.50 per person. Breakfast $1.75.) **Deniz Camping** (tel. 616 6012; fax 616 6008) is to the left of the exit road facing the water. The ebullient Anthia Gurkan, an Englishwoman, is an experienced travel guide who can reserve plane and bus tickets as well as arrange trekking and paragliding adventures. ($2 per person. $2 per tent. $4 per caravan. $4 for a single bungalow. $8 for a double bungalow.)

Food and Entertainment   Eating inexpensively here is a task. Most people eat at the campground cafeterias, where the food is good but pricey (*şiş* $3.50, beer $1.25). **Dippy Dolly's Pancake House,** to the left from the exit road (as you face the water), serves gourmet confections (roughly $3.50). **Çetin Restaurant** (tel. 616 6393), under the Çetin Motel, offers decently priced, delicious meals (chicken *ızgara* $5, casseroles $5). You can relish this juxtaposition or just quench your appetite with beer instead (open daily 8am-11pm). At night, revelers drink, mingle, and dance all night at the **Buzz Bar** (tel. 616 6012), above Deniz Camping. It also serves Turkish ($2.25) and English ($4.50) breakfasts (open daily 7:30am-2am). The **Big Blue Bar Café,** in an upscale fenced-off development to the left of the exit road (facing the water), charges a hefty cover, but the bar's pool alone makes it worth the *lira*. Walk along the coast toward the cluster of paragliding vendors and take a left. Across from the Konıca Store is **Disco Tonoz.** You can put on your platforms and shake your booty on Wednesday nights for free. The party rages daily until 5am.

Sights   Some claim that the tranquil circle of the **Blue Lagoon,** at the tip of the beach, is where the movie of the same name was filmed. They are probably incorrect, but this idyllic bit of land does fill with Speedo-clad beach creatures of another type from dawn to dusk. A quiet dip in these crystal waters, especially on weekday mornings and evenings when it is least crowded, is pure bliss. To reenact the fantasy accurately, you should enter the lagoon from Tabiat Park. Potable water, bathrooms, and showers are available at the site, which is a 20-minute walk from the exit road or a 25¢ *dolmuş* ride (admission 65¢, students 35¢, $2.50 per car, $8.75 per motorcycle). For that death-defying sensation, inquiries about paragliding opportunities from Mt. Baba (1969m) into the Blue Lagoon should be directed at the dozens of vendors sprinkled along the Ölüdeniz coast.

Kaya and **Agia Nikola** Island were thriving Greek Christian communities until they were dispersed by the local Muslim population. Two popular excursions from Ölüdeniz visit the remains of these villages. The larger of the pair is Kaya, 10km away and accessible only by a dirt road. A more popular destination, tiny Agia **Nikola Island** has great swimming, a spine-tingling view of the coast, and the remains of a Byzantine basilica. **Activites Unlimited** (under the name Explora Travel; tel. 616 6316; fax 616 6274), on the main street next to Han Camping, books boat trips to Agia Nikola Island and **Butterfly Valley** for $19.40 including lunch. Visitors to the Butterfly Valley in particular bring reports of having found paradise on Earth. Boats leave from the main anchorage at roughly 10:30am and return at 6pm. Explora also offers comprehensive jeep safaris to **Saklıkent,** the ancient city of **Tlos,**

Patara Beach, Xanthos, and trout farms for $27 per person including lunch (open April-Oct. daily 8am-1pm and 6-11pm).

XANTHOS

Eighty-five kilometers from Ölüdeniz and 22km from Kalkan rest the ruins of the ancient Lycian capital of Xanthos. **Lycian rock tombs** pepper this attractive site, perched above the Eşen (formerly Xanthos) River. Unwilling to surrender during a revolt against the Persians, the Lycians gathered their women, children, and valuables into Xanthos for a final stand. When all hope was lost, they set the city on fire and fought until their last soldier died. Years later, the Romans fortified Xanthos in return for its peoples' support during the Roman invasion of Anatolia; most of the ruins are from this period. Check out the **Roman City Gate,** dedicated to Emperor Vespasian, and the **Roman Theater.** From the theater you can see the remains of the **Roman Acropolis** and a **Byzantine church.** Nearby are the **agora** and a **Byzantine basilica.** The **Xanthian Obelisk** near the agora bears an inscription which describes the Lycian-Athenian battles of the Peloponnesian Wars. At the end of the theater stands the 6th-century BCE Lycian **Tomb of the Harpies,** decorated with a plaster cast of the mythological creatures being summoned to destroy invading armies. To get to Xanthos, take any *dolmuş* running between Fethiye and Kalkan or Kaş, get off at the village of Kınık, and follow the signs to the site (Fethiye-Kınık 1½hr., $2; Kalkan-Kınık 1hr.; $1.90). The bus from Xanthos to Patara costs 75¢.

Ten kilometers southwest of Xanthos are the ancient ruins of **Letoon,** which date from the Roman and early Byzantine periods. Myth has it that Letoon, a Lycian religious sanctuary, was the place where the nymph Leto, mother of Zeus' children Artemis and Apollo, fled Hera's wrath. At the site there are three temples dedicated to each to Leto, Apollo, and Artemis; a function hall; and a pool. Scholars hope that an inscription found on the Leto Temple in Lycian, Greek, and Aramaic will prove as valuable in deciphering Lycian as the Rosetta Stone was in decoding hieroglyphics. There is no guard and no information booth. It is not a good idea to go after sunset.

PATARA

Twenty kilometers farther south (17km west of Kalkan) is the old Lycian port city of Patara. Choked with sand and brush, Patara's imposing ruins lie isolated among a series of seaside hills. Until its harbor silted up, the city was the seat of the Roman governor to Lycia and the site of an oracle to Apollo. Given the size and unwieldiness of the site, most tourists are drawn instead to Patara's vast sand beach. The **Mettius Modestus** triumphal arch, built in 100 CE, rests on the right of the road to the beach. A **necropolis** with numerous sarcophagi surrounds the gate. Along the path from the gateway to the sea lie the ruins of Roman baths, a Christian basilica, the **Baths of Vespasian,** and a theater. Farther back from the beach on the road are two pricey restaurants, one with bathrooms and showers.

To get to Patara, take any bus going from Fethiye to Kalkan, and get off at the turnoff ($1.75; ask the driver for Patara). From there it's six kilometers to the beach. From Kalkan, *dolmuş* leave every 30 minutes and come back at 4 or 5pm ($1.25). From the town, you can walk or take a taxi (roughly $2.50) the last 1500m to the ruins and beach. Minibuses go directly to the beach every morning around 10am from Kalkan and Kaş. From the beach, regular minibuses travel to surrounding cities (every hr. to Kalkan and Kaş until 6:30pm; to Fethiye 5 per day until 5pm). Taxis from Kınık to Kalkan cost roughly $6.50.

Apart from the ruins and nearby beach, the town of Patara consists of little more than pensions, restaurants, and gift shops. **St. Nikolas Pansiyon** (tel. (242) 843 5024, -154), on the main road at the center of town, offers clean, cool rooms with fans. It has a spacious, vine-covered terrace where they serve breakfast and occasionally dinner. All rooms have private baths. ($6.90 per person. Breakfast included.) A little farther from the beach on the main road is **Flower Pansiyon** (tel. (242) 843 5164, -034; fax 843 5078), a friendly establishment with carpeted, lavishly

---

Santa Claus Sure Was One Hip Cat

Next December 25th, when you're roasting chestnuts and frolicking 'neath the mistletoe, spare a moment of reflection for that good-natured Anatolian, the master-of-elves-and-toys, who travels around the world in one night to fill your stocking with goodies (even *Let's Go* can't rival that daytrip). On the very day of his birth in Patara in 270 CE, Saint Nicholas, or Claus as his really close friends called him, is said to have stood up and folded his newborn hands in thankful prayer. Claus's good deeds were many. In one of his travels, he came across a landlord who had not only murdered three young boys but had pickled their little bodies. A hopeless do-gooder, Saint Nick brought the boys back to life and converted the innkeeper. Despite these and other amazing deeds, his fame did not spread across Europe until the 13th-14th centuries, at which time the Dutch coined the white-bearded *Sinterklaas*. The idea of Santa Claus as a bearer of gifts came into being when Nicholas, in another act of kindness, dropped a bag of gold into the window of a poor Anatolian family while they were sleeping. These days, jolly old Saint Nick's belly might not be jiggling like jelly nor his cheeks quite so rosy since the Roman Catholic Church took away his sainthood in 1969 and excised his feast day from the church calendar, claiming that his miraculous works and acts of piety were nothing but old wives' tales. Bah humbug.

---

mosquito-netted rooms and balconies. (Singles $6.90. $5 for back rooms without balconies.) **Rose Pension** (tel. (242) 843 5165) is 100m away and offers the same amenities. ($7.50 per person. Breakfast included.) All three establishments run boat and canoe trips to the islands and Blue Cave, with dinner included, for $18.75-21.25. Patara has no official campsites, but ask about pitching a tent next to one of the restaurants or pensions in town. A large part of the beach is **Caretta-Caretta** sea turtle territory; sleeping there is strictly forbidden.

Despite various myths to the contrary, **Santa Claus** actually grew up right here by the sunny Mediterranean. Born in Patara in the 4th century, St. Nikolaus was famed for his annual gift-giving expeditions. After Santa became Bishop of nearby Myra, he was martyred there. You can visit his birthplace and then check out his church and grave at Myra near the village of Demre. The **Archaeological Museum** in Antalya houses St. Nick's relics—a few bits of bone that his 11th-century grave robbers dropped in their haste to get away (open daily 8:30am-noon and 1pm-5:30pm; admission $1.25, students 65¢).

KAŞ COAST

▓ Kalkan

Kalkan is the quintessential Turkish fishing village. A graceful stone breakwater encloses its harbor, and austere stone houses with wooden balconies huddle around the quay. The outside world has shown its appreciation by making the city a popular vacation stop (especially for Italians and the French), and Kalkan's winding streets are crammed with clothing stores and ceramics boutiques. Advertisements hawking donkey rides and boat trips beckon at every corner. Still, Kalkan's small scale and impressive setting on steep hills overlooking the bay make it a welcome change from larger cities along the coast. Kalkan proper does not have much of a beach; just a bunch of rocks on the left of the harbor. Past this, however, the landscape improves. A short climb leads to a tiny, often deserted pebble beach. Three kilometers along the road to Kaş, beneath a small metal bridge, lies the sandy beach of **Kapıtaş**. It's where blue meets green, sun meets horizon, and Turkish bachelor in leopard-print speedo meets blond gal from the Valley. The best beaches, however, line the coast between Kalkan and Fethiye, especially around Patara.

Orientation and Practical Information   Kalkan, on the main road between Fethiye and Kaş, is serviced by **buses** (Pamukkale office tel. 844 3346), running every 30 minutes between the ports (1½hr. from Fethiye, $2.50; 30min. from Kaş, $1.25). The highway between the two cities hugs the coast every inch of the way, revealing glimpses of distant isles. Buses stop at the top of the village on **Kalkan Caddesi**. The **PTT**, a block down the street, offers **currency exchange** (open daily 8am-midnight). **Postal Code:** 07960. **Telephone Code:** 242.

Accommodations   Rooms above the bus stop in Kalkan are cheaper than those in the center of town. Down the hill from the bus stop, to the left when the road forks, resides **Çelik Pansiyon**, 9 Yalı Boyu (tel. 844 2126). All rooms are immaculately clean and carpeted, and the terrace, where you'll find reception, offers gorgeous views of the harbor. (Singles $8.75. Doubles $15. Triples $18.75. Breakfast included.) For something a little extravagant, try **Daphne Otel** (tel. 844 3380), at Yalı Boyu. If you've been staying at hostels and need a break, here it is—luxurious beds (some with veiled canopies for that honeymoon feeling) in spacious rooms with spotless baths and balconies. (Doubles $25. Smaller doubles $20.75. Breakfast included.) **Holiday Pansiyon**, 33 Süleyman Yılmaz Cad. (tel. 844 3154), at the northeast corner of town, is a family-run establishment in one of the quieter and more idyllic spots in Kalkan. There is also room for 10 guests in a beautiful 150-year-old wood-floored house next to the pension. (Singles $10. Doubles $15.65. Triples $18.75. Breakfast included.) Up the stairs between the Kamıl Koç office and the PTT is **Öz Pansiyon** (tel. 844 3444; fax 844 3152). Don't let the exterior put you off; the rooms within are clean, spacious, and all have private bathrooms. Communal kitchens for your cooking pleasure. (Singles $6.25. Doubles $9.40. Triples $11.25. All-you-can-stuff-in-your-face breakfast $1.65.)

Food   Tourists eat cheaply at the centrally located **Köşk Restaurant** (tel. 844 3046), which lays a sumptuous table of *meze* for $2.25 per plate (open daily 9am-1am). There are several restaurants along the waterfront that charge a bit more (roughly $5.50 for a full meal) for even more sumptuous fare. **Pandora Restaurant**, at the east end of this strip of restaurants, is particularly good. **Belgin's Kitchen** (tel. 844 3614) is across the small amphitheater from Köşk Restaurant. Belgin has created an authentic atmosphere here, complete with rugs, floor tables, and live Turkish music. Full meals go for roughly $4.50 (open daily 10am-1am). Vegetarians try the **Jolly Roger** (tel. 844 3284), down the hill on the extreme right of the fork near the bus stop—the "Scottish Spoken Here" sign will give it away. (Before you get used to the waitress' heavy brogue, you might wonder whether English is spoken here as well.) "Roger" offers veggie options along with plentiful meat dishes (full meal $4.50; open daily 9:30am-1am). Right across the street is the charmingly laid back **Foto'nun Yeri** (Foto's Place; tel. 844 3464). While this sit-on-our-pillows and read-our-makeshift-menus-scribbled-on-postcards joint has a variety of grills, their real specialty is *gözleme*. Every *çişit* you can imagine—honey/banana, potato, chocolate, etc., each for under $2 (open daily 8:30am-midnight). Bars are a-plenty in Kalkan, but the most popular joints are **Bar and Bar Cocktail Bar** and the **Moonlight Bar** (tel. 844 3043), on S. Yılmaz Cad. The best (and only) pastry shop is **Merkez Café** (tel. 844 3053), on the same street as the Bar and Bar, with outdoor seating.

■ Kaş

If you take the square root of Bodrum, add a quantum of Kalkan, and multiply all of the above by sleepy seaside languor, you get Kaş, a luscious little quark of civilization sandwiched between the sea and mountains. The serpentine road from Kalkan to Kaş passes by glittering inlets dotted with pebbly beaches. The town itself is replete with inexpensive, hospitable places to stay, excellent restaurants, and enjoyable bars. A peninsula curves around from one side of the town's harbor, creating a calm, rock-lined lagoon ideal for swimming. Kaş is the place to explore the mountainous, ruin-strewn countryside, take a boat trip, dance to a hodge-podge of Turkish and American pop music in a bar, or wallow on the waterfront, cocktail in hand.

KAŞ

ORIENTATION AND PRACTICAL INFORMATION

Most of the town's activity centers around the small harbor along the main street, **Cumhuriyet Caddesi.** At its west end near the mosque, its name changes to **Hastane Caddesi.** Here it is intersected by **Elmalı Caddesi,** which heads uphill to the bus station. At its east end near the statue of Atatürk, Cumhuriyet is intersected by **Çukurbağlı Caddesi,** which leads to the PTT. From the Atatürk statue, Hükümet Cad. goes above the harbor to two beaches. The street going up the hill behind the tourist office—the one with most of the souvenir shops—is **Uzun Çarşı Caddesi.**

Tourist Office: 5 Cumhuriyet Meydanı (tel./fax 836 1238), to your left as you face the back of the Atatürk statue. English spoken. Area maps sold at bookstores. Open May-Sept. daily 8am-noon and 1-7pm; Oct.-April Mon.-Fri 8am-5pm.

Tourist Agencies: Nearly all agencies offer tours to Kekova. Tour prices vary slightly, so shop around before purchasing a ticket. **Kahramanlar Tourism and Yachting** (tel. 836 1062; fax 836 2402), on Cumhuriyet beyond the mosque, offers numerous options. Buses and cruises and cars (oh my!). **Simena Tours,** 1 Elmalı Cad. (tel. 836 1416), down the street from the *otogar,* books airline tickets in addition to the staple stock of tours to Kalkan, Demre, Patara, Xanthos, Saklıkent, Kekova, and Dalyan. Open daily 8am-8:30pm.

Buses: Station at end of Elmalı Cad., across from Petrol. Pamukkale office (tel. 836 1310). To Antalya (every 30min., 4hr., $5.65); Fethiye (every hr., 2hr., $3.15); Marmaris (8:30am, 10:30am, and 3:30pm, 5hr., $8.75); Bodrum (9am and 4:30pm, 7hr., $11.25); and İzmir (9:30am and 9:30pm, 9hr., $12.50).

International Bookstore: There is a small **used book emporium** a few meters up the hill from the Red Point Bar with an ambience and a bespectacled owner straight out of a Spielberg movie. **Smiley's Restaurant** has a surprisingly large book exchange, and the **Sarıcaoğlu Market** (with the Efes-Pilsen sign), between the Atatürk statue and the mosque, sells and trades books as well.

Laundromat: Habessos Laundry, 5 Uzun Çarşı Antik Sok. (tel. 836 1263), offers a friendly smile with a wash and dry for $6.25 per load. Open daily 8am-midnight.

Hospital: (tel. 836 1185), on Hastane Cad. From the tourist office, 500m past the mosque, before the campground. For **English-speaking health service,** call the town's polyclinic at 836 1014.

Police: (tel. 836 1024), 200m to the left of the tourist office, as you face the water.

PTT: (tel. 836 1430), on Çukurbağlı Cad. Walk down Elmalı Cad. from the bus station, then turn left before the Hacı Baba Restaurant. 200m through the parking lot on the left. Open daily 8:30am-10:30pm. **Currency exchange** desk open 8:30am-5pm. **Postal Code:** 07580.

Telephone Code: 242.

ACCOMMODATIONS

The search for inexpensive accommodations in July and August will test your haggling and shopping skills. The pensions in Kaş are usually very clean and pleasant, but they tend to jack their prices up 20-40% in high season. **Smiley's Restaurant** offers free housing—you just have to dine there. More on this bargain-hunter's dream under Food and Entertainment.

Yalı Pension and Hotel, 50 Hastane Cad. (tel. 836 1870, -1132 for the pension), 1 block to the right of the mosque as you face the water. The hotel is on the right and the pension across the street. Both offer spacious rooms with carpets, couches, and balconies. The pension has slightly smaller rooms and a communal kitchen. Singles $8.75. Doubles $13.75. Triples $17.50. Breakfast $1.90.

Hotel Turquoise (tel. 836 1800), in the narrow street behind the statue (Askerlik Şubesi Yanı Sok.). Turquoise rooms with bathrooms. In-house Turkish textile boutique, and a terrace/bar with a sea view. Singles $12. Doubles $18. Triples $24. Breakfast included. Flash your *Let's Go* book and get a 10% discount.

Kısmet Pansiyon, 17 İlkokul Sok. (tel. 836 1879). From the bus station, follow the directions to the PTT onto Çukurbağlı Cad. Make a left one block after the Benetton store onto Postane Sok; Kısmet is at the top of the street. Bar and reception are on the roof. Roof patio with amazing view. Large, carpeted rooms. Laundry $3.15 per load. Singles $6.75. Doubles $11.25. Triples $15. Breakfast included.

Kaş Camping (tel. 836 1050, -2438), on Hastahane Cad. 100m past the amphitheater, or 500m past the mosque walking from behind the Atatürk statue. Sea view, hills, shade, and grass. Hot water is somewhat unreliable. $2.50 per person. $6.50 per double bungalow. $5.75 per caravan (electricity included). Breakfast $1.75.

FOOD AND ENTERTAINMENT

There's a fruit and vegetable **market** halfway between the bus station and the harbor, one block above the mosque on Elmalı Cad.—Friday is market day. For breakfast, try the **Hacı Babi Pastanesi** (tel. 836 2330), on Elmalı Cad., next to the vegetable market. Locals and tourists alike gather here to chat over plates of primo pastries and junk food. $4.50 will buy you enough sugar, sodium, and cholesterol to make your heart valves flutter with joy (open daily 6:30am-1am). The continental-breakfast set might want to head on over to the laid-back **Moonlight Bar,** across from Kısmet Pension (open daily 8am-1am). **Çınar Lokantası** (tel. 836 2128), between the PTT and Otel Turquoise on Çukurbağlı Cad., offers pleasant atmosphere but is a tad crowded (*kebap* $3; open daily 8am-midnight). If you're looking for Turkish-style home cooking, you can't beat **Oba Restaurant** (tel. 836 1687), on Çukurbağlı Cad., uphill past the PTT on your left. Cheap prices and finger-lickin' good food. Another option is **Smiley's Restaurant** (tel. 836 2812), behind the tourist office. The energetic owner İsmail, a.k.a. Smiley, certainly lives up to his name. He started as a waiter and slowly worked his way up to become the manager of one of the most popular restaurants in town. (Vegetarian specials $3.50-4.50, *kebap* $3.50. *Let's Go* readers get 10% off.) A new development—Smiley set up a charmingly traditional hostel-esque thing upstairs from the restaurant. You can stay in these rather comfy quarters for free on the condition that you eat your meals downstairs. Not bad, eh? And you still get the 10% *Let's Go* discount on your meals.

Eriş Restaurant, Cumhuriyet Meydanı 13 Ortança Sok. (tel. 836 1057), next door to Smiley's. Fancier and pricier than the restaurants along the harbor, but worth it (full meal roughly $5.50). We know you're in Turkey and are desperately fusing with the local culture, but for a relaxing, romantic evening, *the* place is **Chez Evy** (tel. 836 1253), a French restaurant decorated in laudably authentic Turkish decor. Up the street and around the corner from the Red Point Bar, Chez Evy is internationally renowned for its exquiste cuisine (chicken $9.40, salad niçoise $3.75, crepes $1.90-3.75). If your *kebap* threshhold has been saturated walkez-vous to Chez Evy's.

For good music and dancing, try **Mavi Bar** (tel. 836 1834), on the harbor by the tourist office (beer $1.25; open daily 4pm-3:30am). You've probably seen a Red Point Bar in every tourist trap you've visited, but to experience the original, hit the perpetually jam-packed **Red Point Bar** (tel. 836 1605), on the same street as the laundromats, to make nicey-nicey with locals and tourists alike (beer $1.25; open daily 6pm-2:30am). Romantics hit the **Elit Bar,** which has live music and a cozy atmosphere. From the start of the pier, take a right and pass between the teahouses on the shore (beer $1.50; open daily 7pm-2:30am).

SIGHTS

The two beaches of Kaş lie in coves surrounded by rocky cliffs and covered with smooth stones. It takes considerable effort to scramble over the stones, but it's worth it. The entrance to **Küçük Çakil Plajı** (Little Pebble Beach) is at the top of the hill on Hükümet Cad., to your left as you face the harbor (200m left as you exit the tourist office). More determined sunbathers and swimmers frequent **Büyük Çakil Plajı** (Big Pebble Beach), 15 minutes down the road.

Kaş has several historic sights in or near the town. Most impressive is the **Hellenic Theater,** just past the hospital on Hastane Cad. as you leave town. The only intact ancient structure in Kaş, the theater rests on a solitary, elevated perch, overlooking the sea and the Greek island Kastelorizo. You can spend the night in the theater (bring a sleeping bag), but don't count on sleeping much: rowdy young people crowd in after the bars close at 3am and sing and play guitar for most of the night. Follow the footpath behind the theater roughly 50m to get to the 4th-century BCE **necropolis.** Back in town, there's a free-standing **monumental tomb,** also from the 4th century BCE (up Uzun Çarşı Cad. behind the tourist office). If you're lucky enough to be in Kaş on July 1, you should attend the **sea festival** on the harbor. Kaşians celebrate the bounty of the sea by picking up unsuspecting passersby and throwing them into the water, clothes and all. Swimming races are also held.

■ Near Kaş

The farming community of **Demre,** an hour's bus ride east of Kaş ($1.50) on the road to Antalya, sits on a fertile plain sandwiched between the mountains and the sea. The town itself is unattractive, but several interesting sites lie nearby; a long afternoon should take care of them. A short walk from the bus stop brings you to the **Tomb of St. Nikolas,** or **Santa Claus,** housed in a well preserved 4th-century Byzantine basilica (follow signs for "Aya Nicola"). The saint is better known to Turks as Noel Baba. Remembered for his acts of charity, he came to be seen as a protector of sailors and children. In 1087, thieves plundered Santa's tomb, escaping to Bari, Italy, with his bones and a funny red cap. Today, the burial chapel in the basilica houses his simple marble **sarcophagus,** located in a small niche immediately to your right as you enter. St. Nikolas is pictured on the wall above his sarcophagus. Each December 6, the saint's birthday is celebrated with a three-day festival and symposium (basilica open Tues.-Sun. 8am-7pm; admission $1.25, students 65¢). If you stay the night, consider **Şahin Hotel** (tel. (242) 871 5686), on Müze Cad., a few blocks to the left as you leave the bus station. The clean, spacious rooms have 24-hour hot water and there's a shady terrace. ($9.65 per person. Breakfast included.)

The main attraction around Kaş is **Kekova,** a partially submerged Lycian city roughly two hours east. **Excursion boats** visit Byzantine ruins, Kekova, and two fishing villages which flaunt a cliff honeycombed with Lycian tombs and a hill crowned with a half-ruined castle. Both towns are surrounded by a dozen Lycian sarcophagi, some leaning on the village homes (tours $10). The **Blue Caves,** 15km from Kaş and home to the Mediterranean's only **seal colony,** are worth a visit. Try to swim in the mornings before the sea becomes rough. Nearby, 2km after Kalkan, is **Doves Cave,** which can be reached only by swimming. Opposite this grotto, the wide **Güvercin-lik Cave** spouts a cold underwater stream. **Kemer** longs to achieve Spain's Costa del Sol's level of tourist saturation. While it fails to do so, Kemer does offer the only Mexican restaurant on the Turkish Mediterranean, and a plentitude of overpriced, underoccupied hotels. Kemer does have nice beaches, however, and a pleasant pedestrian shopping area if you're out of leather jackets and Benetton accessories.

■ Olimpos

It's hard to say whether Indiana Jones or Han Solo would feel more at home in this remote outpost. The heavenly village of Olimpos, ensconced in a lush, jagged, rocky ravine, is so alien and ragged that it may be difficult to find a stranger place in this galaxy. Whispers from the village's crickets and winds that whip in off the sea twist the daily Muslim prayers into ghostly echoing wails. Enchanting Olimpos is a backpacker's town, and one of the few true budget destinations on the Turkish Riviera.

Originally a powerful **Lycian port city,** Olimpos was subsequently overwhelmed by Greek, Roman, and Byzantine invaders, each of whom left their mark on the town's architecture. As late as the 12th century, Venetian and Genovese **crusaders** used the city as a resting point as they hacked their way to the holy land. At its height, the ancient city was home to more than 30,000 inhabitants.

To get to Olimpos from Kaş, take the Antalya bus and ask to be let off at Olimpos, roughly three hours into the trip. From Antalya, take the Kaş bus and ask to be let off at Olimpos (1hr. from Antalya). From the highway, you can take a taxi to the village ($6.75, negotiable; try to form groups). A one-horse town, Olimpos lacks facilities such as a tourist office, post office, or police station, but you can place international calls from the pensions, mail letters in any neighboring city, and arrange any local sightseeing through your pension owner.

Combine breathtaking scenery, the summer camp you went to when you were twelve, the cast of *Animal House,* and treehouses—yes, treehouses—and you have Olimpos. This is not your typical resort town. Whatever it is, you won't soon forget it. The two best pensions are both owned by a man named Kadir. The first pension you will come to is **Yörük (Nomad) Camping** (tel. (242) 892 1250). Owned by Kadir, Yörük is a bizarre mixture of huts, treehouses, and pillowed shelters for daytime R&R. Table tennis and a wide range of nationalities complete the U.N./summer camp atmosphere. Treehouse accommodations, an excellent dinner, and breakfast are all less than $6 per person. (Small 2- or 3-person cabin $9 per person.) Just down the street is **Kadir Pension** (tel. (242) 892 1110; fax 825 7209). Kadir features treehouses and dinner or breakfast for $6.25 per person and offers nighttime excursions to the Chimaera for $1.25 from both of his pensions. **Gypsy Pension** (tel. (242) 892 1223), past both Yörük and Kadir, is new and closer to the water, but more conventional than its neighbors. ($6.25 per person with shower and bath. Breakfast $2.)

Inexpensive good food, convivial atmosphere, and a marvelous beach are all the entertainment Olimpos offers. Boat trips to the Chimaera and the mountain city ($5.50), as well as trekking, will satisfy your thirst for adventure. The area's archaeological and natural attractions are set off by the beautiful landscape. Moving towards the sea, the pensions thin out and ancient ruins choked with Amazonian vines become more frequent. It's easy to get distracted on the pathways that veer off the road to the beach. Beware of frail footbridges, but don't be daunted—the sights only get better. (Admission to ruins and beach $1.25, students 60¢; keep your ticket, and you only have to pay once for your entire stay.)

In antiquity, Vulcan, god of the forge, was Olimpos' patron deity, due to the town's proximity to the **Chimaera,** a perpetual flame springing from a mountainside seven kilometers away. The ancients thought that this flame was the breath of the Chimaera, a mythical beast that was part lion, part goat, and part serpent. Geologists have yet to come up with a better explanation. In past centuries, the flame was even brighter than it is today, and, according to ancient reports, ships navigated by it. A **Byzantine church** now stands near the site (nighttime tractor tours cost $1.50). The city of Olimpos has only been partially excavated, so the ruins are, in most places, shrouded in vines, shrubs, and flowering bougainvillias. To the left of the beach road, over a small creek, a pathway leads to an ancient mausoleum with two **Greek-inscribed sarcophagi,** suffering the wear of the centuries. Farther left on the path is the better preserved **mosaic house,** an exquisite 5th-century edifice. The floors of the house were entirely covered with intricate tilework, until an earthquake diverted the course of a stream and flooded the building with one meter of water. On the other side of the road to the beach, across the river, is a decrepit **theater** and **medieval walls** which have been damaged by the river and forest.

ANTALYA GULF COAST

■ Antalya

Antalya is Turkey's premier tourist resort, a city of modern white buildings perched atop a cliff. Daily airbuses bring in hordes of tourists from London, Munich, and

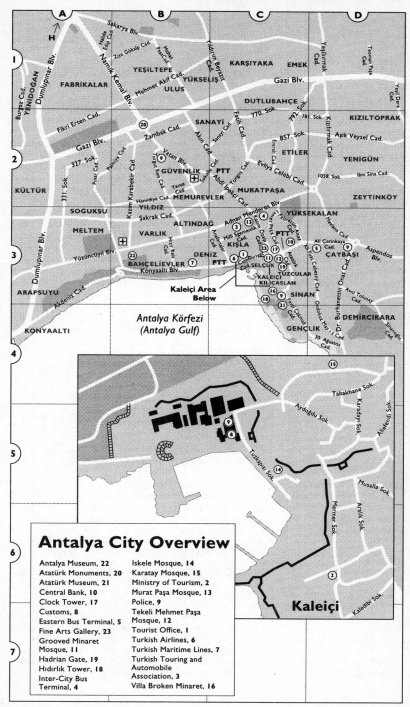

ANTALYA

Antalya City Overview

Antalya Museum, 22
Atatürk Monuments, 20
Atatürk Museum, 21
Central Bank, 10
Clock Tower, 17
Customs, 8
Eastern Bus Terminal, 5
Fine Arts Gallery, 23
Grooved Minaret
Mosque, 11
Hadrian Gate, 19
Hıdırlık Tower, 18
Inter-City Bus
Terminal, 4

İskele Mosque, 14
Karatay Mosque, 15
Ministry of Tourism, 2
Murat Paşa Mosque, 13
Police, 9
Tekeli Mehmet Paşa
Mosque, 12
Tourist Office, 1
Turkish Airlines, 6
Turkish Maritime Lines, 7
Turkish Touring and
Automobile
Association, 3
Villa Broken Minaret, 16

ANTALYA

Amsterdam. Stretching along the bay's edge are the towering, jagged Taurus Mountains. Tourism has been good to Antalya; it is wealthy, sophisticated, and arrogant. Antalya is the capital of the Turkish Riviera, and although it is very touristy, it never descends to the tackiness of Spain's Costa del Sol. People are less friendly here than in inland Turkey, prices are higher, and there is sometimes a "special" price for foreigners—which, in case you were wondering, isn't lower.

ORIENTATION AND PRACTICAL INFORMATION

A new bus station is long overdue and may be ready by the summer of 1997. If so, it will be on Namık Kemal Bulvarı, northwest of the harbor and the old town tourist area, at the Anatolu Kavşağı (Anatolian Crossroads). In the meantime, Antalya's bus station is on the corner of **Adnan Menderes Bulvarı** and **Kazım Özalp Caddesi**. To get to the center of town, exit from one of the bus station's gates on Adnan Menderes Blvd. and take the first left onto Kazım Özalp Cad. After roughly 100m, this street turns into a pedestrian zone. There are several exit gates—make sure you're exiting onto Adnan Menderes. One kilometer farther, at the end of the street, is the intersection with Cumhuriyet Cad. (Republic St.); you will see the red, pointed **Fluted Minaret** (Yivli Minare) on your right and the **clock tower** in front. To the right of the clock tower, a little street runs downhill into the old city. To reach most of our accommodations, it is easier *not* to enter the old city at this point; instead, go left on Cumhuriyet Cad. Take the first major intersection (150m along) to the right. You are now on Atatürk Cad., the city's main street, which is lined with high-class boutiques and leather shops. Roughly 150m down the street, on the right, is the triple-arched Hadrian's Gate. Go through it and take the first left to get to **Hesapçı Sok.** This old street runs for about 1500m, past the **Truncated Minaret** (Kesik Minare) to the Hıdırlık Tower on the seafront with magnificent views of the city, the Gulf of Antalya, and the rugged Taurus Mountains. Most accommodations are scattered along this street.

Tourist Offices: (tel. 241 1747). The **main tourist office** is in a mansion in the old city; it's a challenge to find it. Enter the old city beside the clock tower and walk under the "Welcome" arch. When the road ends after 800m, go left at the Türk Evi Otel. Eventually the road narrows and goes uphill. The tourist office is on your right, opposite the Aspen Hotel. English spoken. Open Mon.-Fri. 8:30am-5:30pm. The **new city's tourist office** (tel. 247 0541, -2) is on Cumhuriyet Cad. Open Mon.-Fri. 8am-6pm, Sat.-Sun. 9am-5pm.

Tourist Police: (tel. 155), on harbor, on a little street to left of Atatürk bust.

Consulates: U.K., Kızılsaray Mah. Dolaplıdere Cad. Pırıltı Sitesi, 1st floor (tel. 247 7000). **Northern Cyprus** (Kıbrıs), Kışla Mah. 35th Sok. Dörteldemir Apt. 11 (tel. 248 9847).

American Express: Pamfilya, #57 30th Ağustos Cad. (tel. 243 1500), near the water at far end. For international cash transfers go to **Koç Bank,** on Atatürk Cad. opposite the Hadrian Gate; to the right with the gate to your back. **Akbank ATM** for AmEx cards is on Kazım Özalp Cad., between the clock tower and bus station.

Flights: (tel. 243 4381, -2), on Cumhuriyet Cad. Offices in same building as smaller tourist office. Open Mon.-Fri. 8:30am-7pm, Sat.-Sun. 8:30am-5:30pm. Direct flights to İstanbul ($65), Ankara ($55), London (1 per week), Amman (2 per week), and Lefkoşa (2 per week). Other connections via İstanbul and Ankara.

Trains: TCDD provides a bus service to Burdur (2hr.) which connects with its train to İstanbul. Through service from Antalya to İstanbul ($12).

Buses: Station at the intersection of Adnan Menderes Blv. and Kazım Özalp Cad., north of the clock tower. Buses to İstanbul (10 per day, 15hr., $20); Ankara (12 per day, 12hr., $16); İzmir (5 per day, 12hr., $16); Rize (2 per day, 30hr., $27); Adana (15 per day, 12hr., $16) via Alanya (2hr.); Anamur (6hr.); Taşucu (8hr.); Mersin (10hr.); and Göreme/Ürgüp/Nevşehir (3 per day, 12hr., $16). To find a cabbie that won't rip you off, go 100m from the station to one of the side streets and hail one there. **Main city bus terminal** is at Meydan, at the intersection of Aspendos Blv. and İbni Sina Cad., 5km from city center (on road to airport).

Dolmuş: *Dolmuş* stop at blue signs marked "D." Run to Museum and Konyaaltı Beach (take *dolmuş* from Konyaaltı Blv.) and to Lale Beach, from the *Doğu Garaj* (East Station; 35¢). To get to Doğu Garaj from Atatürk Cad., take a right onto Cumhuriyet Cad. Walk one block to the Start Hotel, then go right; you'll see *dolmuş* clustered around. The Lale *dolmuş* leaves from 100m down this street, on the right. The former garage is a bazaar; *dolmuş* now leave from streets around it.

Ferries: Turkish Maritime Lines (tel. 241 1120) serves Venice May-Oct. Departs each Wed. and returns Sat. Prices range from $267-600.

English Bookstore: Owl Bookshop, Barbaros Mah. 21 Akarçeşme Sok. (tel. 243 5718). Off Hesapçı Sok. 500m down from the new town, on the left. Selection of new and secondhand books in English. Open daily 10am-1pm and 3-7pm.

Laundromat: Yıkama Laundry, 28 Tabakhane Sok. (tel. 241 1174), beside the Anı Pansiyon. Wash'n'dry $6. **Ünal Laundry,** 43 Hesapçı Sok. (tel. 248 9372), beside the Truncated Minaret. Wash'n'dry $7. Both open daily 8am-10pm.

Hospital: Özel Antalya Kliniği, Işıklar Cad., Apt. No. 55/2 (tel. 243 6651; fax 243 3159). From Cumhuriyet Cad., walk down Atatürk Cad. to the end. Bear left at the park, staying on the main road. The clinic is roughly 1km down, on the left. 24-hr. service includes ambulance and hotel visits. Some English spoken.

PTT: The **main branch** sits a block down Anafartalar Cad., on the left from the Selekler Çarşısı. Open daily 9am-5pm for stamps and currency exchange, 24hr. for phonecalls. The **branch office** is on the harbor. Open daily 8am-6pm. **Smaller branch** is on İsmet Paşa Cad., the continuation of Atatürk Cad. past Cumhuriyet Cad. Open daily 9am-10pm. **Currency exchange** available at both PTTs.

Telephone Code: 242.

ACCOMMODATIONS

There are about 200 hotels and pensions in **Kaleiçi,** the old city. Although historic and well preserved, the old city is touristy and filled with pensions, restaurants, and carpet shops. Unless otherwise stated, prices include private shower and breakfast. Bargaining may be fruitful. The concept of a fixed price hasn't fully taken root.

Sabah Pansiyon, Kaleiçi Kılınçaslan Mah. 60 Hesapçı Sok. (tel. 247 5345, -6). A popular backpackers' hangout. Pleasant courtyard area. Singles $6. Doubles $12-22 with breakfast. Roof, couch, or floor $3. A/C $3. Camping $2.50 per person.

Ninova Pension, Barbaros Mah. 9 Hamit Efendi Sok. (tel. 248 6114). A touch of luxury in a beautifully restored house. Wooden ceilings and floors in large rooms that are as clean as a newly born babe's bottom. Singles $15. Doubles $25.

Anı Pansiyon, 26 Tabakhane Sok., Hesapçı Sok. (tel. 247 0056). This historic home, restored to a high degree of comfort, offers impeccable service. Rooms are smaller than at Ninova. Singles $15. Doubles $25.

Garden Pansiyon, Kılınçaslan Mah. 16 Zafer Sok. (tel. 247 1930). Basic little pension with a slightly wild garden. Singles $10, with bath $15. Doubles $15.

Sen Kaptan Otel/Pansiyon, Kılınçaslan Mah. 65 Hesapçı Sok. (tel. 248 6690). Restored house with a huge shaded garden. Singles $12. Doubles $24.

FOOD AND ENTERTAINMENT

Be sure not to miss the **Tophane Çay Bahçesi** (Battlements Tea Garden), on top of the rampart walls, overlooking the harbor. It's easiest to enter from the park on Cumhuriyet Cad. Half the city comes here to sit and relax (cold drinks 75¢, snacks 75¢-$1.25). For dinner, be careful you don't pay the "tourist price." Try the **Topçu,** 21 Özalp Cad., roughly 50m from the clock tower, in the pedestrian street which leads to the bus station. Veggie fans will enjoy *piyaz* (cold white been salad) and *cacık* (yogurt with cucumbers and mint; $5 each). There are three main eating areas, all in close proximity. **Eski Sebzeciler İçi Sokak** (The Old Inner Street of the Greengrocers) is a narrow, covered alleyway lined with cheap outdoor *kebap* restaurants. It's the place to try the local specialty, *tandır kebap*—mutton roasted in a clay pot. The Old City has dozens upon dozens of restaurants serving Turkish specialties. The outdoor **Favorit Restaurant,** 19 Uzun Çarşı Sok., 100m past the "Welcome to the Old City" sign (on the left), serves, as its specialty, *Ali Nazık kebap*—delicious grilled chopped lamb served in a thick sauce of garlic and eggplants ($4.75). Dozens of crowded, happy, boisterous fish restaurants are crowded at the base of the old city ramparts in the harbor.

There is no shortage of nightlife in Antalya. **Club 29** in the harbor has a highbrow crowd (cover $8 weekends, $6 weekdays). **Olympos,** in the 5-star Falez Hotel near Konyaaltı Beach, includes a laser system, video bar, and occasional live music. **Cinemas** generally show English-language films with Turkish subtitles: **Oscar,** Zafer Sok. in the old city; **Ulusoy,** Kazım Özalp Cad., towards the bus terminal; and **Cultür,** Atatürk Cad., near Police Station and park (all offer 50% ISIC discounts). Antalya is known for its spectacular **waterfalls** *(düdenler)*. The upper falls, accessible by *dolmuş* (30min., 30¢), tumble 11km to the north; the less spectacular lower falls are by Lara Beach. The **Emperyal Casino** (tel. 249 3880) features unlimited food and drinks for a mere $6.25 initial purchase of chips. If you can assemble 15 people, the Ofo Hotel, who runs the casino, will pick you up at your hotel or pension and drive you home later. The flashy casino and low admission price ensure a mixed crowd, so even a backpacker can feel like James Bond at the Emperyal.

SIGHTS

The **Antalya Museum** is among Turkey's more impressive museums. Exhibits range from prehistoric times to the Turkish Republic, featuring the first money, artifacts from the Archaic Era, and finds from Perge, Aspendos, and Side (open Tues.-Sun. 9am-6pm; admission $4, students $2). The museum resides roughly 2½km from town along Cumhuriyet Blv., which changes its name to Konyaaltı Blv. on the way. *Dolmuş* labeled *Konyaaltı/Liman* head left (with your back to the sea) along Cumhuriyet/Konyaaltı Blv. They stop at the large "D" signs. Get off before it heads downhill to the beach; the museum is signposted.

Near the intersection of Cumhuriyet Cad. and the old city entrance, you'll see the red-tinted **Yivli Minare** (Fluted Minaret), dating from the 13th century and virtually the symbol of the city. Down Atatürk Cad., on the right, stands **Hadrian's Gate,** built in 130 CE to commemorate the visit of the emperor Hadrian. Through this gate to the old city, about halfway down Hesapçı Sok., is the **Kesik Minare** (Truncated or Broken Minaret). The ruined mosque beside it was transformed from a Byzantine church by the Seljuks. The structure was actually built as a Roman temple before it was converted into a three-nave basilica in the 4th century CE. At the far end of Hesapçı Sok. is the **Hıdırlık Tower,** believed to have been built as a lighthouse in the 2nd century CE. To its left is the city park. It's a great place to watch the sunset. Founded as Attaleia in the 2nd century BCE by King Attalos II of Pergamon, Antalya is still surrounded by walls built by Greeks, Byzantines, and Seljuks.

■ Near Antalya: Perge

From the extensive remains of ancient Perge (16km from Antalya), it is easy to imagine what life must have been like in this prosperous town of over 100,000 inhabitants. The city was supposedly founded by Greek heroes after the Trojan War, but it did not earn its place in history until it sided with omnipotent boy wonder Alexander the Great. The **stadium,** which seated a crowd of 12,000, has a wall at the far end meant to protect spectators during the wild beast fights that took place here. Against the opposite hill, an impressive **theater** features finely rendered reliefs of Dionysus. Entering through the **Roman gate,** you'll see a large **agora** (market place) to your right. Up ahead, two imposing **Hellenistic towers** mark the beginning of the long colonnaded avenue leading to the **nymphaeum.** In ancient times, water flowed from here into a fountain that flowed the length of the street. Don't miss the remains of the **public baths,** to your left. (Site open in summer daily 8:30am-6:30pm; in off season 8:30am-5:30pm. Theater currently closed for excavation. Stadium free. Admission to main site $2.90, students $1.45.) *Dolmuş* run from the central station in Antalya to Aksu; Perge is a sweltering two kilometer walk from there.

■ Near Antalya: Side

Side (pronounced SEE-deh) contains all the ingredients necessary for a complete Mediterranean coast vacation: Hellenic ruins, parasailing, a fine museum, beautiful sandy beaches, and the self-proclaimed best disco in Europe. Shop for leather goods in the crowded pedestrian streets, study up on ancient history in the 7th-century Roman ruins, and tan under the sun. It's one-stop shopping—Mediterranean style.

Orientation and Practical Information Side can be reached by direct buses from Antalya, but you will most likely (assuming you're not on a package tour) be let off at the highway turn-off in Manavgat. From there, you can catch a *dolmuş* to Side (3km) or walk. Walking has the advantage of taking you past the tourist office. Your best bet is to ask to be let off the *dolmuş* when you see the tourist office on your left (accomplished by yelling out *"İnecek var"*). The **tourist office** (tel. 753 1265) is an inconveniance if you arrive at the *otogar*, but the staff is friendly and somewhat conversant in English—German is much more helpful here (open in summer daily 8am-6pm; in winter Mon.-Fri. 8am-noon and 1:30-5:30pm). To get to the PTT, exit the bus station to the left, turn left when you reach the main road, and go past the Luna Park (Amusement Park). The **PTT** (tel. 753 1796) is centrally located and easy to find. The hospital is just off the main street between Side and the highway, kitty-cornered from the tourist office. For a **medical emergency,** dial 753 1221. **Postal Code: 07330. Telephone Code:** 242.

Accommodations Many pensions line the main road as you walk through a series of gates and arches into town from Manavgat or the bus station. Follow the main drag past the ruins and into the pedestrian shopping street and take a left at the Jungle Bar to get to **Pettino Pansiyon** (tel. 753 1272). One of the nicer places on the Mediterranean Coast, the pension has a beautiful courtyard area with bar and book exchange, vegemite, and excellent rooms with the standard pension ameni-ties. ($10 per person. Breakfast included.) The closest established camping area is the **Seving Pension** (tel. 753 1767), on the left from the center of town, between the first and second gates, off a gravel road. Seving features a bar on a raised plat-form, perfect for watching the waves roll in. ($4 per camping site for 1-3 people. $12 per 1-3 person bungalow room. Breakfast included for bungalows.)

Food and Entertainment No Mediterranean resort would be complete with-out seafood and a kickin' nightlife. Fine seafood can be had throughout the city—in most cases, the better the decor, the more expensive and less inspired the cuisine. Skip the Long John Silver routine and go where the locals go. If you do stay in the touristy part of town, **Pettino Restaurant** (tel. 753 1273), across from the Pettino Pansiyon, offers well prepared Turkish favorites and seafood for not too many *lira*. You can also get a quick meal, or an evening beer or two or three, at the nearby **Blues Bar,** whose Welsh owner often sings and strums the guitar. The **Oxyd Disco,** touted by local pension owners as "the best in Europe," features laser shows, video screens, and screaming house and techno. The cover charge is $5 with the first beer/drink, after that beers are $1.25 and drinks are more.

Sights You'll have no problem finding the ruins. When you enter Side, you'll see the **Nymphaeum** memorial fountain which once had a marble façade depicting punishments administered to those who committed sexual sins or sins against the gods. Fortunately, Side today is as loose as it gets—get down, get dirty; chances are your neighbors are naughtier than you. While most ancient theaters were hewn into the hillsides, the 2nd-century CE **theater** of Side was built on level ground using arches. It's the largest in the area seating 25,000 people (open daily 8:30am-5:30pm; admission $1, students 50¢). Other ruins include two **agoras.** The site is 1500m from the city and can be reached by following the beach to the west. The ancient **Roman baths** now house a great **Archaeological Museum** (open Tues.-Sun. 8am-noon and 1:30-7:30pm; admission $1.65, students 65¢). About 200m to the east stretches the best **beach** in Side, where some tourists unfurl sleeping bags on the sand or in one of the empty wooden shacks. Walk to the right directly out of the bus station about 2km (with the sea to your right) and turn onto the dirt road that leads right to the water (the shacks will be off to the left).

■ Anamur

Anamur is another one of those peaceful Mediterranean cities that provides a pleasant respite from the monster tour groups and overpriced tourist pensions. Well equipped to handle tourists, Anamur combines the best of both worlds: access to uncrowded beaches, water clear as glass, and civilized accommodations and restaurants for the budget traveler. Anamur's charms lie beneath its concrete, hot, and dusty epidermis. In the right spots, it's a serence and uncommercialized town with miles of open beaches. Nearby, a seaside crusader castle and the Roman ruins of Anamarium provide the historic and aesthetic rewards that the city center lacks.

Orientation and Practical Information Buses drop off at the *otogar* in the dusty part of town. From here, **Tourist Information** will provide advice and maps and point out the *dolmuş* stops to take you to the more pleasant parts of town. The *dolmuş* stop to İskele beach, a popular tourist spot, is about 1km behind the *otogar* on the main road (situated to left of Atatürk statue in center of town). To Atatürk's right is the Anamur *dolmuş* stop. The main **tourist office** (tel. 814 3529) is in town, just up the road from the bus station on Bulvar Cad. (open in summer Mon.-Fri. 8am-noon and 1:30-5:30pm, Sat.-Sun. 9am-noon and 1:30-5:30pm; in winter Mon.-Fri. 8am-noon and 1:30-5:30pm). The bus station houses a smaller **tourist office** (open Mon.-Fri. 8:30am-5:30pm). **Buses** run to Alanya (3hr., $5), Antalya (5hr., $6.25), Silifke (3hr., $5), and Mersin (5hr., $6.25). For a **medical emergency,** call the hopital (tel. 814 1086). The **PTT** (tel. 814 1001) is in the bus station (open daily 8:30am-5:30pm, no exchange services Sat.-Sun.). **Telephone Code:** 324.

Accommodations İskele beach, quiet and open, is much more pleasant than Anamur proper, as are the Kale and Anamarium. When you get off at the İskele beach *dolmuş* stop, the first pension you hit is the **Kap Anamur Motel** (tel. (324) 814 2374), on your right as you're facing the pier. The rooms are a cut above your average pension, with towels, soap, balconies, and a roof top terrace. ($10 per person. Breakfast $1.90.) Down this road, past the museum, and across the street is the **Gün Doğmuş Pansiyon** (tel. 814 2336). Doubles prices include breakfast, 24-hour hot water, and modern bathrooms. (Singles $6.90. Doubles $13.75.) Campers have two good options. Follow the main road around the army base to arrive at **Ünlüsek Hotel ve Mocamp** (tel. 814 1973). Dartboards, beach volleyball, and a slide bring out the inner child. Balconies, mosquito prevention devices, bar and restaurant, and beach chairs round out the well appointed package. (Singles $9. Doubles $12. Breakfast included for rooms. $2 per person with tent. $2.50 per person with caravan.) A bit farther is **Yalı Mocamp** (tel. 814 3474), with landscaped campsites and a bar on the beach. The staff is English-impaired, but friendly and willing to patomime. ($4 for 1-5 people including shower, toilet, and electricity. $10 per bungalow double. $15 for triples, quads, and quints with bath.)

Food, Entertainment, and Sights While Anamur is nobody's favorite dining area, it caters to the budget traveler's needs quite nicely. After hours, many of its peaceful, beachfront cafés and tea gardens transform into bopping joints with singing crowds dancing until dawn. Anamur's main drag, İnönü Cad., is home to a variety of restaurants. The **Astor Restaurant** (tel. 816 5610) specializes in fish dishes, but features a wide spectrum of Turkish cuisine. You can sit by the fountain and watch the owner's cute children torment the fish (entrees $1.90-$3.75). **Falmingo Pizza** is the place to be for American-style pizza and hamburgers ($1.90-2.90).

When the sun goes down, İnönü Cad. comes to life. The music is turned up, lanterns and strings of lights flicker, and the street fills with ice cream vendors, souvenir salespeople, and pedestrians looking to enjoy a cool evening. **Yakamaz Bar** has cheap beer, Western music, and dancing; it is one of the few bars where the groups of women are as numerous as the groups of men (no cover, Efes pint $1). Farther down the road, diners linger after dinner at the **Teras Bar and Restaurant,** where regular singers combine traditional Turkic favorites (you'll start with "Güneş Güneş" and end up with "This Could Be the Last Time"). The top of the **Hermes Hotel** also features a terrace bar. The music of choice here is 80s American (Van Halen, Quiet Riot, and Hip-Hop), and the volume goes to 11.

The real sights in Anamur are the popular, but not too populous, beaches and nightlife. The city is not, however, without the requisite historical sights. Right at the water's edge, the **Kale** at Anamur was constructed by the Romans in the 3rd century CE and reconstructed during the crusades. Also on the beach, 12km away, are the modest remains of **Anamarium,** an ancient Roman city originally built by the Phoenicians (admission 25¢). *Dolmuş* (25¢) drop visitors off at the turn-off to Anamarium. From there it's a 2km hike to the ruins.

■ Taşucu

The Turkish Mediterranean Coast is lined with crowded beaches, tourist resorts, and tour groups from Antakya to Antalya. Why such groups avoid Taşucu is a mystery—but one from which you can profit; you can just go, enjoy the beaches, and keep this Utopia to yourself. In addition to providing connections to Kıbrıs (Northern Cyprus), Taşucu is worth visiting in its own right if you don't mind beautiful, uncrowded beaches, great seafood, and some peace and quiet.

The town's main square, where the bus or *dolmuş* will drop you off, looks out onto enticing blue water. The **PTT** (open daily 8am-7pm; no exchange services Sat.-Sun.) and several ferry boat offices that sell tickets for the seabus and ferry to Girne (Kyrenia), Kıbrıs are here. **Fergün** (tel./fax (324) 741 3701) sells tickets for both. The **seabus** has daily departures at 11am and 2:30pm (2½hr., one way $13.75, roundtrip $25, 10% student discount). The **ferry** operates on weekdays (overnight one way $10, roundtrip $17.50, students one way $9.40, student roundtrip $16.25). Contact them to find out the ever-changing Taşucu port tax ($8.50 per entry or departure). Schedules are as likely to change as the taxes. Intercity Antalya-Adana **buses** stop here, as well as buses to or from points to the east.

From the highway, it's a two-minute walk to the sea. To the left, you'll find many pensions, all featuring sunny rooms at similar prices. All of the rooms in the **Tuğran Pansiyon** (tel. (324) 741 4493) have balconies and showers. (Singles $12. Doubles $20.) Two more excellent options are down the road. The **Barış Pansiyon** (tel. (324) 741 2838) offers all the amenities and oceanfront property. There are no singles, so bargain if you're alone. (Doubles $12.50. $17.50.) Across the street, you can't miss the blue and white compound of the **Taşucu Motel** (tel. (324) 741 4952). (Singles $9.40. Doubles $12.50. Triples $15. Breakfast $1.60.)

While Taşucu's seafood is not rock-bottom cheap, it is extremely good. Don't miss the **Taşucu Balık Restaurant** on the main square. For around $8 you can have fresh fish, the best eggplant appetizer you'll probably ever have, and a pint of Efes. Head up the beach, just past Barış, to the **Kordon Café** for ice cream so thick you'll need a knife to cut it.

■ Adana

Adana, Turkey's fourth largest city, is appropriately named after Adanus, the god of weather. The city has a pleasantly balmy Mediterranean climate and fertile countryside surrounding the region. Contemporary Adana is modern and has gained wealth from supplying cotton to the Turkish textile industry and *Adana kebap,* a tasty, spicy beef şiş, to Turkey's hungry mouths. Adana is surprisingly Western due to the nearby U.S. military base at İncirlik.

Orientation and Practical Information   Adana is a large city with few street signs. As you may have guessed, that's not a good combination. The main street is the **E-5 highway,** which runs from the center of town past the bus station and along the Mediterranean coast. In town, the landmarks on the E-5 are the big Akbank building, the overpass, and the minarets of the new Merkez Camii, beside the river. With your back to the bus station, take a right at the Akbank onto Atatürk Cad. The **tourist office** (tel. 359 1994) is 10m ahead. The friendly staff speaks English and will supply you with maps (open Mon.-Fri. 8am-noon and 1-5pm). Continue along Atatürk Cad. and take the first right onto İnönü Cad. to reach many hotels. Past İnönü Cad., Atatürk Cad. changes its name to Saydam Cad. A 10-minute walk along here leads to the Atatürk statue. Beyond the Atatürk statue, down a side street to your left, is the main **PTT** (open 24hr.). You can turn left at the Akbank building onto Atatürk Cad. At the end, if you turn right, you'll reach the railway station (20min.). Opposite the station on İstasyon Cad. is a PTT (open 24hr., exchange services daily 8am-5pm). There is a **small PTT** on İnönü Cad. (open daily 8am-5pm).

To get to the **THY Airlines** office, 1 Stadyum Cad. (tel. 454 1545), make a left out of the tourist office, walk straight, and make the first right after the second traffic circle (open Mon.-Fri. 8:30am-5:30pm, Sat. 8:30am-noon). They don't have service buses to the airport, but around the corner from the big Çetinkaya building, you can catch a *dolmuş* to the airport. From the tourist office, turn right on İnönü Cad. and then left on Zia Paşa Cad. before the Öz Hotel. Past the museum and at the end of the block, across from Hotel Kaza, is the *dolmuş* stop. You can take the one that says "Havaalanı" (airport).

To get to the center of town from the **Merkez Otogar** (bus station), located 5km away along the E-5, cross the road and take an E-5 *dolmuş*. Be sure to cross the road—destination plates read *Barkal* in both directions (every 5min., 25¢). The *dolmuş* depart the E-5 roughly 1km short of the Akbank, one block short of the overpass. Get off here and head for **Kurtulus Meydanı** (Kurtulus Square), across from İnönü Cad. **Taxis** are metered ($5-6). The larger bus companies offer free service to their central offices, clustered around the Akbank on the E-5. It's easiest to buy your ticket in advance from the offices on the E-5. Free service buses will then carry you to the station, 45 minutes to one hour before departure. There is a small **dolmuş station** on the E-5, by the river and opposite the Central Mosque, with services to local towns and villages. *Dolmuş* to Antakya also depart from here (every hr., 3½hr., $1.50), but run along the E-5 first—you can hail them at the Akbank building. *Dolmuş* to Mersin depart from the E-5, near the Akbank.

Currency exchange bureaux (Döviz) cluster around Saydam Cad., the extension of Atatürk Cad., as you exit the tourist office to the right. **Akbank** has an **ATM** and accepts AmEx. For cash transactions, you can go to **Koçbank,** located on the E-5, 100m past Akbank towards the river, on the right.To get to the **U.S. consulate** (tel. 453 9106) on the corner of the Atatürk Park, make a left out of the tourist office and pass through three traffic circles. Foreign-language **newspapers** are sold at **Yolgeçen Kitabevi** on Atatürk Blv. near the railway station, where you can pick up day-old copies of *USA Today* and the *International Herald Tribune*. **Postal Code:** 01122. **Telephone Code:** 322.

Accommodations   Unless you're broke, don't stay in the cheapest hotels, as Adana's worst are pretty bad. An exception is the **Otel Mercan,** 5 Ocak Meydanı, Melekgirmez Çarşısı (tel. 351 2603), which is clean and quite plush for a hotel in its class—all rooms have private bath. Facing the Atatürk statue, look right—it's behind the construction going up. (Singles $7. Doubles $11.75.) **Otel Duygu,** 14 İnönü Cad. (tel. 359 3916), is clean and comfortable with private shower and TV in each room. Some rooms have balconies. Prices posted are very high, but you can show your *Let's Go* guide for last year's rates. (Singles $14. Doubles $23.25. Breakfast

$1.75.) The **İpek Palas,** 103 İnönü Cad. (tel. 351 8741), is similar, as are its prices. It is across the street from Duygu. (Singles $17. Doubles $26. Breakfast $1.50.)

Food, Entertainment, and Sights   Adana's spicy namesake *kebap* will blow you away at **Yeni Onbaşlar,** on Atatürk Cad. opposite the tourist office (open daily 11am-10:30pm), which looks like it hasn't been renovated since the 50s (and that's part of its charm). **Limanı Lokantası,** in the arcade opposite the tourist office, serves standard *lokanta* fare (open daily 6am-9pm).

Walk along the E-5 towards the river to start your tour of the sights. You'll pass the huge **Merkez Camii** (Central Mosque), the "biggest mosque in the Middle East" which is larger than the Taj Mahal. It is still under construction—ask any local when it's likely to be finished, and they'll shrug as only Mediterranean people can. Just before it, the **Archaeological Museum** includes Hittite sculptures, Roman jewelry, and bronze-age pottery (open Tues.-Sun. 8am-noon and 1:30-5pm; admission $1.25). Turn right and follow the river; you'll soon pass a small **Atatürk Museum** (open Tues.-Sun. 8am-noon and 1:30-5pm; admission 60¢), and in five minutes you'll be at the **Roman bridge,** built by Hadrian. Continue past it for five minutes and go right at the government building to reach the **clock tower.** On the right before the clock tower is a park and just beyond it, the **Ulu Camii** (Great Mosque), built in 1541. The park is well shaded, with palm trees and views of the minaret. It's a pleasant place to linger awhile. Past the clock tower is the **Bedesten,** a crumbling but bustling 16th-century market. Continue on to reach **Yağ Camii** (Butter Mosque), an unusual structure dating from 1501. If you follow the road to the right, 50m past the Atatürk statue and right down some narrow streets, you'll find a Catholic church, home to the city's small community of Christians. Just off İnönü Cad. (follow the sign) is a small **Ethnographic Museum** (open Tues.-Sun. 8am-noon and 1:30-4pm; admission $1.25). Outside of town is a dam and huge man-made **lake**— it's none too beautiful, but pleasant tea gardens and restaurants are scattered along its shore. There are innumerable benches, over which the municipality has thoughtfully erected sunscreens. Take a white *dolmuş,* marked "Cemal Paşa" on top and "Göl" on the destination board, from opposite the tourist office. The *dolmuş* will take you all over Adana before stopping at the lake (every 10min., 25¢).

■ Antakya (Hatay)

In Antakya, site of the ancient city of Antioch, the heat and tourist levels subside considerably. The formidable Nur Mountains, which separate Antakya from the rest of Turkey, at one time isolated the city at the end of WWI. Consequently, this area was a part of Syria until 1939 and still retains a considerable Syrian influence. If you're continuing on to Syria, this is a good starting point.

As ancient Antioch, the city was one of the more powerful in the Mediterranean. It was the third largest city in the Roman Empire, after Rome and Alexandria. Seleucus, a general under Alexander the Great, founded the city in 300 BCE and ruled over much of Asia from here. The population swelled to half a million and Antioch became famous for its liberality and debauchery. During Roman rule, the Apostle Peter settled here and gathered the first Christian congregation in a grotto now outside of town. He chose Antioch to curb its excesses.

After a series of earthquakes, the desperate denizens changed the city's name to Theopolis (City of God), in hope that the powers that be would recognize their repentance. The city's importance, both strategic and commercial, made it a prime target for conquest. By the time the Turks got hold of it, Sassanians, Arabs, Byzantines, Crusaders, and Mamluks had all marauded through, and Antioch's glory had been reduced to ruins. A glance at the city's crumbling walls along the surrounding mountain ridge will give you an idea of city's size in ancient time, compared to the population of 150,000 that live here today.

Orientation and Practical Information You'll probably arrive at the bus station, 1km from the center. Nearly all **buses** pass through İskenderun (every 10min., 1hr., $1) and many through Gaziantep (every ½hr., 3½hr., $3.25). They serve Mersin (3 per day, 4hr., $3.75); Urfa (1 per day, 6hr., $9); Kayseri (2 per day, 8hr., $12); Ankara (10 per day, 11hr., $12); Antalya (2 per day, 11hr., $15); İzmir (3 per day, 16hr., $16); Samsun (2 per day, 16hr., $16); İstanbul (9 per day, 17hr., $16); Trabzon (2 per day, 22hr., $19); and Kars (1 per day, 22hr., $25).

Buses to points east (Urfa, Diyarbakır, etc.) leave around 8pm and arrive in the early hours, around 3 or 4am. To avoid this, you can take one of the regular *dolmuş* from the bus station to **Gaziantep** (3hr., $3.50) and change there for hourly connections. Buses head to Aleppo (3 per day, $14) and Damascus, Syria (11am and noon, $21); and to Amman, Jordan (5 per week, $29). Daily departures to major cities in Saudi Arabia (Mecca, Riyadh, Medina, and Jeddah) as well as to Brayda and H. Bartin. You should get your visas ahead of time in İstanbul or Ankara.

To get to the center of town, you should exit the bus station, turn left and left again onto Istiklal Cad. Continue past the Türkiye İş Bankası and Pamukbank ATM to the river (700m). Cross the second bridge into the square with the Atatürk statue, without which we'd all be lost.

The **Archaeological Museum** and the **PTT** keep Atatürk company. The PTT is on the traffic circle, on Atatürk Cad. (open 24hr.). Walk 10 minutes down Atatürk Cad. (to the right of PTT) to reach the **tourist office** (tel. 216 0160) in the park, opposite the circle (open Mon.-Fri. 8am-noon and 1:30-5:30pm). Blue inner-city **buses** (10¢) leave from the center, in front of the Hotel Kent (every 20min., 6am-9pm). **English-language books** and newspapers can be found at **Ferah Koll. Şti.** (open daily 7am-9pm), just past Restaurant Nuri. **Postal Code:** 31050. **Telephone Code:** 326.

Accommodations Head for the **Hotel Saray,** across the river from the square at 3 Hürriyet Cad. (tel. 214 9001). Management offers brand-new rooms with private bath and desk. (Singles $10.50. Doubles $15.25. Breakfast included.) The minaret of the Ulu Camii next door will awaken you at prayer time. The huge, hulking factory-like structure of the **Hotel Güney,** 8 İstiklal Sok. (tel. 214 9713), offers old but clean rooms. (Singles $8.25. Doubles with shower $14.) Heading into town from the bus station, take a left at the fork beside Ata Taxi into the little alley off Istiklal Cad. Cheap, clean, waterless, and minimalist rooms can be found in **Jasmin Hotel,** 14 Istiklal Cad. (tel. 212 7171). (Singles $3.75. Doubles $6.25.)

Food and Entertainment The Hatay region has several local specialties. *İçli köfte,* often referred to as *oruk,* is a hot and spicy meatball covered in thick pastry. *Ekşi aşı* is a variation on this, covered in tomato sauce. For dessert, *künefe* (or *peynirli kadayıf*) is a large *baklava*-style pastry stuffed with white cheese. It isn't easy to get a taste of these regional treats, as Antakya's eateries are simple (though good) *lokanta* and *kebapçı*, and you must hop on a *dolmuş* in order to get to the gourmet center of **Harbiye.** In town, go to **Restaurant Nuri,** 9 Hürriyet Cad., a cheap, authentic, delicious *lokanta* (entrees $1.25; open daily 5am-1:30am). The **Saray Restaurant** (under the hotel of the same name) is similar and almost as good. **Sultan Sofrası,** 18 İstiklal Cad., a *lokanta* with white tablecloths and waiters, occasionally serves local specialties. Large restaurants serve gourmet local and Turkish specialties at low prices.

Sights **Sen Piyer Kilisesi** (St. Peter's Church) is the world's first Christian church. Founded by the Apostle Peter, who preached here along with Paul and Barnabas, the original congregation coined the word "Christianity" to describe their new religion. Although the Christian community here is now tiny, it has never left Antakya, and liturgy is still given here. To get to the church from the bus station, turn left and then make an immediate right onto Istiklal Cad. Follow it one block to the twin gas stations and take a right, continuing 1200m until you see a sign on the right. The church is 250m from the sign. Inner city bus #6 will drop you off near the sign (church open Tues.-Sun. 8am-noon and 1:30-5:30pm; free). The hillside near the church has been a holy spot since pagan times and is riddled with the remains of caves, tunnels, and parts of Antioch's city walls. A path zigzags up from the church to the Hellenistic **fire altar** dedicated to Haron, god of earthquakes. Antakya's **Archaeological Museum** is renowned for its superb collection of Roman mosaics, the second-largest in the world. Dating typically from the 2nd to 4th centuries CE, many of these relics from nearby Daphne represent scenes from Roman mythology (open Tues.-Sun. 8:30am-noon and 1:30-5pm; admission $1.85, students 95¢.)

■ Harbiye

Harbiye, ancient Daphne, with its attractive wooded gorge, has been an excursion spot since Roman times. Legend has it that Antony and Cleopatra were married here. Nowadays it is regarded by locals as the region's premier culinary center. Harbiye provides an excellent opportunity to relax away from the noisier, more crowded Antakya. A favorite tourist spot for years among Syrians and Iranians, Harbiye is beginning to win Western tourists as well with its fresh air, food, and breathtaking views—nearly all of Harbiye's pensions are located on the gorge and most provide balconies and tea gardens to enhance your viewing and relaxing pleasure.

Orientation and Practical Information Harbiye is easily reached by *dolmuş* from Antakya's famed dual gas stations. Leaving Antakya's *otogar,* turn left, and then right. Walk one block to the red and white petrol *ofisi* gas station—another, identical station is across the street. You can grab a *dolmuş* on the side of the street with the first petrol ofisi; they are marked "Harbiye" (every 10min., 25¢). After 10 minutes, you will pass under an arch marked "Harbiye Belediyesi" on Harbiye's main throughfare (some call it Atatürk Cad., others Harbiye Cad.—in any case it's unmarked and locals don't seem to know or care what it's called). After passing the **PTT** on your right (open Mon.-Sat. 8:30am-12:30pm and 1:30-5:30pm), stay on the *dolmuş* until it veers right off the main road. This is Harbiye's restaurant and pension street. Get off at the park after the large pack of off-duty *dolmuş.* All restaurants and pensions will be on this road (Ürgen Cad. for the record, though you won't find a sign). **Postal Code:** 31020. **Telephone Code:** 326.

Accommodations A best bet for all-around services is the **Turistik Hidro Oteli** (tel. 231 4006). T.H.O. features an experienced staff, a fine pension featuring clean rooms with showers and modern bathrooms, an excellent restaurant, and nighttime entertainment. (Singles $12. Doubles $18. Breakfast $3.) The proprietors of the **Huzur Pansiyon** (tel. 231 4219) will probably find you on the street before you find their unmarked pension. ($10 per person. Or, you can rent the whole thing for six people for $25.) Huzur offers use of its kitchen and family room with TV. They are also building a full-service hotel next door for 1997. Numerous other family pensions dot the street as well, with bright signs, usually in Turkish, English, and Arabic.

Food and Entertainment Harbiye specialties *ızgara tavuk* (grilled chicken), *şiş tavuk* (chicken on a skewer), *oruk* (spicy meatball in pastry), and *künefe* (baklava-style pastry with white cheese) are done in a unique style for which Harbiye is duly famous. You can get all the local specialties at the **Hidro Oteli** (see above) on the main road opposite the gorge at the *dolmuş* stop (oruk $2.50, ızgara tavak $3, künefe or peynirli kadayif $1.50). The **Soner Restaurant** (tel. 231 2222) offers similar prices and quality just up the road. Soner also features a regular evening singer. Come early, though, if you wish to avoid the Turkish nightclub scene. **Cafe Defne** offers a beer garden setting under a grape arbor overlooking the gorge (beer $1.50, entrees $1.85-3.75). Try the thick, gooey homemade ice cream at **Dedem Dondurma** on Atatürk Cad., opposite the Büyük Antakya Oteli.

Black Sea Coast

The Black Sea Coast is bountiful and unspoiled and the soft lushness of the country-side profoundly beautiful. The region has long been overlooked by the majority of Turkey's tourists because of its short summer season. Cool breezes and heavy rain-fall nourish this region's forests and thickly cultivated farmland that are more reminiscent of the Northwest United States than a Middle Eastern country. Despite the isolation fostered by adjacent mountain ranges, trading posts such as Sinop, Trabzon, and Amisus (now Samsun) have become commercial centers. They first exported local products and later profited from the silk route trade when Arab invasions blocked the southern passage. The region still supports itself by the export of tea, cherries, and other crops that were the major produce of ancient times. In recent years, commerce with Georgia and other former Soviet republics has brought added prosperity.

■ Trabzon

From its hilltop vantage point over the Black Sea, Trabzon has seen empires rise and fall, preserving a little of each in its architecture and lifestyle. Founded by the ancient Greeks as the port Trapezus, the city is best known as a trade center which attracted merchants from all over the world. Though important in the Greek and Roman periods, Trabzon reached its heyday after Alexis Comneni came to the city in 1204, fleeing Constantinople while the Crusaders sacked it. Comneni dubbed the city Trebizond and made it the capital of his empire. The dynasty he founded became the longest and one of the wealthier in Greek history; its rulers lived off the profits of trade and nearby silver mines. The kingdom held out against the Turks until 1461, even longer than Constantinople, postponing its demise by diplomatically marrying off its daughters, reputedly the most beautiful women in the world.

An industrial region of more than 1.4 million inhabitants, present-day Trabzon has lost much of its romantic appeal as a stronghold of exotic princes. With the influx of impoverished immigrants from the Eastern Bloc came innumerable sex-workers; women traveling alone may be mistaken for prostitutes. A sultry atmosphere traps a rich stink in the city's center, which rains wash away from time to time, leaving the air crystal clear—for a day or so. Trabzon is greener than the cities on the Aegean and Mediterranean; its population is an ethnic bouillabaisse of Turks, Russians, Georgians, and other ex-Soviets. Trabzon may either repulse or bewitch you with its fascinating history, industrial squalor, verdant beauty, and post-Cold War seediness.

ORIENTATION AND PRACTICAL INFORMATION

Tourist Office: (tel. 321 4659), in the southeast corner of the main square's park. Has maps and the dates of the huge highland festivals of late June and late July. Open in summer Mon.-Sat. 8am-5:30pm; in winter Mon.-Fri. 8am-noon and 1-5pm.

Tourist Agencies: Afacan Tour, 40 İskele Cad. (tel. 321 5804), 200m northeast of the main square, can get visas for Georgia ($40 for 1 month, $110 for 3 months) and Russia ($45 for 1 month, $60 for 2 months), and schedules of ships (7-15hr., $30-100) and planes (every Mon., Wed., Fri., $100) to Sochi. Buses to Georgia and other destinations. Afacan Tour also operates daily tours of Trabzon and Sümela ($4); weekend tours of Uzungöl ($11.25) and Ayder ($11.25); ski trips to Zigama (groups of 5 or more, $11.25 per person, ski rental $4.50 per day); and trekking expeditions in the Kaçkars and near Uzungöl.

Consulates: Those interested in traveling to Georgia, Russia, or Iran are probably best off working through a travel agency; applying directly to the consulate is a cheaper, less predictable method. **Georgian Consulate** (tel. 326 2226), opposite Saktur. Visas cost $30 for first month, $19 for each additional month. Visa window open Mon.-Fri. 10am-1pm and 3-6pm. **Consulate of the Russian Federation** (tel. 326 2600), on Aranfil Cad. 200m southeast of the main square. Open

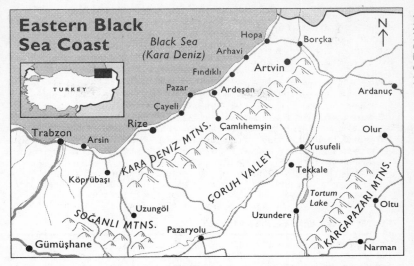

Eastern Black Sea Coast

Black Sea (Kara Deniz)

TURKEY

Tues., Thurs. 9am-noon and 3-5pm. Russian visa requests are more complex; unless you have an invitation from a Russian, go to a travel agency. **Iranian Consulate** (tel. 322 4851), on Boztepe Cad., 1km southwest of the main square.

Flights: THY flies to Ankara (2 per day, 1hr., $36, students $25) and İstanbul (4 per day, 2hr., $47, students $35). Buses leave from the **THY office** (tel. 321 1680, -3446), at the southwest corner of the main square.

Buses: Run from the *otogar* 3km east of the main square to Artvin (5 per day, 4½hr., $6); Samsun (every hr., 6hr., $5.50); Sinop (1 per day, 8½hr., $9); Zonguldak (4 per day, 18hr., $17); Konya (1 per day, 16hr., $15.50); Van (3 per day, 18hr., $22); Urfa (1 per day, 18hr., $9); Antakya (1 per day, 24hr., $17); and Hopa (every hr. 7am-7pm, 3hr., $3.50). **METRO bus lines** heads to Erzurum (1 per day, 6hr., $6.75); Ankara (2 per day, 12hr., $11); İstanbul (3 per day, 18hr., $20, students $15.50); Antalya (1 per day, 20hr., $22, students $20); and Adana (1 per day, 17hr., $20, students $18). Depart from the *otogar,* reachable from the main square via *dolmuş* marked *Otogar* or *Tıp Fak* (50¢). The main way to get back along the Black Sea coast in either direction, or even inland as far as Artvin or Yusufeli, is by coastal *dolmuş.*

Ferries: From June-Sept., **Turkish Maritime Lines** (TML) traces the Black Sea Coast from İstanbul to Trabzon. It leaves İstanbul Mon. at 2pm, stops at Sinop, Samsun, and Giresun, and arrives at Trabzon Wed. at 9:30am. The return voyage leaves Trabzon Wed. at 3pm and arrives in İstanbul Fri. at 1:30pm. Try to purchase tickets a week in advance at the **TML office** (tel. 321 7096), next to the tourist office, which sells tickets for $15-34. 50% student discounts. Open Mon.-Fri. 8am-noon and 1-5pm.

English Bookstores: Derya Kitap-Kırtasiye Pazarlama, 127 Uzun Sok. (tel. 321 1821), has a few English books.

Hospital: Nümune Hospital (tel. 223 4041) is west of downtown on Faik Dranaz Cad. off Kahramanmaraş Cad. Take a *dolmuş* marked "Hastane" or "Nümune" to the Nümune Hospital; get off at the Nümune Durağı.

PTT: Located halfway down Maraş Cad., the street directly west of the main square. Open 24hr. **Postal Code:** 61000.

Telephone Code: 462.

ACCOMMODATIONS

It's difficult to find a decent, quiet hotel here. Most of the cheaper hotels cluster around **İskele Caddesi,** which runs northeast off the main square. They offer cheer-

TRABZON

less, basic rooms, and many have degenerated into semi-brothels. Since the opening of the Georgian border up the coast, Trabzon has been swarming with Russian tourists and shoppers. They fill every hotel and are not shy about socializing well into the night. The secret to a restful stay is to seek out *aile oteli* (family hotels), places that stake their reputations on their healthy atmosphere for children.

Otel Anıl, 10 Güzelhisar Cad. (tel. 321 9566), is a real find. Spic-and-span, carpeted rooms with bath, TV, telephones, and Western toilets. Laundry 90¢ per pair of pants. Singles $12. Doubles $18. Triples $24. Breakfast $1.25.

Erzurum Oteli, 15 Güzelhisar Cad. (tel. 322 5427), next door to the Anil, shares Anil's views of the harbor. Clean doubles have private baths. $5 per person.

Gözde Aile Oteli, 7 Salih Yazıcı Sok. (tel. 321 9579), offers average rooms with showers but no toilets in most. Breakfast and meals available in nearby restaurant. Doubles $9. Triples $13.50. Quads $17.75.

Hotel Benli (tel. 321 1750), 100m east of the main square's south edge. Offers clean, cool, quiet, and odor-free rooms with telephones. Benli's has outworn the luxury status it enjoyed at its opening in 1958, but its price and charm make up for bathless rooms and basic toilets. Singles $5.50. Doubles $9. Triples $13.50.

FOOD AND ENTERTAINMENT

Trabzon's local cuisine is an exotic melange of fresh Black Sea fish, corn, potatoes, and peas from the fertile highlands south of the city. Vegetarians can feast on a well boiled corn on the cob, sold on many street corners for $1.25, or sample the $1 salad bar of **Tad Pizza and Burger** (tel. 321 1238), on the northeast corner of the main square (open daily 11am-9:30pm). West of the square (1½km) along Maraş Cad., you'll stumble upon the **fruit and vegetable market** (open daily 6:30am-9pm). Downhill west of the Luna Park, on the shore, you'll find the **fish market** (open daily 7am-8pm). Several wholesome restaurants with modern decor await along Uzun Sok. (Long Street), a shopping avenue west of the square's south edge that lives up to its name. **Gelik Lokantası** (tel. 326 2445), 1km along at #84, serves the range of dishes you expect from a *lokanta* in an exemplary state of cleanliness. **Uludağ Kebap Salonu** (tel. 321 4120), at #43, dishes out *kebap* with gusto (open daily 7am-10pm). Nearly unknown to tourists is *mantı,* a delicious pasta dish like tortellini served in yogurt and seasoned with garlic, mint, and hot pepper. You can try this traditional family favorite for $1.75 at **Kilim Mantı Salonu,** 46 Uzun Sok. (open Mon.-Sat. 9am-9pm). Or, head to the **Özgür Restaurant** (tel. 321 1319), next to the Özgür Otel on the south end of the central square. Specializing in such comforting foods as pizza ($2.50) and cheeseburgers ($1.25), Özgür is a very pleasant place to eat American when you need a break from *kebap* and *ayran.* For dessert, **Beton Helva,** 21 Uzun Sok. (tel. 321 2550), has 45¢ blocks of *helva,* a sesame seed confection like gritty fudge, and 45¢ glasses of clear grape cider to wash it down. Another curiosity is *aşure,* a fruity oriental pudding, available at **Tad Pizza and Burger** for only 70¢ a bowl.

Cruisers catch the undersea atmosphere at **Blue Sea Bar,** Kemerkaya Mah. Mektep Sok. 51A Sahil Cad. (tel. 322 2733), across the highway from the shore (beer $1.25; open daily 11am-1am). Just off the main square, head for **Kıbrıs Restaurant,** with a pleasant terrace bar overlooking the east side of the square. Tables by the railing have front row seats for the occasional folk dance shows in the square (beers $1.25). Trabzon's long seaside terrace makes for a pleasant stroll; at the west end lies the **amusement park,** featuring rides and a video arcade (admission to park 15¢). Squeaky clean rejuvenation can be had for $3.50, including scrub and massage, at **Sekiz Direkli Hamam,** Pazarkapı Mah. (tel. 322 1012). Constructed by the Seljuks circa 1073 BCE and used until 1916, it was renovated seven years ago with marble and wood paneling (open daily 6am-11pm for both sexes except Thurs. 8am-5pm is reserved for women only). The *hamam* is a mere 2km walk west following Maraş Cad. from the main square to where it turns downhill (follow the signs from there). A taxi costs roughly $2.25 from the tourist office.

Kara Deniz (Black Sea)

Sahil Yolu

Gazipaşa Caddesi

Kale Kapusu Cad.

Reşadiye Caddesi

Keranoğlu S.

Hasan Sokak

CUMHURİYET

Kahraman Maraş Caddesi

Şehit Hava Teğmen Caddesi

İSKANDER PAŞA

Şehit İbrahim Karaoğlanoğlu Cad.

Hükümet Caddesi

İslhane S.

Kasin Sokak

Zağnos Caddesi

Lütfullah Sokak

Tanjant Yolu

Refik Cesur Caddesi

Tanjant Yolu

Zeytinlik C.

Liman (Port)

Limonlu Sokak

Tanjant Yolu

Trabzon Rize Asfaltı

Org. Selahattin Demircioğlu Cad.

Kuzgun Deresi

Tabakhane Deresi

Cephanelik Sokak

İran Caddesi

Osman Kuyono Sokak

Trabzon

Taksim Police, 2
Post Office, 3
Küçük Ayvasıl Kilisesi, 5
Tabakhane Köprüsü, 6
Ortahisar Camii, 8
Yeni Cuma Camii, 7
Santa Maria Kilisesi, 1
(Saint Mary's Church)
Bedesten, 4
Pazarkapı Camii, 9

SIGHTS

The oldest Christian structure in Trabzon is the tiny 7th-century **St. Anne Church.** Head west from the square on Maraş Cad.; it's behind a cluster of newsstands and trees on your left, just before the mosque. At the top of the hill behind the town is **Atatürk Köşkü,** one of Atatürk's villas built at the turn of the century by a rich Greek. Though Atatürk stayed here only two nights in his life, the popular villa is now a museum fat with photographs and paintings of the "Father Turk." *Dolmuş* marked "Atatürk Köşkü" depart from the main square (open in summer daily 8am-noon and 1:30-7pm; in winter 8am-noon and 1-5pm; admission 45¢, students 23¢).

Romantically set in a rose and oleander garden overlooking the Black Sea, the lovely 13th-century **Aya Sofya** church was once part of a monastery. Now a museum, it features fine frescoes and carvings. From the lower end of the square, take a *dolmuş* (25¢) marked "Aya Sofya" (open daily 8am-noon and 1:30-5:30pm; admission $1.25, students 65¢). Within the walls of the old city is the **Ortahisar Camii,** formerly Panagia Chrisokefalos Church, the main basilica of medieval Trebizond. Due north of Ortahisar Camii, on Amasya Sok., is the house where Süleyman the Magnificent, the 16th-century Ottoman sultan, was born. A statue of the turbaned "Grand Turk" stands guard at the newly restored building.

Behind the town rises the hill of **Boztepe.** Check out the remains of the Panagia Theoskepastos convent, and 2.5km farther back into the hills is an Armenian monastery at Kaymaklı with frescoes almost as impressive as those at Aya Sofya. *Dolmuş* to **Rize,** for factory fresh tea, and **Akçaabat,** renowned for its *köfte,* leave frequently from the shore-hugging highway. The most dramatic tourist attraction in the area, however, and one of the more fascinating Byzantine sites anywhere, is the **Sümela Monastery,** 47km southeast of Trabzon, set among lush forested mountains. Established in 385 CE, this cliffside monastery reached its zenith in the late Middle Ages. Monks lived here until the population exchange between Greece and Turkey in 1923. The monastery has been neglected since, although restoration has recently begun. Fire, rain, and vandals have damaged this sublime retreat over the past 72 years. Nevertheless, Sümela is well worth the taxing pilgrimage through the cloud forest. The inspiring beauty of the site and the richness of its history distinguish Sümela as part of the ancient Trabzon that enchanted 19th-century travelers (open in summer daily 8am-5:30pm; in winter Mon.-Sat. 8am-5:30pm; admission $2.50, students $1.25). **Afacan Tour,** on İskele Cad., offers tours to the monastery (depart 11am, $4) as does **Ulusoy Turizm,** 50m uphill from the tourist office on the right (depart 11am, $3.75). For more flexibility, taxis cost $30.

■ East of Trabzon

The towns along this segment of the Black Sea coast are interesting more for their cultural makeup and serene damp atmosphere than for the few historical monuments they house. Most are small, quiet port and industrial towns. The primordial wildlands to the south, a sultry velvet of dense jungle and mist softening the jagged landscape, are even more deeply entrenched in the past. *Yayla,* or highland campgrounds, dapple the mountains, where natives of this region gather from as far away as Holland and Germany to relax and renew their cultural ties. Farther inland, people maintain autonomous, centuries-old traditions, manners, and dress styles from central Anatolia. The best places for campers to find an uncultivated spot are along the beach, by the highway, on *yayla,* or along riverbanks.

■ Uzungöl

Uzungöl, a pristine trout-filled lake hemmed in by steep, fir-packed mountains, is 98km out of Trabzon via Of and Çaykara. The slow and lumpy 20km ride from Çaykara follow a whitewater stream past hillsides of terraced corn and hazelnut trees. Discover the lake as soon as the trademark twin yellow minarets poke into view, and continue 3km upstream by a small dam and out to *yayla.* Between the lake and the dam, a handful of new hotel and restaurant complexes has sprung up to accommodate Turkish families, who come as much for the famous trout and rice pudding as for the scenery. Alcohol is not sold in Uzungöl. Campers either stake their tents for free in the ground upstream from the dam or at some hotels; indoor accommodations tend to be on the expensive side.

Reaching Uzungöl is a scenic adventure. From Trabzon, you cannot reach Uzungöl directly unless you take a daytrip organized by a tourist agency. **Çaykara Tur** (tel. 322 5509) organizes tours that cost roughly $12; they accept phone reservations. Otherwise, you can take a minibus marked "Çaykara" from the office of Çaykara Tur behind Trabzon's Russian bazaar *(Rus Pazari).* The minibuses depart Çaykara every hour on the hour (7:30am-5:30pm, 1½hr., $1.25). Tickets are sold before boarding. From Çaykara, another minibus marked "Uzungöl" (every hr., 75¢) drops passengers off in front of the mosque of the twin minarets.

Majestic cloud-ringed mountains, excellent fishing, and cool climate are reason enough for a visit. Uzungöl boasts neither ancient monuments nor priceless museums. Visitors come here to fish, swim, soak up the scenery, and relax. Uzungöl has some pleasant little pensions around the lake. Perhaps the best bargain is the **Uzungöl Pansiyon** (tel. (462) 656 6129), on the main road between the mosque and the lake. (Free laundry. $3.75 per person with bath. Breakfast $1.) Open all year, the **Sezgin Motel** (tel. (462) 656 6175) has typical well kept rooms for two to four people. ($7.50 per person. Breakfast included.) The cozy three bedroom bungalows at **Orman İşletme Tesisleri** (tel. (462) 656 6010), across the lake, make superb bonding spots for up to eight people. Try to make reservations one week in advance. ($16 per bungalow.) For dinner, the restaurant at the **Sezgin Motel,** across the street from the motel, grills red-spotted trout from their farm ($3.50 per plate of 2 fish), which you can follow up with fresh rice pudding ($1; fixed price $5.65). Near the PTT, **Gülalioğlu Restaurant** offers fresh fish and typical Turkish fare for low prices (full meal $3.15-4.50).

■ Rize

Rize is the tea capital of Turkey. Tourists are often directed to the hills south of town, where the ministry of Agriculture conducts high level R&D in special tea labs, greenhouses, and gardens. Needless to say, there are more teahouses in Rize than Chinese restaurants in Beijing. If tea theory and research isn't your cup of…tea, you may view Rize as merely a necessary overnight stop on the Black Sea highway. If this is the case, you will find Rize to be a very pleasant place to spend a night, look at the ocean and, of course, have a cup of tea.

The main street in Rize is **Atatürk Cad.** All of the rooms are on this street. Restaurants, shops, and teahouses line this and the parallel Camhuriyet Cad. A large tea garden with a fountain is in the west part of town. In fact, all you'll probably see of Rize is packed into a kilometer Atatürk Cad. West of the tea garden, by the mosque, is the **PTT** on the square, near the Atatürk statue (open daily 8:30am-5:30pm; mail service open 8:30am-12:30pm and 1:30-5:30pm). The **tourist office** (tel. (464) 213 0408) is on the fourth floor of the Özel Idare Tessisleri, a building on the shore in the east part of town. They offer a brochure and general information, but their English skills and erratic schedule may cause headaches; you can probably get equally good advice from your pension/hotel manager (open Mon.-Fri. 8:30am-5:30pm). There is a **Turkish Airlines (THY)** office (tel. (464) 213 0591) on Cumhuriyet Cad. (open Mon.-Fri. 8:30am-5:30pm).

Buses leave from the *otogar,* 1km northwest of the town center. There are daily buses to Yusufeli (5hr., $6.75); Kars (9hr., $11.25); Erzurum (9hr., $10); Van (14hr., $16.75); Zonguldak (17hr., $20); and İzmir (23hr., $24.50). More frequent buses go to Artvin (2 per day, 6hr., $5.50); Gaziantep (3 per day, 20hr., $22.25); Antalya (2 per day, 22hr., $24.50); Ankara (2 per day, 14hr., $14.50); Mersin (2 per day, 22hr., $22.25); Bursa (2 per day, 18hr., $42.25); İstanbul (4 per day, 18hr., $42.50); and Samsun (5 per day, 7hr., $9). Most destinations between Trabzon and Hopa are best left to highway *dolmuş* (under $3.50), but if you want to reach Trabzon in better time, with more space, and less cost, **Pamukkale Turizm** buses ($2.25) pass down the coastal highway (every 20min. 8am-8pm).

Budget rooms abound in Rize. **Otel Efes** (tel. (464) 217 7555), two blocks up Atatürk Cad. across from Akbank, is sparkling clean. (All with bath and TV. Singles $15. Doubles $22.50. Triples $30.) For a sea view, try **Otel Turist,** 26 Atatürk Cad. (tel. (464) 217 2009), east of the Otel Efes. Rooms are large, clean, and well furnished, most with bath, balcony, and TV. (Singles $15. Doubles $25. Triples $30. 20% student discount.) For a cheap, excellent meal, try the **Bekiroğlu Restaurant,** 161 Cumhuriyet Cad. (tel. (464) 217 1380), near the Otel Efes (*kebap* $1.75). To reach the **tea lab,** follow the road from the PTT, by the central mosque, about 800m to the hilltop (open daily 10am-5pm).

■ Ayder

Forty kilometers east of Rize in the Hemşin Valley of the Kaçkar range is the mountain resort of Ayder. Pronounced "I dare," it's a popular base for hiking. The organic, timbered houses of this mist-shrouded village look as if they naturally sprouted from the mountainside. On the forested far side of the valley, a slender brook cascades over crags fed by the melting snow at the mountain's peak and joins a roaring stream on the valley floor. The ebullience and colorful dress of the native Hemşin people are as good a reason to visit Ayder as the towering majesty of the site.

If it weren't for the strikingly modern hot springs facility in the center, Ayder would look like an old Alaskan gold-mining town. The one-street village houses a

AYDER

The Hemşin

Travelers in Ayder and the nearby valley may be astonished to discover the Hemşin, an outgoing, merry, sometimes outrageous people that are distinctly different from the often solemn Central Anatolians. The Hemşin are descendants either from a 10th-century Turkish tribe from the original migration or from Heptacomete Christian or pagan tribesmen that spoke a dialect of Armenian. Hemşin are said to have come from Georgia in recent times, and to have lived isolated in the mountains until roughly 150 years ago. Intrepid and independent, they are known for their hospitality, revelry, and jovial drinking of *rakı*. Although many Hemşin have moved to large cities and opened sweetshops for which they are famed, roughly 15,000 still live in the Hemşin Valley. Hemşin women wear brightly colored silk turbans imported from India, perhaps because the valley was once a stop on the silk road. The women's garb stands in stark contrast to the men, who wear dark, drab colors. To attempt to understand the Hemşin mentality, visit one of their *yayla*, or summer villages. These tightly bunched shanty towns are inhabited during summer months by Hemşin who come from as far as Holland and Germany to get in touch with their homeland.

tiny **PTT** by the Ayder Hilton (open daily 9am-5pm). Nearby, a small booth offers **tourist information,** which in terms of Ayder, means a point in one of two directions (open daily 9am-5pm). The booths of two rival **minibus** companies face each other across the main road. Buses run to Çamlıhemşin (10 per day, 30min., 70¢), Pazar (13 per day, 1hr., $1.50), and Rize (4 per day, 1½hr., $2.25). To go to Hopa, catch the Pazar bus and connect from there. Early morning minibuses run up to the *yayla* of Avusor (5km, $1.50), Lower Kavron (7km, $2.25), and Upper Kavron (12km, $2.25). Avusor's annual **festival** falls on August 5; Kavron's happens August 15. Believe it or not, Ayder charges an **admission fee.** Your 50¢ will be collected upon entrance from an attendant in a booth 4km from the center of town. For **trekking information,** you should contact Kardelen Pansiyon or Pirikoğlu.

Because of the proximity of the springs, few hotels have any sort of shower. Most charge the standard price of $4.50 per person, of which 65¢ is easily haggled away. **Otel Altıparmak** (tel. (464) 657 2062), next to the springs facility, has small, new rooms with balconies and good beds. (Singles $5. Doubles $10. Triples $13.75.) For rooms with bath, **Otel Ayder** (tel (464) 657 2039, -40), the big, white, institutional building at the lower end of the main road, has six doubles. The rooms are clean almost to the point of sterility. (Open June-Sept. Singles $5. Doubles with bath $11.25.) In the center of town is the inappropriately named **Ayder Hilton Hotel** (tel. (464) 657 2024). Rooms are clean, but nothing more. (Laundry free. $4.50 per person. Breakfast $1.25. Meals $3.50.) Camping is free beyond the *yayla* and the cluster of buildings above it. That's also where you'll find the **Kardelen Pansion** (tel. (464) 657 2107), the secluded den of Muhammet Önçırak, mountain man and tour guide extraordinaire. Before ascending into the Kaçkars, you should consult the military issue map hanging on his wall. (5 drafty rooms are available June-Aug. $4.50 per person. Group discounts.)

For a wholesome meal, try **Pirikoğlu Lokantası** (tel. (464) 657 2021). The owner is a good source of mountain information (full meal $3.50; open May-Oct. daily 6am-11pm). **Çağlayan Restaurant** (tel. (464) 657 2065), next door, serves alcohol and often features live folk music in the evenings (open daily for dinner). Ayder is a good place to try *muhlama*, a melted mix of cheese, butter, and corn flour that looks like mashed potatoes and behaves like fondue for bread dipping.

There are hot (very hot) **springs** housed in a squat, steaming edifice completed only a few years ago. A dip in the marble bathing pools is an exhausting pleasure; as blood charges through every capillary in your body, you'll come to believe the legends about the curative effects of the water (regular bath $1.90, private bath $7.50; open April-Oct. daily 7am-8pm).

■ Hopa

The Black Sea Highway continues along the coast from Ayder for roughly 60km, finally turning inland at Hopa. Like many of its fellow coastal cities, Hopa is void of tourist diversions, but is not an unpleasant place to spend a night if the need arises. Many stay in Hopa before visiting the Turkish border (with Georgia) in Sarp, just 30km away, or Georgia itself. Due to an extortionist mafia and constant fighting, crossing the border to Georgia is not recommended.

Most of Hopa lies on one of two streets. Several cafés and hotels are on **Cumhuriyet Cad.** and hotels, cafés, and other services are on the parallel **Orta Hopa Cad.**, behind Cumhuriyet. Orta Hopa has Hopa's **PTT**, which provides mail, telephone, and **currency exchange** services (open daily 8:30am-12:30pm and 1:30-5:30pm). Akbank and several others on the same street provide **ATMs** and **currency exchange**. Hopa's *dolmuş* and **bus stations** lie west of the bridge into town. *Dolmuş* and buses travel to Borçka (every 30min., 1hr., 90¢); Artvin (every 30min., 1½hr., $1.75); Yusufeli (every 30min., 3hr., $4); Erzurum (every 30min., 6hr., $4.50); Kars (1 per day, 8hr., $7); Van (3 per day, 12hr., $11.25); Ankara (3 per day, 16hr., $15.50); Adana (1 per day, 18hr., $22.25); İstanbul (1 per day, 20hr., $22.25); İzmir (1 per day, 24hr., $22.25); and Antalya (1 per day, 26hr., $26.75).

Otel Huzur, 25 Cumhuriyet Cad. (tel. (466) 351 4095), bills itself as "your home in Hopa," and indeed it could be. With clean, spacious rooms, A/C, showers, and bathrooms in each room, Huzur's prices are unbeatable. (Singles $3.75, with private bath and shower $6.25. Doubles $8.75, with private bath and shower $10.) **Otel Köşk**, 21 Orta Hopa Cad. (tel. (466) 351 3501), is meticulously clean; most rooms have bathrooms. (Singles $10. Doubles $18.75. Triples $25.) Across the street, **Otel Cihan** (tel. (466) 351 4897) is even more upscale. Rooms on the upper floors, accessible by elevator, have sea views in addition to showers, toilets, phones, and televisions. (Singles $12.50. Doubles $20. Triples $26.25.) Just a few doors down from Otel Huzur, on the waterfront, **Beslen Lokantası** (tel. (466) 351 4957) offers an array of cheap, fresh, and finely prepared dishes (full meal $3.15-4.40).

■ Artvin

Chiseled into the mountain pass is the eerily tranquil town of Artvin, which offers panoramic views of a largely deforested valley. The 15th-century citadel overlooking the highway, which both Georgians and the English sought to control within the last hundred years, receives few tourists since Turkish soldiers still use it. Never mind, though—the nameless road that ribbons 5km up the mountainside to central Artvin puts the tower in its place; the view only gets better.

In vertical terms, the town occupies the space bounded by the hospital above and the bus station below. But the bus station itself is perched 4km up the serpentine road from the valley floor where you get dropped off. To reach it, wait for the municipal bus (roughly every 20min., 55¢) or hop on one of the frequent shuttles. They all go to the center, a main street called İnönü Cad., home to hotels, restaurants, a *dolmuş* lot, a 24-hour **PTT**, and a tea garden. There is a small **tourist office** (tel. (466) 212 3071) in Camii Meydanı, to the right of İnönü Cad. as you walk uphill. It has maps and brochures (open daily 8:30am-12:30pm and 1:30-5:30pm).

Minibuses travel to Hopa (7 per day, 1½hr., $1.50); Rize (roughly every ¾hr. until 5pm, 6hr., $4.50); Kars (daily, 4hr., $5.50); Erzurum (4 per day, 4hr., $5); Tortum (4 per day, $3.50); Trabzon (7 per day, 5hr., $5); Samsun (4 per day, 10hr., $9.25); Ankara (4 per day, 18hr., $14.50); and İstanbul (1 per day, 22hr., $18). **METRO Turizm** offers A/C and beverage service to larger cities for nearly the same prices.

Many of Artvin's hotels feature low prices and good locations, but are also frequented by prostitutes. A trio of clean, cordial, and untainted budget hotels hides down the stairs on the left side of İnönü Cad. as you walk uphill towards the *dolmuş* stop. The **Kaçkar Oteli** (tel. (466) 212 3397) has carpets and showers in every room. Hall bathrooms have toilets. (Free use of washing machine. Singles $5. Doubles $10. Triples $16.75.) **Otel Güven** (tel. (466) 212 1118), next door, offers large rooms, some with panoramic views. Hot water is unreliable, and showers cost $1.25 each, but the management speaks English. ($3.75 per person.)

Watering hole for Artvin's elite, the **Hanedan Restaurant** (tel. (466) 212 7222) has a black bar and a porch with a view of the valley (*kebap* and beer $2.75; open daily 8am-11pm). Bar and view also come with excellent food at **Nazar Restoranı** (tel. (466) 212 1709), at the lower end of İnönü Cad. It's decorated with bizarre posters and features delicious *meze* (open daily 10am-midnight). In the evening, **Çağdaş Gazinosu** presents live music after 8pm (open daily 9am-midnight).

Artvin is close to many *yayla* that locals visit in summer. The plateau of **Kafkasör,** 11km from Artvin, hosts an annual **festival** on the third weekend of June. Traditional dances and other performances take place, but the main events are **bullfights.** The bulls "wrestle" each other like the camels in Manisa, near İzmir. The winner's owner is rewarded and honored. The bull gets nothing. Artvin's Ottoman **hamam** (tel. 212 1158) is just down the street (bath $1.50, massage $1.50, scrub $1; open daily for both sexes 6am-10pm).

■ Yusufeli

The small town of Yusufeli, stretching along the Barhal River, is fast becoming the **whitewater rafting** capital of Turkey. Too dangerous to raft before June, the famous Çoruh River, site of a 1993 rafting championship, passes only 6km away. Yusufeli's dry south side on the Kaçkar range makes it an ideal trekking center.

Most hotels occupy the upstream end of İnönü Cad. which passes the **otogar** lot, **pharmacies,** decent alcohol-free restaurants, and eventually the **PTT** (open daily 7:30am-5pm) at the downstream end of town. The local **hospital** can be reached at 811 2015. Daily **buses** depart Yusufeli for Uzundere (2 per day, 1½hr., $1.25); Tortum (2 per day, 2hr., $2.25); Erzurum (2 per day, 3hr., $3.50); Artvin (5 per day, 1½hr., $2); Hopa (4 per day, 3hr., $3.50); Rize (4 per day, 4hr., $4.50); Trabzon (3 per day, 5hr., $6.75); Kars (1 per day, 4hr., $3.50); Ankara (2 per day, 16hr., $13.50); Bursa (1 per day, 23hr., $20); and İstanbul (2 per day, 23hr., $20).

Otel Keleş (tel. (466) 811 2305), on the corner of İnönü Cad. and Halit Paşa Cad., features quality mattresses in modern, carpeted rooms with shared bath. (Free laundry. $2.25 per person.) The **Hotel Barhal** (tel. (466) 811 3151), on Asma Köprübaşı Cad., stands out for its private baths and river view. (Singles $3.50. Doubles $4.50. Triples $6.75.) Its owner, Sıralı Aydın, is the president of the local **rafting club,** which rents six- and eight-person rafts and equipment at reasonable prices. The **Hotel Çiçek Palas,** 30 Halit Paşa Cad. (tel. (466) 811 2393), off İnönü Cad., offers clean, concrete-floored rooms, shared baths, and use of a stove. ($3.50 per person.)

One of the cleaner and more popular meeting places for tourists and nature lovers is **Çınar Lokantası** (tel. (466) 811 2365), overlooking the river beneath the Hotel Barhal. Its offerings include grilled meat, delicious trout, *rakı,* and vegetarian *meze* like *piyaz, pilaki,* and potato salad (full meal $3; open daily 10am-11pm). Blue inside and out, the **Mavi Köşk Restorant** (tel. (466) 811 2329), downhill from Hotel Barhal off İnönü Cad., is clean and has good food with a well stocked bar (full meal $3.50; open daily 8am-1am).

■ The Çoruh Valley

Yusufeli makes an excellent base for exploring the Çoruh Valley, home to half a dozen 10th-century **Georgian churches.** Begun by Georgians in 730 CE and finished three centuries later, the **İşhan** church (35km from Yusufeli) was enhanced by a Byzantine dome in 1200 CE before its stewardship passed back into Georgian hands. The pilgrimage to İşhan is doubly worthwhile if only for the road's spectacular mountainscapes of tilted strata and ravine-wrinkled cliffs. The façade of the airy **Öşk Vank** (a.k.a. Çamlıyamaç, 50km from Yusufelı) church has been preserved marvelously and features carvings of angels, patrons, and animals. Inside, above the entrance, you'll find a colorful band of frescoed faces next to the image of a church that might be Öşk Vank itself. Of the three other churches, which resemble each other in style and height, **Dörtkilise** (a.k.a. Tekkale, 13km from Yusufeli) is the most accessible. Only 12km high, it features arches as its central theme. From **Tekkale Village** (6km from Yusufeli), a rough, walkable road follows the stream for another 7km to a steep bank 50m below Dörtkilise (Four Churches), whose name refers to four churches that once stood nearby. The ground outside makes good, free camping. Before ascending the Kaçkars, consider staying in Tekkale Village's little-known country pension, **Dörtkilise Resting Camp.**

It's hard to get to the **Barhal church** (a.k.a. Altıparmak, 33km from Yusufeli), now a locked mosque whose main attractions are a few exterior carvings of small crosses, a lion, and a bird. A peek through the slats of the shed left of the entrance will show a finger-tall carving of a human (above and to the right of a semi-circular design above a window left of the entrance). If you travel south toward Haho, you'll pass the pea-green **Tortum Lake,** supposedly formed 630 years ago when the peak of Mt. Hars collapsed into the Çoruh River valley. Locals claim there's a mosque on the lake floor and remnants of an inundated village. The Çoruh's real treat here, however, is **Tortum Falls,** a natural 50m cascade that the government turned into a hydroelectric plant in the 1950s. The **Şelale Tesisleri** restaurant owns a breathtaking view except mid-June through August, when the dam diverts the water.

The falls are easily reached because the Erzurum highway passes within 1km of them. You can tell the driver "Şelale" and sit back to enjoy the view—warped faces of mountain strata like one huge, prehistoric hunk of *baklava* ripped by time. A daily *dolmuş* departs from Yusufeli for each of the three nearby church villages in the afternoon, but doesn't return until morning. **Taxis** tour the area, but aren't cheap (to İşhan $18, Öşk Vank $33, Dörtkilise $6, Barhal $45, and Haho $33). From the village of Uzundere, you can catch cheaper taxis to Öşk Vank and Haho.

Central Anatolia

The high, dry mountain ranges of Central Anatolia form Turkey's bread basket. On top of the mountains' wide plateaus rest some of the more authentic and hospitable villages that this country has to offer. The Aegean and Mediterranean Coasts have been drastically altered by rampant tourism and the Black Sea Coast is suffused with an Eastern European atmosphere—what remains of traditional Turkey is preserved in the sparse, but accessible, mountains of Central Anatolia.

■ Ankara

The former city of Angora, this backward settlement was famous for its wool and little else. That is, until Atatürk declared Ankara Turkey's capital in the 1920s. He brought Europeans to design a modern, European-style city of wide boulevards and parks. To a large extent, however, provincial Anatolia is still found here, balanced atop a number of dramatic hills which rise from the surrounding plains. In the Citadel the way of life remains largely unchanged. The new capital has grown up just to the south, with its main axis, Atatürk Bulvarı, vertically joining the two. Although it lacks the charm of İstanbul, Ankara peers into the soul of modern Turkey. In parts it is quite plush, full of luxury apartments, boutiques, and nightclubs. At other points, it is run-down and dusty, its architecture reminiscent of Eastern Europe. In the summer, sunny weather and 70°F temperatures make Ankara a jewel—a delightful modern complement—to Turkey's other metropolis, old-world İstanbul.

ORIENTATION AND PRACTICAL INFORMATION

The city's main street is **Atatürk Bulvarı,** which runs north-south. At its north end lies the run-down precinct of **Ulus,** centered on the equestrian statue of Atatürk at Ulus Sq. Most of the sights and cheap hotels are here. A couple of kilometers south is **Kızılay,** a clean, up-scale market area. It contains crowded pedestrian precincts lined with bars, cafés, and restaurants. The **University of Ankara** is nearby, and the students lend Kızılay a youthful, cosmopolitan air. It is also a residential and shopping area with some mid-range hotels. Ensconsed 2km south of Kızılay are the wealthy residential areas of **Kavaklıdere** and **Çankaya,** home to most embassies and five-star hotels. Frequent buses run the length of Atatürk Blv. Bus #391 runs from the main gate of the Citadel *(Hisar),* in the north to as far south as the Atatürk Tower via Atatürk Blv. The bus terminal *(otogar)* is 5km west of Kızılay, in **Söğütözü.** The railway station *(gar)* is 1.5km southwest of Ulus Sq.

Tourist Offices: 121 Gazi Mustafa Kemal Blv. (tel. 488 7007 or 231 5572). From the train station's main platform, descend the stairs into the tunnel to Tandoğan Kapalı Çarşı. At the end of the tunnel, turn left onto Gazi Mustafa Kemal Blv., the office will be on the right. Multilingual staff; English spoken. Free city and country maps. Come here to file a complaint with the **tourist police;** the tourist office will serve as your interpreter. Open Mon.-Fri. 8:30am-6:30pm, Sat.-Sun. 9am-5pm; reduced hours in off season. **Airport tourist office** (tel. 398 0348). Open 24hr.

Embassies: Ankara makes a convenient base for securing visas for Eastern Europe, the Middle East, the former Soviet republics, and Central Asia. **Afghanistan,** 88 Cinnah Cad., Çankaya (tel. 438 1121; fax 438 7745). **Albania,** 17 Ebüzziye Tevfik Sok., Çankaya (tel. 441 6105). **Australia,** 83 Nenehatun Cad., Gaziomanpaşa (tel. 446 1180; fax 446 1188). **Azerbaijan,** 20 Cemal Nadir Sok., Çelikler Apt. (tel. 441 2621). **Bulgaria,** 124 Atatürk Cad. (tel. 426 7455; fax 427 3178). **Canada,** 75 Nenehatun Cad. (tel. 436 1275; fax 446 1761). **Czech Republic,** 100 Uğurnuncu Cad., Gaziomanpaşa (tel. 446 1244; fax 446 1245). **Egypt,** 126 Atatürk Blv. (tel. 426 1026; fax 427 0099). **Germany,** 114 Atatürk Blv. (tel. 426 5465; for visas call 468 5906; fax 467 9070). **Great Britain,** 46A Şehit Ersun Cad. (tel. 468 6230). **Greece,** 9-11 Zia Ül-Rahman Cad., Gaziomanpaşa (tel. 436 8860). **Hungary,** 10

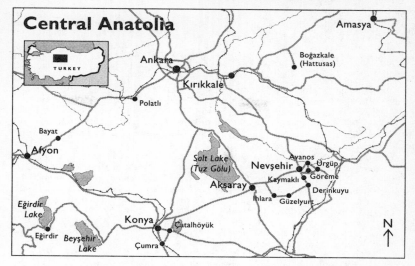

Central Anatolia

Gazi Mustafa Kemal Blv., Kızılay (tel. 418 6257; fax 418 8322). **Iran,** 10 Tahran Cad. (tel. 427 4320; fax 468 2823). **Israel,** 85 Mahatma Gandi Cad. (tel. 446 3605; fax 426 1533). **Jordan,** 18 Dada Kurkut Sok. (tel. 440 2054; fax 440 4327). **Kyrgyzstan,** 11 Boyabat Sok., Eren Apt., Gaziomanpaşa (tel. 446 8408; fax 446 8413). **Lebanon,** 44 Kızkulesi Sok. (tel. 446 7487; fax 446 1023). **Former Yugoslav Republic of Macedonia,** 30/2 Filistin Sok., Gaziomanpaşa (tel. 446 9204; fax 9206). **New Zealand,** 13/4 İran Cad., Kavaklıdere (tel. 467 9056; fax 467 9013). **Northern Cyprus,** 20 Rabat Sok. (tel. 437 6031; fax 446 5236). **Oman,** 63 Mahatma Gandi Cad. (tel. 447 0630; fax 447 0632). **Pakistan,** 37 Iran Cad. (tel. 427 1410, -4; fax 467 1023). **Palestine,** 45 Filistin Sok. (tel. 436 0823; fax 437 7801). **Poland,** 241 Atatürk Blv. (tel. 426 1694). **Romania,** 4 Bükreş Sok., Çankaya (tel. 427 1241; fax 427 1530). **Russia,** 5 Karayağdız Sok., Çankaya (tel. 439 2122). **Slovakia,** 245 Atatürk Blv. (tel. 426 5887; fax 468 2689). **South Africa,** 27 Filistin Sok. (tel. 446 4056; fax 446 6834). **Syria,** 7 Abdullah Devdet Sok. (tel. 440 9657; fax 438 5609). **Turkmenistan,** 28 Kozzo Sok. (tel. 441 7126). **U.S.,** 110 Atatürk Blv. (tel. 468 6110; fax 467 0019). **Uzbekistan,** 14 Ahmet Rasim Sok. (tel./fax 439 2740). **Former Yugoslavia,** 47 Paris Cad. (tel. 426 0354; fax 427 8345).

Banks: All large banks offer **currency exchange.** Slightly better rates are available at the change offices *(döviz)* along Atatürk Blv. in Kızılay. **Vakıf Bank** has an office on the north side of Ulus Sq. and 2 branches on Mustafa Kemal Blv., in Maltepe.

ATMs: Pamukbank's 24-hr. machine at the train station accepts Cirrus and PLUS cards, as well as Visa, Eurocard, and MasterCard. There are other Pamukbank machines half a block south of McDonald's, on Atatürk Bulvarı in Kızılay. **Türkiye İş Bankası** ATMs are scattered around town, but they only take credit cards.

American Express: Head office at 88/1 Cinnah Cad. (tel. 441 5205), but this doesn't deal directly with the public. Go to AmEx's agent, **Türk Express,** 9/4 Cinnah Cad. (tel. 467 7334, -5). **Koç Bank,** 58 Atatürk Blv. (tel. 418 1804) processes AmEx's cash transactions. Open Mon.-Fri. 9am-4pm.

Flights: *Havaş* buses leave from Hipodrom Cad. (next to the train station) and head to the airport, **Esenboğa,** 1 per hour ($3.50). **Turkish Airlines (THY),** 231 Atatürk Blv., Kavaklıdere (tel. 419 2800), offers direct flights to İstanbul (1 per hour 6am-10pm, 1hr.), at least 2 per day to Adana, Diyarbakır, Erzurum, İzmir, and Trabzon (1hr.), and at least 1 per day to Malatya and Van (1½hr.). All domestic flights are $54 or less. Students (14-24) get 25% off. Try to buy tickets two days in advance, because the flights fill up. It is often more convenient and reliable to buy tickets from one of the private travel agencies visible between Kızılay and Bakanlıklar. Open Mon.-Sat. 8:30am-7:30pm, Sun. 8:30am-5:30pm.

Trains: Built in 1937, Ankara's railway station retains the flavor of the era. Faster blue trains *(Mavi Tren)* serve İstanbul (1 per day, 8hr., $6.50) and İzmir (1 per day, 13hr., $6.50). Trains also serve İstanbul (5 per day 8am-10:30pm; 7¼hr. during the day, 9½hr. overnight; $5.50) and İzmir (1 per day, 15hr., $5.50), as well as Adana (1 per day, 12¼hr., $4.50); Kayseri (1 per day, 7½hr., $2.75); Malatya (1-2 per day, 18½-20hr., $4.75); Sivas (2-3 per day, 11½-14hr., $3.75); and Tatvan (3 per week, 31¾hr.). For overnight trains, make couchette reservations the day before. On timetables, İstanbul appears as "Haydarpaşa," İzmir as "Basmane".

Buses: The **terminal** *(Otogar)*, in Söğütözü 5km west of Kızılay, is connected to all points in the city by local buses, *dolmuş*, and taxis. *Dolmuş* (50¢) run when full to Ulus. Their drop-off point is Hisarpark Cad., in the middle of the cheap hotel area. A taxi for the same trip should cost about $5. City buses (25¢) also make the trip. As with İstanbul, scores of companies connect Ankara with nearly every point in Turkey, and buses depart around the clock. Buses (usually 1 per hr.) go to all Turkish cities of significant size: Konya (15 per day, 3hr., $6); İstanbul (8hr., $12); İzmir (8½hr., $12); Kuşadası (3 per day, $14.50); Bodrum (2 per evening, 14hr., $22.25); and Trabzon (2 per day, 12hr., $11). Schedules change.

City Buses: Ankara has a furiously busy, beehive-like bus system. Buses come in three flavors: red, green, and blue. Red and green buses are government-run, blue are private. Buy tickets for red and green buses (25¢) from booths near major bus stops or some street vendors. On the blue buses (25¢), you pay conductors once on board, and they give you change. Conductor sits at desks halfway down the buses. *Dolmuş* within the city cost 30-50¢, depending on distance.

English Bookstores: ABC Bookshop, 1 Selanik Cad., Kızılay (tel. 434 3842), 2 blocks north and ½ block east of the main square. Good selection of English books. Open daily 9am-7pm. The **American Association Library,** 20 Cinnah Cad. (tel. 126 9499), Cinnah Cad. branches off from Atatürk Blv. south of Bakanlıklar. Take any bus marked *Kavaklıdere* from the stop across from the Ulus PTT. Open Sept.-July Mon.-Fri. 1-6pm.

Laundromat: Self-service launderette *(çamaşırhane)* in the Beğendik shopping mall under the Kocatepe mosque. Go up the escalator to the 2nd floor, and take a right; go through the exit at the end of the corridor; turn left. Wash'n'dry $2.75.

Hospital: Bayındır Tıp Merkezi, Kızılırmak Mah. #3-3A 28th Sok. (tel. 287 9000), one of Ankara's best private hospitals. English spoken. **Numune,** Talatpaşa Blv., Samanpazarı (tel. 310 3030), and **Ankara Üniversitesi Tıp Fakültesi,** Tıp Fakültesi Cad., Dikimevi (tel. 319 2160), are the two biggest university hospitals.

PTT: On Atatürk Bulvarı in Kızılay and in Ulus. Both open 24hr. In the train station, open daily 7am-11pm. Poste Restante open Mon.-Sat. 8:30am-5:30pm. Open Mon.-Fri. 8:30am-6:30pm, Sat. 8:30am-12:30pm. **Telephones** at every PTT as well as at the bus and train stations. **Postal Code:** 06443.

Telephone Code: 312.

ACCOMMODATIONS

The two main accommodation centers are Kızılay and Ulus. Kızılay will probably make your memories of Ankara a lot better. This is a clean, upscale residential area of pleasant, modern architecture which is also the city's main shopping district and home to most of its nightlife. Naturally, you may pay more. Ulus, 2km north, is the old part of Ankara. Close to most of the sights but somewhat grim and dusty, it contains a couple dozen of the city's cheaper hotels.

Kızılay

Otel Ertan, 70 Selanik Cad. (tel. 418 4084). Going south along Atatürk Blv., take the fourth left after McDonald's, then the third right onto Selanik Cad. Decent rooms with showers and a garden in front. Peaceful, yet close to the Kızılay nightlife. Singles $11.50. Doubles $17.

M.E.B. Özel Ülkü Kız Öğrenci Yurt, 61 Karanfil Sok. (tel. 419 3715, -3067), between Akay Cad. and Meşrutiyet Cad. off of Atatürk Blvd. Only for women travelers in summer (available July-Sept.), these dormitories provide clean, relatively

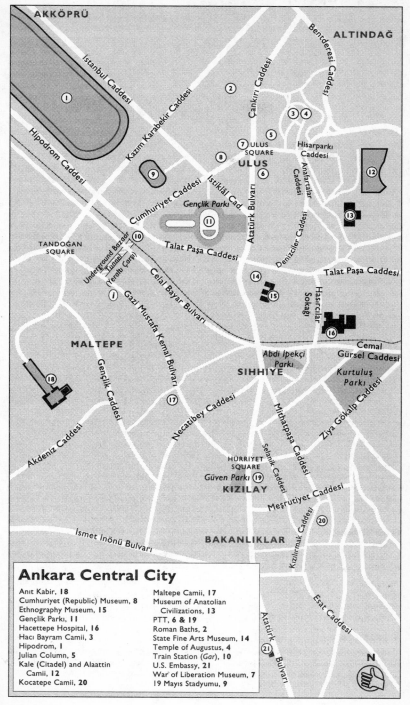

Ankara Central City

Anıt Kabir, **18**
Cumhuriyet (Republic) Museum, **8**
Ethnography Museum, **15**
Gençlik Parkı, **11**
Hacettepe Hospital, **16**
Hacı Bayram Camii, **3**
Hipodrom, **1**
Julian Column, **5**
Kale (Citadel) and Alaattin
  Camii, **12**
Kocatepe Camii, **20**

Maltepe Camii, **17**
Museum of Anatolian
  Civilizations, **13**
PTT, **6 & 19**
Roman Baths, **2**
State Fine Arts Museum, **14**
Temple of Augustus, **4**
Train Station (Gar), **10**
U.S. Embassy, **21**
War of Liberation Museum, **7**
19 Mayıs Stadyumu, **9**

safe lodgings with shared bathrooms/showers and a cafeteria. 24-hr. hot water. Singles, doubles, triples, and quads $10 per person.

M.E.B. Özel Çağdaş Erkek Öğrenci Yurt, 15 Neyzen Tevfik Sok., Maltepe (tel. 232 2954, -5), just north of Kızılay. These coed dormitory lodgings are also available during student summer vacations. From Kızılay, head north on G.M.K. Blvd. They are between G.M.K. Blv. and Gençlik Cad. Singles, doubles, triples, and quads $10 per person.

Ergen Otel, 48 Karanfil Sok. (tel. 417 5906). Recommended by the tourist office, Ergen offers small but clean rooms in the lively Kızılay district. Singles $11.25.

Ulus

To get from the train station to Ulus and its budget hotels, walk straight out along **Cumhuriyet Bulvarı** (a park on your right, a soccer stadium on your left). It's roughly a 20-minute walk—take a taxi if you have a lot of baggage. Continue straight until you reach the equestrian statue, which stands at the center of Ulus. Continue uphill east on Hisarpark Cad. There are hotels off to either side. From Kızılay and the bus station, head north on Atatürk Blvd. The following places are clean, reasonably quiet, and better than some grim alternatives.

Hisar Oteli and Hamam, 6 Hisarpark Cad. (tel. 311 9889 or 310 8128). Rooms at the front suffer from street noise, but have views of old Ankara houses perched on the hills. Large fourth-floor singles have balconies. Cold showers only, but the *hamam* next door costs $2.50. Singles $5.15. Doubles $8.75. Triples $13.75.

Otel Şan, 8 Şan Sok. (tel. 311 0943), from the statue, follow Hisarpark Cad. toward the Citadel and turn right on Anafartalar Cad. It's the 4th street on the left. An old-fashioned hotel with a 1920s feel. Clean and quiet. Showers, kept locked for most of the day, cost $1.50. Singles $8. Doubles $13.75. Triples $17.50.

Otel Taşçıoğlu, 2 Etizafer Sok. (tel. 310 7410), around the corner from the Otel Ulus, visible from Hisarpark Cad. (the second left after the statue). The grim exterior masks a rather charming, cheap hotel. Rooms are very small but clean. Availability of showers is restricted. Hot showers $1.75. Singles $4.75. Doubles $9.50.

Hotel Kale, Anafartalar Cad. 13 Alataş Sok. (tel. 311 3393 or 310 3521), a few doors down from the Otel Şan. A brand-new, clean, and pleasant hotel. All rooms have private shower. Singles $8.75. Doubles $17.50. Breakfast $1.75.

FOOD

The main eating neighborhoods are Kızılay (mid-range restaurants and cafés), Gençlik Park (cheap), the Citadel (upscale-expensive by Turkish standards), and Kavaklıdere (expensive). If restaurant life does not suit your wallet, you'll be placated at the many **supermarkets.** The largest are **Gıma,** on Anafartalar Cad. in Ulus; **Beğendik,** under the Kocatepe mosque in Kızılay (at the south end of Mithat Paşa Cad.); and **Migros,** designated by the *MMM* symbol, on Celalbayar Blv. in Maltepe. Mere steps south and to the right of the Atatürk Tower, **Hoşdere Caddesi** lays claim to many good restaurants, as does the little side street one block south of it.

The Citadel

Several restaurants offer traditional Turkish food. To get to them, do not enter the Citadel via the steps at Hisarpark Cad.—the Citadel is a confusing labyrinth, and hard to navigate. Instead, enter via the gate uphill from the Museum of Anatolian Civilizations. The restaurants are clustered around the main square just inside the gate. All restaurants around here are high-class but reasonably priced. **Kale Washington,** right on the square, on your left, offers tasty fare. You can eat on an open-air, canopied terrace (*imambayıldı* (stuffed eggplant) $2, main courses roughly $4.75).

Kavaklıdere

There are many upscale restaurants here. Several line Noktalı Sok., the road leading uphill on the right of the Sheraton Hotel. $5-7 will get you a main course. These are favored by the employees of the nearby embassies. Nevertheless, the occasional

ANKARA

truly excellent *kebap* place also exists. Hoşdere Cad., steps south and to the right of the Atatürk Tower, is another street of good restaurants. Take the first left off Noktalı Sok. after the Sheraton; **Dürümland,** 9/B Filistin Sok., is 20m down the street to your left. This stand-up joint offers some of the best *döner kebap* you'll taste anywhere ($1.75). If you fancy more than Dürümland's walk-up, stand-up *kebap,* head back to the taxi stand. Below the Chinese Take-away is the **Ayfa Café.** For around $3.75, you can have a good-sized "pizza" (actually just a round Turkish pita with lamb instead of pepperoni) and *çoban salatası* (shepherd's salad).

Kızılay

These streets are crowded with cafés and restaurants. You can barely go wrong here, but it's best to follow the crowds and avoid the more "fast-food" joints. Prices are pretty uniform here. You can expect to pay around $3.75 for salad, entree, and a drink. **Düveroğlu,** 18 Selanik Cad., serves up delicious *İskender kebap* for $2.25 (open daily 10am-1am). The **Coffee Shop,** 1 Selanik Cad., is in the basement of the ABC Bookshop. Great coffee and classical/jazz music is played while Ankara students sip coffee and study for exams (open until 7pm). Everyone even vaguely collegiate seems to head to **Cafe M,** 40 Selanik Cad.—always crowded with hipsters.

Ulus

For slightly more upscale dining, you can hop over to Ulus and try the **Çiçek Lokantası,** 12 Çankırı Cad. Atatürk Blv. becomes Çankırı Cad. north of the equestrian statue. Established in 1932, this white tablecloth restaurant boasts an indoor fountain, and classic black-and-white photos decorate the walls. You will be taken to the kitchen and shown their selection of dishes ($1.50 each), two or three of which make a good meal (open daily 7am-10pm). The **Yavaz Lokantası,** 15 Konya Sok. (tel. 311 8508), is one of Ulus' nicer offerings. This tasteful restaurant offers a quiet "family room" in addition to its main dining area (entrees $2.50-3.75). **Kale Pilsen/ Kale Hamburger** (tel. 311 1125) is just a few doors down from Yavaz. Kale offers standard Turkish café fare at standard Turkish café prices (entrees $1.75-2.50), but in a pleasant marble dining area. As the name suggests, this is a good place to escape the crowded streets for a beer and a burger.

ENTERTAINMENT

Kızılay

When they close up at dusk in Ulus, head south to Kızılay for the evening. Some of Kızılay's streets have been turned into pedestrian zones, many of which are crowded streets lined with bars and cafés. The tree-lined **Yüksel Sok.,** one block south of Kızılay on the left, is crowded with students from Ankara University and the many private and professional schools in the area. To the right is the café laden **Selanik Sok.,** which runs parallel to Atatürk Blv. Pub life is centered on two streets: **İnkilâp Sok.** and **Bayındır Sok.,** two and three blocks to the left, respectively, of Kızılay Sq. as you look south. Bayındır is the livelier. Your best bet is to simply roam the traffic-free streets and pick the crowd you want to hang with. Try **Büyük Ekspress** at No. 11, an always-crowded joint, popular with students, where the beer and conversation flow freely. On the corner of Bayındır and Sakarya Cad. (one block south) is the tiny but happening **Blues Bar,** where they play loud Western (European) music. It's on the second floor of a corner building—you'll hear it before you see it. Also, don't miss **Forza Café and Bar,** across the street from Büyük Ekspress. You can sit inside and watch the Turkish folk singers whose rousing songs earn laughter and applause from the local crowd. If you take a left on this street (Sakarya Cad.), i.e. walk away from Atatürk Blv., for one block, you will reach the **Z-Pub,** another crowded spot where Turkish music is the style. Back on Bayındır, **Major, Nuans,** and **Atesta** are similar. They usually play Turkish music. At the far end of Selanik Cad., just past the Ertan Hotel and close to the Kocatepe Mosque, **Brothers Bar** has a very large, young, yuppie crowd with some hip Turkish tunes. A few doors down, there is a good view of the mosque from quieter, hipper **Tenedo Cafe,** at No. 67. Kızılay starts to quiet down at roughly 10pm during the week, except for some of the bars mentioned above. Prices at all area bars are fairly uniform. A pint of Efes, the local favorite, goes for $1-1.25. Mixed drinks, cognacs, etc. ranges from $1.25-2.

Kavaklıdere

A couple of kilometers south of Kızılay, Kavaklıdere offers much more upscale, less crowded entertainment. Bars are not crammed together as in Kızılay—they are spread out through this residential area and can be hard to find. If bars are not your speed, head to any one of a number of tea houses and pastry shops lining Noktalı Sok. **Paul Boulangerie** and the **Daily News Café** will transport you to a pseudo Greenwich Village as you sip coffee and savor French pastries with a Turkish twist.

Ulus

A stroll through **Gençlik Park** makes a pleasant evening walk. This park is crammed with cheap restaurants. There's also an amusement park and a lake with pleasure boats. Although lone travelers occasionally visit, it's primarily a family scene. The **opera,** located at the Ulus side of the park, may have some performances. If a long day of sightseeing has left you weary and, after returning to your hotel, you've found the shower locked, check out one of the several city **baths. Karaceby Hamamı,** 101 Talat Paşa Blv., Siteler (tel. 311 8447), offers standard bath services (open daily for men 6:30am-10:30pm, for women 8am-7pm; basic fee $2.50). **Marmara Hamamı,** 17 Denizciler Cad. (tel. 324 2527), in Ulus scrubs scrubworthy and scrubbable alike. From the equestrian statue in Ulus Sq., ascend Hisarparkı Cad. towards the citadel, turn right on Anafartalar Cad., then follow Anafartalar until it ends at Denizciler (open daily for men 5am-10pm; for women 6:30am-7pm; bath $2, massage $1).

SIGHTS

Anıt Kabir, Atatürk's mausoleum, is nearly one kilometer long and built on a monumental scale (open daily 9:30am-7pm; free). As you exit the tourist office, walk left (northwest) up Gazi Mustafa Kemal Blv. until you reach Tandoğan Sq. As you approach the square, notice the next major street to your left exiting the traffic circle. This street, Anıt Cad., leads south to the sprawling grounds containing the **mausoleum.** On your right you should see an unmarked entrance guarded by two soldiers, beyond it a road leading uphill. The walk from the gate to the mausoleum entrance takes another 10 minutes. On a hot day, take a taxi ($1.80) from Ulus. At its entrance stand statues of 3 Turkish men and women representing all Turks—one of the women has her face covered to mask the ingrained sorrow caused by Atatürk's death. The broad path from these to the mausoleum is lined with 24 lions. The lions symbolize power and are arranged in pairs according to the Hittite custom. The mausoleum itself is huge and contains **Atatürk's sarcophagus.** There are photos here showing cloud formations shaped like his profile taken after his death, suggesting that his power extends to the supernatural world. Be sure to end your tour with a stop at the gift shop for Atatürk paraphernalia galore: post cards, Atatürk plaques, Atatürk clocks, and $30 18"x30" Atatürk photos.

The **Ethnographic Museum,** 1km south of Ulus off Atatürk Blv., contains a beautiful collection of clothing, calligraphy, ironwork, and woodwork, including some carvings from mosques (open Tues.-Sun. 9:30am-12:30pm and 1:30-5:30pm; admission $3). At the feet of the Citadel, the **Museum of Anatolian Civilizations** is one of Turkey's more famous museums. Walk to the top of Hisarpark Cad., turn right at the Citadel steps (without ascending them), and follow the Citadel boundaries until you get there. Its setting is unique—a restored 15th-century Ottoman *han* (inn) and *bedesten* (covered bazaar). It houses a collection of astoundingly old artifacts which traces the history of Anatolia from the dawn of civilization. The exhibits are not as well-labeled as they could be—the illustrated catalogue ($8) explains all. Expensive guides can be hired for a 1-hour tour. ($20 for a group of 4 or more, $15 for 1-3 persons; fix the price in advance. Open Tues.-Sun. 8:30am-5:30pm. Admission $3.)

The pure white **Kocatepe Mosque,** completed in 1987, shines as one of the world's largest and most beautiful. Billed as a 16th-century mosque utilizing 20th-century technology, it continues the architectural dialogue between the buildings of Sinan, the famous Ottoman architect. Its four columns are reminiscent of Sinan's Selimiye Mosque in Edirne, and the central dome and half-domes recall the Blue Mosque (Sultanahmet Camii, built by Sinan's successor) in İstanbul. Don't miss the stunning interior. The mosque also contains a model of the mosque at Medina—a present from King Fahd of Saudi Arabia to the people of Turkey in 1993. The mosque's courtyard is covered in glass. Underneath it is the large Beğendik supermarket and shopping mall, ultra-modern and air-conditioned. It's an unusual sight, a bizarre juxtaposition of God and mammon. A couple of kilometers farther south soars the **Ataküle Observation Tower.** Bus #391 runs from the Citadel and Ulus to the tower, via Kızılay and Kavaklıdere; bus #613 from Ulus only. From its observation deck, you can literally see all of Ankara (admission 50¢).

There are some Roman ruins in Ankara, though they're in a poor state of preservation and probably aren't worth a lot of your time. They include the Roman Baths, a five-minute walk up Çankırı Cad. from the equestrian statue; the Column of Julian is nearby, as is the **Temple of Augustus,** built in 25 BCE over the site of earlier temples to Cybele (an Anatolian fertility goddess) and to the Phrygian moon god. Later it was converted into a Byzantine church. Nearby are the 15th-century **Hacı Bayram Mosque,** the old **Parliament** (where Turkey was proclaimed an independent republic), and the **zoo** (Atatürk Orman Çiftliği) in an expansive, tree-filled park.

■ Near Ankara

The ruins of **Hattusas,** the once-glorious Hittite capital, lie roughly 200km from Ankara, 30km off the highway to Samsun. The first people to smelt iron, the Indo-European Hittites conquered Anatolia around 2200 BCE. United under a central authority at Hattusas, the Hittites vied with the Egyptians for control of the fertile lands and trade routes of Mesopotamia. The Sea People razed Hattusas shortly after 1200 BCE, but archaeologists have unearthed enough of the ruins to provide a fair representation of the city. The road following the 6km wall that encircles Hattusas first passes by the **Büyük Mabed** (Great Temple) of the Weather God of Hatti and the Sun Goddess of Arinna. A drawbridge over two pools of water granted the only entrance to the original temple. The big, green rock there was a wedding gift from the King of Egypt to his son-in-law, the King of the Hittites. Continuing up the hill and to the right, the road passes the **Aslanlıkapı** (Lion's Gate) and the **Yerkapı** (Earth Gate). The two sphinxes from the Earth Gate are now in İstanbul and Berlin and no longer overlook the 70m-long tunnel, built under the fortifications and used for surprise attacks. The figure carved in relief on the **Kralkapı** (King's Gate), just down the hill, is the Hittite war god. The **Büyük Kale** (Great Citadel) rounds out the tour. The small **museum** in the village of **Boğazkale,** 1km from the site, gives a sense of the area's history (open daily 8am-6pm; admission to museum and ruins $1, to ruins alone 80¢). Your admission ticket is also valid for **Yazılıkaya,** an open air temple with 100 of the 1000 or so gods of the Hittite pantheon represented in base-relief.

To get to Hattusas, take a bus to Sungurlu (2½hr.; $4 from Ankara; frequent buses along the Ankara-Samsun route). The bus will drop you off either on the main highway or in the center of town. To get back to Ankara, flag a bus down on the highway. There are *dolmuş* to Boğazkale that leave from the center of Sungurlu. (Ask someone other than a taxi driver.) Often local taxis function as *dolmuş*. (Bargain with the driver; $2 is a good price.) Otherwise, a private taxi costs $10 for a one-way ride to Boğazkale, $15-20 for a full tour of the ruins. Walking through the ruins—which include the world's first library—takes about half a day.

Like the world's largest diorama, **Boğazkale** portrays modern rural Turkish life perfectly, with its quirks, antiquity, and a population looking to better its lot (over half the population of 2012 leave Boğazakale for eleven months out of the year to work abroad). Amid ancient ruins and a wreath of rolling hills, old men prod their donkeys along while teenagers whiz past on motorcycles. Boğazakale makes a perfectly restful setting for your archaeological exploration.

The closest you can stay to Yazılıkaya is the **Kaleburg Motel** (tel. (364) 452 2189). Gorgeous hilltop views make the Kaleburg an unbeatable preview to a morning's hike through the ruins. All the rooms have balconies and clean bathrooms, and guests can show the proprietor their *Let's Go* guide for a free Turkish breakfast. (Doubles $25.) **Hattusas** (tel. (364) 452 2013) is located right up the hill from the museum. This charming pension boasts 24-hour hot water and lovely views of the countryside from the back rooms which feature large balconies. **Aşıkoğlu** (tel. (364) 452 2004) has welcomed guests for over 35 years. Across from the museum, Aşıkoğlu offers a fine Turkish restaurant and comfortable, clean rooms with toilets and showers. At $15 per person, it's a bit pricey, but well worth the extra money. **Başkent Pansiyon** (tel. (364) 452 2037) features 24-hour hot water, neat and clean rooms, and "slide projection services" for $8.50 per guest, including breakfast. **Atila** (tel. (364) 452 2101) boasts a swimming pool amid its camping space. Clean showers and bathrooms make "roughing it" not so rough. ($3.75 per person.)

■ Konya

In Roman times, St. Paul favored Konya (then called Iconium) with a visit, and sparked the city's transformation into a significant Christian center. In the 11th century, the Seljuks swept through Asia Minor, gaining a formidable reputation in the West and priming the area for later Ottoman conquests. They made Konya Turkey's first capital and replaced its churches with the greatest mosques of the era, most of which survive today. In the 13th century, one of the greater and more well loved Islamic philosophers, Celâleddin Rumi, known to his followers as Mevlâna (our master), came from his birthplace in Balkh, Afghanistan, and settled in Konya. After his death, some of his disciples founded a Sufi order which later became known for its "whirling dervishes," who sought to achieve ecstasy and unity with God through controlled trance-like spinning. Today, Muslims often stop in Konya to visit Mevlâna's tomb before embarking on the pilgrimage to Mecca.

If you are respectful of Konya's religious traditions, you'll find its residents amiable and welcoming—hospitality toward visitors is one of the sect's main principles. You will also experience a different type of "hospitality" from its numerous street carpet hustlers, who will try to lure you to their shops. These middle men get a 30% commission (added on to your price). If you want to buy a carpet, go alone.

ORIENTATION AND PRACTICAL INFORMATION

Konya's main street is roughly 1km long and runs between the turquoise conically towered **Mevlâna tomb** and the circular **Alâaddin Bulvarı**, which runs around the **Alâaddin Tepesi** (Alâaddin Hill) park. The 500m closest to the Mevlâna tomb is called Mevlâna Cad., the other half is Alâaddin Cad. Konya's sights, hotels, and restaurants are clustered within this small area, and finding your way around is easy. The **bus station** *(otogar)* is 3km from town. Frequent trams head from here to Alâaddin Bulvarı (25¢—ask for Mevlâna). The **railway station** is 2km from the center; when you exit, you'll see the road to town, whose start is marked by a roundabout, to your right. If you walk along this street you'll pass Atatürk Stadium and, after 600m, the Atatürk statue. Take the second left onto Atatürk Blv. after the statue, Alâaddin Blv. is roughly 500m farther on. Bear right on Alâaddin Blv., Alâaddin Cad. is the first major right. *Dolmuş* also run the route. To get back to the railway station, take a minibus *dolmuş* marked İstasyon or Gar. Bus #4 to Meram also passes nearby. To get back to the bus station, take any *dolmuş* marked Otogar. The **tourist office,** 21 Mevlâna Cad. (tel. 351 1074; fax 350 6461), across the street from the Mevlâna Müze, provides free maps. Take their accommodation and carpet shop advice with a grain of salt (open Mon.-Fri. 8am-noon and 1:30-5:30pm). **Buses** run to Silifke (7 per day, 3hr., $6), Ankara (15 per day, 3hr., $6), İzmir (10 per day, 8hr.,

$10.50), and Aksaray (11 per day, 2½hr., $4). Nighttime buses run to İstanbul ($11) and Nevşehir/Göreme (3 per day, 4hr., $7.75). There are **pharmacies** scattered all over town; concentrated in the streets off Alâaddin/Mevlâna Cad. The night pharmacy *(nöbetçi)* is posted in all pharmacy windows. The **Sağlık Hastanesi,** Hastane Cad., Iktap Sok. (tel. 233 8204 or 235 6795), is located in the city center. The reception doesn't speak English, but the doctor does. For **medical emergencies** dial 112. There's a **PTT** on Alâaddin Cad. (open 24hr.), and one at the bus station (open daily 7am-11pm). **Postal Code:** 42000. **Telephone Code:** 332.

ACCOMMODATIONS

Finding rooms in Konya is no problem. Many hotels and pensions are clustered in small alleys along the main drag. Rooms in Konya are considerably more expensive than in other cities, and bargains are hard to find as Konya's pension owners seem to operate under a cooperative agreement. Prices range from $10 to $12 per person. The **Otel Çeşme,** İstanbul Cad. 35 Akifpaşa Sok. (tel. 351 2426) offers well kept rooms with bath, fake bricks, and stained glass. (Singles $8.25. Doubles $11.75. Triples $17.50.) A couple of blocks off Mevlana Cad., you can find a peaceful respite from the hey day of Konya at the **Yeni Köşk,** Yeni Aziziye Cad. 28 Kadılar Sok. (tel. 352 0671). The well scrubbed rooms all have showers and there is a safe on the premises. (Singles $9.50. Doubles $14. Triples $24. Quads $32. Breakfast $2.50.) The **Aziziye Oteli** (tel. 352 2287), across from the Aziziye Mosque, caters to a more diehard budget crowd. Reasonably clean rooms, most with private shower (pit toilets down the hall) line broad, atmospheric corridors. Because of its prices, the clientele are primarily working-class Turkish men—women traveling alone may feel uneasy. (Singles $4.75. Doubles $8.25.)

FOOD AND ENTERTAINMENT

The local specialty is *fırın kebap,* a chunk of oven-roasted lamb. With the tourist office on your left and the Mevlâna in front of you, if you go right roughly 100m, passing by the left-hand side of the Balıkçı Otel, then turn right again just before the third roundabout (the one in front of Mevlâna being the first roundabout), you will find a bare brick wall and tacky plastic Pepsi sign which conceal a 150-year-old **Konya house.** They serve some of the best food you'll have in Turkey. Its specialties are *sebzeli çöp kebap* (*kebap* with eggplant, $1.75), *çöp şiş* (some of the best *şiş kebap* you've ever had, $2.25), and *etli yaprak sarması* (meat stuffed grape leaves dipped in yogurt, $1.25). If you want some Western-style coffee, **Ankara Pastanesi,** on Alâaddin Cad., serves a delicious, frothy Nescafé. Coming from the Mevlâna, it's past the post office, on your left. The **Sema** restaurant on İstanbul Cad., under the Otel Çeşme, specializes in *döner kebap* ($2).

If after a day of walking around, your back begins to ache, you can head to the **Şems Mah.,** 7 Serfettin Cad. (tel. 353 0093), in a restored ancient building, beside the Selimiye Mosque (entry $2.50, complete bath'n'massage $6; tip $2-4, depending on service). Nightlife in Konya is restricted to bars in the larger hotels. You may want to try the **Otel Çesme** for some after hours entertainment.

SIGHTS

The interior of the **Mevlâna Tekke** is among Turkey's more spectacular sights. Inside the complex, originally a type of monastery, are the tombs of the Mevlâna and other dervishes, as well as a fascinating museum with hand-written Kur'ans, carpets, dervish garments, and ornate metalwork (open Mon. 10am-6pm, Tues.-Sun. 9am-6pm; admission 60¢, students 15¢). Konya's other major attractions are tame by comparison. They are situated on or around **Alâaddin Tepesi,** which also contains a park and some pleasant tea gardens. Supposedly, this mound contains layers of civilizations stretching back to the Bronze Age. **Alâaddin Camii,** near the hilltop, is an early 13th-century mosque in the Syrian Seljuk style. The mosque re-opened in the summer of 1995 after 11 years of restoration, now sporting a modern decor. The

Seljuks studied astrology here in the reflection of the night sky off the pool in the main chamber. Nearby, on Alâaddin Blv., is the **Karatay Medresesi** (Museum of Tiles). The interior itself is a great example of Seljuk tilework (open Tues.-Sun. 9am-noon and 1:30-5:30pm; admission 60¢). Also on Alâaddin Blv. is the **İnce Minare Medresesi** (Academy of the Slender Minaret). It contains primarily Seljuk and Ottoman stone carvings (open Tues.-Sun. 9am-noon and 1:30-5:30pm; admission 60¢). In the two museums, the buildings are of greater interest than the collections.

Hard to find several blocks south of the hill is the **Archaeological Museum,** which features a 3rd-century sarcophagus illustrating the labors of Hercules (open Tues.-Sun. 9am-noon and 1:30-5pm; admission $1.25, students 60¢). On Atatürk Blv., just off Alâaddin Blv. (the first major left if you're coming from Alâaddin Cad.), you'll find **Atatürk's house**—a small museum of the great man's personal effects (open Tues.-Sun. 9am-4pm; admission 60¢). The **Aziziye Mosque,** a five-minute walk from the Mevlâna (back along Mevlâna Cad., off the main street to the left) is 18th-century Baroque, unusual for Turkey. The windows are larger than the door for extra light, and the dome is self-supporting (without columns). Konya's little bazaar is between the Aziziye Mosque and the PTT. There is an **underground gold bazaar,** about half-way along Mevlâna Cad. You'll see the steps, covered by a glass shelter, leading down. You could also explore the older residential streets east of Mevlâna.

■ Near Konya

A brief trip to **Sille** makes an excellent way to spend a morning. Every 30 minutes, bus #64 leaves from the municipal bus stop (on Alâaddin Cad., across from the PTT) for Sille, 8km away. Arrival in Sille is clear as you leave the mountain roads, descend into the valley, and are let off in the middle of Sille's street. Actually, Sille has several streets, but only this one has stores and a bust of Atatürk, so it's a good point of reference. The **PTT** is ahead and around the corner (open daily 8:30am-5:30pm). There is no tourist office, but you should have no trouble finding your way.

Most visitors come to Sille to visit the **Aya Elena Kilisesi,** a 4th-century Christian church decorated by more recent frescoes (open Tues.-Sun. 9am-4pm, but it will more likely be opened only when you enter the gate and are noticed; admission normally 50¢, but not always collected). The two caves to the left were used as human

---

A Dizzying Poet

Celaleddin Mevlâna Rumi, founder of the order of the Dervishes and perhaps the greatest of all the Persian mystic poets, made his home in 13th-century Konya. Revered both as a poet and a prophet, Rumi is said to have used his spiritual powers to repulse the invasion of Hulegu Khan's Mongol hordes in 1256. For 700 years, the passionate elegance of his verses has inspired readers from İstanbul to Samarkand, Muslim India, Arabia, and Africa. He is not widely known in the West, but English literature has felt his impact through translations made by early 19th-century Orientalists. The prayer-like rhythm of verses such as this one have ravished poets from Goethe to Ginsberg:

> Through Love all that is bitter will be sweet.
> Through Love all that is copper will be gold.
> Through Love all dregs will turn to purest wine;
> Through Love all pain will turn to medicine.
> Through Love the dead will become alive,
> Through Love the king does turn into a slave.

Westerners interested in Sufi-Muslim worship can get a taste of it in its most impassioned form in Rumi, translations of whose poetry are available in the U.S. *I Am Wind, You Are Fire* by Annemarie Schimmel is an excellent introduction to the life and writings of Rumi. Coleman Barks is renowned for his translations.

dwellings. To reach the church, ask the driver to let you off at the Aya Elena Kilisesi sign. There are two. If you are near a manure farm, walk forward until you see the second, identical, sign. At the second sign, the one at the end of the bar lined by a row of garages, look to your left. The church is now partially concealed from view by a house, but it's there. Once you see the church, you might want to follow the road past the second sign.This road takes you up into the hills. About 1km up, there is a flat parking area where you can take in the whole valley. Three kilometers up is a **picnic area** open during daylight hours. If walking in the hills is not your cup of *çay,* take a walk through the city. The streets are shady, the houses old and attractive, and the surrounding mountains are breathtaking.

Çatalhöyük (near the town of Çümra 50km south of Konya) is one of the world's oldest known settlements, dating back to the 8th millennium BCE. An advanced Neolithic community, Çatalhöyük vies with Jericho for the coveted title of "world's first city." Its famous cave drawings and artifacts have been moved to the Ankara museum and to Holland—little remains on site but a few crumbling walls. The tour isn't worthwhile, but the guidebook is on sale at the Mevlâna is. Take a **bus** from Eski Garaj (Old Bus Station) to Çümra (45min.), then ride a taxi the remaining distance (roughly $20 roundtrip, or take a taxi the whole way for $30-45).

■ Eğirdir

Eğirdir rests along a peninsula that juts into the middle of a large, azure lake, surrounded by the Central Taurus mountains. At the peninsula's tip are great views, numerous pensions, delicious fish restaurants, and soft sandy beaches. Discovered by tourists only a decade ago, this fishing town has installed Western amenities but has managed to shield its natural serenity from extravagant tourism.

ORIENTATION AND PRACTICAL INFORMATION

Here in Eğirdir the Seljuks built the world's only walk-through minaret poised atop an archway in the town center. The archway leads east past municipal headquarters to King Croesus's crumbling fortress, with a sign proclaiming EĞİRDİR. Beyond the fortress, a dusty road threads to the shore across from two small islands. The closer one, little more than a tea garden, is called **Canada** (pronounced *JAHN-ah-dah*), which means "adorable island." The larger **Yeşilada** (Green Island) looks a lot like Canada, with rocky shores and verdure, but it hosts half the pensions in Eğirdir. Northwest of the archway, **2nd Sahil Yolu** hugs the lakeshore for several kilometers, passing banks, the post office, the tourist office, and two beaches before it brings you to the usually idle train station. 2nd Sahil Yolu runs west and north along the lakeshore. **Yenimahalle** (New Neighborhood) road begins beside the bus station 100m south of the archway and follows more lakeside past the modern hospital. Due west of the archway lies Eğirdir's permanent market place.

Tourist Office: #13 2nd Sahil Yolu (tel. 312 2098). From the bus station gate (a map stands outside), walk straight and follow the road as it curves to the left. English, French, and German spoken by staff seldom on duty simultaneously. Open Mon.-Fri. 8:30am-noon and 1:30-6pm, sometimes open on weekends.

Trains: (tel. 311 4694), 2km west of town center, off 2nd Sahil Yolu. 1 train leaves for İstanbul at 6pm (12hr.). For Ankara, change in Eskişehir. For İzmir (Tues., Thurs., and Sat., 10hr.), change in Isparta. Open daily 6am-noon and 5pm-7pm.

Buses: (tel. 311 4036), just south of the town center. Buses leave daily for Afyon (5 per day, 3hr., $5); Antalya (7 per day, 3hr., $5); Konya (8 per day, 3½hr., $5); Nevşehir (4 per day, 6hr., $11); İzmir (6 per day, 7hr., $10); Ankara (4 per day, 7hr., $9); and İstanbul (1 per day, 10hr., $13). **Local Buses** leave 7am-10pm every hour from behind the mosque, across the street from the bus station (15¢).

Luggage deposit: Open roughly 6am-8pm at the bus station (65¢).

Hospital *(Hastane)*: **Sağlık Ocağı,** Güney Sahil Yolu (tel. 311 4855).

PTT: 2nd Sahil Yolu (tel. 311 4591), on the way to the tourist office. Information and Poste Restante open 24hr., other services open Mon.-Fri. 8:30am-noon and 1:30pm-5:30pm. **Postal Code:** 32500.
Telephone Code: 246.

ACCOMMODATIONS

Eğirdir offers the complete range of lodging from hotels through pensions and campsites. The hotels tend to be upscale but don't have to break your pocketbook. Yeşilada is the best place to stay, offering lakeside views away from the bustle of town. Unless otherwise stated, all rooms have private showers. Note that on your arrival in Eğirdir, you will be besieged by pension staff trying to hustle you into their pensions. They may not take "no" for an answer—at first. The local tourist authority has also handed down standardized prices, but undercutting by the rival pension owners could save you $2 or $3 a night if you let them bid on you at the *otogar*.

Halley's Pansion (tel. 312 3625), keep right as you enter Yeşilada—100m up. The second oldest pension in town, it is popular with backpackers. An excellent meeting place for bikers, trekkers, and adventurers of all sorts. Come in Sept. to enjoy the grapes from Mehmet's arbor. Free rowboat for guest use. English spoken. Singles $8.75. Doubles $15. Triples $20. Breakfast $1.65. Dinner $5.

Yeşilada Pension (tel. 311 4413), on your left just as you reach Yeşilada, between the ADAC and the Big Apple Pensions. Offers three marble-finish balcony rooms with great views. Next door, the **Big Apple Pension** is nearly identical, but also offers rooms *sans* view. Singles $9.75. Doubles $19. Triples $26. Breakfast $1.65.

ADAC Pension (tel./fax 312 3074). ADAC features a roof terrace, two rooms with balcony, and tours to the National Park and canyon ($7). Free bus station pick-up/drop-off. They won't be at the station, but will come if you call. English spoken. Singles $8.75. Doubles $15. Triples $20. Breakfast $1.65.

Altınkum Plaj Camping. Rent a tent and have access to the camp's electricity and showers. Eğirdir's best beach is here, admission 25¢ for non-campsite dwellers. Roughly 2km past the tourist office; bear right at "major junction" sign. Taxis from town center $1. Changing rooms 50¢. Parking $1.25. $1.25 for tent rental.

FOOD AND SIGHTS

Living in close proximity to such a huge body of water means, of course, that the people of Eğirdir make a mean fish—carp, bass, crayfish, and perch are the local specialties. The pensions of Yeşilada have a limited selection—usually fried perch—cooked with varying degrees of skill. The **Sunshine Restaurant,** at the far end of Yeşilada, should not be missed. Its tables are so close to the lake's edge that if you consume too much *rakı* with your meal, you could topple in (full meal $4-5). A more luxurious meal can be had at the **Kervansaray Restaurant,** next door to the *otogar,* on the lake. A fine wine list and gourmet menu for a truly unique, if pricey, dining experience (entrees $3.75-6.25). **Kemer Lokantası,** by the bazaar on 2nd. Sahil Yolu, features a variety of excellent dishes for low prices (entrees $1.85-3.75).

After hours head for the **Disco Bar** next door to the town's *hamam,* near the Bazaar. Recently opened and undergoing remodeling, it features a music hall, a dancing area, and a full bar with tables on an outdoor terrace overlooking the city.

Eğirdir will not disappoint nature-lovers and adventurers. Twenty-seven kilometers to the east lies **Zindan,** a 1500m-long cave which served the Romans as an open-air temple dedicated to Eurymedon. You should bring a flashlight. Forty kilometers southeast from Eğirdir stand the **Adada ruins,** consisting of an ancient (1st century BCE) temple's fallen columns, sarcophagi, and amphitheater. Only 25km south of town, **Kovada National Park** teams with wildlife and draws butterfly collectors in the spring. Avid walkers can follow a popular stretch of the **King's Road,** by which Lydian rulers once made their way from Ephesus to Babylon.

CAPPADOCIA

The strange grandeur of the ancient province of Cappadocia is sure to make a lasting impression. Volcanic formations shape a striking landscape of cone-shaped monoliths (fittingly called *peribaca*, meaning "fairy chimneys" in Turkish) grouped in valleys and along ridges. The region lies between three volcanoes—Hasan Dağı near Aksaray, Erciyes Dağı near Kayseri, and Melendiz Dağı near Niğde—which once deposited a thick layer of volcanic ash, subsequently hardening into columns of rock called *tufa*, or tuff. Most visitors with only a day or two visit the **fairy chimneys** around Göreme and the spectacular **Open Air Museum,** which contains several churches carved into the rock; the **underground cities** at Derinkuyu and Kaymaklı; and the heavenly **Ihlara Valley.** The region also contains Byzantine chapels and underground habitations that could entertain visitors indefinitely.

GETTING AROUND

Transportation in the region includes minibuses, guided tours, and mountain bike, moped, or car rentals (there are numerous agencies in Ürgüp and Göreme, but it is exorbitant here—$50-60 per day). Biking is an exhilarating way to tackle the area's rudimentary roads. Cycling also allows you flexibility in visiting sites, which are sometimes far apart from one another. Though it is touristy in parts, Cappadocia remains largely rural and conservative; foreigners should expect to be stared at, no matter how appropriately they dress. Freelance camping in the rocks is strictly forbidden. The valley is accessible by **moped** or mountain bike (if you're fit—hills are steep). **Rentals,** available at several agencies around the bus station, are pricey: mopeds and bikes go for $4 per hour, $13 per 4hour, $26 per day. In summer (June-Sept.), an hourly **minibus** (25¢) links Göreme and Ürgüp: its course is Ürgüp-Göreme (via the Open Air Museum) to Zelve-Avanos and back. It departs daily from Ürgüp (main *otogar*) at 20 minutes past the hour, 8:20am-6:20pm. In the same direction, it leaves Göreme (opposite the PTT) at half past the hour, Zelve (main entrance) 40 minutes past, and arrives in Avanos at ten to the hour. It leaves Avanos at 20 minutes past, reaching Zelve on the half-hour, departing Göreme (PTT) at 40 minutes past and arriving in Ürgüp 10 minutes later. If there are a lot of tourists, it may start running in mid-April, but there have been relatively few tourists for several years now. The rest of the year, you have to backtrack to Nevşehir by half-hourly minibus (25¢) from the Göreme bus station, or by the Avanos-Nevşehir bus (catch from outside PTT, same side of the road; leaves a quarter to and a quarter past the hour Mon.-Fri. 7am-6pm, Sat. 7am-5pm; 25¢). From Nevşehir, catch a minibus to Ürgüp (every 30min., 7am-6pm, 50¢). You can get off at either Nevşehir's tourist office or its bus station, and catch the onward connection from the same place.

Because Cappadocia is a relatively small region, Göreme, Nevşehir, and Ürgüp share the same long-distance **bus schedule** and are served by only two intercity bus companies—Nevtur and Göreme. Although some Cappadocia-bound buses terminate in Nevşehir, many carry on to Göreme, Ürgüp, and Avanos as well. Frequent destinations include Ankara (5 per day, 5hr., $7); İstanbul (2 per day, 12hr., $14.50); Konya (3 per day, 4hr., $6.25); Adana (2 per day, 5hr., $6.25); Mersin (2 per day, 5hr., $6.25); and Antalya (2 per day, 11hr., $12.25). One daily bus serves Side (13hr., $12.50); Alanya (14hr., $14.25); Fethiye (15hr., $15.50); İzmir (12hr., $14.50); Pamukkale (11hr., $12.25); Marmaris (15hr., $16.75); Muğla (12hr., $15.75); Eskişehir (8hr., $11); Bodrum (14hr., $16.75); Kuşadası (13hr., $15.75); Selçuk (13hr., $15.75); and Aydın (12hr., $12). For connections to Eastern Turkey, take the bus from Ürgüp to Kayseri (hourly until mid-afternoon, 2hr., $2).

■ Göreme

Göreme has dozens of cone-shaped rocks, roughly 30m high, into which cave-houses have been carved. Many are still inhabited; some have been turned into hotels. Among the cones, there are numerous traditional Turkish rural dwellings. Tourism, however, has changed the face of Göreme—more than sixty pensions have sprung up in the last few years. The main square is full of restaurants and tour agencies, and more pensions are springing up in its narrow back streets. Göreme is a convenient base for exploring rock-hewn churches and the beautiful Rose Valley.

Orientation and Practical Information   If you turn to your right with the bus terminal lengthways behind you, the main road that runs to the mosque will be directly in front of you. You can walk 100m and take a right at the first major intersection to get to the Open Air Museum. The PTT is on the main road at this junction, on your left. Downstairs by the entrance to the Open Air Museum, in the handicrafts building, there is a **PTT** (open daily 9am-5pm) and two **banks** (open daily 8:30am-4pm or later) that cash traveler's checks and give Visa (only) cash advances. The post office also changes money. Göreme's bus station is in the main square and contains the private, hotel-run **tourist office,** which gives information on rooms. The tour agencies in town are also a good source of free information. The **PTT** (open daily 8:30am-12:30pm and 1:30-5:30pm) is in the center of town. Göreme is small, and it's easy to find your way around. To find the **hospital,** you should look for the white H in a blue square on a road sign—it's next to the PTT. **Postal Code:** 50180. **Telephone Code:** 384.

Accommodations   Göreme's pension owners have collectively settled on a price scale: dorm beds $4, singles $5, with bath $7. Your best bet is to pick a room at the bus station's tourist office. The walls are covered with handmade posters for the dozens of pensions. **Tabiat Pension** (tel. (384) 271 2497) has one cave room and several arch rooms surrounding a beautiful garden with patio furniture and a grape arbor. A covered rest area and a common room provide relaxation in the shade. (Turkish breakfast $1.90). The **Melek Otel** (tel./fax 271 2643) is just behind the Hard Duck Café and the Tardelli Pizza Restaurant. Set in a handsomely restored Ottoman house, the Melek has a wide variety of rooms, including some caves. **Paradise Pansiyon** (tel. 271 2248), on the road to the Open Air Museum, has one fairy chimney room; the others are clustered around a courtyard, where a hostel atmosphere reigns. Next door, **Peri Pansiyon** (tel. 271 2136) has rooms in fairy chimneys. Campers should head to **Göreme Dilek Camping** (tel. 271 2396), across from Peri Pansiyon. The campsite and pool are nestled among phallic rock structures. ($4 per site. $7 per tent rental with site. $9 per caravan.)

Food and Entertainment   The **Sedef Café/Bar** is the expatriate's café of choice in Göreme. Sit on the wooden patio in the evening and enjoy traditional Turkish cuisine at its best (entrees $2-4). **Mehmet Paşa,** in the mansion of the former governor of Cappadocia, serves delicious main courses at good prices. Eat on the terrace or in the historic governor's visitors' rooms. The room on the right is the *Salemlik,* or men's room, where affairs of state were discussed. On the left is the *Haremlik,* or women's room, where they gossiped about the men. You can take the first right on the road to the mosque, and then go left. You can look at the rooms for free even if you don't eat here (*köfte* with rice $2.50; spicy Turkish soup with herbs $1.25). The **Orient** (tel. 271 1346), opposite the Yüksel Motel, will entertain your appetite for $2-5 per main course, including vegetarian dishes and a decent *saç tava* ($3). Typical rock valley breakfast items include pancakes with syrup, French toast, yogurt with honey ($1.25), and *menemen,* a Turkish classic (a loose, two-egg omelette of tomatoes, peppers, and spices—only $1.75). The **Rock Valley Pension** has a decent restaurant (full meal $4). In the evening, two bars make every traveler's favorite list. The **Flintstones Bar,** next to Peri Pansiyon, is run by the dashing, and English-Speaking Mustafa, and features an 8-10pm happy hour (Efes by the ½L 63¢

during happy hour, otherwise $1.10). From Flintstone, many escape to the **Escape Bar,** located in a converted donkey barn below the giant fairy chimney with the Turkish flag. Bellydancing is featured at 11pm on two or three nights a week.

Sights The **Rose Valley,** which runs from Göreme to Çavuşin (4km away), makes for a wonderful hike through eerie landscapes of fairy chimneys and bizarre multi-colored rock formations. Tour groups don't come here, so you'll have the place to yourself. From Göreme, you can take the first left on the road to the Open Air Museum. Walk for roughly five minutes, and then go right. You'll be rewarded at this point with your first magnificent vista. Descend into the valley from here. There are several paths through it, but you'll certainly wander off them and get lost from time to time. Eventually you'll end up in the village of **Çavuşin.** The Avanos-Nevşehir bus (every 30min.) or the Avanos-Zelve-Göreme-Ürgüp minibus (every hr., both run June-Sept. only, 50¢) will take you back to Göreme up until 6pm. After that, a taxi from Çavuşin costs roughly $4. You could also take a bus to Çavuşin and walk back to Göreme. From the main road's bus stop, walk into Çavuşin past the town square and take the right-hand fork, which leads to the valley's main path. You may want to leave this path from time to time and head deeper into the valley.

In town, the large fairy chimney with the Turkish flag on top, between the bus station and the huge carpet emporium on the mosque road, is believed to have been used as a **Roman burial ground.** The most impressive concentration of sights in the region is at the **Open-Air Museum,** 1km out of Göreme on the Ürgüp road. The churches here are carved into caves and fairy chimneys. The walls were originally covered in frescoes, and you can still see their remnants. The churches are the legacy of Christianity under the Byzantine Empire. In the 4th century, St. Basil founded one of the first Christian monasteries here, setting down religious tenets that influenced the teachings of St. Benedict and subsequently the Western monastic movement. The church in the hill before the main entrance to the museum is known as **Tokalı Kilise** (Church of the Buckle). Inside the museum are five churches: **Sandal** (Sandal Church), **Yılanlı** (Church of the Serpents), **Barbara, Elmalı** (Church of the Apple, currently closed), and **Karanlık** (the Dark Church, closed for renovations for the last 12 years). Be sure to visit Sandal and Elmalı if they are open. Both contain superb frescoes (museum ticket sales open April-Oct. daily 8am-7pm; once in the site you can wander until one hour before sunset; admission $2, students $1). The former **residence of the Paşa of Göreme** has been opened to the public and its frescoed walls and ceilings restored to their 19th-century splendor.

Guided tours of Cappadocia's major sites are available from several agencies in town. Depending on whether they include museum fees, tours are $15-30, and are a good deal if you want to see a lot. Although the agencies have a price agreement, they often undercut one another, and all give student discounts of roughly 20%. The most expensive tours are not necessarily the best. Most tours do the loop of Göreme, Üçhisar, Pigeon Valley, Derinkuyu, Ihlara, Ağrıkarahan, Kervansaray, and Göreme. Some go off the main road between Derinkuyu and Ihlara to take in **Güzelyurt** (well worth a visit) and the **Crater Lake**—a volcanic crater filled with water.

■ Near Göreme

ÇAVUŞIN

The road north from Göreme to Avanos leads past Çavuşin, known for the ancient hilltop **Church of St. John the Baptist,** formerly a regional pilgrimage site. Its origin is unknown, but it is believed to date from early Christian times. The section to your left as you face the altar contains tombs. You shouldn't walk right to the edge here to see the view—it's unsafe. To reach the church, take the **Göreme-Avanos bus** or minibus and get off at Çavuşin. It's clearly marked. Walk into town past the main square, and take the left fork. Go left and up the hill after the Walnut Restaurant, keeping left at forks. The church is at the end of the path (free). This part of Çavuşin is a bit eerie. Lots of empty, brown Greek mansions create a post-nuclear holocaust effect. The Çavuşin Church, on the main road beside the turn-off to the village (look for the steps leading up to the rock face), has some well preserved frescoes (open daily 8am-7pm; admission $1.25). If you wish to visit the ruins in Çavuşin, your best bet is to make a day trip form Göreme by *dolmuş*. There is no official tourist office here, but the Göreme office will help you coordinate a daytrip.

If you decide to stay in Çavuşin, your choices are few, but not inferior to those in Göreme. The **Green Motel** (tel. (384) 532 7050; fax 532 7032), up the main road just past the town square, provides rooms and camping grounds in a relaxed atmosphere. The multilingual innkeeper will also arrange **horseback riding** and **balloon rides.** The Green Motel's restaurant provides good, cheap Turkish fare at typical Cappadocia prices. (Rooms and camping $8 per person. Breakfast $2.) The **In Pension** (tel. (384) 532 7070; fax 532 7195) provides similarly relaxing and quiet environs in a French-speaking inn. Prices and menus are in French, but the owner assures "all are welcome in my inn." (Singles $4, with shower $6.)

AVANOS

The potters of Avanos have been throwing the red, iron-rich Cappadocian clay since time began. There are roughly a hundred workshops around the area, all with similar prices. There is everything here from high art to American kitsch (there's more of the latter). Avanos itself is a pleasant, European-style town. Its main square contains several pleasant cafés. Above the square are whitewashed Greek buildings—it looks like a village on a Greek island. French is widely spoken in Avanos, and restaurant and pension signs are mainly in French. The **Kızılırmak** (Red River), Turkey's largest, flows through the town. It is from here that the potters take the red clay for their work. At times, the river is a deep red color. Below the square and behind the mosque, there is a wooden footbridge which vibrates as you cross it.

Buses from Göreme run to Avanos every 30 minutes (Mon.-Fri. 7am-6pm, Sat. 7am-5pm). They leave across the road from the Göreme PTT, a quarter to and a quarter past the hour (25¢). During high season you can also take the Ürgüp-Göreme-Zelve-Avanos minibus. To get to the **tourist office** (tel. (384) 511 4360), get off at the first stop in Avanos (open daily 8:30am-5:30pm, sometimes later in peak season). If you walk in the direction of the continuation of the bus route and turn right across the bridge, you'll find yourself on the main street. The square is 250m farther. **ATMs** are numerous at the many branch banks in the Old Town. Just past the square, on the right, is the **PTT.**

Unless you are eager to delve deeply into Avanos' considerable art and pottery scene, you might rather stay in Göreme and visit Avanos as a daytrip. For directions to the town's widely scattered pensions, ask for a map at the tourist office. One that is quite easy to find is the **Hotel Zelve** (tel. (384) 511 4524), on the old town's central square. A large, modern hotel built for the large tour groups, it offers rooms for walk-ins. (Singles $14. Doubles $26). The **Sofa Hotel** (tel. (384) 511 4484; fax 511 489; e-mail http://www.hotels.wec-net.com.tr/data/sofa) is just across the bridge into old town and up the first hill on the left. The hotel offers beautiful rooms decorated in the traditional Turkish style and a small tea garden. (Singles $15. Doubles $20. Breakfast included.) The **Galata Pension** (tel. (384) 511 5146) is owned by a French artist-in-residence. Stay in Galata to taste Avanos' Bohemian side. Galata is on Gazete Sok. in the old town. ($5.75 per person. Breakfast included.)

Atatürk Cad. is full of fine restaurants between old and new town. Specializing in the Central Asian *mantı*, a Turkish ravioli, **Çağlak Restaurant** (tel. (384) 511 3226) provides a Turkic (as opposed to Turkish) feast for under $5 per person. **Sarıkaya** is pricey, but entertaining if you can avoid the tourist bus crowds. Carved into a hillside, Sarıkaya offers Turkish banquets with folklore, music, and dancing for about $10 per person. In the evening, head to the **Peri Bar** on Atatürk Cad., behind the arched black doors, for folk music and dance.

▓ Ürgüp

In Ürgüp, pretty Greek houses are concentrated around bizarre rock formations. Its atmosphere is as different from Göreme as possible. Sophisticated and Western European, it has a dozen ATMs, car rental agencies, and even a Benetton.

Orientation and Practical Information The Ürgüp **tourist office** (tel. 341 4059) is on Kayseri Cad. Inside the garden, it provides maps of the region, extensive bus schedules, and helps arrange tours (open April-Sept. daily 8am-8pm or later; Oct.-March Mon.-Fri. 8am-5pm). The **PTT** is next door to the tourist office (open daily 8:30am-5:30pm). In medical emergencies, call the **hospital** (tel. 341 4031). **Postal Code:** 50400. **Telephone Code:** 384.

Accommodations To get to most accommodations, go left from the bus station, and walk 20m or so to the main square. The directions listed all originate from the Atatürk statue. The main square and the Atatürk statue are also 100m from the tourist office. Turn right as you exit the garden. One hundred and fifty meters up the road, to the right of and behind the Atatürk statue, sits the **Born Hotel** (tel. 341 4756). One of the cheapest places in town, it is a pleasant, basic little pension with ancient wooden staircases and atmospheric rooms. (Singles $6.25. Doubles $9.50. Triples $13.75. Breakfast included.) **Pension Sun** (tel. 341 4493), directly behind the Atatürk statue, manages to contain a large cave (cave rooms available). If you ask in the morning, the family will prepare you a delicious Turkish dinner ($3.50). (Singles $7.50. Doubles $11.25. Triples $15. Breakfast included.) **Hotel Asia Minor** (tel. 341 4645) is a beautiful Greek mansion with reproductions of rock-church frescoes on the lobby walls, and is located 75m up the road to the left, behind the Atatürk statue. Every room is different—some are quite ornate, others plain. Some small rooms are available; they may give a $1 per person discount. (Singles $9.50. Doubles with bath $16.25.) Yet another typical Ürgüp Greek mansion is the **Türkerler Otel** (tel. 341 3354). This one has a swimming pool in front, which detracts from its appearance. (Singles $9.25. Doubles $15. Triples $20. Breakfast included.) **Campers** should ask the driver to stop outside of Ürgüp—look for campsite signs.

Food and Entertainment Stuffed in the courtyard of an antique inn, the **Sofa Restaurant** serves delicious Turkish fare. Or try *kiremit kebap,* which is unique to Ürgüp—lamb with onion, tomato, mushroom, and cheese baked in a clay bowl which retains savory lamb juices ($3.25). Next to the taxi stand in front of Atatürk, **Şömine Café and Restaurant** offers a vast menu of Turkish and Western dishes from *kebap* ($2.25-3.75) to pizza ($2.50-3) as well as a wide selection of local wine and beer. Overlooking the Şomine Café is a second floor restaurant called **Teraslı Uğrak** where one can lounge on the terrace, appropriately enough, and watch the busy square with a fine Turkish menu. If you find yourself still energized after a day of trooping through Ürgüp's narrow, cobblestone streets, head for the **Armağ** disco. Around the corner from the Teraslı Uğrak café, just look for the "born to be free" neon sign over the doors. Disco tunes and Turkish pop precedes a nightly belly dance act. Crowd is half Turkish, half tourist.

The connoisseur may already know that Cappadocia is a major wine-producing region and the industry is centered around Ürgüp. In town, the renowned **Turasan winery,** 100m past the Hotel Hanedan, offers free tours and tasting. For a group of five or more, most travel agencies in town will arrange an impromptu tour for roughly $10 per person. Several specialist wine shops around the main square offer free tastings of a variety of Cappadocian wines. Next door to the tourist office is the town's **museum.** From the bus station, go right, then follow the signs (open April-Oct. daily 8:30am-6pm; admission $2.50, students $1.25).

ORTAHİSAR

The village of Ortahisar surrounds a tall castle hewn from volcanic rock. The **Kale** (Citadel) is at the end of the street leading from the highway to the town square. A tiny town of one main street, Ortahisar is easy to navigate, but a better idea would be to stay in Göreme (have we said this before?) and visit the Kale on a daytrip. There is no tourist office in Ortahisar, but there are few hidden treasures here. About halfway down the street is the **PTT** (open daily 8:30am-5:30pm). International phone calls can be made from one of the three international pay phones outside the PTT. The **hospital** can be reached at (384) 343 3364.

Should you really dig on the Citadel or on the quiet, there are two excellent pension options. The best is **Gümüş** (tel. (384) 343 3127, -3576). Ask for a room on the top floor for some of the finest views in Cappadocia. ($3.75 per person, with bath $5.) A bit farther down the street is the **Dönmez Pansiyon** (tel. (384) 343 3634). Average rooms in a clean, if unspectacular pension. ($8.75 per person. Breakfast included.) Though there is nothing fancy here, the street does have two decent restaurants. The **Gül Çay Evi** provides basic Turkish food, sweets, and tea at low prices. At the end of the street next to the citadel is the **Şato Kafeterya.** An extremely pleasant terrace makes it a nice place to escape the sun and the tourists.

Ortahisar has one real "sight" and two unofficial sights. First, there is the magnificently preserved **Kale** (Citadel). Brave steep staircases and tiny passages lead to the top for a photo-op nobody should miss—360° of Cappadocian beauty (open daily 8am-sundown; admission 50¢, students 25¢). You can shop after your adventure in the **Rose Wine Shop,** just down the street, to the left of the Kale entrance. It offers a wide variety of inexpensive Cappadocian wines for the wine novice or expert. As a final stop, don't miss a sign across from the Kale entrance: it reads "Crazy Ali's Antics." Don't be alarmed—it's only an antique store with an accent.

NEVŞEHİR

Although Nevşehir is not especially interesting, it is the region's transportation hub. Don't stay here if you have time to go on to Göreme, which have nearly as many bus connections. Nevşehir is dusty and lacks the uniqueness of other spots in the valley.

There is one main street in Nevşehir, **Atatürk Bulvarı.** To get here from the bus station, while standing in the main (upper level) bus/car park with the terminal at your back, you'll see **Lale Caddesi** running uphill on your right. You can walk up Lale Cad. for roughly 10 minutes until you reach Atatürk Blv. If you turn left at the intersection, you'll see the tourist office, and beside it, the **state hospital.** The staff at the **tourist office** (tel. (384) 213 3659), at the intersection of Atatürk Blv. and Lale Cad., has maps and brochures (open Mon.-Fri. 8am-5:30pm, Sat.-Sun. 9:30am-5:30pm). *Dolmuş* leave from outside the tourist office for most parts of Cappadocia and stop at the main station (every 30min., 7am-7pm, off season 7am-5pm). Atatürk Blv. has everything you need—restaurants, shops, a Cappadocian tea garden, several **ATMs,** and a 24-hour **PTT. The hospital** can be reached at (384) 213 1200.

KAYMAKLI AND DERİNKUYU

In the villages of Kaymaklı and Derinkuyu, inauspicious passages lead to two of Cappadocia's most spectacular sites. Two stark but well preserved **underground cities,** thought to be more than 3000 years old, lurk beneath the ground in an endless warren of tunnels, rooms, stairwells, and hallways. Throughout centuries of political uncertainty, Christians fled from their villages to the underground cities at times of imminent attack. It is estimated that five to ten thousand people lived here for up to six months at a time. Strict, military-style discipline was imposed and some pillars have holes drilled at the top for chaining transgressors due for torture. It was forbidden for anyone to leave—for any reason—while the cities were occupied, lest their departure give away their location. Strangely enough, **no toilets** have been found in Derinkuyu, though some have been found at Kaymaklı.

The first levels of these cities are believed to have been built by the Hittites around 2000 BCE, either for storage or to escape attack from enemies. Most of the cities were constructed by Christians between 1300 and 1800 years ago. The size and complexity of Kaymaklı—five levels of elaborate passages burrowing down 35m—are mind-boggling, yet Derinkuyu is almost twice as large, with a depth of 120m and 5-km long escape tunnels (now blocked). One of the Derinkuyu passages is even believed to lead back to Kaymaklı. The cities are south of Nevşehir, on the road to Niğde. Kaymaklı is 20km away, Derinkuyu 29km. Derinkuyu, with eight levels excavated so far, is slightly more impressive and offers sizable public rooms and halls, good lighting, and relatively easy access, but you might find the dark, narrow, often unmarked passages of Kaymaklı even more enthralling. In both cities, the tunnels were built low and tortuous to hamper the progress of invaders. Though marked with arrows, the tunnels form a potentially confounding maze, and if you explore extensively you'll almost certainly get lost. Red arrows lead down, blue arrows up. Both cities have unexplored tunnels which are out of bounds, but be careful—some contain traps (such as sudden drops) to deter potential invaders. You shouldn't wander too far off the beaten track. *Dolmuş* run to Nevşehir every 30 minutes (63¢). Bring a sweater; the deeper tunnels can be dank. (Both sites are open daily 8:30am-7pm, off season 8:30am-5pm; admission $1.85, students 95¢.) As with all state museums, a FIYTO card will get you in free.

■ Ihlara

The Ihlara Valley, provider of *lira* to Aksaray, is a true garden paradise hidden in a narrow gorge. You won't even imagine it's there until you literally come up to the edge. For centuries thousands of Greek Christians found this valley a refuge for sedentary life while their nomadic Turkish neighbors grazed their flocks over the grassy plains above. Although the valley is still somewhat off the beaten track, it is becoming more mainstream every year. Nine years ago there were no pensions and no public transport. Now there are a half-dozen pensions and a cliffside restaurant.

GETTING THERE

Getting to Ihlara independently is relatively painless. Three buses per day run to **Aksaray.** The eccentric bus schedule, however, means that it can't be hiked in a daytrip, or even with a single overnight in Ihlara. You should plan accordingly. Buses depart Monday-Saturday from Aksaray's bus station at 11am, 3 and 5:30pm, and arrive at the main square of Ihlara village one hour later. In the other direction, buses depart Ihlara at 7, 7:30am, and 1pm (50¢ each way). Your best option is probably to take the 3 or 5:30pm bus from Aksaray, settle into your pension and have a meal, hike the valley the next day, and leave the following morning. Five daily minibuses connect Aksaray to Nevşehir's bus station (1hr., $2). You can also charter a private *dolmuş* in Göreme's station for $35 to take you to Ihlara and back (8 or 10 passengers). Some of Ihlara's hotels also provide this service for the same price.

On a bus from Aksaray, 10km south from the last turn-off to Ihlara, you'll pass the town of **Selime** pockmarked with the windows and doors of former troglodyte habitations. Selime marks the north end of the Ihlara Valley—hikers sometimes enter here, or at the village of **Yaprakhisar,** around a bend in the road. Ten minutes later, the bus will stop to let passengers off at the main handful of Ihlara's pensions, then continue 1km downhill to the main square of the village.

With the exception of the Star Motel, all pensions reside 1km uphill from the square, near where the bus stops. Except for the excellent restaurant (full lunch $3.50) at the official entrance to the gorge, little food is served outside the pensions. **Hospital:** 453 7006. **Police:** 451 2008. **Postal Code:** 68570. **Telephone Code:** 382.

ACCOMMODATIONS

All accommodations in Ihlara charge per person, not per room. The Akar and Famille pensions offer private *dolmuş* service from Aksaray and will run you to Selime in the morning, from which you can hike through the valley to Ihlara village.

Star Motel (tel. 453 7429), conveniently located on the main square and beside the river. Formerly the River View Hotel. Clean and basic, some rooms have balconies overlooking the fast-moving river, whose sound will lull you to sleep at night and greet you the next morning. The Star's restaurant offers perhaps the best food in town. Tea garden overlooking the river. $6 per person.

Pansion Akar (tel. 453 7018), has clean, comfortable rooms with balconies and private baths. Those at the back have views of Mt. Hasan. The Akar also features a fine restaurant. $8.75 per person. Breakfast included.

Bişkinler Ihlara Pansiyon (tel. 453 7077) has basic rooms, all with hot water, shower, and toilet. Quite a bargain, both in the restaurant and in the pension. $6.25 per person. Breakfast $1.85.

Pansion Anatolia (tel. 453 7440) is basic and clean, with some large rooms. Some singles have balconies. $6 per person.

Pension Famille (tel. 453 7098), where French is spoken rather than English. Offers comfortable rooms in a family home. $6 per person.

HIKING THE VALLEY

The Ihlara Valley properly consists of 14km of the north-south course of the Melendiz River, from Selime to Ihlara village. Most people visit the valley on guided tours from Göreme or Ürgüp—these take tourists on a walk from its "official entrance," near Ihlara's pension cluster, to **Belisırma**, 3km north, where there's a restaurant and a **campsite**. What makes the Ihlara entrance "official" is the admission fee ($1.90), which is only charged to people entering at that point. In reality you have lots of flexibility in visiting the valley. Walking itineraries of 7, 10, and 14km along the valley floor are also easily planned. Hikers often explore the valley by taking a *dolmuş* shuttle to Yaprakhisar or Selime and following the river course 7 or 10km, respectively, south, back to the official valley entrance. The path, which is flat and well worn for most of the way, involves a few scrambles among the boulders north of Belisırma. The full 14km route also begins in Selime but continues 3-4km past the official entrance, looping around to where the valley ends and Ihlara village begins. To do this hike in the opposite direction, you can enter the valley near Ihlara village. If you take the path which runs beside the Anatolia Pension, you'll enter beside a waterfall (admission $1.90).

If walking from Selime, you can take the 7 or 7:30am bus from Ihlara to Aksaray and get off at Selime. Ask the locals to point you to the valley entrance (*vadi girişi*). Walk back at your leisure. The views are best in the downstream direction. In the other direction, you may want to try to time your arrival in Selime to catch the 5:30pm Aksaray-Ihlara bus (be in Selime by 6pm).

The advantage of the **official valley entrance** (unmarked from below) is that it allows tourists to see the highlights of the valley without a hike. There, hundreds of steps painstakingly built up the side of the valley wall provide peerless views and lead directly to the richer churches (signposted, always open, and free of charge). To reach the official entrance from Ihlara's main square, go up the hill towards Aksaray for roughly 1km and take the first main intersection to your right (it's signposted *Ihlara Valley*). From there it's another 2km to the entrance (a conspicuously hotel-like building on your left). Now, like the tour groups, you can buy your ticket, go down the steps, turn left, and walk 3km to get to Belisırma. The walk will take you through beautiful, unspoiled scenery and several frescoed rock churches. Walking from Ihlara to Belisırma, most of the churches will be to your left.

The popular **Sümbüllü** and **Ağaçaltı Churches** flank the official entrance stairs at the valley floor. The Sümbüllü is noteworthy for its rock facade and five deep, arched bays separated by pillars. Spectacular blue and white angels ring the Christ figure on the well preserved dome of the Ağaçaltı. Another 30m south past the Ağaçaltı (to the right after descending the entrance stairs, away from Belisırma) lies the **Pürenliseki Church,** whose faded walls enclose the many martyrs of Sivas. The **Kokar Church,** 70m farther along, celebrates biblical stories with colorful frescoes and ornate, geometrical ceiling crosses. Also worth seeing is the **Yılanlı Church** (Church of the Serpent), which gets its name from a display of Satan's serpents. To reach it, backtrack from the Kokar to the steps at the official valley entrance and cross the wooden bridge. The church lies 100m to your left, up the concrete steps. Inside you'll also find saintly arches framing the geometrically decorated altar.

■ Aksaray

The main reason to visit Aksaray is to catch public transport on to Ihlara. While it's not a destination in its own right, you can easily blow a couple hours here.

Orientation and Practical Information   For orientation's sake, you're lucky to be dropped off at the **bus station** in town. *Dolmuş* from Nevşehir will drop you there, but intercity Nevşehir-Konya buses deposit you instead at a Mobil station on the ring road, 2½km out from the center. Taxis ($1.50) are hassle-free. Ask someone to point the way to the *merkez* (town center). After 500m, you should pass soccer fields on your left. From the bus station, take the exit beside the Pension Çakmak, turn left, and follow the main road 20m to the **main square,** which contains several attractive government buildings and a statue of Atatürk. To reach the tourist office from this square, take the first left—pass the mosque on your left—and walk down this shopping street until it forks. In front of you, you'll see an İmar Bankası. Above it, to the left, is a tiny green sign which reads "Tourist Office." You can enter by a side door, to the left of and past the bank. The tourist office is on the second floor. You'll be ushered into the Director of Tourism's office (tel. 213 24 74 or 212 5651), as only he speaks English (open daily 8:30am-5:30pm). **The police** can be reached at 212 6650, -5211, and -1185). Aksaray is home to a very large, quite modern **hospital** (tel. 213 1043, -5207), located at the entrance to town. The **post office** (PTT) is just off the public garden one block past the main square on the same road as the bus station. Turn right at the garden (open daily 8:30am-5:30pm). **Postal Code:** 68100. **Telephone Code:** 382.

Accommodations   From the bus station, you can exit by the Pension Çakmak, cross the road, and continue down the opposite road. This pair of *pansiyon* are on the first left. The **Aksaray Pansion** (tel. 212 4133) offers large, waterless rooms. Although they vary in size and ambience (some in front have balconies), they all cost the same. (Singles $6.25. Doubles $10. Triples $13.75.) A couple of doors down is the **Hitit Pansion** (tel. 213 1996), where shoes come off at the door and couches decorate the lounge. (Singles $5. Doubles $8.75. Triples $12.50.) There is a comfortable one-star hotel on the main square, **Yuvam Otel** (tel. 212 0024, -5). (Singles $13.75. Doubles $22.50. Triples $25.50.)

Food   Aksaray is not one of Turkey's culinary capitals. One of your best bets is the **Çeşme Lokantası.** With the tourist office and bank at your back, take the right fork. It's 25m down this street, on the right (main courses $1.25-2.25). Across from the tourist office, there is an excellent *pastahane.* Stop there for cookies, *baklava,* and any other Turkish sweet you can imagine.

APPENDICES

GLOSSARY

■ Greek

The table of the Greek alphabet (only 24 letters) below will help you decipher signs. The left column gives you the names of the letters in Greek, the middle column shows the printed lower case and capital letters, and the right column provides the approximate pronunciations of the letters.

alpha	α A	*a* as in father
beta	β B	*v* as in velvet
gamma	γ Γ	before vowels, *y* as in ya-hoo; otherwise a hard *g* as in guest pronounced in the back of the throat
delta	δ Δ	*th* as in there
epsilon	ε E	*e* as in jet
zeta	ζ Z	*z* as in zebra
eta	η H	*ee* as in queen
theta	θ Θ	*th* as in health
iota	ι I	*ee* as in tree
kappa	κ K	*k* as in cat
lambda	λ Λ	*l* as in land
mu	μ M	*m* as in moose
nu	ν N	*n* as in net
ksi	ξ Ξ	*x* as in mix
omicron	o O	*o* as in row
pi	π Π	*p* as in peace
rho	ρ P	*r* as in roll
sigma	σ (ς), Σ	*s* as in sense
tau	τ T	*t* as in tent
upsilon	υ Y	*ee* as in green
phi	φ Φ	*f* as in fog
xi	χ X	*ch (h)* as in horse
psi	ψ Ψ	*ps* as in oops
omega	ω Ω	*o* as in glow

GREETINGS AND COURTESIES

Good morning	ΚΑΛΗΜΕΡΑ	kah-lee-ME-rah
Good evening	ΚΑΛΗΣΠΕΡΑ	kah-lee-SPE-rah
Good night	ΚΑΛΗΝΥΧΤΑ	kah-lee-NEE-khtah
yes	ΝΑΙ	NEH
no	ΟΧΙ	OH-hee
please/you're welcome	ΠΑΡΑΚΑΛΩ	pah-rah-kah-LO
thank you (very much)	ΕΥΧΑΡΙΣΤΩ	ef-hah-ree-STO (po-LEE)
excuse me	ΣΥΓΓΝΩΜΗ	seeg-NO-mee
hello (polite, plural)	ΓΕΙΑ ΣΑΣ	YAH-sas
hello (familiar)	ΓΕΙΑ ΣΟΥ	YAH-soo
OK	ΕΝΤΑΞΕΙ	en-DAHK-see

GREEK

What is your name?	ΠΩΣ ΣΕ ΛΕΝΕ	pos-se-LEH-neh
My name is ...	ΜΕ ΛΕΝΕ	me-LEH-neh ...
Would you like some red wine?	ΜΗΠΟΣ ΘΕΛΕΙΣ ΛΙΓΟ ΚΟΚΚΙΝΟ ΚΡΑΣΙ;	ME-pos THEL-ees LE-go KO-kee-no kra-SEE?
Mr./Sir	ΚΥΡΙΟΣ	kee-REE-os
Ms./Madam	ΚΥΡΙΑ	kee-REE-ah

WHERE?

Where is ... ?	ΠΟΥ ΕΙΝΑΙ;	pou-EE-neh ... ?
I'm going to ...	ΠΗΓΑΙΝΩ ΓΙΑ	pee-YEH-no yah ...
When do we leave?	ΤΙ ΩΡΑ ΦΕΥΓΟΥΜΕ	tee O-rah FEV-goo-meh?
restaurant	ΕΣΤΙΑΤΟΡΙΟ	es-tee-ah-TO-ree-o
post office	ΤΑΧΥΔΡΟΜΕΙΟ	ta-khee-dhro-MEE-o
market	ΑΓΟΡΑ	ah-go-RAH
museum	ΜΟΥΣΕΙΟ	mou-SEE-o
pharmacy	ΦΑΡΜΑΚΕΙΟ	fahr-mah-KEE-o
bank	ΤΡΑΠΕΖΑ	TRAH-peh-zah
church	ΕΚΚΛΗΣΙΑ	eh-klee-SEE-ah
hotel	ΞΕΝΟΔΟΧΕΙΟ	kse-no-dho-HEE-o
room	ΔΩΜΑΤΙΟ	dho-MAH-teeo
suitcase	ΒΑΛΙΤΣΑ	vah-LEE-tsah
airport	ΑΕΡΟΔΡΟΜΙΟ	ah-e-ro-DHRO-mee-o
airplane	ΑΕΡΟΠΛΑΝΟ	ah-e-ro-PLAH-no
train	ΤΡΑΙΝΟ	TREH-no
bus	ΛΕΩΦΟΡΕΙΟ	leh-o-fo-REE-o
ferry	ΠΛΟΙΟ	PLEE-o
ticket	ΕΙΣΙΤΗΡΙΟ	ee-see-TEE-ree-o
hospital	ΝΟΣΟΚΟΜΕΙΟ	no-so-ko-ME-o
port	ΛΙΜΑΝΙ	lee-MA-nee
toilet	ΤΟΥΑΛΕΤΑ	twa-LE-ta
police	ΑΣΤΥΝΟΜΙΑ	as-tee-no-ME-a
archaeology	ΑΡΧΑΙΟΛΟΓΙΑ	ark-ha-o-lo-GEE-a
bar	ΜΠΑΡ	BAR
doctor	ΓΙΑΤΡΟΣ	yah-TROS
right	ΔΕΞΙΑ	dhek-see-AH
left	ΑΡΙΣΤΕΡΑ	ah-rees-teh-RAH
here, there	ΕΔΩ, ΕΚΕΙ	eh-DHO, eh-KEE
open, closed	ΑΝΟΙΧΤΟ, ΚΛΕΙΣΤΩ	ah-nee-KTO, klee-STO

HOW MUCH?

How much?	ΠΟΣΟ ΚΑΝΕΙ;	PO-so KAH-nee
I need	ΧΡΕΙΑΖΟΜΑΙ	khree-AH-zo-meh
I want	ΘΕΛΩ	THEH-lo
I would like ...	ΘΑ ΗΘΕΛΑ	thah EE-the-lah ...
I will buy this one	ΘΑ ΑΓΟΡΑΣΩ ΑΥΤΟ	thah ah-go-RAH-so ahf-TO
Do you have?	ΕΧΕΤΕ	Eh-khe-teh
Can I see a room?	ΜΠΟΡΩ ΝΑ ΔΩ ΕΝΑ ΔΩΜΑΤΙΟ	bo-RO nah-DHO E-nah dho-MAH-tee-o
bill	ΛΟΓΑΡΙΑΣΜΟ	lo-gahr-yah-SMO
newspaper	ΕΦΗΜΕΡΙΔΑ	eh-fee-meh-REE-dha
water	ΝΕΡΟ	ne-RO
good	ΚΑΛΟ	kah-LO
cheap	ΦΤΗΝΟ	ftee-NO

expensive	ΑΚΡΙΒΟ	ah-kree-VO

WHEN?

What time is it?	ΤΙ ΩΡΑ ΕΙΝΑΙ;	tee-O-rah EE-neh?
yesterday	ΧΘΕΣ	k-THES
today	ΣΗΜΕΡΑ	SEE-mer-a
tomorrow	ΑΥΡΙΟ	AV-ree-o
first	ΠΡΩΤΟ	PRO-to
morning	ΠΡΩΙ	pro-EE
evening	ΒΡΑΔΥ	VRAH-dhee
later tonight	ΑΠΟΨΕ	ah-PO-pseh
last	ΤΕΛΕΥΤΑΙΟ	teh-lef-TEH-o

NUMBERS

zero	ΜΗΔΕΝ	mee-DHEN
one	ΕΝΑ	Eh-nah
two	ΔΥΟ	DHEE-o
three	ΤΡΙΑ	TREE-ah
four	ΤΕΣΣΕΡΑ	TES-ser-ah
five	ΠΕΝΤΕ	PEN-dheh
six	ΕΞΙ	E-ksee
seven	ΕΠΤΑ	ep-TAH
eight	ΟΚΤΩ	okh-TO
nine	ΕΝΝΙΑ	en-YAH
ten	ΔΕΚΑ	DHEH-kah
eleven	ΕΝΔΕΚΑ	EN-dheh-kah
twelve	ΔΩΔΕΚΑ	DHO-dheh-kah
thirteen	ΔΕΚΑΤΡΙΑ	DHEH-kah TREE-ah
fourteen	ΔΕΚΑΤΕΣΣΕΡΑ	DHEH-kah TES-ser-ah
fifteen	ΔΕΚΑΠΕΝΤΕ	DHEH-kah PEN-dheh
sixteen	ΔΕΚΑΕΞΙ	DHEH-kah E-ksee
seventeen	ΔΕΚΑΕΠΤΑ	DHEH-kah ep-TAH
eighteen	ΔΕΚΑΟΚΤΩ	DHEH-kah okh-TO
nineteen	ΔΕΚΑΕΝΝΙΑ	DHEH-kah en-YAH
twenty	ΕΙΚΟΣΙ	EE-ko-see
thirty	ΤΡΙΑΝΤΑ	tree-AN-dah
forty	ΣΑΡΑΝΤΑ	sa-RAN-dah
fifty	ΠΕΝΗΝΤΑ	pen-EEN-dah
sixty	ΕΞΗΝΤΑ	ex-EEN-dah
seventy	ΕΒΔΟΜΗΝΤΑ	ev-dho-MEEN-dah
eighty	ΟΓΔΟΝΤΑ	og-DHON-dah
ninety	ΕΝΕΝΗΝΤΑ	en-EEN-dah
hundred	ΕΚΑΤΟ	ek-ah-TO
thousand	ΧΙΛΙΑ(ΔΕΣ)	hil-ee-AH(dhes)
million	ΕΚΑΤΟΜΜΥΡΙΟ	eka-to-MEE-rio

PROBLEMS

Do you speak English?	ΜΙΛΑΣ ΑΓΓΛΙΚΑ;	mee-LAHS ahn-glee-KAH?
I don't speak Greek	ΔΕΝ ΜΙΛΑΩ ΕΛΛΗΝΙΚΑ	dhen mee-LAHO el-leen-ee-KAH
I don't understand	ΔΕΝ ΚΑΤΑΛΑΒΑΙΝΩ	dhen kah-tah-lah-VEH-no
I am lost	ΧΑΘΗΚΑ	HA-thee-ka
I am ill	ΕΙΜΑΙ ΑΡΡΩΣΤΟΣ	EE-meh AH-ross-toss

| Where is my toothbrush? | ΠΟΥ ΕΙΝΑΙ ΤΗΝ ΟΔΟ– ΝΤΟΒΟΥΡΤΣΑ ΜΟΥ; | pou EE-nay teen o-DHON-dho-voo-tsa mou? |
| Help! | ΒΟΗΘΕΙΑ | vo-EE-thee-ah |

■ Turkish

Be aware that certain letters and combinations of letters in Turkish are pronounced differently than the English. Turkish is a phonetic language: each letter has only one sound, and this is always pronounced distinctly. Words are usually lightly accented on the last syllable; special vowels, consonants, and combinations include:

Turkish	English
c	*j* as in jacket
ç	*ch* as in check
ğ	lengthens adjacent vowels
ı	(no dot on the "i") *i* as in hit
i	*ee* as in peace
j	*zh* as in pleasure, or *j* as in French *jadis*
ö	*ö* as in German *könig,* or *eu* as in French *deux*
ş	*sh* as in short
u	*oo* as in boot
â	dipthong of *ea,* or faint *ya*
ü	*ew* as in cue
ay	*eye* as in pie
ey	*ay* as in play
oy	*oy* as in toy
uy	*oo-ee* as in phooey

GREETINGS AND COURTESIES

good morning	*günaydın*	gewn eye-DUHN
good evening	*iyi akşamlar*	ee-YEE ahk-sham-LAR
good night	*iyi geceler*	ee-YEE geh-jeh-LEHR
yes, no	*evet, hayır*	EH-vet, HIGH-yuhr
please	*lütfen*	LEWT-fen
thank you (formal)	*teşekkürler*	tay-shayk-kewr-LEHR
thank you (informal)	*sağol*	SAA-ohl
you're welcome	*bir şey değil*	beer shay DEE-yeel
pardon me	*affedersiniz*	ahf-feh-DEHR-see-neez
hello	*merhaba*	MEHR-hah-bah
good bye (said by a guest)	*allaha ısmarladık*	aw-LAH-huss-small-duck
good bye (said by a host)	*güle güle*	gew-LAY-gew-lay
beautiful, good	*güzel*	gew-ZEHL
okay	*pekiyi*	PEHK-ee-yee
What is your name?	*İsminiz ne?*	ees-meen-eez NEH
Would you like some white wine?	*Biraz beyaz şarap itermi-sin?*	beer-az bay-az sharap ist-aer-me-sin?
My name is ...	*İsmim ...*	ees-MEEM
Mr./Sir	*Bay*	Bye
Ms./Madam	*Bayan*	Bye-AHN

WHERE?

Where is... ?	...nerede?	...NEHR-eh-deh
I'm traveling to...	...ya seyahat ediyorum	...ya say-yah-HAHT eh-dee-OHR-room
How near is it?	Ne kadar yakın?	NEH-kah-dahr yah-KUN
post office	postane	post-aaaah-NEH
museum	müze	mew-ZEH
hotel	otel	oh-TEL
room	yer, oda	OH-da
toilet	tuvalet	too-vah-LET
airport	hava alanı	hah-VAH-ah-lahn-uh
bus	otobüs	oh-toh-BOOS
doctor	doktor	dohk-TOHR
grocery	bakkal	bahk-KAHL
pharmacy	eczane	ej-zaaaah-NEH
bank	banka	BAHN-kah
police	polis	poh-LEES
left, right	sol, sağ	sohl, saah
passport	pasaport	pahs-ah-PORT
train	tren	trehn
ticket	bilet	bee-LET
here, there	burada, orada	BOOR-ah-dah, OHR-ah-dah
open, closed	açık, kapalı	ah-CHUHK, kah-pah-LUH

HOW MUCH?

How much is it?	Kaç para? or Ne kadar?	KACH-pah-rah NEH-kah-dar
I want ...	Őistiyorum	ees-tee-YOH-room...
a double room	iki kişilik oda	ee-KEE kee-shee-leek OH-dah
a twin-bedded room	çift yataklı oda	CHEEFT yah-tahk-LUH OH-dah
I do not want any.	Yok.	YOHK
cheap, expensive	ucuz, pahalı	oo-JOOZ, pah-hah-LUH
bill (as in check)	hesap	hessahp
water	su	soo

WHEN?

What time is it?	Saat kaç?	SAH-aht kahch
yesterday	dün	dewn
today	bugün	boo-GEWN
tomorrow	yarın	YAHR-uhn

NUMBERS

zero	sıfır	SUF-fuhr
quarter	çeyrek	chay-REK
half a...	yarım...	yahr-UHM
one	bir	beer
...and a half	...buçuk	boo-CHOOK
two	iki	ee-KEE
three	üç	ewch
four	dört	duhrt
five	beş	besh

six	*altı*	ahl-TUH
seven	*yedi*	yeh-DEE
eight	*sekiz*	seh-KEEZ
nine	*dokuz*	DOH-kooz
ten	*on*	ohn
eleven	*on bir*	OHN-bir
twelve	*on iki*	OHN-ee-kee
thirteen	*on üç*	OHN-ewch
twenty	*yirmi*	yeer-MEE
thirty	*otuz*	OH-tooz
forty	*kırk*	kirk
fifty	*elli*	ehl-LEE
sixty	*altmış*	ahlt-MUSH
seventy	*yetmiş*	yet-MEESH
eighty	*seksen*	sehk-SEN
ninety	*doksan*	dohk-SAHN
hundred	*yüz*	yewz
thousand	*bin*	been
million	*milyon*	meel-YOHN

PROBLEMS

I don't understand.	*Anlamadım.*	ahn-LAH-mah-duhm
Do you speak English?	*İngilizçe biliyor musunuz?*	EEN-ghee-leez-jeh bee-lee-YOHR-moo-soo-nooz
I don't speak Turkish.	*Türkçe bilmiyorum.*	TEWRK-cheh BEEHL-mee-yohr-oom
I'm lost!	*Yolumu kaybettim!*	YOHL-loo-moo KIGH-bet-tim
I am ill.	*Hastayım.*	hahs-TAH-yuhm
Where's my toothbrush?	*Diş fırçam nerede?*	deesh fir-cham naer-eh-de?
Help!	*İmdat!*	im-DAHT

■ Climate Chart

| Temp in °C Rain in mm | January | | April | | July | | October | |
	Temp	Rain	Temp	Rain	Temp	Rain	Temp	Rain
Athens	12.0	62.0	19	23.0	33.0	6.0	23.0	51.0
Salonika	5.5	44.0	15	41.0	26.5	22.0	17.5	57.0
Ankara	0.0	40.5	11	40.3	23.0	13.5	13.0	24.4
Antalya	10.0	247.5	16	43.3	28.0	2.4	20.0	62.6
İstanbul	5.0	109.0	12	46.0	23.0	34.0	16.0	81.0
Trabzon	6.0	85.2	11	58.4	22.0	37.0	15.0	113.2
Nicosia	10.0	76.0	18	18.0	29.0	1.0	21.0	25.0

■ Holidays and Festivals:

■ Greece

Jan. 1: Feast of St. Basil. Carrying on a Byzantine tradition, Greeks cut a New Year's sweet bread called *Vassilopita,* baked with a coin inside. The person who gets the slice with the coin is that year's lucky person.

Jan. 6: Epiphany. Celebrated in the West as the day the Magi appeared in Bethlehem to greet the baby Jesus; in the Eastern church Epiphany is recognized as the day Jesus was baptized by St. John. In Greece, *kallikantzaroi* (goblins) appear between Christmas and Epiphany. Village bonfires scare them away. At Epiphany, waters are blessed and evil spirits leave the earth. Crosses are thrown into harbors all around Greece and the young men who fetch them are considered blessed.

Jan. 8: Gynaecocracy (St. Domenica's Day/Midwife day). Women of child-bearing age bring gifts to the midwife. In the villages of Komotini, Xanthi, Kilkis, and Serres, women gather in the cafés while men look after the households; the men are allowed to join their wives in celebrations after dusk.

Feb. 1-Feb. 23: Carnival. Three weeks of feasting and dancing before the Lenten fast begins on Feb. 24. Notable celebrations occur in Patras and Cephalonia.

March 25: Greek Independence Day. Commemorates the 1821 struggle against the Turkish Ottoman Empire. Also a religious holiday, the Feast of the Annunciation, when the angel Gabriel told Mary of the Incarnation.

April 25: Good Friday. People carry lit candles in a procession through town or around the church in one of the Greek church's most moving liturgies.

April 27: Easter. The most holy day in the Greek calendar. After a midnight mass that is followed by a meal, celebrations on Easter Sunday typically include feasting on spit-roasted lamb and red-dyed hard-boiled eggs, followed by dancing.

April 23: St. George's Day. Celebration in honor of the dragon-slaying knight. Festivities at Limnos, Chania include horse races, wrestling matches, and dances.

May 1: Labor Day. Also Feast of the Flowers. Wreaths of flowers hung outside people's doors. The odd Communist demonstration.

May 21: Anastenaria. Also called **Feast of St. Constantine and St. Eleni.** Celebrations include fire dancing and walking on burning charcoal. Celebrated in Agia Eleni, Thessaloniki, and Veria.

Early-mid June: The Day of the Holy Spirit. This national religious holiday takes place 40-50 days after Easter and is celebrated differently in each region.

June 3: Pentecost.

Late June to early July: Navy Week. Fishers' and sailors' festivals at various coastal towns. On Volos, a re-enactment of the journey of the Argonauts is staged.

Aug. 15: Feast of the Assumption of the Virgin Mary. Celebration throughout Greece, particularly on Tinos, in honor of Mary's ascent to Heaven.

Sept. 8: The Virgin's Birthday. In some villages an auction is held to determine who will carry the Virgin's icon. The money is used to provide a village feast.

Sept. 14: Exaltation of the Cross. In villages, the altar cross is venerated and paraded through the town while children sing hymns.

Oct. 26: Feast of St. Demetrius. Celebrated with particular enthusiasm in Thessaloniki. The feast coincides with the opening of new wine; i.e., heavy drinking.

Oct. 28: National Anniversary of Greek Independence. Called "*Ohi* Day" in honor of Metaxas's famous "*Ohi*" (No) to Mussolini.

Nov. 17: Commemoration of the rise of the Greek university students against the junta of 1974. Speeches are presented at the University of Athens.

Dec. 24-25: Christmas. As part of the festivities, children traditionally make the rounds singing *kalanda* (Christmas carols).

■ Turkey

Jan. 1: Yılbaşı. New Year's Day.

Jan. 11-Feb. 9: Ramadan (Ramazan). A month-long Islamic holiday during which Muslims abstain from eating, drinking, smoking, and sex between dawn and sunset. Each day's fast is broken with a feast. Only one or two restaurants may be open during the day in the smaller towns and inland, and in such areas it is inappropriate to eat or drink openly during the daytime. The dates for Ramazan change with the lunar calendar, so these dates are only accurate for 1997.

Feb. 28-March 1: Sugar Holiday (Şeker Bayramı). A three-day holiday celebrating the end of Ramazan, an occasion for gift-giving and sweets for children. Eating and drinking in public is encouraged. Banks and holidays close all three days.

April 23: National Sovereignty and Children's Day (Ulusal Egemenlik ve Çocuk Bayramı). Commemorates the first meeting of the Grand National Assembly in Ankara in 1920. An international children's festival is held in Ankara.

May 1: May Day. May 1 is Turkey's labor day; labor protests abound.

April 28-May 1: Festival of Sacrifice (Kurban Bayramı). The most important holiday of the year, this festival recalls Abraham's sacrificial offering of Ismael to God on Mt. Moriah. 2½ million sheep are slaughtered each year in Turkey to honor the faith and piety of Abraham. Offices close for up to a week. The dates for Kurban Bayramı change with the lunar calendar, so these dates only apply for 1997.

May 19: Youth and Sports Day. Mustafa Kemal Atatürk decided to commemorate Turkey's youth and tomorrow's future on this day.

May 27: Constitution Day. Initiated in the 1960s, commemorates the revision of the Constitution during the first military coup.

Aug. 30: Victory Day. Anniversary of the final rout of Western invaders, 1922.

Oct. 29: Republic Day (Cumhuriyet Bayramı). Largest civil holiday commemorates Atatürk's proclamation of the Turkish Republic in 1923. Ubiquitous parades.

Nov. 10: Marks the anniversary of Atatürk's death in 1938. At 9:05am (the time of death), all of Turkey stops for a moment of national mourning; horns are blown.

■ Cyprus and Kıbrıs

Cyprus and Kıbrıs observe not only Greece and Turkey's holidays, respectively, but also hold their own regional and local festivities. Consult the C.T.O. or the T.C.I.O. for more information.

▓ Health Numbers

■ Greece

Agios Vassilios (Patra)

Iamat Pediatric Center—7 Miaoulis	(61) 992 368

Athens

Iamat Center—8 Marni St.	822 9033 - 681 4274
Iamat Center—167, 3rd September St.	(093) 274 385
Iamat Center—15 Markou Botsari St.	867 7916
Iamat Pediatric Center—Afxentiot 7, Kalamaki (near Athens Airport)	984 1499 - 984 8228
Iamat Orthopedic Center—3 Kolofontos	(301) 723 4621
	24 Hours (094) 388 833

Corfu

Hellenic Medical Care—15, Moustoxidoy St.	48 200/1/2/3
Iamat Center—Kapodistria 15	39 850 - 22 073
All Assistance—Mantzaros 10	34 164

Patras

Iamat Center—7 Plila Alonia Sq.	(061) 277 849
Iamat Dental Center—46 Demetriou Ypsilantou	(061) 336 739

Rhodes

Iamat Center—50 Amerikis St.	(241) 29 333

■ Turkey

İstanbul

American Bristol Hospital	(212) 231 4050
Ear Nose Throat Center—Valikonaği Cad. 107/E	(212) 224 8928

İnciraltı-İzmir

Dokuz Eylül University Hostpital	(232) 259 5959

İzmir

Iamat Center—318 Yalı Caddesi, 1 Karşıyaka	(232) 381 7365 - 388 1470

■ Cyprus

Limassol

Iamat Center—28 Aristoteli Valaoriti St.	(5) 381 111

Nicosia

The Nicosia Heart Institute—52 Aeschylou St.	464 245

■ Phone Codes

Greece	30				
Aegina	0297	Kalamata	0721	Paleochora	0823
Agia Galini	0832	Kalambaka	0432	Parga	0684
Agios Nikolaos	0841	Kalavrita	0692	Paros	0284
Agria	0423	Kalymnos	0243	Patmos	0247
Alexandropoulis	0551	Kardamili	0721	Patras	061
Amorgos	0285	Karpathos	0245	Petalidio	0722
Andritsena	0626	Karpenisi	0237	Piraeus	01
Andros	0282	Karystos	0224	Poros	0298
Arachova	0267	Kastoria	0467	Pouri	0422
Astypalea	0243	Kavala	051	Pylos	0723
Athens	01	Kea	0288	Rafina	0294
Cape Sounion	0292	Kellini	0623	Rethymnon	0831
Cephalonia	0671	Kimi	0222	Rhodes	0241
Chalkida	0221	Kithnos	0281	Samos	0273
Chania	0821	Kos	0242	Samothraki	0551
Chios	0271	Kyparissia	0761	Serifos	0281
Chora Sfakion	0825	Kythera	0735	Sifnos	0284
Corfu	0661-3	Lefkada	0645	Sithonia	0375
Corinth	0741	Lesvos	0251	Sitia	0843
Delphi	0265	Lia	0664	Skiathos	0427
Dimitsana	0795	Limni	0227	Skopelos	0424
Edessa	0381	Limnos	0254	Skyros	0222
Epidavros	0753	Litohoro	0352	Sparta	0731
Eritrea	0221	Matala	0892	Symi	0241

Galaxidi	0265	Methoni	0723	Syros	0281
Gythion	0733	Metsovo	0656	Thassos	0593
Hersonissos	0897	Milos	0287	Thebes	0262
Ierapetra	0842	Monemvassia	0732	Thessaloniki	031
Igoumenitsa	0665	Mt. Athos	0377	Tinos	0283
Ikaria	0275	Mycenae	0751	Tripolis	071
Ioannina	0651	Mykonos	0289	Volos	0421
Ios Village	0286	Nauplion	0752	Xilokastro	0743
Iraklion	081	Naxos	0285	Zagora	0426
Isthmia	0746	Neapolis	0734	Zakinthos	0695
Ithaka	0674	Olympia	0624		
Itilo	0733	Osios Loukas	0267		

Turkey **90**

Adana	322	Fethiye	252	Marmaris	252
Ankara	312	Göreme	384	Olimpos	242
Antakya	326	Hopa	466	Ölüdeniz	252
Antalya	242	Ihlara	382	Pamukkale	258
Aphrodisias	256	İstanbul (Euro)	212	Patara	242
Artvin	466	İstanbul (Asia)	216	Pergamon	232
Ayvalık	266	İzmir	232	Rize	464
Bodrum	252	İznik	224	Safranbolu	372
Bursa	224	Kâhta	416	Selçuk	232
Çanakkale	286	Kalkan	242	Taşucu	324
Çeşme	232	Kars	474	Trabzon	462
Datça	252	Kaş	242	Urfa	414
Edirne	284	Konya	332	Ürgüp	384
Eğirdir	246	Kuşadası	256	Yusufeli	466

Cyprus **357**

Agia Napa	03	Nicosia	02	Podromos	0295
Larnaka	04	Pano Platres	05	Polis	06
Limassol	05	Paphos	06		

■ Weights and Measures

1 centimeter (cm) = 0.39 inches	1 inch = 2.54cm
1 meter (m) = 3.28 feet	1 foot = 0.31m
1 kilometer (km) = 0.62 miles	1 mile = 1.61km
1 gram (g) = 0.04 ounces	1 ounce = 28g
1 kilogram (kg) = 2.2 pounds	1 pound = 0.45kg
1 liter (l) = 0.26 gallons	1 gallon = 3.76l
1 Imperial Gallon (U.K.) = 1.2 gallons	1 gallon = .83 Imperial Gallons
$°F = (°C \times 1.8) + 32$	$°C = (°F - 32) \times .56$

Index

★Let's Go 1997 Reader Questionnaire ★

Name: _____ **What book did you use?**_____

Address: _____

City: _____ **State:** _____ **Zip Code:** _____

How old are you? under 19   19-24   25-34   35-44   45-54   55 or over

Are you (circle one)   in high school   in college   in grad school
employed   retired   between jobs

Have you used Let's Go before?   yes   no

Would you use Let's Go again?   yes   no

How did you first hear about Let's Go?   friend   store clerk   CNN
bookstore display   advertisement/promotion   review   other

Why did you choose Let's Go (circle up to two)?   annual updating
reputation   budget focus   price   writing style
other: _____

Which other guides have you used, if any?   Frommer's $-a-day   Fodor's
Rough Guides   Lonely Planet   Berkeley   Rick Steves
other: _____

Is Let's Go the best guidebook?   yes   no

If not, which do you prefer? _____

**Which part of Let's Go do you feel needs most to be improved, if any
(circle up to two)?**   packaging/cover   practical information
accommodations   food   cultural introduction   sights
practical introduction ("Essentials")   directions   entertainment
gay/lesbian information   maps   other: _____

How would you like to see these things improved?
_____
_____

How long was your trip?   one week   two weeks   three weeks
one month   two months or more

Have you traveled extensively before?   yes   no

Do you buy a separate map when you visit a foreign city?   yes   no

Have you seen the Let's Go Map Guides?   yes   no

Have you used a Let's Go Map Guide?   yes   no

If you have, would you recommend them to others?   yes   no

Did you use the internet to plan your trip?   yes   no

Would you buy a Let's Go   phrasebook   adventure/trekking guide
gay/lesbian guide

**Which of the following destinations do you hope to visit in the next three
to five years (circle one)?**   Australia   China   South America   Russia
other: _____

Where did you buy your guidebook?   internet   chain bookstore
independent bookstore   college bookstore   travel store
other: _____